Illuminating Jewish Thought

Faith, Philosophy, and Knowledge of God

Michael Scharf
Publication Trust
Yeshiva University Press
RIETS

מגיד
MAGGID

Netanel Wiederblank

ILLUMINATING JEWISH THOUGHT

Faith, Philosophy, and Knowledge of God

The RIETS Hashkafah Series
Rabbi Daniel Z. Feldman, Series Editor

The Michael Scharf Publication Trust of
Yeshiva University Press

Maggid Books

Illuminating Jewish Thought
Faith, Philosophy, and Knowledge of God

First Edition, 2020

Maggid Books
An imprint of Koren Publishers Jerusalem Ltd.

POB 8531, New Milford, CT 06776-8531, USA
& POB 4044, Jerusalem 9104001, Israel
www.maggidbooks.com

The publication of this book was made possible
through the generous support of *Torah Education in Israel.*

ISBN 978-1-59264-548-0, *hardcover*

A CIP catalogue record for this title is
available from the British Library

Printed and bound in the United States

YOUNG ISRAEL OF RIVERDALE
4502 Henry Hudson Parkway ~ Riverdale, New York 10471

Rabbi Mordechai Willig
718.796.8208

Rabbi Netanel Wiederblank, a rising star on the faculty of our yeshiva, has authored an outstanding hashkafic work "Illuminating Jewish Thought." It is a masterful presentation of the fundamentals of faith, written clearly and annotated thoroughly. The halachic and philosophical works of the Rambam are carefully analyzed. Complementary or opposing views of classical exponents of Jewish thought, such as R. Yehuda Halevi, Ramban, R. Yosef Albo and Abarbanel, are included as well. More recent scholars are also quoted.

The present volume focuses on Redemption. Two others, on belief in Hashem and in Torah, will hopefully follow soon. Rav Wiederblank's comprehensive contribution is invaluable for sincere students of Ikarei Emuna.

Mordechai Willig

בס"ד

תפארת גדליה

YGW

From the Desk of

RABBI AHRON LOPIANSKY

Rosh HaYeshiva

21 Sivan 5776

If the world of halacha is a vast forest, then the world of emunos vdeos can only be described as an unending ocean. In the world of halacha, one at least has the Rambam, Tur and Shulchan Aruch, who define the debate, and the key players thereof. One can describe the parameters of the debate, even if the details are unclear to us. But in the world of emunos vedeos, we do not even have a good definition of the issues, and many times the various opinions seem to occupy different dimensions, talking an entirely different language. This has discouraged many a student from learning these topics; while feeling frustrated that they may be well versed in the minutae of the law, but ignorant about the foundations of Judaism; the very Yesodei Hatorah. Others have taken to cherry picking points to their liking and presenting it as the entirety of Judaism.

Hagaon Rav Nesanel Wiederblank has done an incredible job, creating a full outline of the major points of Emunos Vedeos. I have known him since his youth and I can testify that he has the qualities needed to establish a work such as this. He is a major talmid chacham in shas and poskim, and yet has spent much time delving into these areas. He has a dispassionate analytical mind, yet a heart that is 'yareh vchared' of the dvar Hashem. He constantly bears in mind that the very ground in which he is forging a path, is 'admas kodesh', sacred soil. And above all, he is a true anav, who does not allow arrogance or smugness into the sefer that he has so painstakingly and masterfully put together.

The sefer is an outline, though it is voluminous. Its purpose is to structure the issues and opinions; the seeming internal inconsistencies, and the problems vis a vis the sources; the possible resolution of those questions, and the strengths and weakness of the proffered explanations. He tries to stick to the major opinions, but has included opinions that have become contemporarily popular and/ or controversial.

It is a tremendous zikui harabim, and may Hkb"h grant him the strength and wisdom to enlighten the tzibbur in many areas of Torah, and to reach many talmidim both in person and through his seforim.

With great admiration and deep affection,

Ahron Shraga Lopiansky

YESHIVA OF GREATER WASHINGTON - TIFERES GEDALIAH
1216 ARCOLA AVENUE, SILVER SPRING, MD 20902 ■ 301-649-7077 ■ WWW.YESHIVA.EDU

הרב צבי שכטר
ראש ישיבה וראש כולל
ישיבת רבינו יצחק אלחנן

Rabbi Hershel Schachter
24 Bennett Avenue
New York, New York 10033
(212) 795-0630

מכתב ברכה

העולם רגילים לחלק בין הלכה לבין אגדה,
ורבינו הי' רגיל לומר שאין כ"כ הבדל, שהלכה
באה לפרט איזו פעולות אסורות, איזה מחויבות,
ואיזה מותרות — לא אסורות ולא מחויבות, כמו"כ
במחשבה ובהשקפה — חלק האגדה שבתורה
בא לפרט איזו השקפות מחויבות, ואיזה הן
אסורות, ואיזה מותרות, וידידי יקירי הרב
ר' נתנאל הי"ו, מצעירי הר"מים שבישיבה,
אשר מאוד מצליח בהרבצת התורה, כי תמיד
חוזר למקורות בכל נושא, מוציא כעת ספר
על עניני השקפה — והכל עפ"י מקורות
נאמנים, וברכתי שימצא ספרו חן בעיני
עולם התורה וילמדו ממנו ותרבה הדעת.

צבי שכטר
תשרי תשע"ח

I dedicate this book to my parents, Mr. Jonathan Blank and Dr. Serena Wieder, who have dedicated so much of their lives to me.
אמא *and* **אבא**, *you have no idea how much you have taught me. At every turn in my life I seek to emulate your wisdom, kindness, generosity, and decency. Words cannot describe how much I love you.*

Netanel

In loving admiration of our dear friends
Rabbi Netanel Wiederblank's parents
who have nurtured and encouraged him
מעודו עד היום הזה

Dr. Serena Wieder
world-renowned pioneer in developmental psychology
whose insights and therapeutic innovations
have uplifted thousands of children

and

Jonathan Blank, Esq.
distinguished lawyer, whose pro bono work
on behalf of the Seattle Jewish community
planted the seeds of Torah and Wisdom

Together they have guided Rav Netanel's
critical study of Hashkafa for our times

B'Ahava
Miriam and Allen Schick

וראה בנים לבניך

In gratitude to HaShem,
dedicated with love
to our children's children
Chava Bracha
Moshe Chaim
Golda Chana
Dovid Yisroel
Nesanel Eliyahu
Chana Malka
Shmuel Dovid

Barry & Marcia Wagner Levinson

ברכה והצלחה

Daniel & Raquel Betech
Abraham & Reyna Dayan
Pepe & Margie Cattan
and families

לע״נ

הרב צבי ב״ר שמואל יוסף זצ״ל
נלב״ע כ״א ניסן, שביעי של פסח תשע״ה

ואשתו

אסתר צירל ב״ר יונה ע״ה
נלב״ע ט״ו בניסן, ליל סדר ראשון תשע״ה

ריעדער

אודים מוצלים מאש
הנאהבים והנעימים בחייהם ובמותם לא נפרדו

מאת
אפרים בן ישראל חיים וחיה בת הרב צבי פינשאווער
Kenneth Ephraim and Julie Pinczower
לע״נ

ישראל חיים בן אפרים
פינשאווער ז״ל
Joachim Pinczower

״הולך תמים ופעל צדק ודבר אמת בלבבו״

נולד בגרמניה ד׳ אדר תרפ״ח
וברח לאנגליה בתקופת השואה
וזכה להקים בארה״ב משפחה לתפארת
נפטר כ״ז ניסן תשע״ז

ת.נ.צ.ב.ה.

מאת
אפרים בן ישראל חיים ואשתו חיה פינשאווער
Kenneth Ephraim and Julie Pinczower

Dedicated by Yehoshua and Miriam Grossman

In loving memory of their parents

ר׳ יצחק ב״ר שמואל גרוסמן ע״ה
מרת לאה עטיל בת קלמן קלונימוס ע״ה

ר׳ פנחס אלימלך בן אשר ישעי׳ הלוי גאלדנער ע״ה
מרת בלומא רויזא בת אברהם שלמה ע״ה

Sponsored by
Mrs. Leah Reichmann

Contents

UNIT TWO: AGGADA

UNIT FOUR: KNOWING GOD

Foreword

We are excited to publish this groundbreaking volume (Volume 1 in this series) in Rabbi Netanel Wiederblank's trilogy series, *Illuminating Jewish Thought*. The previous volume (Volume 2 in this series), which explored notions of free will, the afterlife, and the messianic era, has been enthusiastically received by our readers.

The present volume, which deals with faith, philosophy, and knowledge of God, moves from the realm of eschatology to epistemology. Rabbi Joseph Albo divided the fundamentals of Jewish faith into three categories: (1) the existence of God, (2) revelation, and (3) reward and punishment. The previous volume concentrated upon the final category, while the present volume delves into the first and foremost arena of basic belief.

The Talmud (*Shabbat* 31b) records that fear of God is comparable to the key to the outer gate that leads to the inner gates of the Divine palace. While the magnificent majesty of the palace provides the greatest attraction, it is inaccessible to those who do not have the key to open the gate to come inside. This book provides the reader with the keys to enter the inner chambers of religious experience and enlightenment.

Rabbi Wiederblank has a rare gift for elucidating the esoteric and illuminating the incomprehensible. He combines an unshakeable belief in God and Torah with a profound appreciation for philosophical conundrums. His ability to navigate treacherous terrain and extract pearls of perspicacity to inform a religiously resplendent worldview is breathtaking.

Franklin Delano Roosevelt famously declared that "there is nothing to fear but fear itself." In the Jewish tradition, it is fair to state that "there is nothing to fear but God Himself." Our Sages teach us (*Berachot* 33b) that "all is in the hands of God except for the fear of God." In this volume, Rabbi Wiederblank both teaches about the fear of God and demonstrates through his humble and reverential style what it means to be a quintessentially God-fearing personality.

We thank Rabbi Daniel Feldman, the executive editor of the RIETS Press, for providing his trademark standard of excellence in overseeing the publication of this volume. We are also indebted to President Rabbi Dr. Ari Berman for supporting the RIETS Press enterprise, and Rabbi Menachem Penner, Dean of RIETS, for painstakingly ensuring that this magnificent volume would see the light of day. Rosh HaYeshiva Emeritus Rabbi Dr. Norman Lamm ob"m, ybl"c President Emeritus Richard M. Joel, and Dean Emeritus Rabbi Zevulun Charlop have also facilitated every volume published by the RIETS Press.

We hope that Rabbi Wiederblank will have the wherewithal to complete the remainder of this series and to continue to inspire his legions of students and readers with his insight, intelligence, and illumination.

Rabbi Yona Reiss
Director, RIETS Press
Tishrei 5781

Preface

נִפְתְּחוּ הַשָּׁמַיִם וָאֶרְאֶה מַרְאוֹת אֱלֹהִים: (יחזקאל א:א)

The Heavens opened and I saw visions of God.

The opening verse of the book of *Yechezkeil* introduces the prophet's glorious vision. Rambam (*Moreh ha-Nevuchim* 2:47) admonishes us not to read this verse literally: "One should not think that there are gates and doors to the heavens." Rather, there are figurative doors which we must open if we hope to know our Creator.[1] We must learn how to open these doors because the task of knowing God is considered of paramount importance by Rambam and so many of our greatest thinkers. As King David instructs his son Shlomo: דַּע אֶת אֱלֹהֵי אָבִיךָ "Know the God of your father" (*I Divrei ha-Yamim* 28:9). Indeed, Yirmiyahu stresses that only in this accomplishment may a person rightfully take pride: כִּי אִם-בְּזֹאת יִתְהַלֵּל הַמִּתְהַלֵּל, הַשְׂכֵּל וְיָדֹעַ אוֹתִי "Rather, let he that prides himself do so only in this: that he understands and knows Me" (*Yirmiyahu* 9:23).

1. As I explain in the preface to Volume Two, the word "we" here refers to members of the Jewish faith community. Of course, I hope that non-Jews who read this book will find it to be a valuable resource as well. In addition, although male pronouns are generally used, they should not be understood as excluding women, but should be seen as generic.

For those who feel unworthy or unqualified to engage in this noble task, remember Rambam's closing words:

> God is very near to everyone who calls,
> If he calls truly and has no distractions;
> He is found by every seeker who searches for Him,
> If he marchers toward Him and goes not astray.[2]

However, knowing God is more than intellectual knowledge. R. Moshe Chaim Luzatto (Ramchal) powerfully expresses how the study of Torah, and specifically *machshava* (Jewish thought), ignites our soul, allowing us to connect meaningfully to our Creator.

ספר דרך עץ חיים

וזה תראה, כי שנים הם בתבונה אחת נבראו: שכל האדם, והתורה המשכלת אותו. על התורה נאמר (ירמיה כג כט): "הלוא כה דברי כאש נאם ה'". והודיענו בזה, כי אמת הדבר, שהתורה היא ממש אור אחד ניתן לישראל לאור בו, כי לא כחכמות הנכריות וידיעות החול, שאינן אלא ידיעת דבר מה אשר ישיג השכל בטרחו - אך התורה הנה קודש ה', אשר לה מציאות גבוהה בגבהי מרומים. וכאשר יעסוק בה האדם למטה - אור היא אשר תאיר בנשמתו להגיע אותו אל גנזי מרומים, גנזי הבורא יתברך שמו, בדרך הארה ופעולה חזקה .אשר היא .פועלת בה.

And this you will see, that there are two things that were created with one likeness (both function together) – man's intellect and the Torah that gives him the intelligence. Of the Torah it is written, "'Is not My word like fire?' says God" (*Yirmiyahu* 23:29). With these words, God informed us that the Torah is literally a light that was given to enlighten the Jewish people. For it is not like the wisdom of the nations and secular knowledge, which are nothing more than knowledge that the intellect reaches after toiling to understand it. However, the Torah is the holiness of God; it has a supernal existence in the loftiest heights, and when

2. Pines translation, p. 638.

> a man toils in it below, it is a light that illuminates in his soul to elevate him to the treasures on high, the treasures of the Creator, may His Name be blessed.

Torah is more than wisdom – it is light. *Machshava,* learned properly, "illuminates" our lives. Without it, we grope in darkness – not only the darkness of ignorance, but utter darkness in which we are blinded from living a meaningful religious life, and worse, darkness from loving encounters with our Creator (see Rambam, *Hilchot Shechita* 14:16). With Torah, however, Rambam notes in his closing of *Moreh ha-Nevuchim,* those who walk in darkness will see a great light.[3] In the words of Shlomo, ותורה אור, "And Torah is light" (*Mishlei* 6:23). Hence the title: *Illuminating Jewish Thought.*

Rambam writes at the end of his Introduction to *Moreh ha-Nevuchim* that his work "is a key permitting one to enter places the gates to which were locked." Likewise, in a much much smaller sense, the goal of this volume is to help any individual unlock the gates to knowledge of God by presenting the paths of some our greatest teachers and addressing some of the most vexing questions a contemporary Jew faces.

We begin with an introduction where we consider whether these matters should be studied in the first place. In subsequent chapters we consider methodology – how should one go about studying the divine, what sort of sources should we turn to, and how should we interpret them? Later, we consider what a person must believe, and what the implications of false beliefs are. Along the way, we explore the various modes used to arrive at faith, and grapple with challenges to faith, such as those stemming from science.

If this work helps readers acquire a broad and sophisticated knowledge of Jewish thought but leaves them unchanged as people, then the book is an utter failure. Studying *machshava* is not about the acquisition of knowledge. Throughout our journey, we will (hopefully) be inspired by what we, as human beings created in the image of God, can achieve. At the same time, if we are successful, our newfound proximity to God will constantly remind us of our smallness and distance.

---

3. See *Yeshayahu* 9:1.

However, before we begin, I must confess that I should feel petrified writing a book of this nature. The task before me is daunting. As I write in the Preface to Volume Two, I am wholly unqualified to write this book. I have not sufficiently studied the matters I discuss, and, more importantly, I lack the requisite fear of Heaven to teach these topics. That I pontificate upon the most grandiose of levels of knowledge and love of God when I have failed to achieve even the minutest success is the height of hypocrisy. Furthermore, I have no doubt that this work contains numerous errors. Moreover, even if the information presented is accurate, what if it is misunderstood. Rambam in his introduction to *Perek Chelek* records a story that illustrates that, to some degree, it is a teacher's responsibility to teach in a way that will not be misunderstood. There was once a great scholar, the *Tanna* Antigonus of Socho, who taught a very important principle – one should not serve God merely to receive reward, but rather one should serve Him out of love (*Avot* 1:3). Among his pupils were two intelligent people who were troubled by this message. They felt that it only made sense to work hard if one can expect to achieve reward. Their names were Tzadok and Baitus. They misunderstood their teacher. Of course, there will be reward, unimaginable in its greatness. However, ideally one should not be motivated by renumeration. Sadly, their misunderstanding led them to form deviant sects of Judaism that ultimately caused great harm.

In response to this event, Rambam suggests Avot (1:11) teaches, "Scholars, be careful with your words lest you incur the penalty of exile." Rambam writes that Antigonus attempted to teach the people an important lesson. One should seek the truth simply because it is true (see *Hilchot Teshuva,* Chapter 10). But this sophisticated and complex lesson was above the comprehension of some. They would have been better off serving God faithfully, even if they were motivated by the incentives of reward and punishment. True, this is not ideal service, but it is far better than no service at all. Moreover, it does inspire growth, and eventually these people may have reached the goal of service of God out of love. Thus, I wonder, what if instead of bringing the reader close to God I lead him astray? Consideration of the gravity of the topics discussed in this volume should stir within me intense anxiety, and I fear that it does not sufficiently do so. Thus, it is with trepidation that I conclude this small preface with a prayer taken from King David's immortal words:

תהלים קמג:ח

הוֹדִיעֵנִי דֶּרֶךְ זוּ אֵלֵךְ כִּי אֵלֶיךָ נָשָׂאתִי נַפְשִׁי:

> Let me know the path I should walk, for to You I have lifted up my soul.

תהלים קיט:יח–כב

גַּל עֵינַי וְאַבִּיטָה נִפְלָאוֹת מִתּוֹרָתֶךָ... גַּל מֵעָלַי חֶרְפָּה וָבוּז...

> Open my eyes so that I may see wondrous things in Your Torah... Save me from disgrace and contempt...

I owe much gratitude to many people for their contributions to this work. The reader is encouraged to consult the Preface to Volume Two where I acknowledge many of those who brought me to this day and partially attribute the various translations used in this text. Here I wish only to once again thank Rabbis Lopiansky, Willig, Feldman, and Reiss who carefully reviewed and commented on this entire book, and to acknowledge the incredible editing of R. Eliron Levinson, R. Aviyam Levinson, Matt Lubin, and Yoni Rabinovitch. Each of them contributed profoundly to this volume in innumerable ways. Their extraordinary humility and kindness combined with their striking scholarship has taught and inspired me throughout this process. Additionally, I would like to express my appreciation for the Israel Koschitzky Virtual Beit Midrash. I have learned a great deal from their many courses and utilized many of their translations in this volume. Finally, I wish to thank R. Reuven Ziegler, Shira Finson, and Caryn Meltz of Maggid Books for their extraordinary work, as well as the talmidim *who generously and adroitly helped finish the job, including, but not limited to, R. Yitzchok Radner, David Tanner, Yonatan Abrams, and Menachem Gans. May God bless them with opportunities to illuminate the world with the light of His ways.*

Unit One
Introducing *Machshava*

This book seeks to elucidate certain topics in Jewish thought, or *machshava,* such as *emuna* (faith) and Kabbala (Jewish mysticism). In the preface to Volume Two of this series, we offer a working definition of the term *machshava*. In the opening chapters of this volume, we will elaborate on the meaning of this ambiguous term. Specifically, in this unit we will introduce the field of philosophy, and in Unit Two we will analyze the world of Aggada, the non-halachic components of rabbinic literature.

First, however, we must consider whether we should be studying these sorts of topics in the first place. Thus, in Chapter 1, we will explore why we should study *machshava*. In so doing, we will begin to refine our understanding of the term *machshava*. We will examine the value placed upon the study of the non-halachic aspects of Torah by the classical Jewish tradition, and we will discuss the various attitudes towards the study of philosophy. Because this chapter is an introduction, the topics will be dealt with more cursorily, while those later in the book will be dealt with more comprehensively.

In Chapter 2, we will consider whether and under what circumstances a Jew should study philosophy. We do this through introducing Rambam's *Guide to the Perplexed* or *Moreh ha-Nevuchim*. We will define the meaning of philosophy in the Jewish tradition and explore the goals and purposes of such study. Defining "philosophy" is particularly challenging, since the term is used differently in different time periods. Even nowadays, there is no consensus on this topic. In the appendices to Chapter 2, we will examine Rambam's perspective on mysticism and the perception that mystics had on Rambam's philosophy.

In Chapter 3, we will continue our discussion of philosophy by considering the interaction between the text of the Torah and philosophy. Specifically, we will examine how we know when to interpret Scripture allegorically. This question relates to apparent contradictions between Torah and philosophy as well as Torah and science.

Finally, in Chapter 4, we will consider a question that relates to the debates that we will study throughout this book: In every disagreement, does one opinion reflect the truth while the other does not, or are both views somehow correct? We will discuss this question by considering the Talmudic principle of "These and these are the words of the living God."

Chapter One

Why Learn *Machshava*?

Before we can address why one should or should not learn *machshava*, we must define the term. For now, let us define *machshava* as the non-halachic parts of the oral law (i.e., excluding Scripture and Halacha[1] and including Aggada, philosophy, and Kabbala). The importance of studying Tanach is obvious – it is the word of God.[2] The importance of studying Halacha is obvious – we must know what to do.[3] However, it is not at all obvious why one should study *machshava*. Hopefully, as we consider why one should or should not learn *machshava*, we will develop a better sense of what this ambiguous term means.

1. While a positive definition would have been preferable, there is strong precedent for this type of formulation. Almost all of the Geonim and Rishonim, starting with R. Sherira Gaon and R. Shmuel b. Chofni, defined Aggada in the negative, by what it is not. Perhaps they are following in the footsteps of the Yerushalmi *Horiyot* 3:5, זה בעל אגדה שאינו לא אוסר ולא מתיר לא מטמא ולא מטהר.
2. There is a difference in this regard between Torah, which is the direct word of God, and Prophets and Writings, which are somewhat less direct. However, this distinction need not concern us at present.
3. There is much more to the world of Talmud and Halacha than the practical law. This too need not concern us at present.

1.1 REASONS TO STUDY *MACHSHAVA*

After digressing to discuss matters of divine reward and punishment and comparing the views of the rabbis with those of the philosophers,[4] Rambam (1135–1204) concludes his commentary on *Mishnayot Berachot* with the following apology:

> ואין מקום זה מתאים לדבר בו על הענין הזה, אלא שדרכי תמיד בכל מקום שיש איזה רמז בעניני אמונה אבאר משהו, **כי חשוב אצלי להסביר יסוד מהיסודות יותר מכל דבר אחר שאני מלמד**.
>
> Even though this is not the appropriate place to discuss this matter, [I have chosen to discuss it] since any time there is an allusion to matters of faith [such as the nature of providence], I always elucidate, **for it is more important to me to explain one of the principles than any other thing that I teach**.

Rambam justifies his digression by emphasizing the importance of understanding the basic principles of our faith. Likewise, in explaining his organization of *Mishneh Torah*, he writes why he began his halachic work with philosophical matters:

> **מנין המצוות לרמב"ם**
> ספר ראשון: אכלול בו כל המצוות שהן עיקר דת משה רבינו **וצריך אדם לידע אותן תחלת הכל** כגון ייחוד שמו ברוך הוא ואיסור עבודה זרה. וקראתי שם ספר זה ספר המדע.
>
> Book 1: I will include in it all the commandments that are the basic principles of the religion of Moshe, our teacher, **which one needs to know at the outset**. They include recognizing the unity of the Holy One, blessed be He, and the prohibition of idolatry. I have called this book The Book of Knowledge (*Madda*).

---

4. Rambam adds that, for the most part, there is confluence between the rabbis and philosophers:

   ועוד נדבר על משהו מענין זה במסכת אבות, ונראה לך מקצת התאמת דברי גדולי הפילוסופים לדברי חכמים **בכל הענינים**.

Rambam thus informs us of the mandate to explain matters of faith and philosophy in his halachic work. Why? At the most basic level, Rambam's *Hilchot Yesodei ha-Torah* teaches, as its name states, the foundations of the Torah, which are the truths of God and His Torah. If someone fulfills all of the commandments in the Torah to the letter but believes (Heaven forbid) that he is following the commands of the Baal, or if he prays to God but thinks that there are many other such 'gods,' he has completely missed the boat; his observance of *mitzvot* is for naught.[5] But should we really be delving more deeply into these topics, attempting to understand how God runs the world, how He communicates with humanity, etc.? Rambam felt further, lengthy explanation of such principles was valuable. Why might that be? Let us begin with sources in Chazal.

An Essential Aspect of Torah Study

Chazal do not encourage the study of philosophy *per se* (later we shall consider if they discourage it), but they do insist that one pursue non-halachic matters. In numerous places, Chazal stress the importance of studying Aggada, and of not limiting one's Torah study to Halacha:

ספרי עקב פסקא מ"ח

...שלא תאמר למדתי הלכות די לי, תלמוד לומר כי אם שמור תשמרון את כל המצוה הזאת, כל המצוה למוד מדרש הלכות ואגדות...

> ... Lest one say, "It is sufficient that I learned Halachot," the Torah stated, "If you will assiduously keep this *mitzva* completely ..." (*Devarim* 11:22). The phrase "this *mitzva* completely" teaches us that one must learn Midrash, Halacha, and Aggada.

By adding the word "*kol*" (כל המצוה), the verse informs us we should not define the study of Torah narrowly (limited to Halacha). Thus, the

5. Rambam emphasizes this point in his Introduction to *Perek Cheilek,* Ramban, in his Introduction to his commentary on *Iyov.* In Chapter 10 we consider why this is from a hashkafic perspective. See *Koveitz Shiurim* Vol. 2, 47:14, where R. Elchanan Wasserman explains why this would be true from a halachic perspective. In Chapter 11 we analyze whether this is always true and whether there are those who disagree.

first reason to study *machshava* is that doing so constitutes a fulfillment of the *mitzva* of Torah study. In fact, when rabbinic sources define what the *mitzva* of *talmud Torah* encompasses, they always include Aggada.[6] What exactly does Midrash or Aggada add to Halacha? We will present five overlapping themes that are stressed:

(a) *Machshava* ignites the emotional component of our relationship with God. Most importantly, when studied properly it instils fear of God.
(b) *Machshava* facilitates an understanding of God.
(c) *Machshava* guides our *avodat Hashem*, adding meaning to observance of *mitzvot*.
(d) *Machshava* teaches us how to understand our world.
(e) Finally, *machshava* helps us address both internal and external challenges.

1. Fear of Sin

אבות דרבי נתן נוסחא א פרק כט
רבי יצחק בן פנחס אומר כל מי שיש בידו מדרש ואין בידו הלכות לא טעם טעם של **חכמה**. כל מי שיש בידו הלכות ואין בידו מדרש לא טעם טעם של **יראת חטא**.

הוא היה אומר כל שיש בידו מדרש ואין בידו הלכות זה גבור ואינו מזויין. כל שיש בידו הלכות ואין בידו מדרש חלש וזיין בידו. יש בידו זה וזה גבור ומזויין.

R. Yitzchak b. Pinchas says: "Anyone who knows Midrash but does not know Halacha has not tasted the taste of **wisdom**.

6. For example, *Nedarim* (4:3) includes Mikra, Midrash, Halachot and Aggadot. *Sifrei* (306) includes "Mikra and Mishna, Talmud, Halachot and Haggadot." All agree that the well-rounded scholar excels in both Halacha and Aggada. Interestingly, many people feel an affinity to one over the other. While specialization within Torah is encouraged (אין אדם לומד תורה אלא ממקום שלבו חפץ - עבודה זרה יט א), the *Sifrei Eikev* 48 warns against ignoring any genre entirely.

> Anyone who knows Halacha but does not know Midrash has not tasted the taste of **fear of sin.**"
>
> He said: "Anyone who knows Midrash but does not know Halacha is like an unarmed warrior. Anyone who knows Halacha but does not know Midrash is like an armed weakling. Anyone who knows both is like an armed warrior."

This source informs us that Midrash or Aggada teaches fear of sin[7] while Halacha teaches wisdom. Through the metaphor of warrior and weakling, it teaches that Aggada builds strength of character. Aggada transforms a person from a weakling into a driven warrior eager to fight his enemy. Despite his passion, the individual who knows only Aggada lacks a sword with which to fight his enemy. Halacha, notes R. Avraham Yitzchak Bloch (*Shiurei Da'at,* p. 142) in his explanation of this imagery, is precise, like a sharp sword; it informs a person how and when to use the spiritual strength inspired by Aggada.[8]

2. An Understanding of God

The above source seems to indicate that Halacha deals with the intellectual aspects of our religion (*chochma*), while Aggada relates to

7. The term "Midrash" has multiple connotations. The word usually refers to hermeneutic interpretation of Scripture, which can be either halachic (as in *midrashei Halacha*) or aggadic (as in *midrashei Aggada*). Sometimes, the term is used as a synonym for Aggada. In the above source, where it is being contrasted with Halacha, it likely refers to moral or ethical teachings. In the previous source, the terms Midrash, Halacha, and Aggada are used separately, and thus the word Midrash there probably has the first connotation.
8. Many sources stress the value of Aggada in terms of inspiring fear of sin. To cite one example, R. Tzadok writes in *Sichat Malachei ha-Shareit* (p. 8): ההגדות הם המביאים יראה אל לב האדם. *Chazon Ish* (oral communication cited in R. Shlomo Brevda's ימי רצון עמ' כ and קימו וקבלו עמ' לז) suggests, on a simple level, occasional aggadic digressions in the midst of halachic *sugyot* reflects the Amora'im's feeling that they needed to boost their fear of heaven at that juncture.

Judaism's non-intellectual components.[9] However, the next source informs us that Aggada also conveys wisdom; specifically, it teaches us about God:

ספרי פרשת עקב מט

רצונך שתכיר את מי שאמר והיה העולם? למוד הגדה, שמתוך כך, אתה מכיר את הקדוש ברוך הוא ומדבק בדרכיו.

Do you want to know the Creator? Study Aggada. Through this, you will know God and cling to His ways.[10]

The Connection Between the Emotional and Intellectual Value of the Study of Machshava

Of course, the intellectual component of our service of God is closely related to the emotional element described earlier, as Rambam powerfully expresses:

רמב"ם הלכות תשובה פרק י הלכה ו

דבר ידוע וברור שאין אהבת הקב"ה נקשרת בלבו של אדם עד שישגה בה תמיד כראוי ויעזוב כל מה שבעולם חוץ ממנה, כמו שצוה ואמר בכל לבבך ובכל נפשך, **אינו אוהב הקב"ה אלא בדעת שידעהו, ועל פי הדעה תהיה האהבה אם מעט מעט ואם הרבה הרבה, לפיכך צריך האדם ליחד עצמו להבין ולהשכיל בחכמות ותבונות המודיעים לו את קונו כפי כח שיש באדם להבין ולהשיג** כמו שבארנו בהלכות יסודי התורה.

It is well-known and clear that the love of God will not become affixed to a person's heart until he becomes obsessed with it at all times, abandoning all things in the world except for it. This was

9. Along similar lines, Gra (*Mishlei* 25:21) notes that Aggada contains all aspects of *mussar* (it is compared to water, which changes things slowly over time), and in *Mishlei* 8:6 he divides Aggada into two distinct categories: מוסר and סוד (mystical).

10. Later, we shall see numerous sources that stress the inherent value in knowing God. This midrash stresses its value insofar as it facilitates emulating His ways. Gra (*Mishlei* 8:10) implies that this midrash refers specifically to the Aggadot that teach *mussar* (as distinct from those that teach Kabbala; see previous note).

implied by the command ["Love God, your Lord,] with all your heart and all your soul" (*Devarim* 6:5). **One can love God only [as an outgrowth] of the knowledge with which he knows Him. The degree of one's love depends on the degree of one's knowledge! A small [amount of knowledge arouses] a lesser love. A greater [amount of knowledge arouses] a greater love. Therefore, it is necessary for a person to focus himself in order to understand and conceive wisdom and concepts that make his Creator known to him according to the potential that man possesses to understand and comprehend,** as we explained in *Hilchot Yesodei ha-Torah*.

Rambam asserts that to the extent that we know God we can love Him. Increasing one's knowledge of God simultaneously facilitates love and fear of God. He invokes his famous comments from *Hilchot Yesodei ha-Torah*:

רמב"ם הלכות יסודי התורה פרק ב הלכה ב[11]

והיאך היא הדרך לאהבתו ויראתו, בשעה שיתבונן האדם במעשיו וברואיו הנפלאים הגדולים ויראה מהן חכמתו שאין לה ערך ולא קץ מיד הוא אוהב ומשבח ומפאר ומתאוה תאוה גדולה לידע השם הגדול כמו שאמר דוד צמאה נפשי לאלהים לאל חי, וכשמחשב בדברים האלו עצמן מיד הוא נרתע לאחוריו ויפחד ויודע שהוא בריה קטנה שפלה אפלה עומדת בדעת קלה מעוטה לפני תמים דעות, כמו שאמר דוד כי אראה שמיך מעשה אצבעותיך וגו' מה אנוש כי תזכרנו וגו', ולפי הדברים האלו אני מבאר כללים גדולים ממעשה רבון העולמים כדי שיהיו פתח למבין לאהוב את השם, כמו שאמרו חכמים בענין אהבה שמתוך כך אתה מכיר את מי שאמר והיה העולם.

What is the way to cultivate love and fear God? When one contemplates the great wonders of God's works and creations and sees that they are a product of a wisdom that has no bounds or limits, he immediately will love, laud, and glorify [God]. He will yearn with an immense passion to know God, like [King] David

11. English translation adapted from Immanuel O'Levy available at http://www.panix.com/~jjbaker/rambam.html. Generally, translations from *Mishneh Torah* are by R. Eliyahu Touger, first published by *Moznayim* and available at chabad.org.

> said, "My soul thirsts for God, for the living God" (*Tehillim* 42:3). And when one thinks about these matters, he immediately will feel a great fear and trepidation. He will know that he is a low and insignificant creation with hardly an iota of intelligence compared to that of God. Like [King] David said, "When I observe Your heavens, the work of Your fingers...what is man that You are heedful of him?" (*Tehillim* 8:4–5) Based on these ideas, I explain important concepts of the Creator's work as a guide to the discerning individual to love God. Concerning this love, the Sages said that from it one will come to know the Creator.

Rambam writes that contemplation of God's staggering creations ignites fear and love of God. It is noteworthy that Rambam emphasizes that this contemplation does not merely generate love of God but an intense desire to *know* God (מתאוה תאוה גדולה לידע השם הגדול). Frequently we think of the notion of *ta'ava* (desire) as a negative force – Rambam emphasizes it can be positive. Two chapters later, having further described aspects of physics and metaphysics, Rambam further elaborates upon the same point.

> **רמב"ם הלכות יסודי התורה פרק ד הלכה יב**
> בזמן שאדם מתבונן בדברים האלו ומכיר כל הברואים ממלאך וגלגל ואדם וכיוצא בו ויראה חכמתו של הקב"ה בכל היצורים וכל הברואים, מוסיף אהבה למקום ותצמאה נפשו ויכמה בשרו לאהוב המקום ברוך הוא, ויירא ויפחד משפלותו ודלותו וקלותו כשיערוך עצמו לאחד מהגופות הקדושים הגדולים, וכ"ש לאחת מהצורות הטהורות הנפרדות מן הגולמים שלא נתחברו בגולם כלל, וימצא עצמו שהוא ככלי מלא בושה וכלימה ריק וחסר.

> When a man contemplates these matters and recognizes the creations – angels, spheres, man, etc. – and sees God's wisdom in all the formations and creations, his love for God will increase, his soul will thirst, and his flesh will yearn to love God. When he compares himself to one of the great holy bodies, and certainly to one of the holy incorporeal forms, he will fear [God] on account of his lowliness, paucity, and insubstantiality.

> He will see himself as an empty and deficient vessel, full of shame and disgrace.

Perceiving God's profound wisdom as manifest in the physical and spiritual universe can have a powerful effect on a person. Accordingly, Rambam writes that contemplation of physics and metaphysics ignites ardent love and intense fear of God. We are not discussing a dispassionate academic discipline – the study of science and philosophy serves as the basis for a deeply emotional relationship with God.[12] We will explore Rambam's understanding of *ahavat Hashem* and its relationship to wisdom in 10.2.

Maintaining Focus

Many works warn of the danger of placing insufficient focus on the non-halachic aspects of Torah study. For example, in the Introduction to *Chovot ha-Levavot,* R. Bachya ibn Pakuda[13] chastises the Torah scholar who excels in Talmudic jurisprudence but "neglects to investigate the root principles and fundamental precepts of his religion ... without the knowledge of which no precept can be fulfilled." To correct this misdirection, R. Bachya devotes his work to the study of *chovot ha-levavot* or duties of the heart (as opposed to duties of the limbs, i.e., *mitzvot* that have some sort of physical component). Carrying out the *chovot*

12. If they do not, then presumably the study of these disciplines no longer would constitute a fulfillment of *mitzvot* like loving and fearing God, though they might still have some other value. R. Kook, in his Introduction to *Ein Aya* (p. 24), discusses how different paths in the service of God direct a person in the right direction. If practicing a particular *derech* does not bring a person closer to God, then it is either inappropriate for that person, inauthentic, or not being practiced properly.
13. Little is known about the life of this philosopher and *dayan* who lived in Saragossa, Spain, in the first half of the eleventh century. R. Bachya authored (in Arabic) the first systematic approach to divine service in 1040 entitled *Al Hidaya ila Faraid al-Qulub* (Guide to the Duties of the Heart), which was translated into Hebrew by R. Yehuda ibn Tibbon in the years 1161–1180 under the title *Chovot ha-Levavot* (Duties of the Heart). R. Bachya ibn Pakuda should not be confused with R. Bachya b. Asher ibn Halawa (1255–1340) who is also known as Rabbeinu Bachya.

ha-levavot demands a proper understanding of the basis for our belief in God and the nature of His providence, and by addressing these topics, *Chovot ha-Levavot* became a major source for *machshava* as well as a *mussar* work.

Ramchal describes the identical lack of focus in the Introduction to *Mesillat Yesharim*:

> תראה, אם תתבונן בהוה ברוב העולם, כי רוב אנשי השכל המהיר והפקחים החריפים ישימו רוב התבוננם והסתכלותם בדקות החכמות ועומק העיונים איש איש כפי נטית שכלו וחשקו הטבעי.
>
> כי יש שיטרחו מאד במחקר הבריאה והטבע, ואחרים יתנו כל עיונם לתכונה ולהנדסה, ואחרים למלאכות. ואחרים יכנסו יותר אל הקדש, דהיינו, למוד התורה הקדושה. מהם בפלפולי ההלכות, מהם במדרשים, מהם בפסקי הדינים.
>
> אך מעטים יהיו מן המין הזה אשר יקבעו עיון ולמוד על עניני שלמות העבודה, על האהבה, על היראה, על הדבקות, ועל כל שאר חלקי החסידות.
>
> If you reflect upon the current state of affairs in most of the world, you will see most people of quick intelligence and sharp intellect devote most of their thought and interest to the subtleties of wisdom and the depths of analysis, every man according to his intellectual tendency and natural desire.
>
> There are those who toil greatly in studying the creation and nature. Others devote all of their study to astronomy, mathematics, or the arts. There are others who draw closer to the sacred, namely, the study of the holy Torah. Some occupy themselves with halachic analyses, others with Midrash, others with law-decisions.
>
> But few are those who devote thought and study to the matter of perfection of [divine] service: on love of, fear of, and clinging to God, and the other branches of piety.

The above thinkers are not advocating for the study of philosophy as much as for a refocus that includes living a more introspective life and studying what we call *machshava* with the goal of increasing faith, fear of heaven, and closeness to God.

This critique comes up repeatedly in the history of Jewish thought. Two further examples are *Chasidut*[14] and the Mussar Movement.[15] However, it is not simply a matter of emphasis. R. Naftali Tzvi Yehuda Berlin (1816–1893) warns that even the study of Torah can become a destructive force if not rooted in *yira*.[16] R. Kook (1865–1935) likewise warns of the possibility that religion, when improperly understood and practiced, can lead to, and has led to, immorality (*Eider ha-Yakar* 36). While each of the above thinkers preaches different methodologies and solutions, they all stress the importance of the study of what we call *machshava*

---

14. The perceived skewed balance of the mainstream approach to Torah study (with an overemphasis on halachic aspects of Torah at the expense of *yira*) was a central critique raised by early *chasidim*. Consider the following source, written in 1777 by R. Meshulam Fivush, a third generation *chasid*. He bemoans how many people are perceived as great scholars, due to their high level of erudition and knowledge, but do not truly "know" even a small amount of Torah. This paradox stems from a fundamental misdirection in the service of God:

יושר דברי אמת קונטרסים קונטרס ראשון

ובאמת רבים מבני עמינו המדומים בעיניהם ובעיני העולם חכמים גדולים בתורה בנגלה ובנסתר ומדומים ביראה בכל הדברים וסוברים שבאו לקצת תורה ויראה אבל באמת עדיין לא זכו אפילו לידיעה קטנה מתורת אלהינו.

In truth, many of our people who are perceived as great scholars in Torah, both revealed and hidden, think they have achieved some Torah and *yira*, but in truth, they have not merited even a tiny amount of Torah.

Of course, many felt that *chasidim*'s focus on *yira* went too far, a sentiment expressed here by R. Chaim of Volozhin:

נפש החיים שער ד

והן עתה בדורות הללו בעוה"ר נהפוך הוא. הגבוה השפל. שכמה וכמה שמו כל עיקר קביעת לימודם רוב הימים רק בספרי יראה ומוסר. באמרם כי זה כל האדם בעולמו לעסוק בהם תמיד. כי המה מלהיבים הלבבות אשר אז יכנע לבבו להכניע ולשבר היצר מתאוותיו. ולהתיישר במדות טובות. וכתר תורה מונח בקרן זוית. ובעיני ראיתי בפלך א' שכ"כ התפשט אצלם זאת. עד שברוב בתי מדרשם אין בהם רק ספרי מוסר לרוב. ואפי' ש"ס א' שלם אין בו. וטח עיניהם מראות מהבין והשכיל לבותם.

15. See the fifth letter in R. Yisrael Salanter's *Ohr Yisrael*.

16. **העמק דבר דברים ד:ט**

ע"י עסק פלפולה של תורה יכול להגיע לפעמים שנהפך לו לרועץ ח"ו.

to promote *yirat shamayim* and character development. Moreover, they warn that its absence can lead to a perversion of Torah – leaving a person, in the words of *Avot de-Rabi Natan* cited earlier, an armed weakling.

Where to Focus One's Attention

If this is the goal of the study of *machshava,* then not all *machshava* topics are equally vital. Thus, Rambam writes there are subjects that we need not focus on, as they do not lead to this end. One example is excessive contemplation of events surrounding the messianic era:

> **רמב"ם הלכות מלכים פרק יב הלכה ב**
> וכל אלו הדברים וכיוצא בהן לא ידע אדם איך יהיו עד שיהיו, שדברים סתומין הן אצל הנביאים, גם החכמים אין להם קבלה בדברים אלו, אלא לפי הכרע הפסוקים, ולפיכך יש להם מחלוקת בדברים אלו, **ועל כל פנים אין סדור הויית דברים אלו ולא דקדוקיהן עיקר בדת, ולעולם לא יתעסק אדם בדברי ההגדות, ולא יאריך במדרשות האמורים בענינים אלו וכיוצא בהן, ולא ישימם עיקר, שאין מביאין לא לידי יראה ולא לידי אהבה.**

> All of these and similar matters cannot be [clearly] known by man until they occur, for they are obscure in the words of the Prophets. Even the Sages have no established tradition regarding these matters beyond what is implied by Scripture; hence, there is divergence of opinion among them. **In any case, neither the sequence of these events nor their precise details are among the fundamental principles of the faith. One should not occupy himself at length with the Aggadot and Midrashim that deal with these and similar matters, nor should he deem them of prime importance, for they bring one to neither awe nor love [of God].**

Thus, according to Rambam, emphasis should be placed on principles of faith and matters that promote love and fear of God. Likewise, R. Dessler (*Michtav mei-Eliyahu* 4, p. 353) writes that there is no point in studying Aggadot if a person is left unaffected by the study.

The Need to Know God in Order to Fear God

Thus far, we have seen that the study of *machshava* is valuable insofar as it (a) motivates and inspires, igniting the emotional component of our relationship with God and (b) fosters an understanding of God.

These two functions support and build upon each other because one does not develop fear of heaven simply by reading books that discuss fear of heaven. Most Aggadot do not overtly deal with fear of heaven, but the presumption is that studying them naturally enhances our emotional devotion to God. As we saw in Rambam, understanding God leads to the fear of God. Thus, R. Chaim of Volozhin (1749–1821) told his son to be swift in publishing *Nefesh ha-Chaim* – a work largely built upon Kabbalistic sources that does not directly focus on fear of heaven per se – because the book will promote reverence and emotional fervor:

> **הקדמה לנפש החיים**
> ...שיתקבלו דברי בקונטרוס הללו **להשריש יראת ה׳ ותורה ועבודה זכה** בלב ישרי לב המבקשים דרכי ה׳.
>
> [Perhaps heaven will consider me meritorious enough that] my words in these essays be accepted [by people], **so that they implant fear of God, Torah, and unsullied service** [**of God**] in the hearts of those of upright heart who seek God's ways.

Ramchal (1707–1746) goes even further. In the opening line of *Mesillat Yesharim,* Ramchal powerfully expresses the tight connection between **knowledge** of certain principles and **fulfillment** of a person's purpose in the world:

> **פרק א בבאור כלל חובת האדם בעולמו**
> **יסוד החסידות ושרש העבודה התמימה הוא שיתברר ויתאמת אצל האדם מה חובתו בעולמו ולמה צריך שישים מבטו ומגמתו בכל אשר הוא עמל כל ימי חייו.** והנה מה שהורונו חכמינו זכרונם לברכה הוא, שהאדם לא נברא אלא להתענג על ה׳ ולהנות מזיו שכינתו שזהו התענוג האמיתי והעידון הגדול מכל העידונים שיכולים להמצא.

ומקום העידון הזה באמת הוא העולם הבא, כי הוא הנברא בהכנה המצטרכת לדבר הזה. אך הדרך כדי להגיע אל מחוז חפצנו זה, הוא זה העולם. והוא מה שאמרו זכרונם לברכה (אבות ד): העולם הזה דומה לפרוזדור בפני העולם הבא. והאמצעים המגיעים את האדם לתכלית הזה, הם המצוות אשר צונו עליהן האל יתברך שמו. ומקום עשיית המצוות הוא רק העולם הזה.

The foundation of saintliness and the root of perfection in the service of God lie in a person coming to see clearly and to recognize as a truth the nature of his duty in the world and the end towards which he should direct his vision and his aspiration in all of his labors all the days of his life. Our Sages of blessed memory have taught us that man was created for the sole purpose of rejoicing in God and deriving pleasure from the splendor of His presence, for this is the true joy and the greatest pleasure that possibly can be found. The place where this joy may be truly experienced is the world to come, which was created expressly to provide for it. However, the path to this destination is this world, as our Sages of blessed memory have said, "This world is like an antechamber to the world to come" (*Avot* 4:21). The means that lead a person to this goal are the *mitzvot* that we were commanded by God, may His Name be blessed. The place of the performance of the *mitzvot* is this world alone.[17]

In 13.6, we will explain what Ramchal means with respect to the purpose of creation, but for now, suffice it to note that the root of piety and service of God lies in **knowing** (and internalizing) certain things. Only if one knows the purpose of existence will he know how to function properly.

Rambam begins his *magnum opus* with a similar sentiment:

רמב"ם הלכות יסודי התורה פרק א הלכה א

יסוד היסודות ועמוד החכמות **לידע** שיש שם מצוי ראשון, והוא ממציא כל נמצא, וכל הנמצאים משמים וארץ ומה שביניהם לא נמצאו אלא מאמתת המצאו.

17. Translation adapted from www.shechem.org.

> The foundation of all foundations and the pillar of wisdom is to **know** that there is a Primary Being Who brought into being all existence. All the beings of the heavens, the earth, and what is between them came into existence only from the truth of His being.

To be a good Jew, one must **know** certain things – that is why we must study *machshava*. As we shall see throughout this work, Rambam's "knowing" and the Ramchal's "knowing" are not quite the same; nevertheless, that both works begin with the absolute religious imperative to know certain aspects of *machshava* is remarkable.[18]

3. Bringing Meaning to Observance and Life

Studying *machshava* will not affect only our religious worldview; it will affect all of our religious activities. Numerous Rishonim stress the value of understanding the nature of a *mitzva*. For example, Me'iri (1249–1310), in his Introduction to *Beit ha-Bechira*, writes that a *mitzva* will fulfill its purpose (ימשך לו מן המצוה ההיא מה שכיוון נותנה יתברך להמשך ממנה) only if we contemplate its purpose (שיתבונן בענין המצוה).

Along similar lines Rambam writes in *Moreh ha-Nevuchim* 3:51:

> In all cases in which you perform a *mitzva* merely with your limbs – as if you were digging a hole in the ground or hewing wood in the forest – without reflecting either upon the meaning of that action, upon Him whom the commandment proceeds, or upon

18. Many questions must be considered concerning the material that Rambam felt a person must know. For example, Rambam includes the basics of physics and metaphysics in the opening chapters of his great halachic work. Rambam writes that knowing these facts is not just a *mitzva* – it is the "foundation of all foundations." What exactly does Rambam mean when he says we must know these things? Another question: following the above statement, Rambam alludes to one of the four proofs for the existence of God explicated in *Moreh ha-Nevuchim*. Does Rambam believe that one must be able to *prove* the existence of God in order to fulfill the *mitzva* of *anochi* (the *mitzva* of belief)? We return to these questions in Chapter 8.

> the consequence of the action, you should not think that you have achieved the goal.[19]

Ramban likewise stresses the necessity of contemplating the implications of a *mitzva*, arguing that the awareness of the philosophical implications of a *mitzva* is necessary to completely fulfill the *mitzva*.[20] In Unit Ten, we will elaborate on this idea in the context of the reasons for *mitzvot*.

This component of Torah is not limited to *mitzvot*. Non-halachic material, including *mussar*, inspires a person how to live life in a way that studying halachic texts exclusively does not. Hence, so much of Torah is non-halachic. As Ramban (*Bereishit* 1:1) notes, this highlights the fundamental indispensability of the non-halachic portions of Torah. Gra (1720–1797), as quoted by his brother, puts the point very powerfully:

---

19. A similar point may emerge from *Mishneh Torah* as well. R. Mayer Twersky once observed that even though Rambam emphasizes the importance (perhaps requirement) of understanding the reasons for *mitzvot* (*Hilchot Me'ila* 8:6, *Hilchot Temura* 4:13), he does not include this endeavor in his list of areas of study in *The Laws of Torah Study* 1:11. (R. Twersky argued that even though Rambam uses the word ראוי, which might indicate a recommendation and not any obligation, Rambam uses the word ראוי when referring to an obligation that is not formally mandated. It is therefore perplexing that Rambam would omit this obligation from his description of the components of Torah study.)

    This omission might indicate that the requirement to suggest reasons for particular *mitzvot* emerges from the mitzva itself, as opposed to the general obligation to study Torah. Presumably, the reason for this anomaly (usually study stems from the obligation to study Torah) is that the quest for *ta'amei ha-mitzvot* (reasons for *mitzvot*) is speculative, since the Torah generally does not present the purpose of particular *mitzvot*. Thus, Rambam, as we saw above and along the lines of Me'iri, maintains that proper observance of a *mitzva* demands contemplation of the purpose of the mitzva.

20. **דרשת תורת ה' תמימה עמ' קנ (בתוך כל כתבי רמב"ן ח"א מהד' מוסד הרב קוק)**
וידוע כי העושה מצוה בלא כוונה, או מי שלא יתבונן בה, לא עשה בשלמות, אבל המתבונן בה, כגון קנה מזוזה בדינר, קבעה בפתחו **ונתכוון להתבונן בה ובענינה**, הנה הודה ביחוד ובחדוש העולם ובהשגחה, כי יציאת מצרים מורה על כל אלה הוראה שלמה, מלבד שידע כי חסד אלקים רב מאוד על עושי רצונו, שהוציאנו מאותה עבדות לכבוד גדול בזכות אבותינו הקדמונים החפצים ליראה אותו, הנה במצוה קלה הורה בכל שרשי האמונה והשלמות וכו'.

ספר מעלות התורה

ושמעתי מאחי הגאון ז״ל שורש הדבר, שבודאי ליכא למימר שלא יכנסו תחת גדר המצות רק תרי״ג מצות ולא יותר, שאם כן מבראשית ועד בא, אין בהם רק שלשה מצות, גם הרבה פרשיות שבתורה, שאין בהם שום מצוה, וזהו דבר שאין מתקבל, אלא באמת כל דבור ודבור שבתורה, שיצא מפי הגבורה, היא מצוה בפני עצמה.

I heard from my brother (i.e., Gra) that a person should not think that there are only 613 mitzvot. If this were so, then from Bereshit to Bo there would only be three mitzvot. Additionally, there are many parshiyot in the Torah that do not have any mitzva – a notion that is inconceivable. Rather, every utterance in the Torah that emerged from God's mouth is a mitzva in its own right.

4. Understanding the World

In addition, the study of *machshava* helps a person understand our sometimes mysterious world. For example, Ramchal's work *Da'at Tevunot* discusses why evil exists and how there is direction in history.

Ramban, too, makes this point. Having explained that there is indeed an aspect to the problem of evil that we cannot understand, Ramban wonders why we should even study the matter in the first place, since ultimately we must accept divine justice. He answers that this is the attitude of fools. The wise always seek to understand all that can be understood, even if they know they never will complete the task.[21] We must be lovers of wisdom, Ramban asserts.

---

21. **תורת האדם שער הגמול**

ואם תשאל עלינו כיון שיש ענין נעלם במשפט, ונצטרך להאמין בצדקו מצד שופט האמת יתברך ויתעלה, למה תטריח אותנו ותצוה עלינו ללמוד הטענות שפירשנו והסוד שרמזנו, ולא נשליך הכל על הסמך שנעשה בסוף שאין לפניו לא עולה ולא שכחה אלא שכל דבריו במשפט, **זו טענת הכסילים מואסי חכמה**, כי נועיל לעצמנו בלמוד שהזכרנו להיותנו חכמים ויודעי אלהים יתברך מדרך האל וממעשיו, ועוד נהיה מאמינים ובוטחים באמונתנו בנודע ובנעלם יותר מזולתנו.

If you ask: since there is a hidden matter anyway… why bother studying the claims (made by the various characters in the book of *Iyov*) and the secret that we alluded to… **This is the attitude of fools who despise wisdom.** For we shall benefit ourselves through the aforementioned study by becoming wise men who know God in the

Indeed, so much in the world mystifies us. Studying *machshava*, among other things, plays a key role in unlocking the secrets of life. The importance of living a thoughtful and reflective life and the need to unravel its enigmas is powerfully articulated by R. Avraham Yeshaya Karelitz (1878 –1953, known as the *Chazon Ish*) in the opening lines of *Emuna u-Bitachon*:

> **חזון איש אמונה וביטחון א:א**
> אם האדם הוא בעל נפש, ושעתו שעת השקט, חפשי מרעבון תאוני, ועינו מרהיבה ממחזה שמים לרום, והארץ לעומק, הוא נרגש ונדהם, כי העולם נדמה לפניו כחידה סתומה, כמוסה ונפלאה, והחידה הזאת מלפפת את לבבו ומוחו, והוא כמתעלף, לא נשאר בו רוח חיים, בלתי אל החידה כל מעינו ומגמתו, ודעת פתרונה כלתה נפשו, ונבחר לו לבוא באש ובמים בשבילה, כי מה לו ולחיים, אם החיים הנעימים האלו נעלמים ממנו תכלית ההעלם, ונפשו סחרחרה ואבלה וכמהה להבין סודה ולדעת שרשה והשערים ננעלו.
>
> If a person possesses of a sensitive soul, and it is a moment of tranquility free of physical craving, and he scans the heights of the heavens and depths of the earth, he is overwhelmed and astounded. For the world appears as an indecipherable riddle, mysterious and wondrous. This riddle grips his heart and mind. He feels faint, as though lifeless, for he is possessed by this mystery and yearns with his entire soul to solve it. He would opt to pass through fire and water for this [understanding]. What use is life to him, he feels, if this pleasant life is withheld from him?[22]

---

manner in which He acts and in His deeds. Moreover, we shall become believers endowed with a stronger faith in Him than others regarding matters known and unknown (consciously and subconsciously).

22. While *Chazon Ish* is not discussing the study of *machshava per se*, his comments nevertheless are instructive.

5. Responding to Challenges

R. Yosef Dov Soloveitchik (1903–1993) adds another fascinating reason why *machshava* should be studied and included in the curriculum of rabbinical training programs.[23] He boldly claims that had Second Commonwealth Judaism formulated its great moralistic doctrines in a philosophical vernacular, "Christianity would not have been able to boast throughout the ages that it had discovered new ethical horizons." One could add that had the thirteen principles of Rambam, such as the eternity of the Torah and the unique nature of Moshe's prophetic revelation, been formulated at that time, the absurdity of the Christian claims, which Rambam presents *post-facto*,[24] would have been far more apparent *ante-facto*, potentially heading off the schism. Instead, we formulated our ethical teachings and defined the parameters of revelation only in response to Christianity. To the extent possible, R. Soloveitchik argues, we must try to *preempt* challenges instead of *responding* to challenges. The way to do this is through the study of *machshava*.[25]

Thus, in addition to (a) igniting the emotional component of our relationship with God and (b) facilitating an understanding of God, studying *machshava* (c) guides our *avodat Hashem* and (d) gives us a perspective on the world and (e) allows us to answer both internal and external questions.

---

23. See *Community, Covenant and Commitment: Selected Letters and Communications* edited by R. Nathaniel Helfgot, pp. 100–101.

24. *Hilchot Yesodei ha-Torah*, Chapters 7–10.

25. R. Kook also maintained that *machshava* must be included as a component of yeshiva education. In a letter concerning the restoration of the *Sanhedrin*, R. Kook laments that there are many great Torah scholars who are experts in Halacha but lack basic proficiency in matters of *machshava*:

אגרת ת"ב (מחודש טבת תרע"ב, 1912), עמ' ס'

מובן הדבר שההוראות של כל התורה כוללות ג"כ ההוראות הרוחניות של הדעות והאמונות. ועל זה בודאי נהיה צריכים לייסד יסוד מוסד של קביעות לימוד . שהרי ישנם כמה ת"ח גאונים בהלכה, ומ"מ אינם יודעים את המקצוע העיקרי בתורה הנוגע לדעות ואמונות אלא ידיעות שטחיות...

A Transformative Experience

Ultimately, the goal of studying works of *machshava* is not simply to garner information or to understand Jewish philosophy; it is to instruct us how to live our lives, to illuminate our very being, and to connect us to God.

R. Moshe Chaim Luzatto highlights this notion when discriminating between Torah and other forms of wisdom. All other intellectual disciplines convey wisdom, but Torah conveys light. In the words of Yirmiyahu, it is the fire that ignites our soul: "'Is not My word like fire?' says God" הלוא כה דברי כאש נאם ה׳ (*Yirmiyahu* 23:29).

ספר דרך עץ חיים

כי לא כחכמות הנכריות וידיעות החול, שאינן אלא ידיעת דבר מה אשר ישיג השכל בטרחו - אך התורה הנה קודש ה׳, אשר לה מציאות גבוהה בגבהי מרומים. וכאשר יעסוק בה האדם למטה - אור היא אשר תאיר בנשמתו להגיע אותו אל גנזי מרומים, גנזי הבורא יתברך שמו, בדרך הארה ופעולה חזקה אשר היא פועלת בה.

[Torah] is not like the wisdom of the nations and secular knowledge, which are nothing more than knowledge that the intellect reaches after toiling to understand it. However, the Torah is the holiness of God; it has a supernal existence in the loftiest heights, and when a man toils in it below, it is a light that illuminates in his soul to elevate him to the treasures on high, the treasures of the Creator, may His Name be blessed.[26]

In this passage, Ramchal speaks of Torah learning in general, not specifically topics of Aggada or *machshava*. While every Torah topic is divine wisdom and helps a person to better understand God (and thus love and fear Him), the sources we discussed above indicate the singularity of topics in *machshava* in promoting understanding of God.[27]

---

26. Translation adapted from http://dafyomireview.com/article.php?docid=205.
27. In the preface printed at the beginning of every volume of his *Pachad Yitzchak,* R. Yitzchak Hutner explains why this is so:

We close with the words of R. Shlomo Wolbe who makes this point forcefully when addressing the task this work seeks to accomplish:

עלי שור חלק ב עמוד קמה

הלומד ספרי גדולינו העוסקים בהלכות יסודי התורה כדברי מחשבה מופשטת - אינו אלא טועה. אנחנו שואבים מהם *חיות* פנימית, והם מלמדים אותנו ללכת בעקבותיהם להגיע לפנימיות התורה בלבנו ובחיינו בלכתנו באורם.

One who studies the works of our great sages that address the fundamental principles of Torah (such as *Kuzari*, Rambam, Ramban, Maharal, and Ramchal) as abstract thought is erring. We draw inner *life* from them. The authors teach us how to follow in their footsteps and arrive at the inner truth of Torah in our hearts and our lives.

הערה כללית

דאף על גב דבכלליות התורה נוהג הוא החוק שהתלמוד מביא לידי מעשה; מכל מקום, לא הרי הבאה כהרי הבאה. יש הבאה ממקום קרוב, ויש הבאה ממקום רחוק. יש הבאה דרך עפיפה של מהירת הבזק, ויש הבאה בדרך 'אתנהלה לאטי'. דהנה חובות הדעות מתקיימות בכוח ההכרה שבנפש, וחובות הלבבות מתקיימות בכוח התחושה שבהרגשה, וחובות האיברים מתקיימות בכוח העשיה שבגוף, ואילו עסק הלימוד מתקיים הוא בכוח ההשגה שבשכל. ונמצא דבשעה שאנו אומרים שהלימוד מביא לידי קיום, אנו מתכונים באמת לשפע בעל ברכה משולשת. דממקום ההשגה שבשכל, זורמת היא הברכה למקום ההכרה שבנפש, ולמקום התחושה שבהרגשה, ולמקום העשיה שבגוף. וכאן עלינו לחלק בין שני הזרמים הראשונים ובין הזרם השלשי... ומפני שחיי הנפש הפנימיים קרובים יותר אל ההפשטה של אור הנשמה מאשר חיי המעשה החיצוניים, לכן תנועתם של גלגלי החיות הפנימית היא מהירה באין-ערוך מתנועת גלגלי החיות החיצוניות של כלי המעשה. ואשר על כן כשאדם לומד הלכות ציצית, והענין נקלט בכלי השגתו, הרי הדרך מן ההשגה הזו עד מעשה הלבישה של הציצית היא יותר ארוכה מאשר הדרך מן השגת אהבה בשכל עד התעוררות ענין האהבה בתחושתו. כי על כן גם ההשגה וגם התחושה הן מהדברים הנעשים בפנים, ותחומי פעולתם הם תכופים וסמוכים זה לזה. וכשם שמדה זו נוהגת בחובות הלבבות, כמו כן נוהגת היא גם בהלכות דעות. כשאדם רוצה לקיים מצות אמונה על פי דעותיה של תורה, והוא לומד עיקר אחד מעיקרי האמונה וקולטו בהשגתו - הרי השגה זו מעמידתו בתחום האמונה שהיא הקיום, באופן הרבה יותר תכוף מאשר השגה בהלכות סוכה מעמידתו בתחומה של עשיית הסוכה.

To paraphrase, he explains that studying sections of Torah dealing with practical halachot is only indirectly related to the actual performance of those halachot; the study is separate from the actions. When it comes to *mitzvot* of the heart and the mind, however, the study itself – being that it is a practice of the mind and heart – is already associated with the performance of those *mitzvot*.

1.2 THE *MITZVA* TO KNOW GOD: PHILOSOPHY VS. MYSTICISM

Earlier, we saw that the midrash tells us that studying Aggada helps one know God. Let us now consider the nature of the obligation to know God. Rambam acknowledges that there is no explicit verse in the Torah that commands us to know God; rather, Rambam writes (*Hilchot Yesodei ha-Torah* 4:13), five *mitzvot* require us to possess fundamental knowledge of God. These five *mitzvot* are:

1. *Anochi,* "I am Hashem, your God who took you out of Egypt" (*Shemot* 20:2), which demands of us that we know He exists (we shall explain this shortly).
2. *Lo yihyeh,* "You shall have no other gods before Me" (*Shemot* 20:3), which requires us not to consider the thought that there is another divinity aside from God.
3. *Shema Yisrael,* "Hear, Yisrael, Hashem is our God, Hashem is one" (*Devarim* 6:4), which calls on us to know of His oneness and accept His *mitzvot* (see *Sefer ha-Mitzvot, Aseh* 1).
4. *Ahavat Hashem,* "And you shall love Hashem, your God" (*Devarim* 6:5), which obliges us to love Him.
5. *Yirat Hashem,* "Fear Hashem, your God" (*Devarim* 6:13), which demands we fear Him.

Moreover, Rambam defines the Jewish people as those who know God:

> **הלכות עבודה זרה פרק א הלכה ג**
> ...והיה הדבר הולך ומתגבר בבני יעקוב ובנלווים עליהם, ונעשת בעולם אומה שהיא יודעת את ה'.
>
> This concept (monotheism) proceeded and gathered strength among the descendants of Yaakov and those who gathered around them until **a nation that knows God** was formed.

Accordingly, there are many verses that relate the importance of this directive. The following verses are quoted by R. Bachya ibn Pakuda (*Chovot ha-Levavot, Sha'ar ha-Yichud,* Ch. 3) as commanding us to know God:

א. (דברים ד:לט) **וידעת היום והשבת אל לבבך** כי ה׳ הוא האלוקים בשמים ממעל ועל הארץ מתחת אין עוד.[28]

ב. (דברי הימים א:כח) ואתה שלמה בני **דע את אלוהי אביך** ועבדהו בלב שלם ובנפש חפצה, כי כל לבבות דורש ה׳ וגו׳.

ג. (תהילים ק:ג) **דעו** כי ה׳ הוא האלוקים וגו׳.

ד. (תהילים צא:יד) אשגבהו כי **ידע שמי**.

ה. (ירמיה ט:כג) כי אם בזאת יתהלל המתהלל, **השכל וידוע אותי**.

1. **And you shall know and instill in your heart** that Hashem is God in heaven above and on the earth below, there is no other.
2. And Shlomo, my son, **know the God of your father** and serve Him with a complete heart and a willing soul, because God seeks all hearts.
3. **Know** that Hashem is God.
4. I (God) shall elevate him because he **knows My Name**.
5. Rather, let he that prides himself do so only in this: **that he understands and knows Me**.

Different thinkers use these verses to promote divergent educational protocols. Some, like R. Bachya (*ibid.*), argue that these verses inform us of the imperative to philosophically prove the oneness of God. Others, such as R. Shneur Zalman of Liadi (1745–1813), founder and first Rebbe of Chabad, understand these verses to be endorsing the understanding of God through mysticism.[29] And yet others acknowledge that there are multiple avenues by which one can fulfill this *mitzva*. One such thinker is R. Moshe Isserles, better known as Rama (1520–1572), who writes:

---

28. R. Bachya adds that from the verse in *Yeshaya* 44, "ולא ישיב אל לבו ולא דעת ולא תבונה", we infer that the phrase והשבות אל לבבך demands intellectual rigor.

29. תניא קונטרס אחרון על כמה פרקים
משא״כ בסדר ההשתלשלות אף אם משיג המציאות לא עדיף מצד עצמו כלימוד המצות שמשיג ותופס המהות ומעלה עליו כאילו קיים בפועל ממש כמ״ש זאת התורה כו׳ אלא **שידיעת המציאות מההשתלשלות היא ג״כ מצוה רבה ונשאה ואדרבה עולה על כולנה כמ״ש וידעת היום כו׳ דע את אלקי אביך כו׳ ומביאה ללב שלם כו׳ שהוא העיקר והשגת המציאות הוא להפשיט מגשמיות כו׳** רק שזו היא מצוה אחת מתרי״ג והאדם צריך לקיים כל תרי״ג לפי שהן השתלשלות המהות דחיצונית דכלים דאצי׳ לכך צריך להרבות בלימוד כל התרי״ג וקיומן בפועל ממש במחדו״מ שהן בי״ע לברר בירורין אשר שם.

שו"ת הרמ"א סימן ז

אבל לא אסרו ללמוד דברי החכמים וחקירתם במהות המציאות וטבעיהן כי אדרבה על ידי זה נודע גדולתו של יוצר בראשית יתברך... ואף כי למקובלים דעת אחרת בזו - אלו ואלו דברי אלקים חיים. ואף כי חכמי אומות העולם אמרו, כבר אמרו במגילה פ"ק: כל מי שאומר דבר חכמה אף באומות נקרא חכם.

> But they did not prohibit studying the words of the wise and their investigations about the essence of existence and its nature; on the contrary, the greatness of the Creator becomes apparent through their words… And even though the Kabbalists have a different perspective [on the correct way to know God], both views are the words of a living God. And even though these things (i.e., philosophy) were said by the wise men of the nations of the world (i.e., non-Jews), it states in the first chapter of *Masechet Megilla* that anyone who says words of wisdom, even from the nations, is called a "wise man."

The context of Rama's comments is fascinating. He was responding to R. Shlomo Luria, also known as Maharshal (1510–1574), another great sage, who criticized Rama's reference to Aristotle (as well as his poor grammar). Rama responded that everyone agrees to the importance of pursuing what R. Dr. Isadore Twersky called meta-Halacha, that which is beyond Halacha.[30] (When we use the term Halacha in this context we are not simply referring to the practical law, but all matters pertaining to Torah law.) There are two primary avenues to do this – philosophy (i.e. attempting to understand God through the intellect as was done in classical Jewish philosophy) and Kabbala – and Rama argued that both are legitimate.[31] Rama wrote, however, that he prefers

30. See R. Isadore Twersky, "Religion and Law," in *Religion in a Religious Age*, ed. Alexander Altmann (Cambridge, MA: Harvard University Press, 1980), 69–82.

31. Other thinkers besides Rama write about the value of both avenues. See, for example, R. Kook's מאמרי הראיה - לאחדותו של הרמב"ם, which we will quote in section 1.8. Rama, in *Torat ha-Ola*, even attempts to merge philosophy and Kabbala. However, even as most of the great sages pursued some form of meta-Halacha, Prof. Twersky shows that few engaged in both philosophy and Kabbala. That is not to say that Kabbalists lacked awareness of or appreciation for Jewish philosophers. In 2.9, we

philosophy,[32] as it is less dangerous.[33] Rama added, though, that he did not study philosophy from sources containing heresy, but rather from Rambam's *Moreh ha-Nevuchim*. Moreover, he did not pursue these matters during times when others were studying Halacha; instead, he engaged in this quest when others were relaxing, such as on Shabbat and *chol ha-mo'eid*.[34]

What Does Knowing God Mean?

In Chapter 10 we shall better define what Rambam means when he states that a person must know God. For now, let us clarify that, as the above five *mitzvot* indicate, Rambam is not just referring to knowing about God. Were that the case, it would not relate to *mitzvot* such as love and fear which are, at their core, emotions. How then should we define the word *yedi'a* in this context?

I am not aware of a single English word that encapsulates what Rambam means by *yedi'a*. Numerous places in Scripture associate the word *yedi'a* with love.[35] Certainly, knowing about God plays a role, but mere knowledge is insufficient. Consider the following analogy: Imagine I read a profile about another person. The profile contains an immense amount of infor-

---

will see how many Kabbalistic works, such as *Tanya* (Ch. 4) and *Nefesh ha-Chaim* (1:1), quote and incorporate ideas from *Moreh ha-Nevuchim*.

32. Rama's view on the value of philosophy is complex, as can be seen in his formulation in *Yoreh Dei'a* (246:4): "A person should study only Scripture, Mishna, Gemara, halachic decisors (*poskim*), and those that follow them… but a person should not study other branches of wisdom. Nevertheless, it is permitted to study other branches of wisdom occasionally (*be-akra'i*)." We consider this ambiguity in 1.7.

33. Later, we will return to the dangers that lurk in the study of each of these fields.

34. Not everyone agrees with this advice. As we saw in 1.1, many works, from *Chovot ha-Levavot* to *Mesillat Yesharim*, criticize those who focus on the intricacies of the Talmud without devoting sufficient attention to the fundamental sections of Judaism. While most mainstream thinkers stress the necessity of Talmudic analysis, different formulas have been presented to balance these different components.

35. See *Amos* (3:2): רַק אֶתְכֶם יָדַעְתִּי מִכֹּל מִשְׁפְּחוֹת הָאֲדָמָה where Rashi and Metzudot translate ידעתי as אהבתי. Likewise, consider *Bereishit* (18:19) concerning God's selection of Avraham: כִּי יְדַעְתִּיו לְמַעַן אֲשֶׁר יְצַוֶּה אֶת בָּנָיו וְאֶת בֵּיתוֹ אַחֲרָיו. Rashi, citing numerous scriptural precedents, notes the term ידעתי connotes affection, love, and intimacy. Ramban explains the connection between the literal meaning of the word (knowing) and the connotation of the word (loving): אמנם עיקר כולם לשון ידיעה, שהמחבב את האדם ומקרבו אצלו יודעו, ומכירו, meaning that one who cherishes a person and draws close to him *knows* him and becomes familiar with him.

mation, accurately describing the physical and emotional characteristics of the individual. While we might say I know about the individual, we would not say that I *know* the individual. For that, I would need to meet them or at least communicate with them. Likewise, *yedi'a* connotes acquaintanceship and relationship. Consider that the Torah (euphemistically) uses the verb to refer to physical intimacy, as in *Bereishit* 4:1, which clearly has nothing to do with information. We will further discuss the meaning of this term in 8.2.

Why Must We Know God to Love God?

While knowing about God, to the extent humanly possible, does not guarantee love of God, it does play a critical role in the formation of the relationship we all strive to have with Him. Indeed, Rambam stresses that the relationship is defined by this knowledge.

> **רמב"ם הלכות תשובה פרק י הלכה ו**
> אינו אוהב הקב"ה אלא בדעת שידעהו, ועל פי הדעה תהיה האהבה אם מעט מעט ואם הרבה הרבה.

> The degree of one's love depends on the degree of one's knowledge! A small [amount of knowledge arouses] a lesser love. A greater [amount of knowledge arouses] a greater love.

Why is it that knowledge is necessary for love? And why does Rambam maintain that love is contingent upon the degree of knowledge? We will address these problems in 10.1 (based on an analysis of *Moreh ha-Nevuchim* 1:68 and 3:51) and in 10.2 (based on *Sefer ha-Mitzvot* and *Moreh ha-Nevuchim* 3:54). However, in this introductory chapter, it may be helpful to seek a more intuitive answer to these basic questions.

If I love someone, but do not truly understand them, can it be said that I love them? Yes and no. To illustrate, if I am asked whom do I love, I can point to a physical body. However, it is not the physical body that I love – it is the person, and I do not know the person. Still, I can at least identify them. However, with respect to God, that is impossible. He has no body to which I can point. To point to God, I must be able to describe Him and have some frame of reference. Therefore, I must know God to some degree, in order to love Him.

The matter runs deeper. In the above analogy of the human that I do not really know, my love is incomplete. For example, it is possible the person is cruel to others, though he is nice to me. If I knew that, I might not love him. Moreover, I have no appreciation of the object of my love if I lack any understanding of who they are and what they accomplished. Consider the following analogy suggested by my teacher R. Aaron Lopiansky: Imagine the young grandchild of the *gadol ha-dor* (universally recognized Torah scholar). The child loves sitting on the lap of his grandfather and pulling on his long white beard. A powerful bond develops between the two of them, with much time spent frolicking together, before the grandfather passes away when the child is five. Can we say the child knows his grandfather? He knows nothing of the books he authored, the Torah he taught, and the ideas he championed. He knows a sweet man with a white beard, but he does not know the *gadol ha-dor*. Compare this relationship with someone who never met this particular *gadol ha-dor* but has studied all of his writings and read about his accomplishments. Surely, he knows much more about the *gadol* than the young child, though he lacks a certain closeness. Ultimately, the relationship of each of these people with the *gadol ha-dor* is incomplete, albeit for opposite reasons.

Thus, a relationship with God must be rooted in both the experiential and intellectual. Surely it is shaped by our interactions with our Father Who created, raised, supports, and loves us. But, if we have no understanding of God, then our love is lacking because we do not know the recipient of our love. While we will never fully understand Him, to the extent that we study His works, we are able to form a true relationship with Him. Thus, Rambam writes that the degree of love is indeed contingent upon the degree of knowledge.

What Philosophical Topics Are of Interest?

We have already used the word "philosophy" several times, but it may prove helpful to define what exactly we mean. We shall first address this generally, and then more specifically.

In *Mishneh Torah,* for example, Rambam does not write that one must study philosophy. Rather, he instructs us to try to understand God to the best of our ability. The *yesodei ha-Torah* (principles of Torah) provide some sort of definition of what we mean by God, how we know He exists, the nature of that which he created, and how He relates to the universe. All of these principles are referred to in the Torah but can be better understood using the intellect. Thus, by "philosophy" we mean cognizng God through the mind.

Though this is true in a general sense, defining the term "philosophy" precisely proves tricky, as the term has multiple connotations. "Philosophy" could refer to either:

(a) a specific method of inquiry (e.g., rationalism),
(b) a particular set of topics (e.g., metaphysics), or
(c) a particular set of teachings (e.g., Aristotle).[36]

For the moment, let us focus on the second definition of philosophy (a particular set of topics). Philosophers are interested in all sorts of questions. What sort of inquiries interest the traditional thinkers we will be studying in this book? As we note in the preface to Volume Two, the works cited here have a somewhat narrow area of inquiry, because their goal was not pursuing philosophy in general, but rather arriving at an understanding of God. For example, none of these thinkers (as far as I know) would advocate the study of aesthetics (questions like "What makes something art?" or "What is beauty?"), since it has no direct relation to understanding God and improving one's *emuna*.

---

36. In contemporary language, "philosophy" generally is used in one or both of the first two senses. Likewise, in traditional sources, the term "philosophy" refers to both (a) and (b), namely, those areas of study (both in terms of methodology and basic topics) that pertain to the existence of God and His relationship to the universe as well as philosophical prerequisites to such study (e.g., epistemology).

In the *teshuvat ha-Rama* cited above, the term philosophy is used in the first and third sense. Rama contrasts philosophy with Kabbala with respect to methodology, with philosophy referring to the attempt to understand God rationally with the source of information being the intellect (a). The source of Kabbala, on the other hand, is revelation and tradition.

Sometimes, when *poskim* (halachic decisors) discuss "the study of philosophy" they intend the third definition (c), referring specifically to Aristotle's *Prior Analytics*, *Posterior Analytics*, *Physics*, and *Metaphysics*. Thus, when Maharshal prohibits the study of Aristotle he means the study of Aristotle, while Rama permits it as long as it is pursued occasionally (*be-akra'i*) and not studied directly from the source (but rather from Rambam's *Moreh ha-Nevuchim*).

In this volume, the intended meaning of the term "philosophy" will usually be clear from context. When it is not, we shall attempt to clarify.

While this focus might imply a narrow range of interest, it is not always obvious what will bring a person to a greater understanding of God. Rambam, for instance, wrote a treatise on logic and devotes several chapters of *Moreh ha-Nevuchim* to discussing physics. This is because Rambam felt that both of these disciplines are necessary to correctly understand God. Ibn Ezra, cited in the next section, advocates pursuing all wisdom (כל החכמות) in order to know God. Likewise, several sources advocate the study of all "seven branches of wisdom." According to R. Bachya b. Asher, the seven branches include logic (and language), mathematics, geometry, music, astronomy, science, and divine wisdom (i.e., theology).[37] Thus, while frequently thought of as secular subjects, they are valuable insofar as they are not truly secular; that is, assuming they succeed in bringing a person closer to God.

R. Kook may go further than all previous thinkers in this regard, maintaining that everything that exists is a manifest expression of godliness such that all reality is suffused with holiness. Accordingly, R. Kook maintains that there is value to studying everything (including art) to gain a better understanding of the Divine.[38] R. Kook even advocates that "no thought in the world is ever superfluous – **there is nothing that**

37. There are numerous variations of exactly what these seven branches are (see *Sheim ha-Gedolim* 51). R. Bachya (*Avot* 3:18, p. 591 in the *Mosad ha-Rav Kook* edition) lists the following:

א) חכמת ההגיון, ב) חכמת המספר, ג) חכמת המדות, ד) חכמת הטבע, ה) חכמת התכונה, ו) חכמת הניגון, ז) חכמת האלקות.

Moreover, R. Bachya stresses that Torah includes (if one knows how to learn it properly) all branches of wisdom.

רבינו בחיי שמות כה:לא

ועל דרך השכל המנורה בשבעה נרותיה תרמוז לתורה הנקראת אור, שנאמר: (משלי ו:כג) "כי נר מצוה ותורה אור", **והיא כוללת שבע חכמות** ועל כן היו נרותיה שבעה, וששה קנים יוצאים מצדיה כנגד ששה קצוות של עולם התלוים בתורה שנתנה בששה בסיון שהעולם מתקיים בשבילה.

Gra's list (cited in *Kol ha-Tor* 829) differs:

א) חכמת החשבון התכונה והמדידה, ב) חכמת היצירה וההרכבה, ג) חכמת הרפואה והצמיחה, ד) חכמת ההגיון הדקדוק והמשפט, ה) חכמת הנגינה והקדושה, ו) חכמת התיקון והשילוב, ז) חכמת הביגו"ר (בין גשם ורוח) וכחות הנפש.

On the value of pursuing all seven branches of wisdom, see R. Yisrael of Shklov's Introduction to *Pe'at ha-Shulchan* and Netziv's *Kidmat ha-Eimek* and *Ha'ameik Davar Bamidbar* 8:2.

38. This relates to R. Kook's panentheistic outlook (panentheism means that the world exists within God, not to be confused with pantheism: pantheism = all is God; panentheism = all is within God). We will consider his perspective more in 12.2–5.

does not have its place – because all comes out of the Source of wisdom" (*Orot ha-Kodesh* 1:17–18).[39] As Prof. Benjamin Ish-Shalom points out, for R. Kook, every facet of society and expression of culture is a revelation of something holy.[40] Thus, R. Kook charges his readers to see the entire world holistically "through the light of the *shechina*" (*ibid.* 1:83). We elaborate upon this notion in 2.15 when considering the value in studying heretical literature.

1.3 TWO PATHS TO KNOWING GOD: META-HALACHA AND HALACHA

Many sources point to the significance of studying matters beyond Halacha. Even thinkers known for their halachic contribution stressed the importance of non-halachic study. R. Shlomo b. Aderet, or Rashba (1235–1310), besides writing responsa, a commentary on the Talmud, and halachic works, wrote a commentary on Aggada.[41] R. Avraham ibn Ezra (1089–1167), writes that man was created to know God:[42]

---

39. Thus, R. Kook valued even the "problematic" philosophers such as Bergson, Nietzsche, and Schopenhauer.

40. *Rav Avraham Itzhak Hacohen Kook: Between Rationalism and Mysticism*, Albany, NY: SUNY Press, 1993, 81

41. Moreover, without advocating the study of philosophy, Rashba maintains that faith should be rooted in investigation and consideration of alternative possibilities. Thus, when asked to explain what a person should contemplate when reciting *shema*, he responds that the *mitzva* of *shema* demands exploration:

שו"ת הרשב"א חלק ה סימן נה

צריכין אנו להתבונן שאין אמונתו וייחודו מצות אנשים מלומדה שהלימוד שלימדהו והרגי־לוהו עליו יביאוהו להאמין ככה שלא הונח על חקירת דעתו וחכמתו יחויב בהפך כאשר יקרא לרוב האמונות. רק אנחנו חייבים לשמוע ולחקור אחר השמיעה והחקירה שהחקירה האמתית תחויב ותכריע על ככה... וכאן ר"ל באומרו שמע ישראל, כולל ג' ענינים שנצטוינו לשמוע וללמוד כי לולי שנשמע ונלמוד לא נתבונן אליו. ואחרי השמיעה והלימוד וחיקור היטב אם יש ראיה סותרת ח"ו. ואחר שנבא מתוך השמיעה אל החקירה באמת תביאנו החקירה ותכריחנו הכרח אמתי לקבל ולהאמין כי הוא ית' נמצא וכן הוא משגיח על פרטי מעשנו.

We must contemplate that our faith is not rote and unsubstantiated… Rather, we are commanded to listen [to theological teachings] and what we have heard and to study them. For if we do not hear and study them, we never will come to contemplate them, for true investigation will prove our belief… Thus the word "*shema*" indicates that we must do three things: 1) to listen and learn, because without that we cannot contemplate, 2) to thoroughly investigate if there is any counterevidence, and this will lead to 3) acceptance and belief that He exists and oversees our actions.

This citation relates to the broader question concerning the basis for faith, discussed in Unit 3.

42. Likewise, consider the following statement from Rama:

ר׳ אברהם אבן עזרא הושע ו:ג

שנרדפה לדעת את ה׳ כי זה סוד כל החכמות **ובעבור זה לבדו נברא האדם** רק לא יוכל לדעת את השם עד שילמד חכמות הרבה שהם כמו סולם לעלות אל זאת המעלה העליונה וטעם כשחר כי בתחילה ידע המשכיל השם יתברך במעשיו כמו השחר בצאתו ורגע אחר רגע יגדל האור עד שיראה האמת.

We should hurry to know God, for this is the secret of all wisdoms, and **for this reason alone man was created**. But man cannot know God until he studies many disciplines of wisdom, for they all are like a ladder to reach this elevated plane... One first knows God via [studying] His actions...

The Meaning of Ma'aseh Merkava

How can ibn Ezra claim that knowing God is the purpose of man's creation if the focus of Scripture and Talmud does not seem to be the knowledge of God?

Ibn Ezra might respond that the assumption of this question is false. There are numerous verses in Tanach, like those cited above, that emphasize the centrality of knowing God (e.g., *Yirmiyahu* 9:23 "Rather, let he that prides himself do so only in this: that he understands and knows Me"). Likewise, a remarkable Talmudic passage highlights the preeminence of this pursuit when it classifies "*ma'aseh merkava*" as *davar gadol* (a great matter), whereas the dialectics of Abayei and Rava (i.e., the halachic portions of the Talmud) are termed *davar katan* (a little matter):

תורת העולה חלק ג פרק ז

והנה מכל מקום עדיף טפי לחקור על הדברים ולידע אותם במופתים ובמושכלים ע״י חקירה **וזוהי תכלית האדם.**

While one may rely upon tradition, it is preferable to search for the cause of things and know them through proofs and investigation, **and this is the purpose of man.**

תלמוד בבלי מסכת בבא בתרא קלד עמוד א
אמרו עליו על רבן יוחנן בן זכאי שלא הניח מקרא ומשנה גמרא הלכות ואגדות דקדוקי תורה ודקדוקי סופרים וקלין וחמורין וגזרות שוות ותקופות וגמטריאות ומשלות כובסים ומשלות שועלים שיחת שדים ושיחת דקלים ושיחת מלאכי השרת ודבר גדול ודבר קטן **דבר גדול מעשה מרכבה ודבר קטן הויות דאביי ורבא.**

They said regarding R. Yochanan b. Zakkai that he studied all of Tanach, Mishna, Talmud, Halachot, Aggadot…the great matter, and the little matter. **"The great matter" refers to *ma'aseh merkava,* and "the little matter" refers to the debates of Abayei and Rava.**

What exactly is meant by *ma'aseh merkava*? Literally, this term means "the account of the chariot" and refers to the description of God's chariot in the books of *Yeshaya* (Ch. 6) and *Yechezkeil* (Ch. 1, 3, and 10). Broadly speaking, the term refers to the attempt to know and understand God. Thus, many thinkers understand this term as referring to Kabbala. These thinkers maintain that the primary way of understanding God is through mysticism. Rambam also maintains that *ma'aseh merkava* is the means by which we understand God. According to Rambam, however, this is accomplished through philosophy.

Rambam's Understanding of Ma'aseh Merkava

Rambam writes that the first two chapters of *Mishneh Torah* discuss *ma'aseh merkava,* which Rambam understands as referring to divine science,[43] while the next two chapters examine *ma'aseh bereishit,* which Rambam understands as referring to natural science. Rambam notes that the Talmud refers to these topics as *pardeis* (literally "orchard").

43. Earlier Hebrew translations of the *Introduction to Moreh ha-Nevuchim* utilize the term חכמת האלוהות; "divine science" is the translation provided by Prof. Shlomo Pines from the original Arabic.

רמב"ם הלכות יסודי התורה פרק ד הלכה י

כל הדברים האלו שדיברנו בעניין זה, כמר מדלי הם; ודברים עמוקים הם, אבל אינם כעומק עניין פרק ראשון ושני. וביאור כל אלו הדברים שבפרק שלישי ורביעי, הוא הנקרא מעשה בראשית...

These matters have been discussed very briefly here and are deep matters, but not as deep as those discussed in the first two chapters. The matters discussed in these [latter] two chapters are those relating to creation (*ma'aseh bereishit*).

שם הלכה יג

ועייני ארבעה פרקים אלו שבחמש מצוות האלו - הם שחכמים הראשונים קוראין אותן פרדס, כמו שאמרו ארבעה נכנסו לפרדס: ואף על פי שגדולי ישראל היו וחכמים גדולים היו, לא כולם היה בהן כוח לידע ולהשיג כל הדברים על בוריין.

These four chapters have discussed the first five commandments (*anochi, lo yihyeh, shema Yisrael, ahavat Hashem,* and *yirat Hashem*) and are what the Early Sages called *pardeis,* as it is written (*Chagiga* 14b), "Four people went to study *pardeis,* etc." Even though those four people were giants of Israel and very great sages, not all of them had the capability to understand and comprehend these matters.

Next, Rambam explains why even though Chazal call *ma'aseh merkava* a great thing, it should not be studied initially.

ואני אומר שאין ראוי להיטייל בפרדס, אלא מי שנתמלא כרסו לחם ובשר. ולחם ובשר זה, הוא לידע ביאור האסור והמותר וכיוצא בהן משאר המצוות. **ואף על פי שדברים אלו, דבר קטן קראו אותם חכמים, שהרי אמרו חכמים דבר גדול מעשה מרכבה, ודבר קטן הוויה דאביי ורבא, אף על פי כן, ראויין הן להקדימן: שהן מיישבין דעתו של אדם תחילה, ועוד שהן הטובה הגדולה שהשפיע הקדוש ברוך הוא ליישוב העולם הזה, כדי לנחול חיי העולם הבא.** ואפשר שיידעם הכול - **גדול וקטן, איש ואישה, בעל לב רחב ובעל לב קצר.**

> I say that it is not fitting to study *pardeis* unless one first has studied what is metaphorically called "bread and meat," which is the study of *mitzvot:* what is permitted, what is forbidden, and the like. **These matters were called "a little matter" by the Sages, as they have said, "*Ma'aseh merkava* is a great matter, whereas the debates of Abayei and Rava are a little matter." Nevertheless, it still is fitting to study them (*mitzvot*) first, because they settle a man's mind. Furthermore, they are the great good that God gave to this world, [the means] by which we can inherit life in the world to come. It is possible for everyone – adults, children, men, women, those of broad understanding and those of limited understanding – to know these matters.**

In fact, Rambam understands that the study of science and philosophy, when pursued in the proper context, is a fulfillment of the *mitzva* to study Torah. Rambam writes that a person must divide his Torah study into three parts (at least at the beginning of his education[44]). One third should be spent on Scripture, one third on the oral law, and one third on what the Talmud refers to as "*talmud.*"

> **רמב"ם הלכות תלמוד תורה פרק א הלכה יב**
> כיצד היה בעל אומנות והיה עוסק במלאכתו שלש שעות ביום ובתורה תשע, אותן התשע קורא בשלש מהן בתורה שבכתב ובשלש בתורה שבעל פה ובשלש אחרות מתבונן בדעתו להבין דבר מדבר, ודברי

44. Later, Rambam writes:

> במה דברים אמורים, בתחילת תלמודו של אדם; אבל כשיגדיל בחכמה ולא יהיה צריך לא ללמוד תורה שבכתב, ולא לעסוק תמיד בתורה שבעל פה - יקרא בעיתים מזומנים תורה שבכתב ודברי השמועה, כדי שלא ישכח דבר מדברי דיני תורה, ויפנה כל ימיו לתלמוד בלבד, לפי רוחב ליבו ויישוב דעתו.
>
> This pertains to when one first starts to learn Torah, but once he has matured in wisdom, and he no longer needs to learn the written Torah or the oral Torah [as much]. One nevertheless should read occasionally from the written Torah and matters of tradition so that he will not forget any part of the Torah law, and he should devote all his time to learning "*talmud.*"

קבלה בכלל תורה שבכתב הן ופירושן בכלל תורה שבעל פה, **והענינים הנקראים פרדס בכלל הגמרא הן.**

How is division of time done? If one has a profession at which he works for three hours a day, and he learns Torah for nine hours, then of those nine hours, one should learn the written Torah for three, the oral Torah for another three, and for the remaining three one should contemplate what one learnt [in the first six hours] and comprehend how matters can be inferred from one another. The works of the Prophets and the holy writings (Nach) are counted as part of the written Torah, whereas explanations of them are part of the oral Torah. ***Pardeis* is part of *talmud*.**

Rambam understands that this last category, *talmud,* refers to analysis and extrapolation, which includes *pardeis.*[45] Thus, the study of *ma'aseh merkava,* which Rambam understands as referring to divine science or metaphysics, and *ma'aseh bereishit,* which Rambam understands as referring to natural science, constitute a fulfillment of the *mitzva* to learn Torah.[46]

R. Mayer Twersky has argued that the study of contemporary science does not constitute a fulfillment of the *mitzva* to study Torah according to Rambam. We will explore why this may be in 2.9, where we elaborate on Rambam's understanding of *ma'aseh bereishit.*[47]

The Source for Rambam's Understanding of Ma'aseh Merkava

As noted, *ma'aseh merkava* refers to the account of God's chariot depicted in the beginning of *Yechezkeil.* What then is the source for Rambam's scientific/philosophical understanding?

---

45. Proof for Rambam's contention that *ma'aseh merkava* is considered *talmud* can be gleaned from *Mishlei Rabbati,* Ch. 10 (see also *Nefesh ha-Chaim* 4:2).
46. See *Hilchot Rotzei'ach* 5:5–6, where Rambam writes that a father is involved in a *mitzva* when he teaches his son Torah, ***chochma,*** or a trade. In this case, Rambam defines Torah narrowly and does not include *chochma* as part of Torah. This seems to indicate that while the study of *chochma* may constitute a fulfillment of *talmud Torah,* it nevertheless is distinct from essential Torah insofar as it is independently derived.
47. We address Rambam's understanding of *ma'aseh merkava* in Chapter 8.

In *Moreh ha-Nevuchim* Rambam offers an esoteric explanation of the account in *Yechezkeil,* but emphasizes in the Introduction to Book II that it is based on conjecture and may be wrong insofar as it is not rooted in a received tradition or revelation:

> There is the fact that in that which has occurred to me with regard to these matters I followed conjecture and supposition; no divine revelation has come to me to teach me that the intention in the matter in question was such and such, nor did I receive what I believe in these matters from a teacher. But the texts of the prophetic books and the dicta of the Sages, together with the speculative premises that I possess, showed me that things are indubitably so and so. Yet it is possible that they are different and that something else is intended.

Halakhic Man's Perspective on Ma'aseh Merkava

However, philosophy and mysticism are not the only ways to know God. R. Yosef Dov Soloveitchik writes: "Halakhic man's approach to reality is, at the outset, devoid of any element of transcendence" (*Halakhic Man,* p. 17). Rather, Halacha is the blueprint for the *ideal* world.[48] At the same time, the halachic perspective gives man the greatest possible glimpse of God. As R. Lichtenstein writes in summing up R. Soloveitchik's approach:

> Torah study gives the Jew insight – as direct and profound as man is privileged to attain – into the revealed will of his Creator. **Through the study of Halakha – the immanent expression of God's transcendent rational will – man's knowledge of God gains depth and scope.** Further, religious study is a stimulus to the total spiritual personality. Faith can be neither profound nor enduring unless the intellect is fully and actively engaged in the quest for God.[49]

48. **איש ההלכה עמ' 28**
"מהותה של ההלכה שקיבלה מאת הקב"ה היא יצירת עולם אידיאלי והכרת היחס השורר בינו למציאות על כל תופעותיה שרשיה ועיקריה.

49. "R. Joseph Soloveitchik," in *Great Jewish Thinkers of the Twentieth Century*, S. Noveck, ed. (NY, 1963), p. 290.

Thus, the study of Halacha, even more than the study of *machshava,* facilitates a communion with God. According to R. Soloveitchik:

> When a person delves into God's Torah and reveals its inner light and splendor ... and enjoys the pleasure of creativity and innovation, **he merits communion with the Giver of the Torah. The ideal of clinging to God is realized by means of the coupling of the intellect with the Divine Idea that is embodied in rules, laws, and traditions**... However, halachic knowledge does not remain sealed off in the realm of the intellect. It bursts forth into one's existential consciousness and merges with it... The idea turns into an impassioning and arousing experience; knowledge into a divine fire; strict and exacting halachic discipline turns into a passionate love burning with a holy flame. Myriads of black letters, into which have been gathered reams of laws, explanations, questions, problems, concepts and measures, descend from the cold and placid intellect, which calmly rests on its subtle abstractions and its systematic frameworks, **to the heart full of trembling, fear, and yearning and turn into sparks of the flame of a great experience that sweeps man to his Creator.**[50]

Similar to Rambam's description of how contemplation of the universe sparks feelings of fear and yearning, R. Soloveitchik describes how the study of Halacha produces such feelings. Of course, this does not mean there is no value in the study of *machshava*. Indeed, *machshava* comprised a significant component of R. Soloveitchik's teaching and writing. Nevertheless, the study of halachic texts is the primary way of communing with God.

The notion that the study of Halacha creates the closest possible connection to God is rooted in R. Chaim of Volozhin's understanding of *Torah li-shma* (the highest form of Torah study), developed in the fourth section of *Nefesh ha-Chaim.* R. Chaim writes that when we study

50. *Al Ahavat ha-Torah* in *Be-Sod ha-Yachid ve-ha-Yachad,* ed. Pinchas Peli (Jerusalem: Orot, 1976), pp. 410–411; translation adapted from that of R. Ronnie Ziegler https://etzion.org.il/en/14-intellect-and-experience.

Halacha we are clinging to God in the greatest conceivable way since, as the *Zohar* says, "He and His will are one." Torah is the greatest expression of His will. Accordingly, when we study Torah we are connecting to Him.[51] Significantly, it is not the inspirational parts of Torah, such as *Tehillim,* that best facilitate communion with God, but the study of His laws. To support this contention, R. Chaim cites a midrash (Midrash *Shocheir Tov Tehillim* 1) that records King David's request for God to attribute to *Tehillim* the same status as tractates *Nega'im* and *Ohalot.* Implicit in his request is the assumption that the study of these tractates would otherwise be superior to the recitation of *Tehillim.* Moreover, the midrash does not record God's response to King David's request. This implies that, in the final analysis, reciting *Tehillim* is not equivalent to the study of *Nega'im* and *Ohalot.*[52]

For R. Chaim, this midrash indicates that diligent study of the tractates of the oral law is of greater value than the recitation of *Tehillim.* As such, he argues that one cannot define *Torah li-shma* as the study of Torah in order to emotionally cleave to God (as numerous chasidic sources had done[53]). If this were correct, why would reciting *Tehillim* be on a lower level than the intricate tractates of *Nega'im* and *Ohalot*? Rather, the ultimate goal of Torah study is not merely to cleave to the Divine, but

---

51. **נפש החיים שער ד פרק ו**
ויכוין להתדבק בלימודו בו בתורה בו בהקב"ה. היינו להתדבק בכל כחותיו לדבר ה' זו הלכה. ובזה הוא דבוק בו ית' ממש כביכול. כי הוא ית' ורצונו חד כמ"ש בזוהר. וכל דין והלכה מתורה הקדושה. הוא רצונו ית' שכן גזרה רצונו שיהא כך הדין כשר או פסול טמא וטהור אסור ומותר חייב וזכאי.

52. When R. Chaim implies *Tehillim* is on a lower level than the study of Torah, I believe he means the emotional connection to God achieved through the recitation of *Tehillim* is lower than the intellectual connection achieved through Torah study (understanding of God's will). However, R. Chaim agrees that ideal Torah study is not limited to the practical law. Indeed, he emphasizes that even Aggada reflects God's will and therefore constitutes Torah study on the highest level:

נפש החיים שער ד פרק ו
אם הוא עסוק בדברי אגדה שאין בהם נפקותא לשום דין ג"כ הוא דבוק בדבורו של הקב"ה. כי התורה כולה בכלליה ופרטיה ודקדוקיה. ואפי' מה שהתלמיד קטן שואל מרבו הכל יצא מפיו ית' למשה בסיני.

53. It is not entirely clear whom R. Chaim intends to rebuff. There are numerous chasidic sources that equate *Torah li-shma* to *deveikut*. For example, R. Meshulam Fivush b. R. Aharon Moshe ha-Levi Heler of Zaburiz (1740–1795) writes:

to study Torah for its own sake, which brings about the ultimate closeness to God. Thus, R. Soloveitchik writes that the ideal of clinging to God is realized by means of "the coupling of the intellect with the Divine Idea that is embodied in rules, laws, and traditions." Torah study, while intellectually rigorous, must realize itself in the emotional experience of *deveikut*.

יושר דברי אמת קונטרסים קונטרס ראשון

אבל עיקר לימוד התורה לשמה צריך להיות להתדבק בהשי"ת ולהכניע ולהשפיל לפניו ולפני כל, ויותר שילמוד תורה יתדבק יותר בהשי"ת ויתקרב אליו.

Another famous example is the fifth chapter of Tanya. However, R. Chaim's critiques certainly do not relate to the perspective of R. Shneur Zalman of Liadi. For example, R. Chaim writes that, according to the chasidic perspective, it would suffice to fervently recite a single psalm. However, R. Shneur Zalman, in his collection of the laws of Torah study, insists on the indispensability of knowing all of Torah. Indeed, R. Chaim's presentation of *Torah li-shma* is nearly identical to that of R. Shneur Zalman, a point noted by R. Soloveitchik (*Be-sod ha-Yachid ve-ha-Yachad,* p. 410).

While there is conflict between R. Chaim's perspective and that which is attributed to the Besht, R. Chaim's polemic was not primarily against the classical chasidic texts, such as those cited above, which were written by staggering Torah scholars. Rather, it was against an attitude, common among some *chasidim,* that Torah scholarship is unimportant since all that is prized (communion with God) is best accomplished through ecstatic acts. Thus, R. Chaim laments that there are synagogues that do not even have a complete Talmud, since traditional Torah study is not valued. The proofs R. Chaim offers in favor of his version of *Torah li-shma* refute such a perspective.

We should add that chasidic polemics against *mitnagdic* study practices would likewise not apply to the approach set forth by R. Chaim. Consider the following:

יושר דברי אמת קונטרסים קונטרס ראשון

ובאמת רבים מבני עמינו המדומים בעיניהם ובעיני העולם חכמים גדולים בתורה בנגלה ובנסתר ומדומים ביראה בכל הדברים וסוברים שבאו לקצת תורה ויראה אבל באמת עדיין לא זכו אפילו לידיעה קטנה מתורת אלהינו שהיא נקרא תורה ע"ש שמורה הנעלם שהוא השי"ת כמ"ש הקדוש אלהי ר"מ מענדיל הנ"ל ז"ל שאמר בפ׳ [תהלים יט] תורת ה׳ תמימה ר"ל ע"ד צחות שתורת ה׳ דייקא היא תמימה שעדיין לא נגע שום אדם אפי׳ בקצהו כי הם לומדים רק חיצוניות התורה דהיינו שאין במחשבתם להדבק בהשי"ת ולהיות מרכבה לו ולירא ממנו ולאהבה אותו ע"י התורה כמ"ש האריז"ל והובא בס׳ קטן שערי ציון כי הם אינם יודעים כלל מה זה דביקות השי"ת ומה זה אהבה ויראה כי הם סוברים שזה בעצמו הלימוד שלומדים הוא הדביקות והיא האהבה והיראה והאיך אפשר זה הלא ידוע ומפורסם שיש בעו"ה כמה לומדים שהם בעלי ניאוף ר"ל ובעלי עבירות ידועים ואף מאומות יש שלומדים התורה שלנו האיך יתכן שזה יהיה הדביקות בה׳.

While R. Chaim certainly maintains that studying Torah for its own sake constitutes *Torah li-shma,* he likewise insists (*Nefesh ha-Chaim,* Section 4, Chapter 6) that one must consciously learn Torah with the intent to connect to God through the learning.

Thus far, we have considered two basic models of knowing God: through meta-Halacha (philosophy/Kabbala) and through Halacha. The first school of thought proves the indispensability of the Talmud's statement that "the great matter" refers to *ma'aseh merkava* and "the little matter" refers to the debates of Abayei and Rava. How might the second perspective explain the Talmud's statement?

Firstly, even if we accept Rambam's understanding of the Talmudic passage, the statement need not express primacy of the esoteric, as Rambam would have it, but could be understood as saying that *ma'aseh merkava* is a difficult or esoteric discipline, whereas the dialectics of Abayei and Rava are easier to grasp. Thus, the statement does not necessarily assign axiological superiority to *ma'aseh merkava.*

Moreover, other Rishonim reject Rambam's reading altogether. In fact, Ritva (*Sukka* 28a) notes that the fact that the Talmud first lists Tanach, Mishna, Talmud, and Halachot before mentioning *ma'aseh merkava* indicates that these fields are superior to *ma'aseh merkava.* Ritva suggests that the reason the dialectics of Abayei and Rava are referred to as "the little matter" is because they resulted from lack of clarity.[54]

1.4 TORAH AS AN INSTANTIATION OF DIVINE WISDOM

In the previous section, we considered two methods of understanding the Divine: directly, though the study of mysticism and philosophy, or indirectly, through the study of rules, laws, and traditions (*Nega'im* and *Ohalot*). Now, let us consider a third possibility – how the study of the *mitzvot* can lead directly to the greatest possible understanding of God. Many sources indicate that the entire Torah, including the halachic portions, is an instantiation of divine wisdom and a "garment" for abstract truths. This is why the *mitzva* of Torah study (including all of its components) is paramount.

54. דבר קטן הויות דאביי ורבא. פי׳ דבר קטן הוא לגבי מעשה מרכבה שאמרנו, ולגבי הא נמי לא קרי דבר קטן לתלמוד שהרי קדמו לכולם שלא הניח מקרא משנה ותלמוד הלכות ואגדות והם יתד שהכל תלוי בו. אלא הויות דאביי ורבא הם קושיות ותירוצין וספיקות שלהם שלא נתבררו להם מפני שלא ירדו לעומקו של תלמוד כחכמים הראשונים, **ולפי שהיה זה מחסרון ידיעה קרי ליה דבר קטן בחכמת המשנה** אבל גדול הוא מכל שאר חכמות הגוים. וזה הפירוש אמת ונכון לכל המאמין, ולא כמו שפירשו אחרים האלקים יכפר.

R. Yeshaya b. Avraham ha-Levi Horowitz (1568–1630), known as *Shlah* after his work *Shnei Luchot ha-Brit,* expresses this notion in the context of the verse (*Yirmiyahu* 31:30) that predicts the establishment of a new covenant (ברית חדשה). What does this mean in light of the eternity of the Torah? In 25.5, we will offer three interpretations of this problematic phrase; here, we will consider only *Shlah*'s remarkable understanding, as it relates to our discussion. The Torah is eternal. There are, however, *mitzvot* that seem to relate only to our current physical condition. For example, had Adam and Chava not sinned, there would be no need to plow a field. What, then, would be the meaning of the verse prohibiting plowing with an ox and a donkey together?[55] *Shlah* answers that this *mitzva* reflects eternal truths that would have been manifest in a more spiritual fashion had Adam retained his pristine spiritual state. Following Adam's fall, however, this concept was expressed in more physical terms. The ברית חדשה predicted by Yirmiyahu reflects a return to a more spiritual understanding of the eternal truths expressed in the Torah.[56] We elaborate upon this notion in Chapter 12 when introducing Kabbala.

---

55. *Devarim* 22:10

56. **של"ה שער האותיות אות אל"ף אמת ואמונה**

העיקר התשיעי. 'לא יחליף האל ולא ימיר דתו'. לא תחלף תורת משה רבינו ע"ה, ולא תצא תורה מעם השם יתברך זולתה, ולא יהיה בה לא תוספת ולא גרעון, לא בכתב ולא בעל פה. ועל תורת השם יתברך נאמר (דברים יג, א) 'לא תסף [עליו] ולא תגרע [ממנו]'. ומה שנאמר בירמיה סימן ל"א (ל - לא) 'הנה ימים באים נאם ה' וכרתי את בית ישראל ואת בית יהודה ברית חדשה, לא כברית אשר כרתי את אבותם ביום החזיקי בידם להוציאם מארץ מצרים, אשר המה הפרו את בריתי ואנכי בעלתי בם נאם ה'".... **אבל יש עוד פנימיות לדבר זה. כי נודע (ראה לעיל בהקדמת תולדות אדם אות קפה והלאה), כמו שנתגשם האדם כן נתגשמה התורה, כי אילו היה האדם נשאר בכתנות אור בגן עדן, היתה התורה מובנת בענין יותר רוחני, כמו שכתב הפרדס בשער הנשמה (שער ל"א פ"ו), כי איך שייך 'לא תחרש בשור ו[ב] חמר' (דברים כב, י), וכי צריך חרישה בגן עדן, וכיוצא בזה הרבה, אלא שהיה מובן בענין רוחני, מה שנקרא שור וחמור. כן לעתיד שיחזור העולם, תפשוט התורה גשמיותה, ויתקיימו מצוותיה כפי המובן בעת ההיא, וקל להבין. אבל הכל היא זו התורה בעצמה, רק אורה יאיר ביותר, כמו שהאדם יאיר גם כן,** וקל להבין.

Gra offers a similar understanding:

יהל אור כח טור ד - כט טור א

ולעתיד יתגלה הסוד שבתוכו וזהו **התורה חדשה שיתגלה לעתיד.**

Nefesh ha-Chaim 4:27–28 explains that this is because full expression of the Torah's secrets could not be contained in our world as it stands. With the world's purification, however, things will change.

This may be what Ramban means when he declares that before the creation of the world, the Torah existed in the form of black fire (the letters) on white fire (the parchment). The concepts beneath the Torah are eternal, and our version of the Torah (ink on parchment) is the means by which we can tap into these eternal truths. Thus, all wisdom can be ascertained through the study of Torah if one knows how to decode it properly.[57]

R. Shneur Zalman of Liadi (*Tanya,* Ch. 4) explains that this is the meaning of the statement in the *Zohar* that the Torah and the Holy One, blessed be He, are one and the same (אורייתא וקודשא בריך הוא כולא חד):

> פירוש: דאורייתא, היא חכמתו ורצונו של הקדוש ברוך הוא, והקדוש ברוך הוא בכבודו ובעצמו, כולא חד כי הוא היודע והוא המדע וכו׳ כמו שכתוב לעיל בשם הרמב״ם ...וצמצם הקדוש ברוך הוא רצונו וחכמתו בתרי״ג מצות התורה ובהלכותיהן... בכדי שכל הנשמה או רוח ונפש שבגוף האדם תוכל להשיגן בדעתה.

> This means: since Torah is the wisdom and will of the Holy One, blessed be He,[58] it is one with His glory and essence, since He is the Knower, the Knowledge... and the Known, as explained above in Chapter 2 in the name of Rambam...[59] God compressed His will and wisdom into the 613 commandments of the Torah and in their laws... in order that every *neshama,* or even the lower

---

57. **הקדמת הרמב״ן לספר בראשית**
והטעם לכתיבת התורה בלשון זה **מפני שקדמה לבריאת העולם אין צריך לומר ללידתו של משה רבינו כמו שבא לנו בקבלה שהיתה כתובה באש שחורה על גבי אש לבנה.** ... וכל הנמסר למשה רבינו בשערי הבינה הכל נכתב בתורה בפירוש או שרמוזה בתיבות או בגימטריאות או בצורת האותיות הכתובות כהלכתן או המשתנות בצורה כגון הלפופות והעקומות וזולתן או בקוצי האותיות ובכתריהם כמו שאמרו כשעלה משה למרום מצאו להקב״ה שהיה קושר כתרים לאותיות אמר לו אלו למה אמר לו עתיד אדם אחד לדרוש בהם תלי תלים של הלכות עד זו מנין לך א״ל הל׳ למשה מסיני כי הרמזים האלו לא יתבוננו אלא מפה אל פה עד משה מסיני.
58. I.e., the wisdom of Torah expresses God's wisdom; its practical application and laws – e.g., whether or not a particular object is kosher – express His will.
59. These three aspects (knower, knowledge, known), separate and distinct in terms of human intellect, are, as they relate to God, one and the same entity; they all are godliness.

> soul-levels of *ruach* and *nefesh*, situated as they are in the human body, will be able to grasp them with their intellect.[60]

While the above sources capture the notion that Halacha reflects infinite divine wisdom in a mystical sense, R. Yosef Dov Soloveitchik, as noted in the previous section, presented this idea somewhat differently. Like the earlier Kabbalistic sources that argued for a conceptual understanding of *mitzvot* in a way that reveals their eternal truths, R. Soloveitchik, in advocating the Brisker style of learning, offered a different sort of conceptual analysis to reveal the inner truths upon which the law is predicated. As noted, this form of analysis paints a vastly different picture, with halachic man's approach to reality "devoid of any element of transcendence" (*Halakhic Man*, p. 17). At the same time, the halachic perspective gives man the greatest possible glimpse of God.

1.5 THE DEBATE CONCERNING THE STUDY OF PHILOSOPHY: RAMBAM'S VIEW

What Did Chazal Think of Philosophy?

As we have seen, Rambam maintains that the study of philosophy is a *mitzva* insofar as it helps a person know God, love God, and fear God. What did Chazal think of philosophy? There is very little overt discussion of the topic. In one place, however, the Talmud (*Menachot* 64b) curses someone who teaches his child Greek wisdom.[61] This seemingly indicates that Chazal have a very negative attitude towards philosophy and Greek wisdom. In another instance (*Menachot* 99b), the Talmud rules that the study of Greek wisdom is a violation of *bittul Torah*, an inappropriate

60. Translation adapted from that of R. Yosef Wineberg, published and copyrighted by Kehot Publication Society, and available at chabad.org.

61. ת"ר כשצרו מלכי בית חשמונאי זה על זה והיה הורקנוס מבחוץ ואריסטובלוס מבפנים בכל יום ויום היו משלשלין להן דינרין בקופה ומעלין להן תמידין היה שם זקן אחד שהיה מכיר בחכמת יוונית לעז להם בחכמת יוונית אמר להן כל זמן שעסוקין בעבודה אין נמסרין בידכם למחר שלשלו להן דינרין בקופה והעלו להן חזיר כיון שהגיע לחצי חומה נעץ צפרניו בחומה ונזדעזעה ארץ ישראל ארבע מאות פרסה על ארבע מאות פרסה באותה שעה אמרו ארור שיגדל חזיר **וארור שילמד בנו חכמת יוונית.**

interruption from Torah study.[62] Nevertheless, the matter is not actually so clear. The context of *Menachot* 64b indicates that the term "Greek wisdom" does not refer to philosophy but rather to a particular manner of communication.[63] Thus, we cannot necessarily deduce a negative attitude towards philosophy from the Talmud.[64]

62. שאל בן דמה בן אחותו של ר׳ ישמעאל את ר׳ ישמעאל כגון אני שלמדתי כל התורה כולה מהו ללמוד **חכמת יונית** קרא עליו המקרא הזה לא ימוש ספר התורה הזה מפיך והגית בו יומם ולילה צא ובדוק שעה שאינה לא מן היום ולא מן הלילה ולמוד בה חכמת יונית

63. Rashi (*Menachot* 64b) understands the term as referring to **רמזים** (hints or riddles), not philosophy. *Tosafot* (*Menachot* 64b), Me'iri (*Sota* 49a), Rambam (commentary to *Sota* 9:15), Tashbeitz (*Avot* 2:14) and Rivash (45) likewise conclude that Greek wisdom is a form of communication and does not refer to philosophy. The context of *Menachot* 64b supports this translation. See also *Shita Mekubetzet* (*Bava Kama* 83a) for three views on the meaning of the term "Greek wisdom" – hints, astrology, or philosophy.

 Maharal likewise understands that the Talmud's rejection as a repudiation of מליצה או משל, not wisdom in general:

 נתיבות עולם נתיב התורה יד
 ואין סברא לומר כי אף שהחכמה היא חכמה גמורה, מכל מקום אין לו לסור מן התורה כדכתיב והגית בו יומם ולילה.
 ויש להביא ראיה אל סברא זאת ממסכת מנחות (צט ב) שאל בן דמה בן אחותו של רבי ישמעאל כגון אני שלמדתי כל התורה כולה מהו שאלמד חכמת יונית קרא עליו המקרא הזה לא ימוש ספר התורה הזה מפיך צא ובדוק איזה היא שעה שלא מן היום ולא מן הלילה ולמוד בה חכמת יונית, ואם כן מוכח דחכמת יונית אסורה ללמוד מפני שכתוב והגית בה יומם ולילה.
 אבל נראה דחכמת יונית דהתם איידי חכמה שאין לה שייכות אל התורה כלל, כמו חכמה שהיא במליצה או משל וחכמה זאת אין לה שייכות כלל אל התורה וכתיב (יהושע א׳) והגית בו יומם ולילה, אבל החכמות לעמוד על המציאות וסדר העולם בודאי מותר ללמוד. והכי מוכח דפירוש חכמת יונית היינו מליצה ולשון, דבפרק מרובה (ב״ק פב ב) אמרינן באותה שעה. אמרו ארור האיש שיגדל חזרים וארור האדם שילמד את בנו הכמת יונים של בית ר״ג התירו להם לספר בחכמת יונית מפני שקרובים למלכות, ומדאמר לספר שמע מינה שהוא שייך אל הלשון. **ומפני כי דבר זה אין בו תועלת להבין חכמת התורה ולכך אסרוה, אבל דברי חכמה אינו אסור כי החכמה הזאת היא כמו סולם לעלות בה אל חכמת התורה.**
 ועוד כי למה היו קוראין אותו חכמת יונית, אם היא לעמוד על המציאות שהוא בעולם הלא החכמה הזאת היא חכמת כל אדם.

64. The lone usage of the word "philosophy" in the Talmud is similarly equivocal and does not necessarily indicate a negative attitude towards philosophy. It appears in *Shabbat* 116a in a story describing a corrupt judge who was a philosopher:
 אימא שלום דביתהו דרבי אליעזר אחתיה דרבן גמליאל הואי הוה ההוא **פילוסופא** בשבבותיה דהוה שקיל שמא דלא מקבל שוחדא בעו לאחוכי ביה אעיילא ליה שרגא

A more powerful critique of Rambam emerges not from the explicit statements within Chazal, but rather from their silence and apparent disinterest in philosophy. If philosophy is so fundamental, why do we not have a tradition of philosophy as we do concerning the law? R. Yeshaya of Trani or Riaz (c. 1180 – c. 1250) expresses this challenge in the context of the debate about the nature of the oneness of God, a topic we will return to in Chapters 10 and 11. Riaz argues that while we can conclusively demonstrate God's incorporeality, someone who understands Scripture literally and therefore believes God has a body cannot be classified as a heretic. If such an error constituted heresy, the Talmud certainly would have stressed this prohibition. More significantly, the fact that the Talmud does not encourage the study of philosophy indicates that the highest level of faith and a correct conception of God's unity can be achieved based on tradition and through the study of traditional sources. If philosophy was a prerequisite or even a value, the Talmud should have made that point clear.

קונטרוס הראיות לריא״ז מסכת סנהדרין דף צ עמוד א
וכן הדבר ידוע לכל חכמי לב, אבל מי שיטעה בכך ולא ירד לעמקו של דבר ומבין המקראות כפשוטן וסבור שהקדוש ברוך הוא בעל תמונה לא נקרא מין, שאם כן הוא הדבר, איך לא פרסמה תורה על דבר זה ולא גלו חכמי התלמוד להודיע דבר זה בגלוי, ולהזהיר נשים

דדהבא ואזול לקמיה אמרה ליה בעינא דניפלגי לי בנכסי דבי נשי אמר להו פלוגו א״ל כתיב לן במקום ברא ברתא לא תירות א״ל מן יומא דגליתון מארעכון איתנטלית אורייתא דמשה ואיתיהיבת ספרא אחריתי וכתיב ביה ברא וברתא כחדא ירתון למחר הדר עייל ליה איהו חמרא לובא אמר להו שפילית לסיפיה דספרא וכתב ביה אנא לא למיפחת מן אורייתא דמשה אתיתי [ולא] לאוספי על אורייתא דמשה אתיתי וכתיב ביה במקום ברא ברתא לא תירות אמרה ליה נהור נהוריך כשרגא א״ל רבן גמליאל אתא חמרא ובטש לשרגא:
The question we must consider is what is meant by the word "פילוסופא." Does this passage indicate that philosophy should not be studied? Concerning the term "פילוסופא" used in the Talmud, Rashi *Shabbat* 116a translates the term as heretic (*min*); Rashi elsewhere (*Avoda Zara* 54a) translates it as one who possesses gentile wisdom. *Aruch* explains it to mean a stargazer, and *Tosafot* (*Shabbat* 116a) assert that it means a lover of wisdom or a scoffer. The context of *Shabbat* 116a depicts a philosopher as a corrupt judge who presents himself as honest. Thus, the above Talmudic passages do not necessarily indicate that all philosophy or philosophers are bad.

ועמי הארץ על כך שלא יהיו מינים ויאבדו עולמן, הלא כמה אסורים קלים כגון אסור מוקצה וכיוצא בו, חברו חכמים כמה הלכות והרבו כמה דקדוקין להעמיד כל דבר על מכונו, ועל דבר זה שכל האמונה תלויה בו ויש בו כרת בעולם הזה ובעולם הבא, איך לא הורו חכמים על דבר זה בגלוי.

אלא ודאי לא הקפידו לכך, אלא יאמין אדם היחוד כפי שכלו, ואפילו הנשים כפי מיעוט שכלן, שאמר משה ע"ה שמע ישראל ה' אלקינו ה' אחד, ושמע לשון שמועה ולשון קבלה, שעל פי שמועה ועל פי קבלה יאמין דבר זה, ולא נתן משה תורה לישראל אלא בדרך אמונה ובדרך קבלה, וכן חכמי המשנה וחכמי התלמוד לא נתעסקו אלא בדרך קבלה ובדרך אמונה, ולא הורו לדרוש ולחקור על ענין האלהות ועל ענין שאר החכמות כלל, ואם היו יחידים שהיו בקיאין בהם לא היו מורין בהם לרבים, שלא צותה תורה להורות על אלה הדברים.

Someone who errs [in philosophical matters] and does not fully grasp these matters and understands the verses simply, believing that God has an image, is not a heretic. For if it were the case that he is a heretic [as Rambam claims], how is it that the Torah did not publicize this, and why is it that the Sages of the Talmud did not make this matter known and warn women and the uneducated so that they will not be permanently lost?[65] Is it not the case that concerning even light prohibitions, such as *muktzeh* and the like, the Sages composed many rules and articulate many details to establish the matter correctly? How could it be that something like this, a cornerstone of belief [according to Rambam] that carries with it the punishment of being cut off in this world and the next (*olam ha-ba*), was not discussed explicitly?

Chazal clearly did not insist upon a philosophical understanding. Rather, a person can believe in the unity [of God] according to his ability... and believe based on tradition... For Moshe gave the Torah to Yisrael based on tradition and faith. Likewise, the

65. He is referring to Rambam's position that a person with a corporeal understanding of God has no share in *olam ha-ba*.

Sages of the Mishna and Talmud focused entirely on tradition and faith and did not instruct one to investigate or philosophize into questions of God and these forms of wisdom. Even though a few of the Sages were experts in investigating the divine, they did not teach these matters publicly, because the Torah never commanded these things to be studied.

Rambam's Understanding of Why Chazal Do Not Discuss Philosophy

What would Rambam respond to the above challenges? Concerning Riaz's question about *olam ha-ba,* Rambam maintains that the Torah itself warns of the dangers of corporeality, such as in *Devarim* 4:15.[66] In terms of why Chazal do not seem to engage in philosophy, Rambam frequently understands that midrashim allude to philosophical concepts (see, for example, *Moreh ha-Nevuchim* 3:22). It is undeniable, though, that there is little overt philosophy. Why do we not find overt philosophy in midrashim? Why does Rambam rely so heavily on non-Jewish thinkers?

In *Moreh ha-Nevuchim,* Rambam addresses this question. He asserts that originally, we had our own tradition of philosophy. Indeed, King Shlomo alludes to it in his works. Nevertheless, Jewish philosophical teachings never were written down, since this would have violated the prohibition against writing down the oral law[67] (any aspect of our tradition not included in Scripture is considered part of the oral law). Sadly, this philosophical tradition was forgotten due to persecution.[68]

---

66. We address this at length in Chapter 10.

67. *Gittin* 60b: דברים שבעל פה אי אתה רשאי לאומרן בכתב.

68. *Moreh ha-Nevuchim* 1:71:

> Know that many branches of science relating to the correct solution of these problems once were cultivated by our forefathers but were in the course of time neglected, especially in consequence of the tyranny that barbarous nations exercised over us. Besides, speculative studies were not open to all men, as we already have stated; only the subjects taught in the Torah were accessible to all. Even the oral law, as you are well aware, originally was not committed to writing, in conformity with the rule to which our nation generally adhered, "Things which I have communicated to you orally, you must not communicate to others in writing." With reference to the law, this rule was very opportune; for while it remained in force, it averted the evils that happened subsequently,

In fact, there was a great concern that the legal components of the oral law would also be forgotten due to Roman persecution. R. Yehuda ha-Nasi prevented that catastrophe by writing down the legal sections of the oral law, an activity that should have been prohibited but was justified due to the exigencies of the time.[69] No such measures were taken regarding the philosophical tradition due to the concern that writing it down would inevitably cause those not ready to study philosophy to be exposed to unsuitable material, with potentially disastrous results.[70] Thus, we turn to Aristotle to help us arrive at the truth, as Rambam famously writes that we should "accept the truth from whoever utters it."[71] To some degree, with the writing of Torah works like *Moreh ha-Nevuchim*,

> viz., great diversity of opinion, doubts as to the meaning of written words, slips of the pen, dissensions among the people, formation of new sects, and confused notions about practical subjects. The traditional teaching was in fact, according to the words of the law, entrusted to the *Sanhedrin ha-Gadol*, as we already have stated in our works on the Talmud.

69. We will return to the history of the oral law in Chapter 28.
70. In addition, unlike the oral tradition, philosophy could be entirely recreated using the intellect.
71. Towards the beginning of *Shemona Prakim*, his Introduction to *Masechet Avot*, he writes:

> It is important to know, though, that I did not originate the ideas expressed or the explanations offered either in these chapters or in my commentary. Rather, they have been collected from the words of the Sages in the Midrash, the Talmud, and in their other works, as well as from the words of earlier and later philosophers (Jewish and non-Jewish), and from the works of many others. Accept the truth from whoever utters it.

Rambam expresses the same idea at the end of the seventeenth chapter of *Hilchot Kiddush ha-Chodesh* concerning his reliance upon the astronomical calculations made by the Greeks that are necessary to properly sanctify the month:

> ומאחר שכל אלו הדברים, בראיות ברורות הם, שאין בהם דופי, ואי אפשר לאדם להרהר אחריהם - אין חוששין למחבר, בין שחיברו אותם נביאים בין שחיברו אותם גויים: שכל דבר שנתגלה טעמו, ונודעה אמיתתו בראיות שאין בהם דופי - אין סומכין על זה האיש שאמרו, או שלימדו; אלא על הראיה שנתגלתה, והטעם שנודע.

> Since these concepts can be proven in an unshakable manner, leaving no room for question, the identity of the author, be he a prophet or a gentile, is of no concern. For a matter whose rationale has been revealed and has been proven truthful in an unshakable manner, we do not rely on [the personal authority of] the individual who made these statements or taught these concepts, but on the proofs he presented and the reasons he made known.

our crown has been restored to its former glory; the valuable insights of the world of philosophy have been restored to the world of Torah such that it can now be said דִּרְשׁוּ מֵעַל סֵפֶר ה' וּקְרָאוּ אַחַת מֵהֵנָּה לֹא נֶעְדָּרָה, "Seek out of the Book of the Lord and read; not one thing is missing from it" (*Yeshaya* 34:16).[72]

Note that Rambam is distinguishing between knowledge obtained through Torah sources verses non-Torah sources. With respect to knowledge obtained through Torah sources one can trust the claim because it stems from a reputable source. However, when it comes to ideas discovered in non-Torah sources, they are only valuable when conclusively proven.

Likewise, see R. Avraham b. ha-Rambam in *Ma'amar Odot Drashot Chazal*, who stresses accepting truth wherever it can be found and rails against those who are overly reliant upon authority.

72. Rambam refers to this verse to describe how he restored astronomical knowledge to the corpus of Torah. At the end of the seventeenth chapter of *Hilchot Kiddush ha-Chodesh* Rambam writes of the need to turn to Greek sources since our tradition has been lost:

> וטעם כל אלו החשבונות, ומפני מה מוסיפים מניין זה, ומפני מה גורעין, והיאך נודע כל דבר ודבר מאלו הדברים, והראיה על כל דבר ודבר - היא חכמת התקופות והגימטריות, שחיברו בה חכמי יוון ספרים הרבה, והם, המצויים עכשיו ביד החכמים; אבל הספרים שחיברו חכמי ישראל שהיו בימי הנביאים מבני יששכר, לא הגיעו אלינו.
>
> The rationales for all these calculations, and the reasons why this number is added, and why that subtraction is made, and how all these concepts are known, and the proofs for each of these principles are [the subject] of the wisdom of astronomy and geometry, concerning which the Greeks wrote many books. These texts are presently in the hands of the [Greek] Sages. The texts written by the Sages of Israel in the age of the Prophets from the tribe of Yissachar have not been transmitted to us.

However, at the end of the nineteenth chapter of *Hilchot Kiddush ha-Chodesh*, Rambam writes that now that he has restored our astronomical tradition there is no longer any need to use non-Jewish sources since everything can be derived from Torah.

> הרי ביארנו חשבונות כל הדרכים שצריכין להם בידיעת הראייה, ובחקירת העדים, כדי שיהיה הכול ידוע למבינים, ולא יחסרו דרך מדרכי התורה ולא ישוטטו לבקש אחריה בספרים אחרים - "דרשו מעל ספר ה', וקראו - אחת מהנה לא נעדרה" (ישעיהו לד:טז).
>
> Thus, we have explained all the calculations necessary for the sighting [of the moon] and the examination of the witnesses, so that everything will be comprehensible to those of understanding, and they will not lack awareness of any of the Torah's paths. [Therefore,] they will not venture forth in search of it in other texts. "Seek out of the book of God, read it. None of these will be lacking."

This sentiment is reminiscent of Rama's comments cited earlier that there is no longer any need to study Aristotle in the original since Rambam has incorporated the valuable insights from Greek philosophy into the Torah.

How Can We Rely upon the Greeks?

Turning to the Greeks, however, raises another problem: their worldview is fundamentally antithetical to that of the Torah. Indeed, Rambam addresses *Moreh ha-Nevuchim* to a person who sees philosophy and Torah as being irreconcilable and is perplexed as to whether he should follow his intellect, renouncing what the Torah states, or the reverse.

Rambam responds to this challenge by boldly claiming, at least with respect to purely philosophical matters, that there is significant compatibility between Torah and philosophy. In *Moreh ha-Nevuchim* 3:25 he writes:

> When you examine the Torah's view and that of the philosophers, taking into consideration all preceding chapters that are connected with this subject, you will find that there is no other difference of opinion regarding any portions of the universe except that the philosophers believe in the eternity of the universe and we believe in creation.

Rambam writes that with exception of the debate concerning the formation of the universe, where philosophers believe matter is eternal and the Torah teaches that the world was created *ex nihilo*, there is confluence between Torah and philosophy. According to Rambam, the perceived contradictions frequently stem from misunderstanding the Torah.[73] Thus, the major function of *Moreh ha-Nevuchim* is to teach the proper method of biblical interpretation. More importantly, if and when there is conflict, Rambam writes that we must accept the Torah. Thus, when it comes to creation, we reject Aristotle's theory concerning the eternity of matter, as we shall see in 3.3.

1.6 THE DEBATE CONCERNING THE STUDY OF PHILOSOPHY: THE PERSPECTIVE OF RAMBAM'S OPPONENTS

Of course, not everyone agrees with Rambam's position concerning philosophy. The Maimonidean controversies, which revolved around the

73. Mistakes also stem from misunderstanding philosophy; accordingly, much of *Moreh ha-Nevuchim* seeks to correct these misconceptions.

permissibility of the study of philosophy, engulfed numerous communities and raged from 1180, following the publication of *Mishneh Torah,* until 1306. To some degree, resolution was reached around 1235 with Ramban's acknowledgment of Rambam's greatness even as he disagreed with many of his philosophical conclusions. However, the controversy once again flared up at the end of the 13th century and then again in the early 14th century. [74] It finally drew to a close in 1305 when Rashba, Ramban's student, followed his teacher in advancing a form of compromise. Along with the other elders of Barcelona, Rashba signed a fifty year ban (*cheirem*) against the study of Greek philosophy[75] for anyone below the age of 25, lest it lead him astray (see *Teshuvot ha-Rashba* 1:415). Note, however, they did not create a lifetime ban against the study of philosophy, nor did they prohibit the study of Jewish books of philosophy, such as *Moreh ha-Nevuchim.*[76]

Even after the controversy died down, Rambam's view was far from universally accepted. Generally speaking, those who protest the study of philosophy fall into two camps: those who feel it is too dangerous and those who categorically reject philosophy. Let us consider examples of each of these objections.

Studying Philosophy Is Too Dangerous

A modern example of the first camp is R. Elchanan Wasserman (1874–1941), who argues that any form of philosophical speculation is too dangerous nowadays. Thus, even if the Rishonim who maintain that proof plays an important role in faith are correct, their view is relevant only

74. The controversy had four flare ups: (1) following the publication of his *Mishneh Torah* in 1180 until Rambam's death in 1204; (2) centering in Provence around 1230–1235, involving R. David Kimchi, R. Shlomo b. Avraham of Montpellier, Ramban, and others; (3) in the Near East from 1288 to 1290, involving R. Shlomo Petit and R. Yitzchak of Acre; (4) in Christian Spain and Provence around 1300–1306, involving R. Abba Mari b. Moshe Astruc, Rashba, Rosh, and Me'iri. For more on this topic, see *Encyclopedia Judaica* "Maimonidean Controversy" by Prof. Haim Hillel Ben-Sasson.

75. They excluded the study of medicine from the ban, since the Torah grants the license to heal.

76. Thus, they were not going as far as some of the earlier bans. In 1232, for example, the rabbis of northern France issued a total ban on the study of philosophy, including *Moreh ha-Nevuchim* and *Sefer ha-Madda* (the first section of *Mishneh Torah,* which includes philosophical material, as we have seen).

when the dangers of investigation are not serious. Nowadays, even they would concede that inquiry is forbidden (*Koveitz Shiurim,* Vol. 2 47:9). R. Elchanan's words are cited fully in 9.7.

Some go even further, arguing that the Talmud banned even the study of logic (and not just philosophy) due to its danger. R. Yechezkeil Landau (1713–1793), known as *Noda be-Yehuda,* cites the Talmud (*Berachot* 28b) as the basis for the prohibition against studying logic:

> ת"ר כשחלה ר' אליעזר נכנסו תלמידיו לבקרו, אמרו לו רבינו למדנו אורחות חיים ונזכה בהן לחיי העולם הבא. אמר להם הזהרו בכבוד חבריכם **ומנעו בניכם מן ההגיון** והושיבום בין ברכי תלמידי חכמים וכשאתם מתפללים דעו לפני מי אתם עומדים ובשביל כך תזכו לחיי העולם הבא.
>
> Our Rabbis taught: When R. Eliezer fell ill, his disciples went in to visit him. They said to him: "Master, teach us the paths of life so that we may merit the life of the world to come." He said to them: "Be solicitous for the honor of your colleagues, **keep your children away from *higayon,*** and set them between the knees of Torah scholars, and when you pray, know before Whom you are standing. In this way, you will merit the world to come.

What is meant by *higayon*? Rashi (*Berachot* 28b) and Rashbam (*Bereishit* 37:2) understand this to be referring to Tanach;[77] However, R. Landau (*Tzlach, Berachot* 27b), believes that it means logic.[78]

---

77. Why would Tanach be objectionable? In 7.4, we will discuss Rashbam's interpretation, that it refers to the primacy of *drash* over *pshat* with respect to the interpretation of Scripture. Rashi, in *Berachot,* offers a second possibility – *higayon* refers to childish talk (שיחת ילדים). According to R. Tzemach Gaon, it refers to parts of Scripture that might incline a person towards heresy. Presumably, he is referring to *Kohelet,* which Chazal (*Midrash Kohelet* on 2:13) considered hiding due to that very concern (בקשו לגנוז את ספר קהלת שמצאו בו דברים מטין לצד מינות). Though *Kohelet* was canonized, R. Eliezer instructed that children not study the work.

78. **צל"ח (ברכות כז:)**
אני אומר ומה בכך שהוא שייך גם לחכמת התורה כיון שעקרו מתחלה הוקבע לחכמה החיצונית ראוי להתרחק ממנה על דרך עת לעשות לד'. ואני אומר קל וחומר אם מפני תרעומת המינין בטלו מלומר עשרת הדברות בכל יום אף שהוא מצוה רבה לזכור מעמד הר סיני בכל

Significantly, R. Landau agrees that there is value in studying logic; however, sometimes the Torah must be abrogated to ensure its perpetuation. Just as the Talmud (*Berachot* 12a) banned the public recitation of the Ten Commandments, despite the religious benefit of this practice, because heretics were claiming that only the Ten Commandments are mandatory (as opposed to the entire Torah), so too R. Eliezer recommended against the study of logic, despite its value, lest it lead to the study of philosophy, which can lead someone to reject the entire Torah. Thus, R. Landau, like R. Wasserman, bases his objection on the practical concern for heresy, not on fundamental rejection to the study of philosophy.

יום אפילו הכי בטלוהו מפני תרעומת המינין. חכמת הגיון שממשיך אחריו לימוד הפלוסופיא שמזה ממשיך מדחי אל דחי לדחות כל דת התורה קל וחומר שיש להתרחק מזה ומכל הקרוב לזה שימצא ושימצא דשימצא ולכן לעשות הרחקה יתירה מהפלוסופיא האלקית הזהיר ר״א הגדול מנעו בניכם מן ההגיון. אך כדי לחוש גם כן על התורה שידריכו בניהם בלימודים אמיתים ושלא לשגות בדרכי ההטעה שזה עקר פעולת ההגיון נתן להם עצה הגונה הושיבום בין ברכי תלמידי חכמים ומהם ישמעו אופני הלימוד בתורה וסברות הישרות ונכונות והם יורו להם הלימוד הנכון ולהרחיקם מן הפלוסופיא הנזכרת, אמר מנעו מן ההגיון.

Other Acharonim concur with this reading. For example, R. Yaakov Emden in שאלת יעבץ (41) opposes the study of logic based on this Talmudic passage. The context of his remarks is the chastisement of a student who decided to pursue logic and science. He writes that Rambam's view on this topic is not normative. Interestingly, while R. Emden opposes logic and philosophy, he supports the study of science. (He closes the lengthy *teshuva* by asking his student whether he is familiar with any books on alchemy, since חובות הלבבות implies that it is effective, while כוזרי disagrees.)

Remarkably, R. Yaakov ibn Chaviv (c. 1460–1516), organizer of *Ein Yaakov*, comments on the above passage, "Obviously, this does not refer to logic, which is immensely useful in the study of Torah." Likewise, Tashbeitz (מגן אבות לרשב״ץ על אבות ב:יט) writes that the Talmud could not refer to logic, which is valuable. He prefers Rashi's second explanation, which he understands to mean wasting time with frivolous or silly things. Along similar lines, when R. Ya'ir Bachrach discusses what to focus on in a child's education he notes the importance of knowing grammar and offers several examples of necessary rules, but writes that R. Eliezer recommended against children studying the intricacies of grammar insofar as studying them is very time consuming and offers little value:

שו״ת חוות יאיר סימן קכד

...וכן בשוא״ין מ״ש בם דאל״כ ה״ז בור בברכו בציבור על הס״ת או לפני התיבה ברכו בשוא נחה דצ״ל נעה כי באתה אחר תנועה גדולה. **אמנם לידע כל סעיפים וסעיפי סעיפים והיוצאים מן הכללים אין לבלות הזמן בהם כי ידיעתם רבית המבוכה ומעט התועלת ויש שפרשו על זה מ״ש... מנעו בניכם מן ההגיון.**

Categorical Rejection of Philosophy

On the other hand, some thinkers reject philosophy categorically. R. Yehuda ha-Levi, whose view on philosophy is discussed in section 9.1, may reflect this view. Another example of this perspective is Gra, who writes how philosophy, with her fair speech, seduced Rambam away from the proper interpretation of the Torah:

ביאור הגר"א יורה דעה סימן קעט ס"ק יג
והפלסופיא הטתו ברוב לקחה לפרש הגמרא הכל בדרך הלציי ולעקור אותם מפשטן.

> Philosophy, with her fair speech,[79] caused Rambam to err and explain the Gemara allegorically and to uproot it from the simple understanding.

The context of Gra's comments is Rambam's view in *Hilchot Avoda Zara* (11:16) that magic (*kishuf*) is just sleight of hand (see 14.3–5 and 18.9). Gra maintains that Scripture (e.g., *Shemot* 7:12) and Talmud (e.g., *Sanhedrin* 67b) indicate the existence of magic. What caused Rambam to reject the notion? He was seduced by the enticing philosophical notion that the only things that exist are those which can be observed or logically proven.

However, even Gra's denunciation of philosophy does not necessarily reflect a rejection of other forms of wisdom.[80] Instead, Gra objects that Rambam ignored what appears to be the unambiguous message of the Torah (that magic exists in some form) in favor of the philosophical perspective (that true magic does not exist but is merely illusion and sleight of hand).[81]

---

79. This is an allusion to *Mishlei* 7:21, with philosophy being compared to a prostitute who seduces her victim from the path of righteousness.

80. Moreover, he does not utterly reject Rambam's philosophical writings. Indeed, in *Aderet Eliyahu* (*Bereishit* 1:2) he cites *Moreh ha-Nevuchim* and in his commentary to *Mishlei* he invokes the philosophical vocabulary (such as the Aristotelian terms material cause, formal cause, efficient cause, and finite cause) used by Rambam in his book on logic (see *Sefer Mishlei im Bei'ur ha-Gra*, Petach Tikva: 2001, p. 441).

81. Gra's actual position here is complex and nuanced, and a careful reading indicates his primary objection is not to philosophy per se, but to the interpretive methodology employed by those like Rambam who accept the rational conclusions of

philosophy. To better appreciate this we have to consider the entire passage. Gra is commenting on the following halacha which allows for incantations even though they are ineffective to calm the patient, since the patient thinks they are effective.

שולחן ערוך יורה דעה הלכות מעונן ומכשף סימן קעט סעיף ו

מי שנשכו עקרב מותר ללחוש עליו, ואפילו בשבת, **ואף על פי שאין הדבר מועיל כלום** הואיל ומסוכן הוא התירו, כדי שלא תטרף דעתו עליו.

Gra writes that this formulation, which takes for granted that incantations are worthless, follows Rambam's perspective. However, the *pshat* of numerous statements in Chazal contradicts this.

ביאור הגר״א יורה דעה סימן קעט אות יג

> ואע״פ כו׳. הרמב״ם וכ״כ בפי׳ המשנה לפ״ד דעבודת כוכבים אבל כל הבאים אחריו חלקו עליו שהרי הרבה לחשים נאמרו בגמרא והוא נמשך אחר הפלוסופיא הארורה ולכן כ׳ שכשפים ושמות ולחשים ושדים וקמיעות הכל הוא שקר אבל כבר הכו אותן על קדקדו שהרי מצינו הרבה מעשיות בגמ׳ ע״פ שמות וכשפים אמרה איהי מלתא ואסרתה לארבא אמרו כו׳ (שבת פא ב חולין קה ב) ובספ״ד מיתות ובירושלמי שם עובדא דר״א ור״י ובן בתירה וכן ר״ח ור״א דאיברו עיגלא תילתא ור׳ יהושע דאמר שם ואוקמיה בין שמיא לארעא (בכורות ח ב) וכן אבישי בן צרויה (סנהדרין צה א) והרבה כיוצא ואמרו (בספ״ד מיתות חולין ז ב) למה נקרא שמן כשפים כו׳ והתורה העידה ויהיו תנינים וע׳ זוהר שם וכן קמיעין בהרבה מקומות ולחשים רבו מלספר. והפלסופיא הטתו ברוב לקחה לפרש הגמרא הכל בדרך הלציי ולעקור אותם מפשטן **וח״ו איני מאמין בהם ולא מהם ולא מהמונם אלא כל הדברים הם כפשטן אלא שיש בהם פנימיות לא פנימיות של בעלי הפלוסופיא שזורקין אותו לאשפה שהם חצוניות אלא של בעלי האמת:**
>
> This is the view of Rambam, but all those who followed him disagreed, for there are numerous places in the Talmud where incantations are effectively utilized. However, Rambam was drawn after the accursed philosophy and therefore wrote that magic and use of holy names and incantations and demons and amulets are all false. But they already reprimanded Rambam for this assertion since we find many actual stories in the Talmud where holy names and magic is effective (Gra then cites numerous examples of this)… Philosophy, with her fair speech, caused Rambam to err and explain the Gemara allegorically and to uproot it from the *pshat*. **But one should not think that I in any way, Heaven forbid, actually believe in them or what they stand for. Rather, all these things are like the *pshat*, but they also have a *p'nimiut* (hidden deeper meaning), and not the *p'nimiut* that the philosophers ascribe, for they throw out the *pshat* but the *p'nimiut* of the Kabbalists.**

This text obscures the Gra's true understanding of the role of magic, but his objection to Rambam's approach is unambiguous. Rambam ignores *pshat*. The *pshat* of Scripture (e.g., Pharaoh's magicians), Talmud (which state that magicians undermine the divine will – שמכחישין פמליא של מעלה), and *Zohar* all ascribe effectiveness to various forms of magic. Philosophers claim these statements are allegories. But, that is not correct on a level of *pshat*. The philosophers have effectively thrown these sources in the garbage by ignoring their plain meaning.

Philosophy preaches a worldview that at times is at odds with Torah. Moreover, it is seductive, capable of misleading a scholar as great as Rambam.[82]

Despite Gra's rejection of philosophy, he maintains that there is immense value to the pursuit of other wisdoms; however, these wisdoms (unlike the philosophy he rejects) can emerge organically from within Torah. Thus, R. Yisrael of Shklov reports (in his Introduction to *Pe'at ha-Shulchan*) that Gra advocated the pursuit of all seven branches of wisdom, including math, medicine, music, logic, and chemistry,[83] but maintained that they all are contained within Torah.[84]

However, Gra himself acknowledges there is a truer and deeper meaning to these statements. As we shall see in Chapter 7, *drash* and *sod* both reflect deeper and truer interpretations – however, they do not entirely replace the *pshat*. (In contrast to the approach of the philosophers who claim that their allegorical interpretation does entirely replace the *pshat*.) Gra, here, does not indicate what that deeper and truer meaning is. (See 14.12–15 where we discuss the matter.) However, whatever that explanation is it leads Gra to categorically reject any belief in magic.

Thus, while Rambam maintains that there is no such thing as true magic (only slight of hand), many prominent thinkers besides Gra disagree. These include Ramban (*Devarim* 18:9), Rashba (*Shut Rashba ha-Miyuchasot* 283 and *Shut Rashba* 1:413), *Chinuch* (62), *Rivash* (92 where he discusses how to translate שמכחישין פמליא של מעלה), and Nefesh ha-Chaim 3:12 who writes, "כי כל עניני פעולות הכשפים נמשך מהכוחות הטומאה של המרכבה טמאה. והוא ענין חכמת הכישוף שהיו הסנהדרין צריכין לידע. היינו חכמת שמות הטומאה וידיעת עניני כחות המרכבה טמאה בשמותיהם. שע"י יפעלו בעלי הכישופים פעולות וענינים משונים כשמשביעין כחות הטומאה בבחי' הטוב שבו שישפיע בתוכו חיות לעשות נפלאות **היפך סדר כחות הטבעי' והמזלות**." (For more on the topic of magic see 14.5 and 14.12–15.)

82. Gra's precise perspective on philosophy is debated by his students and by scholars. We return to this question in 2.13 when we consider Gra's position that mysticism, using tradition, picks up where Rambam left off. Also, see R. Menachem Mendel of Shklov's Introduction to Gra's commentary on *Avot de-Rabi Natan* and R. Yisrael of Shklov in the Introduction to *Pe'at ha-Shulchan*. For some perspectives among modern scholars see "Philosophy and Dissimulation in Elijah of Vilna's Writings and Legacy." *Revue Internationale de Philosophie* (2018) and *The Genius: Elijah of Vilna and the Making of Modern Judaism* by Eliyahu Stern, Yale University Press, 2013.

83. As noted in 1.2, there are minor differences of opinion as to what is included in the seven wisdoms. According to Gra (*Kol ha-Tor* 829) they are:

    א) חכמת החשבון התכונה והמדידה, ב) חכמת היצירה וההרכבה, ג) חכמת הרפואה והצמיחה, ד) חכמת ההגיון הדקדוק והמשפט, ה) חכמת הנגינה והקדושה, ו) חכמת התיקון והשילוב, ז) חכמת הביגו"ר (בין גשם ורוח) וכחות הנפש.

84. Gra goes even further in his commentary on *Sifra de-Tzniuta*, writing that absolutely all knowledge and history are contained within the Torah.

כה אמר הגר"א כל החכמות נצרכים לתורתנו הקדושה וכלולים בה, וידעם כולם לתכליתם. והזכיר חכמת אלגעברע ומשולשים והנדסה וחכמת מוסיקא ושיבחה הרבה... וביאר איכות כל החכמות ואמר שהשיגם לתכליתם. רק חכמת הרפואה ידע חכמת הניתוח והשייך אליה... ועל חכמת פילוסופיה אמר שלמדה לתכליתה.

So said the Gra: "All knowledge is necessary for our holy Torah and is contained therein." He know them all thoroughly and mentioned them; the wisdom of algebra, trigonometry, geometry, and music which he greatly praised[85]... He explained the value of all wisdom and claimed to have entirely mastered them. Only concerning medicine [did he limit his study.] He knew human anatomy[86]... and the wisdom of philosophy he said that he studied it fully.

Does this mean that Gra maintains that there never is value to pursuing knowledge outside of Torah? The answer to this question is complex and subject to considerable controversy.[87] Gra's student,

---

פירוש הגר"א על ספרא דצניעותא פרק ה

והכלל כי כל מה שהיה והוה ויהיה עד עולם הכל כלול בתורה מבראשית עד לעיני כל ישראל. ולא הכללים בלבד, אלא אפילו פרטיו של כל מין ומין, ושל כל אדם בפרט, וכל מה שאירע לו מיום הולדו עד סופו, וכל גלגוליו. וכל פרטיו ופרטי פרטיו. וכן של כל מין בהמה וחיה, וכל בעל חי שבעולם, וכל עשב וצומח ודומם וכל פרטיהם, ופרטי פרטיהם בכל מין ומין ואישי המינים עד לעולם, ומה שיארע להם ושרשם.

85. On the value of music, see the first footnote in Chapter 12.

86. Why did he limit his study of medicine? R. Yisrael offers a fascinating theory: "He knew human anatomy, but concerning the composition and prescription of medicines which he wanted to learn from doctors, his father told him not to study so as not to diminish his Torah study in case he might need to save lives." In other words, if he had known how to save lives he would have had to do so which would have interrupted his learning. Therefore, he refrained from studying practical medicine.

87. See Raphael Shuchat's "The Debate Over Secular Studies Among the Disciples of the Vilna Gaon," in *The Torah U-Madda Journal*, Vol. 8, 1998, pp. 283–294. Prof. Shuchat claims that despite the earlier claims that Gra valued secular wisdom, with the rise of the *haskala* disciples began to minimize Gra's connection to such studies. What exacerbated the situation was the continued attempt of *maskilim* to use the Gra's position as a precedent in support of secular studies.

R. Baruch of Shklov, writes that his teacher urged him to translate Euclid into Hebrew because a deficit in "other wisdoms" will lead to an even greater deficit in the wisdom of Torah.[88] At the same time, Gra, as noted earlier, clearly maintained that all wisdom is contained within Torah.

How can these statements be reconciled? The answer may be that Gra believes that all wisdom of any value is contained within Torah and can be derived from the study of Torah. However, not everybody succeeds in acquiring this valuable knowledge directly through the study of Torah. Accordingly, studying the works of Euclid may prove valuable with respect to the interpretation of the Torah.[89]

It is worth adding that it was not just Kabbalists who critiqued Rambam's philosophy. Moreover, there were even thinkers who valued secular knowledge but still objected to Rambam's adaptation of Greek and Arabic philosophy. One such thinker was R. Samson Raphael Hirsch. While we will address this issue more fully in Chapter 36, for now, let us briefly note that R. Hirsch critiqued Rambam's attempt to reconcile Judaism with the ideas from without, instead of developing a Jewish Philosophy that arises organically from within (see *The Nineteen Letters*, letter 18). Along similar lines, R. Yosef Dov Soloveitchik in *Halakhic Mind* argues for the need for Jewish Philosophy to emerge from Halacha. According to R. Soloveitchik the great medieval Jewish philosophers such as R. Yehuda ha-Levi and Rambam constructed elaborate philosophical systems but did not systematically draw upon *halachah*

---

88. **הקדמת ר׳ ברוך משקלוב לספר אוקלידוס**
שמעתי מפי קדוש כי כפי מה שיחסר לאדם ידיעות משארי החכמות, לעומת זה יחסר לו מאה ידות בחכמת התורה, כי התורה והחכמה נצמדים יחד ואמר משל לאדם הנעצר יתבלבל שכלו עד כל אוכל תתאב... וצוה לי להעתיק מה שאפשר ללשוננו הקדוש מחכמות, כדי להוציא בולעם מפיהם וישוטטו רבים ותרבה הדעת בין עמנו ישראל.

There are those who claim that R. Baruch misrepresented his teacher's position. Others respond that this seems unlikely since, among other things, the book was published during Gra's lifetime. Either way, there appear to be conflicting accounts about Gra's view towards the study of non-Torah material (see, for example, *Ma'aseh Rav*). While I lack clarity about his actual position on this issue, the approach suggested above may be true regardless of the accuracy of R. Baruch's claim.

89. A similar dialectic can be found when comparing Ramban's Introduction to Torah and his *Drashat Torat Hashem Temima*.

as the primary source. (See "Towards a Philosophy of Halachah" by R. Mayer Twersky, *Jewish Action*, Fall 2003.)

1.7 HOW DO THOSE WHO PROHIBIT PHILOSOPHY JUSTIFY RAMBAM'S PURSUIT?

An interesting question must be considered by those who reject philosophy: how do they understand Rambam's pursuit of philosophy? After the dust of the Maimonidean controversy settled, almost all thinkers acknowledged Rambam's greatness. Thus, Rambam could not simply be dismissed.

Rivash

One approach can be seen in the writings of R. Yitzchak b. Sheishet Perfet, or Rivash (1326–1408). For a number of reasons, Rivash rules that it is prohibited to study philosophy. Firstly, Rivash argues that because it contains heretical ideas, such as the eternity of matter and rejection of divine providence, philosophy should not be studied.[90] Therefore, he permits the study of science, though he maintains that it is not a good use of time, but forbids the study of philosophy. Secondly, he rejects the view that proper faith must be grounded in proof, making philosophy necessary for the fulfillment of the *mitzva* of belief in God. Finally, he invokes the responsa of R. Hai Gaon and Rashba as precedents for prohibiting philosophy, though they may not espouse a position as extreme as Rivash.[91] Having totally proscribed philosophical study, Rivash asks how Rambam could have studied philosophy. His response is comprised of several parts.

---

90. When Rivash refers to philosophy here, he means the teachings of Aristotle.
91. Earlier (1.2), we mentioned Maharshal's chastisement of Rama (quoted in *Teshuvot Rama* 6) for referencing Aristotle (concerning *treifot*). Maharshal cites the above Rivash to support his critique.

שו"ת הרמ"א סימן ו

ואח"כ הראיתני מחכמת אריסטו הערל, מתוך האדים שבארץ כו'. אמרתי, אוי לי שעיני ראו נוסף למה שאזני שמעו, שעיקר המחמד והבושם הוא דברי הטמא, ויהי בפי חכמי ישראל כעין בושם לתורה הקדושה, רחמנא ליצלן מהעון הגדול. ולא אשיב ככל אשר עם לבבי כבר ראיתי דברי רב האי ודברי הרא"ש בתשובה ודברי ר"י בר ששת שהיה מחכמי ספרדים שכתב מהם וסיבתם ומה הגיע אליהם.

Firstly, Rambam mastered all of Torah before studying philosophy, as can be seen from *Mishneh Torah*.[92]

שו"ת הריב"ש סימן מה

ואין להביא ראי' מהרמב"ם ז"ל. כי הוא **למד קודם לכן** כל התורה כולה בשלמות, הלכות ואגדות, תוספת', ספרא וספרי וכולי' תלמודא, בבלי וירושלמי, **כמו שנראה מספר משנה תורה שחבר.**

Do not bring proof from Rambam that the study of philosophy is proper. He **first studied** the entire Torah: Halacha, Aggada, Tosefta, *Sifra, Sifrei,* Talmud Bavli, and Talmud Yerushalmi, **as is clear from *Mishneh Torah*.**

Then Rivash suggests a debatable thesis: Rambam wrote *Moreh ha-Nevuchim* to refute the proofs Aristotle brought concerning the eternity of matter and divine providence.

וכדי להשיב את האפיקורוס, עשה ספר המור', לסתור המופתים והראיות שהביא הפילוסוף לקיים קדמות העולם, וכן בענין ההשגחה. ולפי שהיו בזמנו הרבה מישראל נבוכים בעקרי התורה, מפני מה שלמדו מן החכמה ההיא.

He wrote *Moreh ha-Nevuchim* to refute the philosophical proofs brought to prove the eternity of matter and the absence of divine providence. [This was necessary,] since in his time, there were many Jews who were confused in essential principles of Torah based on their study of philosophy.

92. Rivash's assertion is debatable. While he wrote *Mishneh Torah* before *Moreh ha-Nevuchim,* he clearly studied philosophy well before he wrote *Mishneh Torah,* as can be seen from his commentary on the Mishna and his treatise on logic. Nevertheless, it may very well be the case that he mastered Torah before writing these earlier works and prior to delving deeply into philosophy.

It certainly is true that *Moreh ha-Nevuchim* was written with the intent to help the student struggling to reconcile Torah and philosophy. Rambam writes in the Introduction to *Moreh ha-Nevuchim*: "But the thinker whose studies have brought him into collision with religion, will, as I already have mentioned, derive much benefit from every chapter."

Indeed, he was successful in this respect. Ramban movingly depicts how Rambam ensured that many Jews enamored of philosophy remained faithful. Thus, he writes concerning Spanish and Provençal Jewish intelligentsia in the early 13th century:

> They have filled their bellies with the foolishness of the Greeks ... they ... make fun ... of the trusting souls.... They did not enter profoundly into the ways of our Torah; the ways of alien children suffice for them. **But for the words of [Rambam]**, but for the fact that they live out of the mouth of his works ... **they would have slipped almost entirely.**[93]

Moreover, as Rivash notes, Rambam defends creation and providence in *Moreh ha-Nevuchim*. However, Rivash's claim that Rambam wrote *Moreh ha-Nevuchim* only in order to rebut heretics is problematic. The simple reading of the work – as well as other Maimonidean works – indicates that he valued philosophy intrinsically and encouraged appropriate students to pursue it.[94]

---

93. Cited in *Encyclopedia Judaica* "Maimonidean Controversy" by Prof. Haim Hillel Ben-Sasson, p. 376.
94. Ramban offers a similar argument to that of Rivash to placate the rabbis of northern France and fend off a total ban on the study of Rambam. He suggests that Rambam certainly would oppose the study of philosophy; however, he had no choice:

> Did he trouble himself for your sake, you geniuses of the Talmud? He saw himself compelled and constrained to structure a work which would offer refuge from the Greek philosophers.... Have you ever listened to their words, have you ever been misled by their proofs? (Cited in *Encyclopedia Judaica* "Maimonidean Controversy" by Prof. Haim Hillel Ben-Sasson, p. 376.)

However, Ramban may not have fully believed that this was Rambam's intention. It seems likely that Ramban wrote this in an attempt to restore civility in a fractious debate (מותר לשנות מפני השלום). As we noted earlier, Ramban was quite successful in that regard.

Rivash then suggests another distinction.[95] Unlike most people who consider studying philosophy, Rambam was capable of distinguishing between that which is valuable within Aristotle's views and that which is false. Rivash invokes the example of R. Meir, who studied Torah from *Acheir* (Elisha b. Avuya) despite the latter's heretical beliefs. The Talmud writes that a person generally must ensure that his teachers are righteous. If so, how could R. Meir study Torah from a heretic? The answer is that R. Meir, in his greatness, was able to sift the fine flour from the refuse. The same can be said concerning Rambam.[96] In 2.15 we examine the conditions when a person can follow R. Meir's model.

Nevertheless, Rivash concludes that even Rambam did not emerge unscathed,[97] as some of his theories are false due to the influence of philosophy. These include his position concerning the son of the *Tzorfatit*,[98] *matan Torah*,[99] and whether angels can take on physical

---

95. ויש לומר כמש"א ז"ל (חגיגה טו ב) על רבי מאיר: היכי גמיר תורה מפומי' דאחר וכו'? והית' התשוב': רבי מאיר קרא אשכח ודרש: הט אזנך ושמע דברי חכמים, ולבך תשית לדעתי, לדעתם לא נאמר, אלא לדעתי, כלומר, שרשעים הם, ועכ"ז אמר הט אזנך. ובארו שם: הא בגדול, הא בקטן; כלומר, כשהתלמיד אדם גדול, מותר שיבור הסולת וישליך הפסולת; כמו שאמרו שם: ר"מ רמון מצא, תוכו אכל, קליפתו זרק.

96. Rivash even suggests that Rambam may be alluding to this point at the beginning of his work by quoting the verse that R. Meir used to justify his pursuit (הט אזנך ושמע דברי חכמים, ולבך תשית לדעתי).

97. ועכ"ז לא נמלט הרב ז"ל מהמשך קצת אחר החכמה בקצת המופתים, כגון בבן הצרפתית ובמעמד הר סיני.

98. In *Moreh ha-Nevuchim* 1:42, Rambam writes:

> The word *mavet* signifies "death" and "severe illness," as in "His heart died (*va-yamot*) within him, and he became as a stone" (*I Shmuel* 25:37), that is, his illness was severe. For this reason it is stated concerning the son of the woman of Tzorfat, "And his sickness was so sore that there was no breath left in him" (*I Melachim* 17:17).

Rivash seems to understand this as indicating that Rambam felt that the child did not actually die. Interestingly, in their comments on this passage, Sheim Tov ibn Falaquera, Abarbanel, and R. Kapach all reject this interpretation, assuming that Rambam agrees the child had died. Instead they understand Rambam as saying that had the verse only said that the child died we might have understood that he did not really die, and it therefore added "there was no breath left in him" to unambiguously describe him as actually dead. Indeed, in each of the passages that Rivash highlights as problematic, other commentators of Rambam understood Rambam as taking a less radical approach.

99. See *Moreh ha-Nevuchim* 2:33, where Rambam states that the Jewish people at Sinai heard only an undifferentiated sound and not particular words. We will return to this point in 8.9.

form.[100] Perhaps, posits Rivash, even Rambam did not really believe some of the things he wrote in *Moreh ha-Nevuchim* and wrote them only because he could not fully dissuade followers of philosophy with the undiluted truth.[101]

He then warns that if philosophy harmed great scholars like Rambam and Ralbag (R. Levi b. Gershon), regular people certainly should avoid it.[102]

Another way those who reject philosophy can justify Rambam's study of such subjects is to cite a letter, probably forged,[103] which indicates that Rambam retracted towards the end of his life. Among those who quote this letter are R. Yitzchak Abarbanel (*Avot* 3, towards the end) and R. Moshe Alshakar (*Teshuvot Maharam Alshakar* 117).[104]

1.8 THE BOTTOM LINE

Is there a halachic consensus concerning the monumental question of the permissibility of studying philosophy? In an intriguing manner, Rama addresses it in his glosses to *Shulchan Aruch*. He writes:

שולחן ערוך יורה דעה סימן רמו סעיף ד

הגה: ואין לאדם ללמוד כי אם מקרא, משנה וגמרא והפוסקים הנמשכים אחריהם, ובזה יקנה העולם הזה והעולם הבא, אבל לא בלמוד שאר חכמות (ריב"ש סימן מ"ה ותלמידי רשב"א). **ומ"מ מותר ללמוד באקראי בשאר חכמות,** ובלבד שלא יהיו ספרי מינים, וזהו נקרא בין החכמים טיול בפרדס. ואין לאדם לטייל בפרדס רק לאחר שמלא

100. In *Moreh ha-Nevuchim* 2:42, Rambam maintains that angels cannot take on physical forms. Accordingly, the angels' visit to Avraham (*Bereishit* 18) must have taken place within a dream.

101. ואולי לא היתה כונתו רק באשר לא יוכל להשיב האנשים ההם לגמרי מן הקצה אל הקצה. ובאר להם ענינים מעטים מן התורה בדרך מסכמת אל הפילוסופיא, וגם זה כתבו ברמז ובהעלם. גם במלאכים שנראו לאברהם אבינו ע"ה אמר שהיה במראה הנבוא'.

102. ומעתה, ישא כל אדם קו"ח בעצמו: אם שני המלאכים האלה, לא עמדו רגליהם במישור בקצת דברים, כבודם במקומם מונח; ואם היו גדולי העולם, איך נעמוד אנחנו אשר לא ראינו מאורות, לערכם. וכמה ראינו פרקו עול התפלה, נתקו מוסרות התורה והמצוה מעליהם בסבת למוד אותן חכמות. וכמ"ש רבינו האי גאון ז"ל בתשוב' שכתבתי למעלה.

103. Most of those who quote the letter presumably did not know the letter was forged.

104. The text of the letter, as well as other relevant sources, can be found in a footnote at the end of 2.12.

> כריסו בשר ויין, והוא לידע איסור והיתר ודיני המצות (רמב"ם ס"פ ד' מהל' יסודי התורה).

> A person should study only Scripture, Mishna, Gemara, halachic decisors (*poskim*), and those that follow them. Through this, a person will acquire *olam ha-zeh* and *olam ha-ba*, but a person should not study others branches of wisdom. **Nevertheless, one may study other branches of wisdom occasionally (*be-akra'i*)**, as long as one does not study heretical works. This study (philosophy) is what Chazal called "strolling in the orchard (*pardeis*)." A person should not stroll in the orchard unless he [first] fills his stomach with meat and wine,[105] namely, knowledge of what is permissible and forbidden and the rules of the *mitzvot*.

Rama here does a remarkable thing: he incorporates the views of both Rambam (who maintained that studying philosophy is a *mitzva*) and Rivash (who prohibits the study of philosophy). His compromise allows for its study as a secondary pursuit. R. Yosef Karo (the *Mechaber*), on the other hand, appears to reject Rambam's view. [106]

Of course, Rama is not the final word on the matter, and this question continues to be debated until today.[107] In a situation where a person can be reasonably confident that the pursuit of wisdom outside of Torah will not lead him astray, there is no clear-cut consensus whether such study (for its own sake) is permitted or recommended. (Where a concern of heresy exists, even Rambam would prohibit such study, as we shall see in Chapter 2.)

105. Interestingly, Rama changes Rambam's "bread and meat" to "meat and wine."

106. Most of the *Mechaber*'s formulations in Y.D. 246 are citations of Rambam's *Hilchot Talmud Torah*. However, he entirely leaves out Rambam's understanding of *pardeis*, indicating that he rejected Rambam's view that philosophy plays a role in *Talmud Torah*. Thus, it would seem that R. Yosef Karo rejects Rambam's view while Rama partially accepts it.

107. For a variety of perspectives, see the Introduction of *Leiv Tov* to *Chovot ha-Levavot*.

Chapter Two

Introducing *Moreh ha-Nevuchim*

In the previous chapter, we learned about Rambam's position that the Torah mandates that we know that God exists and demands that we attempt to understand Him to the extent possible. Studying philosophy accomplishes these goals, and, when learned properly, can be considered a fulfillment of numerous *mitzvot*. The above points are made in all of Rambam's major works. However, *Moreh ha-Nevuchim* is where he most comprehensively expresses his philosophy.

In this chapter, we will introduce this great work. Among the questions we will consider are: what are Rambam's prerequisites for the study of philosophy? How do we explain the seemingly conflicting statements within Rambam concerning the role of philosophy vis-à-vis other *mitzvot*? Is intellectual apprehension of God the only goal a person should have or one of many? How does Rambam view those who do not pursue philosophy? How does he view those who excel in philosophy but fail to perform *mitzvot*? How does Rambam recommend becoming the ideal person?

We will also assess Rambam's perspective on apprehension of God – to what extent can we really know God? What are the dangers of pursuing this elusive objective? What are the implications of Rambam's requirement that a person possess an accurate conception of God? Finally, we will evaluate differing approaches to dealing with contradictions within Rambam's writings. In the appendices, we will elucidate Rambam's perspective on Kabbala and Kabbalists' perspective on Rambam. Our first step in exploring *Moreh ha-Nevuchim*, however, will be to identify its audience as well as its stated goals.

Audience

Who was the intended reader of *Moreh ha-Nevuchim*? The work was written in Judeo-Arabic (entitled *Dalālat al-ḥā'irīn*) in the form of a three part letter to his student, R. Yosef b. Yehuda. Of course, the intended audience was not a single person, but anyone torn between following his intellect and following his religion. As Rambam writes in the beginning of the work, there are people facing a troubling dilemma: should a person follow his intellect and thereby "renounce the foundations of the Torah" or should he "turn his back" on his intellect, "while at the same time perceiving that he had brought loss to himself and harm to his religion?"

What type of person would face such a dilemma? An individual who has studied, but not mastered, Torah and philosophy. In Rambam's words, "a religious man who has been trained to believe in the truth of our holy Torah, who conscientiously fulfills his moral and religious duties, and, at the same time, has been successful in his philosophical studies." Someone for whom the study of Torah leaves them perplexed in light of the modern scholarship to which they have been exposed. Someone not dissimilar to a yeshiva and university student of today. (In 1.7, we saw how Ramban writes about the degree to which Rambam was remarkably successful in saving these struggling students from the grips of heresy and restoring their deep faith in Torah.)

The Dual Goals of the Work

The first goal of *Moreh ha-Nevuchim* relates to the above dilemma. The book will guide the perplexed and show that one need not choose between Torah and philosophy. Understood correctly, by definition, there can be no conflict between what the intellect demonstratively proves and what the Torah teaches, since they are both veritable sources of truth.

Rambam writes that he has another goal: to teach Torah, specifically, to clarify the obscure parts of Torah. Indeed, in the Introduction to the Second Book of *Moreh ha-Nevuchim* he writes:

> It was not my intention when writing this treatise to expound natural science or discuss metaphysical systems ... for the books written on these subjects serve their purpose ... But my intention was, as has been stated in the Introduction, to expound Biblical passages which have been impugned, and to elucidate their hidden and true sense, which is above the comprehension of the multitude.

Thus, Rambam writes, he seeks to elucidate the most esoteric sections of the Torah:

> From the Introduction to this treatise, you may learn that its principal object is to expound, as far as humanly possible, the account of the creation, and of the divine chariot, and to answer questions raised in respect to prophecy and to the knowledge of God ... You will invariably find that my exposition includes the key for understanding some allegorical passages of Torah and their esoteric interpretation.

Rambam writes that the physics and metaphysics he presents are intended to help clarify parts of Torah that might otherwise remain inscrutable. In that sense, his work can be seen as a commentary on the Torah. Indeed, the book contains thousands of references to the written and oral law.

A Key that Unlocks Many Doors

While the *Moreh ha-Nevuchim* is occasionally opaque and technical, some find it to be inspiring and exhilarating.[1] It is a work that grants access to new worlds. As Rambam writes at the end of his Introduction:

1. It is said that R. Pinchas of Koretz used to study *Moreh ha-Nevuchim* on the night of Yom Kippur.

"It is a key permitting one to enter places the gates to which were locked. When those gates are opened and those places are entered, the souls will find rest therein, the eyes will be delighted, and the bodies will be eased of their toil and of their labor." And, as Prof. Leo Strauss[2] aptly added, "not merely a key to a forest but is itself a forest, an enchanted forest, and hence also an enchanting forest; it is a delight to the eyes. For the tree of life is a delight to the eyes."

2.1 WHAT IS PHILOSOPHY AND WHEN CAN ONE BEGIN STUDYING PHILOSOPHY?

We opened this chapter by stating that Rambam opines that studying philosophy can be a fulfillment of numerous *mitzvot,* but what do we mean by studying philosophy? After all, Rambam does not write that it is a *mitzva* to study "philosophy." Nowhere does he state that the Torah mandates or even recommends reading works such as Aristotle's *Physics* or *Metaphysics.* Moreover, Rambam does not use the term philosophy when describing the *mitzva* of *anochi* in the first chapter of *Mishneh Torah.* If the *mitzva* is to know God, why are we claiming that according to Rambam studying philosophy can be a fulfillment of numerous *mitzvot*?

To answer this question, we must define the term philosophy. In 1.2, we noted the term "philosophy" generally refers to either:

(a) a specific method of inquiry (e.g., rationalism),
(b) a particular set of topics (e.g., metaphysics), or
(c) a particular set of teachings (e.g., Aristotle).

In this case, we mean all three. (a) When Rambam describes what we know of God, he does so using logic. Moreover, Rambam argues that, although revelation is real, much of what God taught us through revelation can be understood in rational terms.[3] (b) *Moreh ha-Nevuchim*

2. "How to Begin to Study The Guide of the Perplexed," in Prof. Leo Strauss's introductory essay to the Shlomo Pines translation of *Moreh ha-Nevuchim* (University of Chicago Press, 1963).
3. Rambam was not the first rationalist. R. Sa'adya Gaon, in *Emunot ve-Dei'ot,* shows how Judaism is a religion of reason. In fact, an intelligent individual with sufficient time and resources could independently deduce almost all of that which we learned

engages in the study of metaphysics, the branch of philosophy that deals with the first principles of things, including abstract concepts such as being, knowing, substance, cause, identity, time, and space.[4] (c) In *Moreh ha-Nevuchim* Rambam frequently cites and assesses Greek and Arab philosophers, including Aristotle, Plato, Al-Farabi, Avicenna, and his contemporary Averroes.

---

through revelation. R. Sa'adya Gaon was influenced by *kalam*, an Islamic dialectical theology which Rambam felt was less rationally rigorous than philosophy. Accordingly, Rambam sought to improve upon R. Sa'adya Gaon's work in explaining Judaism in rational terms.

4. For example, Rambam spends considerable time considering the nature of matter, time, and substance. Specifically, he rebuffs the views of the Mutakallemim, or professors of Kalam, regarding atomism, time, and space. According to the Mutakallemim the universe is composed of very small parts (atoms). Atoms are indivisible on account of their smallness; such an atom has no magnitude; but when several atoms combine, the sum has a magnitude and thus forms a body. If, therefore, two atoms were joined together, each atom would become a body, and they would thus form two bodies. The original Mutakallemim also believed in the existence of vacuums, i.e., space which contains nothing. Moreover, they believed "time is composed of time-atoms," i.e., of many parts, which cannot be divided because of their short duration.

   In 1:73, Rambam critiques each of these assumptions. He is most critical of this last conclusion. We quote a couple of sentences of this appraisal for purposes of illustration:

   > The Mutakallemim did not at all understand the nature of time... Now, mark what conclusions were drawn from these three propositions and were accepted by the Mutakallemim as true. They held that locomotion consisted in the translation of each atom of a body from one point to the next one; accordingly, the velocity of one body in motion cannot be greater than that of another body. When, nevertheless, two bodies are observed to move during the same time through different spaces, the cause of this difference is not attributed by them to the fact that the body which has moved through a larger distance had a greater velocity, but to the circumstance that motion which in ordinary language is called slow, has been interrupted by more moments of rest, while the motion which ordinarily is called quick has been interrupted by fewer moments of rest. When it is shown that the motion of an arrow, which is shot from a powerful bow, is in contradiction to their theory, they declare that in this case too the motion is interrupted by moments of rest...."

   He also derides the atomists' account of geometry and bodily rotation.

Rambam does all this in order to understand God to the extent possible. Thus, philosophy, for Rambam, plays an oversized role in the service of God. *Moreh ha-Nevuchim* is Rambam's primary venue for expressing his philosophical positions. Nevertheless, scholars debate the extent to which *Moreh ha-Nevuchim* should be seen as a philosophical work. Much of *Moreh ha-Nevuchim* more closely resembles a commentary on the Torah than a work of philosophy. For example, much of his attention is devoted to the explanation of Scripture and an understanding of the reasons for *mitzvot*. We will consider this question extensively in 2.10.

When Can One Begin Studying Philosophy?

Despite the importance of studying philosophy, someone insufficiently prepared will not simply fail to understand; his ill-preparedness likely will cause him to *misunderstand*, potentially leading him astray. Needless to say, the stakes are very high when considering matters such as the existence of God.

Moreover, it is important to stress that while Rambam maintains that a correct conception of God is essential to being Jewish, this can be achieved at a basic level without philosophy. For example, belief in God's incorporeality is a tenet of faith. Knowing how to prove it through philosophy is a noble, yet ultimately less pressing goal.

Rambam writes that the framework for the prerequisites for philosophy can be found in the Talmud (*Chagiga* 11b). There, the Talmud prohibits teaching esoteric wisdom publicly lest someone who is not properly prepared listen in. Even among worthy students, the teacher must be able to give students individual attention to make sure they do not err. Moreover, when it comes to *ma'aseh merkava*, the material cannot be conveyed overtly even to a worthy individual. The student must independently extrapolate the concept from the basic framework set up by the teacher.

Rambam elaborates on this in his Introduction to *Moreh ha-Nevuchim* as well as in *Mishneh Torah*.[5] Following the Talmud, Rambam

5. We already partially cited these texts in 1.3 but return to them due to their fundamentality.

distinguishes between *ma'aseh bereishit,* which he discusses in Chapters 3 and 4, and *ma'aseh merkava,* which he considers in the opening two chapters. Regarding *ma'aseh bereishit* (a category we define in 2.11) the conditions are less restrictive:

רמב״ם הלכות יסודי התורה פרק ד הלכה י
כל הדברים האלו שדיברנו בעניין זה, כמר מדלי הם; ודברים עמוקים הם, אבל אינם כעומק עניין פרק ראשון ושני. וביאור כל אלו הדברים שבפרק שלישי ורביעי, הוא הנקרא מעשה בראשית. וכך ציוו חכמים הראשונים, שאין דורשין גם בדברים האלו ברבים, אלא לאדם אחד בלבד מודיעים דברים אלו ומלמדין אותו.

These matters have been discussed very briefly here and are deep matters, but not as deep as those discussed in the first two chapters. The matters discussed in these latter two chapters are those relating to creation (*ma'aseh bereishit*). Chazal commanded us not to discuss these matters in public. However, one may discuss and teach them to an individual.

Unlike *ma'aseh bereishit,* which can be taught privately, Halacha restricts the explicit teaching of *ma'aseh merkava* entirely:

רמב״ם הלכות יסודי התורה פרק ב הלכה יב
ציוו חכמים הראשונים שלא לדרוש בדברים אלו אלא לאיש אחד בלבד, והוא שיהיה חכם ומבין מדעתו. ואחר כך מוסרין לו ראשי הפרקים, ומודיעין אותו שמץ מן הדבר; והוא מבין מדעתו, ויודע סוף הדבר ועומקו. ודברים אלו דברים עמוקים הם עד למאוד, ואין כל דעת ודעת ראויה לסובלן... לך לבדך, ואל תדרוש אותן ברבים...

Chazal commanded us not to discuss these topics with more than one person, and that person should be wise and capable of independent extrapolation. If one is on that level one presents a rough outline and teaches a small quantity allowing the student to extrapolate and fully understand the profundity of the matter. These topics are extremely deep, and not everyone can understand them… These matters should be yours alone, not taught publicly…

The study of Halacha must precede the pursuit of both *ma'aseh bereishit* and *ma'aseh merkava*:

רמב"ם הלכות יסודי התורה פרק ב הלכה יג

ועִניְיני ארבעה פרקים אלו שבחמש מצוות האלו - הם שחכמים הראשונים קוראין אותן פרדס, כמו שאמרו ארבעה נכנסו לפרדס: ואף על פי שגדולי ישראל היו וחכמים גדולים היו, לא כולם היה בהן כוח לידע ולהשיג כל הדברים על בוריין.

ואני אומר שאין ראוי להיטייל בפרדס, אלא מי שנתמלא כרסו לחם ובשר. ולחם ובשר זה, הוא לידע ביאור האסור והמותר וכיוצא בהן משאר המצוות. **ואף על פי שדברים אלו, דבר קטן קראו אותם חכמים, שהרי אמרו חכמים דבר גדול מעשה מרכבה, ודבר קטן הוויה דאביי ורבא, אף על פי כן, ראויין הן להקדימן: שהן מיישבין דעתו של אדם תחילה, ועוד שהן הטובה הגדולה שהשפיע הקדוש ברוך הוא ליישוב העולם הזה, כדי לנחול חיי העולם הבא. ואפשר שיידעם הכול - גדול וקטן, איש ואישה, בעל לב רחב ובעל לב קצר.**

These four chapters have discussed the first five commandments (*anochi, lo yihyeh, shema Yisrael, ahavat Hashem,* and *yirat Hashem*) and are what the Early Sages called *pardeis,* as it is written (*Chagiga* 14b), "Four people went to study *pardeis,* etc." Even though those four people were giants of Israel and very great sages, not all of them had the capability to understand and comprehend these matters.

I say that it is not fitting to study *pardeis* unless one first has studied what is metaphorically called "bread and meat," which is the study of *mitzvot:* what is permitted, what is forbidden, and the like. **These matters were called "a little matter" by the Sages, as they have said, "*Ma'aseh merkava* is a great matter, whereas the debates of Abayei and Rava are a little matter." Nevertheless, it still is fitting to study them (*mitzvot*) first, because they settle a man's mind. Furthermore, they are the great good that God gave to this world, [the means] by which we can inherit life in the world to come. It is possible for everyone – adults, children,**

men, women, those of broad understanding and those of limited understanding – to know these matters.

Rambam rules that before engaging in esoteric study, one must fill himself with "bread and meat," meaning Halacha. This is important not just because it is important to know what to do, and because it is something that everybody can do, but because the study of Halacha will train a person to think properly.[6]

Does Rambam mean that one first must master all halachic matters ("*Shas* and *poskim*") and only then study philosophy, or does he mean one must have a basic understanding of that which is permitted and prohibited before proceeding? Rambam only explicitly mentions that one must know the practical Halacha (no easy task). R. Shabtai b. Meir ha-Kohen (1621–1662)[7] seems to assume Rambam meant that one must have studied (and presumably know) the entire Talmud ("Shas").[8] R. Elchanan Wasserman (*Koveitz Shiurim* Vol. 2 47:9), which we cite in 9.7, also appears to presume that mastery of revealed Torah is a necessary prerequisite. On the other hand, rabbis like R. Aharon Lichtenstein, who encourage college-age students to pursue science and philosophy because of their religious value, presumably assume a less robust background is demanded.[9] Likewise, chasidic thinkers who support the study of Kabbala for the young and relatively uneducated seemingly accept the latter option (at least with respect to mysticism); see 12.8.

The matter is not so straightforward, though. Both with respect to science/philosophy and with respect to Kabbala, not all explorations are the same. Some questions and texts may be appropriate for someone who has not yet mastered exoteric wisdom, while others demand a more rigorous background. Thus, R. Dovid Beirish Gotlieb (*Yad ha-Ketana*)

6. In *Moreh ha-Nevuchim* (1:32–33), Rambam elaborates upon the dangers of studying philosophy prematurely and suggests a curriculum to prepare a student to study philosophy.
7. Often referred to as *Shach*, the acronym of his masterful commentary on *Shulchan Aruch*, *Siftei Kohen*.
8. *Shach*, Y.D. 246:6
9. See his article in *Judaism's Encounter with Other Cultures* (Northvale, NJ: Jason Aronson, 1997) entitled "Torah and General Culture: Confluence and Conflict."

points out that Rambam requires these comprehensive prerequisites only "*le-tayeil be-pardeis*," i.e., to study *ma'aseh merkava*, but not to study more basic principles of faith.

Other Necessary Preparations

Rambam teaches that God bestowed upon man the means to achieve the highest form of perfection that is possible for a human being, but one will only succeed when properly prepared. We have already seen the necessity to first fill one's stomach with "bread and meat," in other words, a proper understanding of Halacha. However, Torah preparations alone are insufficient. In *Moreh ha-Nevuchim* 1:34 Rambam stresses that one must attain proficiency in logic, algebra, geometry, and astronomy. Logic, in particular, helps one understand the framework and principles of the learning process and avoid distortion of the thought process (*Moreh ha-Nevuchim* 1:5). To prevent error, one's studies must progress in the correct sequence. Thus, in the Introduction to *Moreh ha-Nevuchim*, Rambam adds that a correct understanding of *ma'aseh bereishit* is a prerequisite to *ma'aseh merkava*. He writes: "This is so since natural science borders on divine science, and its study precedes that of divine science in time as has been made clear to whoever has engaged in speculation on these matters."[10]

Intellectual Preparations Are Insufficient

Rambam frequently reminds us that intellectual preparations do not suffice. Even mastery of "*shas* and *poskim*" does not guarantee safety. Elisha b. Avuya (*Acheir*) certainly had filled himself with bread and wine, and yet his venture into *pardeis* led him off a cliff (*Chagiga* 14b). Thus, in his Introduction to *Moreh ha-Nevuchim*, Rambam stresses that intellectual preparation is insufficient; one must genuinely fear God, as the verse says, סוד ה' ליראיו "The secret of God is with those that fear Him" (*Tehillim* 25:14).

Even once one has achieved these impressive prerequisites, Rambam warns of the importance of restraint; while a person is naturally excited to being, a proper student displays modesty and humility in this noble pursuit. Moreover, Rambam in numerous places (e.g., *Moreh ha-Nevuchim* 3:51) stresses that one who is engrossed or even tempted

10. P. 9 of the Pines edition.

by physical pleasures will never progress in understanding God. (Of course, in the third chapter of *Hilchot Dei'ot* Rambam strongly condemns unhealthy, unnecessary, or excessive asceticism.)

In summary, Rambam, in *Moreh ha-Nevuchim* (1:5) enumerates four general prerequisites:

> Man, when he commences to speculate (study philosophy), ought not to embark at once on a subject so vast and important unless he has done the following:
>
> 1. Undergone training in the study of the several branches of science and knowledge,
> 2. Most thoroughly refined his moral character,
> 3. Subdued his passions and desires, the offspring of his imagination;
> 4. When, in addition, he has obtained a knowledge of the true fundamental propositions, a comprehension of the several methods of inference and proof, and the capacity of guarding against fallacies, then he may approach the investigation of this subject.

Intuitively, we understand why character development is necessary, but why is separating from the physical so important to studying these topics? Rambam points to two concerns. The first is the possibility that temptation can unknowingly cause error. Only when a person's singular desire is the quest for truth will he be safe. But if one simultaneously craves other things, such as physical pleasure or honor, these desires may cloud one's judgment and lead one to justify the false beliefs necessary to achieve our yearning. Rambam was well aware that left unchecked, desires pervert our intellectual reasoning. A person may think he is seeking the truth, but, in fact, he is only seeking to justify his agenda. Thus, to correctly apprehend the truth, one must first rid himself of any sort of desire other than to seek truth for the sake of truth. A tall task, but eminently possible.[11]

11. Thus, the Talmud (*Sanhedrin* 63b) observes that subconscious desires were behind any intellectual justifications for idolatry: יודעין היו ישראל בעבודה זרה שאין בה ממש, ולא עבדו עבודה זרה אלא להתיר להם עריות בפרהסיא. In 11.17, we will explore the possibility that desire is also behind the errors of heresy.

Rambam implies that there is a second concern with carnal pleasure. When one seeks to understand non-physical matters, physicality is a barrier. Because the goal is to understand God, and God is non-physical, we must seek to elevate ourselves above the physical as much as possible. This, Rambam writes in *Moreh ha-Nevuchim* 3:51, explains why the Torah stresses that Moshe did not eat or drink while on Sinai. When Moshe reached the pinnacle of divine apprehension at Sinai, naturally (and not supernaturally), food became unnecessary.

2.2 OUR ABILITY TO UNDERSTAND GOD

As we have seen, Rambam assigns great value to the *mitzva* of understanding God. Simultaneously, though, we must consider our limitations in this respect. Rambam writes:

הלכות יסודי התורה פרק א הלכה י
מהו זה שביקש משה רבינו להשיג כשאמר הראני נא את כבודך, ביקש לידע אמיתת המצאו של הקדוש ב"ה עד שיהיה ידוע בלבו כמו ידיעת אחד מן האנשים שראה פניו ונחקקה צורתו בלבו שנמצא אותו האיש נפרד בדעתו משאר האנשים, כך ביקש משה רבינו להיות מציאות הקב"ה נפרדת בלבו משאר הנמצאים עד שידע אמתת המצאו כאשר היא.

והשיבו ברוך הוא שאין כח בדעת האדם החי שהוא מחובר מגוף ונפש להשיג אמיתת דבר זה על בוריו, והודיעו ברוך הוא מה שלא ידע אדם לפניו ולא ידע לאחריו, עד שהשיג מאמיתת המצאו דבר שנפרד הקב"ה בדעתו משאר הנמצאים, כמו שיפרד אחד מן האנשים שראה אחוריו והשיג כל גופו ומלבושו בדעתו משאר גופי האנשים, ועל דבר זה רמז הכתוב ואמר וראית את אחורי ופני לא יראו.

What did Moshe, our teacher, want to comprehend when he requested: "Please show me Your glory" (*Shemot* 33:18)? He asked to know the truth of the existence of the Holy One, blessed be He, to the extent that it could be internalized within his mind, as one knows a particular person whose face he saw and whose image has been engraved within his heart. Thus, this person's [identity] is distinguished within one's mind from [that of] other

> men. Similarly, Moshe, our teacher, asked that the existence of the Holy One, blessed be He, be distinguished in his mind from the existence of other entities, to the extent that he would know the truth of His existence as it is [in its own right].
>
> He, blessed be He, replied to him that it is not within the potential of a living man, a synthesis of body and soul, to comprehend this matter in its entirety. [Nevertheless,] He, blessed be He, revealed [to Moshe] matters that no other man had known before him – nor would ever know afterward – until he was able to comprehend [enough] of the truth of His existence for the Holy One, blessed be He, to be distinguished in his mind from other entities, as a person is distinguished from other men when one sees his back and knows the structure of his body and [the manner in which] he is clothed. This is alluded to in the verse, "You shall see My back, but you shall not see My face" (*Shemot* 33:23).

It goes without saying that as finite creations, we cannot fully understand our infinite Creator. Rambam adds that we are especially limited as long as we remain attached to our physical bodies. Thus, Rambam insists that one must exercise extraordinary caution when attempting to know God.

What emerges is that on the one hand, we are instructed to understand God to the best of our ability. On the other hand, attempting to do so is potentially dangerous. Let us identify two risks.

The Danger of Misunderstanding

The first concern is that when we try to understand God we will make Him human. As finite and limited creatures, we can never fully understand God. Naturally, we tend to imagine God in human terms. For some, this means imagining God has some sort of physical existence. This is obviously wrong. However, there are more subtle errors. Rambam, as we shall see in Chapter 10, writes that ascribing positive character traits to God, such as merciful, contradicts divine unity. R. Kook, in an essay entitled "The Pangs of Cleansing" (*Orot* 5), highlights this danger:

> ... Even attributing to Him intellect and will, even the term divine, the term God, suffers from limitations of definition. Except for the keen awareness that all these are but sparkling flashes of what cannot be defined – these [attributions and terms] will engender heresy... [12]

Due to a human's inherent inability to ever fully understand God, there is a tendency to shrink God down to size, to conceive of Him in ways we can relate to. Doing so can have disastrous consequences. Besides the falsity or the error, R. Kook suggests that an immature understanding of God is a central cause of atheism. R. Kook argues that atheism is frequently the rejection of a misunderstood conception of the Divine. Or, as others put it, the god they reject is not the God in whom I believe.

The Purpose of Anthropomorphisms and the Need to Form a Relationship with God

Just as we err when we make God too human, we can also stray when we make God to non-human. The second concern applies specifically when a person seeks to understand God through philosophy. This hazard is the opposite of the first. Apart from the dangers of error that lurk when we pursue that which is beyond our grasp, a topic we will return to shortly, there is a risk that relating to God in such an abstract manner will hinder our ability to emotionally connect to Him. How does one relate to God when one discovers He has no emotions? It is sometimes easier to love and fear God when He seems more tangible, more real. Grave dangers await an individual who sees God as a concept, forgetting He is an *Elokim chaim,* a living God.[13]

To appreciate this point, we must consider two reasons why the Torah depicts God in a way that could itself be a source of error. Why would the Torah refer to God with positive (e.g., God is kind or merciful),

---

12. Adaptod from the translation of Ben Zion Bokser, "Abraham Isaac Kook: The Lights of Penitence, the Moral Principles, Lights of Holiness, Essays, Letters, and Poems." (New York: Paulist, 1978).
13. Even if the term "living," when used with reference to God, has an entirely different connotation than when used about all other living beings.

emotional (e.g., God's anger), and even physical descriptions (e.g., His outstretched arm) if these depictions are inaccurate?

The first explanation is the straightforward one. We naturally see physical things as more real than non-physical ones. Therefore, the Torah speaks of God in physical terms, despite their falsehood, to reinforce the reality of His existence. (This factor may have been especially necessary in light of the historical considerations.[14]) When understood properly, of course, verses that seem to depict physicality are not meant to be understood as physical characteristics.

The second rationale for anthropomorphisms is more nuanced. Perhaps the Torah uses human parlance, *dibra Torah ke-lashon bnei adam,*[15] not only to ensure that we believe in His existence, but also to enable

---

14. In *Moreh ha-Nevuchim* (1:46), Rambam asks why the Torah uses language that might confuse people and lead them to believe that God has a body. He writes that these descriptions were necessary so that the masses, who feel that only something with a body can exist, would come to belief in God. Of course, this raises other thorny issues. Is it conceivable that the Torah misleads its readers by implying a false conception of God? When was this false portrayal of God corrected? We will examine these concerns in sections 10.8 and 11.4.

15. Many have noted that the Rishonim were the first to use *dibra Torah ke-lashon bnei adam* in this context. For example, the Talmud uses the term to explain why we cannot always extract a law from a repetitive phrase (such as גנוב יגנב), since the Torah sometimes speaks in human parlance, and humans use this sort of repetition (see *Bava Metzia* 94b and *Nedarim* 3a). Numerous Rishonim, though, including Rambam (*Yesodei ha-Torah,* Ch. 1), R. Bachya ibn Pakuda (*Sha'ar ha-Yichud,* Ch. 10), R. Yehuda ha-Levi (*Kuzari* 5:27), and R. Avraham ibn Daud (Introduction to *Emunat ha-Rama*) all use this phrase to justify the anthropomorphisms in Tanach. R. Mayer Twersky argued that fundamentally, the Talmudic usage resembles the medieval usage insofar as both presume that the Torah also intends to address regular people and accordingly accommodates their intellectual frailty.

Why, then, does the Talmud not use the phrase to justify anthropomorphisms? R. Twersky suggested that this question is anachronistic, since the Sages of the Talmud did not feel the need to fight the battle against corporealism. Indeed, Rambam frequently stresses that certain things previously were understood and accepted without the need for a proof, but later, due to deteriorating intellectual conditions, the need to prove or justify them arose. Although belief that God has a body certainly was rampant at the time of Chazal, Chazal apparently felt that among Jews, a more dangerous belief was that of dualism or lack of belief in resurrection. Accordingly, they focused on resolving these issues. Rishonim, due to changing circumstances, turned their attention to addressing questions of corporealism and creation.

us to develop a relationship with Him. This is especially true concerning positive and emotional attributes. As R. Bachya ibn Pakuda writes:

חובות הלבבות שער היחוד פרק י
וכיון שהגענו עד הנה מדברינו, אין צורך לבאר הענין הזה יותר, **מפני שאנו חייבין לרהות ולירא ולהזהר ממנו.**

Now that we have reached this point in our attempt to understand God, there is no need to explain the matter further, **for we have to dread, fear, and be wary from Him.**

As physical creatures, we think in physical terms[16]; accordingly, a person's conception of God can become so intangible that despite its accuracy, it leaves him with nothing left to fear.[17] Therefore, says R. Bachya, at a certain point we have to stop.[18]

---

16. Thus, God conveys His message to prophets using parables.
17. That is not to say that it is permitted to conceive of God in physical terms as a means of creating a relationship with Him. In *Moreh ha-Nevuchim* 1:35, Rambam stresses the importance to teaching the masses about God's incorporeality, even if they cannot understand the proofs for this truth.
18. One might add that the two reasons highlighted above consider the matter from two perspectives. The first reason was particularly relevant for the generation receiving the Torah, who would have had a particularly difficult time relating to an incorporeal God, while the second rationale addresses a perennial problem. Not surprisingly, then, we find R. Bachya ibn Pakuda presents both understandings. We saw above his reference to the second concern, while in *Chovot ha-Levavot* (*Sha'ar ha-Bitachon,* Ch. 6) he writes that anthropomorphisms were particularly necessary for the Jews leaving Egypt because they were steeped in idolatry and unable to relate to that which they could not see. He writes that this is also one reason why the written Torah focuses on physical reward and punishment as opposed to the true, spiritual remuneration. The Jewish people could not envisage a spiritual existence in which the soul is separated from the body. Accordingly, the Torah stresses the corporeal:

    שהעם היו מן הסכלות ומעוט ההבנה בעניין שאיננו נעלם ממה שכתוב בתורה, ונהג הבורא עמהם מנהג האב החומל על בנו הקטן, כשהוא רוצה ליסרו בנחת ולאט, כמו שכתוב (הושע יד) כי נער ישראל ואוהבהו. והאב כשרוצה ללמד את בנו בנערותו והח־כמות אשר יעלה בהם אל המעלות העליונות, אשר לא יבינם הנער בעת ההיא. ואילו היה מפייס אותו עליהם, ואומר לו סבול יגיעות המוסר והלימוד בעבור שתעלה בהם אל המעלות החמודות, לא היה סובל את זה ולא שומע, מפני שאין מבין אותו. וכאשר ייעדהו על זה במה שהוא ערב לו מיד, ממאכל ומשתה ומלבוש נאה ומרכבת נאה והדומה

R. Yitzchak Arama, in *Akeidat Yitzchak* 45, forcefully highlights this danger:

> The revelation [at Sinai] taught [the Jewish people] and left an eternal memory that God looks down from the heavens onto the dwellers of the earth, to pay each person for his actions ... It teaches us that man does not live by philosophical expositions, but only by keeping God's word does he live forever. This is what the divine [Tanna] stated: **"Know what is above you: an eye that sees, an ear that hears, and all your deeds are recorded in a book" (*Avot* 2:1). And even if the masses take this in its literal sense, no harm is done, so long as it brings them to a closer sense of God's providence. For doubt or [abstruse] philosophic discourse takes them away from their simple faith and does not bring them [instead] to any better place; rather they are left losing out from both ends.**[19]

Along similar lines, R. Kook argues that human language cannot capture divine matters. Imagery proves necessary to form a relationship with the Divine: "These images, then, precisely by virtue of their allusive, suggestive, almost numinous quality, induce in the multitude a spirit of fear, awe, trembling, and piety."[20]

In fact, the value of describing God in human terms for purposes of creating a relationship with Him is so obvious, claims R. Yosef Dov

---

לזה, ויועידהו במה שיצער אותו מיד מרעב ועירום ומלקות והדומה להם, ויישב דעתו על מה שיבטח עליו מן הראיות והמורגשות והעדויות הגלויות האמיתיות - יקל מעליו לסבול יגיעת המוסר ולשאת טרחו.

וכאשר יגיע לימי הבחרות, ויחזק שכלו, יבין העניין המכוון אליו במוסרו ויכווין אליו, ותמעט בעיניו הערבות אשר היה רץ אליה בתחילת ענייניו, והיה זה לחמלה עליו.

וכן הבורא יתברך יחל עמו והפחידם בגמול ועונש ממהרים, מפני שידע כי העם כאשר יתקנו לעבודה תגל מעליהם סכלותם בגמול העולם ועונשו, ויכוונו בעבודה אליו, ויתנהגו בה עדיו.

וכן נאמר בכל מה שבספרים מהגשמת הבורא יתברך.

19. Translation adapted from R. Aaron Lopiansky, "The Corporeality Which Never Was," *Dialogue* 5 (Fall 2014), p. 65.

20. *Rabbi Abraham Isaac Kook and Jewish Spirituality* by Lawrence J. Kaplan and David Shatz, p. 48–49.

Soloveitchik, that it is remarkable that Rambam is bothered at all by its usage: "I could never feel sympathy for Maimonides' horror at religious-sensual portrayal."[21]

To summarize, the attempt to try to understand God comes with two grave concerns. The first is we may err in our understanding of God. As finite and limited human beings we can never fully understand God. Instead of recognizing our limitations and limiting our inquiry to that which is within our grasp, we may instead try to fully understand God by depicting Him in a manner that we can conceive of. We may paint God in our own image – imagining that He exists as we exist or that He emotes as we emote.

The second concern is precisely the opposite. It occurs when a person studies philosophy and recognizes that character traits and emotions contradict divine unity. The study of metaphysics can cause a person to conceive of God in such abstract terms that he struggles to have a meaningful relationship with Him. God is no longer a living God but an abstract concept. To avoid this concern the Torah anthropomorphizes God (attributes to God human form and personality), despite the danger of misinterpretation, to inculcate within us the realness of His existence and to aid the establishment of a meaningful relationship.

2.3 WE DO NOT SEEK TO UNDERSTAND GOD'S ESSENCE

If we cannot truly understand God, how can we relate to Him? The midrash offers a fundamental distinction to answer this question. While we cannot possibly understand His essence, we are able to relate to the manner in which He expresses Himself within our world.

שמות רבה (וילנא) פרשת שמות פרשה ג

ויאמר אלהים אל משה, אמר רבי אבא בר ממל אמר ליה הקב"ה למשה שמי אתה מבקש לידע, לפי מעשי אני נקרא פעמים שאני נקרא באל שדי, בצבאות, באלהים, בה', כשאני דן את הבריות אני נקרא אלהים, וכשאני עושה מלחמה ברשעים אני נקרא צבאות, וכשאני תולה על חטאיו של אדם אני נקרא אל שדי, וכשאני מרחם על עולמי אני נקרא ה'.

21. *Worship of the Heart: Essays on Jewish Prayer*, p. 63.

> God said to Moshe, "You request to know My Name? I am known by My actions: sometime I am called *Keil Shakkai*, sometimes *Tzevakot*, sometimes *Elokim*, sometimes the tetragrammaton. When I judge humanity, I am called *Elokim*. When I wage war against the wicked, I am called *Tzevakot*. When I withhold due punishment, I am called *Keil Shakkai*. And when I have mercy on my world, I am called by the tetragrammaton.

The midrash notes that, despite His absolute unity, we perceive God differently at different times.[22] Thus, when Moshe asks what name he should use for God, God responds, "I will be that which I will be."[23]

---

22. R. Bachya b. Asher explains:

רבינו בחיי שמות פרק ג

כונת החכמים במדרש הזה כי אין רבוי ביחוד, ומה ששמותיו יתברך רבים, השכל יודע כי כולם נאמרים לבורא אחד, אבל הפה אינו יכול לכלול אותם בבת אחת במלה אחת כאשר יכלול אותם השכל, ועל כן שמותיו יתעלה רבים, מתרבים ומשתנים לפי הפעולות מצד המקבלים, לא מצדו יתברך.

This is true even with respect to prophets, as noted by R. Chananeil (*Chagiga* 14b). The Talmud there states:

כתוב אחד אומר (דניאל ז) לבושיה כתלג חיור ושער ראשה כעמר נקא וכתיב (שיר השירים ה) קוצותיו תלתלים שחורות כעורב לא קשיא כאן בישיבה כאן במלחמה דאמר מר אין לך נאה בישיבה אלא זקן ואין לך נאה במלחמה אלא בחור.

ר"ח חגיגה יד עמוד א

[הקב"ה] מראה לנביאים כעין דמות באובנתא דליבא (בהבנת הלב), אבל הקב"ה [עצמו] ישתבח שמו אין לו דמות. וזה הדבר מוכיח שאין שם דמות, שאילו היה תמיד [נראה בתואר] אחד - או דמות בחור לעולם או דמות זקן לעולם - [היה מקום לחשוב שזו היא דמותו עצמו], אלא [כיון שהדמות משתנה בא הדבר] ללמדך שאין שם דמות כלל. אלא מה שמראה לנביאים כעין דמות [וכפי] מה שיישר לפניו.

23. Ramban adds that while this name does not capture what He is, He responds to it, and through it we can come close to Him:

רמב"ן שמות פרק ג פסוק יג

ולא יוכל אדם לבא עד עומק דרכיו כן אמר בכאן אהא עם מאן דאהא בשמי שתאמר להם שהוא אהיה כי בו אני עם האדם לחונן ולרחם.

Rambam, however, informs us that there is one name of God, the tetragrammaton (יקוק), that is different in that it refers to His essence and not just a manifestation of His actions:

מורה הנבוכים חלק א פרק סא

כל שמותיו יתעלה הנמצאים בספרים כולם נגזרים מן הפעולות, וזה מה שאין העלם בו אלא שם אחד, והוא יו"ד ה"א וא"ו ה"א שהוא שם המיוחד לו יתעלה, ולזה נקרא שם המפורש, ענינו שהוא יורה על עצמו יתעלה הוראה מבוארת אין השתתפות בה.

Nefesh ha-Chaim (2:2–3) and others write that this midrash teaches us that when we relate to God, we are not relating to His essence, but rather to the manner in which He is manifest in the world.

נפש החיים שער ב פרק ב

אמנם ענין הברכה לו ית"ש. אין הכוונה **לעצמות** אדון יחיד ב"ה כביכול. חלילה וחלילה. כי הוא מרומם מעל כל ברכה. אבל הענין כמ"ש בזו' דקב"ה סתים וגליא. כי **עצמות** א"ס ב"ה סתים מכל סתימין ואין לכנותו ח"ו בשום שם כלל אפילו בשם הוי"ה ב"ה ואפי' בקוצו של יו"ד דבי'.

(ואף גם מה שבז"הק מכנהו ית' בשם אין סוף איננו כנוי עליו ית"ש אלא הכוונה על השגתנו אותו מצד כחות הנשפעים מאתו בהתחברותו ברצונו להעולמות. ולזאת כנוהו א"ס ולא אין ראשית. כי באמת מצד עצמותו ית"ש אין לו לא סוף ולא ראשית. רק מצד השגתינו כחותיו ית'. הלא כל השגתינו הוא רק ראשית. אבל אין סוף להגיע בהשגה להשיג את כחותיו ית' הנשפעים.)

Rambam writes in the next chapter that the forty-two letter name of God also reflects His essence in a different sort of way:

> There also was a name of forty-two letters known among them. Every intelligent person knows that one word of forty-two letters is impossible. But it was a phrase of several words that had forty-two letters in total. There is no doubt that the words had such a meaning as to convey a correct notion of the essence of God, in the way we have stated. This phrase of so many letters is called a name because, like other proper nouns, it represents one single object, and several words have been employed in order to explain more clearly the idea that the name represents, for an idea can more easily be comprehended if expressed in many words... Those two names must have included some metaphysical ideas. It can be proved from the following rule laid down by our Sages that one of the names conveyed profound knowledge: "The name of forty-two letters is exceedingly holy; it can be entrusted only to one who is modest, in the midway of life, not easily provoked to anger, temperate, gentle, and who speaks kindly to his fellow men. He who understands it, is cautious with it, and keeps it in purity is loved above and is liked here below; he is respected by his fellow men, his learning remains with him, and he enjoys both this world and the world to come" (*Kiddushin* 71a).

Others disagree with Rambam, maintaining that no name possibly can capture God's essence; see, for example, *Torat ha-Mincha Shemot* 20 and *Nefesh ha-Chaim* 2:2.

ומה שמושג אצלינו קצת ואנו מכנים ומתארים כמה תארים ושמות וכנויים ומדות. כמו שמצינום בתורה ובכל מטבע התפלה. כולם הם רק מצד התחברותו יתברך אל העולמות והכחות מעת הבריאה להעמידים ולהחיותם ולהנהיגם כרצונו ית"ש.

However, the idea of blessing Him (blessed be His Name) is not [aimed] towards the **Essence** (so to speak) of the One Master (blessed is He) – never ever! – for He is far, far above any blessing. Rather, the idea is as is stated in *Zohar* (*Parshat Emor* 98 and in other places) that the Holy One (blessed be He) is [both] revealed and hidden. For the **essence** of the *Ein Sof*[24] (blessed is He) is the most hidden of the hidden and cannot be assigned any name at all, not even the tetragrammaton (blessed is He)...

(And even the *Zohar*'s reference to Him (blessed be He) with the name *Ein Sof* is not a descriptive name for Him (blessed be His Name). Rather, the intention is relative to how we perceive Him, from the perspective of the forces that are bestowed by Him via His purposeful relationship with the worlds. And for this reason, He is referred to as "*Ein Sof*" (without end) and not "*Ein Reishit*" (without beginning), for in truth, from the perspective of His Essence (blessed be His Name), He has no end and no beginning; [it is] only from our perspective of His powers (blessed be He). All of our understanding is just a beginning, for we can never arrive at a complete understanding of His powers (blessed be His Name) that influence [the world].)

And what we are able to grasp to some small degree and can name and describe with a number of names that are 1) physically descriptive, 2) descriptive of a relationship, 3) descriptive of behavioral qualities, and 4) descriptive of

24. The term *Ein Sof* refers to God and expresses how God is infinite and beyond comprehension. The term literally means unending, as in "there is no end to God."

> **personality qualities, as we have encountered in the Torah and in prayers; all of them only are from the perspective of His (blessed be He) relationship with the worlds and the powers from the moment of the creation, to set them up, to sustain them, and to control them according to His will (blessed be His Name).**

The Tension Between Our Need to Understand and Our Inability to Understand

The tension between our need to understand and our inability to understand is most apparent within the writings of Rambam. On the one hand, we have seen Rambam's assertion that knowledge of God forms the basis for our relationship with Him (see *Hilchot Teshuva*, Chapter 10). At the same time, Rambam stresses the limitations of our ability to understand God.

In *Moreh ha-Nevuchim* (1:58), Rambam writes:

> Praised be He Who, at the moment that the minds glance at His essence, their understanding turns faulty. At the moment of glancing at the necessary correlation between His will and His actions, knowledge turns into ignorance. When the tongues attempt to exalt Him with attributes, all verbosity turns into ineptitude and faultiness.
>
> We longingly strive to come close to Him, but just as we arrive, we realize how far away we are. Accordingly, the greatest praise for Hashem is, as King David said, silence.[25]

Later (*Moreh ha-Nevuchim* 1:59), he adds:

> All the philosophers say that we are dazzled by His beauty, and He is hidden from us because of the intensity with which He becomes manifest, just as the sun is hidden to the eyes that are too weak to apprehend it....The most apt phrase

25. Adapted from the S. Pines translation (Chicago: University of Chicago Press, 1963).

> concerning this subject is the dictum found in *Tehillim* (65:2): "To You silence is praise" לְךָ דֻמִיָּה תְהִלָּה, which is interpreted to mean that silence with regard to You is praise. This is a very profound observation. For whatever was intended to have been expressed by way of exaltation and praise of Him will be found faulty when applied to Him, sensing that the praise is somehow wanting. Accordingly, silence and limiting oneself to the apprehensions of the intellects are more appropriate – just as the perfect ones have enjoined when they said, "Meditate with your heart upon your bed and be silent, *selah*" (*Tehillim* 4:5).

Nefesh ha-Chaim notes that this tension is reflected in the phraseology of every *bracha*, which vacillates between formulations that express proximity to and distance from God.[26] Likewise, Maharal, in his Second Introduction to *Gevurot Hashem*, explains that this is why God is called

---

26. **נפש החיים שער ב פרק ג**

ולכן קבעו אנשי כנה"ג הנוסח של כל ברכות המצות בלשון נוכח ונסתר. תחלתם ברוך אתה הוא לשון נוכח. ומסיימים אשר קדשנו כו' וצונו לשון נסתר. שמצד התחברותו יתברך ברצונו אל העולמות שעי"ז יש לנו קצת השגה כל דהו. אנו מדברים לנוכח ברוך אתה ה' כו'. כי העולמות הם הצריכים לענין התוספת ורבוי ברכה מעצמותו ית' המתחבר אליהם וזהו מלך העולם כמ"ש ברע"מ הנ"ל כד נחית לאמלכא עלייהו ויתפשט על בריין כו' והמצווה אותנו ומקדשנו הוא עצמותו ית' א"ס ב"ה לבדו הסתום מכל סתימין. לכן תקנו בלשון נסתר אשר קדשנו וצונו.

נפש החיים שער ב פרק ד

וטעמו של דבר שנכלל בכל ברכה ב' הבחי' הנ"ל כי יסוד פנת אמונתינו הק', שכל מגמת כוונת לבנו בכל הברכו' והתפלות ובקשו' אך רק ליחידו של עולם אדון יחיד א"ס ב"ה. אמנם לא שאנו מדברים אליו כביכול על עצמותו ית' לבד בבחי' היותו מופשט ומופרש כביכול לגמרי מהעולמו' כענין שהיה קודם הבריאה דא"כ איך נתארהו ח"ו בכל ברכותינו ותפלתינו בשום שם וכנוי בעולם כלל. וגם דאם לא מצד שהראנו יתברך שרצונו להתחבר להעולמות ולאמלכא על בריין כפום עובדיהון, לא היינו רשאים כלל להתפלל לעצמותו יתברך שיתחבר.

Later, *Nefesh ha-Chaim* explains that the entire concept of *mitzvot* relates to our perception of Him rather than to His essence. In reality, He fills all worlds, and our *mitzvot* have no capacity to affect Him. Within our perceived reality, however, He has limited Himself such that we exist and are capable of giving to Him. We will return to this topic in Chapter 35.

ha-Kadosh Baruch Hu,[27] a name which alludes to the inherent gap between our perception of Him and His essence.[28]

2.4 GOING TOO FAR

Thus far, we have seen the roots of a dangerous dialectic: on the one hand, we are commanded to know Him, while on the other hand, we recognize that we cannot understand Him. This tension calls for limits. As Ben Sira warned:

בן סירא ג:כב מובא בתלמוד הבבלי חגיגה י״ג עמוד א
במופלא ממך אל תדרוש ובמכוסה ממך אל תחקור.

> Do not expound upon that which is beyond you, and do not investigate that which is hidden from you.[29]

The warning against going too far first was stressed at *Har Sinai*. Rambam writes (*Moreh ha-Nevuchim* 1:5) that the verse "And the priests and the populace shall not break forth to ascend to Hashem" (*Shemot* 19:24) serves as a general warning against attempting to understand concepts that are beyond us. In fact, Moshe merited his magnificent understanding precisely because he initially showed trepidation

---

27. The word *kadosh* denotes separateness (see Malbim and Ramban to *Vayikra* 19:2 as well as *Tosafot* to *Kiddushin* 3b). See *Nefesh ha-Chaim* 3:5 who elaborates upon this point.

28. ואנחנו תלמידי משה עליו השלום כו׳, **אבל הוא יתברך שקראו חז״ל בשם הקדוש ברוך הוא, ולא נקרא השכל ברוך הוא** [כי חלילה אין על הבורא יתברך שום תוארי החיוב, כאשר האריך בביטול זה המורה לצדקה, כי באמת אינו מושג כלל ואינו נגדר כלל, ואם היה מתואר בחיוב היה מושג במהותו, רק תואריו בשלילה, וזה הוראת שם קדוש] **כי אמיתת עצמו לא נודע, רק שהוא נבדל מכל גשם וגוף ומכל הנמצאים, וע״ז נאמר קדוש ב״ה, שענין קדוש נאמר על מי שהוא נבדל.**

29. Modern scholars debate what exactly Ben Sira meant by this verse. Some, like Martin Hengel in *Judentum und Hellenismus. Studien zu ihrer Begegnung unter besonderer Berücksichtigung Palästinas bis zur Mitte des 2. Jh.s v. Chr.* (WUNT 10; 2nd edition; Tübingen: Mohr, 1973, 243, 258), use this verse to prove that Ben Sira was an anti-Hellenist. According to this view, the above verse is referring to the speculative nature of Greek philosophy. Ben Sira is seen as warning against this kind of speculation. Others disagree and maintain that Ben Sira had a positive attitude towards Hellenistic thought. They understand this verse as warning against esoteric speculations from within Judaism. The above Talmudic passage supports the latter possibility.

about investigating that which was beyond him, as the verse states, "And Moshe hid his face because he was afraid to look toward God." (*Shemot* 3:6).[30]

Questions that Cannot Be Asked

The mishna (*Chagiga* 11b) strictly forbids consideration of four things:

> כל המסתכל בארבעה דברים רתוי לו כאילו לא בא לעולם מה למעלה מה למטה מה לפנים ומה לאחור.
>
> Anyone who speculates upon four things, it would have been better for him if he had not come into the world: 1) what is above, 2) what is beneath, 3) what is before, and 4) what is after.

Ramchal understands that the mishna is banning the contemplation of God's essence.[31] For example, to seek to understand God "before" His creation of the world is to try to understand who He is outside the context of creation. To do so is impossible because, as we have explained, we can relate to Him only as He manifests Himself. Prior to creation, there was no manifestation of the Divine because there was nothing besides Him. The same point can be made about the other three questions.

Rambam (*Moreh ha-Nevuchim* 1:32), in considering the dangers of contemplating that which is beyond us, draws a powerful analogy:

---

30. Rambam alludes to a similar interpretation of the verse in *Hilchot Me'ila* 8:6. Likewise, see R. Bachya b. Asher in his commentary to this verse, who explicates the exegesis of this understanding.

31. **ספר דעת תבונות סימן מו**

מה שצריכים אנו להאמין בזה הוא, כי הוא יתברך שמו, מציאותו נודע לנו ודאי שהוא מוכרח מעצמו, **אך מהותו אי אפשר לנו להשיגו כלל ועיקר; ולא עוד, אלא שכבר אסור לנו איסור עולם להיכנס בחקירה זאת.** וכבר אמרו חכמים, **"המסתכל בארבעה דברים ראוי לו שלא בא לעולם."**

The same point is made by Mabit (*Beit Elokim Sha'ar ha-Yesodot,* Ch. 1) with elaboration. See R. Tzadok's *Sichat Malachei ha-Shareit,* Ch. 3, for a discussion of what specifically is problematic with each of these four questions. See also *Sefer ha-Ikkarim* 2:18.

> You must consider when reading this treatise that cognitive perception, because it is connected with matter, is subject to conditions similar to those to which physical perception is subject. That is to say: if your eye looks around, you can perceive all that is within the range of your vision; however, if you overstrain your eye, exerting it too much by attempting to see an object that is too distant for your eye or by examining writings or engravings too small for your sight, and you force it to obtain a correct perception of them, you not only will weaken your sight with regard to that particular object, but also for those things that you otherwise are able to perceive – your eye will become too weak to perceive what you were able to see before you exerted yourself and exceeded the limits of your vision.
>
> The same is the case with the speculative faculties… If you admit the doubt and do not persuade yourself to believe that there is a proof for things that cannot be demonstrated…or attempt to perceive things that are beyond your perception, then you have attained the highest degree of human perfection…

Remarkably, the highest degree of perfection is achieved when someone knows his limits.

Those Who Went Too Far

Rambam then cites, as a cautionary tale, the episode of the four sages who entered *pardeis*:

> **תלמוד בבלי מסכת חגיגה דף יד עמוד ב**
> ת"ר ארבעה נכנסו בפרדס ואלו הן בן עזאי ובן זומא אחר ורבי עקיבא... בן עזאי הציץ ומת... בן זומא הציץ ונפגע... אחר קיצץ בנטיעות. רבי עקיבא יצא בשלום.
>
> Our Rabbis taught that four entered *pardeis*: Ben Azzai, Ben Zoma, *Acheir*, and R. Akiva… Ben Azzai peered [where he was not meant to] and died… Ben Zoma peered and was injured… *Acheir* became a heretic (lit. cut saplings), and R. Akiva emerged in peace.

Rambam writes:

> [If you respect your limits], you are like R. Akiva, who "entered in peace (the study of these theological problems) and came out in peace." If, on the other hand, you attempt to exceed the limit of your intellectual power... you will be like Elisha (*Acheir*); you not only will fail to become perfect, but also will become exceedingly imperfect.

Rambam continues by noting that when we seek to understand things that are beyond us, we tend to make things up to fill the void: "Ideas founded on mere imagination will prevail over you." Rambam elucidates the Talmud's comparison of knowledge to honey:

> In comparing knowledge to food (as we observed in Ch. 30), the author of *Mishlei* mentions the sweetest food, namely, honey, which has the further property of irritating the stomach and causing sickness. He thus fully describes the nature of knowledge. Though great, excellent, noble, and perfect, it is injurious if not kept within bounds or not guarded properly; it is like honey, which gives nourishment and is pleasant when eaten in moderation but is totally thrown away when eaten immoderately.

In light of this grave danger, one might conclude that the study of philosophy should be shunned. Rambam warns against the folly of such a conclusion:

> It was not the object of the Prophets and our Sages in these utterances to close the gate of investigation entirely and to prevent the mind from comprehending what is within its reach, as is imagined by simple and idle people... The whole object of the Prophets and the Sages was to declare that a limit is set to human reason where it must halt.

R. Sa'adya Gaon likewise writes that the dangers should not dissuade us from appropriately pursuing knowledge of God:

הקדמה לספר אמונות ודעות
ואם יאמר אומר הנה חכמי ישראל הזהירו מזה, ובלבד העיון בתחלת הזמן ותחלת המקום, כאמרם כל המסתכל בארבעה דברים ראוי לו כאלו לא בא לעולם - מה למעלה מה למטה, מה לפנים מה לאחור, נאמר ונעזר באלקים כי העיון האמתי לא יתכן שימנעוהו ממנו, ויוצרנו כבר צוה בו עם ההגדה הנאמנת, כאמרו (ישעיהו ט:כא) הלא תדעו הלא תשמעו הלא הוגד מראש לכם הלא הבינותם מוסדות הארץ.

If one will argue that the Sages warned us against this, especially about investigating the beginning of time and space, as they said: "Anyone who speculates upon four things, a pity for him"... it is inconceivable that they forbade true speculation, as our Creator already has commanded [that we engage in] it, as the verse states: "Do you not know? Have you not heard? Has it not been told to you from the outset? Have you not understood the foundations of the earth?" (*Yeshayahu* 9:21).

But, one may ask, if a person cannot fully understand God, why even try? Regarding this the mishna states:

אבות ב:טז
לא עליך המלאכה לגמור ולא אתה בן חורין להבטל ממנה.

It is not your responsibility to finish the work, but you are not free to neglect it.

In a different context, Ramban (cited in 1.1) writes that only fools who despise wisdom (הכסילים מואסי חכמה) stop searching when they know they cannot complete the task. We benefit immeasurably from everything we do succeed in understanding, even as we acknowledge that we never will finish.

Nevertheless, one must not be reckless. If a person forecasts that studying philosophy might lead him astray he must avoid the subject until he is ready. Accordingly, as noted in 1.6, R. Elchanan Wasserman writes that even those Rishonim (such Rambam and R. Bachya ibn Pakuda) who maintain that belief ideally should be predicated upon proof would agree that it is forbidden should it be the case that such a pursuit would be reckless.

A Process

What emerges from Rambam is that the vital task of understanding God is a process. It begins with preparation, continues with arduous and exhilarating investigation, and concludes with a profound awareness of our own limitations. R. Yisrael b. Eliezer (1700–1760), known as the Ba'al Sheim Tov or the Besht, cited by his student R. Moshe Chaim Ephraim of Sudilkov (1748–1800), powerfully captures this process:

דגל מחנה אפרים בראשית פרשת לך לך

יש שני סוגי אנשים. אחד מיישב בדעתו מאחר ששמעתי שהקב"ה כביכול הוא אין סוף למה לי החקירה בו ומאמין בזה בלי דרישות וחקירות, ואין זה הדרך ישכון אור.

אבל יש סוג שני שאינו מאמין בזה כי אם בדרישות וחקירות, היינו על ידי לימוד תורה, כמו שאמר דוד המלך ע"ה (דברי הימים א כח:ט) "דע את אלהי אביך ועבדהו." מתחילה דע ואחר כך עבדהו ואחר שלומד תורה ומעיין בה שמכיר על ידי התורה גדולת הבורא ברוך הוא וברוך שמו שהוא אין סוף ואז עוזב מלחקור ולדרוש ולהתבונן בענין אלוקות כלל מחמת יראת הרוממות של אין סוף יתברך ויתעלה שהשיג שהוא אין סוף ובאתר דאין סוף מאן יכול וכו'.

There are two types of people. The first type says to himself, "since I have heard that it is impossible to understand God completely, why should I even bother investigating?" He therefore believes without investigation. This is not the proper path.

There is a second type of person who arrives at the same conclusion after searching and investigating (through the study of Torah), as [King] David said, "Know the God of your father and serve Him," first know Him and then serve

Him.[32] Through the study of Torah he recognizes the greatness of the Creator, His infiniteness, and then he abandons his investigation of the Divine due to his fear of the awesomeness of the *Ein Sof*. The person truly realizes that He is infinite, and in the place of that infiniteness, there can be no understanding of Him.

2.5 RAMBAM'S PROHIBITION AGAINST READING IDOLATROUS AND HERETICAL WORKS

Having considered what one may not ask let us consider what one may not read:

הלכות עבודה זרה פרק ב הלכה א

ועניין זה, הוא שהזהירה עליו תורה ואמרה "ופן תישא עיניך השמיימה, וראית את השמש ואת הירח ואת הכוכבים . . . אשר חלק ה' אלוהיך, אותם, לכול העמים" (דברים ד:יט): כלומר שמא תשוט בעין ליבך ותראה שאלו הם המנהיגים את העולם, והם שחלק ה' אותם לכל העמים להיותם חיים והווים ונפסדים כמנהגו של עולם; ותאמר שראוי להשתחוות להן, ולעובדן.

ובעניין זה ציווה ואמר "הישמרו לכם, פן יפתה לבבכם" (דברים יא:טז) - כלומר שלא תטעו בהרהורי הלב לעבוד אלו, להיותם סרסור ביניכם ובין הבורא.

The Torah warns us about this, saying: "Lest you lift your eyes heavenward and see the sun, the moon, and the stars... [and bow down and worship them], the entities which God apportioned to all the nations." This implies that you might inquire with "the eye of the heart" and it might appear to you that these entities control the world, having been apportioned by God to all the nations to be alive, to exist, and not to cease existence,

32. The Besht is not contradicting *na'aseh ve-nishma*, rather he is stating that divine service done without an understanding of the Divine does not compare with service rooted in understanding.

as is the pattern of [the other creations with] the world. Therefore, you might say that it is worthy to bow down to them and worship them.

For this reason, commands: "Be very careful that your heart not be tempted [to go astray and worship other gods]." This implies that the thoughts of your heart should not lead you astray to worship these and make them an intermediary between you and the Creator.

שם הלכה ב

ספרים רבים חיברו עובדי עבודה זרה בעבודתה, היאך עיקר עבודתה ומה משפטה ומעשיה. ציוונו הקדוש ברוך הוא, שלא לקרות באותן הספרים כלל, ולא נהרהר בה, ולא בדבר מדבריה. ואפילו להסתכל בדמות הצורה - אסור, שנאמר "אל תפנו אל האלילים" (ויקרא יט:ד). ובענין זה נאמר "ופן תדרוש לאלוהיהם לאמור, איכה יעבדו" (דברים יב:ל) - שלא תשאל על דרך עבודתה היאך היא, ואף על פי שאין אתה עובד: שדבר זה גורם לך להיפנות אחריה ולעשות כמו שהן עושין, שנאמר "ואעשה כן, גם אני" (שם).

Idolaters wrote many books about their worship: what the main part of their worship is, how it is done, and what the related laws are. God commanded us not to read such books at all and not to think about idols or any related matter. Even to look at a figure (of an idol) is forbidden, as it is written, "Do not turn to idols." Concerning this matter the Torah says, "...And do not inquire about their gods by saying, 'How did these nations serve their gods?'" i.e., do not inquire about the method of worship even if one will not worship, because this leads one to worship and to do as they (the idolaters) do, for it is written, "I will do the same myself."

שם הלכה ג

וכל הלאוין הללו בענין אחד הן, והוא שלא יפנה אחר עבודה זרה; וכל הנפנה אחריה בדרך שהוא עושה בו מעשה, הרי זה לוקה.

All of these transgressions [mentioned so far] are in the same category, namely, that of not turning to idolatry. Anyone who does turn to idolatry and performs the associated acts of worship is flogged.

ולא עבודה זרה בלבד הוא שאסור להיפנות אחריה במחשבה, אלא כל מחשבה שגורמת לו לאדם לעקור עיקר מעיקרי התורה - מוזהרין אנו שלא להעלותה על ליבנו, ולא נסיח דעתנו לכך ונחשוב ונימשך אחר הרהורי הלב: מפני שדעתו של אדם קצרה, ולא כל הדעות יכולות להשיג האמת על בורייו; ואם יימשך כל אדם אחר מחשבות ליבו, נמצא מחריב את העולם לפי קוצר דעתו.

It is not just turning to idolatry in thought that is forbidden; we also are warned not to entertain any thoughts that may lead to uprooting any of the Torah's principles. We are warned not to think these thoughts, turn our attention to them, or allow ourselves to become confused by following the [incorrect] impulses of our hearts. We are enjoined from doing this because man's reasoning is limited, and not all minds can attain the truth with clarity. If a man were to follow his impulsive thoughts, he would destroy the world because of the limitations of his mind [by spreading such opinions amongst others].

כיצד: פעמים יתור אחר עבודה זרה; ופעמים יחשוב בייחוד הבורא, שמא הוא שמא אינו, מה למעלה מה למטה, מה לפנים מה לאחור; ופעמים בנבואה, שמא היא אמת שמא אינה; ופעמים בתורה, שמא היא מן השמיים שמא אינה. ואינו יודע המידות שידון בהן עד שיידע האמת על בורייו, ונמצא יוצא לידי מינות.

What does this mean? Sometimes, he will explore idolatry. At times, he will consider the oneness of the Creator – whether He exists or not, what is in heaven and beneath the ground, what existed before the world was created and what will be after it. Sometimes, he will contemplate whether the prophecies are true or not, and still other times, he will contemplate whether the Torah is heavenly [in origin] or not, and he does not know the principles necessary to arrive at the truth. Consequently, he will become a heretic.

ועל עניין זה הזהירה תורה, ונאמר בה "ולא תתורו אחרי לבבכם ואחרי עיניכם, אשר אתם זונים אחריהם" (במדבר טו:לט) - כלומר לא יימשך כל אחד מכם אחר דעתו הקצרה, וידמה שמחשבתו משגת האמת. כך אמרו חכמים, "אחרי לבבכם", זו מינות; "ואחרי עיניכם", זו זנות. ולאו זה, אף על פי שהוא גורם לאדם לטורדו מן העולם הבא, אין בו מלקות.

The Torah prohibited this by saying, "...And you shall not stray after your mind[33] (lit. your heart) and what your eyes see ..."; that is to say, not to be drawn after his own limited mind and delude himself to think he has arrived at the truth. The Sages said that the words, "your mind" refer to heresy, and the words, "what your eyes see" refer to adultery. Even though this sin [of following incorrect impulses] can prevent a person from meriting the world to come, it does not carry a penalty of corporal punishment.

Explaining Rambam's Behavior in Light of His Restrictions

Rambam rules that one may not study books of idolatry or heretical works lest they lead him astray. Apparently, Rambam does not sanction uninhibited freedom of inquiry. How, then, are we to explain Rambam's own citation of idolatrous works in *Moreh ha-Nevuchim*? And what about Rambam's study of Greek philosophy – how could Rambam violate his own rules?

One possibility is that knowledge of such material sometimes is necessary, such as for purposes of jurisprudence or rebutting heretics. However, one wonders whether this justifies Rambam's behavior as well as the advice he gave others, especially since Rambam implies that the restriction against reading idolatrous works is categorical. In 2.15, we consider Rambam's formulations of the prohibition and specifically whether there may be formal exceptions, such as studying these works *le-havin u-le-horot,* in order to understand and instruct. Here, we analyze the matter in broader strokes.

In truth, there are two questions concerning Rambam's practice, and they may have different answers. Firstly, how do we justify Rambam's

33. The significance of this translation of לבבכם will be explained at the end of 2.5.

assiduous study of Greek and Arabic philosophy given their heretical views? Secondly, how do we understand his citations of idolatrous books if he himself rules that one is prohibited from reading them? The reason why these are different questions is (as noted in 1.5) that Rambam maintains that there is significant consonance between Aristotle and the words of Torah, even though on certain issues they diverge. For example, he urges R. Shmuel ibn Tibbon to study the works of Aristotle and al-Farabi even though Aristotle denied divine providence and al-Farabi denied the immortality of the soul. Presumably, he encourages his student to study these works because, Rambam maintains, they are invaluable with respect to understanding the sciences and logic and therefore play an important role in fulfilling numerous religious obligations, such as believing in and loving God. Of course, they cannot be studied without the proper preparations, as he explains in his commentary on the Mishna (*Chagiga* 2:1) and in *Moreh ha-Nevuchim* (Introduction and 1:32). The same cannot be said about books of idolatry.

Nevertheless, Rambam personally sought out every idolatrous work he could get his hands on. Apparently, he did feel there was some purpose in studying these works. In fact, he utilizes his knowledge of idolatrous rites to explain the purpose of many *mitzvot*.

The Prohibition Against Entertaining Thoughts that Can Result in Heresy

In the above citation, Rambam writes:

> אלא כל מחשבה שגורמת לו לאדם לעקור עיקר מעיקרי התורה - מוזהרין אנו שלא להעלותה על ליבנו.
>
> We also are warned not to entertain any thoughts that may lead to uprooting any of the Torah's principles.

Rambam asks that we draw a delicate balance. On one hand, Rambam maintains that faith ideally should be predicated upon proof, which seemingly calls for the consideration of alternatives. On the other hand, he writes (above; see also *Hilchot Yesodei ha-Torah,* Ch. 1) that consideration of alternatives is strictly prohibited. As R. Sa'adya

Gaon and R. Bachya ibn Pakuda stress, we are to honestly seek to prove what we already know to be true. We shall return to this in Chapters 8 and 11.

It would seem that Rambam intends to restrict any activity that might lead, in a practical sense, to heresy, which would then permit study and thought when it will not lead one to heresy. This definition is supported by his formulation in *Sefer ha-Mitzvot*:

> **ספר המצוות לרמב"ם מצות לא תעשה מז**
> **שהזהירנו שלא לתור אחרי לבבנו עד שנאמין דעות שהם הפך הדעות שחייבתנו התורה** אבל נקצר מחשבתנו ונשים לה גבול תעמוד אצלו והוא מצות התורה ואזהרותיה. והוא אמרו יתעלה (פ' ציצית) ולא תתורו אחרי לבבכם ואחרי עיניכם. ולשון ספרי ולא תתורו אחרי לבבכם זו מינות... ואחרי עיניכם זו זנות.
>
> **We have been commanded not to exercise freedom of thought to the point of believing views opposed to those expressed in the Torah**; rather, we must limit our thought by setting up a boundary where it must stop, and that boundary is the commandments and the instructions of the Torah. This is the intent of the statement, "You shall not stray after your heart and after your eyes." In the language of *Sifrei*, "'You shall not stray after your heart,' – this refers to heresy…, and 'after your eyes' – this refers to licentiousness."

Drs. David Berger and Lawrence Kaplan[34] suggest that Rambam defines the biblical prohibition in terms of *accepting* heretical doctrine rather than entertaining thoughts with the potential of leading to such a doctrine. Thus, assuming that one is adequately prepared and exercises the appropriate humility, as Rambam explains in his commentary on the Mishna (*Chagiga* 2:1) and in *Moreh ha-Nevuchim* (Introduction and 1:32), one may seek proof for the existence of God and His oneness despite the dangers that these pursuits may entail. However, this reading is questionable, since

34. "On Freedom of Inquiry in the Rambam – And Today," *The Torah U-Madda Journal* 2 (1990): pp. 37–50.

Rambam does indeed seem to prohibit even *entertaining* a thought that might cause him to reject one of the Torah's principles: כל מחשבה שגורמת לו לאדם לעקור עיקר מעיקרי התורה--מוזהרין אנו שלא להעלותה על ליבנו.[35] At the same time, this conclusion also appears problematic for who can know with certainty that they will not be affected; or, in the words of Hillel, ואל תאמן בעצמך עד יום מותך, do not have full confidence in yourself until the day of your death (*Avot* 2:4). If one required certainty nobody could study philosophy – an assertion that Rambam would have certainly rejected.

Rather, as R. Mayer Twersky explained, when the Torah says ולא תתורו אחרי לבבכם, the word *leiv* does not mean heart as much as mind.[36] Thus, the verse warns us not to be led astray by our minds. According to Rambam, the verse is admonishing us not to be undisciplined in our thinking and not to gratuitously entertain and conjure up thoughts that undermine our belief in the Torah's principles. In the words of Rambam, one must erect a fence, set limits, and constrain our thoughts (נקצר מחשבתנו ונשים לה גבול). Presumably, the practical implications of this injunction will differ from person to person.

R. Aharon Lichtenstein adds:

> The gap between precept and practice… invites two responses. The first is that the Rambam, and any *gadol* analogous to him, is a rather special case. On the one hand, by virtue of his public position he is presumably under greater pressure to confront alien ideologies he must first master. On the other, by dint of both the range of his knowledge of Torah and the depth of his commitment to it, he is relatively inured to their pernicious influence… The second response relates to the motive and hence, in all likelihood,

35. Seemingly, Rambam permits an intellectual endeavor only if one can be confident that the pursuit will not lead one to reject one of the Torah's principles. This requirement certainly curtails some, but not all, scholarly forays. Accordingly, Rambam would not advise *all* people to seek proof of God's existence, only those that could be confident they would not jeopardize their faith. As noted in 1.6 R. Elchanan Wasserman argued that this standard would indicate that even Rambam would agree that nowadays (or at least in R. Wasserman's time) the study of philosophy is prohibited.

36. Thus, Rambam writes ואם ימשך כל אדם אחר **מחשבות לבו** נמצא מחריב את העולם לפי קוצר דעתו.

the mode of studying aberrant material. With reference to the *pasuk*, "Thou shalt not learn to do in accordance with the abominations of those nations," which presumably addresses itself to study per se, Chazal comment, "You may not learn in order to do but you may learn in order to understand and instruct."[37]

2.6 HOW COULD RAMBAM WRITE *MOREH HA-NEVUCHIM*? HOW SHOULD *MOREH HA-NEVUCHIM* BE READ?

In light of the restrictions against teaching esoteric wisdom publicly described in 2.1, an obvious question arises. By writing *Moreh ha-Nevuchim*, a philosophical work, Rambam publicly taught *ma'aseh merkava*, in violation of the mishna's restriction. Rambam addresses this challenge in his Introduction to *Moreh ha-Nevuchim* (in the section "Directions for the Study of this Work") and offers two justifications or "two precedents." Let us examine each.

Voiding the Torah to Preserve the Torah

Rambam writes: "To similar cases, our Sages applied the verse, 'It is time to do something for the sake of God, for they have abrogated your Torah' (*Tehillim* 69:126)." Chazal understand the verse as saying that at times one must abrogate the Torah to preserve the Torah. To appreciate this answer, let us turn to Rambam's Introduction to *Mishneh Torah*, where he describes the great concern that the oral law would be forgotten due to Roman persecution. R. Yehuda ha-Nasi prevented that catastrophe by partially writing down the oral law, an activity that should have been prohibited[38] but was justified due to the exigencies of the time.[39] The Talmud (*Gittin* 60b) cites the above verse (*Tehillim* 119:126), which calls for the violation of the Torah in order to preserve the Torah, as the basis for this sort of activity.

Thus, Rambam is admitting that writing *Moreh ha-Nevuchim* is indeed a violation of the law. It is justified, however, because refraining from doing so would lead to a greater abrogation. What is the urgency?

37. "Torah and General Culture: Confluence and Conflict" in *Judaism's Encounter with Other Cultures*, p. 280.

38. *Gittin* 60b דברים שבעל פה אי אתה רשאי לאומרן בכתב.

39. We will return to the history of the oral law in Chapter 28.

Rambam explains that there are people who perceive contradictions between Torah and philosophy, which might induce them to reject Torah. Thus, responding to their queries is of utmost necessity.

Let All of Your Acts Be Guided by Pure Intentions

Rambam then offers another justification for writing *Moreh ha-Nevuchim*: "Secondly, they have said, 'Let all of your acts be guided by pure intentions' (*Avot* 2:7).[40] I relied on these two principles while composing some parts of this work."

What exactly is meant by the second principle? How do one's noble intentions justify the violation of a prohibition? Rambam may be alluding to a Talmudic passage that indicates that for the sake of bringing honor to the Torah, one is allowed to reveal its secrets:

> **תלמוד בבלי מסכת מגילה דף ג עמוד א**
> יצתה בת קול ואמרה: מי הוא זה שגילה סתריי לבני אדם? עמד יונתן בן עוזיאל על רגליו ואמר: אני הוא שגליתי סתריך לבני אדם; גלוי וידוע לפניך שלא לכבודי עשיתי, ולא לכבוד בית אבא, אלא לכבודך עשיתי שלא ירבו מחלוקת בישראל.

> A heavenly voice exclaimed: "Who revealed My secrets to people?" Yonatan b. Uziel stood up and declared, "It was I. You are well aware that I did not do it for my own honor or that of my family, but rather for Your honor, so as to prevent the proliferation of dispute."

---

40. In *Iggeret Teiman*, Rambam similarly justifies R. Sa'adya Gaon's prediction of the *keitz* (the time of *mashiach*'s arrival), despite the restriction against doing so:

> As for R. Sa'adya's messianic calculations, there were extenuating circumstances for them, though he knew they were disallowed. For the Jews of his time were perplexed and misguided. The divine religion might have disappeared had he not encouraged the timid and diffused, disseminated, and propagated by word of mouth and pen a knowledge of the Torah's underlying principles. He believed, in all earnestness, that by means of the messianic calculations, he would inspire the masses with hope for the truth. **Verily, all his deeds were for the sake of heaven. Consequently, in view of the probity of his motives, which we have disclosed, one must not decry him for his messianic computations.**

Perhaps the reason for this justification is that the Midrash (*Bereishit Rabba* 9:1) states that the prohibition against publicizing God's secrets is that doing so is a defamation to His honor, as the verse states, "The honor of God is to conceal a matter" (*Mishlei* 25:2). Accordingly, revealing such secrets becomes permitted in order to bring honor to the Torah.[41]

Along similar lines, Maharal writes:

> **ספר באר הגולה באר החמישי פרק א**
> ונכנס עוד לפני ולפנים שלא כדת ושלא כמשפט, לבאר דברים אשר הם כמסו, ואנחנו נגלה. אך בשתים יכפר לנו; האחד, שאין הכוונה פה רק לכבוד השם יתברך, ולכבוד התורה, ולכבוד חכמים, להסיר מהם התלונה. השני, כי נגלה טפח ונכסה עשר טפחים.

> And we will enter the inner chamber without authorization to reveal that which Chazal hid. But there are two atonements for our actions. The first, our intention is only to bring honor to God, the Torah, and the Sages by responding to those who challenge them. The second is that even we as we reveal one handbreadth, we will hide ten.

We shall see shortly that in his second reason, as well, Maharal is following Rambam.

Rambam concludes with an additional factor that relates to the controversy that he anticipated his book would create:

> Lastly, when I have a difficult subject before me – when I find the road narrow and can see no other way of teaching a well-established truth except by pleasing one intelligent man and displeasing ten thousand fools – I prefer to address myself to the one man and to take no notice whatsoever of the condemnation of the multitude. I prefer to extricate that intelligent man from his embarrassment and show him the cause of his perplexity so that he may attain perfection and be at peace.

---

41. This point is made by R. Yehoshua Hartman in his edition of Maharal's *Be'eir ha-Gola, Be'eir Chamishi*, note 74.

Nevertheless, Rambam remains uneasy about his task:

> God, may He be exalted, knows that I have never ceased to be exceedingly apprehensive about writing down those things that I wish to write in this treatise. For they are concealed things; none of them has been written in any book.

Intentional Obscurity

Rambam adds that he is not totally ignoring the injunction against teaching esoteric matters publicly, explaining that by discussing these matters cryptically, he is not in violation of Halacha.[42] In fact, he is imitating God, who described the creation of the world using parables,[43] riddles, and obscure words:

> Therefore, the Almighty began the Torah with the description of the creation, that is, with Physical Science; on the one hand, the subject is very weighty and important, and on the other hand, our means of fully comprehending those great problems is limited. He described those profound truths, which He deemed appropriate to communicate to us, using parables, riddles, and unclear language.[44] Our Sages have said,

42. Earlier, we noted that Rambam states that he is going to offer two justifications for writing *Moreh ha-Nevuchim*. Now, he seems to be offering a third, namely, intentional obscurity. Matt Lubin suggested that the idea of intentional obscurity addresses a different issue relating to the teaching of *ma'aseh merkava*. As we shall see in 2.9, the Mishna requires that it be taught to one person who is fit to be taught, and *even then*, only by way of hinting. Rambam's two justifications allow him to teach it to the masses instead of to one person but do not allow him to dispense with the need to teach it by way of hinting and for the audience to be "fit to hear" such secrets. He therefore wrote (1) obscurely and (2) with contradictions (which we discuss in 2.7) so that only those fit to understand will receive the correct teaching. (This analysis differs from that of Leo Strauss in his introductory essay to the Shlomo Pines translation of *Moreh ha-Nevuchim*, who believes that Rambam's main justification is the insertion of contradictions, since "If you say that something is A, and then proceed to say that it is not A, then you can't be said to have stated anything at all.")
43. We will return to the issue of literalism in the creation narrative in Chapter 3.
44. The Tel Aviv University edition of *Moreh ha-Nevuchim* by Prof. Michael Schwartz translates this sentence as:

> "It is impossible to give a full account of the creation to man. Therefore, Scripture simply tells us, 'In the beginning, God created the heavens and the earth' (*Bereishit* 1:1)."[45] In this manner, they have suggested that this subject is a deep mystery, and in the words of Shlomo, "Far off and exceedingly deep, who can find it out?" (*Kohelet* 7:24). That which is said about creation is communicated using equivocal terms so that the multitude might comprehend them in accord with the capacity of their understanding and the weakness of their understanding, whereas the perfect man, who is already informed, will understand them otherwise.[46]

Here, Rambam alludes to the value of using parables. What emerges from Rambam's Introduction is that figurative language and imagery serves three purposes: 1) to clarify and concretize obscure matters, 2) to obscure the esoteric matters so that unqualified individuals will not understand (while simultaneously conveying the truth to those qualified), and 3) to allow a text to be understood on multiple levels, so that

בשל גודל העניין וחשיבותו הרבה, ומכיוון שיכולתנו קצרה מלהשיג את הגדול שבדברים כפי שהוא, היתה הפנייה אלינו בדברים העמוקים, אשר בהם חייבה החוכמה האלוהית לפנות אלינו, **במשלים, בחידות ובדברים סתומים מאוד.**

45. The precise source Rambam is referring to is unclear. The Schwartz edition cites the following:

מדרשי הגניזה בתי מדרשות תש"ם כרך א עמ׳ רנא: מדרש שני כתובים
להגיד כוח מעשה בראשית לבריות ולהודיעם אי-אפשר, אלא שסתם הכתוב. מכאן אמרו אין דורשין בעריות לשלושה, ולא במעשה בראשית לשניים, ולא במרכבה ליחיד...

46. The last sentence of above passage is adapted from the Pines translation (p. 9). The Friedlander (1919) translation states: "It has been treated in **metaphors** in order that the uneducated may comprehend it according to the measure of their faculties and the feebleness of their apprehension, while educated persons may take it in a different sense." The word "metaphors" in the Friedlander translation, while widely cited, is imprecise. Prof. Michael Schwartz, like Pines, translates this sentence as:

כל הדברים האלה נאמרו **בשמות משותפים** כדי שההמון יפרשו אותם במשמעות שהיא לפי מידת הבנתם וחולשת השׂגתם, ויפרשם השלם היודע במשמעות אחרת.

Likewise, R. Kapach translates it as:

ועשה את הדבור בכל זה **בשמות המשותפים**, כדי שיבינום ההמון לפי עניין שהוא כדי הבנתם וחולשת דעתם, ויבינם השלם שכבר למד באופן אחר.

the uneducated individual will understand it in one way while educated person may take it in a different sense.[47]

2.7 CONTRADICTIONS IN *MOREH HA-NEVUCHIM*

Later in the Introduction, Rambam adds another factor (in the section "On Method"). Rambam writes that there are seven types of contradictions that are found in literary works. These seven can be further divided into two classes; the first class (1–4) consists of apparent contradictions that stem from a misunderstanding of the author's intent.[48] The second class (5–7) consists of real contradictions. Sometimes these exist because the contradiction escaped the notice of the author (6), but other times these contradictions are intentional (5 and 7). Rambam writes that *Moreh ha-Nevuchim* contains contradictions that are the result of design (5 and 7).[49] Let us consider these two types of intentional contradictions.

---

47. In fact, in *Moreh ha-Nevuchim* 1:33, Rambam writes that hiding the truth from the masses, "is the cause of the fact that the Torah speaks in the language of man, as we have made clear." In other words, because the masses would be harmed by overt discussions of esoteric topics, the Torah speaks in the language of man. Presumably, this means that because the masses (at that time) could relate only to a corporeal God, saying that God does not have a body would cause them to question His very existence.

48. They are:
    1. The first cause of contradictions arises from the fact that the author collects the opinions of various men, each differing from the other, but neglects to mention the name of the author of any particular opinion. In such a work, contradictions or inconsistencies must occur, since any two statements may belong to two different authors.
    2. Second cause: The author at first maintains one opinion that he subsequently rejects.
    3. Third cause: The passages in question are not all to be taken literally.
    4. Fourth cause: The premises are not identical in both statements, but for certain reasons they are not fully stated in these passages.

    Tanach, Mishna, and Midrash contain contradictions of this sort. Thus, the Talmud frequently will resolve contradictions by saying that statement A was made regarding X, while statement B was made concerning Y (first cause). Or, A changed his mind (second cause). Or, verse A should not be taken literally (third cause). Or, that verse A is relevant under certain circumstances, while verse B is relevant under different circumstances (fourth cause).

49. Rambam writes: "Any inconsistency discovered in the present work will be found to arise in consequence of the fifth cause or the seventh."

Why would an author intentionally insert a contradiction? He may have educational reasons – things must be taught in steps (5). A teacher initially may have to assume certain inaccurate theories because the student is not yet able to understand the complexity of the truth (such as presuming Newtonian physics until a student is ready to understand relativity). Thus, initially the matter is explained inaccurately according to the capacity of the students, such that they may comprehend it as far as they are required to at first. Later on, the same subject is thoroughly treated and fully developed in its right place.[50] Interestingly, it is not at all clear what Rambam may have had in mind when referring to this type of contradiction.[51]

At other times, the author may be trying to obscure his true intention due to the prohibition of teaching esoteric wisdom to the public (7). For example, sometimes it is necessary to introduce such metaphysical matter as may be partly disclosed but must be partly concealed. Therefore, it may be convenient on one occasion to treat the metaphysical problem as solved in one way and later to treat it as solved in the opposite way.

---

50. In Rambam's words:

> The **fifth** cause is traceable to the use of a certain method adopted in teaching and expounding profound problems. Namely, a difficult and obscure theorem must sometimes be mentioned and assumed as known, for the illustration of some elementary and intelligible subject which must be taught beforehand, the commencement always being made with the easier thing. The teacher must therefore facilitate, in any manner which he can devise, the explanation of those theorems that have to be assumed as known, and he must content himself with giving a general, though somewhat inaccurate, notion of the subject. It is, for the present, explained according to the capacity of the students, so they may comprehend it as far as they are required in order to understand the subject. Later on, the same subject is thoroughly treated and fully developed in its right place.

51. Strangely, Strauss seems to think that none of them actually exist. Ibn Caspi and Asher Crescas, in their commentaries, have noted a few suggestions that are a bit radical. Herbert Davidson ("Maimonides' Secret Position on Creation" in *Studies in Medieval Jewish History and Literature,* ed. Isadore Twersky, p. 17) suggests that an example of such a contradiction can be found in Rambam's discussion of creation. At first, Rambam first presents the "Platonic view" as being against the Torah, but later he writes that *Bereishit* could be interpreted as espousing such a view. Additionally, Daniel Davies in "Method and Metaphysics in Maimonides' Guide for the Perplexed," pp. 103–104, believes that there is a contradiction between 1:68 and 3:21 that is of the fifth type.

This is necessary because the author has the responsibility to endeavor to conceal as much as possible to prevent the uneducated reader from perceiving the truth.

How does inserting contradictions help circumvent this proscription? Presumably, an unprepared reader will dismiss the writer as unintelligent for having included contradictory statements, while the qualified student will recognize the contradiction and perceive the author's true intent. Rambam's solution thereby ensures that only appropriate students derive knowledge from the work.

Rambam also writes in his Introduction that he allows glimpses of these secrets and then conceals them again so as not to violate the prohibition against revelation.

2.8 METHODS OF INTERPRETING RAMBAM

Rambam's resolution to include contradictions in order to avoid the prohibition against publicly teaching esoteric wisdom led to an unintended consequence – fierce debate as to what Rambam really meant. Indeed, R. Shmuel ibn Tibbon, who translated several of Rambam's works, corresponded with Rambam concerning aspects of the book that he did not understand due to unresolved contradictions. Since its publication, great rabbis and scholars have endeavored to understand what Rambam actually meant in *Moreh ha-Nevuchim*,[52] and to this day they debate Rambam's "true" intentions. Naturally, due to the obscurity of his work, people are prone to read their own views into those of this towering figure. Many reasonably insist that any interpreter that always takes Rambam at face value will sometimes be wrong, since Rambam writes that he is, at times, intentionally misleading. However, there are some interpreters who use this idea to justify all sorts of highly speculative theories concerning Rambam's true intentions. Indeed, scholars throughout the ages have come to diametrically opposite conclusions about what Rambam actually meant.

The primary question of interpretation is this: to what extent does Rambam's inclusion of contradictions justify ignoring explicit statements of Rambam when there is no overt statement contradicting

---

52. R. Yosef Shlomo de Medigo wrote in 1597 that he studied eighteen commentaries to *Moreh ha-Nevuchim*.

it. Some interpreters assume that Rambam meant what he said unless there is specific reason to assume that he was obscuring his view. Others presume that Rambam frequently hides his true intentions, and to correctly understand Rambam, one must read between the lines and ignore seemingly unambiguous and uncontested statements. We can categorize the differing views about this specific question and the general interpretation of *Moreh ha-Nevuchim* into three basic schools of thought.[53]

The Rational Esotericists

The Esotericists, which includes both medieval and modern thinkers, argue that Rambam hid his true views on many of the most important issues. Thus, to understand Rambam's perspective, one must ignore many of his traditional (or "*frum*") statements (i.e., statements or ideas that contradict philosophy) since they do not reflect his true beliefs.[54] He wrote them only to protect the naïve, to protect himself from critics, or to avoid the prohibition of publicly teaching esoteric

53. This classification is overly simplistic but sufficient for our purposes. Recently, numerous scholars have suggested different and more subtle divisions. For example, T. M. Rudavsky in *Maimonides* describes three classifications of interpretations of Rambam: radical esoteric, harmonist, and literalist (23–24). Moshe Halbertal, in *Maimonides: Life and Thought*, crystallizes the various interpretations into "four possible readings, differing substantively with regard to the key questions that preoccupy Maimonides" (5). They are the skeptical, the mystical, the conservative, and the philosophical.

54. R. Shmuel ibn Tibbon (c. 1165–1232), the famous translator of *Moreh ha-Nevuchim*, might be an example of this methodology. Ibn Tibbon thought that 3:51 contradicts 3:16–23 concerning providence and disregarded 3:51. We will return to this in Chapter 38. (While R. Shmuel Ibn Tibbon adopted an Esoteric interpretation, his son R. Yehuda Ibn Tibbon preferred a Harmonist approach.) See Dr. Aviezer Ravitzky, "Samuel Ibn Tibbon and the Esoteric Character of The Guide of the Perplexed," *Association of Jewish Studies Review*, 1981, 6: 87–123. Modern expositors of this approach include Dr. Leo Strauss and Dr. Shlomo Pines; see their Introductions to the Pines translation of *The Guide of the Perplexed* (University of Chicago Press, 1963). Modern proponents of this approach tend to go much farther than their medieval predecessors. A history of this school of thought appears in Dr. Aviezer Ravitzky's, "The Secrets of the Guide of the Perplexed: Between the Thirteenth and the Twentieth Centuries," in *Studies in Maimonides* (ed., Isadore Twersky; Cambridge, MA: Harvard University Press, 1990), pp. 159–207.

wisdom. Thus, these "esoteric" commentators believe that we cannot read Rambam plainly, but rather we must look for the secret beneath the surface.[55]

An example of a chapter which, they claim, cannot be read literally would be the concluding chapter of *Moreh ha-Nevuchim* that we will analyze in 10.2. There, Rambam derives from *Yirmiyahu* that the pursuit of kindness and justice is superior to excellence in philosophy. They might suggest that this is contradicted by 3:51 (discussed in 10.1), which indicates that philosophy alone can bring man to true perfection, and it is 3:51 that more accurately reflects Rambam's true intent. As we mentioned earlier, this school of thought buttresses its methodology with Rambam's statement that he is intentionally including contradictions within his work to garble his message and confuse the reader who is not ready to study it.[56]

One problem with this approach is that earlier in the Introduction (in the section "Directions for the Study of this Work"), Rambam implores readers not to distort his words by adding their own interpretation: "I adjure any reader of my book, in the name of God, not to add any explanation even to a single word." This would indicate his opposition to such far-fetched "interpretations." Yet at the same time, Rambam writes: "Should the reader notice any opinions with which he does not agree, let him endeavor to find a suitable explanation, even if it seems far-fetched, in order that he may judge me charitably."[57] The question, however, is whether some of these

55. Proponents of this approach base their methodology on Rambam's seventh cause of contradiction. Interestingly, Strauss, among the most notable of modern esoteric interpreters, maintains that many philosophers, and not just Rambam, hide their true intentions. They do this for two reasons: to protect themselves from the authorities and masses that might be enraged by their seemingly heretical notions and because philosophers recognize that their theories that undermine conventional norms will harm society should they be accepted. Therefore, they conceal their true positions for the benefit of broader society, allowing only rarified individuals to perceive their true intent. While both of these theories are fascinating, their basis in Rambam is far from obvious.

56. Strauss offers numerous examples of contradictions within Rambam to support his method. However, as Kenneth Seeskin shows (in the appendix to *Searching for a Distant God: The Legacy of Maimonides* (Oxford University Press, 2000)), many of these apparent contradictions are not actually contradictions.

57. Are these two statements another example of an intentional contradiction?

explanations have any basis in Rambam's words. Dr. Aviezer Ravitzky sums up the difficulty of this approach: "The cumulative impression of these studies is staggering, to the point of arousing doubts as to whether it is reasonable to suppose that a single author, fitted as he may have been, was capable of such wide-ranging allusion, of such rigor and precision, and of a consistency of approach in such a great number and variety of realms."[58]

The bigger problem with this approach is that it frequently fails to look at Rambam holistically, favoring certain statements while ignoring others, especially those in *Mishneh Torah*. In Chapters 36 and 38 we will consider several examples of this weakness (regarding Rambam's position on sacrifices and providence).

The Religious/Mystical Esotericists

The second school of thought takes the opposite approach, arguing that Rambam did not really believe many of his controversial theories (generally, the ideas that seem to contradict Chazal). These scholars suggest that these ideas were proposed only to rebut heretics and do not reflect Rambam's true belief. This group of thinkers likewise maintains that we cannot read Rambam too literally. (They too were Esotericists.) Rivash's view (cited in 1.7) reflects this way of thinking.

Rivash simply claims that Rambam did not really mean some of his most provocative statements. They were partially disingenuous concessions made to accomplish his laudable goal of restoring the faith of skeptics. While not false, they did not accurately reflect Rambam's true beliefs.

As we shall see (2.12), some thinkers go further arguing for a Kabbalistic reading of *Moreh ha-Nevuchim*. Indeed, many of these writers even argue that Rambam was a closet Kabbalist who presented mystical ideas in philosophical terminology. R. Gershon Chanoch Henech Leiner of Radzyn (1839–1890) was one such thinker.[59] Among his many works,

58. *History and Faith: Studies in Jewish Philosophy*, p. 301.

59. R. Gershon Chanoch was the third rebbe of the Izbetzer dynasty. The first rebbe was R. Mordechai Yosef Leiner, author of *Mei ha-Shiloach*. His son and successor, R. Yaakov Leiner of Izbetz, moved from Izbetz to Radzyn, and the third Rebbe was

R. Gershon Chanoch authored an introductory work to Jewish mysticism entitled *ha-Hakdama ve-ha-Peticha* where he presents a history of Kabbala and highlights over a dozen parallels between Rambam and *Zohar*, some of them uncanny.[60] (While R. Gershon Chanoch claimed this proves that Rambam was in fact a student of Kabbala, we might suggest that this indicates that God reveals His wisdom in multiple ways, such that Rambam arrived at certain truths of Kabbala independently.) Indeed, there are numerous Kabbalistic commentaries on *Moreh ha-Nevuchim*, such as R. Avraham Abulajia's "*Sodot ha-Moreh*."

The common denominator between these first two approaches is the assumption that Rambam does not always mean what he writes. Indeed, as T. M. Rudavsky notes in *Maimonides*, thinkers have read Rambam as a closet Aristotelian, a closet Platonist or Neoplatonist, or even as a closet Kabbalist.[61]

The Harmonists

While the first two schools of thought argued, albeit for radically different reasons, for an esoteric read of Rambam, the third approach seeks a harmonistic reading. Harmonists acknowledge that Rambam included contradictions (he said he would) but consider it a minor aspect of *Moreh ha-Nevuchim*, not its central methodology. Generally, we will take this third approach, which presumes that Rambam can be trusted to say what he means to the extent possible.[62] We still have to deal with apparent contradictions, but we will attempt to solve these without totally discarding either

R. Gershon Chanoch. In addition to expertise in revealed and hidden portions of Torah, R. Gershon Chanoch spoke several languages and studied chemistry, engineering and medicine. He is most well-known for arguing that the cuttlefish was the source for *techeilet* dye.

60. R. Reuven Margoliyot (Vol. 32 and 33 of the journal *Sinai*) argues that the source for a number of halachot in Rambam is the *Zohar*. However, in *Yosef Ometz* (51), *Chida* writes that Rambam clearly did not know about the *Zohar*:

ויש מי שכתב דהרמב"ם יצא לו מדברי הזוהר הקדוש דכן מפורש בזוהר. ולי ההדיוט אינו נראה, דספר הזוהר לא נתגלה אפילו לאחרונים כמו הרשב"א והרא"ש וק"ו שלא נתגלה בימי הרמב"ם.

61. John Wiley & Sons, 2009, p. 23.

62. Thus, in section 10.1 and 10.2, we do not present 3:51 and 3:54 as contradicting one another.

of the statements.[63] This approach has been adopted by many medieval thinkers[64] as well as modern academic scholars.[65] However, even within

63. How would this approach deal with Rambam's admission that there are intentional contradictions in his work? Presumably, Rambam means that there are statements that seemingly contradict each other; however, there is a resolution that does not demand that we entirely disregard either of the two seemingly contradictory statements. Ultimately, Rambam does not intentionally write something that he thinks is false, though certain statements may be misleading or incomplete. The problem with this approach is that it implies that the contradiction is not really a contradiction (since there is a resolution), which would put it in one of the first four categories of "apparent contradictions," rather than in the seventh category which indicates it is a real contradiction.

    To answer this Prof. Ya'ir Lorberbaum suggests a fascinating theory regarding the purpose of Rambam's seventh cause for contradictions. Prof. Lorberbaum argues that when it comes to matters that are extremely profound due to the dialectical nature of expression, some aspect necessarily will be concealed such that each time the topic is discussed a different aspect will be emphasized. According to his view, the seventh cause for contradiction has nothing to do with Rambam attempting to obscure his true intention. ("*'Ha-Siba ha-Shevi'it,' Al ha-Setirot be-Moreh Nevuchim – Iyun mei-Chadash*," *Tarbiz* 69 (2), 5760, pp. 211–237, cited in *shiur* 2 of R. Chaim Navon's series entitled "Introduction to The Guide of the Perplexed.")

    According to this explanation the seventh cause is, in fact, different from the earlier causes insofar as the statements do contradict. Due to limitations of the human intellect there is a need to present the ideas in a dialectical manner of expression – there is no other way for the whole truth to be conveyed simultaneously. (Consider our discussion in Chapter 7, where we address contradictions between *pshat* and *drash* and suggest that sometimes only when an idea is presented in contradictory manners can the scope of the idea be communicated.) At first, this response seems difficult insofar as it makes the seventh cause almost identical to the fifth. In truth, however, it does not. In the fifth cause there is a progression (e.g., Newtonian Physics before relativity). In the seventh there is no progression per se. Rather, the matter must be considered from two seemingly conflicting perspectives in order to arrive at the truth.

64. Such thinkers include Ramban, as we shall see in Chapter 39 when we consider Rambam's view on providence. Another medieval thinker who typifies this approach is R. Moshe b. Shmuel ibn Tibbon. See Dr. Aviezer Ravitzky, "Samuel Ibn Tibbon and the Esoteric Character of The Guide of the Perplexed," *Association of Jewish Studies Review*, 1981, 6: 87–123.

65. Unlike Leo Strauss, Shlomo Pines, and Lawrence Barmen, who maintain that Rambam sides with Aristotelian philosophy when it conflicts with Torah, scholars like Julius Guttman, Harry Wolfson, Arthur Hyman, Marvin Fox and Isadore Twersky maintain (perhaps to differing degrees) that Rambam's view essentially is that of the Torah. In the words of Prof. Isadore Twersky, the goal of Rambam was to demonstrate

this school of thought there is significant variation. In 2.10 we shall present the approach of two *gedolei Yisrael,* R. Kook and R. Soloveitchik, who holistically and (arguably) harmonistically read Rambam's various writings.

2.9 THE NEED FOR EXTRAPOLATION

Besides the attempt to hide esoteric wisdom from the public, there may be another factor behind the ambiguity in parts of *Moreh ha-Nevuchim.* In 2.1, we cited the Talmudic restrictions upon teaching *ma'aseh merkava.* Besides the restrictions concerning who can be taught (e.g., those unprepared), there is a rule that the teacher of *ma'aseh merkava* may teach only *roshei prakim* (lit. chapter headings), forcing the student to fill in the details by means of extrapolation. Accordingly, when Rambam teaches esoteric wisdom, he does not state all points explicitly. Rather, he expects the reader to extrapolate. Needless to say, this makes the process especially challenging.

Let us try to understand this Talmudic requirement. Once a worthy pupil is found, why not teach him overtly? If we are so concerned for misunderstanding, why not demand that everything be spelled out instead?

Two possible solutions seem apparent, both of which may be true. Firstly, this form of communication serves as another barrier preventing the unworthy student from accessing the Torah's secrets. Secondly, esoteric wisdom does not lend itself to full explication; extrapolation is inherently necessary.

To appreciate this second solution, let us consider the example of prophecy where, interestingly, we find the same pattern. Rambam writes that only Moshe was capable of receiving the word of God directly (*Hilchot Yesodei ha-Torah* 7:3). All other prophets understood the divine message through a parable or riddle (*mashal* or *chida),* a process that also involved some sort of extrapolation.[66] Rambam (Introduction to

---

the "inseparability and complementarity of the two apparently discordant but intrinsically harmonious disciplines" of Torah and philosophy. Prof. Twersky highlights the many philosophical passages in Rambam's legal writings and halachic passages in his philosophical writing, all of which underscore Rambam's master plan to harmonize law and philosophy (*Introduction to the Code of Maimonides,* 1980, pp 357–369).

66. While parables and riddles differ from *roshei prakim,* Rambam, as we shall see, partially equates the two insofar as both rely upon extrapolation.

Moreh ha-Nevuchim) compares the process of teaching esoteric wisdom to that of prophecy; in both, there is a need to employ a *mashal* or *chida*.

The reason why prophecy cannot be expressed explicitly seems to be that the recipient is not capable of understanding without a metaphor. God uses the *mashal* or *chida* to concretize an intangible concept, just as a human teacher uses analogies to convey ideas that are too abstract for the student to understand directly.

Yet the need for a *mashal* or *chida* might also reflect the notion that by nature, certain ideas cannot be expressed in finite words. The teacher may not (because it is esoteric) and cannot (because of its complexity) convey the information overtly; rather, he must express *roshei prakim*, leaving the student to recreate the concept independently based upon his master's condensation. Thus, extrapolation is necessary not just in prophecy, but in any transmission of esoteric wisdom.[67] Rambam elaborates in his Introduction to *Moreh ha-Nevuchim*:

> Know that whenever one of the perfect (i.e., a perfected individual) wishes to mention, either orally or in writing, something that he understands of these secrets, according to the degree of his perfection, he is **unable** to explain with complete clarity and coherence even the portion that he has apprehended, as he could do with the other sciences whose teaching is generally recognized. Rather there will befall him when teaching another that which he had undergone when learning himself. **I mean to say that the subject matter will appear, flash, and then be hidden again**, as though this were the nature of this subject matter, be there much or little of it. For this reason, all the Sages possessing knowledge of God the Lord, knowers of the truth, when they aimed at teaching something of this subject matter, spoke of it only in parables and riddles.[68]

67. Why was Moshe able to prophesy without the need for a *mashal* or *chida*? Rambam explains that Moshe prophesied without any intermediary. His closeness to God allowed for direct communication (*Hilchot Yesodei ha-Torah* 7:6). Other prophets prophesied through an angel; accordingly, the message could not be direct.
68. P. 8 of the Pines edition. Rambam elaborates upon this in his Introduction to Section III of *Moreh ha-Nevuchim*.

Rambam distinguishes between teaching about God and teaching other sciences. With respect to other sciences, a competent teacher is capable of transmitting the information he wishes to impart with complete clarity and coherence. Not so when it comes to *ma'aseh merkava.* Here, words cannot convey the idea that the teacher wishes to convey.[69] All the teacher (or author) can hope to do is attempt to trigger the flash of understanding in his student using parables. These lightning bolts of insight will appear, momentarily provide light (understanding), and then disappear, like the *chayot* (a type of angel) depicted in *Yechezkeil* 1:14 (וְהַחַיּוֹת רָצוֹא וָשׁוֹב כְּמַרְאֵה הַבָּזָק).[70] The role of the teacher is to elicit that experience within the student.

In 2.2, we noted that Rambam understands that the purpose of anthropomorphisms in the Torah is to bring the masses to belief in God. R. Kook suggests an additional function that fits nicely with Rambam's explanation of the need for parables in Scripture. R. Kook argues that imagery is necessary because human language cannot capture divine matters. The Torah's language alludes to inexpressible divine secrets, ideas that can be conveyed only though images.[71]

2.10 R. Kook and R. Soloveitchik on Rambam's Relationship with Greek Philosophy

In 1.5, we noted Rambam's belief that, for the most part, Aristotle got things right. However, in 3.3, we will bring an example of Rambam's willingness to diverge from Aristotle with respect to the question of creation. Should this be seen as a minor divergence, with Rambam primarily accepting Greek philosophy as consistent with Torah, or does it

---

69. In a similar fashion, mystical sources teach us that the infinite world of *machshava* (thought) cannot descend to the realm of *dibur* (speech) without some sort of dilution.
70. Along similar lines, in his commentary on the Mishna in *Chagiga*, Rambam writes that the reason for the rule to teach only ראשי פרקים is that the subtlety of these topics is such that any attempt to elucidate the matter explicitly will lead to error. אלא רומזים לו ברמז והוא לומד ודן על פיו מעצמו, וזהו ענין אמרם שונין לו ראשי הפרקים, לפי שיש שם ענינים הנחקקים בנפשות השלמים מבני אדם, וכשמסבירים אותם בלשון וממשלים אותם במשלים פג טעמן ויוצאין מענינן.
71. See *Rabbi Abraham Isaac Kook and Jewish Spirituality* by Lawrence J. Kaplan and David Shatz, p. 48–49.

demonstrate that Rambam adopted a fundamentally different outlook than espoused by Greek philosophy?

The approach we have assumed thus far is closer to the former possibility. Prof. Isadore Twersky powerfully expresses this perspective by describing Rambam's goal to "bring law and philosophy, two apparently incongruous attitudes of mind, two jealous rivals, into fruitful harmony."[72]

On the other hand, R. Kook powerfully argues in favor of the latter option, noting that beneath the façade of common harmony, there is fundamental divergence between Rambam's worldview and the philosophic-Aristotelian one. R. Kook expresses this notion when disagreeing with the historical approach of R. Ze'ev Jawitz (1847–1924),[73] who depicts Rambam's philosophical positions as being heavily influenced by non-Jewish sources. R. Kook, as we shall see, both minimizes the influence that non-Jewish sources had upon Rambam and maximizes the extent to which Rambam's view fundamentally diverges from that of the philosophers.

While R. Kook's view differs from the conventional academic approach and seems at odds with the tone and content of certain passages in Rambam, it is worthwhile to consider insofar as it reflects a profound and possibly correct understanding of Rambam, and it certainly is the way many great Jewish thinkers understood Rambam.[74] Of course,

---

72. Introduction to the Code of Maimonides, 1980, pp 357–369

73. R. Ze'ev Jawitz was born in Kolno to a family distinguished in scholarship and piety. Jawitz excelled in Jewish history. He moved to Israel in 1888, and his writings were published in periodicals such as *Ha'aretz, Pri ha-Aretz* (1892), and *Ge'on ha-Aretz* (2 vols., 1893–1894). He also wrote several textbooks, including *Tal Yaldut* (1891), *ha-Moriya* (1894), *Divrei ha-Yamim le-Am Bnei-Yisrael* (1894), *Divrei Yemei ha-Amim* (1893–1894), and *Neginot Mini Kedem* (1892). His major work is *Toldot Yisrael* (14 vols. 1895–1940).

74. In *Alei Shur* (Vol. 2, p. 145) R. Shlomo Wolbe cites his teacher R. Yerucham Levovitz as saying, "Heaven forbid to consider Rambam a philosopher; the most we can say is that he knew philosophy. He was a *kadosh elyon* (extraordinarily holy)." R. Wolbe understands that *kadosh elyon* indicates that Rambam merited understanding, without Kabbala, the inner truths of Torah.

Interestingly, not all academics agree that *Moreh ha-Nevuchim* should be seen as a philosophical work. As alluded to in 2.8, the matter is subject to considerable debate. Consider the following statement by Prof. Leo Strauss in the introductory essay to the Shlomo Pines translation of *Moreh ha-Nevuchim* (University of Chicago Press, 1963, p. xiv):

one wonders how such a viewpoint can conform with Rambam's statement that the differences are few. The answer is that, while numerically few, these differences reflect a radically different outlook. Specifically, R. Kook notes three basic areas of disagreement: concerning prophecy, creation, and providence.[75] Let us consider each of these carefully.

> The enchanting character of the Guide does not appear immediately. At first glance, the book appears merely to be strange and in particular to lack order and consistency. But progress in understanding it is a progress in becoming enchanted by it. Enchanting understanding is perhaps the highest form of edification. **One begins to understand the Guide once one sees that it is not a philosophic book – a book written by a philosopher for philosophers – but a Jewish book: a book written by a Jew for Jews.** Its first premise is the old Jewish premise that being a Jew and being a philosopher are two incompatible things. Philosophers are men who try to give an account of the whole by starting from what is always accessible to man as man; Maimonides starts from the acceptance of the Torah. A Jew may make use of philosophy, and Maimonides makes the most ample use of it; but as a Jew he gives his assent, where as a philosopher he would suspend his assent.

What Strauss means is that in *Moreh ha-Nevuchim,* Rambam accepts the view of the Torah as true and correct. He is unwilling simply to follow his intellect wherever it takes him. Thus, it is not a true philosophical work, but rather is a religious text. Ironically, although R. Kook and Prof. Strauss differ considerably in their understanding of Rambam, Strauss, like R. Kook, argues that *Moreh ha-Nevuchim* is not a philosophical work and that recognizing this is the key to understanding *Moreh ha-Nevuchim.* (However, as noted in 2.8, Strauss believes that Rambam was a true philosopher. Thus, he maintains that a straightforward reading of *Moreh ha-Nevuchim* does not reflect Rambam's true belief. Thus, the above comment serves as the basis for his esoteric reading of *Moreh ha-Nevuchim,* which R. Kook certainly would reject.)

As discussed in 2.8, many academicians disagree with Strauss's contention. For a critique of this particular point, see *Jewish Philosophy in a Secular Age* (p. 26, n. 8), where Prof. Kenneth Seeskin argues based on *Moreh ha-Nevuchim* 2:25 (concerning corporeality) that Rambam's Judaism as presented in *Moreh ha-Nevuchim* "is transformed to satisfy the needs of philosophy" when the philosophical tenets have been proved. An excellent argument in favor of the notion that *Moreh ha-Nevuchim* is in fact a philosophical work can be found in "The Philosophical Character of Maimonides' Guide – A Critique of Strauss's Interpretation," by Joseph Buijs, *Judaism* 27 (1978): pp. 448–457.

75. **מאמרי הראי"ה לאחדותו של הרמב"ם**

הרמב"ם ז"ל הבדיל הבדלה תהומית שאין למעלה הימנה, בעצם המהות של התורה כלפי חכמת יון, וזאת היא ההבדלה שבין קודש לחול, אחרי אשר קבע הוא ז"ל שלשת יסודות עקריים ששום מעיין בספר המורה לא יוכל לזוז מהם, והם : **האחד**, שהנבואה היא למעלה מכל המושג של השכל האנושי כלו, ומה שלא יושג כלל בשכל האנושי

Prophecy

Rambam's perspective on prophecy is complex; he devotes seventeen chapters of *Moreh ha-Nevuchim* (3:32–48) to the topic. One aspect of his thought on the matter is consistent with the Greek view: Rambam maintains that prophecy is part of a natural process. In *Hilchot Yesodei ha-Torah* (7:1), he writes that both intelligence and moral character are necessary preconditions to prophecy:

> The spirit of prophecy rests only upon the wise man who is distinguished by great wisdom and strong moral character, whose passions never overcome him in anything whatsoever. Rather, his rational faculty always has his passions under control, and he possesses a broad and sedate mind.

What is prophecy? Rambam maintains that prophecy is "a certain perfection in the nature of man"; it is one step beyond what a person can achieve naturally (*Moreh ha-Nevuchim* 2:32). While the steps leading up to prophecy are natural, the last rung is decidedly supernatural. In this

---

הרי הוא נודע בבירור על ידי הנבואה, שהיא דבר ד׳. **השני** הוא יסוד חידוש העולם, שבזה עקר את כל המבט האלילי היוני על כל ההויה כולה, והשיב לנו את ארחות הקודש של התורה שהוא התוכן של המבט היהדותי המקורי על כל ההויה, והוא ההיפוך הגמור מהמבט היוני האחוז בקדמות העולם. ולא כמו שכתב המחבר ז״ל על פי שיטתו, שע״י החוטים הדקים המבדילים והמפרידים בין דעות תורתנו לדעות חכמי יון וערב, עושים אותם רק כמעט לשני הפכים גמורים, לדעת רבינו ז״ל לא רק כמעט שני הפכים גמורים הם, **אלא שני הפכים גמורים לגמרי בהחלט**, כי ההבדל בין המושג של הקדמות וחזיון העולם האלילי, שהם ״אלהא די שמיא וארקא לא עבדו״, לחזיון העולם הישראלי שד׳ אחד ״הוא יוצר כל נוטה שמים לבדו ויוסד הארץ מי אתו״, הוא הבדל כל כך נשמתי עד שאין בו אפילו צד אחד או נקודה אחת ממשית, שאנחנו יכולים לומר עליהם באמת שהם דומים זה לזה. והיסוד **השלישי** הוא יסוד ההשגחה הפרטית במין האדם בכל פרטיו ומעשיו שהוא ההיפך הגמור מכל צביון ההכרה של חכמת יון, אשר אמרה כמאמר הפושעים מעולם, ״עזב ד׳ את הארץ״. כל זה הוא הבדל נורא, וההפכיות הגמורה המתבלטת על ידי שלשת היסודות הללו שקבעם רבינו הגדול בחכמתו ובקדושתו הגדולה להיות חיץ נצח בין הקודש ובין החול, בין חכמת יון האנושית ובין חכמת ישראל האלקית, זו היא הפכיות מוחלטה, שאפילו אם נמצא אי אלו פרטים של דמיון בסגנוני הדברים בין שני אלה, סוף כל סוף קיים ועומד בעינו הדבר, ולא קרב זה אל זה, ולעד יאמר בזה במובן הרוחני וההכמתי כמו במובן הגזעי והטפוסי הלאומי והמסורתי.

respect, Rambam deviates sharply from the Greek perspective.[76] Rambam describes the steps a person can take to prepare himself for prophecy but notes that the final leap to actual prophecy is dependent upon God's will: "It may happen that one who is fit for prophecy and prepared for it will not become a prophet, namely, on account of the divine will." Elsewhere (*Hilchot Yesodei ha-Torah* 7:5), he writes: "Those who sought the prophetic gift were called 'sons of the prophets.' Although they concentrated their minds, the divine spirit might or might not rest upon them."[77]

What does prophecy grant a person that he has not yet achieved? Rambam explains that when the divine overflow reaches a person's **intellect** alone, he is a philosopher. If the overflow reaches a person's **imaginative faculty** as well, he is a prophet.[78] While the precise meaning of this process is obscure, it is clear that this higher level, which reflects a closer connection to God, grants discernment unavailable to someone upon whom the gift has not been bestowed.[79] R. Kook understands

---

76. There are actually two ways to read Rambam. Either the last step is supernatural, or it is natural but God occasionally, supernaturally prevents a person from achieving the natural last step (i.e., prophecy).

77. Some thinkers express this as follows: anything a person can tap into on a regular basis constitutes *teva* or nature. Because prophecy is beyond *teva* it cannot be predicted. Thus, Rambam writes that all stages until prophecy relate to the intellectual faculty, but prophecy, which goes beyond the predictable, requires the imaginative faculty.

78. Rambam writes in *Moreh ha-Nevuchim* (2:37):

> You should know that the case in which **the intellectual overflow overflows only toward the rational faculty and does not overflow at all toward the imaginative faculty** – either because of the scantiness of what overflows or because of some deficiency existing in the imaginative faculty in its natural disposition, a deficiency that makes it impossible for it to receive the overflow of the intellect – **is characteristic of men of science engaged in speculation**. If, on the other hand, **this overflow reaches both faculties** – I mean both the rational and the imaginative – as we and others among the philosophers have explained, and if the imaginative faculty is in a state of ultimate perfection owing to its natural disposition, **this is characteristic of the class of prophets**.

79. As we will explain in 10.1, in the palace analogy (*Moreh ha-Nevuchim* 3:51), Rambam depicts how different people will be closer or farther from the king. The sixth class of people make it to the king's room – an extraordinary intellectual achievement. (They have succeeded in finding a proof for everything that can be proven; they have a true knowledge of God.) But prophets go farther. They interact with the king. How does one arrive at this level? One must "concentrate all their thoughts on God." Rambam

Rambam as saying that prophecy allows one to understand that which is above what can be grasped intellectually. Accordingly, R. Kook argues, Rambam's understanding of prophecy reflects a fundamentally different perspective than that of the Greeks insofar as (a) prophecy is not merely a natural process and (b) it demonstrates the existence of perception inaccessible to the mind but accessible through the spiritual process of prophecy.

Creation

In 3.3, we will examine why Rambam rejects Aristotle's theory of the eternity of matter. R. Kook sees this deviation as reflecting a categorically different worldview. According to Aristotle, the universe exists and operates independently of God's will,[80] while according to Rambam, God is the source for all that exists (see *Hilchot Yesodei ha-Torah,* Ch. 1). Hence, Rambam (*Moreh ha-Nevuchim* 2:24) writes that the entire basis of the Torah is inconceivable according to Aristotle's perspective.[81] Only

---

explains that this pursuit differs from the previous stages which focused on intellectual achievements while this stage is meditative: "This is the worship peculiar to those who have acquired knowledge of the highest truths; and the more they reflect on Him, and think of Him, the more they are engaged in His worship." This idea also relates to why prophets are meant to be leaders: the prophet communicates God's message to the people in a way that a philosopher cannot (*Moreh ha-Nevuchim* 2:37). This, according to Rambam, is the meaning of Yaakov's dream in which angels ascended to heaven and then descended into the world. Rambam understands that the angels are prophets who ascend to the higher spiritual worlds and then bring down God's message to the lower material world where they communicate it to the people.

80. While Aristotle believed (in Rambam's interpretation of him) that the universe is entirely dependent upon God, it is not dependent upon God's *will*. This is why belief in an eternal universe would not be a violation of the first of the thirteen principles (or of the fourth as originally formulated), since God still is *ontologically prior* to the world's creation in Aristotle's view, if not *temporally prior.*

81. Likewise, Rambam writes (*Moreh ha-Nevuchim* 2:25):

> The belief in eternity the way Aristotle sees it – that is, the belief according to which the world exists of necessity, that no nature changes at all, and that the customary course of events cannot be modified with regard to anything – destroys the Torah in its principle, necessarily belies every miracle, and reduces to inanity all the promises and threats that the Torah holds out... If the philosophers would succeed in demonstrating eternity as Aristotle understands it, the Torah as a whole would become void.

if there is creation can there be prophecy, miracles, and the Torah as we understand it. [82]

Providence

While Rambam's perspective on providence is complex (we will treat it extensively in Chapter 38), he clearly maintains that God plays a significant role in running the universe (even if not every person experiences absolute providence). By contrast, the Greek's view denies divine involvement, a view best summarized by the verse in *Yechezkeil* (9:9), "God has abandoned the land."[83] Rambam (*Moreh ha-Nevuchim* 2:25) notes that the possibility of providence is predicated upon creation. Thus, if we accept Aristotle's theory about the eternity of matter:

> In such relation to the universe that He cannot change anything; if He wished to make the wing of a fly longer or reduce the number of the legs of a worm by one, He could not accomplish it.

Rambam maintains that individual providence (*hashgacha pratit*) is appropriate only for man (and not beast) and reflects man's elevated state.[84] Moreover, a person who achieves a more perfected state

---

82. This idea is echoed in the fourth of Rambam's thirteen principles of faith:

פירוש המשנה לרמב"ם מסכת סנהדרין פרק י (הקדמה לפרק חלק)

והיסוד הרביעי הקדמות. והוא, שזה האחד המתואר הוא הקדמון בהחלט, וכל נמצא זולתו הוא בלתי קדמון ביחס אליו, והראיות לזה בספרים הרבה. וזה היסוד הרביעי הוא שמורה עליו מה שנ' מעונה אלהי קדם. ודע כי היסוד הגדול של תורת משה רבינו הוא היות העולם מחודש, יצרו ה' ובראו אחר ההעדר המוחלט.

This text comes from the translation of R. Yosef Kapach, which incorporates changes Rambam made later in life. The earlier editions do not mention that belief in creation is one of the principles (they leave out the last sentence beginning with ודע).

83. See *Moreh ha-Nevuchim* 3:54 and Ramban *Shemot* 13:16.

84. Moreover, Rambam maintains that providence is necessary for divine justice. In *Moreh ha-Nevuchim* (3:17), he writes:

Another fundamental principle taught by the Law of Moshe is this: Wrong cannot be ascribed to God in any way whatever. All evils and afflictions, as well as all kinds of happiness of man, whether they concern one individual person or a community, are distributed according to justice; they are the result of strict judgment that admits no wrong whatever. Even when a person suffers pain in consequence of a thorn

experiences a greater degree of providence. R. Kook argues that Rambam's understanding of God's connection to our world reflects a fundamentally different outlook than that suggested by Greek wisdom.

Beyond the specific differences highlighted by R. Kook, we might add that the fiery, passionate love that Rambam feels is at the heart of religion (see *Hilchot Teshuva,* Ch. 10) hints to an outlook that is inescapably at odds with Aristotle's worldview.

While R. Kook concedes that Rambam appropriates much wisdom from Aristotle, he nonetheless writes:

> He (Rambam) did not follow Aristotle and his Arabic philosophical commentators blindly, but rather investigated, distinguished, and refined matters... and after it became clear that there was no contradiction to the fundamentals of the Torah and he was convinced by them, he did not hide the truth by declaring that they were his opinions, and he determined it proper to explain the written and oral laws in light of them.[85]

R. Kook adds one additional point while addressing a different and equally fascinating question. R. Kook believed that fundamental congruence exists between the rationalist perspective of those like Rambam and the mystical perspective adopted by Kabbalists. After all, the two groups are simply using different but valid tools to understand God. Accordingly, he wonders why the expositors of each position see their opponents in oppositional terms?[86] R. Kook explains that only from the vantage

---

having entered into his hand, although it is at once drawn out, it is a punishment that has been inflicted on him [for sin], and the least pleasure he enjoys is a reward [for some good action]. All this is meted out by strict justice as is said in Scripture, "All of His ways are judgment" (*Devarim* 32:4). We simply are ignorant of the working of that judgment.

85. This citation is from the same essay (לאחדותו של הרמב"ם) referenced above. The translation is adapted from "A Kabbalistic Reinvention of Maimonides' Legal Code: R. Abraham Isaac Kook's Commentary on Sefer Hamada," by James A. Diamond in *Jewish Studies, an Internet Journal,* p. 3.

86. Of course, not all Kabbalists viewed Rambam negatively. As we will show in 2.13, many mystics revered Rambam and borrowed from his philosophical positions. Nevertheless, in Rambam's generation and the generations immediately following,

point of exclusivity will a perspective be taken to its logical conclusion and fully explored. To ensure that all true perspectives were revealed, Providence arranged that the perspectives be seen as antithetical. Once the dust of the dispute settled, however, we can embrace both camps.

R. Kook on Rambam's Sources

R. Kook stresses that we should not see Rambam as stemming from secular sources; the basis for his beliefs is Torah and is rooted in holiness. While it certainly is true that Rambam utilized non-Jewish sources, the wisdom was filtered through the lens of Torah, with Rambam accepting only that which is true. A great person is able to capture the eternal spark even when it is ensconced in rubble, to see that which is good and true even when it is surrounded by that which is false. Rambam's greatness lies in his ability to do just that.[87]

Continuing the tradition evidenced in works such as *Tanya* and *Nefesh ha-Chaim,* R. Kook requires well-rounded scholars to study the works of both camps. Moreover, R. Kook writes that nobody can deny the contribution Rambam's philosophy made in eradicating false beliefs such as corporeality, which was common in his day. Imagine what Jewish thought would look like without Rambam; superstition and falsehood would be even more rampant.[88] Even today, certain people may

---

the two views were generally seen as being fundamentally oppositional. R. Kook addresses why that is.

87. **אורות הקודש חלק א אות יג (יסוד כל המחשבות)**
וכל מה שיתעלה האדם יותר, כל מה ששייכותו היא יותר גדולה לתוכן הפנימי של ההויה והחיים, הרי הוא לוקח מכל מחשבה בין שהיא שלו, בין שהיא של אחרים, את גרעינה הנצחי, ההגיוני, הטוב, הנובע ממקור החכמה, והולך ומתעלה על ידן, והן מתעלות בו.

88. **מאמרי הראיה - לאחדותו של הרמב"ם** ואני תמה איך נוכל להעלים את עינינו מלהחזיק טובה לרבינו הרמב"ם על עבודתו הגדולה בספר המורה. להעמיד את יסוד קדושת האמונה על טהרתו ולהרחיק את ההבלים הנוראים של ההגשמה באלהות מעל גבול ישראל. נקל לנו לתאר מה היה גורל האמונה, לולא עבודתו הקדושה הזאת אשר עבד בה במסירות נפש כל כך ואשר סבל עליה סבלות כל כך נוראה, אשר רק נפש קדושה כנפשו הגדולה היתה יכולה לעבור עליה בכל כך דרך נועם ושלום, ומפעלו זה גרם שב"ה בכלל תמה ונכרתה אמונת טעות זו מלב האומה כולה, ונקבע יסוד בכל לב בעיקר הדת, להאמין באמונה שלמה שהקב"ה אין לו גוף ולא ישיגוהו משיגי הגוף ואין לו שום דמיון כלל. וד' יודע עד איזה מדרגה של הבל והזיה היתה יכולה הטעות של אמונת ההגשמה להגיע לולא בא רבינו להציל את נשמת האמונה ממצולות הטעיה הזאת, ועד כמה היתה הכפירה והשלילה אוכלת אותנו אלמלי היה המצב של האמונה כל כך המוני וגס גם בדורות אשר המדעים וחופש הדעות התפשטו בהמון

be drawn to one particular methodology (rationalism or mysticism) more than another.[89] Accordingly, having sophisticated systems of both varieties proves valuable; a person can say that he is a rationalist and still be a good Jew. After all, Rambam was a rationalist, and all agree that he was a good Jew. Finally, and most importantly, the fact that the Jewish people have accepted Rambam as the greatest of Torah scholars shows that fundamentally he is a great representative of God's will and word. This is true regardless of our position on particular views he may have held.

מאמרי הראיה לאחדותו של הרמב"ם

אין שום ספק שישנם אנשים שדעות מיוחדות פועלות עליהם פעולה טובה, לקשר את לבבם לקדושה ולטהרה לאמונה ולעבודה לתורה ולמצוה, וישנם אנשים אחרים שדוקא דעות אחרות הן מסוגלות לקרב את לבבם לכל הדברים הקדושים והנשגבים הללו. ואם הדעות שנתפרשו בספר המורה התאימו לרוח קדושתו ותוקף אמונתו ודבקות עבודתו הקדושה והאמיתית של הענק הגדול מאור הקודש רבינו הרמב"ם ז"ל, לכל אוצר הטוב והקודש, לכל הזהירות והזריזות לכל הקדושה והטהרה ולכל תוקף יראת השם יתברך ואהבתו, שהיתה תמיד כשלהבת אש קודש בלבבו הטהור, אין שום ספק שרבים מאד הנם בישראל שאלה הדעות עלולות לפעול עליהם את הפעלת הקודש הזאת לטובה. ואם גם ימצאו רבים שאינם יכולים לקשר את מערכי רוחם באמונת אומן עם כל הדעות הנאמרות בספר המורה, הרשות נתונה להם לקשר את מחשבת לבבם גם עם הדעות של גדולי ישראל אשר סללו להם דרך אחרת, אבל חלילה לנו להוציא לעז של חיצוניות וקל וחומר של יוניות וזרות על אלה הדעות, אשר קדשתם רוחו הקדוש של רבינו הגדול הרמב"ם ז"ל.

Without a doubt, some people are affected positively by certain viewpoints that connect their hearts to holiness, purity, faith,

---

במדה כל כך גדולה, והדבקות של קדושת התורה והמסורת היא כל כך רפה בלב המונים רבים, ואיך היתה ההרגשה הכללית כלפי האמונה בכללה לולא קדם רבינו הגדול להופיע עליה באור טהרתו הנפלאה.

89. In *Orot ha-Torah*, R. Kook sees this as expression of the Talmud's dictum (*Avoda Zara* 19a) that אין אדם למד אלא במקום שלבו חפץ.

> service of God, Torah, and *mitzvot*. And there are others whose hearts are drawn to such holy and elevated matters by other viewpoints.
>
> If the opinions expressed in *Moreh ha-Nevuchim* were congenial to the holy spirit, mighty faith, and holy, true service of clinging to God possessed by the great and holy light [that] Rambam [was], if they were congenial to his entire inner treasury of goodness, holiness, exactitude, vitality, sanctity, purity, and the mighty fear and love of God – all of which was a constant flame of holy fire in his pure heart – there can be no doubt that a great many Jews will be positively affected by these opinions and thus drawn to holiness.
>
> On the other hand, many other people cannot forge a connection between their spirit and the opinions put forth in *Moreh ha-Nevuchim*. They have the right to connect the thought of their hearts to the viewpoints expressed by Torah leaders who cleared a different path. But heaven forbid that we disparage Rambam's viewpoints as being outside the realm of Torah, and worse, as Greek wisdom and alien to the Torah, for these viewpoints have been sanctified by Rambam's holy spirit.[90]

How then should one study Rambam? Specifically, how should one relate to concepts in Rambam that seem so foreign to Torah? R. Kook argues that one must judge Rambam favorably and seek to integrate his positions with that of Torah.

> **מאמרי הראיה לאחדותו של הרמב"ם**
>
> בדורותינו וכמה דורות שלפנינו ששקטו הרוחות ושמש הצדקה של הרמב"ם פרשה את אורה על פני כל אופק היהדות, נכנס גם "המורה" בכלל ספרי קודש שהם קניני התורה, וחלילה לנו לנהוג בו מנהג של זלזול, וחובתנו היום לא רק לדון את דבריו לכף זכות, כי

90. *Likutei ha-Re'iyah*; translation adapted from pp. 365–367 of R. Yaacov David Shulman's translation.

אם גם להתעמק בהם ולמצות את מדותיו בתור מדותיה של תורה;
כמו בגופי הלכותיה של תורה ישנם פנים שונים וחילוקי דעות, ואנו
נוהגים לקיים בהם את מדת התורה של עשה אזנך כאפרכסת ושמע
דברי המטהרים ודברי המטמאים, דברי המזכים ודברי המחייבים, דברי
הפוסלים ודברי המכשירים, מפני שכולם נתנו מרועה אחד, אע"פ
שלענין ההלכה למעשה ישנה הכרעה מיוחדת לאחת מן הדעות, כך
מדה זו עצמה נוהגת בהלכות הדעות והאמונות שהעלו חכמי ישראל
המוחזקים לאבות האומה גדולי התורה ואנשי הקודש, חלילה לנו
להקל ראש נגדם, ולהחליט על אחת מדעותיהם שהם דברים חיצונים,
ושהם נדחים מגבול ישראל, וקל וחומר שאסור לנהוג מנהג זה נגד
דעותיו של אביהם של ישראל המאיר עיני הדורות בתורתו חכמתו
וקדושתו, רבינו הרמב"ם ז"ל.

In our days as well as in previous generations, since the controversy over Rambam has died down and his light has spread its rays across the Jewish horizon, his *Moreh ha-Nevuchim* also is to be considered a holy volume of Torah. And heaven forbid that we disparage it in any way. Our obligation today is not only to find some way of justifying Rambam's words, but to delve into them and to relate to his words like we relate to Torah. In Torah law, there are various aspects and differences of opinion, and we apply the dictum, "Make your ears like a spout and listen to the words of those who declare something pure as well as those who declare it impure, those who declare someone innocent as well as those who declare him guilty, those who disqualify something as well as those who approve it – because all of these opinions come from one shepherd (i.e., Moshe)" (*Chagiga* 3a). This is the case even though only one of these opinions is accepted in practice. The same concept applies to the laws of viewpoints and articles of faith that have been posited by the Sages of Israel, who are accepted the forefathers of our nation, great and holy Torah leaders. Heaven forbid that we treat them disrespectfully and conclude that any one of their opinions is drawn from the secular realm, which have no place within Judaism, and in particular we are forbidden to assume such an attitude about the viewpoints of the father of Israel, who has enlightened the

> eyes of all generations with his Torah teachings, wisdom and holiness – Rambam.

In this paragraph R. Kook reveals how his conception of Rambam is sometimes diametrically opposed to the academic approach. He is reading Rambam with an agenda. The holiness and acceptance of Rambam compels him to read Rambam in light of other Torah sources and not the reverse.

There are cases, R. Kook concedes, that this is impossible. Positions where Rambam's view is certainly at odds with the majority of scholarship. In cases like this we can follow the majority position, but must remain respectful of Rambam. Moreover, even if one maintains that there is a certain superiority to the mystical perspective insofar as it stems more directly from God, disparaging the philosophical approach is wholly illegitimate.

> וגם באילו הדעות אשר אנו מוצאים שרבים מחכמי הדורות חולקים עליהן, יכולים אנחנו רק לומר שהננו מוכרעי מוכרעים להחזיק בהדעות שרוב גדולי ישראל נטו אליהן, אבל חס לנו להחליט על דעותיו של רבינו הגדול שהן דעות חיצוניות, חלילה! ואחרי שרבינו הרמב"ם, שתורת ד' היתה מקור חייו, מצא את לבבו נאמן לד' ולתורתו ועמו באלה הדעות, הלא זה הדבר בעצמו הוא הצד המכריע, שאין בהן דבר שיוכל להטיל טינא בלב או לדחות את מי שהוא מקדושת התורה וקדושת ישראל. וההכרעה בזה היא נתונה לפי המצב הנפשי ותפיסת הציורים הרוחניים של כל אחד לפי תכונתו והכל לפי מה שהוא אדם.

> Even when it comes to his opinions that many sages of various generations take exception to, we can say only that we must accept the viewpoint that the majority of Torah leaders tend to. But heaven forbid, heaven forbid, that we come to the conclusion that the viewpoints of the great Rambam are foreign to the Torah!
>
> Since Rambam, whose source of life was God's Torah, found his heart faithful to God, His Torah, and His people by maintaining these views, this itself is proof that there is nothing in them that can raise doubts in anyone's heart or drive anyone

away from the holiness of the Torah and of Israel. What counts in this matter is a person's spiritual state and his grasp of spiritual imagery, for each individual has his own nature. And so, [deciding what to study] must be dealt with on an individual basis.

We will return to the question of whether Rambam's thought is rooted primarily in tradition or whether it mostly derives from foreign sources in 6.3 and 6.4 when we examine how Rambam deals with aggadic statements that are philosophically problematic. However, we close this section with R. Kook's powerful conclusion.

ואין לנו לדבר על רבינו הגדול, שהיה מעניק באמת את החמה המדעית והמוסרית וכל מעלות הקודש והטוהר בקדושתה של תורה, אשר בה הגה יומם ולילה לדבקה על ידו בד׳ אחד, כאילו היה חילוקי לבבות בקרבו, ובמורה היתה עליו רוח אחרת וביתר ספריו רוח אחרת, חלילה! צדיק תמים היה רבינו, כמו שהיה גאון התורה והחכמה כן היה גאון התמימות והאמונה ודבריו כולם וגם דברי הספר הגדול מורה נבוכים ישארו לאור עולם בחכמת ישראל ותורתו כשמש צדקה ומרפא בכנפיה!

We cannot speak [badly] about our great teacher who truly imbued the light of science and ethics with all the attributes of holiness and purity of the holy Torah, which he studied day and night in order that, through them, he would cling to the One God. We cannot say that he had an internal conflict, leading him to write *Moreh ha-Nevuchim* with one spirit and his other works with another – heaven forbid! Rambam was a pure-hearted righteous person. Just as he was a genius in Torah and wisdom, so was he a genius of pure-heartedness and faith. And all of his words, including those of his great *Moreh ha-Nevuchim*, will remain as an eternal light in the wisdom and Torah of Israel, like a generous sun with healing rays.

R. Soloveitchik on Rambam's Fealty to Aristotle

R. Soloveitchik, like R. Kook (though perhaps to a lesser degree), also sees Rambam as fundamentally rejecting Aristotle, despite their many convergences. In *Maimonides – Between Philosophy and Halakhah:*

Rabbi Joseph B. Soloveitchik's Lectures on the Guide of the Perplexed,[91] an entire chapter is devoted to highlighting where Rambam differs from Aristotle. R. Soloveitchik is particularly adamant when countering the claim made by some scholars that Rambam feels Halacha is secondary to philosophy. One place that highlights the falsity of this claim is the closing chapter of *Moreh ha-Nevuchim,* which we will discuss at length in 10.2. There, Rambam stresses that the ultimate objective of man is not simply the intellectual apprehension of God; one must imitate God's actions, which include acts of lovingkindness, justice, and righteousness. Rambam derives from a verse in *Yirmiyahu* that we must act as God does. In so doing, we become God-like and achieve our greatest possible perfection. How does this chapter relate to Rambam's statements that indicate that intellectual achievement supersedes any sort of action? R. Soloveitchik responds by differentiating between two approaches to halachic observance. One approach would be simply to follow the practical law. The higher level, however, is the one identified in the final chapter of *Moreh ha-Nevuchim,* wherein Halacha is a means of identifying with God. According to R. Soloveitchik, Halacha ideally is not about "how to," but about bringing a higher truth into reality.[92]

Like R. Kook, R. Soloveitchik believed that the Torah's attitude is fundamentally antithetical to the Greek conception of the universe, and that a holistic reading of Rambam unequivocally indicates Rambam's unqualified embrace of the Torah's perspective.[93] R. Soloveitchik

91. Ed. Prof. Lawrence Kaplan, Urim Publications, 2016.

92. According to Prof. Kaplan (https://kavvanah.wordpress.com/2016/05/09/rav-soloveitchik-on-the-guide-of-the-perplexed-edited-by-lawrence-kaplan/), R. Soloveitchik counters the claim that Rambam felt that Halacha was secondary to philosophy by noting that Rambam distinguishes between two stages of ethics:

> ... Pre-theoretical ethics, ethical action that precedes knowledge of the universe and God, and post-theoretical ethics, ethical action that follows upon knowledge of the universe and God. Pre-theoretical ethics is indeed inferior to theory and purely instrumental; however, post-theoretical ethics is ethics as the imitation of God's divine attributes of action of Hesed (Loving Kindness), Mishpat, (Justice), and Tzedakah (Righteousness), the ethics referred to at the very end of the Guide, and this stage of ethics constitutes the individual's highest perfection.

93. An example of this line of thinking can be found in the second footnote of *u-Vikashtem mi-Sham.* There, R. Soloveitchik argues that the notion that God does not love the Jewish

powerfully expresses three ways in which Judaism, as understood by all great thinkers including Rambam, differed from the Greeks. (1) The Torah, when describing God's creation of the world and choosing of the Jewish people, ascribes *ratzon* (will) to God. Aristotle rejected creation because the notion that God could "decide" to create the world implies that beforehand He was in some way lacking, and, as such, is irreconcilable with God's perfection. Moreover, God's love for the Jewish people (or for any individual or group) is inconceivable to Aristotle for two additional reasons (2 and 3). Firstly, because it ascribes an emotion to God, and secondly, because the Greeks maintained that anything that is not universal is false.[94] R. Soloveitchik powerfully contrasts the approach of the Torah, as explained by Rambam, with the approach of Aristotle:

> In Aristotelian philosophy… the Prime Mover is aloof from the world and does not long for it. His relationship to the world is that of a teleological and necessary cause, without desire or intention… The Torah, which bases all of Judaism on the principle of creation and providence, but also on the principle of the choseness of the Jewish people, introduced into the center of our world the concept of lovingkindness and of love as a reciprocal process. The creation of the world is the embodiment of God's grace. God's providence of His creatures in general, and His choice of the congregation of Israel in particular, is a manifestation of infinite love.[95]

Ultimately, R. Kook and R. Soloveitchik differ slightly in their readings of Rambam and highlight different areas in which Rambam's views are at variance with Aristotle's. However, both R. Kook and R. Soloveitchik powerfully show how a careful and holistic reading of Rambam yields a picture that is dramatically different than the one typically assumed in the academic setting.

---

people (based on the impossibility of divine emotions) is not only false but heretical due to the numerous references in scripture and Rambam of God's love of the Jewish people.

94. The ancient Greek philosophers Plato, Aristotle and the Stoics believed in a kind of Universalism in which anything that does not apply at all times and for all people is not true.

95. *From There You Shall Seek*, translated by Naomi Goldblum, p. 154.

Understanding Rambam's Admiration for Aristotle

According to the above perspective, one wonders why Rambam frequently expresses such intense admiration for Aristotle. Moreover, is there significance to the fact that Rambam so frequently accepts Aristotle's theories if even on a fundamental level there are significant discrepancies? Ultimately, was Rambam an Aristotelian?

The answer lies in recognizing that Rambam appreciated the Greeks' and Aristotle's immeasurable contribution through their creation of the language of philosophy. This language shaped how we think about and discuss fundamental philosophical matters and theology. Aristotle changed the way in which we think about God, and he revolutionized the way we talk about the Divine.[96] Even when we reject his particular viewpoint, we are affected by his thought process and vocabulary.

To appreciate the nature of this complex relationship let us consider one example from the realm of ethics. In *Hilchot Dei'ot* (Chapters 1 and 2) and in *Introduction to Avot (Shemona Perakim)* Rambam describes that a person should strive for moderation in the realm of character traits, half way between both extremes. While there are certainly sources in Chazal for this notion (as noted, for example, by the commentaries on *Hilchot Dei'ot*), Rambam's formulation and language is taken from Aristotle's *Ethics.*[97] However, Rambam's ideal traits often differ from Aristotle's. For example, Aristotle believes the "middle path" between arrogance and self-deprecation is being proud of one's accomplishments, while Rambam, following Chazal, insists one must be exceedingly humble. Dr. David Shatz notes that this disagreement is a religious one: according to Rambam, a person must be humble because he must recognize that God has given him all those things Aristotle thinks he should be proud of.[98]

---

96. As we noted in 1.5, Rambam maintains that, in fact, there was a Jewish philosophical tradition that was forgotten due to persecution.
97. According to Aristotle, every ethical virtue is a condition intermediate (a "golden mean" as it is popularly known) between two other states, one involving excess and the other deficiency.
98. David Shatz, "Maimonides' Moral Theory" in *The Cambridge Companion to Maimonides,* ed. Kenneth Seeskin, Cambridge: Cambridge University Press, 2005, p. 175. Also, see ההרחקה מגובה-לב ומכעס אל הדרך האמצעית או עד הקצה האחר by R. Elchanan

So, was Rambam an Aristotelian? Yes and no. Rambam maintained that the Greeks were correct in many ways, even as they erred in significant matters. As R. Kook stressed, Rambam did not follow Aristotle blindly, but rather investigated, distinguished, and refined matters, accepting them only when they were consistent with the Torah. What made him an Aristotelian, to the extent that he was one, was his usage of Aristotelian language and methodology, and one should not underestimate the significance of that reality.[99]

To summarize, according to R. Kook and R. Soloveitchik, Rambam uses the language and doctrines of Aristotle to present the ideas of the Torah, just as later thinkers use Rambam's language and doctrines to express their own ideas (even as they often are attributed to Rambam). The numerous citations of Aristotle in Rambam do not imply, as Strauss maintains, that Rambam was a closet Aristotelian.

2.11 HOW COULD *MA'ASEH BEREISHIT* REFER TO SCIENCE? RAMBAM'S SPIRITUAL CONCEPTION OF THE PHYSICAL WORLD

In 1.3, we noted Rambam's statement that the first two chapters of *Mishneh Torah* discuss *ma'aseh merkava,* which Rambam understands as referring to divine science, while Chapters 3 and 4 examine *ma'aseh bereishit,* which Rambam understands as natural science. If *ma'aseh bereishit* is identified as natural science, why does Rambam (based on the

---

Samet in his עיונים בהלכות דעות, which can be found at http://www.daat.ac.il/daat/kitveyet/maaliyot/iyunim2-2.htm.

99. A helpful analogy for understanding Rambam's relationship with Aristotle is suggested by Dr. John Inglis quoting Dr. Ralph McInerny, a scholar of Aquinas, who describes the relationship between Aquinas and Aristotle:

> We find many references to Aristotle in Thomas, we find the invocation of doctrines, the quoting of phrases... He is using the doctrines or language of Aristotle for his own purposes. It is almost as if Aristotle were a language Thomas used to make independent points of his own.

Dr. John Inglis suggests the analogy in *Medieval Philosophy and the Classical Tradition: In Islam, Judaism and Christianity* (Routledge, 2005), p. 203. The same point is made in *The Cambridge Companion to Medieval Jewish Philosophy* edited by Daniel H. Frank and Oliver Leaman.

Talmud in *Chagiga*) require such high standards for its study.[100] While the obligation to conceal the divine sciences is understandable, why is there a need to conceal natural science? Moreover, in what sense should *ma'aseh bereishit* be seen as part of Torah if it simply is science? Would Rambam include all wisdom in Torah?

Rambam partially addresses the first question explicitly:

> **רמב"ם הלכות יסודי התורה פרק ד הלכה יא**
> ומה בין עניין מעשה מרכבה לעניין מעשה בראשית - שעניין מעשה מרכבה, אפילו לאחד אין דורשין בו, אלא אם כן היה חכם ומבין מדעתו, נותנין לו ראשי הפרקים; ועניין מעשה בראשית, מלמדין אותו ליחיד, אף על פי שאינו מבין אותו מדעתו, ומודיעין אותו כל שיכול לידע מדברים אלו. ולמה אין מלמדין אותו ברבים, **לפי שאין כל אדם יש לו דעת רחבה להשיג פירוש וביאור כל הדברים על בוריין.**
>
> What is the difference between the subject matter of *ma'aseh merkava* and the subject matter of *ma'aseh bereishit?* The former is never discussed with even a single person, unless that person is wise and capable of independent extrapolation, and even then, one should only present a rough outline. Creation, on the other hand, may be discussed with one person, even if he is incapable of independent extrapolation, and one may tell him as much as he is capable of understanding. **These matters are not discussed amongst many people, because not everybody has the intellectual capacity to fully understand them.**

One may not teach *ma'aseh bereishit* to a public audience because people in the audience may not understand. Misunderstanding is always undesirable, but concerning *ma'aseh bereishit* the result might be heresy. However, we are still left wondering why the natural sciences would be included in the study of Torah.

---

100. Other thinkers presume *ma'aseh bereishit* refers to the mystical secrets of creation. As such, it is apparent why they must be hidden. But since Rambam seems to assume that *ma'aseh bereishit* refers to the natural sciences it seems perplexing why it would have to be hidden.

It seems that Rambam refers to natural science, he is not necessarily referring to what we call science, but rather to how to see God in the world. One manifestation of this is Rambam's understanding that the spheres and celestial beings contemplate and understand God.[101, 102]

---

101. In *Yesodei ha-Torah* 2:9, he writes:

> כל הכוכבים והגלגלים כולן בעלי נפש ודעה והשכל הם, והם חיים ועומדים ומכירין את מי שאמר והיה העולם כל אחד ואחד לפי גדלו ולפי מעלתו משבחים ומפארים ליוצרם כמו המלאכים וכשם שמכירין הקדוש ברוך הוא כך מכירין את עצמן ומכירין את המלאכים שלמעלה מהן ודעת הכוכבים והגלגלים מעוטה מדעת המלאכים וגדולה מדעת בני אדם.
>
> All the stars and spheres possess a soul, knowledge, and intellect. They are alive, stand, and recognize the One who spoke and [thus brought] the world into being.
>
> Each one praises and glorifies its Creator, according to its greatness and level, just as the angels do. Just as they are aware of the Holy One, blessed be He, they also are aware of themselves and of the angels that surpass them. The knowledge of the stars and the spheres is less than the knowledge of the angels but greater than that of men.

The notion that the celestial bodies praise God may have its roots in Chazal. The Talmud (*Pesachim* 2a) understands the verse, "Praise Him all shining stars" (*Tehillim* 148:3), as indicating that the stars praise God. However, the *Targum* and Midrash *Shocheir Tov* render the verse, "The heavens relate the glory of God" (*Tehillim* 19:2), as "The heavens cause others to relate the glory of God."

102. The distinction between Rambam's understanding and that of contemporary science impacts not only our perception of the universe, but also the lessons that can be drawn from its study.

How should we relate to modern science's rejection of Rambam's cosmological perspective? Rambam writes (*Hilchot Yesodei ha-Torah* 3:9) and attempts to prove (see *Moreh ha-Nevuchim* 2:5) from biblical verses and Chazal that the heavenly spheres have souls, knowledge, and understanding and that they live, stand, and recognize God (Aristotle's position). R. Yaakov Kaminetsky writes (*Emet le-Yaakov al ha-Torah*, 5761, revised edition, pp. 15–16):

> As an aside, we learn from these words of Ramban [on *Bereishit* 1:1], and in particular from what he concluded in the continuation of his words on verse 8, that everything that exists in creation in the entire world, including the sun, the moon, and all the heavenly hosts, are not called "heavens." The "heavens" refer only to things that have no physical bodies, such as angels, *chayot* and the *merkava*. Anything that has a physical body, however, is included in the name "earth" in verse 1... These words of Ramban are what carried me when we saw men descending from a space ship on a ladder onto the surface of the moon. I thought to myself: "What would Rambam, who wrote that the moon has a spiritual form, answer now?" I thought that at that point, Kabbala defeated philosophy, and I comforted myself with the words of Ramban.

Another illustration is Rambam's theory of *tzurot* or forms (see *Yesodei ha-Torah* 4:7, 4:12, 7:1). Like the Greek philosophers, Rambam believed in the existence of non-material, abstract forms. Specifically, every physical object is a compound of matter and form.[103] Rambam's understanding of forms, however, differs in many ways from that of the ancient Greeks. Though a full discussion of this topic is beyond the scope of this work, let us consider one example.

Rambam (*Hilchot Yesodei ha-Torah* 7:1) refers to these entities as holy and pure (הצורות הקדושות הטהורות), whereas for the Greeks they are not holy. Moreover, it should be noted that Rambam interprets statements of Chazal as referring to this world of *tzurot*.[104] Thus, in the Introduction to *Moreh ha-Nevuchim* (cited in section 2.6), Rambam writes that there is a close connection between natural science and the divine science, such that the Torah does not elaborate in the first chapter of *Bereishit*, writing obscurely that in the beginning, God created such-and-such.

In 1.3, we noted that according to Rambam, the study of *ma'aseh bereishit* constitutes a fulfillment of the *mitzva* of Torah study, even if it essentially is the study of science. R. Mayer Twersky has argued that the study of contemporary science would not constitute a fulfillment of the *mitzva* to study Torah according to Rambam.[105]

We are forced to say that what Rambam told us in these chapters (*Hilchot Yesodei ha-Torah*, Ch. 1–4) is neither *ma'aseh merkava* nor *ma'aseh bereishit*. Rather, he wrote those four chapters from his deep mind and from his knowledge of secular wisdom, i.e., not from the wisdom of Torah, but only from philosophy... and Rambam wrote these only as an introduction to the *Mishneh Torah*, while the main part of the book begins with Chapter 5... (Translation adapted from http://hirhurim.blogspot.com/2004/12/rabbis-and-traveling-to-moon.html).

103. Rambam's position largely follows Aristotle's view that every physical object is a compound of matter and form (a doctrine known as "hylomorphism"). This differs from Plato's theory of forms wherein forms exist apart from the material world.

104. See *Torah, Chazal and Science* by R. Moshe Meiselman (Israel Bookshop, 2013), pp. 47–48, for an interesting discussion of this point.

105. When Rambam writes that cosmology is part of *pardeis*, and thus a section of Torah, he is working with the understanding that the celestial spheres and stars are not simply physical objects, but also spiritual creatures that understand God in ways that humans cannot. Their behavior teaches us knowledge that can be considered *talmud Torah*. Since contemporary science views the universe as entirely physical,

Ran's Understanding of Rambam

Ran (R. Nissim b. Reuven, 1320–1376) goes even further in distinguishing what Rambam calls *ma'aseh bereishit* from what we would call science.[106] According to Ran, *ma'aseh bereishit* refers to the spiritual dimension behind physical things that can be known only through revelation (אי אפשר שיודע כי אם בשפע אלהי נבואיי). Of course, this does not resemble what we would consider science. In fact, it is the very opposite! The contemporary meaning of the word "science" includes *only* that which is observable and verifiable through experimentation.[107] According to Ran, we can easily understand why studying *ma'aseh bereishit* constitutes a fulfillment of *talmud Torah*, even if it refers to the natural sciences.

R. Twersky argues, its study cannot be considered *talmud Torah*. While the investigation of cosmology can be valuable from a religious perspective insofar as it can inspire a person, and contemplation of the wondrous creations of God surely can ignite love and fear of God, it does not constitute Torah study in the formal sense.

This distinction is difficult to grasp since even contemporary science can bring a person to a greater understanding of God through the study of His creations. Apparently, R. Twersky understands that what makes *ma'aseh bereishit* a fulfillment of *talmud Torah* is not simply that it is inspirational. Rather, as Rambam indicates in *Hilchot Yesodei ha-Torah* 4:8–9, a person can bind himself to God through the cognition of forms and the other non-physical creations of the cosmos. Accordingly, this study is considered *talmud Torah* and grants a person eternity as Rambam notes there. While contemporary science certainly is valuable, especially if it inspires closeness to and reverence of God, it nevertheless does not afford the same direct connection and therefore would not be considered *talmud Torah* in the formal sense. In Chapter 12, we shall consider the Kabbalistic perspective that everything in the world (even if it is physical) is an embodiment of a divine idea. One wonders if, according to that perspective, studying the world with the goal of seeing that divinity would constitute *talmud Torah*.

106. **דרשות הר"ן הדרוש הראשון**

הנה לפי זה מעשה בראשית היא חכמת הטבע האמיתית, לא אותה שיתפלספו בה המתחכמים, והיא אמיתת ידיעת עצמי הדברים, וזה הוא נמשך ונתלה בנותני הצורות שהם השכלים הנבדלים, ואי אפשר שיודע כי אם בשפע אלהי נבואיי, ולכן תהיה חכמת מעשה בראשית סמוכה ומצרנית למעשה מרכבה, ושניה אליה במעלה, כי שתי אלה החכמות תהיה בהם ההשגה ברוחניים שהם השכלים הנבדלים.

107. Thus, Ran concludes, there is no need to hide science that is derived from observation and experimentation from the masses.

Ran's theory, however, is problematic.[108] It seems difficult to claim that all of Rambam's conclusions concerning *pardeis* stem exclusively from revelation and transmission in light of his explicit declaration that some of his theories come from other sources. In the Introduction to Book 3 of *Moreh ha-Nevuchim,* he writes:

> No divine revelation came to me to teach me that this was the intent of the matter, nor have I received my belief in this respect from any teacher; rather, I have been informed by what I learned from Scripture and the utterances of our Sages, **together with the philosophical principles that I have adopted**, that the matter is as such, without doubt. But it is possible that the matter is otherwise and the meaning is different.

Gra's Rejection of Rambam's Definition

Gra believes Rambam's understanding of *pardeis* was shaped by Greek sources, and accordingly, he sharply criticizes Rambam's position, declaring that Rambam never saw the true *pardeis.*[109] As we saw in 1.6, Gra

---

108. As we noted previously, R. Yaakov Kaminetsky rejected Ran's contention and accepted that Rambam's science, which was based on Greek wisdom, has been disproved.

109. There have been those who questioned the authenticity of these statements of Gra. The quote seems to be accurate, however, as R. Jacob J. Schacter writes in "Facing the Truths of History" *The Torah U-Madda Journal,* Vol. 8 (1998–1999), pp. 215–216:

> This absolute condemnation of philosophy flew in the face of the claim of various *maskilim* who sought to portray the Gaon as one who shared their general openness to worldly wisdom and, this time, some of them even went so far as to claim that it was a forgery. In a letter to Shmuel Yosef Fuenn, Rabbi Zevi Hirsch Katzenellenbogen wrote that he heard from the well-known R. Menasheh of Ilya that the Gaon never wrote these words but they were added later by someone who wanted to falsely present him as an opponent of philosophy. One writer even argued that the verbosity of this gloss proves that it could not have been written by the Gaon whose style was generally distinguished by its brevity and cryptic nature. Also, in an attempt to partially mitigate the harshness of this comment, some printed editions of this commentary simply omit the word "ha-arurah." While one of the Gaon's disciples, R. Israel of Shklov, already noted that later copyists did tamper with the text of some of the Gaon's glosses, it is clear that this statement, like the one written by R. Barukh of Shklov

rejects what he saw as Rambam's total embrace of science and philosophy as teaching us about God, and thus, Gra has a different interpretation of the terms *ma'aseh bereishit* and *ma'aseh merkava.* Commenting on Rama, who cites Rambam's understanding of these terms, he writes:

ביאור הגר"א יורה דעה סימן רמו ס"ק יח
הוא [דברי הרמ"א הם] מדברי הרמב"ם ומפרש שזהו ד' שנכנסו לפרדס ולכך נענשו שהיו כולם רכים בשנים חוץ מר"ע... **אבל לא ראו את הפרדס לא הוא (הרמ"א) ולא הרמב"ם...**

> The opinion of Rama is based on Rambam, who understands thusly the story of the four people who entered *pardeis* and were punished because they were too young, with the exception of R. Akiva... However, neither Rama nor Rambam saw the true *pardeis.*

Gra rejects Rambam's understanding of the esoteric wisdom alluded to in the Talmud. He understands that *pardeis,* as well as *ma'aseh bereishit* and *ma'aseh merkava,* refer to Kabbala.[110, 111]

(concerning the Gaon's positive attitude towards secular studies), is authentic and accurately represents the Gaon's attitude toward this discipline. R. Shmuel Luria, owner of many of the Gaon's writings, testified that he found those very words in the margin of the Gaon's own volume of the Shulhan Arukh written in his own handwriting.

110. Many thinkers agree with this explanation. For example, Ritva (*Sukka* 28a) writes:
דבר גדול מעשה מרכבה. פי' מרכבה העליונה הקדושה שלא נסתכלו בה נביאים מעולם וסודה ידוע לבעלי האמת.

The reference to בעלי האמת is a clear allusion to mysticism.

111. R. Elchanan Wasserman defends Rambam from Gra's critique by referring to Ran's understanding of *ma'aseh bereishit:*

קובץ שעורים חלק ב סימן מז אות יג
מ"ש בביאור הגר"א על הרמב"ם שלא ראה את הפרדס, וכונתו להשיג עמ"ש הרמב"ם, דמעשה בראשית היא חכמת הטבע, ובודאי אם כונת הרמב"ם כפשוטו, הן דברי תימה דמעשה בראשית אלו לומדין בכל הגימנזיות, אבל בדרשות הר"ן דרוש א' פירש היטב עומק כונת הרמב"ם, והכריח כפירושו, יעיי"ש, דיש חכמת הטבע נגלית ונסתרת, וכונת הרמב"ם לחכמה הנסתרת שבטבע וזה א"א להשיג בשכל אנושי כי אם ברוה"ק עיי"ש.

Thus far, we have seen how both rationalist and Kabbalistic thinkers maintain that there is a *mitzva* to know God. Moreover, we have seen that Rambam believes that one fulfills this *mitzva* through the study of philosophy. We also have seen how there are many dangers inherent in the study of philosophy and that some do not approve of such study at all.[112] In Chapter 12, we will return to the question of how the Kabbalists understand the *mitzva* to know God.

2.12 APPENDIX A: RAMBAM'S MYSTICAL SIDE AND HIS POSITION ON KABBALA

Was Rambam a mystic? What was Rambam's position on Kabbala? While related these two positions must be addressed separately.

Was Rambam a Mystic?

To answer this question, we must define the term "mystic."

Rambam was certainly a rationalist who sought to explain all of Torah and every aspect of Judaism rationally. He strongly rejected the notion of magic and the occult (see *Hilchot Avoda Zara,* Ch. 11). As we shall see in 6.4, Rambam worked hard to understand Torah sources in a way which is compatible with this outlook. Moreover, as we shall see in the second half of this section, Rambam did not have, or rejected, Kabbala. Indeed, Rambam's accomplishment in this regard is nothing short of extraordinary. He showed how a person can excel in Torah and live a life of piety and at the same time embrace rationalism. There is nothing in Judaism that cannot be understood rationally. Thus, if we define the mystic as someone who conceptualizes the world non-rationally, then Rambam was certainly not a mystic.

However, the above definition of mystic is not the only way in which the word is used. Usually, a mystic refers to a person who

---

R. Elchanan offers a simple proof for his position: "Certainly, if Rambam meant this literally, it is most startling, since this *ma'aseh bereishit* is studied at every high school." Rather, we must conclude that "Rambam was referring to the wisdom concealed in nature."

112. In 2.13, we shall see that not all Kabbalists viewed Rambam's philosophy so negatively.

experiences a meaningful and intimate encounter with a transcendent being. According to this definition, as we have seen, Rambam certainly qualifies as a mystic. When describing the extent to which a person must love God, Rambam writes: "A person should love God with a very great and exceeding love until his soul is bound up in the love of God. He should constantly be obsessed with this love as if he is lovesick" (*Hilchot Teshuva* 10:3). Of course, love need not be mystical, but for Rambam this love is part of a divine encounter, which should develop into the ultimate encounter – prophecy. Rambam's description of prophecy certainly qualifies as a mystical experience:

רמב"ם הלכות יסודי התורה פרק ז הלכה א

...דעתו פנויה תמיד למעלה קשורה תחת הכסא להבין באותן הצורות הקדושות הטהורות ומסתכל בחכמתו של הקב"ה כולה מצורה ראשונה עד טבור הארץ ויודע מהן גדלו, מיד רוח הקודש שורה עליו, ובעת שתנוח עליו הרוח תתערב נפשו במעלת המלאכים הנקראים אישים ויהפך לאיש אחר ויבין בדעתו שאינו כמות שהיה אלא שנתעלה על מעלת שאר בני אדם החכמים כמו שנאמר בשאול והתנבית עמם ונהפכת לאיש אחר.

His mind should constantly be directed upward, bound beneath [God's] throne [of Glory, striving] to comprehend the holy and pure forms and gazing at the wisdom of the Holy One, blessed be He, in its entirety, [in its manifold manifestations] from the most elevated [spiritual] form until the navel of the earth, appreciating His greatness from them. [After these preparations,] the divine spirit will immediately rest upon him. When the spirit rests upon him, his soul becomes intermingled with the angels called *ishim*, and he will be transformed into a different person and will understand with a knowledge different from what it was previously. He will rise above the level of other wise men, as [the prophet, Shmuel] told Saul: "[The spirit of God will descend upon you,] and you shall prophesy with them. And you will be transformed into a different person (*I Shmuel* 10:6)."

הלכה ב

...וכולן כשמתנבאים אבריהן מזדעזעין וכח הגוף כשל ועשתנותיהם מתטרפות ותשאר הדעת פנויה להבין מה שתראה, כמו שנאמר באברהם והנה אימה חשכה גדולה נופלת עליו, וכמו שנאמר בדניאל והודי נהפך עלי למשחית ולא עצרתי כח.

> When they (prophets other than Moshe) prophesy, their limbs tremble, their physical powers become weak, they lose control of their senses, and thus, their minds are free to comprehend what they see, as the verse states concerning Avraham: "and a great, dark dread fell over him (*Bereishit* 15:12)." Similarly, regarding Daniel it states: "My appearance was horribly changed and I retained no strength (*Daniel* 10:8)."

While prophecy ceased, the Introduction to *Moreh ha-Nevuchim* describes the flashes of light experienced by anyone who properly seeks to understand the Divine in numinous terminology. The purpose of the work is to ignite these illuminations: "My objective is that the concepts of truth will shine for a person as sparks of light, and then disappear," just as described by the prophet Yechezkeil: "The *chayot* ran to and fro, like the appearance of a flash" (*Yechezkeil* 1:14). Indeed, Rambam writes of his own personal quasi-prophetic experience: והבן ענין זה והתבונן כמה מופלא הוא, וראה איך הושגו לי עניינים אלו כעין חזון, "contemplate and understand how marvelous this matter is, and see that I have attained these notions in the likeness of a prophetic revelation" (*Moreh ha-Nevuchim* 3:22).

Moreover, while Rambam rejects the notion of magic, he extensively discusses the nature and existence of spiritual entities such as angels.[113] In fact, Rambam lists ten types of angels in descending order

---

113. In the second chapter of *Hilchot Yesodei ha-Torah*, Rambam explains that everything in the created universe falls into one of three categories:
   (1) Entities composed of matter and form which are subject to generation and degeneration, such as the bodies of man and beasts, plants, and metals.
   (2) Entities composed of matter and form but not subject to generation and degeneration, such as the spheres and the stars. The matter from which they are composed differs from the matter which we encounter in our world.
   (3) Entities which have form but no matter at all, such as angels.

of holiness 1) The holy *chayot,* 2) *ofanim,* 3) *er'eilim,* 4) *chashmalim,* 5) *serafim,* 6) *mal'achim,* 7) the *elohim,* 8) the sons of the *elohim,* 9) *keruvim,* and 10) *ishim.* Remarkably, this ordering parallels the ordering of the *Zohar.*[114]

Rambam describes (and experienced) various transcendent interactions with the Divine. He categorizes and elucidates spiritual creations, while insisting on the absolute rationality of Judaism. Most importantly, as we shall elaborate upon in 10.1, Rambam believed that intellectual achievements alone do not produce true knowledge of God; they must culminate in an emotional relationship and spiritual union with the Almighty. Thus, we could say, Rambam was a rationalist mystic.[115]

What Was Rambam's Position on Kabbala?

In 2.11, we studied Gra's claim that Rambam never saw *pardeis.* It is difficult to imagine Rambam had no awareness of Kabbala. After all, he was familiar with the writings of R. Sa'adya Gaon, who wrote a commentary on *Sefer Yetzira.*[116] In his Introduction to *Perek Cheilek* (first edition; p. 143 n. 27 in the Sheilat edition), Rambam refers to the Kabbalistic work *Shiur Koma* (שיעור קומה), which deals with God's "height." In his youth, Rambam thought that this was a genuine work that was written allegorically. He changed his mind later in life, and in later editions of his Introduction, he crossed out this

114. *Parshat Bo* 43a. Rambam replaces *eilim* with *keruvim,* but that too is consistent with *Zohar Parshat Pinchas* 235a. This point is made by R. Gershon Chanoch Henech Leiner of Radzyn (1839–1890) in his introductory work to Jewish mysticism entitled ההקדמה והפתיחה - עיקרי ושרשי הקבלה, p. 20 (New York, 1949).

115. When I first wrote this chapter I made the same basic point but never would have dreamed of using the term mystic in reference to Rambam. After this book was (mostly) completed, I read R. David Fried's excellent article "Mysticism and its Alternatives: Rethinking Maimonides," on The Lehrhaus (thelehrhaus.com/scholarship/mysticism-and-its-alternatives-rethinking-maimonides) in which he distinguishes between a mystical worldview (which, to some degree, Rambam had) and an enchanted one (which certainly contradicts Rambam's rationalism). The above nomenclature thus reflects Fried's incisive insight.

116. This proof is not decisive, since R. Sa'adya Gaon's commentary (*Kitab al-Mabadi*) interpreted the esoteric work in light of philosophy and scientific knowledge.

reference.[117] Nevertheless, his knowledge of Kabbalistic teachings did not come from genuine tradition; as such, he appropriately rejected them.[118]

To summarize, while Rambam may have been aware of certain Kabbalistic texts, he never received a Kabbalistic tradition from his teachers. Accordingly, he rejected Kabbala entirely, detecting heresy within it.[119]

Ironically, Kabbalists might agree with Rambam's condemnation of Kabbala insofar as it is the appropriate reaction of someone who has not received the Kabbalistic tradition from a reliable source. The truth of Kabbala comes from its pedigree. Taken literally, Kabbalistic texts indeed sound heretical, applying corporeality and other human characteristics to God. When interpreted literally, they contradict the oneness of God, ascribing duality or multiplicity to God.[120] Of course, as we shall see,

117. In a responsum (p. 578 of R. Sheilat's *Igrot ha-Rambam*), he writes that he never thought this work was written by Chazal and that the book should be expunged:
מעולם לא סברתי שזה לחכמים ז"ל, וחלילה להם שיהא להם. ואומנם הוא חיבור אחד מדרשני אדם לא זולת זה. כללו של דבר, מחית זה הכתב והכרתת זכר עניינו - מצוה רבה.

118. The above reading of Rambam differs from the approach adopted by Prof. Menachem Kellner in *Maimonides' Confrontation with Mysticism* (Oxford: Littman Library of Jewish Civilization, 2006). Kellner argues that Rambam was well aware of the dominant mystical or what he calls "proto-Kabbalistic" tradition and sought to refute this worldview. Specifically, Kellner asserts, the Kabbalists invested Halacha, the Hebrew language, and Jewish identity with holiness, and Rambam attempted to dispel this notion. While it certainly is the case that Rambam presents Judaism from a rationalistic perspective that sometimes is at odds with the Kabbalistic perspective, I do not see how Kellner knows that Rambam was aware of the Kabbalistic position that he purportedly is rejecting. Moreover, many of Kellner's arguments demand ignoring certain texts of Rambam that undercut his theory. We elaborate upon this point in Chapter 32 when exploring Rambam's complex position on the chosenness of the Jewish people.

119. I do not wish to imply that had Rambam received such a tradition, he certainly would have accepted it; it is impossible to know.

120. See *Shomeir Emunim ha-Kadmon* of R. Yosef Ergas (1685–1730) (*Vikuach Rishon*, 13):
ועוד אפשר שגם הרמב"ם ראה את ספר יצירה ושאר חיבורי התנאים והיו בעיניו כדברי ספר החתום כי בודאי הגמור סתומים וחתומים הדברים אצל כל אדם שלא קבל פה אל פה המפתחות והתחלות החכמה ופוק חזי מש"כ הרמב"ן בסוף הקדמת פירושו על התורה וז"ל ואני הנני מביא בברית נאמנת היא הנותנת עצה הוגנת לכל מסתכל בספר הזה לבל יסבור סברא ואל יחשוב מחשבות בדבר מכל הרמזים אשר אני כותב בסתרי התורה כי אני מודיעו נאמנה שלא יושגו דברי ולא יודעו כלל בשום שכל ובינה זולתי מפי מקובל חכם לאזן מקבל מבין וכו' ע"ש וכל שכן וקל וחומר דברי ספר יצירה וספר הבהיר ופרקי

legitimate Kabbalists do not interpret these divine descriptions literally and certainly do not deny His incorporeality or unity.[121] One of Rambam's significant contributions, as we shall see in Chapters 10 and 11, is his campaign to root out corporeality, duality, and other heretical beliefs sometimes associated with mysticism from mainstream Jewish thought.

More importantly, Kabbalistic teachings, as the word *kabbala* implies, are known only based on received tradition or revelation.[122] Accordingly, someone who has not received the tradition from an appropriate authority is correct in dismissing it. This is especially true given that Kabbalists often communicate metaphorically and encode certain concepts in terms that at face value are absurd or heretical.[123] Of course, as we shall see, Rambam does not simply reject Kabbala; he presents Judaism in a totally rational fashion.[124] This too is one of Rambam's great contributions, which can be appreciated even by someone who accepts the mystical tradition. With the acceptance of Rambam's greatness, no one can rightfully say that to be a good Jew, one *must* reject rationalism.

ולא עוד אלא כי מי שלא קבל מסורות החכמה הזאת כמו שהעיד על עצמו הרמב"ם שלא היה לו קבלה ממלמד על ביאור סתרי התורה אם יקרא מש"כ בזוהר כמה דברים שמורים גשמות באלהות כגון גולגלתא שערא מצחא אודנין אנפין וכיוצא בלי ספק שיפער פיו לבלי חק נגד הספר ומחברו ואפילו אם יאומת אצלו שרשב"י היה מחברו לא יקבל דבריו תדע שהרי דבר פשוט אצלינו ונתבאר גם כן בגמרא לא יאמת דבריו.

R. Kook (*Shemona Kevatzim* 7:84) elaborates upon this idea as well.

121. While there are different strains of Kabbala, we are referring to the mainstream viewpoints that have been accepted by most of the Jewish people. There always have been, and continue to be, mystical thinkers who espouse illegitimate views or positions that may have seemed reasonable at the time but now are understood to be problematic according to most Jewish thinkers.

122. See, for example, Ramban's comments at the beginning of *Bereishit*, where he writes that the "true" (i.e., Kabbalistic) understanding of the verses was given to Moshe at Sinai and comes to us through him (i.e., Moshe). Nevertheless, many of the great Kabbalists including Arizal and Ramchal, arrived at their understandings through revelations (*giluyim*).

123. According to Gra, the same can be said concerning contradictions between the Talmud and the *Zohar*. R. Chaim of Volozhin (*Keter Rosh Ma'amarim Shonim* 15) cites Gra as stating that there are no discrepancies between the Talmud and the *Zohar*. The perceived contradictions emerge from superficial readings of one or both of the sources.

124. This is not to say that he felt that we can understand everything; rather, acceptance of even the unintelligible ideas is itself rational.

Thus, even though most leading Jewish thinkers embrace Kabbala to some degree and many rituals among both Ashkenazim and Sefardim are rooted in Kabbala, a person who seeks to understand Torah from an entirely rational perspective always can turn to Rambam.

Though it seems Rambam did not have a favorable view of Kabbala (to the extent that he had any view), some disagree. As we mentioned in 2.8, there are those like R. Avraham Abulafia and R. Leiner of Radzyn who see Kabbalistic ideas written in philosophical jargon in Rambam's works.

Other thinkers harmonize their belief in Kabbala with their veneration for Rambam differently. R. Sheim Tov b. R. Avraham ibn Gaon[125] writes that Rambam himself, at least towards the end of his life, studied Kabbala.[126] To support this contention, R. Sheim Tov cites a letter addressed to R. Yosef b. Yehuda, the very same person to whom he addressed *Moreh ha-Nevuchim*.[127] In it, Rambam describes the advantage of Kabbala over philosophy.[128] However, this letter likely

---

125. Born in Spain c. 1287. He was a student of Rashba and authored a number of works on Kabbala, but he is best known for *Migdal Oz*, his commentary on *Mishneh Torah*.

126. **מגדל עוז הלכות יסודי התורה פרק א**

ואני אומר כמה פנים לתורה נסתרים ונגלים והדרך אשר תפס ר"מ ז"ל בזה דומה לדרך שתפס בספר מורה הנבוכים לישב דעת המתפלסף הציקוהו פשוטי המקראות ולכך חברו בלשון הגרי **אבל הוא בעצמו יודע כי דרך האמת נעלמת ואינה נמסרת אלא מפה אל פה ובחשאי יותר מדאי** וכדאיתא בחגיגה כמו שהודיע בהקדמת המורה ובדעתי להביא ראיות אחרות מדברי עצמו בחלק השלישי בעזרת האל ואף שכבר הם כתובות בשאר חבורי בסד"ע ואשר רמז הרב ר"א מקובל מפה אל פה דרך קדש יקרא לשרידים אשר ה׳ קורא. **ולדעתי שר"מ ז"ל ידע בהם בסוף ימיו שאני מעיד שראיתי בספרד ארץ מולדתנו כתוב במגלה של קלף ישן מיושן ומעושן לשון זה. אני משה ב"ר מימון כשירדתי לחדרי המרכבה בינותי בענין הקץ וכו׳, וקרובים היו דבריו לדברי המקובלים האמיתיים** שרמז רבינו הגדול הרמב"ן ז"ל בתחלת פירושו לתורה.

127. Quoted in *Kitvei ha-Rambam u-vno R. Avraham*.

128. **אגרת הרמב"ם לתלמידו (מגילת סתרים)**

התלמיד הנעים החשוב רבי יוסף ברבי יהודה נ"ע שיכניסך הש"י במשכן החיים... כי רוב זמני הייתי נבוך בחקירות הנמצאות לדעת תוכן אמיתתם כפי האפשרי בחק השגגה האנושיות יגעתי ומצאתי מקצת האמן אך באמונה לא מצאתי באמיתיות הכולל מצד החקירה הפילוסופיות ובדרכי מופתיהם אם לא שאומר במה ששנינו הם בלתי צודק אבל עכ"פ צודק כי מה שנתבאר אצלינו מן החכמה לא בא המופת על סותרו אלא בדרכים הגונות מפסידים השכל ומבלבלים. אך אצל חכמי הקבלה האמתיות דרכים מסוקלים מאבני המכשול נועדו בה בקולות נמרץ כל מה שיפול תחת גבול ההשגה האנושיות ובדרך זר דרכו הנביאים והשיגו כל מה שהשיגו מהודעת העתידים ופעלו פעולת זרות

was forged. For a discussion of the history of this letter, see p. 695 of R. Sheilat's *Igrot ha-Rambam.*

2.13 APPENDIX B: HOW DO KABBALISTS UNDERSTAND RAMBAM?

Even as Kabbalists used tradition and revelation to arrive at a conception of God, many expressed an appreciation for Jewish philosophers.[129] Some of the terminology employed in Ramban's Kabbala is rooted in Rambam's formulations. Indeed, many Kabbalistic works, such as *Tanya* (Ch. 4) and *Nefesh ha-Chaim* (1:1), quote and incorporate ideas from *Moreh ha-Nevuchim*. Perhaps the most primary example is the work *Torat ha-Ola*, written by R. Moshe Isserles or "Rama" (1520–1572), who blends Rambam's philosophical system with Kabbalistic traditions.[130]

Several centuries prior to these works, R. Moshe Cordovero (Ramak) wrote: "All that has been written by those who pursue the knowledge of God through human reasoning in the matter of the divine nature is totally correct in negating from His being the attributes and actions."[131] Put differently, Rambam teaches us through philosophy that which the human mind is capable of determining on its own. As such, Rambam's philosophy serves a vital function alongside mysticism in communicating that which is true. As Gra notes, mysticism, using

יוצאות מהמנהג טבעי ומקצת דרכיהם לקחתי גם אני בידיעות טבעי הנמצאות ונודע לי כל ספיקות העצומות שנסתפקתי בהם ונפתחו לפני דלתות הנבוכות ונמסרו בידי מפתחות החכמה והביאור על כל נעלם ממני. והנה משביעך שלא תגלה הסודות האלה הדקים וההערות הנפלאים אלא למי שהוא דק השכל ונקי במעשיו ונדכה בעיניו והולך בדרכי הלימוד והידיעה.

129. Not that Rambam did not have his detractors among Kabbalists (e.g., Gra's critique of Rambam's understanding of *ma'aseh merkava*), but the dominant position, once the dust settled following the initial controversies, was to respect Rambam not only for his halachic works but even for his philosophical writings. One aspect of Rambam's thought that irked Kabbalists was the reasons for *mitzvot* given in *Moreh ha-Nevuchim*. See, for example, *Sefer ha-Emunot* I:1:7a by R. Sheim Tov ibn Sheim Tov. We assess Rambam's *ta'amei ha-mitzvot* in Chapter 36.

130. See especially Section 3, towards the beginning of Ch. 4.

131. *Shiur Koma* (Warsaw, 1885) 34b (No. 67) cited in "Attitudes of the Kabbalists and Hasidim towards Maimonides" in *The Solomon Goldman Lectures*, Vol. 5, ed. Byron L. Sherwin and Michael Carasik (Chicago: Spertus College of Judaica Press, 1990), p. 45.

tradition, picks up where Rambam left off.[132] Ultimately, even if tradition supersedes philosophy in cases of conflict, rationalism continues to serve as one layer in the assimilation of truth.[133]

Examples of How Philosophy and Mysticism Work Together

Let us consider an example that illustrates this subtle phenomenon. Ramban writes that *mitzvot* are for our benefit. After all, it is inconceivable that they can be for God's sake, since He lacks nothing:

> **רמב"ן דברים פרק י פסוק יב**
> מה ה' אלהיך שואל מעמך - נמשך אל לטוב לך - **יאמר איננו שואל מעמך דבר שיהיה לצרכו אלא לצורכך**, כטעם אם צדקת מה תתן לו (איוב לה:ז),[134] רק הכל הוא לטוב לך.

> "What does God ask of you but to fear Him, to follow in His path, to love Him, to serve Him with all of your heart and soul… **for your benefit.**" This verse is telling us that God asks nothing of us for His benefit, [but rather] only for our benefit. As the verse says: "If you have sinned, how have you affected Him; if your iniquities are many, what have you done to Him? If you acted righteously, what have you given Him, and what can He take from your hand?" (*Iyov* 35:6–7).

---

132. **ארחות חיים כתר ראש סימן סא**
פילוסופייא, אמר רבנו **שממקום שמסתיים הפילוסופיא משם ולמעלה מתחיל חכמת הקבלה,** וממקום שמסתיים קבלת הרמ"ק - משם ולמעלה מתחיל קבלת האר"י ז"ל.
How does the above statement square with Gra's strong rejection of philosophy (הפילוסופיה הארורה) cited in 1.6? Presumably, the strong negative language is reserved for cases where philosophy contradicts Torah. Alternatively, it reflects the arrogant attitude common among philosophers that all truth can be discovered using the human mind. As noted earlier, scholars debate Gra's precise attitude towards both philosophy and secular studies.

133. Consider the following analog: Rashbam (*Bereishit* 37:2) writes that we consider the study of *pshat* valuable even though on a normative and even philosophical level *drash* is authoritative. Why? Because both *pshat* and *drash* are means through which God communicates His wisdom.

134. **איוב פרק לה:ו-ז**
אם חטאת מה תפעל בו ורבו פשעיך מה תעשה לו. אם צדקת מה תתן לו או מה מידך יקח.

Elsewhere, Ramban writes that this perspective, which is logically compelling and the approach taken by philosophers such as Rambam,[135] differs from the Kabbalistic approach, which acknowledges that we do in fact give something to God through our service:

רמב"ן שמות פרק כט פסוק מו

יש בענין סוד גדול, כי כפי **פשט** הדבר השכינה בישראל צורך הדיוט ולא צורך גבוה, אבל הוא כענין שאמר הכתוב ישראל אשר בך אתפאר (ישעיה מט:ג), ואמר יהושע ומה תעשה לשמך הגדול (יהושע ז:ט), ופסוקים רבים באו כן, אוה למושב לו (תהלים קלב:יג), פה אשב כי אויתיה (שם יד), וכתוב והארץ אזכור (ויקרא כו:מב).

There is in this matter a great secret, because according to the simple perspective (*pshat ha-davar*), God dwells in Israel for our sake not His. But in truth, the matter is as it says, "Yisrael in whom I am glorified" (which implies that the Jewish people benefit God by bringing Him glory), and Yehoshua says, "What will become of Your great Name?" (which implies that our service glorifies His Name). Many other verses imply [that God has desires] such as "He desired [Zion] as His abode," "Here (in Zion) I will dwell, for I desire it," and "I will remember the land."

"*Pshat ha-davar*" in this case refers to the simple (philosophical) understanding of the matter. This perspective is indeed correct; thus, Ramban presents it without hesitation in *Devarim* 10:12 and elsewhere (such as *Devarim* 4:3). The Kabbalistic explanation, which is known to us only through tradition and does not seem rational, is also true, but on a different plane.[136]

---

135. **מורה הנבוכים חלק ג פרק לא**
והכונה כלה [של המצות] להועילנהו כמו שביארנו מאמרו לטוב לנו כל הימים לחיותנו כהיום הזה.

136. In Chapter 35, we address the seemingly incomprehensible mystical perspective. For our purposes, let us note that Ramban does not maintain that the philosophical approach is supplanted by the mystical one.

Not surprisingly, Kabbalists consider Rambam's contribution valuable, with his positions frequently incorporated into Kabbala. For example, in his *Pardeis Rimonim* (Ch. 7, *Sha'ar Mahut ve-Hanhaga*), Ramak accepts Rambam's philosophical understanding (*Yesodei ha-Torah* 2:10 and *Moreh ha-Nevuchim* 1:68) that in God, "Knower, Knowledge, and the Known is all One."[137]

Rambam's philosophical contributions prove fundamental on another level. Many mystical thinkers, such as Ramchal, agree with Rambam that basic principles of faith can be derived independently of a mystical tradition. A reflection of this is the opening chapter of *Derech Hashem*, a principally mystical work, which parallels and is largely derived from the opening chapter of *Hilchot Yesodei ha-Torah*.

Just as Kabbalists quote thinkers characterized as rationalists, thinkers characterized as rationalists sometimes quote Kabbala. For example, R. Chasdai Crescas cites *Sefer Yetzira* and *Sefer ha-Bahir* and often interprets Scripture and Midrash Kabbalistically.[138]

Contradictions Between Kabbala and Philosophy

What should one do if he encounters a debate between Rambam and Kabbalistic sources? In this case, presumably one would discount the opinion of the Rambam insofar as his position is based on human intellect, which is fallible, while the Kabbalistic source is rooted in revelation. However, it is not so simple. Recall from 1.2 that Rama wrote that the views of Kabbala and philosophy are the words of the living God. How so? As we explained, God expresses Himself to us through multiple means. We can perceive Him by examining the world, through using our intellect, and through the study of His direct teachings. Assuming that we do not err in our analysis, all are valid ways of understanding Him. Thus, when two of these legitimate methods yield contradictory results, our approach

137. R. Micha Berger has noted that while *Leshem*'s Kabbala derives from that of Gra, he also cites heavily from *Moreh ha-Nevuchim*.

138. Harvey, Warren Zev. "Crescas (or Cresques), Ḥasdai ben Judah." *Encyclopaedia Judaica*. Ed. Michael Berenbaum and Fred Skolnik. 2nd ed. Vol. 5.

is to accept that both reflect the truth (i.e., both are the words of the living God) even if we are unable to see their compatibility. The situation is analogous to a debate between *Beit Shammai* and *Beit Hillel*; we see both as reflecting the truth even though they seem irreconcilable (more on this in Chapter 4). Of course, if Rambam arrived at his position using his intellect, he may have erred. On the other hand, even the Kabbalist may have misunderstood the Kabbalistic teaching.

2.14 APPENDIX C: R. KOOK'S VIEW ON INTELLECTUAL FREEDOM AND TOLERANCE IN MODERN TIMES

In 2.5, we saw Rambam insist that we draw a delicate balance with respect to freedom of inquiry. On the one hand, Rambam maintains that faith ideally should be predicated upon proof, which seemingly calls for the consideration of alternatives. On the other hand, he prohibits the study of heretical material (*Hilchot Avoda Zara,* Ch. 2). Moreover, Rambam (*Hilchot Yesodei ha-Torah,* Ch. 1) writes that consideration of alternatives to God's existence is strictly prohibited. As R. Sa'adya Gaon and R. Bachya ibn Pakuda stress, we are to honestly seek to prove what we already know to be true.[139]

A modern thinker who tackles the issue of intellectual freedom and provides a nuanced, seemingly more liberal perspective is R. Kook in "Letter 20." To appreciate this letter, it is helpful to consider its historical context. In the 1903 Zionist Congress, Theodore Herzl suggested the Uganda Proposal, which called for the establishment of a Jewish homeland in Uganda, since settlement in Palestine seemed unrealistic. This triggered a major debate among both religious and secular Zionists. Eliezer Ben Yehuda defended the plan in his periodical *ha-Hashkafa,* where he addressed the accusation that supporters of the plan were rejecting the entire Jewish past:

139. See *Tosafot, Chullin* 57b who distinguishes (in a different context) between questioning out of doubt and questioning in order to prove (שבא לברר הדבר ולהודיע איך ידע שלמה).

> One other claim ... the Zionists of Zion claim about the Ugandists that they... turn their backs on our entire past. There is much hypocrisy in this claim. Let us have no illusions ... we have all turned our backs on our past, and that is our praise and our glory (*ha-Hashkafa,* No. 48, 5665).

Needless to say, this statement aggrieved R. Kook, and he fiercely responded to it in an open letter. However, following his scathing critique, he added the following caveat:

> **אגרות הראי״ה א:יח**
> עם אהבתי ללמוד וללמד את יסודי הדעות שלנו **רחוק אני מלדרוש שלטון על דעותיו של איזה איש שיהיה** שהוא **בימינו** דבר שאינו נשמע.

> Despite my love of learning and teaching the fundamentals of our thought, **far be it from me to demand authority over anyone's opinions**; **nowadays**, it would not be accepted.

This sentence impelled R. Moshe Seidel (1886–1970) to question whether this reflects the ideal Torah position ("*din Torah,*" in his words) or is a concession to the unfortunate reality on the ground. What follows is R. Kook's response (Letter 20). We quote the letter in its entirety (with the exception of the last paragraph, which is cited in 8.12) due to the importance of the matter:

> In reference to my words in the open letter, where I stated that I do not seek to control anyone's opinion, you asked whether this is out of necessity or also the law of the Torah.
>
> Indeed, there is no ambiguity in my language, since I stated "because in **our time** it is unacceptable." So it follows that had it been acceptable, such a requirement would have its place. The issue, however, requires great mountains of study to clarify its boundaries, and since it is impossible for me to write at length I will write briefly and hope it will suffice for someone as discerning as you.

You should know that common sense is always a very important principle in law, be it applied law or legal theory. We therefore always have to reach the core of the truth, and when we see a truth contradicting another truth, there then must be a determining factor, and this will be the place for new study. **Thus, we will see how far the limits of freedom of thought, considered a basic truth by most enlightened men in the world today, extend according to reason. Perhaps you say it has no bounds. That, however, cannot be said**. For one, because we do not have even one virtue in the world which extremism will not harm. Furthermore, the nature of the matter requires that there be a limit to freedom of thought, for if there is no such limit, every person would cast away all obligations of accepted morality until he reaches in his own mind an understanding of what he stands for, and then the earth would be filled with corruption; a total separation between opinions and deeds is impossible, because actions to a small or large extent necessarily stem from opinions. For instance, for a person to accept at heart that there is no wrong in murder is definitely a sin, for if this acceptance flourishes, the existence of the world would be destroyed, and the same is true for other examples. Thus, we learn there is a limit to freedom of opinion, but the difficult issue is to determine this limit.

It follows that the limit is not identical in every society. For example, if a person decides that there is no harm in walking naked in the streets for one who consents to this and calls for people to actually behave in this manner is a sin in our society, and deservedly so, but this would not be a sin among the savages on the islands of Guinea, for example.[140] As there are necessarily differences between societies, the differences are not static, but rather continue to differentiate in accordance with the multitude of conditions. **With regard to religion, there is a marked**

140. See *Moreh ha-Nevuchim* 1:2 and 2:30, where Rambam uses this example to describe a world of convention (*tov ve-ra* as opposed to *emet ve-sheker*).

distinction in this matter between Israel and the rest of the world. Were there a nation in the world whose main being and continued existence as a nation were dependent on a particular idea, then it would be completely legitimate and even obligatory that with regard to that idea there be no freedom of thought within that nation, for that would not be freedom, but laziness in defending itself due to the nervous tendency of a few people. It is true that sometimes individuals should rebel against their nation, when they find that the idea that unites and sustains their nation is harmful to mankind, in which case they must renounce their nation for the truth. If, however, the idea which strengthens the nation is in no way harmful and all the more so if the idea is both beneficial outside its borders and essential for the nation's own existence, then there is no room for tolerance, and someone who is tolerant in this matter deserves the contempt of the whole nation and all mankind.

There is no other nation in the world whose acknowledgement of the name of God, blessed be He, as the Lord of the universe, keeper of the covenant, loving-kindness, and all ways of righteousness, which are attributes of the Holy One, blessed be He, is the basis of its national life, and a unique condition of its restoration to its land and the establishment of its rule. **Israel's conditions are such that it cannot exist without these exalted ideas.** All greatness of soul is associated with a parallel deficiency, and Israel certainly has those deficiencies as well, which lead it to the necessity of the virtue of bearing God's Name as its common identity. Therefore, whoever undermines through thought, and all the more so through deed, the idea which vitalizes the nation, is a traitor to the nation, and his pardon is folly. There is no other nation or people in the world whose national character is connected in the nature of its being with the knowledge of God in its midst and in the world, nor with the tenets of any other faith. Even if there is an exceptional nation which has a base faith, and its faith is national, that faith is surely so small that its very expansion will bring harm to all of mankind.

Furthermore, such a nation cannot possibly survive, because this nation's destruction is imminent and its individual cannot be required to fulfill the duties obligatory to its existence. This is the basis of true zeal of God, the possessors of which are worthy to be given the everlasting priestly covenant[141]; in contrast with the hasty zeal which stems from lack of wisdom and weak character.

In order for us to realize national sovereignty, it is necessary that the powers of the nation reach complete perfection. But in the meantime, to avoid national rule totally is also impossible, because the spiritual character of the nation is, blessed be God, always alive: "David, King of Israel, is alive and enduring." Hence this is the counsel of the Lord, who is wonderful in counsel, and great in wisdom, that the nation's capacity [to control opinion] diminishes to the same extent that the nation's [spiritual] powers weaken, and that **this inability [to control opinion] is a sign of God's will**. There are many ways comes about: sometimes it is a practical obstacle, such as the fear of the state, and the like; sometimes it is a spiritual obstacle, **such as the obligation not to say things which will not be accepted.[142] We accept obstacles such as these gladly because we recognize that it is divine providence in our times**. And this is why we find in the Jerusalem Talmud that Rabbi Shimon bar Yochai was glad that the power to enforce the laws was removed in his time from Israel, "because we are not wise enough to judge." That is what is pertinent to understanding my words.[143]

---

141. A reference to Pinchas; see *Bamidbar* 25:11–13.
142. A reference to *Yevamot* 65b which states that just as it is a *mitzva* to say something (offer chastisement) that will be accepted, so too it is a *mitzva* not to say something (offer chastisement) that will not be accepted. Thus, what the public will tolerate limits what a religious thinker may say. This too is providential.
143. Translation adapted from *Rav A.Y. Kook: Selected Letters*, translated by Tzvi Feldman (Ma'aleh Adumim, 1986).

R. Tamir Granot summarizes R. Kook's position in this letter as follows:

> Rav Kook sees intellectual freedom as a necessary condition for spiritual and intellectual development. Although he applies certain, primarily educational, limitations to it, he embraces the principle that thought must be free. This means that considering every opinion and every possible truth contributes to the development and advancement of understanding.[144]

If this is correct, R. Kook is presenting a vastly different perspective than that of Rambam concerning the scope of intellectual freedom.[145] However, I do not see how the above conclusion emerges from R. Kook's letter (although other sources, as we shall see in 2.15, may indicate that R. Kook did have a greater openness to intellectual freedom, as discussed in the next section).

Superficially, the words of this letter directly address our question of freedom of inquiry. However, in truth, this letter deals with a different issue, namely, tolerance: how should we react to the problematic views that others maintain? Remember, the letter seeks to explain R. Kook's statement that he does not "demand authority over anyone's opinions" (רחוק אני מלדרוש שלטון על דעותיו של איזה איש שיהיה). Moreover, he presents this position as a reflection of our times. In other words, R. Kook acknowledges that his approach differs from the way in which Chazal dealt with dissenting heretical opinions (such as those of the Sadducees). He writes, however, that different times call for different measures. With this in mind, let us summarize the letter.

R. Kook maintains that, like in all matters, there must be a balanced approach in the way in which society responds to dissenting views: there are times when society must not tolerate certain viewpoints (when they undermine society's very essence), and there are times when society

---

144. *Rav Kook's Letters*, Lecture #2b: Letter 20 – On Tolerance, Part 2, http://etzion.org.il/en/lecture-2b-letter-20-tolerance-part-2.

145. Moreover, R. Kook would be asserting the exact opposite of R. Elchanan (cited in 9.7). According to R. Elchanan, there is more of a need to limit intellectual freedom in today's day and age due to the feebleness of our minds. According to R. Kook, though, modernity demands greater freedom of inquiry.

should tolerate such views, even if they are flawed. Moreover, R. Kook maintains that this balance shifts over time.

When it comes to the Jewish people, whose mission is very broad (it is a nation that calls out in the Name of God), it is necessary to eradicate heresy insofar as it undermines its essence. This would explain Chazal's intolerance for heresy. It also helps us understand the holy zealotry of those like Pinchas.[146]

However, "The nation's capacity [to control opinion] diminishes to the same extent that the nation's [spiritual] powers weaken." Thus, in our days, our ability to control opinion is limited. This does not indicate that we are dead – *David melech Yisrael chai ve-kayam* (David, King of Israel, is alive and enduring). Thus, we must create the ideal society given the reality that we inhabit.

Significantly, our inability to control opinion is a sign of God's will (ומניעת היכולת היא לנו לעדה על חפץ ד'), and should be accepted, and even embraced. R. Kook then considers the factors that limit our ability to demand authority. Some are practical. For example, governmental restrictions may not allow us to suppress heretical viewpoints. Even more importantly, antagonizing the proponents of these perspectives will not be effective. R. Kook urges us to follow the Talmud's ruling, "Just as it is a *mitzva* for a person to say something that will be accepted, so too it is a *mitzva* not to say something that will not be accepted" (*Yevamot* 65b). This demands that religious leaders occasionally remain silent; they may not promulgate the Torah's teachings in a way that will make them irrelevant. Thus, unless one wishes to secede entirely from mainstream society (as many religious groups did), one must engage in debate within the marketplace of ideas without imposing one's position upon others.While one might be tempted to see these limitations in a purely negative light (a reflection of our diminished spiritual stature), R. Kook sees them as a reflection of God's hand in history. Therefore,

146. Though Pinchas did not direct his zealotry against heresy, it was appropriate insofar as it was directed against something that undermined the national character. This appropriate zealotry contrasts with the "hasty zeal which stems from lack of wisdom and weak character." It should be remembered that R. Kook suffered greatly from zealots who not only attempted to undermine his agenda but also attacked him personally.

they should be embraced as a manifestation of the divine will. R. Kook brings a fascinating proof for this far-reaching notion from the Yerushalmi:

תלמוד ירושלמי מסכת סנהדרין ז:ב
קודם לארבעים שנה עד שלא חרב בית המקדש ניטלו דיני נפשות מישראל. בימי רבי שמעון בן יוחי ניטלו דיני ממונות מישראל אמר רבי שמעון בן יוחי בריך רחמנא דלי נא חכים מידון.

> Forty years before the destruction of the Temple, capital cases were taken away from Israel (i.e., they no longer were adjudicated). In the times of R. Shimon b. Yochai, monetary cases were taken away from Israel. R. Shimon b. Yochai said: Thank God! We are not wise enough to judge.

Why did R. Shimon b. Yochai celebrate (or at least express gratitude for) our inability to perform a particular *mitzva* – our inability to adjudicate according to Torah law? Because it was God's message that now is not the right time to fulfill this *mitzva*. Of course, one could take this principle too far. One might argue that we should rejoice in our inability to offer sacrifices, since God has made it impossible. Nevertheless, we pray thrice daily for God to restore the Temple service.[147] Likewise, one might have averred that prior to the nineteenth century, the Jews in the diaspora should have been gleeful about their exile and lack of autonomy, as this is a reflection of God's will. Nevertheless, we always have longed for redemption. R. Kook does not address when one should be grateful for his current predicament insofar as it is a reflection of God's hand in history (R. Shimon b. Yochai's approach) and when he should mourn his inability to fully carry out His *mitzvot* (our approach to *galut* prior to the nineteenth century).

To summarize, R. Kook's letter deals with a political question: how should society respond to the heretical claims that some of its members make? This does not relate to Rambam's discussion of the limitations of an individual's intellectual freedom: what books a person

147. R. Kook's perspective on sacrifices is examined in 25.3.

may read and what thoughts a person may consider in his pursuit of the truth. Therefore, R. Kook's discussion, while fascinating, has no bearing on Rambam.

2.15 APPENDIX D: EXCEPTIONS TO THE PROHIBITION TO READ IDOLATROUS AND HERETICAL WORKS

In 2.5, we read that Rambam, in Chapter 2 of *Hilchot Avodat Kochavim*, records two restrictions: (a) upon reading idolatrous works, and (b) upon reading heretical works. In this appendix, we will consider whether there are exceptions to either of these restrictions. Specifically, we will focus on the approaches of three thinkers: Me'iri, Rashbatz, and R. Kook.

Regarding the first restriction, Chazal mention an exception. Commenting on the verse (*Devarim* 18:9) banning emulation of the Canaanite practices, Rashi, citing Chazal,[148] makes an important inference. The verse demands that we may not "learn to do" their abominations, which implies that one may study their abominations to know how grotesque they are.

דברים פרק יח פסוק ט

כִּי אַתָּה בָּא אֶל הָאָרֶץ אֲשֶׁר יְקֹוָק אֱלֹהֶיךָ נֹתֵן לָךְ **לֹא תִלְמַד לַעֲשׂוֹת** כְּתוֹעֲבֹת הַגּוֹיִם הָהֵם:

When you have come to the land the Lord, your God, is giving you, **you shall not learn to do** like the abominations of those nations.

רש"י שם

לא תלמד לעשות - אבל אתה למד **להבין ולהורות**, כלומר להבין מעשיהם כמה הם מקולקלים, ולהורות לבניך לא תעשה כך וכך, שזה הוא חוק הגוים:

You shall not learn to do [like the abominations of those nations]: But you may learn [their practices] **to understand** [**them**] **and to**

148. See *Sifrei* and *Sanhedrin* 68a.

> **teach [them]**, i.e., to understand how degenerate their actions are, and to teach your children, "Do not do such and such, because this is a heathen custom!"

Thus, one exception to the ban against studying idolatrous works is learning about idolatry to know how bad it is. While this ruling might seem narrow, it is significant insofar as it implies that the restriction is not absolute.

Me'iri

Me'iri appears to expand the dispensation in two ways. Firstly, he maintains it applies to heretical works and not just to idolatrous ones. Secondly, he argues that it is not limited to study done in order to accentuate their wickedness. Commenting on R. Akiva's restriction against reading "external works" (ספרים חצונים) (presumably including heretical ones), Me'iri writes that it is only prohibited to study such works in order to follow them.[149] It seems Me'iri thinks the proscription against reading of idolatrous or heretical works applies when turning to them as a means of seeking the truth that may be contained in these books. If, however, one believes that there is untruth contained in these books and is seeking other helpful information, then perusing them would be permissible.

This understanding could certainly justify Rambam's studying these materials. Indeed, R. Abba Mari b. Moshe, a Provençal rabbi from Lunel, made this very suggestion. R. Abba Mari lived in Montpellier from 1303 to 1306, and he was distressed by the prevalence of Aristotelian rationalism, which he felt undermined Torah. Accordingly, he wrote to Rashba asking him to ban the study of philosophy for individuals under the age of 25, which the Rashba did in 1305, as we noted in 1.6 (see *Teshuvot ha-Rashba* 1:415). In soliciting this ban, R. Abba Mari composed a number of letters that were later collected under the title *Minchat Kena'ot* ("Offering of Zealotry"). In one letter, he acknowledges there

---

149. **בית הבחירה (מאירי) מסכת סנהדרין דף צ עמוד א**
ר׳ עקיבא אומר אף הקורא בספרים החצונים ר״ל שלא להבין ולהורות אלא על דעת לילך באמונתם וכבר ידעת מהם שאין מאמינים אלא במה שהעיון נותן וההקש מחייב:

were great people (not necessarily Rambam) who may have studied philosophical works. He claims this was justified because the books were not studied to guide practice (**לא למדו לעשות**) but to understand and instruct (**להבין ולהורות**). Essentially, a person may study a text for two possible reasons: (1) to mold behavior and belief or (2) to acquire practical information. The latter does not necessarily fall under the restrictions prohibiting illicit reading material.[150]

The question we must first examine is whether Rambam subscribes to this understanding of *le-havin u-le-horot*. Next, we must consider if Rambam gives a similar dispensation for heretical works.[151]

---

150. **ספר מנחת קנאות מכתב פד**
אמר הגאון רב החכמים קברנט של פלסופים רמב"ם ז"ל, שאין ראוי לטייל בפרדס עד שימלא כרסו לחם ובשר, ואם הזמן מהשתרע קצר, בן כ"ה שנים לא נס לחה ולא חסר, עוד זמננו גדול מללמוד החכמות, ולא תמו עדיין חולשות הטבע ולא תגבר עלינו השכחה, עלינו בפרצות להציל נפשות בחורי חמד ישראל, אשר לבם כפתח של אולם להבין האמת, ירבו הוראות בישראל ויהיו עמודי עולם, יאמרו יתעסקו הבנים במה שנתעסקו האבות בסדר ישועות ובמס' ברכות ויקיימו מילי דאבות, **ואם מעט הביטו וראו ופנו אל כתבם יתר החכמות, לא למדו לעשות כי אם להבין ולהורות.**

151. R. Yissachar Dov b. Yisrael Leizer Parnass Eilenburg (1550–1623) infers from the Talmud that the dispensation of *le-havin u-le-horot* does not apply to heretical works even if it applies to idolatrous ones. Thus, he argues, Rif, Rosh, and Ritva assume that one cannot study even the valuable ideas from heretical works. As such, he wonders how Rambam could study such works. He suggests that Rambam understood the Mishna's teaching that the eligible individual should know how to refute heretics (דע מה שתשיב לאפיקורוס) as allowing one to study their works to rebut them:
באר שבע מסכת סנהדרין דף ק עמוד ב
כיון דמוכח משמעתין דבספרי מינין אפילו מילי מעלייתא דאית בהו אסור לקרותן, וכמו שפסקו בהדיא הרי"ף והרא"ש והריטב"א שהבאתי לעיל, א"כ קשה על כמה גאוני עולם קמאי דקמאי ובתראי ז"ל, ובראשם הרמב"ם ז"ל, היאך מצאו ידיהם ורגליהם בבית המדרש שלמדו בספרי מינים גמורים כגון אריסטוטלוס ואפלטון ואבן רשד וסייעתם. **ואין ללמוד זכות עליהם מהא דתניא** (סנהדרין לח א) **לא תלמד לעשות אבל אתה למד להבין ולהורות,** משום שזה לא נאמר אלא במילי אחרנייתא, כמו נטיעת קשואין לעיל בסוף פרק ארבע מיתות (שם), וכגון דמות צורת לבנה דרבן גמליאל (ראש השנה כד א), כדפירש רש"י בפרק קמא דעבודה זרה (יח א ד"ה להתלמד) גבי להתלמד עבד כו', אי נמי כגון ההוגה את השם באותיותיו בצנעה להתלמד לפי הגירסא שלפנינו שם בפרק קמא דעבודה זרה (שם), אבל לא גבי ספרי מינים, ולכן סתמו וכתבו הרי"ף והרא"ש והריטב"א לאסור, ולא כתבו שמותר לקרותן להבין ולהורות... ונ"ל שהרמב"ם ז"ל וסייעתו סמכו על המשנה בפ"ב דאבות (משנה י"ד) דקתני רבי אלעזר אומר הוי שקוד ללמוד תורה ודע מה שתשיב לאפיקורוס ודע לפני מי אתה עמל כו', ומייתי לה לעיל בפרק אחד דיני ממונות (לח ב), וא"ר יוחנן עלה לא שנו אלא אפיקורוס עבודה זרה אבל

Finally, we must question if this exception justifies Rambam's engagement with both idolatrous and heretical texts.

Rambam does not explicitly codify the exception of *le-havin u-le-horot,* but he does write that the members of the Sanhedrin must know the ways of idolaters and magicians in order to properly judge them.[152] R. Meir Simcha b. R. Shimshon Kelonymos ha-Kohen of Dvinsk (1843–1926) argues that this is an application of *le-havin u-le-horot.*[153]

Does this dispensation apply heretical works? To answer this we must consider the source for these two prohibitions. Rambam writes that the prohibition to read heretical works stems from **ולא תתורו אחרי לבבכם**, "Do not stray after your hearts" (*Bamidbar* 15:39). Perhaps the prohibition is limited to situations where that concern is realistic.[154] By

---

אפיקורוס ישראל כל שכן דפקר טפי. כתב הרמב"ם בפירוש המשנה (אבות שם) וז"ל ואמרו **אע"פ שתלמוד דעות האומות לדעת איך תשיב עליהם השמר שלא יעלה בלבך דבר מן הדעות ההם**, ודע שמי שתעבוד לפניו יודע צפון לבך, והוא אמרו ודע לפני מה אתה עמל, רצה לומר שיכוין לבו באמונת השי"ת עכ"ל. הרי גילה דעתו מבוארת ומבוררת בכוונת המשנה זו, שצוה התנא שילמוד דעות האפיקורסין ויהא שקוד ללמוד תורה, כדי שידע מה ישיב להם על דעותיהם:

Is this fundamentally different than the principle of *le-havin u-le-horot*? If one adopts an expansive reading of *le-havin u-le-horot,* like Me'iri, then דע מה שתשיב לאפיקורוס might prove more narrow.

152. **רמב"ם הלכות סנהדרין פרק ב הלכה א**

אין מעמידין בסנהדרין, בין בגדולה בין בקטנה - אלא אנשים חכמים ונבונים, מופלאין בחכמת התורה, בעלי דעה מרובה, ויודעין קצת משאר חכמות, כגון רפואות, וחשבון תקופות ומזלות, ואיצטגנינות, **ודרכי המעוננים והקוסמים והמכשפים והבלי עבודה זרה וכיוצא באלו, כדי שיהיו יודעין לדון אותם.**

153. **אור שמח הלכות עבודה זרה פרק ג הלכה ב**

ומפני זה הענין צריכין ב"ד לידע דרכי העבודות כו'. זה נכלל במה שאמרו (סנהדרין סח א) לא תלמוד לעשות כתועבות הגוים ההם כו' (דברים יח:ט) לעשות אי אתה למד אבל אתה למד להבין ולהורות.

154. Of course, as Rambam notes, due to the feebleness of the human mind this concern is almost always relevant:

רמב"ם הלכות עבודה זרה פרק ב הלכה ג

ולא עבודת כוכבים בלבד הוא שאסור להפנות אחריה במחשבה אלא כל מחשבה שהוא גורם לו לאדם לעקור עיקר מעיקרי התורה מוזהרין אנו שלא להעלותה על לבנו ולא נסיח דעתנו לכך ונחשוב ונמשך אחר הרהורי הלב **מפני שדעתו של אדם קצרה ולא כל הדעות יכולין להשיג האמת על בוריו ואם ימשך כל אדם אחר מחשבות לבו נמצא מחריב את העולם לפי קוצר דעתו.**

כיצד? פעמים יתור אחר עבודה זרה; ופעמים יחשוב ביחוד הבורא, שמא הוא שמא אינו, מה למעלה מה למטה, מה לפנים מה לאחור; ופעמים בנבואה, שמא היא אמת שמא

contrast, the prohibition to read idolatrous works emerges from the verse אל תפנו אל האלילים, "Do not turn to the idols" (*Vayikra* 19:4) which forbids even looking at a figure or inquiring about the nature of their service. This source indicates a more categorical prohibition. Indeed, Rambam's language describing the ban on idolatrous works implies the prohibition is unqualified.

רמב"ם שם הלכה ב

ספרים רבים חיברו עובדי עבודה זרה בעבודתה, היאך עיקר עבודתה ומה משפטה ומעשיה. ציוונו הקדוש ברוך הוא, שלא לקרות באותן הספרים כלל, ולא נהרהר בה, ולא בדבר מדבריה.

Idolaters wrote many books about their worship: what the main part of their worship is, how it is done, and what the related laws are. God commanded us not to read such books **at all** and not to think about idols or any related matter.[155]

אינה; ופעמים בתורה, שמא היא מן השמים שמא אינה. **ואינו יודע המידות שידון בהן עד שידע האמת על בוריו, ונמצא יוצא לידי מינות.**

The worship of false gods is not the only subject to which we are forbidden to pay attention; rather, we are warned not to consider any thought which will cause us to uproot one of the fundamentals of the Torah. We should not turn our minds to these matters, think about them, or be drawn after the thoughts of our hearts. **In general, people have limited powers of understanding, and not all minds are capable of appreciating the truth in its fullness. [Accordingly,] were a person to follow the thoughts of his heart, it is possible that he would destroy the world because of his limited understanding.**

What does this mean? Sometimes, he will explore idolatry. At times, he will consider the oneness of the Creator – whether He exists or not, what is in heaven and beneath the ground, what existed before the world was created and what will be after it. Sometimes, he will contemplate whether the prophecies are true or not, and still other times, he will contemplate whether the Torah is heavenly [in origin] or not, **and he does not know the principles necessary to arrive at the truth. Consequently, he will become a heretic.**

155. Generally, a biblical prohibition concerning idolatry applies even if the reason for the prohibition (the concern it may lead to idolatry) is not relevant. The above halacha may imply that this is the case here as well. Evidence for this emerges from the beginning of halacha 3 where he writes: **וכל הלאוין האלו** בענין אחד הן והוא שלא יפנה אחר עבודת כוכבים.

At the same time, Rambam rules that a judge must have familiarity with idolatrous rites in order to adjudicate such cases. Thus, it cannot be a categorical prohibition. However, the dispensation may be limited to situations where knowledge of idolatrous practices is halachically necessary. If that were the case, then Rambam's engagement with these works is problematic. Therefore, it seems reasonable to conclude that Rambam adopted an approach similar to Me'iri with respect to both idolatrous and heretical works.[156]

Rashbatz

A similar but perhaps even more far-reaching justification is provided by R. Shimon b. Tzemach Duran (1361–1444; known as Rashbatz or Tashbeitz) to the mishna in *Pirkei Avot*, "know what to answer an *apikores*":

> **פירוש רשב"ץ מסכת אבות פרק ב משנה יד**
> ומכאן נהגנו היתר בעצמנו ללמוד החכמות ההם כדי שמדברי עצמם נשיבם לומר להם כי אין להם ראיות לסתור דברי תורה ונביאים.
>
> And from here we have allowed ourselves to study these subjects, in order to answer them with their own words, to tell them that they do not have proofs to reject the words of Torah and the Prophets.

---

156. R. Aaron Lopiansky likewise suggested that Rambam only intended to prohibit the reading of idolatrous or heretical works when turning to them as a means of seeking the truth, along the lines of Me'iri. R. Lichtenstein (cited in 2.5) also invokes להבין ולהורות to justify Rambam's practice. R. Yona Reiss suggested that we can discern further evidence for the above suggestion from the third chapter of *Hilchot Teshuva* where Rambam catalogues the causes for loss of *olam ha-ba*. Interestingly, he omits the Mishna's statement that anyone who reads *sefarim chitzonim* (lit. outside books) has no portion in the afterlife. R. Yona Reiss suggested that Rambam's omission was intended to provide the flexibility to allow for reading *sefarim chitzonim* under legitimate circumstances. See *Igrot Moshe* Y.D. 2:111. For an enlightening discussion concerning the practical implications of Rambam's restriction on reading heretical material, see the first three volumes of *The Torah U-Madda Journal*.

Rashbatz continues, emphasizing the need to study heretical works to defend the Torah on *their* terms (**כדי שתצא לנו תשובה נצחת כנגדם מדברי עצמם**). This demands studying their works; knowledge of Torah could not possibly accomplish this.[157]

Tashbeitz asks why studying heretical works to respond to heretics does not violate the Talmud's injunction against reading *sefarim chitzonim* (lit. outside books).[158] He answers that the Talmud only

157. For example, studying Christian texts shows how the person Christians claim to be the messiah did not claim the Torah's laws were no longer binding. He then gives numerous other examples of contradictions in the New Testament.

158. **מגן אבות לרשב"ץ על אבות פרק ב**

ואין זה בכלל מה שאמרו, הקורא בספרים החיצוניים, אין לו חלק לעולם הבא, כי כבר פירשו בגמרא פרק חלק [סנהדרין ק ב], כגון ספרי בן סירא, וכן בירושלמי אמרו [סנהדרין פ"י הל"א כח - א], כגון ספרי בן לענה, והם ספרים מלאים תעתועים כהכרת הפנים. וכמו ספרי הערב מדברי הימים **וכן ספרי מינים שאין בהם חכמה,** אלא אבוד זמן. וכן מה שאסרו ללמוד חכמה יונית, כמו שנזכר בפרק מרובה [ב"ק פג א] ואחרון מסוטה [מט ב], לא אמרו זה על חכמה שהיא על דרך חקירה שכלית, אלא על החכמה שהיתה נוהגת באותו זמן לדבר בלשון רמיזה, כמו שהוא נראה בראשון מחגיגה [ה ב]. ואף חכמה זו מותרת היתה, אלא מפני אותו מעשה הנזכר במנחות פרק ר' ישמעאל [סד ב], ועל אותו מעשה אמרו, ארור המלמד את בנו חכמה יונית והמגדל חזירים. ומה שאמרו בברכות [כח ב] בפרק תפלת השחר מנעו בניכם מן ההגיון אינו חכמת א"ל מנט"ק (כמת הגיון או לוגיק"ה) כי רש"י ז"ל פירש, הגיון שיחה בטלה. ובירושלמי פרק במה אשה [שבת פ"ו מ"ד ז - ד], ר' אבהו בשם ר' יוחנן, מותר אדם ללמד את בתו יונית מפני שהוא תכשיט לה, שמע שמעון בר (בא) [אבא] ואמר, בגין דר' אבהו בעי מלפא בנתיה יונית, הוא תלי לה בר' יוחנן שמע ר' אבהו ואמר, יבא עלי אם לא שמעתי מר' יוחנן.

אבל הספרים המחוברים על דרכי הראיות, אינן בכלל זה, והקורא בהם יקבל מהם האמת וישקוד ללמוד להשיב במה שהוא כנגד התורה וכמו שאמרו על ר' מאיר כשלמד מאלישע אחר, רימון מצא, תוכו אכל, קליפתו זרק, בפרק אין דורשין [חגיגה טו ב]. ואמרו בירושלמי שם, אבל ספרי המירם והספרים שנכתבו מכאן ואילך, כל הקורא בהם כקורא באגרות, מאי טעמא, 'ויותר מהמה בני הזהר עשות ספרים הרבה אין קץ ולהג הרבה יגיעת בשר' [קהלת יב:יב], להגיון נתנם ולא ליגיעה נתנם, ע"כ. ואמרו במדרש קהלת [רבה פרשה יב א [י"ב ד"ה ויותר], כל המכניס בביתו יותר מעשרים וארבעה ספרים מכניס מהומה בתוך ביתו. ופירשו 'עשות ספרים' [קהלת יב:יב], חסר מ"ם, כמו מעשות ספרים, כמו 'השמרו לכם עלות בהר ונגוע בקצהו' [שמות יט:יב], וכן פירש בן גאנ"ח. 'וכמשמרות נטועים' [קהלת יב:יא] הכתוב, שם הוא בשי"ן כנגד משמרות כהונה, הם כ"ד ספרי הקדש. ופירשו מהמה, לשון מהומה לפי שלא אמר מהם. ומה שאמרו כ"ד ספרים, רוצים בזה הם ופירשיהם, וכן כל ספר המחובר בחכמה לפרש עיקרי התורה ממציאות האל ואחדותו והרחקת הגשמות, ושהוא משגיח בעולם ושולח נביאים לצוות ולהזהיר, וגומל ועונש, כל אלו הספרים פירוש התורה הם ומותר לקרותם וכבר אמרו בפרק אין דורשין [חגיגה יא:ב], מקצה השמים ועד קצה השמים אתה שואל, ואין אתה שואל מה למעלה מה למטה, ומה לפנים מה לאחור. אם כן מותר הוא לדרוש ולתור בחכמה בענין זה העולם כולו ממרכז הארץ עד מקיף

prohibited works that lack wisdom and constitute a waste of time.[159] However, when it comes to heretical works that contain wisdom, then a person should follow in the path of R. Meir who studied from the heretic Elisha, taking the good and discarding the bad.[160] The basis of this exception emerges from the Talmud:

חגיגה דף טו עמוד ב

ור"מ היכי גמר תורה מפומיה דאחר והאמר רבה בר בר חנה אמר רבי יוחנן מאי דכתיב (מלאכי ב:ז): "כי שפתי כהן ישמרו דעת ותורה יבקשו מפיהו כי מלאך ה' צבאות הוא?" אם דומה הרב למלאך ה' צבאות יבקשו תורה מפיהו ואם לאו אל יבקשו תורה מפיהו. אמר ר"ל, ר"מ קרא אשכח ודרש (משלי כב:יז): "הט אזנך ושמע דברי חכמים ולבך תשית לדעתי," לדעתם לא נאמר אלא לדעתי. רב חנינא אמר מהכא (תהלים מה:יא): "שמעי בת וראי והטי אזנך ושכחי עמך ובית אביך וגו'" קשו קראי אהדדי לא קשיא הא בגדול הא בקטן. כי אתא רב דימי אמר אמרי במערבא ר"מ אכל תחלא ושדא שיחלא לברא.

How could R. Meir learn Torah from the mouth of *Acheir* (Elisha b. Avuya)? Didn't Rabba b. b. Chana say, "R. Yochanan said,

---

הגלגל העליון, ולא הזהרנו אלא מהספרים שאין בהם חכמה מחכמות הנמצאות. ובזמננו זה אנו שוקדים ללמוד תורה להשיב את שתי האומות הבאות אחר חתימת התלמוד, ואעפ"י שהאומה הראשונה כבר היתה בימי רז"ל, שהם אמרו בפרק ראשון מע"ז [ו ב], לדברי ר' ישמעאל, נצרי לעולם אסור לשאת ולתת עמו, שהיה אומר ג' ימים לפני אידיהן וג' לאחריהן, והן עושין יום אחד בשבת, יום איד. וכן אמרו בתעניות בפרק בשלשה פרקים [כז ב], שאנשי משמר לא היו מתענים במוצאי שבת מפני הנצרים ואעפ"י שדברי שתי האומות הם הבל מעשה תעתועים, כי הם הודו מה שלא הודו המתפקרים הראשונים כי תורתנו היא מן השמים, ואחר שהודו כן, איולת היא להם וכלימה אם אינם מחזיקים בה, ודי להם תשובה לטעותם בזה, **אבל אנחנו חייבים לשקוד על דלתות התורה להשיב להם כנגד טענותיהם**, כמו שמצינו שחכמי יון האחרונים הוצרכו להתחזק להשיב טענות הראשונים שהיו מכחישים התנועה, והרבו ראיות לאמת התנועה, אעפ"י שהיא גלויה ומפורסמת, כדי לבטל טענות המכחישים אותה, כן אנחנו עם שתי האומות, חייבים לשקוד על התורה להכחיש טענותיהם. **ולזה נהגנו היתר בעצמנו לקרות ספר שבושיהם, כדי שתצא לנו תשובה נצחת כנגדם מדברי עצמם.** וכבר ראינו באון גליון אשר הוא ביד הנצרים כי הם טועי' במה שחולקים עלינו שהאיש אשר קראוהו משיח החליף התורה...

159. He then shows how passages in the Talmud that seem to shun the study of philosophy or logic refer only to subjects that are trivial and inane.

160. Recall from 1.7 that Rivash maintained that Rambam was following R. Meir's example.

> 'What is [the meaning of] the verse, "For the lips of a priest shall guard knowledge; and Torah they shall seek from his mouth, for he is an angel of Hashem of Legions (*Malachi* 2:7)"? If the teacher is like an angel of Hashem of Legions, they should seek Torah [teachings] from his mouth, and if not, they should not seek Torah [teachings] from his mouth.'" Reish Lakish said, "R. Meir found a verse and expounded it: 'Incline your ear and hear the words of the Sages, but put your heart to My knowledge (*Mishlei* 22:17).' 'To their knowledge' was not said [in the verse], but rather 'to my knowledge.' R. Chanina said, "[R. Meir derived the permissibility to learn from *Acheir*] from here: "Listen, daughter, and see, and incline your ear and forget your nation and your father's house... (*Tehillim* 45:11)." The verses contradict each other![161] There is no contradiction. The verses [that imply the teacher need not be like an angel refer to when the student] is a *gadol*,[162] and this verse [that implies the teacher must be like an angel refers to when the student] is a *katan*.[163] When R. Dimi came [from Israel], he said, "They say in the West (i.e., Israel, which is west of Babylonia): 'R. Meir ate a date and threw away the pit.'"

Rashbatz's position is fascinating and somewhat mysterious. On the one hand, he insists that the purpose of studying these heretical works is only to rebut the heretics on their own terms, a statement which implies the works have little inherent value. At the same time, he argues that only works containing wisdom should be explored insofar as one can extract the wisdom from the refuse, indicating that these books also contain valuable information. Seemingly, Rashbatz allows incorporating some positive aspects of these works into one's worldview. Regardless, according to Rashbatz the mishna obligates trained individuals to study heretical works in order to carry out a noble task. Of course, if

---

161. R. Yochanan's verse states the teacher must be angelic, while Reish Lakish's and R. Chanina's verses imply one may incline one's ear to learn wisdom from the wicked, while not learning from their ways (see Rashi ibid.).
162. As we shall see, this could be translated as great person or adult.
163. Likewise, this could mean small person or child.

one adopts this broad understanding of *da ma le-hashiv*, one must be extraordinarily careful not to be influenced by these heretical works, as Rambam on this very mishna notes.[164]

R. Kook

R. Kook adopts Rashbatz's openness and takes it further, arguing that certain "great people" are able to learn truths even from heretics.

אורות הקדש חלק א אות יג (יסוד כל המחשבות)
וכל מה שיתעלה האדם יותר, כל מה ששייכותו היא יותר גדולה לתוכן הפנימי של ההויה והחיים, הרי הוא לוקח מכל מחשבה בין שהיא שלו, בין שהיא של אחרים, את גרעינה הנצחי, ההגיוני, הטוב, הנובע ממקור החכמה, והולך ומתעלה על ידן, והן מתעלות בו. איזהו **חכם הלומד מכל אדם, בלא שיור כלל.**

The greater a person is, the greater his relationship to the inner content of existence and life, he can take from every thought – whether it be his or others' – its kernel that is eternal, rational, good, flowing from the source of wisdom. And he goes and rises through them (those thoughts) and they are elevated by him. Who is wise? **He who learns from all people, without any exception at all.**

---

164. **פירוש המשנה לרמב"ם מסכת אבות פרק ב משנה יד**
אמר, למד דברים שבהם תשיב לכופרים מן האומות ותתווכח איתם ותענה להם אם ישאלוך... ועם היותך לומד דעות האומות כדי שתדע איך תשיב עליהם, היזהר שלא ידבק בדעתך דבר מזה, ודע כי אשר תעבוד לפניו ידע צפונותיך.

Learn subjects with which you can respond to the heretics of the nations and argue with them, and respond to them if they ask you... [but] while you are studying the opinions of the nations in order to know how to respond to them, be careful not to allow any of them stick in your own mind, and know that He before Whom you serve knows your hidden [thoughts].

As noted earlier, R. Yissachar Dov Eilenburg also understood that Rambam's justification for studying heretical works was based upon this mishna's instruction to know how to rebut heretics. However, we should note that the simple reading of *Sanhedrin* 38b, where this mishna is discussed, implies that the mishna is instructing one to study Torah in order to combat heresy, not the works of heresy themselves. This understanding is reflected in the commentary of R. Yona and *Tiferet Yisrael* to this mishna.

Elsewhere,[165] R. Kook expounds on the idea that all 'thoughts' have some value in them, and that even heretical positions have something to offer the seeker of truth. However, even R. Kook likely did not advocate such a path to anyone but the greatest scholars, those who are closest to "the inner content of existence and life." After all, the Gemara (*Chagiga* 15b) teaches us that even the great R. Meir was initially not granted the heavenly respect afforded to other Sages due to his having learned Torah from a heretic, even though he was able to extract the 'fruit' from the 'shell.'

While R. Kook and Rashbatz do not invoke R. Meir as a model to explain Rambam, Rivash does, as we saw in 1.7. R. Shabtai ha-Kohen (*Shach*, Y.D. 246:8) wonders why Rambam codifies the Talmud's ruling that one may only study Torah from a teacher that resembles an angel of God while he omits the ruling that a *gadol* may study Torah from a heretic. *Shach* suggests two possible answers:

(1) Only an extraordinarily great person may study from a heretic (or heretical works). Even in Talmudic times, students were not on such a level. Certainly in our times, a worthy person cannot be found. Therefore, Rambam omits this ruling.

(2) We do not accept R. Meir's view and maintain that Torah can never be studied from a heretic.[166]

Either way, at least in contemporary times, studying Torah from a heretical teacher is never permitted according to *Shach*. Therefore, Rambam omitted the ruling. R. Chaim Yosef David Azulai rejects *Shach*'s second answer because Rambam, by studying heretical works, clearly maintained that R. Meir's view is correct. One must therefore conclude that Rambam maintains that it is permitted for someone with extraordinary wisdom and broadmindedness, like R. Meir and Rambam.[167]

---

165. Throughout his *sefer, Orot ha-Emuna*. See esp. page 23.

166. חזינן דאף בימי הש״ס היו קטנים וכל שכן בזמן הזה שכולם נחשבים קטנים כמ״ש אם ראשונים בני אדם אנו כחמורים ולא כחמורו של רבי פנחס בן יאיר כו׳ ואם כן בזמן הזה אין חילוק. והגאון אמ״ו ז״ל תירץ דס״ל מדקאמר ר״ל ר״מ קרא אשכח כו׳ משמע ר״מ סבירא ליה הכי ואנן לא קי״ל כוותיה.

167. **ברכי יוסף יורה דעה סימן רמו**

אך אנן מה נענה דהרמב״ם עביד עובדא בנפשיה ולמד חכמות חיצוניות, וכתב גדול המורים... הריב״ש בתשובה סוף סימן מ״ה, דהרמב״ם סמך על הא דר״מ דבגדול שרי, ולכן בריש ספר

However, had Rambam codified this ruling, people would inappropriately apply it to themselves with disastrous consequences.

> **שער יוסף הוריות דף יב עמוד א**
> כל אחד מחזיק עצמו לגדול הדור שניתנה לו בינה יתירה ואין באחיו גדול ממנו, ומשום הכי לא רצה לכתוב חילוק זה.
>
> Everybody would consider himself the leading sage of the generation to whom special wisdom has been granted, and [think] there is none greater than him among his peers. Therefore, [the Rambam] did not wish to write this distinction.

Rambam, however, knew himself to be worthy and therefore followed R. Meir. Moreover, as Rivash (cited in 1.7) notes, Rambam alludes to this exception in the opening of *Moreh ha-Nevuchim* by citing the verse that R. Meir used to justify his study from Elisha b. Avuya.

Summary

To summarize, Rambam prohibits the study of idolatrous and heretical works. He does not explicitly codify exceptions, except for an allowance for judges to have familiarity with pagan practices so as to adjudicate cases of idolatry. Nevertheless, Rambam frequently cites idolatrous and heretical works. We considered three Talmudic sources which might sanction the study of such works. (1) **להבין ולהורות**, which, according to Me'iri, allows seeking helpful information from these works. (2) **דע מה להשיב לאפיקורוס**, which, according to Rashbatz, allows studying heretical works that contain wisdom in order to refute heretics based

---

המורה כתב הט אזנך וכו׳ ולבך תשית לדעתי, דהוי קרא דדרש ר״מ. ע״ש באורך. וכיון דהרמב״ם סמך על זה, אזדא ליה תירוץ הרב הנז׳ דסבר הרמב״ם דלא קי״ל כר״מ, והדרא קושיא לדוכתא, דאמאי השמיט בחיבורו חילוק זה. ואולי סבר הרמב״ם דהא דאמרו בש״ס הא בגדול הא בקטן, לאו דוקא, אלא בעינן שיהיה גדול בחכמה ודעתו רחבה, כרבי מאיר, אשר רוח בו, שיבור לו לברר אוכל, ולאו גדול בשנים וקטן בשנים. ומשו״ה כיון שהרמב״ם סובר שיהיה לו דעת שלם ורחב לבב, וזה פנת יקרת הדת, לכן השמיט חילוק זה, לסתום הפתח, כי לא רבים יחכמו כר״מ. ואם כה יאמר דגדול שרי, כל אחד ידמה בדעתו כי גדול הוא, וילכד בפח. אבל הרמב״ם איהו גופיה ידע בנפשיה - וכ״ע מודו ליה - כי הוא גדול וידיעתו מכרעת, ונפשו אותה ויעש.

on their very texts. (3) R. Meir, who studied Torah from *Acheir* (Elisha b. Avuya) despite the latter's heretical beliefs.

All three of these exceptions demand that the reader of the heretical material possess expertise in Torah to a degree that the works he is reading pose no threat. The third source is most far reaching but also most circumscribed in that it relates only to those like R. Meir and Rambam.

We should note that the perspectives presented in this section do not necessarily reflect the mainstream viewpoint. Many other thinkers understand the prohibition against studying heresy categorically. Moreover, while analyzing the conditions under which the various thinkers that we surveyed sanctioned the study of heretical material, we encountered differing attitudes towards the value of such study. Most of the sources saw practical (e.g., rebutting heretics) but not inherent value to such study. However, R. Kook disagreed, seeing the value in every thought – the greater the person, the greater his ability to extract the holiness from even the most profane of thoughts.

Chapter Three

Philosophy and the Interpretation of the Torah: When to Interpret Scripture Allegorically?

A major question concerning the scope of philosophy arises when we consider the extent to which we should interpret scripture figuratively in order to resolve philosophical problems raised by a literal rendering of the text. Does doing so imply that Torah is subservient to philosophy? Rambam writes that the primary function of his *Moreh ha-Nevuchim* is to interpret verses that are philosophically problematic. To solve such problems, Rambam generally applies two methods. Frequently, he shows that a word has multiple meanings and argues that the quandary is resolved when we choose one particular definition. On other occasions, Rambam suggests figurative interpretations. Thus, we must define which circumstances warrant non-literal readings. We begin, however, by considering whether non-literal readings ever are warranted.

3.1 THE TORAH, THE PROPHETS, AND THE SAGES ALL USE HYPERBOLE

The Talmud notes that certain verses should not be understood literally, as they are intended to be exaggerations. For example:

דברים פרק ט פסוק א
שְׁמַע יִשְׂרָאֵל אַתָּה עֹבֵר הַיּוֹם אֶת־הַיַּרְדֵּן לָבֹא לָרֶשֶׁת גּוֹיִם גְּדֹלִים וַעֲצֻמִים מִמֶּךָּ עָרִים גְּדֹלֹת **וּבְצֻרֹת בַּשָּׁמָיִם.**

Hear, Israel. Today, you are crossing the Jordan to come in to possess [the land of] nations greater and stronger than you; great cities, **fortified up to the heavens.**

תלמוד בבלי מסכת חולין דף צ עמוד ב
אמר רבי אמי: דברה תורה לשון הואי, דברו נביאים לשון הואי, דברו חכמים לשון הואי... דברה תורה לשון הואי - דערים גדולות ובצורות בשמים...

Says R. Ami: the Torah, the Prophets, and the Sages all use hyperbole... The Torah speaks hyperbolically; for example, "great cities, fortified up to the heavens."

Of course, these are not senseless exaggerations. Hyperbole is a literary tool used when precision will not capture the intended message.[1]

Chazal consider other types of non-literal interpretations. For example, one view in the Talmud (*Bava Batra* 16b) maintains that the story of Iyov is a *mashal* or allegory that never took place. This is true even though the simple reading of the text implies that Iyov was an actual person who lived in a real place.[2]

1. For example, in political cartoons, a cartoonist might exaggerate the mouth of a particular individual. This exaggeration is not senseless; it highlights a particular quality of the featured person.
2. A sophisticated reading of the text, however, highlights the textual (not just theological) motivations for such a position.

The question remains – which parameters justify a deviation from literal interpretation? We begin with R. Sa'adya Gaon's approach and then turn to Rambam.

3.2 THE VIEW OF R. SA'ADYA GAON

R. Sa'adya Gaon addresses the question in the following context: how do we know that the verses promising the resurrection, such as *Daniel* 12:2 and *Yeshaya* 26:19, should be taken literally? Perhaps they should be interpreted allegorically, just as the verses that imply God has a physical body are to be understood figuratively.

R. Sa'adya Gaon considers and rejects four possible avenues that might lead to a rejection of literal resurrection in this case: scientific, philosophical, scriptural (i.e., verses that imply that the dead never will live again), and tradition. He then shows how none of these factors are present with respect to the verses on the resurrection.[3] In the process

---

3. **ספר האמונות והדעות מאמר ז בתחיית המתים**
מצאתי, שהמוצאים אשר יעלו תחלה בראשונה אשר יצאו מהם משכי הטענה על זה, ארבעה אין להם חמישי. וראיתי כל שבוש ששמעתי או חשבתי בו שיהיה טענה על האמונה הזאת, ועמדתי על שבר הכל וביטולו והפסדו, ואז התקימה האמונה הזאת בראיות, מן השלשה ענינים אשר מהם ימשכו המאמינים ראיותם. **והמוצאים הארבעה אשר חקרתי עליהם לראות היש על האמונה הזאת בהם תשובה, הם מוצא הטבע והשכל והכתוב והקבלה.**
והחלותי מן **הטבע**, מפני שקדימתו קדימה עצמית. ואמרתי אולי יתחייב המנע ההודאה בתחיית המתים מפני המנע הטבע לעשות זה, מפני שאין כמו שגדלים בעלי חיים בטבע, ושבים קצתם בטבע, יחיו גם כן אחרי המות בטבע, וכאשר התבוננתי במחשבה הזאת הנחשבת, מצאתיה שאין נתלים בה כי אם האומרים בקדמות או בשניים, מפני שלא יתכן אצלם שיהיו הדברים אלא על דרך המנהגים הנהוגים הנודעים, **אבל המיחדים שמאמינים שהבורא משנה מנהגי הטבע, וישימם בכל עת שירצה כאשר ירצה, אי אפשר להם להמנע מהודות בתחיית המתים מצד הטבע,** שכלם מודים ששלח אליהם נביאיו ובידם אותות מלאות, וגדול מזה בראתו היסודות הראשונו' לא מדבר, ויהיה באור המאמר הזה, שמי שמרחיק תחיית המתים בעת הישועה מפני שהטבע לא יעשה זה, יתחיב להרחיק לעמתו הפוך המטה תנין, והמים דם, ועמוד מי הים והקפאם...
ואחר כן חקרתי במוצא השני אשר הוא המחשב בשכל, ודרשתי אם אמצא לאמונה הזאת מה שיבטל אותה, ולא מצאתי מה שמספק בה כי אם שלשה דרכים. האחת מהם שתהיה היכולת על תחיית המתים מן השקר, וכבר עמדתי על שאיננה כן כאשר בארתי. והשנית שיהיה היכול על זה לא הבטיחם בו, ומצאתיו שהבטיח בו במקומות רבים מן המקרא, אעפ"י שיתכן לסבור בהם סברות רבות עד שיעתקו מענין תחיית המתים אל ענינים אחרים, לא ראיתי העיון מחייב דחות הנראה מהם, בעבור שיתכן שתסבלהו הסברא...
ואחר כן חקרתי במוצא השלישי, והוא הכתוב במקרא. והסתכלתי אולי יש בה מה שמונע תחיית המתים בעולם הזה, ומצאתי ספקות שאפשר שנתלים בה המרחיקים את זה, וראיתי לזכרם הנה ולבטלם. מהם ויזכור כי בשר המה רוח הולך ולא ישוב (תהלים עח:לט). ואמר עוד

of his discussion, he informs us that these four avenues are sometimes legitimate reasons to deviate from the literal interpretation of Scripture and gives examples of each.[4]

Science/Experience

The first reason to reject a literal reading is when it is contradicted by experience. R. Sa'adya Gaon offers an example. The verse (*Bereishit* 3:20) states that Chava was the "mother of all living things." This is contradicted by the observation that women do not give birth to forms of life other than humans. Thus, "all living things" is not to be taken literally, but rather means all human life.

Here, we must consider an obvious objection: why is this different than resurrection? Earlier, R. Sa'adya stated that we do not reject resurrection merely because we have not observed it or cannot explain it scientifically, because we believe in miracles. So why is this different – maybe it was a miracle?

Presumably, the answer is that the verses that describe resurrection indicate that it will be something miraculous and extraordinary; thus, the fact that we have not observed the phenomenon is not a reason to deny the possibility that it will occur. On the other hand, the verse describing Chava as being the mother of all life does not indicate that

---

(שם קג:טו) אנוש כחציר ימיו וגו'. (איוב יד:ב) כציץ יצא וימל וגומר, כי רוח עברה בו ואיננו וגו'. (תהלים כג:טז). ואמר עוד (איוב ז:י) כלה ענן וילך וגו' לא ישוב עוד לביתו וגו' ואמר עוד (שם יד:יב) ואיש שכב ולא יקום ומה שדומה לזה. והתבוננתי כל זה היטב ולא מצאתי אחד מהם שהחפץ בו שהבורא אמר שלא יחיה את המתים אבל כל זה ספור שאין אדם יכול לקום מן הקבר אחר רדתו אליו, ושאינו יכול להנער מן העפר ולשוב אל ביתו...

ואחר כן לא נמנעתי מחקור במוצא הד', אשר הוא העתקת הנביאים וקבלת החכמים. אמרתי אולי אמצא בו תשובה על תחיית המתים, כי דבריהם ז"ל מלאים מזכרה וספורה, וראיתי לזכור מהם דברים מעטים...

4. **ספר האמונות והדעות מאמר ז**

והוא שאנחנו כל בני ישראל מאמינים כי כל אשר בספרי הנביאים הוא כאשר נראה ממשמעו והידוע ממלותיו, אלא מה שהנראה והידוע ממנו מביא אל אחד בארבעה דברים:

א. אם להכחיש מוחש כמו שנאמר על חוה, (בראשית ג:כ) כי היא היתה אם כל חי

כ. או להשיב מה שיש בשכל, כמו שאמר (דברים ד:כד) כי יי אלהיך אש אוכלה

ג. או לסתור דבר אחר כתוב, כמו שנאמר (מלאכי ג:י) ובחנוני נא, אחר שאמר (דברים ו:טז) לא תנסו את יי אלהיכם

ר. או להכחיש מה שקבלוהו קדמוננו, כמו שאמר (שם כה:ג) ארבעים יכנו לא יוסיף, ואמרו רבותינו שהם שלשים ותשע מכה...

this is something unusual; thus, the fact that we have never observed a human giving birth to a non-human justifies a non-literal interpretation.[5] We should note that commentators occasionally debate whether biblical episodes should be understood naturally or supernaturally, with some thinkers expressing the proclivity to minimize miracles. We will return to this issue in Chapter 7.

Philosophy/Logic

The second reason to interpret a verse non-literally is because the literal interpretation is philosophically problematic or illogical. R. Sa'adya Gaon's example is *Devarim* 4:24, which states that God is a consuming fire. Elsewhere,[6] R. Sa'adya Gaon proves that God has no physical substance. Accordingly, it is logically impossible to state that He is a consuming fire. We thus are forced to understand that the verse is referring to God's vengeance, which is like a consuming fire. This understanding is justified in light of other verses that compare anger to fire, such as the verse in *Tzefanya* (1:18), "The entire earth will be consumed by the fire of His wrath."

This sort of exposition does not necessarily imply that all forms of philosophical speculation justify deviation from the literal interpretation.[7] Rather, it seems that R. Sa'adya Gaon is arguing that if a verse is contradicted by unambiguous (syllogistic) logic, there are grounds for reinterpretation.

5. A more far-reaching application of this distinction can be found in ibn Ezra's rejection (at least on a level of *pshat*) of the midrash that Yocheved was born on the way to Egypt (*bein ha-chomot*). He writes that if it were meant literally, it would mean that Yocheved was 130 years old when she bore Moshe. Such a miracle certainly would have been noted by the Torah, as it was when Sara gave birth at the age of ninety. Thus, the rejection of the midrash is textual; it is not rooted in the impossibility of the phenomenon, since miracles are possible. Ramban, however, argues for a literal understanding of the midrash and addresses ibn Ezra's concerns (see Chapter 7 for elaboration).
6. See *Emunot ve-Dei'ot* 2:12.
7. R. Sa'adya Gaon greatly esteemed philosophy, believing that to some degree, the entire Torah could be recreated through philosophy. R. Sa'adya Gaon wrote that "The truth of reliable tradition" is "based on the knowledge of sense perception and the knowledge of reason" (from Alexander Altmann's translation as found in *Three Jewish Philosophers*, New York: Atheneum, 1985, p. 37).

There are those who go much further in using science and philosophy to reinterpret biblical verses. Perhaps the most extreme example (among well-known Rishonim) of this approach can be found in the writings of R. Levi b. Gershon (1288–1344), better known as Ralbag or Gersonides. Ralbag insists that the cessation of the sun's and moon's motion at Giv'on (*Yehoshua* 10:12–14) and the sun's retrogression in the times of Chizkiyahu (*II Melachim* 20:9–11) cannot possibly be literal. In his commentaries on these verses, and in *Milchamot Hashem* (6:2:12), Ralbag rejects the possibility of miracles that affect the celestial domain. Thus, miracles can change the order of events in this world but not the path of the sun. Ralbag's conviction, rooted in his Aristotelian worldview, force him to reinterpret two biblical episodes in a rather forced manner.[8]

Ralbag's questionable exegesis is largely rejected by other thinkers. Rivash,[9] (who praises Ralbag but notes that he was overly influenced by philosophy when explaining these stories), and Maharal[10] both attack Ralbag's approach to these stories. The question of interpretation of these episodes relates to a broader issue concerning the nature of omnipotence, which we deal with in 4.5. This also relates to Rambam's famous comment that he did not reject Aristotle's belief in the eternity of matter based on the verses of *Bereishit*, which we will consider shortly.

Textual Issues

The third reason to reject a literal reading is when the literal meaning of one verse contradicts the literal meaning of another. For example, *Devarim* 6:16 states, "You may not test Hashem, your God." This is contradicted by *Malachi* 3:10, which states, concerning tithes, "You may test me in this." The Talmud (*Ta'anit* 9a) resolves this contradiction by distinguishing between testing God in the realm of charity versus in other areas.

This type of methodology is ubiquitous in the Talmud and Midrash. Sometimes, these sources will reinterpret a verse based on

8. For an excellent article on Ralbag, see "The Scholar Rabbi Levi – A Study in Rationalistic Exegesis" by R. Yitzhak Grossman (*Ḥakirah,* Volume 12).
9. *Teshuvot ha-Rivash* 118
10. Second Introduction to *Gevurot Hashem.*

contradictions, like the aforementioned example. Other times, a text will be reinterpreted based on other textual anomalies or received hermeneutical rules, such as the thirteen principles of R. Yishma'eil. At times, it is difficult to determine the exact motivation for the interpretation.

Tradition

The fourth basis for abandoning a literal interpretation is when such an interpretation contradicts a received tradition. R. Sa'adya Gaon's example is the *halacha le-Moshe mi-Sinai* that when the Torah (*Devarim* 25:3) says that certain sinners receive forty lashes, it really means thirty-nine. We must consider the question of whether this is meant to be the interpretation of the verse or a tradition relevant to the application of the law but not a replacement of the simple understanding of the text. We will return to this question in 7.8 when we consider Rambam's comments in *Moreh ha-Nevuchim* regarding the verse "An eye for an eye."

3.3 RAMBAM ON HOW TO READ THE STORY OF CREATION

Like R. Sa'adya Gaon, Rambam maintained that justification is necessary to deviate from a literal reading:

> In my discussion in the *Guide* of the creation of the world, I pointed out that it necessarily follows that once the doctrine of the production of the universe is accepted, all miracles are possible; therefore the resurrection is also possible. **I believe every possible happening that is supported by a prophetic statement and does not strip it of its plain meaning. I fall back on interpreting a statement [non-literally] only when its plain meaning is impossible, like the corporeality of God.**[11]

11. *Essay on Resurrection*, trans. in Abraham Halkin and David Hartman, *Epistles of Maimonides: Crisis and Leadership* (Philadelphia: Jewish Publication Society, 1985), 209–233, p. 228.

Rambam, like R. Sa'adya Gaon, maintains that there is no basis for a non-literal interpretation of the resurrection prophecies because miracles are possible. Why, in the case of God's corporeality, is a literal read *impossible*? Because corporeality has been *proven* to be false.[12] Thus, Rambam seems to set the bar relatively high with respect to deviating from literalism – it is justified only when the plain meaning is impossible. With this in mind, let us turn to Rambam's perspective on creation.

How Literally Are We to Understand Ma'aseh Bereishit?

Many thinkers highlight the uniqueness of the Torah's first chapter. Indeed, Chazal inform us that the first chapter of *Bereishit* should be viewed differently than the rest of the Torah. Specifically, the Torah's intent is particularly concealed.

> **בראשית רבה (וילנא) פרשת בראשית פרשה ט**
> רבי לוי בשם רבי חמא בר חנינא אמר מתחלת הספר ועד כאן כבוד אלהים הוא הסתר דבר מכאן ואילך כבוד מלכים חקור דבר.
>
> R. Levi in the name of R. Chama b. Chanina said, concerning the beginning of *Bereishit* until the end of the creation of man "It is the glory of God to conceal a matter." Henceforward, "And the glory of a king to investigate a matter."

Maharal explains that we cannot relate to the first chapter of *Bereishit*. This chapter describes the world prior to the creation of man; it is not our world and, as such, we cannot relate.[13]

---

12. Rambam writes (*Moreh ha-Nevuchim* 2:25): "That God does not have a body has been demonstrated; from this, it follows necessarily that everything that in its plain meaning disagrees with this demonstration must be interpreted figuratively, for it is known that such texts are of necessity fit for figurative interpretation."

13. **גבורות ה׳ הקדמות הקדמה א**
במדרש ב"ר (פ"ט) ר׳ לוי בשם ר׳ חמא בר חנינא מתחלת ספר בראשית עד ויכלו כבוד אלהים הסתר דבר מכאן ואילך חקור דבר ע"כ. למה שהיה השגת אדם מתיחסת אל האדם למה שהוא השגתו, מחויב מזה שהדבר שהוא מושג לא יהיה נבדל מכל וכל מן האדם המשיג, שאם היה נבדל לגמרי מן האדם המשיג אין ראוי שיהיה בו השגת האדם. כי כבר אמרנו שההשגה של אדם היא מתיחסת אליו, יחויב מזה שהדבר שהוא נבדל ממנו לגמרי. אחר שהוא נבדל ממנו אין ראוי שיהיה לאדם השגה בו.

Of course, since it is included in the Torah, we must seek to understand it on some level. As we shall see shortly, Ramban averred that unlike the rest of Torah, this chapter is meaningful only on a Kabbalistic level.

Rambam also highlights the chapter's uniqueness and addresses the proper methodology for interpreting this chapter. In his Introduction to *Moreh ha-Nevuchim*, Rambam writes that the Torah uses parables, riddles, and obscure words to describe creation:

> Therefore, the Almighty began the Torah with the description of the creation, that is, with Physical Science; on the one hand, the subject is very weighty and important, and on the other hand, our means of fully comprehending those great problems is limited. He described those profound truths, which He deemed appropriate to communicate to us, **using parables, riddles, and in very obscure words.**[14] Our Sages have said, "It is impossible to give a full account of the creation to man. Therefore, Scripture simply tells us, 'In the beginning, God created the heavens and the earth' (*Bereishit* 1:1)."[15] In this manner, they have suggested that this subject is a deep mystery, and in the words of Shlomo, "Far off and exceedingly deep, who can find it out?" (*Kohelet* 7:24). That which is said about creation is communicated using equivocal

---

14. The M. Friedländer (1903) edition translates the above sentence as "He described those profound truths, which His divine Wisdom found it necessary to communicate to us, in **allegorical, figurative, and metaphorical language.**" However, it seems the more accurate translation is the one cited above from the Pines edition (p. 9). Likewise, the Tel Aviv University edition by Prof. Michael Schwartz translates this sentence as:

    בשל גודל העניין וחשיבותו הרבה, ומכיוון שיכולתנו קצרה מלהשׂיג את הגדול שבדברים כפי שהוא, היתה הפנייה אלינו בדברים העמוקים, אשר בהם חייבה החוכמה האלוהית לפנות אלינו, **במשלים, בחידות ובדברים סתומים מאוד.**

    Likewise, R. Kapach translates the sentence as:

    ומחמת גודל הדבר ורוממותו, ומחמת חוסר יכולתנו להשיג הדברים הגדולים כפי שהם, נאמרו לנו הדברים העמוקים, אשר הוזקקה החכמה האלוהית להודיענו אותם, **במשלים וחידות ובדברים סתומים מאוד.**

15. The precise source Rambam is referring to is unclear. The Schwartz edition cites the following:

    מדרשי הגניזה: בתי מדרשות, תש"ם, כרך א׳, עמ׳ רנא: מדרש שני כתובים.
    להגיד כוח מעשה בראשית לבריות ולהודיעם אי-אפשר, אלא שסתם הכתוב. מכאן אמרו אין דורשין בעריות לשלושה, ולא במעשה בראשית לשניים, ולא במרכבה ליחיד...

> terms so that the multitude might comprehend them in accord with the capacity of their understanding and the weakness of their understanding, whereas the perfect man, who is already informed, will understand them otherwise.[16]

Rambam writes that Scripture's description of creation is incomplete because we could not understand a comprehensive account anyway. Nevertheless, because the topic of creation is fundamental, it cannot be omitted. Therefore, the story uses language and imagery that can be understood in multiple ways, with each person understanding it according to his level.

Rambam does not tell us, however, exactly what words and verses are meant to be understood as *meshalim* and *chidot* (parables and riddles). Likewise, in *Moreh ha-Nevuchim* 2:29, Rambam states that, "Not everything mentioned in the Torah concerning the Account of the Beginning is to be taken in its external sense as the vulgar imagine."[17] By writing that "not everything" is to be taken literally, we can deduce that some things are in fact to be understood in their "external sense."

In 2:29, Rambam offers examples of the complexity involved in translating the first chapter of *Bereishit*. For example, the word *eretz* refers to the four elements in *Bereishit* 1:1, but refers to the element earth in *Bereishit* 1:10. This is not an arbitrary switch; rather, Rambam carefully explains the textual basis for the switch.[18] Rambam's tools of

---

16. Prof. Michael Schwartz translates this sentence as:

    כל הדברים האלה נאמרו **בשמות משותפים** כדי שההמון יפרשו אותם במשמעות שהיא לפי מידת הבנתם וחולשת השׂגתם, ויפרשם השלם היודע במשמעות אחרת.

    Likewise, R. Kapach translates it as:

    ועשה את הדבור בכל זה **בשמות המשותפים**, כדי שיבינום ההמון לפי עניין שהוא כדי הבנתם וחולשת דעתם, ויבינם השלם שכבר למד באופן אחר.

    Contrast these with the M. Friedländer (1903) edition, which has: "It has been treated in **metaphors** in order that the uneducated may comprehend it according to the measure of their faculties and the feebleness of their apprehension, while educated persons may take it in a different sense."

17. Pines translation p. 346.
18. It is based on Rambam's understanding that the phrase "God called object A by the name B" indicates that B is an equivocal term and that in its second appearance in the text, it has a different meaning from its first. Given that the second occurrence of *eretz* (earth) is preceded by "God called the dry land (*yabasha*) *eretz*" (*Bereishit*

interpretation in the first chapter of *Bereishit* are systematic and rooted in the text.[19] In this particular explanation, there is no need to resort to the tools (parables, riddles, and obscure words) referred to above. On the other hand, concerning the word *rakia* (firmament), such tools appear necessary:

> But there is something hidden, as you will see, with regard to the firmament and the thing above it, which is called water. ... If on the other hand, the matter is considered according to its inner meaning and to what was truly intended, it is most hidden. For in that case **it was necessary for it to be one of the concealed secrets so that the vulgar should not know it.** (p. 353 of Pines edition)

Rambam, however, does not explain why it was necessary to hide the true meaning in order to protect the masses. Abarbanel, in his commentary to *Moreh ha-Nevuchim,* suggests that the masses believe that the firmament is something rigid with water above and below it. A literal

1:10), *eretz* in this verse has a different meaning than in verse 1. See "Maimonides' Exoteric and Esoteric Biblical Interpretations in the Guide of the Perplexed," by Sara Klein-Braslavy in *Study and Knowledge in Jewish Thought,* H. Kreisel, ed., (Ben-Gurion University of the Negev, 2006), p. 151.

19. Consider another example cited in Sara Klein-Braslavy's aforementioned article. Concerning the growth of the grass and trees on the third day, Rambam connects the biblical description in *Bereishit* 1:11–12 with *Bereishit* 2:6, "And there went up a mist from the earth" and explains (on the basis of *Bereishit Rabba* 13:1) that the grass and the trees grew after God caused the rain to fall:

> Among the things that you ought to know is that the Sages have made it clear that God only made grass and trees grow from the earth after He had caused rain to fall upon them, and that its saying: And there went up a mist from the earth (*Bereishit* 2:6) is a description of the first state of matters obtaining before the command: Let the earth put forth grass. For this reason Onqelos translates: And there had gone up a mist from the earth. This is also clear from the [scriptural] text itself because of its saying: And no shrub of the field was yet in the earth (*Bereishit* 2:5). (p. 354 of Pines translation)

Rambam writes how this interpretation shows that there is no disagreement concerning the Torah and Aristotelian philosophy. Concerning the understanding of *rakia* (firmament), he indicates potential conflicts with Aristotle.

reading of the text of *Bereishit* might support this view. However, it is false and that is not the true intent of the text.[20] What emerges from these examples is that the usage of parables, riddles and obscure words does not imply a wholesale deviation from the chapter's basic meaning.

The Meaning of "*Yom*" in the Era of Creation and the Age of the Universe

A fascinating instance of an equivocal term is the word *yom,* which generally refers to a unit of time in which the earth completes one rotation with respect to the sun (or, from the perspective of someone on earth, the unit of time in which the sun seems to encircle the earth). Rambam, in *Moreh ha-Nevuchim* 2:30, addresses two objections to using the standard translation with respect to *ma'aseh bereishit.* First, the Torah uses the term *yom* prior to the creation of the sun. Moreover, God created time.[21] If *yom* refers to a unit of time, then the verse (*Bereishit* 1:5) would be making an illogical statement: God created time within time. Accordingly, *yom* in this context is not a unit of time. Since the word *yom* in the context of the days of creation is not referring to a unit of time, one cannot accurately state that God created the world in six days.[22] (Indeed, Rambam maintains that according to Chazal in a number of places,[23] God created everything simultaneously. As such, the words first day, second day, etc. cannot possibly refer to day in the classical sense.[24])

20. Klein-Braslavy shows that in *Bereishit* the word *rakia* is used in two ways: 1) to refer to the heavens and 2) to refer to one of the strata of air in the sublunar sphere.

21. Rambam notes that anyone who maintains that time existed prior to creation is essentially, though perhaps unknowingly, adopting Aristotle's view concerning the eternity of matter.

22. One cannot argue that following the creation of time there were six days since the Torah states "*yom echad*" ("day one" or "first day"). If "*yom echad*" means the first day (or day one) and includes the creation of time, it could not possibly mean day in the sense of a unit of time, for a unit of time cannot possibly include the creation of time.

23. בראשית רבה פרשה א:יד (תיאודור-אלבק, עמ' 12); תלמוד בבלי חגיגה יב,א; חולין ס, א; תלמוד ירושלמי, ברכות, פרק ט', הלכה ז (דף י"ד, ב).

24. Furthermore, Rambam argues that views in Chazal that do not seem to accept this must be adopting the Aristotelian perspective concerning the eternity of matter.

What then does the Torah mean when it describes that which was created on the first, second, third, etc. days? Rambam is not entirely clear on this point, and there are two ways to understand what he says:

(1) The days refer to the chronological stages in which creations emerged (e.g., when the Torah says that grass and trees were created on the third day, it means they emerged during the third stage of creation).
(2) The days depict a hierarchy within the natural world.[25]

---

25. Here is the relevant passage in *Moreh ha-Nevuchim*, as translated by Schwartz (Hebrew) followed by Friedlander (English):

מכאן שהכול נברא יחד, והדברים נבדלו כולם בזה אחר זה, עד שהמשילו זאת לאיכר אשר פיזר זרעים שונים באדמה בדקה אחת, חלקם נבט לאחר יום, חלקם לאחר יומיים, וחלקם לאחר שלושה, בעוד הזריעה כולה היתה בשעה אחת.

Consequently, all things were created together, but were separated from each other successively. Our Sages illustrated this by the following simile: We sow various seeds at the same time; some spring forth after one day, some after two, and some after three days, although all have been sown at the same time.

The above passage seems to indicate that Rambam is not rejecting the simple understanding that the text of the Torah indicates chronological sequence. He is merely rejecting the standard translation of *yom* as a unit of time, the first interpretation above. (According to this understanding, Rambam's view is a lot closer to the traditional understanding of *ma'aseh bereishit.*)

Surprisingly, Abarbanel adopts the second possibility:

אברבנאל בראשית פרשת בראשית פרק א

ויחשוב הרב, שלא היו מלאכות נבדלות בששת הימים, כי ביום אחד ובשעה אחת נברא הכל אצלו. אבל נזכרו אותם הימים במעשה בראשית לרמוז על מדרגות הנמצאים שנעשו כפי הסדר הטבעי. ולא שהיו ימים ממש ולא קדימה זמנית לדבר על דבר ממה שנברא במעשה בראשית. אבל שהיו דברים שאחרי בריאתם באותה שעה שנברא הכל נתגלו ונתראו פעולותיהם אחר כך ושזה גם כן היה ענין יחוד הימים ר״ל להראות פעולות מה שכבר נברא.

Rambam believed that the work of creation was not divided over six days but happened in a single instant. The reason the Torah states there were six days of creation is to indicate the different levels of created beings according to their natural hierarchy. Thus, the Rambam does not understand the word day to be a temporal day and he does not read *ma'aseh bereishit* to be describing the chronological sequence of creation...

It is worthwhile to note that, either way, Rambam's interpretation primarily emerges from internal issues and seeks to address textual problems. Moreover, he argues that his deviation from the literal reading is supported by Chazal.

As R. Y. D. Soloveitchik notes, the implications of this understanding are far-reaching insofar as one cannot make a claim that the Torah tells us anything about the age of the universe or the age of the earth.[26] At most, the Torah informs us of the time since the creation of

---

Abarbanel's comments are perplexing because Rambam writes that the Torah's order of creation does not simply refer to a structural hierarchy within creation but the order of differentiation within creation. (In that sense, Rambam's view resembles that of Rashi who states that everything was created on the first day but emerged over the six days).

However, numerous commentaries attribute the second reading to Rambam and assume that Rambam was rejecting sequence entirely:

- Abarbanel, above, wrote לא קדימה זמנית.
- *Akeidat Yitzchak, Bereishit* 3, states: "the description of creation is not describing the chronological sequence of events; the days simply serve to indicate distinctions in their levels and to inform of the hierarchy of Nature.
- R. Sheim-Tov b. Yosef ibn Falaquera (1225–1295), in his commentary on the above passage from *Moreh ha-Nevuchim*, writes: "The creations of the world prioritization is the result of their nature as to what their purpose and causal relationship is in combining and interacting with other things. Therefore, only in describing their level in reality do we say Day One, Day Two – but not that they were created in this sequence." (The above translations are adapted from R. Micha Berger http://www.aishdas.org/asp/the-rambam-on-time-during-creation.)

Why do they understand Rambam this way? R. Meir Triebitz suggests that they would agree to the first understanding of the above passage in *Moreh ha-Nevuchim*. However, they understood that Rambam, in that passage, is presenting the position of Chazal but not his own. Later in the same chapter, Rambam indicates that Aristotle would have rejected any type of temporal dimension. Thus, even chronological progression is inconceivable. The above thinkers apparently felt that, on this question, Rambam sided with Aristotle. Personally, I find little evidence for their reading. This debate, however, has no bearing on our discussion concerning Rambam's explicit statement that *yom* is not referring to a unit of time.

26. The following citation is from notes of R. Soloveitchik's lectures written by R. Robert Blau and edited by R. Meir Triebitz. (They have been collected into a book, *Notes on Genesis*, which has not been published.)

> Indeed, one of the most annoying scientific facts which the religious man encounters is the problem of evolution and creation. However, this is not the real problem. What actually is irreconcilable is the concept of man as the

Adam.[27] We should note that Ramban rejects Rambam's understanding, writing on *Bereishit* 1:3 that the days referred to in the first chapter of *Bereishit* are literal days.[28] Ramban adds that according to the deeper, Kabbalistic understanding the word *yom* refers to the *sefirot*.[29]

---

bearer of a divine image and the idea of man as an intelligent animal in science. **Evolution and creation can be reconciled merely by saying that six days is not absolutely so, but is indefinite and may be longer. Maimonides spoke of Creation in terms of phases and the Kabbalah in terms of *sefirot*, the time of which may be indefinite**. However, our conflict is man as a unique being and man as a friend of the animal. Science can never explain how being came into being, for it is out of the realm of science, while the Bible is concerned with the problem of *ex nihilo*. Aristotle could not accept evolution because he believed in the eternity of forms. (Lecture XII)

The basic idea of this citation has been included in *The Emergence of Ethical Man*, pp. 4–5.

27. When Chazal (*Sanhedrin* 97a) say the world will exist for six thousand years , this presumably could refer to years from the time of the creation of the universe or from the creation of Adam (as we do in the Rosh ha-Shana prayers, "*ha-yom harat olam*").

28. ודע, כי הימים הנזכרים במעשה בראשית היו בבריאת השמים והארץ ימים ממש, מחוברים משעות ורגעים, והיו שישה כששת ימי המעשה, כפשוטו של מקרא.

In this sentence, Ramban clearly intends to reject Rambam's understanding, though he does not quote him by name.

29. ובפנימיות הענין יקראו ״ימים״ הספירות האצולות מעליון, כי כל מאמר פועל הויה תיקרא ״יום״. והיו שישה, כי לה׳ הגדולה והגבורה.

It is unclear whether Ramban intends for the mystical understanding to supplant the simple interpretation that *yom* is a unit of time or for the mystical interpretation to complement the simple understanding. (In other words, could Ramban also agree there have been more than 5779 years since the creation of the universe?) The certainty of his first statement, and specifically the word ודע, seems to indicate that the latter option is correct. The Kabbalistic explanation adds an additional layer of meaning but is not intended to replace Ramban's initial interpretation that *yom* refers to the standard unit of time. However, R. Meir Triebitz in a personal correspondence to me argues in favor of the former interpretation, writing, "Ramban's understanding of the days as ספירות is his response to the Rambam. He was aware of the difficulty of resolving the creation of time with numbering days, namely how do I begin, and therefore interpreted it as ספירות. Ramban, in my opinion, agrees with the Rambam but offers an alternative Kabbalistic interpretation as he frequently does."

Regardless of Ramban's actual intent, R. Soloveitchik, as cited in footnote 26, argued that, both according to Rambam's reading as well as the Kabbalistic reading, the Torah is not making a claim about the age of the universe.

Why Rambam Accepts Creation Ex Nihilo

Elsewhere in *Moreh ha-Nevuchim*, Rambam returns to the question of literalism in the creation narrative when he addresses a fundamental question: was there true creation in the first place?

As we noted earlier, Rambam writes that the principal goal of his work is to show how to read Scripture in light of philosophy. This issue comes to the fore regarding creation. Aristotle rejected creation *ex nihilo* (out of nothing) in favor of the eternity of matter, meaning that matter always existed; it never was created. Seemingly, the text of the Torah, which describes creation, precludes such a possibility. Rambam, however, writes that he does not reject Aristotle's view on the basis of the text of *Bereishit*, since the text can be understood differently.[30] Indeed, Rambam writes, the verses that imply creation *ex nihilo* are no more numerous than those that imply that God has a body.

Nevertheless, Rambam rejects Aristotle's theory in favor of creation *ex nihilo*.[31] Why? Rambam presents two reasons. Firstly,

30. Consider Rashi's translation of the Torah's first verse: "At the beginning of the creation of heaven and earth, the earth was astonishing with emptiness, and darkness … and God said, 'Let there be light.'"

31. It is important to recognize that the debate about creation is not just one of science or history. It relates to the root of the nature of God's relationship with the world. Philosophers rejected creation because creation implies that God must have will (*ratzon*), that God "decided" to create the world. This notion presents a number of problems. Why would God all of a sudden decide to create the world? It is inconceivable that God created the world because He was in some way lacking prior to creation, for He is perfect. However, if He lacked nothing why create something? The notion of creation appears antithetical to God's perfection. If, however, the universe always existed, and God has nothing to do with it, then the existence of the world does not undermine God's perfection. This argument lies at the center of the argument favoring the eternity of matter, which denies not only the notion of creation, but also the possibility of miracles and prophecy, both of which ascribe *ratzon* to God and contradict His perfection.

    In addressing this query, Rambam stresses that it is impossible to truly understand the cause of something when one exists within that very thing. Imagine an adult who has never seen pregnancy or birth trying to look at himself and extrapolate how he was formed. That would be an impossible task. Even if he was told that he was once a tiny creature living in a sack where he did not eat and where he could not breath, he would reasonably conclude from the nature of his current existence the impossibility of that scenario. Likewise, our ability for us to deduce from within our universe the

Aristotle's view has not been proved definitively: "A mere argument in favor of a certain theory is not sufficient reason to reject the literal meaning of a biblical text." From here, we see the importance of distinguishing between things that are logically coherent but not proved and those that have been proved. Moreover, Rambam rebuffs the arguments in favor of the eternity of matter. [32] Rambam adds that while creation has also not been proved, it is the more compelling option from a scientific perspective.[33]

---

cause of our own existence is limited, especially when doing so demands the impossible – that we know the precise nature and thought process of God.

32. Rambam first responds to the arguments against creation and then argues in favor of creation. Kenneth Seeskin writes that Medieval Aristotelians offer two arguments for the eternity of matter. Firstly, they show that there is something inherent in the nature of the world that makes creation impossible. For example, change always proceeds from something to something else, such as when an acorn develops into a full grown oak tree. If this is true, it is impossible for something to come into being from nothing (*ex nihilo*). Rambam responds (2:17) that given the world as we know it, change does proceed from one thing to something else. But why would one assume the creation of the world had to follow the same pattern? The assumption that it did begs the question: did things always exist as they do now or were they made to be that way?

    The second Aristotelian contention is that there is something inherent in the nature of God that makes creation impossible. If God is perfect, He cannot do anything new, such as bring the world into being, as that would imply change, which itself would indicate that He previously was imperfect and in need of "improvement." Rambam replies (2:18) that for a perfect being, willing something new need not imply change or imperfection. Specifically, if the choice to do something in the future is made independent of external circumstances, it does not indicate imperfection. Moreover, the choice to undertake something new, to the degree that He had intended to do so all along, does not imply that He underwent a change. (Seeskin, Kenneth, "Maimonides", *Stanford Encyclopedia of Philosophy*)

33. Having rejected the arguments in favor of the eternity of matter, Rambam argues in favor of creation. He accepts Aristotle's claim (often used to disprove creation) that everything that is eternal is "necessary" (i.e., a particular thing must be the way it is and could not be otherwise). Since it can be shown that there are features of the universe that are not "necessary," it follows that the universe must have been created. An example of such a phenomenon (cited by Rambam 2:19) is the slowing of spherical motion as one moves closer to the earth (one would have expected the opposite, since the outer spheres are the source for the movement of the inner spheres). Likewise, Aristotle's theory cannot account for why some stars and planets emit more light than others (or why one planet is bigger than another, why one star is closer to the earth than another, etc.). Accordingly,

Secondly, Rambam argues, the basis of the Torah is conceivable only if we reject Aristotle. In other words, if Aristotle were correct, miracles and prophecy would be impossible.[34] Yet the Torah clearly accepts miracles and prophecies. To interpret the Torah figuratively, such that there are no miracles or prophecy, would be an absurdity. Thus, even Rambam agrees that there are limitations to figurative interpretations – certain things are decisive and cannot be reinterpreted.[35]

Rambam notes that Plato's theory, which allows for divine intervention and prophecy even as it denies creation, would not be rejected based on the second reason.[36] Thus, Plato's theory is rejected only because

---

it must be that the universe was created and that God had some unknown reason for the discrepancy in star brightness or distance. Otherwise, every detail of the universe must be logically explicable. As we shall see later in Chapter 32, Rambam writes that now that we have rejected Aristotle's theory on the eternity of matter, we can state that we do not know the reason for God's selection of the Jewish people.

34. Aristotle believed that the universe has its present form as the result of fixed and necessary laws and thus cannot be altered by supernatural forces. As noted earlier, philosophers maintained that the notion of ascribing will (*ratzon*) to God undermines His perfection, which demands that He remain forever unchanged. Just as He could not decide to create the world, He could not decide to change the world or communicate with a human being.

35. Note that Rambam maintains that we know certain philosophical matters, such as the erroneousness of Aristotle's theory, based on Torah. The implication of Rambam's presentation is that the second reason alone is sufficient. Later (2:25), Rambam writes:

> כי אילו הוכח החידוש, ואפילו לפי השקפת אפלטון, היה נופל כל מה שהעזו בו הפילוסופים נגדנו וכן אילו נתקיימה להם הוכחה על הקדמות כפי השקפת אריסטו, היתה נופלת כל התורה ויעבור הדבר להשקפות אחרות.
>
> For if the creation had been demonstrated by proof, even if only according to the Platonic hypothesis, all arguments of the philosophers against us would be of no avail. If, on the other hand, Aristotle had a proof for his theory, the whole teaching of Scripture would be rejected, and we would be forced to other opinions.

In the above quote, Rambam cryptically writes that if creation were proved, even according to the theory of Plato, all of the arguments of the philosophers against us would be void. This statement is perplexing given that Plato denied creation. What could Rambam mean that creation could be proved according to Plato? Perhaps Rambam means that if either creation or even Plato's theory were proved, all of the arguments of the philosophers against us would be void.

36. Rambam considers three approaches to the existence of the world: (i) creation *ex nihilo*, (ii) imposition of form on preexisting matter (Plato), and (iii) the eternity of matter or eternal emanation (Aristotle).

of the first reason (it has not been proved) and could be considered if it were proved,[37] while Aristotle's theory is rejected based on both reasons and thus is rejected entirely. Because of the importance of this text, let us present it in full:

מורה הנבוכים חלק ב פרק כה

דע, שאין בריחתנו מלסבור קדמות העולם מחמת הכתוב אשר נאמר בתורה שהעולם מחודש, לפי שאין הכתובים המורים על חידוש העולם, יותר מן הכתובים המורים על היות האלוה גוף. וגם אין דרכי הביאור נעולים בפנינו ולא נמנעים ממנו בעניין חידוש העולם. אלא יכולים היינו לבאר אותם כדרך שעשינו בשלילת הגשמות, ויתכן שזה היה יותר קל בהרבה, והייתה לנו יכולת רבה לבאר אותם הכתובים ונקיים קדמות העולם, כדרך שביארנו הכתובים[38] ושללנו היותו יתעלה גוף.

ואשר הביא אותנו שלא נעשה כן ולא נסבור כן הם שתי סיבות:

האחת כי זה שאין האלוה גוף - הוכח, וחובה בהחלט לבאר כל מה שפשטו נגד ההוכחה ויוודע שיש לו ביאור בהחלט. וקדמות העולם לא הוכחה, ולכן אין ראוי לדחות את הכתובים ולבארם למען הכרעת השקפה אשר אפשר להכריע הפכה בסוגי הכרעה רבים. זוהי סיבה אחת.

והסיבה השניה כי סברתנו שאין האלוה גוף, אינו סותר לנו מאומה מיסודות התורה, ואינו מכחיש דברי שום נביא, ואין בו אלא מה שמדמים הסכלים שיש בכך נגד הכתוב ואינו נגדו כמו שביארנו, אלא הוא כוונת הכתוב. אבל סברת הקדמות כפי האופן הנראה לאריסטו, שהוא על דרך החיוב, ולא ישתנה טבע כלל ואין דבר יוצא ממנהגו, הרי זה סותר את התורה מעיקרה, ומכחיש את כל הניסים בהחלט, ומבטל כל התקוות שהבטיחה בהן התורה או הפחידה מהן .אלא אם כן נבאר גם את הניסים כדרך שעשו בעלי הסוד המוסלמים, ותהיה התוצאה סוג מן ההזיות.

37. Were that to happen, we would adopt a non-literal reading of *Bereishit*.

38. See *Hilchot Yesodei ha-Torah* 3:4:

כל הגלגלים האלו המקיפין את העולם הן עיגולים ככדור והארץ תלויה באמצע, ויש למקצת מן הכוכבים גלגלים קטנים שהן קבועים בהן ואין אותם הגלגלים מקיפין את הארץ אלא גלגל קטן שאינו מקיף קבוע בגלגל הגדול המקיף. ובהלכות קידוש החודש פי"ד הל' א "הירח עצמו מסבב בגלגל קטן שאינו מקיף את העולם כולו.... והגלגל הקטן עצמו מסבב בגלגל גדול המקיף את העולם.

אבל אם יסבור אדם את הקדמות לפי ההשקפה השניה אשר ביארנו, והיא השקפת אפלטון, והיא שגם השמים הווה נפסדות, הרי אין אותה ההשקפה סותרת יסודות הדת ולא ימשך ממנה הכחשת הניסים אלא אפשרותם, ואפשר לבאר את המקראות לפיה וימצאו לה דמויים רבים בפסוקי התורה וזולתה, שאפשר להתלות בהן ואף ללמוד מהן, אבל אין שום דוחק שיביא אותנו לכך, אלא אילו הוכחה אותה ההשקפה, אבל כיון שלא הוכחה, לא השקפה זו נטה אליה, ולא לאותה ההשקפה האחרת נפנה כלל, **אלא ניקח את המקראות כפשוטם, ונאמר כי התורה הודיעה לנו דבר אשר לא יגיע כוחנו להשגתו, והניסים מעידים על אמתת דברינו.**[39]

We do not reject the eternity of the universe because certain passages in Scripture confirm the creation; for such passages are no more numerous than those in which God is represented as a corporeal being; nor is it impossible or difficult to find for them a suitable interpretation. We might have explained them in the same manner as we did in respect to the incorporeality of God. We should perhaps have had an easier task in showing that the scriptural passages referred to are in harmony with the theory of the eternity of the universe [if we accepted it] than we had in explaining the anthropomorphisms in Scripture when we rejected the idea that God is corporeal.

For two reasons, however, we have not done so and have not accepted the eternity of the universe.

First, the incorporeality of God has been demonstrated by proof: those passages in Scripture that in their literal sense contain statements that can be refuted by proof must be interpreted otherwise. But the eternity of the universe has not been proved; a mere argument in favor of a certain theory is not sufficient reason for

39. Rambam tells us that there are concepts in the Torah that inform us of things we would not have known otherwise. Rambam does not merely show how Torah conforms to philosophy.

rejecting the literal meaning of a biblical text and explaining it figuratively when the opposite theory can be supported by an equally good argument.

Secondly, our belief in the incorporeality of God is not contrary to any of the fundamental principles of our religion; it is not contrary to the words of any prophet. Only ignorant people believe that it is contrary to the teaching of Scripture; but we have shown that this is not the case. On the contrary, Scripture teaches the incorporeality of God.

If we were to accept the eternity of the universe as taught by Aristotle, [namely,] that everything in the universe is the result of fixed laws, nature does not change, and that there is nothing supernatural, we should necessarily be in opposition to the foundation of our religion. We should disbelieve all miracles and signs and certainly reject all hopes and fears derived from Scripture, unless the miracles also are explained figuratively. The Allegorists amongst the Mohammedans have done this and thereby have arrived at absurd conclusions. If, however, we were to accept the eternity of the universe in accordance with the second of the theories that we have expounded above (Ch. 23) and assume, like Plato, that the heavens are likewise transient, we should not be in opposition to the fundamental principles of our religion; this theory does not imply the rejection of miracles, but, on the contrary, would admit them as possible. The scriptural text might have been explained accordingly, and many expressions might have been found in Scripture and in other writings that would confirm and support this theory. But there is no necessity for this expedient, so long as the theory has not been proved. As there is no proof sufficient to convince us, neither theory need be taken as absolute. [**Therefore,**] **we take the text of Scripture literally and say that it teaches us a truth that we cannot prove. And the miracles are evidence for the correctness of our view.**

Critique of Rambam's Deviation from Literalism

There are cases where Rambam is criticized for deviating from the simple reading of the text for philosophical reasons. One example is Rambam's interpretation (*Moreh ha-Nevuchim* 2:42) of the three angels who visit Avraham. Rambam maintains that angels, which are entirely non-physical creatures, cannot take on a physical form. Accordingly, it is impossible that Avraham "saw" them. Therefore, Rambam understands that the entire episode was a dream. In other words, Avraham dreamt he saw three people that turned out to be angels visit him. Ramban (*Bereishit* 18:1) strongly criticizes Rambam's interpretation, writing that "These words contradict the verses and it is prohibited to hear them, let alone to believe in them."

At first glance, this seems to reflect a fundamental debate about the role philosophy plays in the interpretation of Torah. Specifically, Rambam appears to be using philosophy to interpret Scripture non-literally, while Ramban rejects this methodology.

Upon consideration, though, the matter is not so simple. Firstly, Rambam is not suggesting a non-literal interpretation. His elucidation, while arguably forced, does not suggest that any words or phrases are meant figuratively.[40] Secondly, Ramban, in rejecting Rambam's understanding, focuses on textual problems. For example, when exactly does the vision end according to Rambam?[41] Ramban does not focus his critique on Rambam's overall approach to biblical elucidation. That is not to say that there is no fundamental dispute here (hence, the harshness of the critique). However, it relates more to the nature of

40. According to Rambam, the chapter begins with a general statement ("And God appeared to Avraham") followed by a detailed description (the encounter with the guests). Thus, Scripture first states that God appeared to Avraham in the form of a prophetic vision and then explains in what manner this vision took place, namely, that Avraham lifted up his eyes in the vision, "And behold, three men stood by him, and he said, 'If I have found favor in your eyes, etc.'". What follows is the account of Avraham's interactions with the guests in the prophetic vision.

41. Likewise, when Rambam suggests that Yaakov's wrestling with the angel took place in a prophetic vision, Ramban writes: "But if this is the case, I do not know why Yaakov limped on his thigh when he awoke! And why did Yaakov say, 'For I have seen an angel face to face, and [yet] my life has been preserved?'"

prophecy than to the conditions that justify a deviation from the literal interpretation.[42]

Thus, while it certainly is the case that Rambam's philosophical positions color his exegesis, as this case illustrates, his interpretations are rooted in a careful reading of the Torah's text. He certainly does not flippantly suggest non-literal interpretations; as noted earlier, "I fall back on interpreting a statement [non-literally] only when its plain meaning is impossible." Overall, then, Rambam's approach does not seem to differ fundamentally from that of R. Sa'adya Gaon.

3.4 CONTEMPORARY AND MEDIEVAL DEBATE CONCERNING ALLEGORICAL INTERPRETATIONS OF SCRIPTURE

Having seen how Rambam deals with the creation narrative, let us briefly note some of the historical background surrounding the question of when it is justified to deviate from a literal interpretation of the text. This question was one of the key issues in the medieval debate concerning the propriety of studying philosophy.

In 1.6, we mentioned Rashba's role in quieting the Maimonidean controversies by banning the study of Greek philosophy for anyone below age twenty-five. At the same time, a ban was declared against allegorical explanations of Scripture as well. What type of allegorical explanations were banned? Rashba cites some examples:

שו"ת הרשב"א חלק א סימן תטז

כי יאמרו על אברהם ושרה כי הוא חומר וצורה. ושנים עשר שבטי ישראל הם שנים עשר מזלות... ועוד אומרים המנאצים השם כי כלי הקדש המוקדשים האורים והתומים הם כלי האצטורלאב אשר יעשו להם אנשים... כי יאמרו מקצתם כי כל מה שיש מפרשת בראשי' עד מתן תורה הכל משל.

42. Thus, even Ramban must deal with the issue of how a non-physical angel can be seen. Ramban explains that these angels were clothed in a special "created glory" that can be perceived with normal eyes by elevated people – but, Ramban concludes, "I cannot explicate this." The expression "created glory" (*kavod nivra*) actually is used frequently by Rambam and derives from R. Sa'adya Gaon (though he may have meant something different than Ramban).

> They say about Avraham and Sarah that in reality, they symbolize matter and form, that the 12 tribes of Israel are [an allegory] for the 12 planets… [and] that the *Urim* and *Tumim* are to be understood as the astrolabe instrument… Some of them even say that everything in the Torah, from *Beresihit* to the giving of the law, is entirely allegorical.

Here, Rashba bans this sort of allegorical interpretation without offering guidelines for when non-literal interpretations are acceptable. Elsewhere, however, Rashba does offer some parameters. He stresses that it is tradition (תורה שבעל פה) more than anything else that guides us concerning whether we interpret something literally. Nevertheless, even Rashba agrees that conclusive evidence from science and philosophy plays a role in determining if a verse should be understood symbolically, provided such an interpretation does not contradict tradition or normative practice. Thus, his conclusion is very much in line with R. Sa'adya Gaon and Rambam.[43]

---

43. The context of this letter is the Talmud's statement (*Sanhedrin* 97a) that the world will be destroyed:

שו"ת הרשב"א חלק א סימן ט

ודע כי כל חכם מחכמי תורתנו החסידים כשיראה דברי הפלוסופים וישר בעיניו דרכם כשהוא מגיע אצל הכתובים המורים כהפכם פרש אותם בענין שיהיה נאות לחקירה הפילוסופית ומשים ענין המקראות משל. לפי שאין דוחק אותו ענין נבואי או מצוה. אבל כשהוא מגיע אצל חכמי ישראל יפרש המקראות כצורתן ואף על פי שהחכמה הפילוסופית סותרת אותם. כענין תחיית המתים שאין הכתובים מוכרחים בו הכרח נחתך ויש לפרש כל המקראות בדרך משל. כענין המקראות שבאו יותר מבוארים בענין מתי יחזקאל. ואלא שהכריחם הכרח הקבלה המפורסמת באומה. ובמקום הזה יודה שהקבלה תבטל החקירה הפילוסופית. **ואז תהיה לנו הוראה ממנו שאין משגיחין בחקירה כנגד הקבלה. לפי שחכמת השם למעלה מחקירתנו. וככה יקרה לנו מן הדין בכל דבר שיש קבלה ביד הזקנים והזקנות מעמנו.** ולא נסתיר קבלתם רק אחר הקיום שאינו באיפשר חלילה... **כי באמת הרבה כתובים דברו דרך משל אבל כשיהיה הדבר מקובל בידנו למה נבטל הקבלה ואף על פי שתחייב החקירה הפילוסופית ביטולה.** שכן תחייב ביטול קריעת ים סוף ומעמד הר סיני ושאר האותות והמופתים שנעשו לאבות במצרים ובמדבר. וכלל כל התורה שידבר השם עם האדם ויצוה על מניעת החזיר והנבלה והחרישה בשור ובחמור ויצוה על השחיטה מן הצואר וכלל כל המצות כי זה כלו מן הנמנע אצלם. **ועם כל זה אין אנו משגיחין בדבריהם כלל לדעתנו שהחקירה למטה מן**

The great Spanish rabbi, R. Yitzchak Arama (1420–1494),[44] attempts to sum up the divergent views by distinguishing between classes of people with regard to literal and non-literal interpretations (*Akeidat Yitzchak, Bamidbar* 79).[45] The first group (1) errs by interpreting the entire Torah literally. The second group (2) allows for non-literal interpretations, trusting its intellect that demands that certain verses be understood allegorically.[46] This latter group is further divided into (2a) those that are bound by the limits of the Torah's theology and (2b) those who deviate from literalism any time they fail

---

הנבואה באמת... ולא עוד אלא שאף מצד החקירה אין לנו לבטל דבר שחקירת חכם מן החכמים מחייב בטולו אם יש בידינו קבלה על קיומו. ולמה נסמוך על חקירת החכם ההוא ואולי חקירתו כוזבת מצד מיעוט ידיעתו בענין ההוא. ואולי אם יעמוד חכם ממנו יגלה סתירת דבריו וקיום מה שסתר וכמו שקרה לחכמים שקדמו לאפלטון עם אפלטון. ושקרה לאפלטון עם ארסטו תלמידו הבא אחריו ואמר שיש ריב לאמת עמו. ואיני אומר שנסמוך על הדין הזה להכזיב כל מה שיאמר כל חכם כי אילו אמרנו כן היה כסילות באמת. אך אני אומר במקום שיש מצוה או אפילו קבלה אין מדין האמת לבטל הקבלה מפני דברי החכם ההוא מן הצד הזה שאמרתי. ומכל מקום עוד תשאר השאלה במקומה שתשאלני ואנה היא הקבלה הזאת עד שנסמוך עליה להרחיק החקירה ודין השכל האנושי. **אם מצד הכתובים כבר הודינו שיש הרבה כתובים מדברים דרך משל באמת.**

44. R. Arama's approach to philosophy is complex. He frequently includes philosophical interpretations in his commentary to the Torah. At the same time, he was very wary of pursuing philosophy, as can be seen from his work *Chazut Kasha*.

45. As we have seen, Rambam in *Moreh ha-Nevuchim* as well as his commentary on the Mishna (in the Introduction to *Perek Cheilek*) offers a similar classification regarding Aggada, with some telling differences.

46. **עקידת יצחק במדבר שער עט**

הבאים להסתופף בדברי התורה האלהית נחלקו לשלש כתות:

1. האחד, הכת ההמונית המקבלת כל דבריה ככתבן, וחושבין כי מאמר ויתעצב על לבו, וירח ה׳, ויחר אף ה׳, ארדה נא ואראה...
2. והשני, כת בעלי החקירה המביאים כל הדברים האלה והדומים אל מצרף השכל והמחקר. אמנם, אנשי זאת הכת יחלקו לשנים:

a. מהם אנשי דעת ויראת ה׳ שיקבלו המשפט העיוני בכל מה שלא תהרס פינה מפינות התורה, ויפרשו דבריה באופן שיסכימו עימו, כמו שהיה הענין בכל מה שגזרו עליו דברה תורה כלשון בנ״א. אמנם בכל מה שהמשפט השכלי נגד דברי תורה, הנה הם יראים לנפשם, והן לא יאמינו לו ולא ישמעו לקולו, אבל יקיימו דברי התורה ויאמרו כי קצר השכל המשיג הענין ההוא, כמו שעשה הרב המורה לדרוש החדוש...

b. אמנם יש מהם עזי פנים שמטלין דברי תורה מפני הגזרה העיונית, כמו שעשו המכחישים שאינם בני ברית, וגם קצת המתפלספים מני עמנו.

to understand the text. Later, he calls those in the first category (2a) *tznu'im* (modest ones), because they recognize their intellectual limits. According to *Akeidat Yitzchak,* Rambam, by refusing to consider Aristotle's theory concerning the eternity of matter because it contradicts the Torah's tenets, falls into this class (2a). Class 2b errs because it has too much trust in its intellect. Rambam already alluded to this class when he wrote that there are those who interpret all miracles in the Torah allegorically so as not to contradict Aristotle's theory concerning the eternity of matter.

When the ideas of the Torah contradict our intellect, what must we do? *Akeidat Yitzchak* asserts that we must submit to the Torah. As Shlomo said: "I said, 'I shall become wise,' but [I realize that] it (wisdom) is far from me" (*Kohelet* 7:23).

Thus far we have focused upon limitations regarding allegorical interpretations of the non-legal sections of the Torah. For example, Rashba's objection to reading the stories of Avraham and Sarah non-literally or R. Sa'adya Gaon's objection to those who understand references to the resurrection figuratively. However, even more problematic is the suggestion that legal sections of the Torah should be viewed figuratively. (In Ch. 27 we deal with R. Shimon's position in *Sanhedrin* 71a that "there never was and there never will be [a *ben soreir u-moreh*].") For more than two thousand years various groups and individuals have used such techniques to limit the applicability of Halacha while purportedly maintaining their belief in the divinity of Torah. Accordingly, Rishonim also warn us of the dangers of allegorical interpretation of *mitzvot.* Dating back to the days of Philo of Alexandria (c. 20 BCE – 50 CE), there were those who understood the Torah's *mitzvot* non-literally. Initially, many of the debates between hellenized Jews and religious Jews, and later between Jews and Christians, revolved upon this issue. However, even after the dust of those disputes settled, the issue continue to resurface in the medieval period. The problem with this became urgent in the late 13th and early 14th centuries, especially in Languedoc where, Rashba believed, philosophic allegorists such as Levi b. Avraham b. Chaim of Villefranche-de-Conflent were causing great damage to Torah. Most concerning were scholars who offered reasons for *mitzvot* and then limited their application based on the reasons. Accordingly, thinkers such as ibn Ezra,[47] Rashba,[48] *Akeidat Yitzchak* (*ibid.*), and *Sefer ha-Ikkarim* (3:21) all warned against this trend. Some reformers in the modern era argued for a more allegorical interpretation of Halacha, and the issue continues to be explored in certain circles today concerning *mitzvot* that seem illiberal.

---

47. Ibn Ezra cites thinkers who offer figurative readings of *mitzvot* and responds that such interpretations are textually unwarranted. Regarding *Mishlei* the text states that it is a book of allegories, however, concerning the Torah we must presume a literal reading, unless compelled by reason:

אבן עזרא (הפירוש הארוך) שמות פרק יג פסוק ט

והיה לך יש חולקין על אבותינו הקדושים, שאמר כי לאות ולזכרון, על דרך כי לוית חן הם לראשך, וענקים לגרגרותיך (משלי א:ט), גם וקשרתם לאות על ידיך (דברים ו:ח) כמו קשרם על לוח לבך תמיד (משלי ו:כא), גם וכתבתם על מזוזות ביתך (דברים ו:ט), כמו כתבם על לוח לבך (משלי ג:ג). ומהו שיהיה לאות ולזכרון, שיהיה שגור בפיך, כי ביד חזקה הוציאך ה׳ ממצרים. ואין זה דרך נכונה, כי בתחלת הספר כתוב משלי שלמה, והנה כל מה שהזכיר הוא דרך משל, ואין כתוב בתורה שהוא דרך משל חלילה, רק הוא כמשמעו, על כן לא נוציאנו מיד פשוטו, כי בהיותו כמשמעו איננו מכחיש שקול הדעת, כמו ומלתם את ערלת לבבכם (דברים י:טז), שנצטרך לתקנו לפי הדעת.

This critique was leveled against Philo as well. While Philo argued that *mitzvot* must be observed, his philosophical reasons were used by many to obviate the need for practical observance. (This may be one reason why his writings remained popular among Christians but not among Jews.) We will return to this issue in Chapter 36.

48. **שו"ת הרשב"א חלק א סימן תיז**

...עד שאמר אחד מהם דורש ברבים בבית הכנסת כמתמיה מה ראה משה לאסור את החזיר. אם מחמת רוע איכותו החכמים לא מצאו בו רוע איכות כל כך. ואמר אחד מהם שאין הכוונה במצות התפילין להניחם על הראש ועל הזרוע ממש שאין החפץ בזה. רק שיבין ויזכור את השם שמקום התפילין הרמוזין בראש כנגד המוח ובזרוע כנגד הלב שהם כלי ההבנה והזכרון לרמוז שיבין ויזכור לא זולת זה. ומכאן מראין באצבע ששולחין אצבע ומדברין און בכל מצות התורה ופרקו העול מעליהן ואין להם חלק בפשטיהן. וכל איש ואשה הישר בעיניו יעשה. ורבן של אלו כתב כי מה שאמרו מ"ם וסמ"ך שבלוחות בנס היו עומדין אינו אפשר. שכל בעל גוף אי אפשר שיעמוד אלא תחבולה. וענין היה בפנים ומעמידן כזה וכזה אומרים אמור. וכל המחזיק בדברי חכמי ישראל נחשב בעיניהם כסוס כפרד וכחמור. על זה ידווה כל הדווים כי נטו קו תוהו על כל הקוים. ובאמת האנשים האלה אם רוח טועים זה בקרבם ועל זה נשאם לבם. באמת נאצו ה׳ כי יכפרו בתורת אלהינו שנתנה למשה בסיני. ושחתו לכל העם כי יוסיפו על חרון אף עברה וזעם. ויסף עוד להניחנו בגלותנו. ואפילו אחד כי הפושט ידו בזאת מאלה עליו הכתוב אומר כי דבר ה׳ בזה.

Contemporary Applications of Allegorical Interpretations

Returning to the question of allegorical interpretations of non-legal passages of Torah, the debate has resurfaced in contemporary times, especially with respect to questions of Torah and science. Applying the principles of R. Sa'adya and Rambam to questions like the theory of evolution is not always easy. R. Aharon Lichtenstein considers the boundaries:

> But surely we do hold that if, indeed at some point and at some level, faith and reason, *Torah u-Madda,* collide, then it is *Torah ha-ketuva ve-Hamesura,* text and tradition, which prevails. This is, of course, frankly illiberal... [regarding the] series of postulates of liberalism, the foremost being that there is no authority, moral or intellectual, higher than one's rational perception. That liberal position is one which I have said the Newman of the [eighteen] sixties rejected and, of course, so do we.[49]

However, once one has fully accepted the Torah's divine authority and absolute authenticity, the possibility of creative resolutions remains open.

> Confronted by evident contradiction, one would of course initially strive to ascertain whether it is apparent or real to determine, on the one hand, whether indeed the methodology of *Madda* does inevitably lead to a given conclusion and, on the other, whether the received content of Torah can be interpreted or reinterpreted so as to avert a collision.

R. Lichtenstein argues that this reinterpretation includes explaining certain texts as allegorical and even allowing for the contention that the biblical text "intended to convey a moral and spiritual, but not necessarily historical and scientific, truth." While he provides a framework, he does not flesh out the details.

---

49. *Torah u-Madda: Congruence, Confluence and Conflict-* a transcript of a lecture delivered by R. Lichtenstein in 1987 at Yeshiva University and published in a compendium of R. Lichtenstein's articles by Yeshivat Har Etzion, p. 6. This excerpt is cited in "Judaism and Darwinian Evolution," by Baruch Sterman, *Tradition,* Vol. 29, 1, 1994.

How far one is willing to go in this respect depends on two factors: (1) one's tolerance for non-literal interpretations and (2) the extent to which one feels the science that contradicts the simple interpretation of Scripture has been proved. As we saw in our discussion of Rambam, the more one is skeptical about the conclusions that "science" has reached, the less likely he is to reinterpret Scripture.

Not all thinkers are willing to go as far as R. Lichtenstein. Some, like R. Moshe Meiselman in *Torah, Chazal, and Science*, argue that deviating from literalism, at least with respect to issues like evolution, is not in keeping with Rambam's and R. Sa'adya's limitations given that the scientific evidence regarding evolution and the age of the universe is inconclusive. We reconsider both positions in 5.11–5.15 and again in 8.11–8.16 when dealing with contradictions between Torah and science.

The above discussion, which focuses on the role that the human intellect plays in interpreting the non-halachic portions of the Torah, serves as an introduction to Chapter 27, where we will consider the role *sevara*[50] plays in interpreting the legal and non-legal sections of the Torah.

50. The word *sevara,* which plays a major role in legal and ethical norms, defies precise translation. In modern Hebrew, *sevara* generally means conjecture, opinion, or supposition. In the Talmud, however, the term refers to something known to us through logic or reason, or, put more broadly, knowledge acquired through the intellect without proof from Scripture or tradition. However, it is by no means limited to rigorous syllogistic logic; rather, it reflects a human's capacity to use his or her intellect to determine that which is true and that which is right. Frequently, the term is used in contrast to *gemara,* which refers to transmitted knowledge (see *Eiruvin* 60a, *Yevamot* 25b, and *Bava Batra* 77a).

Chapter Four

Eilu ve-Eilu – Multiple Truths or Multiple Possibilities?

This book considers numerous debates relating to fundamental issues of religion. Thus, before continuing, it behooves us to consider how to view debate, especially in the realm of *machshava*.[1] (Not surprisingly, we will encounter debate in this matter as well.) Let us carefully consider the following Talmudic passage:

תלמוד בבלי מסכת עירובין דף יג עמוד ב
שלש שנים נחלקו בית שמאי ובית הלל, הללו אומרים הלכה כמותנו והללו אומרים הלכה כמותנו. יצאה בת קול ואמרה: אלו ואלו דברי אלהים חיים הן, והלכה כבית הלל.

1. In 5.7, we discuss the dispute between the Bavli and the Yerushalmi concerning whether *psak* is appropriate for Aggada. In that vein, we consider the nature and purpose of *psak*. We note that the debate concerning whether *psak* is appropriate may ultimately hinge upon how we relate to the various opinions within a debate, which is the topic of our current chapter.

> For three years, there was a dispute between *Beit Shammai* and *Beit Hillel*, the former asserting, "Halacha is in accordance with our views," and the latter contending, "Halacha is in accordance with our views." A *bat kol* (Heavenly voice) rang out, "These and these are the words of the living God, but Halacha is in accordance with the rulings of *Beit Hillel*."

There is a glaring difficulty with this passage. If the position of *Beit Shammai* reflects "the words of the living God," why does Halacha follow *Beit Hillel*? We will consider a number of approaches to this question.

4.1 THE FRENCH RABBIS AND MULTIPLE TRUTHS

The first is the view of the French Rabbis cited by Ritva:

ריטב"א שם

> שאלו רבני צרפת ז"ל היאך אפשר שיהו שניהם דברי אלהים חיים וזה אוסר וזה מתיר, ותירצו כי כשעלה משה למרום לקבל תורה הראו לו על כל דבר ודבר מ"ט פנים לאיסור ומ"ט פנים להיתר, ושאל להקב"ה על זה, ואמר שיהא זה מסור לחכמי ישראל שבכל דור ודור ויהיה הכרעה כמותם, ונכון הוא לפי הדרש ובדרך האמת יש טעם וסוד בדבר.

> The French rabbis (of blessed memory) asked: how is it possible that both positions could be the words of the living God when one prohibits and the other permits? They answered: When Moshe ascended to receive the Torah, it was demonstrated to him that every matter was subject to forty-nine lenient and forty-nine stringent approaches. When he queried about this, God responded that the scholars of each generation were given the authority to decide among these perspectives in order to establish normative Halacha. (This explanation is correct according to *drash*, but there is also a Kabbalistic secret alluded to here.)

According to the French Rabbis, God refused Moshe's request to resolve certain matters of Halacha. This does not mean that no concrete rulings were issued at Sinai. It does imply, though, that the matters debated in the Talmud, or at least the resolution to the disagreements concerning biblical law that were debated by *Beit Hillel* and *Beit Shammai*, were not given at Sinai.[2] This remarkable theory is based on the Talmud Yerushalmi's description of what happened at Sinai:

תלמוד ירושלמי מסכת סנהדרין פרק ד הלכה ב
אמר רבי ינאי אילו ניתנה התורה חתוכה לא היתה לרגל עמידה מה טעם וידבר יי׳ אל משה אמ׳ לפניו רבונו של עולם הודיעיני היאך היא ההלכ׳ אמר לו אחרי רבים להטות רבו המזכין זכו רבו המחייבין חייבו כדי שתהא התור׳ נדרשת מ״ט פנים טמא ומ״ט פנים טהור מיניין ודגל״ו.

R. Yanai said: Had the Torah been given in clear-cut decisions (*chatucha*),[3] there would be no leg to stand on....[4] Moshe said to

2. This can be understood in two ways: (a) A detailed revelation of the multiple permutations of Halacha i.e., God literally told Moshe all of the options. (b) R. Michael Rosensweig ("Personal Initiative and Creativity in Avodat Hashem," published in *Torah U-Madda Journal*, ed. Jacob J. Schacter, Vol. 1, 1989, pp. 79–83) suggests that the primary thrust of the Sinaitic *mesora* was a revelation of general principles, such that multiple conclusions could be drawn. Consider the following midrash:

   שמות רבה (וילנא) פרשה מא
   ד״א ויתן אל משה, אמר ר׳ אבהו כל מ׳ יום שעשה משה למעלה היה למד תורה ושוכח, א״ל רבון העולם יש לי מ׳ יום ואיני יודע דבר, מה עשה הקב״ה משהשלים מ׳ יום נתן לו הקב״ה את התורה מתנה שנאמר ויתן אל משה, וכי כל התורה למד משה, כתיב בתורה (איוב יא) ארוכה מארץ מדה ורחבה מני ים ולארבעים יום למדה משה? **אלא כללים למדהו הקב״ה למשה.**

   This perspective is developed by *Sefer ha-Ikkarim* and will be discussed in Chapter 28.
3. *Pnei Moshe* understands that the passage is noting the ambiguity with respect to Halacha (בפסק הלכה בלא נטיית דעת לכאן ולכאן). Ridvaz understands this as referring to the manner in which we read *pesukim*. A single correct way was not conclusively revealed even at Sinai but rather left to man to interpret.
4. *Pnei Moshe* explains that the eternality of Torah depends on the possibility of multiple interpretations both of which ultimately are true: "לא היה קיום לעולם דהתורה צריך שתהיה נדרשת פנים לכאן ולכאן כדלקמיה ואלו ואלו דברי אלהים חיים הן." He does not elaborate as to why לא היתה לרגל עמידה. Perhaps he means to say that there would be no room for *talmud Torah*, which of necessity involves creative use of the human intellect and therefore would not be possible without ambiguity. According to *Korban ha-Eida*, if the Torah had been given as a set of clear laws, we would be unable to use it to resolve new questions. The openness to interpretation and extrapolation allows for uncovering the conceptual basis for solving even modern questions: "כלומר, לא היה באפשר להתקיים בה דרוב פעמים הענין משתנה ואיננו כמו שמפורש בתורה." Thus,

> God, "Tell me the normative Halacha." God responded, "Follow the majority; if the majority acquits, then he is innocent, and if the majority convicts, then he is guilty," such that the Torah can be interpreted in forty-nine aspects of purity and forty-nine aspects of impurity...

The Talmud Yerushalmi records that Moshe was frustrated with the Torah's ambiguity. God responded that the ambiguity is essential insofar as it facilitates change and ensures the Torah's timeless relevance without undermining the Torah's eternality and underlying immutability. Moreover, should a debate arise with respect to the Torah's interpretation, there is a clear method of resolution – follow the majority.

According to the French Rabbis, then, both perspectives in a Talmudic debate are equally true in the sense that both emanate equally from the revelation at Sinai and are equally valid interpretations of the Torah. That Halacha follows one particular view reflects that a majority of human scholars understood that this view is correct.[5]

Support for this theory can be found in the Talmud's discussion of a debate whether preparatory acts for a circumcision on Shabbat are permitted if they could have been done before Shabbat. According to R. Eliezer, they are permitted under the general dispensation allowing Shabbat to be violated in order to carry out the circumcision on the eighth day. According to the *Chachamim*, though, doing so would constitute a full-fledged violation of Shabbat and, if done with intent and warning, would be punishable by execution. Halacha follows the opinion of the *Chachamim*, yet the Talmud (*Shabbat* 130a) relates that the inhabitants of R. Eliezer's town acted in accordance with his view and were rewarded for doing so:

---

the ambiguity within the Torah allows Torah to relate to the challenges of each and every generation.

5. While Rambam's view on this matter is quite complex, consider his formulation in his Introduction to his Commentary on the Mishna:
ועל הדרכים האלו נפלה המחלוקת, לא מפני שטעו בהלכות, ושהאחד אומר אמת והשני שקר.

א"ר יצחק עיר אחת היתה בא"י שהיו עושין כר"א והיו מתים בזמנן ולא עוד אלא שפעם אחת גזרה מלכות הרשעה גזרה על ישראל על המילה ועל אותה העיר לא גזרה.

> R. Yitzchak said: There was a city in Israel that followed the view of R. Eliezer and its residents died on time (i.e., they did not die early despite doing an act that according to Halacha should bring about early death). Additionally, there was once a decree by the evil kingdom banning Jews from circumcision, but the decree was not enacted upon that town (i.e., they were rewarded for their devotion to the *mitzva* of circumcision).

How could the inhabitants of R. Eliezer's town be rewarded for following the view that ultimately would be deemed incorrect? While we cannot blame them for following their teacher, one would have expected them to experience some sort of natural spiritual consequence for committing acts that constitute a violation of *Shabbat*.[6] According to the French Rabbis, the question is easily resolved; since the position they followed was equally true and valid, their behavior warrants reward. This concept may explain why minority views are recorded and studied.[7]

Moreover, R. Hershel Schachter (*be-Ikvei ha-Tzon,* pp. 258–9) maintains that numerous rules concerning the determination of Halacha support the French Rabbis' understanding. For example, one may follow a *da'at yachid* (minority opinion) in a time of exigency (*sha'at ha-dechak*)

6. As Ran (cited in 4.9) notes, this question reflects the prevailing approach concerning the ontological value of *mitzvot*.
7. Rishonim (*Eiduyot* 1:5) offer several explanations for this phenomenon. R. Shimshon of Sens (*Tosafot Shantz Eiduyot* 1:5) utilizes the French Rabbis' argument to explain why the Mishna records minority opinions:

   > Although the individual's claims were at first not accepted and many disagreed with him, in other times, many may come to agree with his reasons, and Halacha will follow them. The whole Torah was given to Moshe with aspects of purity and aspects of impurity, and when they asked him how long they should continue to debate, he said to them, "Follow the majority, but both are the words of the living God" (translation adapted from "The History of Halakhah, Views from Within: Three Medieval Approaches to Tradition and Controversy" by Moshe Halbertal, available at http:www.law.harvard.edu/programs/Gruss/halbert.html).

or in matters concerning the laws of *eiruv* or mourning. If one feels the minority position is wrong, then it does not make sense to follow such a position even under difficult circumstances. However, if the view fundamentally is correct, as the French Rabbis maintain, then it seems reasonable that under certain circumstances, that view can be normative.

4.2 OTHER UNDERSTANDINGS OF *EILU VE-EILU*

Others reject the notion of multiple truths. Surely, they argue, one view is "more true" than another. Objectively, something either is pure or impure, not both. If a food is not kosher, how can the fact that a majority of the court deems it kosher make it so?[8] As such, they reject the solution of the French Rabbis.[9] What, then, is meant by *eilu ve-eilu*? Numerous solutions are offered.

Chida 1 – The Dissenting View Helps Us Arrive at the Truth

R. Chaim Yosef David Azulai (1724–1806), known as Chida, understands that each view's truth is manifest insofar as it helps clarify the correct position.

> **פתח עינים מסכת עירובין דף יג עמוד ב**
> אלו ואלו דברי אלהים חיים, אין פירושו דשניהם אמת אלא להיות דאין האור ניכר אלא מתוך החשך, נמצא דהסברא המנגדת תועיל להבין היטב הסברא האמיתית בעצם, ומצד זה קרי בה נמי דברי אלהים חיים. ולעולם דסברא אחת אמת והסברא האחרת אינה אמת.
>
> "These and these are the words of the living God" does not mean that both are correct. Rather, [just as] the light is recognizable

8. As *Chavot Ya'ir* (192) puts it, "זה תמוה כי מה יועיל דבר שבאמת טמא."
9. How would these perspectives explain the normal lifespan and special protection experienced by the inhabitants of R. Eliezer's town? To be sure, they acted correctly by following R. Eliezer, but why were they not harmed by committing an act that objectively is defined as *chillul Shabbat*? Perhaps the reward (protection from the decree against circumcision) was for their exuberance in performing the *mitzva* of circumcision (exuberance deserves reward in its own right). Their long lives indicate that due to the purity of their motivation, they were *supernaturally* protected from natural spiritual harm that ordinarily would have befallen even unintentional violators of Shabbat. In 4.9 we shall see that Ran offers a similar sort of solution.

> only in darkness, [so too] the opposing opinion helps clarify the correct opinion. In that sense, it is called "the word of the living God." Ultimately, however, one opinion is true and the other is not.

According to this perspective, the Talmud's statement is not meant to be understood as saying that even though *Beit Shammai*'s view is the words of the living God (i.e., true), Halacha is in accordance with the rulings of *Beit Hillel*, as the French Rabbis would have it. Rather, *Beit Hillel*'s position is in fact the only true opinion.

The practical value of considering opposing positions, even if they are false, in order to find the truth is highlighted by R. Yaakov b. Yaakov Moshe Lorberbaum of Lissa (1760–1832). In his Introduction to *Netivot ha-Mishpat*, he asserts that there is considerable value in halachic debate, as it contributes to the process of *talmud Torah* (Torah study) by identifying misconceptions, refining authentic views, and honing and sensitizing halachic intuition.[10]

---

10. **הקדמה לספר נתיבות המשפט**

ואף גם זאת אם שהשגיאה והטעות שקר הוא בעצמותו, מ"מ תועלת יש בו לחכמים, ובביאור אמרו חז"ל [גיטין מ"ג ע"א] והמכשלה הזאת תחת ידך, אין אדם עומד על ד"ת אלא אם כן נכשל בו. והענין כי ידוע שהתורה נמשלה למים, וכאשר יפרש השוחה לצלול במים אדירים להעלות הפנינים ואבני יקר בעת השיבולת הולך וסוער, תכהין עיניו מראות, וקשה עליו להשיג ההבדל הדק שבינם ובין אבן החרסית המונח אצלם רשומין כמעט במראה זה לזה, ותחת הספיר מעלה חרס בידו, אולם אחר העלותו, אור עיניו אתו לסמן לעצמו היטב ההפרש שביניהם, עד שכשהוא צולל שוב פעם שנית אבן המטעה לא ימצא עוד, ואם נמצא מיטיב הוא לראות לדעת את הפנינים וכל יקר ראתה עיניו. הרי דליית הדברים המוטעים היה לעזר ולהועיל לבל יטעוהו עוד. הוא הדבר אשר המליצו חז"ל באמרם אי לאו דדלאי חספא לא משכחת מרגניתא תותיה וגם ע"ז יש קבלת שכר מהשמים.

Though halachic errors inherently are false, they nonetheless serve an important didactic function. Indeed, one cannot successfully establish halachic truth without some measure of initial failure. The early stages of halachic analysis resemble a diver who is not yet capable of distinguishing worthless stones from the treasure he wishes to retrieve. More often than not, he surfaces with the former rather than the latter. Once he has analyzed his error, though, he emerges with an enhanced capacity to discern. The very process of failure increases his sensitivity to the nuances that distinguish precious jewels from worthless stones, enhancing his future prospects for success. When he dives again, many of the worthless stones that initially were responsible for his confusion no longer

Chida 2 – There Is Truth to Both Opinions, but They Are Not Equally True

Chida then considers another option:

> נמצא דאלו ואלו דברי אלהים חיים, כי יסודות וטעמי שתי הסברות אמת, רק שבחילוף הנושאים ישתנה הדין.
>
> "These and these are the words of the living God" means that the principles and reasoning of both views are correct; however, depending on the circumstances, the law changes.

He seems to be saying that there is validity to the underlying logic of each view; in that sense, each is "the words of the living God." However, the incorrect view has not applied its logic correctly.[11] Along similar lines, Maharal notes that even if something is pure, it necessarily contains some element of impurity. The opposing opinion correctly picks up on this element, even if its application is incorrect.[12] There is truth to both opinions, though each opinion is not equally true.

Tosafot Rabbeinu Peretz and Dealing with Historical Realities

Another way to understand the meaning of the phrase, "These and these are the words of the living God," can be found in *Tosafot Rabbeinu Peretz*. After quoting the French Rabbis cited by Ritva, R. Peretz notes that this model is not valid for disputes concerning physical reality, such as the Talmudic dispute concerning the dimensions of the altar.

> are present, having already been discarded. Those that remain are unlikely to generate further confusion, inasmuch as the diver has learned to identify the differences between precious and worthless stones. Thus, his initial failure contributes to his ultimate success. As the Rabbis indicate, "If I had not lifted the potsherd, you would not have discovered the pearl underneath it." For this entire process there is a heavenly reward.

Translation adapted from "Elu Va-Elu Divre Elokim Hayyim: Halakhic Pluralism And Theories Of Controversy," by R. Michael Rosensweig, *Tradition* 26:3, 1992.

11. Likewise, see Rashi, *Ketubot* 57a (s.v. *ha ka-mashma lan*).

12. **ספר באר הגולה באר הראשון פרק ה**
שאף אם הדבר טמא, אי אפשר שלא יהיה לו צד בחינה אל טהרה של מה. וכן אם הדבר טהור, אי אפשר שלא יהיה לו בחינה מה של טומאה.

תוספות ר' פרץ עירובין יג עמוד ב

ומ"מ קשה ממעשים שכבר היו, כגון ממזבח דחד מוכח מקרא דהיה ששים וחד מוכח מקרא דהיה עשרים, והתם היכי שייך לומר אילו ואילו דברי אלהים חיים, דהא ליכא למימר הלך אחר רוב חכמי הדור, דהא לא היה אלא בחד ענינא.

וי"ל דגם כולהו לא היה אלא בחד ענינא, אלא חד מוכח מקרא דבדין הי' לו להיות הכי וחד מוכח מקרא דבדין היה לו להיות הכי, **והא דקאמר אילו ואילו דברי אלהים חיים, פי' דמתוך הפסוקים יש משמעות למידרש כמר וכמר, אבל ודאי לא היה אלא בענין אחד.**

This approach [of the French Rabbis] remains problematic concerning events that occurred; for example, concerning the altar, where one opinion proves from Scripture that it was 60 [cubits], and another opinion proves it was 20. How can we say concerning this, "These and these are the words of the living God"? We cannot simply follow the majority of Torah-scholars of the generation, since in reality, only one view corresponds to reality.

[Rather,] everything [only] was one way, but one adduces from a verse that it ought to have been thus, and one adduces from a verse that it ought to have been thus; and **the statement, "These and these are the words of the living God" means that from the verses, one can elicit either meaning. Certainly, however, in point of fact, the reality was only one way.**[13]

According to this view, *eilu ve-eilu* does not mean that both views are correct. Rather, it means that both positions are consistent with the text of the Torah.[14] This understanding is closer to that of the French Rabbis

13. Translation partially adapted from *Leaves of Faith: The World of Jewish Learning*, Vol. 1 by R. Aharon Lichtenstein, p. 67.
14. R. Yaakov Weinberg (*Rav Yaakov Weinberg Talks about Chinuch*) compares *eilu ve-eilu* to the equation $X^2=4$, where both 2 and -2 are correct answers insofar as the equation is accurate when X is replaced by both 2 and -2. Similarly, an interpretation of the Torah is true, on one level, if it explains the text and is consistent with the broader system.

insofar as it allows for both positions to be equally valid on a conceptual plane. In fact, it allows the expansion of the multiple-truth model of *eilu ve-eilu* to include even instances where the debate concerns a matter that relates to a historical reality.[15]

4.3 RAN AND HALACHIC AUTONOMY

Another approach to *eilu ve-eilu* is found in the writings of R. Nissim of Gerona (Ran). Ran (*Drashot ha-Ran, Drasha* 7) argues in favor of halachic autonomy manifest in the system's independence from divine interference. Accordingly, Ran understands the Yerushalmi cited above differently. When God informed Moshe of the options at Sinai and instructed him to choose, He was laying the groundwork for halachic autonomy – the notion that humans are supposed to interpret the Torah using their own feeble minds and follow the conclusion they see as correct. In the event of a dispute, we follow the majority.

The story of *tanur shel achnai*[16] and its climax, "*lo ba-shamayim hee*" (halachic matters are not decided in heaven) illustrate this point:

תלמוד בבלי מסכת בבא מציעא דף נט עמוד ב
תנא באותו היום השיב רבי אליעזר כל תשובות שבעולם ולא קיבלו הימנו אמר להם אם הלכה כמותי חרוב זה יוכיח נעקר חרוב ממקומו מאה אמה ואמרי לה ארבע מאות אמה אמרו לו אין מביאין ראיה מן החרוב חזר ואמר להם אם הלכה כמותי אמת המים יוכיחו חזרו אמת המים לאחוריהם אמרו לו אין מביאין ראיה מאמת המים חזר ואמר להם אם הלכה כמותי כותלי בית המדרש יוכיחו... חזר ואמר להם אם הלכה כמותי מן השמים יוכיחו יצאתה בת קול ואמרה מה לכם אצל ר״א שהלכה כמותו בכ״מ עמד רבי יהושע על רגליו ואמר (דברים ל:יב) לא בשמים היא מאי לא בשמים היא אמר רבי ירמיה שכבר נתנה תורה מהר סיני אין אנו משגיחין בבת קול שכבר כתבת בהר סיני בתורה (שמות כג:ב) אחרי רבים להטות אשכחיה רבי נתן לאליהו א״ל מאי עביד קוב״ה בההיא שעתא א״ל קא חייך ואמר נצחוני בני נצחוני בני...

15. See *Pachad Yitzchak* (*Letters,* 30) cited at the end of 7.6 concerning the Talmudic debate about the shape of the beams in the *mishkan.*

16. A specialized oven whose purity status was debated between the Sages and R. Eliezer.

> On that day, R. Eliezer brought forward every imaginable argument, but the Sages did not accept them. He said to them, "If Halacha accords with me, let this carob tree prove it!" Thereupon, the carob tree was torn a hundred cubits out of its place – others say it was four hundred cubits. "No proof can be brought from a carob tree," they retorted. Then he said to them, "If Halacha accords with me, let the stream of water prove it!" Thereupon, the stream of water flowed backwards. "No proof can be brought from a stream of water," they rejoined. Again he urged, "If Halacha accords with me, let the walls of the house of study prove it"... Again he said to them, "If Halacha accords with me, let it be proved from heaven!" Whereupon a heavenly voice (*bat kol*) cried out, "Why do you dispute with R. Eliezer? In all matters, Halacha is in accordance with him!" But R. Yehoshua arose and exclaimed, "It is not in heaven." What did he mean by this? R. Yirmiyah explained, "The Torah already has been given at Mount Sinai; we pay no attention to a heavenly voice, because You (i.e., God) already wrote in the Torah at Mount Sinai, 'Follow the majority opinion.'" R. Natan met Eliyahu and asked him, "What did God do at that time?" [Eliyahu responded,] "He laughed [with joy], saying, 'My sons have defeated Me, My sons have defeated Me.'"

According to Ran, the miracles and *bat kol* indicated that R. Eliezer was correct and had arrived at the truth. Nevertheless, God demands that the Torah be interpreted independently and that the majority position be followed. Presumably, the majority is more likely to arrive at the truth. But even if it does not, we still follow the majority:

> **דרשות הר"ן הדרוש השביעי**
> שמאחר שהכרעת התורה נמסרה להם בחייהם, ושכלם היה מחייב לטמא, היה מן הראוי שיהיה טמא **אע"פ שהוא הפך מן האמת, שכן מחייב השכל האנושי.** והשאר, אע"פ שאומרים אמת, אין ראויין לעשות מעשה כן בדרכי התורה, כמו שלא טהרו בעל מחלוקתו של רבי אליעזר, אע"פ שניתנה עליהם בת קול מן השמים שהלכה כדבריו.[17]

---

17. Another formulation of this concept is offered by R. Aryeh Leib Heller-Kahane (1745–1812):

> Since the interpretation of the Torah is in their jurisdiction, and their intellects understood that it is impure (*tamei*), it is appropriate that it be deemed *tamei* **even though this is the opposite of truth, because this is what their intellect dictated**. The other view, even though it is true, should not be followed in matters of Torah, just as they did not follow the view of R. Eliezer despite the *bat kol* (heavenly voice) that Halacha follows him.

Some reformers have understood this Talmudic passage and Ran's interpretation thereof as indicating that the Jews' task is to come up with the rules of Halacha and morality on their own. Should their conclusions contradict God's revealed will, they should still accept their own conclusion. Honest consideration of the above sources reveals the falsity of such a derivation. The Sages, along with R. Eliezer, were trying their best to interpret honestly the true intent of the Torah, which is God's words. The majority position understood that R. Eliezer's view contradicted the Torah's intent. They were not claiming one can reject God's words; they were simply playing by God's rules, which demand that we look to the Torah (and not heavenly voices) to determine God's intent.

Ran's theory that Halacha may not accord with the truth prompts a different question: Why are we not concerned with the harmful spiritual consequences that may result from rabbinic error? We will consider this question in 4.9

According to Ran, in what way is the incorrect view the word of God? Ran answers that it is the word of God insofar as God commanded that we follow that view if that is the approach the majority takes. Ran understands that the Torah was given with rules of interpretation. Specifically, it must be interpreted using the intellect, not through prophecy or other divine communication. Therefore, if our intellect indicates that a particular view is correct, then God Himself has told us to follow that

---

הקדמה לספר קצות-החושן

...דידוע דשכל האדם ילאה להשיג האמת בהיות בארץ שרשו, ולזה אמרו [=המלאכים לקב"ה] אתה מבזה תכשיט שלך, כיוון שעיקר הבריאה עבור התורה, והאדם בשכלו האנושי מהנמנע להשיג האמת האמיתי... והיינו 'פיה פתחה בחכמה ותורת חסד על לשונה', משום דתורה שבעל פה ניתנה כפי הכרעת החכמים, אף על פי שאינו אמת, ונקרא תורת חסד.

view, and as such, it reflects the word of God. If we follow the heavenly truth and ignore our own understanding, then we our ignoring the Torah's dictates and contravening the divine will:

דרשות הר"ן הדרוש החמישי
וזה הענין צריך עיון, איך נאמר ששני כתות המחלוקות נאמרו מפי הגבורה, הנה ר' אליעזר ור' יהושע נחלקו, והאחד השיג האמת והשני לא השיגו, ואיך נאמר שיצא מפי הגבורה דבר שאינו אמיתי.

אבל הענין כך הוא, שכבר ידוע שכל התורה שבכתב ושבעל פה נמסרה למשה, כמו שאמרו במגלה (יט ב) אמר ר' חייא בר אבא אמר ר' יוחנן מאי דכתיב (דברים ט:י) ועליהם ככל הדברים וגו' מלמד שהראהו הקב"ה למשה דקדוקי תורה ודקדוקי סופרים ומה שהסופרים עתידין לחדש ומאי ניהו מקרא מגלה. דקדוקי סופרים הם המחלוקות וחילוקי הסברות שבין חכמי ישראל, וכולן למדם משה מפי הגבורה, ומסר בו כלל אשר בו יודע האמת, והוא אחרי רבים להטות (שמות כג:ב), וכן לא תסור מן הדבר אשר יגידו לך (דברים יז:יא). וכשרבו המחלוקות בין החכמים, אם היה יחיד אצל רבים היו קובעים הלכה כדברי המרובים, ואם רבים אצל רבים או יחיד אצל יחיד, כפי הנראה לחכמי הדור ההוא. שכבר נמסרה להם ההכרעה, כאמרו (שם ט - יא) ובאת אל הכהנים הלוים ואל השופט אשר יהיה בימים ההם ודרשת והגידו לך את דבר המשפט, וכו' לא תסור. הרי שנתן רשות לחכמי הדורות להכריע במחלוקת החכמים כפי הנראה להם, ואפילו אם יהיו הקודמים מהם גדולים מהם ורבים מהם, שכן נצטוינו ללכת אחרי הסכמת חכמי הדורות שיסכימו לאמת או להפכו, וזה מבואר בהרבה מקומות.

This matter demands investigation. How could it be that both positions in a dispute were said by God? ... Only one could have arrived at the truth. If so, how can we claim a faulty position emanates from God?

Rather, the matter is to be explained as follows. It is a known fact that the entire Torah, written and oral, was transmitted to Moshe, as the Sages stated, "R. Chiya b. Abba said in the name of R. Yochanan: 'The verse: "And on them (the tablets) was

> written all the words…" teaches that the Holy One, blessed be He, showed Moshe the details prescribed by the Torah and by the Sages, including the innovations they would enact later. And what are those? The reading of the *megilla*'" (*Megilla* 19b). The "details prescribed by the Sages" are halachic disputes and conflicting views of the Sages of Israel. Moshe learned them all from God [without resolution of every controversy]. And [God] also gave him a [guiding] rule through which the truth would be known: "Follow the majority opinion" … as the Sages of that generation saw fit, for the decision had already been delegated to them, as it is written: "And you shall come to the *kohanim*, the *levi'im*, and to the judge that shall be in those days… You shall not deviate[…]." Thus, the Torah has given permission to the wise men of each generation to rule as they see fit in a dispute among the Sages…

R. Moshe Feinstein develops a similar approach in his Introduction to *Igrot Moshe*, where he argues that there is an objective, heavenly truth and a halachic, normative truth. The Torah tells us to follow the halachic truth even as we acknowledge it may not correspond to the objective, heavenly truth.

The above debate may relate to a discussion we will consider in 5.7 concerning the role of *psak* and whether or not *psak* is appropriate for Aggada. Presumably, according to the French Rabbis, *psak* is not about establishing the truth (since both views are equally true), but determining normative practice. Whereas, according to the second school of thought *psak* is the attempt to determine who is right. These two schools of thought would likewise disagree whether *psak* is relevant when there is no practical application to the debate, such as in matters of Aggada. The French Rabbis' understanding of *eilu ve-eilu* may concord with the perspective of the Bavli that *psak* is not relevant in matters of Aggada. There is no point in arriving at *psak* in matters of Aggada, since both positions are equally true. After all, *psak* is necessary in matters of Halacha only to determine normative practice; it should not be seen as the attempt to arrive at the truth, since both positions are equally true. On the other hand, Ran maintains that one position is in fact "more true" than the other. From Ran's perspective, it would make sense to decide matters of Aggada insofar as it allows us to arrive at the truth. This perspective may correspond to the view of the Yerushalmi that *psak* is relevant for non-halachic matters.

4.4 THE QUANTUM MODEL

An additional approach to *eilu ve-eilu* emerges from the Talmud's application of the principle to an actual event:

תלמוד בבלי מסכת גיטין דף ו עמוד ב
כתיב: (שופטים י״ט) ותזנה עליו פילגשו, רבי אביתר אמר: זבוב מצא לה, ר׳ יונתן אמר: נימא מצא לה, ואשכחיה ר׳ אביתר לאליהו, א״ל: מאי קא עביד הקב״ה? א״ל: עסיק בפילגש בגבעה, ומאי קאמר? אמר ליה: אביתר בני כך הוא אומר, יונתן בני כך הוא אומר, א״ל: ח״ו, ומי איכא ספיקא קמי שמיא? א״ל: אלו ואלו דברי אלהים חיים הן זבוב מצא ולא הקפיד, נימא מצא והקפיד...

The verse states: "And his concubine strayed from him,"[18] [What caused him to get angry at his concubine?] R. Evyatar said that he found a fly with her,[19] and R. Yonatan said that he found a hair on her.[20] R. Evyatar came across Eliyahu soon afterwards and said to him, "What is the Holy One, blessed be He, doing?" and he answered, "He is discussing the question of the concubine in Giva." "What does He say?" Eliyahu replied: "[He says], My son Evyatar says such-and-such, and my son Yonatan says such-and-such." R. Evyatar asked, "Can there possibly be uncertainty in the mind of God?" Eliyahu replied, "Both [answers] are the word of

18. This refers to the tragic episode of the concubine in Giva. A certain man became angry with his concubine because "She strayed from him," and she fled from his rage. The Talmud discusses what provoked his anger. The subsequent passage in the Talmud describes the terrible consequences that result from inappropriate anger of this sort.
19. He found a fly in his plate of food.
20. The Talmud later offers two interpretations of what this means. Either it refers to a hair that was found on his plate of food, or it refers to a pubic hair that she did not remove.

> the living God. He found a fly and excused it, and then he found a hair and did not excuse it."

In this remarkable passage, the Talmud tells us that in fact, both R. Evyatar and R. Yonatan were correct about the cause of an actual historical occurrence. Seemingly, *eilu ve-eilu* should not be relevant here. How, then, could Eliyahu apply *eilu ve-eilu*?[21] The answer lies in recognizing that there are two different aspects of what caused the man's anger. R. Evyatar had uncovered the initial cause of the man's anger, while R. Yonatan had discovered the straw that broke the camel's back.[22]

Applying *eilu ve-eilu* to a case like this is very revealing. In this case, each of the protagonists in the debate saw his perspective as being exclusively true. After all, they were debating a historical event – either it was a fly or it was a hair. Thus, R. Evyatar told Eliyahu that it is inconceivable that both views are correct. Eliyahu showed him, however, that both were true in a way that neither had imagined.

This perspective resembles the view of the French Rabbis in that seemingly incompatible options are equally true. However, it differs in the conceptual basis for the truth of each view. While the French Rabbis see the truth-value of each position as stemming from Sinai, despite the fact that in reality they are incompatible, this perspective argues that in fact they are compatible; we simply do not always understand how.[23]

---

21. Perhaps one could invoke R. Peretz's explanation here; however, it fails to explain how God Himself could proclaim both viewpoints. Moreover, R. Peretz's approach would not explain Eliyahu's response.
22. See Gra on *Mishlei* 10:12:

> שנאה תעורר מדנים כי אין דרך האדם לתקוטט מחמת דבר קל ומועט, אך נוטר הוא בלבבו, וכאשר יזדמן עוד דבר, אז תתעורר השנאה הישנה, עד שמתחיל להתקוטט עמו ומזכיר לו הדבר הקל.

The initial anger passed and "*lo hikpid*," but he harbored resentment still until he found the hair and he lost control.

23. While one could argue that this model is not relevant with respect to disputes in Halacha, the fact that the Talmud uses identical language – *eilu ve-eilu* – indicates that they may work in similar ways.

A similar application of *eilu ve-eilu* can be found in *Tosafot* concerning the Talmudic dispute about whether the world was created in the month of *Nissan* or *Tishrei*:

> **תוספות מסכת ראש השנה דף כז עמוד א**
> כמאן מצלינן זה היום תחלת מעשיך - כמאן - כרבי אליעזר... ומה שיסד ר"א הקליר בגשם דשמיני עצרת כר"א דאמר בתשרי נברא העולם ובשל פסח יסד כר' יהושע.
>
> אומר ר"ת דאלו ואלו דברי אלהים חיים ואיכא למימר דבתשרי עלה במחשבה לבראות ולא נברא עד ניסן.
>
> Whose view do we follow when we say on Rosh ha-Shana that "Today is the anniversary of Your creation [of the world]"? That of R. Eliezer, who maintains that the world was created in *Tishrei* (i.e., on Rosh ha-Shana)... [How do we explain] that R. Eliezer ha-Kalir presumed in *Tefilat Geshem* that the world was created in *Tishrei*, while in the prayer recited on Pesach, he followed the view of R. Yehoshua that the world was created in *Nissan*?
>
> R. Tam explained that these and these are the words of the living God, for we can say that in *Tishrei*, God decided to create the world, but He did not actually create it until *Nissan*...

Here, we have another debate about a physical event – when the world was created. *Tosafot* show that it is possible that both views are correct, depending upon how one defines creation. It is possible that those who debated the issue were not aware of this possible resolution and viewed each position as mutually exclusive, while in reality both are correct.

Perhaps we could apply the paradigm of *eilu ve-eilu* described above more broadly and suggest that, with respect to Talmudic debates, both opinions are correct, but from different perspectives. Like R. Evyatar and R. Yonatan, most of the time we are unable to understand the compatibility of both views. From our perspective, they are mutually exclusive –

they cannot both be correct. Even the protagonists of the debate did not see the correctness in their opponents' views. From God's perspective, though, both are fully and equally true, reflecting different perspectives.

R. Shlomo Wolbe (*Alei Shur,* Vol. 2, p. 520) elaborates upon this possibility by proposing an analogue to the notion of legitimate epistemological and ontological pluralism: the paradox of wave–particle duality. Elementary particles exhibit both wave-like and particle-like properties, even though there seems to be no complementarity between these two possibilities. From our perspective, the two options are mutually exclusive – a wave is not a particle and a particle is not a wave. And yet, both models are necessary to explain observed properties of quantum-scale. So too, when we invoke *eilu ve-eilu,* we mean that both possibilities are equally true, even though we cannot solve the paradox of their incompatibility.

To this, we can add another aspect of quantum physics: the essential role of the observer. Just as the properties of these quantum-scale objects differ based on the observer, so too Torah is understood differently, in ways that are equally true, depending on the observer. Science has shown us that, in a certain sense, there is no objective reality. We will elaborate upon this fascinating possibility shortly.

R. Kook and the Unification of Opposites

R. Kook embraces this notion in his theory of the unification of opposites. While two positions may appear oppositional, there is in fact a unity that can be realized with the discovery of "a hidden condition"[24]:

24. Likewise, consider the following remarkable passage.

אורות הקודש חלק א אות יא (ערך הניגודים)

כל הניגודים הנמצאים בהדעות, וכל אותה האפסיות שלפעמים נראה מחוג אחד על חברו, והניגודים הללו מתגדלים ביותר כל מה שהדעות תופסות מקום יותר גדול ברוח האדם, למסתכל פנימי מתראים הם בתואר ריחוקים מקומיים של שתילים, שהם משמשים לטובת רעננותם ושביעת יניקתם, **כדי שכל אחד ואחד יתפתח במילואו, ותהיה הסגולה המיוחדת של כל** והאחדות המתואמה **אחד מחוטבה בכל פרטיה, מה שהקירוב היה מטשטש ומקלקל הכל.** באה רק מתוך זה הריחוק, שרי בפירודא וסיים בחיבורא.

אגרות הראי"ה חלק א אגרת קי עמוד קלג
כעת מונח לפני מכתבו האחרון. ואתפלא, שעל מה שכתבתי בענין אחדות ההפכים, משיב כבודו עלי מהדבר הידוע שאין אפשרות לשני הפכים שיהיו בנושא אחד.

ותמיהני, וכי לזו אנו צריכים. **הלא עיקר הצד של חידוש שבדברי הוא, מה שמצד המחשבה העליונה, הסוקרת את עמקם של דברים, אין במציאות כלל הפכים, וכל מקום שיש הפכים יש שם בודאי איזה תנאי נעלם, שכשיתפרש נמצא ששני המשפטים, שנראו במבטא ובציור הפכים, שאחד מהם הוא בנוי על צד אחד מהמשפט והשני על צד אחר, ונמצא שע"י שני ההפכים יחדיו אנו רואים את המשפט משני צדדיו, ונמצא שאין כאן הפכים בדרך החלט, ומצדם אין כאן נושא אחד, כיון שהיחוסים של הנושא הם שונים.**

ובענין שאנו עסוקים, דהיינו מה שנוגע למצב הדעות, מתפשט זה המשפט על כל הרעיונות הרוחניים, וניגוד אמיתי לא נמצא כי אם במה שנוגע להעובדות ההיסטוריות שהנן מבונות בידיעתנו ע"י הקבלה והמסורת, שגם הן כל מה שהדעות הרוחניות מאירות יותר, נעשות הראשונות יותר מזוקקות ויותר קרובות אל הלב, עד שמגיע האדם גם בהן למדת המדרגה העליונה שבתמימות, אחר ההרחבה היותר בלתי-מוגבלת של חופש המחשבה, ודוקא על ידה.

Your most recent letter is presently before me.[25] I am amazed that your honor responded to what I wrote about the unity of opposites with the known fact that it is impossible for there to be two opposites in one subject.[26]

---

25. R. Kook is responding to R. Shmuel Alexandrov (b. 1865 and apparently murdered by the Germans when they arrived in his town of Bobruisk in 1941), who studied at the Volozhin yeshiva and was ordained as a rabbi yet saw himself as an enlightened freethinker and spent his life searching for a synthesis between these two aspects of his personality. R. Alexandrov rejected R. Kook's notion of uniting opposites, writing: "… this is all imaginary (the possibility of unifying opposites), because regarding absolute divinity, no thought can grasp Him at all, and aside from absolute divinity, there is no room for two opposites on one issue…"
26. The Law of Contradictions: Something cannot be hot and cold or good and bad, etc., simultaneously.

> I was astounded [with your words]. **The main innovation in my words is that from the aspect of higher thought, which scrutinizes the profundity of things, there are no opposites in reality, and whenever there are opposites, there also is some hidden condition that, when it becomes explicit, will show that the two propositions that appeared in an oppositional form and expression are constructed out of different aspects of a single proposition. Thus, through both propositions together, we see two aspects of a single proposition, and thus there are no absolute opposites, and from their aspect there is no one subject, since they have different relations to the subject.**
>
> Regarding the matter at hand, that is, pertaining to differing opinions, this rule extends to all spiritual ideas, and true opposition does not exist except regarding that which pertains to historical facts that we understand through received tradition. There, too, to the degree that the spiritual thoughts enlighten more, the primary ones become more refined and closer to the heart, until a person reaches through them the highest level of simplicity (*temimut*), after the most unlimited broadening of free thought and specifically by way of it.[27]

R. Kook writes that we can examine reality from two perspectives: ours and God's. From our own limited vantage point, certain conclusions are incompatible with others. However, God sees things differently. From His elevated perspective (מצד המחשבה העליונה), there is absolute unity. God perceives the deeper truer reality (עמקם של דברים), and from His perspective, there are no contradictions. When two positions seem to be opposites, there is in fact "some hidden condition" that resolves the apparent contradiction. This resembles the resolutions of Eliyahu (in *Gittin*) and R. Tam (concerning the creation

27. Translation adapted from Elli Fischer, etzion.org.il/en/lecture-13a-letter-44-sections-f-h-unity-opposites.

of the world). R. Kook concedes that concerning historical facts only one thing actually happened.[28]

R. Kook also alludes to the philosophical basis for his conclusion. When it comes to all spiritual ideas (כל הרעיונות הרוחניים), both views emanate from God's oneness, where there can be no contradiction.[29] When we look at the world, we perceive multiplicity – there are so many colors and so many sounds – but we know that they all stem from a single source. So too, the multiple voices within a debate, even when they seem incompatible, must reflect a deeper unity.

R. Dessler takes this one step further, arguing that when it comes to matters of Aggada, there is no true debate. Two views merely reflect two different perspectives. The perception of debate results from our incomplete picture:

מכתב מאליהו חלק ב עמוד רמה
...אולם כלל גדול הוא, כשחז"ל אומרים דעות שונות בעניני אגדה, הרי כולן מאירות אותו נושא מצדדים שונים מבחינות שונות, ואינם מחולקים.

When Chazal offer different approaches in aggadic matters, they simply are different perspectives on a single topic; it does not represent true debate.

---

28. See Rashi, *Ketubot* 57a (s.v. *ha ka-mashma lan*), who writes that when two Amora'im disagree concerning the law, each adducing his own reasoning, there is no falsehood involved – both are the words of the living God. However, when they disagree about what a particular scholar said, i.e., historical reality, then clearly only one view is correct. We will return to and elaborate upon this concept in 4.5, where we consider Maharal's understanding of *shemesh be-Giv'on dom* (*Yehoshua* 10).

29. As the Talmud (*Chagiga* 3b) states, the many opinions of a Torah debate are "All 'given from one shepherd.' One God gave them; one leader, i.e., Moshe, said them from the mouth of the Master of all creation, Blessed be He, as it is written: 'And God spoke all these words.'"
(כולם נתנו מרועה אחד אל אחד נתנן פרנס אחד אמרן מפי אדון כל המעשים ברוך הוא דכתיב [שמות כ:א] וידבר אלהים את כל הדברים האלה).

מכתב מאליהו חלק ג עמוד שנג

והנה מפורש בתיקוני זהר דבעניני אגדה וקבלה לא שייך מחלוקת, והביאור הוא כנ"ל, משום ששני המבטים אמת כל אחד בבחינתו, ואינו חלוק למעשה... ופירוש 'פליגי' בזה, שהוא מופרש וחלוק זה מזה.

It states explicitly in *Tikkunei Zohar* that in matters of Aggada and Kabbala, there is no true debate... Each perspective is true from one vantage point, and there is no practical distinction... The statement "they argue" means that they are different; it does not represent disagreement.

Following this model, we should not disdain debate, but rather should relish it, insofar as it provides us with a more comprehensive vision. This notion is expressed by *Aruch ha-Shulchan*.

הקדמת ערוך השולחן לחושן משפט

וכל מחלוקת התנאים והאמוראים והגאונים והפוסקים באמת למבין דבר לאשורו, דברי אלהים חיים המה, ולכולם יש פנים בהלכה. ואדרבא, זאת היא תפארת תורתנו הקדושה והטהורה, וכל התורה כולה נקראת שירה, ותפארת השיר היא כשהקולות משונים זה מזה, וזהו עיקר הנעימות. ומי שמשוטט בים התלמוד יראה נעימות משונות בכל הקולות המשונות זה מזה.

The debates of Tanna'im, Amora'im, Geonim, and *poskim* are all the words of living God. All of their views have merit from a halachic perspective. In fact, this diversity and range constitute the beauty and splendor of our holy Torah. The entire Torah is called a song, whose beauty derives from the interactive diversity of its voices and instruments. One who immerses himself in the sea of Talmud will experience the joy that results from such rich variety.

R. Kook uses this model to explain Chazal's statement that Torah scholars increase peace in the world. At first, this observation seems troubling, as Torah scholars debate incessantly, endlessly arguing over the minutiae of Halacha. R. Kook explains that we err when we see *machloket* as contradicting *shalom*. In fact, *shalom* demands *shleimut,* which can be achieved only when variant perspectives are considered. Ironically, it is healthy and respectful debate, not uniformity, that promotes true peace.[30]

The remainder of this chapter will be devoted to considering various implications of our discussion of *eilu ve-eilu.*

4.5 THE NATURE OF OMNIPOTENCE: IS GOD BOUND BY LOGIC?

The section that follows is somewhat out of place, but we include it here because our discussion concerning *eilu ve-eilu,* which considers the limitations of logic as well as our ability to independently arrive at the truth, sheds light on another vexing issue: the nature of omnipotence. Let us consider three perspectives concerning whether God is bound by logic.

God Is Bound by Logic

What does omnipotence mean? *Prima facie,* the term indicates that God can do anything. However, the matter is not so simple. Omnipotence cannot mean that God can do anything, because He cannot, for example, destroy Himself. This incapacity does not imply weakness;

---

30. **עולת ראי״ה חלק א עמוד של**

אמר ר׳ אלעזר תלמידי חכמים מרבים שלום בעולם, שנאמר ״וכל בניך לימודי ה׳ ורב שלום בניך,״ אל תקרי בניך אלא בוניך. יש טועים שחושבים, שהשלום העולמי לא ייבנה כי אם על ידי צביון אחד בדעות ותכונות, ואם כן כשרואים תלמידי חכמים חוקרים בחכמה ודעת תורה, ועל ידי המחקר מתרבים הצדדים והשיטות, חושבים שבזה הם גורמים למחלוקת והפך השלום. ובאמת אינו כן, כי השלום האמתי אי אפשר שיבוא לעולם כי-אם דוקא על ידי הערך של רבוי השלום. הרבוי של השלום הוא, שיתראו כל הצדדים וכל השיטות, ויתבררו איך כולם יש להם מקום, כל אחד לפי ערכו, מקומו וענינו. ואדרבא גם הענינים הנראים כמיותרים או כסותרים, יראו כשמתגלה אמתת החכמה לכל צדדיה, שרק על ידי קיבוץ כל החלקים וכל הפרטים, וכל הדעות הנראות שונות, וכל המקצעות החלוקים, דוקא על ידם יראה אור האמת והצדק, ודעת ד׳ יראתו ואהבתו, ואור תורת אמת. על-כן תלמידי חכמים מרבים שלום, כי במה שהם מרחיבים ומבארים ומילדים דברי חכמה חדשים, בפנים מפנים שונים, שיש בהם רבוי וחילוק ענינים, בזה הם מרבים שלום...

ורב שלום בניך, לא אמר גדול שלום בניך, שהיה מורה על ציור גוף אחד גדול, שאז היו הדברים מתאימים לאותו הרעיון המדומה, שהשלום הוא צריך דוקא לדברים אחדים ושיווי רעיונות, שזה באמת מגרע כח החכמה והרחבת הדעת, כי אור הדעת צריך לצאת לכל צדדיו, לכל הפנים של אורה שיש בו, אבל הרבוי הוא רב שלום בניך, אל תקרי בניך, אלא בוניך, כי הבנין יבנה מחלקים שונים, והאמת של אור העולם תבנה מצדדים שונים ומשיטות שונות, שאלו ואלו דברי אלהים חיים, מדרכי עבודה והדרכה וחנוך שונים, שכל אחד תופס מקומו וערכו. ואין לאבד כל כשרון ושלמות כי אם להרחיבו ולמצא לו מקום.

on the contrary, it speaks to His greatness. When we say that God is omnipotent (*kol yachol*), we mean that He can do anything that is theoretically possible. Perhaps this means that God can do only that which is logically possible.[31] Rambam makes this point explicitly in *Moreh ha-Nevuchim* 3:15:

> **We do not ascribe to God the power of doing what is impossible. No thinking man denies the truth of this maxim; only those who have no idea of logic ignore this maxim**... All philosophers consider it impossible for one substratum to have at the same moment two opposite properties... Likewise, it is impossible that God should produce a being like Himself, or annihilate, corporify, or change Himself. The power of God is not assumed to extend to any of these impossibilities.

While Rambam states God cannot violate logic, it would not be precise to state that He is limited by logic, since the inability to violate logic is in no way a limitation – it is an inherent impossibility.[32]

---

31. This definition might solve a problem regarding Ralbag's resolution to the question of the contradiction between free will and divine foreknowledge. Ralbag, as will be explained in 14.3, avers that God does not know in advance the outcome of our free decisions. Many are bothered by this statement. How can Ralbag claim that there is something God cannot do (i.e., know the future)? The answer is that it is impossible to know the future because it does not yet exist and is contingent upon factors such as free will that are as yet indeterminate. Thus, even though God is omnipotent and omniscient, He cannot do that which is logically impossible. If we conclude that free will is logically incompatible with foreknowledge, and we conclude that we have free will, then it necessarily is the case that God does not have foreknowledge with respect to the matters that are contingent upon our free will. He does have the power to know the future, and He may exercise it on occasion; in those instances, however, we will lack free will.
32. There is nothing that can be done that He cannot do. There is no external force that limits Him in any way. Rather, He is unable to do that which is inherently impossible. For example, something cannot exist and not exist simultaneously. Thus, to ask whether God can simultaneously exist and not exist is a meaningless question. To some degree, this whole discussion may be an issue of semantics, except that we shall see that there does seem to be disagreement about this point. Within Rambam's view, it may be worthwhile to distinguish between God's inability to contradict an

This concept is not limited to those typically classified as "rationalist thinkers." Consider the following statement of Rashba:

שו"ת הרשב"א חלק ד סימן רלד

ואצלי, שני חלקים בנמנע. האחד ההכרחי, וישר מצד עצמו, להיות צלע המרובע, גדול מאלכסנו. או מה שהיה, שלא היה, והרבה כיוצא בזה. וזה נמנע גמור, מצד עצמו, לא ישוער בו האפשרות. והשני, לא מצד עצמו, אלא מצדנו, וממניעת החכמה מצד הנמנע בטבע. שלא מצינו סלע מוציא מים, והים יקרע לשעה, וישוב לשעה, ושיעמדו השמש והירח לא יסבבו ולא יזוזו ממקומם, או ישוב השמש לאחרונית, והרבה כיוצא באלו. ותחיית המתים בכללם. ואמנם, אין כל זה נמנע אצלנו, אלא מצד מיעוט חכמת הנבראים כולם, ולאות כחם לשנות המוטבע בחותם הטבע. אבל בחוק הבורא יתברך, אינו נמנע אלא מחויב בחכמתו יתברך, שאין להתייחס לו כלום חסרון ולאות בכח חכמתו, שהוא וחכמתו אחד. ולא ידענו חכמתו, עד שנדע מהותו. ובזה יתקיימו כל הנסים שנעשו, ושעתידים להיות.

To me, there are two types of impossibilities. The first, which is inherently necessary and logical, includes such things as the side of a square exceeding its diagonal, or an event having both occurred and not occurred, and many other similar examples. These things are inherently, absolutely impossible and not conceivably possible. The second, however, is not inherently impossible, but is so from our perspective due to our limited wisdom. We have not seen a rock exude water, the sea temporarily split and subsequently return to its normal state, the sun and the moon remain stationary and cease orbiting, the sun regress in its path, and many other such things, including the resuscitation of the dead. [Yet] these things are impossible only from our perspective due to the limited wisdom of all creatures and their impotence with respect to altering the natural order, but for God, they are not impossible. Indeed, He certainly is able to do such things, for we may not ascribe any deficiency or lassitude to His strength

axiom (such as the law of contradictions) and something that contradicts structural logic (which is conceivable and therefore not necessarily true with respect to God).

> and wisdom, since He and His wisdom are one, and we cannot understand His wisdom until we understand His essence.[33]

Rashba seems to assume that the rules of logic (and geometry[34]) are necessarily true, not a result of God's creation.[35]

This theory prompts a number of questions. Who created these mathematical and logical laws? Is it not God? Assuming it was God, then why can't He break them? *Chazon Ish*, following Rashba, presumes that certain mathematical concepts are necessarily true. In *Emuna u-Bitachon* (missing section after 1:9), *Chazon Ish* writes that there are non-physical necessary truths (יש נמצאים שאין להם לא מידה ולא שטח והם נמצאים בחיוב ולא יצויר בהם העדר והן המושכלות). They are true because the alternative is impossible, not because they were created. He suggests that the basic laws of mathematics fall under this category (כמו ב׳ פעמים ב׳ הם ד׳, וכמו המושכל שהאלכסון עודף על האורך וכיוצא בהן מן המושכלות). He writes these will always be true and cannot be changed (אין עת למציאותן ולא נולדו מעולם ולא ימותו לעולם).

God Could Be Bound by Logic

There are a number of objections that one can raise concerning the notion that God is bound by logic. The first concerns the impossibility

---

33. Thus, according to Rambam and Rashba, God cannot create mathematical impossibilities such as a square whose side exceeds its diagonal. Likewise, Ralbag (*Yehoshua* 4:20) writes that God cannot create a triangle with an angular total other than 180 degrees. See "On Divine Omnipotence and its Limitations," by R. Yitzhak Grossman (*Ḥakirah, the Flatbush Journal of Jewish Law and Thought* Vol. 1) for an excellent article on this topic. The above translation is adapted from that article.
34. Understandably, Rashba was not taking into account non-Euclidean geometry when he said that God could not create a side of a square longer than its diagonal. While contemporary mathematicians may debate Rashba's specific example, his general point is clear and more relevant with respect to logic.
35. Along similar lines, *Avodat ha-Melech* argues that God cannot violate simple mathematics because God cannot do that which is false:

עבודת המלך הלכות תשובה ה:ה

...כאלו נאמר כי שתים פעמים אינו ארבעה במספר שהוא נמנע ואינו בחוק הבורא יתברך שמו (הנמנע הוא שקר ועי׳ תנא דבי אליהו זוטא פ״ג וילקוט האזינו).

of something outside of God (logic) limiting God. To appreciate why this is impossible, let us turn to the opening line of *Mishneh Torah*:

רמב"ם הלכות יסודי התורה פרק א הלכה א
יסוד היסודות ועמוד החכמות לידע שיש שם מצוי ראשון, **והוא ממציא כל נמצא**, וכל הנמצאים משמים וארץ ומה שביניהם לא נמצאו אלא מאמתת המצאו.

> The foundation of all foundations and the pillar of wisdom is to know that there is a Primary Being **Who brought into being all existence**. All the beings of the heavens, the earth, and what is between them came into existence only from the truth of His being.

Rambam writes here that God is the cause for all existence. How, then, can we account for the existence of mathematical or logical laws that seemingly inhibit Him? To this, we can respond that logic and math do not really exist – in other words, God created everything that exists, but the fact that 2+2=4 is not a reality that exists but a necessary truth (but not an existence), and thus, there is still no necessary existence besides Him.[36]

There is a second and far more potent objection to the assumption that God is somehow bound by logic. How can we be sure that the laws of logic actually are laws? After all, the laws of logic are not articulated in the Torah, but something human beings discovered. Moreover, how can we be so presumptuous as to imagine that we can know God sufficiently to claim He cannot violate the rules of logic? Recall from 2.3 that we can perceive God only insofar as He acts in this universe, but we cannot imagine what He can do outside of this universe. Thus, even though we never have encountered examples where 2+2 did not sum to 4, nor can we conceive of such a possibility, how can we presume God could not create such a possibility in a different

36. Interestingly, *Chazon Ish* does refer to mathematical laws as necessarily **existing** (אבל יש **נמצאים** שאין להם לא מידה ולא שטח והם **נמצאים בחיוב** ולא יצויר בהם העדר והן המושכלות, כמו ב׳ פעמים ב׳ הם ד׳). However, the difference between Rambam and *Chazon Ish* is likely semantic.

universe, since we are bound to our perception of God within our universe (or all universes that *we* can conceive of)?[37] Likewise, with respect to logic, even though we cannot imagine the possibility of something both existing and not existing at the same time, how can we be sure that a rule we invented using our own minds is necessarily true and applicable to God?

Perhaps Rambam, Rashba, and *Chazon Ish* mean to say as follows: Even if it were to be the case that God could not violate a particular logical or mathematical axiom, this would in no way imply a deficiency, because when we say God can do anything, we mean He can do anything theoretically possible. Thus, they are not taking a stand on whether or not God can create a triangle where the hypotenuse is longer than the sides, but rather are saying that even if it were the case that God cannot create such a triangle, it is not a contradiction to omnipotence. Rashba, in the aforementioned citation, may be alluding to this point when he concludes, "He and His wisdom are one, and we cannot understand His wisdom until we understand His essence." The simple reading of Rambam, Rashba, and *Chazon Ish*, however, does not lend itself to this explanation. It sounds like they are going further, declaring that God cannot do that which is logically impossible. What, then, is the basis of their assertion?

The answer, it would seem, is remarkable – we should trust our intellect and presume that what seems logically impossible is, in fact, impossible, and, as such, impossible even for God. There are several reasons why this makes sense. Firstly, if we question our logical conclusions, then we should also question the basis of our belief in God.[38] Moreover, once we believe in God, there is no reason to suspect that our minds

37. In fact, such occurrences may have even miraculously occurred in our world, as we shall see shortly when discussing the Talmud's (*Megilla* 10b) statement that the place that the ark (*aron*) occupied is not included in the measurements given for the Holy of Holies in which it was housed. This could mean the ark shrunk or the place it occupied expanded. Either way, it sounds like the laws of mathematics did not operate in the Holy of Holies.

38. See *Sefer ha-Ikkarim* 3:25. This point relates to some of the medieval polemics against Christianity, where Jewish thinkers appealed to logic and rebuffed the Christian thinkers' rejection of logic (e.g., 1 is 3).

(which were created by God) are fooling us.[39] Accordingly, we may suggest that since the laws of logic have been deduced (and universally accepted) using the intellect granted to us by God, we can see these laws as being taught to us by God (a form of quasi-revelation) and trust that He is not misleading us.[40] Just as we are meant to act based on our intellect (to determine that which is right or wrong[41] and to correctly interpret the Torah[42]), and in doing so trust that our intellect is not misguiding us, so

39. It is generally assumed that non-believers trust logic while believers are more suspicious of logical reasoning. Ironically, following our analysis, it is the believer who is less likely to question the correctness of their logical thinking.
40. God conveys His will to mankind in many ways. Prophecy is one. But wisdom, too, is a divine gift: "For God will give wisdom; from His mouth emanate knowledge and discernment" (*Mishlei* 2:6).
41. Numerous sources highlight man's ability to independently determine that which is right or wrong. To cite one example, Rambam writes in *Moreh ha-Nevuchim* 3:17: "He will reward the most pious for all their pure and upright actions, although no direct commandment was given to them through a prophet; and He will punish all the evil deeds of men, although they have not been prohibited by a prophet, if common sense warns against them." Thus, Sodom was destroyed because of her "pride, fullness of bread, and careless ease [that] was in her and in her daughters; she did not strengthen the hand of the poor and needy" (*Yechezkeil* 16:49). The people of Sodom were culpable because they eschewed kindness and generosity, favoring instead a philosophy of "What's mine is mine and what's yours is yours" (*Avot* 5:10). They were not blamed for violating any of the seven Noahide laws. R. Bachya b. Asher makes this point explicitly.

רבינו בחיי בראשית יח:כ

אבל נגמר דינם בעון שהיו מואסים את הצדקה ולא היו משגיחים על ענייהם ועל רעיהם... שהיו מוטלים ברעב... והנביא העיד כן באמרו: (יחזקאל טז:מט) "הנה זה היה עון סדום אחותך גאון שבעת לחם ושלות השקט היה לה ולבנותיה ויד עני ואביון לא החזיקה," וכתיב: (שם נ) "ותגבהנה ותעשנה תועבה לפני ואסיר אתהן כאשר ראיתי." ולפי שהיו תדירין בחטא הזה לכך נגמר גזר דינם עליו, שהרי אין לך אומה בעולם שלא יעשו צדקה אלו עם אלו, ואנשי סדום היו מואסים בה והיו אכזרים בתכלית, **ואע"פ שלא נתנה תורה עדיין, הנה הצדקה מן המצות המושכלות.**

Thus, in his Introduction to the Talmud, R. Nissim Gaon writes: "All *mitzvot* that depend on *sevara* and understanding of the heart are binding upon man from the day on which God created man and upon his progeny forever and ever."
42. Thus, the Talmud asks in three places: "Why do I need a biblical verse to teach me this idea? It is a *sevara*!" (*Bava Kama* 46b, *Ketubot* 22a, and *Nidda* 25a). R. Soloveitchik powerfully expresses the binding power of the intellect in *And From There You Shall Seek*: "What is the role of the intellect? The special importance that Halacha bestows upon reason is so salient that it symbolizes the entire character of the

too we may presume that the laws of logic are necessarily true. Thus, while we can never be absolutely sure that we are not erring (after all, certain rules of mathematics that were assumed to be inviolable have been shown to be false), we still may confidently presume that what seems logically impossible is, in fact, impossible.[43]

God Is Not Bound by Logic

Some thinkers appear to disagree with the view of Rambam, Rashba, and *Chazon Ish*. Let us begin with Maharal's revolutionary thesis. To appreciate his viewpoint, we explore the background of his statement – the stopping of the sun and moon's motion at Giv'on (*Yehoshua* 10:12–14). In responding to philosophers who minimize miracles, he notes that according to Aristotle, miracles are impossible. Thus, the Torah explicitly rejects Aristotelian science. Nevertheless, he acknowledges that there are Jewish scholars, such as Ralbag, that limit miracles based on their understanding of science. Maharal in his Second Introduction to *Gevurot Hashem* asserts that while these thinkers are motivated by a noble cause,[44] they err in their understanding of the sources. Maharal specifically protests Ralbag's insistence on the impossibility of the cessation of the sun and moon's motion at Giv'on and of the sun's retrogression in *II Melachim* 20:9–11.

In his commentaries on these verses, as well as in *Milchamot Hashem* (Book VI Part 2 Chapter 12), Ralbag rejects the possibility of miracles that affect the celestial domain.[45] Ralbag's conviction, rooted in his Aristotelian worldview, creates a serious problem with two biblical narratives that seem to describe just such changes.

---

halakhic approach. Intellect is the final arbiter in all matters of law and judgment" (p. 107). See this author's article "How are we to determine what God wants? Reason, Revelation, or Both" in *Ḥakirah*, Volume 18, Winter 2014, pp. 107–147. In Chapter 27, we expand upon this theme.

43. While Rashba in another *teshuva* (1:9, cited previously in 3.4) highlights the possibility of human intellectual error, he nevertheless maintains that the intellect should be trusted except when contradicted by revelation.

44. They believe that deviation from nature indicates a deficiency in God by implying that the initial laws of nature are flawed and need correction.

45. Ralbag acknowledges that God performs miracles on earth (the sub-lunar realm); he objects specifically to deviations in the celestial domain.

Ralbag creatively reinterprets these passages. For example, concerning the story of the sun's retrogression, he writes: "And it seems to me, because of all this, that this miracle was in the shadow, not in the sun itself."[46] In Chapter 3, we discussed whether scientific and philosophical objections of this sort justify this type of non-literal elucidation of Scripture. Either way, Maharal, like Rivash (Responsa 118) before him, condemns this interpretation, but in the process, he considers a remarkable possibility.

After rejecting Ralbag's reading, Maharal presents an original interpretation of these stories. Instead of simply understanding that the sun indeed stopped (an event that would have been witnessed by the whole world), Maharal suggests the sun stopped from the perspective of the Jewish people but not from the perspective of the rest of the world.[47] This seems logically impossible – how can the sun both move and stand still simultaneously? (Maharal is not referring to an optical illusion; the sun actually stopped and moved at the same time.) Maharal responds that God is not bound by logic. He does not, however, simply state that two contradictory occurrences happened simultaneously within the physical realm (a meaningless and incomprehensible statement); rather, he understands that the supernatural plane, which coexists with the natural plane, is not bound by physical limitations. Thus, in the supernatural realm, the sun can stop even as it continues to move in the natural realm.[48]

---

46. For an excellent article on Ralbag, see "The Scholar Rabbi Levi – A Study in Rationalistic Exegesis" by R. Yitzhak Grossman in *Ḥakirah*, Volume 12.

47. This would explain why these events, which should have been noticed by the entire world, are not recorded outside of the Torah, though this is not Maharal's motivation for postulating this remarkable thesis. However, some sources in Chazal presume that the entire world took note of these miracles. See, for example, *Avoda Zara* 25a and *Esther Rabba* 3.1:

> מראדך בלאדן עובד לחמה היה, והיה רגיל לאכל בשש שעות ולישן עד תשע שעות, ואותו היום שחזר גלגל חמה לאחוריו בימי חזקיהו ישן עד תשע שעות ועמד בארבע שעות, וכיון שנעור משנתו בקש להרג את כל עבדיו, אמר להם הנחתם אותי ישן כל היום וכל הלילה, אמרו לו, לא, אלא שגלגל חמה חזר לאחוריו. אמר להם וכי יש אלוה גדול מאלהי שיכול להחזירו. אמרו לו אלוהו של חזקיהו גדול מאלהיך.

48. **גבורות ה׳ הקדמה ב**

אמנם צריך עיון, אם נעשה נס זה לכל העולם או לא נעשה נס זה רק באופק ההוא כי יש לומר כי ליהושע ולישראל באופק ההוא היה עמידת השמש, ולכל העולם לא עמדה השמש,

This possibility sheds new light on the Talmud's understanding of the placement of the ark in the Temple:

> **תלמוד בבלי מסכת מגילה דף י עמוד ב**
> **ואמר רבי לוי: דבר זה מסורת בידינו מאבותינו: מקום ארון אינו מן המדה.**
>
> R. Levi said, "The following is a tradition we have from our fathers: the place that the ark (*aron*) occupied is not included in the measurement."[49]

וזה יותר פלא, מורה על גבורת השי"ת ונפלאותיו, ואם יאמר איך יתכן דבר זה בציור, כי תלך השמש ותעמוד בפעם אחת, שזהו בעצמו כמו שכתב ברלב"ג שהם שני הפכים בנושא אחד ולא יתקבצו יחד, כבר אמרנו שדבריו לא יצדקו בזה, כי אפשר ויכול להיות שתלך השמש מצד ענינה הנהוג, ותהיה עמידה לה מצד הנס, שיכול להיות לדבר אחד שני דברים הפכים מצד שני בחינות, והטבע דבר מיוחד ושלא בטבע דבר מיוחד, כי אין ספק כי מעלת הנס הבלתי טבעי הוא יותר במעלה ובמדריגה מן הטבע, **ומפני שהם שתי מדריגות מתחלפות, הנה היתה השמש בשני בחינות כפי חלוף המדרגות, תלך מצד הטבע, ותעמוד בצד בלתי טבעי, כי כשם שראוי שתלך מצד הטבע, כך יש בחינה שכלית שבאמצע השמים יש לה עמידה**, כמו שהתבאר, והוא בחינה שכלית, ואין זה טבעי, ולכך היה לה עמידה במדריגה בלתי טבעית. גם ליהושע ועמו שהיו צריכים אל הנס בלתי טבע היתה עומדת, ולשאר העולם אשר אין צריכים לנס היה להם מנהג הטבעי...

ואל יקשה לך, היאך דבר זה אפשר לצייר, שאם נאמר שעמדה השמש ליהושע בלבד, ולכל העולם הלכה, הנה שקעה לעולם מן האופק, וליהושע היתה השמש על האופק, ודבר זה איך אפשר. דבר זה לא קשיא, למי שמבין דברי חכמים ז"ל. כי זה היה ליהושע בענין נסיי מצד המדריגה הבלתי טבעית, שאין דבר זה ענין ושייכות אל הטבע, והיה לה עמידה על האופק מצד הבלתי טבעי, והשקיעה מצד הנהגת הטבע והנסים אין לדבר בהם ולעמוד עליהם מצד טבע, כי הם נסים יוצאים מטבע של עולם. והנה החכמים המדברים מצד הטבע הוא דבר הבאי, כי כלל הדברים כי מעשה נסים הוא, ואין לעמוד עליהם מצד הטבע....

The notion that God can simultaneously carry out opposites is not limited to physical reality:

אלשיך דברים ג:כג

מי א-ל בשמים ובארץ - ...וכן הוא פועל הפכים כאחד, רחמים ודין, מה שאין מלאך יכול...

49. The Talmud proves this from the fact that there were ten *amot* on each side surrounding the ark, yet the Holy of Holies was only twenty by twenty cubits. Rashi explains:

> It did not take up room to reduce the area of the open space on each of its sides. As it is stated: "It had around it an [empty] space of ten cubits on every side." It rested in the middle of the Holy of Holies, and there was a space of ten cubits between it and the walls on each side. And the entire chamber was only twenty by twenty cubits. Thus, it turns out that [the ark] took up no room whatsoever.

The Talmud shows that the same thing is true concerning the *keruvim*.

In other words, space is a constriction of the natural world; miraculous interventions take place within a different reality where space does not constrict.[50] Likewise, Chazal (*Avot* 5:5) state that in the *Beit ha-Mikdash*, the Jews would stand tightly cramped next to each other and yet had room to bow. This does not mean the area of the Temple miraculously expanded or the people miraculously shrank. Rather, when they bowed (an act of self-negation before God), they were not bound by space.[51] Seemingly, Maharal's thesis is at odds with the approach of Rambam, Rashba, and *Chazon Ish*. However, one could argue that this possibility does not violate logic. We will return to this shortly.

As we saw in 4.4, R. Kook frequently employs the notion that opposites can be true simultaneously. Elsewhere, he shows how our very existence depends on this notion and compares one who denies such a possibility to one suffering from intellectual color-blindness.[52] One chasidic leader, R. Gershon Chanoch Henech Leiner of Radzyn (1839–1891), argued that the notion is a fundamental principle of faith.[53]

---

50. The alternative explanations (that the *aron* shrank or the Holy of Holies expanded) seem less reasonable.

51. Likewise, on a supernatural plane, one is not bound by time. (For example, Rashi to *Shemot* 20:1 writes that at the giving of the Torah, all Ten Commandments were uttered at once.)

52. In "Letter 44," R. Kook addresses two perspectives that seem to be at odds. On one hand, "There is nothing but Him," which seems to negate our own existence and the existence of our world, yet it seems that we exist. R. Kook refers to this as the "matter of the *ayin*." He writes:

> It seems to me that there is no need for me to speak with you in detail about the wondrous matter of the *ayin*, and of the conundrum of the unity of opposites. All this derives from a casual look within and an unwavering [look] outward. **The exalted Jewish thought will not tolerate the disunity of opposites**, for how could it be possible for us to see in the entire sensible world that life and all ordered properties are built by the collection and harmonization of opposites – positive and negative, cold and heat, male and female – while the world of ideas is a wilderness, barren and desolate, decomposed and rotten, without connection and relation, only turmoil and confusion. They are certainly mistaken, those who think that there are no opposites and that everything is revealed in one color. This is intellectual color-blindness.

Translation from *Rav A.Y. Kook: Selected Letters*, translated by Tzvi Feldman (Ma'aleh Adumim, 1986).

53. In the next section, we consider whether Maharal would go as far as R. Gershon Chanoch Henech Leiner.

> צריך האדם להאמין באמונה שלימה... שאין שום דבר נמנע מהבורא, וגם דעת האדם היא תמיד ביד הש״י שכמו שאנו בשכל הזה ובידיעתנו והשגתנו הזאת שאי אפשר לשני הפכים בנושא אחד כן יכול לחדש לנו דיעה ושכל אחר והשגה אחרת ונבין ונדע בידיעה גמורה שאפשר להיות שני הפכים בנושא מאחר שהשגתנו ושכלנו וידיעתנו הם נבראים ונסדרים רצון הש״י מה שחלק לנו וסדר לנו ויכול לשנות ולהפך מהפך אל הפך וכמו שנבין עתה בבירור גמור ששנים הם יותר מאחד, כן יכול השם יתברך **להפוך שכלנו ודעתנו שנבין בבירור גמור שאחד הוא יותר משנים.**[54]

> A person must believe with complete faith... that nothing is impossible for God and that even the mind of man is in the hands of God. Just as we know using our minds that two opposites cannot simultaneously be true, God can instill within us a different manner of thinking such that we would be certain that two opposites can simultaneously coexist. This is true because our minds are created and orchestrated by God... Just as we are certain that two is greater than one, **God can change our minds such that we would be certain that one is greater than two.**[55]

54. Cited in the Introduction of שער האמונה ויסוד החסידות published by מכון להוצאת ספרי רבוה״ק מאיז׳ביצא ראדזין.

55. Interestingly, the Rishonim who support the notion that God cannot carry out a mathematical impossibility offer as an example God's inability to create triangles with angular totals other than 180 degrees. As R. Grossman notes in the aforementioned article, with the acceptance of Einstein's General Theory of Relativity, it has been shown that the actual geometry of the universe is not Euclidean. Thus, God does indeed create triangles with angular totals other than 180 degrees. More significantly, contemporary philosophers and mathematicians debate whether mathematics reflects any ontological reality. Formalists reject the perspective of Platonists, who claim that mathematics attempts to discover objective, preexisting truths.

Perhaps the Rishonim who maintain that God cannot violate mathematical norms presume mathematical Platonism. Those that argue that God is not bound by mathematical laws can do so because they adopt a Formalist perspective or because they believe a truly Platonist perspective is impossible because God is the cause of all that exists. The above text presumes the latter possibility.

Another revolutionary chasidic thinker to utilize this notion was R. Tzadok ha-Kohen Rabinowitz of Lublin (1823–1900).[56] R. Tzadok explains that the recognition that God is not bound by logic relates to the question of free will and foreknowledge. Even if these two concepts logically contradict each other, there is no reason to assume that God is bound by logic. In fact, this is how he understands Rambam's resolution of the contradiction[57]:

דברי סופרים ליקוטי אמרים ענין שמשון ד"ה ועוד

וזהו סוד הידיעה ובחירה שתירץ בו האריז"ל בסוף ספר ד' מאות שקל כסף דהידיעה במקום אחר והבחירה במקום אחר ע"ש לשונו וגם בסוף הזוהר חדש מזה ע"ש ובארנוהו במקום אחר דרצה לומר ממש תירוץ הרמב"ם שאין ידיעתנו כידיעתו, ולידיעת השם יתברך אין הבחירה מכחשת כלל אף על פי שהיא היפך הידיעה ואי אפשר לב' הפכים בנושא אחד זהו לגבינו אבל לגבי השם יתברך אפשר וכמ"ש בהקדמת ספר גבורות ד' בענין נס בשני הפכים יעו"ש.

This is the secret of foreknowledge and free will that the Arizal explained: foreknowledge exists on one plane, while freedom exists on another. This is Rambam's solution as well when he says that our knowledge is not like His knowledge, because with respect to God's knowledge, freedom is not contradictory to foreknowledge. This is true even though from our perspective, foreknowledge and free will are opposites, and opposites cannot coexist; this is true only from our perspective. From God's perspective, opposites can exist, as Maharal (cited earlier) explains.

To summarize, we have considered three perspectives concerning the interface between God and logic.

1. Rambam, Rashba, and *Chazon Ish* all maintain that God is bound by the rules of logic that humans discover.

56. Like R. Gershon Chanoch, R. Tzadok was a disciple of the Izbetzer Rebbe, R. Mordechai Yosef Leiner.

57. R. Tzadok, like many Kabbalistic thinkers, sees allusions to his theories in Rambam. In 14.2, we present the straightforward interpretation of Rambam.

2. It is conceivable that God is bound by logic (i.e., the notion would not contradict divine omnipotence), but we cannot be certain of any particular limitation, since (a) we cannot know the extent of His powers and thus cannot say what He cannot do, and (b) we cannot know with certainty that the laws of logic we discover are necessary truths (perhaps something we see as impossible is, in fact, possible).
3. Maharal argues that God is not bound by logic. This idea is developed by a number of chasidic thinkers, including the Radzyner, R. Tzadok, and R. Kook.

4.6 EPISTEMOLOGICAL PLURALISM

Perhaps contemporary physics allows us to conceive of Maharal's thesis in a way that previously was impossible. R. Soloveitchik alludes to this in the opening sentence of "The Halakhic Mind: An Essay on Jewish Tradition and Modern Thought,"[58] where he writes: "It would be difficult to distinguish any epoch in the history of philosophy more amenable to the meditating *homo religiosus* than that of today" (p. 3). What makes our epoch different? (One might have imagined that the ability of science to explain more and more of our universe would make our era less amenable to religion.) Because until recently, it was presumed that there is a single correct way of viewing the world; as such, "philosophy remained the satellite of science until the beginning of the twentieth century" (p. 6). This is because "Both [Aristotle and Newton] adopted a scientifically purified world as the subject matter of their studies" (p. 7), meaning that the universe was simple and orderly, leaving the scientist and philosopher to describe its mechanisms. Today, we no longer are bound by such a model. There is no longer a single, universal, correct model.

Dr. William Kolbrener (*Tradition* 30 (1996), pp. 21–43) summarizes this point as follows:

> The Newtonian philosopher... posited the existence of a universe which was rationally quantifiable and objectively given. The quantum physicist, by contrast, argued against... scientific

58. Written in 1944 but published only in 1986.

> objectivity.... Atomic and subatomic phenomena did not conform to the Newtonian's rationalist map... There was uncertainty... and even worse, quantum physics placed the ostensible objectivity of scientific observation in doubt.... There was no such thing as the innocent observer standing outside or above an ostensibly pure objective reality.... The scientist helped to create his experimental reality; there was no such thing as purely objective data.

Thus, quantum physics showed that:

a. There is no rationally ordered objective world.[59]
b. There is no methodological objectivity.[60]

Perhaps, in light of quantum physics, Maharal's theory (that from one perspective the sun moved while from another it did not) becomes more conceivable. The approaches of Maharal and R. Soloveitchik open the door to a whole new manner of resolving contradictions between Torah and science. We consider this more in 8.14.

59. One could argue that this is going a bit too far. While quantum mechanics does imply that we cannot predict the future perfectly because there is some element of randomness, it does not imply that there is no rationally ordered objective world. It would seem that R. Soloveitchik maintained that the very existence of randomness implies a fundamentally different perspective on the universe than the one posited by all thinkers prior to the twentieth century. While the randomness does not express itself significantly in the operation of the universe, which is highly predictable when dealing with phenomena above the quantum level, conceptually it overturns all previous models of physical reality. Moreover, the fact that relativity and quantum mechanics are fundamentally different theories that have different formulations leaves us with two genuinely incompatible descriptions of reality.

60. We do not need quantum physics to know that we are not objective. However, quantum physics demonstrated that "The human observer is not only necessary to observe the properties of an object, but is necessary even to define these properties" (Fritjof Capra, *The Tao of Physics*, p. 127). In fact, the role of the observer might reflect the lack of a unified, rationally ordered, objective world, since observers can themselves be observed, leading to paradoxes such as that of Wigner's friend. These sorts of questions stimulate the mind but are well beyond this author's field of expertise and are not essential to R. Soloveitchik's thesis.

One possible objection to this approach is that it overstates the extent to which modern physics overturned the notion of a rationally quantifiable and objectively given universe. Quantum physics, while in many ways counterintuitive, does not permit ontological contradictions. We consider this as well in 8.14.

Returning, for a moment, to the question of God and logic, we now can consider a somewhat more nuanced perspective. Initially, we understood Maharal as disagreeing with Rambam's assertion that only a fool would think that God can do the impossible. After all, the most basic rule of logic is what Aristotle called the Law of Contradictions, according to which something cannot be "A" and "not-A" simultaneously. For example, an object cannot be both solid and liquid (i.e., non-solid) at the same time. Maharal seems to indicate that this law does not limit God. However, the matter is not so simple. Maharal does not say that the sun both moved and did not move on the same plane. Rather, in a physical reality the sun continued to move, while in a spiritual reality it did not. Perhaps even Maharal would agree that at least theoretically, God cannot violate logic; however, he urges us to see things more broadly.[61] Or, as R. Soloveitchik put it:

> ... **Epistemological pluralism has not abandoned the realm of logic**. It says only that reason itself leads the physicist, psychologist, philosopher, and *homo religiousus* to a pluralism of viewpoints. The heterogeneity of knowledge, however, is not based upon a manifold of methods employed by theoreticians, but upon the plurality of the objective orders they encounter (pp. 55–6).

4.7 THE ROOT OF TALMUDIC DEBATE

In Chapter 28, we will consider how Talmudic debate arose in the context of the evolution of *Torah she-be'al peh*. In light of our discussion of *eilu ve-eilu*, let us consider the question of what causes some scholars to see things one way and others to see things a different way. Numerous approaches have been suggested.

---

61. If this is the case, Maharal does not go as far as R. Gershon Chanoch Henech Leiner cited in the previous section.

One midrash explains that the revelation at *Matan Torah* was a personal encounter with God, with each individual experiencing the event in a unique manner depending upon his spiritual level. Just as the manna in the desert tasted different to everyone, so too no two people experienced the giving of the Torah in an identical way.

פסיקתא דרב כהנא – פסקא יב אות כה

אנכי י״י אלהיך א״ר לוי נראה להם הקב״ה כאיקונין הזו שיש לה פנים מכל מקום אלף בני אדם מביטין בה והיא מבטת בכולם כך הקב״ה כשהיה מדבר כל אחד ואחד מישר׳ היה אומ׳ עמי הדבר מדבר אנכי י״י אלהיכם אין כת׳ כאן אלא אנכי י״י אלהיך.

א״ר יוסי בר׳ חנינא ולפי כוחן של כל אחד ואחד היה הדיבר מדבר עמו ואל תתמה על הדבר הזה שהיה המן יורד לישראל כל אחד ואחד היה טועמו לפי כוחו התינוקות לפי כוחן והבחורים לפי כוחן הזקנים לפי כוחן.

R. Levi said: The Holy One appeared to them as though He were a statue with faces on every side, with a thousand people looking at her and her looking at them all. So, too, when the Holy One spoke, each and every person in Israel could say, "The divine word is addressing me." Note that Scripture does not say, "I am Hashem, your (plural) God (אלהיכם)," but rather, "I am Hashem, your (singular) God (אלהיך)."

[Moreover,] **R. Yossi b. R. Hanina said: The divine word spoke to each and every person according to his particular power. And do not wonder at this, for when the manna came down for Israel, each and every person tasted it in keeping with his own power.**

While this source does not relate the individualistic Sinaitic experience to halachic debate, R. Shlomo Luria (1510–1573), known as Maharshal, utilizes this idea, employing mystical terminology, to explain the basis of *machloket*:

ים של שלמה הקדמה למסכת בבא קמא

וכל הנמצא בדברי חכמי התורה מימות משה רע״ה עד עתה. הן הן החכמים שאמר הוא עליהן (שם שם, י״א) דברים חכמים כדרבונות. כלם

> נתנו מרועה אחד. ושלא לתמוה על מחלוקתם בריחוק הדיעות, שזה מטמא וזה מטהר. זה אוסר וזה מתיר. זה פוסל וזה מכשיר. זה פוטר וזה מחייב. זה מרחק וזה מקרב. אם דעתם לשם שמים. והראשונים אפילו בבת קול לא היו משגיחים (ב"מ נ"ט ע"ב). וכולם דברי אלקים חיים, כאילו קיבל כל חד מפי הגבורה, ומפי משה... והמקובלים כתבו טעם לדבר, לפי שכל הנשמות היו בהר סיני, וקיבלו דרך מ"ט צינורות. והן שבעה פעמים שבעה, מזוקק שבעתיים. והן הקולות אשר שמעו וגם ראו. וכל ישראל רואים את הקולות הן הדיעות המתחלקות בצינור. כל אחד ראה דרך צינור שלו לפי השגתו. וקבל כפי כח (נשמת עליונו) [נשמתו העליונה], לרוב עילוייה. או פחיתותה, זה רחוק מזה. עד שאחד יגיע לטהור. והשני יגיע לקצה האחרון לטמא. והשלישי לאמצעות, רחוק מן הקצוות והכל אמת והבן.
>
> One should not be astonished by the range of debate and argumentation in matters of Halacha… All of these views are in the category of *divrei Elokim chaim* as if each was received directly from Sinai through Moshe. This is so despite the fact that Moshe never projected opposing perspectives with respect to any one issue. The Kabbalists explain that the basis for this is that each individual soul was present at Sinai and received the Torah by means of the forty-nine paths (*tzinorot*). Each perceived the Torah from his own perspective in accordance with his intellectual capacity as well as the stature and unique character of his particular soul. This accounts for the discrepancy in perception, inasmuch as one concludes that an object is *tamei* in the extreme, another perceives it to be absolutely *tahor*, and yet a third individual argues the ambivalent state of the object in question. All of these are true and sensible views. Thus, the wise men declared that in a debate between true scholars, all positions articulated represent a form of truth.[62]

This depiction brings us back to our discussion of *eilu ve-eilu*. According to Maharshal, Moshe received the Torah through all 49 *tzinorot*, while others received the Torah through fewer *tzinorot*. This does not mean

62. Translation adapted from "Elu Va-Elu Divre Elokim Hayyim: Halakhic Pluralism and Theories of Controversy," by R. Michael Rosensweig, *Tradition* 26:3, 1992.

that their perspectives were partially false (*miktzat sheker*), but rather that they were *emet she'eino gamur* (an incomplete version of the truth) in the sense that each person received only a partial picture, with only Moshe seeing the complete picture. The disputes of the Talmud emerge from the incomplete picture that each side has. With a total vision, we will be able to see the truth in each view.[63]

Without focusing on the differences in each person's inner soul (*shoresh ha-neshama*), Maharal writes that differences emerge from the fact that no two people are alike; therefore, no two people think the same way. People tend to understand things according to their own personal intellectual predilections. Accordingly, the complexity and multifaceted nature of the matters discussed in the Talmud is such that each person's personality will incline him to see a particular piece of the puzzle.[64]

ספר באר הגולה באר הראשון פרק ה

ואמר בעלי אסופות. פירוש, כי אי אפשר שיהיה דעת החכמים על דרך אחד, ואי אפשר שלא יהיה חלוק ביניהם כפי מה שהם מחולקים בשכלם. כי כל דבר ודבר, אי אפשר שלא יהיה בחינה יותר מאחת לדבר אחד. **שאף אם הדבר טמא, אי אפשר שלא יהיה לו צד בחינה אל טהרה של מה. וכן אם הדבר טהור, אי אפשר שלא יהיה לו בחינה מה של טומאה. ובני אדם מחולקים בשכל, ואי אפשר שיהיו כל שכל בני אדם על דרך אחד**, כמו שיתבאר. ולכך כל אחד ואחד מקבל **בחינה אחת כפי חלוק שכלם**. ועל זה קראם 'בעלי אסופות', רוצה לומר שיושבים אסופות ועוסקים בתורה, שאף שהם מחולקים בשכלם, מכל מקום הם מתאספים יחד. וכאשר הם מתאספים יש בהם כל הדעות המחולקות...

63. Based on this, Maharsha (R. Shmuel Eliezer Eidels, 1555–1631) derives the importance of studying Torah among disagreeing groups, because only the debate between discordant positions can lead to the recognition of the truth (*Chidushei Aggadot Chagiga* 3b).

64. In the example of the debate between R. Evyatar and R. Yonatan, we would say that some people naturally see causes in terms of their final cause, while others focus on initial causes.

רק לענין הלכה למעשה אין ספק שהאחד יותר עיקר מן השני. כמעשה ה', אף כי הדבר הוא מורכב, מכל מקום אין זה כמו זה, רק האחד יותר עיקר ... כולם נתנו מן השם יתברך, רק כי אחד מהם יותר עיקר, והוא מכריע, והוא הלכה. מכל מקום אל תאמר כי דבר שאינו עיקר אינו נחשב כלום, זה אינו, כי השומע כל הדעות הרי השיג הדבר כפי מה שיש לדבר בחינות מתחלפות, והרי למד תורה כפי מה שהוא הדבר, שיש לו בחינות מתחלפות. רק לענין הלכה אחד מכריע על השני.[65]

It is impossible for all scholars to understand things in a single, unified way... For even if something is impure, it is impossible that it not contain some element of purity. And so too the reverse. And likewise, it is impossible for the minds of all men to be identical; accordingly, each person understands things according to his own mind...

Yet as a matter of practical Halacha, there is no doubt that one element is more essential than the other... and Halacha corresponds to this element. Yet one should not say that the less essential element is worthless, because one who perceives all the elements of something understands it completely, from all of its different

---

65. R. Michael Rosensweig writes ("Personal Initiative and Creativity in Avodat Hashem" in *Torah U-Madda Journal*, ed. Jacob J. Schacter, Vol. I (1989), pp. 79–83):

> In essence then, what emerges from the Maharal once again, is the doctrine of multiple truths, significant especially outside the area of *pesak,* and related to individual intellect and the capacity of each individual to discern the complexity and subtlety which exists in every aspect of life. Still, how is it possible for there to be multiple truths, but only one *pesak?* The Maharal argues that while there may be multiple truths, all truths are not equal. Life is complex and everything created does obtain of more than one combination of different components. So, for example, it is possible for an object to possess a sense of *tum'ah,* but its sense of *taharah* overwhelms the *tum'ah.* The case of Bet Hillel and Bet Shammai, he argues, is one of those rare occurrences where absolute equality does apply, where the essences of both opinions appear to be of equal strength. But, in most situations, while *pesak halakhah* doesn't deny the *shitat yahid* and considers that it may be possible to rehabilitate it in a different context, there clearly is a decisive determination.

> perspectives, and he has studied Torah according to the thing's true reality. As a matter of Halacha, one overwhelms the other.

Perhaps we should not see this divergence as emerging simply from psychological differences. Some of the time, these differences emerge from an even deeper spiritual differentiation. Why is it, for example, that in the vast majority of cases, *Beit Shammai* rules stringently while *Beit Hillel* rules leniently? R. Shneur Zalman of Liadi (1745–1812) explains how each one's tendencies and perspectives stem from the root of his soul (*shoresh nishmatam*).[66]

Relating to Our Personal Subjectivity

Either way, what are the implications of Maharal's thesis that subconscious aspects of our persona predispose us to adopt a particular position in a complex matter? R. Yisrael Salanter suggests that we must acknowledge the powerful effect our personal makeup and interests have on our decision-making, including the way we view texts. Despite the inevitable effects of our subliminal dispositions, though, we must seek to interpret the Torah as objectively as possible:

> Even with all of this in mind (that Torah learning requires totally unbiased application of purely objective intellect), man, by virtue of being man, though he has the power and ability to flay his intellect so as not to be influenced by his *kochot ha-nefesh* (subliminal dispositions), to the extent that they become sleeping dreamers (dormant and inactive such that they do not break into his intellect

---

66. **אגרת הקדש יג**

בית שמאי ששרש נשמתם מבחינת שמאל העליון, ולכן היו דנין להחמיר תמיד בכל איסורי התורה, ובית הלל היו מבחינת ימין העליון, היו מלמדין זכות להקל ולהתיר איסורי בית שמאי שיהיו מותרים ויוכלו לעלות למעלה.

Stringencies reflect *gevura*. *Beit Shammai*'s soul was rooted in the Supernal "left" (שמאל העליון), while *Beit Hillel*, who derived from the Supernal "right" (ימין העליון), would find arguments for leniency in order to render permissible the things prohibited by *Beit Shammai*, so that these should become released from their prohibitive bonds and be able to ascend. [The word **אסור** means "bound" (i.e., to the *sitra achra*) and hence "prohibited." Its opposite (**מותר**) means "released" and hence "permitted" (adapted from *Lessons In Tanya*).] This idea may emerge from *Zohar* Vol. 3, 245a.

and cause it to err) – with all of this in mind, he is but a human, and his subliminal dispositions lie within him. He is unable to separate them from his intellect. For this reason, man does not have the power to arrive at [a form of] the true [absolute] intellect, totally severed and separated from the subliminal powers of the psyche. Yet the Torah was given to man to judge through following human intellect (in the purest form possible – see *Bechorot* 17b, which states that God says "Do," and He is pleased by whatever results one's efforts produce), and matters are to be clarified through amassing pieces of evidence and weighing them, and to whichever side the weight of the proofs fall, whether due to their quantity or quality, that is how the matter will stand.

[Now,] all human beings are of the same mind regarding [their appreciation of] the quantity of proofs [that may be brought for a position on an issue], provided they understand the proofs as they were intended. But regarding the process of weighing the facts, each human being's spirit differs one from another, and this very process is the one referred to as "*shikul ha-da'at*," the weighing [of facts] by the mind, in which the intellects of human beings differ greatly.

… [T]he cause for their disputes was in the different compositions of each one's *kochot ha-nefesh*, the subliminal dispositional forces of one's psyche [that compels his particular evaluation of things], which no human has the power to sever from his intellect (as mentioned above); and any investigator into the Torah of Hashem can depend upon his own perspective only once he makes all attempts to avoid subjectivism and to exercise his process of assessment while carefully restraining it from exceeding its limits and applying as pure and unbiased an intellect as is humanly possible.[67]

67. *Ohr Yisroel,* translation adapted from Zvi Miller; Feldheim Publishers (May 2005), pp. 44–46.

4.8 THE POSITIVE SIDE OF HAVING FORGOTTEN PARTS OF THE TORAH

In the previous section, we considered how a person's makeup affects the way in which he interprets the Torah. If we assume that Talmudic debate came about to some degree because we forgot certain laws and ideas, it turns out that this loss changed the character of the law by reshaping the Torah in such a way that it subsequently reflected the Sages' individuality.

Let us briefly elaborate. In Chapter 28, we will discuss the debate between Rambam and the Geonim as to whether Talmudic debate emerged as a result of the laws having been forgotten (Geonim[68]) or whether all debates relate to novel matters about which there was no tradition (Rambam[69]). At first glance, one would assume that according to the Geonic view, the existence of debate should be seen in entirely negative terms. After all, it is a result of forgetfulness. Had the law been more carefully preserved, debate would not have emerged, and we would have clarity as well as a pristine understanding of the Torah. However, in light of our previous discussion, one could make the opposite case as

68. This view is expressed by R. Abraham ibn Daud (sometimes known by the abbreviation Ra'avad I) in his *Sefer ha-Kabbala* as well as by R. Nissim Gaon in his *Maftei'ach le-Man'ulei ha-Talmud*. R. Abraham ibn Daud notes that an obvious objection to this approach can be raised: "It is because the rabbis differed on a number of issues that I doubt their words." To this, he responds that the "rabbis never differed with respect to a commandment in principle, but only with respect to its detail; for they had heard the principle from their teachers, but had not inquired as to its details, since they had not been *mishameish* (waited upon) their masters sufficiently." As a case in point, "They did not differ as to whether or not it is obligatory to light the Shabbat candles; what they did dispute was, 'With what it may be lighted and with what it may not be lighted?' Similarly, they did not differ as to whether we are required to recite the *Shema* evenings and mornings; what they differed on was, 'From when may the *Shema* be recited in the evenings?' and 'From when may the *Shema* be recited in the mornings?' This holds true for all of their discussions." (*Sefer ha-Kabbala*, pp. 3–4; translation and summary adapted from "The History of Halakhah, Views from Within: Three Medieval Approaches to Tradition and Controversy" by Moshe Halbertal available at http:www.law.harvard.edu/programs/Gruss/halbert.html.)

69. He elaborates on this view in his Introduction to his commentary on the Mishna. In *Mishneh Torah*, he puts it succinctly:

הלכות ממרים פרק א הלכה ג

דברי קבלה אין בהן מחלוקת לעולם, וכל דבר שתמצא בו מחלוקת בידוע שאינו קבלה ממשה רבינו.

well. While there is certainly a downside to this development (lack of clarity and lack of objectivity), there might also be an advantage, once we assume *eilu ve-eilu*: Debate allows one to perceive multiple correct perspectives. R. Yitzchak Hutner powerfully expressed this notion:

פחד יצחק חנוכה מאמר ג [ג–ד]

פעמים שביטולה של תורה זה הוא קיומה שנאמר אשר שברת יישר כוחך ששברת. מעשה שבירת הלוחות היא מעשה של קיום תורה על ידי ביטולה. והרי אמרו חכמים שאלמלא נשתברו הלוחות לא היתה תורה משתכחת מישראל (עירובין נד). נמצא, איפוא, כי שבירת הלוחות היה בה גם משום השכחת התורה. למדים אנו מכאן חידוש נפלא כי אפשר לה לתורה שתתרבה על ידי שכחת התורה עד כי באופן זה יתכן לקבל יישר כוח עבור השכחת התורה.

ופוק חזי מה שאמרו חכמים כי שלש מאות הלכות נשתכחו בימי אבלו של משה והחזירום עתניאל בן קנז בפלפולו. והרי דברי תורה הללו של פלפול החזרת ההלכות, הם הם דברי תורה שנתרבו רק על ידי שכחת התורה. ולא עוד אלא שכל ענין המחלוקת בהלכה אינו אלא מצד שכחת התורה, ואף על פי כן הלא כך אמרו חכמים אף על פי שהללו מטהרין והללו מטמאין הללו פוסלין והללו מכשירין הללו פוטרים והללו מחייבים וגו׳ אלו ואלו דברי אלקים חיים, ונמצא דכל החילוקי דעות וחילופי שיטות הם הגדלת התורה והאדרתה הנולדות דוקא בכוחה של שכחת התורה.

וחידוש עוד יותר גדול יוצא לנו מכאן, כי מרובה היא מדת הבלטת כוחה של תורה שבעל פה המתגלה במחלוקת הדעות, מאשר במקום הסכמת הדעות. כי הלא בהך דאלו ודאלו דברי אלוהים חיים כלול הוא היסוד כי גם השיטה הנידחית מהלכה דעת תורה היא, אם רק נאמרה לפי גדרי המשא ומתן של תורה שבעל פה. והיינו משום דתורה ניתנה על דעתם של חכמי התורה (לשונו של הרמב״ן, דברים יז, יא) ואם יעמדו למנין אחר כך ויכריעו כהדעה הנידחית, מכאן ואילך תשתנה ההלכה אליבא דאמת (יעוין אור ישראל, פרק ל, בהערה). ונמצא כי מחלוקתם של חכמי תורה מגלה את כוחה של תורה שבעל פה הרבה יותר מאשר הסכמתם. מלחמתה של תורה איננה אופן אחד בין האופנים של דברי תורה, אלא שמלחמתה של תורה היא יצירה חיובית של ערכי תורה חדשים, שאין למצוא דוגמתם בדרי תורה סתם.

Sometimes, the nullification of Torah is its very confirmation, as it is written, "the tablets that you (Moshe) have broken." [God said to Moshe], "May your strength increase because you have broken them." The act of breaking the tablets is an act of establishing the Torah through its nullification. Our Sages have said, "Were the tablets not broken, Torah would not have been forgotten in Israel" (*Eiruvin* 54a); we find, therefore, that the breaking of the tablets contains an aspect of forgetting the Torah. We learn from this an awesome and novel idea: it is possible for Torah to be increased through being forgotten, and it is possible to be blessed with increased strength because of the Torah having been forgotten!

Go out and see what our Sages have taught: three hundred laws were forgotten during the mourning period for Moshe, and Otniel b. Kenaz restored them with his logic and casuistry (i.e., through extrapolation from that which was not forgotten) (*Temura* 16a). And even more than that: every dispute in Halacha stems from the fact that Torah was forgotten, and our Sages nevertheless declared, "Even though these purify and those defile, these invalidate and those permit, these exempt and those obligate, these and those are the words of the living God." Hence, all different opinions and differing views contribute to the growth of Torah and its majesty, which emerge specifically from the power of forgetting Torah.

An even greater novelty emerges here. The power of the oral law is emphasized to a greater extent by disputes rather than by agreement, because "These and those are the words of the living God" includes the principle that even the rejected view in Halacha remains Torah knowledge as long as it was expressed as part of the give-and-take of the oral law. This is because Torah was given to be interpreted by the Sages, and if there will be a vote afterwards and the decision is in accordance with the rejected view, from then on Halacha will be different in truth. Thus, the disputes of the Sages reveal the strength of the oral law more than when they agree.

> The "battles" within Torah are not simply one of many possible ways of (acquiring) Torah, but rather the positive creation of new Torah concepts that cannot be found in the words of Torah… And the two sides that clash in Halacha become partners in the creation of a new Torah concept whose name is "the battle of Torah."[70]

Forgetting the Halacha precipitated the need to consider the law from an intellectual perspective (as opposed to simply accepting the revealed truth), and this necessarily introduces a human component into the divine law. This too can be seen positively, as we have seen.

What emerges, then, is that our Torah, which contains the written and oral law, is rooted in revelation but guided by reason; it is a partnership between God and man. The idea of "These and those are the words of the living God" implies that even as all of Torah is rooted in revelation,[71] God nevertheless makes us partners in the shaping of His law (just as He made us partners in completing His world). Remarkably, this partnership was triggered by forgetfulness.

R. Soloveitchik powerfully expresses the magnitude of this partnership in Chapter 15 of *And From There You Shall Seek*:

---

70. *Pachad Yitzchak, Chanuka* pp. 36–37. Translation partially adapted from R. Shlomo Riskin's *The Living Tree: Studies in Modern Orthodoxy.*

71. Many sources express this far-reaching principle, with the most noteworthy being Yerushalmi's (*Chagiga* 1:8) statement that any ruling expressed by a seasoned student already was stated at Sinai:

> א"ר יהושע בן לוי עליהם ועליהם כל ככל דברים הדברים מקרא ומשנה תלמוד הלכות ואגדות אפילו מה שתלמיד וותיק עתיד להורות לפני רבו כבר נאמר למשה בסיני מה טעמא [קהלת א:י] יש דבר שיאמר ראה זה חדש הוא חבירו משיבו ואומר לו כבר היה לעולמים אשר היה לפנינו.

Interestingly, this passage is frequently quoted in an even more radical way, כל מה שתלמיד ותיק עתיד **לחדש** נאמר למשה מסיני or, "Whatever a seasoned student in the future will **innovate** has already been revealed at Sinai." (This variation is quoted in Netziv's *Kidmat ha-Eimek,* R. Tzadok's *Resisei Layla* 56, and Alshich *Shemot* 20.) Either way, this passage highlights the fact that genuine rootedness in Sinai does not preclude originality.

> What is the role of the intellect? The special importance that Halacha bestows upon reason is so salient that it symbolizes the entire character of the halakhic approach. Intellect is the final arbiter in all matters of law and judgment. The content of the Halacha, whose essence is revelation, is subjugated to the essence of rational cognition.... The background [of the law] is revelation/apocalyptic – both the written and the oral Torah, which were given to Moses at Sinai – the swirl of colors painted upon it is "cognitive/natural" (p. 107).

Seeing the value in debate and the possibility of innovation within the confines of revelation is possible only because "These and these are the words of the living God." We return to explore the tension between revelation and innovation as well as the parameters of plurality in Chapter 28 when discussing the evolution of the oral law.

4.9 RABBINIC ERROR

The Torah (*Devarim* 17:9–11) invests the high court (*Sanhedrin*) that eventually would be in Jerusalem with the authority to interpret the text of the Torah. The verses demand, among other things, that the nation follow the court's rulings.[72] Thus, one might wonder whether we must be concerned that the court erred in its interpretation of the Torah, and, if it did, whether a person can be harmed by following an erroneous ruling.

72. The scope of this *mitzva* is the subject of debate among medieval Jewish thinkers. According to Rambam (*Hilchot Mamrim,* Ch. 1; *Sefer ha-Mitzvot* 164), these verses serve as the source not only for the high-court's judicial and interpretive capacities, but for its legislative capacity as well. Thus, rabbinic ordinances in a certain sense carry the same weight as their biblical counterparts, as the Torah itself commands us to follow rabbinic enactments. Moreover, in certain places (see, for example, his Introduction to *Mishneh Torah*), Rambam implies that this legislative role is not limited to the high-court in Jerusalem. (*Sefer ha-Chinuch* follows this approach in *Mitzva* 496, asserting that the sages in each generation have all three functions.) Ramban (glosses on *Shoresh Rishon* of *Sefer ha-Mitzvot*), however, maintains that these verses do not include rabbinic legislative authority. (Ramban agrees that the sages have the power to legislate, but he argues that these verses do not grant them this authority.) Nevertheless, even Ramban concedes that these verses serve as the basis for the high-court's judicial and interpretive powers.

According to the view of the French Rabbis cited earlier, one could argue that generally speaking, there would be no concern. Even if there was a debate about the correct interpretation of a particular verse, one could reasonably assume that both views were said at Sinai, with God instructing Moshe to follow the majority position. Thus, assuming that the *Sanhedrin* ruled in accordance with one of the forty-nine lenient approaches or forty-nine stringent approaches said at Sinai, one would be safe.[73]

Other understandings of *eilu ve-eilu*, though, could not accept such a solution. For example, we cited Ran's position that one must follow the ruling of the *Sanhedrin* even if its view does not correspond to the absolute truth (it is הפך מן האמת). This prompts an obvious question: will following these erroneous rulings cause any harm? Ran addresses this question as well. To appreciate his analysis, let us consider the matter more broadly.

As noted, the Torah establishes the power of the Sages to interpret the Torah. By placing the yoke of elucidation upon the shoulders of mere mortals, God transferred the Torah into a new domain. It no longer is a purely divine document – man, to some decree, has assumed custody. With human stewardship, however, comes the possibility of error; deviation from the original intent seemingly becomes inevitable. And for the Jew who dreads sin, the prospect of the unknowable transgression becomes terrifying. The fear of rabbinic error proves particularly acute with regard to *chukim*, commandments with no apparent rational motivation. After all, error in something whose very nature supersedes logic seems more likely, less discernible, and potentially more devastating.

Perhaps, however, this apprehension is ungrounded. Maybe there is no harm done when a law, and especially a *chok*, is violated under justifiable conditions, such as a defensible rabbinic error. Who says original

73. This would be true even if one would be obligated to bring a *chatat* based on the original ruling of the *Sanhedrin* that was subsequently overturned (according to the view that *yachid she-asa be-hora'at beit din chayav chatat*). The sacrifice is necessary because the *beit din* perceives the ruling of the earlier *beit din* (or the earlier ruling of the same *beit din*) as incorrect from a halachic perspective regardless of whether it is *divrei Elokim chaim*. (Likewise, *Beit Shammai* would maintain that someone who followed *Beit Hillel* would be liable to bring a *chatat* even if their view reflected *divrei Elokim chaim*.)

intent is decisive? Ran (*Drasha* 11)[74] avers that this dilemma depends upon how one views the ontological value of these commandments. He presents this predicament succinctly:

דרשות הר"ן הדרוש האחד עשר

והנה יש כאן מקום עיון, כי זה ראוי שימשך על דעת מי שיחשוב שאין טעם למצות התורה כלל, אלא כולן נמשכות אחר הרצון לבד, ולפי זה אחר שהדבר מצד עצמו איננו ראוי להיות טמא או טהור דרך משל, אבל מה שטימאתהו או טיהרתהו נמשך אחר הרצון לבד, הנה אם כן לפי זה, הנמשך אחר כל מה שיניחו חכמי הדור, (ש)אי אפשר שיהיו דבריהם על הפך האמת, ואי אפשר שימשך מהענין ההוא בנפשותינו דבר מגונה כלל.

אבל אחרי שאנחנו לא נבחר בזה הדעת, אבל נאמין שכל מה שמנעתהו התורה ממנו, מזיק אלינו, ומוליד רושם רע בנפשותינו, ואף על פי שלא נדע סיבתו, לפי זה הדעת, אם כן כשיסכימו החכמים בדבר אחד טמא שהוא טהור, מה יהיה, הלא הדבר ההוא יזיק אותנו ויפעל מה שבטבעו לפעול, ואף על פי שהסכימו בו החכמים שהוא טהור. ואילו יסכימו הרופאים על סם אחד שהוא שוה, והוא על דרך משל חום במעלה רביעית, שאין ספק שלא תמשך פעולת החום בגוף כפי מה שיסכימו בו הרופאים, אבל כפי טבעו בעצמו. כן הדבר שאסרה לנו התורה מצד שהוא מזיק בנפש, איך ישתנה טבע הדבר ההוא מצד שהסכימו החכמים שהוא מותר, זה אי אפשר, רק על צד הפלא. והיה ראוי אם כן יותר שנמשך בזה על פי מה שתתברר לנו מצד נביא או בת קול, שעל דרך זה נתברר לנו אמיתת הדבר בעצמו.

Behold, we are faced with a great quandary. If one assumes that there is no inherent value in the commandments of the Torah, but rather they simply are meant to be divine rules, then it makes sense that we follow the interpretation of the wise men of one's generation, for it will be impossible that their words would be the opposite of the truth (הפך האמת), and there is no possible harm that can befall us from following their rulings.

74. P. 199 in the Feldman edition, Yerushalayim: Mechon Shelom Yerushalayim, 5734 (1973).

> However, we do not accept this approach; rather, we believe that everything that the Torah prohibited is harmful and leaves a ghastly imprint on our souls, even though we do not know the reason for the commandment. Accordingly, even if the Sages conclude that a particular item is pure, what difference will that make, [for if indeed it is impure,] it still will harm us by its deleterious nature?[75]

Ran here outlines two possibilities. He refers to a great debate that raged between two major schools of thought in medieval Spain regarding the nature of *chukim*.[76] The first position presented by Ran, which may refer to Rambam, concedes that at least the details of these directives do not necessarily reflect ontological truth. Instead, they are designed primarily to instill obedience and submission within us. As such, if the *Sanhedrin*'s error relates to a detail of a *chok*, perhaps there is no need to fear that violations will yield harmful results.[77]

75. For Ran, the problem of rabbinic error is particularly acute, as he accepts the position of Ramban (*Devarim* 17:11) that one is obligated to follow every ruling made by the *Sanhedrin*, even if it declares "of the right that is left and of the left that is right:" "...The Torah, therefore, defined the law that we are to obey the *Sanhedrin*... for it was subject to their judgment that He gave them the Torah, even if it appears to you to exchange right for left." (Though this is based on a midrash [Midrash *Shir ha-Shirim Rabba* 1:18, cited incompletely by Rashi], it seemingly is at odds with the statement of the Yerushalmi [*Horiyot* 2b] that the Sages should be followed only when their position seems correct: "Is it possible that if they told you right is left and left is right you would have to listen to them? The verse teaches we must follow [the Sages] "left and right" – only when they tell you right is right and left is left.") If, as Ramban and Ran seemingly assume, one must unconditionally accept the rulings of the *Sanhedrin*, the consequences of error are even greater, as even those who suspect the ruling to be in error will follow it.
76. We will further explore this debate in Chapter 36.
77. Whom is Ran referring to in this first perspective? Professor Warren Harvey of Hebrew University told me that Ran is referring to Rambam. Seemingly, this cannot be, since Rambam writes that there is a reason for each of the *mitzvot*, *chukim* included. Prof. Harvey, however, argued that since Rambam (*Moreh ha-Nevuchim* 3:26) maintains that *details* of a *mitzva* may be without reason and, presumably, an error made by the *Sanhedrin* would relate to a detail. As such, one could argue that according to Rambam, one need not fear rabbinic error.

    However, one could disagree with Ran's reading of Rambam (or, perhaps, Ran was not referring to Rambam). In fact, Rambam is quite emphatic in *rejecting* the

After explicating the first position, Ran rejects it. Instead, he accepts the position that even obscure commandments (and their details) correspond to metaphysical realities. Accordingly, their violation, even if defensible, is destructive. Thus, eating a piece of non-kosher meat devastates the soul,[78] even if ingested with justification. Having accepted the ontological value of *chukim*, the question of why the individual Jew should not fear rabbinic error becomes acute.

Ran was not alone in his quest to solve this problem. Let us consider the solutions of Ramban, Ran's own solution, and that of *Sefer ha-Chinuch*.

Ramban's Approach

Ramban maintains that *mitzvot* carry inherent metaphysical implications.[79] As such, we would expect him to fear the absolute power of the

positivist view that *mitzvot* have no reasons, vigorously defending their purpose, even if he denies the inherent value of a commandment's minutiae: "He who thinks that there are reasons for the details is as far from the truth as he who thinks that there are no reasons for the basic commandments themselves" (*ibid.*).

Interestingly, Rambam finds a partial ally on this question in Maharal in the seventh and eighth chapters of *Tiferet Yisrael*. While Maharal vigorously denies that any physical harm might be associated with forbidden food, he also rejects the notion that non-kosher is prohibited simply because of metaphysical damage it might cause, for after all, "Is the Torah a medical textbook?" Rather, commandments must be observed simply because they are God's will. This resembles the first position described by Ran above.

78. In addition to the general devastation wrought by violation of the Torah's commandments, when it comes to food-related prohibitions, many sources note that the metaphysical harm (*timtum ha-leiv*) proves particularly injurious because the food becomes a part of the person's physical makeup. See *Shabbat* 145b and 112b and *Mesillat Yesharim*, Ch. 11.

79. For example, in his comments on *Vayikra* 19:1, Ramban writes:

> The intention of the Rabbis [in defining *chukim* as divine decrees for which there is no reason] was not that these are decrees of the King of Kings for which there are no reasons whatever, "For every word of God is pure" (*Mishlei* 30:5). [Rather, they meant] only that *chukim* are like the enactments that a king promulgates for his kingdom without revealing their benefits to the people; the people, not sensing these reasons, entertain questions about them in their hearts but accept them nonetheless out of fear of the government. **Similarly, the *chukim* of the Holy One, blessed be He, are His secrets in the Torah, which the people do not grasp with their intellect as they do in the case**

rabbis, as they may err.[80] Moreover, while there may be some Talmudic sources that imply that if a qualified scholar is confident that the *Sanhedrin* has erred in its ruling that he should not follow this ruling,[81] Ramban maintains that after the matter was debated in the *Sanhedrin* and the

---

> **of *mishpatim* (laws whose rationale is more apparent). Yet they all have a proper reason and perfect benefit.**

Likewise, Ramban (in *Sha'ar ha-Gemul*) asks why the Torah demands a sacrifice only for an accidental sin (*shogeig*) and not for an intentional sin. He responds that an offering is capable of removing the metaphysically deleterious effects of an accidental sin; an intentional transgression, which by definition carries with it a spirit of rebelliousness, cannot be atoned for by a mere sacrifice. Clearly, Ramban believes that sin causes inherent metaphysical damage, so much so that he explains the entire objective of sin-offerings as ameliorating this damage.

80. Many Rishonim are bothered by the story from *Rosh ha-Shana* 25a, which recounts how R. Gamliel instructed R. Yehoshua to appear before him with his walking stick and wallet on the day that R. Yehoshua insisted was Yom Kippur. R. Yehoshua appropriately complied, implying the propriety of following the Sages despite one's personal misgivings. Thus, the Rishonim ask how R. Yehoshua could follow R. Gamliel when his own soul was at stake.

One might be inclined to dismiss the relevance of this story by distinguishing between the Sages' role in setting the calendar and their role in interpreting the Torah generally. In fact, Rambam and Ran make exactly this split, arguing that the court's decision regarding the calendar is valid even if made under faulty pretenses. However, Ramban seems to deny this distinction. He writes in his glosses on *Sefer ha-Mitzvot* (p. 17 in the Chavel edition):

> One may not say, "How can I allow myself to follow the high court, I know with certainty that it is in error?" for this is the commandment [to accept its position even if you know it is wrong]; just as R. Yehoshua acted with R. Gamliel on the day on which Yom Kippur fell out according to his calculation.

Indeed, it is striking that Ramban uses this story as a proof in light of the distinction that Rambam and Ran draw.

81. The Yerushalmi appears to adopt this view explicitly:

תלמוד ירושלמי מסכת הוריות פרק א

יכול אם יאמרו לך על ימין שהיא שמאל ועל שמאל שהיא ימין תשמע להם תלמוד לומר ללכת ימין ושמאל שיאמרו לך על ימין שהוא ימין ועל שמאל שהיא שמאל

The simple reading of the Bavli (*Horiyot* 2a–b) appears so as well. Numerous Acharonim rule that a qualified scholar may not follow the lenient ruling of the *Sanhedrin* if the scholar is confident that the *Sanhedrin* is wrong. This is the ruling of *Cheifetz Hashem* (*Horiyot* 2b), *Be'eir Sheva* (*ad. loc.*), and the *ha-Ketav ve-ha-Kabbala* (*Devarim* 17:11). R. David Zvi Hoffmann cites numerous sources, all of whom address this apparent contradiction:

scholar's view was overruled, the scholar should accept the view of the *Sanhedrin* even if he is confident that it has erred in its ruling.[82] Since

---

שו"ת מלמד להועיל חלק ג (אבן העזר וחושן משפט) סימן פב

דאיתא בהוריות דף ב' ע"ב: הורו ב"ד וידע תלמיד שראוי להוראה ועשה על פיהם דמשכחת לה שהוא שוגג כגון דקא טעי במצוה לשמוע דברי חכמים אפילו למיעבד איסורא, ואלו לדעת הספרי אין זה טעות כלל דהא באמת מצוה לשמוע אל דברי ב"ד הגדול אפילו אמרו על ימין שהוא שמאל וכו' דהיינו שהתירו את האיסור. וכבר עמדו על דבר זה ראשונים ואחרונים ודחקו לתרץ. עיין רא"ם בספר יראים סי' ל"ד, מזרחי על רש"י לתורה, באר שבע על מסכת הוריות, מהר"י אלבו בספר עיקרים ג', כ"ג, רמב"ן בהשגותיו על ס' המצות לרמב"ם שורש א' (וזה דלא כמו שכתב בפירושו על התורה בפ' שופטים), ספר החינוך בפ' שופטים, דרשות להר"ן דרשה י"א, חידושי הר"ן לסנהדרין צ"ט ע"א סוף ד"ה ר' יהודה, בעל עקידה שער מ"ג, אברבנאל בפירושו לפ' שופטים, יפה מראה לירושלמי ברכות פ"א הי"ד, ובאריכות בספר שער יוסף למס' הוריות, וע"ג ספר והזהיר חלק א' צח ומ"ש שם בענפי יהודה בשם רבו.

82. *Sifrei* indicates that one must follow the *Sanhedrin*'s ruling even when confident that it has erred:

ספרי דברים פיסקא קנד

לא תסור מן התורה אשר יגידו לך, מצות לא תעשה, ימין ושמאל, אפילו **מראים בעיניך** על ימין שהוא שמאל ועל שמאל שהוא ימין שמע להם.

Ramban addresses the Talmudic implication that the qualified scholar should not submit to the *Sanhedrin* and responds that that is true only until he has had the opportunity to debate the matter with the *Sanhedrin*. Once he fails to convince the high court, he must follow its ruling even in lenient matters.

השגות הרמב"ן לספר המצוות לרמב"ם שורש א

וזה הוא מה שאמרו (ספרי שם) אפילו אומרין לך על שמאל שהוא ימין ועל ימין שהוא שמאל שכך היא המצוה לנו מאדון התורה יתעלה שלא יאמר בעל המחלוקת היאך אתיר לעצמי זה ואנכי היודע בוודאי שהם טועים והנה נאמר לו בכך אתה מצווה. וכעניין שנהג רבי יהושע עם ר"ג ביום הכפורים שחל להיות בחשבונו כמו שהוזכר במסכת ר"ה (כה א). ויש בזה תנאי, יתבונן בו המסתכל בראשון שלהוריות (ב ב) בעין יפה, והוא שאם היה בזמן הסנהדרין חכם וראוי להוראה והורו בית דין הגדול בדבר אחד להתר והוא סבור שטעו בהוראתן **אין עליו מצוה לשמוע דברי החכמים ואינו רשאי להתיר לעצמו הדבר האסור לו אבל ינהג חומר לעצמו** וכל שכן אם היה מכלל הסנהדרין יושב עמהן בבית דין הגדול ויש עליו לבא לפניהם ולומר טענותיו להם והם שישאו ויתנו עמו ואם הסכימו רובם בבטול הדעת ההוא שאמר ושבשו עליו סברותיו יחזור וינהוג כדעתם אחרי כן לאחר שיסלקו אותו ויעשו הסכמה בטענתו. וזהו העולה מן ההלכות ההם. **ומכל מקום חייב לקבל דעתם אחר ההסכמה על כל פנים.**

This ruling is cited and accepted by *Sefer ha-Chinuch* (496), Ran (*Sanhedrin* 89b), and R. David (*Sanhedrin* 89b). These commentaries note that according to this approach, *Sifrei* and the Yerushalmi need not be in conflict, since the Yerushalmi refers to the situation where the scholar has not yet proffered his arguments. (We are assuming that Ramban in his commentary on the Torah is consistent with his glosses on *Sefer ha-Mitzvot*. R. David Zvi Hoffmann, cited above, assumed a contradiction.)

one must accept the *Sanhedrin*'s view even when positive that it has erred, the concern about rabbinic error is particularly pressing.

There are several aspects to Ramban's solution. The first is to recognize that following the *Sanhedrin* is God's will, and one should not try to outsmart God:

השגות הרמב״ן לספר המצוות לרמב״ם שורש א

כי התורה נתנה לנו ע״י משה רבינו בכתב וגלוי הוא שלא ישתוו הדעות בכל הדברים הנולדים וחתך לנו ית׳ הדין שנשמע לב״ד הגדול בכל מה שיאמרו בין שקבלו פירושו ממנו או שיאמרו כן ממשמעות התורה וכוונתה לפי דעתם. **כי על המשמעות שלהם הוא מצוה ונותן לנו התורה.**

For the written Torah was given to us via Moshe, and it is self-evident that differing views will be expressed in new situations. God established the law for us that we should listen to the high court in all matters, whether they rule based on tradition or because they understand from the text that such is the Torah's intention. **For according to their reading [of the text] God commands and gives us the Torah.**

Thus, one must follow the *Sanhedrin* even if it may have erred because that is what the Torah instructed. While this justifies normative practice, it does not alleviate the concern that the *Sanhedrin* may have erred. Ramban addresses this by noting that God will protect the high court from error and direct it along the proper path:

רמב״ן דברים פרק יז פסוק יא

[לא תסור מן הדבר אשר יגידו לך ימין ושמאל.] ...וחתך לנו הכתוב הדין שנשמע לבית דין הגדול... כי על הדעת שלהם הוא נותן להם התורה, אפילו יהיה בעיניך כמחליף הימין בשמאל, וכל שכן שיש לך לחשוב שהם אומרים על ימין שהוא ימין, כי רוח השם על משרתי מקדשו ולא יעזוב את חסידיו, לעולם נשמרו מן הטעות ומן המכשול.

["You shall not deviate from that which the court tells you right or left."]... Scripture dictated to us that we must listen to the high

> court [even when they appear to err]… because it is on the basis of [the Sages'] understanding that He gave the Torah, even if it appears that they are confusing right and left. And all the more so you should obey them because you should think [contrary to your opinion] that they are [in fact] saying about the right that it is right and about the left that it is left, for the spirit of God rests upon the stewards of His sanctuary and "He will not forsake His devout ones; they will be eternally protected" from error and stumbling.

Thus, God protects the *Sanhedrin* from error. Elsewhere, Ramban notes that this divine assistance is not limited to the *Sanhedrin,* but applies even in the post-Temple period. In explaining the Talmudic statement, "From the day that the Temple was destroyed, even though prophecy was taken away from the prophets, from the Sages it was not taken away" (*Bava Batra* 12a), Ramban writes:

> **חידושי הרמב"ן מסכת בבא בתרא דף יב עמוד א**
> הכי קאמר אע"פ שנטלה נבואת הנביאים שהוא המראה והחזון, נבואת החכמים שהיא בדרך החכמה לא נטלה, אלא יודעים האמת ברוח הקדש שבקרבם.

> This is what it means: Even though the prophecy of the prophets was taken away, meaning prophecies and visions, the "prophecy" of the Sages, which is through wisdom, was not removed. Rather, they (the Sages) know the truth according the divine inspiration (*ruach ha-kodesh)* that is within them.[83]

Thus, there is no reason to fear that the rabbis will not rule in accordance with the ontological truth, since God will guide them through divine inspiration and prevent error.[84] Does this guarantee that no

83. Rashba (*ad. loc.*) expresses similar sentiments.
84. This appears difficult in light of the story of *tanur shel achnai* cited earlier in the chapter, wherein God seemed to side with R. Eliezer against the majority view. How could God allow the Sages to err, and how could the Sages maintain their unequivocally false position? Ramban (*Bava Metzia* 59a) deflects these questions by considering the possibility that the Sages were indeed correct, as they were purveyors of a tradition from Sinai.

court will ever will err? This seems unlikely in light of the Torah's establishment of a *korban* to be brought if the *Sanhedrin* errs and misunderstands the Torah (*par he'eleim davar shel tzibbur*). However, it does alleviate the practical fear of error for the followers of the *Sanhedrin*'s rulings.

In a related context, Ramban (*Devarim* 19:19) writes that God ensures that even court errors will not result in injustice. Addressing the ethical problems relating to a court's fallacious ruling, Ramban wonders why the Talmud rules that an *eid zomeim* (conspiring witness) is punished only when his false testimony *does not* lead to an erroneous punishment. He answers that in the event that the court actually administered a sentence, we should assume that the victim certainly deserved it, even if he did not commit the particular crime with which he was charged, for God never would allow a true miscarriage of justice. Thus, no true harm could stem from a false verdict.[85]

Using a similar line of reasoning, we could address the issue of *par he'eleim davar shel tzibbur*. Perhaps Ramban maintains that the *Sanhedrin*'s incorrect ruling reflects a penalty for iniquity. The Talmud relates instances where scholars are punished by forgetting Torah or making a mistake. Likewise, the corruption of the soul that those who follow the incorrect ruling experience might be a just punishment for

---

According to this theory, the miracles that supported R. Eliezer reflected the eminence of R. Eliezer, not the correctness of his opinion. While this explanation appears forced, it coincides with the extraordinary power Ramban generally accords scholars.

85. **רמב"ן דברים פרק יט פסוק יט**

כאשר זמם ולא כאשר עשה, מכאן אמרו הרגו אין נהרגין, לשון רש"י מדברי רבותינו (מכות ה:) והטעם בזה, בעבור כי משפט העדים המוזמין בגזרת השליט, שהם שנים ושנים, והנה כאשר יבואו שנים ויעידו על ראובן שהרג את הנפש ויבואו שנים אחרים ויזימו אותם מעדותם צוה הכתוב שיהרגו, כי בזכותו של ראובן שהיה נקי וצדיק בא המעשה הזה אילו היה רשע בן מות לא הצילו השם מיד ב"ד, כאשר אמר (שמות כג:ז) כי לא אצדיק רשע אבל אם נהרג ראובן, **נחשוב שהיה אמת כל אשר העידו עליו הראשונים, כי הוא בעונו מת ואילו היה צדיק לא יעזבנו ה' בידם**, כמו שאמר הכתוב (תהלים לז:לג) ה' לא יעזבנו בידו ולא ירשיענו בהשפטו ועוד שלא יתן ה' השופטים הצדיקים העומדים לפניו לשפוך דם נקי, כי המשפט לאלהים הוא ובקרב אלהים ישפוט והנה כל זה מעלה גדולה בשופטי ישראל, וההבטחה שהקב"ה מסכים על ידם ועמהם בדבר המשפט וזה טעם ועמדו שני האנשים אשר להם הריב לפני ה' (פסוק יז), כי לפני ה' הם עומדים בבואם לפני הכהנים והשופטים, והוא ינחם בדרך אמת, וכבר הזכרתי מזה בסדר ואלה המשפטים (שמות כא:ו).

prior wrongdoing.[86] Either way, in his treatment of *eid zomeim,* we see Ramban turning to the supernatural to solve the theological.

Ran's Approach

Ran proposes another option. He too admits the existence of an absolute, unalterable ontological truth, but he asserts that if the Sages follow the biblical guidelines for reaching conclusions, such as following the majority, they most likely will not err. While the possibility of error exists, we need not be concerned about it. Just as we trust doctors despite the possibility of malpractice, we should trust the experts of Torah-interpretation despite the remote possibility of error.[87] Moreover, Ran argues:

> **דרשות הר"ן הדרוש האחד עשר**
> התורה השגיחה לתקן ההפסד שהיה אפשר שיפול תמיד, והוא פירוד הדעות והמחלוקת, ושתיעשה תורה כשתי תורות, ותקנת ההפסד התמידי הזה, כשמסרה הכרעת הספיקות לחכמי הדור, שעל הרוב ימשך מזה תיקון, ויהיה משפטם צודק. כי שגיאות החכמים הגדולים, מועטות ממי שהוא למטה מהם בחכמה, וכל שכן כת הסנהדרין העומדים לפני ה׳ יתברך במקדשו, ששכינה עמהם. **ועם היות שלפעמים אפשר, שעל צד הפלא והזרות, ישגו בדבר מה, לא חששה תורה להפסד ההוא הנופל מעט, כי ראוי לסבול אותו מצד רוב התיקון הנמשך תמיד, ואי אפשר לתקן יותר מזה.**

86. Nevertheless, truly God-fearing sages need not fear error. The notion that God shields the righteous from all spiritual harm, at least that which stems from prohibited foods, can be gleaned from the Talmud (*Shabbat* 112b), which records the miraculous protection afforded even to the donkey of the saintly R. Pinchas b. Ya'ir.

87. At this point, Ran adds an ambiguous phrase, "and certainly (*kol she-kein*) the *Sanhedrin* who stand before God in His temple and the divine presence (*shechina*) rests among them." This appears to imply a measure of concurrence with Ramban's assertion that we should assume that God grants divine assistance to the *Sanhedrin*. Alternatively, Ran may be referring to his earlier elaboration of the dictum, "Whoever judges a correct judgment, the divine presence rests with him." If so, however, the term "*kol she-kein*" is inappropriate, since the divine presence comes only after the verdict, not before it. Moreover, it should not be limited to the *Sanhedrin*. It therefore appears that Ran agrees that God provides special guidance at least to the *Sanhedrin*. Nevertheless, Ran feels that this solution is insufficient, and one still must contend with the possibility of error.

> The Torah made sure to prevent the threat that is constant, namely, division of opinions and practice, such that the Torah would appear like two Torahs [because everybody would be doing different things, each in accordance with his own understanding]. The solution to this constant threat is that the final decision in all matters of doubt was left to the elders of the generation [who would resolve all disputes by following the majority opinion of the *Sanhedrin*]. Most of the time, this will benefit everyone, because their rulings will be correct, as errors among those most wise are much less common than errors among those who are less wise, and certainly when it comes to the *Sanhedrin* who stand before God in His Temple, since His presence is with them. **And even though it is possible, though highly unlikely, that the *Sanhedrin* will err in some way, the Torah was not concerned with the minimal [spiritual] damage that will result [from that error], because it is worthy to bear that harm due to the general value (*tikkun*) that happens all the time. Overall, there is no possibility for greater value (*tikkun*).**

Ran essentially argues that we must look at the big picture, in which the benefits of following the rulings of the *Sanhedrin* across the board, even when we think they might be incorrect, exceed the possible risks entailed by accepting its rulings. Ran compares this to biological processes that generally are helpful and therefore necessary even though at times they are harmful.

What great benefits accrue from following the *Sanhedrin*? Firstly, usually it will be right. Its members are, after all, the wisest and most pious among us. Moreover, its placement in the temple gives it additional divine assistance. And most importantly, explains Ran, we must consider the alternative. If there would be no single method of resolving halachic disputes, everybody would do as he sees fit, and instead of one nation following a single Torah, we would have, as it were, multiple Torahs.[88]

88. To some degree, this is exactly what we suffer from today, as we no longer have a *Sanhedrin* to resolve our disputes.

Still, one wonders why we would not follow R. Eliezer's view in *tanur shel achnai* if we know he was correct. The answer presumably is that the value of *lo ba-shamayim hee* dictates an across the board rejection of heavenly interference in halachic decision-making. Ran explains why this is so earlier in the work. In his fifth *drasha,* Ran writes of the value of having a decisive and readily available means of interpreting the Torah.

דרשות הר"ן הדרוש החמישי
והוא אמרם [ב]בבא בתרא (יב א) חכם עדיף מנביא שנאמר (תהלים צ:יב) ונביא לבב חכמה, מי נתלה במי הוי אומר קטן נתלה בגדול. (וכבר אמרו בב"מ בענין ר"א עמד ר"י על רגליו ואמר לא בשמים היא, מאי לא בשמים היא, כבר נתנה לנו משה על הר סיני וכתוב בה אחרי רבים להטות). והפירוש אצלי הוא, כי החכם יתיר ספקות התורה שהוא יסוד הכל, וישמע אליו הנביא על כרחו, ואם הנביא יעיר לחכם דבר במשפטים שיביאהו מצד נבואתו, לא ישמע אליו כלל.

[ואף אם יסכים היחיד לאמת יותר מן המרובים, יש לו לבטל דעתו אצלם. וכבר אמרו בבבא מציעא (נט ב) בענין ר' אליעזר, עמד ר' יהושע על רגליו ואמר לא בשמים היא (דברים ל:יב), מאי לא בשמים היא, כבר נתנה לנו משה על הר סיני וכתוב בה אחרי רבים להטות]. **הנה ראו כולם שר' אליעזר מסכים אל האמת יותר מהם, וכי אותותיו כולם אמיתים צודקים, והכריעו מן השמים כדבריו, ואף על פי כן עשו מעשה כהסכמתם. שאחר ששכלם נוטה לטמא, אף על פי שהיו יודעים שהיו מסכימים להפך מן האמת, לא רצו לטהר. והיו עוברים על דברי תורה אם היו מטהרים, כיון ששכלם חייב לטמא, שההכרעה נמסרה לחכמי הדורות, ואשר יסכימו הם, הוא אשר צוהו השם יתברך.**

This is what the Sages meant by "A sage is greater than a prophet"… for a sage can resolve the uncertainties in the Torah, which is the foundation of everything, and the prophet must heeds his words no matter what. And even if the prophet will propose a certain argument based on his prophecies, we will ignore him…

And even though it is possible for a single sage to arrive at the truth more than the majority, he should nullify his opinion in favor of the majority… **For everyone perceived that R. Eliezer's**

view accorded with the truth, and they saw the veracity of the wonders performed in his favor and that heaven agreed with his position. And yet they practiced their own position [that was at variance with R. Eliezer's]. For once they all agreed, even though they knew that they were agreeing to a false view, they did not wish to retract. And they would have been in violation of the Torah had they retracted, given that they considered their own view correct, because determination of the law was entrusted to the sages of each generation, and whatever they agree upon is what God commanded [us to keep].

The Approach of Sefer ha-Chinuch

Another solution is found in *Sefer ha-Chinuch* (496). While his solution resembles that of Ran, it is the most practical and least supernatural of the approaches we have considered:

ספר החינוך מצוה תצו

...לא תסור ממנו ימין ושמאל, אפילו יאמרו לך על ימין שהוא שמאל ועל שמאל שהוא ימין לא תסור ממצותם, כלומר שאפילו יהיו הם טועים בדבר אחד מן הדברים אין ראוי לנו לחלוק עליהם אבל נעשה כטעותם, **וטוב לסבול טעות אחד ויהיו הכל מסורים תחת דעתם הטוב תמיד, ולא שיעשה כל אחד ואחד כפי דעתו שבזה יהיה חורבן הדת וחלוק לב העם והפסד האומה לגמרי.** ומפני ענינים אלה נמסרה כוונת התורה אל חכמי ישראל, ונצטוו גם כן שיהיו לעולם כת מועטת מן החכמים כפופה לכת המרובין מן השורש הזה, וכמו שכתבתי שם במצות להטות אחרי רבים.

"One may not deviate right or left [from the ruling of the *Sanhedrin*], even if it tells you that right is left and left is right. In other words, even if the *Sanhedrin* errs ... it is not appropriate to argue with it; rather, we should act in accordance with its mistake, **for it is better to suffer through one mistake and allow for everyone to be under its guidance at all times so as to prevent everyone from going according to his own whim, which will cause a devastation of the religion ... and utter obliteration of the nation.** Because of these risks, the Torah was handed over

> to the Sages for interpretation, and it was commanded that the minority follow the majority.[89]

Here, we have a completely pragmatic approach; if the populace is not subject to the courts, there will be anarchy. Thus, *Sefer ha-Chinuch* surpasses Ran by implying that it is indeed bad for the individual to follow the majority if its ruling is in error. It is necessary for the stability of society, however, to uphold the authority of the *Sanhedrin*.[90]

To summarize, we have considered four possible solutions to the question of why a person can follow the rulings of the *Sanhedrin* with confidence, not worrying that it may have erred[91]:

---

89. *Sefer ha-Chinuch* then shows how this principle explains the story of *tanur shel achnai*:
    ועל דרך ענין זה שעוררתיך בני עליו אפרש לך אגדה אחת שהיא בבבא מציעא בסוף פרק הזהב [נט ב] גבי ההוא מעשה דרבי אליעזר בתנורו של עכנאי המתמהת כל שומעה. אמרו שם, אשכחיה רבי נתן לאליהו וכו׳. אמר ליה מה עביד הקדוש ברוך הוא בההיא שעתא, אמר ליה חייך ואמר נצחוני בני, שהיה שמח הקדוש ברוך הוא על שהיו בניו הולכים בדרך התורה ובמצותה להטות אחרי רבים. ומה שאמר נצחוני בני, חלילה להיות נצחון לפניו ברוך הוא, אבל פירוש הדבר הוא על ענין זה. שבמחלוקת הזה שהיה לרבי אליעזר עם חבריו האמת היה כרבי אליעזר וכדברי הבת קול שהכריעה כמותו, ואף על פי שהיה האמת אתו בזה, ביתרון פלפולו על חבריו לא ירדו לסוף דעתו ולא רצו להודות לדבריו אפילו אחר בת קול, והביאו ראיה מן הדין הקבוע בתורה שציותנו ללכת אחרי הרבים לעולם בין יאמרו אמת או אפילו טועים, ועל זה השיב הבורא ברוך הוא נצחוני בני, כלומר אחר שהם נוטים מדרך האמת שרבי אליעזר הוא היה מכוין בזה את האמת ולא הם, והם באים עליו מכח מצות התורה שצויתים לשמוע אל הרוב לעולם, אם כן על כל פנים יש להודות בפעם הזאת כדבריהם שתהיה האמת נעדרת, והרי זה כאילו בעל האמת נצוח.
90. The idea that the individual must sacrifice for the sake of society does not go as far as the notion of חטא בשביל שיזכה חבירך (sin for the benefit of your friend, i.e., an individual). It is interesting to note, however, that followers of Ramban were more likely to allow for the individual to sin for the sake of his friend than were the *Ba'alei ha-Tosafot*. See *Tosafot*, Ramban, Rashba, and Ritva to *Shabbat* 4a.
91. One might suggest a fifth answer to this question. Perhaps the ruling of the *Sanhedrin* determines the ontological reality. If this were the case, harm never would befall someone who follows its rulings. Ran alludes to, and rejects, this possibility:
    כן הדבר שאסרה לנו התורה מצד שהוא מזיק בנפש, איך ישתנה טבע הדבר ההוא מצד שהסכימו החכמים שהוא מותר, זה אי אפשר, רק על צד הפלא.
    However, this possibility may be extrapolated from Rashba's theory that the Sages' decisions influence the physical world (see *Mishmeret ha-Bayit* 7:3 and *Shach*, Y.D. 189:13, based on the Yerushalmi *Nedarim* 6:8). Accordingly, "The shofar [of the *Sanhedrin* declaring the new month] determines when a woman is likely to menstruate" even if the ruling does not correspond to the lunar reality:

1. No harm will befall someone who follows the rulings of *Sanhedrin* even if they are rooted in a misunderstanding of the Torah (either because *eilu ve-eilu* and the interpretation is also the word of God or because there is no ontological value to the details of *chukim*).
2. Ramban maintains that generally speaking, God will guide the *Sanhedrin* to a correct understanding of the Torah.
3. Ran asserts that the overall benefits of following the rulings of the *Sanhedrin* exceed the possible risks entailed by accepting their rulings.
4. *Sefer ha-Chinuch* suggests that we have no choice but to follow the rulings of the *Sanhedrin,* because if the populace is not subject to the courts, there will be anarchy.

> Since all that *beit din* on earth does, *beit din* in heaven agrees [to], as it says, "[These are the appointed festivals of God, the holy convocations, which you (*beit din*)] shall designate in their proper time" (*Vayikra* 23:4), [which the Talmud interprets to mean] that even [if they are declared] not in their proper time [they are binding]. This is true even in physiological processes ... [Thus,] a child of three years and one day that engaged in intercourse, her hymen does not grow back, [but if the courts] expanded the year (i.e., declared a leap year), her hymen does grow back.

Perhaps, according to Rashba, one who follows the rulings of the rabbis regarding a piece of meat need not worry that he is ingesting a contaminant and thereby tarnishing his soul, since the heavenly court that controls both the physical and metaphysical reality certainly will consent to the verdict of the rabbis and will make the necessary adjustments. However, one could disagree with the above comparison. That the court's ruling can affect physical reality (as stated by the Yerushalmi and Rashba) does not imply that it can affect metaphysical reality (with the possible exception of the declaration of the new month). Accordingly, one still might be concerned about the possibility of an erroneous interpretation of the Torah made by the *Sanhedrin.*

Unit Two

Aggada

Chapter Five

Introducing Aggada

Having introduced philosophy in the previous unit, we now turn to the study of Aggada. Aggada constitutes the non-halachic portions of Talmudic literature, including large portions of the Talmud and Midrash. Aggadic texts form the basis of our knowledge of Chazal's view on non-halachic matters. Thus, we consider why and how to study Aggada.

We consider this topic in three chapters. In Chapter 5, we explore the basis and authoritativeness of Aggada, reflect on why it is so cryptic, and consider whether *psak* is relevant in such matters. In the following chapter, Chapter 6, we turn to Rambam's complex approach towards Aggada. As part of this endeavor, we return to the question of whether Rambam's thought is rooted primarily in tradition or derives mainly from foreign sources.

Finally, in Chapter 7, we focus on the Midrashic interpretations of the Torah. We ponder what the purpose of *drash* and Aggada actually is. We also consider the historicity of Midrashic accounts – when the Midrash explains a particular event, what actually occurred historically? Was it the *pshat*, *drash*, both, or neither? We also discuss the difference between Midrashic interpretations of the narrative portions of Torah, and Midrashic interpretations of the halachic portions of Torah.

5.1 WHY STUDY AGGADA?

The Midrash stresses the imperative to study Aggada – Halacha alone is insufficient:

ספרי פרשת עקב פסקה מ"ח

...שלא תאמר למדתי הלכות די לי, תלמוד לומר כי אם שמור תשמרון את כל המצוה הזאת, כל המצוה למוד מדרש הלכות ואגדות...

> ... so that one should not say: "I learned Halacha; that is adequate for me." For that reason it is written, "If you will assiduously keep this *mitzva* completely" (*Devarim* 11:22). The phrase "this *mitzva* completely" teaches us that one must learn Midrash, Halacha, and Aggada.

We began Chapter 1 with a number of sources highlighting the imperative to study Aggada. Some, like *Avot de-Rabi Natan,* stress that Aggada brings a person to love and fear God. Others, like *Sifrei* 49, focus on the role of Aggada in fulfilling the obligation to know God. We noted how these two goals support and build off each other. Indeed, many of the reasons given in the previous chapters for the study of philosophy also apply to the study of Aggada. In this chapter, we focus on how to study Aggada and begin by considering the extent to which it is binding.

Before beginning, however, let us ponder upon the relationship between Halacha and Aggada. It is complex. Consider the following story (*Bava Kama* 60b). R. Ami and R. Asi were sitting in front of R. Yitzchak Nafcha. One said to him: "Let the master teach Halacha," and the other said, "Let the master teach Aggada." He started to teach Aggada and one student did not let him proceed; he started to teach Halacha and the other student did not let him proceed. He said to them, "I will give you a parable for this matter: a man had two wives, one older and one younger. Since the younger wife plucked out his white hairs, and the older wife plucked out his black hairs, the two of them made him bald." In this story, Halacha and Aggada are portrayed as two wives warring over a single husband. Each one seeks to remake her husband in her own image (the younger wife tried to make her husband look young and the older wife tried to make her husband look old).

This metaphor should not be understood as implying that Halacha and Aggada have conflicting agendas. Nevertheless, it does indicate how disciples of each respective discipline occasionally see them as competing. Indeed, certain Torah scholars excel in the interpretation of Aggada and focus on its study, as their peers pursue Halacha with equal vigor. Ultimately, Halacha and Aggada present two different perspectives on the truth, both of which are necessary for the true servant of God. Thus, Gra (*Mishlei* 25:21) compares Halacha to fire and Aggada to water. In one sense, fire and water are clashing forces, like the two fighting wives from *Bava Kama* 60b. But, in reality, both are life-sustaining forces that complement more than they clash. Thus, in the above story R. Yitzchak Nafcha concludes "I will teach something that will please both of you," and presents an integrated teaching that contains both halachic and aggadic implications. Where the students perceive a clash, the teacher sees unity – "they are all given from one Shepherd" (*Kohelet* 12:11, *Chagiga* 3b).[1]

5.2 IS AGGADA AUTHORITATIVE?

Aggadic teachings from Talmud and Midrash serve as a major source for *machshava*. Just as we turn to Chazal in matters of Halacha, so too we seek Chazal's guidance on non-halachic matters. The question, however, remains: is Chazal's view in non-halachic matters as authoritative as their positions on halachic matters? An important source regarding this inquiry is found in the Yerushalmi:

תלמוד ירושלמי מסכת פיאה פרק ב הלכה ד
רבי זעירא בשם שמואל: אין למדים לא מן ההלכות ולא מן ההגדות ולא מן התוספות אלא מן התלמוד.

1. A similar theme emerges from *Sota* 40a in the story of R. Abahu and R. Chiya b. Abba.

> R. Zeira in the name of Shmuel[2]: we do not learn from Halachot[3], Haggadot, and Tosafot[4], [but rather] only from Talmud.

What concerns us currently is the middle statement, namely, that we do not learn from Aggadot. (The words Haggadot and Aggadot are interchangeable.) The numerous interpretations that have been offered can be broken down into two camps.

Those Who Maintain that Aggada Is Binding

The first camp does not see this statement as undermining Chazal's authority in non-halachic matters. Some in this camp understand the Gemara's statement to mean that we do not derive halachic rulings from aggadic material. Within this understanding, there are those who rule we do not derive halachic rulings at all from aggadic material.[5]

---

2. This may be meant to dispute the previous statement:

    רבי יהושע בן לוי אמר: 'עליהם' - 'ועליהם', 'כל' - 'ככל', 'דברים' - 'הדברים', מקרא משנה תלמוד ואגדה, אפילו מה שתלמיד ותיק עתיד להורות לפני רבו כבר נאמר למשה בסיני. מה טעם "יש דבר שיאמר ראה זה חדש הוא" וגו'? משיבו חבירו ואומר לו: "כבר היה לעולמים".

3. According to Gra and *Pnei Moshe*, this means that we do not apply the principles that emerge from *halacha le-Moshe mi-Sinai* to new cases – אין למדין means we do not extrapolate. According to Rash Sirilio (based on Rashbam *Bava Batra* 130b), this means that we do not necessarily follow statements in the Mishna when they say that the Halacha follows so-and-so.
4. Presumably, this means that we do not derive Halacha from the Tosefta. Many understand that this means that in the event that the Tosefta contradicts the Talmud, we follow the Talmud.
5. This is the view of *Tosafot Yom Tov (Berachot* 5:4) and *Noda be-Yehuda*:

    שו"ת נודע ביהודה מהדורה תנינא יו"ד סימן קסא

    ומה שרצה לומר ללמוד הלכה למעשה מן אגדה ומדברי המדרש במקום שאין הגמרא סותרת לזה וכתב שבירושלמי איתא שאין למדין לא מן הלכות ולא מן אגדות ולא מן התוספתות אלא מן הגמרא. ועל זה נשען מעלתו לומר כי היכי דמן התוספתות נתבאר בדברי הפוסקים שבמקום שאין בגמרא סתירה לדברי התוספתא למדין ממנה, הוא הדין מדברי אגדה היכא דלא מצינו בגמרא סתירה על דברי המדרש למדין מן המדרש דהרי כולהו בני בקתא חדא נינהו. ומתוך כך תמה מעלתו במכתבו סימן ג' על התוי"ט ברכות פ"ה משנה ד' בד"ה ואם הבטחתו שלא רצה ללמוד מן המדרש במה שלא מצינו בגמרא סתירה לזה...

    ואמנם אני אומר דאף דהירושלמי כללינהו יחד מכל מקום לאו בחדא מחתא מחתינהו, ומה ענין המדרש אצל התוספתא? התוספתא עיקרה להלכות, ולזה היה תחלת כוונת

Noda be-Yehuda writes that the reason for this is that the purpose of aggadic statements is to convey ethical teachings, not halachic material. Others[6] contend that this means we are allowed to derive halachic rulings from aggadic material unless it is contradicted by halachic material.[7] Several Rishonim appear to take different positions as well, with some basing Halacha on aggadic statements, while other Rishonim dismiss such halachot.[8] According to both of these understandings, however,

---

מחברם - ור׳ חייא ור׳ אושעיא - המה יסדוה, וכל מגמתם לדיני התורה, ולכן במקום שאין סתירה בדברי הגמרא סומכים על התוספתא. **אבל המדרשים והאגדות, עיקר כוונתם על המוסר ועל הרמזים ועל המשלים שבהם, והכל עיקר הדת, אבל אין עיקר כוונתם על פסקי הלכות, לכן אין למדים מהם לפסק הלכה כלל**, ויפה כתב תוי״ט שם.

6. Including *Pri Chadash* (128:20), *Mayim Chaim* (*Berachot* 5:4, cited by R. Akiva Eiger *ad. loc.*), and many other decisors quoted by R. Ovadya Yosef:

   שו״ת יביע אומר חלק א יורה דעה סימן ד

   (ח) איברא דאמרינן בירושלמי (פ״ב דפאה ה״ד), אין למדין לא מן ההגדות ולא מן התוספות אלא מן התלמוד, ע״ש. וכה״ג כתב בחי׳ הרשב״א מגילה (טו). וכ״כ התוס׳ יו״ט (פ״ה דברכות מ״ד), ע״ש. אכן כבר העלו בזה האחרונים, דלא אמרינן הכי אלא כשיש סתירה לזה מן הש״ס. ודלא כהתוס׳ יו״ט (שם). וכמ״ש הפר״ח (סי׳ קכח ס״ק כ), דמי יוכל לחלוק על המדרש בלא ראיה מהש״ס, ע״ש. וכ״כ בס׳ מים חיים (ברכות שם), והשיג על התי״ט, והובא ג״כ בתוס׳ רעק״א, ע״ש, וכ״כ הגאון באר יעקב (אה״ע סי׳ קיט). ושכ״כ הכנה״ג בכלליו (אות ע), ע״ש. וכ״כ בפשיטות מרן החיד״א בשו״ת חיים שאל ח״א (סי׳ צב), ע״ש. ונהי דאנן קי״ל כדברי התי״ט, שהש״צ אינו עונה אמן אחר הכהנים, אפי׳ הוא מובטח שחוזר לתפילתו, ודלא כהמדרש שהביא התי״ט, וכמ״ש האחרונים. ע׳ בפמ״ג (סי׳ קכח מש״ז ס״ק יד). וכ״פ מהר״ח פלאג׳י בכף החיים (סי׳ טו אות עד). וכ״פ בבן איש חי.(פ׳ תצוה אות טו), ועוד. שאני התם דמשמע להו דסת״מ ברכות (לד) פליגא ע״ד המדרש בזה. וכמ״ש בס׳ באר יעקב שם. וכ״כ בשו״ת לב חיים ח״ג (סי׳ צט, דצ״ג ע״ב), ע״ש. הא לא״ה למדין מן המדרש ואין משיבין. וכן מבואר בס׳ הישר לר״ת, שיש ללמוד מן המדרשים כשאינם מכחישים את התלמוד, שהרבה מנהגים בידינו על פיהם, ע״ש. והובא במחזיק ברכה א״ח (בקונט׳ אחרון סי׳ נא). וע״ע בשו״ת בית שערים (חיו״ד סי׳ תכז), ע״ש. ומכ״ש הפסיקתא שאנו סומכים עליה לפעמים אפי׳ נגד הגמרא דידן, וכמ״ש התוס׳ ברכות (יח), ופסחים (מ:), ע״ש.

7. Proof for the latter possibility is summoned from the Yerushalmi's comparison to Tosefta – just as we derive Halacha from Tosefta if it is not contradicted by other sources, so too we should derive Halacha from Aggada if it is not contradicted by other sources. *Noda be-Yehuda* rejects the comparison, asserting that the purpose of aggadic statements is to convey ethical teachings rather than halachic material. Thus, we cannot derive any Halacha from Aggada. The purpose of Tosefta, on the other hand, is to convey halachic material; however, the Talmud Bavli is the final authority when it comes to Halacha, and in the case of a contradiction, we follow the Talmud Bavli.

8. *Tosafot* frequently derive halachic rulings from Aggada. For example, in *Bava Batra* 74a, *Tosafot* deduce from an obscure story that the dead should be buried while wearing

aggadic material is authoritative (to the extent that is possible) regarding non-halachic matters, just as Talmud is authoritative on halachic matters.

We should note that "authoritative" with respect to non-halachic matters has a different connotation than with respect to halachic matters. There are several reasons for this. Firstly, there frequently are no direct, explicit ramifications that emerge from aggadic texts. Aggadic texts also lend themselves to multiple interpretations. Moreover, they often disagree with each other, in which case one might argue that we accept one perspective over another. What we mean by "authoritative" with respect to aggadic texts is that even a great person may not simply dismiss an aggadic source or claim it is not true. Consequently, even if one accepts the authoritativeness of Aggada, on a practical level, aggadic texts turn out to be less decisive than halachic texts. In 5.4, we shall see that Maharal, who fully endorses the authoritativeness of Aggada, elaborates on this point, arguing that practically, it is difficult to definitively prove anything from Aggada, since one could argue that the text has a deeper meaning.

Even aggadic texts that offer a clear directive are not necessarily normative insofar as they may be understood as offering advice. While the guidance of Chazal must be taken seriously, if a statement is in the realm of advice, it is treated differently than if it is meant normatively. One might claim different times might call for different advice. For example, shopping advice given by Chazal may not be relevant in today's marketplace. Therefore, to the extent that we understand their guidance as advice (as opposed to an elucidation of timeless Torah values), one might conclude that the advice no longer is applicable.[9]

---

tzitzit. Likewise, in *Sanhedrin* 74b, which discusses why Ester didn't allow herself to be killed rather than marry Achashveirosh, *Tosafot* invoke an aggada in *Megilla* 15a that pertains to the discussion. Rashba (*Megilla* 15a) dismisses the proof, averring that we cannot derive halachic material from Aggada (דברי אגדה הן ואין משיבין עליה). See also *Piskei ha-Rosh, Nedarim* 9:2 and *Terumat ha-Deshen* II (*Pesakim u-Ketavim*), No. 108.

9. There are times when it may be unclear whether an aggadic statement is meant as practical advice or as a presentation of eternal Torah values. Let us consider an example pointed out to me by R. Yosef Bronstein. In *Tanna de-Bei Eliyahu*, Ch. 9, it states, "A proper woman (*isha kesheira*) is one who performs the will of her husband." This statement is cited by Rama (*Even ha-Ezer* 10:9). Along similar lines, Rambam writes, "Our Sages commanded ("*tzivu chachamim*")... a woman to honor her

In summary, according to the understandings cited above, the Yerushalmi's statement that we do not learn from Aggadot does not imply that aggadic material is not authoritative regarding non-halachic matters. On the contrary, it may be the case that fundamentally, aggadic passages of the Talmud are fully authoritative with respect to aggadic matters, just as the halachic passages of the Talmud are authoritative on halachic matters.

Those Who See Aggada as Less Authoritative

A number of Geonic statements, however, imply a different understanding of the Yerushalmi's statement that we do not learn from Haggadot:

ר' האי גאון מובא באוצר הגאונים למסכת חגיגה עמוד 59
הוו יודעים כי דברי אגדה לאו כשמועה הם אלא כל אחד דורש מה שעלה על לבו כגון אפשר ויש לומר, לא דבר חתוך, **לפיכך אין סומכים עליהם.**

husband exceedingly... She should carry out all her deeds according to his directives" (*Hilchot Ishut* 15:19–20). To what extent is this mentality binding today? Firstly, we must consider whether Rambam's formulation implies that there is a halachic obligation for a wife to listen to her husband. R. Mordechai Willig notes that the Rambam's usage of the expression "*tzivu chachamim*" always refers to rabbinic advice as opposed to normative law. Therefore, while Rambam understands that Chazal *counseled* a wife to submit to her husband's opinion, this is not an obligatory model for a Jewish marriage. Yet even if there is no halachic obligation for a wife to listen to her husband, we still must consider whether Chazal's statements are meant to convey a certain model for an ideal spousal relationship. A straightforward reading of the above statement certainly has that connotation, and this, in fact, is the approach taken by a number of contemporary thinkers, including R. Avraham Arlinger, former Rosh Yeshiva of Yeshivat Kol Torah (*Birkat Avraham: Ma'amarim ve-Hadrachot* p. 326). R. Aharon Lichtenstein, however, disagrees ("Of Marriage: Relationships and Relations," in *Gender and Relationships in Marriage and Out*, The Orthodox Forum Series, 2007, pp. 2–5). R. Lichtenstein maintains that a different model may be appropriate nowadays because he views the statements in Chazal as practical advice and not as a reflection of timeless Torah values. R. Lichtenstein implies that were it the case that they were meant normatively, even if they were attitudes/values and non-halachic, they would be binding regardless of any societal developments. We elaborate on the notion of Torah values as expressed in aggadic statements in 5.3. R. Bronstein subsequently developed this topic in http://www.thelehrhaus.com/scholarship/she-should-carry-out-all-her-deeds?rq=bronstein.

You should know that aggadic texts are not based on tradition. Rather, each author expounded what he considered to be possible but not necessarily definitive. **Therefore, we do not rely upon them.**

רב שרירא גאון מובא באוצר הגאונים למסכת חגיגה עמוד 60
הני מילי דנפקי מפסוקי (מקרא) [ומקרי] מדרש ואגדה - אומדנא נינהו... **לכן אין סומכים על אגדה.** ואמרו: אין למדין מן האגדות... ונכון מהם, מה שמתחזק מן השכל ומן המקרא - נקבל מהם, ואין סוף ותכלה לאגדות.

These things that are derived from Scripture, called Midrash and Aggada, are *umdena*[10]... **and for that reason, we do not rely upon Aggada**. And they stated: "We do not learn from Aggadot..." And that which is correct in them, namely, that which is supported by logical reasoning or from scriptural text – that we shall accept, and there is no end to Aggadot.[11]

10. The meaning of this statement was a point of contention between R. Azarya de Rossi and Maharal (quoted later). De Rossi understood R. Sherira to be saying that Aggada is mere conjecture and consequently less authoritative and binding than Halacha:
מאור עינים (ווילנא תרכ״ו) אמרי בינה פרק ט״ו עמוד 210
ואמנה אשר יוציאנו מן המצור הזה יהיה הגאון האמתי רב שרירא ז״ל וגם בנו ההולך בדרכיו הגאון רב האי ז״ל במאמרים הביאם בעל המנורה בהקדמתו, וזה כי רב שרירא ז״ל במגלת סתריו על דבר האגדות כתב וז״ל הני מילי דנפקי מפסוקי ומקרו מדרש ואגדה אומדנא נינהו, ורב האי בנו כאשר נשאל מה בין המדרש והאגדה הנכתבים בגמרא והכתובים חוצה לה השיב כי הנקבע בגמרא הוא מחוור ממה שלא נקבע בה.
אשר מאלו נקח שהאגדות בלי ספק אינם הלכה ודאית ומקובלת אבל אומדנא בעלמא מן הממציא אותה, ויש ממנה דבר דבור על אופניו אהוב חביב ונחמד, וממנה גם כן בהפך כי לא כל אדם זוכה ליטול בה את השם כאשר יאונה גם כן ביתר שערי בינה. ...
ובכן עם כל מה שהצענו למעלה בשבח דבריהם ז״ל לא נחדל מלומר כי האגדות אשר תכליתן כפי הוראת תארן מלשון נגד ונפק הוא למשוך את לבות בני האדם אל משמע דברינו, לא בלבד שמיעת האזן כההיא דר׳ במכילתא פסוק (שמות טו:י) נטית ימינך ושיר רבה פסוק (שיר השירים א:טו) הנך יפה רעיתי שבהיותו דורש ראה הצבור מתנמנם וכדי לעוררן אמר אשה אחת ילדה במצרים ששים רבוא בכרס אחד, אבל שמיעת הלב שהוא העקר לקבל את הלמודים ולהמשך על פיהם מן הפחיתיות אל המעלות ובפרט לאהבתו יתברך

11. The cited work of R. Sherira Gaon apparently is not extant, but it is quoted by R. Avraham b. Yitzchak of Narbonne (c. 1110–1179), also known as Ra'avad II, in *Sefer ha-Eshkol*. Since this passage is subject to considerable dispute, we quote it fully:

רבי שמואל הנגיד מבוא לתלמוד ערך הגדה[12]

והגדה הוא כל פירוש שיבא בתלמוד על שום ענין שלא יהיה מצוה, זו היא הגדה. ואין לך ללמוד ממנה אלא מה שיעלה על הדעת. ויש לך לדעת שכל מה שקיימו חז"ל הלכה בענין מצוה שהיא מפי משה רבינו ע"ה שקבל מפי הגבורה אין לך להוסיף עליו ולא לגרוע ממנו, אבל מה שפירשו בפסוקים כל אחד כפי מה שנזדמן לו ומה שראה בדעתו, ולפי מה שיעלה על הדעת מן הפירושים האלו לומדים אותם והשאר אין סומכין עליהם.

ספר האשכול (מהדורת אלבעק: ירושלים תשמ"ד) הלכות ספר תורה דף נט:–ס. עמוד 157 ואמר מר [רב] שרירא הני מילי דנפקי מפסוקי ומקרי מדרש ואגדה אומדנא נינהו, ויש מהן שהוא כך, כגון דברי [ר'] יהודה בענין וזאת ליהודה שאמר ששמעון מוכלל עם יהודה, שהרי מצינו חלקו ביהושע בתוך נחלת יהודה, והרבה יש שאינו כן, כגון מה שאמר ר' עקיבא דמקושש היינו צלפחד, וכגון שאמר ר' שמעון שצום העשירי זה עשרה בטבת, והם הזכירו דעתו של כל אחד ואחד, ואנו לפי שכלו יהולל איש. וכן אגדות שאמרו תלמידי התלמידים, כגון רבי תנחומא ורבי אושעיא וזולתם, רובם אינו כן, ולכך אין אנו סומכין על דברי אגדה. והנכון מהם מה שמתחזק מן השכל ומן המקרא מדבריהם, ואין סוף ותכלה לאגדות.

Subsequently, the Eshkol cites the Geonic position that distinguishes between Aggadot cited in the Talmud and those not cited:

ונשאל ממר רב האיי ז"ל מה הפרש בין ההגדה והמדרש הכתובין בתלמוד שאינן מצויין להסיר שבושן, וההגדות הכתובות חוץ לתלמוד. והשיב כלל זה שכל מה שנקבע בתלמוד מחוור הוא ממה שלא נקבע בו, ואף על פי כן הגדה ומדרש אף על פי שכתובין בתלמוד אם לא יכוונו ואם ישתבשו אין לסמוך עליהם, כי כללינו הוא אין סומכין על ההגדה, אלא מה שקבוע בתלמוד שאנו מוצאין להסיר שבושן ולחזקן יש עלינו לעשות, כי לולא שיש בו מדרש לא נקבע בתלמוד. ומה שאין אנו מוצאין דרך לסלק שבושו נעשה כדברים שאין הלכה. ומה שלא נקבע בתלמוד אין אנו צריכין לכל כך, אלא מעיינין בו אם נכון הוא ויפה, דורשין אותו ומלמדין אותו, ואם לאו אין אנו משגיחין עליו.

This version is from the Albeck Eshkol, though it also is found in the Aurbach version. It is hard to know precisely what this passage means. He clearly is contrasting midrashim that are rooted in Scripture (e.g., that Shimon's portion is inside Yehuda's) and others that are not (e.g., that the *mikosheish* in *Bamidbar* 15:32 was Tzlofchad). Moreover, with respect to the latter category, there is debate (e.g., there are other views regarding the identity of the *mikosheish*). What remains unclear is whether the latter category merely is not in accordance with *pshat*, as Maharal avers, or is less authoritative, as R. Azarya de Rossi maintains. Another ambiguity relates to whether the second category is common or exceptional. The above citation of R. Sherira Gaon indicates that it is common. In the Introduction to *Menorat ha-Ma'or*, however, R. Sherira Gaon is cited as stating that this second category is uncommon.

12. Many scholars believe that this was actually written by R. Sherira Gaon, in which case it would be consistent with his previous remarks.

> Aggada is any commentary that is presented in the Talmud on any topic that is not related to a *mitzva* (i.e., Halacha) – that is Aggada. And you should not accept it unless it is reasonable. You should know that Chazal established Halacha in the context of a *mitzva* based on the teachings of Moshe, who received it from God, and [therefore,] you may not add to it nor detract from it. But what they explained regarding Scripture, each one according to his understanding and what he considered reasonable, we accept what is reasonable based on the text; the rest, we do not rely upon.

Statements such as these may indicate that there is a second camp that contends that the Yerushalmi means to tell us that aggadic statements are less authoritative because they are innovations, and do not reflect a tradition going back to Moshe. Thus, we accept that which is reasonable and are not bound to follow that which we do not understand. Some Geonim also distinguished between Aggadot cited in the Talmud, which are more authoritative, and those cited in other Midrashic texts, which are less authoritative.[13]

Such a position is taken up much later by R. Samson Raphael Hirsch, who sees this difference as being alluded to in the very words that Chazal used to describe these areas of Torah. In his forward to Horeb, he writes:

> There will accordingly be two schools of study engaged in the exposition of the divine law, differing only in the sources from which they draw their knowledge of it. One school will concern itself with the comprehension of the utterances regulating our practical conduct in and for themselves, and of the lessons equally concerned with practice which can be derived from those

13. **אוצר הגאונים למסכת חגיגה עמוד 60**
כל מה שנקבע בתלמוד מחוור הוא ממה שלא נקבע בו, ואף על פי כן, הגדות הכתובות בו בתלמוד, אם לא יכוונו, או אם ישתבשו, אין לסמוך עליהם, כי כלל הוא: אין סומכין על אגדה.
Other thinkers who maintain this distinction are cited in *Encyclopedia Talmudit* Vol. 1, entry "Aggada," footnote 28.

> utterances; and its knowledge will be derived almost exclusively from the tradition which transmits the oral and written Divine utterances and the regulations of the Sages. The other school will concern itself with reflecting and pondering on these laws, and its source of knowledge will be the more or less illuminating power of insight which dwells in each individual religious thinker. The work of the first school lies before us in the שמעתתא made up of things heard (שמע). The work of the second we find in the אגדתא, made up of the ideas which have occurred to each one, of what each one has related (הגיד). Everything belonging to the first school is obligatory, because it emanates from the authority which has power to bind. All that springs from the second school has no power to bind, because it represents only the views of individuals, and can claim recognition only in so far as it is in conformity with what is contained in the work of the first school. The work of the first school, from the very nature of its contents, came to an end with the completion of the Gemara, the collection of the שמעתתא. The production of אגדתא is, however, free and capable of enlargement at all times.

In 5.4, we note that this may not be the only understanding of the above Geonic statements. Maharal claims that all major thinkers, even the Geonim, acknowledged Chazal's authoritativeness even in non-halachic matters. However, even if we take the Geonic statements at face value and presume that many Geonim denied that aggadic statements are authoritative, we must consider whether the Rishonim agree with this sentiment.

It would seem that there is no consensus among Rishonim. Rashi, for example, in numerous places (such as *Bamidbar* 26:24) appears to see Aggada as authoritative.[14] Radak seems to disagree (see, for example, *Yehoshua* 5:14). Rambam and Ramban, as we shall see, both have complex positions on this question, and we consider their positions

14. Concerning the interpretation of R. Moshe ha-Darshan, Rashi (*Bamidbar* 26:24) writes, "ואם אגדה היא הרי טוב ואם לאו...," implying that if it is an aggada, it must be accepted, but if it is only an interpretation of a post-Talmudic figure, as *Siftei Chachamim* deduces, it could be rejected.

in Chapters 6 and 7, respectively. However, over all, most Acharonim tend to embrace the authoritativeness of Aggada in a way that many Geonim and some Rishonim[15] do not. How do we account for this evolution? We will address this question briefly in 5.10.

Why Distinguish?

What basis would there be for distinguishing between the authoritativeness of Chazal on halachic and aggadic matters? The Geonic statements above indicate that the difference lies in the source of Chazal's

---

שפתי חכמים במדבר פרשת פינחס פרק כו

כלומר אם ר׳ משה הדרשן מצא טעם זה בספר אגדה הרי טוב ואיני רשאי לחלוק עליו ואם לאו אומר אני כו׳ כלומר ואם טעמא דנפשיה קאמר אומר אני גם כן טעם אחר מעצמי:

15. A number of Rishonim appear to accept the general approach of the Geonim (though they tend to use more reverential language). Consider, for example, the following quotes taken from *Kuzari* 3:73:

אשר ל׳הגדות׳ יש מהן המשמשות הצעות והקדמות לדעה שהיו מבקשים לחזקה ולאשרה...

ויש שההגדות מספרות על ראיית רוחניים במראה, ואין זה פלא שחסידים כאלה יראו, בכח פרישותם הגדולה וזכוך דעותם... כי דבר זה אפשרי, אם יש אפוא קבלה נאמנה על הדומה לזה, יש להאמין בה...

ויש שההגדות הן משלים שנשאו על סודות החכמות שאסור לגלותם....

אמנם יש הגדות הנראות כנטולות שחר, אך אחרי עיון כלשהו יתברר ענינן...

ולא אכחד ממך, מלך כוזר, כי יש בתלמוד מאמרים שאיני יכול לבארם לך באור מספיק, ואף לא אוכל להראותך באיזה קשר הם עומדים עם העניין שהם דנים בו. מאמרים אלה הוכנסו אל התלמוד על ידי התלמידים אשר השתדלו לשמור על הכלל שהיה בידם ״אפילו שיחת חכמים צריכה תלמוד״ (עבודה זרה יט ב), ומאד היו נזהרים לא לאמר דבר שלא שמעו מרבותם והשתדלו לאמר כל מה ששמעו מפי רבותם, ומה ששמעו מרבותם זהירים היו לאמרו בלשונם ממש, אפילו לא הבינו משמעו, ואז היו אומרים: כך שמענו וקבלנו, ויתכן כי לרב היו בזה כוונות שנעלמו מתלמידיו, כך הגיע מאמר זה אלינו, והננו מזלזלים בו, מפני שאיננו יודעים כוונתו. אולם כל זה רק בדברים שאינם נוגעים לאיסור והתר. **אל נשים אפוא לב למאמרים אלה, וחיבורנו התלמוד לא יגרע מערכו אם נסתפק באפנים נשתמש בכללים שהזכרנו.**

Here are a number of additional statements along similar lines:

רבינו חננאל מסכת חגיגה דף יב עמוד א

אלו כולן מדרשות הן ואין מדקדקין עליהן להשוותן למה שהדעת מתקבלת מהן.

אבן עזרא הפירוש הקצר שמות ב:ט

וסוף דבר, אמרו הגאונים על הדרש אין מקשין בו ולא ממנו:

מגן אבות לרשב״ץ על אבות ב:יג

וכמו שאמרו רז״ל כי הוו רבנן חלישי מגרסייהו, הוו אמרי מילי דבדיחותא, **וזהו ענין האגדות הזרות הנמצאות בתלמוד.**

My appreciation to R. Matt Lubin for pointing these sources out to me.

understanding. Chazal's halachic interpretations of the Torah are Sinaiatic; not so regarding their aggadic elucidations. However, as we shall see in Chapter 28, many Rishonim aver that at least some of Chazal's halachic expositions are novel. For example, Rambam writes in his Introduction to his commentary on the Mishna that we should presume that there is no direct tradition concerning matters in the Talmud about which there is disagreement. Thus, Rambam maintains that many of the halachic *drashot* do not derive directly from tradition but were extrapolated by Chazal. If the latter position is correct, we must once again wonder about the basis for distinguishing between the authoritativeness of Chazal on halachic and aggadic matters. Put differently, why are the halachic conclusions of Chazal, that do *not* stem from tradition, more binding than the aggadic conclusions of Chazal, that also do *not* stem from tradition?

To answer this question, we first must address why we cannot argue with Chazal regarding halachic matters, and then consider whether that reason applies to aggadic matters. Presumably, the authority of Chazal in halachic matters does not lie in Chazal's infallibility. While their ability to correctly understand the Torah certainly is unparalleled, error is conceivable (see 4.9). Moreover, as Rambam explains in the first two chapters of *Hilchot Mamrim*, a court of lower intellectual standing can disagree with a court of superior standing with respect to the interpretation of the Torah. Why, then, can't we argue with Chazal? We address this question in greater depth in Chapter 28, but for the time being, let us briefly introduce the matter. Rambam writes:

> **הקדמה לספר משנה תורה**
> כל הדברים שבתלמוד הבבלי חיבין כל בית ישראל ללכת בהם וכופין כל עיר ועיר וכל מדינה ומדינה לנהג בכל המנהגות שנהגו חכמים שבתלמוד ולגזור גזרותם וללכת בתקנותם, הואיל וכל אותן הדברים שבתלמוד הסכימו עליהם כל ישראל.
>
> Whatever is in the Talmud Bavli is binding upon all of the people of Israel; and every city and town is forced to observe all the customs observed by the Talmud's scholars and to enact their restrictive legislations and to observe their positive legislations. For all those matters in the Talmud received the assent of all of Israel.

Rambam asserts that the authority of the Talmud is rooted in its having been accepted by the Jewish people.[16] Rambam implies that such acceptance grants their rulings the legal status of decisions made by the *Sanhedrin*,[17] whose rulings (both interpretive and legislative) are binding (based on *Devarim*, Chapter 17). Rambam notes that since the Talmud Bavli's completion, there has not been a document or legal body universally accepted by the Jewish people to the same degree. Hence, all post-Talmudic enactments are compulsory only locally, and post-Talmudic rulings are binding only to the extent that their logic is compelling.

With this, let us return to our question. Following Rambam's perspective, why might one distinguish between the halachic and aggadic statements of Chazal? Presumably, the answer is that it is only with respect to halachic rulings that we say that universal acceptance of the Jewish people generates authoritativeness. (This parallels the notion explained in 5.7 that according to R. Bachya, the *Sanhedrin* cannot issue binding rulings concerning non-halachic matters.) Thus, if the difference between Chazal and post-Chazal were rooted in the expertise of Chazal, then perhaps we would not distinguish between halachic and aggadic matters. After all, Chazal were equally expert in both realms. However, since their authority is rooted in acceptance, it is only with respect to normative law that we say that acceptance imparts authority. Concerning Aggada, no such rule exists.

16. Rambam states this explicitly with respect to *gezeirot, takanot,* and *minhagim* (restrictive legislations, affirmative legislations, and customs). Rambam implies in a number of places that universal acceptance also is the basis of the authoritativeness of the Talmud with respect to all of its rulings. For example, the continuation of the above sentence states:

    ואותן החכמים שהתקינו או שגזרו או שהנהיגו או שדנו דין ולמדו שהמשפט כך הוא הם כל חכמי ישראל או רובן, והם ששמעו הקבלה בעקרי התורה כלה איש מפי איש עד משה רבנו.

    Kesef Mishneh (*Hilchot Mamrim* 2:1) sees the Talmud's authority as rooted in the principle of *rov*. We return to this topic in Chapter 28.

17. R. Elchanan Wasserman, among others, suggests that this is because the authority of the Sanhedrin is rooted in the Jewish people and would explain how Rambam knew that the Sanhedrin and *semicha* can be reconstituted (*Kuntrus Divrei Sofrim, Siman 2, Koveitz Shiurim,* Vol. 2, p. 96).

To summarize, there are two reasons why one would argue that the halachic rulings of Chazal are binding whereas their aggadic teachings are not:

1. The Geonim explain that this is because there is a *mesora* (tradition) for their halachic teachings.
2. One could argue that according to Rambam, Chazal's halachic rulings have the binding status of a legal ruling of the Sanhedrin due to national acceptance. Non-legal teachings (Aggada), on the other hand, are not legally binding. Therefore, they can be disputed.

Thus, we have offered a reason to distinguish between the binding nature of halachic and non-halachic Talmudic statements according to Rambam. We have not shown, however, that Rambam actually makes such a distinction. Perhaps Rambam, in contrast to the simple understanding of the Geonim, maintains that Aggada is binding. We address this question in Chapter 6.

Do Aggadic Statements Come from Moshe?

We have seen that numerous Geonim contend that *midrashei Aggada* (as opposed to *midrashei Halacha*) do not necessarily come from God through Moshe.[18] Presumably, even these thinkers concede that some aggadic statements do go back to Sinai. Sometimes, this can be determined by the formulation used in the Talmud. For example, the Talmud states that we have a tradition (*gemiri*) that Avraham was 52 years old when he began converting the people of Charan.[19] The term *gemiri* likely indicates Sinaiatic origin.[20] Likewise, the Talmud states that we

18. As noted, many Rishonim maintain that even when it comes to matters of Halacha, we should not assume that everything stated by Chazal comes *directly* from Moshe.

19. **תלמוד בבלי מסכת עבודה זרה דף ט עמוד א**
וגמירי, דאברהם בההיא שעתא בר חמשין ותרתי הוה.

20. Others, like Netziv, note that *gemiri* may just imply an ancient tradition. The term is used, for example, with reference to events that happened after Sinai; see *Shabbat* 55b, *Yevamot* 17a, and *Sanhedrin* 92b.

have a tradition (*mesora*) that the place of the ark did not occupy space.[21] This formulation also may indicate Sinaiatic origin. Nevertheless, most of the midrashim offer no indication that their basis of information is tradition. This leads numerous Geonim to maintain that the words of Aggada do not necessarily come from God through Moshe.

How are we to know if a particular midrash stems from Sinai (absent an explicit reference)? It is not always easy to know. But Rambam gives us a helpful tool in his discussion of *mashiach*. As we shall see in Chapter 24, there are numerous views in Chazal concerning the details of how *mashiach* will come. Rambam informs us that this alone indicates that even the Sages lacked a tradition about this matter (perhaps reflecting that there are in fact multiple possibilities):

רמב"ם הלכות מלכים פרק יב הלכה ב
וכל אלו הדברים וכיוצא בהן לא ידע אדם איך יהיו עד שיהיו, שדברים סתומין הן אצל הנביאים, **גם החכמים אין להם קבלה בדברים אלו,** אלא לפי הכרע הפסוקים, **ולפיכך יש להם מחלוקת בדברים אלו.**

It is not known how all these and similar matters will occur until they occur, for they are topics sealed off [from definitive knowledge] by the Prophets. **The Sages themselves have no established tradition regarding these matters** beyond what can be derived from the verses; **therefore, they have disagreements in these matters**.

Here, Rambam applies a principle that he articulates in his Introduction to his commentary on the Mishna, namely that debate reflects a lack of tradition. After all, if there were a tradition, the conflicting opinions would accept the tradition and the disagreement would dissipate. Since the Sages have many debates concerning the details of *mashiach*'s arrival, we can conclude that they do not have a tradition on these matters. It

21. **תלמוד בבלי מסכת מגילה דף י עמוד ב**
ואמר רבי לוי: דבר זה מסורת בידינו מאבותינו: מקום ארון אינו מן המדה.

would seem that according to Rambam, all Aggadot that contain debate lack direct Sinaiatic origin.[22]

Thus far, we have considered the Geonic and Maimonidean position that not all midrashim are rooted in tradition going back to Sinai. Others disagree. The Yerushalmi implies that all Aggada was taught to Moshe at Sinai.[23] Accordingly, a number of thinkers affirmed the divine origin of Aggada, among them Radvaz.[24] Likewise, R. Yitzchak Abuhav[25] writes concerning the source for the Talmud's Aggadot: **וקרויין אגדות, והכל ניתן בקבלה,** "and they are called Aggadot; all of them are a received tradition."[26] Later, he emphasizes the extent to which Aggada is binding:

> **מנורת המאור מוסד הרב קוק ירושלים תשכ"א עמוד 100**
> כל מה שאמרו ז"ל במדרשות ובהגדות, חייבין אנו להאמין בו **כמו בתורת משה רבינו עליו השלום,** ואם נמצא בו דבר שיראה לנו שהוא דרך גוזמא או חוץ מן הטבע, יש לנו לתלות בחסרון בהשגת דעתינו, אבל לא במאמרם. והמלעיג על שום דבר ממה שאמרו ז"ל, נענש.

---

22. In the Introduction to his commentary on the Mishna, Rambam applies this principle to halachic debates. Here, he seems to apply it to aggadic sources as well. As we shall see shortly, though, thinkers like R. Dessler maintain that conflicting aggadic opinions should not be viewed as truly disagreeing. Instead, they intend to convey different perspectives. We elaborated on this principle in Chapter 4.

23. ירושלמי מגילה פ"ד ה"א: מקרא ומשנה ותלמוד **ואגדה** ואפי' מה שתלמיד וותיק עתיד להורות לפני רבו כבר **נאמר למשה מסיני.**

24. שו"ת רדב"ז חלק ד סימן רלב (אלף שג): "ונתנה מן השמים כשאר תורה שבעל פה."

25. Little is known about the life of R. Yitzchak Abuhav, who lived in Spain during the 14th century. The author of *Menorat ha-Ma'or* sometimes is referred to as R. Yitzchak Abuhav I, so as not to be confused with R. Yitzchak Abuhav II (rabbi of Castile), the supercommentator on Ramban, who died in 1493. In his preface to *Menorat ha-Ma'or,* R. Yitzchak Abuhav bemoans the lack of focus on aggadic material. He writes that experts in Talmud frequently, "consider it their duty to propose difficult questions and answer them in a witty and subtle manner but leave unnoticed the precious pearls that lie upon the bed of the Talmudic ocean, [namely,] the aggadic passages so rich in beauty and sweetness."

26. מנורת המאור מוסד הרב קוק ירושלים תשכ"א עמוד 14.

> We are required to believe everything that Chazal stated in the Midrashim and Aggadot **just as we are obligated to believe in the truth of the rest of Moshe Rabbeinu's Torah**. If we find something in it that appears to us as exaggeration or supernatural, we should explain it as owing to a lack in our understanding, not their statements. One who denigrates anything they stated will be punished.

Interestingly, while these statements appear to leave little doubt that R. Yitzchak Abuhav rejected the view of the Geonim, in his Introduction he approvingly cites the aforementioned statement of R. Sherira Gaon.[27] Maharsha as well felt so strongly that Aggada was delivered at Sinai that he insisted that his own work on Aggada and Halacha be studied as one unit.[28] Maharal, as we shall see shortly, also may be of the opinion that all aggadic material stems from Sinai. His perspective is also complex, though, as we shall see shortly.

It is possible, however, that this question of whether or not Aggada dates back to Sinai may be merely semantic. When it comes to Halacha, after all, many believe that Moshe did not literally hear every single halachic detail at Sinai, but rather that he received general principles by which Halacha was to be determined (see Chapter 28). Thus

---

27. This fascinating point is made by R. Yitzhak Grossman (http://bdld.info/2011/04/06/Aggadah-authoritative-or-umdena). How can the two statements be reconciled? It seems he understood R. Sherira Gaon's statement was referring to a small minority of Aggadot (כי דבר זה על קצת מהמדרשות שאמרו האחרונים, כגון רבי תנחומא ורבי אושעיא, ועל דברים מעטים מדברי אגדה שבתלמוד, שכתובים באומד), with most Aggadot being extraordinarily profound (אבל רובם הם סודות וחכמות עליונות). Interestingly, as noted by R. Grossman, R. Yitzchak Abuhav's understanding of R. Sherira Gaon is more along the lines of R. Azarya de Rossi, even as his application is totally different. The conclusion according to R. Yitzchak Abuhav, though, is that most Aggadot are authoritative, while a minority is conjecture.

28. **הקדמת המהרש"א לפירושו על הש"ס**
ובאמת הנני רואה עתה מחכמי התלמוד שעשו חיבור אחד מהלכות ואגדות, כי תורה אחת היא לנו, בפירושה של התורה תורת משה. וכמה וכמה דרכי מוסר וחכמה והוראות על פי תורת משה אשר יוצאים לנו מתוך דבריהם מאגדות... ועל כן הנני מבקש מאת כל מעיין שישים לבו לזאת, גם מהיום למרות שעשיתיו שני חלקים, לא יהא מפריד אותם מלעיין בשניהם.

is it possible that just as Moshe was given rules to derive Halacha, and we therefore consider Halacha to be "from Sinai," Moshe was similarly given rules and principles for later rabbis to develop Aggada. Such a position is taken by R. Zvi Hirsch Chajes (Maharatz Chayot; 1805–1855),[29] who, in his *Mevo ha-Talmud,* goes so far as to reconstruct what those principles were based on Chazal's aggadic teachings. In 5.4 we shall see Maharal also adopts a similar approach in explaining the Geonic statements that downplay the Sinaiatic origin of Aggada.

5.3 TORAH VALUES AS EXPRESSED IN AGGADA

What is the purpose of Aggada? In 1.1, we cited a number of sources that expressed how Aggada inspires fear of heaven and allows us to emulate His ways. Aggada is not simply inspiring; it is edifying, insofar as it teaches us, both explicitly and implicitly, how to live as a Jew. In Chapter 27, we consider numerous ways in which we are meant to discover the Torah's values. These include extrapolation from the Torah's stories and *mitzvot* (such as wastefulness from *bal tashchit*), value-driven *mitzvot* (such as *Devarim* 6:18, "*ve-asita ha-yashar ve-ha-tov*"), and the aggadic teachings of Chazal.

One must not underestimate the binding nature of the Torah's values. One reflection of this is the Torah's reference to both a *brit avot*, a covenant established with the forefathers, and *brit Sinai*, a covenant established at Sinai. A covenant implies commitment. *Brit Sinai* refers to our obligation to observe *mitzvot*. What obligations are imposed by *brit avot*? R. Soloveitchik explains that *brit avot* "expresses attitudes, ideals, and sentiments... it guides our feeling and consciousness... it is the backdrop of [*brit Sinai*]; [*brit Sinai*] is the behavioral fulfillment of the truths, values, and Jewish self-awareness established by [*brit avot*]."[30]

---

29. *Hagahot* to *Berachot* 5b, *Megilla* 19b, *Mishpat ha-Hora'a* Ch. 2, *Mevo ha-Talmud* Ch. 3
30. *Man of Faith in the Modern World: Reflections of the Rav*, Vol. 2 (adapted by R. Abraham R. Besdin), p. 68, cited and explained by R. Mayer Twersky in "Masorah and the Role of the Jewish Woman," available at http://www.torahweb.org. See also *Shiurei HaRav: A Conspectus of the Public Lectures of Rabbi Joseph B. Soloveitchik,* edited by Joseph Epstein, p. 51.

The Geonim May Agree that the Messages and Values of Aggadot Are Binding

Let us now return to the Geonic statement in question, "These things that are derived from Scripture, called Midrash and Aggada, are *umdena* (conjecture) … and for that reason, we do not rely upon Aggada as being authoritative." R. Sherira Gaon appears to be referring to Midrashic interpretations of the Torah's texts. The examples cited by R. Hai Gaon support this contention. One example he cites of a non-definitive aggadic statement is the view that the *mikosheish* (gatherer) in *Bamidbar* 15:32 was Tzlofchad. R. Hai Gaon maintains that the view in Chazal that made that assertion did not have a tradition to that effect, and his view therefore is non-definitive. It is not clear, however, that the Geonim would maintain that values derived from Chazal are non-binding. Considering that Chazal are a major source of the Torah's values, a strong case can be made to the contrary. Just as they are our link to Sinai with respect to the Torah's laws, they are the link with respect to the Torah's values.

One reflection of this perspective is R. Ovadya Bartenura's commentary on *Avot* (1:1). He explains that *Avot* begins with the chain of tradition leading back to Sinai in order to demonstrate that tradition is essential to ethics as well.[31] Thus, the prologue to *Avot* demonstrates that the ethics of Chazal derive from Sinai.

Moreover, even if one argues that some of the ethics described by Chazal are not reflective of an uninterrupted chain going back to Sinai, it stands to reason that since Aggada serves as a primary vehicle of our understanding of the Torah's values, the messages it contains are in fact binding. One reflection of this is Rambam's codification of numerous aggadic statements in *Hilchot Dei'ot*.[32] As R. Soloveitchik writes:

---

31. **פירוש הרע״ב על אבות א:א**
אומר אני, לפי **שמסכת זו** אינה מיוסדת על פירוש מצוה ממצות התורה כשאר מסכתות שבמשנה, אלא כולה מוסרים ומדות, וחכמי אומות העולם ג״כ חברו ספרים כמו שבדו מלבם בדרכי המוסר כיצד יתנהג האדם עם חבירו, לפיכך התחיל התנא במסכת זו משה קבל תורה מסיני, לומר לך שהמדות והמוסרים שבזו המסכתא לא בדו אותם חכמי המשנה מלבם אלא אף אלו נאמרו בסיני.

32. On the other hand, many of the ideas in *Hilchot Dei'ot* are not rooted in Chazal. The variety of material in *Hilchot Dei'ot* highlights the complexity of the determining factors that govern proper behavior.

> *Mesora* encompasses not only analytic novella, abstract theories, halakhic formulae and logical concepts ... but also ontological patterns, emotions and reactions, a certain existential rhythm and experiential continuity. Complete transmission of the *mesora* is only possible by means of intimate connection with the previous generation.[33]

The notion of the binding nature of the Torah's values emerges frequently in the writings of R. Soloveitchik and is underscored by many of his students.[34] R. Mayer Twersky eloquently expresses the role of values in ascertaining the divine will:

> *Halakha* is a two-tiered system consisting of concrete, particularized commandments governing our actions as well as abstract, general imperatives governing the matrix of our actions... The Torah legislates not only actions, but also *de'ot* (ethical-moral-religious-intellectual dispositions). It prescribes ritual but also establishes boundaries for the concomitant religious experience.
>
> The reason for halakha's binary system is self-evident. The Torah is not content with ensuring technically correct behavior; it also seeks to mold the human personality. Accordingly, it is concerned not only with our actions but also the etiology and telos of those actions as well. The dual focus of Torah law has important repercussions for the methodology of *pesak*. Any contemplated action or course of action must be evaluated on two levels. We must investigate if it is technically correct and permissible – viz, are any particulars of Torah violated. In addition, we must determine if the proposal is consistent with Torah principles, attitudes, values and concepts. The permissibility or appropriateness of any particular action or initiative can only

33. *Be-Sod ha-Yachid ve-ha-Yachad*, p. 270, cited by R. Mayer Twersky in "Halakhic Values and Halakhic Decisions," *Tradition* 32:3 (Spring 1998).
34. The aforementioned articles by R. Twersky are examples.

> be determined after such a two-pronged analysis – practical and axiological…
>
> It is, however, vitally important that we recognize that the axiological concern is not optional or supererogatory. It is not, in halakhic terminology, merely a *middat hasidut* or *mitsva min ha-muvhar*. Instead it is an integral part of our Torah and tradition, and compliance therewith is mandatory. Accordingly, *hakhmei ha-mesora* transmit and implement both tiers of our *mesora* – viz, the technical-practical as well as the emotional-axiological.[35]

To summarize, the Torah demands adherence not simply to Halacha (narrowly defined), but to the Torah's values. The fact that the Geonim maintained that Chazal's Midrashic understanding of the Torah is not binding does not imply that their presentation of the Torah's values can be ignored.

5.4 MAHARAL ON AGGADA

Perhaps the greatest champion of the Aggadot of Chazal is Maharal. Though he composed halachic works as well, most of Maharal's writings explicate and elucidate aggadic texts in ways both original and highly sophisticated. In his *Be'eir ha-Gola*, Maharal defends Chazal – and specifically Aggada – from critiques that proliferated in his time (many of which still are common). Here, we consider his explanation of the Geonic statements cited earlier that seemingly downplay the authoritativeness of Aggada. First, though, we will examine a little background regarding to whom Maharal was responding. R. Azarya de Rossi (עזריה מן האדומים, 1514–1578), in the fifteenth chapter of *Imrei Bina*, critiques the seeming exaggerations and historical inaccuracies in Aggada. To appreciate this debate, we need to briefly introduce this scholar.

The Italian intellectual known in Hebrew as עזריה מן האדומים is best known for his book *Me'or Einayim*, where he uses critical methods to assess aggadic texts. In *Imrei Bina*, a section of *Me'or Einayim*,

35. "Halakhic Values and Halakhic Decisions," *Tradition* 32:3 (Spring 1998).

he rejects many of the traditional assumptions concerning Jewish history by comparing traditional Jewish sources such as the Talmud with classical historical texts, generally accepting the facts given in the non-Jewish sources over those in the Talmud. R. Azarya de Rossi also relied on the writings of Church Fathers, including Eusebius, Jerome, Augustine, Justin Martyr, and Clement of Alexandria. He also rejected the authoritativeness of *Yosipon*, which was assumed to have been written by Josephus, claiming it was a medieval work that utilized the writings of Josephus but also falsified historical facts. One of his most controversial claims concerned the Jewish calendar that numbers the years from creation; R. Azarya de Rossi argued that this count was a relatively recent Jewish usage, not one that had been utilized by the Talmud or Geonim.

In 1574, even before the printing of *Me'or Einayim* was completed, the rabbis of Venice, headed by R. Shmuel Yehuda Katzenellenbogen, issued a *cheirem* (ban) against owning or reading the book without special permission from the rabbis of the city. Later bans followed. One of the most eloquent challengers of R. Azarya de Rossi, as we shall see shortly, was Maharal.[36] However, we should note that not all traditional Jewish thinkers dismissed R. Azarya de Rossi. His work is cited by *Tosafot Yom Tov* (*Menachot* 10:3), *Minchat Shai* (*Zechariah* 14:5), *Chavot Ya'ir* (*Teshuvot Chavot Ya'ir* 9), and *Ha'ameik Davar* (*Shemot* 28:36).[37] While these citations do not imply endorsement of all of his views, they likely indicate respect for his scholarship.

Maharal's Understanding of the Geonic Statements Downplaying the Authoritativeness of Aggada

How did R. Azarya de Rossi justify his rejection of Talmudic sources? Among other things, he turned to the Geonic statements cited earlier that question the authoritativeness of aggadic teachings and imply that the

36. Much of the above information is taken from Dr. Joseph Dan's "Rossi, Azariah (Bonaiuto) ben Moses dei" in *Encyclopaedia Judaica*. Ed. Michael Berenbaum and Fred Skolnik. 2nd ed. Vol. 17. Detroit: Macmillan Reference USA, 2007.

37. This partial list is taken from an article by Leopold Zunz published in Volume 5 of the journal *Kerem Chemed*. A discussion of this article can be found in a post by R. Gil Student at http://www.torahmusings.com/2006/03/meor-einayim.

words of Aggada are inferior. R. Azarya de Rossi bolsters his claims by finding statements within Chazal that seem to disparage Aggada. Maharal responds to this approach, however, by explaining that R. Azarya de Rossi misunderstood R. Sherira Gaon:

> **באר הגולה באר השישי פרק טו**
> כי הגאון ז"ל בא לומר, שאל יאמר כי כאשר דרשו דבר מן המקרא, והם באמת רחוקים מן לשון המקרא, ועל זה אמר כי הם אומדנא, **רוצה לומר הסברא מחייב זה, רק שסמכו הענין על הכתוב. ואם לא היה הדעת והסברא מחייב אותם, לא היו דורשים אותם מן המקרא.**
>
> For the Gaon stated that one should not say that when they concluded something from Scripture – specifically, when it is clear that the conclusion is very distant from the plain reading of the text – [that they are Sinaitic]. About these *drashot* he stated that they are *umdena* (conjecture). **[By *umdena*] he intended to state that the *sevara* (logic) demanded this conclusion. If the intellect had not independently established the truth of the thought, the author never would have derived it from the text at hand.**

According to Maharal, when R. Sherira Gaon wrote that the exegetical interpretations (*drashot*) of Chazal deviate from the simple reading of the text and are invented (*umdena*), he meant to say that when *drashot* deviate from the simple understanding of the verse, this indicates that Chazal independently discovered the principle and interpret the verse accordingly. The verse does not serve as the true source for the idea. In other words, the Midrashim are not intended to reflect the simple understanding of the verses but still are conveying important religious truths. And because the intellect of the author verifies the truth of the thought, the author is comfortable linking the thought to a particular verse.

Maharal is alluding to an important principle. Even in halachic matters, as we shall see in Chapter 27, we do not derive all laws from the Torah's text. Sometimes, a law is derived from *sevara*. For example, the Talmud (*Sanhedrin* 74a) uses *sevara* to deduce that one must give up his life before committing murder.[38] In fact, in three places (*Bava Kama* 46b, *Ketubot* 22a, and *Nidda* 25a) the Talmud asks, "Why do I need a biblical verse to teach me this idea? It is a *sevara*!" Thus, explains Maharal, when R. Sherira writes that some statements of Chazal are *umdena* (conjecture), he merely is stating that aggadic matters, like halachic matters, are sometimes derived logically. Accordingly, R. Sherira's statement does not in any way denigrate aggadic material.

R. Azarya de Rossi cites a number of additional statements to support his contention that Aggada is to be treated less seriously, such as this one: The Yerushalmi (*Shabbat* 16:1) states, "He who writes Aggada has no portion [in the world to come]." To this, Maharal responds that this is not meant to be disparaging, but rather is a reflection of the prohibition against recording the oral law.[39]

Can Anything Be Proved from Aggada?

Next, R. Azarya de Rossi turns to a statement of R. Nissim Gaon, who said concerning a certain cryptic aggadic passage (*Berachot* 59a):

> הא מלתא אגדתא היא, ובכל דדמיא ליה אמרו רבנן אין סומכין על דברי אגדה.
>
> This story is from the Aggada. Concerning it and all similar things Chazal say: "We do not rely upon Aggada."

---

38. סברא הוא... מי יימר דדמא דידך סומק טפי דילמא דמא דהוא גברא סומק טפי.

39. **וכן הראיה שהביא מהא דאמר (ירושלמי שבת פט"ז ה"א) "הכותבה אין לו חלק," חס ושלום שיאמר דבר כזה על האגדות, שכל סתרי תורה וחכמה צפונים שם, למי שידע להבין.** אבל דבר זה, כי היו רגילים לכתוב אגדות, כי כל הלכות היו רגילים ושכיחים בהם על פה, אבל אגדות לא היו רגילים בה על פה, והיו צריכים לכתוב. ולפיכך תמצא גמרא בכמה דוכתי; (ברכות כג א) גבי רבי יוחנן, כד הוי עייל לבית הכסא, הוי נקט ספר אגדתא והוי יהיב ליה. ועוד (ב"מ קטז א), הוי מפיק ספרא דאגדתא בדברים העשוים להשאיל ולהשכיר. ועוד (גטין ס א) רבי יוחנן הוי מעיין בספר אגדתא בשבתא. ולא תמצא 'ספר הלכות', וזה מפני כי היו רגילים בעל פה בהלכה, ולא היו צריכים לכתוב. אבל אגדה היו כותבים, מפני שלא היו בקיאים בה על פה. ועל זה אמרו שם (ירושלמי שבת פט"ז ה"א) 'הכותבה אין לו חלק', מפני שאסור לעשות ספר חוץ מן כ"ד ספרים, ולפיכך 'אין לו חלק', כלומר שאין לו חלק לעולם הבא, דהוי כאילו מוסיף תורה, כך היה בימיהם. ועתה משום (תהלים קיט:קכו) "עת לעשות לה' הפרו תורתך", לכך כותבין תורה שבעל פה (גיטין ס א).

A similar suggestion can be found in *Shut Radvaz* 4:23.

R. Azarya de Rossi understands R. Nissim as acknowledging that Midrash does not present profound wisdom, but rather was an oratorical tool used to capture the attention of the audience. Maharal rejects this interpretation and offers the following explanation of R. Nissim:

> רק שרוצה לומר שאין לסמוך על דברי אגדה לפרש האגדה כפשוטה.
>
> [R. Nissim Gaon] meant to say that we should not understand Aggada at face value.

In other words, the passage from *Berachot* 59a (which describes God's tears upon seeing a broken world) should not be understood literally or superficially. There is a deeper meaning.

Like Rambam and others, Maharal warns against understanding Midrash literally. He maintains that much of the criticism of Aggada stems from superficial readings. In his defense of Aggada, Maharal suggests a remarkable limitation: a person never can refute something (or definitively prove something) based on an aggadic statement, since the aggadic statement might not be meant literally:

> וזהו בעצמו מה שאמרו אין משיבין באגדה, כי אפשר האומר אותה אמרו על דרך נעלם, ולפיכך אין משיבין ואין מקשין באגדה לפשוטה.
>
> This is precisely what they meant when they said, "We do not ask questions from [or learn from] Aggada," because the author may have intended a hidden meaning. Thus, we may not ask a question based on the simple understanding of an aggadic statement.

Aggadic statements differ from halachic statements. Halachic statements are understood simply unless there is compelling evidence to the contrary.[40] When R. Shmuel ha-Nagid (cited in 5.2) says that we do not learn

---

40. בשלמא בדבר הלכה ודין, הרי אין ראוי לפסוק דין אלא אם כן אין עליו שום סתירה, ואם יש עליו סתירה, אין ראוי לעשות מעשה עליו, ולפיכך יש להקשות. אבל דבר כזה, שאין דין יוצא מזה, לא איסור ולא היתר, אין להקשות ולסתור המאמר, כי אולי לא ימצא תירוץ, ויסתור המאמר עד שיהיה בטל, ומסתמא אינו קשיא, כי לא טעה בעל המאמר.

from Aggada, he means that since Aggada cannot always be understood according to its literal meaning, one cannot refute it, because perhaps the Aggada is being misunderstood. This, according to Maharal, is the meaning of the Yerushalmi (cited in 5.2) that "We do not learn from Aggadot"; we cannot derive definitive proof for an idea from Aggada.[41]

Does the fact that we cannot use Aggada to refute or prove a concept undermine its value? Maharal certainly did not think so. In fact, he frequently uses Aggada to prove his contentions. This does not contradict his resolution, though, because Chazal do use Aggadot to convey meaning. The strength of Maharal's explanations of Aggadot lies in the fact that they are compelling interpretations. (Upon reading one of his interpretations, one frequently concludes that this certainly is what Chazal meant.) Moreover, if there are numerous sources that point in the same direction, one can be confident that he is understanding Chazal correctly. Even more importantly, Maharal generally does not attempt to prove a theory using Midrash. Instead, he tries to understand a midrash on its own terms and then shows that there are other Aggadot that present a similar theme.

Maharal then offers an additional understanding of the Yerushalmi's statement that we cannot learn Halacha from Aggada. The goal of Aggada is to present different perspectives, and thus it cannot be relied

41. Moreover, he adds that the words of Aggada were not analyzed through questions and answers as were the halachic statements of Chazal; therefore, one cannot be certain of their meaning. Hence, אין למדין הלכה מתוך האגדה. In this sense, there is a parallel to the statement אין למדין הלכה מפי משנה – the reason we cannot derive Halacha from a mishna or tosefta also is because it has not been analyzed by the Gemara.

R. Yaakov Kamenetsky, along the lines of Maharal cited earlier, suggests the reason "we cannot refute an aggadic statement" is because the true source for the particular teaching is not necessarily the verse cited. The ideas taught in aggada are known independently and then associated with one verse or another. Thus, if one scriptural source does not work another can be found. (This can be seen as a forerunner for a certain style of Chassidic Torah where the teachings a connected to the verses in a tenuous manner and it is understood that lesson is not truly being derived from the particular verse.)

אמת ליעקב (וישלח לד:יג, עמ' 20)

כלל של 'אין משיבין על הדרוש' אינו משום פחיתותו של הדרוש כלפי הפשט, אלא שהפשט סובב על ביאור הפסוק עצמו, ולכן אפשר להשיב עליו. אמנם, כוונת הדורש אינה אלא להביע איזה רעיון מקורי או חידוש מדעתו, ורק שהוא מסמיכו לפסוק זה. ואם תפריכו מפסוק זה, יסמיך הרעיון לפסוק אחר. ולכן לא שייך להשיבו.

upon normatively, whereas the goal of Halacha is to present the single, normative perspective. Thus, when two Aggadot present an idea differently, they are merely presenting two perspectives.[42]

Heretical Denigrations

Maharal closes with a sweeping condemnation:

> אבל שלא יהיו האגדות דברי תורה כמו שאר תורה שנאמרה מסיני, האומר כך אין לו חלק בעולם הבא. וזה מוכח מכל אשר הביא הוא לראיה, שעל ידי האגדות מכיר בוראו, שהם דברי חכמה אלקית למי שמבין את דבריהם.
>
> But to say that words of Aggada are of lower stature than other words for Torah stated at Sinai [is heretical], and someone who says this has no portion in the world to come. This can be seen from the words [R. Azarya de Rossi himself] cited that through Aggada, a person comes to recognize his Creator, for they are words of divine wisdom to he who understands them.

Maharal concludes that anyone who claims that Aggadot are inferior to other aspects of Torah that were said at Sinai has no portion in the world to come. Seemingly, this statement is consistent with *Menorat ha-Ma'or*, who states that all Aggada is Sinaitic, but at odds with the Geonim who wrote that it is not. Yet the matter is not so simple. Earlier, Maharal explained R. Sherira's statement to mean that ideas of Aggada sometimes are derived independently. Thus, Maharal appears to contradict himself about whether some Aggadot are made up or all Aggadot come from Sinai.

Perhaps the answer is that Maharal does not mean that all Aggadot literally come from Sinai; rather, Maharal means that Aggada is no less Torah than any other portion of Torah, all of which stem from Sinai. However, as we noted, just as halachot sometimes are derived from *sevara*,

---

42. אמנם מה שאמרו אין למידין הלכה מתוך דברי אגדה, ואין משיבין באגדה, הוא עוד דבר חכמה, כי ההלכה הוא הלכה למעשה, ודבר שהוא הלכה למעשה אינו נוטה מן האמת הגמור. אבל דבר שאינו הלכה למעשה, כמו דברי אגדה, דבר זה אף שאינו לגמרי כך, **רק בצד מה בלבד. והנה התורה יש לה כמה פנים, מכל מקום דבר שהוא הלכה למעשה אינו רק פנים אחד.** לכך אמר שאין מקשין ושואלין בדברי אגדה, ואין למדין הלכה מדברי אגדה. וזהו פירוש האמיתי, אין ספק בו.

so too some Aggadot are derived from *sevara*. Nevertheless, ultimately all of Torah, even that which is derived from *sevara,* comes from God.

5.5 WHY IS AGGADA SO CRYPTIC?

Rambam and Maharal stress the importance of discovering the deeper message hidden in aggadic teaching. Accordingly, one wonders why Aggada is frequently written so cryptically. Why can't the teaching be presented more accessibly?

Ramchal addresses this question in his essay concerning Aggada (sometimes printed in the back of *Mesillat Yesharim*). Ramchal writes that when R. Yehuda ha-Nasi decided to record the halachic components of the oral law lest they be forgotten, there also was a concern that the secrets of the Torah would be forgotten. Regarding the Torah's secrets, however, the option of writing them down was not available, since Torah secrets must not be publicized, a concern that does not exist with Halacha.

Why must they not be made public? Ramchal suggests two reasons. It would be dishonorable to God to reveal His secrets to those with bad character traits, even if they are wise. Moreover, because the secrets are so deep, they are likely to be misunderstood by those who are untrained.

To solve this problem, Chazal decided to record these secrets, so that they would not be lost, but they did so figuratively and through riddles, such that only those who were given the keys could unlock their secrets. These keys were carefully guarded and given only to worthy students.[43]

---

43. **מאמר על ההגדות**

הנה כבר ידעת, שמה שהביא לחז"ל לכתוב דברי התורה שבעל פה, אחר היות המקובל אצלם שדברים שבעל פה אסור ללמדם בכתב, היה מה שראו שהיו הדעות הולכות ומתחלשות באורך הגלות וחליפות הזמנים, והזכרון מתמעט והסברא מתקצרת, ונמצאת התורה משתכחת. על כן בחרו משום "עת לעשות לד׳ " לחקוק בספר פירוש המצות כלו, למען ישאר קיים כל הימים, והוא כלל המשנה והגמרא.

והנה התבוננו עוד וראו, שבחששא הזאת שחששו על חלק המצות ראוי היה לחוש גם כן על חלק סתרי התורה ועיקרי האלהיות. אך אין התקון שמצאו לחלק המצות ראוי לחלק הסודות. וזה כי באורי המצות והדינים אין היזק כלל, אם יכתבו בספר בבאור גלוי לכל קורא, אך חלק הסודות אין ראוי שימסר כך לפני כל הרוצה ליטול את השם, לא מצד יקר המושכלות ולא מצד עמקם. אם מצד יקרם, כי אינו כבודו של הבורא ית׳ שימסרו סתריו בידי אנשי מדות רעות, ואפילו שיהיו חכמים מחוכמים. ואם מצד עמקם, שהרי הענינים באמת עמוקים מאד, ולא יצליחו בם אלא אנשים זכי השכל ומלומדים בדרכי העיון היטב,

We should note, however, that not all aggadic statements are equally cryptic. In some cases, such as the Aggadot at the beginning of the sixth chapter of *Bava Batra*, it is more likely that these stories are not meant to be taken literally (see 5.9). In other cases, the matter is debated, while in many cases, Aggadot contain straightforward ethical teachings that can be understood with relative ease (even if they also contain profound truths). Interestingly, Gra writes that specifically in the Aggadot that seem to discuss trivial matters, we find the Torah's greatest secrets.

אבן שלמה ח:כו
האגדות שלפי הנראה ח"ו הם דברים בטלים בהם גנוז כל הסודות.

> The Aggadot that seemingly convey meaningless information (heaven forbid) -- in them are hidden all of the secrets.

Moreover, Gra contends that in the future, these secrets will be revealed:

יהל אור כח טור ד - כט טור א
ולעתיד יתגלה הסוד שבתוכו וזהו התורה חדשה שיתגלה לעתיד.

> In the future, all the secrets therein will be revealed. This is the meaning of the *Torah Chadasha* (new Torah).[44]

Nefesh ha-Chaim (4:27–8) explains that this is because full expression of the Torah's secrets cannot be contained in our world as it stands. With the world's purification, however, things will change.

ואם יפגעו בם שכלים גסים אף בלתי מלומדים בעיונים, יוציאו הענינים האמיתיים היקרים לשבושים ודעות רעות.
על כן גמרו לבצוע את הדין, והיינו לכתוב אותם, למען לא יאבדו מן הדורות האחרונים, אך בדרכים נעלמים ומיני חידות, שלא יוכל לעמוד עליהם אלא מי שמסרו לו המפתחות, דהיינו הכללים שבהם יובנו הרמזים ויפורשו החידות ההן, ומי שלא נמסרו לו המפתחות יהיו לפניו כדברי הספר החתום וכאלו לא נכתבו כלל. והמפתחות האלה השאירום ביד תלמידיהם שקבלום מידם. ואמנם עליהם סמכו שלא ימסרו אלא לתלמידיהם אחריהם הגונים כהם, וכן מדור אל דור.

44. See *Yeshaya* 51:4:
הַקְשִׁיבוּ אֵלַי עַמִּי וּלְאוּמִּי אֵלַי הַאֲזִינוּ **כִּי תוֹרָה מֵאִתִּי תֵצֵא** וּמִשְׁפָּטִי לְאוֹר עַמִּים אַרְגִּיעַ.

5.6 OTHER PERSPECTIVES ON CRYPTIC AGGADOT

Not everyone agrees that all obscure Talmudic tales are meant to convey esoteric information. Some thinkers point out that many midrashim originally were offered as homilies or public discourses. For example, Rashba (*Chidushei Aggadot Berachot* 54b) addresses this issue when explaining the Talmud's discussion of the fantastic height of Og, King of Bashan.

Rashba offers several reasons for why midrashim sometimes present a simple concept abstrusely. He starts by noting that one should not necessarily assume that this indicates that the midrash is relating something esoteric since the presentation may simply be in order to sharpen the minds of those who study it.[45] Moreover, sometimes the obscurity may be to conceal the ideas from people who are not knowledgeable.[46] And finally, exaggerations occasionally serve as a technique to trigger interest. For example, the Midrash (*Shir ha-Shirim Rabba* I 15:3) records that R. Yehuda ha-Nasi once saw that his students were dozing off, so he stated that while the Jews were in Egypt, 600,000 people were born from a single pregnancy. The shocking statement presumably was meant to wake up the students and certainly is not meant literally. The Midrash itself clarifies this point by explaining that there is some truth to the statement in that Moshe Rabbeinu was equivalent to the entire Jewish people, and thus his birth is similar to one pregnancy resulting in 600,000 births.[47]

Should Aggadot Be Understood Literally?

All of the above approaches in Rashba presume that Aggadot frequently utilize hyperbole. Even so, Rashba certainly would agree

---

45. דע, כי באו מהם בלשון עמוק לסיבות רבות, כי לעתים תמצאם ז״ל רומזים עניין פשוט מאד או שאין צורך בו כלל, ועם כל זה יוציאו אותו בלשון זר ועמוק מאד, עד שיחשוב המסתכל שיש בעניין ההוא סוד או עניין שיש צורך להסתירו, ואינו, רק כי לעתים יוציאו אותם בלשון זר מאד כדי לחדד לבות התלמידים.

46. כדי לעוור עיני הכסילים המטילים השיבוש בדברי החכמים בתחילת המחשבה מיד, בצאת הדברים מגדר השגתם ושכלם המועט.

47. כי לעיתים היו החכמים דורשים ברבים ומאריכים בדברי תועלת והיו העם ישנים, וכדי לעוררם היו אומרים להם דברים זרים לבהלם ושיתעוררו משנתם. וזו הסיבה מפורשת להם ז״ל במדרש שיר השירים (שיר השירים רבה א, טו, ג) בפסוק ״הנך יפה רעיתי״ (שיר השירים א:טו), אמרו שם ״רבי היה דורש ונתנמנם הציבור, ביקש לעוררם ואמר: ילדה אשה אחת במצרים ששים רבוא בכרס אחת, והיה שם תלמיד אחד ור׳ ישמעאל בר׳ יוסי שמו, אמר: מאן הות כן מי הייתה זאת? אמר ליה: זו יוכבד שילדה את משה ששקול כנגד ששים רבוא, שנאמר (שמות טו:א) ׳אז ישיר משה ובני ישראל׳״.

that these stories should not be ignored. Rather, we should not be distracted by some of the details, searching instead to understand the story's message.

Rambam, as we shall see in 6.2, likewise denounces those who presume that all events described in Aggadot literally occurred, and while there is disagreement about which texts should be understood literally, this appears to be the mainstream view among Rishonim and Acharonim. However, two points should be made to qualify this summary. Firstly, many scholars understand that the *ba'alei Tosafot* (a) accept that Chazal's aggadic stories are meant to be taken literally and (b) do not seem bothered by the difficulties that this poses.[48] While they may never state this position explicitly, their analyses some of the very strange aggadic stories suggests that the authors of *Tosafot* generally accept these stories at face value.[49] One of the foremost of the *ba'alei Tosafot*, Rashbam, writes explicitly regarding the stories in *Bava Batra* (73a)[50] that they were included in the Gemara to better appreciate God's world. This may indicate that he believes those stories to be literal portrayals of the actual world. The argument that a story must be non-literal because it involves miracles would not faze *Tosafot*, as they might counter that nothing stops God from performing miracles for His faithful servants.[51]

---

48. See E. Urbach, *Ba'alei ha-Tosafot*, pp. 713–715.

49. For example, *Tosafot* (*Avoda Zara* 17a and *Chullin* 7a) are bothered by how Chazal portray inanimate objects as speaking to Eliezer bar Durdai or R. Pinchas b. Ya'ir. In *Avoda Zara, Tosafot* explain that the mountains etc. did not literally speak, but rather לא השיבו לו כך, אלא היה אומר בלבו שכך יוכלו להשיב, א"נ שר של הרים היה משיב כן. Thus, *Tosafot* maintain that the story is literally true, except perhaps for a slight detail. Additionally, *Tosafot* treat contradictions in Talmudic Aggada in the same way they treat contradictions in Halacha (e.g., their comments to *Bava Batra* 16a regarding Avraham's journeys). Furthermore, as already mentioned above, *Tosafot* are willing to base halachot on aggadic sources. One might argue that it would be hard to for them to so if they thought those stories were meant to allude to esoteric concepts and not meant literally. However, this is not a compelling argument since the halachot derived from aggadic texts are generally extrapolated from details that lend themselves to a literal reading.

50. See 5.9.

51. See *Kuzari* 3:73 and this comment by R. Zvi Hirsch Chajes:

Secondly, even among those who interpret Aggada allegorically, some reject the literal meaning of at least some aggadic stories, while others believe that both the esoteric and the superficial meaning of stories intended as parables must be accepted as true.[52] Thus, Gra's comments (quoted above) that the strangest Aggadot hide the deepest secrets in no way contradict another comment of his that even the outer, superficial meaning of the Sages' parables are meaningful and profound.[53] In fact, several of the later commentators consider a rejection of the literal meaning of Chazal's Aggada to be outright heresy.[54]

מבוא התלמוד למהר״ץ חיות פרק כח

באתי לעורר כי לדעת רובי החכמים, ראוי לקחת הדברים כפשוטם, ולהאמין שהם דברים ככתבם, וכן ארעו נסים הללו לצדיקים וקדושים הללו באמת, וכמו שהחוב על איש אשר בשם ישראל יכונה להאמין כי הנסים הכתובים בכתבי קודש המה כפשוטם ונעשו בפועל ממש, כן ראוי וישר להאמין כי שינה ד׳ את הלוך הטבע.

52. See, for example, the commentary attributed to R. Hai Gaon to *Ein Yaakov* on *Bava Batra* 73a, as well as the comments of R. Yaakov Reisher in *Iyun Yaakov* and Maharsha there. See also the comment of R. Chajes quoted in the previous footnote.

53. **ליקוטי הגר״א בתוך משלי ע״פ הגר״א השלם א:ו**

״משל ומליצה״ שניהם בתורה שבכתב. והמשל הוא ספורי התורה, ומליצה הוא הפנימי. וצריך להבין שניהם, שלא להיות מכחיש פשוטי הספורים, אבל להיות מאמין אותם כהויתם, עם שלא תועיל מאוד ידיעתם, דמאי דהוה הוה, אבל דעותינו קצרות מלהשיג תועלת פשוטיהן. ״דברי חכמים וחידותם״ להבין נגליהם ופנימיהם. וזה היתרון הנפלא נמצא לתורה האלוקית על כל חיבור ספרי שאר החכמות והנימוסין שנעשו על דרך משל וחידה, כי מהם שיכונו אל מה שיאמר בהם ולא אל זולתו, ומהם שיכונו אל הפנימי שבהם, והחיצוני הוא דבר רק שאין בו ממש. וזאת התורה - החיצוני והפנימי ממנה, הכל אמת ומכוון. והוא ענין נפלא, לא יאות כלל, אלא אל יכולת החכמה האלהית לבד. וההבדל אשר בין ׳משל׳ ובין ׳חידה׳ שהמשל הוא לקוח מהקדמות ידועות, כמו בתורה שבכתב כל הספורים הם כעין המתנהג בינינו, אבל החידה הוא לקוח מהקדמות שאינם מפורסמות, כמו ׳מעז יצא מתוק׳ (שופטים יד:יד) או בדברי חז״ל - הרבה בר בר חנה (ב״ב עג.) עם שהחיצוני הם בודאי היה אמת אבל לא מפרסמות.

Interestingly, part of this passage is an almost exact quote from R. Yitzchak Arama, *Akeidat Yitzchak, Bereishit Sha'ar* 7, but R. Arama is referring to the text of the Torah, while Gra applies it to the words of the Sages as well.

54. This is implied by the comments referenced in the previous footnotes. R. Shlomo Zalman Auerbach is reported as having forcefully rejected even interpreting Chazal's words as exaggerations, and a similar stance is recorded in the name of *Chazon Ish*:

5.7 *PSAK* IN AGGADA

One last issue related to the authoritativeness of Aggada concerns whether we come to definitive conclusions regarding disputes in Aggada as we do concerning matters of Halacha. In this section, we consider several approaches to this important question.

Psak in Aggada According to R. Bachya ibn Pakuda

R. Bachya ibn Pakuda notes that while the Torah demands that we submit legal questions to the *Sanhedrin*, no such requirement is stated concerning matters of theology. Rather, one should turn inward, and, after having received a correct tradition, utilize one's intellect to arrive at a conclusion.

The basis of R. Bachya's conclusion is the following verse:

דברים יז:ח

כִּי יִפָּלֵא מִמְּךָ דָבָר לַמִּשְׁפָּט בֵּין דָּם לְדָם בֵּין דִּין לְדִין וּבֵין נֶגַע לָנֶגַע
דִּבְרֵי רִיבֹת בִּשְׁעָרֶיךָ וְקַמְתָּ וְעָלִיתָ אֶל הַמָּקוֹם אֲשֶׁר יִבְחַר יְקֹוָק אֱלֹהֶיךָ בּוֹ.

If a matter eludes you in judgment, between blood and blood, between judgment and judgment, or between lesion and lesion (types of *tzara'at*), words of dispute in your cities, then you shall rise and go up to the place Hashem, your God, will choose.

This verse instructs a person to turn to the *Sanhedrin* in the event that a matter of the law is unclear to him. R. Bachya notes what types of things are mentioned with regard to the obligation to turn the high court:

הליכות שלמה הלכות תשעה באב עמ' ת"מ

ונשאל פעם רבנו ע"ד מספר ההרוגים העצום הנראה מדברי חז"ל באגדות החרבן, אם נכון לומר דנקטו לשון הפרזה. והשיב בתוקף דח"ו לומר כן. ובמעשה כעי"ז שהיה אצל רבנו החזון איש ז"ל שפקפק ת"ח אחד בכגון דא, נזהר מיד ממגעו של השואל ביין שהי' על השלחן, והוסיף רבנו שבשעתו הי' הדבר כחידוש בעיני הרואים, אולם נראה שהחזון איש ז"ל בגודל חכמתו ויראתו הבחין באותו שואל שהי' מופלג בתורה ואיש נכבד, שאין תוכו כברו ושאלתו היא מחסרון אמונה, ואכן הוכיח סופו על תחלתו.

In a biography of *Chazon Ish* (*Pe'eir ha-Dor,* Vol. 2, p. 330), there is another version of this story (or perhaps a separate, but similar story), but with the same message.

תורת חובות הלבבות הקדמה תרגום הרב קאפח עמוד י
...דבר הכתוב: "כי יפלא ממך דבר למשפט" וגו', "ובאת אל הכהנים" וגו', "ועשית על פי הדבר אשר יגידו לך" (דברים יז:ח-י). וכאשר תתבונן במה שכלל הפסוק הראשון מעניני הדינים, תמצאם שאלות הצריכות חילוק והגדרה בדרך הקבלה, לא בדרך הלימוד השכלי. הנך רואה שלא הזכיר בכללן ענין מן הענינים הנשגים בשכל, לפי שלא אמר: אם נסתפקת בענין היחוד היאך הוא, ובשמות הבורא ותאריו, וביסוד מיסודות הדת... שתסמוך בהם על זקני חכמי הדת ותשען על מסורת קבלתם בלבד; אלא אמר: פנה אל תבונתך והשתמש בשכלך בכל הדומה לזה אחר שתעמוד עליהן מצד הקבלה הכוללת את כל מצות הדת ויסודיו ופרטיו וחקור עליהם בשכלך והבנתך וכושר שיפוטך, עד שיתברר לך הנכון ויתבטל הבטל...

The verse says that "If a matter eludes you in judgment, between blood and blood, between judgment and judgment, or between lesion and lesion… you shall do according to that which [the high court] tells you." If you consider what subjects are included in the first of these verses, you will find that they are those which need to be particularized, distinguished, and discussed by the method of tradition, not by that of logical demonstration. The verse omits reference to themes on which the intellect can enlighten us. It does not say, for instance, that if you are in doubt concerning the Unity of God – how it is to be understood – or as to the names and attributes of the Creator… and the like, which are fulfilled by the exercise of reason and reflection – you are to accept them on the authority of those learned in Scripture and tradition and rely exclusively on their traditions. On the contrary, Scripture expressly bids you to reflect and exercise your intellect on such themes. After you have attained knowledge of them by the method of tradition that covers all the precepts of the law, you should investigate them with your reason, understanding, and judgment until the truth becomes clear and false notions are dispelled.[55]

55. Translation adapted from Moses Hyamson (Feldheim, New York, 1978), page 31.

R. Bachya understands that the above verse indicates that we must distinguish between matters of Halacha, which are largely dependent upon tradition, and matters of philosophy and theology, which are independently discernible to someone properly trained.[56] Accordingly, one must turn to the high court only to resolve legal doubts concerning matters of tradition. It would seem, then, that according to R. Bachya, there is no such thing as *psak* concerning Aggada – if there were, such matters would have to be resolved by the *Sanhedrin.*

Psak in Aggada According to R. Kook

While the simple reading of *Devarim* 17:8 supports R. Bachya's thesis by indicating that we need to turn to *Sanhedrin* only regarding halachic questions, the Yerushalmi, interpreting the verse using *drash*, derives an obligation to turn to the *Sanhedrin* even concerning aggadic matter, which presumably includes matters of faith.[57] Thus, according to the Yerushalmi, aggadic matters are determined through the same process as matters of Halacha. One could argue, however, that the Bavli (*Sanhedrin* 87a), which does not see a reference to Aggada in this verse, disagrees with the Yerushalmi on this point.[58] Effectively, then, R. Bachya rejects the

---

56. Needless to say, many thinkers strongly disagree with R. Bachya's presumption. Moreover, while R. Bachya's position is reasonable within the rationalist tradition, it is utterly untenable among those who adopt a mystical perspective, whose theology is based upon both tradition and revelations (*giluyim*). Many reject R. Bachya's thesis even regarding non-mystical matters. For example, we have seen that R. Ovadya Bartenura, in his commentary on the first mishna in *Avot*, explains that *Avot* begins with the chain of tradition to make clear that tradition is essential to ethics just as it is essential for matters of Halacha. Thus, the prologue to *Avot* demonstrates that the ethics of Chazal derive from Sinai.

57. **תלמוד ירושלמי מסכת סנהדרין פרק יא הלכה ג**
כי יפלא ממך דבר למשפט מגיד שבמופלא שבבית דין הכתוב מדבר. ממך זה עצה **דבר זו אגדה**. בין דם לדם בין דם נידה לדם בתולים בין דם נידה לדם זיבה לדם צרעת. בין דין לדין בין דיני ממונות לדיני נפשות. בין דין לדין בין הנסקלין לנשרפין לנהרגין ולנחנקין. בין נגע לנגע בין מצורע מוסגר למצורע מוחלט. בין נגע לנגע בין ניגעי אדם לניגעי בגדים ולנגעי בתים. דברי זו השקיית סוטה ועריפת העגלה וטהרת המצורע ריבות אילו הערכים והחרמים והתמורות והקדישות. וקמת וקמת מבית דין ועלית זו העלייה.

58. The Bavli understands the word דבר as referring to הלכה, as opposed to the Yerushalmi, which understands it is referring to אגדה. However, this does not necessarily

Yerushalmi, which mandates *psak* concerning Aggada, in favor of the Bavli, which may reject the notion of *psak* concerning Aggada.

How are we to understand this difference between the Bavli and the Yerushalmi? R. Kook proposes a revolutionary theory: the Bavli reflects a diaspora approach, which focuses on intellect and Halacha, as opposed to the Yerushalmi, which reflects an Israel-based approach, which focuses on prophecy and intuition.[59] Accordingly, R. Kook writes, when Jews return to the land of Israel, we can look forward to the day when we will follow the Yerushalmi in this respect.[60] Indeed, R. Kook believed that the process leading to the return of prophecy was already underway in his day as the Jewish people began returning to their homeland.[61]

---

indicate that the Bavli supports R. Bachya's position, since aggadic matters still might be based on tradition even if aggadic debates are not resolved by the *Sanhedrin*.

59. Interestingly, the great rationalists, such as R. Sa'adya Gaon and Rambam, flourished in the exile, while many of monumental mystics, including R. Shimon b. Yochai and the Arizal, flowered in Israel. (Of course, there are exceptions.)

60. **אגרות הראי"ה קג (מחודש טבת תרס"ח, 1907) עמוד קכו**

והחילוק הוא פשוט, דסדר לימוד שהוא נסמך על שורשי הנבואה וסעיפיה, ההלכות עם האגדות מתאחדות על ידו, ויש עניני קבלה ומסורת בדעות כמו במעשים, וזאת היא דעת הירושלמי, שלא כדעת "חובות הלבבות". אבל בסדר לימוד שבחו"ל, שאינה ראויה לנבואה וממילא אין ענפי רוח הקודש מתלכדים עם ההלכה וניתוחיה, הדעות הינן רק מה שאפשר להוציא מתוך השכל ההגיוני, ואין לעניני האגדות שייכות להלכה ולא שייך עליהם "לא תסור", וזה החילוק טבע את חותם ההבדל בין הבבלי לירושלמי.

לדידן הבבלי עיקר... ומכל מקום, לכל עת שיחדש השם יתברך לב חדש על עמו ויוחזר כח... קדושת ארץ הקודש בגלוי, יגלה האור של הירושלמי מצד סגנונו הקצר והעמוק, שמסתייע ממהלך שכל עליון, וההגדה המקובלת מחוברת בו עם ההלכה בדרך פעולה נסתרת.

R. Kook believed that the Yerushalmi, which was written in a place of prophecy, retains an element where intuition, not just logic, plays a role. (He notes in this letter that this is the reason why there is more Aggada in the Yerushalmi. Many have noted that this is not the case. Presumably, R. Kook means to include Midrashim, such as *Midrash Rabba* and *Midrash Tanchuma*, which were written in Israel.) That Yerushalmi is more strongly rooted in intuition explains why there is less back-and-forth (*shakla ve-tarya*) in Yerushalmi.

61. Accordingly, in a letter concerning the restoration of the *Sanhedrin*, R. Kook writes of the need to establish a yeshiva to promote the study of non-halachic maters and thereby ensure that the sages of the *Sanhedrin* are not simply experts in Halacha, but also masters of Aggada:

Let us elaborate. R. Bachya writes that the reason why there is no need for *psak* in Aggada is because one can rely upon his intellect to determine the truth:

פנה אל תבונתך והשתמש בשכלך בכל הדומה לזה.

Turn to your mind and utilize your intellect for things of this sort.

Put differently, R. Bachya understands that the role of *mesora* in non-halachic matters is less significant.[62] Once one has received the tradition and reached the requisite level of wisdom, one can independently arrive at the truth in non-halachic matters.

R. Kook understands that R. Bachya reflects the diaspora approach to Torah, which relies heavily on the intellect. In Israel, however, where prophecy can flourish, another model reigns supreme. Intellect no longer dominates; rather, it is partially superseded by the divine voice. In such an environment, *psak* in non-halachic matters becomes possible.[63]

The Goal of Psak

Perhaps we can suggest an alternative interpretation of the dispute between the Bavli and the Yerushalmi concerning *psak* in Aggada, one which gets at the heart of the nature of *psak*. Two approaches are conceivable:

(a) *Psak* reflects a practical need to know what to do.
(b) *Psak* is an attempt to arrive at the truth.

אגרות הראי"ה תב (מחודש טבת תרע"ב, 1912) עמוד ס
מובן הדבר שההוראות של כל התורה כוללות ג"כ ההוראות הרוחניות של הדעות והאמונות. ועל זה בודאי נהיה צריכים לייסד יסוד מוסד של קביעות לימוד . שהרי ישנם כמה ת"ח גאונים בהלכה, ומ"מ אינם יודעים את המקצוע העיקרי בתורה הנוגע לדעות ואמונות אלא ידיעות שטחיות...

62. This reflects the Geonic tradition discussed earlier. Nevertheless, R. Bachya, in his Introduction to *Chovot ha-Levavot*, rails against those who overly emphasize the study of Halacha and *chovot ha-eivarim* while neglecting *chovot ha-levavot.*

63. See, also, R. Yosef Gavriel Bechhofer's excellent article "Does Psak Apply to Matters of Hashkafa?" in *The Journal of Halacha and Contemporary Society* (Spring, 2014).

According to the first option (a), when we arrive at a *psak*, we are not necessarily claiming that one position is more correct than the other. After all, "These and these are the words of the living God." Rather, a legal system cannot succeed without standardized normative practices. Accordingly, the Torah offers a means to determine normative law.[64] This perspective may reflect the view in the Talmud that we do not issue rulings concerning matters that have no contemporary relevance, such as *korbanot* (*hilcheta le-meshicha*).[65] While there is immense value in studying these topics, there is no need to issue a *psak*, since the goal of *psak* is practical – to arrive at a normative practice. In cases where normative practice is not relevant, we do not issue *psak*.

The second perspective (b) disagrees. *Psak* is a *cheftza shel Torah* (an aspect of Torah like any other aspect). It is valuable even if there is no normative application. Even as we acknowledge legitimacy in both views in any Talmudic dispute, we must attempt to figure out which

---

64. We follow the majority view, based on the verse אחרי רבים להטות (*Shemot* 23:2).

65. In *Zevachim* 45a, when R. Nachman issues a ruling concerning the laws of *pigul*, R. Yosef questions whether there is a purpose in issuing *hilcheta le-meshicha*. Likewise, in *Sanhedrin* 51b, when R. Nachman issues a ruling concerning the laws of execution, R. Yosef questions whether there is a purpose in issuing *hilcheta le-meshicha*. Generally speaking, however, the Talmud is not bothered by this question. Accordingly, we find four views among the Rishonim regarding how to resolve this apparent contradiction:

1. According to one view in *Tosafot* (*Zevachim* 45a), we never issue *psak* on non-practical matters. All of the rulings in the Gemara that seem to concern non-practical matters actually have some practical application.
2. According to R. Chaim in the above *Tosafot*, R. Yosef's objection is limited to cases where the matter is both non-practical and there is a sin involved (such as *pigul* and execution). Since these matters never will be relevant, since people will not sin in messianic times (see Chapter 24, where we will see that this matter is debated), there is no point in issuing halachic rulings in these matters. Other disputes concerning the *Beit ha-Mikdash* must be resolved, as they will become practical in the future.
3. According to another view in *Tosafot*, it is a debate in the Talmud whether we should issue such rulings.
4. Rashi (*Sanhedrin* 51b) indicates that the Talmud asks the question only regarding disputes over the source for a particular ruling, not in a case where there is a halachic difference between the two opinions.

What emerges is that there is a dispute (either among the Amora'im or the Rishonim) whether we should issue rulings regarding matters that have no practical relevance.

view is more correct. According to this position, we indeed issue rulings regarding matters with no practical relevance.[66]

Perhaps the disagreement between the Bavli and the Yerushalmi about whether the *Sanhedrin* issues *psak* in matters of Aggada hinges upon these two perspectives on *psak*. The Bavli maintains that *psak* relates to determining the normative law. Accordingly, there is no need to issue rulings in matters of Aggada when there is no practical application. This would not apply to all matters of theology, though. As we shall see in the next section, there are practical ramifications of many disputes concerning theology. However, most aggadic disputes do not have practical applications. In cases such as these, the Bavli maintains that the *Sanhedrin* does not issue halachic rulings.[67]

The Yerushalmi, on the other hand, maintains that *psak* is more than practical. Just as there is value in issuing halachic rulings on non-practical halachic matters, so too there is profit in aggadic *psak*. The above dispute may hinge upon the two primary understandings of *eilu ve-eilu* considered in Chapter 4.[68]

5.8 *PSAK* IN AGGADA ACCORDING TO RAMBAM

Rambam writes that we do not follow the halachic process in aggadic disputes that lack practical applications:

---

66. This understanding of the debate concerning *hilcheta le-meshicha* was taught to me by R. Mayer Twersky.

67. Shortly, we shall see that Rambam articulates this position. Interestingly, Rambam also issues *psak* on all matters, even those that have no current practical utility. However, that may because Rambam felt that *psak* is necessary for when they become practically relevant. Thus, even if he espouses position (a), Rambam feels compelled to issue rulings on *hilcheta le-meshicha*.

68. Either way, however, this does not seem to fit with the straightforward words of R. Bachya, who explains that the reason why one is not directed to go to the Sanhedrin for matters of *machshava* is not because it is not normative, i.e., that there is no *need* to go to a Sanhedrin, but rather he emphasizes that it would be inappropriate to do so, because these are questions of logic and reasoning. Thus, while R. Kook's reading might indicate that there should at least be a *psak* in matters of theology that do have practical relevance, such as regarding the fundamentals of faith, Rabbeinu Bachya gives the example of God's unity as not being subject to *psak*.

פירוש המשנה לרמב"ם מסכת סוטה פרק ג משנה ג
וכבר אמרתי לך לא פעם שאם נחלקו חכמים באיזה השקפה ודעה שאין תכליתה מעשה מן המעשים הרי אין לומר שם הלכה כפלוני.

> I already have told you numerous times that if the Sages disagree about a religious matter (a matter of *hashkafa*) that does not have a practical application, **one should not say** that the Halacha follows so-and-so.[69]

Rambam writes there is no need to rule decisively in matters of *hashkafa* since there is no practical halachic relevance to such disputes. This does not mean that Rambam feels that both opinions are equally correct. Rather, aggadic statements such as these still differ from halachic disputes, which are normative and therefore require a final ruling.[70]

In 6.4, we will examine numerous places where Rambam rejects certain philosophical positions in Chazal, arguing that they reflect minority views.[71] At first glance, this formulation indicates that Ram-

---

69. This point is reiterated in a number of places including:

פירוש המשנה לרמב"ם מסכת שבועות פרק א משנה ד
(בנוגע לאיזו עבירה מתכפרת באמצעות איזה קרבן) ומחלוקת זו אין לומר בה הלכה כדברי פלוני, לפי שהוא דבר מסור לה' יתרומם ויתהדר, והם נחלקו בראיות ולמידות מפסוקים שאין מקום זה מתאים להזכיר בו דרכי למודם בהם. וכבר ביארנו שכל סברא מן הסברות שאין בה מעשה מן המעשים שנחלקו בה חכמים **לא נאמר** בה הלכה כפלוני.

משנה מסכת סנהדרין פרק י
... דור המדבר אין להם חלק לעולם הבא ואין עומדין בדין שנאמר (במדבר יד:לה) "במדבר הזה יתמו ושם ימותו" דברי רבי עקיבא. רבי אליעזר אומר: עליהם הוא אומר (תהלים נ:ה) "אספו לי חסידי כורתי בריתי עלי זבח". עדת קרח אינה עתידה לעלות, שנאמר (במדבר טז:לג) "ותכס עליהם הארץ" - בעולם הזה, "ויאבדו מתוך הקהל" - לעולם הבא, דברי רבי עקיבא. רבי אליעזר אומר: עליהם הוא אומר (שמואל א ב:ו) "ה' ממית ומחיה מוריד שאול ויעל"...

פירוש המשנה לרמב"ם מסכת סנהדרין פרק י
כבר הזכרנו לך כמה פעמים שכל מחלוקת שתהיה בין החכמים ואינה תלויה במעשה אלא קביעת סברה בלבד אין מקום לפסוק הלכה כאחד מהם.

70. Earlier, we saw Maharal's thesis that different opinions in aggadic matters reflect different aspects of a broader truth; accordingly, halachic rulings would be inappropriate.

71. For example, the Talmud states that the world will be destroyed. Rambam rejects this view, claiming it is a minority opinion. Likewise, the Talmud states that the

bam maintained that we follow the halachic procedure of following the majority view even in non-halachic contexts. This would contradict his comments above that there is no *psak* concerning aggadic matters. However, as we argue in 6.4, Rambam does not necessarily believe that the majority view is legally binding because it is the majority, as would be the case regarding the majority view in a halachic matter. Rather, he maintains that these views are correct and are accepted due to their correctness, regardless of whether they reflect the majority.[72] Support for this assertion can be garnered from the fact that Rambam does not actually show that a majority of Sages follow one opinion or another. Rather, he simply shows that the position that he is claiming to be the majority view makes more sense.

This might explain why, occasionally, we find statements such as *nimnu ve-gamru* (they voted and concluded) concerning non-halachic matters. For example, the Talmud (*Eiruvin* 13b) records a debate between *Beit Shammai* and *Beit Hillel* whether it would have been better for man had the world not been created. The Gemara concludes that *nimnu ve-gamru* that it would have been better for man not to have been created, but now that man exists, he should scrutinize his ways or analyze his deeds. At first glance, this statement contradicts Rambam's principle that there is no *psak* in aggadic matters. Some, like R. Yehuda b. Eliezer ha-Levi Mintz (c. 1405–1508), have deflected this proof, arguing that there may be practical ramifications from this debate.[73] Others, like Maharsha, understand that *nimnu* does not refer to an actual vote.

In light of our theory above, however, we can suggest that there is a difference between looking to the majority to determine that which seems most logical and following the majority in the formal halachic sense such

purpose of sending away the mother bird when taking her young has nothing to do with preventing cruelty to animals. Rambam rejects this view as a minority opinion.

72. A similar phenomenon is found in Ibn Ezra. See Yehoshua Maori, על משמעות המונח 'דברי יחיד' בפירוש ראב"ע למקרא: ליחסו של ראב"ע למדרשי חז"ל', *Shnaton: An Annual for Biblical and Ancient Near Eastern Studies* 13

73. He explains that this is the reason for the formulations of the second through fourth *berachot* of *birchot ha-shachar* in the negative (his view is cited in *Anaf Yosef*).

that the majority view becomes binding.[74] In fact, this Gemara may be the source for Rambam's tendency to reject certain philosophical views found in Chazal based on the assertion that they do not reflect the majority view.

Theological Discussions Where Psak Is Necessary

We should note, however, that Rambam explains that *psak* is inappropriate only when the theological discussion does not have practical ramifications. In the event that a theological discussion affects practice, *psak* is necessary. Although the theology itself is not subject to *psak,* whether or not a person has certain beliefs does have practical implications. Certain beliefs (most famously, Rambam's thirteen principles of faith) must be held by a person if he wants to be considered a Jew for practical halachic purposes. A person who rejects those principles of faith is a heretic. According to Halacha, a heretic is not considered a Jew for many ritual purposes, such as writing *tefillin,* kosher slaughter, and many instances where Halacha differentiates between Jews and non-Jews. Thus, while the question of God's oneness, for example, is surely not subject to *psak,* the question of whether or not a person who disbelieves in God's oneness is or is not a heretic would be subject to *psak.* Evidence of this is Rambam's ruling (in his commentary on the Mishna[75] and *Hilchot Teshuva*[76]) that certain beliefs are mandatory in order to be considered part of the Jewish people and that someone who lacks these beliefs is halachically labeled a heretic, with all that this categorization entails.[77]

---

74. Maharal (*Derech Chaim* 2:9) arrives at a similar conclusion.

75. Introduction to Chapter 10 of *Sanhedrin*

76. Chapter 3

77. This point undermines a central thesis of Prof. Marc Shapiro's book, *The Limits of Orthodox Theology.* R. Gil Student already noted this in "Crossroads: Where Theology Meets *Halacha* – A Review Essay on *The Limits of Orthodox Theology*" published in *Modern Judaism* 24.3 (2004) 272–295:

> My disagreement with Shapiro revolves around this specific passage in Maimonides and its parallels. He analyzes this section but, according to my understanding, employs an imprecise reading of Maimonides' words that leads to his incorrect conclusions. It is not true, as Shapiro seems to claim, that Maimonides demands a limited pluralism in all theological matters. Maimonides, with his precise and masterly usage of language, specifically writes that there is no need to decide among opinions – to invoke the "halachic process" – when the issue does

An important corollary to this discussion is the question of whether that which characterizes heresy remains fixed or changes based on the consensus view. Some, like *Chatam Sofer* (Y.D. 2:356), maintain that just as in the halachic process there are views that are acceptable before a consensus is reached but become unacceptable subsequently, so too with respect to hashkafic matters that pertain to fundamental beliefs (*ikkarei emuna*). A case in point is the position of R. Hillel (the Amora known as Hillel II), cited in *Sanhedrin* 99a, that there will not be a personal *mashiach*.[78] In 11.2 we shall see that others disagree, arguing that Rambam maintains that anyone who does not believe in the

---

not affect practice. He carefully uses similar wording in all five places in which he discusses this. Never does Maimonides say that there are decisions between views in Halacha and not in Aggada; he always formulates this principle in terms of affecting practice and not affecting practice. According to Maimonides, the question of whether the decision-making process applies to a topic is not a Halacha versus Aggada issue but, rather, a practice versus theory one. Even an aggadic topic is subject to the halachic process if and when it affects practice. Therefore, there are certain areas where Halacha and Aggada – practical and theological Judaism – intersect, and in those cases, where there is a need for practical aggadic conclusions, the halachic process is imposed on Aggada. Shapiro's magnificent edifice rests on this single, crucial issue, and, unfortunately, I believe his foundation to be in error. A careful reading of Maimonides' words yields a conclusion 180 degrees opposite Shapiro's.

78. *Chatam Sofer,* in the above piece, addresses a basic question: what is so fundamental about the thirteen principles of faith such that their denial warrants exclusion from *olam ha-ba*? He answers that it is not the denial of the idea, in and of itself, which is so problematic. Rather, because the thirteen principles have all been accepted, denying them indicates a denial of Torah and its method of interpretation.

Take the example of R. Hillel's understanding that the redemption will come without a personal *mashiach*. When he made this claim, it was understandable. However, after the majority of the Torah scholars ruled that he was wrong, such a position is no longer tenable. To follow such a view indicates a rejection of the principle that Torah matters are decided by the majority position, which is effectively a rejection of Torah. It is the rejection of Torah which warrants exclusion from *olam ha-ba*:

האומר אין משיח וקים לי׳ כרבי הלל הרי הוא כופר בכלל התורה דכיילי אחרי רבים להטות. כיון שרבו עליו חכמי ישראל ואמרו דלא כוותי׳, שוב אין אדם ראוי׳ להמשך אחריו כמו ע״ד משל במקומו של ר״א הי׳ כורתים עצים לעשות פחמין לעשות ברזל לצורך מילה ואחר דאיפסקא הלכתא ע״פ רבי׳ מחכמי ישראל דלא כוותי׳ העושה כן בשבת בעדים והתרא׳ סקול יסקל ולא מצי למימר קים לי כר״א... ועכ״פ הגאולה וביאת המשיח איננה עיקר אבל מי שאינו מודה בו כופר בעיקר של האמנת התורה ודברי נביאים.

thirteen principles is excluded from the Jewish people and loses *olam ha-ba* no matter what the cause for his disbelief. This school of thought maintains that the basis for this seemingly harsh conclusion emerges from Rambam's understanding that immortality is only possible for someone whose conception of God and fundamental beliefs are correct. Loss of *olam ha-ba* is not a punishment, but rather a natural

---

This formulation contradicts what we suggested above and implies that non-halachic matters are in and of themselves subject to *rov*. In contrast, we deduced from Rambam's statements in his commentary on the Mishna that Rambam maintains that there is no need to rule decisively (and therefore no place for *rov*) in matters of *hashkafa* since there is no practical halachic relevance to such disputes. To summarize, we have considered two perspectives of how to understand Rambam's view on *psak\rov* in non-halachic matters:

1. According to *Chatam Sofer* we follow *rov* in all matters, even hashkafic. The thirteen principles were accepted by *rov*. The reason why denial of one of the thirteen principles constitutes heresy is not because of the inherent significance of these principles, but because denial of the principle is, in effect, a denial of Torah since it is a denial of *rov*.
2. We suggested that Rambam opines that there is generally no need to rule decisively (and therefore no place for *rov*) in matters of *hashkafa* since there is no practical halachic relevance to such disputes. Principles of faith are different. Because they are so fundamental, their denial constitutes heresy, and as such has practical implications and is subject to the halachic process. (While Rambam offers no clear explanation of his methodology in composing this list, he describes how he expended much time to compose the list: "I have not composed it in random fashion, but after reflection and conviction and the attentive examination of incorrect views; and after getting to know what things out of all of them it is incumbent upon us to believe, and bringing to my assistance arguments and proofs for every individual section of the subject.")

R. Menachem Mendel Schneerson suggested an even more far-reaching application of *Chatam Sofer*'s principle (see *Likutei Sichot,* Vol. 35, p. 27) writing failure to accept the Besht's conception of God's unity (that in reality nothing else exists besides God) constitutes subtle heresy. However, he notes that prior to the Besht many Torah luminaries indeed presumed that our world exists, though it was created by God. How can he claim that all of those thinkers were heretics? R. Schneerson answers that before the Besht revealed the true nature of God's oneness belief in the true (though dependent) existence of matter was reasonable and non-heretical. Only after the Besht revealed the truth does such belief constitute heresy. (The debate concerning the nature of the Besht's view on panentheism and *tzimtzum she-lo ke-pshuto* need not concern us at present. What we seek from this citation is a radical understanding of the evolving definition of heresy.)

consequence of such fundamental distortions of the truth. This perspective, it would seem, does not allow for any sort of evolution with respect to what constitutes a fundamental belief. We will return to this question and explore Rambam's position in Chapter 11, where we discuss disbelief based on faulty reasoning.

5.9 APPENDIX A: THE RABBA BAR BAR CHANA STORIES

To gain an appreciation of the various approaches to dealing with Aggada, it is instructive to consider some of the various approaches to the stories of Rabba bar bar Chana in the fifth chapter of *Bava Batra*. While these fifteen tales describing Rabba bar bar Chana's marvelous experiences during his voyages and journeys through the desert are unusually fantastic, the methodologies used to understand them shed light on general approaches to Aggada.[79]

The first question to be considered is whether the stories historically occurred in some form or another. The Talmud presents the stories without explicitly stating that that they are meant metaphorically. Thus, some thinkers argue that we must presume that they actually occurred. Nevertheless, it seems inconceivable that they could have occurred literally as presented. This prompts the first solution: hyperbole.

---

79. Interestingly, these tales were used to disparage the Talmud. Spanish historian and physician R. Shlomo ibn Verga (1460–1554) records the following exchange concerning these stories in his *Sheivet Yehuda,* which records a debate between a Christian and Jew before King Alfonso of Portugal:

> **אמר המלך:** יש לי על הדברים אלה השגות, אביאם בסוף ענינגו, ואני אומר שכיוון שמנהג שלכם לומר דברי שקר ושוא כבר הוחזקתם לשקרנים בכל דבר. ואני שמעתי בויכוח אחד, שאתם אומרים בתלמוד שלכם שנמצא צפרדע גדולה כששים בתים, ושתנין בלע אותה, ושבא ‑עורב ובלעו, ודילג על האילן. וכל אלו דברי שקר מפורסם, כפי מה שנתאמת. ועוד אתם אומרים, שבים אוקינוס נפל ברזל ונתגלגל ז׳ שנים ולא ירד לקרקע, מי ראה בעמקי ים אם ירד או לא? ועוד אתם אומרים, כי איש חכם ראה בים שנתגאו גליו, ובין גל לגל שלש מאות פרסאות – וזה שקר, כי כל הים ההוא אינו שלש מאות פרסאות.
> **תשובת היהודי:** כתבו קצת מנבוני לב, שהקדמונים היה מנהגם שכשירצו לקרב העם שישמעו דבריהם היו לוקחים נבל ומנגנים, וכשהעם קרב לערבות הניגון אז היו אומרים מה שנראה להם לתקון הסדר המדיני והישרת הנשמה. והנה קדמונינו, כאשר לא ידעו לנגן, תפסו דרך אחרת, להביא דבריהם בדרך משל ומליצה, והיודע ידע התוכיות. ושני הדברים למדנו בלשון המשורר אשר אמר: ״אטה למשל אזני אפתח בכנור חידתי״.

Indeed, as we saw in 3.1 the Talmud states that the Torah, the Prophets, and the Sages all utilize hyperbole (*lashon havai*). Thus, some opine, we should not be surprised that these stories utilize hyperbole as well. What exactly is meant by *lashon havai*? Presumably, this means that the story fundamentally occurred, but the details are exaggerated. Thus, R. Yeshaya de-Trani the Younger (known as ריא"ז, 1280–1210), an Italian Talmudist and commentator (and grandson of Rid or R. Yeshaya de-Trani the Elder), partially adopts this approach to explain stories like those of Rabba bar bar Chana. R. Yeshaya de-Trani understands that these stories contain exaggerations but also portray miracles.[80]

Thus, this first approach assumes that the stories actually happened, that they reflect God's special providence towards the righteous, even though some of the details may be exaggerated.[81] One difficulty with this approach is that it leaves the reader wondering what is accomplished by these exaggerations. If the purpose of the stories is to convey events and show God's providence, then presumably, this would be better

---

80. ולפי שראיתי מבני פריצי עמינו המלגלגין ובוזין בדברי חכמים, ומלמדין המדרשים לכומרי אומות העולם לתעתע ולהלעיג על תורתנו, באתי לבאר על ענין המדרשין, ומה היתה כוונת חכמי תורתנו בהם. דע והבן, **כי המדרשים הם על שלושה דרכים**, יש מהם שהן **דרך גוזמא**, כמו שאמרו בפרק גיד הנשה **דברה תורה בלשון הבאי**, דברו נביאים בלשון הבאי, דברו חכמים בלשון הבאי, כענין ערים גדולות ובצורות בשמים, וכן ותבקע הארץ לקולם, וכיוצא בהם, **ויש מהם רבים, כדברי רבה בר בר חנה** האמורים בפרק המוכר את הספינה, שהם בדרך גוזמא, שדרך בני אדם לדבר כן.

וגם יש מן המדרשין שהם על דרך **מעשה נסים**, שמראה הקב"ה כחו וגבורתו לחסידיו, ומראה להם מעשים נוראים ומותמהים, כמו שנא׳ בדניאל וראיתי אני לבדי את המראה והאנשים אשר היו עמי לא ראו את המראה, וכן יונה בן אמיתי שבלעו הדג והקיאו, ורבים כיוצא בהם. וכאלה יימצאו רבים בדברי חכמים, כמו שנאמר בפרק חזקת הבתים על ר׳ בנאה, שהיה מציין המערות, וכשהגיע למערת אברהם אבינו, מצא אליעזר עבד אברהם שהיה עומד לפני הפתח, וכל הענין האמור שם. ועוד אומר שם שהיה מגוש אחד שהיה חוטט מערות המתים, וכשהגיע למערת אחד מן החכמים תפשו החכם בזקנו, וכל אותם הענינים מעשה נסים, כמו שהיו נעשים ונגלים לנביאים, מה שאין כן לשאר בני אדם. **ויש מאלה רבים, כמעשים שלרבה בר בר חנה, שהן דברים מותמהין שהיה מראה הקב"ה לחסידיו המאמינים בו בלב בר.**

81. Rashbam likely adopts this approach as well:

רשב"ם מסכת בבא בתרא דף עג עמוד א

אמר רבה אשתעו לי כו׳ - כל הני עובדי דקא חשיב משום **מה רבו מעשיך ה׳** ומהן **להודיע מתן שכרן של צדיקים** לעתיד לבא או לפרש מקראות האמורים בספר איוב המדברים בעופות גדולים ובהמות ודגים גדולים שכל שיחת תלמידי חכמים צריכה תלמוד.

accomplished with a precise rendition. Perhaps R. Yeshaya de-Trani would respond along the lines of Rashba's aforementioned solutions mentioned in 5.6, such as to suggest that the goal is to trigger interest. Alternatively, R. Yeshaya de-Trani might agree that beyond the simple and true reading, there is a secondary message supported by the exaggerated details.

Others question whether we should assume that the stories actually took place. This does not necessarily indicate that we should presume a metaphorical or esoteric interpretation. In 5.6, we cited Rashba's theory that fanciful stories are written in order to sharpen the minds of those who study them or to engage the reader. Some thinkers adopt this view regarding the Rabba bar bar Chana episodes as well, maintaining that they were used to entertain students in order to capture their attention or provide a diversion from the rigors of their demanding studies. R. Yedaya b. Abraham Bedersi (sometimes known as **הפניני**, or Dispenser of Pearls, c. 1270 – c. 1340) [82] adopts this view.[83] Thus, the second approach is to assume that the stories did not happen, nor do they convey particularly meaningful information. Of course, this approach leaves us wondering why the editors of the Talmud would have included numerous pages of such tales.

Ritva espouses a different position. He writes that these stories actually were dreams. When people travel on the sea, they witness extraordinary things. Moreover, contemplating these matters triggers remarkable dreams. The dreams are presented in the Talmud in story form.[84] Thus, Ritva assumes that even though the Talmud does not state

---

82. Cited in the Mechon Yerushalayim edition of *Teshuvot ha-Rashba* Vol. 1 418, p. 221.

83. החלק השלישי כל המאמרים המספרים בשום חדוש יוצא מן המנהג ועל הכלל בשנוי אי זה טבע **שלא ימשך לנו ממנו שום תועלת מבואר** באמונה או שום חזוק, אלא שיזכירו על צד הספור לבד לתועלת הרוחת התלמידים וצורך הכנסתם במלי דבדיחותא להניח מכובד העיון ועמל הגרסא וזה בספורי רבה בר בר חנא וזולתם מהדומים להם רבים, הנה נפרש לזה בודאי ויוציאוהו מגלויו ואף על פי שהוא בלי [ספק] אפשר בחֹק יכולת האל ומבלי שימשך ממנו שום היזק מפורסם באמונה.

84. **ריטב"א מסכת בבא בתרא דף עג עמוד א**

אמר רבה אשתעו לי נחותי ימא וכו'. יש במעשיות שבפרק זה ענינים זרים לבני אדם לפי שלא הורגלו בהם, והם דברים קרובים מאד להיודעים בטבעם, כענין גודל הדגים שבים וגודל סערת גלי הים, **ויש גם במעשיות אלו ענינים נרמזים שלא היו נראין להם במראית העין אלא במראה החלום**, וזה כי כשהחכמים הולכים בים אוקיינוס ורואין שם נפלאות השם יתברך, וגם שהם

that these were dreams, obviously they could not be meant literally.[85] In commenting on the stories, Ritva offers explanations that highlight the wisdom hinted to in the stories.

I believe the dominant approach with respect to Rabba bar bar Chana's marvelous experiences is that regardless of whether the stories actually happened, the purpose of the stories being recorded is to convey profound wisdom. Thus, Gra, who adopts this methodology, sees ethical advice and mystical secrets in these tales.[86] This approach also is adopted by R. Yeshaya b. Avraham ha-Levi Horowitz (known as *Shlah*, תורה שבע״פ כלל יח עמ׳ יז), R. Tzadok (רסיסי לילה עמ׳ 44), and R. Yosef Chaim of Baghdad in his *Ben Ish Chai* (ב״ב עג: ד״ה זמנא חדא), among others. Maharsha also offers allegorical interpretations, but he notes that while the messages are profound, they need not reflect esoteric wisdom.[87]

שם מתבודדים ומחשבים בענינים נוראים ונפלאים, ובעת השינה יראה להם כענין הרהורים ענינים נפלאים מורים על הענין, והגאנים כתבו כי כל היכא דאמרינן הכא לדידי חזי לי במראה החלום היה כשהיה מהלך בים אוקיינוס, ומפני שיש טופלי שקר מלגלגים על דברי רבותינו ז״ל נרמוז בקצת אלו הענינים קצת רמזיהם הקרובים יותר לפשט, וישמע חכם ויוסף לקח.

85. Along similar lines, *Shita Mekubetzet* (*Bava Metzia* 59b) quotes R. Chananeil that it is possible that the miracles that were recorded in the story of *tanur shel achnai* were just a dream and didn't really happen.

86. **יהל אור ביאורים על הזוה״ק עמוד 56**

והסוד גנוז וקבור שם, ולא ידע איש את קבורתו כנ״ל ול״ל רשו לאפקא מינה כו׳ וכמ״ש שם דף ר״פ ע״א ומה דאתמר בך, ולא ידע איש את קבורתו עד היום הזה... והענין כי סוד משה הוא תורתו, הלכה למשה מסיני שהוא הסוד, והוא גנוז ברמז והן הגדות שהן בש״ס כמו המעשים דרבב״ח וסנחריב שהן לפי הנראה ח״ו כמו דברים בטלים ובהן גנוז כל האורה והתורה תורת משה כל רזין דאורייתא. וזה שבקש משה שלא יגנז הסוד באלו הדברים, ולא ניתן לו וזהו מחולל מפשעינו שנעשה חול דברי׳ של חול והוא בפשעינו כמ״ש ויתעבר ה׳ בי למענכם.

In fact, nearly a whole book, *The Juggler and the King* by R. Aharon Feldman, is an elaboration of the Vilna Gaon's interpretation of these stories.

87. **הקדמה לחידושי הלכות, המופיעה בראש פירושו למסכת ברכות**

גם האגדות הזרות לפי פשוטן ורחוקות לפום ריהטא מן השכל לא נתתי לבי לבאר בהם רזים ורמזים בחכמות וסודות נסתרים כי לא נסיתי בהם כאשר גליתי והודעתי כבר וקיימתי בעצמי כבוד אלהים הסתר דבר אך ראיתי שהדברים לא יצאו מפשוטן רק שאמרו זה בדרך משל ומליצה הקרבים לפי פשוטו של דבר כמו ספר משלי שדרשו בו חז״ל דברים הקרובים למשל אל הנמשל כמו שתראה ממני מבואר באגדות דרבב״ח...

Interestingly, he begins his commentary on the stories with the following note:

5.10 APPENDIX B: EVOLVING ATTITUDES TO AGGADA

In 5.2, we considered statements by Geonim and Rishonim that seemed to question the authoritativeness of Aggada. For modern readers trained in yeshiva, these citations seem shocking insofar as they contradict what is without doubt the mainstream view of the contemporary Torah world.

One approach, adapted by Maharal, denies any fundamental change. All of the *chachmei ha-mesora* accept the authoritativeness of Aggada. Is it possible to suggest that while there have always been two schools of thought regarding Aggada, the overall trend has been a shift towards greater deference towards Chazal in non-halachic matters?[88] To address this question we must consider whether there are other examples where views shifted from earlier thinkers to later thinkers.

Though this phenomenon is rare, this is not the only example of such a development. An even more glaring example of this notion emerges from the evolution of Jewish thought regarding the nature of divine providence. As we shall see in Chapters 38 and 39, many Rishonim maintained a more limited approach to providence than many Acharonim.

How is it possible that so many of our greatest thinkers could have erred[89] in this fundamental matter? Additionally, we usually

---

חידושי אגדות מהרש״א ב״ב עג.

אף כי באמת כי אין להכחיש פשטי הדברים כמ״ש (תהילים קז:כג) יורדי הים באוניות עושי מלאכה במים רבים, המה ראו מעשי ה׳ וגו׳ ותרומם גליו יעלו וגו׳ מ״מ יש כאן דברים בגו.

88. What would account for the change? There are probably a number of factors that contribute to this development, including the spread of Kabbala. In 5.17, we cite R. Aharon Feldman: "Kabbalah made it clear that when the Sages spoke, they based themselves on their knowledge of the mysteries of creation." R. Feldman suggests that the increased influence of Kabbala explains why many Rishonim assumed Chazal may have erred in scientific matters, while most Acharonim reject the notion. Conceivably, this could also explain why Acharonim view Aggada as authoritative in a way that many Geonim and Rishonim do not. A second factor for the greater acceptance of aggadic teaching is that later thinkers like Maharal showed the profundity of such teachings in ways that previous thinkers had not.

89. Unless we assume the Rishonim were correct in their time, and the nature of *hashgacha* actually changed.

assume that earlier thinkers had a greater understanding of the Torah than later ones. While the differentiation between Rishonim and Acharonim is not as rigid in aggadic matters as it is in halachic matters, it is still remarkable that the Acharonim's understanding of *hashgacha* would depart so much from earlier approaches. What factors made this revolution possible? Part of the revolution regarding *hashgacha* may relate to the declining influence of Greek philosophy, which may have contributed to some Jewish thinkers' limiting the role of *hashgacha*. However, that does not fully justify the far-reaching shift from Rishonim to Acharonim.

Instead of focusing on historical explanations, I prefer a theological one. Sometimes, the world is not yet ready for certain concepts. The time is not ripe, or other ideas must first develop. Indeed, we find intellectual development in all areas of Torah. Consider, for example, the novel manner in which the Tosafists discovered apparent contradictions within different sections of Talmud and introduced resolutions; the development of the Brisker analytical methodology in the nineteenth and twentieth centuries; the Kabbalistic revelations of R. Shimon b. Yochai and Arizal; and Maharal's innovative approach to Aggada. Likewise, we saw R. Kook develop this idea in 2.10 with respect to the seemingly oppositional approaches of rationalism and mysticism. Thus, even as we uphold the Rishonim's unparalleled mastery of Torah, we do not deny the possibility of development.[90] Essentially, the *chachmei ha-mesora* of each generation apply the received oral tradition – consisting of principles, details, and values – and convey that *mesora* in a way that is at once faithful to the tradition they received and flexible enough to allow for appropriate Torah innovations. Moreover, this process is not merely organic but is influenced and guided by God.

A remarkable expression of the notion that God reveals certain truths only in later generations was suggested by R. Menachem M. Schneerson in addressing the question of why *Chasidut* emerged when it did:

---

90. We will explore the exact nature of human contribution to the oral law in Chapter 28.

There are two explanations given for the fact that *Chasidut* was revealed in these later generations, as opposed to the previous generations, when our people were on a higher spiritual level...

a) Because of the manifold spiritual darkness that has continued to swell in the later generations (and in particular, in the era when *Mashiach*'s approaching footsteps can be heard), it is necessary to tap a higher light, which will enable us to overcome that darkness.
b) To borrow an explanation from the writings of the Arizal (which is quoted as Halacha by the *Magen Avraham* [250:1] and the *Shulchan Aruch* of the Alter Rebbe [250:8])... On Friday, one must taste the foods that are prepared for *Shabbat,* (as alluded to in the phrase: "Those who taste of it merit life"). Similarly, when seeing the entire span of the six millennia as six days, the last generations before the coming of *Mashiach* can be understood as being Friday afternoon, [wee hours] before "the day which is all *Shabbos*." As such, there is drawn down a reflection (at least, a foretaste) of the revelation of *P'nimiyut ha-Torah* which will be made manifest (in a consummate manner) by *Mashiach.*

These two explanations reflect two extremes: According to the first explanation, *Chasidut* was revealed in the later generations because of their lower level. Because of the great spiritual darkness prevalent in these generations, it is necessary that there be a revelation of the higher light of *P'nimiyut ha-Torah.*

According to the second explanation, by contrast, the revelation of *Chasidut* in these later generations is a reflection of the unique positive nature of the present time; it is Friday afternoon, and one can already appreciate a foreshadowing of the revelations of the era of *Mashiach.*[91]

91. *Likkutei Sichot,* Vol. 15, p. 281, translated by Eli Touger.

Sources in Chazal that Seem to Discourage Learning Aggada

In 5.1, we cited a number of statements in Chazal highlighting the importance of studying Aggada. However, some statements in Chazal seem to contradict this notion, such as the Talmud's statement that since the destruction of the Temple, God associates with the world solely via the four cubits of Halacha:

> **תלמוד בבלי מסכת ברכות דף ח עמוד א**
> אמר רבי חייא בר אמי משמיה דעולא: **מיום שחרב בית המקדש אין לו להקדוש ברוך הוא בעולמו אלא ארבע אמות של הלכה בלבד.**
>
> R. Chiya b. Ami said in the name of Ulla: From the day of Temple's destruction, God has in His world only the four cubits of Halacha. [92]

However, when we examine the commentators on this and other similar statements,[93] we find that statements such as these generally are not understood as meaning to denigrate the importance of Aggada. For example, Rambam, in his Introduction to his commentary on the Mishna, derives from the above statement the notion that the purpose of all of creation is to support the person who has perfected himself in wisdom and deed (איש שלם כולל החכמה והמעשה).[94] Clearly, Rambam did not understand the Talmud's usage of the word Halacha to exclude what

92. The continuation of the above passage derives from Ulla's statement the importance of praying in the place of study:
> ואמר אביי: מריש הוה גריסנא בגו ביתא ומצלינא בבי כנישתא, כיון דשמענא להא דאמר רבי חייא בר אמי משמיה דעולא: מיום שחרב בית המקדש אין לו להקדוש ברוך הוא בעולמו אלא ארבע אמות של הלכה בלבד - לא הוה מצלינא אלא היכא דגריסנא. רבי אמי ורבי אסי אף על גב דהוו להו תליסר בי כנישתא בטבריא לא מצלו אלא ביני עמודי, היכא דהוו גרסי.

93. There are other statements of Chazal that superficially might be interpreted as disparaging the study of Aggada. See Maharal (*Be'eir ha-Gola, Be'eir* 6) for an explanation of how these sources are not meant to undermine the importance of Aggada. Also, see R. Zvi Hirsch Chajes' (מהר"ץ חיות) *Mevo ha-Talmud.*

94. הנה נתברר מכל מה שאמרנו, שתכלית כל מה שבעולם ההויה וההפסד הוא איש שלם כולל החכמה והמעשה כמו שביארנו. וכיון שמדבריהם ע"ה אנו לומדים שני הדברים הללו כלומר החכמה והמעשה ממה שביארו וממה שרמזו, בצדק אמרו אין לו להקב"ה בעולמו חוץ מארבע אמות של הלכה.

we call *machshava* or Aggada (quite the contrary). Likewise, *Talmidei R. Yona* (*Berachot* 4a) understand this teaching as telling us that in the absence of the Temple, the primary place of divine manifestation is the place of Torah study.[95]

---

95. כל הקובע מקום לתורתו אויביו נופלין תחתיו, שנאמר, "ושמתי מקום לעמי לישראל וכו'" פי' זה הפסוק נאמר על בהמ"ק שהקב"ה היה משרה שכינתו שם ובזכותו היו ישראל יושבים לבטח, ולא היו מפחדים מהאויבים, **ועכשיו שאין בהמ"ק קיים מקום התורה במקומו כדאמרינן מיום שחרב בית המקדש אין לו להקדוש ברוך הוא בעולמו אלא ארבע אמות של הלכה בלבד,** ולפיכך בזה ינצל מהאויבים, ואפי' מי שאינו יודע אלא מעט יש לו לקבוע באותו מקום וללמוד במה שיודע כדי שיזכה לזה ויחשוב בעניניו ויכנס בלבו יראת שמים ואם אינו יודע כלל, יש לו ללכת לבתי המדרשות שלומדין ושכר הליכה בידו....

אוהב ה' שערים המצויינים בהלכה יותר מבתי כנסיות ומבתי מדרשות... ר"ל שאוהב הקב"ה שערי ציון מכל בתי כנסיות ובתי מדרשות, וכמו שאוהב בהמ"ק יותר מבתי כנסיות ומבתי מדרשות, **כך אוהב השערים המצוינין בהלכה, כלומר, ששם קביעות התורה וההוראות בכל יום, יותר מבתי כנסיות ומבתי מדרשות שלומדים בהם לפי שעה דרשות או פסוק מפני שהמקומות הקבועים הם במקום בהמ"ק כדאמרינן מיום שחרב בית המקדש אין לו להקדוש ברוך הוא בעולמו אלא ארבע אמות של הלכה בלבד,** וכמו שהמקדש חביב יותר מבתי כנסיות ומבתי מדרשות כך מקום קביעות התורה חביב משאר בתי כנסיות ובתי מדרשות שאינם קבועים.

Why, then, is the word "Halacha" used if the intention is Torah study? Maharal writes:

תפארת ישראל פרק ע

וביאור זה, כי אין להקדוש ברוך הוא בעולם הגשמי, באשר הגשמי נבדל מן הקדוש ברוך הוא, ואין ראוי שיאמר בדבר רוחני שהוא גשמי. והדבר אשר הוא להקדוש ברוך הוא, הוא ארבע אמות של הלכה. **פירוש ההלכה הם דברי תורה,** שהם באמת כך פירושם, **לא יטו ימין ושמאל מן האמת. ולפיכך נקרא הלכה, שההולך בדרך אינו נוטה מן היושר לא לימין ולא לשמאל, כך דבר הלכה אינו נוטה מנקודת האמת.**

Excursus

Science and Torah, Part 1

5.11 SCIENTIFIC ERRORS IN CHAZAL

In this book, we address the issue of science and religion in two different places. Here, in our discussion of Aggada, we address the question of statements in Chazal that seemingly are contradicted by science. At the end of Chapter 8, when discussing faith, we address the broader question of contradictions between Scripture and science. While these two investigations overlap, the first is narrower and considers whether the rabbis of the Talmud may have erred with respect to science. The second question is necessarily broader – since God certainly did not err. Instead, the focus is on methodologies of resolution and the certainty of the scientific method.

While nearly everyone agrees that at times (such as the Aggadot in the sixth chapter of *Bava Batra*), aggadic statements should be understood figuratively, the question of how to understand seemingly erroneous scientific statements in Chazal remains. Debate over this inquiry has proliferated over the last few decades; however, the question is not new. As we shall see, Jewish thinkers have grappled with this question for over one thousand years.

This query is relevant to halachic and aggadic statements within the Talmud. We begin with a brief discussion concerning halachic issues and then focus our attention upon aggadic issues (the topic of our chapter).

5.12 HALACHIC ISSUES

An example of a halachic issue is the Talmud's (*Shabbat* 107b) ruling that because lice spontaneously generate,[1] they may be killed on Shabbat. Science has proven that lice do not spontaneously generate.

Numerous approaches have been suggested to solving this problem:

- Some early thinkers question the validity of scientific conclusions.[2] This view would presumably allow the killing of lice on Shabbat. However, it is not clear if any major thinkers would apply this method to incontrovertible deductions, such as the observation that our lice hatch from eggs.[3]

---

1. Rashi (*Shabbat* 12a); see *Meshech Chochma Bereishit* 9:9. R. Moshe Meiselman (*Torah, Chazal and Science,* Chapter 22) argues that Chazal may not have been endorsing spontaneous generation and that the Gemara can be interpreted differently.
2. *Teshuvot ha-Rashba* 1:98 (quoted by Rama Y.D. 57:18 and *Shach* 57:48) writes that despite medical evidence to the contrary, it is inconceivable that the *treifot* enumerated by Chazal could possibly live longer than one year. Rambam disagrees and maintains that even though we follow the *treifot* enumerated by Chazal, it may be the case that today they live longer than one year (see *Hilchot Shechita* 10:12). Rashba's ruling, however, does not definitively imply that we always disregard science when it is contrary to the halachic presumption. The following line allows for the possibility that we may distinguish between rulings based on *halacha le-Moshe mi-Sinai* and other rulings:

   ואם יתחזק בטעותו ויאמר לא כי אהבתי דברים זרים והם אשר ראו עיניהם ואחריהם אלך נאמר אליו להוציא לעז על דברי חכמים אי אפשר ויבטל המעיד ואלף כיוצא בו ואל תבטל נקודה אחת ממה שהסמיכו בו חכמי ישראל הקדושים נביאים ובני נביאים ודברים **שנאמרו למשה מסיני**.
3. R. Moshe Feinstein argues that Rashba would agree that today, certain *treifot* live more than one year:

   שו"ת אגרות משה חושן משפט חלק ב סימן עג

   ליכא בזה שום כפירה בדברי המשנה והגמ' דאדרבה מתקיימין בזה דברי המשנה והגמ' שלא יקשה עלייהו מהמציאות שבדורות האחרונים **שאף הרשב"א אם היה חי וכן עתה שהוא בעולם האמת בגן עדן מודה שיש מקצתן מאלו שמנו במשנה וגמ' שהן טריפות** שיכולין לחיות.

   Seemingly, R. Feinstein is saying that Rashba would concede that Chazal erred. However, this is not necessarily the case, as R. Yitzhak Grossman (http://bdld.info/2011/11/16/terminally-ill-animals-and-dead-horses/) points out. R. Feinstein might be arguing that there must be another resolution to the question (such as that of Rambam) besides Rashba's contention that the scientists are wrong. The solution

- Some have suggested that our lice, which clearly do not spontaneously generate, are different from those described by the Talmud.[4] Thus, the Talmud's statement no longer contradicts clearly observable phenomena. Accordingly, one may not kill a louse on Shabbat nowadays.
- Others propose that the Talmud's ruling is based on the presumption that things not visible to the naked eye do not affect the Halacha. Accordingly, one may kill a louse nowadays.[5]
- Others suggest that Halacha became fixed at the time of Talmud and applies whether or not the basis for the ruling is correct. This view may or may not permit the killing of lice on Shabbat.[6]

---

need not be that Chazal got it wrong. On the contrary, Rashba's stridency implies that he would reject such a solution. For more on this discussion, see *Chazon Ish* E.H. 27:3 and R. Asher Benzion Buchman, "Rationality and Halacha: The Halacha L'Moshe MiSinai of Treifos," in *Ḥakirah,* Volume 4 (Winter 2007), pp. 121–135.

4. There are two versions of this resolution: (1) We are talking about a different species of lice (the Talmudic species perhaps having become extinct). This approach is adopted by R. Moshe Krasner in his work *Sod le-Yireiyav.* (2) The nature of lice has changed (classical *nishtana ha-teva*). See *Tosafot* (*Mo'eid Katan* 11a s.v. *kavra*), who invokes נשתנה הטבע or "nature has changed" to reconcile several places where observable fact contradicts rabbinic contentions. We should add that invoking *nishtana ha-teva* does not necessarily indicate the practical Halacha has changed. R. Moshe Feinstein (שו"ת אגרות משה חושן משפט חלק ב סימן עג אות ד) writes that occasionally the Halacha remains fixed even where the physical reality that was once the basis of the law has changed.
5. See R. Eliyahu Dessler's discussion in *Michtav mei-Eliyahu* (Vol. 4, p. 355) and R. J. David Bleich's analysis in *Tradition* 38:4.
6. Intuitively, one would assume that once we assume that the scientific reality described in the Talmud no longer is relevant, killing lice on Shabbat certainly should be prohibited. However, one still could argue that the Halacha that was established during Talmudic times remains binding even if its basis no longer is justified. The source for such a possibility is the following statement:

סנהדרין דף צז עמוד א

תנא דבי אליהו ששת אלפים שנה הוי עלמא שני אלפים תוהו שני אלפים תורה שני אלפים ימות המשיח ובעונותינו שרבו יצאו מהם מה שיצאו.

The *Tanna de-Bei Eliyahu* teaches: The world is to exist six thousand years. The first two thousand will be desolation (*tohu*); the next two thousand will be Torah; and the final two thousand will be the messianic era, but through our many iniquities, many years have been depleted.

- Finally, some maintain that we should acknowledge that the authors of the Talmud were mistaken in their ruling, and thus we should not kill lice on Shabbat. Of course, their ruling was correct according to their perception of reality. Thus, there was no halachic error, only a scientific mistake. This view would prohibit killing lice on Shabbat.[7]

We will not focus on the halachic aspect of the topic since our present concern is not Halacha.[8]

5.13 THINKERS WHO MAINTAIN THAT CHAZAL MAY HAVE ERRED IN SCIENTIFIC MATTERS

Geonim

In 5.2, we saw numerous sources regarding the authoritativeness of Aggada. Here, we focus on the question of whether they may contain errors concerning scientific realities. The first to deal with this issue were the Geonim, who were addressing the question of whether one should follow medical advice from the Talmud, specifically those found in an extensive discussion of cures in the beginning of the seventh chapter of *Gittin*. R. Sherira Gaon writes:

אוצר הגאונים תשובות שעו גיטין סח:
ודשאלתון למיכתב לכון הני אסואתא דמי שאחזו קורדיקוס מן רב ושמואל עד פסקא דמתניתין, האיך קיבלוהו ופירושו בלשון הגדים.

Some have argued that this means that the rules of Torah are permanently established during the two thousand years of Torah. *Chazon Ish* argues for such a position concerning the determination of *treifot* (but not necessarily other matters).

חזון איש יורה דעה סימן ה
ונמסר לחכמים לקבוע הטרפות ע"פ רוח הקדש שהופיע עליהם, והנה היה צריך להקבע בב' האלפים תורה ... והיו קביעות הטריפות כפי השגחתו ית' בזמן ההוא ... ואפשר דהנתוחים שבזמנינו לא היו מועילים בימים הראשונים.

R. Kook (*Mishpat Kohen* 14) adopts a similar position concerning *kilayim*. The most far-reaching (and largely rejected) application of this principle can be found in R. Moshe Shmuel Glasner's Introduction to his commentary on *Chullin* called *Dor Revi'i*.

7. R. Yitzchak Lampronti's *Pachad Yitzchak* (on צידה) argues that since this might be the case one should be stringent and avoid killing lice on Shabbat.
8. For those interested, three of the most commonly cited sources on this topic among Acharonim are R. Yitzchak Lampronti's *Pachad Yitzchak* (on צידה), *Michtav mei-Eliyahu* (Vol. 4, p. 355, note 4), and *Tosafot Yom Tov* (*Chullin* 9:6).

צריכין אנן למימר לכון דרבנן לאו אסותא אינון ומילין בעלמא דחזונין בזמניהון וכחד חד קצירא אמרונין ולאו דברי מצוה אינון הילכך לא תסמכון על אלין אסותא וליכא דעביד מינהון מידעם אלא בתר דמבדיק וידע בודאי מחמת רופאים בקיאים דההיא מילתא לא מעיקא לה וליכא דליתי נפשיה לידי סכנה. והכין אגמרו יתנא ואמרו לנא אבות וסבי דילנא דלא למעבד מן אילין אסותא אלא מאי דאיתיה כגון קיבלא דקים ליה לההוא דעביד ליה דלית ביה עקתא. וכולהו מילי לא צריכינא לפרושנון וטעמי ליכא לגלואינון אלא מילי דחזיננא דעמיקן עליכון התם.

We must inform you that our Sages were not physicians. They may mention medical matters that they noticed here and there in their time, but these are not meant to be a *mitzva*. Therefore, you should not rely on these cures, and you should not practice them at all unless each item has been carefully investigated by medical experts who are certain that this procedure will do no harm and will cause no danger [to the patient]. This is what our ancestors have taught us: none of these cures should be practiced unless it is a known remedy and the one who uses it knows that it can cause no harm.[9]

R. Sherira Gaon responds that on a practical level, Talmudic cures should not be practiced unless the practitioner knows that they will not cause harm.[10] The reason is that the Sages were not medical experts. Moreover, their advice was not meant to be halachic. At first glance, this position on Talmudic medicine reflects the Geonic position discussed in 5.2 concerning the general authoritativeness of Aggada.

However, we must wonder whether we can extrapolate from the above passage that Chazal erred in scientific matters. Perhaps the approach taken to Talmudic medical advice should be treated differently than other scientific matters. Is the reason that we do not follow Chazal's

9. Translation adapted from "Freedom to Interpret" by R. Aryeh Carmell, p. 5.
10. It is unclear whether this means that if it is known that they will not cause harm that they *should* be practiced or that it is simply permissible but not necessarily recommended.

treatments because they have been refuted based on non-Torah sources and medical advancements, or because of changes in nature (*nishtana ha-teva*) and our inability to precisely follow their directions?

Finally, some[11] have suggested that the cures had their effect on the inner, spiritual level of the affected person and therefore were effective only for the people of the era of the Sages who were on a higher spiritual level. Nowadays, increased physicality does not permit the cures to take effect. According to this view, the opening sentence stating that our Sages were not physicians is not meant to imply that they erred. After all, if they were not physicians, why were they dispensing medical advice? Rather, it indicates that our Sages were not physicians and therefore their medical advice should not be treated in the same manner as a physician's directions. Instead, the Sages were experts in spiritual matters. Accordingly, even their medical advice focuses on the spiritual core of the malady and may not be an appropriate cure for a generation on a lower spiritual plane.

However, the apparent (and most natural) interpretation of the above passage is that Chazal may have erred in scientific matters, as evidenced by the opening statement that our Sages were not physicians. Nevertheless, even thinkers who maintain that Chazal did not err in scientific matters largely concede to the Geonic ruling that one should not practice Talmudic medical advice due to the factors highlighted above (*nishtana ha-teva,* our inability to precisely follow their directions, the understanding that Chazal were treating the spiritual root of the disease, or that the obligation of *ve-rapo yerapei* demands we follow the medical wisdom of our time).

Rambam and R. Avraham b. ha-Rambam's View

One key source in this question is a passage from *Pesachim* 94b that records a debate concerning what happens to the sun at night:

חכמי ישראל אומרים ביום חמה מהלכת למטה מן הרקיע ובלילה למעלה מן הרקיע וחכמי אומות העולם אומרים ביום חמה מהלכת

11. See "The Slifkin Affair – Issues And Perspectives" by R. Aharon Feldman, in *The Eye of the Storm.* Yad Yosef Publications Jerusalem, 2009.

למטה מן הרקיע ובלילה למטה מן הקרקע א"ר ונראין דבריהן מדברינו שביום מעינות צוננין ובלילה רותחין.

> The Sages of Israel say that during the day, the sun travels below the firmament, and at night, above the firmament. And the scholars of the nations say that during the day, the sun travels below the firmament, and at night, below the ground.[12] Rebbi said: Their words seem more correct than ours, for during the day the wellsprings are cool while at night they boil.

Both theories do not seem to coincide with modern science[13]; however, what is relevant for us is the fact that Rebbi acknowledged the correctness of the opinion of the gentile sages in light of scientific evidence. Rambam elaborates: (*Moreh ha-Nevuchim* 2:8)

> It is quite right that our Sages have abandoned their own theory; for everyone treats speculative matters according to the results of his own study, and everyone accepts that which appears to him established by proof.

Rambam's son, R. Avraham, elaborates on this theme in his Introduction to the study of Aggada (printed at the beginning of *Ein Yaakov*), writing that just as we may not show favoritism in judgment and accept the claims of even a wise and righteous person without evidence, so too we may not show favoritism in the pursuit of knowledge and accept the statement of a wise and righteous person without

12. This line has an alternative *girsa* that reads: *le-mata min ha-rakia* (below the firmament) instead of *le-mata min ha-karka* (below the ground). The ramifications of this distinction go beyond the scope of our current discussion.
13. We are presuming that the term "*rakia*" refers to an opaque covering above the earth. While this appears to be the standard translation, R. Moshe Meiselman (*Torah, Chazal and Science,* Chapter 10) notes that some thinkers may adopt alternative translations or read the Gemara non-literally. According to their approaches, it may not be the case that this passage contradicts contemporary science. Later, we will consider the view of R. Menachem M. Schneerson, who likewise maintains that this Talmudic passage does not contradict contemporary science.

evidence.[14] Presumably, this would not apply to matters of tradition, where, as Rambam explains in his Introduction to his commentary on the Mishna, we accept Chazal's rulings unconditionally. Rather, R. Avraham is discussing matters where we have no tradition, and he therefore concludes that if the evidence for a particular theory is not compelling, we are not bound to accept it. Thus, even though the Sages showed incomparable perfection with respect to the interpretation of the Torah, we should not feel compelled to accept their rulings in matters of medicine or science. On the other hand, concerning their interpretation of the Torah, we are bound to accept their conclusions based on the verse, "You shall do according to which they rule" (*Devarim* 17:10).[15]

R. Samson Raphael Hirsch

One last source that reflects the above school of thought and spells out the distinction between Chazal's Torah statements and their scientific ones is to be found in the writings of R. Samson Raphael Hirsch:

> In my opinion, the first principle that every student of Chazal's statements must keep before his eyes is the following: Chazal were the Sages of God's law – the receivers, transmitters, and

14. R. Moshe Meiselman (*Torah, Chazal, and Science*, p. 105, 115) questions the authenticity of some of these comments of R. Avraham b. ha-Rambam.

15. **מאמר על דרשות חז"ל לרבי אברהם בן הרמב"ם**
אמר השי"ת "לא תשא פני דל ולא תהדר פני גדול בצדק תשפוט" וגו'. ואמר "לא תכירו פנים במשפט" וגו'. ואין הפרש בין קבלת אותו דעת להעמידה בלא ראיה, או בין שנאמין לאומרה ונשא לו פנים ונטען לו, כי האמת אתו בלי ספק, מפני שהוא אדם גדול הימן וכלכל ודרדע. שכל זה אינו ראיה אבל אסור.
ולפי הקדמה זו לא נתחייב מפני גודל מעלת חכמי התלמוד ותכונתם לשלמות תכונתם בפירוש התורה ובדקדוקיה ויושר אמריהם בביאור כלליה ופרטיה, שנטען להם ונעמיד דעתם בכל אמריהם ברפואות ובחכמת הטבע והתכונה, [ולהאמין] אותן כאשר נאמין אותן בפירוש התורה, שתכלית חכמתה בידם, ולהם נמסרה להורותה לבני אדם, כעניין שנאמר "על פי התורה אשר יורוך" וגו'.
אתה רואה החכמים, במה שלא נתברר להם מדרך סברתם ומשאם ומתנם, אומרים: "האלהים, אילו אמרה יהושע בן נון לא צייתיה ליה." כלומר לא הייתי מאמין ביה, ואע"פ שהוא נביא, כיון שאין בידו יכולת להודיע העניין בכוונה מדרך הסברא והמשא והמתן, והדרכים שבהם ניתן התלמוד להידרש. ודי בזה ראיה ומופת, ולא נענעין להם עוד, כיון שאנחנו מוצאים להם אומרים שלא נתאמת ולא נתקיימו בגמרא דברי הרפואות.

> teachers of His *torot*, His *mitzvot*, and His interpersonal laws. They did not especially master the natural sciences, geometry, astronomy, or medicine – except insofar as they needed them for knowing, observing, and fulfilling the Torah. We do not find that this knowledge was transmitted to them from Sinai.[16]

As noted before, the simple interpretation of the Geonic passage cited above concords with the view of R. Avraham and R. Hirsch. However, if the Geonic passage reflects a general dismissiveness of Aggada, there may be an important conceptual difference between R. Avraham and R. Hirsch on the one hand and the Geonim on the other. R. Avraham and R. Hirsch appear to fully accept the authoritativeness of general aggadic statements insofar as they pertain to Torah. It is only concerning scientific statements that we consider the possibility of error. On the other hand, the Geonic view may be reflective of a general approach to non-halachic material in Chazal. Of course, as we noted, many thinkers reject the notion that the Geonim were in any way dismissive of Aggada.

5.14 THINKERS WHO MAINTAIN THAT CHAZAL DID NOT ERR IN SCIENTIFIC MATTERS

R. Tam's View

Others seem to disagree with the positions cited thus far that allow for the possibility of rabbinic error in the scientific realm. One view associated with this school of thought is R. Yaakov b. Meir (1100–1171), known as Rabbeinu Tam. He is cited as saying that even though Rebbi (in *Pesachim* 94b, cited above) seemingly conceded that the scholars of the nations are correct regarding the nature of the sun's movement, this, in fact, is not what the Talmud means.

> **שיטה מקובצת כתובות דף יג עמוד ב מתוספות הרא״ש**
> אמר ר״ת ז״ל דאע״ג דנצחו חכמי אומות העולם לחכמי ישראל היינו נצחון בטענות, אבל האמת הוא כחכמי ישראל והיינו דאמרינן בתפילה ובוקע חלוני רקיע.

16. This passage is from a letter written in 1876 to R. Pinchas M. E. Wechsler, published in 1976 in the Jerusalem journal *ha-Ma'ayan*. Translated and adapted by Yehoshua Leiman in *Light Magazine*, Numbers 191–195 (Volume 14:1–5).

> Says R. Tam: Even though the scholars of the nations bested the Sages of Israel, that is with respect to arguments, but the truth is with the Sages of Israel; and that is why we say in the prayers, "*u-Vokei'a chalonei rakia*" ([God who…] splits the windows of the firmament).

R. Tam argues that we should not conclude from the passage in *Pesachim* that we accept the opinion of the wise gentiles when the evidence is compelling. Rather, the Talmud means merely that the evidence seems to support their view; in reality, though, they are wrong. Why would R. Tam interpret the passage in this somewhat strained fashion? It would seem that R. Tam maintains that Chazal cannot be mistaken. Accordingly, his is the only possible interpretation.[17] One example of an early Acharon who decidedly accepts R. Tam's view is R. Menachem Azarya da Fano (1548–1620) known as Rama mi-Pano.[18]

However, this inference – that R. Tam would not accept scientific evidence to contradict Chazal – is debatable. R. Tam never says that Chazal could not have been mistaken on a point of science; he never invokes such a consideration in advancing his interpretation. Rather, his interpretation may have been motivated by the fact that we still recite the liturgical statement "*u-Vokeia chalonei rakia*," ([God who…] splits the windows of the firmament), which assumes the model of the Sages of Israel, implying that their view was not, in fact, rejected. Absent this liturgical evidence, R. Tam may have been perfectly willing to concede that Chazal had been scientifically mistaken.[19] Nevertheless, it certainly is the case that according to R. Tam's reading, the passage from *Pesachim* does not prove that we accept scientific evidence when it contradicts Chazal.

---

17. This does not mean that R. Tam would follow their medical advice. As noted earlier, he might recommend against doing so since we may not know the exact meaning of what they said; moreover, sometimes nature changes (*nishtana ha-teva*), and what once was an effective treatment might no longer helpful.
18. **מאמר אם כל חי ח"א סימן יב**
וכבר הפריז את המדה מי שאמר מן המפרשים שחזרו חכמי ישראל והודו לאומרים כך.
19. David Sidney pointed this out to me.

Rashba, Rivash, R. Chananeil, and Ra'avad

Other Rishonim that seem to maintain that Chazal could not have erred in matters of science are Rashba (*Teshuvot ha-Rashba* 1:98, cited by Rama Y.D. 57:18 and *Shach* 57:48) and Rivash (*Teshuvot ha-Rivash* 447), who rule that despite medical evidence to the contrary, it is inconceivable that the *treifot* (animals certain to die due to fatal injury or defect) enumerated by Chazal could possibly live longer than one year. On one hand, Rashba is quite strident in his opinion that Chazal could not have erred in this regard.[20] On the other hand, Rashba might maintain this position only with respect to halachic matters, and perhaps only in cases where Chazal's assertion about the physical world is rooted in *halacha le-Moshe mi-Sinai* (laws transmitted from Sinai). Thus, with respect to non-halachic matters, Rashba might agree with R. Avraham.[21]

Another Rishon who appears to maintain that Chazal could not have erred in scientific matters is R. Chananeil. In response to an implicit contradiction between the Talmud and certain astronomical teachings, which led some to modify the Talmud, R. Chananeil writes: "Although contemporary astronomers maintain a contradictory view, we pay no attention to them. We are cautioned [to accept]

---

20. ומי שמעיד טעה בכך שלא היה מעולם ... וכיון שכן אפילו יצאו כמה ואמרו כך ראינו אנו מכחישין אותן כדי שיהא דברי חכמים קיימים ולא נוציא לעז על דברי חכמים ונקיים דברים של אלו

וכיוצא בדברים אלו אמרו בההיא אתתא דאמרה ליה לרב אסי אני שהיתי לאחר בעלי עשר שנים וילדתי אמר לה בתי על תוציאי לעז על דברי חכמים וחזרה ואמרה היא רבי לגוי נבעלתי.

וכן בכרות שפכה שנקבו ביציו שאמרו שהוליד ואמר להם רב צא וחזר על בניו מאין הם ולומר שאי אפשר שיהיו דברי חכמים בטלים

וכיוצא באלו אני אומר כאן בבקשה מכם אל תוציאו לעז על דברי חכמים בכל מה שמנו חכמים בטרפיות הודאין ולא עשאום ספק טריפה... אם תשוב ומה נעשה וכבר ראינו בעינינו יתרת ברגל ששהתה שנים עשר חודש זו היא שאמר רבי יהושע בן לוי לרבי יוסי בן נהוראי לא על דא את סמיך כלומר אי אפשר וכאילו אתה מעיד על שראית אותו בעיניך או סבה אחרת יש וכן בכאן אנו שואלין אותו שמעיד מאין אתה יודע ששהתה זו שמא שכחת או שמא טעית או שמא נתחלף לך בזמן או שמא נתחלפה לך בהמה זו באחרת שאי אפשר להעיד שתהא בהמה זו בין עיניו כל שנים עשר חודש.

ואם יתחזק בטעותו ויאמר לא כי אהבתי דברים זרים והם אשר ראו עיניהם ואחריהם אלך. נאמר אליו להוציא לעז על דברי חכמים אי אפשר ויבטל המעיד ואלף כיוצא בו ואל תבטל נקודה אחת ממה שהסמיכו בו חכמי ישראל הקדושים נביאים ובני נביאים ודברים שנאמרו למשה מסיני.

21. We further elaborate upon Rashba's ambivalence towards science in 8.15.

the statements of our masters as they are and not worry about the statements of others."[22] Ra'avad adopts a similar position concerning those who criticized astronomical statements of R. Gamliel. Ra'avad writes that these contemporary astronomers are certainly vastly inferior to R. Gamliel.[23]

R. Menachem M. Schneerson

Earlier, we noted that the views of both the Sages and the scholars of the nations do not seem to coincide with modern science insofar as both positions presume that the sun revolves around the globe. In a letter dated *Rosh Chodesh Kisleiv*, 5736 (November 5, 1975), R. Schneerson argues that, in fact, this Talmudic passage does not contradict contemporary science:

> One of the conclusions of the theory of relativity is that when there are two systems, or planets, in motion relative to each other – such as the sun and earth in our case – either view, namely, the sun rotating around the earth, or the earth rotating around the sun, has equal validity. Thus, if there are phenomena that cannot be adequately explained on the basis of one of these views, such difficulties have their counterpart also if the opposite view is accepted.[24]

Ironically, "modern science," which differs from "Ptolemaic and medieval science," justifies the Talmudic position.[25] In a second letter (on the same date), R. Schneerson reaffirms his "firm belief that

---

22. *Migdal Chananeil*, Leipzig 1876, XCII, cited in R. Isadore Twersky, *Rabad of Posquieres* (Cambridge, 1962), p. 268.
23. **כתוב שם לראב"ד מסכת ראש השנה דף ה עמוד ב**
אמר אברהם: קורא אני על זה ועל כל הלועזים על רבן גמליאל: (ישעיהו ה:כא) הוי חכמים בעיניהם וכנגד פניהם נבונים, כי לא הגיעו לחצי צפרנו ומלעיגים, ואיה כל אותן דברים המופלאים השנויים בברייתא דרבי אליעזר.
24. The letter is available at http://www.chabad.org/therebbe/letters/default_cdo/aid/2046989/jewish/Does-the-Sun-Really-Revolve-Around-the-Earth.htm.
25. The scientific validity of this position was articulated by the great empiricist and teacher of R. Schneerson, Hans Reichenbach. See *Turning Judaism Outward: A Biography of Rabbi Menachem Mendel Schneerson* by Chaim Miller, p. 87.

the sun revolves around the earth." While he argues for the validity of this belief on scientific grounds, it is rooted in the above Talmudic passage.[26]

5.15 MAHARAL ON APPARENT CONTRADICTIONS BETWEEN TORAH AND SCIENCE

Maharal offers a different sort of solution to the problem. One challenge to Chazal that Maharal addresses in *Be'eir ha-Gola* is the claim that Chazal made gross errors in the sciences and history.

באר הגולה, באר השישי פרק א

התלונה הששית, באמרם כי היה נעלם מהם חכמה האנושית, הם החכמות אשר לפי השכל האנושי. ולא שהיה נעלם מהם, רק דברו בהם בתכלית הזרות....

ודבר זה אם היה כך, היה מורה זה על חסרון הידיעה והרחקה מן האמת. ודבר זה הפך מה שהזהירו עליו חכמים

והחכמות שאמרו עליהם שדברו בהם זרות, היא החכמה טבעית וחכמה לימודית. וכבר נתבאר לך, כי כל שהביאום לדבר זה לחשוב על חכמים כך, זהו מה שמצאו בדבריהם שנתנו סבות לדברים טבעים שנתהוים בעולם, והיה נראה להם כי הסבות האלו הם רחוקים שיהיה דבר זה סבה טבעית, ובשביל זה אמרו עליהם שהיו רחוקים מחכמות אלו. אבל אין האמת כך כלל, כי לא באו חכמים לדבר מן הסבה הטבעית, כי קטון ופחות הסבה הטבעית, כי דבר זה יאות לחכמי הטבע, או לרופאים, לא לחכמים. אבל הם ז"ל דברו מן הסבה שמחייב הטבע. והמכחיש דבר זה, מכחיש האמונה והתורה.

The sixth complaint [against Chazal]: they assert that the wisdom available to educated people was unknown to Chazal. Chazal seem not only to ignore human understanding and science, but replace it with strange assumptions...

26. This particular letter does not delineate a general approach to dealing with contradictions between Chazal and science.

Were this the case, it would indicate a lack of knowledge and a disregard for the truth.[27] However, this is the opposite of what our Sages have commanded...

The classes of knowledge regarding which they made strange proclamations are the natural sciences and studied wisdom (such as mathematics). What brought the critics to draw their conclusion are statements by Chazal that provide inconceivable reasons for natural phenomena. As a result of this, they stated about Chazal that they were not educated concerning those categories of knowledge. But this is not the truth in any way, for the Sages did not come to address natural causes, because natural causes are insignificant, worthy only of scientists or physicians but not *chachamim* (wise men). Rather, Chazal addressed the system that underlies and drives nature. And one who rejects this rejects the faith and the Torah.

---

27. If this claim were true, it would be highly problematic; however, he proves that Chazal were very careful to say only that which they were sure about. Thus, even though the simple understanding of the verse "אמור לחכמה אחותי את (משלי ז:ד)" indicates that one should be close to wisdom like a brother to a sister, Chazal understand this as telling us that one should say something only if he is absolutely sure that it is true. Here is the whole paragraph:

ודבר זה אם היה כך, היה מורה זה על חסרון הידיעה והרחקה מן האמת. ודבר זה הפך מה שהזהירו עליו חכמים, ואיתא בפרק חבית (שבת קמה ב) "אמור לחכמה אחותי את" (משלי ז:ד), אם ברור לך הדבר כאחותך שהיא אסורה, אמרהו, ואם לאו, אל תאמרהו. הרי שהם הזהירו שלא יאמר החכם דברים שהם בלתי ברורים, מכל שכן שלא לומר דברים זרים רחוקים, שאף לעינים נראה כי הדבר הוא זר. והפירוש "אמור לחכמה אחותי את", לשון "אחות" מלשון אחוי. ואמר הכתוב שתהיה החכמה מחוברת אליו לגמרי, רוצה לומר ברור בודאי, ואז הדבר ההוא בשכלו ובדעתו בחבור הגמור. אבל דברים שהם מסופקים, ומכל שכן כשהם רחוקים, דבר זה אין לו חבור עמו. וזהו "אמור לחכמה אחותי את", שאין לך חבור יותר כמו אחותך, ולכך פשוט איסורה, כי עריות הם הקרובים אל האדם, ולכך נאסרו. ואמר אם הדבר קרוב לך כמו אחותך, שערוה זאת היא קרובה ביותר, כי אחותו היא עמו כמו בשר אחד לגמרי. אבל האב והבן, או הבת, במה שזהו האב וזהו תולדה, יש להם הבדל, ואינם שוים. אבל האח והאחות הם שוים, לכך לשון "אח" ו"אחות" מלשון אחוי. לכך אם ברור לך הדבר וקרוב לך, כאחותך שהיא אסורה, אמור החכמה, ואם לאו, אל תאמר. הרי כי הם הזהירו שלא יאמר דברים שאינם ברורים, מכל שכן דברים זרים ורחוקים מדעת האדם.

Essentially, Maharal responds that the purpose of Chazal is not to present scientific facts but rather to arrive at deeper truths. Even when they seem to be addressing natural and scientific questions, they are not actually offering natural or scientific explanations. Put differently, their science is not wrong because they are not attempting to explain things scientifically. This answer is premised on an assumption (developed in Chapter 12) that the physical world, as a manifestation of divine wisdom, reflects profundity on many levels. Accordingly, natural phenomena can be explained correctly, though superficially, on a physical level. They also can be understood on a deeper level.

Maharal offers an example of the disparate agendas of scientists and Chazal by turning to a case where the Torah itself seems to offer a false scientific explanation (the cause for the rainbow):

> כמו שהתבאר למעלה שאמרה תורה על אות הקשת (בראשית ט, טז) "וראיתיה לזכור ברית עולם". וחכמי הטבע נתנו סבה טבעית לקשת, כמו שידוע מדבריהם. אבל הדבר הוא כך, שהסבה אשר נתנה התורה הוא הסבה, **שלכל דבר יש סבה טבעית מחייב אותו, ועל אותה הסבה הטבעית יש סבה אלקית, והוא סבת הסבה, ומזה דברו חכמים.**

> As was explained regarding the indicating signal of the rainbow (*Bereishit* 9:16), "And I will see it to be reminded of the everlasting covenant." The scientists offer a natural cause for the rainbow, as is known from their statements. But the matter is thus: the cause given by the Torah is the ultimate cause. **Every effect has a natural cause that directly causes it, but that natural cause has a divine cause, and Chazal made their statements about the [divine] cause of the [natural] cause.**

Maharal readily concedes that the scientists are correct when they assert that the proximate cause of the rainbow is refraction. However, God could have constructed the world in a way that water and light would interact differently. He chose this configuration in order to remind us of the flood.[28] Thus, the scientific understanding of the cause of the rainbow is true, but this is not the interest of the Torah, which offers the deeper truth.[29]

This resolution is reminiscent of what R. Yosef Dov Soloveitchik calls epistemological pluralism, discussed in 4.6.[30] To put it succinctly, R. Soloveitchik maintains that science and religion deal with two different issues and therefore present two different perspectives. Both can be true even if they seem to contradict each other. R. Soloveitchik notes that this model is particularly compelling in light of twentieth-century science (particularly quantum physics), which no longer posits a unified or intuitive view of the world. For example, light is regarded as both a wave and a particle, which would seem to contradict the tenets of Aristotelian logic.

Likewise, R. Kook contends that no scientific evidence should be harmful to religion's foundations for the simple reason that science and

28. This formulation is adapted from R. Yitzchok Adlerstein's translation of *Be'er ha-Gola* (Brooklyn: Mesorah Publications, 2000, p. 209). The translations also are adapted from his work.
29. Interestingly, compare this response to Ramban's (*Bereishit* 9:12) treatment of the rainbow problem:

    "This is the sign of the covenant that I give" – It would seem from this sign that the rainbow that appears in the clouds is not part of the acts of creation, and only now God created something new, to make a rainbow appear in the sky on a cloudy day... But we are compelled to believe the words of the Greeks (ואנחנו על כרחנו נאמין לדברי היונים) that the rainbow is a result of the sun's rays passing through moist air, for in any container of water that is placed before the sun, something that resembles a rainbow can be seen. And when we look again at the wording of the verse, we will understand it thusly. For it says, "I have set my rainbow in the cloud," and it did not say, "I am setting it in the cloud (in the present tense)" as it said, "This is the sign of the covenant that I am giving." And the word, "My rainbow" indicates that the rainbow previously existed.
30. There, we quoted R. Soloveitchik as allowing for competing truths in Aggada, but he appears to advocate such a position regarding Halacha as well. See *Ish ha-Halakha: Galui ve-Nistar*, pp. 28–29. Regarding the application to the question of Halacha and science or observed reality, see "Surrendering to the Almighty" Jewish Press (October 16, 1998) regarding sociologies of men and women, as well as his position regarding '*Nachem*' prayer of after 1967, as quoted by R. J. J. Schacter, "On Changing the Text of Nahem: A Study in Tradition, Truth and Transformation," *Tisha B'av To Go* (Rabbi Isaac Elchanan Theological Seminary) *Av* 5774 (2014).

the Torah have utterly disparate agendas. Science exists to discover the revealed physical reality, to plumb the depths of the created, corporeal universe, while religion relates to the "knowledge of God and morality and their branches in life and actuality in the lives of individuals, the nation, and the world."[31] We elaborate on both of these resolutions in 8.12.

Maharal continues with another example of this phenomenon:

> כי לאדם אל צורתו **ומספר אבריו יש סבה טבעית**, שאין ספק כי יש לדבר זה פועל טבעי, ומכל מקום יש לאותה סבה סבה אלוקית, שעל סבת הסבה אמר (בראשית א, כז) "ויברא אלקים את האדם בצלמו בצלם אלהים ברא אותו"... אמנם גם סבת הסבה שנתנו הם ז"ל, לא עמדו על דבריהם להבין דבריהם, כי רחקו ממנה. וזה כי לקחו דבריהם בהבנה ראשונה, מבלי שנתנו לב להבין אמתת הדברים.

> For regarding a person's form **and the number of his limbs, there is a natural cause.** Every limb and organ serves an important function. Yet there also is a divine cause. About this it states (*Bereishit* 1:27): "God created the man in His image; with the image of God did He create him." However, these critics did not delve into the understandings of Chazal's words; rather, they understood them superficially, without intending to understand the truth of their statements.

Man's physical body shows more than good engineering. It has something to teach us about God and His attributes. Maharal here is alluding to the Kabbalistic notion that the body of man has parallels to the way in which God manifests Himself in the world.[32] Thus, there is a deeper meaning to the limbs of a human. In other words, if we were to ask a biologist about the purpose, function, and form of various limbs we would get one answer. Were we to look to the Torah, we would find a different solution: the 248 limbs (*eivarim*) parallel the 248 positive

---

31. *Igrot* 1, p. 105, *Eider ha-Yakar* pp. 37–38, *Ma'amarei ha-Re'iyah* pp. 10–11. Translation adapted from that of R. Yosef Bronstein.
32. We explain this notion in Chapter 12.

mitzvot, and the 365 sinews parallel the 365 negative *mitzvot*. Maharal then goes on to explain the meaning and significance of the parallelism. To summarize, one can study the body from a medical perspective as well as from a Torah perspective, and both perspectives yield differing but true results.

R. Aaron Lopiansky points out an additional point. God created the world in such a way that we see the sun rising and setting. Primitive man understands the world as he sees it and therefore concludes that we are stationary while the sun is moving. Science, on the other hand, seeks to understand the mechanism. It discovered that even though it seems as though we are stationary, in fact, that is not the case. Does that mean that the first perspective is entirely invalid? No. If God created the world in such a way that we perceive that the sun is encircling us then there is truth to that sensory perspective. Of course, it is not scientifically correct, but even after we understand the mechanism, the non-scientific truth of the sensory perspective remains valid. It is our experiential reality and it was created with design and purpose. God wanted us to feel as though the sun encircles us (and thus the simple reading of Scripture reflects this reality). R. S. R. Hirsch (Collected Writings, Vol. 7, p. 57) powerfully makes this point:

> Jewish scholarship has never regarded the Bible as a textbook for physical or even abstract doctrines. In its view the main emphasis of the Bible is always on the ethical and social structure and development of life on earth; that is, on the observance of laws through which the momentous events of our nation's history are converted from abstract truths into concrete convictions. That is why Jewish scholarship regards the Bible as speaking consistently in "human language;" the Bible does not describe things in terms of objective truths known only to God, but in terms of human understanding, which is, after all, the basis for human language and expression. It would have been inconceivable that the Bible should have intended, for example, Joshua's command "O sun stand still" as implying a biblical dogma confirming or denying the existence of a solar system. The Bible uses human language when it speaks of the "rising and setting of the sun" and not of

> the rotation of the earth, just as Copernicus, Kepler and other such scientists, in their words and writings, spoke of the rising and setting of the sun without thereby contradicting truths they had derived from their own scientific conclusions.

We should note that there are times when Maharal's solution can be easily applied and times when it is less obvious. For example, when the Talmud refers to the spontaneous generation of lice, it seems to be suggesting a physical and not a spiritual explanation of how lice are born. Thus, Maharal's theory would not be useful to justify the seeming scientific error. Furthermore, if the explanations are spiritual, it is curious that they bear such striking resemblance to (incorrect) physical explanations that happened to be prevalent in the ancient world. While there may be truth to the non-scientific sensory experiential reality that lice spontaneously generate, it is not obvious that this reality should determine Halacha. Perhaps Maharal would concede that other answers may also be necessary.

5.16 R. KOOK'S THEOLOGICAL EXPLANATION FOR SCIENTIFIC ADVANCEMENT

R. Kook notes that even if we accept the possibility of scientific error on the part of Chazal, it certainly is part of God's design. God, in His infinite wisdom, reveals certain truths to the world in accordance with His plan for world history.[33] This, for example, explains why certain Kabbalistic truths were revealed only at certain points in history. Likewise, the explosion of scientific understanding over the last few centuries has both practical and theological implications. For example, R. Kook suggests that man thinking he was the center of the universe (an anthropocentric or geocentric model of the universe) was in order to spread the Torah's message of the immense potential and infinite value of a human life. Only recently, when society has come to appreciate mankind's majesty, did God reveal the grandeur of the universe, allowing us to truly appreciate our smallness.

---

33. R. Kook applies the same concept to progress within the moral development within the world.

אגרות הראי"ה איגרת צא

והנה כנסת ישראל היתה צריכה להתעמל הרבה עם כל עובדי עבודה זרה, להבינם שעם גודל הבריאה אין עם כל זאת האדם מבוזה עד שלא יהיה ערך להנהגתו המוסרית, כי אם היצירה המוסרית של האדם היא חשובה מאד יותר מהברואים היותר גדולים בכמותם לאין ערך. אבל לא בנקל עלה הדבר להטביע במקצת חותם ידיעה זו עם השמירה של ההכרה הפנימית של כבוד ד', שהוא גם כן בעיקר היסוד היותר הגדול להשתלמות האנושית, וכל היצירה הכללית בהוה ובנצח, בחיי חומר וחיי רוח. וכל זה העמל היה נדרש, איך להתאים בלב הקטן של האדם את המחזה של גדולת היצירה ושפלות האדם עם חזיון הכרת יד ד' הגדולה, ואיך שהוא נעלה ומרומם מכל הערכים ההסכמיים של כל נוצר, **מה היה אם היה אז ידוע גם כן מכל המון העולמות המעשיים שבציורי המדעים כעת, אז היה כדק נחשב, ומוסרו כאין, ולא היה אפשר להקים בקרבו רוח חיים של גדולה ותפארת כלל. רק עכשיו, אחרי שגם עם הציור שהיה גדול אז לעיניו כבר נלחם ויוכל, שוב אין מבעתים אותו בשום גדולה כמותית לפי האמת.** אבל כל אלה צריכים זמנים והכנות, והציורים הסיפוריים, בין הנמשכים מכח הסקירה על הבריאה מדרך המושכל, בין הבאים מהתגלות יד ד' על ידי נביאיו, צריכים תמיד להיות נושאים עמהם את הכח המאדיר את החיים ואת ההצלחה לאמתתה, ולא להביא לאדם ציד של ידיעות קטועות להשתעשע בהן בשחוק ילדות.

Kenesset Yisrael had to fight strongly against the idol worshippers in order to teach them that despite the greatness of creation, the moral essence of man is much more important than even the greatest creation, beyond measure; a man is not worthless until his moral behavior is valueless. It was not simple to inculcate this matter along with guarding the inner recognition of God's honor, which is also essentially the greatest foundation of human perfection and the creation in general in the present and for eternity, in both material and spiritual life. This labor was necessary in order to implant in the small heart of man the vision of the greatness of creation and the lowliness of man along with the vision of recognition of God's great hand, and how he is elevated and loftier than all agreed upon values of any creation. **If it was then known about the many worlds described by modern science,**

> **man would have considered himself nothing, and his morality would have evaporated; it would have been impossible to raise within him the living spirit of greatness and glory. Only now, after the internalization of man's greatness has struggled and won, man will not reject it even upon encountering any other qualitative and true greatness.** All of these require the proper time and preparation, and the images received – whether gleaned from studying creation with our reason or through revelation of God's hand to His prophets – must always carry with them the power that truly strengthens life and success, and not bring man to bits of knowledge to "play with" as children play.[34]

The same presumably is true if we adopt the approach of changes in nature (*nishtana ha-teva*) to resolve contradictions between Chazal and science. If God changed nature, it was for a purpose. Sometimes, we might suggest a theory for the purpose of these changes,[35] while other times, we may have no idea.

---

34. This translation is taken from *Rav A.Y. Kook: Selected Letters*, translated by Tzvi Feldman (Ma'aleh Adumim, 1986).

35. For example, R. Tzadok argues that the verse גם את זה לעמת זה עשה האלהים (*Kohelet* 7:14) indicates that the world always is marked by parallel and opposite forces. Accordingly, the first stage of Jewish history, typified by miracles and prophets, also experienced *kishuf* (magic/sorcery) and false prophecy. In the second stage, marked by the development of the oral law through the intellect, there was a parallel advancement of wisdom in the non-Torah world, beginning with Greek wisdom and continuing through the various intellectual movements up to and including our times. Thus, we need not be surprised by the lack of genuine magic and sorcery in the modern world; God changed nature to accord with His ultimate plan. R. Tzadok writes:

פרי צדיק דברים פרשת נצבים

> ואם ישתו בני נכר תירושך אשר יגעת בו הענין הוא שבכל פעם שמתגלה בעולם דרך חדש בתורה שבעל פה מתגלה לעומת זה חדשות בחכמות חיצונות באומות. **כמו שמצינו בזמן שמעון הצדיק שהיה משירי אנשי כנסת הגדולה שהם יסדו התורה שבעל פה אז היה כנגדו אלכסנדרוס מוקדון ורבו שהפיצו החכמת יונית שהוא מינות ואפיקורוסות שזה לעומת זה וכמו שנתבאר במקום אחר שבזמן שהיה צריך להיות התגלות התורה שבכתב היה אז חכמת מצרים ואחר כך בבבל היה עוד אשפים וחרטומים לעומת שהיה אז בישראל נביאים.** ובזמן שהתחיל להתפשט חכמת תורה שבעל פה שהוא על הגוון משכל החכמים שבאמת הוא מה שמופיע בהם ה׳ יתברך. התחיל אצלם לעומת זה חכמת יונית שהוא גם כן מה שמחדשים משכלם. ועל זה נאמר ואם ישתו בני נכר שהם האומות

5.17 CONTEMPORARY APPROACHES

R. Aharon Feldman

Let us summarize what we have seen thus far. At least with respect to certain cases, a large group of Rishonim, including R. Tam, Rashba, Rivash, R. Chananeil, and Ra'avad, maintains that at least in certain telling circumstances Chazal did not err with respect to scientific matters. At the same time, other great Jewish thinkers, including R. Sherira Gaon, Rambam, R. Avraham b. ha-Rambam, and R. Hirsch all maintain that Chazal occasionally erred scientifically.[36] These mistakes do not undermine their credibility with respect to other matters of Torah because (a) they never claimed to be experts in science and (b) their scientific statements do not reflect a *mesora* (tradition going back to Sinai).

How is one to relate to such a dispute? Normally, we would leave it at that and not seek to definitively rule on the matter, insofar as there are no obvious practical implications (see 5.8). However, according to R. Aharon Feldman,[37] while there are other Rishonim and Acharonim who side with R. Avraham's view, his opinion is a minority opinion among later thinkers, "one of many which have fallen by the wayside in the course of the centuries and which we no longer follow." R. Feldman writes this despite acknowledging that there are Acharonim who endorse R. Avraham's view, including *Pachad Yizchak* (R. Yitzchak Lampronti, entry "*Tzeida*"), R. Samson Raphael Hirsch (cited above), and R. Dessler (*Michtav mei-Eliyahu,* Vol. 4, p. 355).

העולם תירושך שמרמז לתורה שבעל פה. וכן איתא בתיקונים (תיקון ח׳) ובושה החמה ס״מ וחפרה הלבנה נוקביה דס״מ שהם אומרים שלהם הוא התורה שנמשלה לחמה וכעין שמובא בזוה״ק (ח״ב קפ״ח א) שאמר ההגמון שאצלם הוא השפת אמת שתכון לעד וזה נגד בחינת תורה שבכתב ועל זה אמר ובושה החמה. וחפרה הלבנה הוא מה שמחדשים הם בשכלם ועל זה אומרים שהוא הלבנה שלהם סיהרא דמקבלא משמשא. על זה אומר ואם ישתו בני נכר תירושך. כי מאספיו יאכלוהו הוא נגד אם אתן דגנך וגו׳ שבאמת על ידי האכילה יבואו לדברי תורה והללו את ה׳ ומקבציו ישתוהו הוא נגד התירוש וזהו ישתוהו בחצרות קדשי שיהיה בבחינת היין שזכה משמחו שהיא סוד תורה שבעל פה וכאמור.

36. There may be other great thinkers who maintain this approach as well. See R. Natan Slifkin's "The Sun's Path at Night: Rewriting Jewish Intellectual History: A Review of Sefer Chaim Be'Emunasom," Part 10: The Sun's Path at Night at http://www.rationalistjudaism.com/2009/08/suns-path-at-night.html.

37. "The Slifkin Affair – Issues And Perspectives" in *The Eye of the Storm.* Yad Yosef Publications Jerusalem, 2009.

Why is the possibility of scientific error so intolerable (especially if we consider the possibility that Chazal simply were expressing the scientific assumptions prevalent in their day)? R. Feldman writes: "Kabbalah made it clear that when the Sages spoke, they based themselves on their knowledge of the mysteries of creation. This would give them an accurate knowledge of matters of natural science as well."

An example of this perspective is found in *Leshem Shevo ve-Achlama* by R. Shlomo Elyashiv (known as Leshem, 1841–1926), who writes:

> The main thing is: everyone who is called a Jew is obligated to believe with complete faith that everything found in the words of the Sages whether in Halachot or Aggadot of the Talmud or in the Midrashim, is the word of the Living God, for everything that they said is with the spirit of God that spoke within them, and "The secret of God is given to those who fear Him (סוד ה' ליראיו.)" This is just as we find in *Sanhedrin* 48b that even regarding something that has no application to Halacha and practical behavior, the Talmud asks regarding [the sage] R. Nachman, "How did he know this?" and the reply given is [that he knew this because], "The secret from God is given to those who fear him."[38]

While as far as I can tell, Leshem is not directly addressing scientific statements, he implies that all of the words of Chazal reflect divine wisdom. In 5.2, we considered other thinkers who may be of that view. If this is the case, then it seems reasonable to deny the possibility of error.

At first glance R. Feldman's conclusion is surprising, since we generally do not reject a major school of thought within the Rishonim in favor of Acharonim. R. Feldman explains why this case is different:

---

38. *Dei'a*, Sec. II, *Derush* 4, *Anaf* 19, *Siman* 7 (p. 160). Translation adapted from R. Feldman. Of course, this applies where the Sages are stating a fact, not where their intention is allegorical. This also is the view of *Chazon Ish* in his letters (Section I Letter 15).

> One of the most powerful reasons why R. Avraham's opinion was rejected by most opinions is the introduction of the wisdom of Kabbalah of the Ari Zal in the sixteenth century. This cast the Sages in another dimension. Before then, many authorities had held that the esoteric wisdom described in the Talmud as *Ma'aseh Breyshis* and *Ma'aseh Hamerkava* was science and philosophy. After the introduction of Kabbalah it became clear that these were the *Sefer HaYetzira*, the *Zohar* and the *Tikkunim.*[39] This was accepted by the overwhelming majority of Torah scholars since then.

Along similar lines (though perhaps with slightly different implications), R. Moshe Meiselman (*Torah, Chazal, and Science*) argues that the basis of Chazal's understanding of science is God. Just as Chazal's Torah statements reflect a tradition going back to Sinai (this assumption will be analyzed in Chapter 28), so too their statements concerning science stem from Sinai.[40] Thus, the claim is not that Chazal were experts in science, but that the scientific statements found in the Talmud reflect divine truth.

Three Contemporary Approaches

This controversial topic of Torah and science has exploded over the last few decades. Let us summarize the three major perspectives that have emerged.

- Some, like R. Natan Slifkin,[41] have argued that the view that Chazal erred in scientific matters is an acceptable position

39. See *Leshem Shevo ve-Achlama* (ibid.), where he discusses this change wrought by Kabbala. In Chapter 41, we will consider whether a similar phenomenon took place regarding *hashgacha*, where the dominant view among Acharonim seems to be at odds with the dominant view among Rishonim.
40. "If Chazal make a definitive statement, whether regarding Halachah or realia, it means that they know it to be unassailable" (p. 107). But, if they make a tentative statement, it could potentially be in error.
41. See *The Challenge of Creation: Judaism's Encounter with Science, Cosmology and Evolution* (Zoo Torah/Yashar Books 2006) and his numerous posts on http://www.rationalistjudaism.com/.

with prominent supporters to be found among both Rishonim and Acharonim. Moreover, it is the most reasonable theory in light of scientific advancement. R. Yitzchak Herzog[42] and R. Hershel Schachter[43] (among others) seem to accept this view as well.

- Others, like R. Aharon Feldman (cited above), acknowledge that there is indeed a debate among Rishonim and, to a lesser degree, Acharonim on this matter. However, the perspective that Chazal erred in scientific matters has been largely rejected by Acharonim, to the extent that it no longer is an acceptable position to maintain.[44] (This relates to our discussion concerning *psak* in Aggada in 5.7 and 5.8.)
- Finally, some, like R. Moshe Meiselman (cited above), argue that for the most part, *all* major Jewish thinkers maintain that Chazal did not err in matters of science and that most of what they said is rooted in ancient tradition. R. Meiselman carefully and comprehensively deals with some of the sources cited above that seem to indicate otherwise.

---

42. *Judaism: Law & Ethics*, p. 152 and 166. See, however, *Shut Heichal Yitzchak O.C. 29.*
43. See, for example, *Jewish Action* Winter 2014, https://www.ou.org/jewish_action/12/2014/science-sages/.
44. R. Feldman writes that this was the position of R. Yosef Shalom Elyashiv. R. Feldman also contends that this was the view of R. Shlomo Zalman Auerbach, though this is subject to debate. (see http://bdld.info/2011/11/16/terminally-ill-animals-and-dead-horses/).

Chapter Six

Rambam on Aggada

If a Torah scholar encounters an aggadic statement antithetical to his worldview, what is he to do? In the previous chapter, we considered two options:

(a) In 5.2, we saw a number of statements from some Geonim that implied that Aggada is not binding. As such, perhaps problematic Aggadot can be respectfully dismissed.
(b) Others, as we saw, reject this approach. They maintain that Aggadot, like the halachic statements of Chazal, are binding. This does not imply that a single aggadic statement should overturn one's Weltanschauung. There may be another aggada that disagrees with the first. Moreover, Aggadot should not be understood simplistically; frequently, the superficial understanding is not the correct one. Nevertheless, the option of dismissal is never available according to this view.

What is Rambam's opinion on this topic?

Rambam's view on Aggada is essential to understanding his worldview, yet it is the subject of great debate. Therefore, we devote this chapter to assessing his perspective. As we shall see, it is nuanced and does not fit easily into the above options. To properly address this question we must first consider whether Rambam adopts the Geonic position concerning the authoritativeness of Aggada.[1]

6.1 EVIDENCE THAT RAMBAM ADOPTED THE GEONIC VIEW

Let us begin by considering evidence that Rambam adopted the Geonic view limiting the authoritativeness of Aggada. In 2.7, we saw that in his Introduction to *Moreh ha-Nevuchim,* in a section that discusses "directions for the study of this work," Rambam posits that there are seven types of contradictions found in literary works. These seven can be further divided into two classes; the first class (1–4) consists of apparent contradictions stemming from a misunderstanding of the author's intent. The second class (5–7) consists of real contradictions. Sometimes these exist because the contradiction escaped the notice of the writer (6), but other times these contradictions are intentional (5 and 7). Concerning Chazal, Rambam writes:

> Contradictions occurring in the writings of most authors and commentators... are due to the sixth cause.[2] Many examples of this class of contradictions are found in the Midrash and Aggada; hence the saying: "We must not raise questions concerning the

1. As noted in 5.4, it is not at all clear what the Geonim meant by their statements cited in 5.2. We refer to the "Geonic view" as a typology representative of the simple (though perhaps superficial) reading of the Geonic statements minimizing the authoritativeness of Aggada.
2. "The contradiction is not apparent, and only becomes evident through a series of premises. The larger the number of premises necessary to prove the contradiction between the two conclusions, the greater is the chance that it will escape detection and that the author will not perceive his own inconsistency. Only when from each conclusion, by means of suitable premises, an inference is made, and from the enunciation thus inferred, by means of proper arguments, other conclusions are formed, and after that process has been repeated many times, then it becomes clear that the original conclusions are contradictory or contrary (to one another). Even able writers are liable to overlook such inconsistencies" (ibid.)

> contradictions met within Aggada." You may also notice contradictions in them due to the seventh cause.[3]

The combination of noting the possibility that contradictions may be a result of the sixth cause and his understanding of "We must not raise questions concerning the contradictions met within Aggada" indicate Rambam's acceptance of the Geonic view. The same may be deduced from one of his responsa, where he reiterates the Geonic view that Midrashic material is novel and lacks a tradition going back to Sinai.[4] [5]

6.2 SOURCES THAT INDICATE RAMBAM REJECTED THE GEONIC VIEW

Rambam's view is not so simple, though. While Rambam may not feel compelled to justify every confounding midrash, he shows tremendous esteem for aggadic material. This too can be derived from the Introduction to *Moreh ha-Nevuchim:*

---

3. Intentional contradictions meant to obscure esoteric wisdom that may not be publicized.
4. Rambam writes concerning a Midrashic debate regarding those leaving the *teiva* of Noach that the views in Chazal neither reflect a tradition going back to Sinai nor are based on compelling inferences; rather, they convey the views of individual sages. As such, they are not authoritative:

 תשובות הרמב"ם לר' פנחס הדיין עמ' תסא במהדורות שילת

 ...ולעניין יוצאי תיבה (עיין סנהדרין קח: "למשפחותיהם יצאו מן התבה (בראשית ח:יט) - אמר ר' יוחנן: למשפחותיהם ולא הם") - **כל אותן הדברים - דברי הגדה הן, ואין מקשין בהגדה. וכי דברי קבלה הן או מילי דסברא** וכי מקובלים הדברים מסיני, או שמוכרחים הדברים בדרכי ההגיון?, **אלא כל אחד ואחד מעיין בפסוק כפי מה שיֵרָאה לו בו, ואין בזה לא דברי קבלה, ולא אסור ולא מותר, ולא דין מן הדינין, ולפיכך אין מקשין בהן. ושמא תאמר לי, כמו שיאמרו רבים, וכי דברים שבתלמוד אתה קורא הגדה? - הן, כל אלו הדברים וכיוצא בהן הגדה הן מעניינם** מתוכנם, **בין שהיו כתובין בתלמוד, בין שהיו כתובין בספרי דרשות, בין שהיו כתובים בספרי הגדה**

5. Unlike many of the Geonim, Rambam does not distinguish between aggadic statements in the Talmud versus those not in the Talmud. As noted in the previous chapter, many Geonim maintain that the editors of the Talmud ensured that all aggadic material therein was correct.

פתיחה **לספר מורה הנבוכים**
וכבר יעדנו בפירוש המשנה שאנחנו נבאר ענינים זרים בספר הנבואה, וספר ההשואה, והא ספר יעדנו שנבאר בו ספיקות הדרשות כולם אשר הנראה מהם מרוחק מאד מן האמת יוצא מדרך המושכל והם כולם משלים. וכאשר החילותי זה שנים רבים בספרים ההם וחברתי מהם מעט, לא ישר בעינינו מה שנכנסנו בבאורו על הדרך ההיא, מפני שראינו שאם נעמוד על ההמשל וההעלם למה שצריך העלמתו, לא נהיה יוצאים מן הדרך הראשון ונהי מחליפים איש באיש ממין אחד. ואם נבאר מה שצריך לבארו יהיה זה השתדלותנו בלתי נאות בהמון העם. ואנחנו אמנם השתדלנו לבאר ענייני הדרשות וגלויי הנבואה להמון. **וראינו עוד שהדרשות ההם אם יעיין בם סכל מהמון הרבנים לא יקשה עליו מהם מאומה, כי לא ירחיק הסכל הנמהר הערום מן ידיעת הטבע המציאות, הנמנעות. ואם יעיין בם שלם חשוב לא ימלט מאחד משני דברים, אם שיקחם כמשמעם ויחשוב רע באומר ויחשבהו לסכל ואין בזה סתירה ליסודי האמונה. או שישים להם תוך, וכבר נצל, ויחשוב טוב על האומר, יתבאר לו התוך שבמאמר ההוא או לא יתבאר.**

In our commentary on the Mishna, we stated that we intend to explain strange situations occurring in the Book on Prophecy and in the Book of Harmony. In the latter, we intended to examine all the passages in the Midrash that if taken literally appear to be inconsistent with truth and common sense; they are all to be taken figuratively. Many years have elapsed since I commenced those works. I wrote only a small part of them when I became dissatisfied with my original plan. For I observed that by expounding these passages by means of allegorical and hidden terms, we do not explain anything, but merely substitute one thing for another of the same nature. And if we explained them fully, the results of our efforts would not be pleasant to the greater public. And my sole object in planning to write those books was to make the contents of midrashim and the exoteric lessons of the prophecies intelligible to everybody.

We further have noticed that when an ill-informed religious teacher reads these midrashim, he will find no difficulty; for possessing no knowledge of the factual properties of nature,

> **he will not reject statements that involve impossibilities. When, however, a person who is both religious and well-educated reads them, he cannot escape one of two possible conclusions: either he takes them literally and questions the abilities of the author and the soundness of his mind – doing thereby nothing which is opposed to the fundamental principles of our faith; or he will allow that the passages in question have some secret meaning, and he will continue to hold the author in high estimation, whether he understands the allegory or not.**

Rambam writes that initially he had planned to write a book explaining problematic aggadic statements. Upon reflection, however, he realized that such a work is not as necessary as the work he did write (*Moreh ha-Nevuchim*), which explicates problematic verses in Scripture. For when a person encounters a problematic midrash (i.e., a midrash that if understood literally contradicts science or philosophy), one of three things will happen:

1. Those who are uneducated will not recognize the difficulty and will happily accept the literal understanding of the midrash. They will not be helped by a work explaining these midrashim, since they are not troubled by them in the first place.
2. Some of those who are educated will recognize the problem and dismiss the author of the midrash as foolish. While this approach is *wrong*, it is not heretical, and therefore the need for such a book is not pressing.
3. Some of those who are educated will recognize the problem and will either interpret the midrash so as to resolve the quandary or acknowledge their ignorance as to the true meaning of the midrash. Such people already have adopted the correct path and do not greatly need such a book.

This is in contrast to problematic verses in Scripture, where adopting the first or second approaches is heretical and the third is problematic (in that it leaves many people ignorant of the correct meaning of many verses). Therefore, Rambam chose to write a book explaining philosophically problematic verses.

Here, Rambam adopts a reverential approach towards Aggada, maintaining that midrashim convey profound wisdom, though frequently the correct interpretation is hidden. Either way, Rambam implores us not to dismiss problematic midrashim but instead to uncover their deeper meaning.

6.3 HOW TO READ PROBLEMATIC MIDRASHIM ACCORDING TO RAMBAM

On a practical level, what emerges from Rambam's position concerning midrashim is that problematic midrashim should not cause someone to question basic tenets of faith. Rather, when one encounters a troubling midrash, one must seek to understand it in a way that does not contradict any established principle.[6] If one fails to come up with a compelling alternative explanation, he should acknowledge that he does not understand the author's intent and should presume that there must be a hidden meaning.

Indeed, throughout *Moreh ha-Nevuchim,* Rambam quotes midrashim that allude to the profound philosophical truths that he presents. For example, in 1:60 he writes:

> והסתכל איך אלו העניינים המופלאים האמתיים, אשר עליהם הגיע עיון המעולים שבפילוסופים, מפוזרים במדרשות.

---

6. An example where Rambam himself did so can be found in his response to Ovadya the convert concerning a Talmudic passage that indicates that a person's spouse is predetermined by fate. Rambam first warns Ovadya not to accept aggadic material at face value when it contradicts established principles; he then offers an alternative explanation.

שו״ת הרמב״ם סימן תלו

שאלה על הכל בידי שמים חוץ מיראת שמים תשובה על מה שאמרת אתה כי כל מעשה [בני] האדם אינם בגזירה מלפני הבורא יתעלה הוא האמת שאין בו דופי ולפיכך נותנים לו שכר אם הלך בדרך טובה ונפרעין ממנו אם הלך בדרך רעה וכל מעשה בני האדם בכלל יראת שמים הם וסוף כל דבר ודבר ממעשה בני האדם בא לידי מצוה או עבירה וזה שאמרו רז״ל הכל בידי שמים במנהגו על עולם ותולדותיו וטבעו כגון מיני אילנות וחיות ונפשות ומדעות וגלגלים ומלאכים הכל בידי שמים...

וכל המניח דברים שביארנו שהם בנויים על יסודי עולם והולך ומחפש בהגדה מן ההגדות או במדרש מן המדרשים או מדברי אחד הגאונים ז״ל עד שימצא מלה אחת ישיב בה על דברינו שהם דברי דעת ותבונה אינו אלא מאבד עצמו לדעת ודי לו מה שעשה בנפשו.

We will examine Rambam's somewhat difficult solution in 17.4.

> ...and see how these wondrous and fundamentally true matters, which the greatest of the philosophers addressed, are found scattered among the Midrashic texts.

Rambam elaborates upon his position concerning Aggada in his Introduction to *Perek Cheilek* (the tenth chapter of *Sanhedrin*). There, he also divides those who interpret Aggada into three camps:

1. The first and largest camp understands midrashim literally. Such people lack the wisdom to realize or be bothered by the fact that these explanations are inconceivable. Although they revere the words of the Sages, believing them to contain great wisdom, they in fact denigrate the Sages by making them into fools capable of propounding preposterous theories. It would be preferable for these people to remain silent and refrain from quoting Chazal or to acknowledge that they have no understanding of Chazal's intention.[7]
2. The second group, which also attracts many adherents, likewise understands the words of the Sages literally. These people, however, have studied science and therefore mock the words of Chazal, believing that they themselves know more than our wise Sages. This group is even more foolish than the first group because its members imagine themselves to be smart, in contrast to the first group that acknowledges its simplicity. It realizes that if it had studied true philosophy, it would have realized that theological matters cannot be overtly presented to the masses

7. **הכת הראשונה והם רוב אשר נפגשתי עמהם ואשר ראיתי חבוריהם ואשר שמעתי עליהם, מבינים** אותם כפשטם ואינם מסבירים **אותם כלל,** ונעשו אצלם כל הנמנעות מחוייבי המציאות, ולא עשו כן אלא מחמת סכלותם בחכמות וריחוקם מן המדעים, ואין בהם מן השלמות עד כדי שיתעוררו על כך מעצמם, ולא מצאו מעורר שיעוררם, **ולכן חושבים הם שאין כונת חכמים בכל מאמריהם המחוכמים אלא מה שהבינו הם מהם, ושהם כפשוטם,** ואף על פי שיש בפשטי מקצת דבריהם מן הזרות עד כדי שאם תספרנו כפשטו להמון העם כל שכן ליחידיהם היו נדהמים בכך ואומרים היאך אפשר שיהא בעולם אדם שמדמה דברים אלו וחושב שהם דברים נכונים, וכל שכן שימצאו חן בעיניו. והכת הזו המסכנה רחמנות על סכלותם לפי שהם רוממו את החכמים לפי מחשבתם ואינם אלא משפילים אותם בתכלית השפלות ואינם מרגישים בכך.

and accordingly would understand that the words of Chazal cannot be taken literally.[8]

3. Finally, the third and smallest group[9] has "become aware of the profound wisdom that our Sages possess [by carefully studying their words,] and also is knowledgeable about that which is impossible. Therefore, it understands that words of Chazal that seem implausible mask secrets." As Shlomo said at the beginning of *Mishlei*, [10] the way of the wise is to speak using a *chida* (riddle).[11] It is odd, notes the Rambam, that the second group acknowledges that works like *Mishlei* and *Shir ha-Shirim*, as well as other segments of Scripture, should be understood figuratively (and this is correct).[12]

---

8. והכת השניה גם הם רבים והם אותם שראו דברי חכמים או שמעוהו והבינוהו כפשטו, וחשבו שאין כונת חכמים בכך אלא משמעות פשטי הדברים, ולכן זלזלו בו וגנוהו וחשבו למוזר מה שאינו מוזר, וילעיגו על דברי חכמים לעתים קרובות, וחושבים שהם יותר נבונים מהם ויותר זכי רעיון, ושהם עליהם השלום פתיים חסרי דעת סכלים בכל המציאות, ואינם משיגים שום דבר כלל, ורוב מי שנפל במחשבה זו אותם הטוענים שהם רופאים, וההוזים במשפטי המזלות, לפי שהם לפי דמיונם פקחים חכמים פילוסופים וכמה רחוקים הם מן האנושות אצל הפילוסופים האמתיים. **והם יותר סכלים מן הכת הראשונה ויותר פתים, והם כת ארורה שהתפרצו כלפי אנשים רמי המעלה שכבר נודעה חכמתם אצל החכמים.**

9. He writes that there are so few people like this that it is hard to call them a group.

10. א מִשְׁלֵי שְׁלֹמֹה בֶן דָּוִד מֶלֶךְ יִשְׂרָאֵל. ב לָדַעַת חָכְמָה וּמוּסָר לְהָבִין אִמְרֵי בִינָה. ג לָקַחַת מוּסַר הַשְׂכֵּל צֶדֶק וּמִשְׁפָּט וּמֵשָׁרִים. ד לָתֵת לִפְתָאיִם עָרְמָה לְנַעַר דַּעַת וּמְזִמָּה. ה יִשְׁמַע חָכָם וְיוֹסֶף לֶקַח וְנָבוֹן תַּחְבֻּלוֹת יִקְנֶה. ו **לְהָבִין מָשָׁל וּמְלִיצָה דִּבְרֵי חֲכָמִים וְחִידֹתָם.**

11. A *chida* is something that cannot be understood superficially, as can be seen from the usage of the word in the Shimshon narrative:

    יב וַיֹּאמֶר לָהֶם שִׁמְשׁוֹן אָחוּדָה נָּא לָכֶם חִידָה אִם הַגֵּד תַּגִּידוּ אוֹתָהּ לִי שִׁבְעַת יְמֵי הַמִּשְׁתֶּה וּמְצָאתֶם וְנָתַתִּי לָכֶם שְׁלֹשִׁים סְדִינִים וּשְׁלֹשִׁים חֲלִפֹת בְּגָדִים. יג וְאִם לֹא תוּכְלוּ לְהַגִּיד לִי וּנְתַתֶּם אַתֶּם לִי שְׁלֹשִׁים סְדִינִים וּשְׁלֹשִׁים חֲלִיפוֹת בְּגָדִים וַיֹּאמְרוּ לוֹ חוּדָה חִידָתְךָ וְנִשְׁמָעֶנָּה. יד **וַיֹּאמֶר לָהֶם מֵהָאֹכֵל יָצָא מַאֲכָל וּמֵעַז יָצָא מָתוֹק** וְלֹא יָכְלוּ לְהַגִּיד הַחִידָה שְׁלֹשֶׁת יָמִים.

12. והכת השלישית והם חי ה׳ מעטים מאד עד שאפשר לקרוא להם כת כמו שאפשר לומר על השמש מין, והם האנשים שנתבררה אצלם גדולת החכמים וטוב תבונתם במה שנמצא בכלל דבריהם דברים המראים על ענינים אמתיים מאד, ואף על פי שהם מעטים ומפוזרים בכמה מקומות בחבוריהם הרי הם מראים על שלמותם והשגתם את האמת. וגם נתברר אצלם מניעת הנמנעות ומציאות מחוייב המציאות, וידעו שהם עליהם השלום לא דברו דברי הבאי, ונתברר אצלם שיש בדבריהם פשט וסוד, ושכל מה שאמרו מדברים שהם בלתי אפשריים אין דבריהם בכך אלא על דרך החידה והמשל, וכך הוא דרך החכמים הגדולים, ולפיכך פתח ספרו גדול החכמים ואמר להבין משל ומליצה דברי חכמים וחידותם, וכבר ידוע אצל חכמי הלשון כי חידה הם הדברים שענינים בסודם ולא בפשטם וכמו שאמר אחודה נא לכם חידה וכו׳, לפי שדברי כל בעלי החכמה בדברים הנשגבים שהם התכלית אינם אלא בדרך חידה ומשל, ומדוע נתפלא

R. Avraham b. ha-Rambam, in a piece that offers instructions concerning the study of Aggada (printed at the beginning of *Ein Yaakov*), echoes his father's sentiments and offers numerous examples of how to correctly interpret midrashim. Rambam implies that the correct attitude towards words of Aggada is never to dismiss them; one should presume that Chazal's teachings always convey profound wisdom, and one should interpret them accordingly.

Rambam also notes that scientific impossibility is grounds for the reinterpretation of an aggada. However, we should note that Rambam's idea of what is scientifically impossible may differ from what we would consider impossible. An example of this can be seen Rambam's presentation of the chain of tradition, from Moshe to the culmination of the Talmud, in his Introduction to *Mishneh Torah*. There, he writes that Achiyah ha-Shiloni was among those who left Egypt, and he passed the tradition (oral law) on to Eliyahu.[13] It is clear from the context of that discussion that he believed that this was literally true, which would mean that Achiyah lived an extraordinarily long life (nearly 600 years).[14]

על שחברו את החכמה בדרך משל ודמו אותם בדברים שפלים המוניים, והנך רואה החכם מכל אדם עשה כן ברוח הקדש כלומר שלמה במשלי בשיר השירים ומקצת קהלת, ומדוע יהא מוזר בעינינו לפרש את דבריהם ולהוציאם מפשטן כדי שיהא תואם את המושכל ומתאים לאמת ולכתבי הקדש, **והרי הם עצמם מבארים פסוקי הכתובים ומוציאים אותם מפשוטם ועושים אותם משל והוא האמת,** כפי שמצאנו שאמרו שזה שאמר הכתוב הוא הכה את שני אריאל מואב כולו משל, וכן מה שנ׳ הוא הכה את הארי בתוך הבור וכו׳ משל, ואמרו מי ישקיני מים ושאר מה שאירע כל זה משל. וכן ספר איוב כולו אמר אחד מהם משל היה ולא ביאר לאיזה ענין נעשה המשל הזה. וכן מתי יחזקאל אמר אחד מהם משל היה ורבים כאלה.

13. **הקדמה למשנה תורה**

וזקנים רבים קיבלו מיהושוע, וקיבל עלי מן הזקנים ומפינחס; ושמואל קיבל מעלי ובית דינו, ודויד קיבל משמואל ובית דינו. ואחייה השילוני, מיוצאי מצריים היה ולוי היה, ושמע ממשה, והיה קטן בימי משה; והוא קיבל מדויד ובית דינו. אלייהו קיבל מאחייה השילוני ובית דינו.

14. The Exodus took place in the year 2448 (1313 BCE). Eliyahu began prophesying in 2962 (798 BCE). Rambam seems to accept the tradition that Achiya lived from 2380 to 2964 literally. Why did Rambam feel that this aggadic statement could be literally true? The resolution likely lies in Rambam's position that we will consider in Chapter 24 that exceedingly long lives are not a biological impossibility (as can be seen from the lifespan of the people in the beginning of *Bereishit*). Thus, while Rambam maintains that nature will not change in the messianic era, he also writes that lifespans will increase greatly.

This example illustrates that Rambam was not always so quick to interpret aggadic statements non-literally.

6.4 DID RAMBAM MAINTAIN THAT ONE MAY DISAGREE WITH CHAZAL ON AGGADIC MATTERS?

Generally, Rambam goes to great lengths to show that his conclusions in *Moreh ha-Nevuchim* are derived from, or are at least consistent with, the words of Chazal. This is true especially with respect to his most controversial views. Let us consider a number of examples:

- Rambam's position in 3:54 concerning the superiority of intellectual achievements and knowledge of God over observance of *mitzvot* stems from *Bereishit Rabba*.[15]
- Rambam's assertion in 3:26 that the details of some *mitzvot* do not have reasons but are meant to instill obedience is rooted in *Vayikra Rabba* and *Tanchuma* (more on this in Chapter 36).[16]
- Rambam's cosmological theory in 2:10 that matters in this world are affected by a chain of causation rooted in celestial spheres can be seen in *Bereishit Rabba* (more on this in 40.9).[17]

---

15. **בראשית רבה פרשת נח פרשה לה**
כתוב א׳ אומר (משלי ח) וכל חפצים לא ישוו בה, וכתוב אחד אומר (שם /משלי/ ג) וכל חפציך לא ישוו בה, חפצים אלו מצות ומעשים טובים, חפציך אלו אבנים טובות ומרגליות, ר׳ אחא בשם ר׳ תנחום בר ר׳ חייא חפצי וחפציך לא ישוו בה, (ירמיה ט) כי אם בזאת יתהלל המתהלל השכל וידוע אותי כי אני ה׳ עושה חסד משפט וגו׳.

16. **ויקרא רבה י״ג ותנחומא שמיני פ״ז י״ח**
וכי מה אכפת להקדוש ברוך הוא אם שוחט מן הצוואר או שוחט מן העורף? הוי לא נתנו המצוות אלא לצרף בהן הבריות. שנאמר: כל אמרת אלוה צרופה.

17. **בראשית רבה פרשת בראשית פרשה י**
א״ר סימון אין לך כל עשב ועשב, שאין לו מזל ברקיע שמכה אותו, ואומר לו גדל.
At first glance, this source implies overarching providence. However, Rambam understands that it reflects the theory expressed by philosophers that there is a chain of causation from the spheres down to the growth of every blade of grass such that all causation ultimately is rooted in God's will (Rambam translates *mazal* as star):
ספר מורה הנבוכים חלק ב פרק י
ידוע מפורסם בכל ספרי הפילוסופים כשידברו בהנהגה, אמרו כי הנהגת זה העולם התחתון ר״ל עולם ההויה וההפסד, אמנם הוא בכחות השופעות מן הגלגלים, וכבר זכרנו זה פעמים, וכן תמצא החכמים ז״ל אומרים אין לך כל עשב ועשב מלמטה שאין לו מזל ברקיע שמכה אותו

- Rambam's view that *olam ha-ba* is the disembodied intellect enjoying an entirely spiritual existence derives from the Talmud (see 20.1).[18]

Thus, Rambam did not see himself as recasting the Torah in light of Greek philosophy. Rather, in *Moreh ha-Nevuchim* as in *Mishneh Torah,* Rambam sought to present the eternal and unchanging perspective of the Torah and thereby continue the legacy of Chazal. (In Chapter 2, we considered Rambam's explanation of why we do not find many purely philosophical discussions in the writings of Chazal.)

Nevertheless, Rambam acknowledges that there are times when his position seems to be at odds with that of Chazal. In such cases, Rambam does not simply state that one has the right to disagree with Chazal on matters that are not normative. Instead, he claims that the view he is

---

ואומר לו גדל, שנאמר הידעת חקות שמים אם תשים משטרו בארץ, ומזל יקראו ג"כ הכוכב, תמצא זה מבואר בראש בראשית רבה...

וזהו ענין הטבע, אשר יאמר שהוא חכם מנהיג, משגיח בהמצאת, החי במלאכת מחשבית, משגיח בשמירתו, והתמדתו, בהמציא כחות נותנות צורה הם סבת מציאותו וכחות זנות הם סבת עמידתו ושמירתו הזמן, שאפשר הכוונה הוא זה הענין האלהי המגיע ממנו שתי הפעולות האלו באמצעות הגלגל...

ספר מורה הנבוכים חלק ב פרק מח

מבואר הוא מאד שכל דבר מחודש א"א לו מבלתי סבה קרובה חדשה אותו, ולסבה ההיא סבה, וכן עד שיגיע זה לסבה הראשונה לכל דבר, ר"ל רצון השם ובחירתו, ומפני זה יחסרו הנביאים פעמים בדבריהם הסבות ההם האמצעיות כלם, וייחסו זה הפעל האישי המתחדש אל הבורא, ויאמרו שהוא יתעלה עשאו, וזה כולו ידוע, וככר דברנו בו אנחנו וזולתנו מן המאמתים, והוא דעת אנשי תורתנו כלם...

18. **תלמוד בבלי מסכת ברכות דף יז עמוד א**

העולם הבא אין בו לא אכילה ולא שתיה ולא פריה ורביה ולא משא ומתן ולא קנאה ולא שנאה ולא תחרות, אלא צדיקים יושבין ועטרותיהם בראשיהם ונהנים מזיו השכינה.

Rambam (*Hilchot Teshuva* 8:2) elaborates upon each detail of the metaphor. When the Talmud says there is no eating and drinking, it is telling us that there is no body. When it says that the righteous sit, it means that existence will have no form of strain or effort. The crowns on their heads represent the knowledge that they acquired while in this world and by which they merited *olam ha-ba*. Rambam's view is controversial in two respects. Firstly, contrary to most thinkers, Rambam rejects the existence of a physical body in *olam ha-ba*. Secondly, Rambam focuses on intellectual achievements as the basis for *olam ha-ba*. Rambam derives both of these contentions from the aforementioned Talmudic passage. See Chapters 19 and 20 for elaboration on this topic.

rejecting is a minority one.[19] This technique sometimes proves controversial, since it is not always clear how Rambam knows that the majority view supports his position. Let us consider four examples.

Example 1: Will the World be Destroyed?

The Talmud cites a tradition that the world will be destroyed for a 1000-year period:

מסכת סנהדרין צז עמוד א
אמר רב קטינא שית אלפי שני הוו עלמא וחד חרוב שנאמר ונשגב ה' **לבדו** ביום ההוא.

R. Katina stated: The world will exist for six thousand years, and then for one thousand it will lay in destruction, for it is stated: "On that day, God will be exalted **alone**."

In *Moreh ha-Nevuchim* 2:29, Rambam explains that this is not the only view: "It is the saying of an individual that corresponds to a certain manner of thinking."

Rashba objects:

שו"ת הרשב"א, חלק א סימן ט
ואין אנו רואין בתלמוד חולק עליו.[20]

...and we do not find any dissenting opinion in the Talmud.

---

19. This point is interesting for another reason. At first glance, it would seem to indicate that we resolve non-halachic disputes in a similar manner to halachic ones – namely, accepting the majority position. As we shall see, however, in non-halachic matters, Rambam does not feel compelled to show how he knows a particular position reflects the majority view. Instead, he shows how it is logically compelling. Thus, majority and minority in this context should not be understood in the halachic sense. We elaborate on this point in 5.8.

20. See, however, *Rosh ha-Shana* 31a, where R. Nechemya seems to disagree. Rashi understands that the disagreement concerns the length of the subsequent period. Rambam, however, may have understood a more comprehensive disagreement.

More importantly, Rambam understands that the basis of the dissenting view, which he claims *does* reflect consensus, is in *Kohelet*: "There is nothing new under the sun" (1:9), and that "whatever God does, it shall be **forever**; nothing can be added to it, nor anything taken from it" (3:14).

Example 2: Why Must We Send Away the Mother Bird?

Rashba's challenge above resembles Maharal's critique against Rambam's understanding of the *mitzva* to send away the mother bird before taking her eggs or chicks (*shiluach ha-kein*). The Talmud (*Berachot* 33b) states:

> האומר על קן צפור יגיעו רחמיך - משתקים אותו... מפני שעושה מדותיו של הקב"ה רחמים ואינן אלא גזירות
>
> One who says about a bird's nest: "May your compassion apply here," he is silenced... because he casts all of God's characteristics as being compassionate, while these are nothing more than legal regulations.

In *Moreh ha-Nevuchim* 3:48, however, Rambam writes that the purpose of the *mitzva* is to spare the mother bird pain. Regarding the Talmud's statement, Rambam writes, "It is the expression of one of the two opinions mentioned by us, namely, that the precepts of the Torah have no other reason but the divine will. We follow the other opinion." In other words, there is a debate in Chazal whether or not we are encouraged to seek to understand the reasons for *mitzvot*. Since we follow the view that one should seek to understand the reasons for *mitzvot*, we do not accept the passage from *Berachot*.[21] Maharal (*Tiferet Yisrael*, Chapter 6) objects that we do not find a dissenting opinion in the Mishna.

---

21. Interestingly, Rambam quotes the ruling from *Berachot* in *Mishneh Torah*. *Tosafot Yom Tov* understands that this is because even the perspective that we should seek reasons for *mitzvot* concedes that these are speculative and should not be inserted into the liturgy.

רמב"ם הלכות תפילה ונשיאת כפים פרק ט הלכה ז

מי שאמר בתחנונים מי שריחם על קן ציפור שלא ליקח האם על הבנים או שלא לשחוט אותו ואת בנו ביום אחד ירחם עלינו וכיוצא בענין זה משתקין אותו, מפני שמצות אלו גזרת הכתוב הן ואינן רחמים, שאילו היו מפני רחמים לא היה מתיר לנו שחיטה כל עיקר, וכן לא ירבה בכנוים של שם ויאמר האל הגדול הגבור והנורא והחזק והאמיץ והעיזוז, שאין כח באדם להגיע בסוף שבחיו, אלא אומר מה שאמר משה רבינו עליו השלום.

תויו"ט ברכות ה:ג

דוקא בתפלה **כשאומר בתפלה מחליט הדבר** ולהכי משתקין אותו משא"כ דרך דרש או פשט.

Example 3: Does God Punish a Person in Order to Increase His Reward?

A third example of this phenomenon is Rambam's rejection of *yisurin shel ahava,* which Rambam understands to mean suffering imposed so as to increase reward. Here, too, Rambam dismisses the view as reflecting a minority position:

מורה הנבוכים חלק ג פרק יז

ואנחנו נאמין שכל אלה הענינים האנושיים הם כפי הדין, והאלוה-חלילה לו מעול - לא יענוש אחד ממנו אלא המחויב והראוי לעונש. זהו הכתוב ב'תורת משה רבנו', כי הכל נמשך אחר הדין. ועל זה הדעת נמשכו דברי המון חכמינו - שאתה תמצאם אומרים בבאור: "אין מיתה בלא חטא, ולא יסורין בלא עוון"...

ובאה בדברי החכמים תוספת אחת שלא באה במה שכתוב בתורה, **והוא מאמר קצתם**, יסורין של אהבה. והוא, שלפי זה הדעת אפשר שיחולו באדם מכות ללא פשע קודם, אבל להרבות גמולו.

As for us, we believe that all of human circumstances are according to what is deserved, that He is exalted and above injustice, and that only those among us deserving punishment are punished. This is what is stated in the Torah of Moshe, namely, that everything depends upon that which deserved; and the multitude of our scholars also speak in accordance with this opinion. For you will find them saying explicitly: "There is no death without sin and no sufferings without transgression..."

In the discourse of the Sages, though, there occurs something additional over and above what is to be found in the text of the Torah, namely, **the dictum of some of them** regarding the sufferings of love. For according to this opinion, sometimes misfortunes befall an individual not because of his having sinned before, but in order that his reward should be greater.

Example 4: Do the Stars Affect Our Fate?

A fourth example can be found in his letter to the Jews of Marseilles, where Rambam rejects the notion of astrology and understands statements in Chazal that seem to support astrology as reflecting a minority view[22]:

איגרת לחכמי קהל עיר מארשילייא

ודעתנו עלה מעיקרא היא, שכל דברי החוזים בכוכבים שקר הם אצל כל בעלי מדע. ואני יודע שאפשר שתחפשו ותמצאו דברי יחידים מחכמי האמת רבותינו ע"ה בתלמוד ובמשנה ובמדרשות, שדבריהם מראים שבעת תולדות של אדם גרמו הכוכבים כך וכך. אל יקשה זה בעיניכם, שאין דרך שנניח הלכה למעשה ונהדר אפירכי ואשינויי. וכן אין ראוי לאדם להניח דברים של דעת שכבר נתאמתו הראיות בהן, וינער כפיו מהן ויתלה **בדברי יחיד מן החכמים** ע"ה, שאפשר שנתעלם ממנו דבר באותה שעה, או שיש באותם הדברים רמז, או אמרם לפי שעה ומעשה שהיה.

Our opinion is that the perspective of astrologers is false… I know that it is possible to search and find statements from individual sages in the Talmud, Mishna, and Midrash implying that things that happened to a person were caused by the stars. Do not let this trouble you, for it is not the proper path to abandon practical Halacha in favor of distortions. So too, it is not appropriate for a person to reject knowledgeable statements whose supporting evidence has been substantiated and empty his hands of them and instead rely exclusively on the statements of only one of the Sages. For it is possible that individuals can make mistakes, or that those statements were intended to be a subtle hint, or that he said them in response to a specific, constrained circumstance or situation that occurred.

22. Rambam offers two additional possible explanations: (1) The statements supporting astrology are not meant literally; rather they were intended to convey a secret. (2) The erroneous statements were made due to exigencies of the time. (We will consider this last possibility again in 26.4 when we examine Rambam's *keitz*.)

Rambam's True Motivation for Deviating from the Straightforward Reading of Chazal

Let us consider this pattern. In the above four cases, Rambam's view appears to be at odds with that of Chazal. However, Rambam denies that he is arguing with Chazal; instead, he argues that he is following the majority position within Chazal and rejecting a minority view. It should be noted that in all four cases, logical arguments are a major factor in his rejection of the stated position of Chazal. Additionally, in each of these cases, a superficial reading of the sources in Chazal indicates that the view being rejected by Rambam is the dominant or perhaps the only position, not a minority view.

Yet Rambam presumes a differing majority position; he does not base himself on explicit statements rejecting the minority view, but rather on declarations in the Torah and Chazal that presume principles at odds with the problematic statements. For example, verses concerning divine justice and kindness contradict *yisurin shel ahava*; statements in Chazal that offer reasons for *mitzvot* contradict the statement that *shiluach ha-kein* is simply a *gezeira* (decree); verses that describe the constancy of nature contradict the statement that the world will be destroyed.[23] Regarding his rejection of astrology, besides informing us that the philosophers have proven its falsity, he shows how it contradicts tenets of Torah such as justice and providence.[24]

---

23. As noted, Rambam cites *Kohelet*: "There is nothing new under the sun" (1:9), and that "whatever God does, it shall be **forever**; nothing can be added to it, nor anything taken from it" (3:14) as demonstrating that the world will not be destroyed. Clearly, the minority view, which presumes the world will be destroyed, did not ignore these *pesukim*. Presumably, that view understood these verses differently (multiple possibilities are evident). Once that is the case, how can Rambam assert, based on these verses, that R. Katina is a minority view? Apparently, Rambam understood that since the simple reading contradicts R. Katina, it is justified to state that his view is a minority position.

24. וכל אלו השלוש כיתות של הפילוסופים שאמרו שהכל על ידי הגלגלים והכוכבים ייעשה, יאמרו שזה שיארע לכל אחד ואחד מבני אדם מן המאורעות הוא קרי ואין לו עילה מלמעלה, ולא יועיל בו מולד ולא טבע... ואנחנו בעלי התורה האמיתית לא נאמר שמאורעות בני אדם הם קרי, אלא במשפט, כמו שאמרה התורה "הצור תמים פעלו כי כל דרכיו משפט" וגו'. ופירש הנביא ואמר "אשר עיניך פקוחות על כל דרכי בני אדם לתת לאיש כדרכיו וכפרי מעלליו"...

Thus, in all four cases, a cursory reading of Rambam may indicate that he simply endorsed the position of the philosophers and justified his novel approach by attributing the errant argument to a minority view. However, a careful reading of Rambam, I believe, implies the exact opposite conclusion. Rambam warns of the dangers of considering only solitary statements of midrashim, as they sometimes reflect minority viewpoints. Instead, we must consider the matter more broadly. When we look at the Torah's total viewpoint, we are left with a different conclusion. Thus, while we see that Rambam is unwilling to reject Chazal or offer an opinion at odds with what he perceives as the dominant view, we derive the imperative to subject statements of Chazal to rigorous scrutiny and consider all available sources.

6.5 RAMBAM AND MAHARAL

Sometimes, Rambam and Maharal are presented as taking very different approaches to Aggada. I believe, however, that our analysis has revealed that they are actually quite similar, at least conceptually if not methodologically.[25] Like Rambam, Maharal warns against understanding midrashim literally. Like Maharal, Rambam frequently refers to the statements of Chazal as מאמריהם המחוכמים, wise and profound words, words that only a wicked and foolish person would dismiss. Indeed, even though Maharal occasionally disagrees vehemently with Rambam, Maharal writes that his work *Be'eir ha-Gola* is meant only to add upon the great work of Rambam:

> **מהר"ל באר הגולה תחילת באר הרביעי**
> והנה הרב הגדול שהיה מלא חכמה כים בכל החכמות טבעיות אלקיות למודיות הוא הרמב"ם ז"ל, בהקדמת סדר זרעים האריך בדברים היקרים... להודיע לנו כי דבריהם כולם מחמדים... ודברו בהם כאשר ראוי לחכמים להסתיר הדברים הנעלמים... וכל דבריו בכלל **ופרט** אין צריכים חיזוק סעד ותמך, כי מי יסעוד ומי יתמוך אילנא רבא...

25. For an excellent comparison of Rambam's and Maharal's perspectives on Aggada, see "Maharal's Be'er ha-Golah and His Revolution in Aggadic Scholarship" by R. Chaim Eisen in *Ḥakirah,* Volume 4.

> The great scholar Rambam, who was filled with wisdom in all branches natural and metaphysical, writes wonderful things in his Introduction to the Mishna … where he tells us that all of Chazal's words are precious … and they spoke in a manner befitting wise men, to conceal hidden matters … And all of Rambam's words in general and specific do not need additional support or strength, for who is worthy to support such a mighty tree?

Let us conclude with the advice of R. Dessler, which very much conforms to the approaches of Rambam and Maharal:

> **מכתב מאליהו חלק ד עמוד שנג**
> בדברי אגדה אשר לא נבינם אין אנו מחוייבים ללמוד אותם ולסמוך עבודתנו עליהם, אם כי ברור שהם יסודות התורה. אבל ההלכה שהיא למעשה, הרי מחוייבים הננו במעשה המצוות, אם גם לא נבינם, אבל האגדה, שהיא באה להאיר ללב, הרי כל זמן שאינה מאירה לנו (מפני קטנות השגתנו), אין אנו מחוייבים להתעסק בה, עד שנזכה ונעלה למדרגה שנבין אותה. ויותר מזה, הן באגדות [גנוזים] סודות התורה, וכל זמן שלפי מדרגתנו לא יתגלה לנו הסוד שבמאמר ההוא, אם כן אין בו תועלת בהתעסק בו, מכיון שעל כל פנים אנו משיגים אותו שלא כאמיתתו.
>
> Regarding Aggadot that we do not comprehend, we need not study them and base our worship upon them, though they obviously contain foundational principles of the Torah. We are obligated to keep Halacha, to perform the *mitzvot* whether we understand them or not. Aggada, whose purpose is to illuminate the heart, we need not occupy ourselves with if it does not illuminate for us (due to our dearth of understanding). One day, we will merit understanding it. Moreover, Aggada contains the secrets of the Torah, and as long as the secret is not revealed to us, there is no use in studying it, since anyway we do not understand it correctly.

Chapter Seven

The Relationship Between *Pshat* and *Drash*

In Chapter 5, we introduced Midrash, considered its authoritativeness, and discussed the extent to which it should be taken literally. Let us now turn our attention to the way in which Midrash informs our reading of the text of the Torah and try to understand the complex relationship between *pshat* and *drash*. We shall focus on one specific aspect of this broad question, namely, how *pshat* and *drash* relate to physical reality. By doing this, we hope to gain a broader perspective on the purpose of *drash,* both with respect to the narrative portions of the Torah as well as the legal sections.

7.1 THERE ARE SEVENTY FACES TO TORAH

Chazal frequently express the notion that Torah can be explained on many levels:

במדבר רבה יג:טו

שבעים פנים לתורה.

There are seventy faces to Torah.

מסכת סנהדרין לד עמוד א

כפטיש יפוצץ סלע מה פטיש זה מתחלק לכמה ניצוצות אף מקרא אחד יוצא לכמה טעמים.

"Like a hammer that breaks the rock in pieces" – just as [a rock] is split into many splinters, one biblical verse conveys many teachings.[1]

Moreover, the Torah is written in a way that allows for multiple correct interpretations.[2] In the chapter that follows we will examine the complex relationship between *pshat* and *drash*. Most of the thinkers we shall examine in this chapter will highlight the value if interpreting the Torah on multiple levels, including *pshat, drash,* and even *sod* (mysticism), where each of these methodologies are, more or less, equally valuable. Torah conveys knowledge in many layers with each one reflecting God's voice and His infinite wisdom. In 12.6 we shall consider an alternative perspective. Gra, following the *Zohar,* argues that while there is value in studying all aspects of *pardes* (a term we define in 12.6), there is a hierarchy of interpretation – one begins, as it were, outside the city in the world of

1. Likewise, see the Introduction of Ramban to his commentary on the Torah, where he formulates the notion of the Torah as a divine text formed by infinite combinations of divine names, allowing it to serve as a creative exegetical source of all types of knowledge simultaneously.
2. Radvaz (*Teshuvot Radvaz* 3:643) even posits that the text of the Torah is unencumbered by *nekudot* and *te'amim* – despite the fact that these symbols signal the proper method of public reading of the Torah and are of Sinaitic origin – because their inclusion would inhibit the multiplicity of legitimate possible readings. Ridvaz (Yerushalmi *Sanhedrin* 4:4) understands the Yerushalmi cited in 4.1 as reflecting this notion. Also, consider the following:

שו"ת חוות יאיר סימן קעב

...ואחר שנ"ל שכל בכה"ג ניתן רשות לישב סתירת הפסוקים שלא כתירוצו של הש"ס כי ע' פני' לתורה ולא דמי למלתא דתליא בסברא דא"א לישב קושית הש"ס בסוגיא באופן אחר ממה שתירץ הש"ס אדרבא מחזקינן לתימא למה לא תירץ הש"ס באופן אחר דמרווח מיני' מש"כ פסוקים דסתרי ניתן לדרוש הן חוץ לפשוטן או סמוך לפשוטן... ונחזור לענינינו שלעד"נ שכל סתירת הפסוקים ניתן לדרוש לא לבד לחז"ל רק לכל אדם מבלי שיכחיש דרז"ל. ובדרך אפשר כי כמה פנים לתורה גם בתנאי שלא יחדש בישוב המקראות איזה הלכה וחידוש דין שלא זכרו רז"ל כ"ש נגד קבלת רז"ל זה אין בכוחינו.

pshat. Drash leads a person towards civilization with *remez* representing the city's gate. The end destination is an enchanted city, *sod,* which the individual could not have imagined when he first started upon the road.

7.2 WHAT ACTUALLY HAPPENED: *PSHAT*, *DRASH*, BOTH, OR NEITHER?

Usually, we view these multiple explanations as complementing each other. Nevertheless, one question that bothers many people is how to relate to cases where there is a contradiction between *pshat* and *drash* about what actually occurred. Here, some might say, we cannot simply claim that both are true on different levels, since in the physical world, only one thing happened. Either *pshat* or *drash* corresponds to physical reality; they cannot both have occurred.[3]

In the following sections, we explore this question, first with respect to the narrative sections of the Torah and then with respect to the legal sections.

7.3 PHYSICAL REALITY CORRESPONDS TO *PSHAT*

Let us first examine sources that seem to presume that in the event of a conflict, physical reality at least sometimes corresponds to *pshat*.

Where Was Yocheved Born?

The first source relates to the number of people who went down to Egypt. The verse states that it was seventy, with thirty-three from the family of Leah.[4] The problem is that when we count the enumerated names, we find only thirty-two. The midrash (cited by Rashi) solves the problem by suggesting that Yocheved was born on the way to Egypt.[5] Other resolutions

---

3. In our discussion of *eilu ve-eilu* in Chapter 4, we consider the possibility that both in fact occurred. A model for this counterintuitive model is Maharal's understanding of *shemesh be-Giv'on dom* (*Yehoshua* 10), which we consider in 4.5.

4. **בראשית מו :טו**
אֵלֶּה בְּנֵי לֵאָה אֲשֶׁר יָלְדָה לְיַעֲקֹב בְּפַדַּן אֲרָם וְאֵת דִּינָה בִתּוֹ כָּל נֶפֶשׁ בָּנָיו וּבְנוֹתָיו שְׁלֹשִׁים וְשָׁלֹשׁ:

5. **רש"י שם**
שלשים ושלש - ובפרטן אי אתה מוצא אלא שלשים ושנים, אלא זו יוכבד **שנולדה בין החומות** בכניסתן לעיר, שנאמר (במדבר כו:נט) אשר ילדה אותה ללוי במצרים, לידתה במצרים ואין הורתה במצרים:

have been suggested,[6] but what concerns us is the perspective of ibn Ezra. Ibn Ezra rejects the midrash's answer because if Yocheved was born on the way to Egypt, she would have been 130 years old when Moshe was born. Something this remarkable surely should have been mentioned explicitly in the Torah. After all, when Sarah bore Yitzchak at the age of ninety, the Torah highlights the miracle. The Torah's omission of anything miraculous about Moshe's birth indicates that he was born when his mother still was of normal childbearing age. This forces us to conclude that this midrash does not depict physical reality.[7] Ramban, as we shall see in 7.5, disagrees with ibn Ezra, but let us first consider some other examples of this phenomenon.

Who Actually Died During Makat Bechorot?

Ran (in his eighth *drasha*) asserts that God generally does not intervene supernaturally to affect individuals. For example, sinners are not immediately struck by lightning.[8] Ran uses this principle to deal with the question

---

6. Rosh (*Pesachim* 10:40) suggests that the Torah sometimes rounds up. Besides this instance, he offers the example of *sefirat ha-omer*, where the Torah seems to command us to count fifty days, yet we count only forty-nine days, as well as the punishment of lashes, where the Torah states that the sinner receives forty lashes, while in reality he receives only thirty nine.

   Rashbam offers another possibility:

   רשב"ם בראשית מו:ח

   יעקב ובניו - יעקב מחשבון שבעים נפש כמו שמוכיח לפנינו לפי הפשט כל נפש בניו ובנותיו של יעקב ולאה הכל שלשים ושלש עם יעקב. ורבותינו פירשו זו יוכבד שנולדה בין החומות:

7. One can read ibn Ezra's rejection in one of two ways. (1) Chazal are wrong or (2) Chazal's understanding does not correspond to physical reality. We address this question later.

   ראב"ע בראשית פרשת ויגש פרק מו

   ד"ה ובני דן חושם: ...יש אומר כי מספר שבעים בעבור שהוא סך חשבון כי ששים ותשע היו. וזה המפרש טעה בעבור שמצאנו כל נפש בניו ובנותיו שלושים ושלש. והם שלושים ושתים ובדרש כי יוכבד נולדה בין החומות. גם זה תמה למה לא הזכיר הכתוב הפלא שנעשה עמהם שהולידה משה והיא בת ק"ל שנה. ולמה הזכיר דבר שרה שהייתה בת תשעים. ולא די לנו זה הצער עד שעשו פייטנים פיוטים ביום שמחת תורה יוכבד אמי אחרי התנחמי והיא בת ר"נ שנה וכי אחיה חי כך וכך שנים דרך אגדה או דברי יחיד. והנכון בעיני שיעקב בחשבון וממנו יחל כאילו אמר כל נפש בניו ובנותיו עם נפשו שלושים ושלוש. והראיה על זה...

8. ומכל מקום הדבר מוסכם בין חכמי ישראל, שהעולם הזה התחתון נמסר ונוהג כפי מערכת הכוכבים, אם לא שעבודת השם יתברך תבטל הרושם המתחייב ממנה. ונמשך מזה שאם לא יחזק זכות האדם כל כך שתשתנה המערכת בשבילו, או שיהיה מושגח בהשגחה פרטית דבקה, עד שישים השם יתברך בלבו לעשות איזה פעל יגן בעדו מרעת המערכת, כל עוד שלא יהיה

of why the wicked suffer and righteous prosper.[9] We will analyze this passage in our discussion of providence in 37.8; however, for purposes of our discussion, let us turn to Ran's explanation of a perplexing verse:

במדבר ח:טז–יז

כִּי נְתֻנִים נְתֻנִים הֵמָּה לִי מִתּוֹךְ בְּנֵי יִשְׂרָאֵל תַּחַת פִּטְרַת כָּל רֶחֶם בְּכוֹר כֹּל מִבְּנֵי יִשְׂרָאֵל לָקַחְתִּי אֹתָם לִי. כִּי לִי כָל בְּכוֹר בִּבְנֵי יִשְׂרָאֵל בָּאָדָם וּבַבְּהֵמָה בְּיוֹם הַכֹּתִי כָל בְּכוֹר בְּאֶרֶץ מִצְרַיִם הִקְדַּשְׁתִּי אֹתָם לִי.

> For they are wholly given over to Me from among the children of Israel in place of those that open the womb, all the firstborn of Israel, I have taken them for Myself. For all the firstborn among the children of Israel are Mine, whether man or animal; since the day I smote all the firstborn in the land of Egypt, I have sanctified them for Myself.

In this verse, we are informed that Jewish firstborn were sanctified in Egypt when they were spared from the final plague. But why should the Jewish firstborn owe any extra gratitude to God for sparing them if they were not deserving of death in the first place?[10] In light of his thesis

---

אחד מאלו הצדדים, יתחייב שיענש האדם ההוא, גם כשלא יתחייב אליו כפי מעשיו העונש ההוא. ומפני זה אמרו רבותינו ז״ל בני חיי ומזוני וכו׳. ועל זה הדרך גם כן הוא שאמר ואתם לא תצאו איש מפתח ביתו עד בוקר כיון שניתנה רשות למשחית אינו מבחין בין צדיק לרשע.

9. ובזה הענין יסתלק הספק הגדול, המתמיה בהנהגת העולם, בצדיק ורע לו רשע וטוב לו. והוא שאילו היו השפעים הנמשכים בזה העולם התחתון פרטיים, עד שנאמר שיהיה מתיחד כוכב אחד לבד לאיש אחד, ייחדהו השם יתברך אליו, ויפקידהו לשלם לו כמעשהו, היה בלי ספק ענין זה מתמיה, אבל הענין אינו כן, כי מנהיגי העולם התחתון ענינם כללי, עד שאי אפשר לומר שימשך מהם הטוב תמיד, ולא ימשך מהם הרע לפעמים. כאשר נאמר שאי אפשר לשמש לבשל הפירות ולא תחמם ראש האיש הטוב ההולך בדרך בתקופת תמוז עד שאפשר שיתחדש אליו ממנה חולי כפי הכנתו. וכן כשיהיה איזה דבר רע שופע במקום או באקלים, לא יתחדש הענין שיכה השם יתברך במקל ורצועה איש איש בפרט, אבל שיחדש איזו סיבה מפסדת כוללת, ויגיע ממנה הפסד גם למי שאינו ראוי שיענש בה, אם לא שיחזק זכותו כל כך שיצילהו השם יתברך ממנה בשינוי טבע.

10. ובזה הענין יסתלק ספק גדול שיש לשאול ולומר. הנה השם יתברך צוה שיהיו הלוים מיוחדים לעבודת המשכן תחת הבכורות, ואמר שראוי שיהיה שכר הלוים מוטל על ישראל לפרוע, מפני שזכה בכל בכורות ישראל כאשר ניצולו ממכת בכורות, וכיון שזכה בהם, והם בפשעם נפסלו מעבודתם, ראוי שיהיו שוכרים אחרים תחתיהם. והוא אומרו כי נתונים נתונים המה לי מתוך בני ישראל תחת פטרת כל רחם בכור כל מבני ישראל לקחתי אותם לי, כי לי כל בכור בבני ישראל באדם ובבהמה ביום הכתי כל בכור בארץ מצרים הקדשתי אותם לי, כלומר שביום שהכתי בכורי מצרים שהיו ראויים להענישם, ולא הכה בהם, שלא חטאו ,[ולא הרגתי אותם,

on supernatural intervention, Ran answers that God must have created some sort of condition that affected all firstborn children. Accordingly, it should have killed the Jewish firstborn along with the Egyptians. That the Jews were spared was a miraculous intervention that warrants recognition. Now, argues Ran, a biological condition affecting firstborn children will affect only firstborn of the mother (*peter rechem*), who are biologically distinct insofar as first pregnancies presumably affect the fetus in ways that subsequent pregnancies do not. This explains why the *mitzva* of *pidyon ha-ben* applies only to the firstborn of the mother and not the firstborn of the father, since the sanctification stems from the tenth plague.[11] Ran then notes that his interpretation contradicts the Midrash, which states that the oldest child in every house perished even if he was not biologically a firstborn. He argues, though, that from the perspective of *pshat*, only the firstborn of the mother died.

דרשות הר״ן הדרוש השמיני

אף על פי שאמרו במדרש (תנחומא הקדום בא סי׳ יט) אין בית אשר אין שם מת (שמות יב:ל), אין שם בכור גדול הבית קרוי בכור, **זהו על צד הדרש. אבל כפי פשוטו של דבר,** הבכורות שהיו נתלים בפטרי הרחמים הם שלקו, (ואם היה) [והיה] ביניהם יחס והקשר, אשר מצד היחס ההוא היה ראוי שילקו גם בכורי ישראל, אם יניחם השם לטבעם. ומפני זה אמר השם יתברך, שמפני שהגין בעדם והצילם מן הרע שהיה ראוי לחול עליהם, קידש אותם לו.

Even though the Midrash interprets the verse, "There was no house where a person did not die" to mean that if there was no

---

זכיתי בהם. וזה ענין מתמיה למה זכה בהם מפני שהכה בכורי מצרים,]היהיה ראוי שיאמר המלך לאדם אחד הנה זכיתי בך שתעבוד עבודתי, מאשר הרגתי איש פלוני שהרג את הנפש ולא הרגתי אותך, הנה בלי ספק שאין זה מן הראוי, והנה יראה שיהיה כאן הענין בשוה.

11. אבל התשובה, שאין הפועלים המגיעים בעולם התחתון לאיש איש על ידי סיבות פרטיות, אבל על ידי סיבות כוללות, שאין רצון השם יתברך שישתנה הטבע כפי איש איש, וכשרצה השם יתברך להכות בכורי מצרים, חידש איזה ענין מפסיד ומתיחס לבכורות, כי הבכורות יש יחש ביניהם כולל ומשתף אותם, והוא שאין ספק שאין הרחם אשר לא נולד בו עובר מעולם, באותה התכונה אשר יהיה הרחם אשר כבר נוצרו בו ולדות. ומצד אותו השינוי, יהיה אפשר שיהיה בבכורות כולם הכנה לקבל איזה דבר נעלם ממנו. **ומפני זה היתה מצות קידוש הבכורות תלויה בפטר רחם,** כי הבכורה נותנת יחס והקשר בין הבכורות, ולא הבכורה לאב כלל.

> firstborn, the oldest member of the household was considered a "firstborn," **this interpretation follows the perspective of *drash*, but according to *pshat*,** only those who were the first openings of the womb were smitten, because they had a biological connection. Naturally, the Jewish firstborn also should have suffered, since they shared that biological connection. Therefore, God said that because they were saved, they were sanctified.

The hermeneutical and biological merits of Ran's interpretation need not concern us at present. For our purposes, it is noteworthy that Ran seemingly maintains that at least in this case *pshat* corresponds to physical reality and that only the firstborn of the mother actually died.[12]

Where Were the Twelve Sons of Yaakov Buried?

Another example of this phenomenon relates to the burial of the twelve sons of Yaakov. The midrash states that all of them were buried in Israel. Abarbanel, however, concludes from the textual omission that this midrash does not correspond to physical reality:

> **אברבנאל הגדה של פסח ד"ה ברוך שומר הבטחתו**
> ויקח משה את עצמות עמו ויקברו אותם בשכם...אבל שאר השבטים נקברו במצרים...ועם היות שחז"ל דרשו על והעליתם את עצמותי מזה אתכם שאף שאר השבטים העלו עמהם הוא דרך דרש ופשט הכתוב לא יסבלתו שאמר ויקח משה את עצמות יוסף עמו כי השבע השביע וכו'... ואם היו מעלים עצמות שאר שבטים לא ישתוק הכתוב מלזוכרו...

> And Moshe took the bones of Yosef with him and buried them in Shechem… But the other sons of Yaakov were buried in Egypt… Even though Chazal understand the verse, "And you shall bring up my bones with you" as indicating that the other sons also were buried in Israel, this is from the perspective of *drash*, but the *pshat* of

12. See Ramban (*Shemot* 12:30), who also discusses whether according to *pshat* anyone died besides the firstborn of the mother. It is unclear from this particular discussion, however, whether Ramban would say that *pshat* (when it contradicts *drash*) corresponds to physical reality, as Ran apparently maintains.

> the verse does not tolerate this interpretation... since if Moshe had brought up the other brothers, the verse would have mentioned it.[13]

Methodologically, Abarbanel's point resembles that of ibn Ezra insofar as he presumes that if an important event actually happened as depicted in the Midrash, it would have been mentioned explicitly.[14]

Let us note that unlike Rambam, who frequently is motivated by scientific plausibility when considering whether or not a midrash should be interpreted literally, Ran and Abarbanel are motivated primarily by textual issues.

Thus, ibn Ezra, Ran, and Abarbanel seem to assume that at least in narrative passages, physical reality corresponds to *pshat*. This leads to an obvious problem – what is the purpose of *drash* if it did not actually occur?[15]

7.4 THE PURPOSE OF *DRASH* – THE TORAH'S INNER MESSAGE

We already have seen sources that stress that Aggada teaches us fear of heaven and proper values. There are some who claim that it sometimes resorts to exaggeration in order to do so. For example, R. Zvi Hirsch Chajes (Maharatz Chayot; 1805–1855) writes (Chapter 20 of *Mevo ha-Talmud*):

> The Rabbis... as far as possible... praise the conduct of godly men... to endeavor in every way possible to justify the doings of the good.... It goes without saying that they used exaggeration in the praise of those good deeds of the righteous that are expressly

13. One could argue that Abarbanel is not taking a stand on what actually happened. He is simply stating that according to *pshat* only Yosef's bones were buried in Israel. However, the context and tone indicate that he maintains that in reality only Yosef's bones were buried in Israel.
14. One certainly might question Abarbanel's deduction. Perhaps Yosef's burial is stressed because it is a fulfillment of the oath articulated at the end of *Bereishit* and may relate to Yosef's position in Egypt and his role in burying Yaakov. These issues do not concern us at present.
15. See Chapter 5. As we noted, the Torah itself may, on occasion, utilize hyperbole. See *Chullin* 90b and Rashi to *Devarim* 1:28.

> recorded and employed exegetical methods to show that such persons observed the laws of righteousness to a higher degree than is required… and so endeavored to reveal by exegetical interpretation what the text left unrecorded…. They follow a similar important principle when referring to the evil doings of the wicked; they charge them with all other possible abominable deeds…[16]

As an example of this phenomenon, he cites the passage from the Talmud that states that Eisav violated five major sins on the day he sold the birthright to Yaakov.[17]

Maharatz Chayot's theory concords with what we saw earlier that we should not presume that the stories in Midrash literally occurred. However, an important clarification is in order. The episodes recorded in Midrash are not just thoughtless exaggeration; rather, they are precise metaphors intended to get at the heart of the story. This is true whether or not one presumes that they literally occurred.

Let us consider the above example. One of the five prohibitions that Eisav violated was sleeping with a *na'ara me'orasa* (halachically betrothed maiden). Why do Chazal ascribe this specific sin to Eisav rather than simply stating that he committed adultery? After all, the concept of *eirusin* (halachic betrothal) did not even exist at the time.[18]

The answer, as I heard from my teacher, R. Aaron Lopiansky, is that the concept of *eirusin* highlights an orientation towards the future. Even though the maiden still lives at home, she is considered a married woman based on her future status of entering her husband's home. As we shall see in 18.3, Chazal recognized that the primary point of conflict between Yaakov and Eisav concerned their

---

16. Pp. 162–164 of the English edition (Feldheim, 1952; translated by Jacob Shachter).
17. **מסכת בבא בתרא דף טז עמוד ב**
א"ר יוחנן, חמש עבירות עבר אותו רשע ביום ההוא, בא על נערה המאורסה והרג את הנפש וכפר בתחיית המתים וכפר בעיקר, ושט את הבכורה. בא על נערה המאורסה - כתיב הכא ויבא עשו מן השדה וכתיב התם (פ' תצא) כי בשדה מצאה. הרג את הנפש - כתיב הכא והוא עיף וכתיב התם (ירמי' ד') עיפה נפשי להורגים. כפר בתחיית המתים - דכתיב הנה אנכי הולך למות. כפר בעיקר - כתיב הכא ולמה זה לי וכתיב התם (פ' בשלח) זה אלי ואנוהו, ושט את הבכורה - דכתיב ויבז עשו את הבכורה.
18. See the beginning of *Hilchot Ishut* in Rambam's *Mishneh Torah*.

perception of reality. Eisav saw only the here and now, while Yaakov glimpsed an eternal reality beyond our present one. When Yaakov asked Eisav to sell the birthright, Eisav responded, הנה אנכי הולך למות, "Behold, I am going to die" (*Bereishit* 25:32). According to the Talmud, he meant to say that death is final, that there is nothing besides our meager existence in this world.[19] Ramban explains that this attitude was why Eisav "disparaged" the birthright, arguing, "Eat, drink, and be merry, for tomorrow we will die."[20] To him, giving up on eternity for a good meal seemed like a fair deal. Yaakov disagreed. He argued that there is purpose in existence and direction to history. While the midrash underscores this notion, Ramban demonstrates that it is textually rooted.

Thus, the aforementioned Talmudic passage is meant to get at the heart of the dispute between Yaakov and Eisav. It is not merely hagiographic exaggeration; it is precise imagery intended to convey the deeper message of the stories described in the Torah. Absent Chazal's careful analysis, one might miss the primary message of the text. Indeed, without Chazal, one could cogently argue that Eisav was an innocent victim while Yaakov was a scheming scoundrel. Thus, the interpretation of Chazal proves essential regardless of whether or not it actually happened in a literal sense. More importantly, failure to study Chazal's analysis can cause one to miss the boat completely. For example, without Midrash one might read an entire *parsha* concerning *tzara'at* and miss its central lesson, namely, the evils of *lashon ha-ra*.

Thus, we find that even some of the *pashtanim* (those who explain the Torah using the methodology of *pshat*) assign preeminence to *drash*. Consider Rashbam's programmatic statement:

---

19. **בבא בתרא** דף טז עמוד ב [עשו] כפר בתחיית המתים - דכתיב הנה אנכי הולך למות.

20. **רמב"ן בראשית כה:לד**
ויבז עשו את הבכורה...וזו סיבת בזוי הבכורה, **כי אין חפץ בכסילים רק שיאכלו וישתו ויעשו חפצם בעתם, ולא יחושו ליום מחר.**

רשב"ם בראשית לז:ב

אלה תולדות יעקב - ישכילו ויבינו אוהבי שכל מה שלימדונו רבותינו כי אין מקרא יוצא מידי פשוטו, אף כי עיקרה של תורה באת ללמדנו ולהודיענו ברמיזת הפשט ההגדות וההלכות והדינין על ידי אריכות הלשון ועל ידי שלשים ושתים מידות של ר' אליעזר בנו של ר' יוסי הגלילי ועל ידי שלש עשרה מידות של ר' ישמעאל. והראשונים מתוך **חסידותם** נתעסקו לנטות אחרי הדרשות **שהן עיקר**, ומתוך כך לא הורגלו בעומק פשוטו של מקרא, ולפי שאמרו חכמים אל תרבו בניכם בהגיון, וגם אמרו העוסק במקרא מדה ואינה מדה העוסק בתלמוד אין לך מדה גדולה מזו, ומתוך כך לא הורגלו כל כך בפשוטן של מקראות, וכדאמ' במסכת שבת הוינא בר תמני סרי שנין וגרסינ' כולה תלמודא ולא הוה ידענא דאין מקרא יוצא מידי פשוטו. וגם רבנו שלמה אבי אמי מאיר עיני גולה שפירש תורה נביאים וכתובים נתן לב לפרש פשוטו של מקרא, ואף אני שמואל ב"ר מאיר חתנו זצ"ל נתווכחתי עמו ולפניו והודה לי שאילו היה לו פנאי היה צריך לעשות פרושים אחרים לפי הפשטות המתחדשים בכל יום.

Understand, my beloved, that which our Rabbis taught us, namely, that Scripture should be understood according to *pshat* (אין מקרא יוצא מידי פשוטו). Even though the primary goal of Torah is to teach and inform us – through various allusions in *pshat* – the teachings of Aggada, Halachot, and legal rulings through idiosyncrasies in the text and the thirty-two hermeneutical principles of R. Eliezer and the thirteen of R. Yishma'eil; and the early commentaries, due to their piety, focused on *drash*, for that is primary (accordingly, they were not accustomed to noting the depth of *pshat*); and because Chazal said not to teach one's son too much Scripture (*higayon*), and that focusing on Scripture is not ideal, while focusing on Talmud is ideal, and therefore, they did not focus on *pshat*... Even Rashi, my grandfather, attempted to interpret Tanach according to *pshat*. And I, Shmuel b. R. Meir, debated him (concerning the correct interpretation according to *pshat*), and he agreed with me that if he had time, he would write other interpretations according to the new insights of *pshat* that arise each day.

Rashbam notes that traditional commentaries focus on *drash*. This, he argues, is because it is primary.[21] He even cites a Talmudic passage that he sees as advising parents not to teach their children *pshat*.[22]

Thus, even the presumption that some of the stories contained in Midrash do not correspond to the physical events of this world does not take away from the truth-value of *drash*. What physically happened conveys only that which is external. In Chapter 12, we will consider the *Zohar*'s statement that (according to some) compares *pshat* to a person's clothes. It is the aspect of the person that one first encounters, but it also is the most superficial aspect of a person and does not reflect who he truly is. *Drash* and mysticism attempt to show the *neshama* (soul) of the Torah.

However, even if one views the various methods of interpretation hierarchically, with *pshat* being the lowest,[23] the study of *pshat* remains tremendously valuable. Moreover, *pshat* is profound and should not be confused with a superficial understanding of the text. To appreciate this, consider that Rambam notes in his introduction to *Moreh ha-Nevuchim* that one of the greatest misunderstandings of prophetic texts is the inability to recognize and decipher the multiple levels of meaning, specifically the parables within the text. Rambam maintains that the "vulgar" meaning of the text, like in the verses that imply that God is corporeal, is incorrect but intentional insofar as it proves useful in many respects (we will consider these in 10.8). Thus,

---

21. While I believe this sentiment reflects the prevailing position among the commentators, there may be dissenters. Prof. Mordechai Cohen has argued that R. Sa'adya Gaon, R. Shmuel b. Chofni Gaon and R. Shmuel ha-Nagid all believed that what the Gemara means when it says אין מקרא יוצא מידי פשוטו is that *pshat* is the primary meaning, and the *drash* is secondary.

22. **מסכת ברכות דף כז עמוד ב**

ת"ר כשחלה ר' אליעזר נכנסו תלמידיו לבקרו, אמרו לו רבינו למדנו אורחות חיים ונזכה בהן לחיי העולם הבא. אמר להם הזהרו בכבוד חבריכם **ומנעו בניכם מן ההגיון** והושיבום בין ברכי תלמידי חכמים וכשאתם מתפללים דעו לפני מי אתם עומדים ובשביל כך תזכו לחיי העולם הבא.

Rashbam, following Rashi, understands *higayon* as a reference to the study of Tanach. Some later commentators, such as R. Yechezkeil Landau, understand that it refers to logic.

23. An assertion that many would contest but one seemingly accepted by the *Zohar* and Rashbam.

there is a vast difference between the "vulgar" meaning of the text and what we have been calling *pshat.* Rambam maintains that the "vulgar" meaning is incorrect (but intentionally misleading), whereas *pshat* is correct on one level, even if Scripture also must be studied with an eye towards a deeper meaning of the text.[24]

So far, we have seen that *drash* is meant to convey the truth of Torah on a different level than *pshat. Pshat* or *drash* alone presents an incomplete perspective. Taken together, we get a more comprehensive understanding of the Torah's messages and come closer to understanding God's will. Moreover, we have seen that according to Ran and Abarbanel, in cases of incompatibility, we should presume that *pshat* corresponds to the physical events. We now will consider Ramban's view on this question.

7.5 THE PERSPECTIVE OF RAMBAN

Thus far, we have considered this question in a bifurcated manner, with *pshat* teaching us what happened and *drash* informing us of the deeper meaning. A more sophisticated understanding emerges when we explore the possibility of an integrated approach between *pshat* and *drash.* We will see such an approach in the writings of Ramban.[25] To some degree, this approach undermines the question of what really happened. We

24. Interestingly, Matt Lubin pointed out to me, Rambam and Rashbam adopt almost opposite views. Rashbam believes it is theoretically possible to explain the Torah according to *pshat,* which is correct on some level, but subordinate to *drash.* Thus, it is *drash* alone that determines Halacha. Rambam, as evident from his Introduction to *Sefer ha-Mitzvot,* maintains that אין מקרא יוצא מידי פשוטו implies that even Halacha, to a large degree, is rooted in *pshat. Pshat,* for example, plays a role in determining what is counted among the 613 mitzvot, and whether a particular mitzva is considered מצות של תורה or מדברי סופרים. See שו"ת הרמב"ם סימן שנה and ספר המצוות לרמב"ם שורש ב where Rambam explicates this principle and הלכות שחיטה פרק ה הלכה ג and הלכות מקוואות פרק ח הלכה ו for applications. Indeed, it seems clear from יבמות (יא:) ו(כד.) that אין מקרא יוצא מידי פשוטו and פשט have halachic ramifications (supporting Rambam's view). Perhaps, what Rambam and Talmud are referring to as פשט is not the same thing that רשב"ם is calling פשט. (If this is correct one would have to concede that when Rashbam invokes אין מקרא יוצא מידי פשוטו he is doing so imprecisely.)
25. That is not to say that the aforementioned commentaries would not subscribe to a similar approach.

shall deliberate upon Ramban's perspective in two steps. First, we shall consider why he did not feel that the question of what actually happened is important. Then, we shall attempt to show how *pshat* and *drash* merge to convey meaning in a remarkable way.

With respect to the text of the Torah (as opposed to Midrashim), Ramban stresses that his esoteric explanations do not indicate that the literal stories of the Torah did not occur.[26] What about Midrashim?

Ramban's position on this topic is complex. For example, Ramban defends the Midrash's understanding of Yocheved's birth from ibn Ezra's questions. Yet Ramban does not state categorically that everything in Midrash literally transpired. Nevertheless, he maintains that we should not expect the written Torah to convey the entire story. Many details are left out. Accordingly, the fact that a particular part of the story does not appear in *pshat* does not mean that it did not occur. Ramban writes that this is true especially when it comes to *nissim nistarim* (hidden miracles), which often are omitted from the text.[27, 28]

---

26. For example, even though Ramban explains the Kabbalistic secrets of Gan Eden, he writes in *Sha'ar ha-Gemul*:

ומה שכר ועונש יש לנפשות הצדיקים בגן הזה, דבר זה עיקרו בתורה ופירושו בדברי סופרים שגן עדן מצוי הוא בעולם הזה במקום ממקומות הארץ, ושארבע נהרות יוצאין משם ואחד מהם פרת הסובב ארץ ישראל, **וכל מה שבא בכתוב מפשוטי סדר בראשית הכל אמת אין מקרא** מהן יוצא מידי פשוטו.

27. **רמב"ן בראשית פרשת ויגש פרק מו**

(טו) שלשים ושלש - ובפרטן אי אתה מוצא אלא שלשים ושתים, אלא זו יוכבד שנולדה בכניסתן לעיר, שנאמר (במדבר כו:נט) אשר ילדה אותה ללוי במצרים, לידתה במצרים ואין הורתה במצרים, זו היא שיטת רבותינו (סוטה יב א):

ורבי אברהם השיב ואמר כי זה תימה, אם כן למה לא הזכיר הכתוב הפלא שנעשה עמה שהולידה משה והיא בת מאה ושלשים שנה, ולמה הזכיר דבר שרה שהיתה בת תשעים. ולא די לנו זה הצער עד שעשו הפייטנים פיוטים ביום שמחת תורה יוכבד אמי אחרי התנחמי, והנה היא בת מאתים וחמשים שנה. וכי אחיה השילוני חיה כך וכך שנים, דרך הגדה, או דברי יחיד, אלו דבריו:

והנה פן יהיה חכם בעיניו בסתירת דברי רבותינו, אני צריך לענות אליו. **ואומר, כי על כל פנים יהיה בדבר יוכבד פלא גדול מן הנסים הנסתרים שהם יסוד התורה, כי היא בת לוי עצמו, לא מתיחסת אליו, כמו שכתוב (במדבר כו:נט) אשר ילדה אותה ללוי במצרים. ועוד כתוב (שמות ו:כ) את יוכבד דודתו. והנה אם נאמר כי הוליד אותה בבחרותו כאשר הוליד כל בניו, והיתה לידתה אחר רדתו למצרים מעט, הנה היא בלדת משה זקנה מאד כמנין שאמרו רבותינו או קרוב לו:**

ואם נאמר שנולדה לו אחר שבתו במצרים ימים רבים, והנה נחשוב שהוליד אותה אחר רדתו למצרים חמשים ושבע שנה, והוא יהיה בן מאה שנה, כי ברדתו היה בן מ"ג שנים, והנה יהיו

Essentially, Ramban maintains that the midrash concerning Yocheved's birth does not contradict *pshat,* in which case there is no reason to presume that it is not literarily true. What about in cases where *pshat*

בזה שני פלאים, שיהיה הוא זקן כאברהם אשר הזכיר הכתוב (לעיל יז:יז) הלבן מאה שנה יולד, וכתיב (לעיל יח:יב) ואדני זקן, ותהיה היא זקנה בלדת משה בת ע״ג, ואם נאחר עוד לידתה לסוף ימי לוי, הנה יהיה פלא גדול משל אברהם.

אבל אומר לך דבר שהוא אמת וברור בתורה, כי הנסים הנעשים על ידי נביא שיתנבא כן מתחילה או מלאך נגלה במלאכות השם יזכירם הכתוב, והנעשים מאליהן לעזור צדיק או להכרית רשע לא יזכירו בתורה או בנביאים, וזהו זהב רותח יוצק בפי החכם הזה ממה שהשיב על רבותינו בענין פינחס (במדבר כה:יב) וזולתו במקומות הרבה, ולמה יזכירם הכתוב, **כל יסודות התורה בנסים נסתרים הם.** ועם התורה אין בכל ענינו רק נסים לא טבע ומנהג, שהרי יעודי התורה כולם אותות ומופתים, כי לא יכרת וימות בטבע הבא על אחת מן העריות או האוכל חלב, ולא יהיו השמים כברזל בטבעם מפני זרענו בשנה השביעית, וכן כל יעודי התורה בטובות ההן וכל הצלחת הצדיקים בצדקתם, וכל תפלות **דוד מלכנו וכל תפלותינו נסים ונפלאות, אלא שאין בהם שנוי מפורסם בטבעו של עולם** כאשר הזכרתי זה כבר (לעיל יז:א), ועוד אפרשנו בעזרת השם (שמות ו:ב, ויקרא כו:יא):

והנה אתן לך עד נאמן על מה שאמרתי. ידענו, כי מעת בוא ישראל לארץ עד לדת אדונינו דוד היה כשלש מאות ושבעים שנה. והימים יתחלקו לארבעה דורות, שלמון ובועז ועובד וישי, ויגיע לכל אחד מהם צ״ג שנה, והנה כלם זקנים קרוב לאברהם, והיו מולידים כל אחד בשנת מותו שלא כדרך כל הארץ, כי אין החיים בזמנם מאה שנה. ואם הוליד אחד מהם בבחרותו כמנהג, יהיו האחרים זקנים מאד יותר מאברהם, ויהי בהם הפלא גדול יותר מאד, כי ימי האדם בדור אברהם ארוכים, ובשנות דוד חזרו למחציתם:

ואולי חיו יותר, כי אפשר שהיו לשלמון ימים רבים בבואם לארץ, ולכן נתנו אנשי הקבלה והם חכמי אמת לעובד ימים רבים, והוא נס נסתר נעשה לאבי המלוכה בן הצדקת הבאה לחסות תחת כנפי השכינה. וכן יזכירו באמו ארך ימים רבים:

וכבר פרשתי כי הפלא באברהם איננו כאשר יחשוב החכם הנזכר וזולתו מבעלי המקרא, כי אברהם הוליד את יצחק טרם מותו שבעים וחמש שנה, והנה לא עברו עליו שני חלקים בימיו, והאנשים בכל דור אין הזקנה בהם עד עבור עליהם שלשת חלקי ימותם, כאשר יחשבו הרופאים הילדות והבחרות והאישות והזקנה. ובדורות האלה אשר הימים בהם כשבעים שנה לא יחשבו לו הרופאים זוקן עד אחר ששים:

ועוד כי אברהם הוליד בנים רבים אחרי ארבעים שנה מלדת יצחק, ויהיה הפלא כפלי כפלים. ואם נאמר שהחזירו האל לימי בחורותיו יקשה עליו, כי לא הזכיר הכתוב הפלא הגדול הזה, והוא נס גלוי ומפורסם בהפך מן הטבע:

ומן הידוע כי האנשים בדור הזה, מהם שיולידו בזקנתם עד מלאת שבעים שנה או שמונים שנה ויותר, כפי התקומם בהם הלחות לפי טבעם. וגם הנשים אין להם זמן, וכל עוד היות להן האורח תלדנה, רק התימה באברהם ושרה כאשר פירשתי שם, מפני שלא הולידו בנעוריהם ועתה הולידו זה מזה. ועוד בשרה היה פלא כי חדל ממנה ארח כנשים ואחרי כן לא תלדנה:

והנה אם יהיו ימי יוכבד כימי אביה, ותתקיים בה הלחות עד קרוב לזקנתה כמשפט הנשים, איננו פלא אם תוליד בזמן אשר נתנו לה רבותינו, מפני שרצה האלהים לגאול את ישראל על ידי האחים האלה ולא הגיע הקץ, איחר לידתם ימים רבים עד כי זקנה אמם. ולא יפלא מה׳ דבר:

and *drash* do seem to conflict? To address this question, let us examine several examples.

When Were the Mitzvot Given?

When exactly the *mitzvot* were given seems like a very fundamental question. Remarkably, Ramban presumes that the answer depends upon whether one approaches the issue from a perspective of *pshat* or *drash*. Ramban writes that according to *drash*, all of the *mitzvot* and their details were given at Sinai. According to *pshat*, however, many were given at *ohel mo'eid* (i.e., the *mishkan*), a short time later.[29] This question affects the reading of numerous verses. For example, the opening *pasuk* of the book of *Vayikra* implies that the *mitzvot* described in *Vayikra* were transmitted at *ohel mo'eid* after Moshe had descended from Sinai. According to Chazal (i.e., *drash*), however, this is a repetition of that which already was stated at Sinai.

Ramban notes that the same distinction will determine how to parse the following verse:

ויקרא פרשת צו פרק ז

(לז) זֹאת הַתּוֹרָה לָעֹלָה לַמִּנְחָה וְלַחַטָּאת וְלָאָשָׁם וְלַמִּלּוּאִים וּלְזֶבַח הַשְּׁלָמִים: (לח) אֲשֶׁר צִוָּה יְקֹוָק אֶת מֹשֶׁה **בְּהַר** סִינָי בְּיוֹם צַוֹּתוֹ אֶת בְּנֵי יִשְׂרָאֵל לְהַקְרִיב אֶת קָרְבְּנֵיהֶם לַיקֹוָק **בְּמִדְבַּר** סִינָי:

This is the law for the burnt offering, the meal offering, the sin offering, the guilt offering, the investitures, and the peace offering, which God commanded Moshe on **Mount** Sinai, on the day

28. Why Yocheved bearing Moshe at age 130 is considered a hidden miracle can be understood only in conjunction with Ramban's approach to providence, which we will return to in 39.7.

29. This actually is a dispute in the Talmud (*Sota* 37b). R. Yishma'eil asserts that the general rules were stated at Sinai and the details conveyed at *ohel mo'eid*, while R. Akiva maintains that all details were stated at Sinai, repeated at *ohel mo'eid*, and repeated once again before the Jews entered the land of Israel. Ramban treats the view of R. Akiva as the primary position in Chazal.

He commanded the children of Israel to offer their sacrifices to God in the Sinai **Desert**.

Ramban begins by noting that according to *drash*, all *mitzvot* were given at Sinai.[30] The simple reading of this verse, though, indicates that some *mitzvot* were given at Mount Sinai, while others were given in Sinai Desert, a reference to *ohel mo'eid*.[31]

Ramban frequently refers to this particular discrepancy between *pshat* and *drash*[32] but never seems to be bothered by the question of what actually happened.

---

30. **רמב"ן ויקרא ז:לח**

אשר צוה ה' את משה בהר סיני - **על דרך רבותינו (תורת כהנים בהר פרשה א א) כי כל המצות נאמרו למשה בהר סיני, כללותיהן** ופרטיהן ודקדוקיהן, ונשנו מהן באהל **מועד, והנה מצות ויקרא שנויות:**

31. Ramban suggests two possibilities as to how to explain the verse according to *pshat*. In the first, the verse is distinguishing between certain sacrificial laws that were given at Sinai (those recorded in *Shemot*) and other ones given at *ohel mo'eid*.

ועל דרך הפשט, שיעורו אשר צוה ה' את משה בהר סיני וביום צוותו את בני ישראל במדבר סיני להקריב את קרבניהם לה', כי צוה במלואים בהר סיני וכן בעולה וחטאת, **וצוה במנחה** ואשם ובזבחי השלמים במדבר סיני באהל מועד:

In his second explanation, he notes that the verse's reference to *Har Sinai* may not refer to that which Moshe heard while on the mountain but rather to the position of the Jewish people as they camped besides the mountain, i.e., where they set up the *ohel mo'eid*.

ויתכן כי טעם בהר סיני, במקום הזה לפני הר סיני, והוא באהל מועד, וכן עולת תמיד העשויה בהר סיני (במדבר כח:ו), כי איננו בהר ממש, כי עולת תמיד לא התחילו בה רק באהל מועד, דכתיב וזה אשר תעשה על המזבח וגו' (שמות כט:לח), וכן ויסעו מהר ה' (במדבר י:לג), וכן רב לכם שבת בהר הזה (דברים א:ו):

והטעם בכל אלה, כי ישראל חנו לפני הר סיני בקרוב לו, דכתיב (שמות יט:ב) ויחן שם ישראל נגד ההר, ושם עמדו עד נסעם משם למדבר פארן. והנה עשו אהל מועד והקימו אותו לפני ההר במזרחו, ושם התחילו בעולת התמיד, ובשנה השנית נצטוו על הדגלים והעמידו האהל בתוך המחנות בנסעם. ולפיכך אמר הכתוב בכאן כי זאת התורה לעולה ולכל הקרבנות שצוה השם בהר סיני ביום צוותו במדבר סיני, יגיד כי היה בהר סיני ובמדבר סיני, להודיע שלא היתה בהר ממש במקום הכבוד ששם דיבר עמו עשרת הדברות, ולא במדבר סיני אחרי שנסעו מלפני ההר, **אבל היה במדבר סיני (מלפני) [לפני] ההר, בתחומו וקרוב לו, ושם אהל מועד.** כמו שאמר בתחילת הענין (לעיל א:א) ויקרא אל משה וידבר ה' אליו מאהל מועד, הודיע אותנו עתה מקום אהל מועד:

32. For example, in his Introduction to *Devarim* he writes:

וכבר נאמרו לו כולן בסיני או באוהל מועד.

Was Avraham Actually Thrown into a Furnace?

The context of the next source is Avraham's early history. Ramban discusses where Avraham was born[33] as well as the events that happened prior to his arrival in the land of Canaan. He cites the midrash that Avraham preached monotheism and was given the choice of being thrown into a fiery furnace or renouncing his faith. Avraham, of course, chose the former and miraculously survived the furnace. Ramban then notes that a similar event is recorded in a non-Jewish source, *The Nabataean Agriculture*[34]:

רמב"ן בראשית יא :כח

והענין שקבלו רבותינו בזה הוא האמת, ואני מבאר אותו. אברהם אבינו לא נולד בארץ כשדים... והענין המקובל הזה נמצא גם כן בספר קדמוני הגוים כמו שכתב הרב במורה הנבוכים (ג כט), כי הזכירו בספר "עבודת האכרים המצרים" כי אברם אשר נולד בכותא חלק על דעת ההמון שהיו עובדים השמש, ונתן המלך אותו בבית הסוהר והיה עמהם בתוכחות ימים רבים שם, אחר כך פחד המלך שישחית עליו ארצו ויסיר בני האדם מאמונתם וגרש אותו אל קצה ארץ כנען אחר שלקח כל הונו.

והנה על כל פנים במקום ההוא בארץ כשדים נעשה נס לאברהם אבינו, **או נס נסתר, שנתן בלב אותו המלך להצילו ושלא ימיתנו והוציא אותו מבית הסוהר שילך לנפשו, או נס מפורסם שהשליכו לכבשן האש וניצל כדברי רבותינו:**

The idea that Chazal received is true, and I shall explain it. Avraham was not born in the land of Kasdim… This tradition (that Avraham was thrown into a furnace due to his beliefs) is found also in an ancient text written by **non-Jews**, as Rambam mentioned, called *The Nabataean Agriculture,* which relates that

33. Ramban argues in favor of Charan (as opposed to Ur Kasdim, as Rashi maintains).

34. The Nabataean Agriculture (*Kitab al-Falaha al-Nabatiya* c. 904) is a major treatise on agriculture and superstitions said to be based on ancient Babylonian sources. It was translated from the original Babylonian Aramaic by Abu Bakr Ahmed ibn 'Ali ibn Qays al-Wahshiya (Ibn Wahshiya), a 10th century Iraqi alchemist, agriculturalist, and historian. It is sometimes cited by Rambam and R. Yehuda ha-Levi.

> Avraham was born in Kutta and disagreed with the prevailing opinion of the masses who worshiped the sun. The king incarcerated him, yet he continued debating for many days. Later, the king was afraid that Avraham would cause the people to rebel and deviate from their faith, so he expelled Avraham to the edge of the land of Canaan, after taking all of Avraham's possessions.
>
> Either way (whether we accept the story as recorded in Chazal or as recorded in *The Nabataean Agriculture*), in that place in the land of Kasdim, a miracle happened to Avraham, **either a hidden miracle, that the king saved him and did not kill him, and [instead] let him go free, or an overt miracle, that he was saved from a fiery furnace, as recorded by Chazal.**

Ramban presents two options concerning this famous episode. According to the midrash, Avraham was miraculously saved from the furnace, while according to the non-Jewish source, he was expelled from a dungeon. Ramban appears to treat both options equally.[35] He notes that the two accounts agree more than they differ insofar as both record Avraham's courageous preaching of monotheism, his persecution, and his miraculous salvation. According to the midrash, the salvation was an overt miracle, while according to *The Nabataean Agriculture*, it was a hidden miracle, since despots generally kill those who challenge them rather than simply exiling them.

Ramban then explains why the story's omission from the text of the Torah does not undermine its veracity. If it occurred as recorded in *The Nabataean Agriculture*, then we should not be surprised by its omission, since, as we saw earlier, Ramban maintains that the Torah frequently omits hidden miracles. If the story occurred as Chazal present it, then we do need to answer two questions: (1) why is the miracle not recorded in *The Nabataean Agriculture* and (2) why is it not recorded in

35. One could argue, though, that what Ramban means is that while on a level of *pshat* the non-Jewish source is plausible, the Midrash should be considered a superior source.

the text of the Torah?[36] Ramban responds to the first question by noting that the omission of the overt miracle from *The Nabataean Agriculture* is not surprising, since acknowledgment of the miracle would undermine their religious views. Regarding the second question, Ramban suggests that the reason why the Torah did not include the story is because it did not want to elaborate upon the positions of the idolaters in their disputes with Avraham.[37]

Just as he did in his discussion of the birth of Yocheved, Ramban rejects the presumption that an event's omission from the text implies that it did not actually take place. This is true especially with respect to events that can be considered hidden miracles. The Torah is not meant to be a comprehensive narrative, and as such, aspects of the story are left for the Midrash to fill in. With respect to overt miracles described in the Midrash, however, clarification is needed to justify omission if we are to assume that they literally occurred.

In 7.10, we further consider Ramban's particular approach to Midrash. But regarding the question of what physically happened, Ramban implies that it does not make much of a difference. Thus, he does not feel the need to resolve the discrepancy between *The Nabataean Agriculture* and the Midrash. Instead, just as he did concerning the giving of the *mitzvot,* Ramban simply endeavors to show how both

---

36. That Ramban feels the need to address this question indicates that he generally presumes that all overt miracles that occurred are included in the text. This deduction is supported by his statement that hidden miracles are omitted. Of course, many episodes described in Midrashim but not mentioned in the text are, in fact, overt miracles. This would seem to indicate that Ramban believes that they did not actually happen. However, two limitations of this deduction should be noted. Firstly, what we would intuitively classify as an overt miracle Ramban might classify as hidden, as he does regarding Moshe's birth when Yocheved was 130 years old. Secondly, there may be other factors that explain the omission, such as the one Ramban is about to suggest.

37. ואל יפתה אותך רבי אברהם בקושיותיו שאומר שלא ספר הכתוב זה הפלא, כי עוד אתן לך טעם וראיה בזה ובכיוצא בו (להלן מו:טו). אבל הגויים ההם לא הזכירו זה בספרם לפי שהם חולקים על דעתו, והיו חושבים בנסו שהוא מעשה כשפים כעניין משה רבנו עם המצרים בתחילת מעשיו. ומפני זה לא הזכיר עוד הכתוב הנס הזה כי היה צריך להזכיר דברי החולקים עליו כאשר הזכיר דברי חרטומי מצרים, ולא נתבארו דברי אברהם עימהם כאשר נתבארו דברי משה רבנו בסוף:

approaches are plausible. To further flesh out this point, let us examine another comment of Ramban.

Do Not Eat on the Blood

One of the most obscure transgressions in the Torah is the prohibition of לא תאכלו על הדם, which literally means "Do not eat on the blood." Needless to say, various interpretations have been suggested as to its precise meaning. Ramban, true to form, addresses the question from the vantage points of both *drash*[38] and *pshat*.[39]

Ramban's discussion primarily is halachic, but it also relates to actual events that took place insofar as it will determine the meaning of the following verse:

שמואל א יד:לג

וַיַּגִּידוּ לְשָׁאוּל לֵאמֹר הִנֵּה הָעָם חֹטְאִים לַיקֹוָק **לֶאֱכֹל עַל־הַדָּם** וַיֹּאמֶר בְּגַדְתֶּם גֹּלּוּ־אֵלַי הַיּוֹם אֶבֶן גְּדוֹלָה.

And they told Shaul, saying, "Behold, the people are sinning against God by **eating on the blood**." And he (Shaul) said, "You have transgressed; roll a huge stone to me this day."

---

38. **רמב"ן ויקרא יט:כו**
לא תאכלו על הדם - להרבה פנים נדרש בסנהדרין (סג א), לשון רש"י. והעולה משם לפי הסוגיא, שהם כולם מן התורה, שכלל הכתוב כל אכילת הדם בלאו אחד. **ואם כן, מה שאמר הכתוב בשאול (ש"א יד:לג) הנה העם חוטאים לה' לאכול על הדם, שהיו חוטאים באחד מן השמות הנכללים בלאו הזה, כי היו אוכלים מן הבהמה קודם שתצא נפשה. זהו מה שאמר (שם פסוק לב) ויעט העם אל השלל**, שהוא כעיט הדורס ואוכל, ויקחו צאן ובקר וגו' וישחטו ארצה ויאכל העם על הדם, מרוב השלל בבהמות כשהיו שופכים דמם ארצה היו תולשים אבריהם ואוכלין קודם שימותו:

39. ועל דרך הפשט, הוא מין ממיני הכשוף או הקסמים כי הוא דבר למד מענינו, והיו שופכים הדם ומאספים אותו בגומא והשדים מתקבצים שם כפי דעתם ואוכלין על שולחנם להגיד להם העתידות. **וכאשר היו ישראל עם שאול במחנה ההוא היו מתפחדים מאד מן הפלשתים, ולא היה שאול עושה דבר בלתי שאלת אורים ותומים כמו שנאמר (שם פסוק לו) נקרבה הלום אל האלהים**, והעם היו שואלים בשדים או בכשפים לדעת דרכם ומעשיהם ואוכלים על הדם לעשות המעשה ההוא. ולכך אמר הכתוב ויגידו לשאול לאמר הנה העם חוטאים לה' לאכול על הדם ויאמר בגדתם, לומר הנה השם עשה לכם תשועה גדולה היום ואתם שואלים ללא אלהים, בגידה היא זו. ועוד אפרש איסור מעונן ומנחש (דברים יח:י).

According to the *drash*-understanding of the prohibition, the nation sinned by eating meat after the animal was slaughtered but before it died. According to the *pshat*-understanding of the prohibition, the nation sinned by doing some form of necromancy. Interestingly, Ramban brings textual support from the book of *Shmuel* for both renditions. What actually happened does not seem relevant for Ramban; his goal is to explain Scripture. There is no indication that he maintains that physical reality corresponds to *pshat*. As is often the case, the *pshat* and *drash* of *Vayikra* 19:26 are related to each other and thus flesh each other out. In the incident recorded in *Shmuel*, both the *pshat* and *drash* highlight the nation's insecurity and inability to wait. Ramban feels that, ultimately, it is most important to understand the root of the nation's sinful activity. What actually transpired is less significant.

Thus, we have seen three examples where *pshat* and *drash* present differing accounts of actual events. In all three cases, Ramban describes both versions of the narrative. In none of the cases does he tell us what actually happened, nor does he appear to be bothered by the issue whatsoever.[40] What is important for Ramban is to understand what the Torah is telling us.

7.6 IS IT IMPORTANT TO KNOW WHAT ACTUALLY HAPPENED?

Why is Ramban not concerned with what actually transpired? Certainly, we believe that the events recorded in Scripture actually took place. Doesn't it stand to reason that knowing how they occurred is important? To answer this question, we have to consider Ramban's position concerning the value of the study of *pshat*. First, let us consider another perplexity within the commentary of Ramban.

Until now, we have focused on instances where *drash* deviates from *pshat* in non-halachic areas. Here, we can readily understand the value of viewing a narrative from two perspectives. However, Ramban

---

40. There are many other examples of this phenomenon in Ramban's commentary. For example, in *Bereishit* 25:6 he writes that according to *pshat*, Ketura was not Hagar, while according to *drash*, she was. He then explains the narrative according to both possibilities.

sometimes interprets halachic portions of the Torah according to *pshat*, at variance with the normative law as described by the Talmud (*drash*).[41] Later on, we will explain why the Torah would present a halacha in a way that seems to contradict the normative law; for the time being, let us simply deduce from here that there is value in understanding the text on its own terms even if does not accord with that which we actually do.

If that is true regarding Halacha, we can apply a similar approach to the question of what actually happened. Even if it is the case that the events unfolded as described by the Midrash, it is valuable to study the depiction presented by the written Torah. Likewise, if what actually happened accords with the presentation of *pshat*, studying the Midrash's version nevertheless is inestimably beneficial. It may be that if we actually could figure out what happened, we would try to do so; for the most part, however, we cannot.

To summarize, we are arguing that when interpreting the Torah, we need not be concerned with contradictions between *pshat* and *drash* concerning the exact nature of events that took place. This is not because what happened is unimportant; rather, it is because understanding the text, the word of God, is inherently valuable. Thus, Ramban maintains that when contradictions arise between *pshat* and *drash* or between two midrashim, our primary goal is not to figure out what actually happened, but rather to understand the Torah's underlying message.

---

41. In three places in *Parshat Masei* alone, Ramban suggests such interpretations (*Bamidbar* 34:2, 34:14, and 36:7). There are times when some commentaries attempt to mitigate Ramban's deviation from Halacha. For example, in *Bamidbar* 34:14, Ramban writes that even though the Talmud rules that all 48 Levite cities protect an accidental murderer (like an *ir miklat*), according to *pshat*, only the six *arei miklat* afford this protection. A questioner asked Radvaz how Ramban could contradict Halacha in this regard. Radvaz (*Teshuvot ha-Radvaz* 6:2,138) responds that Ramban is following a view in the Yerushalmi that may accord with this position. The simple reading of Ramban does not support this interpretation, as Ramban does not quote the Yerushalmi and acknowledges explicitly that his view is against Chazal. Nevertheless, even if we accept Radvaz's interpretation, Radvaz acknowledges that Ramban's understanding of *pshat* does not correspond with the normative approach of following Bavli over Yerushalmi:

שו"ת רדב"ז חלק ו סימן ב אלפים קלח

ואע"ג שלא היה ראוי להניח תלמוד שלנו שכתב בשני מקומות דערי הלוים קולטות ולסמוך על הירושלמי מ"מ כדי לקיים פשט הכתוב **לפי שטתו** סמכו על הירושלמי.

R. Yitzchak Hutner (*Letters,* 30) suggests an additional dimension to this perspective. There are times that God hides things and ideas in order to affect the way we serve Him and understand His Torah.[42] To illustrate the difference between our approach to the study of history and the study of Torah, consider the following example. If a historian were to suggest a theory about the shape of the beams of the *mishkan*, and his theory did not correspond to reality, then we would say it is false. From a historical perspective, only one thing happened and there is no

42. הנה ידוע לך שהיו בישראל כמה וכמה גניזות נגנזו הלוחות נגנז המשכן נגנז הארון וכו׳ ובודאי שמכל גניזה היו תוצאות בדרכי התורה ועבודה ומפורש היא הדבר בכתוב בדברי יאשיהו המלך בשעת גניזת הארון שאמר שגניזת הארון הולידה חידוש באופיה של תורה ועבודה והוא הדין והיא המדה בכל הגניזות והנה כשם שאפשר לגנוז חפץ כמו כן אפשר להסתיר ידיעה ועליך לדעת כי בשעה שפלוני אלמוני סובר כי קרשי המשכן נעשו באופן ידוע שונה מכפי שהיתה המציאות באמת הרי זה אינו אלא טועה אבל בשעה שחכם מחכמי המסורה של תשבע״פ שהתורה ניתנה על דעתם ל׳ הרמב״ן שהם הם אנשי עצתו של יוצר בראשית כשהוא סובר שקרשי המשכן נעשו באופן שונה מכפי שהיתה המציאות באמת הרי אין זה אלא גניזה בכוח הדעת כשם שגוף המשכן נגנז לפי רצונו של מקום כמו כן יש מהלך שגם הידיעות על עלינו ובגינו של משכן ידונו לגניזה אלא שבזמן שמקום גניזתו של גוף המשכן הוא בחללא דעלמא הרי גניזת הידיעה על אודות המשכן הוא בכוח הדעת של חכמי המסורה וממילא במקום שהידיעה על אודות פרט אחד מבנין המשכן נוגעת לנו היום להלכה כגוונא דסוגיא דשבת דקרשים שעליך הנך דן אז אם חכם מחכמי המסורה של תשבע״פ לא כיון אל מציאותו של גוף הבנין הרי דוקא ע״י זה כוון לרצונו של מקום מפני שבאופן זה רצונו של מקום הוא לצרף את גניזת הידיעה לגניזת הגוף וממילא ההלכה היוצאת מסברתו של חכם זה **היא היא ההלכה האמיתית וכל מציאות יש לה ואמת שלה וגם המציאות של תורה יש לה אמת משלה והאמת של מציאות תורה הוא** הכוון לרצון השם וכששני האמוראים חולקים באופן עשייתם של קרשי המשכן פירוש מחלקותם הוא כיצד נגלתה לפנינו עכשו תמונת קרשי המשכן מפני שההלכה היוצאת מפלוגתא זו אינה תלויה לגמרי במציאותם של קרשי המשכן אלא באופן גילויים גניזת קדשי כנס״י היא היא גופה של תורה מפני שכל גניזה פועלת היא על מהלך חיי הקדושה בישראל ומחלוקת האמוראים היא כיצד עלינו לדרוש את הפסוקים הדנים בענין זה מפני שדרשות הפסוקים אצל חכמי תשבע״פ הוא הוא רצונו של מקום בגילוי ענין זה בכוח הדעת וכל פרט ממציאות גופו של משכן שחכמי תשבע״פ לא מצאו מקום לדרוש אותו מן הכתובים או מן סברתם אינה אלא גניזה וכשיעמוד ב״ד גדול בחכמה ובמנין מן הב״ד הקודם אשר ע״פ דין יש לו כוח לבטל את דברי הב״ד הקודם וידרוש את הפסוקים באופן אחר המהפך את תמונת הענינים מן הקצה אל הקצה אז נאמר כי רצונו של מקום הוא עכשו לגלות את מה שנגנז מקודם ואלו ואלו הם דברי אלקים חיים כמובן שמקומם היחידי של גניזות אלה וגילויים אלה אינם אלא בכוח הדעת של חכמי תשבע״פ לבד כל דעת אחרת הנמצאת בעולם מופקעת היא מכל המהלך הזה של גילוי וגניזה וממילא אין אנו אומרים עליה אלא אחת משתים או שזה טעות או שזה נכון אבל כל סברותיהם דעותיהם ודרשותיהם של חכמי המסורה של תשבע״פ מופקעים הם מעצם ההבחנה של נכון ובלתי נכון ואין אנו מבחינים בזה אלא הופעה של גילוי או הופעה של גניזה אידי ואידי רצונו של מקום הם אלו ואלו דברי א׳ חיים.

value to the consideration of alternative possibilities. However, when two Talmudic sages debate the shape of the beams of the *mishkan*, as they do in *Shabbat* 98b, there is truth and value to both opinions, not just because the text of the Torah (i.e., God's words) allows for both possibilities, but because, as Ramban stresses, God instructed us to follow their understanding of the Torah.[43] In a sense, then, God has approved any interpretation of one of the *chachmei ha-mesora* (we define this term in the preface to Volume Two). As such, these understandings are inherently valuable. Moreover, they only become possible by God's hiding from us the reality as it physically occurred (since no sage would reject a demonstrable fact). This resembles a similar idea from R. Hutner (discussed in 4.8) in which he articulates how occasionally the forgetting of Torah spawns a proliferation of Torah. Moreover, as we discussed in Chapter 4, both interpretations are intended, even if only one actually occurred. Put differently, the goal of the Torah was not to describe physical reality but to convey deeper truths. The two perspectives on reality help accomplish this. While R. Hutner is discussing two Talmudic opinions describing physical events, the same could be said with respect to discrepancies between *pshat* and *drash* – both are intended; both are meaningful; and both are true – even though only one corresponds to physical reality.[44]

What if We Can Determine What Happened?

What if we can determine what happened? Ramban tells us that we certainly would incorporate this information. A famous example concerns the place of Rachel's burial. Ramban, in his commentary to *Parshat Vayechi (Bereishit* 48:7), writes that Yaakov buried Rachel on the road because he knew prophetically that when the Jewish people would be

43. Commenting on the importance of the commandment to accept the Sanhedrin's interpretation of the Torah, Ramban (*Devarim* 17:11) writes that God gave us the Torah according to their understanding, כי על הדעת שלהם הוא נותן להם התורה. (See 4.9 where we elaborate upon Ramban's approach to the possibility of rabbinic error.)

44. See R. Peretz (cited in 4.3) concerning Talmudic debates regarding physical reality. Also, consider Maharal's approach (cited in 4.5) concerning the stopping of the sun's motion at Giv'on (*Yehoshua* 10:12–14) that the sun both stopped and continued to move simultaneously.

exiled, they would pass Rachel's tomb in "Rama" of Binyamin, hear her weeping, and be comforted. This was written while Ramban still was living in Spain. When he moved to Eretz Yisrael in 1287, he visited Rachel's grave and concluded that the above interpretation is flawed. Accordingly, he offers a new understanding, which affected the interpretation of several verses. His revised view is recorded in *Parshat Vayishlach (Bereishit* 35:16), where he writes:

> **רמב"ן בראשית לה:טז**
> זה כתבתי תחילה, ועכשיו שזכיתי ובאתי אני לירושלם, שבח לאל הטוב והמטיב, ראיתי בעיני שאין מן קבורת רחל לבית לחם אפילו מיל... וכן ראיתי שאין קבורה ברמה ולא קרוב לה... על כן אני אומר שהכתוב שאומר קול ברמה נשמע (ירמיה לא יד), מליצה כדרך משל, לאמר כי היתה רחל צועקת בקול גדול ומספד מר עד שנשמע הקול למרחוק ברמה שהיא בראש ההר לבנה בנימן...
>
> This is what I wrote originally, but now that I have merited, with praise to God, to come to Yerushalayim, I have seen with my own eyes that Rachel is buried less than a *mil* (about a kilometer) from Beit Lechem... Moreover, I have seen that she is not buried in Rama, and that city is not even close [to her burial place]... I therefore assert that the verse that states, "A voice was heard in Rama..." is to be understood figuratively: that her weeping was so loud and bitter that it was heard as far away as Rama, which sits atop the mountain [in the land] of her son Binyamin.

Thus, it is not accurate to state that Ramban does not care what happened. To the extent that we have accurate information about an event, it may affect our interpretation of a verse. However, Ramban maintains that when one encounters a discrepancy between *pshat* and *drash* concerning that nature of an event, the question of what actually happened usually is not relevant. Instead, we should explore the depths of the text according to each interpretation. Moreover, as we shall see later, Ramban maintains that *pshat* and *drash* frequently shed light upon each other, together giving us a total picture of the Torah's message.

7.7 THE VALUE OF STUDYING HISTORY

Thus far, we have assumed that Ramban's disinterest in resolving discrepancies between events as depicted by *pshat* and *drash* does *not* reflect lack of interest concerning what actually happened. However, perhaps one could take a different approach and suggest that Ramban is not troubled by these inconsistencies because it does not really matter how the events actually unfolded.

This concept may relate to sometimes seems like Chazal's position that history is not important in its own right. Rambam presents a similar notion in his comments on R. Akiva's position (*Sanhedrin* 100b) that someone who reads outside books (ספרים החיצונים) has no portion in the world to come. The Talmud suggests that this may include even works like Ben Sira that contain some ethical teachings.[45] Rambam writes that the problem with such works is that they are pointless and a waste of time.[46] Moreover, he includes works of history in this category:

---

45. **סנהדרין דף ק עמוד ב**
[כל ישראל יש להם חלק לעולם הבא... אלו שאין להם חלק לעולם הבא, האומר אין תחית המתים מן התורה , ואין תורה מן השמים, ואפיקורוס.] **רבי עקיבא אומר אף הקורא בספרים** החיצונים-תנא בספרי מינים **רב יוסף אמר בספר בן סירא נמי אסור למיקרי** א"ל אביי מאי טעמא אילימא משום דכתב [ביה] לא תינטוש גילדנא מאודניה דלא ליזיל משכיה לחבלא אלא צלי יתיה בנורא ואיכול ביה תרתין גריצים אי מפשטיה באורייתא נמי כתב (דברים כ:יט) לא תשחית את עצה אי מדרשא אורח ארעא קמ"ל דלא ליבעול שלא כדרכה ואלא משום דכתיב בת לאביה מטמונת שוא מפחדה לא יישן בלילה בקטנותה שמא תתפתה בנערותה שמא תזנה בגרה שמא לא תינשא נישאת שמא לא יהיו לה בנים הזקינה שמא תעשה כשפים הא רבנן נמי אמרוה....

46. Of course, Rambam does not believe that loss of *olam ha-ba* is an appropriate punishment for wasting time. In a formal sense, wasting time is not an egregious sin. Rather, someone who does not value his time lacks the basic values necessary to experience *olam ha-ba*. (To a large degree Rambam understands *olam ha-ba* as a natural consequence of the spiritual accomplishments of this world. More on Rambam's conception of *olam ha-ba* can be found in Chapter 20.) If someone appreciates that they are here to fulfill a higher calling, that there is more to life than pleasure, then they will seek to use their life productively. On the other hand, someone who fritters their days engaged in inane activities demonstrates that they lack an appreciation of why they are here. If they do not value their life here, they forfeit their chance at eternity.

    Rambam's aversion to wasting time also can be gleaned from his explanation of why gamblers are disqualified as witnesses. He writes that gaming is a waste of time; a person should dedicate all of his resources to making the world a better place or himself a better person. Gambling does neither of these:

הקדמת הרמב"ם לפרק חלק

וספרים החיצונים אמרו שהם ספרי מינים. וכן ספר בן סירא, והוא היה איש שחיבר ספרים יש בהם התלים מעניני הכרת פנים אין בהם טעם ולא תועלת, אלא אִבּוּד הזמן בהבל. כגון אלה הספרים הנמצאים אצל הָעֲרָב מסיפור דברי הימים, והנהגת המלכים, וְיִחוּסֵי הָעַרְבִיִּים, וספרי הניגון, וכיוצא בהן מן הספרים שאין בהם חכמה ולא תועלת גופני, אלא אִבּוּד הזמן בלבד.

Sefarim chitzonim (lit. outside books) mentioned in the mishna refers to heretical books. It refers to Ben Sira as well, who was a man who composed books… that have no value other than wasting time with nothingness, like the Arabic books of chronicle, kingly etiquette, and genealogy, as well as books of music and the like that have no wisdom and no bodily value, only a waste of time.

Of course, this passage need not indicate a repudiation of the value of all forms of historical inquiry. To better appreciate this let us turn to Chazal.

Whatever Happened Happened

The following is a telling source on Chazal's perspective regarding the value of studying history:

תלמוד בבלי מסכת יומא דף ה עמוד ב

כיצד הלבישן? - כיצד הלבישן? מאי דהוה הוה! אלא: כיצד מלבישן לעתיד לבוא? לעתיד לבא נמי - לכשיבואו אהרן ובניו ומשה עמהם! אלא: כיצד הלבישן למיסבר קראי? פליגי בה בני רבי חייא ורבי יוחנן, חד אמר: אהרן ואחר כך בניו, וחד אמר: אהרן ובניו בבת אחת.

פיהמ"ש להרמב"ם מסכת סנהדרין פרק ג משנה ג

ואמר המשחק בקוביה, והוא המשחק ב"נרד" ו"סטרנג'" וכיוצא בהם בתנאי שישלם כסף מי שיעשה כך או לא יעשה כך בהתאם לשטת אותו המשחק, **ונאסר זה מפני שהוא מתעסק בעסק שאין בו תועלת לישוב העולם, ויסוד הוא בתורתינו שאין ראוי לאדם להעסיק את עצמו בעולם הזה אלא באחד משני דברים או בחכמה להשלים בה את עצמו, או בעסק שיועיל לו בקיום העולם כגון אומנות או מסחר**, וראוי למעט בזה ולהרבות בראשון כמו שאמרו הוי מעט עסק ועסוק בתורה.

Also, consider his comments in הלכות תשובה פרק ג, where he writes that the purpose of *shofar* is to wake people up from wasting their time (אלו השוכחים את האמת בהבלי הזמן, ושוגים כל שנתם בהבל וריק אשר לא יועיל ולא יציל). Note that he does not focus on sin as much as failure to efficiently use our brief span on this world.

> In what order did Moshe put the garments on Aharon and his sons? [Why is this of interest -] whatever happened already happened? Rather, [the question is] in what order will he put the garments on them in the future. [But why is this of interest -] in the future, too, when Aharon and his sons will come, Moshe will come with them [and tell us]? Rather [the question is] how did he put the clothes on them, [which is important to know in order] to understand the Scriptural account (i.e., interpret the verses)? The sons of R. Chiya and R. Yochanan held different opinions about it. One said that Aharon was clothed first and afterwards his sons; while the other said that Aharon and his sons were clothed simultaneously.

The Talmud appears to be telling us that we are not inherently interested in what happened; *mai de-havei havei* (whatever happened already happened). We are, however, interested in understanding the Torah[47] and gleaning its message. Therefore, if the question of how an event occurred sheds light on the interpretation of a verse, the Talmud rules that it becomes essential that we determine how the event happened. Otherwise, what difference does it make?[48] Gra, in fact, understands *Mishlei* 1:6 as indicating that the stories of the Torah should be viewed as a *mashal*, a parable to teach a deeper lesson. While the events, of course, actually occurred, knowing the history is of little value since **מאי דהוה הוה**. It is the message that is most important.[49] While the scope of the question *mai*

---

47. Another example of this is Ramban's analysis of the burial place of Rachel. Here, the question will determine the correct interpretation of a number of verses.

48. Likewise, see *Shabbat* 96b, where the Talmud discusses what prohibition the wood-gatherer (מקושש עצים) violated (see *Bamidbar* 15:32–36). However, the Talmud indicates that the historical question is not its concern, rather "למאי נפק"מ לכדרב דאמר רב מצאתי וכו' אבות מלאכות ארבעים חסר אחת ואינו חייב מיתה על אחת מהם." In other words, it is important to know what happened only insofar as there is a practical halachic application (whether someone who violates a particular one of the 39 *melachot* is subject to execution).

ליקוטי הגר"א בתוך משלי ע"פ הגר"א השלם א:ו

49. להבין משל ומליצה ועכשיו בא לבאר ענפי הבינה, משל ומליצה שניהם בתורה שבכתב. והמשל הוא ספורי התורה, ומליצה הוא הפנימי. וצריך להבין שניהם, שלא להיות מכחיש פשוטי הספורים, אבל להיות מאמין אותם כהויתם, עם שלא תועיל מאוד ידיעתם, **דמאי דהוה הוה**, אבל דעותינו קצרות מלהשיג תועלת פשוטיהן.

de-havei havei may be a debate among Rishonim,[50] perhaps the phrase also indicates that knowing events of the past is not inherently valuable.[51]

---

50. This question may be the subject of a debate between Rashi and Rosh.

חולין דף יז עמוד א

בעי ר׳ ירמיה אברי בשר נחירה שהכניסו ישראל עמהן לארץ מהו וכו׳.

רש״י: דרוש וקבל שכר הוא שצריכין אנו לעמוד על האמת ואע״פ שכבר עבר.

רא״ש (אות כג): בעי ר׳ ירמיה וכו׳, ופירש״י דרוש וקבל שכר הוא וכו׳, ולא נהירא לי, דדוקא למיסבר קראי דרשינן אע״פ שכבר עבר, אבל לקבוע בעיא בש״ס בדבר שאין בו צורך לא אשכחן, והכי אמרי׳ בפ״ק דיומא (ה ב) כיצד הלבישן וכו׳, כיצד הלבישן [בתמיה] מאי דהוה הוה, אלא כיצד מלבישן לעתיד לבא, לע״ל לכשיבואו אהרן ובניו ומשה עמהן, אלא כיצד מלבישן למיסבר קראי בצוואה כתיב וכו׳. ונר׳ לי דנפק״מ בבעיא זו דר׳ ירמיה לאדם שאסר עצמו באחד מן המינין מזמן ידוע ואילך וכו׳.

The Talmud wonders about the status of a type of meat that was permissible while the Jews were in the desert but prohibited upon their entrance into the land of Israel. Rashi questions the relevance of this discussion, since there appears to be no practical application. Rashi responds by invoking a statement the Talmud uses elsewhere that one is rewarded for studying matters in Torah even if there is no practical application. An example would be the opinion that maintains that the wayward and rebellious child never has and never will exist. Nevertheless, the Torah includes its laws so that we can study them and be rewarded. Presumably, this means that there are lessons that can be derived from the Torah's presentation. When Rashi invokes this notion in *Chullin*, is he informing us that this principle can be applied to any question? This reading is hard to justify, since the Talmud does occasionally ask מאי דהוה הוה. Rosh responds by inventing a practical application to the Talmud's question. While Rosh appears to maintain that there is no value in discovering historical information, he might simply be saying that this sort of query has no place in the Talmud, regardless of its value.

Another place where we find the scope of מאי דהוה הוה debated concerns whether a far-fetched practical application addresses the question of מאי דהוה הוה. The Talmud in *Chagiga* 6b that wonders whether the *olot* offered at Sinai were lambs or bulls. The Talmud wonders what practical application there is to this question. *Tosafot* assume that this is similar to the question of מאי דהוה הוה. The Talmud's first answer is that this question is relevant with respect to determining the verse's cantillation notes. This may parallel the Talmud's answer that understanding Scriptural verses is valuable in its own right. However, the Talmud offers a second answer: the practical difference is if someone vows to bring an *ola* like the *ola* offered at Sinai. Seemingly, this answer undermines the value of the question מאי דהוה הוה, since this sort of answer can be given to any question. Indeed, some Rishonim (see Me'iri and *Yad Rama, Sanhedrin* 15b) offer this sort of answer to explain various questions that the Talmud asks that seem to have no practical application (e.g., *Sanhedrin* 15b and *Avoda Zara* 34a). However, other thinkers presume that these seemingly irrelevant questions must reflect some conceptual question and therefore are valuable. See *Noda be-Yehuda* 2 Y.D. 64.

51. Later, we will suggest that this is not the only way to view מאי דהוה הוה.

The *Zohar* powerfully expresses the notion that there is little value in knowing interesting historical tidbits. Why, for example, does the Torah tell us that Noach's ark landed on Mount Ararat: "Who cares whether it landed on this mountain or that one?" The *Zohar* answers that passages such as these teach us important values and deep secrets. Indeed, we can only perceive the message of the Torah when we dig below the surface.[52] Not only does the *Zohar* tell us that it is inconceivable that the Torah would simply inform us of an irrelevant historical fact, it even curses the person who believes that the verse is merely conveying historical information. Why? Because if that were the case, then "the Torah would not be elevated and would not be truthful." This statement is perplexing. We can understand why it would not be elevated – irrelevant historical data is not holy – but why would it not be truthful? The *Zohar* answers that, in a sense, only something of value is true. Irrelevant historical information is therefore incompatible with "The true

52. **זוהר כרך ג (במדבר) פרשת בהעלותך דף קמט עמוד ב**

דהא אורייתא דאיהי כללא עלאה אף על גב דנפק מנה חד ספור בעלמא ודאי לא אתי לאחזאה על ההוא ספור אלא לאחזאה מלין עלאין ורזין עלאין ולא ללמד על עצמו יצא אלא ללמד על הכלל כלו יצא בגין דההוא ספור דאורייתא או ההוא עובדא אף על גב דהוא נפקא מכללא דאורייתא לאו לאחזאה על גרמיה נפק בלבד אלא לאחזאה על ההוא כללא עלאה דאורייתא כלא נפק.

כגון האי דכתיב (בראשית ח) "ותנח התיבה בחדש השביעי בשבעה עשר יום לחדש על הרי אררט," ודאי האי קרא מכללא דאורייתא נפק ואתי **בספור דעלמא מאי אכפת לן אי שרי בהאי או בהאי דהא באתר חד לישרי**, אלא ללמד על הכלל כלו יצא, וזכאין אינון ישראל דאתיהיב להו אורייתא עלאה אורייתא דקשוט, **ומאן דאמר דההוא ספורא דאורייתא לאחזאה על ההוא ספור בלבד קאתי תיפח רוחיה, דאי הכי לאו איהי אורייתא עלאה אורייתא דקשוט אלא ודאי אורייתא קדישא עלאה איהי אורייתא דקשוט.**

Rambam, when presenting the eighth of the 13 principles of faith (תורה מן השמים), emphasizes the notion that every letter in the Torah conveys profound wisdom:

פירוש המשנה לרמב"ם מסכת סנהדרין פרק י (הקדמה לפרק חלק)

כל אות שבה יש בה חכמות ונפלאות למי שהבינו ה', ולא תושג תכלית חכמתה, ארוכה מארץ מדה ורחבה מני ים.

Accordingly, he writes, all that man can do is pray, גל עיני ואביטה נפלאות מתורתיך, "Open my eyes so that I may glance upon the wonders of Your Torah" (*Tehillim* 119). While Rambam asserts that man can never fully plumb the depths of Torah, in *Moreh ha-Nevuchim* 3:50 he does suggest some fascinating practical explanations of many of the seemingly unimportant passages. (For example, he suggests the Torah presents the genealogy of the descendants of Eisav in order to know that only the progeny of his grandson Amaleik must be destroyed.)

Torah" (*Malachi* 2:6), the Torah that is "perfect… faithful… upright… clear… and pure" (*Tehillim* 19:8).[53]

The priority of the message over the historicity is powerfully expressed by the principle of *ein mukdam u-meuchar ba-Torah* – Scripture is not written in chronological order – whereby precision with respect to historicity is sacrificed in order to better convey the message of the Torah.[54]

Some thinkers (see 7.15) go further and use the Talmudic concept of *mai de-havei havei* (whatever happened already happened) to answer a fundamental question: why is there so little recorded history

---

53. **זוהר כרך ג (במדבר) פרשת בהעלותך דף קמט עמוד ב**
תא חזי מלך ב"ו לאו יקרא דיליה הוא לאשתעי מלה דהדיוטא כ"ש למכתב ליה ואי סליק בדעתך דמלכא עלאה קודשא בריך הוא לא הוו ליה מלין קדישין למכתב ולמעבד מנייהו אורייתא אלא דאיהו כניש כל מלין דהדיוטין כגון מלין דעשו, מלין דהגר, מלין דלבן ביעקב, מלין דאתון, מלין דבלעם, מלין דבלק, מלין דזמרי, וכניש להו וכל שאר ספורין דכתיבין ועביד מנייהו אורייתא, אי הכי אמאי אקרי (מלאכי ב) תורת אמת (תהלים יט) תורת יי' תמימה, עדות יי' נאמנה, פקודי יי' ישרים, מצות יי' ברה, יראת יי' טהורה, משפטי יי' אמת, וכתיב הנחמדים מזהב ומפז רב, אלין אינון מלי דאורייתא, אלא ודאי אורייתא קדישא עלאה איהו אורייתא דקשוט תורת יי' תמימה, וכל מלה ומלה אתייא לאחזאה מלין (אחרנין) עלאין דההוא מלה דההוא ספור לאו לאחזאה על גרמיה בלבד קא אתיא אלא לאחזאה על ההוא כללא קאתי כמה דאוקימנא.
The *Zohar* notes that if it is undignified for a human king to engage in trivial conversation, much less to write it down, it is inconceivable that the Supreme King, the Holy One blessed be He, would include such information in the Torah. While this source seems to indicate that there is no value in knowing this information, in footnote 49 we saw the Gra explain that this means that this is not the primary concern of the Torah. It may nevertheless be valuable on a secondary level.

54. A remarkable reflection of this can be found in *Shabbat* 115b, where the Talmud indicates that the way in which the Torah is written (e.g., the order of events as presented by the text of Torah) has a more powerful effect upon the determination of reality than the manner in which the events actually occurred (e.g., the order of events as they took place historically). Thus, it states that if two tragic events (*puraniot*) that occurred one after another were juxtaposed in the Torah's text, the Jews would be in danger. Ramban (*Bamidbar* 10:35) understands this to mean that if these events are written next to each other, we would become *muchzak be-puraniot* (i.e., the way in which they are written creates the reality of *chazaka*). The fact that historically the events took place one right after another is not relevant; it is the fact that they are written next to each other that will cause the danger. Thus, in the future, when there no longer will be a concern of danger/sin (לעתיד שיהו כל הפורעניות בטלין ולא ידאגו לפורענות ויצר הרע בטל), the text of the Torah will be revised to reflect the historical reality (עתידה פרשה זו שתיעקר מכאן ותכתב במקומה).

in the post-biblical period? True, Talmudic literature relates numerous stories, but there is little interest in systematic history. The answer, they suggest, is that they did not care about history per se. The stories convey the lessons we are meant to learn, the actual historical data is irrelevant.

If this theory is correct, we could explain Ramban's disinterest in resolving the discrepancies between the stories as presented in *pshat* and the stories presented in *drash*. Essentially, we could posit, it does not really matter what happened; *mai de-havei havei*. What matters is what we learn from these stories, and these lessons are gleaned from both presentations.[55]

Yet even if there is some truth to this theory, it does not account for Ramban's disinterest in resolving contradictions between *pshat* and *drash* concerning the most important of events (such as the giving of the Torah) where Ramban clearly is interested in using the text to determine what happened. Moreover, it is certainly an exaggeration to state that Ramban believed history is of no value. Ramban writes that Hashem reveals Himself in history through the miracles done for His people. Ramban (*Shemot* 13:16) stresses the mandate of frequently recalling the actual events of the Exodus, as doing so solidifies our belief in God's existence, His creation of the world, His interaction with the world, and the veracity of prophecy. And knowing past events is not limited to the Exodus. Ramban (*Bamidbar* 33:1) approvingly cites Rambam's theory (*Moreh ha-Nevuchim* 3:50) that the reason why the Torah lists the locations of all of the encampments of the Jews in the desert is because later generations might question the extent of the miraculous protection afforded to the Jews during their sojourns. Thus, by citing the specific locations, the reader will recognize that the Jews actually dwelled in the most inhospitable environment, which would be possible only through supernatural intervention. Finally, Ramban's comments at the beginning of *Parshat Ha'azinu* (*Devarim* 32:7) highlight the importance of viewing past occurrences and current events with an eye towards seeing God's hand and deriving appropriate lessons.[56]

---

55. Along similar lines, see Rabbeinu Peretz *Eiruvin* 13b s.v. *eilu ve-eilu* concerning the Talmudic dispute about the height of the *mizbei'ach* and the application of *eilu ve-eilu* to factual disputes. Likewise, see Gra cited in footnote 49.

56. This is not to say that Ramban would necessarily endorse the study of history using contemporary academic methodology, which seeks secular causation and rejects the possibility of divine causation.

What, then, does *mai de-havei havei* mean? Presumably, it informs us that some details of history are of little value. We cannot extrapolate from the fact that there is no usefulness in knowing the order in which the *kohanim* were dressed during the inauguration (were it not for the fact that this information is relevant to interpreting the verses) that all history is useless. The study of history is especially valuable when it will bring a person to an awareness of God's providential role in world events, or give him a better understanding of who he is and where he should go. Despite his comments in his commentary on the Mishna, Rambam also acknowledges the value of history, as can be seen from his interpretations of the encampments, his historical digressions,[57] and his frequent usage of history to account for numerous *mitzvot* (in the third section of *Moreh ha-Nevuchim*). Nevertheless, Rambam had little use for irrelevant battle chronicles and inconsequential monarchial genealogies.

One might add that the concept of *mai de-havei havei* need not belittle the value of history. Instead it may simply mean that Torah is not the venue to convey history. To appreciate this consider Maharal's comments cited in 5.15. Maharal expressed that Chazal were not doctors and Torah is not meant to convey medical information (thus when it seems to be doing so there must be some deeper meaning). This does not imply that there is no value in studying medicine – it simply means that it is not the Torah's goal. Likewise, one might suggest that *mai de-havei havei* means that Chazal were not historians and Torah is not meant to convey mere historical information information (thus when it seems to be doing so there must be some deeper meaning). This too does not indicate that there is no value in studying history.

This, of course, does not fully answer why we find very few historical words in the post biblical era. We address this question in 7.15.

7.8 RELATING TO *PSHAT* IN HALACHIC TOPICS

Until now, we have focused on the role of *pshat* in narrative sections of the Torah. Here, we can understand the value of studying the story on the respective levels of *pshat* and *drash*. The various

57. Such as Chapter 1 of *Hilchot Avoda Zara* and Chapter 3 of *Hilchot Chanuka*.

renditions present differing perspectives on the same event and thereby give us access to a more complete understanding of the story. What, though, is the role of *pshat* in the legal portions of the Torah? In these cases, the practical Halacha clearly follows the *drash*.[58] Seemingly, there is no reason to consider the *pshat*. Nevertheless, numerous thinkers, including Ramban and Gra,[59] do reflect on the *pshat* of halachic topics, even when the *pshat* differs from the normative Halacha.[60] Accordingly, we must wonder what value there is in considering the *pshat* if it does not accord with Halacha.[61] To address this issue, we will turn to Ramban and Rambam, both of whom see value in explaining and offering reasons for *pshat* understandings even when they are at variance with the normative Halacha as dictated by the *drash*.

---

58. While it is agreed that in cases where the *pshat* and *drash* clash we follow *drash* when determining normative law, *Kesef Mishneh* (*Hilchot Na'ara ha-Me'orasa* 3:6) writes that in the case of a halachic dispute, we accept the view that better conforms with *pshat* (at least when all other factors are equal). Thus, even regarding a halachic topic, *pshat* plays a role in determining normative law. Likewise, Rambam in his halachic code frequently attempts to show how the Halacha emerges from the text of Torah, often citing sources at variance with the ones suggested by the Talmud, insofar as the verses referenced by Rambam better accord with *pshat*.
59. See, for example, *Aderet Eliyahu* to *Shemot*, Chapter 21. To cite one example:
    גר"א שמות כא:ח
    "לו יעדה" הוא הקרי ור"ל שלקחה ליעדה לו ועכשיו אינו רוצה בה. ופשטא דקרא בזימון בעלמא בלא קדושין כי יעידה הוא זימון אבל חז"ל אמרו שהיעידה הוא קדושין...
60. This relates to the concept of *ein mikra yotzei midei pshuto*. This concept generally means that even when Chazal interpret a verse one way (generally in a halachic context), the simple understanding remains valuable. For example, the verse (*Vayikra* 21:9) states "ובת איש כהן כי תחל לזנות את אביה היא מחללת." What is the meaning of את אביה היא מחללת? The Talmud uses these words for a *gezeira shava*. Thus, one might argue that they are no longer true on a literal level. The principle of *ein mikra yotzei midei pshuto* informs us that we still should understand the verse on a level of *pshat* and dishonor the adulteress' father (see *Tosafot, Sanhedrin* 50b ד"ה כשהוא and *Yevamot* 24a and Rashi). We should note that this is not the way Rashbam, cited earlier, was utilizing the principle.
61. Moreover, we must wonder if there is any value in considering the reason for a *mitzva* as presented in *pshat* if the Halacha actually follows the Midrashic explanation, where the reason given for the *pshat* is not relevant.

Ramban's Perspective on Who Eats the Meal Offering

Let us begin with Ramban on the following verses:

ויקרא פרשת צו פרק ז

(ט) וְכָל מִנְחָה אֲשֶׁר תֵּאָפֶה בַּתַּנּוּר וְכָל נַעֲשָׂה בַמַּרְחֶשֶׁת וְעַל מַחֲבַת לַכֹּהֵן הַמַּקְרִיב אֹתָהּ לוֹ תִהְיֶה:

(י) וְכָל מִנְחָה בְלוּלָה בַשֶּׁמֶן וַחֲרֵבָה לְכָל בְּנֵי אַהֲרֹן תִּהְיֶה אִישׁ כְּאָחִיו:

> 9. And any meal offering baked in an oven (*ma'afei tanur*) and any one made in a deep pan (*marcheshet*) or in a shallow pan (*machavat*) belongs to the *kohen* who offers it up; it shall be his.
>
> 10. And any meal offering mixed with oil (*solet*) or dry (*chareiva*) shall belong to all the sons of Aharon, one like the other.

Ramban notes that on the level of *pshat,* the verses inform us that there are two categories of meal offerings (*menachot*):

1. *Ma'afei tanur, marcheshet,* and *machavat* (verse 9)
2. *Solet* and *chareiva* (verse 10)

On the level of *pshat,* verse 9 informs us that the *kohen* who offers the *menachot* in category 1 is entitled to keep the edible parts. Verse 10 tells us that all of the *kohanim* split the edible parts of category 2. Ramban suggests that the reason for this division is that the *menachot* in category 1 require a lot of work to prepare. Accordingly, the *kohen* who did the work is entitled to compensation in the form of the right to eat the offering. The *menachot* in category 2, on the other hand, demand very little work,[62] so all *kohanim* partake equally.

Ramban then notes that according to the midrash and normative Halacha (והקבלה תכריע), in actuality all *menachot* (categories 1 and 2)

62. *Minchat solet* is not baked and *minchat chareiva* does not even have oil or frankincense.

are shared equally among the *kohanim*. The reason for this is to promote peace (ותקנת הכהנים היא ושלום הבית)[63].

Thus, even though Halacha does not follow *pshat*, Ramban offers a reason for the *pshat* understanding of the *mitzva*.[64] Why? Moreover, if the Halacha is that *menachot* are split equally, why does the Torah not say so explicitly? Why does it imply that we distinguish between categories 1 and 2?

The answer, it seems, is that without the *pshat*, we would not have realized the lesson of the *drash*. By telling us what the Halacha should have been were we to follow equitable distribution, the Torah informs us how much we must forgo to promote peace. This lesson would have

---

63. **רמב"ן ויקרא ז:ט**

וכל מנחה אשר תאפה בתנור - **דרך הפשט ידוע בזה, שיצוה בנודר אחת משלש מנחות, מאפה תנור והמרחשת והמחבת, שיהיה לכהן המקריב אותם לבדו. ויאמר בכל שאר המנחות, כגון הנודר מנחה סתם שהוא מביא סלת, ובמנחת הבכורים, שהן בלולות, ובמנחת חוטא וסוטה שהן חריבות, שיהו מתחלקות לכל בני אהרן, כלומר לכל בית אב שלהם. ופירוש וכל מנחה בלולה בשמן וחרבה, מנחה שאין בה אלא סולת, בלולה או חרבה, לא מאלה הנזכרות. ויהיה טעם ההפרש ביניהן, מפני שטרח הכהן באפייתן וראוי להרבות שכרו:**

אבל רבותינו (מנחות עג א) לא רצו בכך, מפני שאמר וכל מנחה בלולה בשמן וחרבה, שכל המנחות שבעולם יכלול זה, שהם כולם בלולות או חרבות. ולכך ראו שפירוש לכהן המקריב אותה, לכהנים הטהורים הנמצאים שם:

וכן מה שאמר, והכהן המקריב את עולת איש, והכהן אשר יכפר בו לו יהיה, כולם לא באו אלא לומר שלא יהיו לבעלים, אבל יהיו בשכר ההקרבה לכהנים הטהורים הנמצאים שם, שכלם הם מקריבים ביד או בצווי, כי היחיד מהם או השנים ושלשה המקריבים ברשות כולם הם עושים ובשליחותם, וכולם עומדים על הקרבן, כחלק היורד במלחמה וכחלק היושב על הכלים יחדיו יחלוקו:

ואחר שאמר שיהיו לכהנים בשכר עבודתם, חזר וביאר וכל מנחה בלולה בשמן וחרבה, שהוא כלל המנחות, לכל בני אהרן המקריבים הנזכרים תהיה איש כאחיו, כלומר לבית אב הטהורים מהם, שכלם הם המקריבים הנזכרים. והזכיר הכתוב למנחות בשמותם, מאפה תנור ומרחשת ומחבת, ואחר כך חזר וכלל לומר איש כאחיו, שלא יהא לזה אלא ממה שיש לזה, ואפילו מנחת הסולת בה יחלוקו:

ואמר הכתוב כי הדין הזה במנחות, וכל שכן בשאר הקרבנות שדמיהן מרובין. **והקבלה תכריע, ותקנת הכהנים היא ושלום הבית.** ויתכן שיהיה שיעור הכתוב כפי הדעת הזו וכל מנחה אשר תאפה בתנור וכל נעשה במרחשת ועל מחבת לכהן המקריב אותה לו תהיה, וכל מנחה בלולה בשמן וחרבה כן, ולכל בני אהרן תהיה איש כאחיו:

64. Another place where Ramban offers a reason for a *mitzva* that accords with *pshat* but not *drash* (i.e., the reason does not accord with normative Halacha) can be found in *Devarim* 23:10.

been lost if the verse were written to accord with normative Halacha.[65] Thus, the discrepancy between *pshat* and *drash* allows the reader to appreciate the central lesson of this *mitzva*.

Sometimes Ramban goes even further, deriving Halacha from *pshat*. One remarkable example of this relates to the verse, כָּל חֵרֶם אֲשֶׁר יָחֳרַם מִן הָאָדָם לֹא יִפָּדֶה מוֹת יוּמָת "Every *cheirem* that is issued on a person shall not be redeemed he shall surely die" (*Vayikra* 27:29). At the end of his *Mishpat ha-Cheirem*, Ramban derives from the simple reading of this verse that a community can create a ban[66] (כָּל חֵרֶם אֲשֶׁר יָחֳרַם מִן הָאָדָם) such that the penalty for violation is death (מוֹת יוּמָת). Even though Chazal appear to understand the verse differently and derive different halachot from this verse, Ramban suggests his understanding, rooted in *pshat*, explains why Shaul felt that his son, Yehonatan, was liable for execution when he violated his father's *cheirem*.

Ultimately, in both narrative and halachic portions of the Torah, *pshat* and *drash* combine to provide us with a more complete understanding of the Torah.[67] Ramban himself makes this point explicitly writing that both are true and rooted in the verse.[68]

---

65. Put differently, the Halacha should have been that the כהן המקריב retains category 1, but פשרה עדיף. This is an example of the phenomenon that *pshat* or *Torah she-bichtav* reflects *din* while *drash* or *Torah she-be'al peh* presents *rachamim*. Another instance of this can be seen in the examples of *peirushim ha-mekubalim* (explanations of verses based on tradition) that Rambam lists in his Introduction to the commentary on the Mishna:
(דברים כה) וקצותה את כפה, שהוא כופר... (ויקרא כא) ובת איש כהן כי תחל לזנות וגו' באש תישרף, שזו הגזירה אין לנו לגזור אותה אלא אם תהיה אשת איש, עכ"פ. וכן גזירת הכתוב (דברים כב), בנערה אשר לא נמצאו לה בתולים שיסקלוה, לא שמענו חולק בה, ממשה ועד עתה, על מי שאמר שזהו לא יהיה אלא אם הייתה אשת איש, והעידו עדים עליה שאחר הקידושים זינתה בעדים והתראה...

This concept is alluded to by Rosh:

רא"ש מסכת בבא קמא פרק ב סימן ב
דפשיטא ליה דהלכתא לגרועי אתא כדאמרינן גבי סוכה אתאי הלכתא וגרעתא לשלישית ואוקימתא אטפח (סוכה ו ב).

There are numerous other examples of this phenomenon. See R. Hershel Schachter's *Eretz ha-Tzvi*, Chapter 2 note 2.

66. A *cheirem* is the upgraded form of *nidduy*.

67. Another example where Ramban employs this form of methodology is *Bamidbar* 15:22.

68. **רמב"ן השגות לספר המצות שרש ב**
מאמרם "אין המקרא יוצא מידי פשוטו", לא אמרו "אין מקרא אלא כפשוטו". אבל יש לנו מדרשו עם פשוטו, ואינו יוצא מידי כל אחד מהם, אבל יסבול הכתוב את הכל ויהיו שניהם אמת.

Rambam's Understanding of an Eye for an Eye

Let us now turn to an illustrative example of this phenomenon in Rambam.

שמות פרק כא:כד

> עַיִן תַּחַת עַיִן שֵׁן תַּחַת שֵׁן יָד תַּחַת יָד רֶגֶל תַּחַת רָגֶל: (כה) כְּוִיָּה תַּחַת כְּוִיָּה פֶּצַע תַּחַת פָּצַע חַבּוּרָה תַּחַת חַבּוּרָה:
>
> An eye for an eye, a tooth for a tooth, a hand for a hand, a foot for a foot, a burn for a burn, a wound for a wound, a bruise for a bruise.

The Talmud informs us that these verses are not to be taken literally. Rather, the punishment for causing bodily injury is a monetary payment. This leaves us with a glaring question: why does the Torah formulate this rule in such a misleading fashion? To answer this question, let us examine one of Rambam's most controversial comments. The context is Rambam's classification of *mitzvot* into 14 categories, the sixth of which is punishments.

מורה הנבוכים חלק ג פרק מא

> הם העונשין, ותועלתן באופן כללי ידועה, וכבר הזכרנוה. אבל פירוטן ודין כל מקרה לא רגיל שנאמר בהן שמע אותם:
>
> עשה עונש כל פושע נגד זולתו באופן כללי שייעשה בו כאשר עשה בשווה, **אם פגע בגוף פוגעים בגופו**, ואם פגע בממון פוגעים בממונו, ויש לבעל הממון למחול ולסלוח. אבל הרוצח דווקא מחמת חומר פשעו אינו נסלח לו כלל, ואין לוקחין ממנו כופר, ולארץ לא יכפר לדם אשר שפך בה כי אם בדם שופכו...

He likewise writes in *Mishpat ha-Cheirem*:

ולא תהיה חותם פינו מפני שרז"ל דרשו המקרא לענין אחר... שאף על פי כן אין מקרא יוצא מדי פשוטו, "אחת דבר אלקים שתים זו שמעתי" (תהלים סב:יב), משמש הכתוב לזה ולזה... צא וראה שהם ז"ל דרשו: "לא יומתו אבות על בנים" (דברים כד:טז), בעדות בנים, "ובנים לא יומתו על אבות", בעדות אבות... ואפילו כן אין מקרא יוצא מידי פשוטו אחת דכתיב: "רק את בניהם לא המית ככתוב בתורת משה: 'לא יומתו אבות על בנים' (מל"ב יד:ו)" הא למדנו שכמה פנים של אמת לתורה.

ומי שהשחית אבר מאבדים לו כמותו, כאשר יתן מום באדם כן ינתן בו. **ואל תטריד את מחשבותך במה שאנו עונשים כאן בתשלומין, כי הכוונה עתה לתת טעם למקראות לא ליתן טעמים לתורה שבעל פה,** עם מה שיש לי בדין זה סברא אשמיענה בעל פה.

והפגעים אשר אי אפשר לעשות כמותן בדיוק דן בהן בתשלומין, רק שבתו ייתן ורפא ירפא. ומי שהזיק בממון יינזק בממונו באותו הערך בדיוק: אשר ירשיעון אלוהים ישלם שנים לרעהו, הדבר אשר לקח ולוקחין כמותו מממון הגנב.

The precepts of the sixth class comprise the different ways of punishing the sinner. Their general usefulness is known and also has been mentioned by us.[69] I will here describe them one by one and point out their nature in detail.

---

69. In 3:35, Rambam summarizes the purpose of this class is deterrence:

The sixth class is formed of precepts regarding fines, e.g., the laws of theft and robbery, of false witnesses; most of the laws contained in the *Book of Shoftim* (of *Mishneh Torah*) belong to this class. **Their benefit is apparent; for if sinners and robbers were not punished, injury would not be prevented at all, and persons scheming evil would not become rarer. They who suppose that it would be an act of mercy to abandon the laws of compensation for injuries are wrong. On the contrary, it would be perfect cruelty and injury to the social state of the country**. It is an act of mercy that God commanded, "Judges and officers you shall appoint for yourselves in all of your gates" (*Devarim* 16:18).

Later (3:41), he writes that there are four factors that determine the nature of a punishment:

1. The greatness of the sin. Actions that cause great harm are punished severely, while actions that cause little harm are punished less severely.
2. The frequency of the crime. A crime that is committed frequently must be put down by severe punishment; crimes of rare occurrence may be suppressed by a lenient punishment considering that they are committed only rarely.
3. The amount of temptation. Only fear of a severe punishment restrains us from actions for which there exists a great temptation, because we have a great desire for these actions, are accustomed to them, or feel unhappy without them.
4. The facility of doing the act secretly, unseen and unnoticed. We are deterred from such acts only by the fear of a great and terrible punishment.

Even though Rambam maintains that punishments are meant as a deterrent, he maintains that the punishment must correlate perfectly. Later (and earlier in 2:29), he elaborates on this principle in his articulation of how the Torah's laws are just and balanced.

> The punishment of one who sins against his neighbor consists of the general rule that there shall be done unto him exactly as he has done: **if he injured someone personally, he must suffer personally**; if he damaged the property of his neighbor, he shall be punished by loss of property. But the person whose property has been damaged should be ready to resign his claim totally or partly. Only towards the murderer must we not be lenient, because of the greatness of his crime, and we must not accept any ransom from him. "And the land cannot be cleansed of the blood that is shed therein except by the blood of him that shed it..."
>
> And one who mutilated a limb of his neighbor must himself lose a limb. "As he has caused a blemish in a man, so shall it be done to him." **You must not raise an objection from our practice of imposing a fine in such cases. For we have set out here to give the reason for the precepts as presented in Scripture, not to give reasons for the oral law.** I have, however, an explanation for the interpretation given in the Talmud, but it will be communicated orally.
>
> Injuries that cannot be reproduced exactly in another person are compensated for by payment; "He shall pay for the [plaintiff's] loss of time and shall cause him to be thoroughly healed." If anyone damaged the property of another, he must lose exactly as much of his own property: "Whom the judges shall condemn, he shall pay double to his neighbor;" namely, he restores that which he has taken and adds just as much [to it] of his own property.

Rambam writes that Torah law demands equitable punishments. If a person intentionally murders, he should be executed; if he damages somebody's property, he should make restitution. What about if he harms somebody's body? In this case, monetary compensation does not fit the crime. Accordingly, the Torah prescribes a punishment of "An eye for an eye." Rambam then notes that the Halacha does not accord with this thesis insofar as it demands monetary compensation for bodily harm. Rambam explains that his purpose in *Moreh ha-Nevuchim* is to give reasons for *mitzvot* as they are presented in the text, i.e., what we have been calling *pshat*; he makes no attempt to give the reasons for the oral law or Halacha.

Thus, Rambam, like Ramban, gives reasons for *pshat* understandings of the text even when they do not accord with Halacha. Here too, then, we must ask: if normative practice does not actually follow *pshat*, why does the Torah formulate the *mitzva* in such a fashion? Moreover, what is the purpose of giving reasons for *mitzvot* according to *pshat* if this is not the way in which they are observed?

Rambam addresses this question in *Mishneh Torah*:

רמב״ם הלכות חובל ומזיק פרק א
החובל בחבירו חייב לשלם לו חמשה דברים, נזק וצער ורפוי ושבת ובושת, וחמשה דברים אלו כולן משתלמים מן היפה שבנכסיו כדין כל המזיקין.

נזק כיצד, שאם קטע יד חבירו או רגלו רואין אותו כאלו הוא עבד נמכר בשוק כמה היה יפה וכמה הוא יפה עתה ומשלם הפחת שהפחית מדמיו, שנ׳ (שמות כ״א:כ״ד - ויקרא כד:כ) ״עין תחת עין״, מפי השמועה למדו שזה שנאמר תחת לשלם ממון הוא.

זה שנאמר בתורה כאשר יתן מום באדם כן ינתן בו אינו לחבול בזה כמו שחבל בחבירו אלא שהוא ראוי לחסרו אבר או לחבול בו כמו שעשה ולפיכך משלם נזקו, והרי הוא אומר (במדבר ל״ה ל״א) ולא תקחו כופר לנפש רוצח, לרוצח בלבד הוא שאין כופר אבל לחסרון איברים או לחבלות יש כופר.

When a person injures a colleague, he is liable to compensate him in five ways: the damages, his pain, his medical treatment, his loss of employment, and the embarrassment he suffered. All five assessments must be paid from the highest quality of property that he owns, as is the law with regard to payment for all types of damages.

What is meant by "the damages"? If a person cuts off the hand or the foot of a colleague, we theoretically consider the injured colleague as a servant being sold in the marketplace and determine his value before the injury and his value afterwards. The person who caused the injury must pay the depreciation in value. This is alluded to in *Shemot* 21:24: "An eye for an eye." The oral tradition interprets תחת, translated as "for," as an indication that the verse requires financial recompense.

The Torah's statement (*Vayikra* 24:20): "Just as he caused an injury to his fellowman, so too an injury should be caused to him," should not be interpreted in a literal sense. It does not mean that the person who caused the injury actually should be subjected to a similar physical punishment. Instead, the intent is that he deserves to lose a limb or to be injured in the same manner as his colleague was, and therefore, he should make financial restitution to him. This interpretation is supported by the verse (*Bamidbar* 35:31): "Do not accept *kofeir* (a ransom) for the soul of the murderer." Implied is that no *kofeir* may be paid for a murderer alone, but *kofeir* may be paid for causing a loss of limb or other injuries.

In *Mishneh Torah,* Rambam reiterates his position that monetary compensation is insufficient in cases where one person causes bodily harm to another; compensation does not correlate with the crime. At the same time, the Torah does not prescribe that the perpetrator be punished with bodily harm. Instead, the Torah allows for the payment of *kofeir.*[70] *Kofeir* is more of an atonement or punishment than compensation. As opposed to murder, where we do not allow the criminal to pay *kofeir* and thereby absolve him of execution, in the case of bodily harm we do allow the criminal to pay *kofeir*. The amount of *kofeir* happens to correlate with the damages caused, but it differs conceptually from compensation paid for property damage.

Thus, the formulation of the Torah reflects the ideal punishment; it teaches us the punishment the criminal deserves, not what he

70. The Talmud (*Bava Kama* 40a) considers two models regarding how to understand *kofeir*; however, either way it differs from standard compensation.

actually gets.[71] The *Torah she-be'al peh* reflects the reality that administering a punishment of bodily injury is impossible or intolerable.[72] This pattern, in which the written law presents the conceptual or ideal law while the oral law lays down the practical law, repeats itself in many places.[73]

However, we still must wonder: are there any practical ramifications of this conceptual framework? Put differently, does it matter that compensation for bodily harm is classified as *kofeir*? Rambam answers in the affirmative in *Hilchot Choveil u-Mazik* 5:6–7, where he exempts the assailant from certain aspects of the payment in the event that there are no witnesses to the assault.[74] Another application relates to which aspects of payment can be collected outside of Israel (*Hilchot Sanhedrin* 5:10).

Thus, we see the importance of studying the *pshat* even in the halachic sections of the Torah, both to gain a conceptual understanding of the law as well as to fully appreciate many practical applications. As with respect to the narrative sections, a complete understanding of

---

71. This is yet another example of the pattern referred to earlier in which the oral law mitigates the harshness of the written law.
72. Among the various reasons for why the Torah does not insist on carrying out the ideal punishment is that it would be impossible to do so. For example, if Reuven strikes Shimon, thereby causing Shimon to lose half of his eyesight, how could we punish Reuven in such a way that he also loses precisely half of his eyesight (see *Bava Kama* 84a where the Talmud offers variations of this argument)? Nevertheless, Rambam in the ensuing halachot writes that although we can find textual allusions not to interpret "An eye for an eye" literally, our definitive knowledge of this understanding comes from tradition.
73. Consider the Ramban discussed in the previous section. Also, see *Shemot* 10:9 and Rashi, Rashbam, ibn Ezra, Shulchan Aruch O.C. 25:5, and *Mishna Berura ad. loc.* Also consider *Shemot* 21:6 with the comments of Rashi and *Meshech Chochma*. We should note, however, that Rambam maintains that *pshat* also plays a large role in determining Halacha. For example, following the above citation, Rambam demonstrates that even on a level of *pshat* an eye for an eye cannot be understood literally. As we noted in a footnote in 7.4, Rambam, especially in *Sefer ha-Mitzvot*, ties pshat to Halacha.
74. See Ra'avad *ad. loc.*, *Choveil u-Mazik* 1:16, and Ramban *Shevuot* 46b s.v. *ha de-tnan.*

the law demands that we integrate the text and tradition, since each one gives us only a partial picture.[75]

75. One might continue to wonder what the *pshat* of the verse is – removal of the eye or compensation? Interestingly, Onkelos translates the verse literally even though he frequently does not translate literally. Perhaps this indicates that he maintains that the literal reading is meant to be *pshat* (which may be the case according to Rambam as well). However, one might suggest that the basis for Onkelos' translation may actually be the following source:

מכילתא דרבי ישמעאל משפטים מסכתא דנזיקין פרשה ח

"עין תחת עין" - ממון. אתה אומר ממון, או אינו אלא עין ממש? היה רבי ישמעאל אומר: הרי הוא: "אומר מכה בהמה ישלמנה ומכה אדם יומת" (ויקרא כד:כא), הקיש הכתוב נזקי אדם לנזקי בהמה ונזקי בהמה לנזקי אדם. מה נזקי בהמה לתשלומין, אף נזקי אדם לתשלומין.

רבי יצחק אומר: הרי הוא אומר: "אם כופר יושת עליו" (שמות כא:ל), והרי דברים קל וחומר: מה במקום שענש הכתוב מיתה לא ענש אלא ממון, כאן שלא ענש מיתה, דין הוא שלא יענש אלא ממון.

רבי אליעזר אומר: עין תחת עין, שומע אני בין מתכוין בין שאינו מתכוין אינו משלם אלא ממון, והרי הכתוב מוציא המתכוון לעשות בו מום שאינו משלם אלא [ממש], שנאמר: "ואיש כי יתן מום בעמיתו" (ויקרא כד:יט).

Commentaries debate exactly what R. Eliezer means and whether the text should include the word *ממש*, or, in its place *ממון*. According to Horowitz and many manuscripts the correct word is *ממש*. This is also the view of the *Pesikta*:

פסיקתא זוטרתא (לקח טוב) שמות פרשת משפטים פרק כא סימן כד

עין תחת עין. ממון, שהיה ר' ישמעאל אומר, ומכה בהמה ישלמנה ומכה אדם יומת (ויקרא כד:כא), מקיש נזקי אדם לנזקי בהמה, מה נזקי בהמה בתשלומין, אף נזקי אדם בתשלומין. וא"ת והא כתיב ואיש כי יתן מום בעמיתו כאשר עשה כן יעשה לו (שם שם יט), ינתן בו ממש, **ר' אליעזר אומר הואיל ונתכוין לתת בו מום אינו משלם ממון אלא נזק ינתן בו ממש, עין תחת עין.**

According to this understanding, R. Eliezer maintains that if one did not intend to injure the other party then one would pay money. If they did, then we would apply an eye for an eye literally, as indicated from the end of the verse: ,ואיש כי יתן מום בעמיתו **כאשר עשה כן ייעשה לו**. Onkelos was a student of R. Eliezer, and his translation may reflect his teacher's view point (see *Megilla* 3a תרגום של תורה אונקלוס הגר אמרו **מפי ר' אליעזר** ור' יהושע). One objection that can be raised on this interpretation is that the Talmud (*Bava Kama* 84a) rejects this understanding of R. Eliezer. (This is not a refutation. Onkelos lived before the Talmud Bavli was written and thus may have had a different understanding of R. Eliezer than the Bavli. Nevertheless, the Talmud's question could be asked upon Onkelos. Certainly, Rambam, who understands that we know that "an eye for an eye" refers to monetary payment based on a tradition and maintains that matters of tradition are not subject to dispute, would disagree with the above analysis.) Regardless, as R. Aviyam Levinson pointed out to me, there are other places where we find Onkelos adopting R. Eliezer's view. Consider two more

One last point is in order concerning the above passage from *Moreh ha-Nevuchim*. Some scholars perceive in Rambam's words dismissiveness towards the oral tradition and a belief that the understanding that "An eye for an eye" refers to compensation was not given along with the written law but was invented sometime later. If so, Rambam would be contradicting his belief – reiterated in numerous places – that this interpretation was given at Sinai along with the rest of the Torah.[76]

Having considered Rambam's elucidation of the law in *Mishneh Torah*, this suggestion becomes patently absurd, as he alludes to his theory presented in *Moreh ha-Nevuchim* and shows how it fits neatly into the halachic framework. This type of error is typical of those who study Rambam's philosophical works without considering his halachic writings.[77]

7.9 THEMATIC AND PHILOSOPHICAL CONTRADICTIONS BETWEEN *PSHAT* AND *DRASH*

Thus far, we have focused on contradictions between *pshat* and *drash* with respect to events that occurred as well as incongruities on halachic levels. Now, let us briefly consider thematic and philosophical discrepancies. Although this is a broad topic, we will suffice with a brief methodological point.

There are times when the midrash does not amplify themes alluded to in the text, but rather seems to contradict them. Let us briefly consider two examples. The text of the book of *Iyov* informs us of Iyov's rectitude. Whatever the cause of his suffering was, it was not sin.

---

examples from a single *parsha*. In *Vayikra* 23:42, he understands the *sukkot* of the verse as referring to the clouds of glory (בְּמְטַלַּת עֲנָנֵי) in accordance with the view of R. Eliezer (*Sukka* 11a, see Maharatz Chayot). In *Vayikra* 21:7, he understands *zona* as referring to someone who is טועה מתחת בעלה (מַטְעֲיָא) in accordance with the view of R. Eliezer (*Yevamot* 61b).

76. **הקדמה לפירוש המשניות**

וזה עיקר יש לך לעמוד על סודו. והוא, שהפירושים המקובלים מפי משה, אין מחלוקת בהם בשום פנים, שהרי מאז ועד עתה לא מצאנו מחלוקת נפלה בזמן מן הזמנים, מימות משה ועד רב אשי בין החכמים, כדי שיאמר אחד, המוציא עין חברו יוציאו את עינו, שנאמר עין בעין, ויאמר השני, אינו אלא כופר בלבד שחייב לתת.

77. See 2.1, where we examine Rambam's prerequisites for studying *Moreh ha-Nevuchim*.

איוב א:א
אִישׁ הָיָה בְאֶרֶץ עוּץ אִיּוֹב שְׁמוֹ וְהָיָה הָאִישׁ הַהוּא תָּם וְיָשָׁר וִירֵא אֱלֹהִים וְסָר מֵרָע.

> There was a man in the land of Utz whose name was Iyov; and that man was whole-hearted and upright, one that feared God and shunned evil.

While the verse attributes no evil to Iyov, with God himself testifying to his goodness, Chazal paint a different picture.

תלמוד בבלי מסכת סוטה דף יא עמוד א
א"ר חייא בר אבא א"ר סימאי, שלשה היו באותה עצה: בלעם, ואיוב, ויתרו, בלעם שיעץ - נהרג, איוב ששתק - נידון ביסורין, יתרו שברח - זכו מבני בניו שישבו בלשכת הגזית...

> R. Chiya b. Abba said in the name of R. Simai: There were three in that plan [to destroy the Jews through the decree that every male child be thrown into the Nile]: Bilam, Iyov and Yitro. Bilam, who devised it, was slain; Iyov, who silently acquiesced, was afflicted with suffering; Yitro, who fled, merited that his descendants should sit in the Chamber of Hewn Stone (on the *Sanhedrin*)...

Here, the midrash, which attributes sin to Iyov and implies that his suffering was meant to punish this sinfulness, contradicts the written text, which states explicitly that Iyov did not sin. Moreover, this conflict affects the entire message of the book of *Iyov*.

Another example (that we will return to in Chapter 29) is the selection of Avraham and the Jewish people. In both cases (*Bereishit* 12:1 and *Devarim* 7:7), the text of the Torah does not offer any reason for God's choice. The implication is that there is no reason that we can or should know. At the same time, midrashim, when interpreting these exact verses, elaborate upon why Avraham was chosen (e.g., his independent discovery of God and his willingness to devote his life to spread God's message) and why the Jewish people were chosen (because of their humility).[78] Here, too, the contradiction has major repercussions, as it defines the character of chosenness and the nature of God's relationship with His people.

How should we deal with contradictions such as these where the biblical text and the oral tradition paint very different pictures? The wrong approach is to entirely supplant the simple reading of the text (which hides the reasons for chosenness and stresses Iyov's rectitude) with the midrash's interpretation. One never can ignore the text; God chose these words for a reason. At the same time, Chazal, whose water we drink thirstily, clearly were highlighting, in one of our examples, the importance of Avraham's early accomplishments – despite the biblical silence.

In situations like this, we are meant to recognize that each perspective presents a partial approach to a challenging issue. Regarding God's choice of the Jewish people, the mixed message points to a duality within chosenness. Rabbinic literature stresses one element of our chosenness, namely, that God selected us because of our outstanding behavior, while the biblical text stresses that our selection transcends our righteousness.

What is the nature of our dual relationship with God? How is it possible that we were chosen for a reason and yet God's choice is beyond reason? The solution can be found when we consider the biblical depictions of our affiliation. The metaphors used to describe God's relationship with Israel brilliantly express the duality of the relationship. Sometimes, Israel is called the son of God.[79] This imagery implies a relationship that transcends merit; a parent need not justify his love for his own child because it is natural, and, to a certain degree, irrational. Moreover, because a progenitor's love does not stem from the rectitude the child but rather from its essence, the relationship never can be broken.[80] Other times, Tanach depicts Israel as the spouse of God.[81] The spousal relationship differs from

78. *Chullin* 89a.

79. See, for example, *Shemot* 4:22 and *Devarim* 14:1.

80. See *Kiddushin* 36a.

81. See, for example, *Yeshaya* 54:5. Rashi, following the Midrash, understands all of *Shir ha-Shirim* as a depiction of the love between God and Israel.

a familial bond in that it initially is formed because of the qualities one spouse finds in the other. Because the union is volitional, it can be broken if one partner fails to live up to expectations. These mixed metaphors are not a contradiction; we are both the child of God and His spouse; we were chosen without a discernable reason and also because of our greatness.

Likewise, with respect to Iyov, Chazal are not saying that his suffering was commensurate with his misdeeds, nor are they indicting Iyov for overt sinfulness (in which case, their understanding would in fact contradict the text). In fact, as R. Chaim Shmuelevitz (*Sichot Mussar* 5733–5) insightfully notes, Iyov's silence in the face of the impending decree of genocide against the Jews was reasonable.[82] Most likely, his protest would not have accomplished very much. Moreover, by remaining silent, he could perhaps minimize the damage or help in some other way. Iyov's compromise seems reasonable. Nevertheless, R. Shmuelevitz explains, Iyov's silence reflected insensitivity. When one is in pain, he cries out even though the cry accomplishes nothing. For not feeling the pain of others, Iyov was sentenced to pain that would cause him to cry out reflexively.

Other resolutions to the above contradictions certainly are possible. The idea, though, is one of perspective. The student of Midrash is not meant to forget the text; to do so not only ignores the direct word of God, but inhibits a full understanding of the intended message of the Midrash.

7.10 APPENDIX: RAMBAN'S UNDERSTANDING OF MIDRASH

In the next two sections we will attempt to understand the numerous statements of Ramban that seem to indicate skepticism concerning midrashim. To this end, we first must get a general understanding of Ramban's goal in his commentary.

82. This idea is also found in R. Yitzchak Zev Soloveitchik's comments printed at the end of בית הלוי על התורה.

The Torah Should Be Understood on Multiple Levels Simultaneously

Much of Ramban's commentary focuses on interpreting Scripture on multiple levels, including *pshat*, *drash*, and *sod* (i.e., Kabbala). Ramban implicitly, and at times explicitly, tells us that the Torah intends these multiple meanings. Each one is rooted in the text. Moreover, it is important to understand which level of interpretation one is dealing with. Let us consider an example.

The third chapter of *Bamidbar* opens with the statement, "These are the descendants of Aharon and Moshe (תולדות אהרן ומשה)." The Torah proceeds to enumerate only the sons of Aharon, omitting those of Moshe. Rashi, citing a midrash, solves this problem by informing us that because Moshe taught Torah to Aharon's sons, it is as though he bore them.[83] Thus, in truth, the verse includes descendants of both Moshe and Aharon.

Ramban understands that this explanation is incorrect on a level of *pshat*. Rather, Ramban writes, Moshe's descendants are in fact referred to later in the chapter when the Torah mentions Amram's family (מִשְׁפַּחַת הַעַמְרָמִי) along with the *levi'im*, which can be referring only to the children of Moshe, as Amram had no other descendants who were *levi'im*.[84]

Ramban then tells us that the textual basis for the midrash's explanation is that Moshe's sons are not mentioned by name as Aharon's are:

> **והדרש סמכוהו** מפני שלא פירש "ואלה שמות בני משה" כאשר עשה בבני אהרן, **לרמוז** כי בני אהרן גם הם תולדות למשה מפני שלמדם תורה:

---

83. ואינו מונה אלא בני אהרן, ונקראו תולדות משה לפי שלמדן תורה, מלמד שכל המלמד חבירו תורה מעלה עליו הכתוב כאילו ילדו.

84. ועל דרך **הפשט**, כי טעם "תולדות אהרן ומשה", לומר שהיו בני אהרן כהנים משוחים נבדלים מן השבט להיותם קדש קדשים, ותולדות משה משפחת העמרמי אשר יזכיר למטה (פסוק כז), כי אין בעמרמי זולתי בני משה נמנים בלוים.

> **And** [**the Sages**] **found a basis for the aggadic teaching** [that the sons of Aharon are the "offspring of Moshe" as well] from the fact that [Scripture] did not specify "These are the names of Moshe's sons" as it did in the case of Aharon's sons. **This is to hint** that Aharon's sons are considered as offspring of Moshe as well, since he taught them Torah.

Ramban concludes by telling us that both explanations are true:

> כי התורה תפרש ותרמוז.
>
> For the Torah explains [explicitly] and hints [at the same time].

Ramban here informs us that *drash* is rooted in the text; however, the basis for *drash* is not explicit statements (which would make it *pshat*), but hints. Often, as in the case above, the midrash intends to address textual idiosyncrasies. Thus, the Midrashic explanation is hinted to (תרמוז) in the text. It is not the case that only the *pshat* is rooted in the text; rather, *drash* seeks to answer certain textual issues that are not significant on a level of *pshat*.

However, significantly, Ramban maintains that it is insufficient to simply demonstrate the scriptural allusion to a midrash, the deeper meaning and significance must also be explained.[85] This is especially true when the simple understanding of the midrash does not seem to be meaningful or is problematic for some other reason. As we note in 12.6, Ramban frequently offers mystical interpretations of midrashim.

Asking Practical Questions on Midrashim

Even though Ramban searches for the deeper meaning of midrashim, it is noteworthy that Ramban frequently asks very practical questions on midrashim and assesses them accordingly. Sometimes he answers these questions, while at other times these questions cause him to offer alternative explanations (at least on the level of *pshat*); sometimes he will do both.

---

85. Examples of this include *Bereishit* 4:22, *Bamidbar* 16:1, and *Devarim* 33:1,

An example of the last option is Ramban's discussion of Yitzchak's suspicion that the person before him attempting to receive a *bracha* was Yaakov and not Eisav. Rashi, citing a midrash, explains that Yitzchak's misgivings stemmed from the petitioner's reference to God's Name (אין דרך עשו להיות שם שמים שגור בפיו). Ramban questions this explanation in light of the fact that Yitzchak perceived Eisav as righteous (a practical question). Ramban then offers a possible defense of the midrash, but he concludes that on a level of *pshat*, Yitzchak's suspicion stemmed from Eisav's voice differing from Yaakov's.[86]

7.11 APPENDIX B: DID RAMBAN THINK ONE CAN DISAGREE WITH CHAZAL?

In 5.2, we considered differing perspectives on the extent to which statements of Aggada are binding. In light of our discussion above, let us consider Ramban's perspective on this matter.

It often is difficult to determine if Ramban's refutations of and skepticism towards a midrash should be seen as indicating (a) a rejection of the midrash (along the lines of the simple reading of the Geonic statements discussed in 5.2), (b) that the story in the midrash did not literally take place (along the lines of Ran in 7.3), or (c) that the questions he has raised against a particular midrash suggest that it should not be considered *pshat*, but not that the midrash is wrong.[87]

---

86. **רמב"ן בראשית כז:כא**
גשה נא ואמשך בני - לשון רש"י, אמר בלבו אין דרך עשו להיות שם שמים שגור בפיו. **וכן בבראשית רבה. ואני תמה,** כי לא היה עשו רשע בעיני אביו, **ואולי** היה חושב בלבו כי בעבור היותו איש שדה ולבו על הציד, איננו מזכיר שם שמים מפחדו שלא יזכירנו במקום שאינו טהור ומבלי כוונה, ונחשב לו זה בעיני אביו ליראת שמים. **ועל דרך הפשט** יהיה זה בעבור טביעות הקול:

87. Along similar lines, we should consider whether the evidence Ramban offers for certain midrashim should be understood as evidence that (a) the explanation given by the midrash is true, (b) that the events described in the midrash actually happened, or (c) that the midrash's explanation is *pshat*. Consider the following example: Ramban wonders why the tribe of Levi was so much smaller than the other tribes. He concludes that the correct explanation is that of the midrash that the tribe of Levi was not persecuted in Egypt. God miraculously caused only the oppressed Jews to multiply. Ramban formulates his thesis as follows:

The comments of Ramban cited in 7.5 might point against the second possibility. Moreover, this option is only relevant with respect to events, but Ramban frequently rejects the interpretations of Chazal in matters where this option is not relevant. Investigation frequently bears out the third option. Consider the following illustrative example:

רמב"ן במדבר ג:מה

תחת כל בכור בבני ישראל - הנה הבכורים נתקדשו להיות לשם מעת שצוה (שמות יג:ב) קדש לי כל בכור בבני ישראל באדם וגו'. והיו בכורים רבים בישראל, ולא נפדו עד הנה, שעדין לא נאמר למי יהיה הפדיון, כי עתה הוא שנתקדשו הכהנים ועדין לא נצטוו במתנות הכהונה. והנה הם עומדים בקדושתן סתם, **ויתכן** שהיתה בהן עבודת הקרבנות כדברי רבותינו (זבחים קיב ב).

> "In place of every firstborn Jew…" Behold, the firstborns were sanctified to God from the time [in Egypt] when God said, "Sanctify every firstborn from man to animal." However, the firstborns were not yet separated until now (about one year later, when the Jews were in the desert) since it was not stated to whom to give the *pidyon* (redemption money), for only now were the *kohanim* sanctified, and the Jews were not yet instructed to give them the priestly gifts. Thus, the firstborns remained sanctified in an unspecified manner, and **it is possible** (יתכן) they brought sacrifices [at Sinai], as Chazal have stated.

The verse indicates that the firstborn were sanctified in Egypt until they were redeemed (over a year later), as described in *Bamidbar* 3:40–51. Ramban speculates what the nature of that sanctification might have been, and then says "it is possible" (יתכן) that they performed the sacrificial service, as Chazal understand (see *Zevachim* 112b).

רמב"ן במדבר ג:יד

ואני חושב, שזה חזוק למה שאמרו רבותינו (תנחומא וארא ו) כי שבטו של לוי לא היו בשעבוד מלאכת מצרים ובעבודת פרך.

When Ramban writes that "this (the small Levite population) supports" the view of Chazal, what is he trying to preclude? Is he rejecting the possibility that (a) the midrash is false, (b) the midrash did not literally happen, or (c) that the midrash is not *pshat*?

The word יתכן (it is possible) implies ambivalence. How should we interpret Ramban's uncertainty? This could mean that (a) Chazal possibly were correct when they said that the firstborn performed the sacrificial service; (b) Chazal's interpretation possibly corresponds to physical reality; or (c) Chazal's understanding possibly corresponds to *pshat* (i.e., Ramban is uncertain whether Chazal's understanding is correct only on a level of *drash* or even on a level of *pshat*). In this context, (b) seems unlikely. Is there any evidence for option (c)?

When we examine other places where Ramban considers this topic, it becomes clear that (a) is incorrect and that (c) is the only possibility. In fact, in two other places he explicitly presumes that the sacrificial service at Sinai was performed by the firstborn.[88] Thus, it is clear that the word יתכן is used because there is very little explicit textual evidence that the sacrificial service initially was performed by the firstborn. Ramban is unsure whether or not it is *pshat*, but he is certain that it is true. In a sense, Ramban is adopting the exact opposite model of Ran – reality accords with the description of the midrash, whether or not it is correct on a level of *pshat*.[89] We will consider this further in 7.13.

---

88. In *Bamidbar* 16:21, Ramban uses the presumption that the sacrificial service originally was performed by the firstborn to explain God's inclination to destroy the entire Jewish people following Korach's rebellion. Elsewhere, Ramban first cites the view of the midrash that the firstborn performed the sacrificial service. He then wonders why they are referred to as נערי בני ישראל and suggests a solution. Then, he writes that, on the level of *pshat*, the sacrificial service was performed by the innocent youth who were firstborn (thus integrating *pshat* and *drash*).

רמב"ן שמות כד:ה

נערי בני ישראל - **הם הבכורות כדברי אונקלוס**, כי הם המעלים העולות והשלמים. **ולא ידעתי למה יכנה הבכורות בלשון נערי**, אולי בעבור שהזכיר הזקנים שהם אצילי בני ישראל, קרא הבכורות נערים, כי הם נערים כנגדם, ירמוז כי לא בעבור מעלתם בחכמה שלחם כי לא היו זקנים, רק מפני הבכורה כי הם המקודשים לקרבנות. **ועל דרך הפשט נערי בני ישראל הם בחורי ישראל** שלא טעמו טעם חטא, שלא נגשו אל אשה מעולם, כי הם הנבחרים בעם והקדושים בהם, כענין שאמרו (ברכות מג ב) עתידין בחורי ישראל שלא טעמו טעם חטא ליתן ריח כלבנון וכו'.

89. Here, too, we must wonder why the Torah does not explicitly depict the physical reality. R. Yehuda Frank ("קונטרס סתרי ומגיני אתה" p. 25) suggests an incisive solution. The first chapter of *Masechet Kala* offers the following derivation of the verse that describes the sacrificial service of the firstborn at Sinai:

There are times, however, where Ramban indicates that he is arguing with Chazal, sometimes referring to their interpretation as "incorrect." (See, for example, *Bamidbar* 25:5 and *Devarim* 31:16.) Here, too, we can argue that he means to say that it is incorrect on the level of *pshat* but may still be correct on the level of *drash*. The simple reading of such comments of Ramban, though, indicates that to some degree he is accepting the Geonic perspective that the views of Chazal on non-halachic topics are not necessarily binding.

Let us consider an example. Moshe tells Pharaoh that Pharaoh will give the Jews animals to sacrifice when they leave Egypt (*Shemot* 10:25). Ramban asserts that this statement is meant rhetorically. Though he acknowledges that Chazal indicate otherwise, he nevertheless rejects their interpretation.[90] In this case, Ramban cannot be saying that the interpretation of Chazal is incorrect only on a level of *pshat*, because Ramban rejects the interpretation that Pharaoh gave the Jews actual sacrifices on theological grounds (it would be inappropriate to accept sacrifices from the wicked), not textual grounds.[91] It thus appears that he is disagreeing with

---

כל המפנה עצמו מעבירה ולא עשאה אפילו הוא ישראל ראוי הוא לעלות עולה ככהן גדול שנ׳ וישלח את נערי בנ״י ויעלו עולות.

By referring to those who performed the sacrificial service as נערי בני ישראל, the verse teaches us a remarkable lesson. If this is correct, Ramban's approach here parallels his thesis cited earlier concerning the distribution of *menachot*, namely, that by deviating from a literal description, the Torah conveys fundamental lessons.

90. **רמב״ן שמות י:כה**

גם אתה תתן בידינו זבחים ועולות - לא אמר משה דבר זה על מנת להעשות, ולא עשה כן כלל, אבל הם דברי חיזוק. יאמר כי תכבד מאד יד ה׳ עליו ועל עמו, עד כי גם זבחים ועולות וכל אשר לו יתן בעד נפשו. ובאמת כי כאשר אמר להם (להלן יב:לב) וברכתם גם אותי, היה נותן ברצונו כל מקנהו לכפר עליו, אבל לא עלה על דעת משה לעשות זבח רשעים תועבה (משלי כא:כז), כי ה׳ חפץ דכאו, לא לכפר עליו, רק להענישו ולנער אותו ואת כל חילו בים. **ורבותינו אמרו** (מכילתא פרק יג, תנחומא בא ז) כי "כאשר דברתם" (להלן יב:לב) הוא על מאמרם גם אתה תתן בידינו זבחים ועולות. **אולי רצו לומר** שרמז להם לתת ככל אשר אמרו, לא שלקחו ממנו כלל, או זבחים ועולות להם כדי שיצאו, לא להקריבם עליו. **וגם זה אינו נכון:**

Ramban first rejects the possibility that the Egyptians sent sacrifices, then notes that this is the view of Chazal, then offers a possible justification (אולי רצו לומר), and finally rejects this solution (וגם זה אינו נכון).

91. Another possible example concerns the sin of Moshe in *Bamidbar*, Chapter 20:

רמב״ן במדבר כ:ח

החטא במשה ואהרן במי מריבה אינו מתפרסם בכתוב. ורש״י פירש (בפסוקים יא, יב) מפני שצוה אותם ודברתם אל הסלע - ולא אמר והכיתם, שאלו דברו היה הקב״ה מתקדש לעיני כל

the interpretation of Chazal.[92] In the next section, we consider one further source within Ramban's writings that may shed light on this discussion.

7.12 APPENDIX C: RAMBAN'S STATEMENT CONCERNING AGGADA IN THE DISPUTATION OF BARCELONA

One pertinent source concerning the extent to which Ramban maintains that statements of Aggada are binding is his famous debate. The Disputation of Barcelona (July 20–24, 1263) was held at the royal palace of King James I of Aragon in the presence of the king, his court, ecclesiastical dignitaries, and knights. It pitted Dominican Friar Pablo Christiani, a convert from Judaism to Christianity, against Ramban. What follows is an excerpt from Ramban's transcription of the debate.

ויכוח הרמב"ן

חזר פראי פול וטען כי בתלמוד אמרו שכבר בא המשיח, והביא אותה הגדה שבמדרש איכה בההוא גברא דהוא (רדי) וגעת תורתיה. עבר חד ערבי ואמר ליה, בר יהודאי בר יהודאי, שרי תורתך שרי פדנך שרי קנקנך, דאיתחרב בית המקדש. שרא תורתיה שרא פדניה שרא

העדה ואומרים ומה סלע זה שאינו שומע ואינו מדבר מקיים דברו של הקב"ה אנו על אחת כמה וכמה. **ודברי אגדה הם, אבל לא נתחוורו**, כי מאחר שצוה קח את המטה יש במשמע שיכה בו, ואלו היה רצונו בדבור בלבד מה המטה הזה בידו. וכן במכות מצרים שאמר (שמות ז:טו) והמטה אשר נהפך לנחש תקח בידך, והוא להכות בו, ולפעמים יאמר נטה את ידך, ורצונו לומר להכות במטה, כי הכתוב יקצר בדבר הנשמע. ואין הנס גדול בדבור יותר מההכאה, כי הכל שוה אצל הסלע. ועוד למה אמר בזה (דברים לב:נא) מעלתם בי. והצוואה בדבור אל הסלע הזה הוא מה שנזכר במעשה, צוה שיאמרו והיא שומעת כי השם יוציא מים מן הסלע הזה, כדרך כי היא שמעה את כל אמרי ה׳ (יהושע כד:כז), וכן עשו כמו שאמר (פסוק י) ויקהילו משה ואהרן את הקהל אל פני הסלע ויאמר להם וגו׳, והנה הסלע שומעת באמרו כן לכולן.

Ramban firsts sites Rashi's view that the sin of Moshe was that he hit the rock instead of speaking to the rock. Ramban notes that this interpretation is based on Chazal but does not make sense for a number of reasons. The questions Ramban asks would indicate the interpretation is wrong, and not just incorrect on a level of *pshat*. His language אבל לא נתחוורו also supports this notion.

92. R. Mayer Twersky understood based on sources such as these that Ramban maintains that one may argue with Chazal in non-halachic contexts. We might add that Ramban does not simply dismiss the interpretation of Chazal. Rather, he argues it is inconsistent with other Torah sources. In that sense, he is doing something similar to Rambam as discussed in 6.4.

קנקניה. געת זמן תנינית. אמר ליה, אסור תורתך אסור פדנך אסור קנקנך, דאיתיליד משיחכון.

ואען ואומר: **איני מאמין בהגדה זו [כלל]** אבל ראיה היא לדברי.

אז זעק אותו האיש (ואמר): ראו שהוא מכחיש בספרים שלהם.

אמרתי: **באמת שאיני מאמין שנולד המשיח ביום החורבן, וההגדה הזאת או שאינה אמת או שיש לה פירוש אחר מסתרי החכמים.** אבל אקבל אותה כפשטה כאשר אמרת, כי ראיה היא לי. הנה היא אומרת כי ביום החורבן אחרי שנחרב (הבית) בו ביום נולד המשיח. אם כן אין ישו משיח כאשר אמרתם, שהוא קודם החורבן נולד ונהרג, ולידתו קרוב למאתיים שנה קודם החורבן לפי האמת, ולפי חשבוניכם ע״ג שנה. אז נשתתק האיש...

Friar Pul (i.e., Pablo) then reverted [to the original topic], arguing that they say in the Talmud that the Messiah already has come. He quoted the homily in the Midrash on Lamentations concerning a [Jewish] farmer whose cow lowed while he was plowing. A passing Arab called to him, "Israelite, Israelite, untie your cow, untie your plow, take apart your plowshare, for the Temple has been destroyed." So he untied the cow, untied the plow, and disassembled the plowshare. The cow then lowed a second time. The Arab said to him, "Tie your cow, tie your plow, tie your plowshare, for your Messiah has been born."

I responded, "**I do not believe in this aggada at all**, but [in any case] it is a proof to my words."

Friar Pul shouted, "See, he [himself] is renouncing their [sacred] books!"

I elaborated, "**Truly, I do not believe that Messiah was born on the day of the [Temple's] destruction. Either this homily is not true or it has another meaning, [which lies] among the secrets of the Sages**. Yet [even if] I would accept its literal meaning as you have expressed it, then it is a proof for my contention, for this [midrash] relates that the Messiah was born on the day of the destruction, after that event. If so, the Nazarene could not be the Messiah as you have said, for he was born and was killed before the destruction. According to the truth, his birth took place about two hundred years before the destruction, and according to your reckoning, [it occurred] seventy-three years [before the destruction]." The man thereupon was silenced…

חזר אותו האיש ואמר כי בתלמוד מפורש שרבי יהושע בן לוי שאל לאליהו מתי יבוא המשיח, והוא ענה אותו: שאל למשיח עצמו. (אמר) והיכן הוא?(אמר) בפתח דרומה (של רומא) בין החולים. הלך שם ומצאו. ושאל לו כו׳. אם כן כבר בא, והוא ברומה, (והוא ישו המושל ברומה).

עניתי לו: והלא מפורש מכאן שלא בא, שהרי שאל לאליהו מתי יבוא. וכן שאל אליו בעצמו מתי אתי מר. אם כן לא בא עדיין. אבל נולד כפי פשוטי אלו ההגדות, ואיני מאמין בכך.

...קמתי ואומר: שמעו עמים כולם. פראי פול שאלני אם כבר בא המשיח שדברו בו הנביאים, ואמרתי שלא בא. והביא ספר אגדה שאמר בו כי ביום שחרב בית המקדש בו ביום נולד. **ואמרתי אני שאיני מאמין בזה.**

(דעו כי) אנחנו יש לנו שלושה מינין של ספרים, האחד הוא הבב"ליה וכולנו מאמינים בו אמונה שלמה. והשני הוא נקרא תלמוד, והוא פירוש למצוות התורה, כי בתורה יש תרי"ג מצוות ואין בה אחת שלא נתפרשה בתלמוד, ואנחנו מאמינים בו **בפירוש המצוות.** עוד יש לנו ספר שלישי הנקרא **מדרש, רוצה לומר שרמ"וניש.** כמו שאם יעמוד ההגמון ויעשה שרמון (אחד), ואחד מן השומעים היה טוב בעיניו וכתבו. **וזה הספר מי שיאמין בו טוב, ומי שלא יאמין בו לא יזיק.**

[Friar Pul] reverted [to the original theme] and said that it is explained in the Talmud that R. Yehoshua b. Levi asked Elijah [the prophet], "When will Messiah come?" He answered him, "Ask Messiah himself." He said, "Where is he?" [Elijah] replied,

> "At the gate of Rome, among the sick." So [R. Yehoshua b. Levi] went there, and he found him. He asked him, etc. Thus, he had already come, and he is the Nazarene, who rules in Rome.
>
> I retorted, "Is it not clearly written here that he has not come? Did [the rabbi] not ask Elijah, 'When will he come?' Similarly, [the rabbi] asked the Messiah, 'When will the master come?' Thus, he had not yet come, although according to the literal meaning of these homilies, he already was born; **but I do not believe in that**."
>
> … I got up and said: "Listen everybody. Friar Pul asked me if the Messiah described by the Prophets already has come, and I said that he did not come. And he cited a book of Aggada that states that on the day the Temple was destroyed he was born. And I said that I do not believe in that. Know that we have three types of literature: the first is Scripture, which we all believe in with complete faith. The second is Talmud, which is an explanation of the commandments of the Torah, for in the Torah there are 613 commandments, and every one of them is explained in the Talmud, and we believe in it **with respect to the explanations of *mitzvot*** (i.e., Halacha). The third is called Midrash, meaning sermons. Imagine that the bishop would arise and deliver a sermon and one of the listeners thought well of it and wrote it down. **Concerning this sort of book, if someone believes in it, fine, and if he does not, there is no harm.**[93]

Ramban was asked a question based on midrashim that indicate that *mashiach* has already come. He responded by saying he does not believe in that Aggada. Later, he clarifies that either the Aggada is false or it has an esoteric meaning. Later on, he is asked a similar question and again he responds that he is not bothered by such sources, as they are not authoritative. He writes that there are three sorts of texts: Scripture, Halacha, and Midrash (which Ramban translates into Latin as sermons) – the first two

93. Translation partially adapted from that of Hyam Maccoby in *Judaism on Trial Jewish-Christian Disputations in the Middle Ages*, pp. 102–146.

are binding, while the third is not. Moreover, he does not distinguish between midrashim in the Talmud and those quoted by other sources.

Seemingly, he accepts the view of the Geonim that Aggada is not binding. It is also noteworthy that he translates Midrash as sermon. However, we must ask whether Ramban actually believed what he said or said it merely to defend the faith. In other words, perhaps he felt that Aggada is authoritative but that any explanation he would have given for such passages would not have been accepted by his interlocutors, and as such, he dismissed these statements.[94]

R. Ari Yizchak Shevet[95] notes that this question has been debated for centuries with three schools of thought emerging. Some claim that Ramban's statements concerning Aggada do not reflect his own attitude towards Aggada.[96] R. Charles Chavel (in his notes to p. 308 of *Kitvei ha-Ramban*), for example, cites R. Mordechai Alisberg, who wrote that it is obvious that Ramban did not mean what he said.[97] This is the position of R. Dr. Isadore Twersky as well,[98] who writes that in light of Ramban's general approach of using midrashim to show the depth of Halacha, it is clear that he could not mean what he said here. Moreover, whenever Ramban encounters a midrash that is halachically problematic, he does

94. If this were the case, it seemingly would violate Maharshal's theory (ים של שלמה מסכת בבא קמא פרק ד) that one may not distort the Torah even to save one's own life. Perhaps one could counter that here, the safety of the entire community was at stake; this argument, though, would not conform to Maharshal's proof for his theory from the story in which the rabbis taught the Roman emissaries even laws that discriminate between Jews and non-Jews despite the fear that doing so would endanger the nation. Maharshal might respond that here, Ramban's intention was not to save his own life, but rather to prevent an even greater misrepresentation of the Torah.

95. In an article entitled תוקפם המחייב של מדרשי חז"ל גישתו של הרמב"ן לאור הוויכוח בברצלונה in צוהר, יא תשס"ב (pp. 49–68).

96. Ramban would not have been first to do this. In a debate in 1240, R. Yechiel of Paris, one of the Tosafists, adopted the same position concerning Aggada, even though it is almost certain that this does not reflect his true attitude.

97. ברור הדבר שאלו הדברים שאמרן הרמב"ן בפיו ביטלן בלבו... ברור שאלו הדברים נתנו מקום לקלי הדעת לבלי להאמין לכל דברי ההגדה והמדרשים... ובכל זה לא חש לכל זה כלל, בראותו את עצמו נלחץ למען הצלת כל הדת.

R. Chavel himself is unsure.

98. *Rabbi Moses ben Nachman: Explorations in His Religious and Literary Virtuosity*, Introduction, p. 7 (Cambridge, Mass.: Harvard University Press, 1983).

not dismiss it as non-binding, as he does here, but instead attempts to explain it (see, for example, *Chiddushei ha-Ramban Ketubot* 61a).

The second school of thought argues that we must take Ramban at his word. They point out that Ramban publicized his record of the debate only two years after it took place. Why would he publicize a text that contains a major theological error? Moreover, Ramban expresses his position with such vehemence that the implication is that he believed what he was saying (איני מאמין בהגדה זו [כלל], או שאגדה זו אינה אמת, ואיני מאמין בכך). These proofs could be rebuffed considering the value of recording an accurate transcription.

R. Ari Yizchak Shevet offers a compromise position by distinguishing between different types of midrashim. When Ramban refers to "sermons," he is not necessarily referring to all Aggada.

Perhaps the simplest solution is that Ramban certainly believes that all midrashim are true in the sense that they contain profound wisdom. However, many midrashim should be understood allegorically or, at the very least, not in their plain sense. (Therefore, one may choose whether or not to accept them in the way in which they are being presented.) If this is the case, a perplexing midrash never can undermine accepted principles, such as the notion that *mashiach* has not come. Should someone cite such a midrash to refute an accepted principle, the defender of the faith is justified in dismissing it, as it certainly is false in the sense that it is being cited; the defender need not cite an alternative explanation in his defense. In this sense, midrashim are different than Scripture or halachic texts where, as Ramban explains, a defender certainly would have to justify any counter-evidence. As we saw in 5.4, this thesis is rooted in Maharal.[99]

99. Yoni Rabinovitch noted that a difficulty with this explanation is that Ramban writes: "וההגדה הזאת או שאינה אמת או שיש לה פירוש אחר מסתרי החכמים," which implies two different solutions and not just one. Interestingly, when Friar Pul questions him regarding *Yeshayahu* 53 (the suffering servant) Ramban responds, "According to the truthful meaning it is only speaking of the Jewish people in general. The prophet continually calls them 'Yisrael My servant' 'Yisrael My servant'." In other words, "servant" frequently refers to the Jewish people collectively, not an individual and certainly not the Messiah. Friar Pul then cites a midrash which understands the prophecy as referring to the Messiah. Ramban

7.13 APPENDIX D: INSTANCES WHERE THE *DRASH* INFORMS US OF THE PHYSICAL REALITY

In this chapter, we have considered numerous cases where some thinkers have argued that in cases where *pshat* and *drash* offer disparate accounts of what happened, *pshat* corresponds to physical reality, while *drash* is intended to help us understand the deeper meaning of the events described in the text. There may be cases where the reverse is true, namely, that the *drash* corresponds to what actually happened. In 7.10, we considered an example of this possibility in Ramban's commentary.

An illustration of this phenomenon in Chazal concerns the date in which the walls of Yerushalayim were breached during the destruction of the first *Beit ha-Mikdash*. The verse in *Yirmiyahu* (52:7) reports that this took place on the 9th of Tammuz. The Talmud Bavli (*Ta'anit* 28b) asks how this fits with the mishna that states that the walls were breached on the 17th of Tammuz. It replies that during the destruction of the first *Beit ha-Mikdash*, the walls were breached on the 9th, while during the destruction of the second *Beit ha-Mikdash*, the event took place on the 17th.

The Talmud Yerushalmi, however, records a different solution. In reality the walls were destroyed on the 17th, as described in the mishna. However, the verses record the perception and memory of the people, who remembered the event as having taken place on the 9th.[100] In other words,

---

responds: "It is true that our Rabbis, their memory is for a blessing, in their works of Haggada, have a midrash that it is about the Messiah; however, they do not state that he is killed by his enemies." In other words, even the Midrashic explanation cannot possibly be referring to Jesus. He then pledges to explain the midrash elsewhere. He fulfills the promise in an essay entitled באור על פרשת הנה ישכיל עבדי where he reiterates that the collective explanation (i.e., that the servant refers to the entire Jewish people) is correct (הנכון בפרשה הזאת שהיא על ישראל כלו), however, he proceeds to explain what the midrash actually meant. Why did he feel compelled to explain the midrash in this instance and not in the example mentioned in the text? Was it because this midrash is more authoritative and less easily dismissed? Or, perhaps, because the prophecy of the suffering servant was so frequently used in anti-Jewish polemics that he felt more of a need to explain Chazal.

100. **תלמוד ירושלמי מסכת תענית פרק ד ה"ה**
והובקעה העיר כתיב בתשעה לחדש הובקעה העיר ואת אמר הכין אמר ר' תנחום בר חנילאי קילקול חשבונות יש כאן.

what really happened is recorded in the oral law, while Scripture records the people's perception. Why is their inaccurate perspective recorded? *Korban ha-Eida* explains that it grants meaning to the story. It conveys the confusion and chaos experienced by the Jews at the time of the destruction; they even lost track of time. Moreover, by including the error in the text, the verse highlights that God too experienced the pain, as it were.[101] Had the verse written only the accurate date, we would not be aware of the degree of trauma that the people (and God) experienced. Conversely, if we had only the written record of the 9th, we would be unaware of the history. Together, Scripture and tradition portray the full truth.[102]

7.14 APPENDIX E: RED LINES AND LIMITS TO *PSHAT*

Are There Limits?

Thus far, we have seen many commentaries offer interpretations that differ from Chazal, in the words of Rashbam cited above (7.4), לפי הפשטות המתחדשים בכל יום, "according to the new insights of *pshat* that arise each day." One question that arises relates to whether there are limits? Consider the possibility we alluded to earlier (7.4), could one argue that in the story of *Parshat Toldot* Yaakov is the duplicitous villain? I believe a careful reading of the *pesukim* does not allow for such a reading. But, let's imagine, a person studies the text to the best of their ability and arrives at such an unfathomable conclusion.[103] Could they say my interpretation is correct on a level of *pshat* since it is supported by the text of the Torah?

---

101. **קרבן עדה**
מרוב הצרות טעו בחשבונות ולא רצה המקרא לשנות ממה שסמכו הם לומר כביכול אנכי עמו בצרה

102. Interestingly, as noted in 8.14, R. Kook uses this notion to explain why scientific inaccuracy might be implied by the text of the Torah. He suggests this happens when it will facilitate the furthering of Scripture's message. Just as a mistake in history is recorded to highlight the plight of the Jews, so too an inaccuracy in science may be included to bring us to a greater appreciation of God's might.

103. While traditional commentaries debate the degree to which we should see Yaakov's actions in this episode as righteous and Eisav's as villainous (see, for example, *Bechor Shor* who presents Eisav in a reasonably positive light), no traditional commentaries, as far as I know, depict Yaakov as a scoundrel.

I believe the answer is no. To appreciate this, let us draw an analogy from Rambam's treatment of creation *ex nehilo* discussed in 3.3. The predominant scientific and philosophical viewpoint in Rambam's era rejected creation, accepting instead the Aristotelian notion that matter is eternal. Rambam (*Moreh ha-Nevuchim* 2:25) rejects this position not because of the text of *Parshat Bereishit*, which could conceivably be read in a way that is consistent with the Aristotelian position, but for two other reasons. Firstly, Aristotle's view has not been proved definitively. Secondly, and this is what is relevant for our discussion, Rambam argues that the basis of the Torah is conceivable only if we reject Aristotle.[104] There are limits. Rambam is informing us that when considering the appropriateness of an interpretation, there are more than textual limitations.

I believe the same thing can be said about certain basic Torah principles that we know from Chazal, such as the rectitude of Yaakov.[105] This does not mean Yaakov was perfect. Chazal themselves criticize some of his decisions. But there is no question that he was a *tzaddik* chosen by God to carry on the legacy of Avraham and Yitzchak.[106]

104. This is because if Aristotle were correct, miracles and prophecy would be impossible. (Aristotle believed that the universe has its present form as the result of fixed and necessary laws and thus cannot be altered by supernatural forces.) Yet the Torah clearly accepts miracles and prophecies. To interpret the Torah figuratively, such that there are no miracles or prophecy, would undermine more than the first chapter of *Bereishit*.

105. This idea was conveyed to me by many of my teachers, including R. Aaron Lopiansky and R. Moshe Stav. R. Stav cited the Introduction of the *Sefer ha-Chinuch* as an expression of this idea: "Among the fundamentals of the Torah is to believe that the true explanation of the Torah is the traditional received explanation that is in our hands from the early Sages of Israel. And anyone who explains about it something that is **the opposite of their intention** is [expressing] a mistake and a completely void thing." R. Stav understood that this allows for explaining matters differently than Chazal, but never the opposite of Chazal.

106. R. Shalom Carmy ("Homer and the Bible" Tradition 41:4 [Winter 2008], 1–7) offers a different type of critique on this sort of approach:

> "One manifestation of this 'new irreverence' is the proliferation of interpretations, presented in the lingo of pop psychology, purporting to take the Avot and other sanctified biblical personalities down from their pedestal, and bring them down to earth. In Israel this is called Tanakh be-govah einayim. 'Bible at eye level' sees the Avot as dysfunctional guys very much like the ones in our society. For people like me, precisely because we want psychological insight to animate our religious life and do not want to treat biblical characters as "petrified statues of ossified

Two Examples of Red Lines

An illustration of the principle emerges from a debate concerning Nimrod. Chazal portray Nimrod as the epitome of evil. Among other things, he attempts to fight God through the tower of Bavel and kill Avram in a fiery furnace. His very name, which comes from the root *mered* or rebel, alludes to his primary objective – to rebel against God. (Who else could the most powerful person on earth rebel against?)

However, the text of the Torah (*Bereishit* 10:9), *gibor tzayid lifnei Hashem,* is ambiguous. Ibn Ezra translates this phrase as meaning "a mighty hunter in the presence of God." This understanding allows ibn Ezra to suggest a positive conception of Nimrod: "Nimrod was the first to show mankind's might over the animals for he was a 'mighty hunter.' The phrase 'before God' tells us that Nimrod would build altars to God and sacrifice the animals that he caught to God. This is the straightforward reading of the text (*derech ha-pshat*); however the midrash chooses a different reading." Ibn Ezra notes that his explanation differs from Chazal, but insists it is right on a level of *pshat.*

Ramban disagrees: "How can he be correct? He has transformed the *rasha* into a *tzaddik*! Our Sages know from the earliest tradition that Nimrod was evil." Ramban's principle contention is not textual. He asks no textual questions upon ibn Ezra, as he frequently does. Instead, he asserts that ibn Ezra has crossed the line cited above.

But why does Ramban contest ibn Ezra's rejection of the midrash when Ramban himself regularly does the very same thing, explaining a verse according to *pshat* in a way that varies from *drash*? This Ramban, it would seem, alludes to an important principle in *parshanut* (biblical exegesis). While not every interpretation of Midrash may be the result of a tradition, nevertheless there are some basic and uncontested ideas, such as Nimrod's wickedness, that reflect tradition and cannot be questioned,

tsidkut" (R. Lichtenstein's phrase), the results are disappointing. The tragedy is not only that they shrink the Avot to our size, but that, failing to recognize the shaping religious personalities of our tradition in their magnificence we lose the aspiration to live religiously passionate lives ourselves. We subject ourselves to the casual deterministic assumptions, clichéd depictions of emotion, typical of the therapeutic outlook at its dreariest, and adopt a philosophy that cannot grasp the dramatic, absolute, momentous solemnity of the moral-religious life.

even on a level of *pshat*. How did Ramban know this? Why is it different from the specific interpretations of the *pesukim* which Ramban frequently rejects, at least on a level of *pshat*? The answer seems to be that basic uncontested assumptions in Chazal *must* reflect a tradition.[107] Thus, even though Ramban's explanation of the above verse differs from that of Chazal, it is in keeping with the basic premise that Nimrod was wicked.[108]

Does ibn Ezra fundamentally disagree with Ramban and maintain that one can argue with a tradition of Chazal even on a level of *pshat*? Certainly not. Thus, often when ibn Ezra is inclined to disagree with Chazal, he prefaces his maverick ideas with qualifications such as the following **ואם דברי קבלה נקבל ומדרך סברא אין זה נכון**, "if the interpretation of Chazal is based on tradition, we accept it, but if it is not, then it is incorrect" (*Bereishit* 22:5). Likewise, in many places, such as *Shemot* 15:22, ibn Ezra states explicitly that he withdraws his explanation if it is the case that it argues with a tradition of Chazal (**ואם קבלה היא ששבעה ענני כבוד היו נניח סברתינו ונסמוך על הקבלה**). Thus, both Ramban and ibn Ezra agree that one may explain a verse differently from an interpretation of Chazal, but not when it disagrees with a tradition of Chazal. In this particular case they disagree whether or not there is a tradition, with Ramban maintaining that the uncontested assumption of Chazal that Nimrod was wicked must reflect a tradition and ibn Ezra rejecting that contention (perhaps because of Nimrod's relative unimportance on a level of *pshat*).[109] Clearly, whether or not an idea in Chazal is a tradition is not always clear-cut. However, what is most relevant

---

107. This may parallel Rambam's contention in his Introduction to the Mishna concerning uncontested halachic assumptions.

108. Interestingly there are other red lines that seem to bother ibn Ezra much more than Ramban. Earlier we considered how Ramban interprets halachic texts in manners that are not consistent with the practical Halacha. Ibn Ezra in a number of places, especially his famous letter on Shabbat, seems less inclined to do that.

109. Interestingly, R. Yoram Bogacz discovered a midrash that is consistent with ibn Ezra's understanding of Nimrod (presumably neither Ramban nor ibn Ezra had access to this particular source):

מדרש בראשית רבתי ממשה הדרשן

...שלאדם הראשון לא הותרה לו בשר תאוה, ולא הותר לו אלא עשבים ופירות... אבל לנח התיר... ואף על פי כן לא רצה נח ובניו לאכול מהם... כשעמד נמרוד אמר, "הקדוש ברוך הוא התירם לנו. מפני מה אין אנו אוכלין מהם?!" התחיל לצוד ולאכול. הדא הוא דכתיב גִּבֹּר צַיִד לִפְנֵי ה׳, שעשה מצותו של הקדוש ברוך הוא וצד ואכל.

for us is Ramban's contention, which has been largely accepted, that basic assumptions of Chazal, especially when they relate to fundamental matters, should not be discarded even when interpreting on a level of *pshat*.[110]

Let us consider one more example of a possible red line. R. Soloveitchik maintained that there is no "*pshat*" in *Shir ha-Shirim*:

> The allegorical character of the Song of Songs is a firm principle of the Halakhah, upon which are founded both the physical sanctity of the scroll of Song of Songs as not to be touched (*Yadayim* 3:5), and the sanctity of the name Shelomoh, occurrences of which in the Song of Songs are interpreted allegorically as appellations for God. The aggadic tradition also interprets the Song of Songs symbolically.... The book cannot be interpreted according to *pshat*. In all of the rest of the Torah, we are permitted to interpret the verses according to either the Midrashic reading or the plain sense... In this case, the symbolic method is the only one we can use. Anyone who explains this book, in accordance with the literal meaning of the words, as referring to sensual love, defiles its sanctity and denies the Oral Torah.[111]

---

110. Ramban's comments here must also be considered within the broader debate between him and ibn Ezra (who is but one leading member of an entire exegetical school), which, among other things, concerns the value and role of Chazal in *parshanut ha-mikra*. Either way, it is not my claim that all great thinkers strictly speaking abide by the above red line. Consider the Izbetzer's interpretation of the Zimri-Pinchas episode (of course, he was not interpreting on a level of *pshat*). Rather, this guideline, rooted in Ramban, reflects the mainstream and generally accepted approach. It is certainly one that ordinary people should seek to follow.

111. *From There You Shall Seek*, translated by Naomi Goldblum, pp. 151–153. See *Nefesh Harav* page 289–290 and https://www.ou.org/torah/parsha/vayigdal-moshe/parshas-behaaloscha-2/. In what sense is this work different from other biblical allegories, which should be understood as having a *mashal* and *nimshal*? Clearly, the fact that human love is used to allegorize our relationship with the Divine reflects the reality that the powerful emotions between people is the best vehicle to portray the love between the Jewish people and God.

    To appreciate what the Rav was saying, we can compare his statement to Rambam's comments about *Mishlei* in his Introduction to *Moreh ha-Nevuchim*. There, Rambam explains that biblical metaphors generally offer insight on two levels: "The parables of the Prophets are similar [to a golden apple overlaid in silver]. Their *pshat* [represented by the silver overlay] contains wisdom that is useful in many

Generally, when *pesukim* speak allegorically, there is a *mashal* – the vehicle of the message being conveyed – and the *nimshal,* which is the message being conveyed. This is not the case for *Shir ha-Shirim.* While Rashi, Rashbam, and ibn Ezra all elucidate the verses according to *pshat,* they see the *pshat* as an allegory. What R. Soloveitchik claimed is that the assertion that on a level of *pshat Shir ha-Shirim* is a collection of love poems, entirely lacking in religious content, is false. Regarding such a basic and uncontested issue, the position of Chazal reflects a tradition which cannot be debated, even on a level of *pshat.* Hence, R. Akiva (Tosefta *Sanhedrin* 12:10) said if someone treats *Shir ha-Shirim* as a love-song, he has no portion in the world-to-come.

R. Soloveitchik compares this to Rambam's idea that when there is a tradition to the correct understanding of a particular verse, then all other interpretations are false. "In these cases, only the *derasha* exists; the plain meaning has been completely abolished. To interpret literally… 'an eye for an eye'… constitutes denial of our tradition."[112] Of course, this does not mean one may ignore the literal reading. As we have seen, Rambam (*Hilchot Choveil u-Mazik,* Ch. 1 and 5) derives significant halachic and philosophical lessons from the Torah's referring to this particular monetary payment as a penalty. Likewise, the fact that God chose to allegorize His relationship with the Jewish people through romantic human affection teaches us a great deal about the nature of religious love. Thus, even when the Halacha (according to R. Soloveitchik) places methodological limitations on *pshat,* one can never ignore the text.

---

respects, among which is the welfare of human societies, as is shown by the *pshat* of *Mishlei* and of similar sayings. Their deeper meaning [comparable to the golden core] contains wisdom that allows a person to apprehend the truth as it is." Perhaps R. Soloveitchik intended to contrast *sefarim* like *Mishlei* which convey wisdom and truth on multiple levels, to *Shir ha-Shirim.* Do not say that on a simple but true level *Shir ha-Shirim* is Shlomo's profession of love towards a woman and on a deeper level it reflects the relationship between the Jewish people and God, rather the only true level of interpretation is the *nimshal.* Of course, to understand the *nimshal* one must understand the *mashal.* Hence, Rashi, Rashbam, and ibn Ezra all carefully elucidate the *mashal* independently of the *nimshal.* If that is indeed what R. Soloveitchik intended, it would seem that there are those who disagree. Consider R. Yitzchak Arama's Introduction to *Shir ha-Shirim* who writes: "ומעתה נבאר המגלה הזאת לפי חמר המשל כי הוא **דבר ראוי ונאות** ואח"כ נבא אל הנמשל."

112. Ibid. p. 153.

Conclusion

On a practical level, this means that anyone who engages in the valuable pursuit of discovering novel interpretations of Scripture must be wary of going too far. Even if one accepts the view that the non-halachic words of Chazal are not binding and even if one simply claims his interpretation is true only on a level of *pshat*, an explanation that deviates from fundamental and universal assumptions made by Chazal is wrong and intolerable.

To be sure, there is no clear line. Great people may debate whether a particular interpretation is tenable. However, the values, worldview, and basic assumptions of Chazal are not the inventions of mortals but traditions stemming from Sinai. As such, they are sacrosanct and uncontestable on any level of interpretation. Of course, the above analysis will not always provide clear-cut guidelines. Some of the traditional commentators display remarkable creativity explaining Scripture in a way that deviates substantially from Chazal.[113] I cannot tell you whether a particular interpretation has crossed the line. Such a decision often requires the intuition of a *gadol*. However, ultimately, we must always treat the words of Chazal with reverence and accept that there are even limits on *pshat*.[114]

7.15 APPENDIX F: HISTORY IN THE POST-BIBLICAL PERIOD

Why is there so little recorded history in the post-biblical period? True, Talmudic literature relates numerous stories, but expresses little interest in systematic history. It is not just the Talmud that omits this course of study. Dr. Yosef Hayim Yerushalmi in *Zakhor: Jewish History and Jewish Memory* (University of Washington Press, Seattle 1982) notes that the

113. Consider the following examples: Ralbag (and Drashot ha-Ran) contends that the people did not sin with the tower of Bavel; God's motivation was actually to ensure the dispersal of humanity in order to guarantee its survival in the event of a major catastrophe; Rambam understands that angels did not visit Avraham when he was sick, but that the episode took place in a dream; Rashbam argues that the brothers did not sell Yosef, but rather left him in the pit and the Midianites sold him to the Ishmaelites; ibn Ezra asserts that Yocheved could not have been born on the way down to Egypt and that several of the plagues, including the first, affected Jew and Gentile indiscriminately, and Ralbag claims that there were no real walls in the splitting of the sea.

114. I would like to thank the following people who contributed to my understanding explicated in Appendix E: Rabbis Yitzhak Grossman, Matt Lubin, and Doni Zuckerman.

Rishonim for the most part do not engage in the study of history. He notes that the lack of interest in history in the medieval period cannot be attributed to the lack of Talmudic material, since medieval Jewry "blazed new paths in philosophy, science, linguistics, secular and metrical Hebrew poetry, none of which had precedents in the Talmudic history. Only in historiography, a field in which Islamic civilization excelled and forged an important tradition, did a similar interaction fail to take place" (33).[115]

In 7.7 we considered the possibility that the answer to this question lies in the Talmudic concept of *mai de-havei havei* (whatever happened already happened). Essentially, this is Yerushalmi's solution. "The modern effort to reconstruct the past," writes Yerushalmi, "begins at a time that witnesses a sharp break in the continuity of Jewish living and hence also an ever-growing decay of Jewish group memory. In this sense, if for no other, history becomes what it had never been before – the faith of fallen Jews." That is not to say that Jews did not believe the events happened. Rather, instead of approaching history from a dispassionate academic perspective, Jewish thinkers would look to the past to cement their relationship with God and shape their belief in Him and His people. Yerushalmi calls this "memory," not history. In 7.7 we considered why such an approach does not fully answer the question.

Another thinker to address this question at around the same time as Yerushalmi was R. Shimon Schwab. In an article originally published in *Mitteilungen* (Dec. Mar. 1984–85) and reprinted in *Selected Writings* (Lakewood, N.J., 1988, pp. 232–235), R. Schwab notes that even though "the story of Chanukah is described in detail in the Book of Maccabees," in Chazal there are "only a few scant references to this epic drama." Moreover:

> We have no authentic description by our Tanaim of the period of the Churban, the Jewish war against the Romans, the destruction of the Jewish state, the revolt and the downfall of Bar Kochba, except for a few Haggadic sayings in Talmud and Midrash. For

115. Yerushalmi deals with the handful of possible exceptions, such as *Yosippon, Seder Olam,* and *Sefer ha-Kabbala*. While in the early-modern period Jewish historical works began to emerge, Yerushalmi claims that their authors largely were influenced by non-Jewish sources, or, later, were traditionalist responses to those works.

> our historical knowledge we have to rely on the renegade, Josephus Flavius, who was a friend of Rome and a traitor to his people.
>
> Come to think of it, since the close of the Tanach at the beginning of the Second Beis Hamikdash, we have no Jewish history book composed by our Sophrim, Tanaim and Amoraim. The prophets and the Anshei Knesses HaGedolah have recorded all the events of their days as well as all previous periods. When prophecy ceased, the recording of Jewish history stopped at the same time. Why did our great Torah leaders not deem it necessary to register in detail all the events of their period just as the Neviim had done before them?

R. Schwab suggests a fascinating answer – to record history would be a violation of *lashon ha-ra*:

> There is a vast difference between history and storytelling. History must be truthful; otherwise it does not deserve its name. A book of history must report the bad with the good, the ugly with the beautiful... the guilt and the virtue... It cannot spare the righteous if he fails, and it cannot skip the virtues of the villain.

Essentially, only with God's directive can we record the unflattering truths of history. (This may relate to another fascinating position of R. Schwab concerning the controversy regarding the chronology of the kings of Persia. Modern scholarship assumes that the Persian empire spanned approximately 206 and that the Second Temple stood for approximately 585 years. Chazal, on the other hand, presume the Persian empire lasted only 52 years with the Second Temple standing for just 420 years. In a 1962 essay R. Schwab maintained that the rabbis had intentionally obscured "the missing years" in order to prevent calculating the time of the coming of *mashiach*, see *Daniel* 11:2. However, in a 1991 revision of his 1962 work, R. Schwab recanted his position expressing uncertainty on the matter.) R. Schwab's theory, while interesting, raises a number of questions. How can one transmit a *mesora* if it is not entirely truthful? How do we explain the numerous stories in the Talmud that do, in fact, portray great people negatively?[116] R. Yaakov Kamenetsky (*Emet le-Yaakov, Bereishit* 37:18) appears to disagree with R. Schwab's theory, maintaining that history about those who are no longer alive would not formally violate *lashon ha-ra* and is appropriate when there is significant value.[117]

Another approach to why historical details of the Chanuka story are not recorded in Chazal can be found in R. Shlomo Brevda's להודות ולהלל (adapted into English as *The Miracles of Chanukah*). He suggests that Chazal deliberately concealed much of the Chanuka story to protect us from reading potentially harmful material. As a precedent, he cites Ramban's comments to *Bereishit* 12:2. Ramban inquires about the many missing details in Avraham Avinu's life story, from when he is born at the end of *parshat Noach* until Hashem tells him to leave his home (beginning of *parshat Lech Lecha*) when Avraham is 75 years old (*Bereishit* 12:4). Ramban answers that the Torah is not fond of discussing idolatrous ideology. Avraham fled Ur Kasdim for the land of Canaan because of the opposition and abuse that he faced there for believing in Hashem. The Torah wished to avoid speaking about the heretical beliefs of those that opposed Avraham and to skip the religious debate between him and the people of Ur Kasdim. Ramban adds that this is also the reason the Torah does not elaborate on the advent of idolatry in the generation of Enosh, merely alluding to it.

R. Brevda notes that the principle that the Torah refrains from discussing foreign philosophies may also be found in the comments of *Chasid Ya'avetz* to *Pirkei Avot* 5:2. *Chasid Ya'avetz* asks why the Torah did not discuss the huge miracle of Avraham's being saved from the furnace in Ur Kasdim. He answers that the Torah refrained from sharing Avraham's history because Avraham had been arguing with the people of Ur Kasdim using logical arguments, like any philosopher would, and

116. See *Nefesh ha-Chaim – Perakim* Ch. 8 regarding the incident of R. Amram Chasida recorded in *Kiddushin* 81a ונראה הגם שהקב"ה חס על כבודן של צדיקים, עם כל זה קבעוה להאי עובדא בתלמוד, להורות לנו דרכי ה' הישרים. See, also, *Chavot Yair* 152 who reinterprets the harsh statements of numerous Sages in ways that make them seem gentle.

117. See *Brachot* 19a *"kol ha-misaper acharei ha-meit k-eelu misaper acharei ha-even."* Negative speech about the dead would violate the *cheirem kadmonim* recorded in *Shulchan Aruch* O.C. 606:3. Presumably, it would only be appropriate when there is a value (i.e., it is *le-to'elet*) and not in violation of the *cheirem*.

Hashem wants us to follow His commands for His sake because they are His commands, not because the *mitzvot* make sense to us logically. Likewise, details of the Chanuka story were omitted because the religious danger they pose. While this theory can be used to explain some of the historical omissions, it does not seem to fully account for the general disinterest in history that marks the post-biblical period. Moreover, one might question the degree to which these sources fully answer our question since Avraham's early history is discussed, to some degree, in the Oral Law. (See Chapter 29 where we return to the question of the Torah's omission of Avraham's discovery of God.)

Let us add three additional factors for consideration. First, perhaps the Talmud focuses mainly on wisdom that is inherently valuable (Torah) or that has some sort of practical utility (e.g. medicine). Dr. Yerushalmi wonders why the Rishonim were interested in science and philosophy but not history. Here too, we might respond that these fields, especially when studied the way in which the Rishonim studied them (see 2.9), are inherently valuable. Linguistics too, especially when used to understand and interpret Torah, is intrinsically important. History does not have that same inherent value (it is *mikreh* using Maharal's formulation). While important, insofar as it teaches us important lessons and is even a reflection of God's plans, it lacks the same significance. Thus, while many sources derive instruction from past events, history, in and of itself, lacks the same stature.[118]

Secondly, but along similar lines, from our very inception God instructed us that we are (or can be) above history (צא מאצטגנינות שלך – see *Nedarim* 32a and Rashi to *Bereishit* 15:5). History focuses on secular causation, but the Jewish people merit unique providence (see Ramban *Bereishit* 28:12 and Chapters 38 and 39 of this series). If history reflects nature (טבע), we exist above nature (למעלה מן הטבע).[119] Or, as the Talmud states on *Shabbat* (156a), *ein mazal l-Yisrael,* which seems to mean that Jews are not always bound by fate, and can, at times, rise above the natural (and supernatural) forces that would otherwise shackle a person's

118. As we noted in 7.7 the concept of מאי דהוה הוה need not belittle the value of history. Instead, it may simply mean that Torah is not the venue to convey history.
119. See, for example, *Tiferet Yisrael,* Ch. 2.

destiny. While the above ideas in no way preclude the study of history, they partially explain its lack of prominence.[120]

Finally, as we have noted in a number of places (see 2.10), Providence arranges that certain perspectives develop at particular points in history. Even if traditional Jewish scholars never engaged in Jewish History it is not necessarily the case that the Torah disapproves of such pursuits (see *Chullin* 7a). In fact, the value of honest scholarship by those steeped in Torah knowledge and fear of Heaven is particularly valuable when one considers the anti-Torah bias certain historians have demonstrated. In fact, Dr. Michael A. Meyer notes the anti-traditional agenda employed by many Jewish historians of the 18th and 19th century:

> The use of Jewish historiography to undermine the acceptability of prevalent religious norms continued well into the nineteenth century. The movement for religious reform in Judaism, which burgeoned in Germany during this period, employed historical criticism to loosen the hold of various orthodox beliefs and practices.... Geiger himself had once written that one primary purpose of Jewish historical scholarship was "to prove that everything that presently exists at some point came into being and [therefore] possesses no binding force."[121]

However, theirs was not the only perspective. Indeed, the last century and a half has seen numerous exceptional Torah scholars pursue the study of history, from R. Yitzhak Isaac Halevy (1847–1914) to R. Dr. Isadore Twersky (1930–1997) to R. Dr. Haym Soloveitchik (b. 1937), to name just a few. Regardless of whether some of the early

---

120. The above ideas are frequently emphasized by Maharal. Interestingly, his student, R. David Gans (1541–1613) was a rare example of a pre-modern Jewish historian. His history entitled *Tzemach David*, includes two parts, the first containing the annals of Jewish history, the second those of general history. The introduction to the second section justifies authoring a "profane" subject like general history, showing that it can even be studied on Shabbat.

121. "The Emergence of Jewish Historiography: Motives and Motifs," *History and Theory*, Vol. 27, No. 4, Beiheft 27: Essays in Jewish Historiography (Dec., 1988), pp. 160–175.

traditional Jewish historians were merely responding to the challenges laid down by reformist historians, thinkers such as these have shown us that we need not be scared of history. On the contrary, a robust understanding of our past offers insight and perspective that generates a better understanding of our past, present, and future. Indeed, as R. Tzadok (cited in 8.13) notes, studying history serves as one of the most extraordinary tools to deepen our *emunah*.

Like all disciplines, the study of history can be used for good or bad. It can be a tool to liberate the Jew from tradition by historicizing it, or to create a new attachment to the past by highlighting the eternality of our living Torah.

Unit Three

Belief in God

In this unit, we will consider various ways by which a person can attain and maintain faith in God. We will begin with Rambam's perspective, examining the nature and necessity of philosophical proofs. Then, we explore non-philosophical approaches, with a focus on R. Yehuda ha-Levi. Specifically, we will ponder whether experiential knowledge is preferable to philosophical knowledge. In both chapters of this unit, we will consider the applicability of Rambam and R. Yehuda ha-Levi in our contemporary world.

Chapter Eight

The *Mitzva* of Knowing and Believing in God According to Rambam

In this chapter, we will examine Rambam's understanding of the *mitzva* of *emuna* (faith). Recall that in 1.2, we elucidated Rambam's position (*Hilchot Yesodei ha-Torah* 4:13) that knowing God is mandated by five *mitzvot*: *anochi*, *lo yihyeh*, *shema Yisrael*, *ahavat Hashem*, and *yirat Hashem*. In 1.3, we assessed Rambam's understanding of *ma'aseh merkava* as referring to philosophy or divine science. We described the limits of our understanding of God as well, noting that while we can and should try to understand God to the best of our ability, we cannot comprehend His essence. Finally, having considered (in Chapter 2) the importance of a correct conception of God, we now turn to Rambam's position on the place of philosophy vis-à-vis the *mitzva* of *emuna* and the extent to which philosophical achievements are integral to achieving our purpose in life.

8.1 THE BASICS OF BELIEF

Rambam begins his *magnum opus* with the following passage:

רמב"ם הלכות יסודי התורה פרק א הלכה א

יסוד היסודות ועמוד החכמות **לידע** שיש שם מצוי ראשון, והוא ממציא כל נמצא, וכל הנמצאים משמים וארץ ומה שביניהם לא נמצאו אלא מאמתת המצאו. ואם יעלה על הדעת שהוא אינו מצוי, אין דבר אחר יכול להימצאות. ואם יעלה על הדעת שאין כל הנמצאים מלבדו מצויים, הוא לבדו יהיה מצוי ולא ייבטל הוא לביטולם: שכל הנמצאים צריכין לו; והוא ברוך הוא אינו צריך להם, ולא לאחד מהם. לפיכך אין אמיתתו כאמיתת אחד מהם. הוא שהנביא אומר "וה' אלוהים אמת" (ירמיהו י:י) - הוא לבדו האמת, ואין לאחר אמת כאמיתו. והוא שהתורה אומרת "אין עוד מלבדו" (דברים ד:לה), כלומר אין שם מצוי אמת מלבדו כמותו. המצוי הזה - הוא אלוה העולם, אדון כל הארץ. והוא המנהיג הגלגל בכוח שאין לו קץ ותכלית, בכוח שאין לו הפסק, שהגלגל סובב תמיד, ואי אפשר שיסוב בלא מסבב; והוא ברוך הוא המסבב אותו, בלא יד ולא גוף. **וידיעת דבר זה מצות עשה, שנאמר "אנוכי ה' אלוהיך"** (שמות כ:ב; דברים ה:ו).

The foundation of all foundations and the pillar of wisdom is to **know** (*leida*) that there is a First Being Who brought into being all existence. All existing things, whether celestial, terrestrial, or belonging to an intermediate class, exist only through His true existence. If one would imagine that He does not exist, no other being could possibly exist. If one would imagine that no other entities aside from Him exist, He alone would continue to exist, and the nullification of their [existence] would not nullify His existence, because all the [other] entities require Him and He, blessed be He, does not require them nor any one of them. Therefore, the truth of His [being] does not resemble the truth of their [being]. This is implied by the prophet's statement (*Yirmiyahu* 10:10): "And Hashem, God, is true" – i.e., He alone is true and no other entity possesses truth that compares to His truth. This is what [is meant by] the Torah's statement (*Devarim* 4:35): "There is nothing else aside from Him" – i.e., aside from Him, there is no true existence like His.

> This entity is the God of the world and the Lord of the entire earth. He controls the sphere[1] with infinite and unbounded power. This power [continues] without interruption, for the sphere is revolving constantly, and it is impossible for it to revolve without someone causing it to revolve. And He, blessed be He, causes it to revolve without a hand or any [other] corporeal dimension. **The knowledge of this concept is a positive commandment, as it says (*Shemot* 20:2): "I am Hashem, your God...."**

There are many things a Jew must believe. In Chapter 11, we will consider Rambam's thirteen principles of faith and why their acceptance is indispensable. Here, however, Rambam writes that belief – or, more precisely, knowledge – of God's existence is foundational. Before getting into the details, let us summarize this passage.

1. One must **know** There is a First Being (God).
2. He brought into being all existence.
3. All other existents are contingent, depending upon His existence. Put differently, God necessarily exists (it could not be otherwise), while other existents accidentally exist (they happen to exist).[2] For example, I exist; however, my existence is not necessary; it is contingent upon His willing me to exist. Moreover, while I happen to exist, it could have been otherwise. Indeed, there was a time that I did not exist and there may be a time when I no longer will exist.
4. Various verses express this principle. For example, "And Hashem, God, is true" means that it is necessarily true that God exists. No other being necessarily exists. Therefore, He alone is true and no other entity possesses truth that compares to His truth. Thus, "There is nothing else besides Him" that necessarily exists.

---

1. A reference to the Aristotelian notion of crystalline spheres.
2. It is helpful to refer to "conceivable worlds" to clarify modal terms and concepts. Thus, if something is necessarily true, it is true in all conceivable worlds.

5. If it could be supposed that He does not exist, no other being could possibly exist.
6. The verse "I am Hashem, your God" expresses this *mitzva*.[3] Thus, we are instructed to believe in/know of His necessary existence.[4]

---

3. Is there a place where the Torah explicitly expresses that God's existence is necessary? Here, Rambam mentions, "There is nothing else aside from Him" (*Devarim* 4:35). Elsewhere, Rambam writes how God conveyed the necessity of His existence to Moshe at the burning bush where He calls Himself (*Shemot* 3:14) *Eh-yeh Asher Eh-yeh* ("I will be that which I will be" or "I am that I am"). In *Moreh ha-Nevuchim* (1:63), Rambam explicates the meaning of this appellation:

 > The first noun which is to be described is *Eh-yeh*: the second, by which the first is described, is likewise *Eh-yeh*, the identical word, as if to show that the object which is to be described and the attribute by which it is described are in this case necessarily identical. **This is, therefore, the expression of the idea that God exists, but not in the ordinary sense of the term: or, in other words, He is "the existing Being which is the existing Being," that is to say, the Being whose existence is absolute.**

 This understanding is likely the intent of *Targum Yonatan* and R. Sa'adya Gaon as well. In *Hilchot Yesodei ha-Torah* (above), Rambam implies that it emerges from the words of אנוכי ה' אלוהיך. However, he does not explain precisely how this demand is implied by these words. Perhaps this emerges from how the spelling of the word Hashem (tetragrammaton) refers to God's eternal existence (היה הוה ויהיה). Thus, אנוכי ה' means "I necessarily exist." We should note that the notion that the tetragrammaton refers to God's necessity and eternality is halachically normative. *Tur* (O.C. 5) and *Shulchan Aruch* (O.C. 5:1) state that each time one mentions the name "Hashem," one should think about its meaning based on its pronunciation (He is the master of everything, אדון כל) and its spelling (היה הוה ויהיה). Gra (O.C. 5, based on R. Yona) maintains that having both intentions in mind is only necessary during the first verse of *Shema*.

4. Rambam does not explain how this verse, which seems to be a statement, expresses an obligation to believe in the above principles. Ramban (*Shemot* 20:1), who more or less follows Rambam's understanding, explicates how the statement implies an obligation:

 > אנכי ה' אלוקיך: הדיבור הזה מצוות עשה, אמר אנכי ה', יורה ויצוה אותם שידעו ויאמינו כי יש ה', והוא אלהים להם, כלומר הווה, קדמון, מאתו היה הכל בחפץ ויכולת, והוא אלהים להם, שחייבים לעבוד אותו.

 By saying "I am Hashem," God is demanding that we believe in His existence, eternity, that He is the source for all that exists, and is all-powerful. Ramban notes an additional point not mentioned by Rambam. By adding *Elokecha*, your God, God is instructing us to serve Him. Ramban continues:

 > ואמר אשר הוצאתיך מארץ מצרים, כי הוצאתם משם תורה על המציאות ועל החפץ, כי בידיעה ובהשגחה ממנו יצאנו משם, וגם תורה על החדוש, כי עם קדמות העולם לא ישתנה

8.2 "TO BELIEVE" OR "TO KNOW"

Let us return to Rambam's striking formulation. "The foundation of all foundations and the pillar of wisdom is to **know** that there is a First Being Who brought into being all existence… The **knowledge** of this concept is a positive commandment, as it says (*Shemot* 20:2): 'I am Hashem, your God.'" Apparently, to be a proper Jew, one must *know* (לידע) certain things. Knowing these things is mandated by the *mitzva* of *anochi* (*Shemot* 20:2).

The term לידע implies more than simple belief without understanding. Thus, Rambam includes the basics of physics and metaphysics in the opening chapters of his great halachic work; this information facilitates a correct conception of God and has a role in the proper fulfillment of the *mitzva* of *anochi*.[5] Rambam writes that knowing the information contained in the beginning of this chapter is not just a *mitzva* – it is the foundation of all foundations (יסוד היסודות).

What exactly does Rambam mean when he says we must *know* these things? In *Moreh ha-Nevuchim*, Rambam offers four proofs for the existence of God. Does this mean Rambam believes one must be able to *prove* that God exists to fulfill the *mitzva* of *anochi*?

To address this question, let us analyze the very first *mitzva* of *Sefer ha-Mitzvot*. It is important to note that Rambam wrote his *Sefer ha-Mitzvot* in Arabic (with Hebrew letters), and there is some debate how to translate the Arabic word אעתקאד in Rambam's formulation of *anochi* in *Sefer ha-Mitzvot*.[6] R. Shmuel ibn Tibbon (c. 1150 – c. 1230) translates the Arabic into Hebrew as follows:

דבר מטבעו, ותורה על היכולת, והיכולת תורה על הייחוד, כמו שאמר (ט:יד) בעבור תדע כי אין כמוני בכל הארץ. וזה טעם אשר הוצאתיך, כי הם היודעים ועדים בכל אלה. וטעם מבית עבדים - שהיו עומדים במצרים בבית עבדים, שבויים לפרעה, ואמר להם זה שהם חייבין שיהיה ה׳ הגדול והנכבד והנורא הזה להם לאלהים, שיעבדוהו, כי הוא פדה אותם מעבדות מצרים, כטעם עבדי הם אשר הוצאתי אותם מארץ מצרים (ויקרא כה:נה).

By adding that He took us out of Egypt, God informs us that He has a will and is involved in the world. Moreover, by emphasizing that we were enslaved in Egypt, God justifies, as it were, His right to our service – we were slaves to Pharaoh and He redeemed us to be His servants.

5. See *Sheim Tov*'s comments to *Moreh ha-Nevuchim* 2:1.
6. The same ambiguity exists in *Moreh ha-Nevuchim* 1:50. There, he writes: דע, המעיין בספרי זה, שהאעתקאד אינו העניין הנאמר אלא העניין המצטייר בנפש כאשר מקבלים כאמת

ספר המצוות לרמב"ם מצות עשה א
המצוה הראשונה היא הצווי אשר צוונו **להאמין** האלוהות והוא שנאמין שיש שם עלה וסבה הוא פועל לכל הנמצאות והוא אמרו ית', "אנכי י"י אלהיך."

> The first *mitzva* is the commandment that He commanded us to **believe in** (להאמין) the Divinity. That is, that there is a Transcendent Essence that is the cause of everything that exists. God articulated [this *mitzva* with the words]: "I am Hashem, your God" (*Shemot* 20:2).

While ibn Tibbon translates the word **אעתקאד** as להאמין (to believe), R. Yosef Kapach (1917–2000) and R. Chaim Heller (1880–1960) believe the correct translation should be: "to **know**."[7] Evidence for this is the aforementioned citation from *Mishneh Torah* (which was originally written in Hebrew) where Rambam uses the word **לידע** when describing the *mitzva* of *anochi*. Likewise, in the list of *mitzvot* found at the beginning of *Mishneh Torah*, he states:

מצוה ראשונה ממצות עשה, **לידע** שיש שם אלוה, שנאמר "אנוכי ה' אלוהיך" (שמות כ:ב; דברים ה:ו).

> The first of the positive commandments is the *mitzva* to **know** that there is a God, as [*Shemot* 20:2] states: "I am Hashem, your God."

Thus, it seems reasonable to conclude there is no *mitzva* of *emuna*; rather, *anochi* demands knowledge of God's existence.

R. Soloveitchik's Understanding of the Word לידע

In 1.2, we showed that the word *yedi'a* means much more than knowing about God. *Yedi'a* connotes acquaintanceship and relationship. Consider

---

שהוא כך כפי שהצטייר. See note 15 to the *peticha* of the Schwartz edition of *Moreh ha-Nevuchim* for an analysis.

7. It seems that the Arabic could mean either one, making the question one of Rambam's intent.

that the Torah uses the verb to refer to physical intimacy, which clearly has nothing to do with information.

R. Yosef Dov Soloveitchik (*Al ha-Teshuva*, p. 196; *On Repentance*, p. 131) adds that the word לידע should not be translated as "to understand," as if to imply that a person is obligated to philosophize about the nature of God's existence. As we will explain in 10.4–5, we cannot understand God. Rambam does not maintain that there is a *mitzva* to be a philosopher or theologian. What does לידע mean? R. Soloveitchik suggests an unconventional understanding of the word – the *mitzva* mandates constant awareness of His existence: "A level of consciousness never marred by inattention." On the other hand, the term להאמין or "to believe" implies no prohibition against inattentiveness. Thus, the word לידע demands that a person be:

> In a state of perpetual affinity, of constant orientation, God should become a living reality that one cannot forget for a minute. This keen awareness of the existence of God should constitute the foundation of our thoughts, ideas, and emotions in every kind of situation and under all conditions. Everything else inevitably depends upon this supreme article of faith.

R. Soloveitchik notes that this understanding mirrors the use of the word in *Mishlei* (3:6), which instructs us, בכל דרכיך דעהו, "In all of your ways, know Him." This means that we must know Him in all that we do. Powerful evidence for this translation can be gleaned from Rambam's usage of the word אעתקאד in the context of the obligation to fear God.[8]

---

8. R. Mayer Twersky pointed out that the Rambam uses the same Arabic word אעתקאד when describing the *mitzva* of fearing God. Ibn Tibbon translates this as follows:

ספר המצוות לרמב"ם מצות עשה ד

והמצוה הרביעית היא **שצונו להאמין יראתו** יתעלה ולהפחד ממנו ולא נהיה ככופרים ההולכים בקרי אבל נירא ביאת ענשו בכל עת והוא אמרו יתעלה, "את י"י אלהיך תירא (ואתחנן ו)."

R. Kapach notes that the phrase להאמין יראתו, makes no sense (how can one believe in fear). He therefore translates the phrase as לקבוע בדעתנו יראתו יתעלה. However, ibn Tibbon's translation reflects his rule in which he consistently translates the same Arabic words into the same Hebrew words (a rule that R. Kapach does not follow). Since Rambam uses the word אעתקאד here (באעתקאד כ׳ופה תעאלי) and ibn Tibbon

How does this constant awareness bring a person to "**know** that there is a First Being Who brought into being all existence"? R. Soloveitchik suggests that if a person lives with this awareness, he will see God everywhere and will truly know that there is a First Being:

> A man goes outdoors on a fair summer's day and sees the whole world blossoming; that man comes "to know" that there exists a Primary Being Who is the originator of all that there is; in every budding flower, in every rose opening its petals, in every ray of light and in every drop of rain – "to know that there is a Primary Being and that He is the Originator of all that is."

R. Soloveitchik continues, explaining that it is not simply nature that yields this knowledge; all encounters, when perceived thoughtfully, accomplish this goal, from seeing God's hand in current events to reflecting on the health of one's children.

Regardless of whether one accepts R. Soloveitchik's interpretation, R. Soloveitchik highlights an important point with respect to this passage: Rambam does not state that fulfillment of this *mitzva* demands the study of philosophy. Thus, while it certainly is the case that the pursuit of philosophy can indeed constitute a fulfillment of the *mitzva* and perhaps reflects the most ideal way of fulfilling it, the *mitzva* does not demand that we philosophize. It simply demands that we "**know** that there is a First Being Who brought into being all existence." Ultimately, there may be many ways to arrive at this knowledge.

8.3 *YEDI'A* AND *EMUNA*

Other Rishonim explicitly formulate the *mitzva* of *anochi* as encompassing both *yedi'a* and *emuna*. Ramban (*Shemot* 20:1), for instance, writes:

---

translates אעתקאד as להאמין, he must translate the phrase as להאמין יראתו. However, if we accept R. Soloveitchik's understanding that אעתקאד connotes constant awareness, then the usage of אעתקאד in both the first and fourth *mitzva* makes perfect sense. Indeed, the continuation of *mitzva* four supports this idea, אבל נירא ביאת ענשו בכל עת, which highlights that constant awareness is definitional to the *mitzva*.

אנכי ה' אלוקיך: הדיבור הזה מצוות עשה, אמר אנכי ה', יורה ויצוה אותם שידעו ויאמינו כי יש ה'...

> "I am Hashem, your God." This statement is a positive *mitzva*. When God says "I am Hashem," this instructs them (Bnei Yisrael) to **know** and **believe** that God exists ...[9]

Interestingly, R. Elazar Menachem Man Shach (1899–2001) asserts that Rambam also accepts the need for both *yedi'a* and *emuna*. This understanding is rooted in the ibn Tibbon translation of *Sefer ha-Mitzvot* as well as the widespread usage of the word *emuna*. Yet, as clearly indicated by *Mishneh Torah*, Rambam understands that the Torah demands we must **know** (*leida*) that God exists. R. Shach argues that God's existence is intuitive and obvious, since nothing else can account for the existence of this complex world. Thus, concerning the existence of God we must have *yedi'a*. What, then, is the role of *emuna*? R. Shach cites R. Chaim Soloveitchik as maintaining that *emuna* begins when the intellect ends.[10] Later, he cites *Beit ha-Levi*[11] (end of *Parshat Bo*) as supporting this position.[12]

---

9. Likewise, *Sefer ha-Chinuch* (*Mitzva* 25) initially uses the word *emuna* (**להאמין** שיש לעולם אלו-ה אחד שהמציא כל הנמצא) and later adds the word *yedi'a* (**תדעו ותאמינו** שיש לעולם אלוה).

10. **אבי עזרי הל' תשובה ה:ה**

והנה **מאז ומתמיד הייתי מתפלא למה מכנין למצוה זו אמונה, הרי בפשוטו שזהו מהמושכלות הראשונות,** דאי אפשר לעולם בלי מנהיג. וגם מבשרי אחזה אלקי. והחכמה הנפלאה שבכל יצור קטן, אין להעריך, ומכל שכן, החכמה ביצירת האדם. ואיך אפשר שכל זה הוא בלא מנהיג. והרי הרמב"ם הנ"ל כתב לידע את ה', הרי זו ידיעה, ובכתוב נאמר וידעת היום והשיבות אל לבבך כי ה' הוא אלקים, ולמה זה נקרא אמונה? ובספר המצות במצוה א' כתב היא הציווי אשר צונו בהאמנת האלהות. ושאלתי את זאת **למרן הגאון הגדול רבי יצחק זאב סאלאווייציק זצ"ל, ואמר לי שגם הוא עמד על זה ושאל זאת לאביו הגר"ח זצ"ל,** ואמר לו, שודאי עד כמה ששכל האדם מגעת הוא מושכל **ואין זו אמונה והיא ידיעה.**

Interestingly, this formulation is reminiscent of R. Nachman of Breslov cited by R. Dessler:

מכתב מאליהו ח"ג עמ' 177

ר' נחמן כתב שבמקום אשר שם גבולו של השכל - שם מתחילה האמונה.

11. Written by R. Yosef Dov Soloveitchik, father of R. Chaim.

12. אח"ז הראוני שבספר בית הלוי סוף פרשת בא כתב כן, שאמונה היא על מה שאין השכל משיג זאת ע"ש בדבריו הנעימים.

R. Shach writes that R. Chaim's son, R. Yitzchak Zev Soloveitchik (known as the Brisker Rav), understood that the need for the *mitzva* of *emuna* stems from our inability to fully understand or even define God. Our minds are limited by time and space; therefore, there cannot be a *mitzva* of *yedi'a* concerning that which does not exist in time and space.[13] At that point, there is a *mitzva* of *emuna*.[14] Thus, with regard to God's existence there is *yedi'a*, whereas with regard to His nature, there is *emuna*.[15]

We might add another point. According to Rambam, God's existence can be proven (and is intuitive); therefore, knowledge of His existence is categorized as *yedi'a*. However, the Torah enjoins us to believe in other things that cannot be philosophically proven, such as the veracity of Torah. This we know based on tradition and is categorized as *emuna*.

The idea that faith contains two aspects, knowledge and belief, fits nicely within Rambam's writings. As we mentioned, Rambam writes in the first chapter of *Hilchot Yesodei ha-Torah* that we can know of God's existence directly, because it can be proven. How do we know that the Torah is true? There is no formal philosophical proof for the truth of Torah. Rather, in the eighth chapter of *Hilchot Yesodei ha-Torah*,

13. Indeed, Rambam writes that we cannot know anything about God Himself. We can only relate to His actions. (Thus, only negation of characteristics or descriptions of His actions are accurate.) The proofs for God justify saying that God is, they cannot show **what** God is (see *Moreh ha-Nevuchim* 1:51–59). Thus, we can have **knowledge** that He is; we can have no knowledge of Him. Indeed, Rambam's proofs do not begin with a conception of God and then prove that such a being exists. Instead, they begin with the universe and prove there must be a prime cause (there is movement so there must ultimately be an unmoved mover). Thus, our knowledge of God stems from how He relates to us (He is the cause for the movement we experience). We cannot know Him even as we can perceive the effects of His existence.

14. It would seem that R. Chaim is not stipulating that there is a *mitzva* of *yedi'a* independent of the *mitzva* of *emuna*. Rather, *yedi'a* does not qualify as a *mitzva* because it is so obvious. Therefore, the mitzva of *emuna* only really begins where the point of obviousness (*yedi'a*) ends.

15. **אבי עזרי הל' תשובה ה:ה**
והסביר לעצמו הענין, **ששכל האדם הלוא מוגבל הוא בזמן ובמקום**, ומה שהוא למעלה מן הזמן והמקום, שאין שם מקום לשכל האדם, אז חלה עליו חובת האמונה.

Rambam gives a different reason as to how the Jewish people came to such belief.[16]

This does not mean belief in the Torah's veracity is irrational. Quite the opposite: Rambam maintains that the Torah asks of us to act rationally, and Rambam shows that it is highly rational to believe in the Torah. However, our knowledge of that which we know based on tradition differs from that which we actually can prove. For example, it is rational to believe that a man named George Washington once lived and was the first president of the United States. While this fact cannot be philosophically proven, it can be known with certainty based on the plethora of evidence documenting his existence. Likewise, our belief in revelation is both rational and certain even if it cannot be proven in the same manner as the existence of God.

---

16. Rambam writes:

> The Children of Israel did not believe in Moshe [solely] because of the signs he presented, for someone who believes [in a prophet solely] because of the signs he presents is tainted, for it could be that his signs are performed by means of spells and witchcraft. All the signs that Moshe performed in the wilderness were done according to the needs of the moment, not to bring proof to his prophecies… It was the assembly at Mount Sinai that made them believe in Moshe, when our eyes, and no one else's, saw, and our ears, and no one else's, heard, and Moshe drew near to the darkness, and the voice spoke to him, and we heard it saying to Moshe, "Moshe, Moshe, go tell them such-and-such." In connection with this it is written, "God spoke with you face to face." And it also is written, "God did not make this covenant with our fathers [alone], but with us, even us." From where is it known that the assembly at Mount Sinai was the proof that the prophecy of Moshe was true and that he was not speaking basely? It is derived from the verse, "Behold, I come to you in a thick cloud, that the people may hear when I speak with you and believe in you forever." From this we see that prior to the assembly at Mount Sinai, their belief in Moshe was not one that would have lasted forever, but rather was a belief that left room for discussion and thought.

Rambam here addresses only how the generation at Sinai arrived at certainty concerning the Torah's truth. Presumably, subsequent generations know of the Torah's truth because the details of the revelation were passed down faithfully from generation to generation. Either way, even though Rambam writes that a person retains a modicum of doubt even after witnessing miracles, national revelation leaves a rational person with no doubts. Nevertheless, because this cannot be proven, it constitutes *emuna*, not *yedi'a*.

Accordingly, there are two types of faith: we must know that which can be proven in the formal philosophical sense (the first four *ikkarei emuna*[17, 18]), and we must believe that which cannot be proven in the formal philosophical sense (the last nine *ikkarei emuna*). Both components of faith, however, are justified by rational analysis.

8.4 THE IMPORTANCE OF PROOF

While the matter certainly is debated (as we shall see), many Jewish thinkers emphatically argued in favor of seeking proof for the existence of God if one is capable of doing so. Thus, R. Bachya ibn Pakuda declares, "It would show want of zeal for anyone to rely on tradition alone who can obtain certainty by method of rational demonstration."[19] In *Chovot ha-Levavot*, R. Bachya first demonstrates God's existence

---

17. We have not included the fifth *ikkar* (the prohibition against idolatry) because, as we shall see in 10.9, Rambam sees the primary focus of the prohibition against idolatry as the prohibition against using intermediaries to serve God. Thus, one can have a correct conception of God and still be in violation of idolatry. It is only through the Torah, not the intellect, that we know that it is wrong to serve God through intermediaries.
18. That is not to say that *all* aspects of the first four *ikkarim* can be proven. For example, in Rambam's amended version of his Commentary on the Mishna (found in R. Kapach's edition), he includes belief in creation *ex nihilo* as part of the fourth *ikkar*:

    והיסוד הרביעי הקדמות. והוא, שזה האחד המתואר הוא הקדמון בהחלט, וכל נמצא זולתו הוא בלתי קדמון ביחס אליו, והראיות לזה בספרים הרבה. וזה היסוד הרביעי הוא שמורה עליו מה שנ׳ מענה אלהי קדם. ודע כי היסוד הגדול של תורת משה רבינו הוא היות העולם מחודש, יצרו ה׳ ובראו אחר ההעדר המוחלט, וזה שתראה שאני סובב סביב ענין קדמות העולם לפי דעת הפילוסופים הוא כדי שיהא המופת מוחלט על מציאותו יתעלה כמו שביארתי ובירתי במורה.

    As we shall discuss, Rambam believes that the truth of creation *ex nihilo* cannot be proven. We *know* it through the Torah, though scientifically speaking it is the more compelling model as well. Thus, while God's antiquity, the primary theme of the fourth *ikkar*, is provable and therefore qualifies as *yedi'a*, an aspect of the *ikkar*, creation *ex nihilo*, is not provable and would be considered *emuna*.

    Interestingly, in the ibn Tibbon translation of Rambam's commentary on the Mishna, which reflects an earlier translation prior to Rambam's writing *Moreh ha-Nevuchim*, Rambam omitted reference to creation in the fourth *ikkar*. Perhaps this is the reason why Rambam originally did not include belief in creation as part of the fourth principle – because it cannot be proven.
19. *The Duties of the Heart* tr. Moses Hyamson (Jerusalem: Feldheim, 1970), V. 1, p. 33

philosophically in his *Sha'ar ha-Yichud*. Then, he turns to discover God in nature in his *Sha'ar ha-Bechina*. He concludes, "The examination of the wisdom manifested in the universe which the Creator called into being, is the most direct and surest road to a realization of His existence and reality."[20]

Rambam informs us of how Avraham first became aware of God's existence:

רמב"ם הלכות עבודה זרה פרק א הלכה ב–ג
אבל צור העולמים לא היה שום אדם שהיה מכירו ולא יודעו אלא יחידים בעולם כגון חנוך ומתושלח נח שם ועבר, ועל דרך זה היה העולם הולך ומתגלגל עד שנולד עמודו של עולם והוא אברהם אבינו.

כיון שנגמל איתן זה התחיל לשוטט בדעתו והוא קטן והתחיל לחשוב ביום ובלילה והיה תמיה היאך אפשר שיהיה הגלגל הזה נוהג תמיד ולא יהיה לו מנהיג ומי יסבב אותו, כי אי אפשר שיסבב את עצמו, ולא היה לו מלמד ולא מודיע דבר אלא מושקע באור כשדים בין עובדי כוכבים הטפשים ואביו ואמו וכל העם עובדי כוכבים והוא עובד עמהם ולבו משוטט ומבין עד שהשיג דרך האמת והבין קו הצדק מתבונתו הנכונה, וידע שיש שם אלוה אחד והוא מנהיג הגלגל והוא ברא הכל ואין בכל הנמצא אלוה חוץ ממנו, וידע שכל העולם טועים ודבר שגרם להם לטעות זה שעובדים את הכוכבים ואת הצורות עד שאבד האמת מדעתם, ובן ארבעים שנה הכיר אברהם את בוראו, כיון שהכיר וידע התחיל להשיב תשובות על בני אור כשדים ולערוך דין עמהם ולומר שאין זו דרך האמת שאתם הולכים בה.

The Eternal Rock was not recognized or known by anyone in the world, with the exception of [a few] individuals: for example, Chanoch, Metushelach, Noach, Sheim, and Eiver. The world continued in this fashion until the pillar of the world – the Patriarch Abraham – was born.

20. Ibid., p. 125.

> **After this mighty man was weaned, he began to explore and think. Though he was a child, he began to think [incessantly] throughout the day and night, wondering: How is it possible for the sphere to continue to revolve without having a director (*manhig*) or someone controlling it? Who is causing it to revolve? Surely, it does not cause itself to revolve.**
>
> He had no teacher, nor was there anyone to inform him. Rather, he was mired in Ur Kasdim among the foolish idolaters. His father, mother, and all the people [around him] were idol worshipers, and he would worship with them. [However,] his heart was exploring and [gaining] understanding.
>
> Ultimately, he appreciated the way of truth and understood the path of righteousness through his accurate comprehension. He realized that there was one God who controlled the sphere, that He created everything, and that there is no other God among all the other entities. He knew that the entire world was making a mistake. What caused them to err was their service of the stars and images, which made them lose awareness of the truth.
>
> Abraham was forty years old when he became aware of his Creator. When he recognized and knew Him, he began to formulate replies to the inhabitants of Ur Kasdim and debate with them, telling them that they were not following a proper path.

Rambam's version of Avraham's proof is, in brief, one of the four proofs that Rambam offers for the existence of God in *Moreh ha-Nevuchim*. The spinning spheres in Rambam's formulation reflect Rambam's Aristotelian conception of the universe.[21] While we would no longer phrase this argument in terms of spinning spheres, the basic argument continues to

21. *Chovot ha-Levavot* 1:6 frames the argument as follows: just as it is obvious that a poem on paper was intentionally written and not simply the result of spilled ink, so too the complex world must be the work of a creator.

be used today. (The contemporary scientific viability of this approach is considered in 8.13.)[22]

That Avraham arrived at awareness of God's existence through a teleological argument[23] (also known as an argument from design) is actually recorded in a midrash:

בראשית רבה (וילנא) פרשת לך לך פרשה לט א
אמר רבי יצחק משל לאחד שהיה עובר ממקום למקום, וראה בירה אחת דולקת אמר תאמר שהבירה זו בלא מנהיג, הציץ עליו בעל הבירה, אמר לו אני הוא בעל הבירה, כך לפי שהיה אבינו אברהם אומר תאמר שהעולם הזה בלא מנהיג, הציץ עליו הקב"ה ואמר לו אני הוא בעל העולם...

R. Yitzchak says: To what may this be compared? To a man who was traveling from place to place[24] and saw an illuminated[25]

---

22. In *Moreh ha-Nevuchim* 3:27–28, Rambam adds that Avraham's proofs were passed down to Yitzchak and Yaakov but forgotten during the Egyptian enslavement. While in Egypt, the majority of Jews adopted the pagan beliefs of the Egyptians. Thus, when the Jews were redeemed, it became necessary to establish a system of belief that went beyond philosophical proofs, since such proofs can be forgotten. Various *mitzvot* of the Torah serve that purpose.
23. R. Mayer Twersky has noted that in his two-part question (How is it possible for the sphere to continue to revolve without having anyone controlling it? Who is causing it to revolve?) Rambam is alluding to both the cosmological (why is there something rather than nothing; there must have been something that started it all) and teleological argument (the argument from design). Perhaps the simpler reading of Rambam, however, is that there is no argument from design here at all. This is one linear cosmological argument.
24. Why is this detail relevant? R. Aaron Lopiansky has suggested that it reflects Avraham's journey. As Rambam notes, it was a long process, beginning when he was three and culminating at the age of forty. In fact, despite his youthful questions, Avraham continued to serve idolatry (והוא עובד עמהם). Thus, Avraham was wandering from place to place searching for the truth until he found it.
25. This can be translated either as "illuminated" or "burning." Either way, we must wonder what it adds to the proof. If we choose "illuminated," the text highlights that God did not just create the world, but also continues to sustain it. This is supported by the continuation of the midrash, which calls God a *manhig* (director). If we translate the word as "burning," the passage might imply that even in destruction there is guidance and direction. *Tzaddik ve-ra lo* may leave us bewildered, but does not imply that there is no *manhig*. After all, it is a beautiful palace that is burning.

> palace. He wondered, "Is it possible that the palace lacks a director (*manhig*)?" The director of the palace looked out and said, "I am the director of the palace." So Avraham our father said, "Is it possible that the world lacks a director (*manhig*)?"[26] The Holy One, blessed be He, looked out and said to him, "I am the Sovereign of the Universe."

Like Rambam, the midrash emphasizes that consideration of the universe, whether the rotating spheres or the illuminated palace, demonstrates not just that there was a creator but that there is a *manhig* who continues to direct our world. In *Moreh ha-Nevuchim* 2:19, Rambam explains the prophet Yeshayahu (40:26) as offering this sort of argument, telling the people: "Lift up your eyes on high and see who created these."

So far, we have seen Rambam utilize a proof for God in order to prove His existence to a non-believer (in this case, a younger Avraham). But would such proofs also have value to someone who already believes in God? Rambam averred that ideally, a person should be able to prove the existence of God; as we saw, *anochi* demands that we *know* that God exists. In fact, Rambam argues that when a person knows through a logical proof that God exists, it is as though this knowledge was received directly from God insofar as the knowledge is direct (and not through an intermediary). In that sense, this knowledge is superior to our knowledge of other *mitzvot*, which we received through an intermediary (Moshe).

Rambam uses this distinction between direct knowledge through reason and indirect knowledge through a prophetic intermediary such as Moshe to offer a fascinating interpretation of a passage in the Talmud (*Makkot* 23b–24a). The Talmud states that the first two of the Ten Commandments were heard directly by the Jewish people, as opposed to the subsequent commandments, which God told Moshe and Moshe in turn related to the Jewish people. Rambam, however, understands that this

26. The midrash here refers to God as a *manhig* (director). Interestingly, Rambam, above, uses the very same word (אפשר שיהיה הגלגל הזה נוהג תמיד ולא יהיה לו **מנהיג**... וידע שיש שם אלוה אחד והוא **מנהיג** הגלגל והוא ברא הכל). In fact, it may be that the midrash's use of this word conveyed to Rambam the nature of Avraham's ruminations.

cannot be taken literally, as it is inconceivable that the Jewish people could hear the direct word of God, since they were not on the level of prophets, and prophecy is, by definition, impossible for someone who lacks a high degree of spiritual, moral, and intellectual perfection.[27, 28]

---

27. This idea is expressed in the Talmud, which states:

נדרים דף לח עמוד ב

אמר רבי (יונתן) [יוחנן] אין הקב"ה משרה שכינתו אלא על חכם גבור ועשיר ועניו, וכולם ממשה וגו'.

Rambam in *Iggeret Teiman* understands that these qualities reflect moral perfection:

רמב"ם אגרת תימן

ואחד מן התנאים שיש אצלנו ידועים לכל נביא - שיהיה בתכלית המדע ואז ינבא אותו הקב"ה. **לפי שהוא עיקר אצלנו שאין הנבואה שורה אלא על חכם וגיבור ועשיר. וביארו, שאפילו גיבור שיהיה כובש את יצרו, ועשיר - עשיר בדעתו.**

The Talmud's proof text for *ashir* (עשיר - "פסל לך" פסולתן שלך יהא) would seem problematic for Rambam. Moreover, the redundancy poses a problem for Rambam (why would the Talmud need to mention חכם as well as עשיר?).

28. While other thinkers, such as Ran (דרשות הר"ן הדרוש החמישי), R. Albo, and R. Crescas, believe that *Matan Torah* was an exception to the general rule that only wise people who have perfected their character can experience prophecy, Rambam maintains that this principle can have no exceptions.

Rambam expresses this position in a number of places:

הדקמת הרמב"ם לפרק חלק

והיסוד הששי הנבואה. והוא, לדעת שזה המין האנושי יש שימצאו בו אישים בעלי כשרונות מפותחים מאד ושלמות גדולה, ותתכונן נפשם עד שמקבלת צורת השכל, ויתחבר אותו השכל האנושי בשכל הפועל, ויאצל עליהם ממנו אצילות שפע, ואלה הם הנביאים, וזוהי הנבואה וזהו ענינה. וביאור היסוד הזה בשלימות יארך מאד, ואין מטרתינו פירוט כל יסוד מהם וביאור דרכי ידיעתו, לפי שזה הוא כללות כל המדעים, אלא נזכירם בדרך הודעה בלבד, ופסוקי התורה מעידים בנבואת נביאים רבים.

הלכות יסודי התורה פרק ז הלכה א

מיסודי הדת, לידע שהאל מנבא את בני האדם; ואין הנבואה חלה אלא על חכם גדול בחכמה, גיבור במידותיו, ולא יהיה יצרו מתגבר עליו בדבר בעולם אלא הוא מתגבר בדעתו על יצרו תמיד, בעל דעה רחבה נכונה **עד מאוד.**

ספר מורה הנבוכים חלק ב פרק לב

אבל הפתיים מעמי הארץ א"א זה אצלנו, ר"ל שינבא אחד מהם אלא **כאפשרות הנבא חמור או צפרדע**

In this last source, where he equates the possibility of an unperfected person prophesying to the possibility of a frog prophesying, we see the extent to which Rambam sees this principle as axiomatic.

An important question remains to be considered: how can we say that God was unable to allow unworthy people to prophesy – doesn't that contradict divine omnipotence? We consider this question in 4.5.

Rather, the Talmud means that the truth of the first two commandments, namely, the existence of God and His unity, can be derived independently using logic.[29] Since there is no need for prophecy to arrive at these principles, our knowledge of them is direct and, in that sense, identical to that of Moshe's. This contrasts with the rest of the Torah, which we know only through Moshe. Rambam writes:

ספר מורה הנבוכים חלק ב פרק לג

יתבאר לי שבמעמד הר סיני לא היה המגיע למשה מגיע לכל ישראל, **אבל הדבור למשה לבדו ע"ה,** ולזה בא ספור עשרת הדברות כלו ספור היחיד הנפרד, והוא עליו השלום ירד לתחתית ההר ויגד לבני אדם מה ששמע, אמרה התורה אנכי עומד בין ה' וביניכם, ואמר ג"כ משה ידבר והאלהים יעננו בקול, ובביאור אמרו במכילתא כי כל דבור ודבור היה משיבו להם כמו ששמע, וכתוב בתורה גם כן בעבור ישמע העם בדברי וגו', מורה כי הדבור היה לו והם ישמעו הקול ההוא העצום לא הבדל הדברים, ועל שמע הקול ההוא העצום

---

29. With this, *Meshech Chochma* (*Shemot* 20:2) resolves Ramban's challenge on Rambam's inclusion of *anochi* as a *mitzva*. Rambam in *Sefer ha-Mitzvot* proves that *anochi* is a *mitzva* because the Talmud states that the first two utterances were uttered by God and are included in the 613 *mitzvot*:

ספר המצוות לרמב"ם מצות עשה א

ובסוף גמר מכות (כג ב, כד א) אמרו תרי"ג מצות נאמרו לו למשה בסיני מאי קראה תורה צוה לנו משה כלומר מנין תור"ה והקשו על זה ואמרו תורה בגימטריא הכי הואי שית מאה וחדסרי הואי והיתה התשובה אנכי ולא יהיה מפי הגבורה שמעום. הנה כבר התבאר לך כי אנכי י"י מכלל שש מאות ושלש עשרה מצות והוא צווי באמונה כמו שבארנו:

Ramban objects that the first two utterances, according to Rambam's own formulation, contain five *mitzvot*:

השגות הרמב"ן לספר המצוות שם

ועם כל זה ראיתי לבעל ההלכות שלא ימנה אותה מצוה בכלל תרי"ג. **ובדבור לא יהיה לך מניעות רבות לא יהיה לך לא תעשה לא תשתחוה להם ולא תעבדם. ואם כן יהיה מפי הגבורה חמש ומפי משה שש מאות ושמנה, לא מניין תור"ה.**

Accordingly, the Talmud should have said that five *mitzvot* were stated by God and 608 by Moshe. However, Rambam's understanding of the Talmud in *Moreh ha-Nevuchim* resolves this question, since it is not the words of the first two utterances that were stated by God, but the truth of the first two commandments that can be derived independently using logic, making it as if they were heard directly from God. (God's unity is referred to in the verse *shema Yisrael*, which is not in the Ten Commandments. Perhaps Rambam is referring to the prohibition against idolatry, which is predicated upon His unity.)

אמר כשמעכם את הקול, **ואמר קול דברים אתם שומעים, ולא אמר דברים אתם שומעים**, וכל מה שבא משמע הדברים, אמנם הנרצה בו שמע הקול, ומשה הוא אשר ישמע הדברים ויספרם להם, זהו הנראה מן התורה ומרוב דברי החז״ל.

אלא שיש להם גם כן מאמר כתוב בהרבה מקומות מן המדרשות והוא בתלמוד גם כן, **והוא אמרם אנכי ולא יהיה לך מפי הגבורה שמעום, רוצים בזה שהם הגיעו אליהם כמו שהגיעו למרע״ה, ולא היה מרע״ה מגיעם אליהם, וזה ששתי אלו השרשים, ר״ל מציאות האל ית׳, והיותו אחד, אמנם יושג בעיון האנושי וכל מה שיודע במופת, משפט הנביא בו ומשפט כל מי שידעהו שוה, אין יתרון,** ולא נודעו שני השרשים האלה מצד הנבואה לבד, אמרה התורה אתה הראת לדעת וגו׳, אמנם שאר הדברות הם מכת המפורסמות והמקובלות לא מכת המושכלות.

It is clear to me that what Moshe experienced at the revelation on Mount Sinai was different from that which was experienced by all the other Israelites, for Moshe alone was addressed by God, and for this reason the second person singular is used in the Ten Commandments. Moshe then went down to the foot of the mount and told his fellow men what he had heard. As it states, "I stood between God and you at that time to tell you the word of God" (*Devarim* 5:5). And it further states, "Moshe spoke, and God answered him with a loud voice" (*Shemot* 19:19). In the *Mechilta*, our Sages say distinctly that he brought to them every word as he had heard it. Furthermore, the words, "In order that the people hear when I speak to you" (*Shemot* 19:9) show that God spoke to Moshe, and the people heard only the mighty sound, not distinct words. It is to the perception of this mighty sound that Scripture refers in the passage, "When you hear the sound" (*Devarim* 5:20); it further states, "You heard a sound of words" (*ibid.* 4:12), and it is not said, "You heard words"; and even where the hearing of the words is mentioned, only the perception of the sound is meant. It was only Moshe who heard the words, and he reported them to the people. This is apparent from Scripture and from the utterances of our Sages in general.

> There is, however, an opinion of our Sages, frequently expressed in the Midrashim and found also in the Talmud, to this effect: The Israelites heard the first and the second commandments from God, **i.e., they learnt the truth of the principles contained in these two commandments in the same manner as Moshe, and not through Moshe. For these two principles, the existence of God and His Unity, can be arrived at by means of reasoning, and whatever can be established by proof is known by the prophet in the same way as by any other person; he has no advantage in this respect. These two principles were not known through prophecy alone.** The verse states, "You have been shown to know that," etc. (*Devarim* 4:34). But the rest of the commandments are of an ethical and authoritative character and do not contain [truths] perceived by the intellect.

We return to Rambam's surprising theory in 8.9; however, the above interpretation certainly highlights the importance of proving the existence of God using logic. We therefore have seen that both R. Bachya and Rambam believe that understanding a philosophical proof for God's existence is integral to fulfilling the *mitzva* of "knowing God." Does this mean that anyone who is unable to understand or accept such a proof does not fulfill this crucial *mitzva,* even if he believes in God and prays to Him daily? We will discuss this problem in section 8.6, but we must first explain what Rambam's philosophical proof is.

8.5 THE PROPOSITIONS OF RAMBAM'S PROOFS AND HIS POSITION ON CREATION

In the previous section, we cited Rambam's understanding of Avraham's derivation of the existence of God: "How is it possible for the sphere to continue to revolve without having anyone controlling it? Who is causing it to revolve? Surely, it does not cause itself to revolve."[30] Rambam formulates the proof differently than the midrash, which presents Avraham's derivation as "There cannot be a building (*bira*) without a

---

30. This proof (הגלגל סובב תמיד) is presented in *Hilchot Yesodei ha-Torah* as well:
רמב"ם הלכות יסודי התורה פרק א הלכה ה

director (*manhig*)." The different formulation reflects Rambam's Aristotelian conception of the universe (as discussed in 2.11).[31] While Rambam offers four proofs for the existence of God in *Moreh ha-Nevuchim,* he chooses to succinctly present this one in the *Mishneh Torah,* perhaps because it is the simplest.

The proof is fully developed in the beginning of the second part of *Moreh ha-Nevuchim,* where Rambam lays out the proof in twenty-six steps.

Rambam prefaces his proofs for the existence, unity, and incorporeality of God with twenty-five metaphysical and physical propositions which, he writes, already have been proven. To this, he adds a twenty-sixth proposition, the eternity of matter, which he thinks is wrong but nevertheless will presume for purposes of his proof:

> Twenty-five of the propositions that are employed in the proof for the existence of God, or in the arguments demonstrating that God is neither corporeal nor a force connected with a material being, or that He is One, have been fully established, and their correctness is beyond doubt. Aristotle and the Peripatetics[32] who followed him have proved each of these propositions. There is,

המצוי הזה הוא אלהי העולם אדון כל הארץ, והוא המנהיג הגלגל בכח שאין לו קץ ותכלית, בכח שאין לו הפסק, שהגלגל סובב תמיד ואי אפשר שיסוב בלא מסבב, והוא ברוך הוא המסבב אותו בלא יד ובלא גוף.

שם הלכה ז

אלוה זה אחד הוא ואינו שנים ולא יתר על שנים, אלא אחד, שאין כיחודו אחד מן האחדים הנמצאים בעולם, לא אחד כמין שהוא כולל אחדים הרבה, ולא אחד כגוף שהוא נחלק למחלקות ולקצוות, אלא יחוד שאין יחוד אחר כמותו בעולם, אילו היו אלוהות הרבה היו גופין וגויות, מפני שאין הנמנים השוין במציאותן נפרדין זה מזה אלא במאורעין שיארעו בגופות והגויות, ואילו היה היוצר גוף וגוייה היה לו קץ ותכלית שאי אפשר להיות גוף שאין לו קץ, וכל שיש לגופו קץ ותכלית יש לכחו קץ וסוף, **ואלהינו ברוך שמו הואיל וכחו אין לו קץ ואינו פוסק שהרי הגלגל סובב תמיד, אין כחו כח גוף,** והואיל ואינו גוף לא יארעו לו מאורעות הגופות כדי שיהא נחלק ונפרד מאחר, לפיכך אי אפשר שיהיה אלא אחד, וידיעת דבר זה מצות עשה שנאמר ה׳ אלהינו ה׳ אחד.

31. Significantly, however, Rambam also uses the term *manhig* (at least with respect to the *galgal*), both in *Hilchot Yesodei ha-Torah* and in *Hilchot Avoda Zara.*

32. The Peripatetic school of philosophy in Ancient Greece followed Aristotle. The name derives from the *peripatoi* (colonnades) of the Lyceum in Athens where the members met.

> however, one proposition that we do not accept, namely, the proposition affirming the eternity of the universe, but we will admit it for the present, because by doing so we shall be enabled to clearly demonstrate our own theory.

Aristotle believed in the eternity of matter, meaning that the world always existed; it was not created. His position was widely accepted in medieval times by philosophers. In fact, Rambam (e.g., *Moreh ha-Nevuchim* 1:50) and Ramban (e.g., *Drashat Torat Hashem Temima*) frequently state that the eternity of matter is one of the core beliefs that the Torah seeks to eradicate. Likewise, in *Moreh ha-Nevuchim* 2:13, Rambam writes that the foundation of the entire Torah is that God created matter and time: "It is undoubtedly the fundamental principle of the Law of Moshe, our teacher; it is next in importance to the principle of God's unity" (יסוד תורת משה רבינו ע"ה בלי ספק והיא שניה ליסוד היחוד).[33] In 3.3, we explored why exactly Rambam sees the eternity of matter as counter to the Torah.

---

33. There, he writes that Avraham disseminated this notion when he called God אל עולם:

> Among those who believe in the existence of God, there are three different theories regarding the question of whether the universe is eternal or not.
>
> First Theory. -- **Those who follow the Law of Moshe, our Teacher, maintain that the whole universe, i.e., everything except God, has been brought by Him into existence out of non-existence. In the beginning, God alone existed, and nothing else**; neither angels, nor spheres, nor the things that are contained within the spheres existed. He then produced from nothing all existing things such as they are, by His will and desire. **Even time itself is among the things created...**
>
> This is the first theory, and it undoubtedly is a fundamental principle of the Law of Moshe, our teacher; it is next in importance to the principle of God's unity. Do not follow any other theory. **Avraham, our father, was the first that taught it, after he had established it by philosophical research. He proclaimed, therefore, "the Name of Hashem, God of the universe"** (*Bereishit* 21:33): and he previously had expressed this theory in the words, "Possessor of heaven and earth" (*ibid.* 19:22).
>
> .... All who follow the Law of Moshe, our teacher, and Avraham, our father, and all who adopt similar theories, assume that nothing is eternal except God, and that the theory of creation *ex nihilo* includes nothing that is impossible, whilst some thinkers even regard it as an established truth.

Likewise, in *Hilchot Avoda Zara* (cited above), Rambam writes that Avraham taught the world the notion of creation *ex nihilo*.

Given Rambam's rejection of the eternity of matter, why does Rambam state that his proof actually presumes the eternity of matter? This is not because Rambam accepts Aristotle's theory. Rather, Rambam makes this assumption because if one assumes that the world was created, there is no need to prove the existence of God; it is taken for granted.[34] Thus, he shows how the existence of God can be proven even if one fully accepts the Aristotelian conception of the universe, including the eternity of matter. By doing this, Rambam's proof becomes "acceptable to all."

Moreover, the concession makes the proof stronger because it does not presume something that cannot be proven. As we noted in 3.3, Rambam believes that from a scientific and philosophical perspective, creation *ex nihilo* is the more compelling option; however, it cannot be definitively proven (*Moreh ha-Nevuchim* 1:71–73).[35] Thus, any proof for God that presumed creation would not be absolutely conclusive.

Rambam makes these points clearly in *Moreh ha-Nevuchim* 1:71 where he explains:

> Such being the nature of this theory, how can we employ it as an axiom and establish on it the existence of the Creator? In that case, the existence of God would be uncertain: if the universe had a beginning, God does exist; if it be eternal, God does not exist. The existence of God thus would remain either an open question, or we should have to declare that the creation has been proved, and compel others by mere force to accept this doctrine, in order thus to be enabled to declare that we have proved the existence of God. Such a process is utterly inadmissible. The true method, which is based on a logical and indubitable proof, consists, according to my opinion, in demonstrating the existence of God, His unity, and His incorporeality by such philosophical arguments as are

---

34. Interestingly, today many scientists do exactly that. They presume that the world was created (big bang theory) but remain agnostic or atheistic. We return to this issue in 8.13.

35. This no longer is the case. From before Aristotle until the middle of the twentieth century, the question of whether the universe always existed was debated. However, in the twentieth century, as evidence for the big bang mounted, all of this changed dramatically.

founded on the theory of the eternity of the universe. **I do not propose this method as though I believed in the eternity of the universe, for I do not follow the philosophers on this point, but because by the aid of this method these three principles, viz., the existence of God, His unity and His incorporeality can be fully proved and verified irrespective of the question whether the universe had a beginning or not. After firmly establishing these three principles by an exact proof, we shall treat the problem of creation and discuss it as fully as possible**...

My method, as far as I now can explain it in general terms, is as follows. The universe either is eternal or had a beginning. If it had a beginning, there must necessarily exist a being that caused the beginning. This is clear to common sense, for a thing that has a beginning cannot be the cause of its own beginning; another must have caused it. Therefore, [we must conclude that] the universe was created by God. If, on the other hand, the universe is eternal, it could in various ways be proved that apart from the things that constitute the universe, there exists a being that is neither body nor a force in a body and that is one, eternal, not preceded by any cause, and immutable. That being is God. You see that the proofs for the existence, the unity and the incorporeality of God must vary according to the propositions admitted by us. Only in this way can we succeed in obtaining a perfect proof, whether we assume eternity or the creation of the universe.

For this reason, you will find in my works on the Talmud,[36] **whenever** I have to speak of the fundamental principles of our religion, or to prove the existence of God, that I employ arguments that imply the eternity of the universe. I do not believe in that eternity, but I wish to establish the principle of the existence of God by an indisputable proof and should not like to see this most important principle founded on a basis that everyone could shake or

36. This is a reference to the halacha quoted above from *Hilchot Avoda Zara.*

> attempt to demolish, and which others might consider as not being established at all…

Rambam here indicates that the halacha cited at the beginning of this section assumes the eternality of the universe. Presumably he is referring to the words "the sphere continuously revolves" (שהגלגל סובב תמיד), which implies that it always has been revolving.[37]

Having introduced the proofs, let us briefly summarize what they actually are. Each of the four proofs begins with some observed characteristic of the world (e.g., motion), invokes the principle that an infinite regress is impossible (there cannot be an infinite number of movers), and concludes that a first principle must exist (there must be an unmoved mover). The first is derived from motion, the second from the composition of elements, the third from necessity and contingency, and the fourth from potentiality and actuality (causality). We refrain from elaboration due to their complexity. Dr. Arthur Hyman summarizes the first proof as follows:

> Maimonides begins his first proof, that from motion, by noting that in the sublunar world things constantly move and change. These sublunar motions, in turn, are caused by celestial motions which come to an end with the motion of the uppermost celestial sphere. The motion of that sphere is caused by a mover that is not moved by another mover. This mover, called the Prime Mover, is the last member in the chain of causes producing motion. Maimonides uses the following example as an illustration. Suppose a draft of air comes through a hole, and a stick is used to push a stone in the hole to close it. Now the stone is pushed into the

37. This idea is echoed in Rambam's Commentary on the Mishna in the fourth of the *ikkarei emuna*:
והיסוד הרביעי הקדמות. והוא, שזה האחד המתואר הוא הקדמון בהחלט, וכל נמצא זולתו הוא בלתי קדמון ביחס אליו, והראיות לזה בספרים הרבה. וזה היסוד הרביעי הוא שמורה עליו מה שנ׳ מענה אלהי קדם. ודע כי היסוד הגדול של תורת משה רבינו הוא היות העולם מחודש, יצרו ה׳ ובראו אחר ההעדר המוחלט, **וזה שתראה שאני סובב סביב ענין קדמות העולם לפי דעת הפילוסופים הוא כדי שיהא המופת מוחלט על מציאותו יתעלה כמו שביארתי ובירתי במורה.**

> hole by the stick, the stick is moved by the hand, and the hand is moved by the sinews, muscles, etc., of the human body. But one must also consider the draft of air, which was the reason for the motion of the stone in the first place. The motion of the air is caused by the motion of the lowest celestial sphere, and the motion of that sphere, by the successive motions of other spheres. The chain of things moved and moving comes to an end with the last of the celestial spheres. This sphere is set in motion by a principle which, while it produces motion, is itself not moved. This is the Prime Mover, which for Maimonides is identical with God.
>
> Maimonides then turned to the nature of the Prime Mover. Four possibilities exist: Either the Prime Mover exists apart from the sphere, and then either corporeally or incorporeally; or it exists within the sphere, and then either as distributed throughout it or as indivisible. It can be shown that the Prime Mover does not exist within the sphere, which rules out the last two possibilities, nor apart from it as a body, which rules out the third. Hence, it exists apart from the sphere and must be incorporeal. Maimonides shows, further, that there cannot be two incorporeal movers. Thus, it has been established that the Prime Mover exists, is incorporeal, and is one.[38]

8.6 CORRECT UNDERSTANDING AND CERTAINTY, EVEN WITHOUT PROOF

Even as Rambam advocates for the importance of being able to prove God's existence, it is not the case that philosophical proof is necessary for the basic fulfillment of the *mitzva* of *anochi*. Rambam explicates this distinction in *Moreh ha-Nevuchim* 1:50, where he describes the *mitzva* of *emuna* (or *yedi'a*).

Rambam begins by noting that simply saying something is not the same as knowing it:

---

38. "Maimonides, Moses." *Encyclopedia Judaica*. Ed. Michael Berenbaum and Fred Skolnik. 2nd ed. Vol. 13. Detroit: Macmillan Reference USA, 2007, p. 391.

> When reading my present treatise, bear in mind that by "belief"[39] we do not understand merely that which is uttered with the lips, but also that which is apprehended by the soul, the conviction that the object [of belief] is exactly as it is apprehended.

Rambam elaborates: Some people claim that it is enough to say that which is true (e.g., recite *shema Yisrael*), "as if the object of the law (Torah) was to seek forms of expression, not subjects of belief." But this is wrong: "**For belief is possible only after the apprehension of a thing**; it consists in the conviction that the thing apprehended has its existence beyond the mind [in reality] exactly as it is conceived in the mind." Thus, even if a person were to correctly say that God is one, but he does not understand the direct implications of what he is saying, he has accomplished nothing. Essentially, one must understand that which he says.

What does Rambam mean when he writes that we must understand the direct implications of what we are saying? Rambam shows how a corollary of His oneness is that God has no attributes.[40] Thus, "Those who believe that God is One and [simultaneously] that He has many attributes declare the unity with their lips and assume plurality in their thoughts." In other words, saying that He is One when reciting *shema Yisrael* is of little value if one believes that He has attributes, because having attributes contradicts oneness. Rambam suggests a remarkable comparison: saying He is one but yet has attributes "is like the doctrine of the Christians, who say that He is one and He is three, and that the three are one." In other words, it makes no sense.

39. According to R. Yosef Kapach and R. Chaim Heller, this should be translated as "knowledge." Prof. Pines translates it as belief.

40. Attributes are problematic for a number of reasons. If they are accidental qualities, then they would imply that He changes (e.g., He sometimes is kind and sometimes is jealous). Change is impossible for God because that would indicate that He is imperfect in His original form. Even unchanging attributes contradict oneness by introducing multiplicity – there is Him and His attributes. If they are definitional, then they imply that these defining characteristics exist outside of Him, which cannot be since He is the source for all existence. See the first chapters of *Hilchot Yesodei ha-Torah* and *Moreh ha-Nevuchim* 1:50–60 for an elaboration of this concept. While Rambam writes that these concepts are simple and apparent for anyone who pursues philosophy, many modern readers find them far from obvious.

Let us return to our question. According to Rambam, what is necessary to fulfill the *mitzva* of *anochi*? Rambam has told us that a person must have a correct conception, "For belief is only possible after the apprehension of a thing." Rambam (*Moreh ha-Nevuchim* 1:50) also demands certainty:

> Belief is possible only after the apprehension of a thing; it consists in the conviction that the thing apprehended has its existence in reality exactly as it is conceived in the mind. If, in addition to this, we are convinced that the thing cannot be different in any way from what we believe it to be, and that no reasonable argument can be found for the rejection of the belief or for the admission of any deviation from it, then there is certainty.

However, he does not demand that a person be able to prove that which he knows to be true – certainty is possible without the ability to formally prove. Those capable of doing so, however, should strive for proof. To do this, Rambam writes that a person needs to "renounce desires and habits, follow reason, and study what I am going to say."

In 8.10, we will see that not everyone agrees that uncertainty is equated with failure to believe.

8.7 DOES EVERYONE AGREE THAT BELIEF IS A *MITZVA*?

As we have noted, Rambam argues that belief in God, or, more precisely, knowledge of God, is a *mitzva*. Others disagree. In fact, Rambam's argument in favor of enumerating *anochi* as a *mitzva* is a response to *Halachot Gedolot*'s[41] omission of the *mitzva*. Ramban, in his glosses to the first *mitzva* in Rambam's *Sefer ha-Mitzvot*, defends the view of Behag,[42] though in his commentary on the Torah (*Shemot* 20:2),

41. *Halachot Gedolot* (also known as Behag) is a work on the *mitzvot* from the Geonic period. There is some debate as to its author; R. Avraham ibn Daud wrote in *Sefer ha-Kabbala* (M. J. C. i. 63), "R. Simeon Kayyara wrote his work in the year 741."

42. Ramban acknowledges that *Makkot* 23b indicates that *anochi* is in fact a *mitzva*. However, he argues that the Talmud's understanding is an *asmachta*, an allusion in the text for something that does not qualify as a formal biblical *mitzva*. Moreover, as we noted earlier, were it to be the case that it served as a genuine proof, then it

he writes that he prefers Rambam's position. One of the strongest challenges to Rambam's view was penned by R. Chasdai Crescas (1340–1410) in the preface to *Ohr Hashem*, where he offers three rationales for rejecting Rambam's position[43]:

---

would in fact undermine Rambam's thesis, since the first two utterances, according to Rambam's own formulation, contain five *mitzvot*. In an earlier footnote, we noted that *Meshech Chochma* demonstrates that this question is invalid according to Rambam's understanding of the Talmud as elucidated in *Moreh ha-Nevuchim* 2:33.

43. ואולם היות שרש התחלות התורה האלהית היא האמונה במציאות האל יתברך הוא מבואר בעצמו תהיות התורה מסודרת ומצווה ואין ענין להיותה אלהית זולת היות המסדר והמצוה האל יתברך ולזה טעה טעות מפרסם מי שמנה במצוות עשה להאמין מצירות האל יתברך וזה כי המצוה מן המצטרף ולא יצויר מצוה בזולת מצוה ידוע ולזה כאשר נניח אמונת מציאות האל יתברך מצוה כבר נניח אמונת מציאות האל יתברך קודמת בידיעה לאמונת מציאות האל ואם נניח ג״כ אמונת מציאות האל הקודמת מצוה יתחייב גם כן אמונת מציאות האל קודמת וכן לבלתי תכלית וכל זה בתכלית הביטול ולזה הוא מבואר שאין ראוי למנות אמונת מציאות האל במצוות עשה וכבר יראה מפנים וזה שכבר יראה מהוראת שם המצוה וגדרה שלא תפל אלא בדברים שיש לרצון ובחירה מבוא בהם אמנם אם האמונה במציאות האל היא מהדברים שאין לבחירה ורצון מבוא בהם יתחייב שלא תפל הוראת שם המצוה בה וזה ממה שנחקר בו במה שיבוא בגזרת הצור ואיך שיהיה למה שהוא מבואר היות האמונה הזאת שרש והתחלה לכל המצוות אם נמנה אותה במצוה יתחייב שתהיה התחלה לעצמה וזה בתכלית הביטול אמנם הביאו אל זה ר״ל למנות השרש הזה מצוה המאמר שבסוף גמרא מכות אמרם תרי״ג מצות נאמרו למשה בסיני מאי קראה תורה צוה לנו משה והקשו תורה בגימטריא שית מאה וחד סרי הוו והשיבו אנכי ולא יהיה לך מפי הגבורה שמענום וחשבו מפני זה שאנכי ולא יהיה לך שתי מצוות ולזה מנו אמונת מציאות האל במצוה והוא מבואר שלא יתחייב זה לפי שהמכוון שם שהשם הנקרא כן הוא האלוה והמנהיג אשר הוציאנו מארץ מצרים ולזה הטיב הרב רבינו משה ז״ל לפי דרך זה בספר המצוות שלו שמנה המצוה הראשונה בהאמנת האלוהות והוא שנאמין שיש שם עלה וסבה הוא הפועל לכל הנמצאים והוא אמרו אנכי ה׳ אלהיך הנה פרש שם האלהות היותו פועל לכל הנמצאים ויהיה לפי זה אמרו אשר הוצאתיך מארץ מצרים כדמות ראיה על זאת האמונה וזה שמשם נעמוד על יכלת השם וכי המציאות כלם בערכו כחמר ביד היוצר ולזה כבר תפל זאת המצוה על האמונה שהוא אשר הוציאנו מארץ מצרים אלא שהדרך הזה מבאר הנפילה בעצמו וזה שאמרם אנכי ולא יהיה לך כבר יראה שהוא כולל כל הדיבור הנמשך לאהבי ולשמרי מצותי לפי שכבר ישתתפו אלה השני דיבורים בדקדוק לשון מדבר בעדו כאמרו אנכי ה׳ אשר הוצאתיך על פני כי אנכי ה׳ אלהיך לאהבי ולשמרי מצותי ולפי ששאר הדברות נמשכות בדקדוק לשון מדבר בנסתר כאמרו כי לא ינקה ה׳ כי ששת ימים עשה ה׳ שבת וינפש הסכימו שאנכי ולא יהיה לך מפי הגבורה ולפי שכל המחברים מוני האזהרות ראו למנות לא תעשה לך פסל ולא תשתחוה להם בשתי אזהרות והוא האמת בעצמו הנה אם היה שנמנה אנכי במצוה יהו שלש ששמענו מפי הגבורה ויהיה תרי״ד ואם נחשב לא יהיה לך אלהים באזהרה שלא להאמין האלוהות לזולתו כמו שכתב הרב יעלו לתרט״ו ולזה ראוי שנאמר שלא היתה הכונה באמרם אנכי ולא יהיה לך מפי הגבורה שמענום שיהיה כל אחד מצוה אבל למה ששניהם נשתתפו בלשון מדבר בעדו כמו שקדם הוא שבארנו שמפי הגבורה שמענום ויתחייב ששתי האזהרות שבדבור לא יהיה לך שהם לא תעשה לך פסל וכל תמונה

1. Commanding faith seems illogical – if one already believes, the commandment is superfluous, and if he does not believe, he will take no heed of such a *mitzva.*
2. Beliefs cannot be fairly commanded, since they are not voluntary.[44]
3. Rambam's understanding of *Makkot* 23b–24a, which serves as the legal basis for his position, is questionable.

How would Rambam respond to these arguments? Regarding the third critique, Rambam's understanding of the passage in the Talmud remains the simpler one. How might Rambam respond to the first two objections?

What the Mitzva of Emuna Demands of Us

Commentators suggest a number of approaches to address the first of R. Crescas's critiques. The first possibility argues that the *mitzva* of *anochi* demands more than simply belief. For example, R. Yitzchak Abarbanel (1437–1508) in *Rosh Amana,* Ch. 7, notes that Rambam (*Hilchot Yesodei ha-Torah,* Ch. 1) does not simply understand that *anochi* demands belief or knowledge of God's existence – it requires that we have some sort of understanding of God. As explained earlier, we must know that God necessarily exists and is the basis for all else that exists.[45] R. Crescas challenged that if one already believes in God, then the commandment is superfluous. The response is that this is not true, since someone may "believe in God," but not be fulfilling the *mitzva* of *anochi.* (For example, they know He exists but do not appreciate that He necessarily exists.) Moreover, even someone who already believes can strengthen his faith through further contemplation and deliberation. As we noted, Rambam

ולא תשתחוה להם אשר שמענום מפי הגבורה ישלימו לתרי״ג עם התרי״א אשר שמענום מפי משה.

44. This point specifically relates to R. Crescas's perspective on free will, which we explore in 15.4.

45. אבל כוונת הרב הגדול בכל דבריו הוא שהעיקר הראשון והמצוה הראשונה הוא שנאמין שהאלוה ב״ה שכבר ידענו שהוא נמצא, מציאותו הוא היותר ראשון ויותר שלם אשר בכל המציאות, שמציאותו אינו אפשר מצד עצמו כיתר הנמצאים אבל הוא מחויב המציאות מצד עצמו כו׳ וכבר התבאר שהמחויב הוא כי הוא אינו צריך במציאותו לזולתו וכל מה שזולתו צריך במציאותו אליו לפי שהוא נותן המציאות וקיום לכל הנמצאים כו׳

maintains that ideally a person should seek proof for the existence of God.[46] Thus, there is much that the *mitzva* of *anochi* demands of the believer; the *mitzva* is far from superfluous.

A similar approach argues that *emuna* demands more than knowledge of His necessary existence. R. Menachem Mendel Schneerson, also known as the *Tzemach Tzedek* (the third Rebbe of the Chabad Lubavitch chasidic movement; 1789–1866), defends Rambam by arguing that a Jew must feel and appreciate that God's exaltedness goes beyond that which we can possibly understand.[47] Essentially, R. Schneerson accepts R. Crescas's critique that there is no need for a *mitzva* to believe in that which can be easily seen, intuited, or proven. If it can be demonstrated that God necessarily exists, then there is no need to command that one must believe He necessarily exists. However, *emuna* is to believe that He is greater than we can imagine.[48] Moreover, one might add that *anochi* demands that we must believe in Him with our entire being, not just with our intellect. Our hearts and minds must unite in our belief/knowledge of His existence as they did when He revealed himself at Sinai.

A different line of reasoning is followed by others, who argue that the primary obligation of "*anochi Hashem*" is not belief in God per se, but acceptance of His sovereignty,[49] which differs from commanding belief.

---

46. This idea is developed by Maharam Shick (*Taryag Mitzvot* No. 25).

47. **דרך מצותיך מצות האמנת אלקות מה, א**

והעולה מדבריו (הר״י אברבנאל בספר ראש אמנה) שציווי ההאמנה אינה על מציאות האל כי ע״ז לא נצרך לציווי כי כבר ידענו שהוא נמצא כמשי״ת רק הציווי הוא ההאמנה שמציאותו הוא היותר שלם כו׳, אמנם מה שביאר החכם הנז׳ ענין שלימות מציאותו שהוא מחוייב המציאות הנה ע״פ דרך הקבלה הוא בענין אחר כמשי״ת לפנינו אי״ה כי גם על היותו מחוייב המציאות א״צ לאמונה כי הוא נכלל בכלל הידיעה שכבר ידענו זה שיש בורא המחי׳ העולם וממילא שהוא מחוייב המציאו׳ כמו שביאר בעצמו ענין מחוייב המציאות שהוא זה **אלא האמונה היא שהוא ית׳ רם ונשגב למעלה מעלה ממדריגת החכמה.**

48. Or, as we cited earlier from R. Nachman of Breslov, *emuna* begins where the intellect ends.

49. This is the explanation of Ramban (to Rambam's *Sefer ha-Mitzvot, Asei* 1) and R. Ovadya Seforno in his Introduction to *Ohr Amim*. See also Maharal, *Tiferet Yisrael*, Ch. 37.

השגת הרמב״ן לספר המצוות עשה א׳

אמר הכותב האמונה הזאת בדבור הזה לא נפלאת היא ולא רחוקה היא וכן בדברי רבותינו ז״ל מפורש שהוא קבלת מלכותו יתע׳ והיא אמונת האלהות. אמרו במכלתא [והוב׳ ברמב״ן ל״ת ה] לא יהיה לך אלהים אחרים על פני למה נאמר לפי שהוא אומר אנכי י״י אלהיך משל למלך

A final approach in explaining the *mitzva* of *anochi* is that it demands that we believe that He who is Creator of the universe is identical to the God who brought us out of Egypt and gave us these laws in the Torah.[50] Perhaps we could respond to R. Crescas' objection by saying that one can indeed decide to hold such a belief, because it involves associating something one already knows or believes in (i.e., God's existence) with the experience of Sinai.

Is Belief Voluntary?

Likewise, with respect to R. Crescas's second point, as we have seen, Rambam maintains that a person can, in fact, be drawn to false ideologies. While these erroneous beliefs may be tempting, a person is capable of searching honestly and arriving at the truth. As Rambam writes (*Hilchot Avoda Zara* 2:1) concerning idolatry:

> The Torah commands: 'Be very careful that your heart not be tempted [to go astray and worship other gods]' (*Devarim* 11:16). This implies that the thoughts of your heart should not lead you astray to worship these and make them an intermediary between you and the Creator.

The Torah commands us to not allow our thoughts to cause us to stray. Apparently, we have the capacity to prevent such thoughts from causing us to stray. This notion is underscored by Rambam's formulation of the violation of *lo yihyeh*:

> **הלכות יסודי התורה פרק א הלכה ו**
> וידיעת דבר זה מצות עשה שנאמר אנכי ה׳ אלהיך **וכל המעלה על דעתו שיש שם אלוה אחר חוץ מזה עובר** בלא תעשה שנאמר: ״לא

שנכנס למדינה אמרו לו עבדיו גזור עליהם גזירות אמר להם לאו כשיקבלו מלכותי אגזור עליהם גזירות שאם מלכותי אינן מקבלים גזרותי היאך מקיימין כך אמר המקום לישראל אנכי י״י אלהיך לא יהיה לך אלהים אחרים על פני אני הוא שקבלתם עליכם מלכותי במצרים אמרו הן כשם שקבלתם מלכותי קבלו גזירותי לא יהיה לך.

50. Ran, *Drashot ha-Ran*, *Drasha* 9 and R. Yosef Albo, *Sefer ha-Ikkarim* 1:14.

יהיה לך אלהים אחרים על פני" וכופר בעיקר שזהו העיקר הגדול שהכל תלוי בו.

> The knowledge of this concept is a positive commandment, as it says (*Shemot* 20:2): "I am Hashem, your God." **And whoever permits the thought to enter his mind that there is another deity besides this God** violates a prohibition, as it is said, "You shall have no other gods before Me," and denies the essence of religion – this doctrine being the great principle upon which everything depends.

Rambam's formulation of the negative commandment is striking. Rambam does not simply write that anyone who thinks there is another god is in violation of the prohibition. He writes, "Whoever permits the thought to enter his mind." Rambam alludes to the objection to commanding belief by highlighting the extent to which we control our thoughts. In 2.1, we cited Rambam's assertion that we must abstain from the pleasures of this world and focus all of our energy on the quest to find God if we hope to succeed. We have only ourselves to blame if our half-hearted attempt ends in failure. Thus, Rambam frequently stresses that we must choose between assessing reality honestly and allowing our hearts to control our minds. This, in essence, is the *mitzva* of *emuna*.

8.8 THE DANGERS OF SEEKING "PROOF"

In 9.7, we shall see that many thinkers prefer faith based on tradition over faith based on proof. One obvious reason for this is that the pursuit of proof may lead to heresy. After all, what happens if proof is not found? This did not concern Rambam, who felt that if the seeker of proof is properly prepared and motivated, he will not flounder (see 2.1 on what constitutes proper preparation).

Even if one succeeds in finding proof, though, other dangers lurk. In Chapter 9, we will explore *Kuzari*'s critique of faith that is based on proof. Among other things, he notes that faith that is based on proof may yield intellectual knowledge of God's existence but not a relationship with God. Moreover, *Kuzari* notes that sometimes, knowledge rooted in the mind is far more tenuous than faith rooted in the heart (see 9.1).

A historical observation that reflects this concern was made by R. Yosef Ya'avetz (known as *Chasid Ya'avetz*; 1440–1508[51]), who was among those expelled from Spain in 1492. He notes that among those who were put to the ultimate test, those whose faith was rooted in philosophical proof (whom he compares to a tree with many branches but shallow roots) failed, whereas the ignorant (whom he compares to a tree with deep roots but few branches) remained steadfast. It was they who were willing to sacrifice their lives and fortunes for God.[52] History has shown us that "proof" does not always yield conviction.[53]

R. Yitzchak Hutner noted that it is for this reason a Jew is taught to say *shema* while still a child,[54] well before he can understand the philosophical implications of the verse. We hope that faith becomes deeply implanted within the child in a way that is deeper than (though later supplemented by) cognitive knowledge.[55]

8.9 APPENDIX A: RAMBAM'S CONCEPTION OF WHAT ACTUALLY HAPPENED AT *MATAN TORAH* AND HIS UNDERSTANDING OF HOW WE KNOW THE TORAH IS TRUE

In 8.4, we referred to Rambam's understanding of what the Jews heard at Sinai. His mysterious comments warrant elaboration, but before

---

51. He was a student of Abarbanel and colleague of R. Yitzchak Arama. He is not to be confused with R. Yaakov Emden.

52. **אור החיים פרק שני**
אליכם אישים אקרא מגלות ספרד אני אשר גורשנו בעונותינו הרבים והעצומים, ורוב המתפארים בחכמה ובמעשים טובים **כלם המירו את כבודם ביום מר,** והנשים ועמי הארץ מסרו גופם וממונם על קדושת בוראם. ולטוש אתה המעיין את עין שכלך במשנה [אבות ג:יז] כל שמעשיו מרובים מחכמתו למה הוא דומה וכו'.

53. Rambam certainly was aware of this danger, frequently describing how genuine contemplation of the Divine leads to a powerful and unbreakable emotional bond that even the strongest winds cannot uproot (see, for example, *Hilchot Yesodei ha-Torah,* Ch. 2, and *Hilchot Teshuva,* Ch. 10).

54. Rambam, *Hilchot Talmud Torah,* Ch. 1.

55. **ספר הזיכרון למרן בעל פחד יצחק עמ' ד'**
שהוא טעם למה שחוזרין שמע ישראל עם הילד דוקא בעוד שהוא תינוק... שהתפיסה בקבלת עול מלכות שמים לא תהיה מבוססת על הבנה שכלית גרידא, אלא על תשתית ויסוד הנפש, שהיא בגדר למעלה מן השכל.

beginning, let us note Rambam's warning that trying to understand what exactly happened at *Matan Torah* may be impossible:

ספר מורה הנבוכים חלק ב פרק לג

> ודעהו וזכרהו, שאי אפשר שיכניס אדם עצמו למעמד הר סיני ביותר מזה השיעור אשר זכרוהו שהוא מכלל סתרי תורה. ואמתת ההשגה ההיא ואיך היה הענין בה, נעלם ממנו מאוד כי לא קדם כמותו ולא יתאחר, ודעהו.
>
> Know this and remember it, that it is impossible for any person to expound the revelation on Mount Sinai more fully than our Sages have done, since it is one of the secrets of the Torah. It is very difficult to have a true conception of the revelation and what occurred in it, for there never before has been, nor will there ever be again, anything like it. Know this.

Rambam informs us that the journey upon which we are about to embark is perilous; we must tread carefully. Indeed, Rambam writes in *Moreh ha-Nevuchim* (1:5) that the verse concerning *Matan Torah* (*Shemot* 19:24) that states, "The priests and the populace shall not break [their formation] to ascend to God, lest He wreak destruction upon them" serves as a general warning against attempting to understand concepts that are beyond us. Moshe merited his magnificent understanding because he initially showed trepidation about investigating that which was beyond him, as the verse states, "And Moshe hid his face, for he was afraid to look at God" (*Shemot* 3:6).

With this qualification in mind, let us consider a startling interpretation of Rambam from *Moreh ha-Nevuchim* (2:33). Earlier, we cited the Talmud's statement (*Makkot* 23b–24a) that the first two of the Ten Commandments were heard directly by the Jewish people, as opposed to the subsequent commandments, which God told Moshe and Moshe in turn related to the Jewish people. We also saw Rambam's position that this cannot be taken literally, as it is inconceivable that the Jewish people could hear the direct word of God, as they were not on the level of prophets. Rather, the Talmud means that the truth of the first two commandments, namely, the existence of God and His unity, can be derived independently using logic. Since there is no need for prophecy to arrive at these principles, our knowledge of them is direct, and in that sense, it is identical to Moshe's. This is in contrast to the rest of the Torah, which we know only through Moshe. What then did the Jewish people hear at Sinai? Rambam responds that they heard an undifferentiated "*kol*" (sound). Moshe deciphered this *kol* and transmitted it to the Jewish people.

This revolutionary explanation seems to contradict a fundamental principle of faith that Rambam explicates elsewhere. Rambam writes that the basis of our faith in Moshe and his Torah is not the miracles that the Jews witnessed in the desert, since miracles may leave a person with a twinge of doubt (as they may be sorcery). Rather, the experience at Sinai, where we heard God communicate directly to man, forms the basis of our faith in Torah, since the experience of prophecy is unmistakable.

In and of itself, this does not contradict his comments in *Moreh ha-Nevuchim*. In *Moreh ha-Nevuchim,* he writes that our knowledge concerning the existence of God and His oneness stems from logic; however, our confidence in the divinity of Torah, as explained in *Mishneh Torah,* rests on revelation. Rather, the seeming inconsistency emerges from his description in *Mishneh Torah* of what we witnessed at Sinai. In *Mishneh Torah,* he writes:

הלכות יסודי התורה פרק ח:א

משה רבנו לא האמינו בו ישראל מפני האותות שעשה שהמאמין על פי האותות יש בליבו דופי שאפשר שייעשה האות בלאט וכישוף אלא כל האותות **שעשה במדבר**, לפי הצורך עשאן לא להביא ראיה על הנבואה צרך להשקיע את המצריים קרע את הים והצלילם בו צרכנו למזון הוריד לנו את המן צמאו בקע להם את האבן כפרו בו עדת קורח בלעה אותם הארץ וכן שאר כל האותות.

ובמה האמינו בו במעמד הר סיניי שעינינו ראו ולא זר ואוזנינו שמעו ולא אחר האש והקולות והלפידים והוא ניגש אל הערפל והקול מדבר אליו **ואנו שומעים משה משה לך אמור להם כך וכך** וכן הוא אומר "פנים בפנים דיבר ה' עימכם" (דברים ה:ד) ונאמר "לא את אבותינו כרת ה' את הברית הזאת" (דברים ה:ג).

ומניין שבמעמד הר סיניי לבדו, היא הראיה לנבואתו שהיא אמת שאין בו דופי--שנאמר "הנה אנוכי בא אליך בעב הענן, בעבור ישמע העם בדברי עימך, וגם בך יאמינו לעולם" (שמות יט:ט): מכלל שקודם דבר זה, לא האמינו בו נאמנות שהיא עומדת לעולם, אלא נאמנות שיש אחריה הרהור ומחשבה.

The Children of Israel did not believe in Moshe [solely] because of the signs he presented, for the belief of someone who believes [in a prophet solely] because of the signs he presents is tainted, for it could be that his signs are performed by means of spells and witchcraft. All the signs that Moshe performed in the wilderness were done according to the needs of the moment, not to bring proof to his prophecies. There was a need to sink the Egyptians, so Moshe split the sea and drowned them in it; the Children of Israel needed food, so Moshe brought down the manna for them; they needed water, so Moshe split the rock for them; Korach and his followers rebelled, so Moshe opened up the ground and they were swallowed up. The same principle applies with all the other signs.

It was the assembly at Mount Sinai that made them believe in Moshe, when our eyes, and no one else's, saw, and our ears, and no one else's, heard, and Moshe drew near to the darkness, and the voice spoke to him, and we heard it saying to Moshe, "Moshe, Moshe, go tell them such-and-such." In connection with this it is written, "God spoke with you face to face." And it also is written, "God did not make this covenant with our fathers [alone], but with us, even us."

From where is it known that the assembly at Mount Sinai was the proof that the prophecy of Moshe was true and that he was not speaking basely? It is derived from the verse, "Behold, I come to you in a thick cloud, that the people may hear when I speak with you and believe in you forever." From this we see that prior to the assembly at Mount Sinai, their belief in Moshe was not one that would have lasted forever, but rather was a belief that left room for discussion and thought.

Here, Rambam writes that the entire Jewish people heard and understood Hashem's voice, in contrast with his comments in *Moreh ha-Nevuchim* where Rambam states that we heard only the undifferentiated "*kol*."

The answer to this riddle lies in recognizing what Rambam in *Mishneh Torah* says we heard. He writes that the Jewish people heard, "Moshe, Moshe, go tell them such-and-such." Rambam does not say that we heard, "I am Hashem, your God…" In that sense, he is totally consistent with his comments in *Moreh ha-Nevuchim*. In fact, the words "Moshe, Moshe, go tell them such-and-such" do not appear in any verse in the Torah. How does Rambam know that the Jews heard these words? The answer can be discerned in the following verse:

שמות יט:ט

וַיֹּאמֶר יְקֹוָק אֶל מֹשֶׁה הִנֵּה אָנֹכִי בָּא אֵלֶיךָ בְּעַב הֶעָנָן בַּעֲבוּר יִשְׁמַע הָעָם בְּדַבְּרִי עִמָּךְ וְגַם בְּךָ יַאֲמִינוּ לְעוֹלָם.

> And God said to Moshe, "Behold, I am coming to you in the thickness of the cloud in order that the people hear when I speak to you, and they also will believe in you forever."

The verse does not say we will believe because God will address us; rather, it states we will believe because we will hear God conversing with Moshe. In this verse, the Torah relates that the Jewish people hearing God speak to Moshe is the basis for our eternal belief in the veracity of Moshe's prophecy, which is precisely what Rambam writes.

Perhaps Rambam means to say that when they heard the "*kol*," they perceived, "Moshe, Moshe, go tell them such-and-such." While they could not understand the specific words that made up the "*kol*," they understood that these were words directed towards Moshe with the intention that he relate them to the rest of the people. This experience was unmistakable; unlike miracles, which may be attributed to magic, the Jews heard the voice of God and understood the unambiguous message: "Moshe, Moshe, go tell them such-and-such."[56]

---

56. Essentially, we are suggesting that the Jewish people understood this critical lesson through extrapolation. The notion that extrapolation is a fundamental element of

Conceivably, we can go even further and suggest that the Jews heard the actual words "Moshe, Moshe, go tell them such-and-such" from God. This does not contradict Rambam's axiom that unworthy people cannot receive prophecy, because prophecy is defined by the transmission of content, not practical instructions.[57]

Rambam's approach to *Matan Torah* was sharply criticized by other Rishonim. In fact, after writing why he feels it is inappropriate

---

prophecy is expressed by Rambam in a number of places. Rambam in the seventh chapter of *Hilchot Yesodei ha-Torah* maintains that only Moshe was capable of directly receiving the word of God. All other prophets understood the divine message through a *mashal* or *chida*, a process that involves some sort of extrapolation. In that sense, the prophetic experience of the Jewish people at Sinai, which also involved extrapolation, was more similar to general prophecy than at first appears.

57. Perhaps we can find a paradigm for such an explanation by considering a problematic component of Rambam's thesis. If only the righteous can prophesy, how do we explain Bilam?

In *Moreh ha-Nevuchim* (2:45), Rambam enumerates ten levels of prophecy, with the first two levels being a type of sub-prophecy. In the first level, divine assistance motivates an individual to perform a great action. This spirit is sometimes called "the spirit of God" or "holy spirit." Examples include Yosef's success in Egypt, Moshe hitting the Egyptian, the acts of the *Shoftim*, and David's actions after being appointed by Shmuel.

The next level is known as *ruach ha-kodesh*. The difference between *nevua* and *ruach ha-kodesh* explains the difference between *Nevi'im* and *Ketuvim*:

היא שירגיש האדם כאלו דבר מה חל בו, וכוח אחר עבר עליו שמדובבו, ואז ידבר בדברי חכמה, או תהילה, או בדברי תוכחת מועילים, או בדברים מדיניים או אלוהיים, וכל זה בהקיץ ובמצב של שימוש החושים כרגיל, וזהו שאומרים עליו **שהוא מדבר ברוח הקדש.**

ובכיוצא בזה מרוח הקודש חיבר דוד תלים, וחיבר שלמה משלי וקוהלת ושיר השירים. וכן דניאל ואיוב ודברי הימים ושאר הכתובים, בכיוצא בזה מרוח הקודש נתחברו. ולפיכך נקראים כתובים, כוונתם שהם כתובים ברוח הקדוש, ובפירוש אמרו מגילת אסתר ברוח הקודש נאמרה.

This category can take place when the recipient is awake as well as through a dream, as opposed to true prophecy which, according to Rambam, takes place only when the prophet is asleep, with Moshe being the sole exception:

ואין ספק כי מעלה זו למטה ממעלת אשר נאמר בהם בחלום אדבר בו. ולפיכך הסכמת כל האומה לסדר ספר דניאל מכלל כתובים לא מן הנביאים. ולפיכך העירותיך כי סוג זה של נבואה אשר באה לדניאל ושלמה, ואף על פי שנראה בהן מלאך בחלום, הרי הם בעצמם לא מצאו שהיא נבואה בהחלט, אלא חלום המודיע דברי אמת, והרי הוא מסוג מי שמדבר ברוח הקדש, וזו היא המעלה השניה.

Rambam writes that Bilam falls under this category:

to study Greek philosophy, Rivash (*Teshuvot ha-Rivash* 45) asks how Rambam could have engaged in such a pursuit. His answer is twofold, as noted in 1.7. Firstly, Rambam was capable of distinguishing between that which is valuable and that which is false. Rivash invokes the example of R. Meir, who studied Torah from *Acheir*.[58] Secondly, Rambam wrote *Moreh ha-Nevuchim*, which utilizes Greek philosophy, to refute the heretics of his day. Nevertheless, even Rambam, asserts Rivash, did not emerge unscathed. One example cited by Rivash of philosophy's pernicious influence upon Rambam can be seen in his treatment of *Matan Torah*.

Thus, let us conclude by once again remembering Rambam's warning: "It is impossible for any person to expound the revelation on Mount Sinai... since it is one of the secrets of the Law." Nevertheless, to the extent that we can, we must attempt to understand it, for it is the basis of our faith.

ודע כי גם בלעם מן הסוג הזה היה בזמן כשרותו, ולעניין זה רצה באומרו וישם ה׳ דבר בפי בלעם, כאלו אמר כי ברוח ה׳ ידבר, ועל עניין זה אמר הוא על עצמו שומע אמרי אל.

With this, Rambam answers the question we raised earlier: how could Bilam prophesy if he was not righteous? The answer is that he was not a true prophet. (It also is interesting to note that even Bilam experienced only the "holy spirit" when he was still *kasher*. The question is: when did he stop being righteous? Seemingly, it is after all of his pronouncements. Presumably, he loses this status only when he advises Balak to seduce the Jewish people.)

What emerges clearly is that while full prophecy requires moral and intellectual perfection, God still communicates to humans through these quasi-prophetic means even if they are unworthy. Examples of instances where God communicates with unworthy people through non-prophetic means are Hagar and Avimelech. Based on the distinction between quasi-prophecy and true prophecy, we can understand how the Jewish people were able to hear "Moshe, Moshe, go tell them such-and-such," even if they were not able to decipher the *kol*. To understand the content of the Ten Commandments may have required the moral and intellectual perfection of a prophet, but, as we have seen, certain forms of divine communication are available even to unworthy individuals.

58. Elisha b. Avuya was a brilliant Torah scholar who adopted a heretical worldview and thereafter was referred to as *Acheir* ("the other one").

8.10 APPENDIX B: DO DOUBTS AUTOMATICALLY CLASSIFY A PERSON AS A HERETIC?

In 8.6, we cited Rambam's view that fulfillment of the *mitzva* of *anochi* demands certainty; a person must be "convinced that the thing cannot be different in any way from what we believe it to be and that no reasonable argument can be found for the rejection of the belief or for the admission of any deviation from it; then the belief is true."

Likewise, in a statement following the thirteen principles of faith, Rambam implies that doubt categorizes a person as a heretic:

> וכאשר **יפקפק** אדם ביסוד מאלו היסודות הרי זה יצא מן הכלל וכפר בעיקר ונקרא מין ואפיקורוס וקוצץ בנטיעות.
>
> If a person **doubts** one of these fundamentals, he leaves the nation and is a denier of the basic principle and is called a heretic and a denier...

Moreover, he writes in *Mishneh Torah*:

> **רמב"ם הלכות יסודי התורה פרק א הלכה ו**
> **וכל המעלה על דעתו** שיש שם אלוה אחר חוץ מזה, עובר בלא תעשה שנאמר לא יהיה לך אלהים אחרים על פני, וכופר בעיקר שזהו העיקר הגדול שהכל תלוי בו.
>
> Anyone who **considers the thought** that there is another deity transgresses a negative commandment, as [*Shemot* 20:3] states: "You shall have no other gods before Me" and denies a fundamental principle [of faith], because this is the great principle [of faith] upon which all depends.

Thus, when Rambam writes that a person should seek proof for the existence of God, the act of proving does not stem from uncertainty, but is an attempt to prove what he already knows.[59]

---

59. As noted in 2.3 and 2.5, a valid proof must consider the possibility of an alternative solution. Thus, Rambam writes that for purposes of proving the existence of God, one may imagine that God does not exist.

Not everyone agrees that all forms of questions and doubt automatically classify a person as a heretic.[60] A dissenting view emerges from Rashi's understanding of the famous story concerning Hillel's attitude towards a person who sought conversion on condition that he be taught only the written law:

תלמוד בבלי מסכת שבת דף לא עמוד א

תנו רבנן: מעשה בנכרי אחד שבא לפני שמאי, אמר לו: כמה תורות יש לכם? אמר לו: שתים, תורה שבכתב ותורה שבעל פה. אמר לו: שבכתב - אני מאמינך, ושבעל פה - איני מאמינך. גיירני על מנת שתלמדני תורה שבכתב. גער בו והוציאו בנזיפה. בא לפני הלל - גייריה, יומא קמא אמר ליה: א״ב ג״ד, למחר אפיך ליה. אמר ליה: והא אתמול לא אמרת לי הכי? אמר לו: לאו עלי דידי קא סמכת? דעל פה נמי סמוך עלי!

There once was a gentile who came before Shammai. The gentile asked: "How many Torahs do you have?" Shammai responded: "Two – one written and one oral." The gentile retorted, "I believe you about the written law, but not about the oral law; convert me on condition that you teach me the written Torah." Shammai scolded him and repulsed him in anger. When he went before Hillel, he accepted him as a convert. On the first day [of teaching him], Hillel taught him א, ב, ג, ד; the following day, he reversed the order to him. "But yesterday you did not teach them to me thus," [the gentile] protested. "Must you then not rely upon me [as to what the letters are]? Then rely upon me with respect to the oral law as well," Hillel replied (i.e., there must be certain reliance upon authority before anything can be learnt at all).

Why did Shammai dismiss the potential convert? Rashi explains that Shammai simply was carrying out the law that we cannot convert

60. If one accepts the fourth approach (see 11.4) to Rambam's understanding of *tinok she-nishba,* it is conceivable that even Rambam agrees to the distinction that follows.

someone unless he accepts the entire Torah. Certainly, someone who rejects the oral law rejects many principles of Torah:

How, then, could Hillel convert the person? Rashi answers:

> וסמך על חכמתו שסופו שירגילנו לקבל עליו, דלא דמיא הא לחוץ מדבר אחד - שלא היה כופר בתורה שבעל פה, אלא שלא היה מאמין שהיא מפי הגבורה, והלל הובטח שאחר שילמדנו יסמוך עליו.
>
> [Hillel] relied on his wisdom that in the end, he would accustom him to accept [the oral law], for it is not the same as [accepting the Torah] "except for one thing," for he did not deny the oral law; rather, he did not believe that it comes from God, and Hillel was sure that, following his instruction, [the gentile] would rely on him.

Rashi distinguishes between denial or כפירה (which would invalidate the conversion) and lack of belief (which does not disqualify conversion). In other words, Hillel understood that this person simply saw no reason to believe in the oral law. Hillel was confident, however, that his disbelief stemmed from not having been shown evidence for its existence. Thus, Hillel converted him knowing that he would accept a valid argument when presented.

On a practical level, we might not share Hillel's keen insight into other people's motivation. Thus, because it is difficult to tell whether a person's lack of belief stems from denial or is rooted in not having been taught, we will not accept a convert who does not actively express belief. Nevertheless, we see from here that not all questioning or even expressions of denial reflect heresy.[61] The litmus test will be whether a person accepts the truth when it is shown to him.[62] (Of course, there may be

61. In terms of Halacha, see *Shach* (Y.D. 268:23). Practically, of course, we would not presume such clairvoyance.
62. This parallels *Chazon Ish*'s view that a person has the status of *tinok she-nishba* as long as he would be convinced to believe in God and Torah if an appropriate attempt to convince him were made:

חזו"א יו"ד סי' א אות ו

differences between denial of God and other fundamental principles of faith. We consider this in Chapter 11.)

Rashash (R. Shmuel Strashun; 1794–1872) outlines the ramifications of Rashi's understanding:

> נ"ל כונתו דכופר לא מיקרי אלא אחר החקירה בכל חלקי הסותר, אבל זה לא חקר ולא נוכח אלא שלא היה מאמין וכו' לכן הובטח שלאחר שיברר אליו אמיתת הדברים ישוב מאמין.
>
> The term "heretic" applies only after investigation of all possibilities, but this [gentile] did not investigate, nor was he convinced of anything. Rather, he simply did not believe. [Hillel] therefore was sure that after he clarified the truth of the matter for him, he would believe.

According to Rashash, a person who denies based on lack of education is not classified as a heretic. This relates to our discussion of *tinok she-nishba* in 11.10.

Thus, it would appear that Rambam maintains that doubts constitute heresy, while according to Rashi, this may not be the case.

R. Kook's Distinction Between Agnosticism and Atheism

Another important position on this question can be found in the letters of R. Kook.

ותינוק שנשבה בין העכו"מ דינו כישראל ושחיטתו מותרת, שהוא בחזקת שאם יודי־עוהו וישתדלו עמו כשיעור ההשתדלות שהוא ראוי לשוב, לא יזיד לבלתי שב, אמנם אחר שהשתדלו עמו והוא מזיד וממאן לשוב, דינו כמומר. ושעור ההשתדלות תלוי לפי התבוננות הדיינים כאשר יופיע רוח קדשם בהכרעת דינו. ומה שנחלקו אחרונים ז"ל בצדוקים בדורות האחרונים אי חשיבי כאנוסים היינו בהכרעת שיעור הידיעה שיודעים ממציאות ישראל ושאבותיהם פירשו מהם ונותנים כתף סוררת, אי דיינינן להו כשעור ידיעה למחשב מזיד או לא ואכתי אנוסים הם ובאמת צריך לדון על כל איש ואיש בפרט... וכמו כן אותו שאבותיו פרשו מדרכי הצבור והוא נתגדל ללא תורה דינו כישראל לכל דבר, ונמי צריך למוד שיעור ידיעתו אי לא חשיב מזיד, ואותו שדיינינן ליה כאנוס זוכין עירוב עבורו.

חזו"א עירובין פז:יד

ותינוק שנשבה בין העכו"ם דינו כישראל ושחיטתו מותרת שהוא בחזקת שאם יודיעוהו וישתדלו עמו כשיעור ההשתדלות שהוא ראוי לשוב לא יזיד לבלתי שב.

אגרות הראי"ה אגרת כ

ולענין דינא. דע, שאע"פ שאיסור גמור וחולי רע הוא, אפילו מי שמסתפק ומהרהר על דברי האמונה השלמה, **מכל מקום לא מצינו שדנו חז"ל דין אפיקורוס, כי אם על הכופר, דהיינו המחליט ההיפך.** וההחלטה של ההיפך אי אפשר שתמצא כלל בישראל בין שום אדם שלא יהיה רשע גמור ומשקר במזיד. כי הרשעה היותר גדולה לא תוכל כי אם להטיל דופי של ספק לחלושי הדעות, וכיון שכן מי שמעיז פנים לאמר שהוא כופר בבירור, הרי הוא רשע מוחלט, שבצדק היה ראוי לדונו בכל הדינים המפורשים, ואין כאן טענת לבו אונסו כלל. ואם הייתה הכפירה שבדורנו בעלת אמת, היתה תמיד טוענת טענת ספק, והיו מבררים לה בנקל ספקותיה, אבל היא משקרת בזדון, וטוענת טענת ודאי, בשעה שאפילו ליותר חלושים בדעת אי אפשר כלל שתבוא כי אם למדת ספק, והרי היא עסוקה ברשע של רדיפה בעזות מצח, על כן היא חייבת כל הדינים, שבידי אדם ובידי שמים, לפי הערך של המכשלה שהיא עושה. ופרטי הדברים מובן שצריכים אריכות גדולה של ספרים רבים לבאר. ודבר זה ברור, שמי שבא לידיעה איך שכל המינות, ביחש לישראל, איננה כי אם טענה של ספק גרועה, המתלקטת מחסרון ידיעה וחסרון רגש ומעוט מוסר, מיד הוא נעשה שלם באמונה ויראת ד׳ באמת, וכל מה שיהיה יותר דבק בתלמידי חכמים, דורשי א-להים באמת, כן יתעלה מעלה מעלה, להיות ממולא באמונה של חסן חכמת ודעת. "כל כלי יוצר עליך לא יצלח וכל לשון תקום אתך למשפט תרשיעי, זאת נחלת עבדי ד׳ וצדקתם מאתי אמר ד׳".

As for the law, you should know that even though it is utterly prohibited and diseased for one to doubt and wonder about matters of perfect faith, **we do not find the Sages applying the law of heresy [in such a case], but only in the case of a non-believer, that is, one who definitely affirms the opposite**. And absolute belief in the opposite can be found in Israel only amongst those who are inherently wicked and deliberate liars, because even the greatest evil [influence] can only cast a doubt in weak-minded persons; therefore, someone who dares to say unequivocally that he is an atheist is completely wicked and is fit to be judged according to all the explicit laws [relating to a heretic], since there is no justification for the argument that he was compelled to think thusly. And if the atheistic idea in our generation was

> genuine, it always would claim uncertainty, and its doubts could be clarified easily; but it lies deliberately and claims certainty at a time when even the most weak-minded are at most doubtful [of the existence of God]. The atheistic idea is in brazen pursuit of malice and is thus liable to all the laws in the hands of man and heaven in accordance with the harm it does.
>
> Clarification of the details of this law would, of course, require many lengthy books. This is clear: whoever reaches the understanding that any denial of faith, in relation to Judaism, is nothing but a feeble argument of doubt, a combination of a lack of actual knowledge, lack of feeling, and shortcoming in virtue, immediately will become whole with his faith and God-fearing. The more he attaches himself to Torah scholars, true seekers of God, the more he will be exalted and filled with an unshakable faith of wisdom and knowledge: "No weapon formed against you shall succeed, and every tongue that rises against you at law, you shall condemn. Such is the lot of the servants of God, such is their triumph through me, declares God."[63]

R. Kook distinguishes between agnosticism, which is intellectually plausible, and atheism, which is intellectually implausible (how could anyone be certain that there is no God?) and therefore inexcusable (אין כאן טענת לבו אונסו כלל), dishonest, and malicious.[64] Agnosticism,

---

63. This translation is adapted from *Rav A.Y. Kook: Selected Letters*, translated by Tzvi Feldman (Ma'aleh Adumim, 1986).

64. Elsewhere, R. Kook writes about the holiness and redeeming value of atheism. In an essay entitled "The Pangs of Cleansing," R. Kook notes that the source of atheism is an immature understanding of God. (The god they reject is not the God I believe in.) The value, and even holiness, in atheism is that by forcing us to confront their challenges, it refines our belief.

> The greatest impediment to the human spirit, on reaching maturity, results from the fact that the conception of God is crystallized among people in a particular form going back to childish habit and imagination....
>
> The tendency of unrefined people to see the divine *essence* as embodied in the words and in the letters alone is a source of embarrassment to humanity, and **atheism arises as a pained outcry to liberate man from this narrow and alien pit**....

on the other hand, while certainly prohibited, is viewed more as a sickness (חולי רע). As such, ostracism is inappropriate.

R. Kook's statement that we do not find the Sages applying the law of heresy with respect to someone who has doubts concerning matters of faith is somewhat baffling in light of Rambam's position cited in 8.6.[65] Perhaps R. Kook deduced that Rambam declared a person a heretic only if he categorically **stated** a heretical position.[66] Such a possibility may be supported from *Hilchot Teshuva.*

רמב"ם הלכות תשובה פרק ג הלכה ח

שלשה הן הנקראים אפיקורסין: **האומר** שאין שם נבואה כלל ואין שם מדע שמגיע מהבורא ללב בני האדם; והמכחיש נבואתו של משה רבינו; **והאומר** שאין הבורא יודע מעשה בני האדם. כל אחד משלשה אלו הן אפיקורוסים. שלשה הן הכופרים בתורה: **האומר** שאין התורה מעם ה' - אפילו פסוק אחד אפילו תיבה אחת, אם אמר 'משה אמרו מפי עצמו' הרי זה כופר בתורה; וכן הכופר בפרושה, והוא תורה שבעל פה, והמכחיש מגידיה, כגון צדוק ובייתוס; **והאומר** שהבורא החליף מצוה זו במצוה אחרת וכבר בטלה תורה זו, אף על פי שהיא היתה מעם ה', כגון ההגרים. כל אחד משלשה אלו כופר בתורה.

Three are called heretics: One who **says** that prophecy does not exist and there is no information that reaches the human mind from the Creator; one who denies the prophecy of Moshe; and one who **says** that the Creator does not know of human actions. Each of these three is a heretic. Three are deniers of the Torah: One who **says** that the Torah is not from God – even one verse

---

The violence of atheism will cleanse away the dross that accumulated in the lower levels of religious faith, and thereby will the heavens be cleared and the shining light of the higher faith will become visible, which is the song of the world and the truth of the world.

Whoever recognizes the essence of atheism from this perspective embraces the positive element in it and traces it back to its origin in holiness....

65. One solution is that when R. Kook writes "the Sages," he is referring exclusively to Chazal and did not intend to include Rishonim. This proposition seems unlikely, because while he may not have felt bound by Rambam's view (especially if there are others who argue), he also would not have been so dismissive.

66. See R. Chaim Hirschensohn, in *Musagei Shav ve-Emet*, p. 81.

> or one word, if he **says** that 'Moshe said it on his own,' he denies the Torah; similarly, one who denies its interpretation, which is the Oral Law, and [one] who opposes those who recount it, such as Tzadok and Baitus; and one who **says** that the Creator replaced one *mitzva* with another *mitzva* and that this Torah has been superseded, even if it was from God, as the Muslims say. All three of these are deniers of the Torah.

Thus, it might be argued that only one who *says* heretical statements is deemed a heretic. (R. Kook acknowledges that doubting is prohibited; he simply claims that it does not give the person the legal status of heretic.)

While this solution is tenable within the *Mishneh Torah*, it seems untenable within the commentary on the Mishna. After listing the thirteen principles of faith, Rambam writes the following:

> **וכאשר יהיו קיימים לאדם כל היסודות הללו ואמונתו בהם אמתית, הרי הוא נכנס בכלל ישראל**, וחובה לאהבו ולחמול עליו וכל מה שצוה ה׳ אותנו זה על זה מן האהבה והאחוה, ואפילו עשה מה שיכול להיות מן העבירות מחמת תאותו והתגברות יצרו הרע, הרי הוא נענש לפי גודל מריו ויש לו חלק, והוא מפושעי ישראל. וכאשר יפקפק אדם ביסוד מאלו היסודות הרי זה יצא מן הכלל וכפר בעיקר ונקרא מין ואפיקורוס וקוצץ בנטיעות, וחובה לשנותו ולהשמידו ועליו הוא אומר הלא משנאיך ה׳ אשנא וכו׳.[67]

> **And when the person will believe all these fundamentals and his faith will be clear in them, he enters into the nation of Israel** and it is a *mitzva* to love him, have mercy on him, and act towards him according to all the ways God commanded us regarding loving one's neighbor. And even if he did all of the sins in the Torah due to desire and from his physical aspect conquering him, he will be punished for his sins, but he still has a share in the world to come and is among the sinners of Israel. If, however, he **doubts** one of these fundamentals, he leaves the nation and is a denier of the fundamentals and is called a heretic, a denier, etc., and it is a *mitzva* to

67. The Hebrew text above is taken from the R. Kapach translation.

> hate him and to destroy him. And regarding him it is said, "Behold, will not the enemy of God be my enemy?" (*Tehillim* 139:21).

Here, Rambam emphatically claims that actual belief is necessary to be included among the Jewish people and have a share in the world to come. Doubt, on the other hand, classifies a person as a heretic. Of course, Rambam's position here is startling and difficult to accept, especially regarding those who make honest mistakes or who do not know any better. We investigate the matter in Chapter 11.

Whether one adopts the view of Rambam, Rashi, or R. Kook (or maintains that there is no dispute), on a practical level it is important not to confuse unresolved questions with heresy. A thinking person frequently will be left flummoxed; but he need not be afraid of these feelings. Instead, they should prompt further investigation and honest explorations. R. Aharon Lichtenstein powerfully expresses this notion:

> What I received from all my mentors, at home or in yeshiva, was the key to confronting life, particularly modern life, in all its complexity: the recognition that it was not so necessary to have all the answers as to learn to live with the questions.[68]

68. "The Source of Faith Is Faith Itself," *The Jewish Action Reader*, Vol. 1, Union of Orthodox Jewish Congregations of America, New York, 1996.

Excursus

Science and Torah, Part 2

8.11 EVIDENCE FOR GOD'S EXISTENCE IN LIGHT OF CONTEMPORARY SCIENCE AND CONTRADICTIONS BETWEEN SCRIPTURE AND SCIENCE

We begin this section by analyzing contemporary evidence for the existence of God. Specifically, we examine two approaches taken by contemporary thinkers as to whether proof is still possible. Next, in 8.14–6, we consider instances where contemporary science seems to contradict Torah. Specifically, we analyze three general approaches to dealing with such contradictions.

First, however, a disclaimer: a comprehensive presentation on these topics would require scientific and philosophical expertise, both of which I lack. Instead, I hope to present some sources that I personally have found helpful when considering these weighty topics.

Introducing the Two Perspectives

Earlier, we cited the midrash that Avraham initially arrived at an awareness of God's existence through the simple argument that if there is a building, there must have been a builder. Rambam and other medieval thinkers developed this idea and presented proofs for the existence of God. Modernity has challenged this enterprise for two reasons. The first stems from the philosophical rejection of medieval proofs. In the 18th century, philosophers attacked the viability of the cosmological argument.[1] Secondly, contemporary science has offered an alternative solution (evolution) as to how life can exist even if God does not.

Thus, for more than a century, those engaged in philosophy of religion have been divided into two main camps over the question of what constitutes the epistemological basis for belief in God. The first camp deemphasizes and sometimes outright rejects the search for proof, seeing it not only as invalid but inappropriate and unnecessary. As we shall see in Chapter 9, this attitude is not new and not simply a reaction to the debunking of scholastic proofs for God's existence. *Rishonim*

1. Specifically, David Hume questioned both the presumption of causation assumed in the argument (that causation is an objective, productive, necessary relation experienced as power that holds between two things) and the Causal Principle (that every contingent being has a cause of its being – this lies at the heart of the argument). Later, Immanuel Kant averred that by identifying the Necessary Being, the cosmological argument rests upon the ontological argument, which he questions. More significantly, Kant claimed to have rendered the idea of both proofs and disproofs of God impossible. For more on the history of the cosmological argument, see Dr. Bruce Reichenbach's "Cosmological Argument" in *The Stanford Encyclopedia of Philosophy*.

   Prof. Leo Strauss, the German-Jewish political philosopher who was not orthodox, made two pertinent points relevant to this discussion. Firstly, without rejecting modern science, Struass, following thinkers like Friedrich Heinrich Jacobi, critiqued the commonly made but unfounded philosophical conclusion that "scientific knowledge is the highest form of knowledge" (*Jewish Philosophy and the Crisis of Modernity*, ed. Kenneth Hart Green, Albany, NY: State University of New York Press, 1997, p. 99). Strauss argues that Hobbes, Spinoza, and later Enlightenment thinkers frequently overstep their bounds when they depreciate pre-scientific knowledge in the name of science.

   More importantly, Strauss contended that if orthodoxy claims to *know* that the Torah is God's word recorded by Moshe and that the miracles recorded in the Torah are true then Spinoza may have refuted orthodoxy. But the case is entirely different if orthodoxy limits itself to asserting that it *believes* the aforementioned things, i.e. that they cannot claim to possess the binding power peculiar to the known. (See *Spinoza's Critique of Religion*, trans. Elsa M. Sinclair, New York: Schocken, 1965, p. 29, where Strauss argues what would be necessary for a "genuine refutation of orthodoxy." My appreciation to Jeffrey Bloom for pointing this out to me.)

   The validity of Strauss's defense rests upon the nature of *emuna*. Rambam appears to demand that a Jew *know* that God exists. As we have seen and shall continue to see, other sources appear to define *emuna* differently. Even if they demand certainty, the basis of faith need not be science and philosophy. We explore this proposition in Chapter 9.

argued that philosophical proofs should not serve as the foundation of belief even when these proofs were unchallenged. Instead, they embraced other modes of achieving faith, such as experiential knowledge. As we shall see in 9.6, however, some religious thinkers, including R. Soloveitchik, have conceded that in the post-Kantian world, "proof" no longer is possible. We consider this first school of thought in 8.12.

Other contemporary thinkers, however, continue to emphasize proof. Many in this camp scaled down their claims from having "proofs" that yielded *certainty* to amassing a cumulative weight of converging lines of evidence that yields a high degree of *probability* or at the very least showing that it is rational to believe in God, even if it cannot be shown that it is irrational not to believe in God. We consider this second school of thought in 8.13.

8.12 THE FIRST SCHOOL OF THOUGHT – PROOF NO LONGER IS POSSIBLE

We begin by considering the perspective of believers who maintain that God's existence cannot be proven. These believers emphasize that the reality that we can no longer prove God's existence in the way that Rambam did does not imply that belief is no longer rational. Rambam himself, in *Moreh ha-Nevuchim* 1:32, writes of the importance of accepting that some true ideas cannot be proven:

> The same is the case with the speculative faculties… **If you admit the doubt and do not persuade yourself to believe that there is a proof for things that cannot be demonstrated**… or attempt to perceive things that are beyond your perception, then you have attained the highest degree of human perfection…

Rambam argues that we must honestly acknowledge our intellectual limitations. While Rambam felt that the existence of God can be proven, we must consider the possibility that in light of what we have discovered in science and philosophy, this is not the case. Our inability to prove does not indicate that the notion is false.

According to this first approach, belief in God remains compelling in the modern world, but is not based on the types of proofs that were once offered to establish the existence of God. In the modern world, the religious person should seek other means to know that God exists. We consider these means in 9.2.

It should be stressed that this group of thinkers would not agree that science or philosophy have refuted religion in any way. There is nothing in modern science that disproves the existence of God. However, we no longer can turn to science and philosophy, as we once did, to prove the existence of God.

Thus, even as R. Soloveitchik conceded that "proof" no longer is possible in the post-Kantian world, he writes in *The Lonely Man of Faith*: "I have never been seriously troubled by the problem of the Biblical doctrine of creation vis-à-vis the scientific story of evolution at both the cosmic and the organic levels" (p. 7). In 8.14 we consider why science did not bother R. Soloveitchik. Now, however, let us turn to the second school of thought concerning proof for the existence of God in the modern world.

8.13 THE SECOND SCHOOL OF THOUGHT – SCIENCE STILL CAN SERVE AS THE BASIS FOR BELIEF IN GOD

Not all contemporary religious philosophers and scientists accept the above concession. This brings us to the second school of thought, which argues that we still can turn to science and philosophy to demonstrate that belief is the most reasonable worldview insofar as it alone can explain everything we observe. While the arguments they offer may lack the elegance of the medieval syllogistic proofs, they nevertheless are powerful evidence for God's existence.

Some in this camp have argued that the cosmological argument is not dead (though it needs some reformulation). Let us begin by briefly considering the validity of the critique upon the cosmological argument for the existence of God.

Why Does Anything Exist?

Instead of conceding that modern physics dispenses with the need for God, the opposite case can be made. Until the middle of the twentieth century, one could deny that the existence of the universe was proof that God exists by simply claiming that the universe always existed. However, with powerful scientific evidence supporting the big bang theory, this is no longer plausible. Accordingly, with universal scientific acceptance that our universe is not eternal, it is easier than ever to prove the existence of God.

In fact, with all that modern science has taught us, there still are many questions that cannot be fully answered without resorting to God. First and foremost, why does anything exist? What started the process that caused our universe to come into existence? The big bang theory does nothing to answer these questions. Rather, it describes the process by which our universe developed following the big bang. What triggered the big bang in the first place is not addressed. Likewise, the theory of evolution does nothing to address these questions. Rather, it seeks to explain how life on earth could naturally evolve from simpler building blocks. It does not consider the root of existence.

One response to this argument is to speculate that there may have been something beforehand or that our universe is part of something bigger. Dr. Stephen Hawking, for example, suggests that our universe is part of a much larger, perhaps infinitely large, multiverse. Thus, there may have been many bangs, scattered through space and time, that naturally sprouted many universes.[2]

Of course, there is no evidence for the existence of these additional universes. Moreover, the additional universes of the multiverse lie beyond our powers of observation, and, for the foreseeable future, cannot be investigated. Hypothesizing that they exist seems to reflect a newfound willingness among some scientists to set aside the need for

2. Indeed, the starting point to presume the existence of a multiverse is the presumption that God does not exist. If God does not exist how do we account for two seemingly impossible things: (1) why does anything exist (addressed previously) and (2) even if one somehow accounts for existence in general, how do we explain our existence. To solve this scientists and philosophers created the multiverse. Thus, John Leslie (1989), Derek Parfit (*Universes*, London: Routledge, 1998), and J. J. C. Smart (*Our Place in the Universe: A Metaphysical Discussion*, Oxford: Blackwell, 1989), and others argue vigorously that the fact that our universe meets the extremely improbable yet necessary conditions for the evolution of life, supports the thesis that there exist very many universes. Roger White in "Fine-Tuning and Multiple Universes" (NOÛS 34:2, 2000, pp. 260–276) offers a powerful critique to this theory.

experimental confirmation, "breaking with centuries of philosophical tradition of defining scientific knowledge as empirical."[3]

Some scientists have suggested that quantum physics allows for matter to spontaneously generate out of nothing.[4] However, as Dr. Paul Davies notes,[5] even if we accept these theories, a much tougher problem now looms: "What is the source of those ingenious laws that enable a universe to pop into being from nothing?" The solution, in effect, simply kicks the can down the road.

Even if one gets over this hump and somehow accounts for the existence of the world, there are numerous things that evolution cannot explain. There is, for example, no concrete evidence for the possibility that life can evolve from non-life (animate from inanimate).[6] Likewise, there is no theory that explains the evolution of consciousness.[7, 8]

---

3. *Nature* Dec. 2014, "Scientific Method: Defend the integrity of physics," by George Ellis and Joe Silk.
4. In his book *The Grand Design* Hawking argues that "Because there is a law such as gravity, the universe can and will create itself from nothing… Spontaneous creation is the reason there is something rather than nothing, why the universe exists, why we exist. It is not necessary to invoke God to light the blue touch paper and set the universe going" (180). This befuddling theory still leaves one wondering what accounts for the laws that allow spontaneous creation.
5. http://www.theguardian.com/commentisfree/belief/2010/sep/04/stephen-hawking-big-bang-gap.
6. Even if one accepts the validity of the famous experiment in which an electric current was run through a soup of organic molecules and some amino acids were found, this does not explain evolution of life, since amino acids are chemicals, not life, and attempts to create life have failed. (See *The Devil's Delusion* by David Berlinski.)
7. As Ron Rosenbaum writes in "The Dangerous Mysteries of Consciousness: We still need answers" (http://www.slate.com/articles/life/the_spectator/2009/11/the_dangerous_mysteries_of_consciousness.single.html), these questions are much more problematic than something like the irreducible complexity of the human eye because "There is nothing that will explain why matter in a certain form will go "mental." This point has been cogently argued by non-believing philosophers such as Raymond Tallis in "The Unnatural Selection of Consciousness," (http://philosophypress.co.uk/?p=485) and Colin McGinn in *The Mysterious Flame: Conscious Minds in a Material World*. For possible (though, in my opinion, uncompelling) responses to this problem, see the works of David Chalmers, Daniel Denett, Douglas Hofstadter, and Susan Blackmore.
8. Ramban (*Bereishit* 1:1) writes that the term *bara* signifies creation of something out of nothing. (This happened only at the beginning of creation. Subsequently things emerged from other things.) Interestingly, there are three times that the Torah uses

God of the Gaps

This sort of evidence has been rejected by some atheists, such as Richard Dawkins, as unconvincing insofar as it only supports the existence of the "God of the gaps."[9] They claim that if God exists only based on gaps in science, and the gaps in scientific knowledge keep on getting smaller, then it can be predicted that any basis for God's existence eventually will disappear.

This critique appears flimsy for many reasons. Most notably, these "gaps" are not minor holes, but major questions that science does not appear to be on the verge of answering. Frequently, evolutionists' faith in their theory does not appear very scientific.[10]

Another critique offered against the contemporary argument of design is, "Who designed the designer?" While this question dates back to David Hume, it is popularly known as "The Ultimate Boeing 747 gambit," a term introduced by Richard Dawkins in Chapter 4 ("Why there almost certainly is no God") of his 2006 book *The God Delusion*.[11]

---

the word *bara* in the first chapter of *Bereishit*. These three usages correspond to the three unanswerable questions mentioned above: the explanation for the existence of anything, of life, and of consciousness. (The parallel is not perfectly precise, since the second *bara* corresponds to animal life as opposed to cellular life; however, the parallel still is noteworthy.)

9. This notion was first articulated by Henry Drummond in his Lowell Lectures on *The Ascent of Man* and was explicated during World War II by the German theologian Dietrich Bonhoeffer (who was killed by the Nazis). He wrote: "...how wrong it is to use God as a stop-gap for the incompleteness of our knowledge. If in fact the frontiers of knowledge are being pushed further and further back (and that is bound to be the case), then God is being pushed back with them, and is therefore continually in retreat. We are to find God in what we know, not in what we don't know" (*Letters and Papers from Prison*, pp. 310–312). In *The God Delusion*, Richard Dawkins dedicates a chapter to criticism of the God-of-the-gaps fallacy.

10. Consider the following example from Darwinist/atheist Richard Dawkins' *The Blind Watchmaker*: "Cumulative selection, once it has begun, seems...powerful enough to make the evolution of intelligence probable, if not inevitable" (p. 146). As Ron Rosenbaum points out in an article written for Slate Magazine, (http://www.slate.com/articles/life/the_spectator/2009/11/the_dangerous_mysteries_of_consciousness.single.html), "seems powerful enough" does not sound very scientific.

11. Astrophysicist Fred Hoyle is reported as having stated that the "probability of life originating on Earth is no greater than the chance that a hurricane, sweeping through a scrapyard, would have the luck to assemble a Boeing 747." According to Dawkins,

Chazon Ish addresses this claim in *Emuna u-Bitachon* (missing section after 1:9). After showing that God's existence is necessary because no other cause could account for the universe, he addresses this important critique.[12] *Chazon Ish* writes that if one asks what caused the Creator, we would answer that the Creator always existed. But if we are happy with that solution, why not say that the world always existed?

Chazon Ish answers that physical things are limited both in space and time, and thus they must have a beginning. Non-physical things, on the other hand, need not have a beginning. An example of a non-physical thing that need not have a beginning, because it is necessarily true, is the mathematical truth that 2x2=4.[13]

Another straightforward response to the "God of the gaps" objection was formulated by Dr. Alvin Plantinga[14] in a recent *New York Times* interview:

> Some atheists seem to think that a sufficient reason for atheism is the fact (as they say) that we no longer need God to explain natural phenomena – lightning and thunder for example. We now have science.

---

this logic is self-defeating, as the theist must now account for God's existence and explain whether or how God was created.

12. ויש מבעלי דמיון השואלים מה נרוויח אם נסכים שיש להעולם ממציא, אחרי שהננו מוכרחים להסכים שבורא עולם נמצא ואין עת להתחלתו ומציאותו נצחית והרי הדרא קושיא לדוכתה (והרי חוזרת הקושיה למקומה): איך אפשר לנמצא בלא הויה?
אבל אין לדמיון בינה כי כל נמצא שיש לו מידה וקצב אורך ושטח אנו מציירים בדעתנו העדרו וכל הנמצאים בסוג הזה בהכרח שיש עת למציאותם ויש להם התחלה וכל שיש לו התחלה יש לו הויה וכל שיש לו הויה יש לו מהוה.
אבל יש נמצאים שאין להם לא מידה ולא שטח והם נמצאים בחיוב ולא יצויר בהם העדר והן המושכלות, כמו ב׳ פעמים ב׳ הם ד׳, וכמו המושכל שהאלכסון עודף על האורך וכיוצא בהן מן המושכלות שאין למושכל מושגים ממושגי גוף ואין עת למציאותן ולא נולדו מעולם ולא ימותו לעולם. ואין מציאותן נרגשות רק בנשמה שניתן לאדם להבין ולהשכיל ונמצא כזה הוא מציאותו יתברך, ממציא כל הנמצאים, אך אין ליצור שום מושג ממהותו כי הוא יתברך בעל כח ובעל בחירה יודע כל יצוריו ויודע מעשיהם ויודע צורכם וכל המתרחש עמהם ומהוה את כל הנעשה בכל העולמות ברצונו יתברך כי כל הנעשה ברצונו יתברך קשורה ואין כל פעולה זולתו יתברך.
13. We address this point more extensively in 4.5. I believe this point still precludes Hawking's spontaneously generated universes, which still requires the existence of fields of some sort from which matter can emerge.
14. Plantinga is an emeritus professor of philosophy at the University of Notre Dame and former president of the American Philosophical Association.

> As a justification of atheism, this is pretty lame. We no longer need the moon to explain or account for lunacy; it hardly follows that belief in the nonexistence of the moon (a-moonism) is justified. A-moonism on this ground would be sensible only if the sole ground for belief in the existence of the moon was its explanatory power with respect to lunacy. (And even so, the justified attitude would be agnosticism with respect to the moon, not a-moonism.) The same thing goes with belief in God: Atheism on this sort of basis would be justified only if the explanatory power of theism were the only reason for belief in God. And even then, agnosticism would be the justified attitude, not atheism.[15]

That is not to say that these questions conclusively prove the existence of God either. In the aforementioned article, Plantinga notes that there are a large number – maybe a couple of dozen – of "pretty good theistic arguments." While none is conclusive, each, or at any rate the whole bunch taken together, is about as strong as philosophical arguments ordinarily get.[16]

---

15. http://opinionator.blogs.nytimes.com/2014/02/09/is-atheism-irrational/?_r=0.
16. One such argument that Plantinga offers is fine-tuning:

> Scientists tell us that there are many properties our universe displays such that if they were even slightly different from what they are in fact, life, or at least our kind of life, would not be possible. The universe seems to be fine-tuned for life. For example, if the force of the Big Bang had been different by one part in 10 to the 60th, life of our sort would not have been possible. The same goes for the ratio of the gravitational force to the force driving the expansion of the universe: If it had been even slightly different, our kind of life would not have been possible. In fact the universe seems to be fine-tuned, not just for life, but for intelligent life. This fine-tuning is vastly more likely given theism than given atheism.

There is a huge amount of literature discussing various philosophical proofs for God. Two contemporary books that go through almost all of the arguments that have been made by philosophers to date are J. L Mackie's *The Miracle of Theism* and, from a more analytical perspective, J. H. Sobel's *Logic and Theism: Arguments for and against Beliefs in God*. However, both of these authors reject all philosophical proofs for God. Authors who do a good job defending one or more of these arguments as valid include Richard Swinborne, Alvin Plantinga, William Lane Craig, and Peter van Inwagen.

Epistemological Consistency

These sorts of evidence-based arguments lack the elegance of the syllogistic proofs offered by Rambam.[17] Thus, a person may still say that he wants definitive proof. Such a person must consider whether he is being epistemologically consistent. Is that the attitude with which he approaches other questions?[18] Does he always demand absolute

17. R. Shalom Carmy puts the dilemma as follows:

> Despite what you hear from the bastions of academia, such arguments are alive. Some scientists continue to regard the intricacies of the human eye and other wondrous phenomena as evidence of a directing intelligence. Recent philosophers have devoted attention to the so-called anthropic principle, which argues that natural evolution is unlikely to have produced creatures capable of uncovering the laws of nature. Nevertheless, it is undeniable that the revolution in biological thinking originating with Darwin has enabled scientists to devise plausible naturalistic explanations of unusual biological facts. Philosophical naturalists firmly believe that they will eventually produce compelling explanations of all such phenomena. Insofar as the arguments revolve around the probability that a particular event could have happened according to one story or the other, conclusiveness is lacking. The straightforward briskness of the inkwell argument is not available to us. ("A Religion Challenged by Science: – Again? A Reflection Occasioned by a Recent Occurrence" by R. Shalom Carmy, *Tradition* 39.2, Summer 2005, p. 2.)

18. Oxford professor Richard Swinburne in *Is There a God?* (Oxford University Press: 2010) makes a similar point in his book's epilogue. Having articulated numerous arguments supporting the existence of God, he concludes:

> I reach the end of this book with some dissatisfaction. I am well aware of objections other than the ones which I have discussed which can be made to almost every sentence which I have written… I am also aware of counter-objections which can be advanced to turn against every objection to my views, and also of the need for qualifications and amplification of most of the assertions in this book. Argument and counter-argument, qualification and amplification, can go on forever. New experiments can always be done to test Quantum Theory, new interpretations can be proposed for old experiments, forever. And the same goes for interpretations of history or theories of politics. But life is short and we have to act on the basis of what such evidence as we have had time to investigate shows on balance to be probably true.

In an earlier work, he puts it as follows: "There is quite a chance that if there is a God, he will make something of the finitude and complexity of a universe. It is very unlikely that a universe would exist uncaused, but rather more likely that God would exist uncaused. The existence of the universe…can be made comprehensible if we suppose that it is brought about by God" (*The Existence of God*, Oxford: Clarendon Press. 1979, 131–132). Put differently, attributing the creation of the universe to God is

proof?[19] To summarize what we have seen so far, the second school of thought maintains that (1) there are reasonable, if not conclusive arguments in favor of the existence of God, and (2) the demand for absolute proof is not epistemologically warranted, especially in light of the other options.

To these two points we can add a third: Plantinga concludes:

> I don't think arguments are needed for rational belief in God. In this regard belief in God is like belief in other minds, or belief in the past. Belief in God is grounded in experience, or in the *sensus divinitatis*, John Calvin's term for an inborn inclination to form beliefs about God in a wide variety of circumstances.

We consider experiential arguments in Chapter 9 when considering the views of R. Yehuda ha-Levi and R. Soloveitchik, who also preferred experiential awareness to philosophical knowledge. However, now let us consider why, from a philosophical perspective, this direction is rational.

When it comes to neutral matters (such as whether or not there is a teapot that orbits the Sun somewhere in space between the Earth and Mars), it may make sense to argue that it is irrational to believe that something exists until it is proven (Bertrand Russell's argument against belief). But, when it comes to something like the existence of God, which, for many people, is intuitive, and which explains our existence more simply than any alternative theory, then it may be

---

more reasonable than merely attributing it to brute fact, devoid of explanation. While this inductive cosmological argument is less powerful than a deductive cosmological proof, which would make it "incoherent to assert that a complex physical universe exists and that God does not" (119), it is nevertheless quite compelling.

19. R. Dessler suggests that when a person says that he will not believe without philosophical proof, he merely is looking for an excuse not to believe.

מכתב מאליהו ח"ג עמ' 177

טעות היא לחשוב שיכולים להשיג את האמונה המוחלטת ע"י חקירות שכלייות ופילוסופיה, הרי השכל משוחד ע"י כל מיני נגיעות. הרצון מטה את השכל לאן שהוא חפץ. **כשהאדם פונה אל שכלו, בטרם התעמק בתורה, וביסס את אמונתו על קבלת אבות ואמונת חכמים, ורוצה ששכלו יהיה השופט הבלעדי על עניני אמונה - סימן הוא שאינו רוצה להאמין, לכן פונה אל שופט משוחד שיורה לו כרצונו.** השכל גם מוגבל, כי המחשבה מיוסדת על ציורים גשמיים שהם מוגבלים...

rational to accept His existence even if it cannot be definitively proven. Put differently, the question of theism verses atheism depends upon whom the philosophic burden of proof lies. Atheists claim that it lies entirely upon theists – if it cannot be proven, then presumably it does not exist. Theists can respond that given our intuitive belief and experiential connection to God, it is rational to presume His existence when there is ample evidence (though no definitive proof) that He exists. This argument, while subtle, goes much further than the God of the gaps.

To summarize, those who argue against belief in God are unable to account for the existence of numerous phenomena, such as existence, life, and consciousness. As such, these phenomena, at the very least, demonstrate that belief in God is the most reasonable worldview insofar as it alone can explain everything we observe.[20] Certainly, when these scientific arguments for the existence of God are combined with the other arguments that we shall explore in the next chapter, a person can be left with certain knowledge (*yedi'a*) about the existence of God. A sophisticated, believing Jew need not buy into the dogma that contemporary science and philosophy have demonstrated that belief is no longer rational. If anything, the opposite is the case.

---

20. Swinburne summarizes this argument as follows:

> Scientists, historians, and detectives observe data and proceed thence to some theory about what best explains the occurrence of these data. We can analyze the criteria which they use in reaching a conclusion that a certain theory is better supported by the data than a different theory--that is, more likely, on the basis of those data, to be true. Using those same criteria, we find that the view that there is a God explains *everything* we observe, not just some narrow range of data. It explains the fact that there is a universe at all, that scientific laws operate within it, that it contains conscious animals and humans with very complex intricately organized bodies, that we have abundant opportunities for developing ourselves and the world, as well as the more particular data that humans report miracles and have religious experiences. In so far as scientific causes and laws explain some of these things (and in part they do), these very causes and laws need explaining, and God's action explains them. The very same criteria which scientists use to reach their own theories lead us to move beyond those theories to a creator God who sustains everything in existence. (*Is There a God?* pp. 1–2)

Am I Being Honest?

At the beginning of 8.11, I readily acknowledged my ignorance in the fields of science and philosophy, which makes me question the value of the previous section. While I attempted to be honest in studying the question and presenting my findings, in reality, I am dabbling in fields way above my head.[21] As such, it seems highly presumptuous of me to dismiss the theories of brilliant thinkers such as Stephen Hawking, as I did in the previous section. Moreover, in a world where expertise in the relevant academic disciplines is unattainable for almost all people (how many people have a chance at understanding quantum mechanics?), perhaps we should throw up our hands and exclude any scientific considerations when considering the question of *emuna*. The more honest thing to do, it would seem, is to acknowledge that since there are intelligent people on both sides of the equation and we are in no position to evaluate their debate, we should ground our *emuna* on other factors, leaving science out of the equation.

Perhaps this is so. However, I believe there is value in considering these matters. Yeshayahu's exhortation, "Lift up your eyes on high and see who created these" (40:26), continues to ring true. That the arguments in favor of God's existence seem to me far more intuitive and reasonable (e.g., why should anything exist?), and the justifications given by atheists (e.g., spontaneous creation, multiverse, etc.) seem counterintuitive and implausible has a powerful impact upon my *emuna*. That is true even though I concede that (a) I am not an expert in the fields I am assessing, and (b) Even as I attempt to be intellectually honest, the basis of my intuition is likely affected by my preconceived notions. Finally, while I find the arguments in the previous section powerful, they are not the primary source for my belief in God. I discuss my personal approach to faith in 9.2.

21. Indeed, this relates to another major difference between the medieval intellectual milieu and that of today. It may have been conceivable in Rambam's time for an intelligent person to achieve mastery in science and philosophy (along with Torah) such that one could recommend (as Rambam does) that ambitious and intelligent people conquer these disciplines in order to fulfil the *mitzva* of *emuna* in the most ideal fashion. However, this is no longer the case. Today, most scientists master only a small subset of knowledge and rely upon experts, to the extent that it is necessary, regarding other areas.

Seeing God in History

When seeking external evidence for the existence of God, one should not limit himself to science. R. Tzadok, for example, stresses knowing God through history by studying the miracles that He has done for the Jewish people throughout their existence:

ספר הזכרונות מצות עשה אנוכי

ולא מיציאת מצרים בלבד יוכל האדם להבחין ולדעת בירור אמונה זו אלא מכל הניסים והנפלאות שנעשו לאבותינו ולנו.

> And not just through the Exodus can a person recognize and know the certainty of faith; rather, from all the miracles and wonders that have been done to our fathers and us.

Fundamentally, seeing God in history should not differ from seeing God in any other part of nature. Indeed, some scholars have seen divine intervention as the only possible explanation for Jewish continuity throughout a long and bitter exile.[22] Likewise, the establishment of the State of Israel is among the most improbable events in human history, all the more so for having been predicted millennia in advance.[23]

Why Science Turns Some People Towards God and Others Away from God

Let us consider one last point concerning scientific evidence for the existence of God. It seems surprising that the study of science can yield diametrically opposite conclusions concerning belief in God, with some seeing science as the means by which to discover and prove the existence of God and others using science to rid humanity of this (in their view) archaic notion.

This phenomenon is not new:

---

22. See, for example, *The Meaning of History* by Nikolai Berdiaev, Meridian Books (1962, c1936).
23. See R. Soloveitchik's *Kol Dodi Dofeik*.

דברים ד:יט
וּפֶן תִּשָּׂא עֵינֶיךָ הַשָּׁמַיְמָה וְרָאִיתָ אֶת הַשֶּׁמֶשׁ וְאֶת הַיָּרֵחַ וְאֶת הַכּוֹכָבִים
כֹּל צְבָא הַשָּׁמַיִם וְנִדַּחְתָּ וְהִשְׁתַּחֲוִיתָ לָהֶם...

And lest you lift up your eyes to heaven and see the sun, the moon, and the stars – all the host of heaven – and be drawn away to prostrate yourselves before them and worship them...

ישעיה מ:כו
שְׂאוּ מָרוֹם עֵינֵיכֶם וּרְאוּ מִי בָרָא אֵלֶּה.

Lift up your eyes on high and see, who created these?

Here, we have the identical activity yielding diametrically opposite results. The first verse describes how examining the celestial bodies will lead to idolatry; the second urges a person to examine those same entities in order to see God. In fact, the very same verb (תִּשָּׂא\שְׂאוּ) is used. What differentiates the person who considers the universe and arrives at God from the person who arrives at atheism or idolatry? Perspective.[24] That different people, even world-renowned scholars and specialists, arrive at such differing conclusions when examining identical evidence highlights that there is more at play than a dry, academic question. The stakes are so high that objectivity proves elusive. (We return to this question in 11.7.) With this in mind, we turn to consider various approaches to dealing with contradictions between Torah and science.

---

24. R. Moshe Shapiro notes that the second verse begins with the *rashei teivot* שמע, indicating that if one looks from the perspective of hearing, then one will find God. However, if one looks only with his eyes, he will end up with heresy. How so? The sense of sight provides for an instantaneous picture. Not so with the sense of sound, where a single sound conveys no meaning. Instead, sounds make up syllables, syllables make up words, words make up sentences, and only then is there meaning. Thus, if one looks at the world as it is (sight), he will not discover God. However, if he perceives the process – he asks what caused it to be this way, what preceded this, what started it all (תאמר שהבירה זו בלא מנהיג) – then he will see God.

8.14 CONTRADICTIONS BETWEEN SCIENCE AND RELIGION: THE FIRST SCHOOL OF THOUGHT – DENYING THE PROBLEM

For many, science is not the solution but the problem. Modern science has raised new challenges to religion. In this section, we briefly consider solutions. In what is an oversimplification of a complex topic, let us consider three basic approaches to resolving contradictions between Torah and science.

The first school of thought repudiates the notion of seeking resolutions because it denies the possibility of a contradiction. One reason why scientific claims do not trouble some religious believers is that science seeks to answer different sorts of questions and does not claim to address the ultimate questions. Sir Peter Medawar put it as follows:

> [There exist] questions that science cannot answer and that no conceivable advance of science would empower it to answer. These are the questions that children ask – the "ultimate questions"… I have in mind such questions as: How did everything begin? What are we all here for? What is the point of living?[25]

How does one deal with cases where the Torah does appear to make scientific statements that are at odds with science? This first school of thought argues that despite superficial appearances, there is no contradiction. There are various formulations of this resolution that we consider presently.

Maharal

In 5.15, we considered Maharal's understanding that the purpose of the Torah and Chazal is not to present scientific facts but to arrive at deeper truths. Even when they seem to be addressing natural and scientific questions, they are not actually offering natural or scientific explanations. One example Maharal uses to illustrate this theory is the Torah's explanation for

25. *The Limits of Science,* Harper and Row 1984 p. 86. As Brian L. Silver wrote in *The Ascent of Science* (Oxford University Press, 2000, p. 25), "Personally, I find that the faith-versus-science controversy has the smell of past centuries. I am happy to follow Bacon and agree to a separation of forces…"

the rainbow. When the Torah offers an explanation of the rainbow, it is not addressing the scientific question of what causes the rainbow (reflection, refraction, and dispersion of light in water droplets), but rather the reason behind this reason. Essentially, Maharal maintains that when the Torah or Chazal offer explanations for physical phenomena, such as the rainbow, they are not attempting to transmit the scientific explanation, but rather to give the spiritual elucidation of a physical phenomenon.

Put differently, Maharal avers that many of the seeming contradictions between Torah and science emerge from a superficial understanding of Torah. A central goal of Maharal in all of his writings is to highlight the complexity of aggadic teaching and to demonstrate that a nuanced read often yields a very different conclusion than a cursory understanding. This approach is especially true with respect to contradictions between Torah and science where the tension surfaces from the presumption that the Torah is offering natural causes to physical phenomena.

R. Soloveitchik

There is another related theory of Maharal, explicated in 4.5, that is relevant here as well. Recall that Ralbag saw the story of the cessation of the sun and moon's motion at Giv'on (*Yehoshua* 10:12–14) as contradicting his scientific understanding that rejects the possibility of miracles that affect the celestial domain. Ralbag resolved the problem by reading the text in a way that did not contradict his worldview. After rejecting Ralbag's forced reading, Maharal presents a remarkable interpretation of the story. Instead of simply understanding that the sun indeed stopped (an event that would have been witnessed by the whole world), Maharal suggests that the sun stopped from the perspective of the Jewish people but not for the rest of the world. The supernatural plane, which coexists with the natural plane, is not bound by physical limitations.

In 4.6, we considered R. Soloveitchik's thesis that contemporary physics allows us to conceive of Maharal's radical notion in a way that previously was impossible.[26] He writes in the opening sentence of *The Halakhic Mind* that "it would be difficult to distinguish any epoch

26. R. Soloveitchik does not cite Maharal, but his theory can be used to explain Maharal in a novel manner.

in the history of philosophy more amenable to the meditating *homo religiosus* than that of today." Until the 20th century, scientists and philosophers posited that the universe was simple and orderly. Today, we no longer are bound by such a model. What has changed? R. Reuven Ziegler summarizes R. Soloveitchik's theory:

> For centuries, science and philosophy had walked hand-in-hand, with philosophy following science's lead in adopting a single way of viewing the world. Medieval and early modern philosophy had been beholden to Aristotelian and Newtonian science, respectively, in determining the questions to be asked and the methods of answering them. This forced religious philosophy either to justify religion in rationalist-instrumentalist terms or to reject rationality altogether.
>
> However, twentieth-century science (particularly quantum physics) no longer posits a unified or intuitive view of the world. For example, light is regarded as both a wave and a particle, which would seem to contravene the tenets of Aristotelian logic. Since science has adopted a stance of epistemological pluralism, admitting a multiplicity of models and sources of knowledge, philosophy must follow suit. The quantitative scientific model must no longer be regarded as the sole cognitive method of viewing the universe. This opens the way for establishing religion as an autonomous domain of knowledge and truth.[27]

Maharal's approach opens the door to a whole new manner of resolving contradictions between Torah and science. R. Soloveitchik writes (*The Halakhic Mind,* pp. 55–6):

> Epistemological pluralism has not abandoned the realm of logic. It says only that reason itself leads the physicist, psychologist, philosopher, and *homo religiosus* to a pluralism of viewpoints.

27. http://etzion.org.il/en/23-lonely-man-faith-continuation-part-6a-autonomy-faith.

> The heterogeneity of knowledge, however, is not based upon a manifold of methods employed by theoreticians, but upon the plurality of the objective orders they encounter.

Torah presents one perspective on the universe. Science presents another. The fact that we cannot relate the two no longer necessarily implies that one is wrong, since they both may reflect the truth from different perspectives.[28] Dr. William Kolbrener powerfully summarizes R. Soloveitchik's conclusion: "Quantum physics rescued the philosopher of religion from his slavish attachment to the objectivity of Newtonian science."[29] Thus, R. Soloveitchik writes in the opening to *Lonely Man of Faith* that "I have never been seriously troubled by the problem of the Biblical doctrine of creation vis-à-vis the scientific story of evolution at both the cosmic and the organic levels."

R. Kook

R. Kook offers a number of resolutions to the seeming contradictions between Torah and science. In *Eider ha-Yakar*, he focuses on archeological issues. In Letter 91, which we will analyze presently, he deals with the age of the universe.[30] For purposes of clarity, we will divide and categorize the different elements of his solution.

---

28. Galileo wrote: "Both the Holy Scriptures and nature originate in the Divine Word.... [T]wo truths can never contradict one another" (cited in *The Galileo Connection* by Charles E. Hummel, p. 95).

29. R. Mordechai Kornbluth noted that the formulation may be going too far in that it implies that quantum physics permits ontological contradiction, when in fact that may not be the case. Rather, quantum physics' relevant argument is, "If one formulates things in an intuitive way, he might see a contradiction, but if he formulates them more carefully, he will see that it all works out." For example, light sometimes acts as a wave (e.g., diffraction) and sometimes as a particle (e.g., the photoelectric effect); there is no contradiction once one formulates it as "quantized electromagnetic waves" (e.g., a 2.45 GHz microwave can put out a wave whose energy is ten, twenty, or thirty microelectronvolts, but it is physically impossible to have one whose energy is fifteen microelectronvolts).

30. In 3.3 we analyzed Rambam's perspective on the age of the universe.

Concordance

First, R. Kook highlights the surprising concordance between Torah and science. For example, concerning the age of the universe and prehistoric man, he notes the compatibility between traditional sources and contemporary science:

אגרות ראיה איגרת צא

ועל דבר מנין שנות היצירה ביחש להחשבונות הגיאולוגיים בזמנינו. כך היא הלכה רווחת, שהיו כבר תקופות רבות קודם למנין תקופתנו הוא מפורסם בכל המקובלים הקדמונים, ובמדרש רבה "שהיה בונה עולמות ומחריבן", ובזוהר פרשת ויקרא שהיו כמה מיני אנשים חוץ מאדם שנאמר בתורה.

> It long has been an accepted concept, noted by all of the early Kabbalists, that there were many eras that preceded our own, as the Midrash states, "He created worlds and destroyed them" and the *Zohar* writes that there were types of men different from Adam, who is described in the Torah.[31]

According to this approach, the opening chapters of *Bereishit* do not record the years of existence of the universe (since there were previous worlds that were destroyed), but the history of our civilization. Likewise, the fossil record may reflect previous worlds and (based on the *Zohar*) different types of man.

Scientific Inaccuracy

Next, he questions the certainty of certain scientific conclusions.

אם כן אותן החפירות מורות לנו, שנמצאו תקופות של ברואים, ואנשים בכללם, אבל שלא היה בינתים חורבן כללי, ויצירה חדשה, על זה אין מופת מוכיח, כי אם השערות פורחות באויר, שאין לחוש להן כלל.

---

31. This translation is adapted from *Rav A.Y. Kook: Selected Letters*, translated by Tzvi Feldman (Ma'aleh Adumim, 1986).

> These excavations indicate that there were eras of creations – including man – but that there was no mass destruction between these eras. But these are assumptions that are up in the air, with no conclusive proof, and one need not be concerned with them.

Later, he elaborates by noting that scientific advancement often entails the rejection of earlier theories that were held with strong conviction.

> אבל על כל פנים אין שום סתירה לשום דבר מן התורה מכל דעה מחקרית שבעולם כלל, אלא שאין אנחנו צריכים לקבל השערות לודאיות, אפילו יהיו מוסכמות הרבה, כי הן כציץ נובל, שעוד מעט יתפתחו יותר כלי הדרישה, ותהיינה כל ההשערות החדשות ללעג ולקלס, וכל החכמות הנעלות שבימינו לקטנות המוח, ודבר אלקינו יקום לעולם.

> In any event, there is no contradiction between anything in the Torah and the opinions of the scientists. For we do not have to accept assumptions as axioms, even if many people agree to them; they are like withering grass, for in a short time, methods will develop further and all of the new theories will be ridiculed, and all the great wisdom of today will be considered small-mindedness – but the word of God endures forever.

Non-literalism

Next, R. Kook questions the literalism that is the basis of the supposed contradictions:

> אבל באמת אין אנו נזקקים לכל זה, שאפילו אם היה מתברר לנו שהיה סדר היצירה בדרך התפתחות המינים גם כן אין שום סתירה, שאנו מונים כפי הפשטות של פסוקי תורה, שנוגע לנו הרבה יותר מכל הידיעות הקדומות, שאין להן עמנו ערך מרובה. והתורה ודאי סתמה במעשה בראשית, ודברה ברמיזות ומשלים, שהרי הכל יודעים שמעשה בראשית הם מכלל סתרי תורה, ואם היו כל הדברים רק פשוטם איזה סתר יש כאן, וכבר אמרו במדרש "להגיד כח מעשה

בראשית לבשר ודם אי אפשר, לפיכך סתם הכתוב בראשית ברא אלקים".

But in truth, we do not need all of this. For even if it was conclusively proven that creation took place through development of species, there would be no contradiction [with the Torah]. For we count according to the simple explanation of the words of the Torah, which is more relevant to us that other sources, which are of little value for us. And the Torah certainly concealed the story of creation and spoke in hints and allegories. All know that creation is one of the secrets of the Torah; if we were to understand the matter according to the literal meaning, what secret would there be here? The Midrash already states: "To recount the power of creation to flesh and blood is impossible; the Torah therefore concealed the matter with the words, 'In the beginning, God created.'"

R. Kook here paraphrases Rambam (cited in full in 3.3), who explains that Scripture's description of creation is incomplete because we could not understand a comprehensive account anyway. Nevertheless, because the topic is fundamental, it could not be omitted. Therefore, the story uses language and imagery that can be understood in multiple ways, with each person understanding it according to his level.

Later, R. Kook incorporates Ramban's (*Bereishit* 1:1) understanding that the only way to correctly understand the opening chapters of *Bereishit* is mystically. A simplistic understanding of these chapters is impossible.[32]

32. That is not to say that it should be understood non-literally. Ramban simultaneously writes that the literal understanding is true as well; that understanding, though, teaches very little helpful information. Thus, Ramban notes, it would have sufficed for the Torah to have stated simply that in six days, God created heaven and earth, and on the seventh day He rested. The details, such as what was created on the first and second days, are meaningful only when understood mystically. We considered Ramban's view on whether the word *yom* in the first chapter of *Bereishit* should be understood literally in 3.3.

R. Kook offers an example of the type of flexibility that would allow for the compatibility between Torah and science. When the Torah states, "And God formed," or "And God did," this need not be understood as directly doing, but should be interpreted as "And God orchestrated." Essentially, the Torah is communicating in an abbreviated form. He offers an example where the terms are used as such. Concerning the building of the *Beit ha-Mikdash*, the verse states, "Then Shlomo built." Of course, Shlomo did not do the actual building:

> ואין אומרים ששלמה צוה לשרים והשרים להנמוכים מהם, והם להאדריכלים והאדריכלים לאומנים והאומנים לעושי המלאכה הפשוטים, מפני שהוא דרך ידוע, וגם איננו עקרי.
>
> We do not say that Shlomo commanded his officers, and they commanded their subordinates, and they commanded the architects, and they commanded the craftsmen, and they commanded the simple laborers – for this is a well-known process; and it also is tangential.

Likewise, with respect to creation, the unambiguous intention of the verse is that God orchestrated the creation. How He carried out His will remains undefined and is subject to multiple interpretations. This flexibility allows one to embrace aspects of evolution without undermining Scripture.

To be sure, the Torah was not always understood this way. However, the fact that scientific discovery impels novel interpretations need not undermine their credibility. A genuine Torah scholar always will discover new understandings of Torah, some of which may be stimulated by outside sources. Moreover, as explained in 5.15, God, in His infinite wisdom, reveals certain truths to the world in accordance with His plan for world history. Thus, just as the scientific advancements were made at a particular point in history for a particular purpose, so too the original Torah elucidations inspired by these discoveries were revealed at a particular time in order to further that goal.

R. Kook adds that the newly discovered science opens our eyes to the infinite wisdom manifest in God's creation. The complexity, when viewed correctly, does not undermine faith – it solidifies it.

The Torah's Goal

Despite offering numerous solutions to the problem of Torah and science (it almost seems like he is throwing the book at you), it seems that the root of R. Kook's approach lies in a different sort of distinction, which is why he can be grouped with the first school of thought, along with Maharal and R. Soloveitchik.

> והעיקר היא הידיעה העולה מכל הענין לדעת ד׳, וחיי המוסר האמיתי.
>
> The main point [of the Torah and its discussion of creation] is the conclusion that emerges from the discussion – to know God and true moral life.

According to R. Kook, no scientific evidence should be harmful to religion's foundations for the simple reason that science and the Torah have utterly disparate agendas. Science exists to discover the revealed physical reality, to plumb the depths of the created corporeal universe, while religion relates to the knowledge of God and morality and their application in the lives of individuals, the Jewish nation, and the world.

Indeed, the *Zohar* we cited in 7.7 highlights this point when it wonders why the Torah tells us that Noach's ark landed on Mount Ararat: "Who cares whether it landed on this mountain or that one?" (מאי אכפת לן אי שרי בהאי או בהאי דהא באתר חד לישרי). This question, and many like it, take for granted that the goal of the Torah is not to convey scientific or historical information, but, as the *Zohar* states, that which is holy. Moreover, when we encounter passages such as these, we much scratch below the surface because they too teach us important values and deep secrets. The *Zohar* unambiguously declares that someone who sees only scientific information in a particular verse is not merely incorrectly interpreting that particular verse but misrepresenting the character of the Torah (ומאן דאמר דההוא ספורא דאורייתא לאחזאה על ההוא ספור בלבד קאתי תיפח רוחיה, דאי הכי לאו איהי אורייתא עלאה אורייתא דקשוט).

Assessing the First School of Thought

This first school of thought attempts to tackle the problem without modifying Torah or science. This point, while powerful indeed, does not attempt to deal with the more practical details of reconciling scientific observations with the verses of the Torah. As such, it leaves some thinkers unsettled. How, practically, does one resolve the contradiction? This is probably why R. Kook offers numerous solutions.

The latter two approaches, on the other hand, tackle this question by either rejecting (to some degree) the mainstream conclusions of the scientific community (the second school of thought) or by modifying the simple understanding of the Torah in light of scientific discoveries (the third school of thought). Before presenting these approaches, though, it might be helpful to consider what type of people are plagued by questions of Torah and science.

What Difference Does it Make?

The first approach offers a theological reason why questions of Torah and science should not bother the true believer. However, there is another, less philosophical reason why many thinkers are not bothered by apparent contradictions between Torah and science: What difference does it make?

Imagine that Reuven concludes that science has unequivocally demonstrated that the universe is many billions of years old. Reuven also happens to be confident that this perspective is incompatible with the Torah. If Reuven has some level of uncertainty about the veracity of the Torah, then this problem will trouble him insofar as it seems to undermine the Torah's credibility. Reuven may be drawn to modify his understanding of Torah to make it compatible with science. He might, for example, read *Bereishit* allegorically, or show that the term "day" has no meaning prior to the creation of the celestial bodies, or consider the possibility that time moved more slowly in the early "days" of creation, or that the term "day" can refer to a long and undefined period of time. Or Reuven might seek to show that the scientific conclusions about ancient history are, in fact, inconclusive.

If, however, Reuven is absolutely firm in his belief in Torah, if he harbors no doubts about its veracity and divinity, then he will not be troubled by the question of the age of the universe because it does not affect his life in any way; it makes no practical difference. It is a curiosity, and if an answer emerges, it would be interesting to know, but Reuven will not lose sleep over the question nor will he be motivated to seek a solution (except, perhaps, to help people who are in fact bothered by the question). This is true even though Reuven is no intellectual slouch. Some theological questions do bother him; and he seeks solutions to such difficulties. The answers to some philosophical questions will affect the way Reuven lives his life or thinks about God. But not this one. It does not affect the way he prays or the way he thinks of prayer. It is like the myriad inane philosophical questions that can be debated endlessly with brilliant arguments in favor of both positions that provide little interest to most religious thinkers.

While he may wonder about these questions, Reuven realizes, as Maharal (*Tiferet Yisrael* Ch. 6) emphasizes, that it is unrealistic to expect to be able to answer every question. While having answers is nice, not being able to solve every query does not undermine the validity of the system, especially if it is so compelling in other ways. Along similar lines, R. Mayer Twersky ("The Rav's Unwritten Work," *Jewish Action* Fall, Fall 2013) addresses why R. Soloveitchik never sought to reconcile apparent contradictions between the dicta of modern science and Torah, such as the age of the world or the fossil record: "As for the vexing questions involving the fossil record and the like, which pose external challenges and thus did not fall within the Rav's purview, I believe that we can transpose an insight that the Rav was wont to share during his shiurim. When confronted with a question regarding his analysis, the Rav would immediately intuit whether the question represented a possible refutation of his explanation. When it did not, the Rav did not feel compelled to answer it in order to justify his interpretation. If the truth of his explanation was overwhelmingly clear, questions were just that – questions, but not potential refutations. On such occasions the Rav would say, "*Men shtarbt nisht fun a kasha*" ("One does not die from a question"). Similarly, the Rav was convinced that if Jews understood Judaism – its way of life and philosophy – any question would be just that, a question and no more."

Thus, for the person who has a speck of doubt about the Torah's authenticity, the question of the age of the universe is practical – it demands a solution or at least investigation. For the person who has no doubts, this question, while perhaps interesting, is not pressing. Such a person will feel little need to amend his understanding of Torah (without compelling internal evidence). Moreover, he will not be drawn to rejecting powerful scientific arguments. He will sleep soundly, confident that there is a solution out there which, when discovered, will be interesting to read about.

Of course, not all believers are like Reuven. Some people, even those who are firm in their faith, seek a solution to the question not because they wonder about the Torah's veracity but because they seek to understand the truth; they seek to understand the world around them and to understand the Torah's opening chapter. After all, answering this question certainly constitutes a fulfillment of Torah study insofar as it offers insight into the meaning of a section of Torah. Thus, there are two groups of people who desire a more tangible solution to the problems raised by science: someone plagued by doubt concerning the Torah's veracity, and someone seeking to correctly understand *Parshat Bereishit*. We now consider some models for solutions.

8.15 THE SECOND SCHOOL OF THOUGHT – CHALLENGING THE VALIDITY OF SCIENTIFIC CONCLUSIONS

The second school of thought questions the validity of the scientific conclusions that contradict the Torah. These sources frequently stress the distinction between scientific conclusions that are more speculative and those that relate to observed phenomena.

In 3.3, we saw Rambam reject the prevailing views on the eternity of matter since they were not scientifically proven. In 8.14, we noted R. Kook's caution against accepting all conclusions said in the name of science. Another important authority that adopts this methodology is Rashba.

Rashba

Rashba lambasts the hubris sometimes expressed by scientists who fail to acknowledge their limitations. There are many things that science cannot explain. Scientists are human and subject to error. Often times, dogma accepted by the scientific community of one generation is discarded by the next. Plato rejected the wisdom of his predecessors, and his student Aristotle rebuffed the understanding of his teacher.[33] Rashba urges moderation. It would be foolhardy to reject all that science teaches us. However, when we know something based on the Torah, we must not be so quick to modify our understanding of Torah in light of science, since there is a reasonable possibility of scientific error.[34] (We elaborate upon Rashba's ambivalence towards science in halachic contexts in 5.14.)

R. Menachem M. Schneerson

A modern variation of this approach can be found in the letters of R. Schneerson. Before citing his work, it is worth noting that R. Schneerson presents his information from the perspective of someone knowledgeable in the fields of science. In a different letter (cited in 5.14), he reminds his reader that he studied science for four years in Berlin and four years in Paris and remains up-to-date.

Like R. Soloveitchik, R. Schneerson notes that advancements in science make science far more amenable to religion. In a 1971 letter to the Association of Orthodox Jewish Scientists, he writes:

---

33. **שו"ת הרשב"א חלק א סימן ט**
ויותר מזה אני רואה מן התמה בדבריהם שהם באמת מודים שאין חקירתם משגת לאמתת טבע הנמצאות כי יש לכל גוף מן הנבראים סגולות לא נודעו להם סבותם. כמשיכת האבן השואבת את הברזל בלי שידבק גוף לגוף ואחר כן ישוטט הברזל אחר מקום הסדן הקבוע בשמים ויפנה אליו ולפניו ינוח. היש דבר יוצא מגדר הטבע יותר מזה שיתנועע בעל גוף דומם בלי אמצעות גוף אחר מניעו ושיהפך הברזל פניו אל הסדן. באמת אם סופר זה לארסטו היה מכזיבו בלי ספק לולי שנתפרסם הענין פרסום רב. ואחר שהתקיים אצלו הענין הוא חוזר לבקש מן הטענות ומתחכם עליהם.... ולא עוד אלא שאף מצד החקירה אין לנו לבטל דבר שחקירת חכם מן החכמים מחייב בטולו אם יש בידינו קבלה על קיומו. ולמה נסמוך על חקירת החכם ההוא ואולי חקירתו כוזבת מצד מיעוט ידיעתו בענין ההוא. ואולי אם יעמוד חכם ממנו יגלה סתירת דבריו וקיום מה שסתר וכמו שקרה לחכמים שקדמו לאפלטון עם אפלטון. ושקרה לאפלטון עם ארסטו תלמידו הבא אחריו ואמר שיש ריב לאמת עמו.

34. ואיני אומר שנסמוך על הדין הזה להכזיב כל מה שיאמר כל חכם כי אילו אמרנו כן היה כסילות באמת. אך אני אומר במקום שיש מצוה או אפילו קבלה אין מדין האמת לבטל הקבלה מפני דברי החכם ההוא מן הצד הזה שאמרתי.

> Contemporary science no longer lays claim to absolutes; the principle of probability now reigns supreme... Need one remind our orthodox Jewish scientist, who still feels embarrassed about some "old fashioned" Torah truths in the face of scientific hypotheses, that Heisenberg's "principle of indeterminacy" has finally done away with the traditional scientific notion that cause and effect are mechanically linked, so that it is now quite unscientific to hold that one event is inevitably a consequence of another, but only most probable? Most scientists have accepted this principle of uncertainty (enunciated by Werner Heisenberg in 1927) as being intrinsic to the whole universe. The 19th century dogmatic, mechanistic, and deterministic attitude of science is gone. The modern scientist no longer expects to find Truth in science. The current and universally accepted view of science itself is that science must reconcile itself to the idea that whatever progress it makes, it will always deal with probabilities; not with certainties or absolutes.[35]

At first glance, this paragraph resembles R. Soloveitchik's theory of epistemological pluralism rooted in the fact that twentieth-century science (particularly quantum physics) no longer posits a unified or intuitive view of the universe. But, in fact, R. Schneerson draws a very different conclusion. R. Soloveitchik sees modern physics as allowing for the possibility of multiple true perspectives. R. Schneerson argues that in light of contemporary science, we can fully embrace traditional teachings concerning the physical nature of the universe. In 5.14, we considered how R. Schneerson uses the discoveries of Drs. Hans Reichenbach, Albert Einstein, and Werner Heisenberg to justify geocentrism. Likewise, in the above letter he lambasts the apologetic attitude taken by some Orthodox Jewish thinkers who feel the need to reinterpret Torah to conform to contemporary science.

R. Schneerson articulates his position on the age of the universe in "A letter on Science and Judaism." R. Schneerson argues that the discovery of fossils is by no means conclusive evidence of the great antiquity of the earth. His first reason relates to our limited knowledge of prehistoric conditions:

35. http://www.chabad.org/library/article_cdo/aid/112235/jewish/Apologetics.htm.

> In view of the unknown conditions which existed in "prehistoric" times, conditions of atmospheric pressures, temperatures, radioactivity, unknown catalyzers, etc., etc. as already mentioned, conditions that is, which could have caused reactions and changes of an entirely different nature and tempo from those known under the present-day orderly processes of nature, one cannot exclude the possibility that dinosaurs existed 5722 years ago, and became fossilized under terrific natural cataclysms in the course of a few years rather than in millions of years, since we have no conceivable measurements or criteria of calculations under those unknown conditions.

In the aforementioned letter to The Association of Orthodox Jewish Scientists, he adds that the reality that contemporary science no longer lays claim to absolutes proves particularly important concerning speculation about the world's early conditions:

> Certainly in such realms as the origin of the universe, the origin of life on earth, and the origin of the species, where theories are based on speculative extrapolation, and even more so in the realm of pure science, where everything is based on assumed premises (IF we assume that, etc., then it follows, etc.) – scientists do not deal with certainties.

Elsewhere, R. Schneerson expresses disillusionment with academic claims to objectivity, noting how motives and personal bias sometimes influence what is presented as objective study.[36]

Returning to "A letter on Science and Judaism," R. Schneerson adds additional reasons why the fossil record does not undermine the traditional view concerning the age of the universe:

> (b) Even assuming that the period of time which the Torah allows for the age of the world is definitely too short for fossilization (although I do not see how one can be so categorical), we can still readily accept the possibility that God created ready fossils,

36. See *Turning Judaism Outward: A Biography of Rabbi Menachem Mendel Schneerson* by Chaim Miller, pp. 86–87.

> bones or skeletons (for reasons best known to Him), just as He could create ready living organisms, a complete man, and such ready products as oil, coal or diamonds, without any evolutionary process.

R. Schneerson, likes others before him, allows for the possibility that God created the world in a way that makes it look older than it really was. Adam, for example, on the first day of creation did not look like an infant. He was created with the form of a person who already had lived for many years. The same might have been true about the rest of the world. This argument, while plausible, leaves one wondering why God would have created a world that looks like it was billions of years old. R. Schneerson addresses this as well.

> As for the question, if it be true as above (b), why did God have to create fossils in the first place? The answer is simple: We cannot know the reason why God chose this manner of creation in preference to another, and whatever theory of creation is accepted, the question will always remain unanswered. The question, Why create a fossil? is no more valid than the question, Why create an atom? Certainly, such a question cannot serve as a sound argument, much less as a logical basis, for the evolutionary theory.

Here, R. Schneerson alludes to an argument found in *Moreh ha-Nevuchim* (2:25) concerning various questions a person can ask regarding why the world was created in one particular way and not another:

> We answer to all these questions[37]: He willed it so; or, His wisdom decided so. **Just as He created the world according to His will, at a certain time, in a certain form, and we do not**

37. Questions such as: why has God inspired a certain person and not another? Why has He revealed the Torah to one particular nation and at one particular time? Why has He commanded this and forbidden that? Why has He shown through a prophet certain particular miracles? What is the object of these laws? And why has He not made the commandments and the prohibitions part of our nature, if it was His object that we should live in accordance with them?

> **understand why His will or His wisdom decided upon that peculiar form, and upon that peculiar time**, so too we do not know why His will or wisdom determined any of the things mentioned in the preceding questions.

R. Schneerson next turns to the gaps in the theory of evolution:

> What scientific basis is there for limiting the creative process to an evolutionary process only, starting with atomic and subatomic particles – a theory full of unexplained gaps and complications, while excluding the possibility of creation as given by the Biblical account? For, if the latter possibility be admitted, everything falls neatly into pattern, and all speculation regarding the origin and age of the world becomes unnecessary and irrelevant.
>
> It is surely no argument to question this possibility by saying, why should the Creator create a finished universe, when it would have been sufficient for Him to create an adequate number of atoms or subatomic particles with the power of colligation and evolution to develop into the present cosmic order? The absurdity of this argument becomes even more obvious when it is made the basis of a flimsy theory, as if it were based on sound and irrefutable arguments overriding all other possibilities.

Another contemporary thinker with a background in both Torah and science who defends the Torah against science by questioning the legitimacy of scientific conclusions is R. Moshe Meiselman in *Torah, Chazal, and Science.*

8.16 THE THIRD SCHOOL OF THOUGHT – OFFERING RESOLUTIONS

The third approach attempts various forms of resolution. Generally, proponents of this school do one of two things. Either they show how many traditional sources surprisingly correspond to contemporary scientific teachings, or they show how Scripture could be read such that it does not contradict contemporary scientific thought (or both). While the two tactics differ substantially, they align in their acceptance of science[38] and their attempt to highlight compatibility.[39] In 8.14, we saw R. Kook employ both of these methods.

Traditional Sources that Correspond to Contemporary Science

The first variation is to show how many traditional sources surprisingly correspond to contemporary scientific teachings. For example, one approach to dealing with scientific evidence for a much older world and the evolution of man is proposed by R. Yisrael Lifshitz (1782–1860), author of the *Tiferet Yisrael*, in *Derush Ohr ha-Chaim* (found in *Mishnayot Nezikin* after *Masechet Sanhedrin*). He cites aggadic texts, such as the Talmudic statement (*Chagiga* 13b) that "there were 974 generations before Adam," that are compatible with the existence of Neanderthals.[40] Likewise, he writes he was delighted when he received the news of fossil discoveries insofar as they confirmed traditional Torah teachings that God created many worlds and destroyed them before the creation of our world.

He writes:

> ...Regarding the past, R. Abahu states at the beginning of *Bereishit Rabba* that the words "and it was evening, and it was morning" (in the apparent absence of the sun) indicate that "there was a series of epochs before then; the Holy One created worlds and destroyed them, approving some and not others."
>
> The Kabbalists expanded upon this statement and revealed that this process is repeated seven times with each *shemita* achieving greater perfection than the last...They also tell us that

---

38. E.g., dinosaurs or Neanderthals once lived; their bones were not buried simply to give the impression of an older world.
39. E.g., evolution is compatible with *Bereishit*.
40. ולפע"ד שאותן הבני אדם שהיו בעולם הקדום שנקראין פר"א פרפאדעמיטען בל"א, ר"ל הבני אדם שהיו בעולם קדום בריאת אדם הראשון העכשויי, הן הן התתקע"ד דורות שנזכרו בשבת וחגיגה, שהיו נבראים קודם בריאת העולם העתיי.

we are now in the midst of the fourth of these great cycles of perfection…[41]

We are enabled to appreciate in full the wonderful accuracy of our holy Torah when we see that this secret doctrine, handed down by word of mouth for so long and revealed to us by the sages of the Kabbala many centuries ago, has been borne out in the clearest possible way by the science of our generation.

The questing spirit of man, probing and delving into the recesses of the earth, in the Pyrenees, the Carpathians, the Rocky Mountains in America, and the Himalayas, has found them to be formed of mighty layers of rock lying upon one another in amazing and chaotic formations, explicable only in terms of revolutionary transformations of the earth's surface.

Probing still further, deep below the earth's surface, geologists have found four distinct layers of rock, and between the layers fossilized remains of creatures. Those in the lower layers are of monstrous size and structure, while those in the higher layers are progressively smaller in size but incomparably more refined in structure and form.

Furthermore, they found in Siberia in 1807, under the eternal ice of those regions, a monstrous type of elephant, some three or four times larger than those found today…

Similarly, fossilized remains of sea creatures have been found within the recesses of the highest mountains, and scientists have calculated that of every 78 species found in the earth, 48 are species that are no longer found in our present epoch.

We also know of the remains of an enormous creature found deep in the earth near Baltimore, seventeen feet long and eleven feet high. These also have been found in Europe and have been given the name "mammoth." Another gigantic creature whose fossilized remains have been found is that which is called

41. R. Moshe Newman adds that many paleontologists also consider there to have been four eras: the Precambrian, Paleozoic, Mesozoic, and Cenozoic.

"Iguanodon," which stood fifteen feet high and measured ninety feet in length; from its internal structure, scientists have determined that it was herbivorous. Another creature is that which is called "Megalosaurus," which was slightly smaller than the Iguanodon but was meat-eating.

From all this, we can see that all that the Kabbalists have told us for so many years about the repeated destruction and renewal of the earth has found clear confirmation in our time.[42]

Some modern thinkers take this further, showing how the verses of the Torah hint at scientific knowledge that has been discovered only recently.[43] Some scientists have specifically turned to Kabbalistic interpretations of the Torah to highlight the commonality between Torah and contemporary science.[44]

Others find this approach dangerous. Earlier, we noted Maharal's warning against simplistically and superficially interpreting midrashim. Likewise, R. Kook, after highlighting the complementarity between science and Torah concerning the age of the universe (such as the Kabbalistic teaching that there were many eras that preceded our own and the Midrashic statement that He created worlds and destroyed them), warns: אלא ששם צריך להשכיל יפה את המליצות העמוקות, **הצריכות ביאור רחב מאד מאד**, "But one must contemplate well the deep allegories, **which demand extensive explanation**." Kabbalistic teachings allusively convey esoteric wisdom and should not necessarily be seen as presenting scientific information.

Along similar lines, concerning the question of evolution, R. Shalom Carmy writes:

42. Translation adapted from http://ohr.edu/ask_db/ask_main.php/238/Q1/.

43. For examples of this perspective, see Gerald Schroeder, *The Science of God* (New York: Broadway Books, 1997) and *Genesis and the Big Bang: The Discovery of Harmony Between Modern Science and the Bible* (New York: Bantam Books, 1990); and Andrew Goldfinger, *Thinking About Creation: Eternal Torah and Modern Physics* (Northvale, NJ: Jason Aronson, 1999), Chaps. 7, 9, and 25.

44. See "Kabbalah, Science and the Creation of the Universe," by Dr. Nathan Aviezer, *Jewish Action,* Fall 2004.

> What challenges does the idea of natural selection pose for religious believers? Why is it such a controversial matter for so many? Many would immediately complain that scientific natural history differs from the account of natural history that would be derived from a literal reading of Genesis. Much ink has been spilled in the effort to demonstrate that Genesis, when read properly, teaches no more and no less than the most up to date theory. I prefer not to devote space to this literature, having suggested elsewhere that it is neither honest nor religiously beneficial to study Torah as a series of oracular pronouncements about natural science intended for an ingenious, sophisticated interpreter living millennia later.[45]

Contemporary Scientific Theories Are Compatible with Scripture

The second tactic that proponents of the third approach employ is to show that contemporary scientific theories are in fact compatible with Scripture. Based on science, we see how our initial understanding of Torah (from which the contradiction emerged) was wrong. Shortly after Darwin's theory was published, R. Samson Raphael Hirsch wrote:

> If the notion of evolution were to gain complete acceptance by the scientific world, Judaism would call upon its adherents to give even greater reverence to God, Who in His boundless creative wisdom, needed to bring into existence only one amorphous nucleus and one law of "adaptation and heredity" in order to bring forth the infinite variety of species that we know today.[46]

In this passage, R. Hirsch does not explain how the beginning of *Bereishit* is compatible with the theory of evolution, although presumably

45. "Natural Selection: Science or More Than Science?" *The Commentator*, August 31, 2005. Also, see "A Religion Challenged by Science: – Again? A Reflection Occasioned by a Recent Occurrence" by R. Shalom Carmy, *Tradition* 39.2.

    See also R. Kook's *Igrot ha-Re'iyah* #91 (English in Tzvi Feldman, *Rav A.Y. Kook: Selected Letters* 3–10).

46. *Collected Writings* [English], Vol. 7 (New York, 1997), 264.

he felt such a reading was possible. He does not, however, inform us of how he would read the text.[47]

R. Aharon Lichtenstein considers the boundaries of such reinterpretation. On one hand, the veracity of Torah always is maintained. Once one has fully accepted the Torah's divine authority and absolute authenticity, the possibility of creative resolutions remains open.

> Confronted by evident contradiction, one would of course initially strive to ascertain whether it is apparent or real to determine, on the one hand, whether indeed the methodology of *Madda* does inevitably lead to a given conclusion and, on the other, whether the received content of Torah can be interpreted or reinterpreted so as to avert a collision.[48]

R. Lichtenstein argues that this reinterpretation includes explaining certain texts as allegorical and even allowing for the contention that the biblical text "intended to convey a moral and spiritual, but not necessarily historical and scientific, truth."[49] While he provides a framework, he does not flesh out the details.

Along similar lines, some religious scientists have argued that one can embrace a form of guided evolution and still maintain the beliefs mandated by Halacha. One example of such a thinker is Prof. Nathan Aviezer, who writes:

---

47. Consider Rambam's comments in *Moreh ha-Nevuchim* 2:24 that if the eternity of matter would be proven to be correct, he would have no problem interpreting the text of *Bereishit* to accord with that theory. (We considered Rambam's comments in 3.3.) Indeed, many Rishonim interpret Scriptural texts presuming concepts like the active intellect and Aristotelian cosmology. See "Is there Science in the Bible? An Assessment of Biblical Concordism," in *Tradition* 41:2, where Dr. David Shatz considers arguments both for and against this sort of approach.
48. *Torah uMadda: Congruence, Confluence and Conflict* – a transcript of a lecture delivered by R. Lichtenstein in 1987 at Yeshiva University in conjunction with the institution's *Torah uMadda* project, published in a compendium of R. Lichtenstein's articles by Yeshivat Har Etzion, p. 6. Cited in "Judaism And Darwinian Evolution," by Baruch Sterman, *Tradition*, Vol. 29, 1, 1994.
49. The last point resembles R. Kook's approach cited earlier.

Both Darwin and Rav Hirsch viewed evolution as the mechanism used by God to produce the animal kingdom. Particularly interesting is Rav Hirsch's statement that the evolution of the animal kingdom is even more impressive than producing every species by a separate act of divine creation. Although it is impressive to make a beautiful pair of shoes, it is much more impressive to make a factory that automatically takes raw materials and from them produces "endless forms" of shoes "most beautiful and most wonderful."

Rav Hirsch stresses that God works within the laws of nature (*olam keminhago noheg*). This important principle explains how God interacts with His world. It follows from this principle that no scientific discovery can cast doubt on the existence of God.

We now return to Dawkins' assumption that there is only one explanation for the animal kingdom and the origin of the universe. On the basis of this erroneous assumption, Dawkins concluded that a scientific explanation proves that the explanation of divine intervention must be wrong, leading him to gleefully declare that "God has been kicked out."

We have seen that both Rav Hirsch and Darwin reject Dawkins' assumption. They write that the scientific explanation illustrates how God causes the phenomena of nature to occur. This provides an immediate reply to Dawkins' assertion that "God has been kicked out" by scientific explanations. Science and belief march together.

In fact, the opposite of Dawkins' conclusion is true. We expect God to have created the universe through the laws of nature because He does everything through the laws of nature. Therefore, the recent discovery of Hawking and Krauss that the origin of the universe can be explained by combining quantum theory with string theory actually serves as a confirmation of how God operates.[50]

---

50. The above quote is taken from *Jewish Action*, Spring 2015. Elsewhere, Dr. Aviezer fleshes out the details of the concordance. For example, he understands the six

It is beyond the scope of our current discussion to assess this particular argument. We cite it as an illustration of the school of thought that maintains that there is nothing in contemporary science that contradicts the views of the Torah.

The extent to which this reasonably can be done often hinges on the extent to which biblical and aggadic texts can be understood non-literally, a topic discussed by Rishonim at length. We considered the matter in Chapter 3 regarding Scripture and Chapter 5 concerning Aggada.

What if None of These Approaches Works?

What is one to do if he is bothered by the problem but finds none of the above approaches compelling? I believe that the answer is that it is acceptable to leave the question unanswered, and, in fact, this approach proves superior to accepting solutions that do not seem intellectually honest. The fact that a person cannot answer every question does not undermine the credibility of the Torah. Indeed, it is presumptuous to assume that one should be able to answer every question concerning the Torah, such that if there is a question that he cannot answer, he must call into question the validity of the entire system. At times, we must concede that God's ways are mysterious and the true understanding of Torah is elusive. Perhaps if he studies more Torah and internalizes its values to a greater degree, the person will discover an answer that satisfies him. In the meantime, he must continue faithfully.

A powerful example of this form of humility emerges from a lecture by R. Aharon Lichtenstein concerning a related question (the seeming immorality of the *mitzva* of destroying Amaleik):

> I recall in my late adolescence there were certain problems which perturbed me, the way they perturb many others. At the time, I resolved them all in one fell swoop. I had just read Rav Zevin's book, *Ishim Ve-shitot*. In his essay on Rav Chayim

days of creation as referring to large periods of time. The evolutionary framework applies except where the word *bara* (create) is used. See his *In the Beginning, Biblical Creation and Science* and *Fossils and Faith: Understanding Torah and Science.*

> Soloveitchik, he deals not only with his methodological development, but also with his personality and *gemilut chasadim* (acts of kindness). He recounted that Reb Chayim used to check every morning if some unfortunate woman had placed an infant waif on his doorstep during the course of the night. (In Brisk, it used to happen at times that a woman would give birth illegitimately and leave her infant in the hands of Reb Chayim.) As I read the stories about Reb Chayim's extraordinary kindness, I said to myself: Do I approach this level of *gemilut chasadim*? I don't even dream of it! In terms of moral sensibility, concern for human beings and sensitivity to human suffering, I am nothing compared to Reb Chayim. Yet despite his moral sensitivity, he managed to live, and live deeply, with the totality of Halakha – including the commands to destroy the Seven Nations, Amaleik and all the other things which bother me. How? The answer, I thought, was obvious. It is not that his moral sensitivity was less, but his *yirat Shamayim*, his *emuna*, was so much more. The thing to do, then, is not to try to neutralize or de-emphasize the moral element, but rather to deepen and increase the element of *yirat Shamayim*, of *emuna*, *d'veikut* and *bittachon*.[51]

While not identical, the questions of the morality of the destruction of Amaleik and the seeming contradictions between Torah and science share certain parallels. God gives us an innate sense of morality, and yet commands us to destroy a nation "from child to suckling babe" (*I Shmuel* 15:3). As R. Lichtenstein points out earlier in the above piece, "Although generally such an act would be considered immoral, it assumes a different character when God, from His perception and perspective, commands it." One's moral intuition does play a role in determining the propriety of a particular act, but not when it contravenes the dictates of the divine command.

51. "Being Frum and Being Good: On the Relationship Between Religion and Morality," adapted by R. Reuven Ziegler, published in *By His Light: Character and Values in the Service of God.*

Likewise, God communicates to us through His creation. Exploring science can allow us to see God. We are entrusted to use our intellect to understand Him through His creation. When that understanding contradicts (in our perception) the explicit word of God, though, we must abandon our explorations in favor of what is a more direct divine communication.[52] Ultimately, if a person really believes in the divinity of the Torah, the fact that he cannot (yet) reconcile it with science need not test his *emuna*.

What Is Really Behind "Scientific Heresy"?

Why is it that some people are incredibly bothered by the questions posed by science and others, even highly intelligent and thoughtful religious thinkers, are not? Certainly, there are many answers to the question (see above 8.14 and 8.15). However, R. Kook, when discussing why people leave the faith due to "scientific heresy" (the claim that science disproves Torah), suggests a provocative solution. If religion had properly fulfilled its function of spreading "the knowledge of God on the land" by guiding humanity's moral development, the "scientific heresy" would soon lose its basis, as people would realize the shallowness of the supposed contradictions. (In this context, R. Kook points to the Catholic Church as being particularly guilty of suppressing man's moral development.) The true reason behind modern man's exodus from religion does not lie in the irresolvable contradictions between religion and science, for, as we have noted, there are solutions. Rather, R. Kook (*Eider ha-Yakar*, 36) contends, the destructive and immoral behavior perpetrated in the name of religion is the basis for the "moral heresy" (the claim that belief in God and loyalty to religion have hindered rather than helped man's moral state) that caused so many people to abandon religious belief and practice.[53] Indeed, R. Kook argues that it is "moral heresy" that really is behind "scientific heresy."

52. See Ramban's *Drashat Torat Hashem Temima*, where he elaborates upon this theme.
53. This point is beautifully developed by R. Yosef Bronstein in an unpublished essay entitled "Scientific Developments in the Thought of Rav Kook."

Chapter Nine

The *Mitzva* of *Emuna* According to R. Yehuda ha-Levi

In Chapter 8, we considered the value of philosophical proof for the existence of God. In this chapter, we consider the pitfalls of this approach as well as the advantages and disadvantages of other approaches generally, and specifically in the modern world.

We begin by considering the *mitzva* of *emuna* according to R. Yehuda ha-Levi (*Kuzari*) and then examine the *mitzva* according to a number of other thinkers, including R. Kook, R. Shneur Zalman of Liadi, and R. Soloveitchik.

9.1 *EMUNA* ROOTED IN PROPHECY, A RELATIONSHIP, AND EXPERIENCE

Introducing R. Yehuda ha-Levi

In this chapter, we consider the approach of R. Yehuda b. Shmuel ha-Levi (Rihal) to faith. It may prove helpful to first introduce this great thinker. Rihal was born in 1075 in Toledo, Spain. In his youth, Rihal studied under R. Yitzchak Alfasi (Rif) and befriended Ri Migash (Rambam's teacher). Rihal became a great poet and moved to Granada to be closer to R. Moshe ibn Ezra. Rihal studied medicine, which provided him with both a livelihood and inspiration. He married and had one daughter (who, according to legend, married R. Avraham ibn Ezra).

Besides *Kuzari,* Rihal composed poetry including numerous odes expressing his love of Israel and his longing to live there. He eventually journeyed to the Holy Land, though it is unclear whether he ever reached his final destination. Legend relates[1] that when he knelt down to kiss the stones of Israel and proclaim "*Tziyon ha-lo tish'ali*" (the opening of one of the *kinot* recited on *Tisha be-Av* composed by Rihal), he was trampled by an Arab horseman.

Rihal's most important work is *Kuzari* or *The Book of Argument and Proof in Defense of the Despised Faith* (Kitab al Khazari).[2] The work is based upon a story that reached Spain in the tenth century but took place in the eighth century. The Khazar people lived on the shores of the Caspian Sea. Legend has it that the king of the Khazars dreamt the same dream as his general; they were told, "Your way of thinking is indeed pleasing to the Creator, but not your way of acting." This dream led the king to convene a debate. Initially, the Jewish position is not sought; instead, the king first considers and rejects Aristotelian philosophy, Christianity, and Islam. Eventually, a Jewish sage (the *chaveir*) is sought, since, as the king notes, the basis of Islam and Christianity can be found in Judaism. The king is convinced of the correctness of Judaism and converts (described at the beginning of Book 2). The conversation

---

1. R. Gedaliya ibn Yachya (c. 1515 – c. 1587) records the story in his historical work entitled *Shalshelet ha-Kabbala.*
2. *Kuzari* originally was written in Arabic. There are numerous translations into Hebrew and English. A highly readable rendition of *Kuzari* into English was written by R. N. Daniel Korobkin and published by Feldheim. The Hartwig Hirschfeld edition (New York, 1905) is the basis for much of the translation that follows. Therefore, the translations that follow do not line up exactly since they are two independent translations from Arabic. I have included the Hebrew and English with the hope that between the two, a truer conception of the original will emerge. Some of the translations and ideas that follow are based on the *shiurim* of R. Itamar Eldar available at etzion.org.

with the *chaveir* continues for five books until the *chaveir* announces his departure to the Holy Land.

Avraham's Discovery of God

In 8.4, we cited the midrash that offers a teleological proof for the existence of God:

> **בראשית רבה (וילנא) פרשת לך לך פרשה לט**
> אמר רבי יצחק משל לאחד שהיה עובר ממקום למקום, וראה בירה אחת דולקת אמר תאמר שהבירה זו בלא מנהיג, הציץ עליו בעל הבירה, אמר לו אני הוא בעל הבירה, **כך לפי שהיה אבינו אברהם אומר תאמר שהעולם הזה בלא מנהיג, הציץ עליו הקב"ה ואמר לו אני הוא בעל העולם...**
>
> R. Yitzhak says: To what may this be compared? To a man who was traveling from place to place and saw an illuminated palace. He wondered, "Is it possible that the palace lacks a director?" The director of the palace looked out and said, "I am the director of the palace." So Avraham our father said, "Is it possible that the world lacks a director?" The Holy One, blessed be He, looked out and said to him, "I am the Sovereign of the Universe."

While this midrash highlights the value of proof, informing us that Avraham first came to the awareness of God's existence based on a teleological argument, it does not end there. Instead, Avraham's initial search led to a conversation with God – it developed into a relationship. This idea brings us to the position of Rihal, who argues that the undeveloped awareness of God's existence, established through philosophical proof, falls short of the Torah's expectation vis-à-vis our relationship with God.[3]

---

3. Rihal was not the first to critique this approach (see, for example, R. Nissim Gaon's *Megillat Setarim*), nor was he the last (as we shall see later); however, his position is among the most developed.

God of Avraham Versus God of Aristotle

Rihal contrasts the person who believes in God solely based on philosophical proof with the person who has a relationship with God, or, in *Kuzari*'s words (4:17), the difference between someone who believes in "the God of Aristotle" and someone who serves "the God of Avraham."

Before examining the details of this distinction, let us paint the comparison in broad strokes. Aristotle believed in God. Aristotle writes in Book 12 of *Metaphysics*, "there must be an immortal, unchanging being, ultimately responsible for all wholeness and orderliness in the sensible world." God embodies absolute perfection. He is "the unmoved mover," perfectly beautiful, indivisible, and contemplating only the perfect contemplation. He, by definition, lacks will (*ratzon*). He could not create the world, because that would imply that something was initially lacking. Instead, He is simply "the unmoved mover." Clearly, such a God cannot hear prayer. He does not converse with prophets. He does not interact with the world.

Avraham's God is totally different. He speaks to man. He cares about the world and is involved in the world. He destroys the city of Sodom and redeems the Jewish people from bondage. And, most importantly, He loves Avraham (*Devarim* 4:37) and Avraham loves Him (*Yeshayahu* 41:8).[4] With this in mind, let us consider some of the distinctions between these two forms of belief that Rihal highlights.

God's Name

Kuzari understands that the concept of an intimate relationship with God was Avraham's great innovation. It is reflected in his referring to God using the *sheim havaya* (tetragrammaton), an actual name, as opposed to simply referring to Him as God or *Elokim*.[5] *Elokim* is the God of Aristotle; He is abstract and totally impersonal; there is no relationship. It is the God of creation [בראשית ברא אלוקים]. The *sheim havaya* is a personal

4. It is important to stress that Rihal is primarily criticizing Aristotle's conception of God, not Rambam's.

5. As we shall see, Avraham was not the first to use the *sheim havaya*, but his relationship with God was like no other that preceded him.

name, not just a title or description. Just as we refer to a friend by his personal name, Avraham refers to God by the *sheim havaya*.[6]

כוזרי ד:טז

אמר הכוזרי: הנה נתבאר לי ההפרש בין השמות 'אלוהים' וה', והבינותי מה רב המרחק בין 'אלוהי אברהם' ובין אלוהי אריסטו: כי לה' יתעלה משתוקקים בני אדם שהשיגוהו בחוש ועל יסוד עדות ראיה, ואלו ל'אלוהים' נוטים על פי הקש הגיוני.

The Khazar king: Now I understand the difference between *Elokim* and the tetragrammaton, and I see how much the God of Abraham is different from the God of Aristotle. Man yearns for the tetragrammaton as a matter of love, taste, and conviction, while knowledge of *Elokim* is the result of philosophical speculation.

כוזרי ד:א

אמר החבר... אין שם מדויק יותר וחשוב יותר מן השם הנכתב באותיות 'יוד הא ואו הא' יתברך ויתרומם! זה הוא שם פרטי, בו רומזים לאלוה, לא בתואר המקום, כדרך שרומזים לכל מתואר בלתי ידוע, ולא בתארים [נוספים על עצמותו], ולא בהכללה, כבשם הכללי 'אלוהים', כי אם בשם המיוחד לו, שכן הוא נקרא ה' על דרך הייחוד. כאילו שאל שואל: מי הוא 'אלוהים' שיש לעבדו, השמש, או הירח, או השמים, או המזלות, או אחד הכוכבים, או האש, או הרוח, או המלאכים, הרוחניים או זולתם, כי הלא לכל אחד מאלה פעולה משלו ושלטון משלו, וכל אחד מהם סיבה להתהוות דברים ולהאפסם? ועל זה באה התשובה: ה'!, כאלו

6. Moreover, the tetragrammaton is more intimate insofar as it reflects God's essence, while the rest of the names of God are descriptive of the way in which we perceive His actions.

כוזרי ב:ב

אמר החבר: כל שמות האלוה (חוץ מן השם המפורש) הם סיפורים ותארים נוספים [על עצמותו] שכולם שאולים מההתפעליות שהנבראים נפעלים מגזרותיו וממעשיו.

The *Chaveir*: All names of God, save the tetragrammaton, are predicates and attributive descriptions, derived from the way His creatures are affected by His decrees and actions.

אמרת: פלוני! וקראת לו בשם פרטי, ראובן ושמעון למשל, בתנאי שעל ידי השמות ראובן ושמעון תיוודע אמיתת עצמותם.

> The *Chaveir*: ... A more exact and loftier name is to be found in the form known as the tetragrammaton. This is a proper noun by which we refer to God, not in association with location or other attributes, and [this name] formerly was unknown.[7] If He commonly was styled "*Elokim*," the tetragrammaton was used as a special name. This is as if one asked: Which God is to be worshipped – the sun, the moon, the heaven, the signs of the zodiac, any star, fire, a spirit, or celestial angels, etc.; each of these, taken singly, has an activity and force, and causes growth and decay? The answer to this question is: "Hashem," just as if one would say: A. B., or a proper name, as Reuven or Shimon, supposing that these names indicate their personalities.

R. Soloveitchik and The Lonely Man of Faith

R. Soloveitchik develops Rihal's idea in *The Lonely Man of Faith* when explaining the two different creation narratives. The first chapter of *Bereishit* describes the creation of man very differently from the second chapter. R. Soloveitchik sees this as reflecting two different archetypes, Adam I (the person described in *Bereishit*, Chapter 1) and Adam II (the person described in *Bereishit*, Chapter 2). The first chapter refers to God as *Elokim* (**בראשית ברא אלוקים**), whereas the second chapter introduces the tetragrammaton. Thus, Adam I relates only to the cosmic God; Adam II, on the other hand,

> Studies [the universe] with the naiveté, awe and admiration of the child who seeks the unusual and wonderful in every ordinary thing and event ... He looks for the image of God not in the mathematical formula or the natural relational law but in every beam of light, in every bud and blossom, in the morning breeze and the stillness of a starlit evening (p. 23).

7. Before Avraham.

Adam I uses his practical intellect and scientific ability to comprehend the forces of nature and his technological ability to bend them to his will. Adam II, on the other hand, does not have such a grandiose self-image; he is humble, realizing that he was created from the dust of the earth. He allows himself to be overpowered and defeated by God. While Adam I maintains some distance from God, relating merely to the divine endowment of creativity, Adam II has a "genuine living experience" of God and is preoccupied with Him, as evidenced by the metaphor of God breathing life into his nostrils. "*Elokim*" denotes God as the source of cosmic dynamics, while the tetragrammaton indicates personal, intimate communion between God and man. Adam I is satisfied by an impersonal encounter with the former (the cosmic experience), while Adam II craves the latter (the covenantal experience).

The Shortfalls of Philosophical Proof – a Clockmaker Is Not the Same as a Personal God

It is not simply that philosophical demonstration fails to yield a relationship with God; it fails to prove the existence of a God with which a relationship even is possible. Philosophy can prove that there is a deity, but it does not demonstrate that He hears us and interacts with us. This can be known only through prophecy.

כוזרי ד:ג

אמר הכוזרי: ואיך אקרא בשם מיוחד את שאין לרמוז עליו וכל ראייתי עליו מפעולותיו היא.

The Khazar king: How can I individualize a being if I am not able to point to it and can prove its existence only by its actions?

אמר החבר: **יש ויש עליו רמז: בעדות הנבואה ובראית הלב! כי הבאת הראיות מתעה, וממנה נולדו המינות והשיטות הנפסדות...**

אולם דרכי הבאת הראיות שונות זו מזו מהן שבאו בדיוק רב ומהן שקיצרו בזה, והמדויקת ביותר היא דרך הפילוסופים, ואותם הביאה דרך זו לידי אמונה באלוה אשר אינו לא מרע ולא מיטיב

לנו ולא יודע דבר על תפילותינו ועל קרבנותינו, על עבודתנו או על מרינו, וכן לידי אמונה שהעולם קדמון כקדמות האלוה, ולכן אין אצל הפילוסופים שם פרטי לאלוה, שם בו ירמזו לו לבדו. רק איש ששמע את דבר האלוה ומצוותו ואזהרתו והודעתו כי הוא גומל טוב לעובדיו ועונש על המרי יקראהו בשם פרטי, ככינוי מיוחד למי שדיבר אליו וברר לו כי הוא שברא את העולם אחר ההעדר. הראשון בין האנשים מסוג זה היה אדם, שלא היה מכיר את האלוה לולא דיבר האלוה עימו ויעד לו גמול ועונש ובחר לו את חוה, שיצרה מאחת מצלעותיו, כך נתברר לו לאדם כי האלוה הוא בורא העולם, ואליו פנה אדם בדיבור ואותו תאר בתארים ולו קרא בשם ה׳.

The *Chaveir*: **It can be designated by prophetic or visionary means. Demonstration can lead astray. Demonstration was the mother of heresy and destructive ideas....**

There are differences in the ways of demonstration, of which some are more extended than others. Those who go to the utmost length are the philosophers, and the ways of their arguments led them to teach of a Supreme Being who neither benefits nor injures and knows nothing of our prayers, offerings, obedience, or disobedience and that the world is as eternal as He. None of them applies a distinct proper name to God, except he who hears His address, command, or prohibition, approval for obedience, and reproof for disobedience. He bestows on Him some name as a designation for Him who spoke to him, and he is convinced that He is the Creator of the world from nothing. The first man never would have known Him if He had not addressed, rewarded, and punished him and had not created Chava from one of his ribs. This gave him the conviction that this was the Creator of the world, whom he designated by words and attributes, and called out in the Name of Hashem (the tetragrammaton).

Kuzari then describes the history of how His Name became known and how it became forgotten.

לולא כל זה היה אדם מתארו רק בשם 'אלוהים', כי לא היה מתברר לו אם אלוה אחד או רבים, אם יש לו ידיעה בפרטים אם לא. אחרי אדם באו קין והבל, אשר ידעו את האלוה בראשונה מתוך מה שמסר להם אביהם ואחרי כן גם מתוך התגלות בה נגלה גם להם. אחריהם בא נח, ואחריו אברהם ויצחק ויעקב ועוד, עד משה והנביאים שאחריו, וכל אלה קראוהו ה', כי כולם זכו להתגלות. אשר לבני העם שהאמינו בקבלה שקבלו מאלה, הם קראוהו ה' על היות מצותו והנהגתו נתונות לבני אדם.

Without this, Adam would have been satisfied with the name *Elokim*, neither perceiving what He was, whether He was a unity or many, nor whether He was cognizant of individuals or not. Kayin and Hevel were made acquainted with the nature of His being by the communications of their father as well as by prophetic intuition. Then Noach, Avraham, Yitzchak and Yaakov, Moshe and the Prophets called Him Hashem, as did the people, having been taught by tradition that His influence and guidance were with men.

Sacrifice

The person who believes in God based on philosophy (someone who serves "the God of Aristotle"), for example, rarely will give his life for that which he knows to be true. Imagine a king who threatened to kill anyone who did not declare his belief in a statement that is clearly false. (For example, that the hypotenuse of a triangle sometimes is longer than the sum of its sides.) Even a person who is certain that this is false would not necessarily give up his life for that which he knows to be true; doing so is irrational, as it accomplishes nothing. So too with respect to someone who knows of God's existence only through philosophy – his intellectual awareness of God's existence would not necessarily move him to sacrifice for God. God is a concept, a true idea. Nothing more. Not so for someone who has a relationship with God. God is not a concept; He is the object of the person's greatest love. He naturally inspires sacrifice.[8] Moreover, the type of deity that speculation yields remains uninvolved in the world and does not demand sacrifice.

8. Some thinkers explain that philosophical speculation usually will not inspire sacrifice because the belief remains knowledge external to the person; it never becomes part

כוזרי ד:טז

מי שהשיגו בחוש בא לידי מסירות נפש מתוך אהבת האלוה ולידי הנכונות למות עליה. ואלו ההקש מראה רק זאת: כי חובה היא לרומם את האלוה כל שעה שאין הדבר מזיק ואין סובלים צער עליו. אין להאשים אפוא את אריסטו על הלגלוג שלגלג על טקסי עבודת האלוה, מאחר שהוא מסופק אם האלוה יודע בזה

> A relationship with God invites its votaries to give their lives for His sake and to prefer death to His absence. Speculation, however, makes veneration a necessity only as long as it entails no harm, but it does not encourage one to bear pain for His sake. I would, therefore, excuse Aristotle for thinking lightly about the observation of the law, since he doubts whether God has any cognizance of it.

Accordingly, we can understand why Avraham alone was tested. This notion is explicated by R. Yitzchak Arama regarding the purpose of a *nisayon*, specifically the binding of Yitzchak. Avraham's willingness to sacrifice his beloved son reflects that his connection to God was not rooted only in the cerebral knowledge of God's existence, but rather was an intimate relationship animated by love and fear.[9]

As we noted in 8.8, a historical observation that reflects this concern was made by R. Yosef Ya'avetz, who notes that among those who were put to the ultimate test the faith, those whose faith was rooted in philosophical proof failed, while the ignorant remained steadfast. It was

---

of him. In the words of Blaise Pascal (1623–1662), "The metaphysical proofs for the existence of God are so remote from human reasoning, and so complicated, that they make little impact, and, even if they did help some people, it would only be for the moment that they see such demonstration, because an hour later they would be afraid they had made a mistake" (Penses, 542).

9. **עקידת יצחק בראשית שער כא (פרשת וירא)**
ואולם ישאר שהוא מהמין השני והוא כדי שיוציא המנוסה שלמותו אל הפועל ויושלם בו שכלו ודעתו משני פנים. האחד מצד הענין המצוה ההיא הכללית והוא שיוציאהו בה לגמרי **ממדרגת פילוסוף טבעי למעלת תורני אלהי כי בדרך הפילוסופים אין סכלות גדולה מזו** והוא מבואר שלא יעשה האדם כך עד שיקיים בנפשו חיוב השמיעה אל עצה ומצוה עליונה למעלה מהשכל האנושי **באהבתו ויראתו** כי הממאן והמסרב בה יגיעהו מהעונש רע ומר ממות ומשכל, אשר לא ישוער זה בחק השכל העיוני הפילוסופי כמ"ש ראשונה **וכמו שכבר התחיל זה עמו במצות מילה** כי על כן אמר התהלך לפני והיה תמים (בראשית י"ז) כמו שאמרנו שם.

they who were willing to sacrifice their lives and fortunes. History has shown us that "proof" does not always yield conviction.

To summarize, there are two reasons that someone who accepts only the God of Aristotle would not give up his life for his belief:

1. A person whose faith rests entirely on reason will lack the will to sacrifice his life for his belief.
2. Even if such a person could muster the wherewithal to offer his life, he would not do so, because it is irrational. The nature of faith built entirely upon logic would not demand sacrifice. On the contrary, sacrifice would represent the height of irrationality. For such a person, God is a concept, something that exists, but, like a triangle, not something that demands sacrifice.

Avraham's Transition

Kuzari does not contradict the midrash cited at the beginning of this section; he echoes it. The midrash informs us that Avraham initially recognized God through speculation (תאמר שבירה זו בלא מנהיג). *Kuzari* agrees, writing that this was Avraham's initial point of view until God spoke to him. As soon as this took place, he gave up all his speculations and strove only to develop his relationship with a personal God. Having established this relationship (reflected by *sheim havaya*), Avraham looked back upon his earlier proofs and recognized their inadequacy. The notion of a philosophical proof, *Kuzari* explains, is laughable for the person who has experienced the passionate embrace of his beloved (God) and has been overwhelmed by His presence.

כוזרי ד:כז

ויתכן כי העיון הזה שמצאנו ב'ספר יצירה' היה עיונו של אברהם אבינו שעה שכבר נתבררו לו אחדות האלוה ורבונותו אך טרם זכה להתגלות, אולם לאחר שזכה להתגלות עזב את כל ההקשים ולא ביקש מעם האלוה כי אם להיות לו לרצון, אחרי אשר למדו האלוה מה הוא הרצון, במה יושג ובאיזה מקום. וכבר דרשו החכמים על מאמר הכתוב 'ויוצא אותו החוצה': 'צא מאצטגנינות שלך!', כלומר עזוב חכמת הכוכבים וכל חכמת טבע מסופקת.

Perhaps this was Avraham's point of view when divine power and unity dawned upon him prior to the revelation accorded to him. As soon as this took place, he gave up all his speculations and strove only to gain the favor of God, having ascertained what this was and how and where it could be obtained. The Sages explain the words, "And He (God) brought him (Avraham) outside" (*Bereishit* 15) thus: "Give up your horoscopy!" This means: Forsake astrology as well as any other doubtful study of nature.

Kuzari on Philosophy

To fully appreciate Avraham's innovation, we must consider Rihal's attitude towards philosophy generally. Rihal lyrically expresses his negative attitude towards philosophy in a poem, "And don't be fooled by wisdom of the Greeks, which bears flowers but no fruit" (cited in *Yehuda Halevi* by Hillel Halkin, Knopf, 2010, p. 133). Yet, while Rihal sometimes is classified as an anti-rationalist, he does not categorically reject philosophy. He contends that given their tools, philosophers fared quite well:

כוזרי א:סג

אין לבוא בטענות, הואיל והם אנשים שלא קבלו חכמה או דת בירושה, שהרי הם יונים, ויון הוא מבני יפת יושבי הצפון

There is an excuse for the philosophers. Being Greek, science and religion did not come to them as inheritances. They belong to the descendants of Yefet, who inhabited the north.

Given their lack of divine tradition and exposure to revelation, the Greeks had to rely exclusively upon speculation in searching for wisdom and truth. Those of them who were humble and intellectually honest acknowledged this limitation.

כוזרי ד:יג

אכן הפילוסופים אם אמנם רחקו כל הרחק הזה מהשגת האלוה לפי הנבואה אין להאשימם על כך כי אל חכמת האלוהות לא היה להם מבוא כי אם דרך ההיקש ההגיוני וההיקש לא הביאם כי אם למה שאמרנו ואכן אותם מהם האוהבים להודות על האמת יאמרו לבעלי התורה

> דברים שאמר סוקרטס (לבני עירו) חברי האזרחים חכמת אלוהות זו אשר לכם אין אני מכחישה אולם אומר אני כי איני מכירה כי אני יודע רק בחכמה האנושית.

> We cannot blame philosophers for missing the mark, since they arrived at this knowledge purely by way of speculation, and the result could not have been different. The most sincere among them speak to the followers of a revealed religion in the words of Socrates: "My friends, I will not contest your theology. I say, however, that I cannot grasp it; I understand only human wisdom."

The intellect is a powerful gift bestowed by God capable of guiding a person to live a virtuous life.

כוזרי ה:יד

> אך בכל הדעות הללו נפלו ספקות ואין הסכמה בין פילוסוף לחברו. על כל פנים אין להאשימם על כך, אדרבה, יש לשבחם על ההישגים שהשיגו בכוח ההפשטה שבהיקשיהם ועל שכיוונו אל הטוב וייסדו את החוקות השכליות ומאסו בתענוגי העולם הזה.

> They are full of doubts, and there is no consensus of opinion between one philosopher and another. Yet they cannot be blamed, nay, they deserve thanks for all they have produced in abstract speculations. For their intentions were good; they observed the laws of reason and led virtuous lives.

The Jewish people, on the other hand, have something even the greatest philosophers lacked – revelation. Thus, while philosophical speculation may yield proof of God's existence, it does not generate a correct conception of the Almighty. Moreover, revelation not only produced wisdom, but allowed for the formation of a relationship with the Divine. Thus, Avraham, after independently concluding that God necessarily exists, was granted something much greater – a personal bond with the Almighty.[10]

---

10. To fully appreciate this point, we must explore the notion of the *inyan Eloki*, the divine influence that the Jewish people enjoy, and its connection to prophecy. We consider this topic in Chapter 31.

While Rihal is not discussing mysticism, it is interesting to note that Gra suggests a similar correlation between philosophy and mysticism. Mysticism, which is rooted in revelation, begins where philosophy, which is rooted in the intellect, leaves off.[11] Philosophers need not be wrong (though frequently Rihal and Gra maintained that they were); rather, they present a limited and incomplete perspective on the universe. But when philosophers overstep their boundaries and attempt to utilize the tools of science/philosophy in matters of religion and theology, they are sure to err. (Thus, Rihal distinguishes between logic, where the methodology of philosophy yields truth, and speculation, where philosophers fall short.) The same holds true in the legal realm:

> **כוזרי ב:מח**
> אלה וכל הדומים להם הם החוקים השכליים, אך הללו אינם כי אם הצעות והקדמות לתורה האלוהית, הקודמות לה בטבע ובזמן, אשר בלעדיהן לא תיתכן כל הנהגה בכל חברה מחברות בני אדם, עד כי גם חברת שודדים לא ייתכן שלא תקבל שלטון הצדק בדברים שבינם לבין עצמם בלא זה לא תתמיד חברותם.
>
> These are the rational laws, being the basis and preamble of the divine law, preceding it in character and time, and being indispensable in the administration of every human society. Even a gang of robbers must have a kind of justice among them if their confederacy is to last.

Rihal in the above passage paraphrases Chazal's aphorism *derech eretz kadma la-Torah,* or "proper ethical behavior preceded Torah" (*Vayikra Rabba* 9:3). The intellect is capable of deriving rational laws. These laws are indispensable in the administration of society. The Torah's divine laws build upon these rational laws (revelation begins where the

---

11. **ארחות חיים כתר ראש סא**
פילוסופייא, אמר רבנו **שממקום שמסתיים הפילוסופיא משם ולמעלה מתחיל חכמת הקבלה,** וממקום שמסתיים קבלת הרמ"ק - משם ולמעלה מתחיל קבלת האר"י ז"ל.
We explored this topic more fully in 2.13.

intellect ends) to create not merely a just society but a divine society that encourages communion with the Almighty. However, "The divine law cannot become complete until the social and rational laws are perfected" (*Kuzari* 2:48).

9.2 EXPERIENTIAL KNOWLEDGE OF GOD'S EXISTENCE AND APPLYING *KUZARI* IN THE MODERN WORLD

For *Kuzari*, this relationship-based approach to faith is largely rooted in prophecy. Where does that leave us in the post-prophetic world? The answer is that it continues. Even in our world, we continue to encounter God.

One powerful manner in which a person encounters God is through the study of Torah. R. Dessler argues that the most powerful and definitive proof for the existence of God emerges from the study of Torah.[12]

Knowledge that God exists through the study of Torah differs from knowledge that He exists through philosophical proof, but it is no less certain. While this sort of connection to God may not convince someone who has not experienced it, once one has encountered God through Torah study, he will be left with no doubts about His existence.

---

12. **מכתב מאליהו ח״ג עמ׳** 177

התעלות באמונה פנימית באה ע״י התעמקות בתורה עצמה (לימוד בעיון) ולא ע״י חקירות השכל מופשטות. טעות היא לחשוב שיכולים להשיג את האמונה המוחלטת ע״י חקירות שכלייות ופילוסופיה, הרי השכל משוחד ע״י כל מיני נגיעות. הרצון מטה את השכל לאן שהוא חפץ. כשהאדם פונה אל שכלו, בטרם התעמק בתורה, וביסס את אמונתו על קבלת אבות ואמונת חכמים, ורוצה ששכלו יהיה השופט הבלעדי על עניני אמונה - סימן הוא שאינו רוצה להאמין, לכן פונה אל שופט משוחד שיורה לו כרצונו. השכל גם מוגבל, כי המחשבה מיוסדת על ציורים גשמיים שהם מוגבלים. אבל האמונה הבאה מפנימיות האדם - אין שולטות עליה הגבלות אלו. ר׳ נחמן כתב שבמקום אשר שם גבולו של השכל - שם מתחילה האמונה. אמנם חוייבנו לברר את אמונתנו ע״י השכל - כדברי החובות הלבבות, אכן הגישה לא תהא ״מה שאני מבין בשכלי אקבל...״ אין הכונה שיסמוך על שכלו בלבד, כי בזה לא יוכל להגיע אף פעם אל בירור האמת, כי הוא משוחד מרצונותיו, וגם מוגבל. גדר בירור האמונה ע״י השכל הוא: אחרי שנתיישבה כבר האמונה בלבו ע״י קבלת אבות, וע״י למוד התורה והכרת גדולתה וגדולת חכמינו, יעסוק אדם לקרב אל שכלו את יסודות האמונה, לבררם לעצמו בבירור שכלי.

Torah study is not the only way to arrive at experiential knowledge of God's existence. *Mitzva*-observance in general, and genuine prayer and careful observance of Shabbat in particular, are particularly powerful factors in instilling faith.[13] However, even many of our everyday experiences can bring about this same awareness.

Is Experiential Knowledge a Cop-out?

At first glance, seeking experiential awareness for the existence of God seems like a cop-out in light of science. However, this may not be the case when we consider what it is that "science" purports to demonstrate. Philosopher Gary Gutting in *Debating God: Notes on an Unanswerable Question,*[14] succinctly presents the issue in a "conversation" with himself:

> **G.G.**: O.K., but at least aren't believers who appeal to religious experience and metaphysical arguments admitting what popular atheism so insistently claims: There's simply no evidence for God's existence, and that alone warrants atheism?
>
> **g.g.**: There's no *scientific* evidence, but there are other sorts of evidence.
>
> **G.G.**: I suspect that most atheists think scientific evidence – evidence that ultimately appeals only to empirically observable facts – is the only sort of evidence there is.
>
> **g.g.**: That may be their assumption, but how do they show that it's correct? It certainly isn't supported by scientific evidence, since that tells us about only what *is* empirically observable. The question is whether there is anything else.[15]

13. See *Alei Shur,* Volume 1 Chapter 3.
14. http://opinionator.blogs.nytimes.com/2014/10/13/ and reprinted in *Talking God: Philosophers on Belief* by Gary Gutting (W. W. Norton & Company, Nov 22, 2016).
15. This relates to the comments of Dr. Alvin Plantinga (cited in 8.13) that despite the numerous scientific and philosophical arguments that can be offered to support the existence of God, "I don't think arguments are needed for rational belief in God. In

Gutting notes the methodological error frequently made by atheists and agnostics when they disregard all evidence except that which is based on empirically observable facts. Scientific evidence does not support the assumption that nothing exists besides that which is empirically observable. Interestingly, Ramban offers the same critique against the ancient Greek philosophers:

רמב״ן ויקרא טז:ח

כי היינו צריכים לחסום פי המתחכמים בטבע הנמשכים אחרי היוני אשר הכחיש כל דבר זולתי המורגש לו, והגיס דעתו לחשוב הוא ותלמידיו הרשעים, כי כל ענין שלא השיג אליו הוא בסברתו איננו אמת:

> We need to close the mouths of they who make themselves wise in nature, who follow the Greek (Aristotle) who denied whatever he could not apprehend with his senses; He arrogantly assumed, he and his wicked disciples, that anything not grasped by his reasoning is not true.[16]

As we have seen, seeking this sort of experiential knowledge is not just a secondary option in the event that one concludes that traditional proofs no longer are valid. Rather, experiential awareness serving as the basis for belief in God is epistemologically superior to logical certainty insofar as it fosters a relationship.

While we may have presented Rihal and Rambam as having two opposing views of how one is to arrive at faith in God, the path of "experiential knowledge" is not necessarily anti-rational or non-philosophical; it simply relies on a different type of knowledge than abstract logical proof. In today's philosophical climate, this path might even be the more rational one. Abstract logical proofs of God are now seen as fraught with

---

this regard belief in God is like belief in other minds, or belief in the past. Belief in God is grounded in experience" (http://opinionator.blogs.nytimes.com/2014/02/09/is-atheism-irrational/?_r=0).

16. Ramban, in other places (e.g., his commentary to *Bereishit* 9:12), acknowledges the contribution of the Greeks in the scientific realm. His objection is to their denial of everything not scientifically verifiable.

complications and potential logical problems, whereas experience itself is a rational basis for knowledge.[17]

The Greatest Source of Faith Is God Himself

R. Aharon Lichtenstein powerfully expresses this idea in an essay entitled "The Source of Faith Is Faith Itself," where he discusses the basis for his own personal belief:

> The greatest source of faith, however, has been the God Himself...
>
> Encounter, of course, has been varied. In part, it has been channeled – primarily through the learning of Torah (this is no doubt an aspect of "the light within it," of which our Sages spoke) but also through prayer and the performance of *mitzvot*; or, if you will, by the halachic regimen in its totality. In part, it has been random – moments of illumination while getting on a crowded bus or watching children play in a park at twilight. Obviously, it has also been greatly varied in intensity. In its totality, however, whatever the form and content, it has been the ultimate basis of spiritual life.[18]

A person whose heart is open will encounter the Almighty in everyday events. Simple things like seeing children play can evoke a powerful emotional experience – something that gives a person faith that God exists.

What if I Don't Experience God?

Of course, such experiences can help someone only if he experiences them. When it comes to philosophical evidence, one can attempt to rationally convince the skeptic. But experiential knowledge helps only

---

17. See R. Shalom Carmy, *Notes from ATID: Forgive Us, Father-in-Law, for We Know Not What to Think: Letter to a Philosophical Dropout from Orthodoxy* (Jerusalem: Atid, 2004), esp. pp. 14–17.
18. *The Jewish Action Reader*, Volume 1, Union of Orthodox Jewish Congregations of America, New York, 1996.

those who have it (or are open to having it). R. Lichtenstein addresses the problem:

> This will obviously provide little guidance for those to whom attaining encounter is precisely the problem. To those "struggling to develop faith" one can, however, proffer first the reassuring assertion of the religious significance of the quest per se, as in the footsteps of Abraham, they have already become seekers of God; second, the prospective hope of successful resolution, as "The Lord is good unto them that yearn for Him, to the soul that seeketh Him" (*Eicha* 3:25); and third, the counsel to focus persistently, in terms of Coleridge's familiar distinction, upon faith rather than belief, upon experiential trust, dependence and submission more than upon catechetical dogmatics. Intellectual assent is normative and essential; but, at the personal level, it is generally not the key. In the final analysis, the primary human source of faith is faith itself.

On a practical level, one can seek activities that promote faith. This is especially true for someone who already believes but seeks to deepen his *emuna*.[19] Thus, the *mitzva* of *anochi* demands that a person look for ways to solidify his faith, whether through seeking logical proof, studying history, or attending a *kumzits* (a group of people who join to sing spiritually moving songs).

How Do We Know that We Are Not Delusional?

Of course, R. Lichtenstein notes that one could question the validity of these experiences. Perhaps these emotions stem from neurons triggered in the brain by certain types of stimuli. How do we know that we are not delusional?

> At the level of rational demonstration, this is, of course, patently circular. I hold no brief for Anselm's ontological proof and I

19. In general, proofs for God have been sought by people who already believed and were seeking to strengthen their faith.

> recognized the theoretical possibility of self-delusion long before I had ever heard of Feuerbach. Existentially, however, nothing has been more authentic than the encounter with Our Father, Our King, the source and ground of all being. Nothing more sustaining, nothing more strengthening, nothing more vivifying.

The answer to this question is two-fold. At a certain point, we have to trust our gut (as we do for almost every other decision in our life) – when something continuously feels authentic, we can trust that it is authentic. This is especially true when the feeling of connection to God feels more real than any other feeling.[20] Moreover, these types of experiences contribute to belief, but they are not its only foundation. These powerful emotions join the myriad of other factors that point to the existence of God.[21]

---

20. R. Lichtenstein elaborates upon this point in *Mevakshei Panecha: Sichot im ha-Rav Aharon Lichtenstein* (a Hebrew book that records conversations between R. Chaim Sabato and R. Lichtenstein), p. 20.
21. Another objection stems from the fact that devout practitioners of other religions experience similar numinous sensations. Idolaters claim to have experienced powerful transcendent religious experiences, yet the Torah tells us that idolatry is utterly false. To fully address this question, one would need to fully consider the Torah's perspective on other religions, which is an interesting question, but beyond the scope of this chapter.

    A brief response to this question, however, is in order. This objection would be more troubling if one's faith were entirely based upon these inexpressible feelings. However, as we have seen, the Torah insists that faith also be rooted in the intellect. The logos portion of Judaism is so persuasive that it bolsters the feelings as legitimate. This is not true for any other religion. The emotion an individual experiences when serving idolatry may reflect his need to connect with a transcendent being. There is a degree of truth in his feeling, but it is misguided. Using his intellect, an individual can appreciate the falseness of idolatry and redirect his sentiment towards the True God.

    Consider the following analogy: When considering the suitability of a particular spouse, the intangible emotional attraction surely plays a role. However, the intelligent individual makes sure that there are rational reasons to expect this relationship will work. Feelings alone are insufficient reason to marry. The same holds true with respect to our relationship with God. Even if our emotional

What emerges from the above is that faith often is personal. Unlike the philosophical proofs described in Chapter 8, the arguments considered in this chapter might prove absolutely compelling to the one who experiences them yet remain unconvincing to another who does not. Allow me, then, to deviate momentarily from this book's general format and discuss my personal path to faith.

What Inspires Me

I am fortunate to spend most of my days studying and teaching Torah. This produces an exhilarating intellectual thrill and, on a practical level, teaches me how to live my life. But it also does much more. While I cannot say that every time I learn I feel this way, sometimes the profundity, depth, and brilliance of Torah overwhelm me, leaving me feeling small in the presence of something great. More importantly, the heart can decipher truth with a sense of certainty that the mind sometimes lacks.

---

attachment defines our bond with our Creator, it is anchored in belief that goes beyond mere "feelings."

This notion need not reject the religious experiences of non-Jews. Torah Judaism is not the only correct means for humans to serve God. The reason why we are not meant to proselytize is because there are valid methods for non-Jews to connect to God other than Judaism. Thus, when a numinous experience overwhelms a non-Jew while practicing his religion, that feeling may be entirely authentic and even true, assuming his religion is monotheistic. If, however, the non-Jew's religion violates the Noachide Laws then it is not only false but also destructive (see *Derech ha-Techiya* where R. Kook writes of the grave dangers that arise when raw spirituality is unrestrained by the intellect). In 11.9 we consider the question of whether a non-Jew is held accountable for "accidental" idolatrous beliefs.

For further investigation see: (1) R. Soloveitchik's "Confrontation," where he explains that interfaith dialogue is "absurd" because religious experiences do not lend themselves to "universalization": "The word of faith reflects the intimate, the private, the paradoxically inexpressible cravings of the individual for and his linking up with his Maker. It reflects the numinous character and the strangeness of the act of faith of a particular community which is totally incomprehensible to the man of a different faith community." And (2) R. Kook's essay *Derech ha-Techiya* where he considers the nature of spirituality in paganism. For further elaboration on R. Kook's somewhat radical perspective see *Shemona Kevatzim* 2:276, "*Talelei Orot*" (*Ma'amarei ha-Re'iyah*, 22–23), and *Igrot ha-Re'iyah* 1, 142.

Ultimately, then, it is the beauty of Torah more than any sort of philosophical argument that generates certainty of its divinity.

Other contributors to faith include:

- Examination of the extraordinary providence I have experienced in my life. So many unlikely events, from the way I found my wife to how I ended up teaching in Yeshiva University, leave me no doubt that my Father in heaven is lovingly guiding me. The "smaller" acts of providence are no less inspiring. When I find my lost keys as soon as I pray (but not before) I am often overwhelmed by the awareness of the extent to which He listens.
- Consideration of the moral perfection that I see that my teachers have reached through Torah. Living a life filled with genuine altruism is exceedingly rare. Yet the remarkable character development found in *Gedolei Yisrael* that I personally have witnessed and been the beneficiary of testifies to the unmistakable truth and divinity of the Torah.
- Contemplation of the complexity of the human body and the astonishing story of the Jewish people leave me awestruck. Studying biology, physics, and history allow us glimpses of God's power and inscrutability in a very tangible way. Studying philosophy and considering some of the arguments outlined in 8.9 turn this visceral emotion into cerebral certainty.
- Finally, encounters with God in prayer, in song, while watching my children play or reading them a book, are like no other emotional experiences. These experiences, in conjunction with the factors mentioned above, leave me with certainty that He is constantly watching, guiding, and protecting me.

Of course, this is (part of) my own personal basis for belief. These reasons may not resonate with others. Many people may not at all relate to my experiences. All that is fine. As we have noted, there are many pathways to forge a relationship with the Almighty. Each of us must search – around us and deep within us – to find and connect to our Creator.

9.3 RESPONDING TO THE PROBLEM OF EVIL

A number of the above sources write that the superiority of experiential proof for God's existence over philosophical proof is that a person with experiential knowledge will not be swayed by questions. Someone whose knowledge is based on science naturally will have doubts if he cannot answer questions based on science. But when a person has a relationship with someone, there is no doubt that the other exists. Two people can reasonably debate whether a metal box can fly, but if one goes outside and sees a 747 take off, all doubts dissipate, regardless of what questions remain. Likewise, someone who experiences God's immanence may have all sorts of unanswered questions, but the questions do not undermine his faith.

This approach addresses not only scientific objections concerning the existence of God, but also other powerful theological problems. For example, Ramban notes that for the most part, it is not scientific conundrums or philosophical speculations that turn people away from faith. The primary reason why people deny God's existence or His providence is the problem of evil. Witnessing or experiencing agony "pains the heart and distresses the mind."[22] This is not just a philosophical quandary or scientific enigma; it is the visceral response to seeing injustice – to watching a child writhe in pain, to seeing the righteous beaten and the wicked flourish.

The fact that it is an emotional more than intellectual question that causes people to question God indicates the importance of an emotional and not just intellectual response. Thus, in 14.12–14.19 we will return to this issue and consider some of the more intellectual solutions proposed to the problem of evil. Presently, however, we shall consider the question from a more emotional perspective.

Even the Righteous Struggle with the Suffering of the Innocent – the Tumultuous Inner Life of the Servant of God

The problem of evil plagues even those closest to God. It is, in a sense, an unanswerable question. Hence, our greatest leaders, such

---

22. **רמב"ן הקדמה לאיוב**

ויש דבר מכאיב הלבבות ומדאיב המחשבות, ממנו לבדו נמשכו כל הדורות לכפירה גמורה, והוא הראות בעולם משפט מעוקל וצדיק ורע לו רשע וטוב לו ... זה שורש המרי בכל המורדים מכל אומה ולשון.

as Yirmiyahu (12:1), Chabakuk (1:13), and Kohelet (8:14) wrestled with it. At first glance, this is surprising. One might have expected that witnessing the suffering of the righteous would pose no problem for the person who fully believes in divine justice and providence. Indeed, this was the attitude of Iyov's friends. However, it was not the attitude of our great Prophets. Faith does not always guarantee tranquility.

R. Soloveitchik (*Halakhic Man* footnote 4) rails against this popular attitude:

> And that which appears in the sermons of these preachers in a primitive, garbled form, at times interwoven with a childish naiveté and superficial belief, is refined and purified in the furnace of popular "philosophy" and "theology" and becomes transformed into a universal religious ideology which proclaims: If you wish to acquire tranquility without paying the price of spiritual agonies, turn unto religion! If you wish to achieve a fine psychic equilibrium without having to first undergo a slow, gradual personal development, turn unto religion. And if you wish to achieve an instant spiritual wholeness and simplicity that need not be forged out of the struggles and torments of consciousness, turn unto religion!
>
> ... [T]his ideology is intrinsically false and deceptive. That religious consciousness in man's experience which is most profound and most elevated, which penetrates to the very depths and ascends to the very heights, is not that simple and comfortable. On the contrary, it is exceptionally complex, rigorous, and tortuous. **Where you find its complexity, there you find its greatness.**

R. Soloveitchik rejects those who inappropriately embrace simplicity to shield themselves from the vicissitudes of the struggle. In striving to avoid the darker depths of the human psyche, such a person shuns the reality of redemption. If a person has never experienced darkness, he will not appreciate the illumination when it arrives.

Likewise, when the Prophets wrestled with the injustice they perceived in the world, they did not dismiss their emotions due to their appreciation of divine fairness. Yet even as these righteous individuals struggled with these questions, they did not lose their faith. How? Let us consider the experience of Asaf.

The Story of Asaf in Tehillim 73

Like any sensitive soul, Asaf struggled with the seeming injustice of our world; his emotional turmoil was so powerful that he nearly was swept away: "My feet almost turned away, in an instant my steps would have slipped" (2). Why? Because he "would see the tranquility of the wicked" (3), the prideful people who steal from the innocent to consume so much bounty that their eyes bulge in fatness. Those who worry not of divine retribution; after all, "How does God know, and is there knowledge in the Most High?" (11). And seemingly they are right – since they continue to prosper while "I was plagued all the days" (14).

How does Asaf resolve his crisis of faith? He comes to the Temple: once Asaf enters "the sanctuaries of God" his problems dissipate (17). How? The answer lies in *Kuzari*'s secret. The *Beit ha-Mikdash* is a place where we can connect to God, where we embrace our Lover. We still may not have all the answers, but we also do not have any doubts. Evidence to the contrary no longer triggers doubts because we are certain of the truth.[23]

23. While I have interpreted the arrival at the Temple as spawning an experiential and spiritual transformation (see, for example, *Tehillim* 27), many of the commentaries understand that Asaf received answers to his questions when he arrived at the *Beit ha-Mikdash*. He was reminded (or learned) that eventually the wicked are punished and righteous prosper:

רש״י תהלים עג:יז

עד - אשר באתי: אל מקדשי אל - אשר בירושלים, וראיתי מה שאירע בסנחרב ואז הבינותי לאחרית הרשעים שהוא לאבדון ואמרתי אך כל הטובה הבאה להם חלקות הם שהקב״ה מחליק להם הדרך שלהם שתהא נוחה וחלקה למען לא יתנו לב לשוב אליו ויאבדו.

אבן עזרא שם

עד - עתיד תחת עבר כאילו ידבר על זמן עומד כאשר פירשתי וטעם מקדשי אל ששם כהני השם וחכמי ישר׳ והם גלו זה הסוד והוא אבינה לאחרית׳ כי לא הובא האדם בעולם הזה להתענג בו או להיותו מלך או עשיר רק שתהיה אחריתו טובה וזה הוא שכר נפשות הצדיקים.

I Have Not Seen a Righteous Man Forsaken and His Offspring Seeking Bread

Let us consider one last powerful expression of this idea. King David makes a startling assertion: נַעַר הָיִיתִי גַּם זָקַנְתִּי וְלֹא רָאִיתִי צַדִּיק נֶעֱזָב וְזַרְעוֹ מְבַקֶּשׁ לָחֶם, "I was young, I also aged, and I have not seen a righteous man forsaken and his offspring seeking bread" (*Tehillim* 37:25). Surely, David had seen the righteous suffer; much of *Tehillim* describes his own suffering. What does he mean?

The answer is, as we have seen, that David knew the truth of God's justice and kindness, and accordingly, he was confident that any evidence to the contrary could not possibly be true. Whatever suffering exists is but a temporary aberration. Like Asaf, he knew that in the end there would be justice.[24]

רד"ק שם

עד אבוא. תרתי בלבי לדעת זאת בעמל גדול ולא מצאתי, עד שבאתי במחשבות לבבי אל מקדשי אל, והוא עולם המלאכים והרוחות, כי שם סוף השכר והגמול הקיים, כי טוב העולם הזה אינו עומד, אבל באחרית והוא עולם הנפשות בו יבחנו הטובים והרעים, וזהו שאמר אבינה לאחריתם.

מצודת דוד שם

עד אבא - לא הבנתי דרכי ה' עד אשר באתי אל המקדש ואל הכהנים המתבודדים שם בעיון החכמה ואת פיהם שאלתי ואדע מלין יענוני ואבינה לאחרית הרשעים שאיננה טובה.

Along similar lines, in 18.9, we present the interpretation of R. Shlomo Fisher (*Drashot Beit Yishai* 23 note 5, pp. 180–181), who understands that this verse is referring to the afterlife. But we must wonder why he needed to go to the Temple to discover this secret. If the notion of the afterlife was well-known in the biblical era, this Psalm makes little sense. But, suggests R. Fisher, because in the biblical period the concept of *olam ha-ba* was known only to elite sages and priests, it makes sense that it is only in the *Beit ha-Mikdash* that Asaf could find solace.

24. When Asaf goes to the *Beit ha-Mikdash*, he is comforted because he is able to see the big picture, אָבִינָה, לְאַחֲרִיתָם, "I see their end" (17). And for the true believer, the end is always near, כְּרָגַע, "in a moment" (19). Our perception of reality is but a dream from which we soon will awaken (20). Malbim adds a remarkable point:

מלבי"ם תהלים לז:כה

נער הייתי גם **זקנתי ובחנתי תולדות הימים**, ולא ראיתי שיהיה הצדיק נעזב **עד שזרעו יהיה מבקש לחם**, כי לא יעזב לעולם, ואם לא הצליח הוא יצליחו בניו, כי ראיתי את הצדיק אשר. (כו) כל היום חונן ומלוה עד שנעשה עני ע"כ, בכ"ז זרעו לברכה ותשוב ההצלחה ביד בניו, וצדקת אביהם תהיה ברכה לבניו...

The verse stresses that now that I (David) have aged, I have never saw the progeny of the righteous seek bread. Surely, I have witnessed the *tzaddik* struggle in the short term; but his suffering bore fruits in the long run.

Of course, as we have noted, David's inner spiritual life was tormented. He feels, on occasion, abandoned and betrayed. He experiences injustice and hypocrisy. However, ultimately David tells us that when one lives life with the perspective of God's lover, one will see answers where others see questions. Thus, David declares, **כִּי אֵין מַחְסוֹר לִירֵאָיו כְּפִירִים רָשׁוּ וְרָעֵבוּ וְדֹרְשֵׁי יְקֹוָק לֹא יַחְסְרוּ כָל טוֹב**, "There is no want to those who fear Him. Young lions suffer want and are hungry, but those who seek God lack no good" (*Tehillim* 34:10–11). Where did David come up with the preposterous idea that those who fear God never are hungry? From his own tragic experience.

This epiphany strikes him when doing that which was right forces him to flee Sha'ul's hateful wrath. He was all alone, feigning madness, drooling spit, and fighting for his life (**בְּשַׁנּוֹתוֹ אֶת טַעְמוֹ לִפְנֵי אֲבִימֶלֶךְ וַיְגָרְשֵׁהוּ וַיֵּלַךְ**).[25] This predicament might have led any reasonable person to conclude that indeed there are times when a *tzaddik* is abandoned. But David concluded **כִּי אֵין מַחְסוֹר לִירֵאָיו**, those who fear Him are never left wanting. How? Because, when all alone and feigning madness, he was given bread by a stranger.[26] Ultimately, it is a question of perspective. In truth, there never was a *tzaddik* who was abandoned **נֶעֱזָב**, though certainly there was good reason for him to feel abandoned **נֶעֱזָב**. If one has trust, then even when presented with evidence to the contrary, the trust does not dissipate. This, writes *Kuzari*, is the nature of experiential knowledge of God's existence.

9.4 R. KOOK ON *EMUNA*

As we shall see in 9.7, some thinkers present two paradigms for arriving at *emuna*: proof and tradition. However, when comparing Rihal to those who value philosophical evidence, we are not simply comparing proof with tradition. Rihal does not say that belief in God should emerge

---

25. **שמואל א כא:יד**
וַיְשַׁנּוֹ אֶת טַעְמוֹ בְּעֵינֵיהֶם וַיִּתְהֹלֵל בְּיָדָם וַיְתָיו עַל דַּלְתוֹת הַשַּׁעַר וַיּוֹרֶד רִירוֹ אֶל זְקָנוֹ:

26. **רד"ק תהלים לד:י**
כי אין מחסור ליראיו, ואמר זה לפי שהוא היה גולה בין פלשתים ואין לו שם יודעים ומכירים אותו שיתנו לו לחם לאכול, ולפי שירא את ה' לא חסר טרפו.

from tradition. Rather, he advocates belief that is rooted in a relationship and experience.

Likewise, R. Kook writes that there are two valid ways to arrive at faith (Rambam and Rihal). And like many thinkers, R. Kook sees Rihal's approach as superior. However, R. Kook does not simply compare philosophy with tradition. Rather, R. Kook compares knowledge arrived at from *outside,* such as the cosmological proof for God's existence in which a person looks outside himself[27] and arrives at a philosophical proof for the existence of God, and organic belief that comes from *intuition* ("ישרות הלב והנטיה הישרה").[28]

Following his logic, if someone simply believes in God because his parents told him that God exists (tradition), he is no better than someone who believes because of a compelling philosophical reason, since this knowledge too is external. If, however, his upbringing fosters an intuitive belief, then he is serving God on this elevated platform. Likewise, if a philosophical argument brings a person to an innate and natural awareness, then that person also is serving God on this elevated platform. As we saw, Rihal himself understands that Avraham followed this path (he initially discovered God philosophically but then a relationship ensued). Likewise, Rambam frequently writes about how philosophical ruminations ignite a passionate love of God (e.g., *Hilchot Yesodei ha-Torah* 2:1).

---

27. One could argue that this critique would not apply to ontological arguments. Generally speaking, however, Rishonim did not offer ontological arguments. (There is some debate concerning one of Rambam's proofs.) Nevertheless, it is hard to argue that ontological proofs qualify as ישרות הלב והנטיה הישרה, in which case they too would be inferior.

28. **עין איה על ברכות דף ד ע"ב**

הנה השלמות האנושי, בפרט הישראלי, אפשר הוא להשיגו ע"י שני דרכים. הא', היא דרך החכמה וההתפלספות, עד שיכיר את האמת מתוך מופתים חותכים. והב', **הוא דרך התמימות והמשרים, מצד ישרות הלב והנטיה הישרה, שממנה באה האמונה השלמה.** ובצדק שבח בכוזריי את דרך התמימות יותר מדרך המחקר ע"פ דרכי החכמה... והנה החילוק הוא בין השלמות המושגת, מצד המשרים והאמונה ביושר הלב לבין הבאה מצד המחקר, כי הנטי' הטבעית שבלב היא דבר עצמי בנפש האדם, וא"צ דבר מחוצה לה שיעיר אותה אל שלמותה, אבל ההשגה והחכמה הם דברים נבדלים מהאדם, וצריך הערה חיצונה להעיר אותו על השלמתו. ובודאי משובחת ההשלמה הדבקה בעצם יותר מהבאה מחוץ, אע"פ שיש בה קנין מ"מ אינה דבקה כ"כ בנפש המשתלם, כמו השלמות שבא מצד עצם טבע הלב.

9.5 *EMUNA PSHUTA* AND R. SHNEUR ZALMAN OF LIADI

Some chasidic thinkers refer to "*emuna pshuta*" or simple faith: faith which is not rooted in rational demonstration.[29] The faith of those who have *emuna pshuta* is deeply rooted. Frequently, the faith of a person who cannot tell you why they believe is far more powerful than that of the individual armed with innumerable arguments supporting his belief.

What is the nature of *emuna pshuta*? Simple faith is not simplistic,[30] but it is available to those who are simple (i.e., have not studied philosophy or Kabbala). A simple person accepts things as true without trying to understand them. When it comes to understanding God, the more we try to understand Him, the more we are bringing Him down to our level of cognition when, in fact, He is totally beyond comprehension. Thus, in a sense, the simple person's conception of God is truer than that of someone sophisticated who tries to understand God and thereby limits Him. This is certainly true when it comes to those who try to comprehend God using philosophy where their comprehension of God comes entirely through their own limited intellect. Approaching God philosophically limits a person to that which he can understand independently. On the other hand, studying God through His Torah gives us a better glimpse.

This is how the founder of Chabad, R. Shneur Zalman of Liadi (1745–1812), put it: If we follow the philosophical model, then a person

29. **מאמרי אדמו"ר הזקן מהגר"ז פרשת כי תשא**
הנה ישראל הם מאמינים בני מאמינים בה' אחד **באמונה פשוטה** בלי שום טעם ודעת המושג ומובן על מה ולמה ואיך כו' ומה שנלאו חכמי המחקר בספריהם הפלוסופים וקצר מצע שכליהם להשיג אפס קצהו א' מיני אלף אלפי אלפים כו' הוא יסוד פשוט וכלל מונח קבוע בלב כל איש מבית ישראל מקרב ולב עמוק כיתד שלא תמוט באמונה קבועה וחזקה ואפי' כל הרוחות שבעולם אין מזיזות כלום...

30. Dr. Norman Lamm powerfully expressed this notion in his essay, "Faith and Doubt," which appeared in *Tradition* 9 (1967, pp. 14–51):

> Moreover, the most aggressive proponents of simple faith were not necessarily simple souls. Perhaps the most radical exponent of emunah temimah in fairly modern times was the Hasidic Zaddik, R. Nachman Bratzlaver; yet one need but read his writings and the writings about him by his leading disciple and biographer to realize that he was an extraordinarily complicated man who had suffered the worst torments of doubt, who had studied Maimonides' Guide, and who had struggled valiantly in order to achieve the blessed temimut which he recommended over the theological sophistication for which he had such contempt. Simple faith is not the same as simple-mindedness.

with philosophical training will have greater faith than someone who lacks such training. However, once we acknowledge that even the greatest philosopher will not understand God's essence (something Rambam agrees to), then someone who acknowledges that he cannot truly understand God has the truest knowledge of God – even if he doesn't know any philosophy.

In a sense, someone without a philosophical outlook has an advantage when it comes to faith. The simpleton who lacks the inclination to figure things out from a scientific or philosophical perspective views the world through the perspective of faith. Things are true because they are true; there is no attempt to understand why. The nature of someone intelligent is to withhold belief until he understands. Thus, concerning God, we should all follow the path of simpletons.[31]

In Hebrew, the term *tam* (תם) has two meanings. It can mean simpleton in the sense of foolish. But it also can refer to someone intelligent who realizes the truth and beauty in simplicity. A chasidic saying attributed to R. Naftali Zvi Horowitz of Ropshitz (1760–1827) reflects this:

> גדולה התמימות מהחכמה, אבל כמה חכם האדם צריך להיות כדי להיות תמים.

---

31. **ליקוטי אמרים [תניא] פרק יח**
הנה החכמה היא מקור השכל וההבנה והיא למעלה מהבינה שהוא הבנת השכל והשגתו והחכמה היא למעלה מההבנה וההשגה והיא מקור להן **וזהו לשון חכמה כ״ח מ״ה שהוא מה שאינו מושג ומובן ואינו נתפס בהשגה עדיין** ולכן מתלבש בה אור א״ס ב״ה **דלית מחשבה תפיסא ביה כלל ולכן כל ישראל אפילו הנשים ועמי הארץ הם מאמינים בה׳ שהאמונה היא למעלה מן הדעת וההשג׳ כי פתי יאמין לכל דבר וערום יבין וגו׳ ולגבי הקב״ה שהוא למעלה מן השכל והדעת ולית מחשבה תפיסא ביה כלל הכל כפתיים אצלו יתי** כדכתיב ואני בער ולא אדע בהמות הייתי עמך ואני תמיד עמך וגו׳ כלומר שבזה שאני בער ובהמות אני תמיד עמך ולכן אפי׳ קל שבקלים ופושעי ישראל מוסרים נפשם על קדושת ה׳ על הרוב וסובלים עינוים קשים שלא לכפור בה׳ אחד ואף אם הם בורים ועמי הארץ ואין יודעים גדולת ה׳. וגם במעט שיודעים אין מתבוננים׳ כלל ואין מוסרי׳ נפשם מחמת דעת והתבוננות בה׳ כלל. אלא בלי שום דעת והתבוננות רק כאלו הוא דבר שאי אפשר כלל לכפור בה׳ אחד בלי שום טעם וטענה ומענה כלל והיינו משום שה׳ אחד מאיר ומחיה כל הנפש ע״י התלבשותו בבחי׳ חכמה שבה שהיא למעלה מן הדעת והשכל המושג ומובן.

When he writes חכמה כ״ח מ״ה, he means the faculty of the unknown – מה means "what," reflecting that which we cannot comprehend.

> *Temimut* (simplicity) is greater than wisdom, but how wise does a person have to be to be *tamim*.

To summarize, even as R. Shneur Zalman of Liadi extols the superiority of "simple faith," he paints a rather sophisticated understanding of the value of simple faith.[32]

9.6 R. SOLOVEITCHIK'S APPROACH TO *EMUNA*

R. Soloveitchik (*The Halakhic Mind*, p. 118, note 58) expresses the weakness of philosophical proofs for the existence of God.

> The problem of evidence in religion will never be solved. The believer does not miss philosophic legitimization; the skeptic will never be satisfied with any cognitive demonstration… in some cases *homo religious* is so overwhelmed by the import of his experience that he very distinctly perceives the reality of his object. He is fully conscious of the existence of the transcendental order.

Philosophical arguments generally are presented to two classes of people: the skeptic and the believer. However, R. Soloveitchik explains, they are of little value to either. They do not usually convince the skeptic. Why not? As we noted in 8.13, philosophical arguments generally do not prove that God exists. At best, they offer the most compelling explanation to justify the existence of the world and its phenomena.

---

32. The above understanding of *emuna pshuta* does not exempt a person from the obligation to understand the Divine to the best extent possible. Indeed, R. Shneur Zalman insists that this responsibility is more important than all other *mitzvot*. Thus, while he extols the value of simple faith, he insists that one not satisfy themselves with a simple understanding of God.

תניא קונטרס אחרון על כמה פרקים

משא״כ בסדר ההשתלשלות אף אם משיג המציאות לא עדיף מצד עצמו כלימוד המצות שמשיג ותופס המהות ומעלה עליו כאילו קיים בפועל ממש כמ״ש זאת התורה כו׳ אלא **שידיעת המציאות מההשתלשלות היא ג״כ מצוה רבה ונשאה ואדרבה עולה על כולנה כמ״ש וידעת היום כו׳ דע את אלקי אביך כו׳ ומביאה ללב שלם כו׳ שהוא העיקר והשגת המציאות הוא להפשיט מגשמיות כו׳** רק שזו היא מצוה אחת מתרי״ג והאדם צריך לקיים כל תרי״ג לפי שהן השתלשלות המהות דחיצונית דכלים דאצי׳ לכך צריך להרבות בלימוד כל התרי״ג וקיומן בפועל ממש במחדו״מ שהן בי״ע לברר בירורין אשר שם.

However, someone who says he will not believe until he has definitive proof will not be convinced, since he always can claim that there may be another possibility.[33]

The second audience philosophical proofs attempt to reach is those who already believe. R. Soloveitchik notes that such proofs do not really help these people. They already feel the passionate embrace of their beloved (God); their certainty is unmistakable as they already are overwhelmed by His presence. What need is there for philosophical proof? Both in "The Lonely Man of Faith" (p. 52) and "*u-Vikashtem mi-Sham*" (p. 133), R. Soloveitchik approvingly quotes Kierkegaard's pointed remark on this subject:

> Does the loving bride in the embrace of her beloved ask for proof that he is alive and real? Must the prayerful soul clinging in passionate love and ecstasy to her Beloved demonstrate that He exists? So asked **Soren Kierkegaard** sarcastically when told that Anselm of Canterbury, the father of the very abstract and complex ontological proof, spent many days in prayer and supplication that he be presented with rational evidence of the existence of God.[34]

Like *Kuzari*, R. Soloveitchik maintained that even if a philosophical proof is flawless, it does not produce a truly religious person. Thus, he writes in "*u-Vikashtem mi-Sham*" that "Man cannot come to God on his own, through the initiative of his own spirit" (p. 40) and that "such rationalism, which emerges from time to time in philosophical religious thought, lowers prophecy to the level of a pedagogical tool" (p. 126).

---

33. In 8.13, we considered whether this response is intellectually honest or psychologically driven. Either way, the evidence will not compel them.

34. Likewise, in *The Halakhic Mind* (p. 120), he writes:

> The certainty of the realness of God does not come about as a corollary of logical premises, as a leap from the realm of logic to the realm of ontology, from an assumption to a fact. It is, on the contrary, a transition from an immediate apprehension to a thought ... from being overwhelmed by the Presence of God to an awareness of His existence.

This is not to say that there is not incredible value in seeing God in the world. Rambam (*Hilchot Yesodei ha-Torah,* Ch. 2) powerfully describes the passionate religious experience triggered by examining God's marvelous creation. However, it is not dispassionate philosophical speculation that ignites the fire. This is true even with respect to the "proofs" in *Moreh ha-Nevuchim*:

> Maimonides' position in the *Guide* is that the dynamics of the world lead to the idea that there is a God, but this does not have the status of a demonstrative proof. God does not serve as a theoretical explanation of the cosmos. Rather, my apprehension of God follows immediately, not indirectly, from my apprehension of the cosmos.[35]

To summarize, R. Soloveitchik maintains that in the post-Kantian world, definitive syllogistic proof of the variety that Rambam offers no longer is possible. Accordingly, R. Soloveitchik describes the type of experiential awareness championed by *Kuzari*, not just because proof no longer is possible, but because experiential awareness is superior. Moreover, R. Soloveitchik maintains that even Rambam's approach (especially in *Mishneh Torah*) differs from the philosophical approach that *Kuzari* is rejecting.

R. Soloveitchik nevertheless argues that even if proof is impossible, it is philosophically rational to believe in God.[36] How can God's existence be rationally known if it cannot be proven? R. Soloveitchik responds that the subjective consciousness of the presence of God can serve as the basis of rational belief in God, what he calls "ontological awareness." He writes:

---

35. Lawrence J. Kaplan, ed., *Maimonides: Between Philosophy and Halakhah: Rabbi Joseph B. Soloveitchik's Lectures on the Guide of the Perplexed at the Bernard Revel Graduate School* (1950–51) (Brooklyn: Urim Publications, 2016), p. 106.
36. See Shubert Spero's "Rabbi Joseph Dov Soloveitchick and Belief in God" in *Modern Judaism* 19.1 (1999), pp. 1–20), where he demonstrates that from the published works of R. Soloveitchik one can draw a philosophically defensible position as to the epistemological basis of an individual's belief in Judaism.

> If there is a world, if there is being at all ... then there is a God who is the ground of existence and its source. If there is an 'I,' if man exists then there is a living personal God who fills this self-awareness. It is impossible to think, to speak and to deliberate about existence without living and feeling the source of existence ... the religious consciousness feels and lives God in the very midst of the ontological awareness. Without Him there is no existence, no reality.... The ontological awareness which evinces movement, direction and volition is itself awareness of God. Man unites with God by seeking out the nature and quality of existence.[37]

In fact, even though the earlier quotes from R. Soloveitchik indicate that he rejects Rambam's position that seeks proof, in truth R. Soloveitchik maintains that Rambam's view is more nuanced, identifying this "ontological awareness" with Rambam's *mitzva* (described in the beginning of *Hilchot Yesodei ha-Torah*): to "know that there is a primary existent who brings into existence and who is the ground of all other existents. And all that is in heaven and earth and in between do not exist except by the truth (the reality) of His existence . . . and the primary existent is God of the universe, master of all the earth." R. Soloveitchik declares:

> Creation is the separation of something from the lap of the infinite. The ongoing existence of the world apart from God is impossible. The unmediated ontological awareness acknowledges there is no existence without God.
>
> Divinity is pure being who brings all into existence and encompasses all. God's relationship to the world is not summed up merely by the terms "cause and effect," but rather by a constant outpouring of being. The relative creature is hewn out of the Rock of the Absolute. There is no existence without God and

---

37. "*u-Vikashtem mi-Sham,*" pp. 6–9, *Hadarom*, No. 47 (New York, 1978), p. 8 (Hebrew) Translation by Shubert Spero, "Rabbi Joseph Dov Soloveitchick and Belief in God," *Modern Judaism* 19.1 (1999), p. 4.

no reality that is not grounded in God. Therefore, God draws after Himself the creature who feels the emptiness and dependence of his own finitude and yearns for an existence that is complete and whole.[38]

9.7 APPENDIX: ADDITIONAL APPROACHES TO FAITH

In this appendix we will briefly examine some other perspectives on *emuna*, specifically regarding the question of whether a person should seek proof. In Chapter 8, we noted Rambam's position concerning the importance of logically proving the existence of God. Rambam was not the only thinker who stressed the value of proof. R. Bachya ibn Pakuda notes that not all people are endowed with the cerebral capabilities to prove the existence of God intellectually. However, those that are capable of doing so must do so. God has given them the gift of the intellect; failure to use it is scornful. Moreover, belief based upon proof is far more powerful and real.

ספר חובות הלבבות הקדמה

מי שבכח שכלו והכרתו לעמוד על ברור מה שקבל, ועכבוהו מלעיין בו בשכלו העצלות והקלות במצוות האל ובתורתו, הוא נענש על זה ואשם על אשר התעלם ממנו...(אבל) אם לא היית יכול להגיע אל ענין זה מדרך שכלך... וכן, אם היתה דעתך קצרה והכרתך חלושה מהשיג אליו, לא היית נענש על פשיעתך...

אבל, אם אתה איש דעת ותבונה, שתוכל לעמוד בהם על ברור מה שקבלת מהחכמים בשם הנביאים משרשי הדת וקוטבי המעשים, אתה מצווה להשתמש בהם, עד שתעמוד על הענין ויתברר לך מדרך הקבלה והשכל יחד. ואם תתעלם ותפשע בדבר, תהיה כמקצר במה שאתה חייב לבוראך יתברך... ומן הדין לעיין במה שיושג מדרך השכל ולהביא עליו ראיות במופת ששקול הדעת עוזרו, למי שיש לו יכולת לעשות כן.

Whoever has the mental capability to demonstrate that which he received (through tradition), and due to laziness or disregard for the Torah and *mitzvot* failed to do so, shall be punished for his

38. "*u-Vikashtem mi-Sham,*" p. 29, n. 9; p. 69, n. 4.

> oversight… But if he was unable to do so through his intellect, he will not be punished for his failure…
>
> But, if you are a wise man and capable of doing so, you are commanded to use your mental faculties until you can demonstrate what you have received through proof as well. And if you are derelict in this, you have fallen short of what you are obligated to your Creator… One is required to investigate and prove whatever he is capable of proving.

Indeed, two major sections of *Chovot ha-Levavot* describe how to arrive at certain knowledge of God's existence. In the first section, *Sha'ar ha-Yichud*, he uses philosophy, and in the second section, *Sha'ar ha-Bechina*, he uses nature.

Along similar lines, *Sefer ha-Chinuch* writes that the study of philosophy allows one to fulfill the *mitzva* of *emuna* most completely.[39] R. Yosef Albo uses even stronger language – investigation is an obligation for those capable:

ספר העיקרים א כד
בעל דת חייב לחקור על דתו.

> A religious person is required to investigate (i.e., to attempt to prove) his religious beliefs.

It should be stressed that the notion that belief ideally should be rooted in evidence and not simply in tradition is not limited to philosophers. For example, Maharsha writes:

---

39. **ספר החינוך מצוה כה: מצות האמנה במציאות השם יתברך**
ועניין ההאמנה הוא, שיקבע בנפשו שהאמת כן. ושאי אפשר חילוף זה בשום פנים. ואם יושאל עליו ישיב לכל שואל שזה יאמין לבו, ולא יודה בחילוף זה אפילו יאמרו להרגו, שכל זה מחזיק וקובע האמנת הלב כשמוציא הדבר מן הכח אל הפועל, רצוני לומר כשמקיים בדברי פיו מה שלבו גומר. **ואם יזכה לעלות במעלות החכמה, ולבבו יבין ובעיניו יראה במופת בלתי זה, אז יקיים מצות. נחתך שהאמונה הזאת שהאמין אמת וברור אי אפשר** להיות דבר **עשה זו מצוה מן המובחר**

מהרש"א ראש השנה דף לב עמוד א
[צריך] לידע במופת וידיעת השכל.

One must know with proof and intellectual discernment.

Rama uses particularly striking language, ruling that while one may rely upon tradition, it is preferable to search for the cause of things and know them through proofs and investigation for "this is the purpose of man."

תורת העולה חלק ג פרק ז
עדיף טפי לחקור על הדברים ולידע אותם במופתים ובמושכלים ע"י חקירה וזוהי תכלית האדם.

It is preferable to investigate matters and demonstrate them through proofs using the intellect – this is the purpose of man.

R. Yeshaya b. Avraham ha-Levi Horowitz (1568–1630, known as *Shlah*[40]) takes a similar approach.[41] Likewise, in *Reishit Chochma,* R. Eliyahu de Vidas (1518–1587) writes of the advantage of faith based on knowledge:

סוף שער היראה על פסוק ותהי יראתם אותי מצות אנשים מלומדה נראה שצריך האדם לחקור ולידע באמיתות למי הוא עובד ולמי הוא ירא, כענין מה שצוה דוד המלך ע"ה לשלמה בנו ע"ה, דע את ה' אלהי אביך ועבדהו. והטעם כי העובד דרך מצות אנשים מלומדה, פעם יעשה ופעם לא יעשה, ואין לבו תקוע באמונה, **ואם יבא גוי או**

---

40. *Shlah* is an acronym for *Shnei Luchot ha-Brit,* a work written by R. Horovitz.

41. **של"ה (שמות, וארא, נר מצוה)**
וכן נצטוינו לידע דבר זה בידיעה אמיתית, ולא די באמונה מצד הקבלה, רק ידיעה בלב מצד ההשגה, כמו שנאמר (דברים ד:לט), וידעת היום והשבות אל לבבך כי הוי"ה הוא האלהים בשמים ממעל ועל הארץ מתחת אין עוד. הוי"ה הוא האלהים זהו מציאת הש"י, בשמים ממעל ועל הארץ מתחת זהו השגחתו בעליונים ובתחתונים, אין עוד זה מורה על יכולתו. כי אין בלתו להיות בעל יכולת במוחלט, כי הוא יתברך יכול על כל היכולים, וברצונו יתברך נותן יכולת למי שירצה, וברצונו נוטל. **וכל זה צריך לידע בלב ולהשיג נוסף על קבלת האמונה.**

אחר כמוהו ויסתור לו אמונתו מכח ראיות וקושיות, אפשר שינוצח, אמנם העובד בידיעת לבו לא ינוצח בשום פנים וכו'.

> **It appears that a person is required to investigate and know with certainty Whom he is serving and revering,** as David commanded his son Shlomo, "Know the God of your father and serve Him" (*I Divrei ha-Yamim* 28:9). And the reason for this is that if one serves by rote, sometimes he will serve and sometimes he will not, and his heart is not set in faith. **And if someone else will attempt to destroy his faith through proofs and questions, he might falter. But one who serves through knowledge never will be defeated.**

Here we have a counter-argument to those who rely entirely upon experiential faith: a person may not always feel inspired, but logic is unchanging. Moreover, the challenges of others will not shake his faith, as he will have ready responses.

Of course, the manner in which *Shlah* and *Reishit Chochma* sought to *know* that God exists differs from that of Rambam. But all of these thinkers share the view that it is insufficient to believe just because one was told that God exists. Even the inner conviction that emerges from experience is insufficient. Rather, we must find ways to solidify that which we have been taught. Moreover, belief is not meant to be a leap of faith that is not rationally grounded. Instead, a person should seek to intellectually ground his *emuna*.

While some, like R. Sa'adya Gaon and R. Bachya ibn Pakuda, write that faith based on tradition is important only until one arrives at knowledge based upon proof, other thinkers write that ideally, faith always should be based on these two pillars. There are distinct advantages to faith rooted in tradition that do not necessarily follow from faith based on philosophy. The position of R. Shlomo Luria (1510–1574) is an example of this approach.

מהרש"ל על הסמ"ג מצוה ב':

מ"ע להאמין וכו'. פירוש, **צריך שניהם, אמונה וקבלה.** כי אמונה על דרך התולדה שמגודל בה כל ימיו מנעוריו, ומ"מ אף שנשתקע

באמונת שמים, אין יוצא בה ידי חובתו, **אלא כששמע וקבל בלבו הקבלה שהיא המופת על הראיה.** כמו שהביא אח"כ דברי רבינו סעדיה. וכן כתב בעל הנצחון, שאין אדם יוצא באמונה אא"כ למד ספר מדע.

ומ"מ קשה לסמוך על המופת לבד, אם לא שיהא אמונה תקועה בלבו מן התולדה, אז מספיק הראיה, אף שיש ספרים הרבה. וסיוע לזה, שמע ישראל וגו' שאמרו בני יעקב לאביהם כדאיתא בגמ'. וגם לבני יעקב היה האמונה על דרך התולדה מנעוריהם, אלא שהיה מסופק בהם, שלא ידע אם היה מופת להם מספיק לפי דעתם, לכך אמרו לו שמע ישראל, כשם שאין בלבך וכו' וק"ל.

It is a *mitzva* to believe – this means that one requires both faith and acceptance. For faith means that which one was raised with from his youth; yet, even if one becomes deeply entrenched in this faith, **he has not fulfilled his obligation until his heart accepts that faith through proof**...

Nevertheless, it is difficult to rely on proof alone; rather, one must first have faith planted in his heart from his youth, for then the proof will be sufficient. And support for this can be found in the story of Yaakov's children, who declared: "Hear, Yisrael [that we believe in the unity of God]." Yaakov did not doubt that they believed in the unity of God, but rather was unsure if they believed simply because they were taught thusly or because they had proved it as well.

Not all thinkers advocate seeking proof. R. Yeshaya de-Trani the Younger, or Riaz (partially cited in 1.5) writes that nowhere in the Torah does it instruct us to seek proof. The depths of a person's faith and his willingness to give his life for what he knows to be true certainly do not demand philosophical proof. Rather, we are told to believe, and ideally this is accomplished through tradition:

פסקי ריא"ז סנהדרין דף צ עמוד א

וכן צוה עלינו רבן של נביאים ע"ה שמע ישראל ה' אלקינו ה' אחד, ולא אמר להשכיל ולהתבונן בידיעת האלקים בדרך החכמה אלא להאמין

היחוד על פי השמועה ועל פי הקבלה כמו שאנו מקובלין כל התורה והמצות, כעניין שנאמר צדיק באמונתו יחיה.

The greatest of the prophets (i.e., Moshe) commanded us, "Hear, Yisrael, Hashem is our God, Hashem is one" (*Devarim* 6:4). He did not say that we should contemplate knowledge of God through philosophical inquiry, but rather listen (*shema*) and accept through tradition, just as we accept the rest of the Torah and *mitzvot* through tradition. And the verse states, "A righteous man lives through his faith" (*Chabakuk* 2:4).

R. Elchanan Wasserman writes that although in medieval times scholars debated whether one should seek proof for the existence of God through the study of philosophy, this debate no longer is relevant. He asserts that no one would argue that one should pursue philosophy to arrive at belief in God if the chances of philosophy leading someone astray also are very high (as they are today). Even Rambam writes that it is permitted to study philosophy only if one is a God-fearing person who has filled his stomach with meat and wine (we discussed the nature of this restriction in 2.1). Moreover, no one could possibly claim that philosophical proof is indispensable for the basic fulfillment of the *mitzva*, since every thirteen-year-old boy and twelve-year-old girl is commanded to believe despite their inability to engage in philosophical speculation.

קובץ שעורים ח"ב סימן מז:ט

מ"ש כ"ת כי נראה מדברי הקדמונים שנחלקו אם מותר להתעסק בפילוסופיה, באמת כן הוא שנמצאו בין הקדמונים מתירין, ומדברי חובות הלבבות בהקדמתו נראה שהיא מצוה - דע את אלקי אביך - שהאמונה תהא ע"י ידיעה, והחולקין אמרו שהמאמין מפני קבלה מהאבות זוהי מצות אמונה, **אבל למעשה אצלנו אין שום נ"מ ממחלוקת זו,** כי הדבר פשוט כי גם לדעת המתירין אין ההיתר אלא היכא דלא שכיח היזיקא, היינו באנשים שמילאו כרסם בבשר ויין - כלשון הרמב"ם - ואשר יראתם קודמת לחכמתם, שכל הרוחות שבעולם לא יזיזום ממקומם, באלו אמרו שמצוה להן לברר האמונה ע"י חקירה, אבל לא באנשים פחותי ערך

כמונו, אשר הסכנה עצומה לנטות ולטעות, ולעולם לא יעמוד אדם במקום סכנה.

ותדע, שהרי מצות האמונה היא לנער מבן י״ג שנה ולנערה בת י״ב, היעלה על הדעת לאמר שהתורה חייבה לכל מנער ועד זקן טף ונשים שיהיו כולם פילוסופים כאריסטו, ואין הקב״ה בא בטרוניא עם בריותיו, אלא ברור שלא דברו בעלי השיטה הנ״ל אלא מיחידי סגולה, אשר אינם מצויים כלל בדורותינו:

It appears from the medieval scholars that there is a dispute if one is permitted to study philosophy… However, **there is no practical outgrowth of this debate**, because it is obvious that those who allow it do so only if there is no reasonable concern for [spiritual] damage, meaning for those who already have mastered the Torah and are filled with fear of God, such that there is no way they would be led astray. For such people there is (according to this view) a *mitzva* to clarify their *emuna* through proof. But for those of lower stature (such as us), where there is danger of being led astray, there is no such *mitzva*.

This is clear from the fact that every thirteen-year-old boy and twelve-year-old girl is obligated to believe, and it is inconceivable that the Torah obligates every person to be a philosopher like Aristotle. God does not demand unreasonable things from us. Thus, it is obvious that even those who mandated the study of philosophy did so only for exceptional individuals of the type that are not to be found in our times.

While R. Wasserman does not explicate why times have changed, he lived during a time when many Jews were abandoning their faith due to the prevailing zeitgeist that saw religion as irrational. Moreover, we saw R. Soloveitchik presume that in the post-Kantian world, proofs no longer make sense.

One final point made by Prof. Shubert Spero concerning those who oppose philosophical proofs:

This group claimed that holding God to be an inferred entity was not only invalid but inappropriate and unnecessary. It was invalid because the "proofs" in their classic form had already been indisputably refuted by Hume and others. It was inappropriate because logical *certainty*, even if it could be achieved, was intellectually coercive and as such not compatible with the voluntary commitment to God demanded by religion. It was unnecessary because if those involved with this question would properly analyze their consciousness, they would find that they already believed in God! Instead, those in the camp maintained, God in the first instance is not a cognitive abstraction that comes as the conclusion of a syllogism but a living reality that is immediately encountered or experienced by the total person. Although this position had always been implicitly held by mystics, saints, and prophets, this group now argued that the omnipresence of God implied an immanentism such that unmediated religious experience was open "to all who call upon Him in truth."[42]

42. Ibid., pp. 1–2.

Unit Four
Knowing God

In this unit, we continue to consider various ways by which a person can know and believe in God. According to Rambam, the primary goal of the study of philosophy is to know God. Therefore, in Chapter 10, we will elaborate on Rambam's understanding of the nature of the *mitzva* to know God. Next, in Chapter 11, we will explore what happens if a person has a false conception of God. For example, if one concludes that God has a physical body based on a literal reading of the text of the Torah, would one be considered a heretic? Finally, in Chapter 12, we will turn briefly to mystical approaches to knowing God.

Our focus on Rambam in Chapters 10 and 11 reflects Rambam's unique stature and the complexity of his position, which is frequently misrepresented. However, we should acknowledge that Rambam's view differs from the approach adopted by many Rishonim.[1] While our

1. For example, in the previous chapter, we saw Rihal argue that knowledge of God is not increased through philosophical investigation as He cannot be grasped by reasoning at all, but through revelation, and it is only such a God that one comes to love and serve (4:15–16). Ultimately, knowledge of God can only come by tradition of revelation, not philosophy. To better appreciate this consider that in 1.2 we noted that some Rishonim deduce from King David's instruction to his son Shlomo: דַּע אֶת אֱלֹהֵי אָבִיךָ "Know the God of your father" (*I Divrei ha-Yamim* 28:9) the importance of knowing God. Rihal (5:21) labels this the Karaite view:

introduction to Kabbala in Chapter 12 partially addresses the lacuna, due to space concerns, this book fails to present the perspective of many Rishonim and Acharonim on this weighty topic. Hopefully the discussion here will trigger further investigation and analysis that encompasses more viewpoints.

> Leave also alone **the argument of the Karaites**, taken from David's commandment to his son "Know the God of your father and worship him." They conclude from here that a complete knowledge of God must precede His worship. As a matter of fact, David reminded his son to receive from his father and ancestors the belief in the God of Avraham, Yitzchak, and Yaakov, whose providence was with them, and who fulfilled His promises.

Of course, we should not confuse "the argument of the Karaites" with that of Rambam. Rambam never claimed that knowledge of God must precede divine worship. Nevertheless, the focus of Kuzari's service of God does not emphasize using the intellect to understand God.

Chapter Ten

Rambam's Ultimate Goal

10.1 RAMBAM'S PALACE ANALOGY

To better understand the role of philosophy in Rambam's thought, let us consider his palace analogy from *Moreh ha-Nevuchim* (3:51).

Rambam asks us to imagine a city with a palace in the center. The city's populace contains many types of people who vary in their proximity to the palace and the king within:

1. Some people remain outside the city.
2. Others have entered the city, but their backs are to the palace courtyard (they are headed in the wrong direction).
3. Others face the palace courtyard but cannot see the courtyard.
4. Others enter the courtyard.
5. Others enter the palace antechamber.
6. Some are in the king's room.
7. And some actually converse with the king.

In this metaphor, the different levels of closeness to the king and his palace correspond to different levels of understanding God.

The people in group one have no conception of the Divine, neither based on speculation nor received by tradition. Rambam writes that such people are below the rank of mankind but above the rank of monkeys, since they have the form and shape of a person and a mental faculty above that of monkeys.

The next group of people has a conception of God, but it is false. They have adopted their false doctrines either due to great mistakes in their own speculation or because others have taught them these false beliefs. Despite their desire to come close to God, they recede more and more from Him (metaphorically walking away from the palace). Such people are far worse than those in the first class.

What kind of people is Rambam alluding to with this second group? Presumably, those who mistakenly believe God has a physical form. As we shall see in Chapter 11, belief in divine corporeality is the most problematic of all possible mistakes one who believes in God can make. Rambam claims it is worse than idolatry (*Moreh ha-Nevuchim* 1:36),[1] because idolatry, according to Rambam, primarily means serving God through intermediaries (we will elaborate on this in 10.9). Thus, an idolater may have a correct conception of God, even as he serves God inappropriately.[2] The person who believes in a corporeal God, on the other hand, has an incorrect conception of God. In a sense, he is serving a god that does not exist, while ignoring the One who does.[3] Despite the egregiousness of this error, it was quite widespread during the time of Rambam. Moreover, many understood that the Torah adopted such a conception. Hence, a major goal of *Moreh ha-Nevuchim* is to refute this belief.

Rambam's words, however, remain puzzling. In what way are the people of the second group "far worse" than the first? One would have expected those in the second group to be better insofar as they at least

---

1. והיאך יהיה מצב מי שקשורה כפירתו בעצמותו יתעלה, והוא בדעתו הפך מכפי שהוא, כלומר: שאינו לדעתו מצוי, או שלדעתו הוא שנים, או שסבור שהוא גוף, או שהוא לדעתו בעל התפ־עלויות, או שמיחס לו איזו מגרעת שהיא, הנה זה בלי ספק יותר חמור מעובד עבודה זרה על דעת שהיא אמצעי או מטיבה או מרעה לפי דמיונו.
2. Rambam presumably would agree that a heretical idolater who actually believes in the divinity of another being or multiple beings would be worse than (or at least as bad as) someone who believes in a corporeal God.
3. Along similar lines, Rambam writes that one who thinks that God has positive attributes is an unconscious atheist, since he "has abolished his belief in the existence of God without being aware of it" (*Moreh ha-Nevuchim* 1:60). If we follow Rambam's thesis to its logical conclusion, we would conclude that any misconception of God is worse than idolatry. We will elaborate on this point in 10.7.

believe in God (they are "inside the city"). After all, in the analogy, the first group is not merely comprised of idolaters who inappropriately worship the true God – they have no conception of the Divine.

Perhaps the answer is that the second group is worse because it should know better; we do not blame the first group, as its members are not truly human, whereas we denounce the second group, since its errors are unforgivable.

This resolution is inconceivable, however, as Rambam acknowledges that even the second group may not be responsible for its errors, which emerged "because of their following the traditional authority of one who had fallen into error." In other words, even the members of the second group may innocently have been led astray. Another baffling feature of the second group is Rambam's ruling that "They are those concerning whom necessity *at certain times* impels killing them." Why does he say that this class may be killed – he did not mention extermination concerning the first class? Furthermore, what does he mean when he says "at certain times" we should kill them? Since Rambam rules in numerous places[4] that heretics *always* are to be pushed into a pit and should not be saved from one (when possible), why does he say this class is killed only at certain times? (We should stress that all halachot concerning the killing or punishing of heretics are no longer applicable and should not be observed.[5])

The answer to all these questions emerges from the final words of the passage: "They are those concerning whom necessity *at certain times* impels killing them and blotting out the traces of their opinions **lest they lead others astray**." Rambam implies that they are not inherently worse than the first class, but rather are more dangerous for society than the first class in that they may be more likely to lead others astray by spreading their false beliefs.

---

4. Such as his Introduction to *Perek Cheilek* and *Hilchot Eidut* 11:10 where he writes: "Our Sages had no need to list informers, *apikorsim*, and apostates among those who are not acceptable as witnesses … These deserters of the faith should be pushed into a pit and should not be saved from one; they will not receive a portion in the world to come."
5. See *Chazon Ish* (Y.D. 2:16).

Here, Rambam may be alluding to his *tinok she-nishba* principle. Rambam writes that just as we do not blame a second generation Karaite because his false beliefs stem from his false education, so too the corporealist errs "because of his following the traditional authority of one who had fallen into error." However, even though we do not fault these poor souls, we cannot ignore them either, due to the danger they pose. Accordingly, necessity requires that "at certain times," we must kill the people of this class in order to prevent them from misleading others. Rambam's language parallels his statement in *Hilchot Mamrim* (3:3), where he writes concerning the *tinok she-nishba*: "It therefore is appropriate to motivate them to repent and to draw them to the power of the Torah with words of peace until they return to the bulwark of Torah, and *one should not rush to kill them.*"[6] Here too, Rambam acknowledges that at times, we must kill them, not because they are deserving of execution, but because of the danger they pose. Nevertheless, because they fundamentally are innocent, we do not "rush" to do so, hoping instead that they will return. We will discuss this radical recommendation in 11.10; for now, let us continue with the analogy.

The third group is the masses of religious people who observe the Torah but are ignorant.

The fourth group is those who devote themselves exclusively to the study of the practical law. They have proper beliefs, but they arrive at these beliefs based on tradition alone rather than investigating or attempting to prove them.

Those who have investigated maters of theology have entered the antechamber (the fifth group). There are many different levels within this group; some have entered further into the palace, while others remain in the vestibule. This is the level of the *chachamim*.

Those who have succeeded in finding a proof for everything that can be proven, who have a true knowledge of God (so far as a true knowledge can be attained[7]), are together with the king in the same room (the sixth group).

---

6. This line is omitted in the censored printings of Rambam.
7. See *Moreh ha-Nevuchim* 2:24.

The Final Leap

Once a person is in the room with God, as it were, is there further room for growth? What happens next is nothing short of extraordinary.

The next step, unlike the previous stages, is not primarily intellectual advancement – the individual has already achieved what can be achieved intellectually – it is a communion with God. To move forward, a person must abandon all that is in this world[8] and dedicate himself exclusively to the pursuit of understanding God. This is the level of the prophets.[9] Thus, there are fundamentally two steps in the service of God: understanding God and then connecting to (or uniting with God).[10]

Rambam stresses that this form of connecting to God is only appropriate if it follows the appropriate and necessary intellectual preparations:

> **ספר מורה הנבוכים חלק ג פרק נא**
> וכבר ביארה התורה כי העבודה הזו האחרונה (ההתייחדות אליו) אשר העירונו עליה בפרק זה, לא תהיה אלא לאחר ההשגה.

> The Torah has explained that the latter service (connecting to God), that which we have explained in this chapter, must only take place after a correct understanding of God.

There are two reasons for this: (1) Connecting to God is only valuable when one has a correct conception about God. Thus, those who frequently mention God, but err in their conception, are distant even from

---

8. In 2.1, we explained why this sort of separation is necessary.
9. In 2.10, we saw how Rambam (*Moreh ha-Nevuchim* 2:37) explains that in all the steps leading up to prophecy the divine overflow reaches a person's **intellect** alone, and he is classified as a philosopher. If the overflow reaches a person's **imaginative faculty** as well, he is a prophet. Moreover, all of the intellectual steps leading up to prophecy are natural and automatic. The final step, the initiation of prophecy, is not. The transcendent connection made with God in this final stage is supernatural.
10. הנה נתבאר כי המטרה אחר ההשגה, ההתייחדות אליו.

the palace courtyard. (2) The *process* of investigating and arriving at a correct conception of God must proceed connecting to God.[11]

How does one take this leap? One must "concentrate all his thoughts on God." Rambam explains that this pursuit differs from the previous stages which focused on cerebral achievements; this stage is meditative (בהתבודדות וההתייחדות): "This is the worship peculiar to those who have acquired knowledge of the highest truths; and the more they reflect on Him, and think of Him, the more they are engaged in His worship." Somebody at this phase does nothing other than contemplate upon the Divine; Rambam emphasizes that any distractions impede this stage.

Like group five, group seven also has many different levels. The greatest of all prophets, Moshe, achieved such proximity to God that the Torah states, "He was there with God" (*Shemot* 34:28). He could

---

11. אבל מי שחושב בה׳ ומרבה לזכרו בלי ידיעה, אלא שהולך אחר סתם דמיון מסוים או אחרי דעה שקבל מזולתו, הרי הוא לדעתי עם היותו מחוץ לחצר ורחוק ממנו, אינו זוכר את ה׳ באמת ואינו חושב בו. כי אותו הדבר אשר בדמיונו, ואשר הוא מזכיר בפיו, אינו מתאים למצוי כלל, אלא הוא מוצר שיצרו דמיונו, כמו שביארנו בדברינו על התארים.

It is not entirely clear whom Rambam is referring to in this passage. On the one hand, he seems to be discussing someone with an errant conception of God, hence ואשר הוא מזכיר בפיו אינו מתאים למצוי כלל. Nevertheless, the beginning of the sentence does not state that his conception is mistaken; only that it emerges from his imagination or has been taught by others. In other words, he has not arrived at his conception correctly. The next sentence supports this possibility:

> אלא ראוי לעסוק במין זה של עבודה אחר ההכרה השכלית, וכאשר תשיג את ה׳ ופעולותיו כפי שמחייב השכל, אחר כך תעסוק בהתייחדות אליו.

Here Rambam emphasizes that the second step (לעשוק בהתייחדות אליו) must follow the first step (ההכרה השכלית). Those who seek to connect to God without having first undergone the requisite intellectual preparations stray regardless of the technical accuracy of their divine connection. Subsequently, Rambam again emphasizes that it is the process and not just the results:

> **הזירוז תמיד** על ההשגות השכליות לא על הדמיונות, כי המחשבה בדמיונות אינה נקראת דעה, אלא נקראת העולה על רוחכם.

Rambam writes that there are two forms of thought that we must not confuse:

1. הזירוז תמיד על ההשגות השכליות
2. המחשבה בדמיונות

Only the first is called דעה, with the latter called העולה על רוחכם. Rambam implies that the latter is wrong not just when their conclusions are false (though that will almost inevitably be the case), but because of failure in the process.

converse with God whenever he wanted. His level was so exalted that he did not need to eat or drink.

These levels[12] correspond not just to knowledge of God, but also to love of God:

וכבר ביארנו פעמים מספר כי האהבה כפי ערך ההשגה.

> We have explained many times that the degree of love (for God) corresponds to the degree of understanding (of God).

We elaborate upon Rambam's understanding of *ahavat Hashem* in 10.12.

What Is Actually Happening in the Final Stage?

A perplexing principle which a student of Rambam encounters is the connection Rambam makes between love of God and intellectual apprehension of God. Surely, apprehension of God may be helpful in facilitating love, but why is it essential?[13] Also, why are love and apprehension of God are associated with and defined by pleasure[14] and joy?[15] Moreover, why is active, uninterrupted contemplation of the Divine

---

12. It is somewhat unclear if Rambam is referring to the various levels within the seventh group or the seven levels of Rambam's analogy. I believe the latter is correct; thus, Rambam agrees that love of God is possible along each rung, depending upon knowledge of Him.

13. In 1.2, we presented a more intuitive answer to this pressing question. Here, we will consider a more esoteric solution.

14. In *Sefer ha-Mitzvot*, Rambam refers to this pleasure in the very definition of the mitzva of loving God. Moreover, he writes that the study of Torah will automatically breed love:

    ספר המצוות לרמב"ם מצוות עשה ג

    היא שצונו לאהבו יתעלה **וזה שנתבונן ונשכיל מצותיו ופעולותיו עד שנשיגהו ונתענג בהשגתו תכלית התענוג וזאת היא האהבה המחוייבת.** ולשון סיפרי "לפי שנאמר 'ואהבת את ה' א-להיך' איני יודע כיצד אוהב את המקום תלמוד לומר 'והיו הדברים האלה אשר אנכי מצוך היום על לבבך' שמתוך כך אתה מכיר את מי שאמר והיה העולם." הנה כבר בארנו לך כי **בהשתכלות תתאמת לך ההשגה ויגיע התענוג ותבא האהבה בהכרח.**

15. Indeed, Rambam (*Moreh ha-Nevuchim* 3:51) writes that because of the great joy Moshe experienced due to his comprehension, he did not need to eat or drink while on Mount Sinai.

so important? Finally, why is the degree of love contingent upon the degree of knowledge?[16]

The answers to these questions can be found when we recall what happens when one reaches the final stage. Rambam describes the level of connection the *avot* and Moshe reached with God:

ספר מורה הנבוכים חלק ג פרק נא
וזאת ג"כ מדרגת האבות, אשר הגיע קרבתם אל הש"י עד שנודע שמו בהם לעולם, "אלהי אברהם אלהי יצחק ואלהי יעקב וגו', זה שמי לעולם," **והגיע מהתאחד דעותם בהשגתו** שכרת עם כל אחד מהם ברית קיימת, "וזכרתי את בריתי יעקוב וגו'," כי אלו הארבעה ר"ל האבות ומשה רבינו, **התבאר בהם מן ההתאחדות בשם, ר"ל השגתו ואהבתו...**

The Patriarchs likewise attained this degree of perfection; they achieved such a degree of closeness to God that, through them, His Name became known in the world. Thus, we read in Scripture: "The God of Abraham, the God of Isaac, and the God of Jacob.... This is My Name forever" (*Shemot* 3:15). **Their minds were so unified with the knowledge of God**, that He made a lasting covenant with each of them: "Then will I remember my covenant with Jacob," etc. (*Vayikra* 26:42). For it is known from statements made in Scripture that these four, viz., the Patriarchs and Moses, **experienced unity with the Name of God, that is, with knowledge of and love for Him**...

Rambam emphasizes the union (התייחדות) achieved between the individual who has reached this rarified state and God. In this context, Rambam also emphasizes the intense joy experienced by those in this state.[17]

16. Rambam expresses this idea in numerous places. For example, we just read from *Moreh ha-Nevuchim* 3:51, "We have explained many times that the degree of love (for God) corresponds to the degree of understanding (of God)."

17. **מורה הנבוכים חלק ג פרק נא**
יש מהם מי שהגיע מרוב השגתו ופנותו מחשבתו מכל דבר זולתי האלוה ית' עד שנאמר בו "ויהי שם עם יי" - וישאל ויענה וידבר וידובר עמו במעמד ההוא המקודש; ומרוב **שמחתו** במה

In this context, Rambam is describing a leap forward in the service of God. I believe this leap can be understood in two ways (emotional and spiritual), and both are correct:

1. The leap is emotional. Once one knows God, he can love God. Emotional connection comes only after intimate knowledge. Hence, in this step, Rambam emphasizes emotion (אהבה, שמחה, נועם). An emotional connection to God is impossible prior to the intellectual understanding of God because the person does not know God and is attempting to connect to an entity he does not understand and may not even exist (if his conception is false).
2. The leap is spiritual. Once a person knows God, his soul can connect to God, which creates a spiritual unity between him and God. Rambam indicates (*Hilchot Yesodei ha-Torah* 4:8–9) that a person can bind himself to God through the cognition of forms and the other non-physical creations of the cosmos. In fact, it is through that transcendental union that the soul achieves eternity.[18] To better understand this, Prof. Gideon Freudenthal suggests we need to consider another chapter in *Moreh ha-Nevuchim* – 1:68.[19] There, Rambam explains that the intellect can become one with the abstract form it is actively cognizing. If the same sort of thing

---

- שהשיג "לחם לא אכל ומים לא שתה" - כי התחזק השכל עד שנתבטל כל כח עב שבגוף רצוני לומר מיני חוש המישוש.

One of these has attained so much knowledge, and has concentrated his thoughts to such an extent in the idea of God, that it could be said of him, "And he was with the Lord," (*Shemot* 34:28); during that holy communion he could ask Him, answer Him, speak to Him, and be addressed by Him. He exulted in his level of understanding to such a degree that "he did not eat bread nor drink water" (ibid.), for his intellect dominated to the point where all coarser functions of the body, especially those connected with the sense of touch, were in abeyance.

18. There, Rambam explains that the *nefesh* (the soul) of a person (and its *tzura* or form) is able to know and comprehend knowledge which is above matter (i.e., non-material), know the Creator of all things, and thereby exist forever (יודעת ומשגת הדעות הפרודות מן הגולמים ויודעת בורא הכל ועומדת לעולם ולעולמי עולמים).
19. Prof. Gideon Freudenthal develops elements of what follows in "The Philosophical Mysticism of Maimonides and Maimon," in *Maimonides and His Heritage*, ed. Idit Dobbs-Weinstein et al. (Albany: SUNY Press, 2009), pp. 113–152.

can be said with respect to active, uninterrupted cognition of God, then we could say that a certain type of unity is achieved between the intellect of the person thinking of God and God. Of course, this does not mean the person literally merges with God. However, there is an unparalleled unity of consciousness that can be best described as love and is associated with intense joy.[20] The

20. While explaining a notion he set forth in *Hilchot Yesodei ha-Torah* (1:10) regarding God that, הוא היודע והוא הידוע והוא הדעה עצמה הכל אחד, "He is the Knower, He is the Subject of Knowledge, and He is the Knowledge itself. All is one," Rambam emphasizes that this oneness differs from human knowledge, which is not the person but external to the person. Nevertheless, even when it comes to human knowledge, a degree of unity can be achieved between the form or essence of the object the human is actively cognizing and the human intellect. In *Moreh ha-Nevuchim* 1:68 he elaborates:

> Man, before comprehending a thing, comprehends it in potentia (δυνάμει) when, however, he comprehends a thing, e.g., the form of a certain tree which is pointed out to him, when he abstracts its form from its substance, and reproduces the abstract form, an act performed by the intellect, he comprehends in reality (ἐνεργείᾳ), and the intellect which he has acquired in actuality, is the abstract form of the tree in man's mind. For in such a case the intellect is not a thing distinct from the thing comprehended. It is therefore clear to you that the thing comprehended is the abstract form of the tree, and at the same time it is the intellect in action: and that the intellect and the abstract form of the tree are not two different things, for the intellect in action is nothing but the thing comprehended, and that agent by which the form of the tree has been turned into an intellectual and abstract object, namely, that which comprehends, is undoubtedly the intellect in action. All intellect is identical with its action: the intellect in action is not a thing different from its action, for the true nature and essence of the intellect is comprehension, and you must not think that the intellect in action is a thing existing by itself, separate from comprehension, and that comprehension is a different thing connected with it: for the very essence of the intellect is comprehension. In assuming an intellect in action you assume the comprehension of the thing comprehended.

However, this unity only takes place when the intellect is actively cognizing upon the form of this object. Otherwise, his intellect exists only in potential. (In the Aristotelian tradition, knowledge is understood as the unification of the knowing subject with the known object.) Thus, before a person comprehends a thing, he comprehends it in potential, but when he succeeds in comprehending the essence of the thing (such as a tree), he abstracts its form from its substance and reproduces the abstract form in his mind. He has acquired the thing in actuality (the abstract form

crowning religious experience takes place along with the ultimate intellectual experience, and the result is intense joy, the emotional bond we call love, an extraordinary degree of divine providence,[21] and prophecy.

The Connection Breaks when We Disengage

Following the palace analogy in 3:51, Rambam writes the following encouraging but petrifying remark:

> כי השכל הזה אשר שפע עלינו מאתו יתעלה, הוא המגע אשר בינינו לבינו. והבחירה בידך, אם תרצה לחזק את המגע הזה ולעבותו - עשה, ואם תרצה להחלישו ולדקקו לאט לאט עד שתפסקהו - עשה.
>
> ואין המגע הזה מתחזק אלא בהפעלתו באהבתו וההליכה בכוון זה כמו שביארנו, והחלשתו ודקותו תהיה **בהתעסק מחשבתך במה שזולתו...**
>
> **ודע, כי אף אם היית החכם בבני אדם באמיתת המדע האלוהי, הרי בשעה שאתה מרוקן את מחשבתך מה׳ ומתעסק בכל ישותך באכילה הכרחית או בעסק הכרחי, הנך מפסיק אותו המגע אשר בינך ובין ה׳,** ואינך עמו אז, וכן אין הוא עמך, כי אותו היחס אשר בינך ובינו כבר נפסק בפועל באותה השעה.

---

of the tree in man's mind). When this happens, the intellect is not a thing distinct from the thing comprehended. Moreover, Rambam maintains that it is forms, as it were, that exist in the oneness of God. Therefore, a person can bind themselves to God through the cognition of forms. This is why Rambam stresses in *Hilchot Yesodei ha-Torah* 4:8–9 that the intellect, through great exertion, is able to comprehend that something can exist even though it has no matter (such as an angel). Accordingly, a human can understand that God (who is certainly incorporeal) can exist, and therefore, it is through the intellect that a person can bind themselves to God. It is this knowledge that lasts even after a person has lost his materiality (i.e., he has died) as Rambam explains in *Hilchot Teshuva* 8:2–3. Essentially, as Dr. Lawrence Kaplan observes, it is only the intellect – itself a form – that, for Rambam, is able to cognize the forms, and therefore only the intellect is able to serve as the bond between man and God. See *Rabbi Abraham Isaac Kook and Jewish Spirituality,* NYU Press, 1994, p. 54.

21. This unity is achieved when a person is actively contemplating the Divine. Otherwise, it is known only in potential (the sixth level).

> The intellect that emanates from God onto us is the link that joins us to God. You have it in your power to choose to strengthen that bond or to weaken it gradually until it breaks.
>
> The bond will become strong only when you employ it (the intellect) in the love of God and seek that love; it will be weakened when **you direct your thoughts to other things...**
>
> **You must know that even if you were the wisest man in respect to true knowledge of God, you break the bond between you and God whenever you turn your thoughts entirely to the necessary food or any necessary business**; at that time, you are not with God, and He is not with you, for that relationship between you and Him is interrupted at those moments.

Rambam guided us through the gates of the palace, past the antechamber, and into the throne room. Now, with these frightening words, Rambam teaches us how to commune with our Creator. As we have seen, Rambam informs us that there are two distinct categories, which are frequently confused: (a) true knowledge of God and (b) a bond with God. The first is intellectual; the second is experiential. When we busy ourselves in the material world, we may not forget our true knowledge of God, but, generally speaking, our bond with Him weakens and breaks. How do we strengthen our knowledge of God? Through thoughtful study of Torah and philosophy. How do we strengthen our bond with Him? In 10.3, we will consider the practical advice Rambam gives.

Where This Chapter Leaves Us

Over all, 3:51 emphasizes the prominence of the intellect in Rambam's thought. While intellectual knowledge alone is insufficient, the subsequent emotional development builds upon the intellectual preparation. The chapter, however, does not seem to value *mitzvot.* Some have gone so far as to claim Rambam thinks that serving God in other ways, such as through adherence to His commandments, is not vital for the ideal person – all that God truly asks of us is our minds. However, this is a misunderstanding of Rambam's position, as will become evident once we examine another place where Rambam considers a hierarchy of human perfection.

10.2 RAMBAM'S SURPRISING UNDERSTANDING OF THE ULTIMATE PERFECTION

Rambam's focus on intellectual achievement might lead one to the conclusion that intellectual attainments along with their emotional responses are the ultimate goal. This, however, would be an incorrect understanding of Rambam. To appreciate this, we must examine Rambam's conclusion to *Moreh ha-Nevuchim.*

In this chapter Rambam analyzes a verse from *Yirmiyahu* (9:22–23):

> כֹּה אָמַר יְיָ אַל יִתְהַלֵּל חָכָם בְּחָכְמָתוֹ וְאַל יִתְהַלֵּל הַגִּבּוֹר בִּגְבוּרָתוֹ אַל יִתְהַלֵּל עָשִׁיר בְּעָשְׁרוֹ. כִּי אִם בְּזֹאת יִתְהַלֵּל הַמִּתְהַלֵּל הַשְׂכֵּל וְיָדֹעַ אוֹתִי כִּי אֲנִי יְיָ עֹשֶׂה חֶסֶד מִשְׁפָּט וּצְדָקָה בָּאָרֶץ כִּי בְאֵלֶּה חָפַצְתִּי, נְאֻם יְיָ.
>
> Thus says God: "Let not the wise man glory in his wisdom, nor the mighty man in his might, nor the rich man in his riches. Rather, let he that prides himself do so only in this: that he understands and knows Me, that I am God who exercises kindness, justice, and righteousness on the earth, because these I desire," says God.

Our Ultimate Goal Is Not Just Intellectual – Rambam's Interpretation of Yirmiyahu 9

In 1.3, we saw R. Bachya and ibn Ezra refer to the *mitzva* of knowing God (*yedi'at Hashem*). One source they cite to substantiate this requirement is the above verses. Now, let us consider Rambam's understanding of these verses as presented in the conclusion of *Moreh ha-Nevuchim* (3:54).

Rambam enumerates four types of perfection towards which a human can strive:

1. Material perfection – a person can acquire wealth or possessions. Because it relies upon transient materials, this form of perfection

remains entirely external to the person and can be lost at any moment.

2. Physical perfection – a person can become strong or healthy, capable of performing great physical feats. This perfection is shared with animals, as they also can be fast or strong.
3. Character perfection – a person can develop excellent *middot*. Most *mitzvot* aim to achieve this goal. However, if a person were all alone, this level of perfection would not be actualized, since it relates to interactions with other people. Thus, even this perfection is not inherent, but rather is a means to the fourth perfection.[22]
4. Intellectual perfection – true perfection is intellectual perfection, which allows a person to reach an understanding of the Divine. Through this, a person achieves eternity.[23]

The aforementioned verses in *Yirmiyahu* allude to these four perfections, and teach us that one should take pride only in the fourth:

1. כה אמר ה׳ אל יתהלל חכם בחכמתו refers to the third perfection[24]
2. ואל יתהלל הגבור בגבורתו refers to the second perfection
3. ואל יתהלל עשיר בעשרו refers to the first perfection
4. כי אם בזאת יתהלל המתהלל השכל וידוע אותי refers to the fourth perfection

22. Later, we will clarify exactly what sort of perfection Rambam is referring to here. When he states that most *mitzvot* relate to this category, he is referring to his thesis developed in *Moreh ha-Nevuchim* 3:27 that the first aim of *mitzvot* is "the establishment of good mutual relations among men by removing injustice and creating the noblest feelings." In his commentary on the Mishna (*Sanhedrin* 3:3), he refers to this goal as *tikkun olam*. In *Mishneh Torah* (*Hilchot Temura* 4:13), he notes that sometimes even ritual *mitzvot* fall under this category.
23. We will elaborate upon Rambam's focus on intellectual accomplishments vis-à-vis *olam ha-ba* in 20.3.
24. Rambam explains why character perfection is referred to as *chochma*: "By the expression, 'the wise man in his wisdom,' he means the man of good moral principles. For in the eyes of the multitude, who are addressed in these words, he is likewise a great man." In other words, this verse is addressing the misconception of the masses who venerate wealth, followed by might, followed by moral virtue, which they conflate with wisdom. The prophet informs them that they have skewed their priorities and inverted the path towards perfection.

Lest one conclude that Rambam's elevation of intellectual achievements (the fourth perfection) above *mitzvot* (the third perfection) is his own innovation, Rambam cites a midrash that expounds the verse and likewise concludes that the fourth perfection indeed is greater than the third.

> **בראשית רבה (וילנא) פרשת נח פרשה לה**
> כתוב א' אומר (משלי ח) וכל חפצים לא ישוו בה, וכתוב אחד אומר (משלי ג) וכל חפציך לא ישוו בה, חפצים אלו מצות ומעשים טובים, חפציך אלו אבנים טובות ומרגליות, ר' אחא בשם ר' תנחום בר ר' חייא חפצי' וחפציך לא ישוו בה, (ירמיה ט) כי אם בזאת יתהלל המתהלל השכל וידוע אותי כי אני ה' עושה חסד משפט וגו'.
>
> In one place, Scripture says, "And all things that are desirable (*chafatzim*) cannot be compared to her (wisdom)" (*Mishlei* 8:11); and in another place, it states, "And all things that you desire (*chafatzecha*) cannot be compared to her (wisdom)" (*Mishlei* 3:15). "Things that are desirable" (*chafatzim*) refers to the performance of *mitzvot* and good deeds (מצות ומעשים טובים), while "things that you desire" (*chafatzecha*) refers to precious stones and pearls. R. Acha in the name of R. Tanchum explained: "Both things that are desirable (*chafatzim* – *mitzvot* and good deeds) and things that you desire (*chafatzecha* – precious stones and pearls) cannot be compared to her (wisdom), as the verse says, 'But let he that prides himself do so only in this: that he understands and knows Me.'"

This midrash underscores the value of wisdom, particularly knowledge of the Divine, over performance of *mitzvot*.

Rambam's Shocking Conclusion

Rambam then notes that the verse does not stop with its admonition to *know* God. Knowing God's actions is insufficient – we also must emulate God's actions. Thus, the verse concludes, "'I am God, who exercises kindness, justice, and righteousness on the earth, because these I desire,' says God." After stressing the importance of knowing God, the verse concludes that just as God does acts of kindness, justice, and righteousness, we must perform acts of kindness, justice, and righteousness.[25] This reminds us of the *Sifrei* cited by Rambam in *Sefer ha-Mitzvot* that highlights that contemplation leads to love, which in turn leads to emulation of His ways.[26] Rambam does not write that this is a fifth and ultimate perfection; instead, it is a part of the fourth perfection. This indicates that ethical behavior is a reflection of having achieved the appropriate knowledge of God, since this knowledge is not limited to a person's brain but has affected his whole being. Proof for Rambam's understanding of the verse can be found in *Shabbat* 127a, where the Talmud states that greeting guests is greater than communing with the Divine; thus, Avraham interrupted his conversation with God to greet his guests.

This brings Rambam to the conclusion of his masterful work:

> ואח"כ השלים הענין ואמר כי באלה חפצתי נאם ה', ואמר בחסד במשפט וצדקה חפצתי נאם ה', ר"ל שכוונתי שיצא מכם חסד משפט וצדקה בארץ, כמו שבארנו בי"ג מדות, כי הכוונה להדמות בהם ושנלך על דרכם. **א"כ הכוונה אשר זכרה בזה הפסוק, הוא באורו, ששלמות האדם אשר בו יתהלל באמת, הוא להגיע אל השגת השם כפי היכולת, ולדעת השגחתו בברואיו בהמציאו אותם והנהיגו אותם, איך היא, וללכת אחרי ההשגה ההיא בדרכים שיתכוין בהם תמיד לעשות חסד ומשפט וצדקה, להדמות בפעולות השם**, כמו שבארנו פעמים בזה המאמר:

> The prophet thus concludes, "'Because these I desire,' says God," i.e., My object [in saying this] is that you shall practice lovingkindness, justice, and righteousness on the earth. In a similar manner, we have shown (1:14) that the object of the enumeration of God's thirteen attributes is the lesson that we should acquire similar attributes and act accordingly. **The object of the above verse, therefore, is to declare that the perfection in which man can truly glory is attained when he acquires – as far as humanly**

25. Rambam highlights the verse's use of the word *aretz*. This informs us of God's providence in the world. We will return to this topic in Chapter 38.

26. תן הדברים האלה על לבך, **שמתוך כך אתה מכיר את מי שאמר והיה העולם ומדבק בדרכיו**.

> **possible – the knowledge of God, His providence, and the manner in which His providence influences His creatures in their production and continued existence; and he expresses this knowledge of God in ways that continually show loving-kindness, justice, and righteousness–imitating the ways of God.** We have explained this many times in this treatise.

From here, we see that despite Rambam's frequent focus on intellectual achievements and knowledge of God, these alone are insufficient; they must lead to kindness, justice, and righteousness. In and of itself, this is unsurprising. What is remarkable is the implication that perfection in the realm of behavior is superior to intellectual perfection. This not only contradicts what Rambam said earlier in this chapter, but conflicts with numerous statements throughout *Moreh ha-Nevuchim*. Consider 3:27, for example, where he writes: "Clearly, this second perfection (perfection of the soul) certainly does not include any action or good conduct, but only knowledge."

This question has vexed many thinkers, but it seems the solution lies in recognizing that Rambam does not mean that kindness, justice, and righteousness inherently constitute a higher perfection. As noted, they do not constitute a fifth perfection that is superior to knowledge of God. Rather, one who engages in acts of kindness, justice, and righteousness demonstrates that he has acquired a correct knowledge of God; his understanding has integrated into his very essence, affecting his mind, body, and soul. Just as cognition that fails to produce love implies erroneous cognition, so too comprehension that is not manifest in generosity is insufficient comprehension.

What is the precise flaw of such a person? Rambam answers that such a person has failed to become Godly, as evidenced by the verse in *Yirmiyahu*. Even though God is "Knower, Knowledge, and the Known" (*Yesodei ha-Torah* 2:10 and *Moreh ha-Nevuchim* 1:68), seemingly indicating that one should engage exclusively in the intellectual realm in order to be Godlike, this verse declares otherwise. The perfected individual must exercise kindness, justice, and righteousness because God expresses these same qualities in His relationship with us. One's intellectual achievement is complete only if, like God's, it is reflected in one's relationships with others. In fact, the formal halachic mandate for such behavior is derived from our obligation to be like Him (*Hilchot Dei'ot,* Ch. 1). Therefore, if a person reaches the heights of intellectual achievement but remains aloof – failing to engage in acts of kindness – his failure to be Godlike implies he is far from true perfection. With this understanding, we see that Rambam is not contradicting himself with his surprising conclusion, but rather unifying his remarkable works.

Two Types of Chesed

One obvious challenge to Rambam's reading remains – what is the difference between the third perfection, moral virtues, and the fourth perfection, which also seems to include moral and character perfection (kindness, justice, and righteousness)?

One possible solution is to suggest that the third perfection mentioned earlier cannot be referring to *middot* such as kindness. The third perfection refers to character traits that allow a person to succeed in society while allowing society to function smoothly and fairly. This contrasts with the Godlike qualities of kindness, justice, and righteousness, which are inherently valuable. This explanation is problematic because it is difficult to claim that moral virtues only refer to the practical traits needed for the smooth functioning of society, especially since Rambam indicates that most *mitzvot* aim to achieve this goal.

Instead, R. Soloveitchik differentiates between two approaches to halachic observance and moral virtue. The third perfection reflects pre-theoretical ethics. At this stage, which is no small accomplishment, a person simply follows the practical law and acts justly and kindly. He does not contemplate or appreciate the significance of his actions, and his kindness is not a reflection of a broader vision. When someone has achieved the fourth perfection, Halacha and kindness become a means of identifying with God.[27] According to R. Soloveitchik, ideally Halacha is not just about "how to," but about bringing a higher truth into reality. Prof. Lawrence Kaplan summarizes R. Soloveitchik's distinction:

27. *Maimonides – Between Philosophy and Halakhah: Rabbi Joseph B. Soloveitchik's Lectures on the Guide of the Perplexed,* edited by Prof. Lawrence Kaplan (Urim Publications, 2016), p. 51.

> Pre-theoretical ethics, ethical action that precedes knowledge of the universe and God, and post-theoretical ethics, ethical action that follows upon knowledge of the universe and God. Pre-theoretical ethics is indeed inferior to theory and purely instrumental; however, post-theoretical ethics is ethics as the imitation of God's divine attributes of action of Hesed (Loving Kindness), Mishpat (Justice), and Tzedakah (Righteousness), the ethics referred to at the very end of the Guide, and this stage of ethics constitutes the individual's highest perfection.[28]

Indeed, R. Soloveitchik emphasizes that Rambam chose the elucidation of the verse in *Yirmiyahu* to conclude his majestic work because it highlights the vast difference between his philosophy and that of Aristotle. Aristotle argues that theoretical perfection is intrinsic while the ethical act is only of instrumental significance. According to that view, Halacha and even acts of kindness would be secondary by definition. It would never be described as Godly. The theoretical world of contemplation is where one achieves true perfection and where he best mimics God. "Did Rambam simply follow in Aristotle's footsteps and provide the latter's ideas with appropriate biblical proof-texts?" No! The verse in *Yirmiyahu* and Rambam's concluding chapter emphasize that true perfection means following God by pursuing *chesed, mishpat,* and *tzedaka.*

Rambam[29] powerfully expresses this when describing the meaning of Yaakov's dream. The angels (prophets) ascend the ladder (comprehend God in the greatest manner humanly possible) and then descend to contribute to the world.[30] However, the prophet's contribution is

28. https://kavvanah.wordpress.com/2016/05/09/rav-soloveitchik-on-the-guide-of-the-perplexed-edited-by-lawrence-kaplan/.
29. *Moreh ha-Nevuchim* 1:15.
30. R. Eli Hadad in "Shiur #08: Ascent For The Sake Of Descent" (etzion.org.il/en/ascent-sake-descent) notes that this, according to Rambam, is the difference between the philosopher and the prophet. The philosopher remains aloof and disengaged from the world's problems. The prophet, having achieved that same intellectual accomplishment, uses his knowledge to help society. R. Hadad notes that this lesson emerges directly from the study of science and philosophy: "Anyone who contemplates the deeper meaning of the natural processes, recognizing God as their first cause, is

qualitatively different from the individual who has not perceived God. Ascending the ladder does not merely grant intellectual comprehension of God or convey practical directions of how to perfect society; it transforms the individual into a Godlike being.

10.3 A (REASONABLE) PATH TO PERFECTION

We have seen Rambam underscore the value of emulating God's acts of kindness, justice, and righteousness. What about other *mitzvot*? We will analyze Rambam's understanding of *mitzvot* in Unit 10, but for now, let us return to his comments in *Moreh ha-Nevuchim* 3:51. There, Rambam describes the value of thinking about God and constructs a hierarchy of those who do so, with the highest level as someone whose mind never wanders from contemplating the Divine. How does a regular person reach such a lofty state? Is a person supposed to sit around philosophizing all day? Rambam writes that proper fulfillment of *mitzvot* can bring a person to such a plane:

> ודע כי כל מעשה העבודות הללו, כקריאת התורה והתפלה ועשיית שאר המצוות, אין תכליתן אלא שתוכשר בהתעסקות במצוותיו יתעלה מלעסוק בענייני העולם, כאלו התעסקת בו יתעלה לא בזולתו.
>
> You must bear in mind that all religious acts, such as reading the Torah, praying, and the performance of other *mitzvot*, serve exclusively as the means of causing you to occupy and fill your mind with the precepts of God and free it from worldly business; for you are thus, as it were, in communication with God and undisturbed by any other thing.

Rambam does not seem to be referring to all *mitzvot*. As we saw in 10.1, many *mitzvot* aim to perfect society. Here, Rambam is referring to *mitzvot bein adam la-makom* (between man and God) – these *mitzvot* serve to focus a person on the Divine. However, this will happen only if a person actually directs his thoughts:

---

neither able nor permitted to remain in the realm of speculative knowledge. He must draw practical conclusions that demand of him that he act in a similar manner."

ולכן אם אתה מתפלל בנענוע שפתיך ופניך אל הקיר ומחשב בממכרך ומקחך, וקורא את התורה בלשונך ולבך בבניין ביתך מבלי להתבונן במה שאתה קורא, **וכן כל זמן שאתה עושה מצווה אתה עושה אותה באבריך,** כמי שחופר גומה בקרקע או חוטב עצים מן היער מבלי להתבונן בעניין אותו המעשה ולא ממי בא ולא מה תכליתו, אל תחשוב שהגעת אל תכלית, אלא תהיה אז קרוב למי שנאמר בהם 'קרוב אתה בפיהם ורחוק מכליותיהם.'

> **But if you pray with the motion of your lips with your face toward the wall but simultaneously think of your business; if you read the Torah with your tongue while your heart is occupied with the building of your house**, and you do not think of what you are reading; **if you perform the commandments only with your limbs**, like those who are engaged in digging in the ground or hewing wood in the forest, without reflecting on the nature of those acts, or by Whom they are commanded, or what is their purpose, then do not think you have arrived at the goal (of *mitzvot*). Rather, you are like those about whom Scripture says, "You (God) are near in their mouth, yet far from their kidneys (i.e., thoughts)" (*Yirmiyahu* 12:2).

At the end of 10.1, we saw Rambam distinguish between two spheres: (a) true knowledge of God and (b) a bond with God. The first is intellectual; the second is experiential. When we busy ourselves in the material world, we may not forget our true knowledge of God, but, generally speaking, our bond with Him weakens and breaks. How do we strengthen our knowledge of God? Through thoughtful study of Torah and philosophy. How do we strengthen our bond with Him?

Rambam proposes a plan. As a first step, a person should focus on God when reciting *shema* and *shemoneh esrei*. When, over the course of many years, he succeeds in this endeavor, he should learn to focus fully when reciting other *berachot* and studying Torah. His thoughts during these moments should be removed entirely from worldly affairs.

When a person has practiced this successfully for many years, he may continue to think of worldly matters while engaged in them, such as while eating, drinking, or bathing, and while conversing with his wife, little children, or others. But when engaged in the performance of all religious duties, a person should direct his mind exclusively to what he is doing. Moreover, when he is lying awake in bed, he should be careful not to squander such precious moments on anything but contemplation (העבודה השכלית).[31]

Later, Rambam discusses an even higher level achieved by the most extraordinary of people, who succeed in constantly contemplating the Divine even when engaged in worldly affairs. Accordingly, their bond with God will never break. We will return to this service of the pious in Chapter 38 where we will analyze Rambam's assertion that such people experience constant and absolute providence from God.

10.4 NEGATIVE THEOLOGY AND THE PROBLEM WITH DIVINE ATTRIBUTES

In *Moreh ha-Nevuchim* (1:50–60), Rambam proves that attributing positive attributes to God, whether essential or accidental, contradicts His oneness and incorporeality. For example, saying that God is kind, merciful, all-knowing, or all-powerful introduces plurality insofar as it implies that these qualities are separate attributes. This contradicts His oneness because it indicates that there is Him, on the one and, and His kindness, mercy, power, or knowledge, on the other hand.

Moreover, Rambam writes, it contradicts logic. If we were to say that God is "the most knowledgeable being," then we would be placing God into two genera, the genus of "beings" and the genus of "those that are knowledgeable," and doing so indicates that those genera exist prior to, and are more inclusive than, God Himself (1:52).

Furthermore, if we try to avoid that conclusion by saying God is a composite of two things (e.g., knowledge and God), there would have to be something that keeps them together, which would indicate that

31. In his commentary to *Avot* 3:4, Rambam explains that this is the intention of the mishna which states:

חנניה בן חכינאי אומר הניעור בלילה והמהלך בדרך יחידי והמפנה לבו להבטלה הרי זה מתחייב בנפשו.

פירוש המשנה לרמב"ם מסכת אבות פרק ג

הנעור בלילה לבטלה, ומי שיתבודד בנפשו, גם כן לא לתכלית, אלא לבטלה, וכן המפנה לבו מדרכי העולם, לא להשגת אמת, אלא לבטלה.

there is a cause ontologically prior to God (besides for already having compromised God's oneness).[32] In addition, it is false to say that He is the wisest or most powerful being, since that would indicate that God's wisdom or power resembles ours (1:56–57).

Accordingly, one can describe God only through negative attributes, i.e., expressing our knowledge of God by describing what He is not, rather than by describing what He is. For instance, while it is not technically accurate to say that God exists, it can be said that God is not non-existent. Likewise, we should not say that "God is wise"; but we can say that "God is not ignorant," in the sense that God has some properties of knowledge.

Of course, saying that someone is not ignorant is not much of a compliment. Therefore, despite the problematic nature of attributes, from a religious perspective, we need to be able to describe and relate to God. After all, we are commanded to love Him, fear Him, and pray to Him. Accordingly, we are called upon to declare His oneness when reciting *shema*. Likewise, the Torah frequently describes God using positive attributes. Rambam has two ways of understanding the attributes used to describe God in the Torah and in our prayers.

The first way is known as "negative theology." Since it is inaccurate to say "God is One," when we say *shema*, we mean to state that "there is no multiplicity in God's being." In other words, positive statements should be understood as disguised negations. For example, "God is powerful" should be understood as, "God is not lacking in power." The negative formulation has an additional advantage: "God is powerful" implies that we have insight into God's essence, which is false, while "God is not lacking in power" does not.[33]

Alternatively, attributes can be seen as describing the way in which we perceive His relation to the world rather than descriptions of Him. Rambam calls these "attributes of action," and examples include references to God as merciful or angry. These are neither negations nor

32. *Moreh ha-Nevuchim,* Introduction to Book 2, Premise 21.

33. However, in *Moreh ha-Nevuchim* 1:58, Rambam maintains that even negations are not entirely precise because they imply complexity (God is neither this nor that).

descriptions of His essence. Instead, they describe the effects of divine activity. Dr. Kenneth Seeskin puts it as follows:

> We can say that God is merciful to the extent that the order of nature (what God created) exhibits merciful characteristics and angry to the extent that it is harsh toward things that do not take proper care of themselves. The point is not that God possesses emotions similar to ours but that the effects of God's actions resemble the effects of ours.[34]

This distinction allows for a profound understanding of an otherwise perplexing conversation. Upon *Har Sinai,* Moshe asks God, הַרְאֵנִי נָא אֶת כְּבֹדֶךָ, "Please show me Your glory!" (*Shemot* 33:18). God responds, וְרָאִיתָ אֶת אֲחֹרָי וּפָנַי לֹא יֵרָאוּ, "You will see My back, but My face shall not be seen" (ibid. 23). What do the terms "face" and "back" mean in the context of Moshe's request to understand God's glory? Moshe cannot see God's "face," meaning perceive His essence, but he can see His "back," meaning Moshe would be able to perceive and describe God by relating the consequences or effects that flow from Him. (Looking at the wake of a boat is a helpful analogy.)[35]

---

34. Seeskin, Kenneth, "Maimonides", The Stanford Encyclopedia of Philosophy (Spring 2014 Edition), Edward N. Zalta (ed.), http://plato.stanford.edu/archives/spr2014/entries/maimonides/.

35. In *Hilchot Yesodei ha-Torah* (1:10), Rambam offers a somewhat different explanation of the episode:

> What did Moshe, our teacher, want to comprehend when he requested: "Please show me Your glory" (*Shemot* 33:18)? He asked to know the truth of the existence of the Holy One, blessed be He, to the extent that it could be internalized within his mind, as one knows a particular person whose face he saw and whose image has been engraved within his heart. Thus, this person's [identity] is distinguished within one's mind from [that of] other men. Similarly, Moshe, our teacher, asked that the existence of the Holy One, blessed be He, be distinguished in his mind from the existence of other entities, to the extent that he would know the truth of His existence as it is [in its own right].
>
> He, blessed be He, replied to him that it is not within the potential of a living man, a synthesis of body and soul, to comprehend this matter in its entirety. [Nevertheless,] He, blessed be He, revealed [to Moshe] matters that no other man had known before him – nor would ever know afterward – until he was

Is a Relationship Possible

Many wonder – is love possible? How can a person love God when they can never truly know Him and can barely say anything about Him that is precise or accurate?

Notwithstanding our inability to understand His essence or accurately describe Him using positive traits, Rambam, as we have seen, emphasizes that our limited knowledge of Him serves as the basis for our powerful relationship. When Rambam describes King David and other *tzaddikim*'s love for God, one gets the impression that the more a person recognizes his inability to understand God, the more he yearns for closeness.[36] While it may strange or unlikely that one could have a passionate relationship with an inscrutable being, the very fact that Rambam clearly enjoyed such intimacy attests to the fact that it is indeed possible. (If it feels like love and smells like love, then it is love, even if it differs from the types of love we commonly experience with people.) Moreover, we must seek to know Him more and more and through that achieve greater closeness, for as Rambam writes כי האהבה כפי ערך ההשגה, the degree of love corresponds to the degree of understanding.

Additionally, the *Zohar* (*Acharei Mot* 56) adds that *ahavat Hashem* is a gift from Heaven. Fear of God is attainable through hard work; it is in our hands. Not so with respect to love. Rather, when a person toils to cultivate a relationship with God, then God assists him to love.[37]

Finally, praising God by describing Him, despite God being fundamentally indescribable, is a religious necessity, but one should understand that the praise is indirect (i.e., it describes His actions and not Him) and remember that His essence is unknowable. Ultimately, as King David noted, the greatest form of praise we can offer is silence: לְךָ דֻמִיָּה תְהִלָּה, "To You, silence is praise" (*Tehillim* 65:2).[38]

---

able to comprehend [enough] of the truth of His existence for the Holy One, blessed be He, to be distinguished in his mind from other entities, as a person is distinguished from other men when one sees his back and knows the structure of his body and [the manner in which] he is clothed. This is alluded to in the verse, "You will see My back, but My face shall not be seen" (*Shemot* 33:23).

36. See, for example, *Hilchot Teshuva* 8:7 and the citations at the beginning of 10.2.

37. See *Michtav mei-Eliyahu,* Vol. 2, p. 120.

38. Quoted in *Moreh ha-Nevuchim* 1:49.

Does God Love Us?

The above presentation may leave a person with the impression that God does not love us. Not, of course, because He hates us, but because any emotion, including love, is antithetical to His oneness. In the second footnote of *u-Vikashtem mi-Sham* (*From There You Shall Seek*), R. Yosef Dov Soloveitchik seeks to rid the student of Rambam of this "stumbling block" (*michshol*). Indeed, such a claim is not only false; it is heretical: "Anyone who says that Judaism commands the individual to love God but does not promise him reciprocal love is a heretic" (Ibid., p. 154). R. Soloveitchik argues that even a rudimentary knowledge of Scripture and Rambam highlights the erroneousness of this reading. Thus, multiple verses attest to God's love for us (e.g., *Devarim* 10:15, 18, 23:6, *Yeshayahu* 63:9, *Malachi* 1:2). A special blessing said before Shema declares His love for us, beginning with "Eternal love" and ending with "He who loves His nation Israel." Rambam frequently mentions God's eternal love:

רמב"ם הלכות עבודה זרה פרק א הלכה ג
ומאהבת ה' אותנו ומשמרו את השבועה לאברהם אבינו עשה משה רבינו רבן של כל הנביאים ושלחו, כיון שנתנבא משה רבינו ובחר ה' ישראל לנחלה הכתירן במצות.

Because of God's love for us, and to uphold the oath He made to Avraham, our patriarch, He brought forth Moses, our teacher, the master of all prophets, and sent him [to redeem the Jews]. After Moses, our teacher, prophesied, and God chose Israel as His inheritance, He crowned them with *mitzvot*.

רמב"ם הלכות תשובה פרק ז הלכה ו
גדולה תשובה שמקרבת את האדם לשכינה... אמש היה זה שנאוי לפני המקום משוקץ ומרוחק ותועבה והיום הוא אהוב ונחמד קרוב וידיד... ולא עוד אלא שמתאוים להם...

Teshuva is great for it draws a man close to the *Shechina*... *Teshuva* brings near those who were far removed. Previously, this person

> was hated by God – disgusting, far removed, and abominable. Now, he is **beloved** and desirable, close, and dear... Moreover, God desires them (his *mitzvoth*)...

Rambam calls the second book of *Mishneh Torah* "The Book of Love" (*Sefer Ahava*), reflecting the loving relationship between God and the Jewish people.

Thus, according to R. Soloveitchik, Rambam's view differed substantially from that of Aristotle's. Love, in Aristotelian philosophy, is one-way; the world yearns for the Prime Mover, but there is no reciprocal love. Judaism, according to Rambam, definitively rejects such a notion. Even as it denies positive traits, the reciprocal love between us and our Creator is at the heart of divine service.[39]

The Kabbalistic Approach to Negative Attributes

At first glance, Rambam's approach, which denies that God has any true attributes, seems distinct from the Kabbalistic approach, which focusses on His attributes (the *sefirot*). However, this is not necessarily the case. Many Kabbalistic sources emphasize that God's true essence is reflected in the term *Ein Sof*.[40]

---

39. R. Soloveitchik, as far as I can tell, does not explain how God can experience love. The simplest resolution is to suggest that these expressions of love as attributes of action. However, R. Soloveitchik emphasizes that God's love is reciprocal and divine expressions of love that do not reflect true love does not seem to be reciprocal. However, how is true love possible for an existent that feels no emotion?

 Presumably, the meaning of the word love when used with respect to God differs from the word when used with respect to humans. Nevertheless, the term is accurate, and as such, it can accurately be described as reciprocal. Even if these expressions of love reflect attributes of action insofar as He does acts of love for us and we respond with expressions of love towards Him. This perspective fundamentally differs from the Aristotelian one in which God remains an unmoved mover – totally uninvolved in the universe.

40. The term *Ein Sof* expresses how God is infinite and beyond comprehension. The term literally means unending, as in "there is no end to God."

תיקוני זוהר הקדמה דף יז עמוד א

פתח אליהו ואמר רבון עלמין דאנת הוא חד ולא בחושבן. אנת הוא עלאה על כל עלאין סתימא על כל סתימין לית מחשבה תפיסא בך כלל. אנת הוא דאפיקת עשר תקונין וקרינן לון עשר ספירן לאנהגא בהון עלמין סתימין דלא אתגליין ועלמין דאתגליין, ובהון אתכסיאת מבני נשא. ואנת הוא דקשיר לון ומייחד לון. ובגין דאנת מלגאו, כל מאן דאפריש חד מן חבריה מאלין עשר אתחשיב ליה כאלו אפריש בך.

Eliyahu opened and said: Master of the world (a reference to *Ein Sof*). You are One, but not in number (when we use the term one with reference to You we are not referring to the number one in the number system, i.e., something that be counted). You are He Who is highest of the high, most hidden of the hidden; no thought can grasp You at all. You are He who dispatched ten rectifications (*tikkunim*), which we call ten *sefirot* (emanations), to conduct the hidden worlds which are not revealed and the revealed worlds. And with them, You conceal Yourself from humankind. (The created worlds could not handle the light from the *Ein Sof*. They would be negated. With respect to the *Ein Sof*, nothing else can exist. Thus, the *sefirot* allow for our existence, and allow us to relate to Him, though not His essence.) And You are He Who binds them and unifies them. (Do not think that there is plurality within God since each *sefira* reflects a different characteristic, because You bind them and unify them.) And because You are within [them], anyone who will separate one among these ten *sefirot* from its fellows is considered as if he made a separation within You (since all of *sefirot* stem from the same source, the *Ein Sof*).

The passages that follow this, continue to emphasize God's oneness and our inability to relate to or grasp His essence (ולית בך דידע כלל), and that the plurality implied by the various descriptions and names do not accurately reflect His essence where there is absolute unity (וכל ספירן כל חד אית ליה שם ידיע, ובהון אתקריאו מלאכיא, ואנת לית לך שם ידיע). Moreover, we have no way to grasp or relate to this unity, for there is nothing comparable to it (ובך לית דמיון ולית דיוקנא מכל מה דלגאו ולבר).

The *sefirot* serve to hide Him, and because He is hidden, as it were, we can exist. Thus, even as we relate to Him through His emanations, we constantly remember that they are not Him.

As R. Shneur Zalman of Liadi notes, there is fundamental agreement between the Maimonidean and Kabbalistic approaches:

תניא שער היחוד והאמונה פרק ח

והנה מה שכתב הרמב"ם ז"ל שהקב"ה מהותו ועצמותו ודעתו הכל אחד ממש, כן הענין ממש בכל מדותיו של הקב"ה ובכל שמותיו הקדושים והכינויים שכינו לו הנביאים וחז"ל כגון: חנון ורחום וחסיד וכיוצא בהן... אין רצונו וחכמתו ומדת חסדו ורחמנותו וכו' מוסיפים בו ריבוי והרכבה חס ושלום במהותו ועצמותו, אלא הכל אחדות פשוטה ממש, שהיא היא עצמותו ומהותו, וכמו שכתב הרמב"ם ז"ל, שדבר זה אין כח בפה לאמרו, ולא באוזן לשמעו, ולא בלב האדם להכירו על בוריו, **כי האדם מצייר הכל כמו שהוא בו**, אבל באמת הקב"ה הוא רם ונישא וקדוש ומובדל ריבוא רבבות עד אין קץ ותכלית מדרגות הבדלות מערך וסוד ומין כל התשבחות והמעלות שיוכלו הנבראים להשיג ולצייר בשכלם.

Regarding what Rambam has said – that the Holy One, blessed be He, His essence and being, and His knowledge are completely one, a perfect unity and not a composite at all – this applies equally to all the attributes of the Holy One, blessed be He, and to all His holy names, and the designations which the Prophets and Sages, of blessed memory have ascribed to Him, such as gracious, merciful, beneficent, and the like… His will and His wisdom and His attribute of kindness and His mercy and His other attributes do not add plurality and parts (God forbid) to His essence and being, but all of the above constitute an absolutely perfect unity, which is His very being and essence. As Rambam wrote, "This [form of unity] wherein God's knowledge and so on is one with God Himself is beyond the capacity of the mouth to express, the ear to hear, and the heart of man to comprehend clearly." **For man visualizes things as they are in him.** But in truth, the Holy One, blessed be He, is "high and exalted" and "Holy is His Name" (the word holy, קדש, reflects His being separate, exalted, and

> ultimately inaccessible). That is to say, He is holy and separated many myriads of degrees of separations ad infinitum, above the quality, type or kind of praises and exaltation which creations can grasp and conceive in their minds.

Humans can only relate to entities that are in some way like them. Thus, we anthropomorphize God. *Sefirot* give us the tools to appropriately and constructively do that. However, ultimately we must realize that the *sefirot* are not Him, and despite our conception of God, in reality, God can have no desire, thought, word, attribute, or action. Like Rambam, many Kabbalists argue that the attributes used to describe and relate to God do not reflect His true essence. However, many Kabbalists go further than Rambam insofar as they reject even the possibility of negative attribution. Thus, they proclaim, we can say nothing at all about God's essence. While studying the *sefirot* proves valuable, a person must realize it tells us nothing about His true self, which is entirely beyond comprehension.

To better appreciate this, consider that according to the Arizal, the first act of creation, the *tzimtzum* or self-withdrawal of God, created the "empty space" that allows for the world to exist. Moreover, many chasidic sources stress that *tzimtzum* is only the illusionary concealment of God's eternal light, the *Ohr Ein Sof*.[41] In other words, like Rambam, positive

41. Many thinkers, including R. Dessler, argued that even Gra agreed with this notion and denied *tzimtzum mamash* (the notion that God actually limited Himself). Others, including the final Lubavitcher Rebbe, argued that the question of *tzimtzum mamash* was the central debate between *mitnagdim* and chasidic thinkers. In a letter dated 19 *Shevat*, 5699, he argued that there exists a fundamental debate concerning two issues:
    a) Should the concept of *tzimtzum* be understood literally or not, i.e., are we speaking about a withdrawal of the light, or merely its concealment? *Chasidim* argued for the latter while many *mitnagdim* preferred the former.
    b) Did the *tzimtzum* affect merely God's light, or did it affect also the Source of light, [i.e., that He Himself has withdrawn or is hidden from our world]? *Chasidim* argued for the former while many *mitnagdim* preferred the latter.

    Chasidim maintain the concept of *tzimtzum* should not be interpreted literally insofar as it affects only God's light, but not the Source of light. Moreover, it affects only the lowest level of the light which existed before the *tzimtzum*. According to the Lubavitcher Rebbe, *Mitnagdim* disagreed with these premises, though varied in the degree to which they dissented. For more on this topic, see R. Tzvi Einfeld's *Torat ha-Gra u-Mishnat ha-Chasidim.*

attributes are fundamentally false in the ultimate sense, even if they are essential insofar as they allow us to understand and relate to Him.

The Need for Positive and Negative Descriptions

If positive descriptions are false, why are they so pervasive? The answer, as R. Dessler explains, is that one must simultaneously relate to God on two levels. If we do not anthropomorphize God, we will not fear Him, love Him, or even truly appreciate that He exists. Danger lurks when God becomes an impersonal being more similar to a concept than an entity. Thus, at times, we must think of God in terms that inspire fear and love. Humans are inspired by tangible and concrete images. For example, if we compare our smallness with His bigness, then we can hope to fear Him. If we consider only negative traits we will remain distant and unloving. For this reason, the Torah describes Him positively – as merciful, just, kind, and even angry.[42] When people think they do not need these sorts of descriptions, they are denying their humanity and will fail to properly fear and love God. This notion helps explain the most shocking anthropomorphism – that man is created in the image of God. This image conveys the idea that man is endowed with the capability to emulate the attributes exhibited by God as He runs the world.[43]

---

42. **מכתב מאליהו חלק ג עמוד רנח**
אין כל סתירה בין שני אופני ההשגה, שתיהן נצרכות במקומן, ומתאחדות בתכליתן, כולן ניתנו לנו לצורך עבודתנו. יסוד הוא אצלנו שאין הנפש מתפעלת אלא על ידי ציורים חיוביים, כגון ציור גדלות ה׳ מול קטנותנו, כי הנפש לא תתפעל למעשה כי אם בהרגישה את הענינים באופן מוחשי, ולשם כך נדרשות לנו השגות מעין אלו. לעומת זאת נדרשת לנו ההשגה השלילית, המופשטת, כדי להצילנו מהגשמת הבורא חס וחלילה, ולגלות לנו את חסרוננו וקטנות ערכנו מול הבורא ית״ש, חסרון שאינו רק באופן יחסי אלא באופן מוחלט.

43. יש השגות חיוביות ושליליות. השגה חיובית כיצד? כבודו יתברך מתגלה לנו בדרך ציור על פי כחותינו ומדותינו אנו. כשאנו קוראים להקב״ה חסיד, רחמן, גבור, בעל חימה וכו׳ מסתכלים אנו בו יתברך בבחינה חיובית. תארים אלו יש להם מובן ביחס אל מדותינו וכוחותינו אנו. וכך נאה לנו, כי עלינו לחקור ולהתבונן ולצייר לעצמנו את הנהגתו יתברך, על פי המדות והכחות אשר שם בנו, הרי לשם כך ניתנו כדי לחשוב ולהתבונן על ידם. ועל זה נאמר ״בצלם אלקים עשה את האדם,״ שהוא נברא בכחות גשמיים ורוחניים המקבילים למדות העליונות המתגלות בהשגחתו והנהגתו יתברך את הנבראים.
השגה שלילית כיצד? זו הידיעה הברורה שאחר כל האמור בו יתברך אין המחשבה תופסת בו כלל. כך הזכירו ב״פתח אליהו״ (שבתקוני זוהר), ואמרו שם שכל הספירות, אופני גילויי מדותיו יתברך, אינן אלא מסתירות את אמיתת מהותו, וכן ביאר הרמב״ם בחלק א׳ פרק נ״ח מהמורה, שלא ניתן לנו להשיג את מהותו יתברך, ועל כן אין נכון על פי השכל לייחד לו תוארים חיוביים

At the same time, if we corporify Him, we will be left with a false conception. We must appreciate that these anthropomorphisms are false. They contradict His unity and attempt to describe something fundamentally indescribable. At best, they are negations, analogies, or descriptions of our perception of the way in which He relates to us, even as they are absolutely necessary for the service of God. Essentially, we must simultaneously appreciate these two realities. We must relate to His descriptions as positive and negative. We are capable of granting these two perspectives their proper place.

To appreciate this, consider two descriptions used to describe how God judges on Rosh ha-Shana: (a) He judges each person individually, and (b) He judges the entire world simultaneously. Why are these two contradictory descriptions necessary? Because individually, each would leave us with a false impression. When humans examine many things at once, they necessarily do so superficially and impersonally. Thus, if we were told that God judges everyone instantaneously, we would feel the judgment lacks inimitable scrutiny. Chazal therefore inform us that we are judged individually, as a shepherd counts his sheep. Of course, the analogy is not only coarse, but false. God does not exist in time, and therefore, the notion that judgment is a process in which He looks at one person after another is unthinkable. Certainly, He judges everyone concurrently.

Thus, to correctly appreciate Rosh ha-Shana, we must simultaneously hold onto both images.[44] Likewise, we must remember His transcendence and immanence, that He lacks nothing and that we give

---

כלל, אלא תארים שליליים. למשל, כשאומרים שהוא נמצא, הענין הוא שאינו נעדר. תכלית הגישה השלילית הזאת לפי הרמב"ם שם היא, ליישר את השכל אל אמונת האחדות הגמורה, כי אם נשתמש בתארים חיוביים, יש מקום לטעות שנמצאים בו יתברך ההרכבה, ההשתנות, והריבוי, מה שאינו כן בתארים השליליים המרחיקים את הריבוי, וגם מדגישים כמה אנו רחוקים מכל השגה במהותו יתברך הנעלמת מכל הנבראים.

המטשטש את הגבולים נופל בטעויות חמורות, העלולות לגרור אחריהן גם מכשולים מעשיים. 44.

למשל אומרת הגמרא (ר"ה ט"ז) שבראש השנה כל באי עולם עוברים לפניו כבני מרון, ופירש אחד אחד, ואף על פי כן כולם נסקרים בסקירה אחת... זו בחינה שלילית, ללמד את השכל, שידיעתו יתברך היא למעלה מהזמן, ולא שייך אצלו זה אחר זה... ומי שרוצה להשיג מסקנות חיוביות מן ההשגה השלילית, לחשוב כביכול, שאם הוא בסקירה אחת הרי אי אפשר שתהיה ההשגחה על כל פרט ופרט ממש, הרי זה טועה טעות עוד יותר חמורה. הוא רוצה להכניס כביכול לעולמנו השגה השייכת רק מחוץ לעולמנו - למעלה משורש השגתנו. עליו נאמר, (חגיגה י"א), המסתכל מה למעלה מה למטה וכו' ראוי לו שלא בא לעולם. גילוי למעלה

Him joy when we serve Him. There are no contradictions; only multiple images that when carefully considered allow one to achieve a powerful relationship with his Maker.[45] When people perceive contradiction, they are looking at things too concretely or simplistically – failing to accord each perspective its proper place.

Those Who Allow for Positive Characteristics

It would appear that there are those who disagree with Rambam. Among others,[46] R. Shimon b. Tzemach Duran (1361–1444; known as Rashbatz or Tashbeitz) in the fifth chapter of the first section of *Magen Avot* appears to maintain that certain positive characteristics or descriptions do not contradict His unity or incorporeality. For example, we can accurately state that He exists. This can be understood positively. Whereas Rambam presumes this should be taken negatively – He does not not-exist. Moreover, His existence is necessary and the source for all else that exists.

Another example, He is one. (This can be understood positively. Whereas Rambam presumes this should be taken negatively – He has no multiplicity or complexity.) However, His oneness differs from any other oneness because He is inherently one. (A oneness that cannot contain multiplicity.)

Moreover, the *Sheim ha-Meforash* (יקוק) reflects this essence. (Rambam appears to agree to this, see *Moreh ha-Nevuchim* 1:62.) As opposed to other names, such as *Elokim, Shakai, A-donai,* all of which reflect His actions.

מהמדרגה שעומדים בה אינו אלא הסתר, ועל כגון דא אמרו, שיש דברים שהמסתכל בהם עיניו כהות, הם גורמים לו הסתר במקום גילוי.

45. ערבוב תחומים זה הוא שורש התמיהות שאנו נתקלים בהם במחשבתנו, ומקור הבעיות שלכאורה פתרונן רחוק מהשגתנו, כגון, איך ליישב הסתירות הכרוכות בגדרי הענינים ההפכיים, צמצום מול בלתי בעל תכלית, בחירה מול סבה ומסובב וכדומה. עלינו לדעת ולהכיר שהציור החיובי הוא הגילוי הנכון לפי מדרגתנו, ואמיתי לפי מציאותנו, היינו האור המשתקף מעל גבי ההסתר, וההשגה השלילית היא ניצוץ מלמעלה מעולמנו, שתכליתה לברר לנו את הגבלותינו וקטנותנו. רק עירבוב שני התחומים יוצר את הבעיות...

46. Ralbag, R. Crescas, R. Albo all, to differing degrees, rejected Rambam's position on positive attributes.

Tashbeitz initially agrees that characteristics like "wise" should be understood as negations, as Rambam maintains. Then he considers that they could be understood positively in a way that does not imply multiplicity (i.e., saying God is wise need not imply that there is Him and His wisdom) since His wisdom, which is unlike our wisdom, stems from Him.[47]

Tashbeitz also maintains that relational statements (על צד הה צטרפות) do not imply complexity or multiplicity.[48] For example, statements like, "God is exalted above all else," need not be understood as negations because they say nothing about Him and only describe His relationship to other things.

On the other hand, saying, "God is eternal," cannot be understood positively, since it implies He exists within time. Rather, it should be understood as a negation, precluding change.

While Tashbeitz's views seem to be fundamentally at odds with Rambam's, Tashbeitz seems to understand that he and Rambam fully agree about God's oneness, unity, and simplicity. Their debate is in the field of logic and, to some degree, semantics: What are the logical implications of God's oneness, unity, and simplicity vis-à-vis positive attributes? In a sense, it is more of a debate in the realm of logic than Torah or theology.

Did the Jewish People Accept Rambam?

In light of his opposition to attributes, Rambam in *Moreh ha-Nevuchim* (1:59) expresses reservations about *piyyutim* (liturgical poems) that describe God in great detail. While these poems in and of themselves do not contradict Rambam's position, insofar as they can be seen as negations or attributes of action, they run contrary to the spirit and tone of his view. R. Soloveitchik in *Halakhic Man* captures how the Jewish people, who generally embraced such poems rejected Rambam's view:

---

47. אבל הקל יתברך אינו כבנ"א, כי מהשגתו עצמו נשפע מאצילותו ברצונו, ויכלתו זה המציאות, א"כ חכמתו שהיא השגתו ורצונו ויכלתו כולם הם עם עצמותו דבר אחד, אין שם תוספת וריבוי.

48. Examples include גדול ה׳ מכל האלהים and אל עליון על כל הארץ.

> Halakhic man never accepted the ruling of Maimonides opposing the recital of *piyyutim*, the liturgical poems and songs of praise. Go forth and learn what the *Guide* (1:59) sought to do to the piyyutim of Israel! "Thus what we do in prayer is not like what is done by the truly ignorant who spoke at great length and spent great efforts on prayers that they composed and on sermons that they compiled.... This kind of license is frequently taken by poets and preachers or such as think that what they speak is poetry, so that the utterances of some... contain rubbish and perverse imaginings." Nevertheless, on the High Holidays the community of Israel, singing the hymns of unity and glory, reaches out to its Creator. And when the Divine Presence winks at us from behind the fading rays of the setting sun and its smile bears within it forgiveness and pardon, we weave a "royal crown" of praise for the *Atik Yomin,* the Ancient One (the hymn *Keter Malchut* by R. Shlomo ibn Gabirol). And in moments of divine mercy and grace, in times of spiritual ecstasy and exaltation, when our entire existence thirsts for the living God, we recite many *piyyutim* and hymns, and we disregard the strictures of the philosophical midrash concerning the problem of negative attributes. The Halakha does not deem it necessary to reckon with speculative concepts and very fine, subtle abstractions on the one hand and vague feelings, obscure experiences, inchoate affections, and elusive subjectivity on the other. It determines law and judgment in Israel. (58–59)

10.5 IF WE CANNOT UNDERSTAND WHY EVEN TRY?

The Maimonidean and Kabbalistic teachings above leave us with mixed messages. We are told there is no way to truly understand God. Any perception we may have of Him is intrinsically false. Concurrently, we are urged to devote our entire life to understanding Him; we should direct every act we perform towards achieving that end.[49] Clearly, our inability to conceive of Him does not imply we should not try. But, we wonder, why?

---

49. **שמונה פרקים לרמב"ם פרק ה**
ראוי לאדם להעביד כוחות נפשו כולם לפי הדעת, כפי שהקדמנו בפרק אשר לפני זה, ולשים לנגד עיניו תכלית אחת, והיא: השגת ה׳, יתפאר ויתרומם, כפי יכולת האדם, רצוני לומר: ידיעתו.

For now, let us consider two answers: (1) There are things we can understand, and (2) the pursuit of the elusive and even unreachable goal is valuable in its own right.

What We Can Know

We cannot fully understand God. In a sense, we cannot even partially understand Him. Moreover, attributing positive attributes to God, whether essential or accidental, contradicts His oneness and incorporeality. At the same time, Rambam believes there is a *mitzva* to know God. But if we cannot actually know what God is, only what He is not, where does that leave us regarding the *mitzvot* of *yedi'at Hashem, anochi,* and *yichud Hashem*?

The answer is that while we never can know His essence, there are basic truths that are knowable and that we must know. As Rambam explains in the opening chapter of *Hilchot Yesodei ha-Torah,* these include His existence, His oneness, His being the cause for all that exists, and His incorporeality. Thus, there is much that we can learn about God. Moreover, our knowledge of God, though limited, will stay with us forever. As such, pursuing it is of utmost value.[50]

R. Soloveitchik (*Al ha-Teshuva,* pp. 195–201) adds a fascinating addendum to this point. Because it is impossible to really "know" God, Rambam means that we are obligated to constantly recognize God's existence and emulate His ways.[51] This explanation is

וישים פעולותיו כולן, תנועותיו ומנוחותיו וכל דיבוריו, מביאים אל זאת התכלית, עד שלא יהיה בפעולותיו בשום פנים דבר מפועל ההבל, רצוני לומר: פועל שלא יביא אל זאת התכלית.

50. Several Jewish philosophers who succeeded Rambam (such as Ralbag, R. Yosef Albo, and R. Chasdai Crescas) address this question in greater detail explaining how a scholar who recognizes that he only has a 'negative' understanding of God is closer to the truth than the simpleton who has never thought about God at all (and thus has also never ascribed to Him any attributes). R. Albo (*Sefer ha-Ikkarim* 2:30), for example, suggests that although it is technically true that God is neither "foolish" nor "wise," He is surely more not-foolish than He is not-wise. Thus, they argue, one can know a lot about God without ascribing any positive quality to God.

51. The notion that "knowing God" may refer to emulating His ways can be seen in *Mishlei* (3:6), "In all your ways know Him." Radak (*Yirmiyahu* 9:23) likewise understands the words וידוע אותי to refer to *imitatio dei*:

buttressed by the concluding chapter of *Moreh ha-Nevuchim*, as we explained in 10.2.[52]

Most importantly, we must note that any understanding of God's negative attributes is meaningless without first recognizing that He does exist. This is stated by R. Soloveitchik:

> The entire phenomenon of negative cognition is only possible against a backdrop of affirmative cognition. For we negate with respect to the Creator all of the attributes that we have affirmed with respect to created beings. Therefore, in order to arrive at the negation, we must engage in an act of affirmation. The act of negation is reconstructed out of the very substance of affirmation. And what constitutes affirmative cognition if not the cognition of the cosmos – the attributes of action? Moses prayed that these attributes be communicated to him, and his petition was granted. Indeed, we are all commanded to occupy ourselves with the understanding in depth of these attributes, for they bring us to the love and fear of God, as Maimonides explains in the Laws of the Foundations of the Torah (II, 2). First we cognize in positive categories God's great and exalted world, and afterward we negate the attributes of created beings from the Creator. (*Halakhic Man*, pp. 11–12)

The Value in the Chase

R. Nachman of Breslov powerfully expresses the dilemma we have been considering:

בהשכל וידוע אותי - פירוש בהשכל אותי וידוע אותי. והשכל האל הוא שישכיל כי הוא אחד קדמון ואינו גוף והוא בורא הכל ומשגיח על הכל ומנהיג כל העולם בחכמתו עליונים ותחתונים, **וידיעת האל היא ללכת בדרכיו** לעשות חסד משפט וצדקה כי כן עושה אותם הוא.

Radak writes that we are obligated both to philosophically understand God (to the best of our ability), as indicated by the word *haskeil,* and to know God in the sense of emulating his ways (*yado'a oti*).

52. It is interesting to consider whether R. Soloveitchik's comments should be seen as a radical *reinterpretation* of the first *mitzva* of Rambam or as an *additional* component to *Hilchot Yesodei ha-Torah* 1:1. See our elaboration in 8.2.

> **ליקוטי מוהר"ן תורה כד א**
> דע שיש אור, שהוא למעלה מנפשין ורוחין ונשמתין, והוא אור אין סוף. ואע"פ שאין השכל משיג אותו, אעפ"כ רדיפה דמחשבה למירדף אבתריה. ועל ידי הרדיפה, אז השכל משיג אותו בבחי' מטי ולא מטי. כי באמת אי אפשר להשיג אותו, כי הוא למעלה מנר"נ.
>
> Know that there is a light higher than *nefesh, ruach,* and *neshama.*[53] This is the light of the *Ein Sof*. Even though the intellect cannot grasp this light, the racing of the mind nevertheless pursues it. And through that pursuit, the intellect is able to grasp it in an aspect of "reaching and not reaching" (*matei ve-lo matei*). For the truth is, it (the intellect) cannot grasp it (the light of the *Ein Sof*) because it is higher than the *nefesh, ruach,* and *neshama.*

The precise meaning of this Kabbalistic idea need not concern us at present. What relates to us is that the notion *matei ve-lo matei* reflects that the experience of trying to understand God, even while knowing we can never fully succeed, brings us close to Him. The chase, as it were, is valuable in and of itself, and it yields fruits we would never taste if we would not pursue the unreachable goal.

In a similar vein, the Besht offers a profound insight that dovetails with Rambam's palace analogy. We can react to our inability to comprehend the Divine in one of two ways; we can give up, or we can investigate to the extent possible, even as we appreciate we will never truly know the King. The second approach will allow us to enter the King's palace, traverse splendid rooms and delight in their beauty, and continue until we reach the point where we can go no further. The first approach will leave us forever outside the palace, not even truly knowing what we cannot know.[54]

---

53. These terms refer to the three lower elements of the soul. There are two higher levels (*chaya* and *yechida*) to which human's generally cannot relate.

54. **כתר שם טוב חלק ראשון ג**
מהבעש"ט ביאר הלואי אותי עזבו ותורתי שמרו (ירושלמי חגיגה א,ז). פי' כי הידיעה שלא נדע. אמנם יש ב' סוגים שלא נדע. א' מיד שאינו נכנס לחקור ולידע מאחר דא"א לידע. ב' שחוקר ודורש עד שידע שא"א לידע. והפרש בין זה לזה מלה"ד שנים שרוצים לידע את המלך וא' נכנס בכל חדרי המלך ונהנה מאוצרי והיכלי המלך ואח"כ לא יוכל לידע המלך והשני אמר מאחר

Of course, as we stressed in 2.4, we must know our limits. Trying to understand what cannot be understood can have grievous consequences. However, if we are aware of our limitations, then there can be no greater task than pursuing this elusive goal.

10.6 THE IMPLICATIONS OF A MISTAKEN CONCEPTION OF GOD – IS SOMEONE WHO BELIEVES THAT GOD IS MERCIFUL A HERETIC?

Having established the problematic nature of positive attributions, we must wonder how the Torah treats a person who calls God merciful and means it in the simple sense, unaware that such a statement contradicts His unity. This is similar to the topic of Chapter 11 where we will consider how Rambam views a person who believes God has a body based on the simple reading of the Torah. However, these issues must be addressed separately because Rambam clearly considers corporeality heresy while his view on positive attributions is far less clear. While Rambam unambiguously maintains that positive attributions are false, he does not explicitly discuss the implications of such an error. Thus, we are left wondering, what is the status of a person who erroneously believes God is merciful based on the simple reading of the Torah. Do we consider such a person a heretic, since he is essentially, though unknowingly, denying God's unity? Or, is this error qualitatively different? Perhaps there is a difference between someone who believes God has a body and someone who believes He is merciful?

To solve these quandaries, we will begin with evidence that belief in positive characteristics is equivalent to belief in corporeality and therefore would constitute heresy. We will then consider evidence to the contrary and suggest a resolution.

Evidence that Belief in Positive Characteristics Constitutes Heresy

Rambam states that someone who thinks God has positive attributes is an unconscious atheist; he "has abolished his belief in the existence of God without being aware of it" (*Moreh ha-Nevuchim* 1:60). Who would

שא״א לידע המלך לא נכנס כלל לחדרי המלך ולא נדע מיד. ובזה יובן ודאי בשני סוגים הנ״ל. אותי עזבו מלידע שא״א מ״מ הלואי אותי עזבו מתוך החקירה והידיעה אחר שתורתי שמרו.

be included in this category? Rambam writes: "I do not merely declare that he who affirms attributes of God has insufficient knowledge concerning the Creator, admits some association with God, or conceives Him to be different from what He is; but I say that he **unconsciously** loses his belief in God." In other words, we cannot say that someone who believes God has positive attributes believes in God but simply is making a mistake; rather, he does not believe in God, because the "god" he believes in does not exist. Rambam explains:

> For he whose knowledge concerning a thing is insufficient understands one part of it while he is ignorant of the other as, for example, a person who knows man possesses life but does not know man possesses understanding. But in reference to God, in whose real existence there is no plurality, it is impossible that one thing should be known, and another unknown. Similarly, he who associates an object with [the properties of] another object conceives a true and correct notion of the one object and applies that notion also to the other; while those who admit the attributes of God do not consider them as identical with His essence but as extraneous elements. Again, he who conceives an incorrect notion of an object must necessarily have a correct idea of the object to some extent. He, however, who says that taste belongs to the category of quantity has not, in my opinion, an incorrect notion of taste, but is entirely ignorant of its nature, for he does not know to what object the term "taste" is to be applied.

Rambam offers an imaginative illustration of his principle. Imagine someone who has never seen an elephant asks his friend to describe one. His friend replies that an elephant is an animal with one leg and three wings that lives in the depth of the sea. It has a transparent body and the face, form, and shape of a man; it speaks like a man, sometimes flies in the air, and sometimes swims like a fish. Would we say the first person now knows what an elephant is, but his understanding is inaccurate? Or would we say he has no conception of what an elephant is, since there is no connection between his understanding of an elephant and what an elephant actually is? Clearly the latter. Rambam maintains that the same is true if someone believes God has a physical body or positive characteristics. A being with positive characteristics is so fundamentally different than one without them that a mistake in this regard indicates a lack of belief in the true God.

Further proof for this conclusion emerges from *Moreh ha-Nevuchim* 1:50. Rambam writes that part of belief is understanding the direct implications of what one believes. Thus, "Those who believe God is one and that He has many attributes declare the unity with their lips and assume plurality in their thoughts." In other words, their saying that He is one when they recite *shema Yisrael* is of little value because they believe He has attributes, and having attributes contradicts oneness. Here, Rambam indicates that denial of divine attributes is absolutely fundamental.[55] It would seem, then, that applying positive attributes to God is equivalent to believing that He has a body.

Evidence that Belief in Positive Characteristics Does Not Constitute Heresy

There is, however, counter evidence to the above conclusion. When enumerating the thirteen principles of faith in his commentary on the Mishna, Rambam includes rejection of incorporeality but does not include belief that God has no attributes among the basic principles a Jew must believe to be considered Jewish.[56] This indicates that this belief is not as fundamental as incorporeality, especially since belief in positive

55. Moreover, the presentation of 1:50–52 indicates that the attribution of essential characteristics and accidental characteristics are equally problematic (even though one contradicts oneness and one contradicts incorporeality).

56. The second principle states:

    אחדותו יתעלה. והוא, שזה עלת הכל אחד, לא כאחדות המין ולא כאחדות הסוג, ולא כדבר האחד המורכב שהוא מתחלק לאחדים רבים, ולא אחד כגוף הפשוט שהוא אחד במספר אבל מקבל החלוקה והפיצול עד בלי סוף, אלא הוא יתעלה אחד, אחדות שאין אחדות כמוה בשום פנים, וזה היסוד השני מורה עליו מה שנ׳ שמע ישראל ה׳ אלהינו ה׳ אחד.

    The unity of God: Meaning to accept that this is the quintessential idea of oneness. It is not like the oneness of a pair (i.e., pair of shoes – one group) and not one like a species. And not like man that has many individual [members], nor like a body that is one unit but divisible into many different parts until no end (every part being divisible). Rather, God is one and there is no other oneness like His. This is the second principle and is taught in the verse, "Hear Israel, Hashem is our God, Hashem is one" (*Devarim* 6:4).

attributes certainly was widespread, and, like incorporeality, would have needed to be dispelled. While this evidence could be deflected by stating that the presentation in the commentary on the Mishna is not meant to be comprehensive, his omission of the problematic nature of characteristics of God from *Mishneh Torah* as well points to the conclusion that attribution of characteristics is *not* heretical.[57]

More significantly, in *Moreh ha-Nevuchim* 1:35, Rambam appears to allow for the non-education of the masses about the inapplicability of positive attributes to God while simultaneously insisting upon educating the masses about His incorporeality:

> As for discussion **concerning attributes and the way they should be negated with regard to Him and the meaning of the attributes that may be ascribed to Him... all these are obscure matters.** In fact, they are truly the mysteries of the Torah and the secrets constantly mentioned in the Prophets and in the dicta of the Sages, may their memory be blessed. They are the matters that ought not to be spoken of except in chapter headings, as we have mentioned, and only with an individual such as has been described.
>
> **On the other hand, the disavowal of (1) the corporeality of God, (2) His having a likeness to created things, and (3) His being subject to affections are matters that ought to be made clear and explained to everyone according to his capacity** and ought to be inculcated... in children, women, ignoramuses, and those of defective natural disposition, just as they adopt the notion that God is one, that He is eternal, and that none but He should be worshipped. **For there is no profession of unity unless God's corporeality is denied.**[58]

57. Rambam does not discuss God's lack of attributes in the areas of *Mishneh Torah* that discuss God (*Hilchot Yesodei ha-Torah*) or in the context of what one is required to believe and who is considered a heretic (*Hilchot Teshuva*).

58. Adapted from Pines translation, Vol. 2, p. 81. In *Moreh ha-Nevuchim* 1:46, Rambam explains why the Torah describes God in terms that may cause a person to believe that He has a body. He suggests that it was necessary in order to bring the masses to belief

Here, Rambam groups the inapplicability of divine attributes with a number of other "secrets of the law" and states that it is only to be explained (indirectly) to one who is fully proficient in all of the necessary antecedents to studying *ma'aseh merkava* (see 2.1). Meanwhile, divine incorporeality is to be taught to every man, woman, and child as a foundation of the faith.

10.7 THE DIFFERENCE BETWEEN HALACHIC HERESY AND PHILOSOPHICAL HERESY

It seems that the resolution to the above contradiction is to distinguish between what halachically constitutes heresy and what theologically constitutes heresy. As we explained in 5.7, Rambam maintains that there are practical halachic ramifications that emerge from espousing heretical beliefs. These include the validity or usability of the *tefillin* written by a heretic, his ritual slaughtering (*shechita*), and the wine he touches. In Rambam's halachic works, when describing what constitutes heresy, he omits attribution of attributes to the Divine. This implies that Rambam maintains that even if someone were to incorrectly ascribe positive attributes God, his *shechita* would be valid, the *tefillin* he writes kosher, and the wine he touches permitted. In his philosophical work, however, Rambam stresses the highly problematic repercussions of such belief, equating the error of positive characteristics with corporeality. Thus, it appears they are philosophically equivalent even as we distinguish halachically.

Of course, the problem with this resolution is that it does not seem to make sense. Since there does not seem to be a logical difference between ascribing physicality to God and ascribing attributes to Him (since both errors, according to Rambam, logically contradict His unity), why should we distinguish between the two in Halacha? What would account for the distinction?

The solution lies in the distinction between how we know He does not have a physical body and how we know He has no positive attributes. The Torah frequently warns against corporeality, such as in

---

in a single God. This appears to contradict his statement in 1:35, which does not allow for such a concession regarding incorporeality. We will address this question in 11.4.

Devarim 4:15.[59] In fact, Rambam stresses that we know of His incorporeality not through philosophical speculation, but from the Torah itself:

רמב"ם הלכות יסודי התורה פרק א הלכה ח

הרי מפורש בתורה ובנביאים שאין הקב"ה גוף וגוייה שנאמר, "כי ה' הוא האלהים בשמים ממעל ועל הארץ מתחת," והגוף לא יהיה בשני מקומות. ונאמר, "כי לא ראיתם כל תמונה." ונאמר, "ואל מי תדמיוני ואשוה," ואילו היה גוף היה דומה לשאר גופים.

> Behold, it is explicitly stated in the Torah and the Prophets that the Holy One, blessed be He, is not [confined to] a body or physical form, as [*Devarim* 4:39] states: "Because Hashem is God in the heavens above and the earth below," and a body cannot exist in two places [simultaneously]. Also, [*Devarim* 4:15] states: "For you did not see any image," and [*Yeshayahu* 40:25] states: "To whom can you liken Me and I will be equal?" Were He [confined to] a body, He would resemble other bodies.

Moreover, according to Rambam, while Onkelos intentionally removed anthropomorphisms that could be incorrectly interpreted as implying corporeality, he did not remove references that could be interpreted as ascribing positive characteristics to God. Rambam writes that one of the reasons why belief in corporeality is particularly inexcusable is Onkelos' clarification. It seems that Rambam maintains that since we know of the falseness of attributes only through logic, such an erroneous belief, egregious as it may be, does not halachically constitute heresy.[60]

---

59. In fact, there is a negative prohibition that stresses God's incorporeality:

דברים ד:טו-יח

(טו) וְנִשְׁמַרְתֶּם מְאֹד לְנַפְשֹׁתֵיכֶם כִּי לֹא רְאִיתֶם כָּל תְּמוּנָה בְּיוֹם דִּבֶּר יְקֹוָק אֲלֵיכֶם בְּחֹרֵב מִתּוֹךְ הָאֵשׁ.
(טז) פֶּן תַּשְׁחִתוּן וַעֲשִׂיתֶם לָכֶם פֶּסֶל תְּמוּנַת כָּל סָמֶל תַּבְנִית זָכָר אוֹ נְקֵבָה.
(יז) תַּבְנִית כָּל בְּהֵמָה אֲשֶׁר בָּאָרֶץ תַּבְנִית כָּל צִפּוֹר כָּנָף אֲשֶׁר תָּעוּף בַּשָּׁמָיִם.
(יח) תַּבְנִית כָּל רֹמֵשׂ בָּאֲדָמָה תַּבְנִית כָּל דָּגָה אֲשֶׁר בַּמַּיִם מִתַּחַת לָאָרֶץ.

60. Interestingly, Rambam writes (*Moreh ha-Nevuchim* 1:52) that the only reason why anyone would think God has positive characteristics is from the verses in the Torah that imply as much.

Additionally, it is relatively easy to understand, on some level, the error of corporeality. Every typical 12 or 13 year-old child can believe in an incorporeal God. However, understanding why positive attributes contradict divine unity proves quite complex. As such, fulfilment of the *mitzva* of *emuna* on a basic level, an obligation incumbent upon every 12 or 13 year-old child, could not necessitate a rejection of positive attributes.

An interesting question that remains is whether the above distinction between the errors of corporeality and positive attribution reflect an inherent difference between these two mistakes (even though, from a strictly logical perspective, they both contradict divine unity) or it simply is a practical difference. Possibilities abound. Is this distinction indicative of a difference between the practical effects of having people believe in a corporeal God as opposed to a God with attributes, the first possibility being more harmful because it constitutes a greater misrepresentation of the Divine? Or, perhaps the difference lies in the fact that regular people are capable of understanding that God has no physical body but are incapable of understanding the problematic nature of positive attributes and emotions. Alternatively, there may be a greater need for more people to imagine God has emotions in order to have an emotional relationship with Him themselves and to fear divine wrath in order to desist from sin. Either way, the Torah's distinction between these two types of errors, as reflected in the Halacha, guides both the individual and society to the greatest possible perfection.

Whether or not we accept that there might be some theoretical difference between the mistaken belief in divine corporeality and divine attributes, a significant question remains. Even if a person who believes in divine attributes is not a heretic with regards to Halacha, does his incorrect belief (and therefore *dis*belief) in God cause him to lose his share in the afterlife? If we posit that belief in divine attributes is a less serious misrepresentation of God than corporealism, then the person in question might still be saved from being eternally cut off from the Jewish people.

However, to fully understand the answer to this question, we must know whether the consequences of a false belief concerning God are entirely naturalistic or are at least partially retributive. If the former, it should not matter whether a person's beliefs are the result of negligence or are entirely inadvertent. If the latter, exculpability is relevant. We will discuss this question at length in Chapter 11.

10.8 MISLEADING STATEMENTS THAT PROMOTE POLITICAL WELFARE

The distinction between halachic heresy for believing in corporeality and theological heresy for believing in positive attributes sheds light on another problematic passage in *Moreh ha-Nevuchim*. In 3:28, Rambam writes that even though ascribing emotions to God implies He can change and, as such, contradicts His oneness, the Torah itself ascribes emotions to God in order to accomplish important societal goals. He writes:

> ממה שראוי שתתעורר עליו הוא, שתדע כי ההשקפות הנכונות אשר בהן תושג השלמות הסופית, לא נתנה תורה מהן אלא תכליתן, וקראה להיות בהן בדעה באופן כללי, והוא: מציאות ה׳ יתעלה, ויחודו, וידיעתו, ויכולתו, ורצונו, וקדמותו. ואלה כולן תכליות סופיות, לא יתבארו בפירוט ובהגדרה, אלא לאחר ידיעת השקפות רבות.
>
> **וכן גם קראה התורה להיות בדעה בדברים אשר סבירתן הכרחית בתקינות המצבים המדיניים. כגון זה שאנו בדעה, שהוא יתעלה יחרה אפו על מי שמרד בו, ולפיכך חובה לירוא ולפחד ולהשמר מן המרי.**
>
> You should be aware, among other things, that the Torah's commands regarding the proper perspectives (through which one can attain perfection) spell out only the end goal. And the Torah calls for belief in them in a generic way – that is, to believe in the existence of the deity, may He be exalted, His unity, His knowledge, His power, His will, and His eternity. All these points are ultimate ends, which can be made clear in detail and well-defined only after knowledge of many perspectives.
>
> **Likewise, the Torah also calls for the adoption of certain beliefs which are necessary for the sake of political welfare. For instance, it is our belief that He, may He be exalted, will be**

violently angry with those who disobey Him, and therefore it is necessary to fear, dread, and take care not to disobey [Him].

Rambam writes that the Torah aims to bring individuals and society to perfection. To do this, the Torah teaches two types of beliefs: (1) beliefs that are true and (2) beliefs that help perfect society. The former are taught because they are true and therefore must be known, for one can achieve perfection only if one has them (e.g., belief in God, His unity, and His power). The latter are promulgated because they are helpful for the perfection of society. For example, if a person believes that God will be violently angry at him if he sins, he is unlikely to sin. Therefore, the Torah writes that God's wrath flares against idolaters. Now, is it actually true that God gets angry with idolaters? No. God cannot experience emotion. However, this false belief is useful and therefore is expressed in the Torah. Of course, it is hoped that those capable will study philosophy and discover that, in reality, God does not get angry.

At the end of 3:28, Rambam indicates that this type of misrepresentation never would be employed concerning corporeality, since belief in incorporeality falls under the first class of beliefs:

> Let us sum up what we have said concerning belief as follows: in some cases a *mitzva* communicates a correct belief, which is the only thing aimed at – for instance, the belief in the unity and eternity of the Deity and in His incorporeality.[61] In other cases, the belief is necessary for the abolition of reciprocal wrongdoing or for the acquisition of a noble moral quality. Examples of this include the belief that He, may He be exalted, has a violent anger against those who do injustice, as the verse says: "And My wrath shall flare, and I will kill, etc." (*Shemot* 22:23), and the belief that He, may He be exalted, responds instantaneously to the prayer of someone wronged or deceived: "And when he cries out to Me, I will hear, for I am gracious (*Shemot* 22:26).[62]

---

61. For example, the purpose of the *mitzva* of saying *shema* is to instill belief in His oneness.
62. The inaccuracy in this verse is presumably that God does not respond instantaneously. Rambam, however, is not discounting the notion that God responds to prayer, as we shall see in Chapter 38.

It seems Rambam is saying the Torah will insinuate an incorrect belief to maintain or enhance society. However, it does so only when such a belief does not contradict the first aim of the Torah, which is to bring individuals to perfection. Consequently, it follows that belief that God experiences emotions, such as graciousness or wrath, does not prevent an individual from achieving perfection. It seems Rambam believes that a person who commits such intellectual errors does believe in God, even if his beliefs regarding God logically contradict His unity. In other words, a person who believes in a corporeal God cannot actually be said to believe in God at all,[63] but one who believes that God can get angry still can be said to believe in God, though his beliefs are grossly mistaken. This difference supports our earlier distinction between halachic and philosophical heresy but seems hard to reconcile with *Moreh ha-Nevuchim* 1:60.

One could reject this understanding by arguing that there is no difference between these beliefs, and Rambam understands that the Torah actively teaches disbelief in God for the sake of promoting political wellbeing. Support for such a position can be garnered from Rambam's statement in 1:46 (which we will elaborate upon in 11.4) that the Torah is written in a way that can be understood as implying that God is corporeal so as to bring people to belief in God. If that is correct, then our distinction between corporeality and positive attributes, which we proposed to explain 3:28, has little basis.

This position, however, seems inconceivable. Firstly, Rambam frequently states that the primary goal of Torah is to bring individuals to perfection, with only the secondary goal of bringing society to perfection.[64]

---

63. Just like the person who believes that an elephant is an animal that looks like a man and lives in the sea.

64. For example, he writes in 3:27:

> The true Torah, which as we said is one and besides which there is no other Torah, viz., the Torah of our teacher Moshe, has for its purpose to give us the twofold perfection. **It aims first at the establishment of good mutual relations among men by removing injustice and creating the noblest feelings.** In this way, the people in every land are enabled to stay and continue in one condition, and everyone can acquire his first perfection. **Secondly, it seeks to train us in faith and to impart correct and true opinions when the intellect is sufficiently developed.** Scripture clearly mentions the twofold perfection

Thus, because belief in corporeality prevents an individual from achieving perfection, it never would be taught by the Torah. Moreover, Rambam explicitly differentiates in 3:28 between beliefs such as incorporeality ((1) above), which the Torah teaches to promote individual perfection, and beliefs that are politically expedient errors (2), such as divine emotions.

Thus, 1:46 should be understood differently than 3:28. In 1:46, Rambam writes that there is a purpose in writing in such a way that the Torah could be *misunderstood*[65] as referring to God's physical body, since this will bring the masses to belief in His existence.[66] While such an understanding is devastating in the long run, there still is value in bringing the masses to belief in a corporeal god, as it serves as a stepping-stone to the correct conception of God. In 3:28, Rambam writes that the Torah teaches that God experiences emotion because it will bring society to perfection by discouraging sinful behavior. While mature students of Torah will grow to appreciate the truth, the false understanding is meant to be no more than a short-term fix. (We will investigate this distinction further in 11.4.)

10.9 RAMBAM'S CONCEPTION OF IDOLATRY

Many *mitzvot* relate explicitly to the Torah's ban on idolatry. Rambam, in the third section of *Moreh ha-Nevuchim,* adds that many additional *mitzvot,* such as the Torah's injunction against rounding the edges of the head (*pei'ot*) or mixing meat and milk, also are rooted in the Torah's drive

---

> and tells us that its acquisition is the object of all the divine commandments: "And God commanded us to do all these statutes, to fear Hashem, our God, for our good, always, that He might preserve us alive as it is this day" (*Devarim* 6:24). **Here, the second perfection is first mentioned because it is of greater importance, being, as we have shown, the ultimate aim of man's existence.**

The same idea is expressed in his Commentary on the Mishna (*Sanhedrin* 3:3) and the final halacha of *Hilchot Temura.*

65. After all, Rambam devotes almost the entirety of Section I of the *Moreh ha-Nevuchim* to showing that the corporealist reading of various words or passages in Tanach is incorrect.

66. As Leo Strauss writes in his Introduction to the Shlomo Pines edition of the *Guide,* "Generally stated, the literal meaning of the Bible is not corporealistic... the corporealistic meaning is not the only meaning, it is not the deepest meaning, it is not the true meaning, but it is as much intended as the true meaning" (pp. xxxv-xxxvi).

to weed out idolatry. In fact, the goal of uprooting idolatry is a major focus on the Torah's *mitzvot.*[67] It therefore behooves us to understand Rambam's position on this matter as it relates to the discussion above.

In 10.1, we mentioned Rambam's remarkable statement that someone who understands that God has a physical body is worse than one who serves idols. To appreciate Rambam's intention, we must consider Rambam's understanding of what idolatry is and what its origins are.

רמב"ם הלכות עבודה זרה פרק א הלכה א

בימי אנוש, טעו בני האדם טעות גדול ונבערה עצת חכמי אותו הדור ואנוש עצמו מן הטועים היה, וזו היתה טעותם, אמרו הואיל והאלהים ברא כוכבים אלו וגלגלים להנהיג את העולם ונתנם במרום וחלק להם כבוד והם שמשים המשמשים לפניו ראויין הם לשבחם ולפארם ולחלוק להם כבוד, וזהו רצון האל ברוך הוא לגדל ולכבד מי שגדלו וכבדו, כמו שהמלך רוצה לכבד העומדים לפניו וזהו כבודו של מלך, כיון שעלה דבר זה על לבם התחילו לבנות לכוכבים היכלות ולהקריב להן קרבנות ולשבחם ולפארם בדברים ולהשתחוות למולם כדי להשיג רצון הבורא בדעתם הרעה, וזה היה עיקר עבודת כוכבים, וכך היו אומרים עובדיה היודעים עיקרה, לא שהן אומרים שאין שם אלוה אלא כוכב זה, הוא שירמיהו אומר, "מי לא ייראך מלך הגוים כי לך יאתה כי בכל חכמי הגוים ובכל מלכותם מאין כמוך ובאחת יבערו ויכסלו מוסר הבלים עץ הוא" (ירמי' י:ז-ח), כלומר הכל יודעים שאתה הוא לבדך אבל טעותם וכסילותם שמדמים שזה ההבל רצונך הוא.

During the times of Enosh,[68] humanity made a great mistake, and the wise men of that generation gave thoughtless counsel.[69] Enosh himself was one of those who erred.

67. He writes this in many places. His formulation in his Introduction to *Perek Cheilek* (fifth principle) is ורוב התורה באה להזהיר על זה. We should add that Rambam in numerous places indicates that more than irradiating idolatry (in the narrow sense) the Torah seeks to uproot heresy. See 1:36 and 3:51. Thus, while idolatry, according to Rambam does not necessarily entail heresy, it is dangerously close.
68. According to the traditional chronology, Enosh, the grandson of Adam, lived from the year 235 after creation to the year 1140.
69. Note that it was not the commoners who instigated this error, but the wise men.

> Their mistake was as follows. They said that God created stars and spheres with which to control the world. He placed them on high and treated them with honor, making them servants who minister before Him. Accordingly, it is fitting to praise and glorify them and to treat them with honor. [They perceived] this to be the will of God, blessed be He, that they magnify and honor those whom He magnified and honored, just as a king desires that the servants who stand before him be honored. Indeed, doing so is an expression of honor to the king.
>
> After conceiving of this notion, they began to construct temples to the stars and offer sacrifices to them. They would praise and glorify them with words and prostrate themselves before them because they would – according to their false conception – be fulfilling the will of God.
>
> This was the essence of the worship of false gods, and this was the rationale of those who worshiped them. They would not say that there is no other god except for this star.
>
> This message was conveyed by Yirmiyahu, who declared (*Yirmiyahu* 10:7–8): "Who will not fear You, King of the nations, for to You it is fitting. Among all the wise men of the nations and in all their kingdoms, there is none like You. They have one foolish and senseless [notion. They conceive of their] empty teachings as wood"; i.e., all know that You alone are God. Their foolish error consists of conceiving of this emptiness as Your will.

Rambam rarely includes history in his *Mishneh Torah*. In this case, he does so because understanding the history of *avoda zara* is necessary to comprehend the nature of the prohibition. To appreciate how this is so, let us consider Rambam's thesis. Rambam asserts that those who initiated idolatry had a correct conception of God. Their error lay in the manner in which they suggested He be served. Instead of serving Him directly, they saw fit to serve His magnificent creations. Rambam continues to explain that this error proliferated throughout the world and led people to have a false conception of God, with only a handful of people continuing to serve God properly. This dreadful path continued until Avraham independently recognized the truth and began to spread God's message. Moreover, Avraham realized that serving intermediaries was what led people to their false beliefs: "What caused them to err was their service of the stars and images, which made them lose awareness of the truth" (*Hilchot Avoda Zara* 1:3).

Rambam maintains that while serving the sun with the belief that it is god certainly constitutes idolatry,[70] possessing a correct conception of God while simultaneously worshipping intermediaries, as in the case of Enosh's generation, also constitutes *avoda zara*:

> **רמב"ם הלכות עבודה זרה פרק ב הלכה א**
> **עיקר** הצווי בעבודת כוכבים שלא לעבוד אחד מכל הברואים לא מלאך ולא גלגל ולא כוכב ולא אחד מארבעה היסודות ולא אחד מכל הנבראים מהן **ואע"פ שהעובד יודע שה' הוא האלהים והוא עובד הנברא הזה על דרך שעבד אנוש ואנשי דורו תחלה הרי זה עובד כוכבים.**
>
> The **essence** of the commandment [forbidding] the worship of false gods is not to serve any of the creations: not an angel, a sphere, a star, one of the four fundamental elements, nor any entity created from them. **Even if the person worshiping knows that Hashem is the [true] God and serves the creation in the manner in which Enosh and the people of his generation worshiped [the stars] originally, he is considered to be an idol worshiper.**

Moreover, in *Moreh ha-Nevuchim* 1:36, Rambam writes that even after the generation of Enosh, the primary form of idolatry continued to be

70. In fact, technically speaking, simply believing the sun is a god would not constitute *avoda zara*. To violate the formal prohibition, there must be some sort *avoda* (act of worship), though a declaration of belief might suffice (see *Hilchot Avoda Zara* 3:4). Someone who believes the sun is god but does not actually serve it is classified as a *min* and perhaps a *mechareif u-megadeif* (see *Hilchot Avoda Zara* 2:6) but has not formally violated the prohibition of *avoda zara*.

the service of God through intermediaries, as opposed to a belief in the divinity of other beings:

> ואתה יודע שכל מי שעבד עבודה זרה, לא עבדה מתוך הנחה שאין אלוה זולתה, ולא דימה אדם מעולם בדורות שעברו, ולא ידמה מן העתידים, שהצורה שהוא עושה מן המתכות או מן האבנים והעצים, אותה הצורה בראה את השמים והארץ והיא המנהיגה אותם. ולא עבדום אלא על דרך שהם דמות לדבר שהוא אמצעי בינינו לבין ה'.

> You must know that idolaters when worshipping idols do not believe that there is no God besides them, and no idolater ever did assume that any image made of metal, stone, or wood created the heavens and the earth and still governs them. Idolatry is founded on the idea that a particular form represents the intermediary between God and His creatures.

Rambam then cites numerous verses to support his contention.[71] This explains how the Jewish people continued to struggle with idolatry even after they knew of God's existence. According to Rambam, there is no inherent contradiction between belief in God and *avoda zara*. In fact, Rambam argues that the Torah's prohibition against idolatry is a **safeguard** to prevent people from arriving at false beliefs.

In short, Rambam maintains that a person with a correct conception of God still can be in violation of idolatry. This is because he thinks idolatry primarily consists of serving God through intermediaries and/or worshipping anything other than God even while acknowledging the existence of the one true God. Thus, an idolater may have a correct conception of God even as he inappropriately serves other beings. We can now understand why, as mentioned previously, Rambam

71. It should be noted, however, that the simple reading of many passages in Tanach contradicts this understanding, and the majority of commentators likely to do not share Rambam's view of idolatry (see, for example, Ramban to *Shemot* 20:3). For Rambam, however, such passages in Tanach emphasizing the beliefs inherent idolatry should be understood hyperbolically (as *melitzot*).

maintains that a person who believes that God has a physical body is far worse than the idolater.[72] Even though he worships God incorrectly, the idolater nonetheless possesses a correct conception of God. The person who believes in a corporeal God, on the other hand, has an incorrect conception of God. As we explained earlier, since he serves and believes in a nonexistent god while ignoring the true God, he is worse than the individual who accepts God's incorporeality but worships intermediaries.

Idolatry Is a Waste of Time and Energy

Another theme Rambam frequently stresses when describing the perniciousness of idolatry (in the event that it is not associated with a theological error) is that it is a colossal waste of time and resources.[73] Idolatry and the erroneous beliefs associated with idolatry (e.g., magic), distract and mislead practitioners from focusing on that which is valuable and effective and can occasionally lead to a society's implosion.

---

72. **מורה הנבוכים חלק א פרק לו**
והיאך יהיה מצב מי שקשורה כפירתו בעצמותו יתעלה, והוא בדעתו הפך מכפי שהוא, כלומר: שאינו לדעתו מצוי, או שלדעתו הוא שנים, או שסבור שהוא גוף, או שהוא לדעתו בעל התפ־עלויות, או שמיחס לו איזו מגרעת שהיא, הנה זה בלי ספק יותר חמור מעובד עבודה זרה על דעת שהיא אמצעי או מטיבה או מרעה לפי דמיונו.

73. **איגרת הרמב״ם לחכמי קהל עיר מארשילייא**
וזו היא שאבדה מלכותנו והחריבה בית מקדשנו והאריכה גלותינו והגיעתנו עד הלום. שאבותינו חטאו ואינם, לפי שמצאו ספרים רבים באלה הדברים של דברי החוזים בכוכבים, **שדברים אלו הם עיקר עבודה זרה**, כמו שביארנו בהלכות עבודה זרה, **טעו ונהו אחריהן, ודימו שהם חכמות מפוארות ויש בהן תועלת גדולה, ולא נתעסקו בלמידת מלחמה ולא בכיבוש ארצות, אלא דמו שאותן הדברים יועילו להם**. ולפיכך קראו אותם הנביאים סכלים ואווילים. ודאי סכלים ואווילים היו, ואחרי התוהו אשר לא יועילו הלכו.
רמב״ם הלכות חמץ ומצה פרק ז הלכה ד
וצריך להתחיל בגנות ולסיים בשבח, כיצד מתחיל ומספר שבתחלה היו אבותינו בימי תרח ומלפניו כופרים **וטועין אחר ההבל** ורודפין אחר ע״ז, ומסיים בדת האמת שקרבנו המקום לו והבדילנו מן התועים וקרבנו ליחודו.
מורה הנבוכים חלק ג פרק ל
וכאשר נתפרסמו הדברים הללו [דברי הצאבה (מין ע״ז)] עד שנחשבו לאמת, ורצה ה׳ יתעלה ברחמיו עלינו למחות את הטעות הזו מלבנו, ולסלק היגיעה מגופותינו בביטול אותם המעשים **המיגעים שאינן מועילים**, ונתן לנו התורה על ידי משה רבנו.
My appreciation to Gabriel Gross for pointing these sources out to me.

10.10 RAMBAM'S VIEW ON PRAYING TO ANGELS

Because Rambam understands the prohibition against idolatry as rooted in serving intermediaries, the prohibition against idolatry also disallows serving angels. This can be seen in the fifth of Rambam's thirteen principles of faith, enumerated in his Introduction to *Perek Cheilek*:

> והיסוד החמישי שהוא יתעלה הוא אשר ראוי לעבדו ולרוממו ולפרסם גדולתו ומשמעתו. ואין עושין כן למה שלמטה ממנו במציאות מן המלאכים והכוכבים והגלגלים והיסודות וכל מה שהורכב מהן, לפי שכולם מוטבעים בפעולותיהם אין להם שלטון ולא בחירה אלא רצונו יתעלה, ואין עושין אותם אמצעים להגיע בהם אליו, אלא כלפיו יתעלה יכוונו המחשבות ויניחו כל מה שזולתו. וזה היסוד החמישי הוא האזהרה על עבודה זרה, ורוב התורה באה להזהיר על זה.
>
> The fifth principle is that God, blessed be He, is worthy that we serve Him, glorify Him, make known His greatness, and perform His commands. But we should not do thus to those that are below Him in the creation, not to the angels, stars, planets, or anything else. For it is their nature to act as they do; they do not wield independent power, nor do they have freedom of choice to act other than in the manner Hashem desires. Also, it is not fitting to serve them as intermediaries to God. Only to God should you incline your thoughts and your actions. This is the fifth principle, and it warns against idolatry; and most of the Torah warns against this.

That Rambam includes serving angels in the prohibition against idolatry follows naturally from his conception of the prohibition of idolatry. However, an obvious problem emerges. There is no prohibition against asking a person to pray on one's behalf. Indeed, in *Bereishit* 20:7, God instructs Avimelech to return Sara in such a way that Avraham would pray on his behalf. Why is asking an angel to bring one's prayers before God different than asking a person to pray on one's behalf?

Rambam, in the above citation, indicates that the distinction lies in understanding that humans have free will, while angels do not. Thus, asking a human to pray is no different than asking him to water one's garden. It does not constitute serving God through an intermediary. Angels, on the other hand, lack freedom.[74] [75]

The simple reading of this text indicates that all prayers to angels would be heretical. This leads some to understand that Rambam would

74. Praying to angels resembles the idolatry started by Enosh (and those who followed him). Enosh realized the sun that he served as an intermediary lacked freedom. He nevertheless served it as a means of glorifying God. Petitioning an angel, which likewise lacks free will, is essentially identical. (Remember, according to Rambam, the sun is also "alive.") What would Rambam say about a person who petitions angels because he thinks they do have free will? Is this a form of idolatry or not? Would Rambam distinguish by saying that since the person erroneously believes angels have free will his petitioning would not constitute idolatry since his request (according to his false understanding) is no different from requesting help from a human? If this would not constitute idolatry, would worshipping the sun as an intermediary while believing (mistakenly) that the sun has free will be in violation of idolatry? It is hard to believe that it would not. (Idolaters certainly believed that serving the sun was beneficial, though it is not clear if, according to Rambam, they believed it had free will.) Regardless, praying to angels is wrong. If the petitioner believes (correctly) that angels lack free will, then it constitutes idolatry. And if the petitioner believes (incorrectly) that they have free will, then at the very least he is making a major theological error and is possibly in violation of the Torah's proscription of idolatry.

75. One objection to Rambam's theory is the two examples in the Torah where it sounds like people made requests of angels: Lot (*Bereishit* 19:18–20) and Yaakov in his *bracha* to Yosef's children (*Bereishit* 48:16). Numerous commentaries on Scripture show how these verses should not be understood as prayers to angels.

While Rambam in the above passage indicates angels do not have free will, in *Moreh ha-Nevuchim* 2:7 he indicates that they do, writing, "for the spheres and the intellects apprehend their acts, **choose freely**, and govern" (אבל הגלגלים והשכלים משיגים פעולותיהם **ובוחרים** ומנהיגים). However, this type of choice is irrelevant in our context because their freedom is unlike human freedom: we can choose to do the wrong thing, while the "intellects and spheres are not like that, but always do that which is good, and only that which is good is with them… and all that they have exists always in perfection in practice." This can be seen from the beginning of the fifth chapter of *Hilchot Teshuva* where Rambam derives from Scripture that only humans have the capacity to choose between good and evil. According to Rambam, הֵן הָאָדָם הָיָה כְּאַחַד מִמֶּנּוּ לָדַעַת טוֹב וָרָע, means "the human species became singular in the world with no other species resembling it in the following quality: that man can, on his own initiative, with his knowledge and thought, know good and evil, and do what he desires." Thus, what Rambam means in *Moreh ha-Nevuchim* 2:7 is that angels have the conceivable ability to choose. This is similar to what he writes in Moreh ha-Nevuchim 3:17 that "all the species of animals move in virtue of their own will." Rambam there explains this is not meaningful free will, therefore it is permitted to slaughter animals to eat.

ban prayers such as the stanza *barchuni le-shalom* from the Friday night song *Shalom Aleichem*, which addresses angels and asks for a blessing, and the passage in Ashkenazi *selichot* (beginning with *machnisei rachamim*) in which angels are asked to bring a person's prayers before God.[76] This is especially problematic with respect to *barchuni le-shalom*, which is recited weekly by most Torah-observant Jews.

Some argue that these petitions indeed constitute heresy according to Rambam.[77] If one draws this conclusion, one might also wish to infer that normative Halacha does not accept Rambam's position in this regard, since these prayers commonly are recited. However, it seems troubling to conclude that most Jews are heretics according to Rambam. Moreover, in light of Rambam's rulings elsewhere, it is not at all clear that he would deem these prayers heretical. In fact, Rambam himself seems to sanction certain types of petitions to angels.

רמב"ם הלכות תפילה ונשיאת כפים פרק ז הלכה ה
וכל זמן שיכנס לבית הכסא אומר קודם שיכנס, "התכבדו מכובדים קדושים משרתי עליון **עזרוני עזרוני שמרוני שמרוני** המתינו לי עד שאכנס ואצא שזה דרכן של בני אדם."

Whenever one enters the bathroom, before entering, he should say [to the angels that accompany him]: "Be honored, holy, honorable ones, servants of the Most High. **Help me. Help me. Guard me. Guard me.** Wait for me until I enter and come out, as this is the way of humans."

76. A full treatment of this question lies beyond the scope of this chapter. See Maharal (*Netivot Olam, Netiv ha-Avoda,* Ch. 12), *Teshuvot Chatam Sofer* (O.C. 166), *Teshuvot Mahari Brona* (275), *Shibbolei ha-Leket (Rosh ha-Shana* 282), *Mor u-Ketzi'a* (O.C. 3), and R. Raphael Stohl's excellent article in *Yeshurun* (Volume 27) entitled שיטת הרמב"ם באמירת מכניסי רחמים, pp. 808–814.

77. See *Ishei Yisrael* (*Siddur ha-Gra*) on *Barchuni*. See also *Keter Rosh* 93 regarding R. Chaim of Volozhin's objection. See also *Sha'arei Rachamim* 26, who mentions R. Chaim of Volozhin's objection and the *siddur Eizor Eliyahu* who cites R. Chaim's objection (from *Keter Rosh*) and that R. Naftali Hertz ha-Levi from Yafo in his *siddur* (סידור הגר"א בנגלה ובנסתר) was not convinced that Gra objected. See also *Siddur R. Yaakov Emden* on *Machnisei Rachamim*.

Rambam rules that before going to the bathroom, one should address the angels that accompany him and ask them, "Help me. Help me. Guard me. Guard me." This ruling (based on *Berachot* 60b) seems to support the notion that certain types of petitions to angels are appropriate and seems to contradict Rambam's ruling in his commentary on the Mishna.

The solution to this quandary rests in a subtle distinction: Rambam prohibits only worshipping angels as a religious service. As he writes in *Hilchot Avoda Zara* 2:1 (cited above), שלא **לעבוד** אחד מכל הברואים לא מלאך ולא גלגל ולא כוכב. Likewise, in his commentary on the Mishna, he bans service (לעבדו), such as glorifying them (ולרוממו), or using them as intermediaries to reach God (אמצעים להגיע בהם אליו).[78]

It seems, then, that asking angels to help and guard a person does not constitute service (*derech avoda*). This may be why the above request concludes with שזה דרכן של בני אדם, "as this is the way of humans."[79] In other words, one simply is acting courteously towards the angels as opposed to worshiping them.[80] Perhaps the purpose of this request is

78. This distinction emerges internally from within Rambam. For example, Rambam seems to rule that one may not publicize the greatness of a star (שהוא יתעלה הוא אשר ראוי לעבדו ולרוממו **ולפרסם גדולתו** ומשמעתו ואין עושין כן למה שלמטה ממנו במציאות מן המלאכים **והכוכבים**). However, he certainly would not ban a mere description of the size, power, beauty, or purity of a star, because this does not constitute worship. Worship is only when serving **them** (i.e., the stars), as the initial idolaters did (לשבחם ולפארם ולחלוק להם כבוד). A similar distinction emerges from *Mishneh le-Melech*'s understanding of *Hilchot Avoda Zara* 3:6.

79. Another way to understand this phrase is that the need to relieve oneself reflects the weakness and frailty of the human condition.

80. Additionally, R. Yehuda b. Yakar (in his commentary to the *siddur*) and R. Meir ha-Me'ili of Narbonne (in the book *Milchemet Mitzva*, printed in the back of his *Sefer ha-Me'orot* on *Masechet Berachot*) explain that the phrase *shimruni* should be translated as "wait for me," not "guard me." According to this interpretation, there is no petition to an angel at all. While this is not the ordinary translation of the word *shamar*, a precedent can be found in *Bereishit* 27:11, "ואביו שמר את הדבר." (While this renders the next phrase, המתינו לי, redundant, it is very likely that Rambam's text of the Talmud did not include this phrase, as it is missing from the Bodleian MS. Huntington 80).

Another possible interpretation is put forth by R. Manoach, an early commentator on Rambam, who writes that this prayer is not directed to angels, but to certain intellectual faculties. By saying this "prayer" before entering the lavatory, a person actually is reinforcing (to himself) that he should not be fully using his rational

to remind a person of the angels that constantly accompany him, i.e., God's protection of him.

What remains unclear is whether Rambam would ban prayers like *barchuni le-shalom* and *machnisei rachamim*. Certainly with respect to *barchuni le-shalom,* a strong case can be made that it should be permitted. Just like it is good manners to address one's accompanying angels and ask them to "help me" and "guard me" before relieving oneself, it is likewise permissible, when bidding farewell to the angels that have accompanied a person home on Friday night, to tell them "Go in peace and bless me." The value of singing *shalom aleichem* is not for the angels (they do not need our hospitality), but to remind us that there are angels that accompany us as we enter our home on Shabbat evening.

The permissibility of *machnisei rachamim* is more ambiguous. This prayer, prima fascia, reflects a petition towards an intermediary, which Rambam would certainly forbid. Nevertheless, one might suggest that it too is meant to reinforce awareness in the cosmic order whereby angels bring our prayers before God. By reminding the angels to do their job, we remind ourselves of our own insignificance and dependency.[81] As such, the statement is not *derech avoda* and therefore permissible.

10.11 APPENDIX A: RAMBAM'S PERSPECTIVE ON EXPUNGING INNOCENT HERETICS AND THE PURPOSE OF PUNISHING WRONGDOERS

In 10.1, we examined Rambam's statement that those with a false conception of God (the second group in the palace analogy) are worse than those who deny God entirely (the first group). We suggested that Rambam means they are more dangerous to society than the first class in that they may lead others astray by spreading their false beliefs. There is no such fear concerning the first class. Rambam goes further, writing that under certain circumstances, it may be necessary to kill the people of this class in order to prevent them from misleading others. In other words, even though people

---

faculties while in there (presumably because one is not permitted to study Torah in the bathroom) but at the same time does not want to abandon them completely.

81. Whether Rambam would have agreed to such a notion is irrelevant. Our question is whether Rambam would have viewed a prayer with this intention as heretical.

of this class are not necessarily responsible for their false doctrines–after all, their teachers have misinformed them–they pose a grave danger to society, and thus it is necessary, at times, to exterminate them.

We should stress that this law no longer is relevant. One reason for this is expressed by *Chazon Ish*.[82]

Rambam's comments in *Moreh ha-Nevuchim* (3:51) correspond to his theory concerning *tinok she-nishba*, which states that those not responsible for their false beliefs are not deemed heretics (a category with certain halachic ramifications), since they cannot be fully blamed for their errors. We will present Rambam's view on this matter in section 11.10, where we shall see how Rambam distinguishes between these innocent heretics and other types of heretics. For example, we do not ostracize the *tinok she-nishba*, but instead warmly try to bring him near and teach him the truth. Here, however, let us note that Rambam also writes that even though they are innocent, sometimes there still is a need to eliminate such people lest they mislead the rest of the community. This particular point is omitted from most printed editions of Rambam.

רמב"ם הלכות ממרים פרק ג הלכות א-ג
מי שאינו מודה בתורה שבעל פה אינו זקן ממרא האמור בתורה, אלא הרי זה בכלל האפיקורוסין ומיתתו בכל אדם.

---

82. **חזון איש יורה דעה סימן ב' סוף סעיף ט"ז**
ונראה דאין דין מורידין אלא בזמן שהשגחתו ית' גלויה כמו בזמן שהיו נסים מצויין ומשמש בת קול, וצדיקי הדור היו תחת השגחה פרטית הנראית לעין כל, והכופרין אז הוא בנליזות מיוחדות בהטיית היצר לתאוות והפקרות, ואז היה ביעור רשעים גדרו של עולם שהכל ידעו כי הדחת הדור מביא פורעניות לעולם ומביא דבר וחרב ורעב בעולם, אבל בזמן ההעלם שנכרתה האמונה מן דלת העם אין במעשה הורדה גדר הפרצה אלא הוספת הפרצה שיהיה בעיניהם כמעשה השחתה ואלמות ח"ו וכיון שכל עצמנו לתקן, אין הדין נוהג בשעה שאין בו תיקון ועלינו להחזירם בעבותות אהבה ולהעמידם בקרן אורה במה שידינו מגעת.
Rambam presumably would not have agreed to this as he implies that these principles applied in his days, even though they too were a time of divine hiddenness. See also *Igrot Moshe* O.C. 4:91:6 who takes for granted that the laws of מורידין ואין מעלין would not apply to followers of the Conservative movement, even though they are considered heretics. He also implies they would have a share in the world to come insofar as they are not responsible for their heresy, and are considered a *tinok she-nishba*, a concept we will discuss in Chapter 11.

מאחר שנתפרסם שהוא כופר בתורה שבעל פה מורידין אותו ולא מעלין והרי הוא כשאר כל האפיקורוסין והאומרין אין תורה מן השמים והמוסרין והמומרין, שכל אלו אינם בכלל ישראל ואין צריך לא לעדים ולא התראה ולא דיינים אלא כל ההורג אחד מהן עשה מצוה גדולה והסיר המכשול.

במה דברים אמורים באיש שכפר בתורה שבעל פה במחשבתו ובדברים שנראו לו, והלך אחר דעתו הקלה ואחר שרירות לבו וכופר בתורה שבעל פה תחילה כצדוק ובייתוס וכן כל התועים אחריו, אבל בני התועים האלה ובני בניהם שהדיחו אותם אבותם ונולדו בין הקראים וגדלו אותם על דעתם, הרי הוא כתינוק שנשבה ביניהם וגדלוהו ואינו זריז לאחוז בדרכי המצות שהרי הוא כאנוס ואע״פ ששמע אח״כ שהוא יהודי וראה היהודים ודתם הרי הוא כאנוס שהרי גדלוהו על טעותם כך אלו שאמרנו האוחזים בדרכי אבותם הקראים שטעו, **לפיכך ראוי להחזירן בתשובה ולמשכם בדברי שלום עד שיחזרו לאיתן התורה ולא ימהר אדם להרגן.**

A person who does not acknowledge the validity of the oral Torah is not the rebellious elder mentioned in the Torah. Instead, he is one of the heretics and should be put to death by any person.

Once it becomes well-known that such a person denies the oral Torah, he may be pushed [into a pit] and may not be helped to climb out. He is like all the rest of the heretics who say that the Torah is not of divine origin, those who inform on their fellow Jews, and the apostates. All of these are not considered as members of the Jewish people. There is no need for witnesses, a warning, or judges for them to be executed. Instead, whoever kills them performs a great *mitzva* and removes a stumbling block [from the people at large].

To whom does the above apply? To a person who denies the oral Torah consciously, according to his perception of things. He follows his frivolous thoughts and his capricious heart and denies the oral Torah on his own, as did Tzadok and Baitus and those who erred in following them.

> The children of these errant people and their grandchildren whose parents led them away, and those born among the Karaites and raised with their beliefs, are considered as a child who was captured [by gentiles] (*tinok she-nishba*) and raised by them (gentiles). Such a child may not be eager to follow the path of *mitzvot*, for it is as if he is compelled not to. Even if he later hears that he is Jewish and sees Jews and their faith, he is considered as one who is compelled against observance, for he was raised according to their mistaken path. This applies to those whom we mentioned who follow the erroneous Karaite path of their ancestors. **It therefore is appropriate to motivate them to repent and to draw them to the power of the Torah with words of peace until they return to the bulwark of Torah, and one should not rush to kill them.**[83]

We should note that there are those that argue that Rambam's ruling that "one should not rush to kill them" should not be understood as implying they should ever be killed. According to a number of prominent Acharonim, including R. Eliyahu Mizrachi (1455–1526, Responsa 57), Rambam maintained that the Karaites should never be harmed, provided they are not acting antagonistically.[84] R. Mizrachi cites a letter of Rambam to support his claim.[85] Even

83. This last phrase is absent from the Vilna edition of Rambam but appears correct in light of manuscript evidence.

84. **שו"ת רבי אליהו מזרחי (הרא"ם) סימן נז**
ואין לדקדק ממאמר "אל ימהר אדם להורגם" מכלל שראוי להורגם אחרי שהשתדל להחזירם בתשובה ולא רצו לשמוע, שהרי כבר דמה אותם לתנוק שנשבה לבין הגוים שאינו בן מות כלל ואף על פי שלא רצה לשוב בתשובה מדקאמר הרי הוא כאנוס ואנוס פטור ממיתה כדנפקא לן מההוא פרט לאנוס.

85. **תשובות הרמב"ם סי' תמט**
ובזאת יכון לנו לכבדם וללכת לשאול בשלומם אפי' בבתיהם ולמול את בניהם ואפי' בשבת ולקבור מתיהם ולנחם אבליהם.... דהנהו מילי דר' טרפון במינים דכפרי בעיקר נינהו ודמו להנהו דדרשי בהו חכמי' הרחק מעליה דרכך ואל תקרב אל פתח ביתה זו המינות והרשות ודמיאן להנהו דאיתמר עליהו המינים והמשומדים מורידין ולא מעלין אבל הני דהכא כל אימת דלא פקרי בחציפותא לא חשבינן להו כוותיהו ופלגינן להו יקרה ומלינן לבנייהו בשבתא כל שכן בחולא היכא דגזיר להו גזירתא דידן ועביד להו מילה ופריעה דדילמא נפיק מנייהו זרעא מעלייא והדרי בתשובה.

if we understand Rambam more literally, this need not imply that Rambam viewed Karaites as heretics, as many claim (see Radvaz and Maharit discussed in 11.10). While the letter of the law does not dictate they should be killed, Rambam may understand that sometimes people are punished for the betterment of society. In fact, Rambam maintains that the primary purpose of all punishments carried out by human beings is deterrence. (This contrasts with divine justice, which necessarily is perfect.) Under current consideration is to what extent an individual may be sacrificed for the betterment of society. On the one hand, the individual is in fact guilty of heresy. On the other hand, he is not at fault, since he has been misguided.

Another source that highlights the Torah's perspective on punishments meted out by courts is *Moreh ha-Nevuchim* 3:35. Rambam classifies all *mitzvot* into 14 categories, the sixth being punishments. Rambam then summarizes the purpose of this class:

> הקבוצה הששית כוללת את המצוות התלויות בעונשין, כגון דין גנב וגזלן, ודין עדים זוממין, ורוב מה שמנינו בספר שופטים. **ותועלת אלה פשוטה וברורה, לפי שאם לא יענש המזיק לא יסתלקו הנזקים כלל, ולא ירתע כל מי שזומם להרע.** ולא כקלות דעת מי שדימה כי זניחת העונשין רחמים על בני אדם, אלא היא עצם האכזריות עליהם והפסד סדר המדינה, אלא הרחמים מה שציווה בו יתעלה: שופטים ושוטרים תתן לך בכל שעריך.

> The sixth class comprises the commandments concerned with punishments, such as laws concerning thieves and robbers and laws concerning false witnesses – in fact, most of the matters we have enumerated in the *Book of Judges* (*Sefer Shoftim*). **The utility of this is clear and manifest, for if a criminal is not**

In this letter, Rambam advocates not only pitying love and toleration, but honor, respect, and friendship. Some scholars question the authenticity of the letter. Dr. Isadore Twersky, *Introduction to the Code of Maimonides* (Yale UP, 1980, p. 85) and R. Kapach (in his comments to *Chullin* 1:2) both accept the authenticity of the letter. R. Yitzchak Shilat, on the other hand, argues it is a forgery (*Igrot ha-Rambam* pgs. 668–669).

> **punished, injurious acts will not be abolished in any way, and none of those who scheme evil will be deterred.** Not like the weak-minded suppose that the abolition of punishments would be merciful on men. On the contrary, this would be cruelty itself on them as well as the ruin of the order of society. Mercy is to be found in His command, may He be exalted: "You shall appoint judges and officers in all of your gates" (*Devarim* 16:18).

Rambam writes that the purpose of punishments is deterrence – the threat of punishment deters people from engaging in illegal acts. He does not mention restitution or retribution. Elsewhere, Rambam writes that this is true not just with respect to punishments of individuals, but also with respect to nations.[86] However, a balance always must be maintained between protection of the individual and promoting

86. Thus, he writes in *Moreh ha-Nevuchim* 3:41:

> The section on judges also includes the commandment to blot out the memory of Amaleik. The same way one individual is punished, so too a whole family or a whole nation must be punished in order that other families shall hear and be afraid and not accustom themselves to practice mischief, for they will worry they may suffer in the same way as those people have suffered; and if there be found among them a wicked, mischievous man, who cares neither for the evil he brings upon himself nor for that which he causes to others, he will not find anyone in his family ready to help him in his evil designs.

Rambam does not mean we sacrifice justice for the sake of deterrence. Only one deserving of death is punished. (Even in the case of Amaleik, Rambam, *Hilchot Melachim,* Ch. 6, maintains that peace must be offered before war commences.) Rather, societal benefit is one of the factors in determining who is punished. Later in Chapter 41, he writes that there are four factors that determine the nature of a punishment:

1. The greatness of the sin. Actions that cause great harm are punished severely, while actions that cause little harm are punished less severely.
2. The frequency of the crime. A crime that is committed frequently must be put down by severe punishment; crimes of rare occurrence may be suppressed by a lenient punishment.
3. The amount of temptation. Only fear of a severe punishment restrains us from actions for which there exists a great temptation, because we have a great desire for these actions, are accustomed to them, or feel unhappy without them.
4. The facility of doing the act secretly, unseen and unnoticed. We are deterred from such acts only by the fear of a great and terrible punishment.

societal perfection.[87] Thus, initially we draw the Karaite near, hoping he will repent; we should not rush to kill him despite the danger he poses. Nevertheless, at a certain point, another course of action may be necessary.[88]

---

87. In *Moreh ha-Nevuchim* 3:34, Rambam writes:

> The Torah does not take into account exceptional circumstances; it is not based on conditions that rarely occur. Whatever the Torah teaches, whether it be of an intellectual, moral, or practical character, is founded on that which is the rule and not on that which is the exception. **It ignores the injury that might be caused to a single person through a certain maxim or a certain divine precept.** For the Torah is a divine institution, and [in order to understand its operation,] we must consider how in nature, the various forces produce benefits that are general but in some solitary cases cause injury as well.

88. In this case, there may be an additional factor. The primary reason we maintain warm relations with the Karaites is our hope they or their progeny will return. Thus, if they are causing more harm than good, a different stance must be taken:

תשובות הרמב״ם (מהדו׳ בלאו כרך ב סי׳ תמ״ט)

אלה הקראים השוכנים פה וכו׳ ראויים הם לחלקם מחלקי הכבוד להתקרב אצלם במעשה יושר ולהתנהג עמהם במדת הענוה ובדרך האמת והשלום כל זמן שגם הם ינהגו עמנו בתמימות ויסורו מהם עקשות פה ולזות שפה מלדבר תועה על חכמי הרבנים שבדור וכ״ש כשישמרו לשונם מלהתלוצץ ומלהלעיג בדברי רבותינו ע״ה הקדושים התנאים...ובזאת יכון לנו לכבדם וללכת לשאול בשלומם אפי׳ בבתיהם למול את בניהם ואפי׳ בשבת ולקבור מתיהם ולנחם אבליהם. וראיה לדבר הוא דתנן בגיטין פר׳ הנזקין בסופו, מחזיקין ידי גוים בשביעית אבל לא ידי ישראל, ושואלין בשלומם מפני דרכי שלום...ותניא לא ילך אדם בביתו של גוי ביום אידו ליתן לו שלום וכו׳, ש״מ דשלא ביום אידו מותר ללכת בביתו ולשאול בשלומו ומעשים רבים בתלמוד יוכיחו...ואם בעובדי ע״ז כן קל וחומר במי שכופר בכל חוקי הגוים ומודה בא-ל יתעלה שמו שמותר לנו לשאול בשלומם ואפי׳ בבתיהם...ואם נפש אדם לומר האי דר׳ טרפון שאיתיה במס׳ שבת (קטז.) וכו׳ שאפי׳ רדף רודף אחריו להורגו ורץ נחש אחריו לנשכו אל יכנס בבתיהם וכו׳, האי לא קשיא מידי, דהנהו מילי דר׳ טרפון במינים דכפרי בעיקר נינהו וכו׳ ודמיאן להנהו דאיתמר עליהו המינים והמשומדים מורידין ולא מעלין, אבל הני דהכא כל אימת דלא פקרי בחציפותא לא חשבינן להו כוותיהו **ופלגינן להו יקרה ומלינן לבנייהו בשבתא וכו׳ דדילמא נפיק מנייהו זרעא מעלייא והדרי בתשובה.** והכי אשכחינן ליה לרבי׳ האיי גאון זצ״ל דאמר הכי, ולעניין מילה מעולם לא נמנעו רבותי׳ ע״ה מלמול את בניהם של קראים בשבת **כי אפשר שיחזרו אל המוטב** ואין מעבירין עליהם...ותניא מפרנסין עניי גוים עם עניי ישראל מפני דרכי שלום ומבקרין חולי גוים עם חולי ישראל וכו׳ כל שכן אלו שהן מתולעת יעקב.

Interestingly, R. Shilat disagrees with R. Kapach and argues that this letter is a forgery.

10.12 APPENDIX B: RAMBAM'S FIERY PASSION AND HIS UNDERSTANDING OF THE *MITZVA* OF LOVING GOD

In the final sections of 10.1, we considered Rambam's description of how the pinnacle of divine service involves a transcendent experience that results in passionate love of God. However, it is equally clear that Rambam does not believe that only someone who has reached that level loves God. Rather, as we saw in 3:51, knowledge of God at every level is associated with love: "The degree of love corresponds to the degree of understanding." Rambam stresses this alliance in his halachic works as well when explicating the various methods of achieving love:

> **ספר המצוות לרמב"ם מצות עשה ג**
> והמצוה השלישית היא שצונו לאהבו יתעלה וזה **שנתבונן** ונשכיל מצותיו ופעולותיו עד שנשיגהו ונתענג בהשגתו תכלית התענוג וזאת היא האהבה המחוייבת.
>
> And the third command is that we are commanded to love God. This means we must **contemplate** and consider His *mitzvot* and His actions in order that we may understand Him and take supreme pleasure in understanding Him; this is the love that is commanded.
>
> **הלכות יסודי התורה פרק ב הלכות א–ב**
> והיאך היא הדרך לאהבתו ויראתו: בשעה **שיתבונן** האדם במעשיו וברואיו הנפלאים הגדולים, ויראה מהם חכמתו שאין לה ערך ולא קץ - מיד הוא אוהב ומשבח ומפאר ומתאווה תאווה גדולה לידע השם הגדול, כמו שאמר דויד "צמאה נפשי, לאלוהים - לאל חי" **וכשמחשב** בדברים האלו עצמן, מיד הוא נרתע לאחוריו, ויירא ויפחד ויידע שהוא בריה קטנה שפלה אפלה, עומד בדעת קלה מעוטה לפני תמים דעות.
>
> What is the way to cultivate love and fear God? When one **contemplates** the great wonders of God's works and creations and sees that they are a product of a wisdom that has no bounds or limits, he immediately will love, laud, and glorify [God]. He will yearn with an immense passion to know God, like [King] David said, "My soul thirsts for God, for the living God" (*Tehillim* 42:3).

> And when one **thinks** about these matters, he immediately will feel a great fear and trepidation. He will know that he is a low and insignificant creation with hardly an iota of intelligence compared to that of God.

> **רמב"ם הלכות תשובה פרק י הלכה ו**
> דבר ידוע וברור שאין אהבת הקב"ה נקשרת בלבו של אדם עד **שישגה בה תמיד** כראוי ויעזוב כל מה שבעולם חוץ ממנה, כמו שצוה ואמר בכל לבבך ובכל נפשך, **אינו אוהב הקב"ה אלא בדעת שידעהו, ועל פי הדעה תהיה האהבה אם מעט מעט ואם הרבה הרבה, לפיכך צריך האדם ליחד עצמו להבין ולהשכיל בחכמות ותבונות המודיעים לו את קונו** כפי כח שיש באדם להבין ולהשיג כמו שבארנו בהלכות יסודי התורה.

> It is well-known and clear that the love of God will not become affixed to a person's heart until **he becomes obsessed with it at all times**, abandoning all things in the world except for it. This was implied by the command ["Love God, your Lord,] with all your heart and all your soul" (*Devarim* 6:5). **One can love God only [as an outgrowth] of the knowledge with which he knows Him. The degree of one's love depends on the degree of one's knowledge! A small [amount of knowledge arouses] a lesser love. A greater [amount of knowledge arouses] a greater love. Therefore, it is necessary for a person to focus himself in order to understand and conceive wisdom and concepts that make his Creator known to him according to the potential that man possesses to understand and comprehend**, as we explained in *Hilchot Yesodei ha-Torah.*

One cannot help but be swept up in the fiery passion of Rambam's description. Any thought that Rambam was a dry, dispassionate intellectual is immediately dispelled. Though each of the above formulations is distinct with subtle but significant differences, all three associate love of God with knowledge of God, and inform us that the path to – and the result of – loving God is contemplation of His ways and the study of Torah. According to Rambam, intellectual knowledge becomes intellectual love, and intellectual love triggers a thirst for more knowledge in an unending spiral of growth towards perfection.[89] Contemplation and study can trigger intensely passionate reactions. Thus, study and contemplation are not merely intellectual pursuits, but can be emotional experiences, which, as Rambam stresses, are associated with pleasure. In *Sefer ha-Mitzvot,* the commandment to love God is defined as this very pleasure: ונתענג בהשגתו תכלית העונג וזוהי תכלית האהבה המצווה, "And the pleasure one experiences in meditating upon Him is the epitome of pleasure, **and this is the essence of the love that is commanded.**"[90] Likewise, in *Hilchot Yesodei ha-Torah,* Rambam describes how contemplation leads one to praise and glorify the Almighty. Later (*Hilchot Yesodei ha-Torah* 4:12), Rambam elaborates:

> בזמן שאדם מתבונן בדברים האלו ומכיר כל הברואים... ויראה חכמתו של הקב"ה בכל היצורים וכל הברואים, מוסיף אהבה למקום **ותצמאה נפשו ויכמה בשרו** לאהוב המקום ברוך הוא.
>
> When a person considers these things and recognizes all of the creations… and perceives God's wisdom in all creatures and all creations, he loves God even more, and **his soul will thirst and his flesh will long** to love the blessed God.

Note how Rambam describes not just an intellectual and emotional experience, but one with physical reverberations as well – "his soul will thirst and his flesh (*besaro*) will long to love the blessed God."[91] Interestingly, Rambam in 3:51 writes: "And because of Moshe's great **joy** in that which he comprehended, he did not eat bread or drink water [while

---

89. Both nature and Torah are ways in which we perceive God and His will. Hence, sometimes Rambam emphasizes nature while elsewhere he stresses Torah.

90. This follows the Kapach translation. The ibn Tibbon translation is even more forceful: וזאת היא האהבה המחוייבת "and this is the love that is commanded."

91. Rambam is borrowing the phraseology of *Tehillim* 63:2. I do not know whether he intends this literally (i.e., to describe an emotional and intellectual reaction so strong that it has physical manifestations) or figuratively. Either way, the words convey the intensity of the longing a person should experience for his Creator.

on *Har Sinai*] for his intellect attained such strength that all the gross faculties in the body ceased to function."[92]

In *Sefer ha-Mitzvot*, Rambam informs us of the source in Chazal for this understanding of the *mitzva* of *ahavat Hashem*, loving God:

ספרי דברים פיסקא לג

״והיו הדברים האלה אשר אנכי מצוך היום על לבבך״. רבי אומר: למה נאמר? לפי שנאמר: ״ואהבת את ה׳ אלוקיך בכל לבבך״, **איני יודע כיצד אוהבים את המקום**, תלמוד לומר: ״והיו הדברים האלה אשר אנכי מצוך היום על לבבך״ - תן הדברים האלה על לבך, **שמתוך כך אתה מכיר את מי שאמר והיה העולם ומדבק בדרכיו**.

"And these things that I command you this day shall be upon your heart" – Rebbi said: Why was this said? Because it is written, "You shall love Hashem, your God with all your heart" – **I do not know how one loves God**. Therefore, it says, "And these things that I command you this day shall be upon your heart" – meaning, place these things upon your heart **such that you thereby will recognize He Who spoke and the world came into existence, and you will cleave to His ways**.

While all of the above sources emphasize the importance of the intellectual component in achieving love of the Divine, two practical points stand out. First, for love to be achieved, cerebral study must breed an emotional bond. Thus, contemplation and meditation must accompany study. Second, the value of diversification. One must study Torah, understand *mitzvot*, observe nature, explore science, and pursue philosophy. God speaks in many languages, and to experience love we must seek to understand them all.

92. Rambam implies that Moshe's not eating was not supernatural as much as a natural consequence of his connection to God. This state resembles Ramban's conception of *olam ha-ba* described in Chapter 19. Remarkably, Rambam implies that it was the joy associated with his comprehension that facilitated this achievement.

Chapter Eleven

Rambam's Perspective on Disbelief Resulting from Faulty Reasoning

In Chapter 1, we noted Rambam's insistence on the importance of maintaining correct theological positions. Rambam, therefore, organized what he saw as the thirteen basic principles of Jewish faith. They are presented in his commentary on the Mishna in his Introduction to *Perek Cheilek* (the tenth chapter of *Masechet Sanhedrin*).[1]

Rambam was the first to compose such a list, which prompts one to wonder why nobody had done so before. While this chapter is not the appropriate location to elaborate upon this question, it is worth

1. In a footnote in 5.8, we presented two approaches concerning the significance of these 13 principles. We suggested that these beliefs were significant in and of themselves, such that their denial constitutes heresy. However, we noted that others (see *Shut Chatam Sofer* Y.D. 2:356) maintain that it is not necessarily the case that all 13 are inherently significant. The reason their denial constitutes heresy is that denying ideas that have been accepted by the majority of the Sages constitutes a denial of Torah and, as such, renders the denier a heretic.

noting that Rambam also was the first to organize and systematize Halacha in his *Mishneh Torah*,[2] where he organizes rulings previously stated in a disorganized fashion throughout the Talmud.[3] Many of the classical commentaries understand the thirteen principles in the same vein. Just as Rambam wrote *Mishneh Torah* as a response to ignorance and inaccuracy in the field of Talmud and Halacha (as he explains in the work's Introduction), he codified the principles of faith as a response to ignorance and inaccuracy in matters of faith. In both cases, Rambam maintains that he was, for the most part, organizing material rooted in tradition and not innovating novel material.[4]

---

2. Both of the above statements are not technically precise. Prof. Marc Shapiro notes that there were some lesser-known earlier lists of beliefs. Likewise, there were some earlier codes (such as *Halachot Gedolot* dating from the Geonic period and attributed to R. Shimon Kayyara, who lived in the first half of the 8th century). However, no other author came close to the Rambam's comprehensiveness and influence. Thus, in a very real sense, Rambam was the first in both of these endeavors.
3. In his introduction to *Mishneh Torah,* Rambam writes that his decision to codify Jewish law was primarily a response to a contemporary need. Specifically, due to the complexity of Talmudic literature and the vicissitudes of the time, few people were able to arrive at the correct halachic conclusions. By organizing all of Jewish law, *Mishneh Torah* addressed that problem. For more on Rambam's motivation, see *Introduction to the Code of Maimonides (Mishneh Torah)* by R. Dr. Isadore Twersky (Yale University Press, 1980), pp 61–81.

   While Rambam does not explicitly state his motivation for compiling a list of core beliefs, R. Mayer Twersky suggested that, here too, codification is a response (and concession) to a national crisis. In an environment where tradition and belief are vibrant, parents need not explicate to their children the core beliefs by which they live and take for granted. However, when principles and values are challenged, articulation and codification become necessary. Matt Lubin added that this explains why Rambam (as noted in the next footnote) had to work so hard to uncover the principles. If these principles were well known and universally accepted, why was unearthing them so difficult? Part of the answer may be that, in codifying the principles, Rambam sought to explicate what had always been taken for granted. Mining a work for its implicit assumptions proves difficult, and determining what beliefs are fundamental is challenging. Thus, while the source material for Rambam's rulings in *Mishneh Torah* is generally explicit Talmudic statements, the precise basis of each of the principles of faith is less clear.
4. Rambam offers no clear explanation of his methodology in composing this list. However, he insists that the reader contemplate his ideas carefully for he, too, expended much time to gather the information contained in his work.

Our present concern, however, is to understand Rambam's position concerning the importance of correct beliefs. To do this, we must consider Rambam's definition of a heretic and an accidental heretic, terms which, as we shall see, have halachic as well as philosophical implications.

At the outset, one is troubled by the notion of an accidental heretic. Why would we brand a person who arrives at heretical views after an honest search as a heretic if his error is reached through no fault of his own? On the other hand, if we claim that there is no such thing as accidental heresy (i.e., we conclude that accidental heresy is not considered heresy), then we are, it would seem, claiming there is almost no such thing as heresy, since most people arrive at heretical beliefs without malicious intent. Especially troubling is determining the status of a person who arrives at false beliefs through a misunderstanding of the Torah. For example, what happens if a person believes that God has a physical body based on a literal understanding of "for with a mighty hand God took you out of Egypt" (*Shemot* 13:9) and other similar verses?[5]

פירוש המשנה לרמב"ם מסכת סנהדרין פרק י

וכבר הארכתי בדברים מאד ויצאתי מענין חבורי, אלא שעשיתי כן לפי שראיתי שזה תועלת באמונה לפי שאני אספתי לך דברים רבים מועילים המפוזרים בחבורים רבים וגדולים, היה בהם מאושר. וחזור על דברי אלה פעמים רבות, והתבונן בהם היטב. ואם תשלה אותך מחשבתך שכבר הבנת עניניו מפעם אחת או עשר, ה' יודע שבשקר השלתה אותך. ואל תמהר בו לפי שני לא כתבתיו איך שנזדמן אלא אחר התבוננות וישוב הדעת ועיון בדעות נכונות ובלתי נכונות, וסכום מה שצריך להאמין מהם ובירורו בטענות וראיות על כל ענין וענין, ומאת ה' אשאל לנחותיני בדרך האמת.

I find that I have prolonged my remarks very much and have departed from the main thread of my thesis. But I have been obliged to do so because I consider it advantageous to religious belief. For I have brought together for you many useful things scattered about in many collections of books. Therefore, find happiness in them, and repeat my discourse many times over, and ponder it well… And so do not go through it hurriedly for I have not composed it in random fashion, but after reflection and conviction and the attentive examination of incorrect views; and after getting to know what things it is incumbent upon us to believe, and bringing to my assistance arguments and proofs for every individual section of the subject.

5. Many of the insights that follow come from R. Raphael Stohl, though the conclusions articulated here may differ from his. Additionally, Gabriel Gross's excellent unpublished paper, "Infants in the Talons of Eagles: Inadvertent Heresy in Maimonidean Thought and Interpretation," which I read after writing this chapter, was very helpful.

11.1 RAMBAM'S DEFINITION OF A HERETIC

After listing the thirteen principles of faith in his Introduction to *Perek Cheilek*, Rambam writes:

> **וכאשר יהיו קיימים לאדם כל היסודות הללו ואמונתו בהם אמתית, הרי הוא נכנס בכלל ישראל**, וחובה לאהבו ולחמול עליו וכל מה שצוה ה׳ אותנו זה על זה מן האהבה והאחוה, ואפילו עשה מה שיכול להיות מן העבירות מחמת תאותו והתגברות יצרו הרע, הרי הוא נענש לפי גודל מריו ויש לו חלק, והוא מפושעי ישראל. וכאשר יפקפק אדם ביסוד מאלו היסודות הרי זה יצא מן הכלל וכפר בעיקר ונקרא מין ואפיקורוס וקוצץ בנטיעות, וחובה לשנאותו ולהשמידו ועליו הוא אומר הלא משנאיך ה׳ אשנא וכו׳.
>
> **And when a person believes all these fundamentals and his faith in them will be genuine, he enters into the nation of Israel**, and it is a *mitzva* to love him, have mercy upon him, and act towards him according to all the ways God commanded us regarding love and brotherliness. And even if he did all of the sins in the Torah due to desire of the emotions and from his evil inclination conquering him, he will be punished for his sins, but he still has a share in the world to come and is among the sinners of Israel. If, however, he **doubts** one of these fundamentals, he has left the nation and has denied the fundamentals and is called a heretic, a denier, etc., and it is a *mitzva* to hate him and to destroy him. And regarding him it is said, "Behold, will not the enemy of God be my enemy?" (*Tehillim* 139:21).

This startling idea is restated in the third chapter of *Hilchot Teshuva*. Rambam's statement seems very harsh. He seems to conclude that anyone who does not believe in these thirteen principles is excluded from the Jewish people and loses *olam ha-ba*, no matter what the cause for his disbelief. In fact, Ra'avad raises this very objection. Ra'avad comments on the following halacha:

> **רמב״ם הלכות תשובה פרק ג הלכה ז**
>
> חמשה הן הנקראים מינים: האומר שאין שם אלוה ואין לעולם מנהיג, והאומר שיש שם מנהיג אבל הן שנים או יותר, והאומר שיש שם רבון

> אחד אבל שהוא גוף ובעל תמונה, וכן האומר שאינו לבדו הראשון וצור לכל, וכן העובד כוכב או מזל וזולתו כדי להיות מליץ בינו ובין רבון העולמים כל אחד מחמשה אלו הוא מין.

> Five types of people are classified as *minim* (heretics): one who says there is no God nor ruler (or director) of the world; one who accepts the concept of a ruler, but maintains that there are two or more; one who accepts that there is one Master [of the world] but maintains that He has a body or form; one who maintains that He was not the sole First Being and Creator of all existence; one who serves a star, constellation, or other entity so that it will serve as an intermediary between him and the eternal God. Each of these people is considered a heretic.

Ra'avad comments:

> ולמה קרא לזה מין וכמה גדולים וטובים ממנו הלכו בזו המחשבה לפי מה שראו במקראות ויותר ממה שראו בדברי האגדות המשבשות את הדעות.

> Why has he called such a person (who believes in a corporeal God) a heretic? There are many people greater than and superior to us[6] who adhere to such a belief on the basis of what they have seen in verses of Scripture and even more people adhere to such a belief on account of what they have seen in the words of those Aggadot that corrupt correct opinion about religious matters.

Ra'avad claims that we cannot deem disbelief resulting from a faulty reading of Scripture or even a faulty understanding of Aggada as heresy. Accordingly, if someone concludes that God has a body due to his

6. Alternatively, this could be translated as "greater than and superior to him (Rambam)." R. Mayer Twersky advocated the translation in the text. In 11.11 we consider to whom Ra'avad might be referring.

misunderstanding of Torah, he cannot be classified as a heretic. As we shall see in section 11.9, others agree with Ra'avad on this matter.

In *Moreh ha-Nevuchim* 1:36, cited in 11.6, Rambam addresses this challenge writing that if we were to excuse those who believe in a corporeal God, we also would have to excuse the idolater. In both cases, the error emerges from faulty comprehension or faulty education.[7] We will present a number of approaches to Rambam's perspective on the innocent heretic in general and to this passage specifically.

Summary of the Four Approaches

Despite the fundamentality of this issue, I remain uncertain about Rambam's true position. Thus, several options will be presented. As we shall see, each perspective will have advantages as well as drawbacks. Our goal in this chapter is to try to understand Rambam, though his view may not be normative. Due to the confusing nature of the treatment, let us outline in advance the various possibilities we will consider:

- The first approach accepts the simple understanding of the passage from the Introduction to *Perek Cheilek*: Any denial (even if the person is blameless) of *any* of the thirteen principles automatically excludes a person from the Jewish people and *olam ha-ba*.
- The second approach distinguishes between principles: A false conception of God (or denial of the first five principles) automatically excludes a person from the Jewish people and *olam ha-ba* (even if the person is blameless). However, blameless denial of the other eight principles does not exclude a person from the Jewish people and *olam ha-ba*. (He would be categorized as a *tinok she-nishba*.)

7. The equation between corporeality and idolatry is consistent with Rambam's view that *avoda zara* merely is a mistaken practice (serving God through intermediaries), not a mistaken belief (see 10.9). R. Mayer Twersky noted that if one were to adopt the approach of Ramban (*Shemot* 20:3) that *avoda zara* is a rejection of monotheism (by acknowledging some sort of partnership or *shituf* with God), it would not make sense to equate idolatry to corporeality. According to this perspective, one could argue that idolatry is worse, and it would make more sense to pardon the corporealist than the idolater.

- The third approach distinguishes between repercussions: Any denial of any of the thirteen principles automatically excludes a person from *olam ha-ba,* but blameless denial of any of the thirteen principles does not exclude a person from the Jewish people because he would be categorized as a *tinok she-nishba. Tinok she-nishba* is a status that determines how we relate to the person; it has no bearing on his afterlife.
- The fourth approach categorically limits the scope of the passage from the Introduction to *Perek Cheilek*: Truly blameless denial of *any* of the thirteen principles does *not* exclude a person from either *olam ha-ba* or the Jewish people. Rambam's statements excluding heretics from *olam ha-ba* or the Jewish people is referring to people who should have known better and are negligent.

11.2 FIRST APPROACH: THE "*NEBECH APIKORES*" IS BOTH EXCLUDED AND DENIED *OLAM HA-BA*

As noted, the simple reading of Rambam implies that anyone who does not believe in the thirteen principles is excluded from the Jewish people and loses *olam ha-ba* no matter what the cause for his disbelief. We wondered what would account for the harshness of this conclusion, especially since we generally assume that a person is not held accountable for sins that are beyond his control (*oneis rachmana patrei*; see *Zevachim* 108b).

Perhaps Rambam maintains that with respect to basic tenets of belief, it does not matter whether someone's error is innocent. True, a person may be blameless; however, when it comes to false conceptions of God (or perhaps all thirteen principles of faith), an innocent heretic also is deemed a heretic, with all that the term implies. The simple reading of the aforementioned passage likewise implies that one must believe in the principles to have a portion in *olam ha-ba*.[8]

---

8. וכאשר יהיו קיימים לאדם כל היסודות הללו ואמונתו בהם אמתית, הרי הוא נכנס בכלל ישראל, וחובה לאהבו ולחמול עליו וכו׳, ואפי׳ עשה מה שיכול להיות מן העבירות מחמת תאותו והתגברות יצרו, הרי הוא נענש לפי מריו **ויש לו חלק**, והוא מפושעי ישראל.

The most famous expositor of this position is R. Chaim Soloveitchik, who is said to have claimed that according to Rambam: "נעביך א אפיקורוס איז אויך א אפיקורוס," "*Nebech apikores*" (an unfortunate heretic) still is an *apikores* (heretic)." However, R. Soloveitchik's position does not appear in any of his published writings. Not surprisingly there is significant ambiguity as to what he actually opined. One possibility is that he favored the first approach, which we are about to develop. Other students, as we shall see in 11.6–7, maintained that he espoused the fourth approach.

Why Consider the Accidental Heretic a Heretic?

Why consider the accidental heretic a heretic? The likely rationale for this thesis is that in Rambam's view, which we explained in 10.6, belief in corporeality does not constitute belief in God whatsoever, because such a god does not exist. Thus, like the idolater, the corporealist prays to and worships a figment of his own imagination. Rambam deems such a person an accidental heretic insofar as he thinks that he believes in God while, in fact, he does not. In fact, the deity he believes in has nothing to do with God due to the centrality of incorporeality in defining God.

Still, we may object, it is not his fault. Why should he be punished? The answer, according to this view, is that Rambam maintains that the disembodied intellect achieves immortality through knowledge of non-physical beings garnered in this world. As such, a correct conception of God is a natural and necessary prerequisite to achieving *olam ha-ba* (as explained in Chapter 20). Thus, loss of *olam ha-ba* is not a punishment, which would be unfair, but rather a natural consequence.

Two Texts that Indicate that the Afterlife is Predicated Upon a Correct Understanding of God

Let us examine two texts that explain and seem to support this notion. In the first, Rambam defines the term *nefesh* or soul. The *nefesh* of a human being does not depend upon his body; even after death, when the body ceases to function, the *nefesh* continues to exist in a state that we refer to as *olam ha-ba*. This contrasts with what Rambam calls *neshama*, which is not the soul but the life force that all living beings share[9]; this life force ceases upon death.

Rambam writes that our unique *nefesh* is what allows us to understand non-physical things. Lower forms of life lack this ability. Man alone was given the intellectual capacity to recognize that even something non-physical can truly exist.[10] Thus, only man has the ability to believe in God. Moreover, Rambam implies that this ability to know God is what allows a person to experience eternal life.

הלכות יסודי התורה פרק ד הלכות ח–ט

נפש כל בשר, היא צורתו שנתן לו האל. והדעת היתרה המצויה בנפשו של אדם, היא צורת האדם השלם בדעתו; ועל צורה זו נאמר בתורה "נעשה אדם בצלמנו כדמותנו" (בראשית א:כו), **כלומר שתהיה לו צורה היודעת ומשגת הדעות שאין להם גולם,** עד שיידמה להן. ואינו אומר על צורה זו הניכרת לעיניים, שהיא הפה והחוטם והלסתות ושאר רושם הגוף, שזו תואר שמה.

ואינה הנפש המצויה לכל נפש חיה, שבה אוכל ושותה ומוליד ומרגיש ומהרהר. אלא הדעה – שהיא צורת הנפש, ובצורת הנפש הכתוב מדבר. ופעמים רבות, תיקרא זו הצורה נפש ורוח; ולפיכך צריך להיזהר בשמות, שלא תטעה: וכל שם ושם, יילמד מעניינו.

אין צורת הנפש הזאת מחוברת מן היסודות, כדי שתיפרד להם, ואינה מכוח הנשמה, עד שתהא צריכה לנשמה כמו שהנשמה צריכה לגוף; אלא מאת ה', מן השמיים היא. לפיכך כשייפרד הגולם שהוא מחובר מן היסודות, ותאבד הנשמה מפני שאינה מצויה אלא עם הגוף וצריכה לגוף בכל מעשיה, לא תיכרת הצורה הזאת, לפי שאינה צריכה לנשמה במעשיה – **אלא יודעת ומשגת הדעות הפרודות מן הגלמים, ויודעת**

---

9. As in *Bereishit* (7:22):

כֹּל אֲשֶׁר נִשְׁמַת רוּחַ חַיִּים בְּאַפָּיו מִכֹּל אֲשֶׁר בֶּחָרָבָה מֵתוּ׃

> Everything that had ***nishmat chaim*** (breath of the spirit of life) in its nostrils, of all that was on the dry land, died.

Rambam's distinction between *nefesh* and *neshama* does not correspond to the Kabbalistic understanding of these terms.

10. An angel is an example of a non-physical being. Rambam adds that by understanding beings like angels, a person, despite his body, can resemble angels.

בורא הכול, ועומדת לעולם, ולעולמי עולמים. הוא שאמר שלמה בחכמתו, "וישוב העפר על הארץ, כשהיה; והרוח תשוב, אל האלוהים אשר נתנה" (קוהלת יב:ז).

The soul (*nefesh*) of all flesh (including animals) is the form that it was given by God. The extra dimension that is found in the soul of man is the form of man who is perfect in his knowledge. Concerning this form, the Torah states: "Let us make man in our image and in our likeness" (*Bereishit* 1:26), meaning, **granting man a form that knows and comprehends ideas that are not material**, like the angels, who are form without body, until he can resemble them. [This statement] does not refer to the form of the body perceived by the eye – i.e., the mouth, the nose, the cheeks, and the remainder of the structure of the body. This is referred to as *to'ar* (appearance).

It is not the soul found in all living flesh that allows it to eat, drink, reproduce, feel, and think. Rather, knowledge is the form of this [dimension of] soul and it is concerning this form of the soul, that the verse states: "In our image and in our likeness." Frequently, this form is referred to as *nefesh* or *ru'ach*. Therefore, one must be careful regarding these names, lest another person err regarding them. Each name reveals its characteristics.

The form of this soul (*nefesh*) is not a combination of the fundamental [elements] into which it ultimately will decompose, nor does it come from the *neshama* so that it would require the *neshama*, as the *neshama* requires the body. Rather, it is from God, from heaven. Therefore, when the matter [of the body], which is a combination of the fundamental [elements], decomposes, and the *neshama* ceases to exist – for [the *neshama*] exists only together with the body and requires the body for all its deeds – this form (*nefesh*) will not be cut off, for this form does not require the *neshama* for its deeds. **Rather, it knows and comprehends knowledge that is above matter, knows the Creator of all things, and exists forever**. In his wisdom, Shlomo [gave this description]:

> "The dust will return to the Earth as it [originally] was, and the *ru'ach* will return to God who granted it" (*Kohelet* 12:7).

Possessing knowledge of the non-material, and especially of God, makes one non-material and, therefore, allows for eternality.[11] To better appreciate this, we must turn to another text, in which Rambam describes *olam ha-ba*. His description is based on the following Talmudic passage:

> **תלמוד בבלי מסכת ברכות דף יז עמוד א**
> העולם הבא אין בו לא אכילה ולא שתיה ולא פריה ורביה ולא משא ומתן ולא קנאה ולא שנאה ולא תחרות, אלא צדיקים יושבין ועטרותיהם בראשיהם ונהנים מזיו השכינה.

> In *olam ha-ba*, there will be no eating and drinking, no procreation, no commerce, no jealousy, no enmity, and no rivalry – but rather the righteous will sit with crowns on their head and enjoy the radiance of the *shechina* (divine presence).

11. What is so important about knowledge of the non-material? The answer is complex and rooted in Rambam's conception of the spiritual world and the means by which we can connect to God. To appreciate this, consider Rambam's description of prophecy in *Moreh ha-Nevuchim* (2:36). Rambam writes that a human being, due to his physicality, cannot directly connect to God. Rather, between God and the material world there are a series of non-material intellectual beings ("separate intellects") that have some sort of effect upon the material world. The active intellect refers to the lowest of these intellectual beings. Thus, Rambam writes: "Know that the true reality and essence of prophecy consist in its being an overflow overflowing from God, may He be cherished and honored, through the intermediation of the active intellect, toward the rational faculty in the first place and thereafter toward the imaginative faculty." In other words, there is a path that starts with God, passes through the separate intellects, and concludes with prophecy. A similar thing, though on a lower level, happens when a person considers and understands all non-material beings. While it might feel like thinking of God, Rambam understands that this sort of knowledge emanates from the active intellect and creates within man a type of intelligence that is eternal. To appreciate this, let us return to Rambam's distinction between *nefesh* and *neshama*. Rambam distinguishes between two kinds of intelligence; one is material and therefore dependent upon the body; the other is non-material and is a direct emanation from the active intellect. Rambam writes that this latter form of intelligence results from efforts of the *nefesh* to attain knowledge of the pure intelligence of God.

Rambam elaborates upon each detail of the metaphor. When the Talmud says there is "no eating and drinking," it is telling us that people will exist without a physical body. When it says that "the righteous sit," it means that their existence requires no form of strain or effort. The "crowns on their heads" represent the *knowledge* that they acquired while in our current physical world and by which they merited *olam ha-ba*. Rambam here focuses on intellectual achievements as the basis for *olam ha-ba*. Finally, when it says they "enjoy the radiance of the *shechina*," it refers to understanding God in a way that cannot be achieved as long as a person has a physical body:

הלכות תשובה פרק ח הלכות ב-ג
וכן זה שאמרו עטרותיהן בראשיהן **כלומר דעת שידעו שבגללה זכו לחיי העולם הבא מצויה עמהן** והיא העטרה שלהן כענין שאמר שלמה בעטרה שעטרה לו אמו, והרי הוא אומר ושמחת עולם על ראשם ואין השמחה גוף כדי שתנוח על הראש כך עטרה שאמרו חכמים כאן **היא הידיעה,** ומהו זה שאמרו נהנין מזיו שכינה **שיודעים ומשיגין מאמתת הקב"ה מה שאינם יודעים והם בגוף האפל השפל.**

כל נפש האמורה בענין זה אינה הנשמה הצריכה לגוף **אלא צורת הנפש שהיא הדעה שהשיגה מהבורא כפי כחה והשיגה הדעות הנפרדות ושאר המעשים** והיא הצורה שביארנו ענינה בפרק רביעי מהלכות יסודי התורה היא הנקראת נפש בענין זה.

Similarly, when they said that the righteous people have crowns on their heads, **they were referring to the knowledge by which they inherited a place in the world to come**. This knowledge remains with them, and that is their crown, as Shlomo said, "…with the crown that his mother crowned him" (*Shir ha-Shirim* 3:11). It also is written, "…and everlasting joy shall be upon their head" (*Yeshaya* 35:10) – this is not physical pleasure that they will receive, but rather the crown of the sages, i.e., knowledge. When they said that they will benefit from the radiance of the divine presence, **they meant that they will know and understand the existence of God in a manner that they could not while in their gloomy and paltry bodies.**

> Whenever the word "*nefesh*" is mentioned in this context, it refers not to the soul which needs the body, but **the form (*tzura*) of the soul (*nefesh*) which is the intelligence by which it attained knowledge of the Creator according to its intellectual power, and by which it attained knowledge of the non-concrete intelligences (separate bodies) and other works of God**, even it is the form which we have explained in the fourth chapter of *Hilchot Yesodei ha-Torah*. It is called "*nefesh*" with respect to this matter.

Rambam here reiterates his position that immortality is attained through the acquisition of knowledge of non-physical beings, especially the Creator. Furthermore, immortality is the continued life of the disembodied intellect, making the afterlife a simple and almost natural process. That is not to say that intellectual achievements are the only factor determining a person's place in the afterlife; Rambam frequently stresses good deeds (מעשים טובים) when determining who merits *olam ha-ba* (as discussed above in section 10.2). Rather, according to this theory, a correct conception of God is a natural and necessary prerequisite to achieving eternity.

To summarize, if this is the correct reading of Rambam (a presumption we question in 20.3), then someone who believes that God has a body cannot, by definition, experience *olam ha-ba*. This should not be seen as a punishment; after all, it is not his fault. It simply is a reality. Thus, Rambam (*Moreh ha-Nevuchim* 1:35) stresses the importance of ensuring that even young children have a proper conception of God. After all, eternality necessarily demands a proper conception of God, for without an accurate perception, the disembodied intellect cannot continue to exist without a physical body.[12]

---

12. If this indeed is the correct reading of Rambam, then Rambam's position appears highly problematic. For example, Chazal (*Sanhedrin* 110b) assume infants have a portion in *olam ha-ba* despite lacking a correct conception of God.

Some contemporary thinkers presume that R. Chaim's "*nebech apikores*" theory (the first approach) is normative. (See, for example, R. Shimshon Dovid Pincus's *Bereichot be-Cheshbon*, towards the end.) Interestingly, these very same thinkers reject the notion that *olam ha-ba* depends entirely on the acquired intellect. Presumably, though, the two points are linked.

An example of this first approach to Rambam'a view on accidental heresy can be found in the writings of Abarbanel.[13] He explains with an analogy. Just as someone who swallows poison thinking that it is food inevitably will be harmed despite not deserving it, so too the natural consequence of disbelief is to not partake of immortality.

Problems with the First Approach

One problem with this first position is that it seems to contradict Rambam's extension of the *tinok she-nishba* principle to matters that relate to the thirteen principles of faith. Rambam's position is explicated in 11.10, but, briefly put, Rambam maintains that a person who does not acknowledge the validity of the oral law is deemed a heretic and punished accordingly. However, this is true only if he "denied the oral law consciously, according to his perception of things," such as the first generation of Karaites. The "children of these errant people and their grandchildren whose parents led them away and those who were born among these Karaites and raised according to their conception are considered as children captured and raised by them." Since they are not responsible for their false beliefs, the legal consequences of heresy are not applied to them.

---

13. Abarbanel first cites the perspective that someone who arrives at false beliefs due to a misunderstanding of the Torah is not deemed a heretic. He rejects this view comparing the consequences of such disbelief to ingesting poison. Even if a person wishes to eat something healthy, they will nevertheless die if it is poison. Likewise, if someone tries to apprehend the truth by studying Torah, but ends up with a false conclusion on a fundamental principle of faith, they too shall die.

ראש אמנה פרק יב

אבל זה עם ההתבוננות מבואר הנפילה, דלדבריו כל כופר בכל עיקר לא לכוונה יהיה בעל העולם הבא. וגם אמונת צדוק ובייתוס שהם יבינו הדברים בתורה ובנבואה כפשטן, ויחשבו שהכוונה בהם מה שיבינֵיהו תהיה בלתי חולקת על ההצלחה האמיתית, לא נאמר שהם כופרים ומינים. ויהיה אפשר כפי זה שימצא איש בלתי מאמין בשום עיקר מהעיקרים ובשום אמונה מאמונות התורה ולא יקרא מין ולא כופר אם שהביאוהו אל זה סכלות ועורון והיותו בלתי מבין כוונת התורה.

והדברים האלה כולם לא יסבלם האמונה התוריית ושכל הישר. לפי שהדעת הכוזב, כשיהיה בעיקר מעיקרי האמונה כבר יסיר הנפש מהצלחתו האמיתית, ולא יביאהו לחיי העוה"ב, אע"פ שלא יעשה אותה בכוונה למרוד. כי כמו שהסם המות כשיאכל האדם אותו יכלה רוחו, ונשמתו אליו יאסוף, אע"פ שנאמר שאכל אותו בחשבו שהיה מאכל בריא ונאות, כן הכפירה ואמונה הכוזבת בענין עיקרי הדת, יגרשו נפש האדם וימנעוהו מירושת העולם הבא בלא ספק.

Thus, even though the second-generation Karaite denies one of the thirteen principles by rejecting the authority of the oral law, he is not treated as a heretic because he is not held responsible for his false beliefs; he simply was falsely educated from youth. This seems to contradict the assumption of the first approach that we classify a person as a heretic even if it is not his fault. Put differently, Rambam cannot be claiming that all heretics are by definition excluded from the Jewish people since he explicitly excuses certain types of heretics when they are not responsible for their error.

In the following sections, we present two ways to reconcile Rambam's position on *tinok she-nishba* with the notion that *olam ha-ba* is by definition impossible for the person with a false conception of God. Following this, we propose an alternative understanding of Rambam's position on the innocent heretic.

11.3 SECOND APPROACH: DIVIDING THE *IKKARIM*

One way to solve the *tinok she-nishba* problem is to suggest the following distinction. As Abarbanel asserts, Rambam automatically classifies as a heretic anyone who makes a major error concerning his *basic conception of God*. Thus, we cannot extrapolate from *tinok she-nishba,* which is a principle stated concerning mistakes in the conception of Torah, since Rambam might not apply this classification to mistakes in the conception of God. Specifically, this perspective would distinguish between the first five principles of faith[14] and the subsequent eight.[15] Regarding the

14. 1. The existence of God, who is perfect in every way and is the Primary Cause of all that exists
    2. God's absolute unity
    3. God's non-corporeality
    4. God's eternity
    5. The imperative to worship God exclusively
15. 6. Prophecy
    7. The primacy of the prophecy of Moshe
    8. The divine origin of the Torah
    9. The immutability of the Torah
    10. God's omniscience and providence
    11. Divine reward and retribution
    12. Mashiach and the messianic era

first five principles, Rambam maintains *nebech apikores* is an *apikores,* but concerning errors in the principles that do not imply a false conception of God, we consider the possibility of *tinok she-nishba.*[16]

At first, this option is quite compelling. After all, why is it that Rambam treats the believer in a corporeal god so harshly? Because he essentially is worshiping something that does not exist. True, he may not be at fault, but as we explained earlier, that is irrelevant concerning such beliefs, because one must necessarily have a correct conception of

13. Resurrection of the dead

16. Evidence for such a distinction may emerge from Rambam's differentiation between מין and הכופרים בתורה:

פירוש המשנה לרמב"ם מסכת חולין פרק א

ואמרו הכל שוחטין, ואפילו ישראל משומד, ויש לכך תנאים ואז תהיה שחיטתו מותרת, האחד שלא יהא עובד עבודה זרה, לפי שאמרו משומד לעבודה זרה משומד לכל התורה כולה. והשני שלא יהא מחלל שבת בפרהסיא לפי שהכלל אצלינו מחלל שבת בפרהסיא הרי הוא כגוי לכל דבריו. ושלא יהיה מין.

ומינים אצל חכמים הם הכופרים מישראל, אבל אמות העולם הרי קוראים לכופריהם בסימן היחס ואומרים מיני גוים. והם בני אדם אשר טמטמה הסכלות את שכלם והחשיכו התאוות את נפשם ופקפקו בתורה ובנביאים עליהם השלום מתוך סכלותם, ומכחישים את הנביאים במה שאין להם בו ידיעה, ועוזבים את המצות מתוך זלזול, והכת הזו היא כת של ישוע הנצרי ודואג ואחיתופל וגחזי ואלישע אחר וכל ההולך בשטתם שם רשעים ירקב. ויוודע שהאדם מן הכת הזו כגון שנראה מתבטל ממצוה מן המצות מתוך זלזול בלי שישיג באותו המעשה הנאה. האנשים הללו אשר זה תיאורם אסור לאכל משחיטתם, וכך אמרו תנו רבנן שחיטת מין לעבודה זרה פתו פת כותי יינו יין נסך ספריו ספרי קוסמים פירותיו טבלים בניו ממזרים. וכן מתנאי המשומד הזה שמותר לאכל משחיטתו שלא יהא צדוקי ולא ביתוסי והם שתי הכתות אשר החלו להכחיש את התורה שבעל פה כמו שבארתי באבות, ונעשה האמת אצלם הבל, ונתיבות האור חשך אפלה, בארץ נכוחות יעול, והם שקוראים אותם אנשי זמנינו היום מינים בסתם, **ואינם מינים לפי אמונתם אלא דינם לענין ההריגה כלומר המתחיל את השטה הזו בראשונה מדעתו הנפסדת כדין המינים, כלומר שמותר להרגם היום בזמן הגלות לפי שהם המבוא אל המינות האמתית.** ודע כי מסורת בידינו מאבותינו כפי שקבלוהו קבוצה מפי קבוצה כי זמנינו זה זמן הגלות שאין בו דיני נפשות אינו אלא בישראל שעבר עברת מיתה, אבל המינים והצדוקים והביתוסים לכל שינוי שיטותיהם הרי כל מי שהתחיל אותה השטה תחלה ייהרג לכתחלה כדי שלא יטעה את ישראל ויקלקל את האמונה, וכבר נעשה מזה הלכה למעשה באנשים רבים בכל ארץ המערב. **אבל אלו אשר נולדו בדעות אלה וחונכו על פיהן הרי הם כאנוסים ודינם דין תינוק שנשבה לבין הגוים שכל עברותיו שגגה כמו שבארו, אבל המתחיל הראשון הוא מזיד לא שוגג.** וכן מן המקובל בידינו המפורסם למעשה כי האדם שעושה עברה שהוא חייב עליה מיתת בית דין כיון שאין אנו יכולים היום לדון דיני נפשות מחרימין אותו חרם עולם בספרי תורות אחרי שמלקין אותו ואין מתירין אותו לעולם.

Rambam mentions *tinok she-nishba* regarding Sadducees and Karaites. Perhaps this is because they are אינם מינים לפי אמונתם.

God in order to be admitted to the afterlife. This rationale would not pertain to denial of *mashiach* (the twelfth principle) or resurrection (the thirteenth principle). Moreover, we might add that we are more likely to blame someone for errors in the first principles because their veracity can be proven, whereas subsequent principles are known to us only via revelation.[17]

This approach would resolve the question (asked by Radvaz, as will be discussed below in 11.9) regarding the Talmudic sage R. Hillel, who denied personal *mashiach*.[18] Seemingly, Rambam would have ruled that R. Hillel was a heretic for denying the twelfth principle; but how could Rambam classify a Talmudic sage as a heretic? If, however, Rambam distinguishes between false conceptions of God and other errors, the question dissipates, since R. Hillel's error was innocent insofar as it stemmed from a misunderstanding of the Torah.

Support for the Second Approach

Possible support for this distinction emerges from 3:28 where Rambam differentiates between beliefs necessary for ultimate perfection and beliefs necessary for political welfare:

17. If this is the primary reason for the distinction, we might distinguish between the first four and subsequent principles, as Rambam in *Moreh ha-Nevuchim* proves these principles. The fifth principle, which excludes the service of intermediaries, is known to us through revelation, like the subsequent eight. Additionally, we might also not be able to include part of the second principle, which, in the version that the Rambam changed after writing *Moreh ha-Nevuchim*, includes the belief that God created the world from nothing. As we noted in Chapter 3, Rambam maintains that this cannot be definitively proven philosophically.
18. R. Hillel, known as הלל נשיאה or Hillel II (so as not to be confused with Hillel the Tanna), was a fifth-generation Amora and held the office of *Nasi* of the *Sanhedrin* between 320 and 385 CE. In *Sanhedrin* 99a, R. Hillel states that the future redemption will not involve a messianic figure. Specifically, he says "אין משיח לישראל." Rashi explains that this does not mean that there will not be a redemption, but rather "הקב"ה בעצמו יגאלם בלי שליח." *Teshuvot Chatam Sofer* (2:Y.D. 356) demonstrates that this is the only possible explanation of this passage. Even given this caveat, R. Hillel's position violates Rambam's twelfth principle of faith, and anyone who accepts his view is a heretic.

> ...in regard to the correct opinions through which the ultimate perfection may be obtained, the Law has communicated only their end and made a call to believe in them in a summary way – that is, to believe in the existence of the deity, may He be exalted, His unity, His knowledge, His power, His will, and His eternity. All these points are ultimate ends, which can be made clear in detail and through definitions only after one knows many opinions. In the same way, the Law also makes a call to adopt certain beliefs, belief in which is necessary for the sake of political welfare. Such, for instance, is our belief that He, may he be exalted, is violently angry with those who disobey Him and that it is therefore necessary to fear Him and to dread Him and to take care not to disobey.

This paragraph supports the second approach by articulating the necessity of belief in His existence, His unity, His knowledge, His power, His will, and His eternity. On the other hand, this passage does not mention the necessity of belief in such things as the Torah or the resurrection.

This passage would fully validate the distinction suggested by the second approach if it corresponded to the first five principles of faith. However, it does not. While this passage articulates the necessity of belief in His existence, His unity, His knowledge, His power, His will, and His eternity, this does not definitively support the second approach because it does not correspond Rambam's principles of faith.[19] Rambam's list of 'ultimate-perfection' truths includes items which are not found in the principles at all (i.e., divine will) as well as beliefs which appear in the final eight principles (i.e., divine knowledge).[20] Moreover, non-corporealism is not mentioned at all among the necessary truths. Thus, this passage cannot serve as the basis for a distinction between the earlier and later principles of faith.

---

19. Gabriel Gross alerted me to this point.

20. The later eight principles of faith do not correspond to the second group of political beliefs either. The two examples of political truths mentioned by Rambam, namely the fact that God grows angry with sinners and (later in 3:28) that He responds immediately to petitionary prayer, do not appear anywhere in the list of principles.

Problems with the Second Approach

The clearest reason to reject the second approach is that the classic example of *tinok she-nishba* is a baby taken captive and raised by idolaters. Such a child certainly would deny basic principles concerning God. Clearly, then, a false conception of God does not preclude a person from the category of *tinok she-nishba*. Yet Rambam seems to agree that a *tinok she-nishba* does not have the halachic status of heretic. Moreover, the palace analogy from *Moreh ha-Nevuchim* 3:51 (as we saw in 10.1) does seem to apply the *tinok she-nishba* exemption to those who believe in a corporeal god.

Another problem with the second approach (as well as the first approach) is that Rambam writes in his Introduction to *Perek Cheilek* that someone who lacks belief in any of the thirteen principles is to be hated and destroyed, "חובה לשנאותו ולהשמידו." We must wonder why a person who innocently maintains a false conception of God should be excluded from the community of Israel and hated. Even if such a person cannot attain *olam ha-ba,* why should he deserve such enmity in this world?[21]

Most importantly, this approach is rooted in a distinction between the first five principles and the latter eight. Nowhere does Rambam make this distinction; he seems to equate all thirteen principles. Put differently, this theory (approach 2) is forced to concede that Rambam's statement in the Introduction to *Perek Cheilek* (cited above) that it is a *mitzva* to hate anyone who does not believe in these thirteen principles is not a categorical statement referring to all deniers, since it does not include those classified as *tinok she-nishba*. Rather, concerning the final eight principles, it means those who inexcusably violate these principles. Once we are forced to read the statement that way concerning the final eight principles, why not assume that the limitation applies to all thirteen principles? The same can be said concerning his comments in *Hilchot Teshuva*. Thus, approach 1 is problematic because it fails to account for *tinok she-nishba,* and approach

21. While this objection can be neutralized by responding that the animosity stems from the fear that people with problematic beliefs will lead others astray (Rambam frequently stresses this concern, such as in 3:51), this solution does not seem to account for the unmitigated enmity and lack of allowance for *tinok she-nishba*.

2 is problematic because it relies on a distinction contradicted by the simple reading of Rambam.

11.4 ADDITIONAL PROBLEMS FOR THE FIRST TWO APPROACHES

Another major problem for these two approaches is Rambam's theory in *Moreh ha-Nevuchim* 1:46 as to why the Torah describes God in terms that may cause a person to believe that He has a body. As we shall see, the following passage can be read in two different ways, which has significant implications concerning our question at hand.

> כך אירע בהודעת ה׳ יתהדר ויתרומם להמון **בכל ספרי הנביאים וגם בתורה**, כאשר הביא אותנו הצורך להורות ולהדריך את כולם על מציאותו יתעלה, וכי לו השלמויות כולן, כלומר: שאינו רק מצוי בלבד, כמו שהארץ מצויה והשמים מצוים, אלא מצוי, חי, יודע, יכול, פועל, ושאר מה שראוי להאמין במציאותו ויתבאר זה.
>
> **לפיכך הודרכו המחשבות על שהוא מצוי - בדימויי הגשמות; ושהוא חי - בדימויי התנועה. כי לא יבין ההמון דבר שמציאותו ודאית אמת שאין בו פקפוק כי אם הגוף**, וכל שאינו גוף, אלא שהוא בגוף, הרי הוא מצוי, אלא שהוא גרוע במציאות מן הגוף, מחמת שהוא זקוק במציאותו לגוף. אבל מה שאינו גוף וגם לא בגוף, אינו דבר מצוי כלל בשום אופן בראשית עיונו של אדם, ובפרט בדמיונו.
>
> וכן לא ישכיל ההמון מעניין החיות זולת התנועה, וכל שאינו בעל תנועה רצונית מקומית אינו חי, ואף על פי שאין התנועה מעצמות החי אלא מקרה חיובי לו. וכן ההשגה הידועה אצלנו היא בחושים, כלומר: השמע והראות. וכן אין אנו יודעים ומבינים העברת העניין מלב כל אחד ממנו ללב אדם אחר אלא על ידי הדיבור, והוא הקול שמחתכים אותו השפתיים והלשון ויתר כלי הדבור.
>
> וכאשר הודרכו מחשבותינו גם על היותו יתעלה משיג, ושיש עניינים מגיעים מאתו אל הנביאים שיביאום אלינו, תארוהו לנו שהוא שומע ורואה, עניינו שהוא משיג את הדברים הללו הנראים ונשמעים ויודע אותם. וכן תארו לנו שהוא מדבר, עניינו שמגיעים עניינים מאתו יתעלה

אל הנביאים, וזהו עניין הנבואה, ועוד יתבאר זה בתכלית הביאור. ולפי שאין אנו מבינים המצאתנו את זולתינו כי אם בעשותנו אותו בפועל, לפיכך תיארוהו שהוא עושה.

וכך גם כיון שאין ההמון מכיר דבר חי כי אם בעל נפש, תארוהו לנו גם שהוא בעל נפש, ואם כי שם נפש משותף כמו שנתבאר העניין שהוא חי.[22]

The same is the case with the information concerning the Creator given to the ordinary classes of men in **all prophetic books and in the Torah.** For it was necessary to teach all of them that God exists and that He is in every respect the most perfect Being; that is to say, He exists not only in the sense in which the earth and the heavens exist, but He exists and possesses life, wisdom, power, activity, and all other properties that our belief in His existence must include, as will be shown below. **The minds of the multitude accordingly were guided to the belief that He exists by imagining that He is corporeal and to the belief that He is living by imagining that He is capable of motion.** Because ordinary men consider only the body as fully, truly, and undoubtedly existing, while something that is connected with a body but is itself not a body, although believed to exist, has a lower degree of existence on account of its dependence on the body for existence. That, however, which is neither itself a body, nor a force within a body, is not existent according to man's first notions and is above all excluded from the range of imagination.

In the same manner, motion is considered by the ordinary man as identical with life; what cannot move voluntarily from place to place has no life, although motion is not part of the definition of life, but rather an incidental property connected with it.

---

22. The Hebrew text here is from the R. Kapach translation.

> The perception by the senses, especially by hearing and seeing, is best known to us; we have no idea or notion of any other mode of communication between the soul of one person and that of another other than by means of speaking, i.e., by the sound produced by lips, tongue, and the other organs of speech. When, therefore, we are to be informed that God has a knowledge of things, and that communication is made by Him to the prophets, who convey it to us, they represent Him to us as seeing and hearing, i.e., as perceiving and knowing those things that can be seen and heard. They represent Him to us as speaking, i.e., that communications from Him reach the prophets; that is to be understood by the term "prophecy," as will be fully explained. God is described as working, because we do not know any other mode of producing a thing except by direct touch. He is said to have a soul in the sense that He is living, because all living beings are generally supposed to have a soul; although the term soul is, as has been shown, a homonym.

Rambam writes that the reason why the Torah uses language that might confuse people and lead them to believe that God has a body is that these descriptions are necessary to bring the masses to belief in God. Since the multitude presumes that only something with a physical body really exists, the Torah uses words that can be understood as referring to the body of God. That is not to say that their interpretation is correct. It is wrong. The first sixty chapters of *Moreh ha-Nevuchim* are devoted to demonstrating that the correct interpretation of Scripture does not imply divine corporeality.[23] Rambam writes, however, that there is a purpose in writing in such a way that the Torah could be misunderstood as referring to God's physical body, since this mistake will bring the masses to belief in His existence.

---

23. Moreover, our knowledge of His incorporeality is not known to us only through philosophy, but also by explicit texts of the Torah:

הלכות יסודי התורה פרק א הלכה ח

הרי מפורש בתורה ובנביאים שאין הקב״ה גוף וגוייה שנאמר כי ה׳ אלהיכם הוא אלהים בשמים ממעל ועל הארץ מתחת, והגוף לא יהיה בשני מקומות, ונאמר כי לא ראיתם כל תמונה, ונאמר ואל מי תדמיוני ואשוה, ואילו היה גוף היה דומה לשאר גופים.

Now, if it is the case that someone who believes in God's corporeality is axiomatically excluded from the Jewish people and can have no share in the world to come, then the Torah's misleading statements are highly problematic.

One could deflect this objection by noting that even if we presume that *olam ha-ba* is definitionally impossible for someone who believes in a corporeal God, there still is value in bringing the masses to belief in a corporeal god, as it serves as a stepping-stone to the correct conception of God. As Rambam writes elsewhere (*Moreh ha-Nevuchim* 3:32), it is impossible to instantaneously go from one extreme to another. Accordingly, bringing the masses to belief in a corporeal god was a necessary evil.

The problem with this resolution is that it would mean that most of the Jewish people at this time were not truly Jews (המורדין הכופרין פחותין הן מן הגוים), that it was a *mitzva* to hate them (חובה לשנאותו), an obligation to kill them (מיתתו בכל אדם... מורידין ולא מעלין), and that they had no portion in the world to come. Moreover, this was true not just for one generation but, as Rambam notes, for the entire period of the Prophets. This seems highly unlikely, especially when the Prophets say that there were times when the masses of people followed in the way of God.[24]

If, however, we conclude that believing in a corporeal god excludes someone from the Jewish people and denies him *olam ha-ba* only if the mistake is inexcusable, then we can understand why there is value in initially bringing people to belief in a corporeal god. Put differently, if we reject the entirely naturalistic approach to the afterlife and presume that defensible heresy does not constitute heresy, then *Moreh ha-Nevuchim* 1:46 can be understood as saying that in the biblical period when, as Scripture indicates, most people struggled with idolatry, it may have been impossible for many people to conceive of an incorporeal God. Indeed, even belief in a single corporeal God proved to be a challenge. To combat this and eventually bring the masses closer to belief in God, the Torah is written in a way that can be understood as referring to a corporeal God. At some point, this no longer was the case. In 1:36, Rambam implies that human

24. There is one view in the Talmud that the generation who received the Torah had no portion in *olam ha-ba*; however, no body claims that this was true throughout the period of the Prophets.

progress, the development of philosophical tools, and the translations of Onkelos and Yonatan b. Uziel ensured that all (or nearly all) people now are capable of believing in an incorporeal God. When Rambam writes that a corporealist necessarily is a heretic, he is referring exclusively to this later period. This reading would be at odds with the first approaches.

However, *Moreh ha-Nevuchim* 1:46 need not be a refutation of the naturalistic approach to the afterlife. One can read *Moreh ha-Nevuchim* 1:46 in a way that mitigates the above objections. Perhaps Rambam simply means that the Torah implies that God has a body as a temporary and short-term measure. Initially (בראשית עיונו של אדם), it is difficult to conceive of something that exists with no tangibility. However, once a person arrives at the conviction that He exists, he must immediately move onto the next stage, where he is taught of God's incorporeality. Nobody should be left in that first stage, believing in a falsehood. Thus, even if we assume that a correct conception of God is a prerequisite for the afterlife, there is value in bringing the masses to belief in a corporeal god, as it serves as a provisional stepping-stone to the correct conception of God.[25]

To summarize: There are two ways to interpret Rambam's controversial thesis in *Moreh ha-Nevuchim* 1:46. The first reading presumes that belief in an incorporeal God was impossible for many people (the masses) during the biblical and prophetic period. Accordingly, Scripture is written in a way that implies God's corporeality, since it will, at the very least, bring these people to belief in one God, even if a false one. At some point, this no longer was necessary. Rambam in 1:36 writes that currently, tools like *Targum Onkelos* make believing in an incorporeal God indefensible. When Rambam writes that a corporealist necessarily is a heretic he is referring to this period. This reading would be in disagreement with Abarbanel's thesis.

The second reading of *Moreh ha-Nevuchim* 1:46 assumes that Scripture's use of corporeal terms was meant as a short-term fix. Because

25. Rambam compares this to the circuitous route the Jews took when they first left Egypt. A direct path towards their destination would have been much quicker, but the specter of military engagement, at this stage, would have frightened the Jews into returning to Egypt (*Shemot* 13:17). Likewise, when it came to teaching fundamentals of faith, the direct path would not have been the fastest. This stage, however, may have been only short-term.

the generation leaving Egypt (as well as those throughout the biblical and prophetic period) could not initially relate to an incorporeal God, it was necessary to first introduce them to a corporeal god. Once that was done, they could immediately be taught the truth. This reading would be consistent with Abarbanel's thesis.

11.5 THIRD APPROACH: DISTINGUISHING BETWEEN LOSS OF *OLAM HA-BA* AND EXCLUSION FROM THE JEWISH PEOPLE

A third resolution to solve the *tinok she-nishba* quandary is to distinguish between two applications of the status of heretic. One application is that the heretic is excluded from the Jewish people, and there is a *mitzva* to hate him. Another application is the loss of *olam ha-ba.* According to this approach, while it is true that a *tinok she-nishba* loses his share in *olam ha-ba,* he is not to be treated as a heretic in interpersonal halachic contexts.

How would this approach deal with the passage from the Introduction to *Perek Cheilek* that someone who denies any of the thirteen principles is *both* excluded from the Jewish people and denied *olam ha-ba,* seemingly equating these two consequences of heresy? One would have to conclude that this passage cannot be referring to a *tinok she-nishba* since a *tinok she-nishba,* despite rejecting one of the principles, remains part of the Jewish people and is to be loved. However, it still may be the case that a *tinok she-nishba* loses his share in *olam ha-ba.* Thus, it is only concerning *olam ha-ba* that one would claim accidental heresy constitutes heresy (*nebech apikores* is an *apikores*).

The rationale for this distinction would be, as explained earlier, that *olam ha-ba* is, by definition, inaccessible to someone with false beliefs. However, there is no reason why the *tinok she-nishba* would be excluded from the Jewish people, since he is not responsible for his false beliefs. Rather, we would seek to help him see the truth.

At first glance, this distinction appears reasonable, since in *Hilchot Teshuva,* Rambam writes that someone with false beliefs has no portion in the world to come but does not mention that he is excluded from the Jewish people. Thus, we can suggest that the exclusion from *olam ha-ba* in *Hilchot Teshuva* is categorical, whereas the exclusion from both the

Jewish people and *olam ha-ba* described in the Introduction to *Perek Cheilek* would not apply to *tinok she-nishba*.[26]

When Did Most Jews Learn of the Resurrection?

In his "Treatise on Resurrection" Rambam explicitly states that the masses were taught of the resurrection (one of the thirteen principles of faith) in the time of Daniel only after belief in the possibility in miracles (and a rejection of Sabian theology) had been firmly cemented among the people.[27] Thus, it seems clear that most Jews could not have possibly believed in all thirteen principles of faith until the time of Daniel. It is inconceivable that most Jews, until this time, were precluded from the afterlife.[28]

Seemingly, this question refutes the first and third approach. The second approach remains plausible, however, as we have noted, it has its own difficulties.

Evidence that the Innocent Heretic May Have *Olam ha-Ba*

Further evidence against the third solution emerges from the laws of testimony. Chazal list a number of people that are invalid witnesses, and heretics are not included in this list. Yet, Rambam rules that they are invalid. Why are they not listed? Rambam explains that their exclusion need not be stated because if non-Jews are excluded from giving testimony, then certainly heretics are excluded, since unlike non-Jews, they are killed and have no portion in *olam ha-ba*.

הלכות עדות פרק יא הלכה י

המוסרין והאפיקורוסין **והמינים** והמשומדים לא הוצרכו חכמים למנות אותן בכלל פסולי העדות שלא מנו אלא רשעי ישראל. אבל אלו המורדין הכופרין פחותין הן מן הגוים, שהגוים לא מעלין ולא

---

26. The question from *Moreh ha-Nevuchim* 1:46 would be less problematic according to this approach since, at the very least, the masses of the Jewish people of the biblical period would be considered Jews. However, it remains troubling to conclude that the multitude of Jewish people for this considerable period would lose eternality.

27. והתמיד העניין כן, עד שנתחזקו אלו הפינות והתאמתו בהמשך הדורות, ולא נשאר ספק בנבואות הנביאים ובחידוש המופתים. ואחרי כן ספרו לנו הנביאים מה שהודיעם ה׳ יתעלה מעניין תחיית המתים, והיה קל לקבלו.

28. My appreciation to R. Avrohom A. Elias for pointing this out to me.

מורידין ויש לחסידיהן חלק לעולם הבא, ואלו מורידין ולא מעלין ואין להם חלק לעוה״ב.

> Our Sages had no need to list informers, infidels, **heretics**, and apostates among those who are not acceptable as witnesses. For they listed only the wicked among the Jewish people. These rebellious deserters of the faith are inferior to the gentiles, for while gentiles need not be saved from a pit, they should not be pushed into one, and the pious among them will receive a share in the world to come. However, [these deserters of the faith] should be pushed into a pit and not saved from one, and they will not receive a portion in the world to come.

Now, Rambam rules (*Hilchot Avadim* 6:6) that a Karaite who has the status of *tinok she-nishba* can, at times, serve as a valid witness.[29] The

---

29. **רמב״ם הלכות עבדים פרק ו הלכה ו**

כל שטר שיש עליו אפילו עד אחד כותי פסול חוץ מגיטי נשים ושחרורי עבדים שהן כשרין בעד אחד ישראל ועד אחד כותי והוא שיהיה כותי חבר, ובזמן הזה שהכותים כעכו״ם לכל דבריהם אנו למדין מהן לצדוקין **שהצדוקין בזמן הזה כמו כותי באותו הזמן** קודם שגזרו עליהם שיהיו כעכו״ם לכל דבריהם.

> Any legal document that is signed by even one witness who is a Kuti is not acceptable, with the exception of bills of divorce for women and bills of release for slaves, provided the Kuti is known to be precise in his observance. In the present age, when the Kutim are considered as gentiles with regard to all matters, we apply the laws stated with regard to them to the Sadducees. **For the Sadducees in the present era are considered like the Kutim of the previous era**, before it was decreed that they would be considered like gentiles.

The basis of my inference is that the "Sadducees in the present era," i.e. Karaites, deny the validity of the oral law. One could reject my inference by arguing that Rambam only validates a Karaite who is a believer in the oral law. Moreover, the fact that a second Jewish witness signed on the *get* indicates that the second witness knows that this particular Karaite is a believer, otherwise he would not have signed. This reading seems questionable since, as Rambam informs us, the whole premise of the Karaite faith is denial of the oral law. If the witness accepted the oral law, he would not be Karaite. We should note, however, that there are thinkers, such as Radvaz, who disagree with our inference in Rambam. To resolve our question they suggest that Rambam must be discussing a case where the Karaite renounced his faith in front of the witness he is signing with; however, he is still considered a Karaite since he did not publicly formally renounce his faith (שקבל עליו דברי חברות בפני זה הישראל אשר

implication, then, is that such a person might also have a share in the world to come. In light of this passage, it seems reasonable that the *tinok she-nishba* exception applies not just with respect to his inclusion in the Jewish people, but also with respect to *olam ha-ba*. Further evidence for this possibility can be gleaned from *Hilchot Shechita*.[30]

(חתם עמו דאי לאו דחבר הוא לא הוה מחתים ליה מקמיה אבל לא קבל עליו בפני שלשה). *Igrot Moshe* EH 1:82 s.v. *v-aminah* also presumably disagrees with my understanding of Rambam, though he does not address how to read the Rambam. Accordingly, the above understanding is presented tentatively, and with hesitation.

30. **רמב"ם הלכות שחיטה פרק ד הלכות יד-טז**

> אם היה משומד לע"ז או מחלל שבת בפרהסיא **או מין והוא הכופר בתורה ובמשה רבינו כמו שבארנו בהל' תשובה הרי הוא כגוי** ושחיטתו נבלה... אלו הצדוקין והביתוסין ותלמידיהן וכל הטועים אחריהן שאינם מאמינים בתורה שבע"פ שחיטתן אסורה, ואם שחטו בפנינו הרי זו מותרת, שאין איסור שחיטתן אלא שמא יקלקלו וכו'.
>
> If he was an apostate because of worship of false deities, one who violates Shabbat in public, **or a heretic who denies the Torah and [the prophecy of] Moshe, our teacher, as we explained in *Hilchot Teshuva*, he is considered as a gentile**, and [an animal] he slaughters is a *neveila* (i.e., not kosher)... These Sadducees, Baitusim, their disciples, and all that err following their path and do not believe in the oral law – their slaughter is forbidden. If, however, they slaughtered [an animal] in our presence, it is permitted. For their slaughter is forbidden only because it is possible they blunder.

In *halacha* 14, Rambam refers to *Hilchot Teshuva* when classifying heretics as non-Jews, and then, in *halacha* 16, states that this classification does not apply to a *tinok she-nishba* (we will demonstrate shortly that הצדוקין והביתוסין ותלמידיהן must be referring to people who qualify as *tinok she-nishba*). Accordingly, the passage in *Hilchot Teshuva*, which states that heretics have no portion in *olam ha-ba*, cannot be referring to *tinok she-nishba*, as implicit in Rambam's language in *Hilchot Shechita*. What appears to emerge from this is that Rambam links both applications of being a heretic (exclusion from the Jewish people and loss of *olam ha-ba*). This may be why he did not need to explicate that the heretics in *Hilchot Teshuva* are excluded from the Jewish people. If this is true, then there is less support for R. Chaim's theory from *Hilchot Teshuva*.

One cannot deflect this proof by saying that הצדוקין והביתוסין ותלמידיהן refers to the original Sadducees, which were certainly not *tinok she-nishba*, since they would be heretics whose *shechita* is invalid, as indicated in *Hilchot Shechita* 4:14 and *Hilchot Teshuva* 3:8. It must be the case (as *Chasdei David, Chullin* 3a notes) that הצדוקין והביתוסין ותלמידיהן refers to contemporary Sadducees and their students who are classified as *tinok she-nishba*. That צדוקין can refer to contemporary deniers of the oral law (and, therefore, classified as *tinok she-nishba*) can be seen from הלכות עבדים פרק ו הלכה ו.

Let us review. The linchpin of the first three approaches is that *olam ha-ba* is definitionally impossible for the individual who lacks a correct conception of God. However, Rambam does not say this anywhere. In places where Rambam writes heresy results in exclusion from the afterlife (*Commentary on the Mishna* – Introduction to *Perek Cheilek* and *Hilchot Teshuva*), he does not seem to be referring to a *tinok she-nishba*.[31] Ultimately, we do not have an explicit statement asserting that a *tinok she-nishba* does or does not have a share in the world to come. This leaves the door open for the fourth approach, that, in theory, a *tinok she-nishba* does have a share in the world to come.

11.6 FOURTH APPROACH: IT *IS* HIS FAULT

Having questioned the first three approaches, let us consider a radical conclusion. We have already established that Rambam cannot be referring to a *tinok she-nishba* when he writes that one who does not believe in the thirteen principles of faith is excluded from the Jewish people and the afterlife. Perhaps, then, a *tinok she-nishba* would not only be included in the Jewish people (as Rambam states explicitly), but also potentially be the beneficiary of *olam ha-ba*.

In other words, heresy does not, in and of itself, warrant loss of *olam ha-ba* – if someone cannot be blamed for his or her false beliefs then experiencing *olam ha-ba* remains possible. When Rambam writes that deniers are excluded from the afterlife, he refers to those who should have known better. Accordingly, even someone with false beliefs could merit *olam ha-ba*.

Why would someone with false beliefs experience *olam ha-ba*? Firstly, because justice dictates that someone who served God to the best of his ability, who engaged in acts of kindness and sacrificed for God's sake should be rewarded for his efforts and piety. Moreover, the

---

Another way to reject this proof is to distinguish between errors concerning God and other errors concerning fundamental principles. Perhaps only a *tinok she-nishba* who, at least, believes in the correct God is accepted into *olam ha-ba*. However, we have shown that such a distinction also lacks support.

31. In the Introduction to *Perek Cheilek*, he writes that deniers of the 13 principles are excluded from the Jewish people, which clearly does not apply to the *tinok she-nishba*. In *Hilchot Teshuva* he writes that corporealists have no portion in the afterlife, but in *Hilchot Shechita* he indicates that *Hilchot Teshuva* is not referring to the *tinok she-nishba*.

mishna states, and Rambam echoes both in his commentary on the Mishna and in *Hilchot Teshuva* 3:5, that every Jew by dint of his Jewishness has a share in *olam ha-ba*. The only way for one to lose that share is to lose one's Jewishness, and a *tinok she-nishba*, as Rambam writes explicitly, does not lose his Jewishness.

Of course, this understanding rejects the notion that *olam ha-ba* is definitionally impossible for the individual who lacks a correct understanding of God.[32] Rather, there is an aspect of *olam ha-ba* that emerges by dint of being Jewish and "portions" of *olam ha-ba* available for those who devoutly serve Him even if they err in their conception of Him. Whether Rambam can subscribe to such a view depends on the manner in which one interprets the Maimonidean texts cited in 11.2. Their simple understanding certainly implies that Rambam maintains that the eternity of the soul demands a correct understanding of God. If that reading is correct, one is forced to accept one of the first three approaches cited above. Of the three, I believe the third is most compelling. However, as argued above and in Chapter 20, it is not implausible to suggest that Rambam would agree that the *tinok she-nishba* who serves God to the best of his ability would have a portion in *olam ha-ba*.[33]

Clearly, this matter is complex, and it is unlikely that we can conclusively demonstrate the veracity of any of the approaches. However, let us consider six factors that support this approach. (Some of these points have already been made, but, for purposes of clarity, bear repetition.)

1. Rambam's Reason Why Corporealists Are Heretics

The strongest proof for the approach that follows is from *Moreh ha-Nevuchim* 1:36, where Rambam addresses the claim that believers in a corporeal god should not be held responsible for their beliefs. Rambam

32. See *Sanhedrin* 110b that considers five views regarding at which stage a Jew can have a share in *olam ha-ba*: conception, birth, circumcision, speech, and when the child says *amen*. Obviously, at none of these stages will the individual have a correct conception of God.

33. Gabriel Gross, in his essay referenced in footnote 2 of this chapter, suggests a revolutionary resolution to this quandary: Rambam changed his mind. Gabriel shows that Rambam's position on the impossibility of *olam ha-ba* for the accidental heretic may have evolved over time, with his final position allowing for the possibility of admission.

writes that if we were to excuse those who believe in a corporeal god, we ought to excuse idolaters as well since, in both cases, the error emerges from faulty comprehension or faulty education.

ספר מורה הנבוכים חלק א פרק לו

ואם יעלה בדעתך שיש ללמד זכות על מאמיני הגשמות בשל היותו חונך כך או מחמת סכלותו וקוצר השגתו, כך ראוי לך להיות בדעה בעובד עבודה זרה, מפני שאינו עובד אלא מחמת סכלות או חנוך, מנהג אבותיהם בידיהם.

ואם תאמר כי פשטי הכתובים הפילום בשבושים אלו, כך תדע שעובד עבודה זרה לא הביאוהו לעבדה כי אם דמיונות ומושגים גרועים. נמצא שאין התנצלות למי שאינו סומך על בעלי העיון האמיתיים אם היה קצר יכולת עיונית. ואיני חושב לכופר מי שלא הוכח לו שלילת הגשמות, אך חושב אני לכופר מי שאינו קובע בדעתו שלילתה. ובפרט עם מציאות תרגום אנקלוס ותרגום יונתן בן עזיאל עליהם השלום, אשר הרחיקו את הגשמות תכלית ההרחקה.

If you think that there is an excuse for those who believe in the corporeality of God on the ground of their training, their ignorance, or their defective comprehension, you must make the same concession to the worshippers of idols. Their worship is due to ignorance or to childhood training; "They continue in the custom of their fathers" (*Chullin* 13a).

If, however, you should say that the literal interpretation of Scripture causes men to corporealize God, you ought to know that an idolater is similarly impelled to his idolatry by imaginings and defective representations. Accordingly, there is no excuse for one who does not accept the authority of men who inquire into the truth and are engaged in speculation if he himself is incapable of engaging in such speculation. I do not consider those men as heretics who are unable to prove incorporeality, but I hold those to be so who do not believe it, especially when they see that *Targum Onkelos* and *Targum Yonatan* avoid [in reference to God] expressions implying corporeality as much as possible.

Rambam writes that the reason these heretics have no excuse is that they should have accepted the position of the true philosophers (בעלי העיון האמיתיים). Rambam forcefully implies that the person is responsible insofar as he fails to utilize the tools available to him, choosing instead to independently discover the truth when he is incapable of doing so (שאין התנצלות למי שאינו סומך על בעלי העיון האמיתיים אם היה קצר יכולת עיונית.). Rambam assumes that a person is capable of being aware of his own limitations. However, if these tools are not available, then to some degree, the errors are excusable (התנצלות).

Rambam's answer does not seem to correspond to the assumption made in the first three approaches that such a person's exclusion from the next world is a natural consequence. Thus, if one of the first three approaches is correct, Rambam should have responded that *olam ha-ba* is by definition impossible for someone with an incorrect conception of God. Instead, Rambam answers that the person is in fact to blame for his erroneous beliefs. The implication is that he is considered a heretic because of his negligence.[34]

2. Rambam's Theory of Biblical Anthropomorphism

With this, we can understand Rambam's theory in 1:46 that there is value in "guiding the masses" to belief in a corporeal god. For the multitude of Jews during the biblical period, there was no choice but to imply that

34. One could deflect this proof by distinguishing between two different issues. Here, Rambam is justifying his harsh treatment of corporealists. The reason that they are excluded from the afterlife, though, is that such an existence is definitionally impossible for someone with such an erroneous belief. Nevertheless, the simple reading of the passage accords with the above analysis. To appreciate this, consider the immediately preceding paragraph where Rambam explains that the reason why God is angry and unforgiving towards the corporealist is since, in effect, he denies God's existence: "Such a person is undoubtedly worse than he who worships idols in the belief that they, as agents, can do good or evil. Therefore, bear in mind that by the belief in corporeality or in anything connected with corporeality, you would provoke God to jealousy and wrath, kindle His fire and anger, and become His foe, His enemy, and His adversary in a higher degree than by the worship of idols." Rambam in this context is not explaining why the people should treat the corporealist harshly; he is explaining why God treats him harshly. Therefore, it would seem that his explanation relates to the corporealist's exclusion from the afterlife.

god is corporeal. With time, however, belief in God became widespread and the true philosophers (בעלי העיון האמיתיים) taught that God has no body.[35] Moreover, even though a literal translation of certain verses may support corporeality, readily available tools like *Targum Onkelos* show that these passages should not be understood literally.[36] Anyone who fulfills his obligation of *shnayim mikra ve-echad targum* (studying the weekly *parsha* with *Targum Onkelos*) will not err. Thus, in Rambam's time, people no longer have an excuse for belief in a corporeal god – accordingly, they are deemed heretics and excluded from the world to come.[37]

Thus, Rambam writes, just as we would not excuse an idolater for his false beliefs, we cannot excuse a heretic for his false beliefs. This is true with respect to corporeality. What about other basic principles of *emuna*? Here, Rambam writes that sometimes, such as in the case of second- and third-generation Karaites, we apply the principle of *tinok she-nishba* and do not treat them as heretics. We see their error as excusable (even if they have encountered rabbinic Jews).[38] To clarify, we are not claiming that the *tinok she-nishba* is not a heretic; we are claiming that

35. Moreover, our knowledge of God's incorporeality, as Rambam notes in *Yesodei ha-Torah* 1:8, is not just through philosophy (in which case, we might excuse error), but through the text of the Torah (e.g., *Devarim* 4:15) and through reliable tradition. Rambam means that it was the philosophers who proved God's incorporeality. Regular people need not understand the proofs as long as they accept the conclusion. Moreover, without the education of the "true philosophers," we might not know how to reconcile the verses that imply incorporeality with those that negate it.

36. For example, *Targum Onkelos* on the words וירד ה' (*Shemot* 19:20), which literally means that God descended, is ואיתגלי ה', which means that God was revealed. Ramban (*Bereishit* 46:1) notes that Onkelos does not always seem to remove implications of corporeality and suggests that one can resolve the discrepancies only based on Kabbala.

37. Rambam does not inform us as to when this shift took place. It would appear that it was after the prophetic period, since Rambam notes that the Prophets continued to describe God in seemingly corporeal terminology.

38. This essentially is *Chatam Sofer*'s answer concerning R. Hillel's denial of a personal messiah. Recall that Radvaz asks that according to Rambam, R. Hillel is a heretic for his denial of a personal messiah. *Chatam Sofer* (cited earlier) answers that at the time, the question of whether or not there would be a personal messiah had not yet been resolved. Accordingly, R. Hillel's mistake would not make him a heretic, since his error was excusable. Subsequently, though, the matter was resolved. Thus, Rambam is correct in characterizing anyone who denies a personal messiah as a heretic.

he is not *treated* as a heretic regarding exclusion from the Jewish people and loss of *olam ha-ba*.

Accordingly, if someone truly is blameless, even Rambam would not treat him as a full-fledged heretic. Proof for this position can be derived from Rambam's extension of the *tinok she-nishba* principle to matters that relate to the thirteen principles of faith such as the veracity of the oral law. When Rambam writes that we do not excuse a person for his false conception of God, it is because he should have known better.

Moreover, as we noted in 11.5, Rambam states that the masses were taught of the resurrection (one of the thirteen principles of faith) only in the time of Daniel after belief in the possibility in miracles had been firmly cemented among the people. Thus, it seems clear that most Jews could not have possibly believed in all thirteen principles of faith until the time of Daniel. Since it is inconceivable that most Jews, until this time, were precluded from the afterlife, it seems reasonable to conclude that only those that are blameworthy are excluded.

3. The Principles of Faith Include Non-Salvific Truths

As we have noted, some of the thirteen principles of faith (especially the first four or five) relate to a correct conception of God. As such, we can readily understand their fundamentality if we adopt a naturalistic approach to the afterlife. However, the latter principles, and especially ideas such as the messiah or resurrection, do not appear particularly salvific. Their inclusion implies that the importance of these principles of faith lies not in their naturalistic fundamentality, but in their religious significance. A person who denies the resurrection loses *olam ha-ba* not because *olam ha-ba* is definitionally impossible for such a person, but because the Torah teaches that there will be a resurrection, and its rejection implies either denial of God's ability to perform miracles (Rambam emphasizes this point in his letter on the resurrection) or denial of our tradition that promises the resurrection. Either one of these possibilities justifies exclusion from the Jewish people and the afterlife. However, when the denial does not stem from either of these options, as is the case with the *tinok she-nishba*, then there is no reason to exclude the denier.[39] Once we acknowledge that this is the case for the 12th or 13th principle, there is little reason not to assume that it is also the case for the rest, since Rambam in no place distinguishes between them.

4. Why Hate the Heretic?

Rambam obligates the believer to hate and destroy the individual who lacks belief in any of the thirteen principles, "חובה לשנאותו ולהשמידו." If the consequences of the rejection are in any way naturalistic, this reaction is troubling, since there will be times, as Rambam acknowledges, that a person is blameless in their rejection. But if we are correct in assuming that Rambam vilifies only the individual whose heresy stems from malfeasance, then Rambam's ruling becomes much more palatable. As such, Rambam instructs us to respect the *tinok she-nishba* (שראוי לחלק להם כבוד).

---

39. According to *Chatam Sofer*, however, denial of the messiah, in and of itself, is not the problem. The issue is a rejection of Torah (which promises a messiah) that causes someone to lose *olam ha-ba*.

שו״ת חתם סופר חלק ב (יורה דעה) סימן שנו

...אך א״א לי בשום אופן להאמין שיהי׳ גאולתינו א׳ מעיקרי הדת ושאם יפול היסוד תפול החומה חלילה ושנאמר אלו הי׳ ח״ו חטאנו גורמים שיגרש אותנו גירוש עולם וכדס״ל לר״ע בעשרת השבטים שהם נדחים לעולם המפני זה רשאים הם לפרוק עול מלכות השמים או לשנות קוצו של יו״ד אפי׳ מדברי רבנן חלילה אנחנו לא נעבוד ה׳ לאכול פרי הארץ ולשבוע מטוב׳ לעשות רצונך אלקי חפצתי ועכ״פ ועל כל אופן עבדי ד׳ אנחנו יעשה עמנו כרצונו וחפצו ואין זה עיקר ולא יסוד לבנות עליו שום בנין אך כיון שעיקר יסוד הכל להאמין בתורה ובנביאים ושם נאמר גאולתינו האחרונה בפ׳ נצבים ובפ׳ האזינו כמ״ש רמב״ן שם והרבה מזה בדברי נביאים **אם כן מי שמפקפק על הגאולה הלז הרי כופר בעיקר האמנת התורה והנביאים.**

והנה ר׳ הלל בפ׳ חלק צ״ט ע״א אמר אין משיח לישראל פירש״י אלא הקב״ה בעצמו יגאלם בלי שליח ופי׳ זה מוכרח הוא דאל״ה אדמקשה לי׳ רב יוסף מעני רוכב על החמור דיש לדחות דקאי על נחמי׳ כמ״ש רמב״ן סוף פי׳ שיר השירים ולא דחאו מדברי זכרי׳ שיצאו מים חיים מבית ה׳ וראיה זו כ׳ הרא״בע סוף זכרי׳ ע״ש אע״כ מזה אין ראיה דודאי גם לר׳ הלל יש גאולה אלא שאין משיח מלך **וגם בזה לית הלכתא כוותי׳ והאומר אין משיח וקים לי׳ כרבי הלל הרי הוא כופר בכלל התורה דכיילי אחרי רבים להטות כיון שרבו עליו חכמי ישראל ואמרו דלא כוותי׳ שוב אין אדם ראוי׳ להמשך אחריו** כמו ע״ד משל במקומו של ר״א הי׳ כורתים עצים לעשות פחמין לעשות ברזל לצורך מילה ואחר דאיפסקא הלכתא ע״פ רבי׳ מחכמי ישראל דלא כוותי׳ העושה כן בשבת בעדים והתרא׳ סקול יסקל ולא מצי למימר קים לי כר״א. והא דתני׳ במס׳ עדיות למה נישנו דברי היחיד ע״ש מילתא אחריתי כמובן ואין להאריך **ועכ״פ הגאולה וביאת המשיח איננה עיקר אבל מי שאינו מודה בו כופר בעיקר של האמנת התורה ודברי נביאים....**

5. Positive Characteristics

In 10.6, we saw Rambam states that someone who thinks that God has positive attributes is an unconscious atheist; he "has abolished his belief in the existence of God without being aware of it" (1:60). Further proof for this conclusion emerges from *Moreh ha-Nevuchim* 1:50. Rambam writes that part of belief is understanding the direct implications of what one believes. Thus, "Those who believe that God is one and that He has many attributes declare the unity with their lips and assume plurality in their thoughts."

However, as we have seen, when enumerating the thirteen principles of faith in his commentary on the Mishna, Rambam includes rejection of incorporeality but does not include belief that He has no attributes among the basic principles a Jew must believe to be considered Jewish. This indicates that this belief is not as fundamental as incorporeality, especially since belief in positive attributes certainly was widespread, and, like incorporeality, would need to be dispelled. Likewise, omitting from *Mishneh Torah* the problematic nature of characterizing God also points to the fact that attribution of characteristics is *not* heretical.

More significantly, in 1:35, Rambam appears to insist upon educating the masses about divine incorporeality, but to allow for non-education about the inapplicability of positive divine attributes. Rambam here groups the inapplicability of divine attributes with a number of other "secrets of the law" and states that it is only to be explained (indirectly) to one who is fully proficient in all of the necessary antecedents to studying *ma'aseh merkava* (see 2.1). Divine incorporeality, meanwhile, is to be taught to every man, woman and child as a foundation of the faith.

According to the first three approaches taken above, the discrepancy between positive attributes and corporeality proves troubling since fundamentally the mistakes are identical. However, according to the fourth approach, the solution is simple. While the errors are philosophically identical, the basis by which we know that He does not have a physical body differs from the basis by which we know the falseness of positive attributes. The Torah frequently warns against corporeality, such as in *Devarim* 4:15. Rambam stresses that we know of His incorporeality not through philosophical speculation, but from the Torah itself. Moreover, according to Rambam, while Onkelos intentionally removed anthropomorphisms that could be incorrectly interpreted as implying corporeality, he did not remove references that could be interpreted as ascribing positive characteristics to God. Additionally, it is relatively easy to understand, on some level, the error of corporeality. Every typical twelve or thirteen year-old child can believe in an incorporeal God. However, understanding why positive attributes contradict divine unity proves quite complex. As such, fulfillment of the *mitzva* of *emuna* on a basic level, an obligation incumbent upon every 12 or 13-year-old child, could not necessitate a rejection of positive attributes.

If we accept the first three views, this distinction is quite problematic since loss of *olam ha-ba* is a natural consequence of a mistaken belief about God. However, according to the fourth view, it makes perfect sense. The Torah itself distinguished between the two errors. Since loss of *olam ha-ba* is a Torah imposed punishment (and not a natural consequence) it only applies to corporeality and not positive attributes.

6. R. Hillel

In 11.3, we referenced the question Radvaz asks on Rambam from the Talmudic sage, R. Hillel, who denied personal *mashiach*. Seemingly, Rambam would have ruled that R. Hillel was a heretic for denying the twelfth principle; but how could Rambam classify a Talmudic sage as a heretic? If, however, we adopt the fourth approach, the solution is simple. R. Hillel's error did not stem from negligence. Clearly, R. Hillel was unaware of a tradition concerning the meaning of the prophecies in the Prophets about a personal messiah, and a consensus had not yet been reached. As such, he was excused. All this points to the notion, accepted by the fourth approach, that the heretic's exclusion stems from malfeasance and is not the naturalistic consequence of a false belief.

While some of these six arguments are compatible with the second and third approaches taken as a whole, in my view, they support the fourth approach.[40]

40. To these six arguments, Gabriel Gross, in the aforementioned essay, added two more: (1) Rambam's statement in 2:28 (cited in 11.3) that knowledge of divine will is necessary for human perfection despite his rejection of the possibility of demonstrating novel divine will. (2) Rambam's insistence, following *Mishnat Rabi Eliezer,* that Noachides can achieve immortality only through acceptance of revelation. (We address this point in 20.6.)

Objections to the Fourth Approach

As noted earlier, the primary objection to the fourth approach is implicit the two texts cited in 11.2 that imply that the afterlife is definitionally impossible for the person with an incorrect conception of God.

An additional objection to this approach is that Rambam seems to categorically classify those who deny any of the thirteen principles as not having a portion in *olam ha-ba*. He does not state that this is true only if he is responsible for his error. For example, in the third chapter of *Hilchot Teshuva* (3:14), after listing the twenty-four classes of people that have no portion in *olam ha-ba* (such as *minim, apikorsim,* and *kofrim*) he writes:

> כל אחד ואחד מארבעה ועשרים אנשים אלו שמנינו - אף על פי שהן ישראל, אין להן חלק לעולם הבא.
>
> Any of the twenty-four individuals listed above will not receive a portion in the world to come, even though he is Jewish.

It sounds as though he is saying that such people lose *olam ha-ba* under all circumstances. However, as we have seen, this may not be the case.[41]

One troubling element of this thesis is that the person who believes in a corporeal god is not intentionally distorting the truth. Why, then, do we hold him accountable, even if it is true that he could have known better? (This may be part of Ra'avad's objection.) It seems that Rambam believes that major theological errors that could have been

41. In *Hilchot Shechita,* he refers to *Hilchot Teshuva* when classifying heretics as non-Jews and immediately afterwards writes that this classification does not apply to a *tinok shenishba*. In addition, internally within *Hilchot Teshuva* there may be reason to presume he is referring only to *meizidim* (willful violators), at least with some of the twenty-four people listed that lose *olam ha-ba*. For example, one of the twenty-four people to lose *olam ha-ba* is someone who separates himself from the community (הפורש מדרכי ציבור): "A person who separates himself from the congregation of Israel and does not fulfill *mitzvot* together with them, does not take part in their hardships, or join in their [communal] fasts, but rather goes on his own individual path as if he is from another nation and not [Israel]." In this case, it seems reasonable that only someone classified as *meizid* would be included (though how exactly to define *meizid* in this context is unclear). If that is the case, then it is not far-fetched to presume others on the list are *meizid* as well.

avoided reflect subconscious wickedness.[42] As Rambam writes in *Hilchot Avoda Zara* (2:5), foolish mistakes are not innocent mistakes (והמינים הם התרים אחר מחשבות ליבם בסכלות).[43]

Likewise, Rambam (*Hilchot Mamrim* 3:3) writes that we characterize a first-generation Karaite as a heretic because "He follows after his frivolous thoughts and his capricious heart and denies the oral Torah on his own, as did Tzadok and Baitus and those who erred in following them." Since they should have known better – after all, they were taught about the truthfulness of the oral law – their errors reflect wickedness. This may not be conscious malevolence. Rather, Rambam maintains that a person is responsible to accept the truth if he is capable of doing so. Various factors may encourage a person to disregard the truth and choose falsehood. Should he do so, he is held accountable. However, the Karaites' children never were educated. Thus, about them we conclude: "The children of these errant people and their grandchildren whose parents led them away, and those born among these Karaites and raised according to their conception, are considered as a child who was captured (*tinok she-nishba*) and raised by them (i.e., non-Jews)."[44]

---

42. This does not mean that we treat such mistakes as intentional (*meizid*). At times, the Torah prescribes a *chatat* for someone who accidentally (*shogeig*) serves idolatry. Yet Rambam categorizes idolatry as an inexcusable offense. (In fact, he compares incorporeality to idolatry in this regard: just as idolatry obviously is inexcusable, so too corporeality.) Rambam thus maintains that errors of this sort are Halachically accidental (*shogeig*), since the violator does not knowingly violate the Torah's law, but also asserts that they are egregious, because anyone who honestly searches will come to the correct conclusion. However, any time an honest search would not necessarily lead to the truth, we exempt the person and classify him as a *tinok she-nishba*.

43. Rambam's assumption is presumed by the verse, as understood by Chazal, to which Rambam alludes in this line:

במדבר טו :לט

וְלֹא תָתֻרוּ אַחֲרֵי לְבַבְכֶם.

This injunction presumes that we have the power not to stray after our hearts. Chazal (*Sifrei*; see Rashi on this verse) understand this as a reference to heresy (ולא תתורו אחרי לבבכם - זו מינות). Thus, the Torah views heresy as allowing the heart to control the mind – something we are capable of avoiding.

44. A more explicit example of this phenomenon can be found in *Moreh ha-Nevuchim* 3:41. Rambam divides sins into four classes: (1) involuntary transgressions, (2) sins committed in a state of ignorance, (3) sins done knowingly, and (4) sins

done spitefully. Rambam, based on Chazal, includes the idolater in the fourth class. He presumes that there can be no accidental sinning in this regard (at least in a world where monotheism has been spread); we do not say that the idolater innocently arrived at false conclusions. Rather the idolater's intentions are malicious.

מורה הנבוכים חלק ג פרק מא

עושה ביד רמה הוא המזיד המתחצף ומתפרץ ועובר בפרהסיא, וכאילו אינו עובר לעצם התאותנות או להשגת מה שמנעה אותו התורה מלהשיגו מחמת רוע מדותיו בלבד, **אלא מפני שהוא מתנגד לתורה ומתקומם נגדה, ולפיכך אמר עליו את ה' הוא מגדף**, והוא נהרג בלי ספק. **ודבר זה לא עושהו אלא מתוך השקפה שנתגבשה לו להתקומם בה נגד התורה. ומשום כך בא הפירוש המקובל 'בעבודה זרה הכתוב מדבר'**, לפי שהיא ההשקפה הנוגדת את יסוד התורה. כי בהחלט לא יעבוד כוכב אלא מי שהוא בדעה עליו שהוא קדמון, כמו שביארנו בחיבורינו כמה פעמים.

וכך הוא הדין לדעתי בכל עברה הנר' ממנה סתירת התורה **וההתקוממות נגדה**, ואפי' אכל לדעתי אדם מישראל בשר בחלב או לבש שעטנז או גלח פאת ראש מתוך בזיון וזלזול מחמת השקפה המתפרש ממנה שאינו מאמין אמתת התורה הזו, הרי זה לדעתי את ה' הוא מגדף, ונהרג כהריגת כופר לא הריגת עונש, כאנשי עיר הנדחת שנהרגים הריגת כפירה לא הריגת עונש, ולפיכך ממונם נשרף ואינו ליורשיהם כשאר הרוגי בית דין.

If a person sins presumptuously, such that in sinning, he shows impudence and seeks publicity, if he does not sin only to satisfy his appetite; if he does what is prohibited by the Torah, not only because of his evil inclinations, **but in order to oppose and resist the Torah; such a person "reproaches God"** (*Bamidbar* 15:30), and undoubtedly must be put to death. **None will act in such a manner but such as have conceived the idea to act contrary to the Torah. According to the traditional interpretation, therefore, the above passage speaks of an idolater who opposes the fundamental principles of the Torah; for no one worships a star unless he believes that the star is eternal, as we frequently have stated in our work.**

I think that the same punishment [viz., sentence of death] applies to every sin which involves the rejection of the Law, **or opposition to it**. Even if an Israelite eats meat [boiled] in milk, or wears garments of wool and linen, or rounds the corners of his head, out of spite against the Law, in order to show clearly that he does not believe in its truth, I apply to him the words, "he reproacheth the Lord," and [I am of opinion] that he must suffer death as an unbeliever, though not for a punishment, but in the same manner as the inhabitants of a "city misled to idolatry" are slain for their unbelief, and not by way of punishment for crime; wherefore their property is destroyed by fire, and is not given to their heirs, as is the case with the property of other criminals condemned to death.

However, this derivation is not entirely clear, since we do allow some unintentional idolaters to bring a *chatat*, indicating that we see their actions as *shogeig*. Perhaps, then, all Rambam is saying is that any intentional idolatry falls into the fourth category of sin rather than the third. Nevertheless, the above citation still proves our point

Thinkers who Appear to Adopt the Fourth Approach

R. Shlomo of Chelm (1716–81) in *Mirkevet ha-Mishneh* maintains that according to Rambam the corporealist loses *olam ha-ba* because he should have known better, and not because it is an inherent impossibility (as presumed by the first three approaches).[45] A similar approach also emerges from Ramban (*Bava Metzia* 71b; this is his own position and not an explanation of Rambam).

R. Moshe Shternbuch (*Teshuvot ve-Hanhagot* 2:460) goes one step further, suggesting that even R. Chaim might agree to this thesis. He suggests that even if R. Chaim maintains that someone misled by Scripture is considered a heretic, someone who never was educated at all (as frequently is the case today) is considered a *tinok she-nishba*.[46] Presumably, the logic for such a distinction is, as we have argued, that we do not see the individual who understands Scripture literally as blameless, because, as Rambam writes, he should have studied *Targum Onkelos*.

---

because it indicates that idolatry and heresy are considered intentional (*meizid*) when people foolishly follow their hearts, as he writes elsewhere:

רמב"ם הלכות עבודה זרה פרק ב הלכה ה

ישראל שעבד עבודה זרה - הרי הוא כגוי לכל דבר, ואינו כישראל שעבר על עבירה שיש בה סקילה; ומשומד לעבודה זרה, הרי הוא משומד לכל התורה כולה. וכן המינים מישראל, אינן כישראל לדבר מן הדברים... **והמינים, הם התרים אחר מחשבות ליבם בסכלות**, בדברים שאמרנו, עד שנמצאו עוברים על גופי תורה להכעיס, **בשאט בנפש ביד רמה; ואומרין, שאין בזה עוון.**

An Israelite who worshiped idolatry is to be treated as a gentile in all respects, and not as an Israelite who violates a prohibitive commandment punishable by stoning. A convert to idolatry is rebellious against the whole scope of the Torah. Likewise, infidels (*minim*) among Israel are not to be judged as Israelites in any respect... **The infidels are they that absorb themselves in the swerving fancies of their heart about the foolish matters** previously mentioned, until they ultimately transgress by stepping upon the vitals of the Torah with spite, **soul-sickening and high-handedness, and proclaim that therein lies no iniquity.**

45. **מרכבת המשנה (חעלמא) הלכות תשובה פרק ג הלכה ז**
שהוא גוף. ובהשגות. ותמהני דודאי כל מין בדעתו שהאמת אתו ומ"מ אין לו חלק לעוה"ב דחמיר שגגת אמונה זרה דהו"ל למידק ולמה יגרע אמונת הגשמה משאר אמונה זרה.

46. **תשובות והנהגות כרך ב סימן תס**
ובשם הגר"ח מבריסק ידוע שאין טענת אונס בכפירה, דסוף כל סוף הוא אפיקורס, אבל דבריו באחד שמשתבש מפסוקים, **אבל מי שלא קיבל חינוך כלל ודאי ראוי לרחם עליו ולקרבו,** ועובדא היא שהרבה נתעוררו היום לתשובה ב"ה.

Thus, according to R. Chaim, many contemporary non-believers would be fully categorized as *tinok she-nishba.*

R. Meir of Narbonne (ha-Me'ili)[47] is among the first to adopt this line of thinking. In *Ma'amar Meishiv Nefesh,*[48] he cites numerous sources in Chazal that, when understood literally imply, that God has a body. He argues that it is inconceivable that Rambam maintains that someone who understands these literally is deemed a heretic. This would make most of our nation heretics. Would Rambam believe that we should kill most of the Jewish people? Certainly, Rambam would agree that someone who killed such a pure Jew would be deemed a murderer. Indeed, Rambam himself admits (*Hilchot Yesodei ha-Torah* 2:10) that these matters cannot be understood. Rather, Rambam means that someone who rejects tradition and comes to this conclusion on his own is deemed a heretic. In this case, he has no excuse for his error. While this approach differs somewhat from the approach suggested earlier (based on 1:36) that in Rambam's time anyone who believed in a corporeal god would be considered a heretic, the conceptual understanding of Rambam is identical to that suggested in the fourth approach (that only inexcusable heresy constitutes heresy).[49]

---

47. 1190–1263, author of *Sefer ha-Me'orot* (Halachic material on *Berachot, Chullin,* and *Seider Mo'eid*). He died in Toledo, Spain. For more biographical material, see *Judeo-Christian dialogue in Provence as reflected in Milhemet mitzva of R. Meir Hameili* by William K. Herskowitz, Yeshiva University, 1974.

48. Published in *Yeshurun,* Vol. 27, pp. 92–99, edited by William K. Herskowitz.

49. R. Yosef Bronstein showed me that a number of the approaches explicated above are advanced by contemporary scholars. R. Tuvia Katzman (*ha-Ma'ayan, Chanuka* 5772) prefers the second approach, namely, that a false conception of God (or denial of the first five principles) automatically excludes a person from the Jewish people and *olam ha-ba* (even if the person is blameless). However, blameless denial of the other *ikkarim* does not exclude a person from the Jewish people and *olam ha-ba.* (He would be categorized as a *tinok she-nishba.*)

R. Avraham Ross (in a response to the above article published in *ha-Ma'ayan, Tishrei* 5773) argues in favor of the third approach that any denial of any of the thirteen principles automatically excludes a person from *olam ha-ba,* but blameless denial of any of the thirteen principles does not exclude a person from the Jewish people because such a person would be categorized as a *tinok she-nishba.*

R. Yisrael Yosef Rappaport (*le-Tshuvat ha-Shana,* p. 331) suggests that this question hinges on the correct text of Rambam concerning whether one should kill a *tinok*

11.7 R. ELCHANAN WASSERMAN'S VARIATION

A modern variation of the above approach can be found in the writings of R. Elchanan Wasserman. R. Elchanan also noted that R. Chaim's approach seems to contradict the concept of *tinok she-nishba*. Moreover, it seems unfair. His solution is similar to the fourth approach insofar as it exonerates anyone who honestly errs. R. Elchanan seems to maintain that even R. Chaim would accept his explanation.

ביאורי אגדות על דרך הפשט יב:ח[50]

שמעתי בשם כ׳ מו״ר הגר״ח הלוי זצ״ל מבריסק בדעת הרמב״ם, **כי הכפירה לא שייך שוגג דהא מ״מ אינו מאמין וא״א להיות בכלל ישראל בלא אמונה...ולכאו׳ דבריו מוכרחין שהרי כל הכופרים וכל עובדי ע״ז הם מוטעין.** ואין לך מוטעה יותר מהמקריב בנו למולך והוא חייב מיתה.

אבל קשה דהא תינוק המוטל בעריסה ג״כ אין לו אמונה, ומ״מ הוא בכלל ישראל, ותינוק שנשבה לבין העכו״ם מביא קרבן של שגגתו ואין דינו כמומר, **ומוכח דאנוס רחמנא פטרי׳ גם בחסרון אמונה.**

וי״ל לפי המבואר למעלה (שם סי׳ א׳) כי יסודי האמונה מוכרחין ודעת האדם מצד עצמה לא תתן מקום לכפירה, ורק רצון האדם לפריקת עול מטה את שכלו לטעות בדברים פשוטים ומוכרחים וע״כ שגגתו עולה זדון. אבל האומר מותר לעבור ע״ז הוא שוגג ופטור ממיתה כיון שסבור שעושה ברשות התורה.

---

she-nishba. Recall that the Vilna edition of Rambam implies that he should not be killed. R. Rappaport understands that this suggests that they are not heretics. This, he claims, is the view of *Chazon Ish*. However, manuscript editions of Rambam state ולא ימהר אדם להרגן. R. Rappaport understands this indicates that they are, in fact, heretics. He reports that this was the view of R. Yitzchak Zev Soloveitchik. However, we noted in 10.11 that the manuscript text does not necessarily indicate that they are heretics. Rather, Rambam understands that they may be killed due to the danger they pose to society.

50. *Bei'urei Aggadot Al Derech ha-Pshat* is printed at the end of some editions of his *Koveitz He'arot* on *Yevamot*.

I have heard in the name of R. Chaim Soloveitchik of Brisk regarding the view of Rambam that **all heresy is not considered *shogeig* (accidental) because in the final analysis, he does not have *emuna*, and it is impossible to be part of the Jewish people without *emuna*... Seemingly, his view is compelling, because all heretics and idolaters err only unintentionally**. There is no greater mistake than someone who offers his son to *molech*,[51] and yet he is liable for execution (i.e., we don't treat him as *shogeig* even though his sin does not seem like a willful rejection of the truth but a misunderstanding of the truth). [Rather, it must be the case that lacking faith automatically excludes a person from the Jewish people.]

But we cannot conclude that someone without faith automatically is excluded from the Jewish people, because a baby also does not have faith, yet he certainly is part of the Jewish people. Likewise, a baby taken captive by idolaters brings a sacrifice for his sins (i.e., he is considered a *shogeig*), and he is not treated as an apostate. **From here we see that we apply the principle that "God excuses all those coerced" even to matters of faith**. (This seems to contradict R. Chaim.)

The answer is in accordance with what we explained earlier, namely, that the principles of faith are in and of themselves simple and compelling. It is only a person's desire to throw off God's yoke that causes his intellect to err and deny that which is obvious. Accordingly, such errors are considered intentional violations. But someone who [believes in God and Torah, but] says that it is permissible to serve idolatry is considered *shogeig* and exempt from execution, since he thinks that his acts are in accordance with the Torah (i.e., he is not denying Torah).

51. A ritual in which a person marches his child between two fires. There is a debate in the Talmud (*Sanhedrin* 64a–b) regarding whether or not the ritual automatically constitutes idolatry.

R. Elchanan Wasserman interprets Rambam following his general theory relating to the possibility of heresy and denial of God. He argues that conceivably, a truly innocent heretic, someone who arrived at his conclusions after a genuine search, certainly would not be culpable even according to Rambam. However, no such person exists. The truly honest search always will lead to God; how else would it be fair to command belief in God?

R. Elchanan arrives at this far-reaching conclusion after considering a number of basic questions concerning the *mitzva* of *emuna*. R. Elchanan wonders how the Torah could legislate belief in God if such belief is not really in a person's control. Moreover, knowledge of God's existence clearly is not achieved so simply; after all, someone as wise as Aristotle did not maintain correct beliefs in this regard. How can the Torah demand that every Jewish twelve-year-old female and thirteen-year-old male have this belief? The answer, R. Elchanan asserts, is that anyone who considers the matter honestly will arrive at the truth of God's existence.[52] Likewise, Rambam holds the "innocent" heretic responsible for his negligence because he is not really innocent; he could have known better.[53] How does a person turn to heresy; what causes man to err? His desires and passions:

---

52. Proof for R. Elchanan's thesis can be found in the Talmud (*Zevachim* 12b). The Talmud queries about a case in which a person designates a *chatat* and subsequently denies the existence of God (המיר דתו), which disqualifies him from bringing a *korban*, and then returns to his faith in God. Do we say that his *korban* is invalid, since for a time it could not be brought (דיחוי)? The Talmud concludes that this might not be דיחוי because he has it in his power to repent (בידו לחזור). This case differs from a situation where a person designated a *chatat*, went mad, and then regained his composure. In this case, the *korban* is invalid, since it is not in his power to regain his faculties. Now, we must ask why the first case is considered בידו לחזור if, in his current state, he has come to the erroneous conclusion that God does not exist. If his position reflects a truly honest mistake, it is not in his power to realize the error of his ways. If we accept R. Elchanan's conclusion, though, the question dissipates. His erroneous belief merely reflects giving in to his desires and allowing his cravings to control his beliefs. Thus, just as it is in his control to tackle his desires, so too, if he exerts himself, he can overcome his heretical inclinations and honestly arrive at the truth.
53. What, then, does Ra'avad hold? According to R. Elchanan, Ra'avad partially forgives even the heretic who errs following an honest search. He could have avoided error

> The fundamentals of faith in and of themselves are simple and compelling for any person who is not a fool. It is impossible to doubt their truth. This holds, though, only provided that a person is not bribed, that is, that he is free of this-worldly lusts and desires. Thus, heresy is not rooted in a breakdown of reason in and of itself, but rather in a person's desire to satisfy his lusts, which distorts and blinds his reason. We now understand the Torah's admonition (*Bamidbar* 15:39): "And you shall not stray after your heart" – this refers to heresy (*Berachot* 12b). This means that a person is admonished to suppress and control his desires in order that his reason be free from the distortions they cause so that he may recognize the truth... Heresy has no place in man's reason, but rather in his desires and lusts.[54]

Of course, R. Elchanan does not believe that idolaters or heretics are conscious of this motivation. Rather, as the Talmud tells us concerning idolatry – which people served with devotion and sacrifice – subconscious forces often produce skewed decisions.[55] Nevertheless, even if a person is unaware of his motivation, he is held accountable to the degree that he had the ability, through contemplation and introspection, to arrive at the truth.

Indeed, in 2.1 we saw Rambam (*Moreh ha-Nevuchim* 1:5) warn that temptation can unknowingly cause error. Only when a person's singular desire is the quest for truth will he be largely protected from error. As long as a person simultaneously craves other things, such as lust or honor, these desires may cloud his judgment and lead him to justify the false beliefs necessary to achieve his yearning. Rambam emphasizes that, left unchecked, desires pervert our intellectual reasoning. A person may think he is seeking the truth, but, in fact, he is only justifying their agenda. Thus, to correctly apprehend the truth, one must first rid

---

by better controlling his desires, but because his mistakes were honest, he is not deemed a heretic.

54. *Dugma'ot le-Bei'urei Aggadot Al Derech ha-Pshat* No. 1. Translation adapted from David Strauss.

55. **סנהדרין דף סג עמוד ב**

אמר רב יהודה אמר רב: יודעין היו ישראל בעבודה זרה שאין בה ממש, ולא עבדו עבודה זרה אלא להתיר להם עריות בפרהסיא.

oneself of this sort of desire. He must seek truth for the sake of truth. While difficult, Rambam maintains that, with hard work, a human being is capable of reaching this state.

Is R. Elchanan's Theory Still Relevant Today?

R. Yehuda Amital (*Jewish Values in a Changing World*) objects to R. Elchanan's general approach, at least in the modern context:

> I believe that Rabbi Wasserman's explanations do not suffice. Many people come to a secular outlook not in order to satisfy their desires, but rather because of their dedication to ideals that may, at times, even demand great sacrifice. It is difficult to pin all disbelief on following after one's desires.[56]

What would R. Elchanan respond? Would he say that times are different and it no longer is true that an honest search automatically yields belief in God? Or would he say that even today, the honest seeker would conclude that God exists? Since his argument rests upon the eternal *mitzva*

---

56. In 11.6, we saw R. Shternbuch suggest that R. Chaim maintains that someone who never was educated at all (as frequently is the case today) is considered a *tinok shenishba* with respect to all forms of heresy. R. Aharon Lichtenstein considers a similar approach in *Mevakshei Panecha* (cited in an article available at http://yediah.blogspot.com/2012/01/reading-mevakshei-panecha-part-4-final.html.):

> Rav Elhanan Wasserman said that faith [in God] is simple and easy. However the *Yetzer Hara* interferes and keeps man from worshipping God. I do not accept these words. Firstly, to my mind, that is factually untrue. Secondly, this argument is somewhat insulting. It argues that were it not for bad urges, others too would aspire to faith. True that our natural senses may bring a person to believe, but to argue that it is easy and simple, were it not for our urges, I cannot agree with that. A certain effort is required for one to arrive at belief. The concept of faith is complex. Specifically, one cannot give one answer that one can say with certainty that it will convince every denier.

One might respond that R. Elchanan is not claiming that it is easy. Arriving at the truth in spite of the various urges proves exceedingly difficult, just as the attraction to idolatry in the ancient world, which Chazal understood was subconsciously rooted in sexual desire, was extraordinarily powerful. R. Elchanan simply is saying that it is possible to arrive at the truth.

of *emuna,* he presumably would contend that even today, an honest search will yield belief in God.[57]

What about R. Amital's challenge? In a recent *New York Times* interview, Dr. Alvin Plantinga was asked why so many presumably intelligent philosophers are atheists in light of the powerful arguments that can be mounted against atheism. Essentially, this is R. Elchanan's question as to how someone as brilliant as Aristotle could deny God. Remarkably, he gives the same answer:

> I'm not a psychologist, so I don't have any special knowledge here. Still, there are some possible explanations. Thomas Nagel, a terrific philosopher and an unusually perceptive atheist, says he simply doesn't *want* there to be any such person as God. And it isn't hard to see why. For one thing, there would be what some would think was an intolerable invasion of privacy: God would know my every thought long before I thought it. For another, my actions and even my thoughts would be a constant subject of judgment and evaluation.
>
> Basically, these come down to the serious limitation of human autonomy posed by theism. This desire for autonomy can reach very substantial proportions, as with the German philosopher Heidegger, who, according to Richard Rorty, felt guilty for living in a universe he had not himself created. Now there's a tender conscience! But even a less monumental desire for autonomy can perhaps also motivate atheism.[58]

Is R. Elchanan's Theory Relevant for All 13 Principles?

Another question one might ask is to what extent R. Elchanan's theory applies to all thirteen principles. Firstly, why should desires trigger denial of incorporeality? A person who believes in a physical God may still

57. Indeed, R. Amital's description of the great sacrifice made for heretical ideals was even more apt during R. Elchanan's time than our own, and yet he still maintained his position.
58. http://opinionator.blogs.nytimes.com/2014/02/09/is-atheism-irrational/?_r=0.

punctiliously observe the Torah. Moreover, even if we accept that the honest searcher always concludes that God exists, will he always conclude that there will be a resurrection or that every word in the Torah comes from God? Belief in God can, to some extent, be shown logically. Not so concerning the resurrection.

To this, R. Elchanan responds that the honest search concludes not just in the necessity of God's existence, but in the veracity of the Torah. This second component demands belief in all thirteen principles. However, even R. Elchanan concedes that concerning certain beliefs, we allow for *tinok she-nishba* when it comes to reasonable errors.[59] The question then remains: to which principles are we willing to apply this exception? Perhaps as the world becomes more secular, the list expands.

Earlier Thinkers Who Disagree with R. Elchanan's Theory

Despite the cogency of R. Elchanan's argument, other great thinkers disagree. In Ramban's Introduction to his commentary on *Iyov* he notes that the primary reason why people deny God's existence or His providence is suffering and the problem of evil. Witnessing or experiencing agony is not only painful, but the central cause of heresy:

> ויש דבר מכאיב הלבבות ומדאיב המחשבות, ממנו לבדו נמשכו כל הדורות לכפירה גמורה, והוא הראות בעולם משפט מעוקל וצדיק ורע לו רשע וטוב לו... זה שורש המרי בכל המורדים מכל אומה ולשון.

> There is a matter that pains the hearts and distresses the mind. In every generation people were drawn to absolute heresy from it **alone**. And it is seeing injustice, the righteous suffer and the wicked prosper... This is the root of all remissness from every nation and every language.

59. R. Elchanan presumes that a person is expected to recognize, on his own, that God must have left instructions for His creatures and to seek out the bearers of that divine tradition. Unfortunately, such a person may be fooled by some other religion's leaders into believing the wrong beliefs (*tinok she-nishba*).

Ramban implies that it is both witnessing the innocent suffer as well as being plagued by the philosophical problem of evil, and not the desire for pleasure, that leads to heresy.[60]

Along similar lines, R. Sa'adya Gaon considers the various causes for heresy, outlining eight triggers. Like R. Elchanan, many stem from intellectual laziness, justification of a life free of obligation, and arrogance. However, R. Sa'adya Gaon also considers the possibility that a person's rejection stems from the lousy arguments sometimes offered by believers and incoherent defenses of religion. R. Sa'adya Goan appears open to the possibility that the root of heresy is sometimes intellectual.[61] Accordingly, in *Emunot ve-Dei'ot* he seeks to correct these errors.

---

60. On one hand, Ramban writes that it is the question of evil, not the desire for pleasure, that leads to heresy. At the same time, one wonders whether Ramban is referring to the intellectual problem of suffering or the emotional pain (מכאיב הלבבות ומדאיב המחשבות) that witnessing suffering triggers.

61. ספר האמונות והדעות הקדמה

ואסמיך לדברים אלה מה שעלה בדעתי בסבות, אשר הפילו בכפירה ובכזב וברוח מהאמנת האותות והעיון באמונות, כי אני רואה מהם שמונה, הם נמצאות הרבה:

1. תחלתם כובד הטורח על טבע בני אדם, וכאשר ירגיש הטבע בענין שבא עליו לחזק אותו ולאמצו בראיה ומשתמש בה בענין התורה הוא בורח ומפחד מזה. ובעבור זה אתה רואה הרבה בני אדם אומרים: האמת כבדה. ומהם אומרים: האמת מרה. והם רוצים בחירות ובורחים ממנה, ועליהם אמר הכתוב (יחזקאל י״א ט״ו) רחקו מעל י״י לנו היא נתנה הארץ למורשה. ולא הבינו הפתאים כי אם ילכו לרצון הטבע בברחם מהעמל והיגיעה ישארו רעבים ונענים בבטול הזרע והבנין.
2. והשנית הסכלות הגוברת על רבים מהם והוא מדבר בלשון האולת וחושב בלבו העצלה ואומר מבלי מחשב, אין דבר, וכן במצפונו. ובאלה הוא אומר (הושע י׳ ג׳) כי עתה יאמרו אין מלך לנו כי לא יראנו את י״י והמלך מה יעשה לנו. ואינם חושבים כי כאשר הם מדברים בקצת האולתות האל והגבוהות ימותו ויאבדו.
3. והשלישית נטות האדם למלאת תאוותיו במאכל ומשתה, ומשגל, ובקנין, והוא ממהר לעשות זה בזריזות בלי מחשבה, ובהם אומר הכתוב (תהלים נ״ג ב׳) אמר נבל בלבו אין אלהים וגו׳. ולא חשב כי כאשר יעשה זה בחליו ובבריאותו ויאכל כל מה שיתאוה, וישגל כל אשר ימצא, ימות ויאבד.
4. והרביעית הקיצה בעיון ומיעוט התישבות בעת השמע והמחשב ומספיק לו המזער ויאמר כבר עיינתי ולא יצא לי כי אם זה, ובהם אמר הכתוב (משלי י״ב כ״ז) לא יחרוך רמיה צידו וגו׳. ופירוש רמיה הקץ לא יגיע לחפצו, ולא ידעו כי אם ינהגו בזה בענין תאותם לא תשלם להם.
5. והחמישית עזות וגאוה שגוברים על האדם, ולא יודה כי יש חכמה נעלמת ממנו ולא מדע עמד לפניו, ובהם אמר הכתוב (תהלי׳ י׳ ד׳) רשע בגובה אפו בל ידרוש וגו׳, ולא הרגיש כי הטענה הזאת לא תועילהו בעשות טבעת ולא בכתיבת אות.

The above two sources do not address the question of whether the denier should be blamed; they simply observe the complexity of disbelief. Another earlier commentator who appears to have a radically different position than R. Elchanan is R. Abba Mari ha-Yarchi, in *Minchat Kena'ot,* Ch. 14 (*Mossad ha-Rav Kook* ed. *Teshuvot ha-Rashba,* Vol. 1, p. 257). In discussing the heresies of Aristotle, he writes that Aristotle himself was not at fault for his heretical beliefs because he could not have known better.[62]

11.8 *CHAZON ISH*

Another great thinker who appears to reject R. Chaim's understanding of Rambam is *Chazon Ish. Chazon Ish* derives from Rambam's treatment of *tinok she-nishba* that Rambam maintains that anyone who would be convinced to believe in God and Torah given an appropriate attempt does not have the status of heretic.[63] Thus, non-observant Jews today, for the most

---

6. והששית מלה שישמענה האדם בשם אחד מן המכחישים והגיעה אל לבו ותמחצהו ויעמוד כל ימיו במחצו, ובו אומר (משלי י"ח ח') דברי נרגן כמתלהמים וגו', ולא חשב כי אם לא יגן על עצמו מהחום והקור יביאוהו אל המות.
7. והשביעית ראיה חלושה שמע אותה מאחד מן המיחדים והוא חושב כי הכל הוא כן ויהיו משחקים עליהם ומלעיבים בם, ולא העלה במחשבתו כי סוחר הבגדים היקרים אם איננו בקי בקפולם לא יפחית זה הבגדים מאומה.
8. והשמינית אדם שיש בינו ובין קצת המיחדים שנאה ומביאו זה עוד לשנוא אלהיו, ובהם הוא אומר (תהלי' קי"ט קל"ט) צמתתני קנאתי כי שכחו דבריך צרי, ולא ידע הכסיל ששונאו לא יוכל להגיע ממנו מה שהגיע הוא מעצמו, כי אין ביכולת משנאו להתמיד עליו הענוי המכאיב עדי עד. אך מי שהיה מנהגו חלוף הדעות, כאשר חשב בפסוקים מהמקרא, וראה בהם מה שהרחיקו או שהתפלל לאלהיו ולא ענהו ושאל ממנו ולא נתן לו. או שראה רשעים שלא נקם מהם. או שהיה תמה איך תעמוד לכופרים מלכות, או שראה המות אוסף את הבריות וכולל אותם, או שענין האחדות והנפש וענין הגמול והעונש לא עלה בשכלו. אלה כלם והדומה להם אני עתיד לזכור כל א' מהם במאמר אשר הוא ממנו, ובשער הראוי לו, ואדבר עליו כפי היכולת, ואקוה שאגיע בו אל תקות המנהגים בזה בע"ה.

62. This treatment of philosophers (which is very different than R. Elchanan's, who accuses Aristotle of bias against the truth) may be similar to that of R. Yehuda ha-Levi in *Kuzari,* as discussed in 9.1.

63. **חזו"א (יורה דעה סימן א אות ו)**
ותינוק שנשבה בין העכו"מ דינו כישראל ושחיטתו מותרת, שהוא בחזקת שאם יודיעוה וישתדלו עמו כשעור ההשתדלות שהוא ראוי לשוב, לא יזיד לבלתי שב, אמנם אחר שהשתדלו עמו והוא מזיד וממאן לשוב, דינו כמומר. ושעור ההשתדלות תלוי לפי התבוננות הדיינים כאשר

part, would have the status of *tinok she-nishba*. Not only do we not kill them, but we are obligated to love them.[64] Moreover, he shows that the concept of *tinok she-nishba* is not the innovation of Rambam but rather emerges from the Talmud.[65] This will be discussed further in 11.10, Appendix B.

11.9 APPENDIX A: THINKERS WHO EXCUSE DISBELIEF BASED ON FAULTY REASONING

Earlier, we cited R. Chaim's understanding of Rambam that disbelief based on faulty reasoning constitutes heresy, and we questioned this reading of Rambam. Even if one accepts the conventional interpretation, though, Rambam's view is not unanimous; Ra'avad (cited in 11.1) disagrees. Later thinkers accept Ra'avad's critique and expand it.[66]

יופיע רוח קדשם בהכרעת דינו. ומה שנחלקו אחרונים ז״ל בצדוקים בדורות האחרונים אי חשיבי כאנוסים היינו בהכרעת שיעור הידיעה שיודעים ממציאות ישראל ושאבותיהם פירשו מהם ונותנים כתף סוררת, אי דיינינן להו כשעור ידיעה למחשב מזיד או לא ואכתי אנוסים הם ובאמת צריך לדון כל איש ואיש בפרט ... וכמו כן אותו שאבותיו פרשו מדרכי הצבור והוא נתגדל ללא תורה דינו כישראל לכל דבר, ונמי צריך למוד שיעור ידיעתו אי לא חשיב מזיד, ואותו שדיינינן ליה כאנוס זוכין עירוב עבורו.

חזון איש עירובין סימן פז אות יד

ותינוק שנשבה בין העכו״ם דינו כישראל ושחיטתו מותרת שהוא בחזקת שאם יודיעוהו וישתדלו עמו כשיעור ההשתדלות שהוא ראוי לשוב לא יזיד לבלתי שב.

64. **חזון איש יורה דעה סימן ב אות כח**

ובהגהות מיימוניות פ״ו מהלכות דעות כתב, דאין רשאין לשנאותו אלא אחר שאינו מקבל תוכחה. ובסוף ספר אהבת חסד, כתב בשם הגר״י מולין, דמצוה לאהוב את הרשעים מהאי טעמא, והביא כן מתשובת מהר״ם מלובלין סי׳ יג, כי אצלנו הוא קדם תוכחה, שאין אנו יודעים להוכיח ודיינין להו כאנוסים ולכן אי אפשר לנו לדון בזה לפטור מן היבום, וכן לשאר הלכות.

65. **חזון איש יורה דעה סימן ב אות יח בהג״ה**

ותימא דאמר מכות ח: דישראל גולה ע״י כותי ואי דינו במורידין איך יתכן שגולה, ואין לומר בכותי חבר דאמר שם דאם לטיי׳ פטור משום דאינו עושה מעשה עמך וע״כ לומר דאין דברי הר״מ אלא בראשונים אבל דורות הבאים אינם במורידין וכמו שסיים הר״מ שם, וגמ׳ דמכות בדורות אחרונים ולפ״ז אפשר דזה שדינו להורידו באמת דינו כמומר לכל דבר דהכופר בתורה שבע״פ אין לו חלק גם בתורה שבכתב שהרי עיקר פירושה בעל פה ומה בצע בפירושים שוא ושקר, וכל דברי הר״מ בפ״ד מהלכות שחיטה בקראים משום רבניהם נחשבים כשוגגים, וכן הא דהכשירו בגמ׳ שחיטת כותי ג״כ משום דהבנים כשוגגים, וכן מסתבר שהרי מבואר בגמ׳ מכות שם שהם כשרים לעדות וכן אמרו גיטין י׳ ב׳ ואי דינם במורידין לא מסתבר כלל שיהיו כשרים לעדות.

Rashi (*Chullin* 132b s.v. *she-eino modeh be-avoda*) also seems to accept the thesis of *tinok she-nishba*. (This presumption resolves Ritva's challenge. *Chatam Sofer* has an alternative, though very difficult, solution.)

66. A similar position may emerge from Rashi *Shabbat* 31a, as we explained in 8.12.

These thinkers maintain that we excuse the person who makes an honest mistake in interpreting the Torah to imply that God has a physical body.[67] Let us cite three presentations of this perspective.

Radvaz (1479–1573) was asked how to deal with a preacher who publicly taught that Moshe was divine in some sense. Here is his response:

שו"ת רדב"ז חלק ד סימן קפז

ולא מצאתי טעם לפוטרו מן העונש זולת מפני שהוא טועה בעיונו ותקנתו קלקלתו. ולא עדיף האי ממי שטועה באחד מעיקרי הדת מחמת עיונו הנפסד שלא נקרא בשביל זה כופר. **והרי הלל היה אדם גדול וטעה באחד מעיקרי הדת שאמר אין להם משיח לישראל שכבר אכלוהו בימי חזקיהו.** ומפני זה הטעות לא חשבוהו כופר ח"ו דאם לא כן איך היו אומרים שמועה משמו. והטעם מבואר **כיון שאין כפירתו אלא מפני שחושב שמה שעלה בעיונו אמת ואם כן אנוס הוא** ופטור. אף הכא נמי טועה בעיונו הוא.

I have found no basis for exempting him from punishment other than that he has erred in his thinking, such that what should have brought him to greater perfection has brought him to ruin. He is no better than one who has erred in one of the fundamental religious principles on account of his deficient understanding, which does not make him a heretic. Surely, Hillel was a great man, and he erred in one of the fundamental principles of our religion when he said that Israel has no messiah, for the messiah already was consumed in the days of Chizkiyahu.[68] But Hillel was not

67. It seems conceivable that these thinkers would not exonerate certain mistakes. For example, would Ra'avad excuse a person who does not believe in God in the same manner in which he forgives the person who believes God has a body based on a literal understanding of a midrash? Perhaps all thinkers would concede that there are certain parameters for inclusion in the Jewish people which are not waived even in the event of guiltless errors.

68. Sanhedrin 98b cites the following opinion:

דרבי הילל דאמר: אין משיח לישראל, שכבר אכלוהו בימי חזקיה.

R. Hillel said, "There is no messiah for the Jewish people, because they have already enjoyed him in the days of Chizkiyahu."

Rashi explains:

> regarded as a heretic, God forbid, on account of this error, for if so, how did they report traditions in his name? The reason is clear: **since his heresy stems from thinking that the results of his speculation are true, he is regarded as if he were coerced, so he is exempt**. Here, too, [the preacher] has erred in his thinking.[69]

Radvaz argues that just as in all other areas of Halacha we exempt someone coerced (*oneis*) from punishment, so too we exempt this sinner. Since his heresy stems from thinking that the results of his speculation are true, he is regarded as if he were coerced.

Radvaz goes further than Ra'avad, since one could have argued Ra'avad critiques Rambam's position only concerning corporeality, because there are Torah sources that seem to support the error. He would not apply this dispensation to theological positions explicitly contradicted by even a superficial reading of the Torah. However, Radvaz maintains that since the dispensation of *oneis* applies in all areas of Torah, it is relevant here as well.

R. Yosef Albo (1380–1444) in *Sefer ha-Ikkarim* takes a similar stance when trying to justify the many great sages who made major theological errors.[70] He writes that every Jew must believe that everything written in the Torah is absolutely true. Therefore, anyone who denies anything stated in the Torah is a heretic.[71] However, if someone fully accepts all that is in the Torah but misunderstands its content, then he is not a heretic.

אין משיח לישראל - שחזקיה היה משיח ועליו נאמרו כל הנבואות אצמיח קרן לבית ישראל ועמד ורעה בעוז ה׳.

69. Translation adapted from "How to relate to one who has lost his faith" by R. Yehuda Amital in *Jewish Values in a Changing World*.

70. ללמד זכות על חכמי ישראל המדברים בזה וכיוצא בו.
See, however, *Sefer ha-Ikkarim* 2:16, which indicates that R. Albo may not apply this standard to all beliefs.

71. כל איש ישראל חייב להאמין שכל מה שבא בתורה הוא אמת גמור, ומי שכופר בשום דבר ממה שנמצא בתורה, עם היותו יודע שזהו דעת התורה, נקרא כופר, כמו שאמרו רבותינו ז״ל בפרק חלק (סנהדרין צט א), שכל האומר כל התורה כולה מפי הגבורה חוץ מפסוק אחד שאמרו משה מעצמו, עליו נאמר כי דבר ה׳ בזה (במדבר טו:לא), והוא בכלל האומר אין תורה מן השמים.
This appears to be true even regarding someone who "accidentally" didn't believe in the Torah, such as a literal *tinok she-nishba* among non-Jews. The Radvaz may

ספר העיקרים מאמר ראשון פרק ב

אבל מי שהוא מחזיק בתורת משה ומאמין בעקריה, וכשבא לחקור על זה מצד השכל והבנת הפסוקים הטהו העיון לומר שאחד מן העקרים הוא על דרך אחרת ולא כפי המובן בתחלת הדעת, או הטהו העיון להכחיש העקר ההוא להיותו חושב שאיננו דעת בריא תכריח התורה להאמינו, או יחשוב במה שהוא עקר שאיננו עקר ויאמין אותו כשאר האמונות שבאו בתורה שאינם עקרים, או יאמין אי זו אמונה בנס מנסי התורה להיותו חושב שאיננו מכחיש בזה שום אמונה מן האמונות שיחויב להאמין מצד התורה, **אין זה כופר**, אבל הוא בכלל חכמי ישראל וחסידיהם, אף על פי שהוא טועה בעיונו, והוא חוטא בשוגג וצריך כפרה.

> If a person upholds the law of Moshe and believes in its principles, yet when he undertakes to investigate these matters with his reason and scrutinizes the texts, he is misled by his speculation and interprets a given principle otherwise than it is taken to mean at first sight; or if he denies the principle because he thinks that it does not represent a sound theory that the Torah obligates us to believe; or if he erroneously denies that a given belief is a fundamental principle, even though he believes it as he believes the other principles of the Torah that are not fundamental principles; or if he entertains a certain notion in relation to one of the miracles of the Torah because he thinks that he is not thereby denying any of the doctrines that are obligatory upon us to believe by the authority of the Torah – **a person of this sort is not an unbeliever**. He is classed with the sages and pious men of Israel, though he holds erroneous theories. His sin is due to error and requires atonement.

Note that R. Albo does not conclude that the person who accidently holds false beliefs is given full reprieve. He too needs atonement like any accidental sinner (חוטא בשוגג). However, he is not classified as a heretic.

Thus, R. Albo's view differs from that of Rambam even if we accept the fourth approach. According to Rambam, with respect to fundamental

agree to this principle as well, meaning that everyone quoted so far would excuse a mistaken heretic only insofar as that heretic still believes in the Torah.

matters of faith, a person is either an *oneis* (someone coerced, i.e., *tinok she-nishba*) or a heretic and, therefore, excluded from the Jewish people and the afterlife. R. Albo, on the other hand, allows for a middle ground. When a person's false beliefs stem from negligence, he is deemed an accidental sinner (חוטא בשוגג). He requires atonement, but the Torah does not classify him as a heretic.

A modern variation of this position can be found in the writings of R. Kook, who appears to take for granted that we accept the position of Radvaz. When several important rabbis attacked R. Moshe Glasner because of his support for Zionism, R. Kook defended him. One of his arguments was that even if one thinks R. Glasner to be in error, he is no worse than an accidental heretic, whom we do not classify as a heretic. Accordingly, he still must be accorded respect:

> **מאמרי הראי״ה** 55–57
>
> ואפ׳ אי יהיבנא להו טעותייהו, שהדעה שהדר״ג ס״ל כוותה הוא דעה שהיא ח״ו נגד אמתתה של תורה, האיך יש להם רשות לדבר עליו עתק, הלוא דברי הרדב״ז בתשובה הם מפורשים, שאפי׳ מי שטועה ח״ו בדבר מעיקרי התורה מחמת עיונו פטור מעונש, שמפני שחושב שמה שעלה בעיונו הוא אמת, וא״כ, אנוס הוא... וחלילה לבזותו אפ׳ אם הטעות היא בעניין של עיקר.
>
> Even if you assume (incorrectly) that he is in error – that the position that R. Glasner has adopted runs counter, God forbid, to the truth of the Torah – how are you permitted to speak about him with such arrogance? Surely, the words of Radvaz in his responsum are explicit, that even one who errs, God forbid, in one of the fundamental principles of the Torah on account of his speculation is exempt from punishment. Because he thinks that the results of his speculation are true, he is regarded as if he were coerced… Heaven forbid that he should be humiliated, even if he has erred about a fundamental principle.

Non-Jewish Idolaters

Our focus, thus far, has been on Jews. What about non-Jews? Clearly, the Torah expects non-Jews to believe in God and shun polytheism. Idolatry is one of the seven Noahide Laws and the Talmud states that according to Torah law, a non-Jew who serves idolatry is executed. How is the non-Jew supposed to know that idolatry is wrong? What if he sincerely errs and concludes that there is more than one god?

The Talmud (*Bava Kama* 92a)[72] indicates that a non-Jew is subject to execution only because he could have or should have known otherwise:

תלמוד בבלי מסכת בבא קמא דף צב עמוד א
מכאן לבן נח שנהרג, שהיה לו ללמוד ולא למד.

> From here (God's instruction to Avimelech [*Bereishit* 20:7]), we derive that a Noahide is executed because he should have learned and did not learn.

Rambam codifies this by noting that even though a non-Jew is not executed if he accidentally (*shogeig*) violated the law, violations that stem from ignorance of the law are considered negligence and the perpetrator is held accountable:

רמב"ם הלכות מלכים פרק י הלכה א
בן נח ששגג באחת ממצותיו פטור מכלום... במה דברים אמורים בשגג באחת ממצות ועבר בלא כוונה, כגון שבעל אשת חבירו ודמה שהיא אשתו או פנויה, אבל אם ידע שהוא אשת חבירו ולא ידע שהיא אסורה עליו, אלא עלה על לבו שדבר זה מותר לו, וכן אם הרג והוא לא ידע שאסור להרוג, הרי זה קרוב למזיד ונהרג, ולא תחשב זו להם שגגה מפני שהיה לו ללמוד ולא למד.

> A gentile who inadvertently violates one of his commandments is exempt from all punishment... When does the above apply? When he inadvertently violates a command without sinful intention; for example, a person who engages in relations with his colleague's wife under the impression that she is his own wife or

72. See also *Makkot* 9a. Note that the explanation of Rashi as well as R. Menachem Me'iri there may indicate that they disagree with Rambam regarding a non-Jew who had no knowledge of the laws of Noach altogether.

> unmarried. If, however, one knew that she was his colleague's wife, but did not know that she was forbidden to him, or it occurred to him that this act was permitted, or one killed without knowing that it is forbidden to kill, he is considered close to having sinned intentionally and is executed. This is not considered as an inadvertent violation. For he should have learned the obligations incumbent upon him and did not.

What if nobody told the gentile that idolatry is wrong? Rambam implies that every human being is capable of independently deriving the seven Noahide laws, which reflect basic morality.[73]

> **רמב"ם הלכות מלכים פרק ט הלכה א**
> על ששה דברים נצטווה אדם הראשון: על ע"ז, ועל ברכת השם, ועל שפיכות דמים, ועל גילוי עריות, ועל הגזל, ועל הדינים, אע"פ שכולן הן קבלה בידינו ממשה רבינו, **והדעת נוטה להן,** מכלל דברי תורה יראה שעל אלו נצטוה, הוסיף לנח אבר מן החי...

> Six precepts were commanded to Adam: (1) the prohibition against worship of false gods, (2) the prohibition against cursing God, (3) the prohibition against murder, (4) the prohibition against incest and adultery, (5) the prohibition against theft, and (6) the command to establish laws and courts of justice. Even though we have received all of these commands from Moshe **and,**

73. One wonders the extent to which this is true regarding the details of the laws. For example, do we expect every individual to figure out that his mother's daughter is prohibited to him, but not his father's daughter? Or, perhaps, the notion that incest is wrong is intuitive, even if the details are not. Moreover, one wonders if Rambam maintains that all people can independently ascertain these directives, or that wise people could figure them out.

Another important question to consider is whether non-Jews must observe these laws because they are divinely ordained. In 20.6 we discuss Rambam's distinction between *chasidei umot ha-olam* (the pious among the gentiles) and *chachmei umot ha-olam* (the wise among the gentiles), with the former observing the seven Noahide laws because God commanded them in the Torah and the latter observing them because wisdom dictates that they be observed. We also consider whether *chachmei umot ha-olam* have a share in *olam ha-ba* and whether they are superior to *chasidei umot ha-olam*.

> **furthermore, they are concepts that intellect itself tends to accept**, it appears from the Torah's words that Adam was commanded concerning them. The prohibition against eating flesh from a living animal was added for Noach…

Nevertheless, Abarbanel notes that generally when the Torah chastises non-Jews for their moral lapses, it rarely focuses on idolatry (certainly when referring to non-Jews not living in the land of Israel). While this does not imply any degree of legitimacy to idolatry (it is false and prohibited by God), it may imply a degree of tolerance. Conceivably, this thesis would explain the following verse which points to a distinction between how God views a non-Jew serving idolatry (even if it is utterly false) and a Jew doing the same:

> **דברים ד:יט**
>
> וּפֶן תִּשָּׂא עֵינֶיךָ הַשָּׁמַיְמָה וְרָאִיתָ אֶת הַשֶּׁמֶשׁ וְאֶת הַיָּרֵחַ וְאֶת הַכּוֹכָבִים כֹּל צְבָא הַשָּׁמַיִם וְנִדַּחְתָּ וְהִשְׁתַּחֲוִיתָ לָהֶם וַעֲבַדְתָּם אֲשֶׁר חָלַק יְקֹוָק אֱלֹהֶיךָ **אֹתָם לְכֹל הָעַמִּים** תַּחַת כָּל הַשָּׁמָיִם:
>
> And lest you lift up your eyes to heaven, and see the sun, and the moon, and the stars, all the host of heaven, **which Hashem your God assigned to all peoples** under the entire heaven, and be drawn away to prostrate yourselves before them and worship them.

Superficially, this verse seems to legitimize idolatry for non-Jews. Of course, such a reading is inconceivable insofar as the Torah prohibits idolatry for non-Jews. That is why this verse is always understood differently (e.g., the celestial bodies were given to illuminate or God allows non-Jews to be misled and perceive the sun and moon as gods).[74]

---

74. See Rashi, Rashbam, and Rambam, Chapter 2 of *Hilchot Avoda Zara*. Interestingly, Ramban understands this verse as referring to the reality that non-Jews are, to some degree, under the domain of their national angel (*sar*). Thus, God has, in a sense, handed them over to their *sar*:

    רמב"ן דברים ד:יט-כ

    וכבר פירשתי (ויקרא יח:כה) אשר חלק ה' אלהיך אתם לכל העמים - כי לכולם כוכב ומזל וגבוהים עליהם מלאכי עליון, כגון הנאמר בדניאל שר מלכות פרס ושר מלכות יון, ובעבור

However, Abarbanel cites the above verse in his comments on the book of *Yona* in a way that implies that it does indicate a degree of forbearance allowed to non-Jews in the realm of idolatry in the event that they did not know better. To appreciate this, we must consider whether the inhabitants of Ninveh were idolaters. At the end of the book, Yona feels dejected by God's decision to spare the city. God criticizes this response: "You had pity for the gourd, something you did not work for, nor grew; which came up in a night and perished in a night. And should I not have pity on Ninveh, the great city, wherein are more than one hundred and twenty thousand people **that cannot discern between their right and their left**; and also much cattle" (*Yona* 4:11). What does the bolded phrase mean? According to Rashi and Radak, it refers to children. Had God destroyed the city, the children, who could not have known better, would have suffered. Yona should have had compassion on them. Abarbanel, however, understands that the above verse refers to the adults who, to some degree, did not know better.

If we accept this understanding, we must consider what the inhabitants of Ninveh were doing wrong. Specifically, were they idolaters? This too is subject to debate. According to ibn Ezra (1:2), they were not (he deduces this from 3:3 which refers to the city as **עִיר גְּדוֹלָה לֵאלֹהִים**). However, Abarbanel assumes that they were.[75] With this, Abarbanel explains why Yona was so perturbed that God spared

---

כן יעשו להם אלהים מהם ויעבדום. ואמר ואתכם לקח ה' - כי אתם חלק השם, לא תקימו עליכם שר או עוזר זולתו. כי הוא הוציא אתכם מכור הברזל, שהייתם בתוך מצרים בכור אש ועצים, והוציא אתכם משם כנגד שריהם שעשה בהם שפטים, ולולי שהפילם לא הייתם יוצאים כי היו הם במעלתם שלא תצאו, והנה עשה כל זה כדי שתהיו לו נחלה ותהיו לשמו הגדול סגולה מכל העמים.

However, the fact that they are governed by their *sar* does not lend any legitimacy to their serving their *sar*.

75. **אברבנאל יונה ד:יא**

ידע בין ימינו לשמאלו ובהמה רבה שלא אמר זה על התינוקות כדברי המפרשים כי הנה בעיר הנדחת היו נדונים התינוקות בחטאת אביהם כי הם איברי האדם וחלקו, אבל אמר זה אל אנשי נינוה כולם שהיו בתוך העיר הרבה משתים עשרה רבוא אדם מבלי תורה **ולכן בענין הע"ז לא ידעו בין ימינם לשמאלם** והם כבהמה רבה, אמנם ישראל שעמדו על הר סיני ונצטוו על הע"ז ושמעו מפי הגבורה לא יהיה לך אלהים אחרים על פני אין ראוי לפוטרן בענין הע"ז כמו לאנשי נינוה.... ולכן [נינוה] לא נתחייבו כליה מפאת אמונותיהם במה שלא נצטוו עליו...

Ninveh after they repented. He answers that this is because they remained idolatrous, only repenting from their immoral behavior.[76] While such repentance would have been unacceptable for Jews, who should have known better, it was acceptable for the people of Ninveh.[77] Most relevant to our discussion is that Abarbanel cites the aforementioned verse in *Devarim* to justify Ninveh's lack of culpability.[78]

This idea may reflect itself in Halacha as well. The Talmud (*Chullin* 5a) rules that we do not accept the sacrifice of a Jewish idolater (*mumar la-avoda zara*), but we do accept the sacrifice of a non-Jewish idolater. Why distinguish between the two; after all, the Torah equally forbids Jew and non-Jew from idolatry? Though this law emerges from scriptural analysis, Abarbanel's thesis beautifully explains why the Torah might differentiate, insofar as this halacha also reflects forbearance allowed to non-Jews in the realm of idolatry.[79]

It seems to me, however, that even Abarbanel would not fully exonerate idolatrous non-Jews. It seems hard to imagine that only those non-Jews who happen to know that God commanded the Seven Noahide Laws are responsible to keep them. Rather, idolatry is less egregious for non-Jews, in the event that they do not know that God prohibited it. Therefore, they are more likely to be punished for moral lapses which are entirely inexcusable (see Ramban *Bereishit* 6:13).[80] Either way, we see

---

76. This relates to Abarbanel's general approach to Yona in which the prophet is primarily concerned about Ashur's role in the punishment of the Jewish people.

77. והרעה שנזכרה כאן היא חולי שבעצבון לבו נפל וחלה חולי ורעה גדולה ובקש למות, והיה זה לפי שיונה חשב שלא תשוב הגזרה מעליהם כ"א כשישובו מדרכם הרעה באמונות ובמעשים אבל כשראה שהחזיקו בע"ז שלהם ולא עשו תשובה במה שבינם למקום שהוא העיקר אלא במה שבינם לחבריהם ושעכ"ז נחם השם על הרעה נתקיים במחשבתו שהיה משוא פנים בדבר, כי הנה העבודה זרה הוא היותר חמור שהיה ביניהם והם לא שבו ממנו ולמה אם כן נחם השם על הרעה אשר דבר לעשות להם אין זה אלא שהוא נושא להם עון ופשע...

78. **אברבנאל יונה פרק ד**

 וא"ת שהם עובדים ע"ז ושלא שבו ממנה הנה הם כדמות ב"ח בלתי מדברים כי אחרי שאין להם תורה ולא נצטוו בה **וחלק השם צבא השמים לכל העמים ומפני זה אין ראוי שיענשו עליה.**

79. See *Achiezer* 3:67 for an alternative explanation of this halacha.

80. Regardless, as we have seen, Abarbanel's understanding of *Devarim* 4 does not seem to reflect the mainstream approach. Moreover, from a textual standpoint it is not any more satisfying, because even Abarbanel concedes that the Torah bans idolatry from non-Jews, therefore, the term אֲשֶׁר חָלַק יְקֹוָק אֱלֹהֶיךָ אֹתָם לְכֹל הָעַמִּים is still not precise.

Abarbanel uphold that basic principle that people are held accountable only for evil perpetrated in the event that they should have known better, and that fundamentally this holds true even with respect to idolatry.

11.10 APPENDIX B: *TINOK SHE-NISHBA*

The Talmud (*Shabbat* 68b) introduces the concept of *tinok she-nishba bein ha-nochrim*, an infant who was captured and consequently raised among gentiles.[81] Such a person never was taught even the basic concepts of Jewish faith, such as the laws of *Shabbat*. Accordingly, he is treated differently than a Jew who violates the Torah after having been educated in its ways. For example, a regular Jew would have to bring a sin-offering (*chatat*) for every accidental violation of *Shabbat*, whereas a *tinok she-nishba* brings only one. The complex details of this category need not concern us at present. Instead, let us present Rambam's expansion of this principle.

Rambam's eighth principle of faith declares that not only is the written Torah the word of God transmitted through Moshe, but that this is true of the oral Torah as well:

> **וכן פירושה המקובל גם הוא מפי הגבורה, וזה שאנו עושים היום צורת הסוכה והלולב והשופר והציצית והתפילין וזולתם היא עצמה הצורה שאמר ה׳ למשה ואמר להו, והוא רק מוביל שליחות נאמן במה שהביא**
>
> Similarly, the explanation of the Torah was received from God, and this is what we use today to know the appearance and structure of the *sukka, lulav, shofar, tzitzit, tefillin*, etc. And all this God said to Moshe and Moshe told to us. And he is trustworthy in his role as the messenger…

In Chapter 28, we shall see which aspects of the oral law were given to Moshe and which evolved throughout the generations. All agree, however, that certain interpretations of the written Torah were given through Moshe, which Rambam calls *peirushim ha-mekubalim*, such as

81. כלל גדול אמרו בשבת, כל השוכח עיקר שבת, ועשה מלאכות הרבה בשבתות הרבה, אינו חייב אלא אחת; כיצד? **תינוק שנשבה לבין הנכרים**, וגר שנתגייר בין הנכרים, ועשה מלאכות הרבה בשבתות הרבה - אינו חייב אלא חטאת אחת.

the meaning of the words *sukka* and *totafot* (i.e., *tefillin*). Thus, if someone denies that these interpretations come directly from God through Moshe, he has the status of a heretic with all that it implies, as described in 11.1.[82] This law is codified in *Mishneh Torah*:

רמב"ם הלכות ממרים פרק ג הלכות א-ב

מי שאינו מודה בתורה שבעל פה אינו זקן ממרא האמור בתורה, אלא הרי זה בכלל האפיקורוסין ומיתתו בכל אדם. מאחר שנתפרסם שהוא כופר בתורה שבעל פה - מורידין ולא מעלין, כשאר המינים והאפיקורוסין והאומרין אין תורה מן השמים והמוסרים והמשומדים: כל אלו אינן בכלל ישראל.

A person who does not acknowledge the validity of the oral Torah is not the rebellious elder mentioned in the Torah. Instead, he is one of the heretics and should be put to death by any person. Once it becomes well-known that such a person denies the oral Torah, he may be pushed into a pit and may not be helped to climb out. He is like all the rest of the heretics who say that the Torah is not of divine origin, those who inform on their fellow Jews, and the apostates. All of these are not considered as members of the Jewish people.

Rambam then adds that there is an exception:

רמב"ם הלכות ממרים פרק ג הלכה ג

במה דברים אמורים באיש שכפר בתורה שבעל פה במחשבתו ובדברים שנראו לו, והלך אחר דעתו הקלה ואחר שרירות לבו וכופר בתורה שבעל פה תחילה כצדוק ובייתוס וכן כל התועים אחריו, אבל בני התועים האלה ובני בניהם שהדיחו אותם אבותם ונולדו בין הקראים וגדלו אותם על דעתם, הרי הוא כתינוק שנשבה ביניהם וגדלוהו ואינו

82. Conceivably, one could argue that denial of certain details referred to in Rambam's principles of faith does not constitute heresy. Thus, while denying the divinity of Torah (the focus of the eighth principle) is considered heresy, denying the divinity of the oral law is not. However, *Hilchot Mamrim* 3:1 implies that denying the divinity of the oral law does, in fact, constitute heresy.

> זריז לאחוז בדרכי המצות שהרי הוא כאנוס ואע״פ ששמע אח״כ [שהוא יהודי וראה היהודים ודתם הרי הוא כאנוס שהרי גדלוהו על טעותם] כך אלו שאמרנו האוחזים בדרכי אבותם הקראים שטעו, לפיכך ראוי להחזירן בתשובה ולמשכם בדברי שלום עד שיחזרו לאיתן התורה [ולא ימהר אדם להרגן].
>
> To whom does the above apply? To a person who denies the oral Torah consciously, according to his perception of things. He follows his frivolous thoughts and his capricious heart and denies the oral Torah on his own, as did Tzadok and Baitus and those who erred in following them.
>
> The children of these errant people and their grandchildren whose parents led them away, and those born among the Karaites and raised according to their conception, are considered as a child who was captured (*tinok she-nishba*) and raised by them (i.e., non-Jews). Such a child may not be eager to follow the path of *mitzvot*, for it is as if he was compelled not to. Even if he later hears that he is Jewish and sees Jews and their faith, he is considered as one who is compelled against observance, for he was raised according to their mistaken path. This applies to those whom we mentioned who follow the erroneous Karaite path of their ancestors. It therefore is appropriate to motivate them to repent and to draw them to the power of the Torah with words of peace until they return to the bulwark of Torah.[83]

Essentially, we do not consider anyone whose heresy is excusable as a heretic. Rambam, as we saw in 10.1, reiterates this principle in numerous places.[84] Recall that in 11.8 we referred to *Chazon Ish*'s proof that Rambam's expansion of *tinok she-nishba* emerges directly from the Talmud.

---

83. This follows the text in the Vilna edition of Rambam. There is a missing line, which we discussed in 10.11.

84. **פה״מ חולין א:ב**
אבל אלו אשר נולדו בדעות אלה וחונכו על פיהן הרי הם כאנוסים ודינם דין תינוק שנשבה לבין הגוים שכל עברותיו שגגה כמו שבארו, אבל המתחיל הראשון הוא מזיד לא שוגג.

The scope of *tinok she-nishba* has been debated since Rambam's time. In 10.11, we cited the approach of R. Eliyahu Mizrachi (1455 – 1526, Responsa 57) who understands that Rambam fundamentally did not see Karaites as heretics. The numerous places where Rambam maintains that Karaites have the halachic status of Jews certainly support this claim. For example, besides those mentioned above, Rambam rules that Karaites do not render wine prohibited via handling as Rambam maintained other heretics do.[85] In addition, R. Eliyahu Mizrachi cites Rambam's letter supporting the circumcision of Karaite children, in which Rambam advocates treating Karaites respectfully (שראוי לחלק להם כבוד), though the authenticity of this letter has been questioned by some scholars.[86] R. Eliyahu Mizrachi downplays the line in *Mishneh Torah* where Rambam rules that "one should not rush to kill" Karaites. If one maintains that our relationship with Karaites should be cordial, how could we ever kill them? R. Eliyahu Mizrachi responds that this line cannot be taken literally, since Rambam has already compared them to someone compelled to sin, who is certainly not liable for death (שהרי כבר דמה אותם לתנוק שנשבה לבין הגוים שאינו בן מות כלל ואף על פי שלא רצה לשוב בתשובה מדקאמר הרי הוא כאנוס ואנוס פטור ממיתה). It is not clear how he understood Rambam. It is inconceivable that Rambam included a literary flourish without any legal weight in his halachic work. In 10.11, we explained that this ruling does not fundamentally detract from Rambam's ruling that Karaites are not heretics. Instead, it reflects the position that innocent people must occasionally be expunged to protect society from their pernicious influence.

---

85. תשו' הרמב"ם סי' שע"א. In addition, R. Avraham b. ha-Rambam cites this ruling in the name of his father:

שו"ת רבי אברהם בן הרמב"ם סימן פ

...בדבר יין הקראים והשיב בכתיבת ידו. תשובה אם היה הקראי מאנשי היראה והדקדוק באמונתם משביעים אותו על היין שלא העסיק בו גוי ולא גויה ולא שפחה שאינה טבולה ואחר כך מותר לשתותו. וכך פסק אבא מארי זצ"ל ואם אין התנאים הנזכרים אסור לשתותו.

86. Dr. Isadore Twersky, *Introduction to the Code of Maimonides* (Yale UP, 1980, p. 85) and R. Kapach (in his comments to *Chullin* 1:2) both accept the authenticity of the letter. R. Yitzchak Shilat, on the other hand, argues it is a forgery (*Igrot ha-Rambam*, pp. 668–669). See Gabriel Gross's aforementioned essay for much more on this topic.

Other scholars understand Rambam's statements regarding the expunging of Karaites as indicating Rambam fundamentally continues to view Karaites as being heretics. Two thinkers to adopt this view were R. David ibn Zimra (1479–1573) [87] and R. Moshe de-Trani (1505–1585).[88]

The Shulchan Aruch and Rama both seem to accept a more expansive interpretation.[89] Others, such as R. Shabtai ha-Kohen, appear to accept the more narrow application propounded by Radvaz.[90]

---

87. **שו"ת רדב"ז חלק ב סימן תשצו**
וכבר כתבתי שאסור להתחתן בהם מן התורה כי מי שכופר בתורה שבעל פה חייב מיתה בידי אדם איך יהיה מותר לקחת את מי שמחוייבת מיתה. וכ"ת מפני שכתב הרמב"ם ז"ל בהלכות ממרים שאלו אנוסים הם כיון שגדלו אותם אבותם על אמונתם וכו' הרי הוא ז"ל כתב אין ממהרין להרגן משמע שאם הזהירו אותם ועדיין עומדין במורדן הורגין אותם אם ידינו תקפה והרי אשה זו שהוא רוצה ליקח עדיין עומדת במרדה להחזיק בכפרות שלהם וא"כ איך ישאנה.
If one should not rush to kill them, then when should they be killed? Radvaz understands that Rambam means that we do not initially kill them, preferring to educate them instead. However, once reasonable attempts to educate do not yield improvement, they would revert back to the status of heretic. Moreover, Radvaz distinguishes between the Karaites of his time and those who lived during Rambam's life. Thus, when Rambam wrote that they were like *tinok she-nishba,* he was referring only to those who lived in his own time:
אבל הנמצאים בזמננו זה אם היה אפשר בידינו להורידן מצוה להורידן שהרי בכל יום אנו מחזירין אותם למוטב ומושכין אותם להאמין בתורה שבעל פה והם מחרפין ומגדפין את בעלי הקבלה ואין לדון את אלו בכלל אנוסים אלא כופרים בתורה שבע"פ.
According to Radvaz, Rambam's dispensation no longer applied in his day. Interestingly, Baruch Mazor notes that Radvaz lived relatively shortly after the inter-communal strife between the Karaites and the Rabbanites in Egypt reached one of its peaks, in the 1460s. Moreover, "nowhere else, at any time, were the relations between the Karaites and the Rabbanites as strained as in Cairo" at this juncture despite greater Rabbinate efforts to achieve reconciliation between the two communities than in other major Jewish centers of the time. ("Sa'īd ibn Dāud al-'Adanī: His role in fifteenth century Judeo-Arabic literature," Harvard, PhD Dissertation 1975, p. 47.)
88. *Shut Mabit* 1:37 and 38. He rules, for example, that the wine they touch is prohibited.
89. See Y.D. 2:8–9, 159:3, 385:6; E.H. 4:37; and O.C. 385:1.
90. *Shach* (Y.D. 2:24, 159:6). Radvaz's view is also cited by R. Moshe Feinstein (אגרות משה אהע"ז ח"ד סימן נ"ט). However, in *Igrot Moshe* O.C. 4:91.6 R. Feinstein implies that followers of the Conservative movement are considered *tinok she-nishba* and would have a share in the world to come insofar as they are not responsible for their heresy. R. Asher Weiss (שו"ת מנחת אשר ח"א סימן י) is surprised that R. Feinstein would cite Radvaz if his view is rejected by Shulchan Aruch and Rama.

R. Yaakov Ettlinger (1798–1871) was one of the first to apply the principle *tinok she-nishba* to the modern non-observant Jew.[91] This point also can be found in the writings of R. Kook and R. Meir Simcha of Dvinsk.[92]

11.11 APPENDIX C: WERE THERE GREAT PEOPLE WHO BELIEVED IN A CORPOREAL GOD?

Ra'avad (cited in 11.1) refers to Aggadot that corrupt correct opinion about religious matters. To which Aggadot is he referring? While we do not know what he specifically had in mind, there are many texts when understood literally imply a corporeal God. For example, *Berachot* (6a) describes the *tefillin* that God dons.[93]

---

91. In fact, it is one of three reasons that he offers why they should not be treated as heretics:

שו"ת בנין ציון החדשות (סי' כג)

פושעי ישראל שבזמנינו לא ידענא מה אדון בהם, אחר שבעו"ה פשתה הבהרת לרוב, עד שברובם חלול שבת נעשה כהיתר... ומה גם בבניהם אשר קמו תחתיהן, אשר לא ידעו ולא שמעו דיני שבת, שדומין ממש לצדוקין דלא נחשבו כמומרים אעפ"י שמחללין שבת מפני שמעשה אבותיהן בידיהם, והם כתינוק שנשבה לבין עובדי כוכבים, כמבואר (סי' שפ"ה).

92. **אגרות ראיה סוף אגרת רסו**

כל השנאות כולן וחומרי דיניהן הנם נאמרים רק במי שברי לנו שקיימנו בו מצוות תוכחה. וכאשר אין לנו בדור הזה ולא בכמה דורות שלפנינו, על פי עדות רבי עקיבא, מי שיודע להוכיח. על כן נפל פותא בבירא (עי' רש"י שבת סו) וכל ההלכות הנוטות לרוגז ושנאת אחים, נעשות הן כפרשת בן סורר ומורה עיר הנדחת ובית המנוגע, למ"ד לא היו ולא עתידין להיות, ונכתבו משום דרוש וקבל שכר.

משך חכמה דברים כב:ד

לכן אסור לשנוא איש כזה, רק מי שהוא בעצמו סר מרע וצדיק תמים בדרכיו, אבל קשה למצא כמותו וע"ז אמרו (סוכה מה:) ראיתי בני עליה והמה מועטים, לכן כתיב אחיך.

93. Interestingly, when commenting upon that particular passage, R. Chananeil shows that when prophets perceive God, they generally see Him as a human. Moreover, the sources that describe people "seeing" God do not refer to physical sight but perception (ראיית הלב) and understanding (אבנתא דלבא). Indeed, he claims that there is nowhere in the whole Talmud that indicates that God has some sort of physical image:

ספר אור זרוע חלק א הלכות קריאת שמע סימן ז

אמר רבין בר רב אדא אמר ר' יצחק מנין שהקב"ה מניח תפלין שנא' נשבע ה' בימינו ובזרוע עזו... **פר"ח** זצ"ל שהקב"ה מראה כבודו לנביאיו וחסידיו **באבנתא דלבא** כדמות אדם יושב דכתיב ראיתי את ה' יושב על כסאו וכתי' ואראה את ה' יושב על כסאו וכמי שיש לו רגלים דכתי' ותחת רגליו כמעשה לבנת הספיר וכיון שנודע לנו כי מתראה לנביאים כענין הזה נתברר לנו כי זה הראי' האמורה בראיית הלב ולא בראיית העין היא כי לא יתכן להאמר בראיית העין שנראית דמות להקב"ה שנאמר ואל מי תדמיון אל ומה

To whom is Ra'avad referring when he writes that there were people greater than us (or greater than Rambam[94]) who believed in a corporeal god? It is not clear. In Chapter 3 of *The Limits of Orthodox Theology*, Dr. Marc Shapiro lists a number of Torah scholars who purportedly subscribed to corporealism. Indeed, there are various reports that French medieval Torah scholars subscribed to some sort of corporeality. However, as Dr. Ephraim Kanarfogel points out, evidence of anthropomorphic views amongst the medieval Torah scholars of France comes from detractors rather than proponents, which, therefore, creates an exaggerated picture of its popularity.[95] Saul Zucker (*Ḥakirah*, Volume 9, winter 2010, pp. 15–43) claims that a review of the sources in Shapiro's book reveals that there are only three known, identifiable corporealists among the Torah scholars of northern France during the entire period of the Rishonim (R. Moshe Taku, R. Shlomo Simcha of Troyes, and R. Avraham b. Azriel).[96]

דמות תערכו לו אלא ראי׳ בלב הוא. כך יתכן לומר שאפשר לאדם לראות בראיית הלב דמות כבוד בראש ועליו תפלין והאומר **ראיתי ראיית הלב** כדכתיב ולבי ראה הרבה חכמה ודעת וכך כוונתו **ולא ראיית העין** ממש שהנה בפירוש אמר הכתוב ודברתי על הנביאים וביד הנביאים אדמה מלמד שמראה לנביאיו דמיון שיכול לראות **אבל ראי׳ ממש ח״ו שיש מי שיעלה על דעתו וכי ר׳ יצחק חולק על התורה שנאמר כי לא יראני האדם וחי** ובא ר׳ יצחק ואמר כי נראה הקב״ה. ועוד הא כתיב ויראו את אלהי ישראל ותחת רגליו וגו׳ הנה מראה הכתוב שראו ומקרא אחר כתי׳ כי לא ראיתם כל תמונה קשו קראי אהדדי נפרקי׳ לא קשיא האי קרא דכתיב ויראו את ה׳ ראיית הלב והא דכתיב כי לא ראיתם כל תמונה ראיית העין ומצאנו לשון הקודש שקורא בענין הזה ראי׳ שנאמר וירא יעקב כי יש שבר במצרים ויעקב לא היה במצרים כ״א בארץ כנען וכהנה רבות **ולמביני דעת יראי שמים פחות מזה די להם להבין ולידע שאין בכל התלמוד מודיע שיש בישראל נותן דמות לבוראנו יתעלה שמו וזכרו...**

94. As we noted in 11.1, וטובים ממנו could mean "superior to us" or "superior to him (i.e., Rambam)."

95. See make it Ephraim Kanarfogel for stylistic consistency, Ephraim, "Varieties of Belief in Medieval Ashkenaz: The Case of Anthropomorphism."

96. Another possibility is that he is referring to R. Daniel the Babylonian, who, in a correspondence with R. Avraham b. ha-Rambam (see *Milchamot Hashem*, ed. Margoliyot, pp. 20–29), argues that God could appear in a physical form if He chose to do so. However, from a historical perspective, it seems far-fetched to assume that Ra'avad was referring to this.

And it still is debatable to what extent any of these thinkers was a true corporealist.[97] For example, regarding R. Moshe Taku, R. Aaron Lopiansky has shown that even though he vehemently rejects Rambam's approach to anthropomorphism, arguing that any type of reasoned discussion of God Himself is impossible due to the limitations of human reason, he does not seem to concede that God has a body.[98]

One possibility is that Ra'avad is referring to Rashi, since there are places where Rashi implies that God has a body. However, in light of other statements made by Rashi (e.g., Rashi *Shemot* 15:6, 19:18, 31:17, 20:11, *Devarim* 30:3, *Yeshayahu* 22:13, and *Yechezkeil* 1:3), this conclusion is not compelling. In all of these cases, Rashi argues that anthropomorphisms are metaphors.[99]

Let us consider one comment of Rashi that is cited as an example of his belief in corporeality. On the verse: "And Pharaoh shall not listen to you, and I shall place My hand upon Egypt, and I shall take out my host, my people, the Children of Israel, from the land of Egypt with great judgments" (*Shemot* 7:4). Rashi comments: "'My hand' – An actual hand (*yad mamash*) with which to smite them." Some cite this as proof that Rashi believed that God had a body (see, for example, Dr. Marc Shapiro, *The Limits of Orthodox Theology*, p. 57). However, as R. Moshe Ben-Chaim points out, it is preposterous to assume that Rashi understood that there literally was an actual hand that smote the Egyptians.[100] Moreover, as R. Natan Slifkin shows from Rashi *Shemot* 2:5, when Rashi writes "an actual hand," he might not be referring to a bodily hand, but rather that

97. Even these thinkers are not necessarily full corporealists. For example, R. M. M. Kasher (*Torah Shleima* in the back of the volume on *Parshat Mishpatim*) shows that R. Moshe Taku agrees that God does not have a body, but He could appear as a body if He so wished. Others, such as Professors Efraim Urbach and Marc Shapiro, have argued that R. Moshe Taku was a corporealist. Subsequently, other scholars have shown that this may not be the case and have marshaled evidence that he was not a corporealist: See David Sedley's "Rav Moshe Taku: non-Rationalist Judaism," *Reshimu* 3 (July 2009).
98. "The Corporeality Which Never Was," *Dialogue* 5 (Fall 2014).
99. Often Rashi is more troubled by phrases that seem undignified than those that are corporeal.
100. "God's Hand," Jewish Times, Vol. 4 No. 16 (January 21, 2005).

the verse was written as referring to a literal meaning of the word, albeit in an allegorical sense.[101]

More importantly, Prof. Ephraim Urbach (cited by R. Slifkin) stresses that the literal elucidations that Rashi frequently offers do not necessarily mean that he understood the Talmudic passages literally, but was merely quoting these earlier sources in their original metaphors.[102] Put differently, we must understand the goal of Rashi – to explain the text. As such, Rashi's usage of the imagery is no different than the text upon which he is commenting. Rashi makes this point explicitly in his Introduction to *Shir ha-Shirim*: "And even as the Prophets communicated using metaphors and similes, one must explain the metaphor as well, in the order of the verses."[103]

Returning to our question, we do not really know to whom Ra'avad was referring. For all we know, he may have been referring to some Torah scholars that he knew personally who are lost to history. Moreover, he may have exaggerated their scholarship for emphasis. While it seems abundantly clear that there must have been some significant corporealists, as per Ra'avad's comment, it is noteworthy that few, if any, clear-cut examples have been found. Presumably, this points to the strength of the *mesora* and the extent to which problematic views have been weeded out.

---

101. Natan, Slifkin. "Was Rashi a Corporealist?" *Ḥakirah,* Volume 7 (Winter 2009), pp. 81–105.
102. R. Slifkin himself is inclined to assume that Rashi was a corporealist. In a response article, "No, Rashi Was Not a Corporealist," Saul Zucker questions this conclusion.
103. Along similar lines, when *Tosafot* comment upon Aggadot, their goal is not to address questions from the outside (e.g., philosophical problems), but to explicate how the text they are analyzing is consistent with other texts.

Chapter Twelve

Knowing God Through Kabbala

Kabbalistic teachings present a vast and complex perspective on how the universe functions and how God relates to His creations. What then is the best way to introduce Kabbala?

One way is to summarize the nature and evolution of this web. However, I am unqualified to do this – to properly encapsulate these teachings I would have to understand the nuances of Kabbala, which I do not. Moreover, this sort of summarization does not accurately open a window into the poetry and profundity of Kabbala. Nor will it instruct us how to better live our lives. Instead, the aim of this chapter is to introduce Kabbala by briefly contemplating two very basic questions: how do we know God, and how should we relate to our world? Of course, a single chapter certainly cannot adequately introduce Kabbala. Hopefully, however, it will provide some taste and context.

Before we begin, a note of clarification. In this chapter, we speak of Kabbala as though it is a single entity with a single perspective. This is not the case. There are many perspectives conveyed within the world of Kabbala that are, at times, at odds with each other. For purposes of this brief introduction, though, we will portray a single unified vision that reflects the perspectives of a wide range of thinkers.

How Do We Know God?

We have seen how both rationalistic and Kabbalistic thinkers maintain that there is a *mitzva* to know God. Moreover, we have seen that Rambam believes that one fulfills this *mitzva* through the study of Torah and philosophy. What method do Kabbalists prescribe for fulfilling this *mitzva*?[1] Naturally, Kabbalists understand that we are supposed to know God through Kabbala. Unlike philosophy, these Kabbalistic ideas are not independently discoverable, but were passed down orally from Moshe Rabbeinu (see Ramban *Bereishit* Ch. 1) or were made known through later revelations (*giluyim*).[2] Indeed, Kabbalists emphasize that the great advantage that Kabbala has over philosophy is the access to truths that the mind cannot independently discover through logic and reasoning.[3]

As we noted in 2.2, these teachings do not relate to God's essence (or *Ein Sof*) which, by definition, cannot be understood by human beings. While we cannot understand God's essence, Kabbala does seek to describe Him in various ways so that we may better relate to Him. Accordingly, as we shall see, God is depicted in human terms (like in Scripture, but with much more detail). Moreover, the various ways in which we perceive Him are described through various symbols and metaphors, such as God's masculine and feminine personifications.

Should these descriptions perhaps be taken literally? Is it conceivable that Kabbalists disagree with divine incorporeality? While there may be lines that sound corporealistic, I do not believe that any mainstream Kabbalists ascribe to such a view. Moreover, Kabbalists frequently stress this notion. For example, Ramban (*Kitvei Ramban*, Vol. 1, p. 345), writing to the Torah scholars of France, states that all

1. We should note that while Kabbalists have a different understanding of the *mitzva* of knowing God, this is not necessarily because of their rejection of philosophy (some did, while others did not). Rather, they believe Kabbala provides a better description of God and His ways than philosophy can offer. See the first *mitzva* in *Sefer Chareidim*.
2. Many of the great Kabbalistic thinkers experienced revelations, including R. Shimon bar Yochai, Arizal, and Ramchal.
3. See Ramchal's debate between a philosopher and a Kabbalist which emphasizes this point.

Kabbalistic thinkers agree that Scriptural and aggadic references to God's form should not be taken literally. In fact, R. Chaim Vital, in a paragraph printed at the end of some editions of *Eitz Chaim,* and Ramchal, in *Choker u-Mikubal,* emphasize that this is the case for all Kabbalistic thinkers. Of course, there were (and are) Kabbalists who maintained problematic views. However, their views are not mainstream. To illustrate, let us consider but one text from Arizal's commentary on the *Sifra de-Tzniuta* (a section of *Zohar* found at the end of *Parshat Teruma*). The *Zohar* associates the various ways in which we perceive God (i.e., various emanations) to various colors. Arizal warns that a person must not understand these descriptions literally – the mystical system of colors does not imply any corporeality in God:

> אל יפתוך רמי הקומה קרואי שאול האומרים כי שם מראות וגוונים במקום הנאצלים העליונים עבר עליהם המים הזדונים ויחפו דברים אשר לא כן על אדוני האדונים כי אין שם גוון ולא מראה רואה ואינו נראה (ע"ג) המתגאה על גאה.
>
> הן אמת כי שרשם למעלה. ותוצאותם הימה כי שם נגלו את אשר כבר עשוהו השרשים העליונים כי כח הגוונים לבן ואדום וירוק ושחור וזלתו שם דרכי הכוחות כולם ויגלו מהארץ העליונה מאותם ארזי' אשר נטעו בה לעשות ענף ולשאת פרי והוציא ההוא אפריון כגוונא דידהו
>
> Do not let the proud ones who are destined for hell seduce you into thinking that the emanated divine realms are comprised of actual colors, for the waters of iniquity have washed upon those who falsify words of description upon the Lord of Lords. For there is no color or visual representation there that refers to Him Who sees and is not seen, who is exalted over the proud.
>
> True, the root of these colors is from above. The effect of these elevated roots is below, for there is manifest that which the elevated roots have done, where the force of the colors white, red, green, black, and the rest reveal from the upper universe from the cedars planted in it to produce branches and bear fruits, each fruit according to its colors.

In this paragraph, we find Arizal referring to people who must have understood this Kabbalistic notion of divine colors literally. He refers to them as arrogant and destined for hell.

With this in mind, let us briefly consider two paths to discover aspects of God. The first, through the study of Torah, is predictable; the second, through the study of the human form, is more surprising.

12.1 RELATING TO THE TORAH'S STORIES

In the course of advocating the study of *machshava* in Chapter 1, we demonstrated the importance of analyzing the non-halachic sections of Torah. Of course, this can be derived from the fact that so much of Tanach, as well as Talmudic literature, is non-halachic. As Ramban (*Bereishit* 1:1) notes, this indicates the fundamental indispensability of the non-halachic portions of Torah.

To truly appreciate the value of these sections of Torah, though, we must search beneath the surface. We developed this point in Chapter 7 when we discussed the relationship between *pshat* and *drash,* and explicated the value of pursuing both realms. Here, we shall consider a remarkable passage from the *Zohar* that warns against shallow and superficial understanding of the Torah's stories (and *mitzvot*). Kabbala, like Midrash, seeks to understand the deeper meaning of the Torah. In one sense, it goes one step deeper than *drash*. (Though, as we noted in Chapter 7, it frequently is powerfully rooted in the text of the Torah.)

זהר ח"ג פ' בהעלותך דף קנב ע"א

ר"ש אמר, ווי להאוא ב"נ דאמר דהא אורייתא אתא לאחזאה ספורין בעלמא ומלין דהדיוטי, דאי הכי אפילו בזמנא דא אנן יכלין למעבד אורייתא במלין דהדיוטי ובשבחא יתיר מכולהו, אי לאחזאה מלה דעלמא, אפילו אינון קפסירי דעלמא (שרים ושלטונים, ד"א) אית בינייהו מלין עילאין יתיר, אי הכי נזיל אבתרייהו ונעביד מנייהו אורייתא כהאי גוונא. אלא כל מלין דאורייתא מלין עילאין אינון ורזין עילאין...

אורייתא... כיון דנחתת להאי עלמא אי לאו דמתלבשא בהני לבושין דהאי עלמא לא יכיל עלמא למסבל. ועל דא האי ספור דאורייתא לבושא דאורייתא איהו, מאן דחשיב דההוא לבושא איהו אורייתא

ממש ולא מלה אחרא, תיפח רוחיה ולא יהא ליה חולקא בעלמא דאתי. בגין כך אמר דוד (תהלים קיט:יח) גל עיני ואביטה נפלאות מתורתך, מה דתחות לבושא דאורייתא.

תא חזי אית לבושא דאתחזי לכולא, ואינון טפשין כד חמאן לבר נש בלבושא דאתחזי לון שפירא, לא מסתכלין יתיר. חשיבו דההוא לבושא גופא, חשיבותא דגופא נשמתא.

כהאי גוונא אורייתא אית לה גופא, ואינון פקודי אורייתא דאקרון גופי תורה. האי גופא מתלבשא בלבושין דאינון ספורין דהאי עלמא. טפשין דעלמא לא מסתכלי אלא בההוא לבושא דאיהו ספור דאורייתא, ולא ידעי יתיר ולא מסתכלי במה דאית תחות ההוא לבושא. אינון דידעין יתיר לא מסתכלן בלבושא אלא בגופא דאיהו תחות ההוא לבושא. חכימין עבדי דמלכא עילאה אינון דקיימו בטורא דסיני לא מסתכלי אלא בנשמתא דאיהי עיקרא דכולא אורייתא ממש, ולזמנא (ולעלמא) דאתי זמינין לאסתכלא בנשמתא דנשמתא דאורייתא.

R. Shimon said: Woe to the person who says that the Torah came to tell simple stories and folklore, for if this were the case, one could make a Torah that would be even better. And if Torah was meant to tell us the way of the world, the nobility have better works, so why not use them? Rather, all matters of Torah are elevated concepts and lofty secrets…

The Torah… when it entered this world, if it did not dress itself in the clothes of this world (i.e., the stories and human language), the world would be unable to bear it. Thus, the stories of the Torah are the clothing of the Torah. Anyone who thinks that the clothing of the Torah is the true Torah and that there is nothing deeper, may his spirit be blown, and he has no potion in the world to come. Therefore, David said, "Open up my eyes and let me see the wonders of your Torah," namely, that which is beneath the garments of Torah.

Come and see that there are garments that are visible to all, and the fools, upon seeing a well-dressed person, do not look further

> (judging the person by the clothing he is wearing). They think that the clothing is the body of a person, and the body of a person is his soul.
>
> Likewise, the Torah has a body, and it is the *mitzvot* of the Torah that are called *gufei Torah*. This body is dressed in clothing, the stories of this world. The fools of the world look only at the clothing and do not consider what is beneath the clothing. Those that know more do not look at the clothing, but rather at the body beneath the clothes. The wise ones, the servants of the Elevated King, and those that stood at Mount Sinai, look only at the soul of the Torah, because this is the actual core of the Torah. In the world to come, we will see the inner soul (נשמתא דנשמתא) of the Torah.

The *Zohar* warns against perceiving the stories of the Torah as mere folktales; better stories can be found in secular folklore.[4] Rather, the stories

---

4. This notion is reminiscent of Ramban's comments at the beginning of *Bereishit* (1:1), where he is troubled by Rashi's question (citing R. Yitzchak) of why the Torah needs to begin with *Bereishit*. Ramban asks that it certainly is necessary to convey the fundamental principle that God created the world, so what is R. Yitzchak's question? He answers that the statement in the Ten Commandments כי ששת ימים עשה ה׳ את השמים ואת הארץ את הים ואת כל אשר בם וינח ביום השביעי would have been sufficient to convey the message that God created the world. R. Yitzchak therefore wonders why it is necessary to convey the details about what was created each of the seven days of creation, if these verses anyway can be understood only through mysticism, and the mystical interpretation cannot be discerned through the study of the text. Thus, the text seemingly serves no purpose:

רמב״ן בראשית א:א

בראשית ברא אלהים - אמר רבי יצחק לא היה צריך להתחיל התורה אלא מהחודש הזה לכם שהיא מצוה ראשונה שנצטוו בה ישראל... ויש לשאול בה, כי צורך גדול הוא להתחיל התורה בבראשית ברא אלהים, כי הוא שורש האמונה, ושאינו מאמין בזה וחושב שהעולם קדמון, הוא כופר בעיקר ואין לו תורה כלל. **והתשובה, מפני שמעשה בראשית סוד עמוק אינו מובן מן המקראות, ולא יוודע על בוריו אלא מפי הקבלה עד משה רבינו מפי הגבורה, ויודעיו חייבין להסתיר אותו, לכך אמר רבי יצחק שאין להתחלת התורה צורך בבראשית ברא, והספור במה שנברא ביום ראשון ומה נעשה ביום שני ושאר הימים, והאריכות ביצירת אדם וחוה, וחטאם וענשם, וספור גן עדן וגרוש אדם ממנו, כי כל זה לא יובן בינה שלימה מן הכתובים,** וכל שכן ספור דור המבול והפלגה, שאין הצורך בהם גדול, ויספיק לאנשי התורה בלעדי הכתובים האלה, ויאמינו בכלל בנזכר להם בעשרת הדברות (שמות כ:יא) כי ששת ימים עשה ה׳ את

of the Torah convey profound wisdom, with the physical manifestations acting as a cloak for the eternal concepts.[5]

The *Zohar* decries superficial understandings of the Torah, or, at the very least, presuming that the simple meaning is the only intended meaning.[6] The *Zohar* is not necessarily advocating ignoring the simple meaning of the Torah entirely in favor of allegorical interpretations. In fact, Ramban, the great Kabbalist, devoted incredible energy to understand *pshat*. Rather, the *Zohar* means that mystical explanations supplement the simple meanings of the text. At the same time, the *Zohar* is contemptuous towards understanding the stories superficially. Likewise, in 7.7, we saw how the *Zohar* seeks broader significance in every detail of the Torah; for instance, concerning Noach's ark landing on Mount Ararat, the *Zohar* wonders, "Who cares whether it landed on this mountain or that one?" (While we elaborated more upon this issue in Chapter 7 in the context of the relationship between *pshat* and *drash*, we return to focus on the role of Kabbalistic interpretations of Scripture in 12.6.)

Had the Torah not cloaked itself in the garments of this world, the world could not survive. But, the *Zohar* cautions, we should not be fooled by the external raiment and thereby fail to perceive the inner truth. Thus, the *mitzvot* reflect the body of Torah. This body is cloaked in the stories of this world. Fools see only the clothing. Those that know a little more perceive the body. Those who are wise recognize

---

השמים ואת הארץ את הים ואת כל אשר בם וינח ביום השביעי, ותשאר הידיעה ליחידים שבהם הלכה למשה מסיני עם התורה שבעל פה.

5. Maharal explains that this is true not just with respect to the stories, but, as we saw in *Shlah*, with respect to *mitzvot* as well:

ספר תפארת ישראל פרק יג

ואף על גב דהוא לא אמר שהתורה היא לבוש למלין עלאין רק בשביל הספורין שהם בתורה, שלא יבזה אותם האדם. מכל מקום בכלל הזה גם כן מצות התורה. שאי אפשר שיהיה בעולם החמרי הזה רק בגוף, והם המצות הגשמיות. וכמו שברא האדם שיהיה בו הצלם האלהי הנבדל, כך זאת תורת האדם, עם שכל דבריה דברים עליונים, הם עומדים בדברים הגשמיים. וכאשר משיג בדברים הגשמיים, הלא הדברים ההם נמשכים אל הדברים שהם סודי התורה, וכאילו האדם דבק באותו שכל האלהי, כי התורה היא אחת.

6. This danger is particularly relevant in academic settings, where simplistic and superficial understandings frequently are presumed.

the soul. Finally, in future times, the inner soul will be revealed. One must attempt to understand the soul of the story and not be satisfied with the external cloak.[7]

Based on this idea, Radvaz (3:643) suggests a remarkable interpretation of the dialogue between Moshe and the angels when Moshe ascended *Har Sinai* to receive the Torah. The Talmud (*Shabbat* 88b–89a) records that when the angels objected to the Torah being given to humans, Moshe responded that Torah addresses people who must fight their base desires to choose what is right. Clearly, then, the Torah was meant for humans and not angels. This point seems so obvious that Radvaz wonders what the angels could possibly have been contending. He suggests that, as we have seen, the Torah can be understood on many levels, even as God's names. The angels implored God to leave Torah in that supernal state, that it not be cloaked in the worldly raiment necessary to allow it to be meaningful to mortals. Of course, God accepted Moshe's argument, and the Torah's eternal ideas were translated into human language.[8] Nevertheless, if we exert ourselves to understand, we can discover some of the deeper layers. In future times, even more layers will become discernable. In fact, as we note in 25.5, *Shlah*

7. *Pardeis Rimonim* (R. Moshe Cordevero 1522–1570) notes that this is why Halacha stresses the importance of studying the weekly *parsha* without skipping any words – because even the seemingly insignificant words convey profound truths:

> וזהו מן הנמנע כי וודאי דברי תורה הם משיבת נפש וראיה ממה שחוייבנו בהשלמת התורה שנים מקרא ואחד תרגום ואפילו עטרות ודיבון וזה מורה על שלימות התורה ושיש לה פנימית והעלם ורוחניות וחיות וכן פירש ר׳ שמעון בפרשת בהעלותך (דף קנב) וז״ל רש״א ווי לההוא בר נש דאמר דהא אורייתא אתא לאחזאה ספורין בעלמא ומילין דהדיוטא. דא הכי אפילו בזמנא דא אנן יכלין למעבד אורייתא במלין דהדיוטא ושבחא יתיר מכלהו. אי לאחזאה מילי דעלמא אפי׳ אינון קפסירי דעלמא אית בינייהו מלין עלאין יתיר. אי הכי נזיל אבתרייהו ונעביד מנייהו אורייתא כה״ג. אלא כל מלין דאורייתא מילן עילאין אינון ורזין עילאין.

Indeed, Kabbalistic texts frequently elaborate upon the verses that seem least important. If on a level of *pshat* these verses seem insignificant, we must turn to *sod* to recognize their import. (Rambam in *Moreh ha-Nevuchim* 3:50 offers non-mystical explanations of these sorts of verses, writing: "There are in the Torah portions that include deep wisdom but have been misunderstood by many people; they therefore require explanation…")

8. My appreciation to R. Jordan Ginsberg for this insight.

understands the ברית חדשה (new covenant) described in *Yirmiyahu* 31:30 as referring to a new understanding of Torah that we will discover in messianic times. Although Torah in its current instantiation relates to physical reality, its commandments emanate from a more refined, purely spiritual level of reality (see 1.4). At this level, the Torah is the repository of profound and eternal spiritual truths. While these truths manifest themselves in our world in the form of commandments and prohibitions that regulate our worldly existence, these eternal truths will become revealed again in the messianic era.

12.2 THE GODLINESS IN THE HUMAN FORM

Many people have seen an image of a human body with extended arms and legs with points referring to the ten *sefirot*. What is this meant to depict? The *sefirot* reflect the different modes in which God relates to the world. But what does that have to do with a human image?

To begin, we must realize that for Kabbalists, the human body is not just a physical object; it reflects great secrets.[9] First and foremost, this is alluded to in the notion of man being created in the image of God. Of course, this does not mean that God has a physical body in any sense. But it does refer to the idea that by considering the human form, one can arrive at an understanding of the Divine. Hence, prophets perceived God with human-like qualities.[10] An expression of this notion

9. Considering the holiness of even the physical components of the human body, it is not surprising that numerous chasidic thinkers emphasize the significance of serving God through the limbs of the body. We will return to this point shortly.

10. בראשית רבה פרשת בראשית פרשה כז notes two examples of this phenomenon. The first, from *Daniel* 8:16 (וָאֶשְׁמַע קוֹל אָדָם בֵּין אוּלָי), is less striking in that it seems to be referring to an angel. The second, from the Merkava vision of Yechezkeil, is more telling:

יחזקאל א:כו

וּמִמַּעַל לָרָקִיעַ אֲשֶׁר עַל רֹאשָׁם כְּמַרְאֵה אֶבֶן סַפִּיר דְּמוּת כִּסֵּא וְעַל דְּמוּת הַכִּסֵּא דְּמוּת כְּמַרְאֵה אָדָם עָלָיו מִלְמָעְלָה:

We should note that this analogy notwithstanding, the commentaries on these verses warn us not to understand this analogy too literally. (Indeed, *Targum* on the verse in *Yechezkeil* does not even translate the word *adam*.) For example, R. Yosef Caspi understands that the *adam* depicted here is not a manifestation of God Himself, but a manifestation of expressions of God.

can be found in Ramban's comments concerning the *mitzva* of washing a *kohen*'s hands prior to Temple service.[11]

An important manifestation of this concept is alluded to in the verse, וּמִבְּשָׂרִי אֶחֱזֶה אֱלוֹהַּ, "And from my body, I see God" (*Iyov* 19:26).[12]

ר' יוסף כספי מעשה המרכבה

זה האדם, כולל השניים והשכל הפועל, **ואינו האל יתברך בכללו**, כי לא ימשילוהו לעולם, רצוני, אותו הסבה הראשונה, כמו שכתב המורה ז"ל, פרק ז משלישי; אבל זה האדם - וזה הכלל - השניים והשכל הפועל, ואין השם בכלל זה, **כי לא ימשילוהו באדם או זולתו.** אבל נכון להם לצייר השכל הנפרד בכלל הכולל השנִיים והשכל הפועל, שהוא האיש, והאל הוא הראש, והשכל הפועל - שיתכן הרגליים על דרך משל.

Thus, while we cite these verses as manifestations of how contemplation of the human can give us a better understanding of God, we must remember, as R. Yeshaya de-Trani writes on the above verse, that ultimately there is no true analogy and all comparisons are inaccurate:

ואין לאדם לחקור ולהרבות דברים בעניין זה, כי אין ליבינו מכיל מאלף אלפים וריבי רבבות אחד מעניין גודל האלהות, והמהרהר בזה נוטל חייו מן העולם, ועל זה אמרו חכמים (חגיגה יא ב): האומר מה למעלה ומה למטה, מה לפנים ומה לאחור, ראוי לו שלא בא לעולם, מפני שמהרהר בכבוד השכינה. סוף הדברים, כמה יסמוך ויאמין כל אדם **כי אין דמות לבורא, לא דמות ולא תמונה**, ואין לו חקר מרוב דקותו והעלמו; ומה שנדמה לנביאיו הוא דמיון נוצר לפי שעה, שיאמין הנביא כי הבורא שולח אותו ומאתו יבוא הקול אליו.

11. **רמב"ן שמות ל:יט**

ורחצו אהרן ובניו וגו'... ועל דרך האמת, בעבור היות ראש האדם וסופו הידים והרגלים, כי הידים למעלה מכל גופו בהגביהו אותן, והרגלים למטה, והם בצורת האדם רמז לעשר הספירות שיהיה כל גופו ביניהם, וכמו שאמרו בספר יצירה (פרק ו) כרת לו ברית בין עשר אצבעות ידיו ובין עשר אצבעות רגליו במלת הלשון ובמלת המעור, לפיכך נצטוו משרתי עליון לרחוץ הידים והרגלים.

Ramban notes that the hands and feet are the extremities of the human body (when a person is standing with his hands raised). The ten fingers and ten toes allude to the ten *sefirot*, with the body between them. As it says in *Sefer Yetzira*, God created a covenant between the ten fingers, with the circumcision of the tongue, and between the ten toes, with the *brit mila*. Therefore, the priests must wash their hands and feet.

12. The entire verse reads:

וְאַחַר עוֹרִי נִקְּפוּ זֹאת וּמִבְּשָׂרִי אֶחֱזֶה אֱלוֹהַּ.

And when after my skin this is destroyed, and I see God from my flesh.

According to the simple understanding of this verse, Iyov accuses his friends of tormenting him with their harsh words despite his painful skin inflammation. His skin condition attests to God's judgement against him. Thus, "I see [the judgment of] God from my flesh." As Rashi comments:

"ואחר עורי נקפו זאת" - והם אינם נותנים לב לגואלי אלא אחר מכת עורי נקפו ונקרו הקניטה והרדיפה הזאת שאמרתי שהיא לי כנוקף וחותך בעורי כמו (ישעיהו י) ונקף סבכי היער. "ומבשרי" - אני רואה משפטים. "אלוה" - ל' משפט ויסורין.

The *Zohar* understands this verse to mean that a person can "see" or understand God by examining his own body.[13]

Ramban (*Sha'ar ha-Gemul*), likewise, describes how many of the physical things in our world allude to and reflect lofty mystical concepts. This, in fact, was the uniqueness of Gan Eden, where everything reflected esoteric truths, allowing Adam to reach supernal wisdom by observing its contents.[14] To appreciate this, consider the following analogy. A skilled technician can view the text and images that appear on a computer monitor and extrapolate what is behind those representations. So, too, when Adam saw the rivers and trees in the garden, he perceived profound truths. Moreover, he apprehended that these physical creations were merely expressions of these truths. And this is not limited to *Gan Eden*; R. Yosef Karo[15] explains everything in the human body has a parallel in the upper worlds.[16, 17]

This reality has practical implications. The Talmud (*Shabbat* 118b) teaches that a person must not get out of bed undressed. "Why must I cover myself if I am alone in the room?" The standard explanation is

---

13. **זוהר כרך א (בראשית) פרשת לך לך דף צד עמוד א**
פתח אידך ואמר (איוב י"ט) ומבשרי אחזה אלוק מאי ומבשרי ומעצמי מבעי ליה אלא מבשרי ממש, ומאי היא, דכתיב (ירמיה י"א) ובשר קדש יעברו מעליך וכתיב (בראשית י"ז) והיתה בריתי בבשרכם דתניא בכל זמנא דאתרשים ב"נ בהאי רשימא קדישא דהאי את מניה חמי לקודשא בריך הוא, מניה ממש, ונשמתא קדישא אתאחידת ביה, ואי לא זכי, דלא נטיר האי את, מה כתיב (איוב ד') מנשמת אלוק יאבדו דהא רשימו דקודשא בריך הוא לא אתנטיר ואי זכי ונטיר ליה שכינתא לא אתפרש מניה.

14. אבל סוד הענין הזה שהדברים כפולים, כי גן עדן וארבע נהרותיו ועץ החיים ועץ הדעת אשר נטע שם האלהים, וכן הכרובים ולהט החרב המתהפכת גם עלה התאנה והחגורות וכתנות העור, כולם כפשוטם וכמשמעם, אמת הדבר ויציב הענין, ולסוד מופלא הוא כי הם כציורי דבר להבין עוד ענין עמוק במשל כמו ששנינו (ר"ה כ"ד א') דמות צורות לבנות היו לו לרבן גמליאל בעליה בטבלא בכותל שבהן מראה את ההדיוטות כזה ראיתם או כזה ראיתם, כי כן מלאכת הקדש במשכן בשלשת מקומותיו, חצר ואהל ולפנים מן הפרוכת, ובמקדש עזרה והיכל ודביר, וכל אשר בכל מקום ומקום מן הכלים וציורי הכרובים כולם להבין סודות מעשה עולם העליון והאמצעי והשפל, ורמזי הוית כל המרכבה שם, **וכל הנבראים עצמם ביצירתן בדמות נבראו, כמו שאמרו בספר יצירה סימן לדבר ועדים נאמנים עולם שנה ונפש.**

15. The work *Maggid Meisharim* records R. Yosef Karo's conversations with a *maggid*.

16. **מגיד מישרים אור ליום שבת יום ראשון לחנוכה**
וכי האי גוונא הוי בבר נש ברזא דמבשרי אחזה אלוה דליכא מידי בבר נש דלית ליה דוגמא לעילא.

17. Ramchal (*Derech Hashem*) extends this to literally every physical object, though, as we shall see, there is a distinctiveness to the human form.

simple: a person must be aware that God's glory fills the whole world – the whole world, including one's bathroom. Being in the presence God demands modesty.[18] However, *Shlah* adds a powerful nuance.[19] A person's limbs, including the *brit mila*, allude to elevated concepts; they are manifestations of God. Accordingly, they should not be exposed, for one brings honor to God by hiding His glory as expressed in one's limbs.[20] Thus, we are constantly in the presence of God, not just because His Shechina fills the world, but because our own bodies express His being.

Maharal frequently cloaks Kabbalistic ideas in non-Kabbalistic terminology. This is how he elucidates the aforementioned topic:

ספר תפארת ישראל פרק ד

וידוע כי העולם הזה הגשמי הוא כמו מלבוש אל עולם הנבדל. וכמו שהמלבוש מתואר בו הלובש, לא באמתתו של הלובש, רק כפי המלבוש יתואר בו הלובש, אף שאינו באמתתו. וכן יתואר השם יתברך בעולם הגשמי מצד עולם הגשמי. ונאמר על האדם שהוא בצלם אלוקים... כי כאשר יתבונן האדם בציור גופו יכול האדם לעמוד לדעת את השם יתברך.

It is known that this world is like a cloak for the elevated world. Just as clothing provide a descriptive shape of the wearer without revealing his true essence, so too God can be understood, though not truly, through examining the physical world. It is said of man that he is created in the image of God… for when a person contemplates the form of his physique, a person can come to know God.[21]

18. See *Ta'anit* 11a, *Chagiga* 16a, and *Shulchan Aruch* O.C. 2:2.

19. **של"ה מסכת חולין פרק דרך חיים תוכחת מוסר**

ואל יעמוד ממטתו ערום ולא ילבש חלוקו אף מיושב, אך יקח חלוקו ויכניס בו ראשו וזרועותיו בעודו שוכב, ואז בקומו יהיה מכוסה, כמו שהיה מתפאר רבי יוסי (שבת קיח ב), מעולם לא ראו קורות ביתי שפת חלוקי. ואל יאמר הנני בחדרי חדרים בבית אופל, מי רואני ומי יעידני, כי מלא כל הארץ כבודו, אשר לפניו חשיכה כאורה, אמן. הטעם לזה, **כי אברי האדם רומזים לדברים עליונים, כמו שאמר איוב (איוב יט:כו) 'ומבשרי אחזה אלוה', אף כי הברית הקדוש, ולכן אין ראוי לגלותם, כי כבוד אלהים הסתר אבריו.**

20. Based on *Mishlei* 25:2, "כְּבֹד אֱלֹהִים הַסְתֵּר דָּבָר וּכְבֹד מְלָכִים חֲקֹר דָּבָר."

21. With this, Maharal explains the following:

תלמוד בבלי מסכת יבמות דף מט עמוד ב

א"ר שמעון בן עזאי כו'. תני, שמעון בן עזאי אומר: מצאתי מגלת יוחסין בירושלים, וכתוב בה: איש פלוני ממזר מאשת איש, וכתוב בה: משנת ר' אליעזר בן יעקב קב ונקי, וכתוב בה: **מנשה**

With this, Maharal explains why the Talmud writes that the 248 positive *mitzvot* correspond to the 248 limbs of a human.[22] Maharal warns against taking the approach of physicians, who maintain that the limbs of a human are natural, like the limbs of animals. In truth, he writes, the number 248 is not accidental. Positive *mitzvot*, corresponding to our physical bodies, bring a person to spiritual perfection.

In 5.15, we saw that Maharal believes that the biological statements found in Chazal are meant to offer spiritual explanations (as opposed to scientific ones) of physical phenomena. He thus explains why the Talmud offers a spiritual reason for why a person's fingers are shaped as they are.[23]

הרג את ישעיה. אמר רבא: מידן דייניה וקטליה, אמר ליה, משה רבך אמר: בכי לא יראני האדם וחי, ואת אמרת: ואראה את ה׳ יושב על כסא רם ונשא! משה רבך אמר: דמי כה׳ אלהינו בכל קראנו אליו, ואת אמרת: הדרשו ה׳ בהמצאו! משה רבך אמר: ואת מספר ימיך אמלא, ואת אמרת: זוהוספתי על ימיך חמש עשרה שנה! אמר ישעיה: ידענא ביה דלא מקבל מה דאימא ליה, ואי אימא ליה אישוייה מזיד, אמר שם איבלע בארזא. אתיוה לארזא ונסרוה, כי מטא להדי פומא נח נפשיה, משום דאמר: חובתוך עם טמא שפתים אנכי יושב. **מכל מקום קשו קראי אהדדי! ואראה את ה׳ - כדתניא: כל הנביאים נסתכלו באספקלריא שאינה מאירה, משה רבינו נסתכל באספקלריא המאירה.** דרשו ה׳ בהמצאו - הא ביחיד, הא בצבור. ויחיד אימת? אמר רב נחמן אמר רבה בר אבוה: אלו עשרה ימים שבין ראש השנה ליום הכפורים. את מספר ימיך אמלא - תנאי היא; דתניא: את מספר ימיך אמלא.

Because Moshe was on a higher level of prophecy, he did not need a parable to understand God. Indeed, as the level of prophecy descended, images of God became more ornate and humanlike.

22. **ספר תפארת ישראל פרק ד**

ונתן להם עוד רמ״ח מצות עשה, שהם קנין מעשה, שעל ידם קונה מעלה ושלימות, כנגד חלק המציאות השני, שהוא האדם. שנמצא באדם קנין מעלה, שלא תמצא בחלק הראשון, שאין בו קנין כלל, רק נשאר על מה שנברא עליו. והאדם בלבד יש בו קנין מעלה. והאברים של אדם הם שלימות צורת האדם. כי אל תחשוב כמו שחשבו קצת בני אדם, והם הרופאים, כי האברים של אדם הם טבעיים כמו שאר בעלי חיים. כי אין הדבר כך כלל, כי רופאי אליל המה, לא ידעו באמת תאר האדם ואיבריו, שכולו אלהי. ולפיכך האיברים שלו הם שלימות האדם, ועל ידי אבריו - שהם רמ״ח - נברא בצלם האלהים, ומצד הזה הוא מלך בתחתונים, שנאמר (בראשית א:כו) ״נעשה אדם בצלמנו וגו׳ וירדו בדגת הים ובעוף השמים״. ולפיכך מספר המצות - שהם שלימות האדם - כמספר אבריו, שהם גם כן שלימות ומעלת האדם, עד שהוא בצלם אלהים על ידי רמ״ח אבריו. ושלימות ומעלת המצות נמשך אחר השלימות הזה מה שהאדם נברא בצלם אלהים, שעל ידי זה האדם הוא שלימות כל התחתונים.

23. **ספר באר הגולה באר השלישי פרק א**

פרק קמא דכתובות (ה א), דרש בר קפרא, מאי דכתיב (דברים כג:יד) ״ויתד תהיה לך על אזנך״, אל תקרא ״אזניך״, אלא ׳אזנך׳, שאם ישמע אדם דבר שאינו הגון, יניח אצבעו לתוך אזניו. והיינו דאמר רבי אלעזר, מפני מה אצבעותיו של אדם משופעות כיתידות. מאי טעמא,

In fact, Maharal adds, this very point serves as the primary distinction between scientific knowledge, which is based on observation and, therefore, limited to the physical, and the knowledge of our Sages, which stems from tradition and, therefore, applies to the eternal.[24]

This understanding has implications on our attitude towards the physical world, a topic we deal with shortly.

12.3 THE PURPOSE OF ANTHROPOMORPHISMS

In the previous section, we considered how examination of the human being affords us a glimpse of the Divine. Now, let us consider why God chose this method of "communication." In addition, let us explore how Kabbalists understand verses that seem to ascribe physical qualities to God.

To better grasp the purpose of Kabbala's use of human imagery to portray the Divine, let us compare the approaches of Rambam and Kabbala with respect to the Torah's anthropomorphisms. Rambam

---

אילימא משום דמתחלקים, כל חד וחד למילתא עביד. דאמר מר, זו זרת, וזו קמיצה, זו אמה, זו אצבע, זו גודל. אלא מאי טעמא משופעות כיתידות, שאם ישמע האדם דבר שאינו הגון, יניח אצבעו לתוך אזנו. תנא דבי רבי ישמעאל, מפני מה אוזן כולו קשה, והאליה רכה, שאם ישמע האדם דבר שאינו הגון, יכוף האליה לתוכו, עד כאן.

... אמנם מה שלא היה כסוי לאוזן בעצמו, כמו שהוא לעינים ולפה. אם יאמרו לך הרופאים או בעלי טבע דברים טבעים לזה, אל תאבה להם ואל תשמע להם, כי רופאי אליל המה, לא ידעו בחכמת היצירה והבריאה כלום. אבל דבר זה הוא, מפני שהאוזן הוא משמש הקבלה בלבד, כמו שהתבאר למעלה. ושלימות הקבלה בעצמו שיהיה פתוח לקבל, ולא שיהיה לו סתימה בעצמו של אוזן שנברא לקבלה, כי יהיו שני הפכים בנושא אחד. ואמנם יש לו סתימה חוץ מן הכלי, עד שהוא כמו צמיד פתיל עליו. ולפיכך האוזן שהוא כלי הקיבול, ראוי שאין בו סתימה בעצמו. והדברים האלו הם דברי חכמה מאוד.

24. **ספר באר הגולה באר החמישי פרק ד**

וכאשר תבין את זה, אז תבין מעלת צלם האלקי שבאדם. והפלסופים לא ראו והביטו רק הטבע כמו הרופאים לא ידעו ולא יבינו רק הטבע, ולכך לא עמדו על הבריאה הזאת הוא האדם, כי יצירת האדם בפרט, הכל הוא ענין אלקי, ולא טבעי. ומעתה איך תשתפכנה אבני קודש בראש כל חוצות (איכה ד:א), מושלכים רמוסים תחת רגלי האדם, נתונים למרמס, עד שהאדם מואס בם הדריסה עליהם. **והם אבנים יקרות, יותר משוהם וישפה ספיר גזרתם. ואין חכמתם דומה לחכמת חכמי האומות, כי חכמי האומות, אף כי היו חכמים, היה חכמתם שכל האנושי. אבל חכמינו, חכמתם חכמה פנימית, סתרי החכמה, מה שידעו על פי הקבלה מרבם, ורבם מרבם, עד הנביאים, ועד משה רבינו עליו השלום.** לכן עיני עיני הורידו כנחל דמעה אל תתנו פוגת לכם, איך נחשבו דברי יקר להבל אין חפץ בו. ואם לא שלא יתעללו בהם אנשים שאין ראוי להם לפרש סתרי החכמה, היה ראוי להוסיף פירוש בדברים אלו, למען דעת כל עמי הארץ כי אין חכמה זולת חכמתם. והוא יתברך יכפר בעדנו, אמן.

devotes much of the first section of *Moreh ha-Nevuchim* to dealing with instances where the Torah uses words to describe God or His actions that denote corporeality. Rambam's general approach is to argue that these words, when used to describe God, have completely different meanings than when they are used to describe humans – they are homonyms. (At the same time, Rambam offers evidence for the accuracy of the secondary definition of the term from other places in Scripture where the secondary definition clearly is intended.) This is what Rambam means in his Introduction (cited in 3.3) when he writes that the Torah uses "equivocal language," namely, language that can be understood in two ways. Why was the Torah imprecise? Why didn't it use language that unequivocally expressed the intended meaning? The answer, as we have seen, is that the simplistic understanding is valuable insofar as it is necessary to bring the masses, who initially are incapable of imagining an incorporeal being, to belief in God. Thus, according to Rambam, these passages can be understood in two ways, either incorrectly by the uninitiated, or correctly by those properly trained.

Kabbalists, as we have seen above, agree that these corporeal terms are not meant literally. At the same time, though, they are not mere homonyms. Instead, they serve a symbolic function. They depict a supernal truth about the Divine that otherwise is inexpressible. The ear and the eye, masculinity and femininity, left and right, are all means of expressing spiritual qualities of God that cannot be expressed differently.[25] As *Shlah* writes,[26] it is not the case that the

25. See "Rav Kook and the Jewish Philosophical Tradition," by Lawrence J. Kaplan, pp. 49–50, in *Rabbi Abraham Isaac Kook and Jewish Spirituality*, who notes the above distinction and considers the position of R. Kook that there is not necessarily fundamental disagreement between Rambam and the Kabbalists in this regard.

26. **שני לוחות הברית, תולדות אדם, בית אחרון (אות לב)**
נמצא כל התוארים הנזכרים בו ית' עין אוזן רגל יד וכן כולם, גם ענין זיווג חבוק נשוק, אב ואם, בן ובת, חמיו חמותו, והרבה כאלה כל אלו הם לשון קודש שמם עצמיים שלהם בקדושה, ואחר כך בהשתלשלות הוא בשאלה, עד שאפילו הגשמיים נקראים בשמות אלו בשאלה, ואז מובן כי אדרבה כל אברי פרקי מרכבה שמותם בו יתברך בעצם והוא אדם העליון, ושמות כחות אברים שלנו הוא בשאלה ונקראים כן על שם שהם סימן למה שלמעלה, כראובן בן יעקב שהוא סימן, כמו שכתב בעל האורה. והקב"ה ברא אדם תחתון

Torah "borrows" human terminology to describe the Divine, but just the opposite: the true "*yad*," for example, refers to a concept in God that, when applied to our physical human existence, describes a hand. Thus, the literal meaning of the verse should be embraced insofar as it conveys profound secrets. In fact, as we shall see in 12.6, the Kabbalistic explanations frequently correspond to the literal reading of the text.

12.4 THE INNOVATION OF *CHASIDUT*

From one perspective, when considering the Kabbalistic worldview, the least ideal means of seeking God is through examining the physical world, since the physical world is, as it were, the most remote manifestation of God. To appreciate this, we must go back to the beginning of creation. Prior to creation, God is referred to as the *Ein Sof*; meaning the Being that has no end. We cannot truly relate to Him as such. While He did not change through creation, creation involved God creating something finite out of the infinite, which allows for our existence. Some Kabbalistic texts speak of an ongoing contraction of divine power or revelation as it streams into this finite world, such that when it reaches our world, there is nearly total concealment.[27] Along similar lines, the writings of Arizal describe a dramatic leap from infinite to finite called *tzimtzum* (contraction).[28] Either way, we would not expect to look for God in the most distant emanation of God – in our world.

בו סימנים לאדם העליון להיותו מרכבה במציאת אמתתו, יש דברים ועניינים פנימיים דקים רוחניים בתכלית והם פרקי מרכבה אשר מהם מתפשט האור והשפע לקיום הנמצא הזה העושה בדמותו והם נקראים ידים רגלים עינים אזנים, לא שמהות יד כמהות יד, או תבנית יד כתבנית יד, חלילה שהרי כתיב (ישעיה מ:יח) ואל מי תדמיון אל וגו׳, ואין ביני ובינינו דמיון כלל מצד העצם והתבנית. ואמנם נתקן ונעשה בדמות הזה, להורות שאם יזכה לטהר אחד מאבריו ולהשלימו במצות התלויות בו, יהיה האבר ההוא כדמיון מרכבה וכסא הכבוד לדבר ההוא העליון הפנימי הנקרא בשם זה, אם עין עין, אם יד יד, אם רגל רגל, וכן שאר האברים

27. There are many places where this notion is discussed. One accessible presentation is in *Tanya, Sha'ar ha-Yichud ve-ha-Emuna*, Ch. 4.

28. These ideas are not merely esoteric wisdom; many Kabbalistic texts stress the practical guidance that emerges from these teachings. For example, the notion of *tzimtzum* teaches modesty and the value of remaining understated and even hidden.

Nevertheless, even our world comes from God and thus allows us to perceive Him. In fact, it is precisely because of His contraction that we are able to perceive Him at all.[29] Thus, the *Zohar* states, "There is no place void of Him."[30] This idea became one of the major themes of chasidic thought. Instead of focusing on His distance from our physical world (His transcendence), *Chasidut* focuses on His presence in our world (His immanence). Everywhere we look, we can (if we open our eyes) see Him – as the Maggid of Mezeritch (R. Dov Ber b. Avraham, 1704?-1772)[31] writes:

לקוטי אמרים אות רסג

...ולית אתר פנוי מיניה, והכל מלא מחיות הבורא ברוך הוא. נמצא כל מה שרואה הוא רואה רק חיות הבורא הנמשך בו.

> There is no place devoid of Him; all is filled with the life of the Creator. Thus, in everything one sees, he is seeing the life of God that is drawn through it.

In fact, many thinkers, among them R. Kalonymus Kalman Shapira of Piaseczno (1889–1943), see this idea as the central pillar of all of *Chasidut*.

---

29. R. Soloveitchik (*Halakhic Man* note 61) expresses this dichotomy:

> The attribute of *tzimtzum* expresses itself in two ideas: concealment and disclosure. On the one hand, God sustains the cosmos through concealing and hiding His glory, and were He to reveal Himself, then all would revert to chaos and the void, for who can withstand the splendor of His excellence when He comes forth to overawe the earth? It is the concealment of the divine countenance which brings into being all existence. On the other hand, the Almighty gives life to and sustains all existence through the disclosure of His glory, for He is the root and source of reality, and the concealment of the divine countenance would result in the destruction of the world and the negation of reality. Only the act of disclosure creates. This powerful antinomy, "splendid in its holiness", is practically the central axis of Chabad doctrine. Concealment and disclosure – both equally sustain the cosmos, but both equally cause it to revert back to nothingness and naught.

Some thinkers, such as R. Nachman of Breslov (*Likutei Moharan* 1:64:1), see a paradox in this notion of *tzimtzum*.

30. **תקוני זוהר דף קכב ע"ב**

לית אתר פנוי מיניה.

31. The Maggid of Mezeritch was one of the major disciples of R. Yisrael Ba'al Sheim Tov, the founder of *Chasidut*.

It also was a major cause for the controversy surrounding *Chasidut* insofar as the idea can be misconstrued as being pantheistic or corporealizing God.[32] However, as we noted, these ideas are rooted in earlier sources.[33] The innovation is more in terms of focus.[34]

---

32. **ספר מבוא שארים לר' קלונימוס קלמיש שפירא מפיסצ'נה הי"ד פרק ג**
ויסוד תורת הבעל שם טוב זצ"ל נכללת בהפשט אשר גלה בקדשו על הפסוק מלא כל הארץ כבודו.
רבים אף רבים בתורה הרבו לרדוף את הקדוש ישראל בשביל זה, באמרם שחס ושלום מגשם הוא בזה את כבוד של מעלה, אבל העיר וקדיש אשר מן שמיא נחית קדושינו הבעש"ט זצ"ל ידע שלא לבד שאינו מגשם חס ושלום, רק עוד מרבה ומגלה את כבודו יתברך בזה, ולא רק פשט ושכל אומר בזה רק את השחר שלפני המשיח ממרום העיר, ואם לא יתנו להקדים את השחר, ולא יתרגל העולם בהארת השחר, אז את השמש של המשיח חס ושלום מפריעים מלעלות, לכן הכריז בקדשו ואמר לא בלבד שבתוך כל דבר מדברי העולם, חיות אלקית נמצא, ועל חיות הזה גשם הארץ סובב ומסתיר, רק גם הגשם וגם הארציות רק לנו כגשם נראה, **ובאמת הכל אלקות**, וצריכים רק עינים לראות וגוף המתקדש, ואז **כשאתה מסתכל על העולם, אתה מביט על אלקים ואלקים עליך**, מלא כל הארץ כבודו, אף הארציות הלבוש והכלים מלאים הארת כבודו יתברך הם, והוא הראשית של ומלאה הארץ דעה וכו'... שגם הארץ תמלא דעה את ה'.

33. While some see this idea as innovated by chasidic thinkers, it can be traced back to non-Kabbalistic sources in Chazal and is explicated by non-chasidic thinkers as well. As the Nazir (R. David Cohen, student of R. Kook, 1887–1972) showed:
קול הנבואה עמ' קכג - קכז
אמנם, **לחז"ל** במדרשים: "אין מקום פנוי בלא שכינה" "הוא מקומו של עולם ואין העולם מקומו". **ובזוהר:** "לית אתר פנוי מיניה, איהו מסובב כל עלמין, איהו ממלא כל עלמין, איהו מחיה להון, הה"ד: ואתה מחיה את כולם." **ולרמ"ק:** "הכל בו, והוא בכל, וחוץ הכל". גם **רס"ג באמונות ודעות** (סוף מאמר שני, ובפירוש לספר היצירה), איך יעלה בשכלנו, הימצאו בכל מקום, עד שלא יהיה מקום ריק ממנו, וכמו שאמר: "הלא את השמים ואת הארץ אני מלא נאם ה'". ואחריו **בשיר היחוד:** "סובב הכל, ומלא את כל, ובהיות הכל, אתה בכל, אין עליך ואין תחתך, ואין מקום ריק ממך ונחדל". **ובספר הנצחון:** "ברוך הוא, שממציא חיים כולם, ועל כן נקרא: חי עלמא, כי הוא חיותם, ועל זה ארז"ל: "הוא מקומו של עולם ואין העולם מקומו".
יש שאמרו (שו"ת חכם צבי) אלוהי"ם = הטבע... ובחכמה הפנימית, והחסידות: **אלהי"ם בגימ' הטב"ע.** אך שם זה אינו אלא אחד משמות הקודש, המורה על גבורה וצמצום. **אמנם השם המיוחד, שם העצם, הוא למעלה מהטבע**... ראשית דבר שיטת החסידות, מיסודו של **ר' ישראל בעש"ט**, הוא, שהאין סוף ב"ה ממלא כל עולמים, ומסבב, ובתוך, ולית אתר פנוי מיניה, ואפילו בדברים הנמוכים, בכל יש האלוקות, המחיה הכל, והכל מלא מחיות הבורא ב"ה. והבעל שם טוב נסמך אל רב סעדיה גאון. וכן בחסידות **חב"ד**... גם בספר **נפש החיים לר"ח מוולוז'ין בשער ג'**, תלמיד הגר"א: שהוא מקומו של עולם, והוא המקום האמיתי, הסובל ומקיים העולמות והבריות כולם... והוא נסמך על הרמב"ם... ההתנגדות לחסידות היתה משום שדבר זה נתפרסם להמון, ואין הדבר אמור אלא לחכם ומבין מדעתו. ובדורות האחרונים יפה לנו מאוד כל שיחתם של תלמידי הגר"א יחד עם תלמידי הבעש"ט.

34. That is not to say that there is no disagreement concerning theological matters between *Chasidim* and *Mitnagdim*. One major disagreement relates to the nature of

12.5 THE KABBALISTIC APPROACH TO THE PHYSICAL WORLD

The discussion described in the previous sections regarding our orientation towards the physical world relates to a fundamental question concerning physical actions and spiritual achievements. Maharal writes:

ספר תפארת ישראל פרק ט

הפילוסופים אשר זכרנו למעלה, יתנו שם ותפארת אל השכל, ועל ידי המושכלות יקנה האדם הנצחיות, ויעשו המעשים הישרים והטובים כמו תכונה וסולם, אשר יגיע בהן אל המושכלות. ומזה הסולם נפלו.

> The philosophers that we mentioned earlier give recognition and glory exclusively to the intellect, believing that through intellectual achievements, a person can achieve eternity (*olam ha-ba*).[35] They consider ethical acts and good deeds like a ladder to reach intellectual achievements. And from this ladder they (i.e., the philosophers) fell.

According to Maharal, the philosophers erred by claiming that doing good deeds is only secondary to intellectual achievement.[36] Their focus on the intellect ignores the fact that we humans are physical as well as

---

tzimtzum – was there true *tzimtzum* or just the appearance of *tzimtzum* such that in reality there is nothing devoid of God? The latter perspective, sometimes called panentheism (not to be confused with pantheism, which posits that the universe and the Divine are ontologically equivalent), was adopted by many chasidic thinkers, most notably R. Shneur Zalman of Liadi, and appears to differ from non-chasidic Kabbalistic sources. However, as noted in the previous footnote, a case can be made that there is little significant disagreement. (R. Kook adopted and developed the panentheistic approach; his student, the Nazir, sought to minimize the magnitude of his teacher's innovation.) On the difference between pantheism and panentheism, see *The Philosophical Quest: Of Philosophy, Ethics, Law and Halakhah* by R. J. David Bleich, pp. 60–61.

35. We will discuss this contention in Chapter 20.

36. Maharal's critique of philosophers does not imply a lack of veneration for Rambam and respect for *Moreh ha-Nevuchim*. Maharal calls Rambam "the great rabbi – who was filled like the sea with wisdom in all natural, theological, and scholastic disciplines" (*Be'eir ha-Gola, Be'eir* 4, p. 49).

spiritual creatures.[37] The *mitzvot*, many of which involve physical activities alongside intellectual involvement, elevate the human and allow him to achieve his full potential.

Likewise, the author of *Iggeret ha-Kodesh* blames Aristotle's pernicious influence upon Rambam for Rambam's negative attitude[38] toward marital relationships.[39] Maharal explains why the Talmud treats

---

37. Maharal argues that the philosophical worldview is highly elitist:

> לפי דבריהם לא תהיה רק לאחד או לשנים בדור, וכי בשביל אלו העולם נמצא.
>
> According to the philosophers (who value only abstract cognitive activity), there could be only one or two people in a generation who could achieve greatness. (Rambam, in fact, seems to adopt this position in his Introduction to his commentary on the Mishna.) Maharal considers this conclusion illogical.

38. For example, in *Moreh ha-Nevuchim* (2:36), Rambam approvingly cites Aristotle's negative view.

> After these introductory remarks you will understand that a person must satisfy the following conditions before he can become a prophet: ... There must be an absence of the lower desires and appetites, of the seeking after pleasure in eating, drinking, and cohabitation: and, in short, every pleasure connected with the sense of touch. (**Aristotle correctly says that this sense is a disgrace to us**, since we possess it only in virtue of our being animals; and it does not include any specifically human element, whilst enjoyments connected with other senses, as smell, hearing, and sight, though likewise of a material nature, may sometimes include [intellectual] pleasure, appealing to man as man, according to Aristotle. This remark, although forming no part of our subject, is not superfluous, for the thoughts of the most renowned wise men are to a great extent affected by the pleasures of this sense, and filled with a desire for them. And yet people are surprised that these scholars do not prophesy, as if prophesying be nothing but a certain degree in the natural development of man.)

However, consider Rambam's comments in *Hilchot Isurei Bi'a* 21:9 and 11 and *Hilchot Dei'ot*, Ch. 5.

39. *Iggeret ha-Kodesh*, attributed to Ramban, is a small work dealing with marriage. Many question the accuracy of this attribution. R. Chaim Dov Chavel included *Iggeret ha-Kodesh* in the second volume of his *Collected Writings of the Ramban* (Mosad ha-Rav Kook, Jerusalem 5724/1964) and discusses the authorship of this important work, concluding that while probably not written by Ramban himself, it does appear to have originated from his students and likely is based upon his teachings. *Iggeret ha-Kodesh* states:

> ואין הדבר כאשר חשב הרב המורה ז"ל במורה הנבוכים בהיותו משבח לארסט"ו על מה שאמר כי חוש המשוש הוא חרפה לנו. חלילה, אין הדבר כמו שאמר היוני, לפי שדעתו היוני יש שמץ מינות שאינו מורגש, שאלו היה מאמין שהעולם מחודש בכוונה לא היה אומר כך זה היוני הבליעל. אבל כל בעלי התורה מאמינים שהשם ברא את הכל כפי מה שגזרה חכמתו, ולא ברא

physical relations, in the proper context, as a holy endeavor, appropriately discussed in holy texts. With this, he responds to those who denigrate the Talmud's discussion (*Bava Metzia* 84a) of a seemingly lewd topic.[40]

דבר שיהיה גנאי או כיעור, שאם יאמר שהחבור הוא דבר של גנאי, הנה כלי המשגל הם כלי הגנות, והרי השי"ת בראם במאמרו דכתיב (דברים לב) הוא עשך ויכוננך ואז"ל במסכת חולין (נו ב) שברא הקב"ה כונניות באדם. ובמדרש קהלת (ב:יב) אמרו אשר כבר עשוהו מלמד שהוא ובית דינו נמנו על כל אבר ואבר והושיבוהו על כנו. ואם כלי המשגל גנאי, היאך ברא הש"י דבר שיש בו משום חסרון או גנות חלילה, אלא פעולותיו של הקב"ה תמימות שנאמר (שם לב) הצור תמים פעלו. [ואומר וירא אלקים את כל אשר עשה והנה טוב מאד].

One of the objections raised to the possibility that the work actually was written by Ramban is the fact that in explaining the prohibition against restricted relationships, Ramban's tone in some places somewhat resembles that of Rambam (see *Vayikra* 18:6). However, even if Ramban did not write the letter, it likely is written by one of his students. Moreover, the central idea of *Iggeret ha-Kodesh* can be found in Ramban as well (see *Vayikra* 18:19).

The root of the disagreement between Rambam and Ramban lies in understanding the nature of the physical body. For Rambam, the physical body is blood and bones, whereas for Ramban, as we have seen, it is a reflection of our Creator. Thus, the potential for spiritual achievement by means of the physical body is naturally greater. Nevertheless, even for Rambam, physical pleasure is not entirely base; he too allows for its elevation when properly directed. Consider, for example, Rambam's comments in *Hilchot Yom Tov* 6:18 (אין זו שמחת מצוה אלא שמחת כריסו). Rambam, in that context, distinguishes between positive physical pleasure, where one includes others in their celebration, and base physical pleasure, where one focuses entirely on his own family.

40. Maharal first notes that the act of intimacy can be a spiritual and not just a physical act. Then he notes that a person might find the Talmud's discussion of intimacy strange. He responds that such a reaction reflects the Aristotelian (and later Christian) perspective which sees intimacy as base. However, the Torah sees things differently. In fact, the continuity of the world depends upon procreation. Clearly, there is nothing inherently bad about intimacy.

חידושי אגדות למהר"ל בבא מציעא דף פד עמוד א

...ומה שאמר האהבה דוחקת הבשר פי' כי איש ואשה, דהיינו חבורם יחד, הוא מן הש"י, שהוא המאחד את שניהם יחד על ידי שם י"ה, וזה דוחה הגשמי, הוא הבשר, כי החבור האלקי גובר על זה...

כל דבר זה נראה זר לכתוב זה בתלמוד... דע כי באו ללמד לנו ענין נפלא. כי הרבה מחכמים, והם החוקרים בשכלם על הנמצאי' שהם אומרים כי זה חרפת אדם ובשתו וכלימתו חבור איש ואשתו, עד שאמרו בהסכמה מוחלטת חוש המשוש חרפה הוא לנו. ודבר זה באו להרחיק חכמי', כי לא יסבול דבר זה הדעת, כי יהיה יסוד כל, אשר הוא קיום העולם שהוא פריה ורביה, יהיה נבנה על דבר גנאי וחרפה, וכאשר היסוד הוא רעוע

Thus, we see how the Kabbalistic approach to the holiness of the body expresses itself as an entire approach to the physical world. In Chapter 20, we will see how this debate relates to the disagreement between rationalists and Kabbalists as to whether there is a physical body in *olam ha-ba*. Rambam argues that it is inconceivable that there will be a physical body in *olam ha-ba*, while Ramban maintains that there will be.

Two Perspectives

Interestingly, we find two seemingly contradictory perspectives in Kabbalistic and especially chasidic texts concerning our relationship to the world. Some urge us to withdraw from the world and have nothing to do with the *alma de-shikra* (world of falsehood), while others write of elevating the physical world through spiritual involvement in it. While it is tempting to see this as a debate reflecting opposing schools of thought, the resolution cannot be so simple since we frequently find the same thinkers stressing both aspects. For example, we saw *Iggeret ha-Kodesh* describe the holiness of intimacy; at the same time, he writes that the pious should attempt to minimize pleasure when engaging in this activity. Likewise, Maharal describes how our belief in the sanctity of this world explains the Talmud's positive attitude towards the physical, yet at the same time, he writes how the physical and spiritual realms are opposites and absolutely incompatible:

ספר נצח ישראל פרק טו

וזה כי כל דבר שהוא בעולם הזה, שהוא עולם גשמי, אין לו שייכות אל הנבדל מן הגשמי, מפני שחלקו בעולם הגשמי בלבד, ואין דבר אחד שייך לשני דברים שהם מחולקים. כי העולם הזה הגשמי מחולק ונבדל מן עולם הבלתי גשמי.

This is because everything in this world, which is the physical world, has no connection to that which is elevated from the

---

כל אשר נבנה עליו הוא נופל. ולכך ראוי להרחיק את דעת זה, כי אין בחבור איש עם אשתו שום דבר רע כלל.

> physical, due to its connection to the physical, since one thing cannot belong to two categories, and the world of the physical is separate from the non-physical world.

The resolution to this puzzle is complex, but, perhaps, its root lies in recognizing that the Kabbalistic perspective allows for holiness in this world exclusively through performance of *mitzvot* or, at the very least, secular acts done with an elevated intention. For an example of this distinction, consider Ramban's perspective on intimacy discussed in 12.9. There we shall see how Ramban argues that the act is inherently holy when done in the context of a *mitzva*.

Moreover, even within the context of a *mitzva*, the sanctity is not fully automatic and is defined by intent. Thus, the same Shabbat meal eaten by two people may have profoundly differing religious implications depending upon the intent each party has.

The Mystery of the Showbread

Another fascinating insight that highlights this difference between the rationalistic and mystical perspective on physicality follows. In *Moreh ha-Nevuchim* 3:26–49, Rambam suggests reasons for the Torah's *mitzvot*, offering rationales even for enigmatic commandments (*chukim*) such as *sha'atneiz* (the prohibition against wearing garments made of wool and linen combined) and the red heifer. However, when it comes to the *lechem ha-panim* (the showbread), Rambam admits ignorance:

> **ספר מורה הנבוכים חלק ג פרק מה**
> והצורך למזבח הקטורת ומזבח העולה וכליהם מבואר, **אבל השלחן והיות עליו הלחם תמיד לא אדע בו סבה, ואיני יודע לאיזה דבר איחס אותו עד היום**

> The use of the altar for incense and the altar for burnt-offering and their vessels is obvious; **but I do not know the object of the table with the bread upon it continually, and up to this day I have not been able to assign any reason to this commandment.**

What makes the showbread so mysterious?[41]

R. Moshe Stav once showed me that a clue can be found in the *Shabbat zemer* "*Ki Eshmera Shabbat*," where R. Avraham ibn Ezra writes:

> רָשַׁם בְּדָת הָקֵל חֹק אֶל סְגָנָיו. בּוֹ לַעֲרֹךְ לֶחֶם פָּנִים לְפָנָיו. עַל כֵּן לְהִתְעַנּוֹת
> בּוֹ עַל פִּי נְבוֹנָיו. אָסוּר לְבַד מִיּוֹם כִּפּוּר עֲוֹנִי.

> Engraved in God's law is a *chok* (decree) for His priests – to arrange showbread before Him. Therefore, fasting on [Shabbat] is prohibited, as explained by His Sages; except for on Yom Kippur.

In this poem, ibn Ezra alludes to the mysteriousness of the showbread, calling it a *chok*. Then he writes that the law of the showbread serves as the reason for the prohibition against fasting on Shabbat. How?

To answer these questions, we must remember a highly unusual element of the showbread's service. Generally, when it comes to Temple service, the sacrifices brought inside the Temple structure, and therefore in close proximity to the Holy of Holies, were not eaten. Thus, the inner altar was used only for incense. Any sacrifice whose blood is brought inside was not eaten. For example, a regular *chatat* (sin offering) is consumed by *kohanim*, while a *chatat penimit* (inner sin offering),[42] which is brought inside, is entirely burnt. Rambam understands that this stems from the sacrifice's proximity to the divine presence (see *Moreh ha-Nevuchim* 3:46). Thus, the holiness of the *korban*, as reflected by being offered inside, precludes the possibility of eating it. Put differently, physical ingestion contradicts holiness, such that the holiest sacrifices may not be consumed. If this is the case, Rambam is left with a mystery: the showbreads were brought inside, reflecting intense holiness, and yet were entirely consumed.[43] This apparent inconsistency within the

41. Ramban (*Shemot* 25:24) as well as *Sefer ha-Chinuch* 97 offer reasons for this law.
42. פר העלם דבר של ציבור, פר הכהן המשיח, ופר ושעיר של יום הכיפורים.
43. Only the cups of *levona* were offered upon the altar.

laws of sacrifices is the reason for Rambam's admission that he cannot understand the reason for the showbread.[44]

Ibn Ezra, aware of the enigma, concludes that the secret of the showbread is that physical activities, such as eating, do not contradict holiness. On the contrary, activities such as eating can elevate us spiritually in a manner that purely spiritual activities cannot. The *lechem hapanim* demonstrate this and therefore teach us that we may not fast on Shabbat, the holiest day of the week.[45]

12.6 KABBALISTIC INTERPRETATIONS OF SCRIPTURE

In Chapter 7, we considered two layers of Torah interpretation – *pshat* and *drash*. In 12.1, we read how the *Zohar* is contemptuous towards understanding the stories superficially. While *pshat*, when properly studied, is certainly not superficial, and *drash* further seeks to plumb the depths of Torah, *sod* (lit. secret) takes this one step further. Let us briefly consider the role of mysticism, or *sod*, in the elucidation of the Torah with a focus on Ramban. Before considering Ramban's perspective on *sod*, however, let us briefly introduce the relationship between *pshat*, *drash*, and *sod*. In 12.1, we considered the *Zohar*'s comparison of *pshat* to a person's skin or clothes, which are the most superficial aspects of a person and do not reflect who he truly is. *Drash* is the second step after *pshat* in grasping the Torah's concealed mysteries. Ultimately, however, one seeks to understand the upper worlds through the study of Torah:

רמב"ן בראשית א:א
תדע כי על דרך האמת הכתוב יגיד בתחתונים וירמוז בעליונים

44. This may relate to the interpretation (see *Vayikra Rabba* 32:3) that the *mitzva* of the showbread caused the blasphemer to blaspheme.

45. Another manifestation of this concept can be seen in Rashi's understanding of *neshama yeteira*:

רש"י מסכת ביצה דף טז עמוד א
נשמה יתירה - רוחב לב למנוחה ולשמחה, ולהיות פתוח לרווחה, ויאכל וישתה ואין נפשו קצה עליו.

Perhaps Rashi is informing us that the tension between physical pleasures and spirituality need not exist on Shabbat. (see *Teshuvot ha-Rashba* 7:349)

> You should understand that according to the way of truth (i.e., the Kabbalistic understanding of the Torah), Scripture **describes** lower matters and **alludes** to the upper realm.

In this cryptic statement, Ramban is alluding to the parallelism between the upper and lower worlds. One can understand the upper worlds by studying the lower worlds because, as we have seen, the lower worlds and the stories of the Torah cloak the deeper truth. The explicit discussions of lower matters allude (*yirmoz*) to these deeper truths.[46] Thus, the Kabbalistic explanations of the Torah are described, as in the above passage, as "the path of truth" or "at the inner core of the matter" (פנימיות הענין).[47]

As noted earlier, this deeper meaning does not devalue the simple explanation of the text. Because Torah relates to this world, it communicates on a level of *pshat*. Because Torah allows a person to transcend this world, it also communicates on a level of *sod* (or *emet*). Put differently, the reason why Ramban stresses the importance of *pshat* is that we live on this world and are physical creatures. Thus, *pshat* relates to a greater degree to the realm we inhabit.

Pardeis

With this in mind we can better understand the relationship between the various levels of interpretation. The acronym "*Pardeis*" refers to the four primary approaches to biblical exegesis:

Pshat (פְּשָׁט) – simple meaning.
Remez (רֶמֶז) – hinted meaning.
Drash (דְּרַשׁ) – exegetical meaning.
Sod (סוֹד) – mystical meaning.

---

46. In 2.9, we explained why esoteric wisdom cannot be expressed explicitly insofar as the infinite ideas cannot be limited by finite words.

47. For example, concerning the word "day" (*yom*) in the first chapter of *Bereishit*, Ramban writes:

רמב"ן בראשית א:ג
ובפנימיות הענין יקראו "ימים" הספירות האצולות מעליון, כי כל מאמר פועל הויה תקרא "יום".

Because each of these layers is divine, studying each of them proves valuable. As such, Gra penned three different commentaries on *Megillat Ester,* one following *pshat,* a second following *remez* and *drash,* and a third following *sod.*

To better understand the relationship between these layers, we once again turn to metaphor. *Mishlei* 1:20–1[48] refers to four places from which wisdom, or Torah, calls forth. Gra understands these verses as depicting the four levels of *Pardeis. Pshat* is represented by someone far outside of a city (*ba-chutz*) in the wilderness. *Drash* is depicted as a road (*rechov*), since Halacha (literally to go or to walk) which emerges from *derash,* leads a person from the wilderness to the city. *Pshat* is distinct from the other forms of interpretation (unlike the other three, it does not relate directly to the city) since it deals with the text on its own terms and needs no additional knowledge. However, *pshat* also forms a pair with *drash* insofar as it is exoteric.

Remez and *sod* also form a pair, with *remez* serving as the gateway to *sod.* A city gate (*petach ha-sha'ar*) portrays *remez* since, by alluding to the deeper truth, *remez* grants access to the city (*ir*), which is the world of *sod.* Let us take a step back and consider what this insight conveys. In Chapter Seven we considered a number of thinkers who maintained that *pshat, drash,* and *sod* were all, more or less, equal methodologies of interpreting Scripture. Torah conveys knowledge in many layers with each one reflecting God's voice and His infinite wisdom. Gra, following the *Zohar,* take a decidedly different approach. While there is value in studying all aspects of *pardes,* there is a hierarchy of interpretation—one begins outside the city in the world of *pshat. Drash* leads a person towards civilization with *remez* representing the city's gate. The end destination is an enchanted city, *sod,* which the individual could not have imagined when he first started upon the road.

גר"א משלי א:כ

התורה נחלקת לשנים שהם ארבע. והם פשט וסוד, ובכל אחד שנים. בסוד: סודות עצמן ורמז הוא פתח השער לסודות. ובפשט: דרש ופשט. וזהו "חכמות בחוץ" לאותן העומדים בחוץ עדיין אינו מראה

---

48. **משלי א:כ-כא**
חָכְמוֹת **בַּחוּץ** תָּרֹנָּה **בָּרְחֹבוֹת** תִּתֵּן קוֹלָהּ: בְּרֹאשׁ הֹמִיּוֹת תִּקְרָא **בְּפִתְחֵי שְׁעָרִים בָּעִיר** אֲמָרֶיהָ תֹאמֵר:

להם רק הפשט... "ברחובות" שהוא הדרוש שמרחיב ההלכה שם תתן קולה... "בראש הומיות תקרא" בפתחי שערים הוא רמז שהוא פתח השער, ואח"כ "בעיר" שהוא בפנימיות התורה אז תאמר להם כל אמריה וסודותיה:

The Torah has two general levels of meaning, which form a total of four levels.[49] One is *pshat*, or the simple meaning, the other is *sod*, or the secrets hiding beneath the surface. *Sod* includes a sub-level, *remez*, meaning hint or insinuation. This includes various forms of codes or other indications that there is indeed something beneath the surface. *Remez* is thus the gateway to *sod*. *Pshat* also includes a sublevel, *drash*. The verse in *Mishlei* refers to knowledge singing outside the city, which refers to those who still stand outside the city of *sod* and see only *pshat*… The verse then refers to the streets, which represents *drash* which is an expansion of Halacha… [this leads to] *remez*, which is a gate… which leads to the city of *sod* that is the inner world of *sod*.

In another remarkable metaphor, *Zohar* (2:99a–b) portrays Torah as a beloved woman slowly revealing herself to her lover: Initially, she calls out. If he does not notice, she sends messengers. When the timid young man finally approaches, he has passed the first barrier, and she converses from behind a concealing curtain, corresponding to the level of "*drasha*," and afterward through a thin veil, at the level of "*aggada*." Finally, if he perseveres, the layers drop and she reveals her deepest secrets:

זוהר כרך ב (שמות) פרשת משפטים
קריב לגבה שריאת למללא עמיה מבתר פרוכתא דפרסא ליה מלין לפום ארחוי עד דיסתכל זעיר זעיר ודא הוא דרשא, לבתר תשתעי בהדיה מבתר שושיפא דקיק מלין דחידה ודא איהו הגדה.

לבתר דאיהו רגיל לגבה אתגליאת לגביה אנפין באנפין ומלילת בהדיה כל רזין סתימין דילה וכל ארחין סתימין דהוו בלבאה טמירין מיומין קדמאין, כדין איהו בר נש שלים בעל תורה ודאי מארי דביתא דהא כל רזין דילה גליאת ליה ולא רחיקת ולא כסיאת מיניה כלום.

49. Verse 20 refers to the first pair and verse 21 the second.

> When he comes close to her, she begins to speak to him from behind a curtain – words he can understand, until he begins to slowly look at her. This is *drasha*.[50] Then she begins to convey riddles to him from an even thinner screen. This is *aggada*.[51]
>
> Once he has grown accustomed to her, she reveals herself to him face to face and relates to him all her concealed mysteries and all the concealed ways, which were hidden in her heart from primeval days. Thus, he becomes a complete human being and a definite master of Torah, the master of the house, to whom all her secrets are revealed and from whom nothing is distanced or covered.

Sod is not just another layer beyond *pshat* and *drash* – it is the Torah's song;[52] it is her (Torah's) language of love; it is her splendor.[53] It is what she exposes only to those whom she can trust. It is her holy secrets.

Textual Underpinnings of Mystical Interpretations

We should not assume, though, that these mystical explanations are unrelated to the text of the Torah. Quite the reverse, Ramban frequently shows how Kabbalistic explanations, which he calls *derech ha-emet* (the approach of truth), stem from and best accord with the most literal reading of the verses.[54] This reflects itself not just in textual

---

50. When he begins to think about her words, he has gone from *pshat* to *drash*.
51. As we saw in Chapter 5, Aggada often conveys wisdom discursively and in riddles (see 5.9).
52. The poetry of works like the *Zohar* is incredibly inspiring. Remarkably, R. Yisrael of Shklov reports (in his Introduction to *Pe'at ha-Shulchan*) that Gra used to say that most of the inner meanings of Torah and the secrets of the songs of the *levi'im* and the secrets of the *Tikkunei Zohar* cannot be understood without knowledge of music theory. As we saw in 1.6, music is one of the seven wisdoms that Gra claimed was necessary to properly understand Torah.
53. *Zohar* literally means splendor or radiance.
54. Ramban and ibn Ezra frequently show how *pshat* is closely connected to the mystical interpretation. See, for example, Ramban and ibn Ezra to *Shemot* 6:2. Rashbam occasionally adopts this approach as well; see, for example, *Shemot* 3:15.

interpretations; Kabbalistic concepts allow for a more symbolic, but less metaphorical interpretation of the Torah. Let us consider one of many examples.

רמב"ן דברים כב:ו

ולשון זו האגדה עצמה הוזכרה בילמדנו (תנחומא שמיני ח) בפרשת זאת החיה, וכי מה איכפת לו להקב"ה בין שוחט בהמה ואוכל או נוחר ואוכל כלום אתה מועילו או כלום אתה מזיקו, או מה איכפת לו בין אוכל טהורות או אוכל טמאות, אם חכמת חכמת לך (משלי ט:יב), הא לא נתנו המצות אלא לצרף את הבריות, שנאמר (תהלים יב:ז) אמרות ה' אמרות טהורות, ונאמר כל אמרת אלוה צרופה, למה, שיהא מגין עליך. הנה מפורש בכאן שלא באו לומר אלא שאין התועלת אליו יתעלה שיצטרך לאורה כמחושב מן המנורה, ושיצטרך למאכל הקרבנות וריח הקטרת, **כנראה מפשוטיהם.**

The midrash asks: "What does God care whether we slaughter an animal from the front of its neck or the back? Does it harm Him or help Him… Rather, *mitzvot* are given to purify man…" Behold, the midrash is coming to teach us that the purpose of *mitzvot* is not because He needs the light, as one might have understood from the *mitzva* of the *menora,* or that He needs the food of the sacrifices and the aroma of the incense offering, **as would appear to be the case from the simple understanding of the verses.**

Ramban writes that the simple understanding of the Torah is that God enjoys the *korbanot*. Consider, for example, the following verse:

במדבר כח:ב

צַו אֶת בְּנֵי יִשְׂרָאֵל וְאָמַרְתָּ אֲלֵהֶם אֶת **קָרְבָּנִי לַחְמִי לְאִשַּׁי רֵיחַ נִיחֹחִי** תִּשְׁמְרוּ לְהַקְרִיב לִי בְּמוֹעֲדוֹ:

Command the children of Israel and say to them: "My offering, **My food for My fire offerings, a spirit of satisfaction for Me,** you shall take care to offer to Me at its appointed time."

Of course, the notion that God enjoys the meat of a *korban* is absurd. The midrash cited by Ramban addresses this issue and explains that God does not benefit from our *mitzvot*. Rather, *mitzvot* benefit us by purifying us. The way Ramban understands this midrash is that *mitzvot* instill within us ethical values and moral sensitivity. For example, when slaughtering an animal, one must slaughter from the front of the neck, which minimizes the animal's pain. This restriction thus makes us more compassionate and prevents us from becoming cruel, which might otherwise happen when killing an animal. Thus, the *mitzvot* are not for God (God does not benefit from our slaughtering in the front as opposed to the back), but rather for us (we become sensitive).[55] Ramban writes that this midrash corrects the simple understanding of the verses, which implies that God benefits from our *mitzvot*. Ramban, in fact, concludes that this concept is universally accepted.[56]

The matter is not so simple, though. Concerning the purpose of the *Beit ha-Mikdash*, Ramban writes:

רמב"ן שמות כט:מו
יש בענין סוד גדול, כי כפי **פשט** הדבר השכינה בישראל צורך הדיוט ולא צורך גבוה, אבל הוא כענין שאמר הכתוב ישראל אשר בך אתפאר (ישעיה מט:ג), ואמר יהושע ומה תעשה לשמך הגדול (יהושע ז:ט), ופסוקים רבים באו כן, אוה למושב לו (תהלים קלב:יג), פה אשב כי אויתיה (שם יד), וכתוב והארץ אזכור (ויקרא כו:מב):

There is in this matter a great secret, because according to the simple perspective (*pshat ha-davar*), God dwells amongst us for our sake, not for His sake. But in truth, the matter is as it

55. והביא ראיה מן השוחט מן הצואר והעורף לומר שכולם לנו ולא להקב"ה, לפי שלא יתכן לומר בשחיטה שיהא בה תועלת וכבוד לבורא יתברך בצואר יותר מהעורף או הניחור, אלא לנו הם להדריכנו בנתיבות הרחמים גם בעת השחיטה. והביאו ראיה אחרת, או מה איכפת לו בין אוכל טהורות והם המאכלים המותרים, לאוכל טמאות והם המאכלים האסורים, שאמרה בהם התורה (ויקרא יא:כח) טמאים המה לכם, ורמז שהוא להיותנו נקיי הנפש חכמים משכילי האמת. ואמרם אם חכמת חכמת לך, הזכירו כי המצות המעשיות כגון שחיטת הצואר ללמדנו המדות הטובות, והמצות הגדורות במינין לזקק את נפשותינו, כמו שאמרה תורה (שם כ:כה) ולא תשקצו את נפשותיכם בבהמה ובעוף ובכל אשר תרמוש האדמה אשר הבדלתי לכם לטמא, א"כ כלם לתועלתנו בלבד. וזה כמו שאמר אליהוא (איוב לה:ו) אם חטאת מה תפעל בו ורבו פשעיך מה תעשה לו, ואמר (שם פסוק ז) או מה מידך יקח.

56. וזה דבר מוסכם בכל דברי רבותינו.

> says (*Yeshaya* 49:3), "Yisrael in whom I am glorified" (which implies that the Jewish people benefit God by bringing Him glory), and Yehoshua says (*Yehoshua* 7:9), "What will be with Your great Name" (which implies that our service glorifies His Name)... and [*Tehillim* 132:14 states] "Here (in the Temple) I will dwell, for I desire it," and it says, "And I will remember the land" (*Vayikra* 26:42).

"*Pshat ha-davar*" in this case refers to the simple (philosophical) understanding of the matter. This perspective is indeed correct; thus, Ramban presents it without hesitation above and elsewhere (such as *Devarim* 4:3 and 10:12). The Kabbalistic explanation, which is known to us only through tradition and does not seem rational, is true as well and, as we have seen, conforms to the literal understanding of the text. Thus, Ramban concludes with a number of verses that highlight this seemingly untenable concept.

Of course, while the Kabbalistic understanding accords with the literal interpretation of the verses, it does not understand them simplistically. Nobody would imagine that God enjoys the meat of sacrifices in the same manner as a human enjoys a good steak. The true meaning of this explanation is indeed a great secret and has nothing to do with the superficial understanding of the verse.[57] Nevertheless, the Kabbalistic explanation does accord with the literal understanding of the words in a manner that the Midrash's interpretation does not.

Mystical Interpretations of Midrash

Just as *sod* is necessary to account for the literal understanding of the verses, it sometimes is necessary to explain problematic midrashim. Thus, Ramban responds to difficulties in certain midrashim by arguing that they should not be understood literally, but rather as conveying Kabbalistic concepts. For example:

---

57. In 13.6, we elaborate upon this seemingly incomprehensible mystical perspective. For our purposes, let us note that Ramban does not maintain that the philosophical approach is supplanted by the mystical one.

רמב"ן שמות יט:יג
במשוך היובל המה יעלו בהר - הוא שופר של איל, ושופר אילו של יצחק היה (פדר"א לה). לשון רש"י.

ולא הבינותי זה, כי אילו של יצחק עולה הקריב אותו, והקרנים והטלפים הכל נשרף בעולות (זבחים פה ב). אולי גבל הקב"ה עפר קרנו והחזירו למה שהיה.

אבל לפי דעתי האגדה הזו יש לה סוד, ואמרו שזה הקול הוא פחד יצחק, ולכך אמר (פסוק טז) ויחרד כל העם אשר במחנה, ולא השיגו דבור בגבורה הזאת זולתי קול (דברים ד:יב):

"When the ram's horn sounds they may ascend the mountain." Rashi understands that the word הַיֹּבֵל refers to a *shofar* of a ram [for in Arabia, they call a ram "*yuvla*"]. And this *shofar* was from Yitzchak's ram (i.e., the ram that Avraham sacrificed instead of Yitzchak).

I do not understand this, because Yitzchak's ram was offered as an *ola,* where the Halacha is that even its horn would be burnt. Perhaps, [according to Rashi,] one might claim that God reconstituted the *shofar*.

But in my opinion, the aggada cited by Rashi (*Pirkei de-Rabi Eliezer,* Ch. 31) should be understood as conveying a secret. It is teaching us that this *kol* (the sound that emanated during *Matan Torah)* is a reference to *Pachad Yitzchak* (Yitzchak's dread of God). Hence, the verse says that the people receiving the Torah were petrified (*charada*) and did not perceive speech within this demonstration of might (*gevura*), only sound (*kol*).

Here, we see that Ramban presumed that Rashi understood the midrash literally. Ramban questions this literal understanding of the midrash. Although he offers a possible resolution, he prefers a Kabbalistic, non-literal understanding of the midrash.[58] Briefly reading the above passage

58. Perhaps this cryptic statement can be understood in light of Ramban's explanation of *Pachad Yitzchak* in *Bereishit*.

also highlights one aspect of Ramban's mystical interpretations of Scripture. Ramban identifies opaque and idiosyncratic words or phrases that appear in numerous places (e.g., *Pachad Yitzchak*) and shows how they relate to each other to convey the deeper meaning of the episode.[59] More specifically,

---

רמב"ן בראשית לא:מב

ופחד יצחק היה לי... לשון רש"י. וכן דעת אונקלוס כי פחד יצחק אלהיו, דדחיל ליה יצחק. ורבי אברהם אמר... וישבע יעקב בפחד אביו יצחק (פסוק נג), במי שיצחק מתפחד ממנו... ועל דרך האמת יבא הלשון כפשוטו ומשמעו, והוא מדת הדין של מעלה...

Ramban first notes that the classical commentaries understand the words *Pachad Yitzchak*, the dread of Yitzchak, as referring to God whom Yitzchak feared. However, the Kabbalistic explanation understands the reference more literally as a reference to *middat ha-din*, God's attribute of justice. (The very notion of *Pachad Yitzchak* is another example of a Kabbalistic notion that emerges from a more literal reading of the verse.) Thus, the verse which states לוּלֵי אֱלֹהֵי אָבִי אֱלֹהֵי אַבְרָהָם וּפַחַד יִצְחָק הָיָה לִי כִּי עַתָּה רֵיקָם שִׁלַּחְתָּנִי, refers to God's attribute of justice which was responsible for Yaakov's salvation. Here we see the verse alluding to the Kabbalistic notion that each of the *Avot* reflect different *middot* of God, and different ways to serve God, with Avraham reflecting *chesed* and Yitzchak *gevura*. Moreover, we see Yaakov, who represents *tiferet*, incorporating these two paths. Why does Yaakov mention this now? Yaakov is offering gratitude that incorporated both *chesed* (God bestowed kindness upon him and saved him from Lavan even if he was undeserving) and *din* (by chastising Lavan for his unworthy behavior). While on a *pshat* level we simply have two references to God (אֱלֹהֵי אַבְרָהָם and פַּחַד יִצְחָק), the mystical interpretation hones in on the word *pachad*, interprets it literally, and then derives a remarkable understanding of the verse.

Returning to Ramban's explanation of the shofar from Yitzchak's ram, Ramban understands that the dread experienced by the Jewish people (**ויחרד** כל העם אשר במחנה) refers to service of God with the *midda* of *din*, the *midda* of *gevura*. Ramban picks up on the association of three things in this verse, *charada*, *shofar*, and *kol*. As in, **וְקֹל שֹׁפָר** חָזָק מְאֹד **וַיֶּחֱרַד** כָּל הָעָם אֲשֶׁר בַּמַּחֲנֶה (*Shemot* 19:16). Dread (*charada*) of God was not simply something experienced by Yitzchak at the *akeida*, but throughout his life (e.g., **וַיֶּחֱרַד** יִצְחָק חֲרָדָה גְּדֹלָה עַד מְאֹד, *Bereishit* 27:33). This parallelism is alluded to by the shofar of Yitzchak, since a shofar is meant to inspire dread, אִם יִתָּקַע שׁוֹפָר בְּעִיר וְעָם לֹא **יֶחֱרָדוּ** (*Amos* 3:6). Ramban then adds that this divine message was conveyed not through speech but through *kol*, as stressed in *Devarim* 4:12 which stresses the notion of communication through sound and not words: **וַיְדַבֵּר** ה׳ אֲלֵיכֶם מִתּוֹךְ הָאֵשׁ **קוֹל** דְּבָרִים אַתֶּם שֹׁמְעִים וּתְמוּנָה אֵינְכֶם רֹאִים זוּלָתִי **קוֹל**.

59. Another example of where Ramban understands a midrash as alluding to a Kabbalistic idea is here:

רמב"ן דברים לג:א

ולזה הסוד נתכוונו רבותינו במדרש שאמרו בבראשית רבה...

As we noted in 7.5, Ramban frequently attempts to adduce the deeper meaning behind midrashim. We should also note that Rambam frequently understands midrashim

Ramban employs textual methodologies to build a Kabbalistic dictionary of Kabbalistic ideas, which he uses to explain textual nuances. So, according to Ramban, Kabbala emerges from the text and sheds light upon the text.

12.7 THE DANGERS OF KABBALA

In 1.7, we examined Rivash's harsh critique of philosophy. Interestingly, he expresses uncertainty concerning Kabbala as well. Despite inheriting the intellectual tradition of Ramban,[60] Rivash was hesitant about what he saw as perversions of Kabbala in his generation. Thus, he lambasts those who study Kabbala without receiving the tradition from a qualified teacher. Rivash then adds another concern, the misapplication of Kabbala. He is especially concerned about meditations on *sefirot* while praying:

שו"ת ריב"ש סימן קנז

וגם הודעתיך, כי מורי הרב רבי פרץ הכהן ז"ל, לא היה כלל מדבר ולא מחשיב באותן הספירות. גם שמעתי מפיו, שהרב רבי שמשון מקינון ז"ל, שהיה רב גדול מכל בני דורו... והוא היה אומר: אני מתפלל לדעת זה התינוק; כלומר, להוציא מלב המקובלים, שהם מתפללים פעם לספירה אחת ופעם לספירה אחת, כפי עניין התפילה.

I already have told you that my teacher, R. Peretz ha-Kohen, did not speak of or recognize *sefirot*. I heard from him that R. Shimshon from Kinon, who was an outstanding rabbi... used to say, "I pray like a child."[61] He meant to negate the perspective of the Kabbalists, who sometimes pray to one *sefira* and sometimes pray to a different *sefira* based on the type of prayer.[62]

---

as alluding to esoteric concepts. Thus, *Moreh ha-Nevuchim* is replete with citations of midrashim that are used to substantiate his philosophical understandings. Indeed, as we explained in Chapter 6, Rambam believed that any time an aggada seemed to be describing something impossible, one should assume that it is alluding to a deeper truth that the author has intended to keep hidden.

60. Rivash was a student of Ran, who was a link in the Spanish tradition going back to Ramban.

61. Maharshal (*Teshuvot Maharshal* 98) explains this to mean that even after he had studied all of the great mystical secrets, when he prayed, he prayed like a child, meaning he did not contemplate the *sefirot* while praying.

62. Along similar lines, R. Yechezkeil Landau understands the Talmud in *Berachot* as warning against thinking of *sefirot* while praying.

Rivash even quotes someone who claimed (facetiously) that those who consider the ten *sefirot* (while praying) are worse than the Christians who serve only three (the trinity).

Rivash then writes that he once asked a genuine Kabbalist (Don Yosef ibn Shushan) how Kabbalists think of one *sefira* when they make one *bracha* and another *sefira* when making a different *bracha*. The Kabbalist answered that prayer always is addressed directly to God; however, just as a person who needs bread might ask the king to direct the minister of bread to give him bread, and he would not request that the king ask the minister of wine to give him bread, so too we consider the particular *sefirot* relevant to our request.[63] Rivash assents to this answer (*ve-hinei tov me'od*) but concludes that it still is better to address God directly, allowing God to decide how best to respond. Later, he quotes Ran's hesitancy concerning Ramban's Kabbala. Rivash concludes:

> ולזה אני אומר, שאין לסמוך בדברים כאלו אלא מפי חכם מקובל, ועדיין אולי.

> And about this I say that one should not rely on these things unless he hears them from an accepted sage (חכם מקובל), and even then, only maybe (ועדיין אולי).

Some have detected in the words ועדיין אולי (and even then, only maybe) that Rivash was opposed to all Kabbala and not just abuse of Kabbala; though, in light of the rest of this responsum, this conclusion is

---

צל"ח מסכת ברכות דף כח עמוד ב
ולהרחיקם מן כת המקובלים שלא יכוונו בתפלתם רק פירוש המלות, הזהירם ואמר וכשאתם מתפללים דעו לפני מי אתם עומדים, לומר להם שלא יכוונו לשום מדה וספירה רק דעו לפני מי אתם עומדים, והוא מקור שממנו מקבלים כל אחד שפעו, והוא ישפיע לכל מדה נכונה בחסדו ובגבורתו וברחמיו, אבל אתם לא תכוונו רק אליו לבד ולא תדעו דבר רק לפני מי אתם עומדים.
Additionally, R. Landau waged a fierce battle to ban the recitation of *le-sheim yichud* (see *Noda be-Yehuda* Y.D. 93). Indeed, that prayer which longs for the unification of *kudsha brich hu* and *shechintei* highlights the dangers of the incorporation of overtly mystical prayers for those uninitiated insofar as it can be misunderstood as implying a form of duality.

63. See *Nefesh ha-Chaim* 2:4, who answers Rivash's question somewhat differently.

questionable.[64] Nevertheless, Rivash's caution concerning the dangers of Kabbala warrants attention. Superficial unguided interpretations of Kabbalistic texts can lead a person to believe in a corporeal God and to other heretical beliefs. These dangers bring us to our next issue – restrictions on the study of Kabbala.

12.8 APPENDIX A: ARE THERE AGE RESTRICTIONS ON KABBALA?

Just as there are prerequisites for the study of philosophy (discussed in 2.1), there are prerequisites for the study of mysticism. Primarily, one must be firmly grounded in the revealed Torah, particularly the Talmud. R. Shabtai ha-Kohen (*Shach*) writes that Kabbala may not be studied until one has filled his stomach with Talmud. Moreover, he cites some opinions that one should wait until age forty.[65] Interestingly, *Shach* himself lived only until the age of 40 or 41, yet R. Chaim Yosef David Azulai (Chida) reports he was a great Kabbalist.[66] In fact, many of the great Kabbalists died before the age of forty, including the Arizal (38), Ramchal (37), and R. Nachman of Breslov (38); fortunately, they did not observe this restriction. R. Moshe Kordevero (who lived until 48) writes (*Ohr Ne'erav* 3:1) that one may begin studying mysticism at the age of twenty. Of course, just because the study of Kabbala at an early age may be appropriate for extraordinarily pious and gifted students does not mean it is correct for everybody.

---

64. See *Teshuva mei-Ahava* (Introduction to Vol. 1) and *Chavot Ya'ir* (210, towards the end) for more on Rivash's position.

65. **ש"ך יורה דעה סימן רמו ו**
גם המקובלים ושאר האחרונים הפליגו בדבר שלא ללמוד חכמת הקבלה עד אחר שמילא כריסו מהש"ס ויש שכתבו שלא ללמוד קבלה עד שיהא בן **ארבעים שנה** כמ"ש בן ארבעים לבינה בשגם שצריך **קדושה וטהרה וזריזות ונקיות** לזה ורוב המתפרצים לעלות בחכמה זו קודם הזמן הראוי קומטו בלא עת כמ"ש כל זה בד' חכמי האמת.

66. *Shach* on *Shulchan Aruch* demonstrates not only total mastery of Talmud and Rishonim but also awareness of all the contemporary rabbinic works. Chida writes (*Sheim ha-Gedolim*) that *Shach* could not possibly have had access to all of those works unless he used holy names (*sheimot ha-kedoshim*), as he was fleeing from the Cossacks when writing his monumental commentary.

Shach notes that more important than any technical age restriction is the requirement of holiness and purity of heart and mind (קדושה וטהרה). Much like Rambam admonished that fear of Heaven precedes the study of philosophy (see 2.1), *Shach* warns that danger lurks for one who engages in the esoteric without appropriate character development (זריזות ונקיות). Proof for this can be seen in the Talmudic story (*Chagiga* 14b) in which four scholars attempted to study esoteric wisdom. Three out of the four were harmed in their pursuit, since they were intellectually unprepared, emotionally ill-suited, or lacked the appropriate level of saintliness. Only R. Akiva entered in peace and left in peace.

As noted, the framework for the prerequisites for such study goes back to the Talmud (*Chagiga* 11b), which prohibits teaching esoteric wisdom publicly lest someone who is not suited listen in. Even among worthy students, the teacher must be able to give students individual attention to make sure they do not err. Moreover, when it comes to *ma'aseh merkava*, the material cannot be conveyed overtly even to a worthy individual. The student must independently extrapolate the concept from the basic framework set up by the teacher.

Thus, many fought hard to curtail the public and premature teaching of Kabbala. Gra (*Mishlei* 21:17) warns of the dire consequences of beginning prematurely:

> והיינו, שהלחם הוא הלכות, ו"יין ושמן" הם אגדות שהן רמז וסודות, והרוצה להלך בגדולות ונפלאות ואיננו רואה לקיים [קודם] הדינים וללמוד אותם, "לא יעשיר", כי "איזהו עשיר, השמח בחלקו" ואינו הולך בגדולות ונפלאות, קודם שממלא כריסו בלחם, שהוא "לבב אנוש יסעד". ואי אפשר לבא לסודות כי אם על ידי זה, ולכן "לא יעשיר", שלא יהיה לו כלום.

> At first one must learn Halachot and fulfill them, because they are like bread that satiates, and only afterwards may one toil in the secrets, which are compared to wine and oil. Whoever switches the order will not succeed and will lose everything.

These comments should be considered in light of Gra's battle against *Chasidut*. One of the chief charges leveled against early *Chasidut* was the claim that *chasidim* were violating the Talmud's restrictions concerning the promulgation of esoteric wisdom. A century earlier, there were others who fought hard against publicly teaching Kabbala, especially in the aftermath of the Shabtai Tzvi tragedy.[67]

How would those who seem to push the limits respond? Firstly, one must differentiate between different sorts of study. For example, much of the *Zohar* resembles other forms of Midrashic literature and should be distinguished from more esoteric Kabbala.[68] In fact, some thinkers maintain that *Zohar* can be understood according to *pshat* and *sod*, just like any *midrash Aggada*. Moreover, there is a difference between simply reciting passages of *Zohar* (a practice common in many Sefardic communities) and the study and analysis of Kabbalistic texts.

The Popularization of Kabbalistic Concepts

Nevertheless, it cannot be denied that some communities and thinkers have advocated the study of Kabbala at early ages for all Jews. This is especially common in certain chasidic communities. Some have suggested (see R. Yaakov Tzemach's Introduction to *Eitz Chaim*) that, as *mashiach* approaches, the appropriate age should be reduced.[69] Indeed, R. Yitzchak of Komarno writes (*Notzeir Chesed, Avot* 4:20):

> ולו עמי שומע לי בדור הזה שהמינות גובר היו לומדין עם תינוק בן תשעה שנים ספר הזוהר והתיקונים להגות בהם והיה יראת חטאו קודמת לחכמתו ויתקיים.

> If only my nation would listen to me, in this generation when heresy is powerful, they would teach a nine-year-old *Zohar* and

67. Many historians presume that Gra's intense opposition to *Chasidut* stemmed from a suspicion that some *chasidim* were closet Sabbateans.

68. This idea is said in the name of R. Yisrael Meir Kagan ha-Kohen, the *Chofeitz Chaim*.

69. Moreover, the study of Kabbala, and especially *Zohar*, will bring the redemption. See רעיא מהימנא דף קכד: where it says: ובגין דעתידין ישראל למטעם מאילנא דחיי דאיהו האי ספר הזהר יפקון ביה מן גלותא ברחמי.

> the *Tikkunim* such that his fear of sin would precede his wisdom and thereby endure.

This debate did not originate in the seventeenth or eighteenth century. Indeed, attitudes concerning the appropriateness of publicly referring to Kabbalistic concepts have evolved such that one can clearly discern a broader trend in which mystical secrets that once were the domain of elite scholars have become known to the masses.

An example of this shift in attitude can be seen concerning the concept of transmigration of the soul (*gilgul neshamot*). Whenever Ramban refers to the concept, he does so through oblique allusion (*sod ha-ibur*).[70] Ramban felt that any elaboration would be a violation of the restrictions against the public teaching of mysticism. However a few generations later, thinkers such as R. Bachya b. Asher (*Bereishit* 38:1) present this idea with no such compunctions. A number of centuries later (especially following the Arizal[71]), the concept is referred to openly (even in non-mystical works such as *Mishna Berura*[72]). Of course, though, there is a big difference between referring to a Kabbalistic concept and endorsing its study for the masses. Hence, the issue of the proper age to study Kabbala (if it is to be studied at all) continues to divide groups of Jews even today.[73]

---

70. See Ramban on *Bereishit* 38:8 and *Devarim* 25:6.

71. The Arizal felt that what originally were secrets (*nistarot*) now are revealed (*niglot*). An expression of this attitude can be found in R. Yaakov Tzemach's Introduction to *Eitz Chaim*:

    גילוי חכמה זאת עתה בדורות גרועות הוא כדי שיהיה לנו מגן עתה לאחוז בלבב שלם באבינו שבשמים, כי באותן הדורות הקודמים היו אנשי מעשה וחסידים, והמעשים טובים היו מצילין אותן מפי המקטריגים, עתה רחוקים אנו משרש העליון כמו השמרים בתוך החביות, מי יגן עלינו אם לא קריאתינו בחכמה הזאת הנפלאה והעמוקה. ובפרט על דרך שכתב הרב [האר"י] ז"ל שהנסתרות נעשו עתה כמו נגלות, כי בדור הזה מושל הזנות ומלשינות ולשון הרע ושנאה שבלב, ונתפשטו הקליפות באופן שמתבייש האדם לנהוג דברי חסידות, והשם יגן עלינו וימחול לעונינו, אכי"ר.

72. See *Sha'ar ha-Tziyun* 622:5:

    כי האדם חושב כמה פעמים לייאש את עצמו שאין יכול לתקן בשום אופן ועל כן יתנהג תמיד באופן א׳, ואם יגזור עליו הקב"ה למות ימות. אבל טעות הוא, שסוף דבר יהיה... ויבא עוד פעם ופעמים לעולם הזה... לתקן...

73. Divergent views can be found between those who are Ashkenazi versus Sefardi and Chasidic versus Litvishe.

12.9 APPENDIX B: RAMBAN ON INTIMACY

In 12.5, we noted positive and negative descriptions of intimacy in *Iggeret ha-Kodesh* and Maharal. The same discrepancy emerges from Ramban. In one place, explaining the prohibition against restricted relationships, Ramban's perspective on intimacy appears highly negative:

> **רמב"ן ויקרא יח:ו**
> ודע כי המשגל דבר מרוחק ונמאס בתורה זולתי לקיום המין, ואשר לא יולד ממנו הוא אסור, וכן אשר איננו טוב בקיום ולא יצלח בו תאסור אותו התורה.
>
> Know that sexual intercourse is distanced and disgusted by the Torah besides for when it is done to preserve the species, and is prohibited when done in a way that cannot lead to procreation or that would yield defective offspring.

Ramban here explains that the reason for the Torah's prohibition against incest, pederasty and bestiality is that such a union will not lead to healthy procreation. However, in presenting his argument, he implies that the goal of intimacy is entirely procreation.

However, when we look elsewhere in Ramban, we clearly see that the matter is not so straightforward. Consider Ramban's translation of the words *she'eir, kesut,* and *ona* (*Shemot* 21:9). Rashi understands that *she'eir* refers to a husband's responsibility to provide food for his wife, *kesut* refers to his obligation to cloth his wife, and *ona* describes his conjugal responsibilities. Ramban, however, shows how all three words relate to intimacy, at least on a level of *pshat*. If *she'eir* refers to the husband's formal conjugal obligations, then what does *ona* mean? Ramban understands that *ona* (lit. her time) describes when the couple unites "at a time of love" (עת דודים).[74] Moreover, Ramban, in the above

74. This particular phrase comes from the book of *Yechezkeil* and literally means a time of lovemaking.

יחזקאל טז:ח
וָאֶעֱבֹר עָלַיִךְ וָאֶרְאֵךְ וְהִנֵּה עִתֵּךְ עֵת דֹּדִים וָאֶפְרֹשׂ כְּנָפִי עָלַיִךְ וָאֲכַסֶּה עֶרְוָתֵךְ וָאֶשָּׁבַע לָךְ וָאָבוֹא בִבְרִית אֹתָךְ נְאֻם אֲדֹנָי יְקוִק וַתִּהְיִי לִי:

passage (when translating the word *she'eir*), alludes to his comments in *Bereishit* 2:24 where he explains why the Torah describes the union between husband and wife as their becoming "one flesh" (**והיו לבשר אחד**). The phrase, according to Ramban, refers to the notion that the union between husband and wife is closer than any other possible relationship, even the bond of blood relatives.[75]

The potential for holiness in intimacy can also be found in Ramban's rationale for the Torah's prohibition of sleeping with a *nidda*:

רמב"ן ויקרא יח:יט

וכל שכן שתזיק לשוכב עמה **אשר תדבק גופה ומחשבתה בו ובמחשבתו.**

[The reason why] it will harm someone to sleep with someone who is a *nidda* is that [**during sexual relations**] **with her, her body and thoughts unite with him and his thoughts.**

---

75. **רמב"ן בראשית ב:כד**

והנכון בעיני, כי הבהמה והחיה אין להם דבקות בנקבותיהן, אבל יבא הזכר על איזה נקבה שימצא, וילכו להם, ומפני זה אמר הכתוב, בעבור שנקבת האדם היתה עצם מעצמיו ובשר מבשרו, ודבק בה, והיתה בחיקו כבשרו, ויחפוץ בה להיותה תמיד עמו. וכאשר היה זה באדם, הושם טבעו בתולדותיו, להיות הזכרים מהם דבקים בנשותיהם, עוזבים את אביהם ואת אמם, ורואים את נשותיהן כאלו הן עמם לבשר אחד. וכן כי אחינו בשרנו הוא (להלן לז:כז), אל כל שאר בשרו (ויקרא יח:ו). הקרובים במשפחה יקראו "שאר בשר". והנה יעזוב שאר אביו ואמו וקורבתם, ויראה שאשתו קרובה לו מהם.

What appears to me as correct is that domestic and wild animals have no commitment to their females, but rather the male copulates with any female he should chance upon and then goes on his way. And it is because of this that the verse states that on account of the fact that the female of man was "bone of his bones and flesh of his flesh," she would be in his bosom as part of his own body, and he would desire her to be with her constantly. And just as this was with Adam, so it was integrated into the nature of his progeny, that the males would be committed to their wives, abandoning their fathers and mothers, and viewing their wives as if they were one flesh with them… Familial relatives are called שאר בשרו. And so he will leave the שאר [flesh] of his father and mother and their kinship and will realize that his wife is even closer to him than they are.

For a more thorough treatment of Ramban's understanding of intimacy, see "Nahmanides and Rashi on the One Flesh of Conjugal Union: Lovemaking vs. Duty," by James A. Diamond, in *The Harvard Theological Review* Vol. 102, No. 2 (Apr., 2009), pp. 193–224. The above translation is taken from that article, p. 233.

Ramban writes that the unity achieved during the sexual act is far more profound than the physical act. In this sentence, Ramban alludes to a central thesis of *Iggeret ha-Kodesh* that intimacy is called *yedi'a* (lit. knowledge) because the union between husband and wife during intimacy is much deeper than their physical connection, and is therefore best allegorized by the word *yedi'a*.[76]

Thus, while Ramban frowns upon intimacy not rooted in holiness, the act (when performed nobly) produces a profound physical and spiritual union between husband and wife. However, as Ramban alludes to and as *Iggeret ha-Kodesh* explains, it is not just about husband and wife connecting. The Talmud (*Nidda* 31a) teaches that the creation of a child is a partnership between the husband, the wife, and God. Accordingly, intimacy, which is the catalyst of that creation, also has within it the ability to connect to and partner with God. Consequently, intimacy can be anything from a base, animalistic, and hedonistic act to a giving act of love that unites the couple with God.

Indeed, this distinction emerges from the word Ramban uses to describe the act of intimacy. When discussing sexually abhorrent behavior in his commentary on the Torah, Ramban uses the term ביאה or משגל; whereas, when describing the positive union between husband and wife, he uses the term חיבור.[77] (The author of *Iggeret ha-Kodesh* likewise uses the term חיבור when referring to the act done in the context of holiness.)

---

76. וכבר ידעת שלא נקרא האדם יודע דבר פלוני עד שנדבק המשכיל במושכל.

The author of *Iggeret ha-Kodesh* adds that the term connotes not just union between husband and wife, but also includes the *shechina*:

פי׳ כשהאדם מתחבר לאשתו בקדושה שכינה ביניהם, תמצא בשם האיש יו״ד ובשם האשה ה׳ הרי זה שמו של הקב״ה מצוי ביניהם. אבל אם לא נתכוונו לחבור קדושה אלא למלאות האשה שהוא. תאותם ומתוך התאוה והחמוד נתחממו כאש, יו״ד של שם האיש וה׳ של שם י״ה מסתלק מביניהם ונשאר אש ואש...

עליון. כי בהתחבר האדם לאשתו ומחשבתו נדבקת בעליונים, הרי אותה המחשבה מושכת אור למטה והוא שורה על אותה טפה שהוא מתכוין עליה ומהרהר בה...

77. This point is made by Dr. James A. Diamond in "Nahmanides and Rashi on the One Flesh of Conjugal Union: Lovemaking vs. Duty," in *The Harvard Theological Review* Vol. 102, No. 2 (Apr. 2009), p. 209, note 38. He argues that the former connotes one-sided sex, while the latter connotes a coming together which occurs when all the elements of *she'eir, kesut,* and *ona* are present.

The root of the disagreement between Rambam and Ramban regarding intimacy (referred to in 12.5) lies in their differing perspectives on the nature of the physical body. For Rambam, the physical body is blood and bones; whereas for Ramban, as we have seen, it is a reflection of our Creator. Thus, contends Ramban, the potential for spiritual achievement by means of the physical body is incalculable. Do not see the physical as profane, Ramban informs us, for even before man was tainted by sin, when he lived in the Garden of Eden, he had a physical body. Moreover, before man can enjoy the ultimate spiritual bliss of *olam ha-ba,* his body will be restored. Furthermore, argues the author of *Iggeret ha-Kodesh,* it is inconceivable that the act would not have the possibility for holiness, because it was created by God.[78] Thus, while man, using his free will, has the ability to taint this sanctified activity, fundamentally it is holy.[79]

78. דע כי חבור זה הוא ענין קדוש ונקי כשיהיה הדבר כפי מה שראוי ובזמן הראוי ובכוונה הנכונה. ואל יחשוב אדם כי בחבור הראוי יש גנאי וכיעור ח"ו. שהחבור הראוי נקרא ידיעה, ולא לחנם נקרא כך כאמור (ש"א א) וידע אלקנה את חנה אשתו. וזהו סוד טפת הזרע כשהיא נמשכת ממקום הקדושה ובטהרה נמשכת הדעה [והחכמה] והבינה והוא המוח. ודע שאלו לא היה בדבר קדושה דולה לא היו קוראין אל החבור ידיעה....
אבל כל בעלי התורה מאמינים שהשם ברא את הכל כפי מה שגזרה חכמתו, ולא ברא דבר שיהיה גנאי או כיעור, שאם יאמר שהחבור הוא דבר של גנאי, הנה כלי המשגל הם כלי הגנות, והרי השי"ת בראם במאמרו....

79. אין בכל אברי האדם מצד הבריאה דבר קלקול או כיעור כי הכל בחכמה עליונית דבר מתוקן וטוב ונאה, אבל האדם בהיות סכל מביא כיעור בדברים שאין בהם כיעור מתחלה...

The fonts used in this book are from the Arno family